Koren Talmud Bavli
THE NOÉ EDITION

SHABBAT • PART SIX

Steinsaltz Center

KOREN

I0809465

תלמוד בבלי

KOREN TALMUD BAVLI

THE NOÉ EDITION

שבת

SHABBAT

Daf 115a through Daf 137b

COMMENTARY BY

Rabbi Adin Even-Israel Steinsaltz

EDITOR-IN-CHIEF

Rabbi Dr Tzvi Hersh Weinreb

SENIOR CONTENT EDITOR

Rabbi Dr Shalom Z Berger

EXECUTIVE EDITOR

Rabbi Joshua Schreier

•

STEINSALTZ CENTER

KOREN PUBLISHERS JERUSALEM

Supported by the Matanel Foundation

Koren Talmud Bavli, The Noe Edition
Vol. 2.6: Tractate Shabbat, Daf 115a through Daf 137b
Paperback, ISBN 978-965-7765-31-9

First Hebrew/English paperback edition, 2019

Koren Publishers Jerusalem Ltd.
PO Box 4044, Jerusalem 91040, ISRAEL
PO Box 8531, New Milford, CT 06776, USA
www.korenpub.com

Steinsaltz Center

Steinsaltz Center is the parent organization of institutions established by Rabbi Adin Even-Israel Steinsaltz

PO Box 45187, Jerusalem 91450 ISRAEL
Telephone: +972 2 646 0900, Fax +972 2 624 9454
www.steinsaltz-center.org

Hardcover design by Ben Gasner

This book was published in cooperation with the Israel Institute for Talmudic Publications.

הִנֵּה יָמִים בָּאִים, נְאֻם אֲדֹנָי יֱהוִה, וְהִשְׁלַחְתִּי רָעָב בָּאָרֶץ,
לֹא־רָעָב לַלֶּחֶם וְלֹא־צָמָא לַמַּיִם, כִּי אִם־לִשְׁמֹעַ אֵת דִּבְרֵי יהוה.

Behold, days are coming – says the Lord God – I will send a hunger to the land, not a hunger for bread nor a thirst for water, but to hear the words of the Lord. (AMOS 8:11)

The Noé edition of the Koren Talmud Bavli
with the commentary of Rabbi Adin Even-Israel Steinsaltz
is dedicated to all those who open its covers
to quench their thirst for Jewish Knowledge,
in our generation of Torah renaissance.

This beautiful edition is for the young, the aged,
the novice and the savant alike,
as it unites the depth of Torah knowledge
with the best of academic scholarship.

Within its exquisite and vibrant pages,
words become worlds.

It will claim its place in the library of classics,
in the bookcases of the Beit Midrash,
the classrooms of our schools,
and in the offices of professionals and business people
who carve out precious time to grapple with its timeless wisdom.

For the Student and the Scholar

DEDICATED BY LEO AND SUE NOÉ

Steinsaltz Center

Executive Director, Steinsaltz Center

Rabbi Meni Even-Israel

Managing Editor

Rabbi Jason Rappoport

Senior Content Editor

Rabbi Dr. Shalom Z. Berger

Translators

Amy Fay Kaplan Benoff
Betzalel Philip Edwards
Rabbi Elli Fischer
Gila Hoch
Stephen Lauber
Elie Leshem
Rabbi Eli Ozarowski
Gavriel Reiss
Yosef Rosen
Jay Shapiro
Rabbi Ami Silver
Eliana Kinderlehrer Silver
Avi Steinhart
Amiel Vick
Rabbi Abe Y. Weschler

Editors

Mali Brofsky
Rabbi David Jay Derovan
Rabbi Dov Karoll
Rabbi Yaakov Komisar
Rabbi Adin Krohn
Rabbi Jason Leib
Sally Mayer
Rabbi Jonathan Mishkin
Rabbi Noam Shapiro
Rabbi Michael Siev
Rabbi David Strauss

Copy Editors

Aliza Israel, *Coordinator*
Bracha Hermon
Shira Finson
Ita Olesker
Nechama Unterman

Language Consultants

Dr. Stephanie E. Binder, *Greek & Latin*
Rabbi Yaakov Hoffman, *Arabic*
Dr. Shai Secunda, *Persian*
Shira Shmidman, *Aramaic*

KOREN

Design & Typesetting

Raphaël Freeman, *Design & Typesetting*
Dena Landowne Bailey, *Typesetting*
Tani Bayer, *Jacket Design*

Images

Eliahu Misgav, *Illustration*
Yehudit Cohen, *Image Acquisition*

Digital Edition

Raphaël Freeman, *Team Leader*
Eliyahu Skoczylas, *Senior Architect*
Tani Bayer, *User Interface Design*
Dena Landowne Bailey, *Concept*
Rabbi Hanan Benayahu, *Concept*
Laura Messinger, *Commercial Liaison*

Introduction by the Publisher

The Talmud has sustained and inspired Jews for thousands of years. Throughout Jewish history, an elite cadre of scholars has absorbed its learning and passed it on to succeeding generations. The Talmud has been the fundamental text of our people.

Beginning in the 1960s, Rabbi Adin Even-Israel Steinsaltz שליט״א created a revolution in the history of Talmud study. His translation of the Talmud, first into modern Hebrew and then into other languages, as well the practical learning aids he added to the text, have enabled millions of people around the world to access and master the complexity and context of the world of Talmud.

It is thus a privilege to present the *Koren Talmud Bavli*, an English translation of the talmudic text with the brilliant elucidation of Rabbi Steinsaltz. The depth and breadth of his knowledge are unique in our time. His rootedness in the tradition and his reach into the world beyond it are inspirational.

Working with Rabbi Steinsaltz on this remarkable project has been not only an honor, but a great pleasure. Never shy to express an opinion, with wisdom and humor, Rabbi Steinsaltz sparkles in conversation, demonstrating his knowledge (both sacred and worldly), sharing his wide-ranging interests, and, above all, radiating his passion. I am grateful for the unique opportunity to work closely with him, and I wish him many more years of writing and teaching.

Our intentions in publishing this new edition of the Talmud are threefold. First, we seek to fully clarify the talmudic page to the reader – textually, intellectually, and graphically. Second, we seek to utilize today's most sophisticated technologies, both in print and electronic formats, to provide the reader with a comprehensive set of study tools. And third, we seek to help readers advance in their process of Talmud study.

To achieve these goals, the *Koren Talmud Bavli* is unique in a number of ways:

- The classic *tzurat hadaf* of Vilna, used by scholars since the 1800s, has been reset for great clarity, and opens from the Hebrew "front" of the book. Full *nikkud* has been added to both the talmudic text and Rashi's commentary, allowing for a more fluent reading with the correct pronunciation; the commentaries of *Tosafot* have been punctuated. Upon the advice of many English-speaking teachers of Talmud, we have separated these core pages from the translation, thereby enabling the advanced student to approach the text without the distraction of the translation. This also reduces the number of volumes in the set. At bottom of each *daf*, there is a reference to the corresponding English pages. In addition, the Vilna edition was read against other manuscripts and older print editions, so that texts which had been removed by non-Jewish censors have been restored to their rightful place.
- The English translation, which starts on the English "front" of the book, reproduces the *menukad* Talmud text alongside the English translation (in bold) and commentary and explanation (in a lighter font). The Hebrew and Aramaic text is presented in logical paragraphs. This allows for a fluent reading of the text for the non-Hebrew or non-Aramaic reader. It also allows for the Hebrew reader to refer easily to the text alongside. Where the original text features dialogue or poetry, the English text is laid out in a manner appropriate to the genre. Each page refers to the relevant *daf*.

- Critical contextual tools surround the text and translation: personality notes, providing short biographies of the Sages; language notes, explaining foreign terms borrowed from Greek, Latin, Persian, or Arabic; and background notes, giving information essential to the understanding of the text, including history, geography, botany, archaeology, zoology, astronomy, and aspects of daily life in the talmudic era.
- Halakhic summaries provide references to the authoritative legal decisions made over the centuries by the rabbis. They explain the reasons behind each halakhic decision as well as the ruling's close connection to the Talmud and its various interpreters.
- Photographs, drawings, and other illustrations have been added throughout the text – in full color in the Standard and Electronic editions, and in black and white in the Daf Yomi edition – to visually elucidate the text.

This is not an exhaustive list of features of this edition, it merely presents an overview for the English-speaking reader who may not be familiar with the "total approach" to Talmud pioneered by Rabbi Steinsaltz.

Several professionals have helped bring this vast collaborative project to fruition. My many colleagues are noted on the Acknowledgements page, and the leadership of this project has been exceptional.

RABBI MENACHEM EVEN-ISRAEL, DIRECTOR OF THE STEINSALTZ CENTER, was the driving force behind this enterprise. With enthusiasm and energy, he formed the happy alliance with Koren and established close relationships among all involved in the work.

RABBI DR. TZVI HERSH WEINREB שליט"א, EDITOR-IN-CHIEF, brought to this project his profound knowledge of Torah, intellectual literacy of Talmud, and erudition of Western literature. It is to him that the text owes its very high standard, both in form and content, and the logical manner in which the beauty of the Talmud is presented.

RABBI JOSHUA SCHREIER, EXECUTIVE EDITOR, assembled an outstanding group of scholars, translators, editors, and proofreaders, whose standards and discipline enabled this project to proceed in a timely and highly professional manner.

RABBI MEIR HANEGBI, EDITOR OF THE HEBREW EDITION OF THE STEINSALTZ TALMUD, lent his invaluable assistance throughout the work process, supervising the reproduction of the Vilna pages.

RAPHAËL FREEMAN, EDITOR OF KOREN, created this Talmud's unique typographic design which, true to the Koren approach, is both elegant and user friendly.

It has been an enriching experience for all of us at Koren Publishers Jerusalem to work with the Steinsaltz Center to develop and produce the Koren Talmud Bavli. We pray that this publication will be a source of great learning and, ultimately, greater *avodat Hashem* for all Jews.

Matthew Miller, Publisher
Koren Publishers Jerusalem
Jerusalem 5772

Contents

Shabbat Part Six **183**

Image Credits **310**

For the vocalized Vilna Shas layout, please open as a Hebrew book.

Introduction to **Perek XVI**

This chapter mainly deals with a single question: How is one to conduct oneself when a fire breaks out on Shabbat? The *halakha* maintains that it is prohibited to extinguish a fire on Shabbat, even in a situation of great financial loss. Therefore, the question arises: What is permissible to do in the case of a fire? Under what conditions is it permissible to rescue materials from a fire on Shabbat?

The decrees instituted by the Sages with reference to rescuing objects from a fire on Shabbat are the source of many of the questions pertaining to this matter. These decrees are based upon the concern that if one is permitted to evacuate his goods, he may, in his panic, perform the kind of extinguishing that is biblically prohibited, both because of his preoccupation with the act of evacuation and because people become panicked when their property is at stake. Therefore, the Sages permitted the rescue of domestic utensils and even foodstuffs in only limited quantities. Additionally, there is discussion of the numerous details related to permissible methods and stratagems that enable the rescue of more than the very minimum fixed by the law.

Another question related to rescuing materials from a fire is the problem of sacred writings and other holy objects. Because of their sanctity, the Sages permitted many procedures for rescuing them that may not be performed for other objects. According to many opinions, the Sages went to great extremes to grant permission in this matter, ruling leniently even when there are risks of violating rabbinic prohibitions, and sometimes even biblical prohibitions, because of their great concern for salvaging a wide variety of sacred materials.

The detailed explication of what one is permitted to and prohibited to rescue from a fire on Shabbat, the enumeration of the types of holy objects that are worthy of rescue, and guidelines for how to conduct oneself in the event of a fire are the main topics of this chapter.

Incidentally, as is typical of talmudic discourse, there are discussions of other subjects related to the chapter's central theme.

מתני׳ כׇּל כִּתְבֵי הַקֹּדֶשׁ מַצִּילִין אוֹתָן מִפְּנֵי הַדְּלֵיקָה, בֵּין שֶׁקּוֹרִין בָּהֶן וּבֵין שֶׁאֵין קוֹרִין בָּהֶן. אַף עַל פִּי שֶׁכְּתוּבִים בְּכׇל לָשׁוֹן טְעוּנִים גְּנִיזָה. וּמִפְּנֵי מָה אֵין קוֹרִין בָּהֶם – מִפְּנֵי בִּיטּוּל בֵּית הַמִּדְרָשׁ.

MISHNA With regard to **all sacred writings, one may rescue them from the fire**[N] on Shabbat, **whether they are read** in public, e.g., Torah or Prophets scrolls, **or whether they are not read** in public, e.g., Writings scrolls. This ruling applies **even though they were written in any** foreign **language.** According to the Rabbis, those scrolls are not read in public, but they are still sacred and require burial.[H] **And why** does **one not read** the Writings on Shabbat? **Due to suspension** of Torah study **in the study hall.**[N] People came to the study hall at specific times on Shabbat to hear words of *halakha*, and other texts were not allowed at those times.

גמ׳ אִיתְּמַר: הָיוּ כְּתוּבִים תַּרְגּוּם אוֹ בְּכׇל לָשׁוֹן, רַב הוּנָא אָמַר: אֵין מַצִּילִין אוֹתָן מִפְּנֵי הַדְּלֵיקָה, וְרַב חִסְדָּא אָמַר: מַצִּילִין אוֹתָן מִפְּנֵי הַדְּלֵיקָה. אַלִּיבָּא דְּמַאן דְּאָמַר ״נִיתְּנוּ לִקְרוֹת בָּהֶן״ – דְּכוּלֵּי עָלְמָא לָא פְּלִיגִי דְּמַצִּילִין. כִּי פְּלִיגִי – אַלִּיבָּא דְּמַאן דְּאָמַר ״לֹא נִיתְּנוּ לִקְרוֹת בָּהֶן״. רַב הוּנָא אָמַר: אֵין מַצִּילִין – דְּהָא לֹא נִיתְּנוּ לִקְרוֹת בָּהֶן, רַב חִסְדָּא אָמַר: מַצִּילִין – מִשּׁוּם בִּזְיוֹן כִּתְבֵי הַקֹּדֶשׁ. תְּנַן: כׇּל כִּתְבֵי הַקֹּדֶשׁ מַצִּילִין אוֹתָן מִפְּנֵי הַדְּלֵיקָה, בֵּין שֶׁקּוֹרִין בָּהֶן בֵּין שֶׁאֵין קוֹרִין בָּהֶן, אַף עַל פִּי שֶׁכְּתוּבִין בְּכׇל לָשׁוֹן. מַאי לָאו ״שֶׁקּוֹרִין בָּהֶן״ – נְבִיאִים, וְ״שֶׁאֵין קוֹרִין בָּהֶן״ – כְּתוּבִים, אַף עַל פִּי שֶׁכְּתוּבִין בְּכׇל לָשׁוֹן, דְּלֹא נִיתְּנוּ לִקְרוֹת בָּהֶן, וְקָתָנֵי ״מַצִּילִין״, וּתְיוּבְתָּא דְּרַב הוּנָא!

GEMARA It was stated that *amora'im* debated the status of sacred writings **written in** Aramaic **translation or in any** other **language. Rav Huna said: One may not rescue them from the fire** on Shabbat. **And Rav Ḥisda said: One may rescue them from the fire** on Shabbat. The Gemara adds: **According to the one who said** that sacred writings written in other languages **may be read, everybody** agrees that **one may rescue** them. **Where they argue** is **according to the one who said that they may not be read.**[N] **Rav Huna said: One may not rescue** them, **as they may not be read.** Whereas **Rav Ḥisda said: One may rescue** them **due to disgrace to sacred writings** that will result. **We learned** in the mishna: With regard to **all sacred writings, one may rescue them from the fire** on Shabbat **whether they are read** in public **or whether they are not read** in public, **even if they are written in any** foreign **language. What, is it not** that the phrase: **"That they are read"** is referring to the books of the **Prophets, and** the phrase: **"That they are not read"** is referring to the **Writings? Even though these are** books **written in any** foreign **language, which may not be read, it is taught that one may save them.** This then is **a conclusive refutation of** the opinion of **Rav Huna.**

אָמַר לָךְ רַב הוּנָא: וְתִסְבְּרָא?! אֵימָא סֵיפָא: טְעוּנִין גְּנִיזָה. הַשְׁתָּא אַצּוֹלֵי מַצִּילִינַן, גְּנִיזָה מִיבָּעֵי?! אֶלָּא, רַב הוּנָא מְתָרֵץ לְטַעְמֵיהּ, וְרַב חִסְדָּא מְתָרֵץ לְטַעְמֵיהּ. רַב הוּנָא מְתָרֵץ לְטַעְמֵיהּ: בֵּין שֶׁקּוֹרִין בָּהֶם – נְבִיאִים, וּבֵין שֶׁאֵין קוֹרִין בָּהֶם – כְּתוּבִים, בַּמֶּה דְּבָרִים אֲמוּרִים – שֶׁכְּתוּבִין בִּלְשׁוֹן הַקֹּדֶשׁ, אֲבָל בְּכׇל לָשׁוֹן – אֵין מַצִּילִין, וַאֲפִילּוּ הָכִי – גְּנִיזָה בָּעוּ. רַב חִסְדָּא מְתָרֵץ לְטַעְמֵיהּ: בֵּין שֶׁקּוֹרִין בָּהֶן – נְבִיאִים, וּבֵין שֶׁאֵין קוֹרִין בָּהֶן – כְּתוּבִים, אַף עַל פִּי שֶׁכְּתוּבִין בְּכׇל לָשׁוֹן – נַמִי מַצִּילִין, וְהָכִי קָאָמַר: וּמֶקֶק שֶׁלָּהֶן טְעוּנִין גְּנִיזָה.

Rav Huna could have **said to you: And** do **you understand** the mishna that way? **Say the latter clause** of the mishna, which states: They **require burial.** This is unnecessary, as **now,** that it was mentioned that **we rescue them** from the fire, **is it necessary** to say that they require **burial? Rather,** the mishna must be emended. **Rav Huna reconciles** the mishna **in accordance with his reasoning, and Rav Ḥisda reconciles** the mishna **in accordance with his reasoning. Rav Huna reconciles** this **in accordance with his reasoning: Whether they are read** is referring to the **Prophets, and whether they are not read** is referring to the **Writings. In what** case **is this statement said? It is** in a case **where they are written in the holy tongue, but** if they are not written in Hebrew but **in any** other **language,** they are **not rescued** from the fire on Shabbat, **and even so, they require burial. Rav Ḥisda reconciles** the mishna **in accordance with his reasoning: Whether they are read** is referring to the **Prophets, and whether they are not read** is referring to the **Writings, even if they are written in any language** other than Hebrew, they are **also rescued. And this is what** the mishna **is saying: And even the decayed** sections of parchment **require burial.**

NOTES

One may rescue them from the fire – מַצִּילִין אוֹתָן מִפְּנֵי הַדְּלֵיקָה: In the Jerusalem Talmud it is explained that the *halakha* is in accordance with Rabbi Shimon's opinion that, in general, extinguishing a fire is prohibited by rabbinic and not by Torah law. Therefore, it is permitted to douse a fire in order to rescue sacred books.

Suspension of Torah study in the study hall – בִּיטּוּל בֵּית הַמִּדְרָשׁ: In the Jerusalem Talmud it is stated, and Rabbi Neḥemya stated below, that the decree against reading the Writings on Shabbat was issued to underscore the sanctity of the day. If one is prohibited to read the sacred Writings, people will certainly refrain from reading other books, contracts, and additional business documents.

They may not be read – לֹא נִיתְּנוּ לִקְרוֹת בָּהֶן: It is a matter of dispute whether or not sacred writings translated from Hebrew into other languages may be read in public. Some *tanna'im* held that it is permitted to read the Greek translation of the Torah in public. However, the translations of other books of the Bible may neither be written nor read in public.

HALAKHA

Burying sacred writings – גְּנִיזַת כִּתְבֵי קֹדֶשׁ: Scrolls of the sacred writings that have become worn must be treated with proper respect. Consequently, they are not thrown into the garbage, but are buried. Books of *halakha* and *aggada* are included in the category of sacred writings. Once they were allowed to be written, their status is that of sacred writings in this regard (*Tosafot*; Rambam *Sefer Ahava, Hilkhot Tefillin UMezuza VeSefer Torah* 10:3; *Shulḥan Arukh, Yoreh De'a* 282:5).

BACKGROUND

Translations of the Bible – תַּרְגּוּמֵי הַמִּקְרָא:

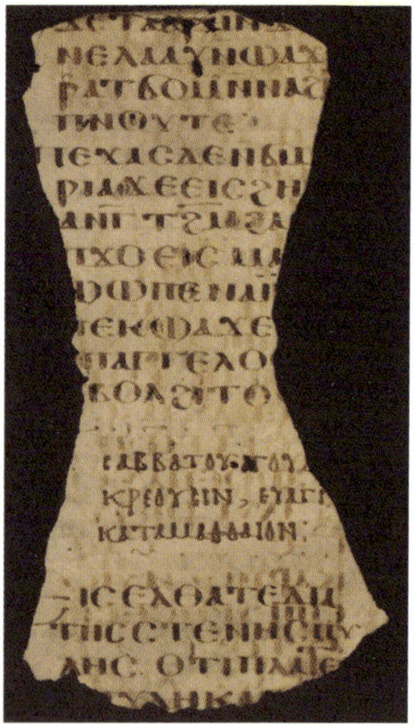

Section of the Bible translated into Coptic, from the talmudic period

Section of the Bible in ancient Hebrew script, from the Dead Sea Scrolls

Section of the Bible translated into Judeo-Greek, Second Temple period

מֵיתִיבִי: הָיוּ כְּתוּבִים תַּרְגּוּם וְכָל לָשׁוֹן מַצִּילִין אוֹתָן מִפְּנֵי הַדְּלֵיקָה, תְּיוּבְתָּא דְּרַב הוּנָא! אָמַר לָךְ רַב הוּנָא: הַאי תַּנָּא סָבַר נִיתְּנוּ לִקְרוֹת בָּהֶן. תָּא שְׁמַע: הָיוּ כְּתוּבִין גִּיפְטִית, מָדִית, עִיבְרִית, עֵילָמִית, יְוָנִית, אַף עַל פִּי שֶׁלֹּא נִיתְּנוּ לִקְרוֹת בָּהֶן – מַצִּילִין אוֹתָן מִפְּנֵי הַדְּלֵיקָה, תְּיוּבְתָּא דְּרַב הוּנָא! אָמַר לָךְ רַב הוּנָא: תַּנָּאֵי הִיא; דְּתַנְיָא: הָיוּ כְּתוּבִין תַּרְגּוּם וּבְכָל לָשׁוֹן – מַצִּילִין אוֹתָן מִפְּנֵי הַדְּלֵיקָה, רַבִּי יוֹסֵי אוֹמֵר: אֵין מַצִּילִין אוֹתָן מִפְּנֵי הַדְּלֵיקָה.

The Gemara **raises an objection** from that which was taught in a *baraita*: If **they were written in** Aramaic **translation** or in **any language**[H] other than Hebrew, **they are rescued from the fire** on Shabbat. And this is a **conclusive refutation** of the opinion of **Rav Huna,** who states that these are not rescued. **Rav Huna** could have **said to you: This *tanna* holds** that sacred writings not written in Hebrew **may not be read,** whereas Rav Huna holds in accordance with the opinion of the *tanna* who holds that they may be read and therefore may be rescued. **Come** and **hear** another proof from that which was taught in a different *baraita*: Sacred writings that **were written** in **Coptic,** Egyptian; **Median;** *Ivrit*, i.e., ancient Hebrew script; **Eilamitic;** or **Greek**[B] **are rescued from the fire** on Shabbat, **even though they may not be read.** This is a **conclusive refutation** of the opinion of **Rav Huna,** who holds that they are not rescued. **Rav Huna** could have **said to you: This is** a dispute between ***tanna'im*, as it was taught** in a *baraita*: If **they were written in** Aramaic **translation or in any language** other than Hebrew, **one may rescue them from the fire** on Shabbat. **Rabbi Yosei says: One may not rescue them from the fire.**

אָמַר רַבִּי יוֹסֵי: מַעֲשֶׂה בְּאַבָּא חֲלַפְתָּא שֶׁהָלַךְ אֵצֶל רַבָּן גַּמְלִיאֵל בְּרִיבִּי לְטִבֶרְיָא, וּמְצָאוֹ שֶׁהָיָה יוֹשֵׁב עַל שֻׁלְחָנוֹ שֶׁל (יוֹחָנָן הַנָּזוּף) וּבְיָדוֹ סֵפֶר אִיּוֹב תַּרְגּוּם וְהוּא קוֹרֵא בּוֹ. אָמַר לוֹ: זָכוּר אֲנִי בְּרַבָּן גַּמְלִיאֵל אֲבִי אָבִיךָ שֶׁהָיָה עוֹמֵד עַל גַּבֵּי מַעֲלָה בְּהַר הַבַּיִת, וְהֵבִיאוּ לְפָנָיו סֵפֶר אִיּוֹב תַּרְגּוּם, וְאָמַר לַבַּנַּאי: שַׁקְּעֵהוּ תַּחַת הַנִּדְבָּךְ! אַף הוּא צִוָּה עָלָיו וּגְנָזוֹ. רַבִּי יוֹסֵי בְּרַבִּי יְהוּדָה אוֹמֵר: עֲרֵיבָה שֶׁל טִיט כָּפוּ עָלָיו. אָמַר רַבִּי: שְׁתֵּי תְשׁוּבוֹת בַּדָּבָר, חֲדָא – וְכִי טִיט בְּהַר הַבַּיִת מִנַּיִן?! וְעוֹד: וְכִי מוּתָּר לְאַבְּדָן בַּיָּד?! אֶלָּא: מַנִּיחָן בִּמְקוֹם הַתּוּרְפָּה, וְהֵן מַרְקִיבִין מֵאֲלֵיהֶן. מַאן תַּנָּאֵי?

Rabbi Yosei said: There was **an incident involving** my **father, Ḥalafta, who went to the esteemed Rabban Gamliel** of Yavne in **Tiberias, where he found him sitting at the table of Yoḥanan HaNazuf and in his hand** there was **a translation of the book of Job, and he was reading** from **it.** Yoḥanan **said to** Rabban Gamliel of Yavne: **I remember Rabban Gamliel, your father's father, who was standing on top of a step on the Temple Mount. And they brought before him a translation of the book of Job, and he said to the builder: Bury this** book **under the course of bricks.** When he heard of that incident, Rabban Gamliel of Yavne **ordered that it** be buried **and he buried it.**[N] **Rabbi Yosei, son of Rabbi Yehuda, says** that on the Temple Mount **they overturned a large bowl of mortar on it. Rabbi** Yehuda HaNasi **said:** There are **two responses to this** that prove that it did not happen: **One, from where would they get mortar on the Temple Mount?** Construction on the Temple Mount was performed with other materials, not with mortar. **And furthermore, is it permitted to** actively **destroy** even sacred writings that are not read, **with one's hands? Rather,** at the very least **they leave them in a neglected place,** where they are likely to decompose quickly, **and they decay on their own.** The Gemara seeks to clarify: **Who are the *tanna'im*** who dispute this *halakha* according to Rav Huna?

HALAKHA

If they were written in Aramaic translation or in any language – הָיוּ כְּתוּבִים תַּרְגּוּם אוֹ בְּכָל לָשׁוֹן: Sacred writings written in any language must be rescued from fire on Shabbat. In contemporary times, when writing and printing the Oral Torah is permitted, all those texts are significant and are rescued from a fire. The dispute between Rabbi Huna and Rabbi Ḥisda took place in an era when the Oral Law was not written, and if it was, it was prohibited to read or study these writings (*Tosafot*; Rosh; Ran; *Shulḥan Arukh, Oraḥ Ḥayyim* 334:12).

NOTES

Burial of the book of Job – גְּנִיזַת תַּרְגּוּם אִיּוֹב: The translation of the book of Job was buried not because it was flawed; rather, because initially it was one of those matters that was supposed to remain unwritten. Writing it would be in violation of the decree prohibiting writing oral matters. Although it was not prohibited to translate Job orally or even to standardize that translation, writing it was only permitted much later.

אילימא תנא קמא דרבי יוסי – ודילמא בהא קמיפלגי, מר סבר: ניתנו לקרות בהן, ומר סבר: לא ניתנו לקרות בהן. אלא: רבי יוסי ותנא דגיפטית.

If we say it is the **first *tanna*** who disagrees with **Rabbi Yosei,** that is not necessarily so, **and perhaps they are disagreeing about this: This Master,** the first *tanna,* **holds** that books written in other languages **may be read; and this Master,** Rabbi Yosei, **holds** that **they may not be read,** and their dispute is unrelated to the dispute between Rav Huna and Rav Ḥisda. **Rather,** it is the dispute between **Rabbi Yosei** and **the** first ***tanna,*** who spoke **about** books written in **Coptic.** According to that *tanna,* even books that may not be read are rescued, whereas Rabbi Yosei holds that they are not rescued.

תנו רבנן: הברכות והקמיעין אף על פי שיש בהן אותיות של שם, ומעניינות הרבה שבתורה – אין מצילין אותן מפני הדליקה, אלא נשרפים במקומן [הן ואזכרותיהן]. מכאן אמרו: כותבי ברכות כשורפי תורה. מעשה באחד שהיה כותב בצידן, באו והודיעו את רבי ישמעאל, והלך רבי ישמעאל לבודקו. כשהיה עולה בסולם הרגיש בו, נטל טומוס של ברכות ושיקען בספל של מים. ובלשון הזה אמר לו רבי ישמעאל: גדול עונש האחרון מן הראשון.

The Sages taught in a *baraita:* **The blessings** that are written **and the amulets,**[H] **even though there are the letters of the Name** of God **in them** and **matters that** appear **in the Torah** are mentioned in them, they **are not rescued from the fire; rather, they burn in their place, they and the names** of God contained therein. **From here** the Sages **said: Writers of blessings** are **like burners of Torah** scrolls, as it is prohibited to rescue these texts from the fire on Shabbat even though it is likely that they will be destroyed. There was **an incident involving one who was writing** pages with blessings[H] **in Sidon. They came and informed Rabbi Yishmael** of his actions, **and Rabbi Yishmael went to examine him** to determine if the report was true. **When** Rabbi Yishmael **was ascending the ladder** to confront him, the scribe **sensed his** presence, **took a bundle** [***tomos***][L] **of blessings, and submerged it in a basin of water** to conceal it from Rabbi Yishmael. **And in these words Rabbi Yishmael said to him:** The **punishment** for **the latter** action is **greater than** the punishment for **the former.** Although it is prohibited to write blessings, destroying them is a greater violation.

בעא מיניה ריש גלותא מרבה בר רב הונא: היו כתובין בסם ובסיקרא בקומוס ובקנקנתום בלשון הקדש, מצילין אותן מפני הדליקה או אין מצילין? תיבעי למאן דאמר "מצילין", תיבעי למאן דאמר "אין מצילין". תיבעי למאן דאמר "אין מצילין"; הני מילי – היכא דכתיבי תרגום ובכל לשון, אבל הכא דכתיבי בלשון הקדש – מצילין. או דילמא: אפילו למאן דאמר "מצילין" – הני מילי – היכא דכתיבי בדיו, דמיקיים. אבל הכא, כיון דלא מיקיים – לא? אמר ליה: אין מצילין. והא רב המנונא תנא "מצילין"! אמר ליה: אי תניא – תניא. מאי תניא? אמר רב אשי, כדתניא: אין בין ספרים למגילה אלא שהספרים נכתבים בכל לשון, ומגילה עד שתהא כתובה אשורית, על הספר ובדיו.

The Exilarch raised a dilemma before Rabba bar Rav Huna: If the sacred scrolls **were written in** yellow-tinged **arsenic, or red paint, in gum, or in copper sulfate,**[H] types of ink which may not be used to write Torah scrolls; however, the scrolls were written properly **in the holy tongue,** does **one rescue them from the fire** on Shabbat **or does one not rescue** them? The Gemara adds: This **dilemma is raised according to the one who said** that **one rescues** sacred writings written in other languages; and this **dilemma is raised according to the one who said** that **one does not rescue** them. The Gemara elaborates. This **dilemma is raised according to the one who said** that **one does not rescue** them: Perhaps **that** applies specifically in a case **where** they **are written in** Aramaic **translation and in any** foreign **language; however, here, where they are written in the holy tongue, one rescues** them. **Or perhaps even according to the one who said** that **one rescues** them, **that applies** specifically in a case **where** they **are written in ink that endures; however, here,** since the script **does not endure,**[N] they are **not** rescued. Rabba bar Rav Huna **said to him: One does not rescue them.** The Exilarch said to him: **Didn't Rav Hamnuna teach** in a *baraita* **that one saves them.** Rabba bar Rav Huna **said to him: If it was taught** in a *baraita,* **it was taught,**[N] and I retract my statement. The Gemara asks: **What** is the *baraita* that **was taught** on this matter? **Rav Ashi said, as it was taught** in a *baraita:* **The only** difference **between the books** of the Bible **and the Megilla** of Esther **is that** the **books are written in any language** and are valid, **and the Megilla** is only valid **if it is written in Assyrian script,**[H] the familiar square Hebrew script, **on a** parchment **scroll, and in ink.** Apparently, other sacred books need not be written in ink.

HALAKHA

And the amulets – וְהַקְּמֵיעִין: There is a difference of opinion with regard to rescuing amulets from a fire on Shabbat that were written for a sick person whose life is not in danger (*Mishna Berura*). Some authorities hold that it is prohibited to write amulets at all, and they are therefore not rescued, even in modern times (Rashba). Other commentaries assert that just as it was permitted write blessings, so too were amulets permitted (*Tur*), and they are therefore rescued. Later authorities ruled in accordance with the first opinion (*Baḥ*; Maharshal; Rambam *Sefer Zemanim, Hilkhot Shabbat* 23:27; *Shulḥan Arukh, Oraḥ Ḥayyim* 334:14).

Rescuing pages with blessings – הַצָּלַת טוֹפְסֵי בְּרָכוֹת: In modern times, when it is permitted to write the Oral Torah, all sacred writings are rescued from the fire on Shabbat. Therefore, pages with the blessings that the Sages instituted for daily recitation are also rescued (Rambam *Sefer Zemanim, Hilkhot Shabbat* 23:27; *Shulḥan Arukh, Oraḥ Ḥayyim* 334:12).

Scrolls that are written not with black ink – סְפָרִים הַכְּתוּבִים שֶׁלֹּא בִּדְיוֹ: Sacred books in the Hebrew language, in Assyrian script (Rambam), even though they are not written with black ink, are rescued from fire on Shabbat (Rambam *Sefer Zemanim, Hilkhot Shabbat* 23:27; *Shulḥan Arukh, Oraḥ Ḥayyim* 334:12).

The Megilla is only valid if it is written in Assyrian script – וּמְגִילָּה עַד שֶׁתְּהֵא כְּתוּבָה אַשּׁוּרִית: A Megilla is only valid if it is written on parchment or hide that was treated with gallnuts in black ink, like a Torah scroll. If it was written with copper sulfate ink, it is valid after the fact (Rambam *Sefer Zemanim, Hilkhot Megilla* 2:9; *Shulḥan Arukh, Oraḥ Ḥayyim* 691:1).

LANGUAGE

Bundle [*tomos*] – טוֹמוֹס: From the Greek τόμος, *tomos,* meaning part of a book, a tome, or a volume.

NOTES

Since the script does not endure – כֵּיוָן דְּלָא מִיקַּיֵּים: The Sages determined that writing with a quill and copper sulfate is a full-fledged act of writing on Shabbat, because it endures, as opposed to writing with fruit juice, which does not. Nevertheless, there is a distinction between the *halakhot* of Shabbat and the *halakhot* governing the writing of a Torah scroll. On Shabbat, a significant labor is required, and writing that endures, even temporarily, meets that criterion. However, a Torah scroll must be written in a manner that ensures that the writing will endure for a long time (Rashba).

If it was taught, it was taught – אִי תַּנְיָא תַּנְיָא: This expression appears throughout the Talmud and usually indicates that a Sage who heard the *baraita* consequently reconsidered his own statement. Another explanation of this phrase is that the Sage is saying: I heard this *halakha* from my rabbi and I stand by it. However, other Sages are free to rule in accordance with the *baraita* (Rashi in tractate *Nidda*).

HALAKHA

Which books are rescued from the fire on Shabbat – אלו ספרים מצילין מן הדליקה בשבת: A book that is an aggregate of eighty-five letters in complete words or that has the name of God written in it must be rescued from a fire on Shabbat. The *halakha* is in accordance with the opinion of Rav Huna, who was greater than Rav Ḥisda. In modern times, even translations of the Bible are rescued, as are all sacred books (Rambam *Sefer Zemanim, Hilkhot Shabbat* 23:28; *Shulḥan Arukh, Oraḥ Ḥayyim* 334:12).

BACKGROUND

Signs – סימניות:

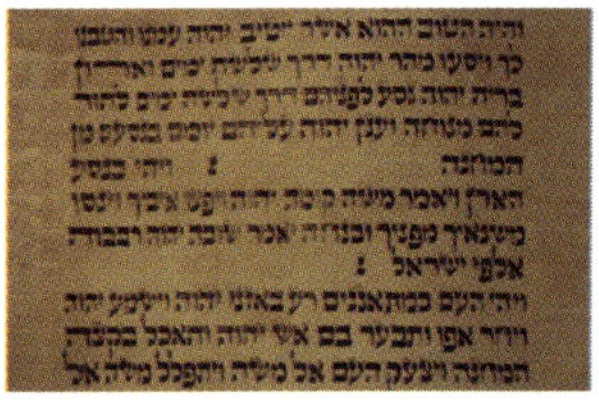

Portion of "And when the Ark traveled" (Numbers 10:35) as it appears in a Torah scroll with signs before and after it

בעא מיניה רב הונא בר חלוב מרב נחמן: ספר תורה שאין בו ללקט שמונים וחמש אותיות, כגון פרשת "ויהי בנסע הארון" מצילין אותה מפני הדליקה, או אין מצילין? אמר ליה: ותיבעי לך פרשת "ויהי בנסע הארון" גופה! היכא דחסר פרשת "ויהי בנסע" – לא קמיבעיא לי, דכיון דאית ביה הזכרות, אף על גב דלית ביה שמונים וחמש אותיות – מצילין. כי קא מיבעיא לי – ספר תורה שאין בו ללקט, מאי? אמר ליה: אין מצילין.

Rav Huna bar Ḥaluv raised a dilemma before Rav Naḥman: With regard to **a Torah scroll in which there is not** enough **to compile** from it **eighty-five** complete **letters** written properly and in order, which is the minimum measure determined by the Sages for a Torah to maintain the sanctity of a Torah scroll, **as in the portion of: "And when the Ark traveled"** (Numbers 10:35–36), **does one rescue it from the fire** on Shabbat **or does one not rescue** it? Rav Naḥman **said to him: And raise a dilemma** with regard to **the portion of: "And when the Ark traveled," itself,** i.e., does one rescue it on Shabbat if it is missing a single letter? Rav Huna bar Ḥaluv answered: In a case **where the portion of: "And when the Ark traveled," is incomplete, it is not a dilemma for me, as since it contains names** of God, **even though there are not eighty-five letters in it, it is rescued.** However, the case **where it is a dilemma for me is** with regard to **a Torah scroll in which there is not** enough **to compile** from it eighty-five complete letters; **what** is the ruling? Is it rescued on Shabbat or not?[H] Rav Naḥman **said to him: It is not rescued.**

איתיביה: תרגום שכתבו מקרא, ומקרא שכתבו תרגום, וכתב עברית – מצילין מפני הדליקה; ואין צריך לומר תרגום שבעזרא ושבדניאל ושבתורה. תרגום שבתורה מאי ניהו – "יגר שהדותא" – ואף על גב דלית בה שמונים וחמש אותיות, כי תניא ההיא – להשלים.

Rav Huna bar Ḥaluv **raised an objection to his** opinion from that which we learned: A verse that is originally written in Aramaic **translation that was written** in the language of **the Bible, and** a verse that is originally written in the language of **the Bible that was written** in Aramaic **translation, and** a Torah that was written in ancient **Hebrew script, one rescues** them **from the fire** on Shabbat. **And, needless to say,** one saves the verses written in Aramaic **translation that are in** the book of **Ezra, and that are in** the book of **Daniel, and that are in the Torah. What are the** verses originally written in Aramaic **translation in the Torah?** It is the verse: "And Laban called it **Yegar Sahaduta,** and Jacob called it Gal Ed" (Genesis 31:47), **and** apparently, it is rescued, **even though there are not eighty-five letters in it.** Rav Naḥman answered him: That is no proof, as **when that** *baraita* **was taught,** it was in a case where the Aramaic verse is counted **to complete** the total of eighty-five letters, but it is not independently significant.

איבעיא להו: הני שמונים וחמש אותיות, מכונסות או מפוזרות? רב הונא אמר: מכונסות. רב חסדא אמר: אפילו מפוזרות. מיתיבי: ספר תורה שבלה, אם יש בו ללקט שמונים וחמש אותיות, כגון פרשת "ויהי בנסע הארון" – מצילין, ואם לאו – אין מצילין. תיובתא דרב הונא! תרגמה רב חסדא אליבא דרב הונא – בתיבות.

A dilemma was raised before the Sages: With regard to **these eighty-five letters** that allow one to rescue a Torah scroll, is that specifically when they **are juxtaposed, or** even when they are **scattered? Rav Huna said:** Only when they are **juxtaposed. Rav Ḥisda said: Even** when they are **scattered.** The Gemara **raises an objection** from that which we learned: With regard to **a Torah scroll that is worn, if there is** enough **to compile** from it **eighty-five** complete **letters as in the portion of: "And when the Ark traveled," one rescues** it from the fire, **and if not one does not rescue** it. The term: To compile, indicates that the letters are not juxtaposed, and this is a **conclusive refutation** of the opinion of **Rav Huna. Rav Ḥisda interpreted** it **according to** the opinion **of Rav Huna:** Indeed, the *baraita* is referring to a case where the letters are scattered, but they are juxtaposed **in** the form of **words.** In that case, even Rav Huna agrees that it is a sacred book. Rav Huna and Rav Ḥisda only disagree in a case where isolated letters are scattered.

תנו רבנן: "ויהי בנסע הארן ויאמר משה" פרשה זו עשה לה הקדוש ברוך הוא סימניות מלמעלה ולמטה, לומר

Apropos the portion: "And when the Ark traveled," the Gemara cites that which **the Sages taught** in a *baraita*. It is stated: **"And when the Ark traveled and Moses proclaimed:** Rise up, God, and Your enemies will scatter and those who hate You will flee from before You." **And The Holy One, Blessed be He, made signs**[B] in the Torah **for this portion, above and below,** i.e., before and after it, in order **to say**

Perek **XVI**
Daf **116** Amud **a**

שאין זה מקומה. רבי אומר: לא מן השם הוא זה, אלא מפני שספר חשוב הוא בפני עצמו.

that this is not its place, as the previous portion does not discuss the nation's travels. **Rabbi** Yehuda HaNasi **says: It is not for that** reason that signs were inserted. **Rather,** the signs are there **because** this portion **is considered a book unto itself.**

כְּמַאן אָזְלָא הָא דְּאָמַר רַבִּי שְׁמוּאֵל בַּר נַחְמָן אָמַר רַבִּי יוֹנָתָן: ״חָצְבָה עַמּוּדֶיהָ שִׁבְעָה״ – אֵלּוּ שִׁבְעָה סִפְרֵי תוֹרָה. כְּמַאן – כְּרַבִּי.

The Gemara asks: **According to whose** opinion is **that** which **Rabbi Shmuel bar Naḥman said** that **Rabbi Yonatan said,** that with regard to the verse: "With wisdom she built her house, **she carved its seven pillars"** (Proverbs 9:1), **these are the seven books of the Torah? According to whose** opinion? It is **according to** the opinion of **Rabbi** Yehuda HaNasi, as by his count there are seven books of the Torah: Genesis; Exodus; Leviticus; Numbers until: "And when the Ark traveled"; the portion: "And when the Ark traveled," which is considered its own book; the remainder of Numbers; and Deuteronomy.

מַאן תַּנָּא דִּפְלִיג עֲלֵיהּ דְּרַבִּי – רַבָּן שִׁמְעוֹן בֶּן גַּמְלִיאֵל הוּא, דְּתַנְיָא, רַבָּן שִׁמְעוֹן בֶּן גַּמְלִיאֵל אוֹמֵר: עֲתִידָה פָּרָשָׁה זוֹ שֶׁתֵּיעָקֵר מִכָּאן וְתִכָּתֵב בִּמְקוֹמָהּ. וְלָמָּה כְּתָבָהּ כָּאן – כְּדֵי לְהַפְסִיק בֵּין פּוּרְעָנוּת רִאשׁוֹנָה לְפוּרְעָנוּת שְׁנִיָּה. פּוּרְעָנוּת שְׁנִיָּה מַאי הִיא? ״וַיְהִי הָעָם כְּמִתְאוֹנְנִים״. פּוּרְעָנוּת רִאשׁוֹנָה – ״וַיִּסְעוּ מֵהַר ה׳״; וְאָמַר רַבִּי חָמָא בְּרַבִּי חֲנִינָא: שֶׁסָּרוּ מֵאַחֲרֵי ה׳. וְהֵיכָן מְקוֹמָהּ? אָמַר רַב אַשִׁי: בִּדְגָלִים.

Who is the **tanna who disagrees with Rabbi** Yehuda HaNasi? **It is Rabban Shimon ben Gamliel. As it was taught** in a *baraita* that **Rabban Shimon ben Gamliel says: In the future, this portion will be uprooted from here,** where it appears, **and will be written in its** proper **place. And why was it written here,** even though it discusses the travels of the children of Israel, and the portion before it does not? It is **in order to demarcate between the first punishment and the second punishment. What is the second punishment** that appears immediately afterward? It is the verse: **"And the people complained** wickedly in God's ears, and God heard and became angry, and the fire of God burned in them and it consumed the edge of the camp" (Numbers 11:1). What is **the first punishment?** It is the verse: **"And they traveled from the mountain of God** [*mehar Hashem*] for three days" (Numbers 10:33), **and Rabbi Ḥama, son of Rabbi Ḥanina, said: That they turned from after God** [*me'aḥarei Hashem*][N] and hurriedly fled Mount Sinai. The Gemara asks: **And** if so, **where is** the proper **place** for this paragraph? **Rav Ashi said: In** the portion of the **flags,** where there is a description of the manner in which the Jewish people traveled through the desert.

אִיבַּעְיָא לְהוּ: הַגִּלְיוֹנִין שֶׁל סֵפֶר תּוֹרָה מַצִּילִין אוֹתָן מִפְּנֵי הַדְּלֵיקָה, אוֹ אֵין מַצִּילִין אוֹתָן מִפְּנֵי הַדְּלֵיקָה? תָּא שְׁמַע: סֵפֶר תּוֹרָה שֶׁבָּלָה, אִם יֵשׁ בּוֹ לְלַקֵּט שְׁמוֹנִים וְחָמֵשׁ אוֹתִיּוֹת, כְּגוֹן פָּרָשַׁת ״וַיְהִי בִּנְסֹעַ הָאָרוֹן״ – מַצִּילִין, וְאִם לָאו – אֵין מַצִּילִין. וְאַמַּאי? תֵּיפוֹק לֵיהּ מִשּׁוּם גִּילָּיוֹן דִּידֵיהּ! בָּלָה שָׁאנֵי.

A dilemma was raised before the Sages: With regard to **the blank folios** of parchment **of a Torah scroll,** does **one rescue them from the fire** on Shabbat, **or** does **one not rescue them from the fire?**[H] **Come and hear** a resolution to this from that which we learned: With regard to **a Torah scroll that is worn, if there is** enough **in it to compile eighty-five** complete **letters as in the portion of: "And when the Ark traveled," one rescues** it from the fire, **and if not one does not rescue** it. If even the blank folios are rescued, **why** would one not rescue a Torah scroll with fewer than the requisite number of letters? **Derive** that this scroll may be rescued **due to its blank folios. The Gemara** answers: A Torah scroll that **is worn is different,** because at that point its sanctity is negated, and its blank folios are not sacred. Therefore, one may rescue the scroll only if it contains eighty-five letters.

תָּא שְׁמַע: סֵפֶר תּוֹרָה שֶׁנִּמְחַק, אִם יֵשׁ בּוֹ לְלַקֵּט שְׁמוֹנִים וְחָמֵשׁ אוֹתִיּוֹת, כְּגוֹן פָּרָשַׁת ״וַיְהִי בִּנְסֹעַ הָאָרוֹן״ – מַצִּילִין, וְאִם לָאו – אֵין מַצִּילִין. וְאַמַּאי?! תֵּיפוֹק לֵיהּ מִשּׁוּם גִּילָּיוֹן דִּידֵיהּ! מְקוֹם הַכְּתָב לָא קָמִיבַּעְיָא לִי, דְּכִי קָדוֹשׁ – אַגַּב כְּתָב הוּא דְּקָדוֹשׁ, אֲזַל כְּתָב – אָזְלָא לָהּ קְדוּשָּׁתֵיהּ. כִּי קָמִיבַּעְיָא לִי – שֶׁל מַעְלָה וְשֶׁל מַטָּה, שֶׁבֵּין פָּרָשָׁה לְפָרָשָׁה, שֶׁבֵּין דַּף לְדַף, שֶׁבִּתְחִלַּת הַסֵּפֶר שֶׁבְּסוֹף הַסֵּפֶר. וְתֵיפוֹק לֵיהּ מִשּׁוּם הַהוּא! דְּגַיְיז וּשְׁדִי.

Come and hear a different resolution from that which was taught in another *baraita*: With regard to **a Torah scroll that was erased, if there is** enough **in it to compile eighty-five** complete **letters as in the portion of: "And when the Ark traveled," one rescues** it from the fire, **and if not, one does not rescue** it. **And why** is that so? **Derive** that this scroll may be rescued **due to its blank folios,** as the erased section is surely no less significant than the blank folios of the scroll. The Gemara answers: That is not so. In a case where **the place of the writing** is erased **it is not a dilemma for me, as it is sacred due to** the **writing.** If the **writing is gone, its sanctity is gone. When it is a dilemma for me is** with regard to the blank portions that are **above and below, that are between** one **section** and another **section, that are between** one **page** and another **page, that are at the beginning of the scroll,** and **that are at the end of the scroll.** The Gemara asks again: **Derive** that this scroll may be rescued **due to that** area that is blank, whose sanctity remains. The Gemara replies: There, it is referring to a case **where** the blank area **was cut and thrown** out, and all that remains is the place of the writing.

NOTES

That they turned from after God – שֶׁסָּרוּ מֵאַחֲרֵי ה׳: In *Tosafot* a different interpretation is cited: Rashi, in tractate *Ta'anit*, explains that the verse: "And they traveled from the mountain [*mehar*] of the Lord" (Numbers 10:33) can be interpreted: "And they traveled quickly [*maher*] from the Lord," meaning that they fled from God.

HALAKHA

Rescuing blank folios – הַצָּלַת גִּלְיוֹנִים: Blank portions of a Torah scroll that were excised or portions of the parchment that were erased (*Magen Avraham*) are not rescued from the fire on Shabbat. This dilemma remained unresolved in the Gemara. Consequently, the Rif, the Rosh, and the Rambam all rule stringently in this regard (Rambam *Sefer Zemanim, Hilkhot Shabbat* 23:27; *Shulḥan Arukh, Oraḥ Ḥayyim* 334:20).

HALAKHA

Blank folios with regard to rendering hands ritually impure – **הַגִּלְיוֹנִים לְעִנְיַן טוּמְאַת יָדַיִם**: The blank portions of a Torah scroll, like the scroll itself, render one's hands ritually impure, as the Sages deemed these spaces integral parts of the Torah scroll (Rambam *Sefer Tahara, Hilkhot She'ar Avot HaTumot* 9:6).

The scrolls of heretics, one does not rescue – **סִפְרֵי הַמִּינִין אֵין מַצִּילִין אוֹתָן**: Texts written by heretics and idolators are not sacred. They are burned along with the divine names written in them. Needless to say, they are not rescued from a fire on Shabbat (Rambam *Sefer HaMadda, Hilkhot Yesodei HaTorah* 6:8 and *Sefer Ahava, Hilkhot Tefillin UMezuza VeSefer Torah* 1:13; *Shulḥan Arukh, Oraḥ Ḥayyim* 334:21 and *Yoreh De'a* 281:1).

Entering a house of idolatry to save one's life – **כְּנִיסָה לְבֵית עֲבוֹדָה זָרָה לְהַצִּיל עַצְמוֹ**: It is permitted for a Jew to escape danger by entering a temple of idolatry. Some authorities state that when Jews are being persecuted, it is prohibited to do so (*Kol Bo*). This *halakha* is based on the statement of Rabbi Tarfon (*Shulḥan Arukh, Yoreh De'a* 157:3 and in the comment of the Rema).

NOTES

Scrolls of heretics – **סִפְרֵי מִינִין**: This category includes both Jewish sacred books written by heretics and sectarian writings. The latter contained verses from the Bible with the name of God (*Me'iri*).

Scrolls of heretics are like blank folios – **סִפְרֵי מִינִין הֲרֵי הֵן כְּגִלְיוֹנִים**: Even though these were written texts, the Sages likened them to blank folios of Torah scrolls, which are devoid of sanctity. Consequently, they are not rescued from destruction and one may even actively destroy them (*ge'onim*; Rashi).

To make peace…these who impose jealousy and hatred – **לַעֲשׂוֹת שָׁלוֹם...הַלָּלוּ שֶׁמַּטִּילִין קִנְאָה וְאֵיבָה**: This statement refers to the Christians, who claimed that God was fed up with the Jewish people and chose the Christians to replace them as His people. This explains the expression: Who impose jealousy, and hatred, and conflict between the Jewish people and their Father in Heaven (Maharsha).

תָּא שְׁמַע: הַגִּלְיוֹנִין שֶׁל מַעְלָה וְשֶׁל מַטָּה, שֶׁבֵּין פָּרָשָׁה לְפָרָשָׁה, שֶׁבֵּין דַּף לְדַף, שֶׁבִּתְחִלַּת הַסֵּפֶר שֶׁבְּסוֹף הַסֵּפֶר – מְטַמְּאִין אֶת הַיָּדַיִם. דִּילְמָא – אַגַּב סֵפֶר תּוֹרָה שָׁאנֵי.

Come and **hear** a different resolution from what we learned in a mishna: The Sages decreed that **the blank folios** that are **above and below, that are between** one **section and** another **section, that are between** one **page and** another **page, that are at the beginning of the scroll,** and **that are at the end of the scroll render the hands** that touch them **ritually impure.**[H] Apparently, the blank folios have the sanctity of a Torah scroll. The Gemara replies: That is not a proof, as **perhaps** when it is **part of the Torah scroll, it is different,** and in those circumstances the sanctity of the Torah extends to the blank portions. When they stand alone they have no sanctity.

תָּא שְׁמַע: הַגִּלְיוֹנִין וְסִפְרֵי מִינִין אֵין מַצִּילִין אוֹתָן מִפְּנֵי הַדְּלֵיקָה, אֶלָּא נִשְׂרָפִין בִּמְקוֹמָן הֵן וְאַזְכְּרוֹתֵיהֶן. מַאי לָאו – גִּלְיוֹנִין דְּסֵפֶר תּוֹרָה? לֹא, גִּלְיוֹנִין דְּסִפְרֵי מִינִין. הַשְׁתָּא סִפְרֵי מִינִין גּוּפַיְיהוּ אֵין מַצִּילִין, גִּלְיוֹנִין מִבַּעְיָא?! הָכִי קָאָמַר: וְסִפְרֵי מִינִין הֲרֵי הֵן כְּגִלְיוֹנִים.

Therefore, **come** and **hear** a different resolution from that which was taught in another *baraita*: With regard to **the blank folios and the** Torah **scrolls of heretics,**[NB] **one does not rescue**[H] **them from the fire; rather, they burn in their place, they and the names** of God contained therein. **What, is this not** referring to the **blank folios** of a **Torah scroll?** The Gemara rejects this: **No,** it is referring to **the blank folios of the scrolls of heretics.** The Gemara is surprised at this: **Now,** with regard to **the scrolls of heretics themselves, one does not rescue** them; is it **necessary** to say that one does not rescue their **blank folios?** Rather, **this is what it is saying: And the scrolls of heretics are like blank folios.**[N]

גּוּפָא: הַגִּלְיוֹנִים וְסִפְרֵי מִינִין אֵין מַצִּילִין אוֹתָם מִפְּנֵי הַדְּלֵיקָה, רַבִּי יוֹסֵי אוֹמֵר: בַּחוֹל קוֹדֵר אֶת הָאַזְכָּרוֹת שֶׁבָּהֶן וְגוֹנְזָן, וְהַשְּׁאָר שׂוֹרְפָן. אָמַר רַבִּי טַרְפוֹן: אֲקַפַּח אֶת בָּנַי, שֶׁאִם יָבֹאוּ לְיָדִי שֶׁאֲנִי אֶשְׂרוֹף אוֹתָם וְאֶת הָאַזְכָּרוֹת שֶׁבָּהֶן, שֶׁאֲפִילּוּ אָדָם רוֹדֵף אַחֲרָיו לְהוֹרְגוֹ, וְנָחָשׁ רָץ לְהַכִּישׁוֹ – נִכְנָס לְבֵית עֲבוֹדָה זָרָה, וְאֵין נִכְנָס לְבָתֵּיהֶן שֶׁל אֵלּוּ. שֶׁהַלָּלוּ מַכִּירִין וְכוֹפְרִין, וְהַלָּלוּ – אֵין מַכִּירִין וְכוֹפְרִין. וַעֲלֵיהֶן הַכָּתוּב אוֹמֵר ״אַחַר הַדֶּלֶת וְהַמְּזוּזָה שַׂמְתְּ זִכְרוֹנֵךְ״.

Apropos the scrolls of heretics, the Gemara analyzes **the matter itself.** With regard to **the blank folios and the** Torah **scrolls of the heretics, one does not rescue them from the fire. Rabbi Yosei says: During the week, one cuts the names** of God contained **therein and buries them, and burns the rest. Rabbi Tarfon said** in the form of an oath: **I will bury my sons** if I fail to do the following, **that if** these books **come into my possession I will burn them and the names** contained **therein. As even** if **a person is pursuing him** with the intent **to kill him, and a snake is hurrying to bite him, one enters a house of idolatry**[H] **and does not enter the houses of these** heretics. The reason is **that these** heretics **are aware** of the greatness of the Creator manifest in the Torah and its mitzvot, **and** nevertheless, they **deny** the existence of God; **whereas these** idolators **are not aware, and** that is the reason that they **deny** the existence of God. **And with regard to the** heretics, **the verse says: "And behind the door and the doorpost you place your memory"** (Isaiah 57:8). Although they remember the word of God, they treat it contemptuously, as if casting it behind the door.

אָמַר רַבִּי יִשְׁמָעֵאל: קַל וָחוֹמֶר, וּמַה לַּעֲשׂוֹת שָׁלוֹם בֵּין אִישׁ לְאִשְׁתּוֹ אָמְרָה תּוֹרָה: שְׁמִי שֶׁנִּכְתַּב בִּקְדוּשָּׁה יִמָּחֶה עַל הַמַּיִם. הַלָּלוּ שֶׁמַּטִּילִין קִנְאָה וְאֵיבָה וְתַחֲרוּת בֵּין יִשְׂרָאֵל לַאֲבִיהֶן שֶׁבַּשָּׁמַיִם – עַל אַחַת כַּמָּה וְכַמָּה, וַעֲלֵיהֶם אָמַר דָּוִד ״הֲלֹא מְשַׂנְאֶיךָ ה׳ אֶשְׂנָא וּבִתְקוֹמְמֶיךָ אֶתְקוֹטָט תַּכְלִית שִׂנְאָה שְׂנֵאתִים לְאוֹיְבִים הָיוּ לִי״. וּכְשֵׁם שֶׁאֵין מַצִּילִין אוֹתָן מִפְּנֵי הַדְּלֵיקָה, כָּךְ אֵין מַצִּילִין אוֹתָן לֹא מִן הַמַּפּוֹלֶת וְלֹא מִן הַמַּיִם וְלֹא מִדָּבָר הַמְאַבְּדָן.

Rabbi Yishmael said: The fact that the names of God in the scrolls of heretics may be burned can be derived through an ***a fortiori*** inference: **Just as to make peace between a husband and his wife,** the **Torah says: My name that was written in sanctity shall be erased in the water** in the framework of the ordeal of the *sota*; **these,** the heretics, **who impose jealousy, and hatred,**[N] **and conflict between the Jewish people and their Father in Heaven, all the more so** it is proper to erase God's names because of them. **And with regard to** heretics, **David said: "For I hate those who hate You, God, and I fight those who rise against You. I hate them with the utmost hatred, they have become enemies to me"** (Psalms 139:21–22). **And just as they,** the scrolls of heretics, **are not rescued from the fire, neither are they rescued from a rockslide, nor from water, nor from** any other **matter that destroys them.**

BACKGROUND

Scrolls of heretics – **סִפְרֵי הַמִּינִים**: The heretics were members of various dissenting sects that existed during the time of the Mishna. The reference in this context is specifically to the Chrisitian sects. Rabbeinu Ḥananel writes: The heretics who existed at that time had not yet developed the customs that they practice today. Rather, they were misguided. Some of them observed the Torah while others did not, yet they all read it. Rabbeinu Ḥananel describes a period in the history of Christianity during which it was not yet a distinct religion. During that period, its believers had broken away from Judaism, but some of them still observed the Torah and its mitzvot. As a result, there were different attitudes toward them. This period lasted over one hundred years.

בעי מיניה יוסף בר חנין מרבי אבהו: הני ספרי דבי אבידן, מצילין אותן מפני הדליקה או אין מצילין? אין ולאו ורפיא בידיה. רב לא אזיל לבי אבידן, וכל שכן לבי נצרפי. שמואל, לבי נצרפי – לא אזיל, לבי אבידן – אזיל. אמרו ליה לרבא: מאי טעמא לא אתית לבי אבידן? אמר להו: דיקלא פלניא איכא באורחא, וקשי לי. ניעקריה! דוכתיה קשי לי. מר בר יוסף אמר: אנא מינייהו אנא, ולא מסתפינא מינייהו. זימנא חדא אזיל, בעו לסכוניה. רבי מאיר הוה קרי ליה און גליון, רבי יוחנן הוה קרי ליה עוון גליון.

Yosef bar Ḥanin raised a dilemma before Rabbi Abbahu: With regard to **these books of the house of Abidan,** does **one rescue them from the fire or** does **one not rescue** them? There were sacred Jewish texts in that house, which were used in debates and discussions on matters of faith. Rabbi Abbahu did not give him a clear answer but said **yes and no, and** the matter was **uncertain to him. Rav would not go to the house of Abidan**[B] for conversation, **and all the more so** he would not go **to the house of Nitzrefei,**[L] the Persian fire-temple. **Shmuel, to the house of Nitzrefei he did not go,** but **to the house of Abidan he did go.** The gentile scholars **said to Rava: Why did you not come to the house of Abidan?** He evaded their question with an excuse and **said to them: There is a certain palm tree on the road, and** that makes the path **difficult for me.** They said to him: **We will uproot it.** He said to them: Nevertheless, the resulting pit in **its place** will be **difficult for me. Mar bar Yosef said: I am** one **of them,** we are friends, **and I do not fear them.** Still, **one time he went** and argued with them and **they sought to endanger his** life. **Rabbi Meir would call** the Christian writing, the Evangelion, the **wicked folio** [*aven gilyon*]; **Rabbi Yoḥanan** called it the **sinful folio** [*avon gilyon*].

אימא שלום דביתהו דרבי אליעזר אחתיה דרבן גמליאל הואי. הוה ההוא פילוסופא בשבבותיה

The Gemara relates: **Imma Shalom, the wife of Rabbi Eliezer, was Rabban Gamliel's sister. There was a** Christian **philosopher** [*pilosofa*][L] **in their neighborhood**

BACKGROUND

The house of Abidan – בי אבידן: According to the tradition of the *ge'onim*, the house of Abidan was a well-known courtyard in which there were books of knowledge from all the nations. Scholars and wise men from all nations gathered there to discuss wisdom. The house of Nitzrefei served a similar purpose. However, it was also a temple for idol worship. Therefore, it was appropriate for Shmuel to attend meetings and discussions in the house of Abidan, which he considered as a forum for philosophical debates, but he would never enter the house of Nitzrefei, which was devoted to idolatry. There were other Sages who thought that the debates were problematic and dangerous, and it was preferable to refrain from participation in those forums.

LANGUAGE

The house of Abidan and the house of Nitzrefei – בי אבידן ובי נצרפי: These two names are difficult. Some commentaries think that the confusion in the Gemara is intentional. The house of Abidan may derive from the Iranian compound bag-dān, meaning container of the god, i.e., a temple. The meaning of the house of Nitzrefei is more elusive. It has been suggested that the term means house of burning, from the Semitic root *srf,* and refers to a Zoroastrian fire temple. However, it now seems more likely that it originated from a Parthian word meaning Nazarene, an ancient name for Christians, and refers to some sort of Christian church.

Philosopher [*pilosofa*] **– פילוסופא:** From the Greek **φιλόσοφος**, *philosophos*, meaning lover of wisdom. It was used to describe scholars who studied science and philosophy.

Perek **XVI**
Daf **116** Amud **b**

דהוה שקיל שמא דלא מקבל שוחדא. בעו לאחוכי ביה; אעיילא ליה שרגא דדהבא, ואזול לקמיה, אמרה ליה: בעינא דניפלגי לי בנכסי דבי נשי. אמר להו: פלוגו. אמר ליה, כתיב לן: במקום ברא ברתא לא תירות. אמר ליה: מן יומא דגליתון מארעכון איתנטלית אורייתא דמשה, ואיתיהיבת עוון גליון, וכתיב ביה: ברא וברתא כחדא ירתון.

who disseminated about himself **the reputation that he does not accept bribes. They wanted to mock him** and reveal his true nature. **She** privately **gave him a golden lamp,**[N] **and** she and her brother **came before him,** approaching him as if they were seeking judgment. **She said to** the philosopher: **I want to share** in the inheritance **of my father's estate. He said to them: Divide** it. Rabban Gamliel **said to him: It is written in our** Torah: **In a situation** where there is a **son, the daughter does not inherit.** The philosopher **said to him: Since the day you were exiled from your land, the Torah of Moses was taken away and the *avon gilyon* was given** in its place. **It is written in** the *avon gilyon*: **A son and a daughter shall inherit alike.**

למחר הדר עייל ליה איהו חמרא לובא. אמר להו: שפילית לסיפיה דעוון גליון וכתב ביה: אנא לא למיפחת מן אורייתא דמשה אתיתי [ולא] לאוספי על אורייתא דמשה אתיתי. וכתיב ביה: במקום ברא ברתא לא תירות. אמרה ליה: נהור נהוריך כשרגא! אמר ליה רבן גמליאל: אתא חמרא ובטש לשרגא.

The next day Rabban Gamliel **brought** the philosopher **a Libyan donkey.** Afterward, Rabban Gamliel and his sister came before the philosopher for a judgment. **He said to them: I proceeded to the end** of the ***avon gilayon*****, and it is written: I,** ***avon gilayon*****, did not come to subtract from the Torah of Moses, and I did not come to add to the Torah of Moses. And it is written there. In a situation** where there is a **son, the daughter does not inherit. She said to him: May your light shine like a lamp,** alluding to the lamp she had given him. **Rabban Gamliel said to him: The donkey came and kicked the lamp,** thereby revealing the entire episode.

"ומפני מה אין קורין כו'". אמר רב: לא שנו אלא בזמן בית המדרש, אבל שלא בזמן בית המדרש – קורין. ושמואל אמר: אפילו שלא בזמן בית המדרש אין קורין. איני?! והא נהרדעא אתריה דשמואל הוה, ובנהרדעא פסקי סידרא בכתובים במנחתא דשבתא! אלא, אי איתמר הכי איתמר; אמר רב: לא שנו אלא במקום בית המדרש, אבל שלא במקום בית המדרש – קורין.

We learned in the mishna: **And why** does **one not read** the Writings on Shabbat? **Due to suspension** of Torah study **in the study hall. Rav said: They only taught** that it is prohibited to read from the Writings on Shabbat **during the hours of** study in **the study hall; but** when it is **not during the hours of** study in **the study hall, one may read** them. **And Shmuel said: Even** when it is **not the hours of** study in **the study hall one may not read** from the Writings on Shabbat. The Gemara asks: **Is that so? Wasn't Neharde'a Shmuel's place** where he was the rabbi of the town, **and in Neharde'a they concluded** their **regular** weekly **discourse with Writings**[H] **on Shabbat afternoon. Rather,** if a dispute **was stated** in this matter, **it was stated as follows: Rav said: It was only taught** that there is a prohibition **in a place** where there is a **study hall** nearby that people can attend; **but not in a place** where there **is a study hall, one may read** Writings.

NOTES

She gave him a golden lamp – אעיילא ליה שרגא דדהבא: The Maharsha explains that Rabbi Eliezer and Imma Shalom did not actually bribe the philosopher. They merely showed him items that would have been appropriate as bribes. They did not actually give him anything.

HALAKHA

Concluded the regular weekly discourse with Writings – פסקי סידרא בכתובים: The Sages issued a decree prohibiting to read the books of the Writings on Shabbat during the time of a generally attended regular lecture in the study hall. This was intended to prevent absence from the study hall (Rambam *Sefer Zemanim, Hilkhot Shabbat* 23:19).

HALAKHA

One may rescue the casing of a Torah scroll – מַצִּילִין תִּיק הַסֵּפֶר: One may rescue the casing of a Torah scroll and the casing of other sacred writings from a fire on Shabbat, along with the scroll encased therein. The casing of phylacteries may be rescued along with the phylacteries. Doing so is permitted even if there is money in the casing (Rambam *Sefer Zemanim, Hilkhot Shabbat* 23:28; *Shulḥan Arukh, Oraḥ Ḥayyim* 334:15).

One flays the Paschal lamb – מַפְשִׁיטִין אֶת הַפֶּסַח: If the fourteenth of Nissan occurs on Shabbat, the Paschal lamb is sacrificed just as it would be on a weekday. Consequently, the entire hide of the lamb is flayed in same manner as it is done on a weekday. The *halakha* is in accordance with the majority opinion (Rambam *Sefer Korbanot, Hilkhot Korban Pesaḥ* 1:16).

וּשְׁמוּאֵל אָמַר: בֵּין בִּמְקוֹם בֵּית הַמִּדְרָשׁ בֵּין שֶׁלֹּא בִּמְקוֹם בֵּית הַמִּדְרָשׁ, בִּזְמַן בֵּית הַמִּדְרָשׁ – אֵין קוֹרִין, שֶׁלֹּא בִּזְמַן בֵּית הַמִּדְרָשׁ – קוֹרִין. וְאָזְדָא שְׁמוּאֵל לְטַעְמֵיהּ, דִּבְנְהַרְדְּעָא פָּסְקִי סִידְרָא דִּכְתוּבִים בְּמִנְחָתָא דְּשַׁבְּתָא.

And Shmuel said: Whether it is in the place of the study hall or it is not the place of the study hall, one may not read anywhere **when it is during the hours of** study in **the study hall;** but **when it is not during the hours of** study in **the study hall, one may read. And Shmuel follows his** line of **reasoning** stated elsewhere, as **in Neharde'a they** would **conclude their** studies with **Writings on Shabbat afternoon.**

רַב אָשֵׁי אָמַר: לְעוֹלָם כִּדְאָמְרַן מֵעִיקָּרָא, וּשְׁמוּאֵל כְּרַבִּי נְחֶמְיָה. דְּתַנְיָא: אַף עַל פִּי שֶׁאָמְרוּ כִּתְבֵי הַקֹּדֶשׁ אֵין קוֹרִין בָּהֶן – אֲבָל שׁוֹנִין בָּהֶן וְדוֹרְשִׁין בָּהֶן, נִצְרַךְ לְפָסוּק – מֵבִיא וְרוֹאֶה בּוֹ. אָמַר רַבִּי נְחֶמְיָה: מִפְּנֵי מָה אָמְרוּ, כִּתְבֵי הַקֹּדֶשׁ אֵין קוֹרִין בָּהֶן – כְּדֵי שֶׁיֹּאמְרוּ: בְּכִתְבֵי הַקֹּדֶשׁ אֵין קוֹרִין, וְכׇל שֶׁכֵּן בִּשְׁטָרֵי הֶדְיוֹטוֹת.

Rav Ashi said: Actually, the dispute is **as we stated initially, and Shmuel said** what he said **in accordance with** the opinion of **Rabbi Neḥemya. As it was taught** in a *baraita*: **Although** the Sages **said** with regard to **sacred writings** that they **may not be read** on Shabbat, **one may study** the midrash on **them and teach them** before the congregation; if **one requires a verse** that is written in the Writings, **he brings** a book **and looks in it. Rabbi Neḥemya said: Why did they say** that **sacred writings are not read**[N] **on** Shabbat? **So that** people **will say: Sacred writings may not be read, all the more so** that is the case with **ordinary documents,** i.e., contracts and letters. If so, according to Rabbi Neḥemya, reading any sacred writings on Shabbat is prohibited so that people will refrain from reading non-sacred documents on Shabbat. It was not prohibited to encourage attendance the study hall. Shmuel himself does not hold in accordance with the opinion of Rabbi Neḥemya.

מתני׳ מַצִּילִין תִּיק הַסֵּפֶר עִם הַסֵּפֶר. וְתִיק הַתְּפִילִּין עִם הַתְּפִילִּין, וְאַף עַל פִּי שֶׁיֵּשׁ בְּתוֹכָן מָעוֹת. וּלְהֵיכָן מַצִּילִין אוֹתָן? לְמָבוֹי שֶׁאֵינוֹ מְפוּלָּשׁ, בֶּן בְּתֵירָא אוֹמֵר: אַף לִמְפוּלָּשׁ.

MISHNA One may rescue the casing of a Torah **scroll**[H] from a fire on Shabbat together **with the Torah scroll, and the casing of phylacteries along with the phylacteries, even if they have money inside them.**[N] **And to where may one rescue them? Into an alley that is closed,** which, if it is surrounded on three sides, is considered to be a private domain by Torah law. **Ben Beteira says: Even into an open** alley.

גמ׳ תָּנוּ רַבָּנַן: אַרְבָּעָה עָשָׂר שֶׁחָל לִהְיוֹת בְּשַׁבָּת מַפְשִׁיטִין אֶת הַפֶּסַח עַד הֶחָזֶה, דִּבְרֵי רַבִּי יִשְׁמָעֵאל בְּנוֹ שֶׁל רַבִּי יוֹחָנָן בֶּן בְּרוֹקָה, וַחֲכָמִים אוֹמְרִים: מַפְשִׁיטִין אֶת כּוּלּוֹ. בִּשְׁלָמָא לְרַבִּי יִשְׁמָעֵאל בְּנוֹ שֶׁל רַבִּי יוֹחָנָן בֶּן בְּרוֹקָה – דְּהָא אִיתְעֲבִיד לֵיהּ צוֹרֶךְ גָּבוֹהַּ. אֶלָּא לְרַבָּנַן – מַאי טַעְמָא? אָמַר רַבָּה בַּר בַּר חָנָה אָמַר רַבִּי יוֹחָנָן: דְּאָמַר קְרָא ״כֹּל פָּעַל ה׳ לַמַּעֲנֵהוּ״. וְהָכָא, מַאי ׳לַמַּעֲנֵהוּ׳ אִיכָּא? רַב יוֹסֵף אָמַר: שֶׁלֹּא יַסְרִיחַ. רָבָא אָמַר: שֶׁלֹּא יְהוּ קׇדְשֵׁי שָׁמַיִם מוּטָלִין כִּנְבֵלָה.

GEMARA Apropos the mishna, the Gemara cites that which **the Sages taught** in a *baraita*: If **the fourteenth** of Nissan **occurs on Shabbat,** and the Paschal lamb is offered but not roasted until Shabbat ends, **one flays the Paschal** lamb[NH] **up to the breast** to enable removal of the parts of the animal that are offered on the altar on Shabbat. One flays the rest of the animal after Shabbat. Further skinning is only to facilitate eating the animal, therefore, it does not override Shabbat; this is **the statement of Rabbi Yishmael, son of Rabbi Yoḥanan ben Beroka. And the Rabbis say: One flays it in its entirety.** The Gemara asks: **Granted, according to** the opinion of **Rabbi Yishmael, son of Rabbi Yoḥanan ben Beroka,** who said one may flay only part of the animal, the *halakha* is understandable. **Since it has** already **been used for its divine purpose** of having its blood sprinkled on the altar, the animal no longer should be flayed. **But according to the Rabbis, what is the reason** for their opinion? **Rabba bar bar Ḥana said** that **Rabbi Yoḥanan said: The verse states, "All that the Lord has made is for His sake"** (Proverbs 16:4), meaning that a prohibited action is only permitted if its performance honors God. The Gemara asks: **And here, what** manifestation of **for His sake is there** in flaying the remaining hide from the Paschal lamb? **Rav Yosef said:** The Rabbis permitted removing the entire hide so **that** the sacrifice **will not putrefy. Rava said:** The Rabbis permitted removing the entire hide so **that the sacred sacrifices will not be left** in disgrace **like** a half-stripped **animal carcass** left unattended.

NOTES

Reading sacred writings – קְרִיאָה בִּכְתְבֵי הַקּוֹדֶשׁ: There were different customs in different communities for the period following the afternoon prayer on Shabbat. In some locations, the Talmud was not studied because Moses died at that hour of the day. When a Sage dies, regular yeshiva study is suspended in his honor. In other communities, only the recitation of tractate *Avot* was permitted.

Even if they have money inside them – וְאַף עַל פִּי שֶׁיֵּשׁ בְּתוֹכָן מָעוֹת: The problem with money in this context is not the prohibition of moving objects that are set-aside. Rather, the concern is that, when rescuing the object on Shabbat, one might carry it to a prohibited domain or four cubits in the public domain (Ramban).

One flays the Paschal lamb – מַפְשִׁיטִין אֶת הַפֶּסַח: In *Tosafot*, the question is raised: Why did the Sages specifically choose the Paschal lamb as in the focus of this discussion? The same issue could have been raised with regard to all communal offerings on Shabbat. Several answers were proposed. First, Paschal lambs were so numerous that they created an impression that they were animal carcasses cast aside. Second, since the meat of the Paschal lamb was to be eaten, the Sages permitted flaying its hide. Another possible answer is that on the contrary: Even though the Paschal lamb is an individual offering sacrificed on Shabbat, the Sages permitted flaying it as they did with communal offerings.

מַאי בֵּינַיְיהוּ? אִיכָּא בֵּינַיְיהוּ: דְּמַנַּח אַפְתּוֹרָא דְּדַהֲבָא, אִי נַמִּי – יוֹמָא דְּאַסְתָּנָא. וְרַבִּי יִשְׁמָעֵאל בְּנוֹ שֶׁל רַבִּי יוֹחָנָן בֶּן בְּרוֹקָה, הַאי "פָּעַל ה' לַמַּעֲנֵהוּ" מַאי עָבֵיד לֵיהּ? שֶׁלֹּא יוֹצִיא אֶת הָאֵימוּרִין קוֹדֶם הַפְשָׁטַת הָעוֹר. מַאי טַעְמָא? אָמַר רַב הוּנָא בְּרֵיהּ דְּרַב נָתָן: מִשּׁוּם נִימִין.

The Gemara asks: **What is** the practical difference **between them?** The Gemara answers: **There is** a practical difference **between them when** the Paschal lamb **is laid on a golden table.** In this case, there is indeed a concern that the carcass will putrefy, although there is no element of disgrace. **Alternatively,** there is a practical difference on **a day with a** cold **northern wind.** In this case, there is no concern that it will putrefy but there is a concern of disgracing the sacrifice. The Gemara asks: **And what does Rabbi Yishamel, son of Rabbi Yoḥanan ben Beroka, do with the** verse, "All **that the Lord has made is for His sake**"? The Gemara answers: He uses it to permit removing part of the hide, **as** if it was **not** for this verse, it would have been possible **to remove the sacrificial parts** offered on the altar **before removing the hide** by puncturing the hide of the animal and removing the fats through the opening. The Gemara asks: **What is the reason** that the Torah prohibited doing so? **Rav Huna, son of Rav Natan, said: Because of the hairs,** so that they do not become entangled in the sacrificial parts and distort them.

אָמַר רַב חִסְדָּא אָמַר מָר עוּקְבָא: מַאי אֲהַדְרוּ לֵיהּ חַבְרַיָּיא לְרַבִּי יִשְׁמָעֵאל בְּנוֹ שֶׁל רַבִּי יוֹחָנָן בֶּן בְּרוֹקָה – הָכִי קָאָמְרִי לֵיהּ: אִם מַצִּילִין תִּיק הַסֵּפֶר עִם הַסֵּפֶר – לֹא נַפְשִׁיט אֶת הַפֶּסַח מֵעוֹרוֹ? מִי דָּמֵי? הָתָם – טִלְטוּל, הָכָא – מְלָאכָה! אָמַר רַב אַשִׁי: בְּתַרְתֵּי פְּלִיגִי; פְּלִיגִי בְּטִלְטוּל, וּפְלִיגִי בִּמְלָאכָה. וְהָכִי קָאָמְרִי לֵיהּ: אִם מַצִּילִין תִּיק הַסֵּפֶר עִם הַסֵּפֶר – לֹא נְטַלְטֵל עוֹר אַגַּב בָּשָׂר?!

Rav Ḥisda said that **Mar Ukva said: How did the members of the group respond to Rabbi Yishmael, son of Rabbi Yoḥanan ben Beroka? This is what they said to him: If one may save** the **casing of a** Torah **scroll along with the** Torah **scroll,** why **may one not strip the Paschal** lamb **of its skin?** Here too, in the case of skinning the Paschal lamb, once part of the action is permitted one should be able to perform the entire act. The Gemara is surprised at this: **Are they comparable? There,** in rescuing the casing of the scroll, only **moving** is involved, which is prohibited by rabbinic law; whereas **here,** in the case of the Paschal lamb, the act of flaying is a **prohibited labor** by Torah law. **Rav Ashi said: They are disagreeing with regard to two** issues: **They disagree with regard to moving** the hide along with the flesh, **and they disagree with regard to the labor** of flaying the animal. **And this is what they said to him: If one may rescue** the **casing of the Torah scroll along with the Torah scroll,** will **we not move** the **hide** of the Paschal lamb **together with the flesh**[N] of the sacrifice? The sacrifice should be moved with its skin so it does not putrefy.

NOTES

Hide together with the flesh – עוֹר אַגַּב בָּשָׂר: The Ramban explains that this discussion is based on the assumption that the hide may be moved because it could be used as a cushion on Shabbat. However, the flesh may not be moved since it may be eaten only that night. Although our version of the text does not exactly correspond to this interpretation, it helps to explain the subsequent discussion in the Gemara.

Perek **XVI**
Daf **117** Amud **a**

מִי דָּמֵי?! הָתָם – נַעֲשָׂה בָּסִיס לְדָבָר הַמּוּתָּר, הָכָא – נַעֲשָׂה בָּסִיס לְדָבָר הָאָסוּר. אֶלָּא, הָכִי קָאָמְרִי לֵיהּ: אִם מַצִּילִין תִּיק שֶׁל סֵפֶר עִם הַסֵּפֶר, וְאַף עַל פִּי שֶׁיֵּשׁ בְּתוֹכוֹ מָעוֹת, לֹא נְטַלְטֵל עוֹר אַגַּב בָּשָׂר? מִי דָּמֵי?! הָתָם – נַעֲשָׂה בָּסִיס לְדָבָר הָאָסוּר וּלְדָבָר הַמּוּתָּר, הָכָא – כּוּלּוֹ נַעֲשָׂה בָּסִיס לְדָבָר הָאָסוּר! אֶלָּא, הָכִי קָאָמְרִי לֵיהּ: אִם מְבִיאִין תִּיק שֶׁיֵּשׁ בְּתוֹכוֹ מָעוֹת מֵעָלְמָא לְהַצִּיל בּוֹ סֵפֶר תּוֹרָה, לֹא נְטַלְטֵל עוֹר אַגַּב בָּשָׂר?!

The Gemara asks: **Are they comparable? There,** with regard to the Torah scroll, the casing **is a base for a permitted object,** i.e., the scroll itself, which may be moved on Shabbat; whereas **here,** with regard to the hide of the Paschal lamb, the skin **is a base for a prohibited object,**[N] i.e., the flesh of the sacrifice, which may not be moved until nightfall because it may not be eaten until night. **Rather, this is what they said to him: If one may save** the **casing of the Torah scroll along with the scroll, even if there is money inside it,** why then **may one not move** the **hide together with the flesh?** The Gemara asks: **Are they comparable? There,** with regard to the Torah scroll, the casing **becomes a base for a prohibited object and a permitted object;** whereas **here,** with regard to the hide, **it is entirely a base for a prohibited object. Rather, this is what they said to him: If one may bring a casing that has money inside it from outside** in order **to save a Torah scroll in it,** why **may one not move** the **hide together with the flesh?**

NOTES

Base for a prohibited object – בָּסִיס לְדָבָר הָאָסוּר: The Sages permitted moving the flesh of the Paschal lamb on Shabbat because deference to God supersedes the prohibition against moving it. Nevertheless, in principle, the flesh of the sacrifice is still considered to be a prohibited object vis-à-vis the hide which is its base (Rabbi Elazar Moshe Horovitz).

והיא גופה מנלן? אילימא דמדהיכא דאית ביה לא שדי להו – איתויי נמי מייתינן, מי דמי?! התם – אדהכי והכי נפלה דליקה, הכא – אדהכא והכי לישדינן! אלא אמר מר בר רב אשי: לעולם כדאמרינן מעיקרא, ודקא קשיא לך "הכא טלטול והכא מלאכה" – כגון דלא קבעי ליה לעור.

The Gemara asks: **And from where** do we derive **this** ***halakha*** **itself?** As it is not stated in the mishna, from where do we derive that it is permitted on Shabbat to bring a casing containing money from the outside in order to save a Torah scroll? **If you say** that **from** the fact **that** in a situation **where** the casing has money **in it one does not throw it** away but brings it out with the casing, when the casing is outside and has money in it, one may also **bring** the money **along with it; is it comparable? There,** with regard to the Torah scroll's casing with money inside, if one tarries in order to empty the money from the case, **in the meantime the fire might catch** the Torah scroll and burn it; whereas **here,** with regard to bringing in the casing, **in the meantime he could have thrown it away. Rather, Mar bar Rav Ashi said: Actually,** it is **as we said initially.** The Sages equated carrying the Torah casing with flaying the hide of the Paschal lamb. **And** as for **what was difficult for you,** that **here,** with regard to the Torah casing, **moving** alone is involved, whereas **here,** with regard to a Paschal lamb, a prohibited **labor** is involved, it can be explained as referring to a case **where one does not need the hide** of the Paschal lamb. Therefore, he is exempt.

והא אביי ורבא דאמרי תרוייהו: מודה רבי שמעון בפסיק רישיה ולא ימות! דשקיל ליה בברזי.

The Gemara asks: **But Abaye and Rava both said: Rabbi Shimon concedes in** cases categorized as **cut off its head and will it not die,** i.e., an action with an inevitable consequence. When an action has an inevitable consequence, even Rabbi Shimon, who normally exempts a person for performing an action with an unintended consequence, maintains the one is liable. Rather, we must say **that one flays it strip by strip,** and thereby he does not benefit from the hide. It therefore does not constitute the prohibited labor of stripping the hide.

"ולהיכן מצילין אותן וכו'". היכי דמי מפולש, היכי דמי שאינו מפולש? אמר רב חסדא: שלש מחיצות ושני לחיין – זהו מבוי שאינו מפולש, שלש מחיצות ולחי אחד – זהו מבוי המפולש. ותרוייהו אליבא דרבי אליעזר, דתנן: הכשר מבוי, בית שמאי אומרים: לחי וקורה, ובית הלל אומרים: או לחי או קורה, רבי אליעזר אומר: שני לחיים.

We learned in the mishna: **And to where may one rescue them?** Into an alley that is closed, which, if it is surrounded on three sides, is considered to be a private domain by Torah law. Ben Beteira says: Even into an open alley. The Gemara asks: **What are the circumstances** of an alley that is **open,** and **what are the circumstances** of an alley that is **not open? Rav Ḥisda said:** An alley that has **three walls and two posts** at its entrance **is an alley that is not open;** one that has **three walls and one post is an alley that is open. And they both,** the first *tanna* and ben Beteira, disagree in the mishna **in accordance with the opinion of Rabbi Eliezer,**[N] **as we learned** in a mishna: For **preparation of an alley** to permit carrying within it on Shabbat, **Beit Shammai say** the alley must have **a post** on the side of the entrance **and a beam** over the entrance. **And Beit Hillel say: Either a post or a beam**[BH] is sufficient. **Rabbi Eliezer says:** In order to permit carrying, **two posts** are required.

אמר ליה רבה: שלש מחיצות ולחי אחד מפולש קרית ליה?! ועוד, לרבנן נציל לתוכו אוכלין ומשקין! אלא אמר רבה: שתי מחיצות ושני לחיין – זהו מבוי שאינו מפולש, שתי מחיצות ולחי אחד – זהו מבוי המפולש.

Rabba said to him: Did you call an alley that has **three walls and one post open?** Even if Rabbi Eliezer does not permit carrying there, it is still not considered to be open but closed. **And furthermore, according to the Rabbis,** if this is so, **let us rescue food and drinks** by carrying them **there**[N] as well. Since the Sages only permitted carrying in an alley that is not open, and because, according to all opinions, it is permitted to carry in a closed alley, one should also be allowed to save food and water, and not only a Torah scroll, by carrying them there. **Rather, Rabba said:** An alley that has **two walls and two posts** at both entrances to the alley **is an alley that is not open.** If it has **two walls and one post, it is an alley that is open.**

NOTES

In accordance with the opinion of Rabbi Eliezer – אליבא דרבי אליעזר: Why did Rav Ḥisda interpret the mishna contrary to the accepted ruling, in accordance with the rejected opinion of Rabbi Eliezer? The commentaries explain that there are reasons that render difficult establishing the mishna in accordance with the opinion of ben Beteira, who permitted carrying the Torah scroll casings even in an open alley. Therefore, the Sages were forced to establish the mishna in accordance with the opinion of Rabbi Eliezer, even though that is not the *halakha* (Rashba; *Tosafot*).

Let us rescue food and drinks by carrying them there – נציל לתוכו אוכלין ומשקין: Why did Rabba ignore the question that he himself raised (see *Tosafot*)? The Ramban answers that Rabba explains that even according to Rabbi Yehuda, two partitions alone do not create a full-fledged private domain because it remains similar to a public domain. Consequently, it is not permitted to rescue everything into that area (see Rashba).

BACKGROUND

A beam and posts – קורה ולחיים: Pictured is an alleyway that has sideposts on either side of the entrance. These are two protrusions that serve as a symbolic partition. The picture also shows a crossbeam over the entrance to the alleyway.

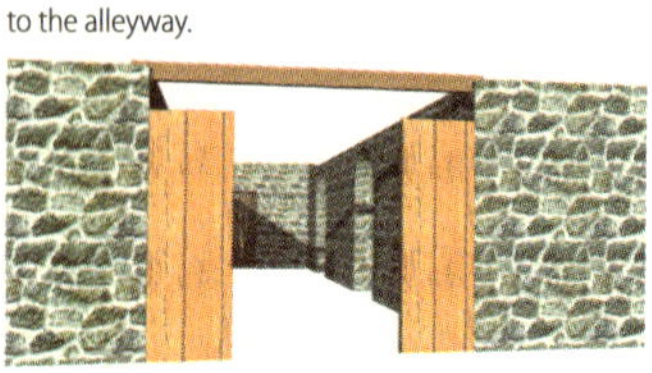

Alleyway with two sideposts and a crossbeam

HALAKHA

Preparation of an alley…either a post or a beam – הכשר מבוי...או לחי או קורה: It is permitted to carry inside an alleyway surrounded by three walls with the fourth side open, provided one places a sidepost at its entrance or a crossbeam above the entrance to the alleyway, in accordance with the opinion of Beit Hillel. A post is defined as any object of any width that is at least ten large handbreadths high (Rabbi Akiva Eiger; Rambam *Sefer Zemanim*, *Hilkhot Shabbat* 17:2; *Shulḥan Arukh*, *Oraḥ Ḥayyim* 363:3, 14).

וְתַרְוַיְיהוּ אַלִּיבָּא דְּרַבִּי יְהוּדָה, דְּתַנְיָא: יָתֵר עַל כֵּן אָמַר רַבִּי יְהוּדָה: מִי שֶׁיֵּשׁ לוֹ שְׁנֵי בָתִּים בִּשְׁנֵי צִדֵּי רְשׁוּת הָרַבִּים עוֹשֶׂה לֶחִי מִיכָּן וְלֶחִי מִיכָּן, אוֹ קוֹרָה מִיכָּן וְקוֹרָה מִיכָּן – וְנוֹשֵׂא וְנוֹתֵן בָּאֶמְצַע. אָמְרוּ לוֹ: אֵין מְעָרְבִין רְשׁוּת הָרַבִּים בְּכָךְ.

And both of them hold **in accordance with the opinion of Rabbi Yehuda. As it was taught** in a *baraita*: **Furthermore,**[N] **Rabbi Yehuda said: One who has two houses** opposite each other **on two sides of the public domain,** if he chooses, **he may** create a private domain for himself in the area of the public domain. He may **place a** ten-handbreadth high **post from here,** perpendicular to the public domain. This creates a symbolic wall which, in the *halakhot* of alleyways, has the legal status of a wall. **And** he may place **an** additional **post from here,** on the other side, and that has the same legal status as if he closed the public domain on all of its sides. **Or,** he can implement a different solution appropriate for alleyways by placing **a beam** extending **from here,** from one end of one house, to the end of the house opposite it. This creates a symbolic partition across the width of the street. **And** he may place **a beam** extending **from here,** from the other side of the house. According to Rabbi Yehuda, in that way, one is permitted to **carry** objects **and place** them **in** the area **between** the symbolic partitions, as he would in a private domain. The Rabbis **said to him: One may not establish an *eiruv* in the public domain in that** way.

אָמַר לֵיהּ אַבָּיֵי: לְדִידָךְ נַמִּי, לְרַבָּנַן נַצִּיל לְתוֹכוֹ אוֹכָלִין וּמַשְׁקִין!

Abaye said to Rabba: According **to your** opinion **too,** according **to the** opinion of the **Rabbis** cited in the mishna who agree with Rabbi Yehuda and permit carrying in an alley that is closed, let **us** also **save food and drinks** by carrying them **there.**

NOTES

Furthermore – יָתֵר עַל כֵּן: In the same *baraita*, Rabbi Yehuda speaks of a case in which there are two houses on opposite sides of the public domain, and their upper floors extend over the public domain and connect, rendering the area beneath them a private domain. Rabbi Yehuda then adds that even in a case where there are no building extensions overhead, the addition of a post and a beam can also transform that area into a private domain. Rabbi Yehuda's rationale is that by Torah law an area becomes a private domain with only two walls, and the post and beam are only placed there as a conspicuous indication that the area is indeed a private domain (Rashi).

Perek **XVI**
Daf **117** Amud **b**

אֶלָּא אָמַר רַב אַשִׁי: שָׁלֹשׁ מְחִיצוֹת וְלֶחִי אֶחָד – זֶה מָבוֹי שֶׁאֵינוֹ מְפוּלָּשׁ, שָׁלֹשׁ מְחִיצוֹת בְּלֹא לֶחִי – זֶהוּ מָבוֹי הַמְפוּלָּשׁ. וַאֲפִילּוּ לְרַבִּי אֱלִיעֶזֶר דְּאָמַר ״בָּעֵינַן לְחָיַיִם״, הָנֵי מִילֵּי – לְאוֹכָלִין וּמַשְׁקִין, אֲבָל לְסֵפֶר תּוֹרָה – בְּחַד לֶחִי סַגִּי.

Rather, Rav Ashi said: The Sages in the mishna disagree with regard to the opinion of Rabbi Eliezer: **Three walls and one post is an alley that is closed; three walls without a post** at all **is an open alley. And even according to Rabbi Eliezer, who said we need two posts,** one post being insufficient, **those words** were stated to permit one **to** move **food and drinks, but for** the purpose of moving **a Torah scroll,**[H] **one post is sufficient.**

מתני׳ מַצִּילִין מְזוֹן שָׁלֹשׁ סְעוּדוֹת, הָרָאוּי לְאָדָם – לְאָדָם, הָרָאוּי לַבְּהֵמָה – לַבְּהֵמָה. כֵּיצַד: נָפְלָה דְלֵיקָה בְּלֵילֵי שַׁבָּת – מַצִּילִין מְזוֹן שָׁלֹשׁ סְעוּדוֹת, בְּשַׁחֲרִית – מַצִּילִין מְזוֹן שְׁתֵּי סְעוּדוֹת, בְּמִנְחָה – מְזוֹן סְעוּדָה אַחַת. רַבִּי יוֹסֵי אוֹמֵר: לְעוֹלָם מַצִּילִין מְזוֹן שָׁלֹשׁ סְעוּדוֹת.

MISHNA **One may rescue food for three meals**[H] from a fire on Shabbat. One may rescue food **that is suitable for a person for a person;** and one may rescue food **that is suitable for an animal for an animal.**[N] **How so?** If **a fire ignited on Friday night** before the Shabbat evening meal, **one may rescue food for three meals.** If a fire ignited **in the morning,** after the Shabbat evening meal has been eaten and before the meal of Shabbat day, **one** may only **rescue food for two meals.** If a fire ignited **in the afternoon,** one may rescue **food for one meal. Rabbi Yosei says: One may always rescue food for three meals,** which is the measure that the Sages permitted without distinguishing between the times of day.

גמ׳ מִכְּדִי בְּהֶיתֵּרָא קָטָרַח, נַצִּיל טְפֵי! אָמַר רָבָא: מִתּוֹךְ שֶׁאָדָם בָּהוּל עַל מָמוֹנוֹ, אִי שָׁרֵית לֵיהּ – אָתֵי לְכַבּוֹיֵי. אָמַר לֵיהּ אַבָּיֵי: אֶלָּא הָא דְּתַנְיָא, נִשְׁבְּרָה לוֹ חָבִית בְּרֹאשׁ גַּגּוֹ – מֵבִיא כְּלִי וּמַנִּיחַ תַּחְתֶּיהָ, וּבִלְבַד שֶׁלֹּא יָבִיא כְּלִי אַחֵר וְיִקְלוֹט, כְּלִי אַחֵר וְיִצָּרֵף. הָתָם מַאי גְּזֵירָה אִיכָּא? הָכָא נַמִּי, גְּזֵירָה שֶׁמָּא יָבִיא כְּלִי דֶּרֶךְ רְשׁוּת הָרַבִּים.

GEMARA The Gemara asks: **Now, since one is exerting** himself to move **permitted** objects, **let us rescue more.** Why was he allowed to rescue food for only three meals? **Rava said: Since a person is agitated about his property, if you permit him** to move more, **he will come to extinguish** the fire. **Abaye said to him: Rather, that which was taught** in a *baraita*: If **one's barrel broke atop one's roof** on Shabbat, **he may bring a vessel and place it under** the barrel to salvage its contents, **and** this is permitted **provided that he does not bring another vessel** and place it on the ground **to catch** the liquid that flows out of the barrel. Similarly, one may not bring **another vessel and attach** the vessel next to the roof so that the liquid from the barrel will pour into it. **There, what decree** applies to prohibit saving it in any other way? Rava said to him: **Here, too,** it is **a decree** issued due to the concern **lest one bring** the additional **vessel through the public domain,** which is prohibited.

HALAKHA

Three walls and a single post…but for a Torah scroll, etc. – שָׁלֹשׁ מְחִיצוֹת וְלֶחִי אֶחָד...אֲבָל לְסֵפֶר תּוֹרָה וכו׳: On Shabbat, one may rescue from a fire sacred writings that are written in ancient Hebrew in Assyrian script by taking them into an alley that is enclosed on three sides with walls and has a sidepost. This rule applies even if no merging of alleyways was established, in accordance with the opinion of Rav Ashi (Rambam *Sefer Zemanim, Hilkhot Shabbat* 17:2, 23:26; *Shulḥan Arukh, Oraḥ Ḥayyim* 334:17, 363:1, 3, 14).

One may rescue food for three meals – מַצִּילִין מְזוֹן שָׁלֹשׁ סְעוּדוֹת: One may rescue sufficient food from a fire for the meals that one must eat on Shabbat. At night, prior to the first meal, one may rescue enough food for three meals. In the morning, one may rescue enough for two meals. In the afternoon, one may rescue only enough for one meal. This applies to the people whose house is on fire. Those who live nearby may rescue whatever they want from their homes, if they are concerned that the fire will spread to their houses (*Tosafot*; Rosh; Rambam *Sefer Zemanim, Hilkhot Shabbat* 23:21; *Shulḥan Arukh, Oraḥ Ḥayyim* 334:1).

NOTES

Food that is suitable for an animal for an animal – הָרָאוּי לַבְּהֵמָה לַבְּהֵמָה: Although an animal is not obligated to eat three meals on Shabbat, since the Sages declared that one may not eat until he has fed his animals, one should prepare food for three meals for his animals as well (*Tiferet Yisrael*).

גופא, נשברה לו חבית בראש גגו – מביא כלי ומניח תחתיה, ובלבד שלא יביא כלי אחר ויקלוט, כלי אחר ויצרף. נזדמן לו אורחין – מביא כלי אחר וקולט, כלי אחר ומצרף. ולא יקלוט ואחר כך יזמין, אלא יזמין ואחר כך יקלוט, ואין מערימין בכך. משום רבי יוסי בר יהודה אמרו: מערימין.

Apropos this *baraita*, the Gemara discusses **the matter itself: If one's barrel broke atop one's roof** on Shabbat, **he may bring a vessel and place it under** the barrel to salvage its contents, **and** this is permitted **provided that he does not bring another vessel** and place it on the ground to **catch** the liquid, **another vessel and attach** the vessel next to the roof. If **guests happen** to come **to him**[H] and he needs more to drink, **he** may **bring another vessel and catch** the liquid, and **he** may **bring another vessel and attach** it. **And one may not catch** the liquid **and then invite** guests; **rather,** one must first **invite** guests, **and afterward catch** the liquid. Until he invites guests, there is no need for the beverage, and he will be catching the liquid in a prohibited manner. **And one may not employ artifice in this** by inviting guests expressly for the purpose of rescuing his wine. **In the name of Rabbi Yosei bar Yehuda, they said:** One may even **employ artifice.**

לימא בפלוגתא דרבי אליעזר ורבי יהושע קמיפלגי; דתניא, אותו ואת בנו שנפלו לבור, רבי אליעזר אומר: מעלה את הראשון על מנת לשוחטו, והשני עושה לו פרנסה במקומו, בשביל שלא ימות. רבי יהושע אומר: מעלין את הראשון על מנת לשוחטו, ואינו שוחטו, ומערים ומעלה את השני. רצה – זה שוחט, רצה – זה שוחט.

The Gemara suggests: **Let us say** that Rabbi Yosei bar Yehuda and the Rabbis **disagree in the dispute** between **Rabbi Eliezer and Rabbi Yehoshua, as it was taught** in a *baraita*: With regard to **it and its offspring**[N] **that fell into a pit**[H] on a Festival, **Rabbi Eliezer says: One may raise the first in order to slaughter it, and** then **slaughter it; and** with regard to **the second one, one may provide it sustenance in its place** in the pit **so that it will not die. Rabbi Yehoshua says: One may raise the first in order to slaughter it, and** then reconsider and **not slaughter it, and one may employ artifice** and say that he reconsidered and wants to slaughter the other, **and raise the second. If he** so **desires, he slaughters this** one; **if he** so **desires, he slaughters that** one.

ממאי? דילמא עד כאן לא קאמר רבי אליעזר התם – דאפשר בפרנסה, אבל הכא דלא אפשר – לא. ועד כאן לא קאמר רבי יהושע התם – משום דאיכא צער בעלי חיים, אבל הכא דליכא צער בעלי חיים – לא!

The Gemara rejects this: **From what** does that conclusion ensue? **Perhaps Rabbi Eliezer only stated** that he may not raise the second animal **there,** in a case **where it is possible** to save the animal by **feeding** it in the pit; **however, here,** in the case of the barrel, **where it is impossible to** save it by **feeding** it in the pit, **no,** he would permit doing so. Perhaps even he agrees that it is permitted to employ artifice in this case. **And** similarly, perhaps **Rabbi Yehoshua only said there** that one may employ artifice **because there is** an issue of the **suffering of living beings, but here, where there is no** issue of the **suffering of living beings,** perhaps he did **not** permit employing artifice.

תנו רבנן: הציל פת נקיה אין מציל פת הדראה. פת הדראה – מציל פת נקיה. ומצילין מיום הכפורים לשבת – אבל לא משבת ליום הכפורים, ואין צריך לומר משבת ליום טוב, ולא משבת לשבת הבאה.

The Sages taught in the *Tosefta*: If **one rescued** sufficient **fine bread** for his needs, **he may not** then **rescue coarse bread** [*hadra'a*],[L] bread made from flour and bran. However, if one rescued **coarse bread,** he may then **rescue fine bread.**[H] **And one may rescue** bread **on Yom Kippur for** the purpose of **Shabbat; however,** one may **not** rescue bread **on Shabbat for** the purpose of **Yom Kippur. And, needless to say,** one may not rescue bread **on Shabbat for** the purpose of **a Festival, and** one may **not** rescue bread **on Shabbat for** the purpose of **the next Shabbat.**[H]

תנו רבנן: שכח פת בתנור וקידש עליו היום – מצילין מזון שלש סעודות, ואומר לאחרים: בואו והצילו לכם. וכשהוא רודה – לא ירדה במרדה אלא בסכין. איני?! והא תנא דבי רבי ישמעאל: "לא תעשה כל מלאכה" – יצא תקיעת שופר ורדיית הפת, שהיא חכמה ואינה מלאכה! כמה דאפשר לשנויי משנינן.

And **the Sages taught:** If **one forgot bread in the oven and** did not remove it until **the day** of Shabbat **was sanctified,**[H] **he may rescue** enough **food** for **three meals** from the oven. **And, one may say to others: Come and rescue** bread **for yourselves. And when one removes** the bread from the oven, **he may not remove** it in the usual manner **with a baker's paddle, but** he removes it in an unusual manner, e.g., **with a knife.** The Gemara asks: **Is that so? Didn't the school of Rabbi Yishmael teach** that it is stated: "And the seventh day is Shabbat for the Lord, your God, **you shall not perform any labor"** (Exodus 20:10), and the emphasis on the word labor **excludes blowing the shofar and removing bread, which is a skill and not a labor,** and which therefore is not prohibited on Shabbat. If by Torah law removing bread on Shabbat is permitted, why may one not remove it in the usual manner? The Gemara answers: Nevertheless, **as much as it is possible to alter** the manner in which one removes bread from the oven **one alters,** to emphasize that the day is Shabbat.

HALAKHA

If a barrel on top of one's roof breaks…if guests happen to come to him – נשברה לו חבית בראש גגו...נזדמן לו אורחין: When a barrel breaks on one's roof, it is permitted to bring a vessel, even if it is very large (*Mishna Berura*), and place it beneath the broken barrel to catch the contents pouring out; attaching it to the broken barrel is prohibited. If guests arrive, it is permitted to catch the liquid even by attaching a vessel to the broken barrel. However, one may not employ artifice and invite guests for this purpose. This ruling is in accordance with the unattributed mishna. If one caught the liquid in a prohibited fashion and afterward invited guests, it is permitted to drink it. According to the Rambam, it is permitted to employ artifice in this case, even *ab initio* (*Magen Avraham*; Rambam *Sefer Zemanim, Hilkhot Shabbat* 22:16; *Shulḥan Arukh, Oraḥ Ḥayyim* 335:2–3).

It and its offspring that fell into a pit – אותו ואת בנו שנפלו לבור: If a mother animal and its offspring fell into the same pit on a Festival, one may raise one of them in order to slaughter it, and then employ artifice to raise the second one, using an excuse for preferring the second animal, e.g., it is fatter (*Mishna Berura*). Then, he may slaughter either animal. The *halakha* is in accordance with the opinion of Rabbi Yehoshua in his dispute with Rabbi Eliezer (Rambam *Sefer Zemanim, Hilkhot Yom Tov* 2:4; *Shulḥan Arukh, Oraḥ Ḥayyim* 498:10).

Rescuing types of bread – הצלת מיני פת: One who rescued coarse bread from a fire on Shabbat may return to the house to rescue fine bread. However, if one rescued fine bread, it is prohibited to return to the fire to rescue coarse bread (Rambam *Sefer Zemanim, Hilkhot Shabbat* 23:25; *Shulḥan Arukh, Oraḥ Ḥayyim* 334:3).

Rescuing for the purpose of another day – הצלה לצורך יום אחר: One may rescue food from a fire on Yom Kippur that occurs on Friday for the purpose of eating it on Shabbat. On Shabbat, it is prohibited to save food from a fire to eat it on Yom Kippur, a Festival, or the following Shabbat. On Yom Kippur, one may rescue sufficient food for a single meal, to be eaten at night after Yom Kippur (Jerusalem Talmud; Rambam *Sefer Zemanim, Hilkhot Shabbat* 23:25; *Shulḥan Arukh, Oraḥ Ḥayyim* 334:4).

One forgot bread in the oven and the day of Shabbat was sanctified – שכח פת בתנור וקידש עליו היום: If one forgot bread in an oven and Shabbat began, it is permitted to remove enough bread for the three meals of Shabbat, provided that this bread is the only food that he has on Shabbat. One may invite others who have no other food to eat, to come and remove bread from the oven according to their needs. However, one must remove the bread in an atypical manner, e.g., with a knife. If it is impossible to do so atypically, one may remove it in the typical manner (Ran; Rambam *Sefer Zemanim, Hilkhot Shabbat* 22:1; *Shulḥan Arukh, Oraḥ Ḥayyim* 254:5).

NOTES

It and its offspring – אותו ואת בנו: Although in the Torah, the prohibition of "it and its offspring" (Leviticus 22:28) is phrased with masculine pronouns, most of the Sages rule that the essential prohibition refers to a mother animal and its offspring. Other authorities extend the prohibition to a father animal and its offspring, in cases where the paternity of the animal is clear. In terms of the prohibition, it is irrelevant whether the mother animal or the offspring is slaughtered first.

LANGUAGE

Coarse bread [*hadra'a*] – הדראה: The origin of this word is not entirely clear. Some commentaries suggest that it originates in Hebrew and an antonym of *hadar*, beauty (Rashi). Other authorities assert that it is from *deira'on*, disgrace (Rashash). Some linguists have found a similar root in the Aramaic *hadra'a*, meaning bran bread. According to the *Arukh*, the origin of the word is perhaps the Latin hordeum, meaning barley or buckwheat.

אָמַר רַב חִסְדָּא: לְעוֹלָם יַשְׁכִּים אָדָם לְהוֹצָאַת שַׁבָּת, שֶׁנֶּאֱמַר: "וְהָיָה בַּיּוֹם הַשִּׁשִּׁי וְהֵכִינוּ אֵת אֲשֶׁר יָבִיאוּ" – לְאַלְתַּר. אָמַר רַבִּי אַבָּא: בַּשַּׁבָּת חַיָּיב אָדָם לִבְצוֹעַ עַל שְׁתֵּי כִכָּרוֹת, דִּכְתִיב: "לֶחֶם מִשְׁנֶה".

Rav Ḥisda said: A person should always rise early on Friday in order **to prepare** all of the **expenditures for Shabbat,**[H] **as it is written** with regard to the collection of the manna: **"And it shall be on the sixth day,**[N] **and they will prepare that which they have brought"** (Exodus 16:5), indicating that the children of Israel would begin preparing the food for Shabbat **immediately** upon collecting the manna in the morning. Apropos manna, the Gemara mentions other matters derived from it. **Rabbi Abba said: On Shabbat a person is obligated to break** bread[H] in his meal **over two loaves** of bread, **as it is written:** "And it happened on the sixth day, they collected **double the bread,** two *omer* for each one" (Exodus 16:22).

אָמַר רַב אַשִׁי: חֲזֵינָא לֵיהּ לְרַב כָּהֲנָא דְּנָקֵט תַּרְתֵּי וּבָצַע חֲדָא, אָמַר "לָקְטוּ" כְּתִיב. רַבִּי זֵירָא הֲוָה בָּצַע אַכּוּלָּהּ שֵׁירוּתֵיהּ. אֲמַר לֵיהּ רָבִינָא לְרַב אַשִׁי: וְהָא מֶיחֱזֵי כְּרַעַבְתָנוּתָא! אֲמַר לֵיהּ: כֵּיוָן דְּכָל יוֹמָא לָא עָבֵיד, וְהָאִידָּנָא הוּא דְּקָעָבֵיד – לָא מֶיחֱזֵי כְּרַעַבְתָנוּתָא. רַבִּי אַמִּי וְרַבִּי אַסִּי כִּי מִיקְּלַע לְהוּ רִיפְתָּא דְּעֵירוּבָא – שָׁרוּ עִילָּוֵיהּ, אָמְרִי: הוֹאִיל וְאִיתְעֲבִיד בָּהּ חֲדָא מִצְוָה – לִיתְעֲבִיד בָּהּ מִצְוָה אַחֲרִינָא.

Rav Ashi said: I saw that Rav Kahana took two loaves in his hand **and broke one,** not both at once. **He said** in explanation that **it is written:** "They **collected** double the bread," meaning that one collects and holds two loaves together, but need not break both. **Rabbi Zeira would break** off a piece that would suffice for **his entire meal.**[NH] **Ravina said to Rav Ashi: Doesn't that appear like gluttony?** Rav Ashi **said to him: Since on every** other **day he does not do** this **and now he is doing** so, **it does not appear like gluttony. Rabbi Ami and Rabbi Asi, when the bread from the** *eiruv* **would happen** to become available **to them, they would begin** and recite the blessing over **it.**[NH] They **said** in explanation: **Since one mitzva was performed with it, let an additional mitzva be performed with it.**

"כֵּיצַד, נָפְלָה דְּלֵיקָה כו'". תָּנוּ רַבָּנַן: כַּמָּה סְעוּדוֹת חַיָּיב אָדָם לֶאֱכוֹל בַּשַּׁבָּת? שָׁלֹשׁ, רַבִּי חִידְקָא אוֹמֵר: אַרְבַּע. אָמַר רַבִּי יוֹחָנָן: וּשְׁנֵיהֶם מִקְּרָא אֶחָד דָּרְשׁוּ, "וַיֹּאמֶר מֹשֶׁה אִכְלוּהוּ הַיּוֹם כִּי שַׁבָּת הַיּוֹם לַה' הַיּוֹם לֹא תִמְצָאֻהוּ בַּשָּׂדֶה". רַבִּי חִידְקָא סָבַר: הָנֵי תְּלָתָא "הַיּוֹם" – לְבַר מֵאוֹרְתָא, וְרַבָּנַן סָבְרִי: בַּהֲדֵי דְּאוֹרְתָא. תְּנַן: נָפְלָה דְּלֵיקָה בְּלֵילֵי שַׁבָּת –

We learned in the mishna that one may rescue food for three meals on Shabbat. **How so? If a fire ignited** before the meal on Shabbat evening, one rescues food for three meals; if a fire ignited Shabbat morning, he rescues food for two meals; if a fire ignited in the afternoon, he rescues food for one meal. With regard to meals on Shabbat, **the Sages taught** in a *baraita*: **How many meals is a person obligated to eat on Shabbat?**[H] **Three. Rabbi Ḥidka says: Four. Rabbi Yoḥanan said: And both of them derived** their opinions **from one verse: "And Moses said: Eat it today, for today is Shabbat for God, today you will not find it in the field"** (Exodus 16:25). **Rabbi Ḥidka holds: These three** mentions of the word **today** allude to the number of meals on Shabbat **besides the evening** meal, as Moses spoke on Shabbat morning. **And the Rabbis hold** that these three mentions **include the evening** meal. **We learned** in the mishna: If a **fire ignited on Shabbat evening,**

NOTES

And it shall be on the sixth day – וְהָיָה בַּיּוֹם הַשִּׁשִּׁי: With the statement, "And it shall be," the Torah indicates that the people should begin preparations, "they will prepare" (Exodus 16:5), immediately when the day begins. An alternative interpretation is that since they did not collect the manna at night, the Torah teaches that preparations began with its collection in the early hours of the morning (Ritva).

He would break off a piece that would suffice for his entire meal – בָּצַע אַכּוּלָּא שֵׁירוּתֵיהּ: Some commentaries explain that Rabbi Zeira would break all of the loaves that he prepared for the meal (Rashba).

When the bread from the *eiruv* would happen to become available to them, they would begin and recite the blessing over it – כִּי מִיקְּלַע לְהוּ רִיפְתָּא דְּעֵירוּבָא שָׁרוּ עִילָּוֵיהּ: Some commentaries explain that Rabbi Ami and Rabbi Asi would do so specifically with the bread of the joining of cooked food [*eiruv tavshilin*] (*ge'onim*).

HALAKHA

A person should always rise early to prepare all of the expenditures for Shabbat – לְעוֹלָם יַשְׁכִּים אָדָם לְהוֹצָאַת שַׁבָּת: One should rise early on Friday morning to prepare what is needed for Shabbat. Even if one has servants, it is preferable that he honor Shabbat by participating in the preparations (*Shulḥan Arukh, Oraḥ Ḥayyim* 250:1).

A person is obligated to break bread, etc. – חַיָּיב אָדָם לִבְצוֹעַ וכו': During the Shabbat meal, one recites the blessing while holding two loaves of bread and then breaks one of them. This practice is in accordance with the custom of Rabbi Kahana (Rambam *Sefer Zemanim, Hilkhot Shabbat* 30:9; *Shulḥan Arukh, Oraḥ Ḥayyim* 274:1, 289:1).

He would break off a piece that would suffice for his entire meal – בָּצַע אַכּוּלָּהּ שֵׁירוּתֵיהּ: At the Shabbat meal, it is a mitzva to break off a slice of bread sufficient for one's entire meal. According to Rabbi Zeira, this is a display of affection for the Shabbat meal (*Shulḥan Arukh, Oraḥ Ḥayyim* 274:2).

When the bread from the *eiruv* would happen to become available to them, they would begin and recite the blessing over it – כִּי מִיקְּלַע לְהוּ רִיפְתָּא דְּעֵירוּבָא שָׁרוּ עִילָּוֵיהּ: Bread that was used to make the joining of the courtyards for Shabbat should be eaten at the Shabbat morning meal, as per the custom of Rabbi Ami and Rabbi Asi (*Shulḥan Arukh, Oraḥ Ḥayyim* 394:2 and in the comment of the Rema).

How many meals is a person obligated to eat on Shabbat – כַּמָּה סְעוּדוֹת חַיָּיב אָדָם לֶאֱכוֹל בַּשַּׁבָּת: One is obligated to eat three meals on Shabbat. One should make certain to eat the third meal, even if doing so requires extra effort (Rambam *Sefer Zemanim, Hilkhot Shabbat* 30:9; *Shulḥan Arukh, Oraḥ Ḥayyim* 291:1).

מַצִּילִין מְזוֹן שָׁלֹשׁ סְעוּדוֹת, מַאי לָאו – דְּלָא אֲכַל? לָא, דַּאֲכַל. ״שַׁחֲרִית מַצִּילִין מְזוֹן שְׁתֵּי סְעוּדוֹת״, מַאי לָאו דְּלָא אֲכַל? לָא, דַּאֲכַל. ״בְּמִנְחָה, מַצִּילִין מְזוֹן סְעוּדָה אַחַת״,

one rescues food for three meals. What, is this not referring to a situation where **he has not** yet **eaten** any meals? Apparently, one is obligated to eat only three meals on Shabbat. The Gemara rejects this: **No,** it is referring to a situation where **one** already **ate** one meal. Three meals still remain, in accordance with the opinion of Rabbi Ḥidka, who requires four meals. The Gemara challenges this from the continuation of the mishna: If a fire ignited in the **morning, one may** only **rescue food for two meals. What, is it not** referring to a situation where one **has not** yet **eaten** one's morning meal and the obligation is to eat only three meals, one at night and two during the day? The Gemara rejects this: **No,** it is referring to a situation where **one has** already **eaten** the morning meal. The Gemara challenges this from the continuation of the mishna: If a fire ignited **in the afternoon,** one may rescue **food for one meal.**

מַאי לָאו דְּלָא אֲכַל? לָא, דַּאֲכַל. וְהָא מִדְּקָתָנֵי סֵיפָא ״רַבִּי יוֹסֵי אוֹמֵר: לְעוֹלָם מַצִּילִין מְזוֹן שָׁלֹשׁ סְעוּדוֹת״ מִכְּלָל דְּתַנָּא קַמָּא שָׁלֹשׁ סְבִירָא לֵיהּ! אֶלָּא מְחַוַּורְתָּא, מַתְנִיתִין דְּלָא כְּרַבִּי חִידְקָא.

What, is it not referring to a situation where one **has not** yet **eaten** the afternoon meal and the obligation is to eat only three meals? The Gemara rejects this: **No,** it is referring to a situation where **one has** already **eaten.** The Gemara challenges this: **From** the fact that **it is taught in the latter clause** of the mishna: **Rabbi Yosei says: One may always rescue food for three meals, by inference,** even the **first** ***tanna*** **holds** that the obligation is to eat **three** meals, as there is no dispute with regard to the number of meals on Shabbat. **Rather, it is clear** that the **mishna is not in accordance with** the opinion of **Rabbi Ḥidka.** According to the *tanna'im* in the mishna, one is obligated to eat three meals on Shabbat.

וְהָא דִּתְנַן: מִי שֶׁיֵּשׁ לוֹ מְזוֹן שְׁתֵּי סְעוּדוֹת – לֹא יִטּוֹל מִן הַתַּמְחוּי, מְזוֹן אַרְבַּע עֶשְׂרֵה – לֹא יִטּוֹל מִן הַקּוּפָּה. מַנִּי? לָא רַבָּנַן וְלָא רַבִּי חִידְקָא! אִי רַבָּנַן – חֲמֵיסַר הָוְיָין, אִי רַבִּי חִידְקָא – שִׁית סְרֵי הָוְיָין! לְעוֹלָם רַבָּנַן, דְּאָמְרִינַן לֵיהּ: מַאי דְּבָעֵית לְמֵיכַל בְּאַפּוֹקֵי שַׁבְּתָא – אַכְלֵיהּ בְּשַׁבְּתָא.

And that which we learned in another mishna: **One who has** sufficient **food for two meals** in his possession **may not take** food **from the charity plate**[N] that is distributed to the poor. He is not considered needy and would be taking food at the expense of people who are worse off than he. And one who has **food for fourteen** meals, enough meals for an entire week, **may not take** money **from the charity fund.**[H] The Gemara asks: In accordance with **whose** opinion is this mishna? Apparently, it is **neither** in accordance with the opinion of **the Rabbis nor** in accordance with the opinion of **Rabbi Ḥidka. If** it were in accordance with the opinion of **the Rabbis,** they maintain that **they are fifteen** meals that are eaten in a week, two each day, evening and morning, and three on Shabbat. **If** it were in accordance with the opinion of **Rabbi Ḥidka, they are sixteen** meals that are eaten in a week, twelve during the six days of the week and four on Shabbat. The Gemara rejects this: **Actually,** the mishna is in accordance with the opinion of **the Rabbis,** but **we say to him: That which you want to eat at the conclusion of Shabbat,** Saturday night, **eat** it as the third meal **on Shabbat.**

לֵימָא רַבָּנַן הִיא וְלָא רַבִּי חִידְקָא? אֲפִילּוּ תֵּימָא רַבִּי חִידְקָא, דְּאָמְרִינַן לֵיהּ: מַאי דְּבָעֵית לְמֵיכַל בְּמַעֲלֵי שַׁבְּתָא – אַכְלֵיהּ לְאוּרְתָּא. וְכוּלֵּי יוֹמָא דְּמַעֲלֵי שַׁבְּתָא בְּתַעֲנִיתָא מוֹתְבִינַן לֵיהּ?! אֶלָּא, הָא מַנִּי – רַבִּי עֲקִיבָא הִיא, דְּאָמַר: עֲשֵׂה שַׁבַּתְּךָ חוֹל, וְאַל תִּצְטָרֵךְ לַבְּרִיּוֹת.

The Gemara asks: **Let us say** that **this** mishna **is** in accordance with the opinion of **the Rabbis and not** in accordance with the opinion of **Rabbi Ḥidka.** The Gemara rejects that approach: **Even if you say** that it is in accordance with the opinion of **Rabbi Ḥidka,** the mishna can be understood, **as we can say to him: That which you want to eat on Shabbat eve,** Friday afternoon, **eat at night** on Shabbat instead. The Gemara asks: **And do we have a person sit** and **fast all day on Shabbat eve?** According to this suggestion, he would not eat at all on Friday. **Rather,** we must say: In accordance with **whose** opinion is **this** mishna? **It is** in accordance with the opinion of **Rabbi Akiva, who said: Make your Shabbat** like **a weekday**[H] **and do not be beholden to** other **beings.** It is preferable to eat two meals on Shabbat as he does during the week if he can thereby avoid taking charity.

NOTES

One who has sufficient food for two meals may not take food from the charity plate – מִי שֶׁיֵּשׁ לוֹ מְזוֹן שְׁתֵּי סְעוּדוֹת לֹא יִטּוֹל מִן הַתַּמְחוּי: The Sages ruled that one may not receive assistance from charity unless he is truly in need. Although they stated that it is appropriate for one who needs help to avail himself of that help rather than suffer, it remains preferable to avoid receiving charity. Consequently, the Sages set different criteria for eligibility to receive charity, and it was incumbent upon the poor to take no more than the measure for which he is eligible.

HALAKHA

Who is fit to receive charity – מִי רָאוּי לְקַבֵּל צְדָקָה: A poor person who has enough food for two meals may not take from the charity plate from which food is distributed to the needy. In addition, one who has food to last a week, i.e., fourteen meals, may not take money from the charity fund (Rambam *Sefer Zera'im, Hilkhot Mattenot Aniyyim* 9:13; *Shulḥan Arukh, Yoreh De'a* 253:1).

Make your Shabbat like a weekday – עֲשֵׂה שַׁבַּתְּךָ חוֹל: A person who is especially needy and has no collateral to enable him to take a loan to cover Shabbat expenses should make his Shabbat like a weekday and not be beholden to other beings. According to Rabbi Akiva, it is preferable for a person to refrain from honoring Shabbat with food and drink than to receive charity. Nevertheless, one who has available means must make every effort he can to honor Shabbat (Rambam *Sefer Zemanim, Hilkhot Shabbat* 30:7; *Shulḥan Arukh, Yoreh De'a* 253:1, *Oraḥ Ḥayyim* 242).

וְהָא דִּתְנַן: אֵין פּוֹחֲתִין לְעָנִי הָעוֹבֵר מִמָּקוֹם לְמָקוֹם מִכִּכָּר בְּפוּנְדְּיוֹן מֵאַרְבַּע סְאִין בְּסֶלַע. לָן – נוֹתְנִין לוֹ פַּרְנָסַת לִינָה, וְאִם שָׁבַת – נוֹתְנִין לוֹ מְזוֹן שָׁלֹשׁ סְעוּדוֹת. לֵימָא רַבָּנַן הִיא וְלָא רַבִּי חִידְקָא! לְעוֹלָם רַבִּי חִידְקָא, כְּגוֹן דְּאִיכָּא סְעוּדָה בַּהֲדֵיהּ, דְּאָמְרִינַן לֵיהּ: הָא דְּאִיכָּא בַּהֲדָךְ – אַכְלֵיהּ. וְכִי אָזֵיל בְּרֵיקָן אָזֵיל?! דִּמְלַוִּוינַן לֵיהּ סְעוּדָה בַּהֲדֵיהּ. מַאי ״פַּרְנָסַת לִינָה״? אָמַר רַב פָּפָּא: פּוּרְיָא וּבֵי סַדְיָא.

And that which we learned in another mishna: **One gives no less** charity **to a poor person who is traveling from place to place**[H] **than a loaf** worth **a pundeyon,**[NBL] one forty-eighth of a *sela*, when the standard price of grain is **four se'a for a sela. If he sleeps** there, **one gives him money for sleeping; and if he spends Shabbat** in that city, **one gives him food for three meals. Let us say** that is in accordance with the opinion of **the Rabbis and not** the opinion of **Rabbi Ḥidka.** The Gemara rejects this: **Actually,** it is in accordance with the opinion of **Rabbi Ḥidka.** When it says that if the poor traveler spends Shabbat there one gives him food for three meals, it is referring to a case **where there is** one **meal** that he brought **with him, for we say to him: This** meal **that you have with you, eat it.** The Gemara is surprised at this: **And when he goes, does he go** empty-handed, with no food. The Gemara answers: **We** provide **him** a **meal** to **accompany** him when he leaves. The Gemara asks: **What** is the meaning of **money for sleeping? Rav Pappa said:** It means that one provides his sleeping needs, i.e., **a bed and cushions.**

תָּנוּ רַבָּנַן: קְעָרוֹת שֶׁאָכַל בָּהֶן עַרְבִית מְדִיחָן לֶאֱכוֹל בָּהֶן שַׁחֲרִית, שַׁחֲרִית – מְדִיחָן לֶאֱכוֹל בָּהֶן בְּצׇהֳרַיִם, בְּצׇהֳרַיִם – מְדִיחָן לֶאֱכוֹל בָּהֶן בְּמִנְחָה. מִן הַמִּנְחָה וְאֵילָךְ שׁוּב אֵינוֹ מֵדִיחַ, אֲבָל כּוֹסוֹת וְקִיתוֹנִיּוֹת וּצְלוֹחִיּוֹת – מֵדִיחַ וְהוֹלֵךְ כׇּל הַיּוֹם כּוּלּוֹ, לְפִי שֶׁאֵין קֶבַע לִשְׁתִיָּה.

The Sages taught in a *baraita*: With regard to **bowls from which one ate in the evening** on Shabbat, **he may rinse them** in order **to eat from them in the morning.** Bowls from which one ate in the **morning, he may rinse them to eat from them in the afternoon.** Bowls from which one ate **in the afternoon, he may rinse them to eat from them in the afternoon.** However, **from the afternoon onward, one may no longer rinse them** because there is no further need for these bowls on Shabbat, and it is prohibited to make preparations on Shabbat for a weekday. **However,** with regard to **cups, and ladles, and flasks,** which are vessels used for drinking, **one rinses them**[H] **all day long because there is no fixed** time **for drinking,** and one does not know when he will drink again.

אָמַר רַבִּי שִׁמְעוֹן בֶּן פָּזִי אָמַר רַבִּי יְהוֹשֻׁעַ בֶּן לֵוִי מִשּׁוּם בַּר קַפָּרָא: כׇּל הַמְקַיֵּים שָׁלֹשׁ סְעוּדוֹת בְּשַׁבָּת נִיצּוֹל מִשָּׁלֹשׁ פּוּרְעָנִיּוֹת: מֵחֶבְלוֹ שֶׁל מָשִׁיחַ, וּמִדִּינָהּ שֶׁל גֵּיהִנָּם, וּמִמִּלְחֶמֶת גּוֹג וּמָגוֹג. מֵחֶבְלוֹ שֶׁל מָשִׁיחַ – כְּתִיב הָכָא ׳יוֹם׳ וּכְתִיב הָתָם ״הִנֵּה אָנֹכִי שֹׁלֵחַ לָכֶם אֵת אֵלִיָּה הַנָּבִיא לִפְנֵי בּוֹא יוֹם וגו׳״. מִדִּינָהּ שֶׁל גֵּיהִנָּם – כְּתִיב הָכָא ׳יוֹם׳ וּכְתִיב הָתָם ״יוֹם עֶבְרָה הַיּוֹם הַהוּא״. מִמִּלְחֶמֶת גּוֹג וּמָגוֹג – כְּתִיב הָכָא ׳יוֹם׳ וּכְתִיב הָתָם ״בְּיוֹם בֹּא גוֹג״.

Rabbi Shimon ben Pazi said that **Rabbi Yehoshua ben Levi said in the name of bar Kappara: Anyone who fulfills** the obligation to eat **three meals on Shabbat is rescued from three punishments: From the pangs of the Messiah,** i.e., the suffering that precedes the advent of Messiah, **and from the judgment of Gehenna, and from the war of Gog and Magog.** The Gemara derives that one is rescued **from the pangs of Messiah** by means of a verbal analogy. **It is written here,** with regard to Shabbat, **day:** "Eat it today" (Exodus 16:25). **And it is written there,** with regard to Messiah, day: **"Behold, I am sending you Elijah the prophet before the coming of the** great and awesome **day** of God" (Malachi 3:23). The Gemara derives that one is rescued **from the judgment of Gehenna** by means of a verbal analogy. **It is written here,** with regard to Shabbat, **day,** as cited above. **And it is written there,** day: **"That day will be a day of wrath,** a day of trouble and distress, a day of destruction and desolation, a day of darkness and blackness, a day of cloud and thick fog" (Zephaniah 1:15), which is interpreted as referring to the punishment of Gehenna. The Gemara derives that one is rescued **from the war of Gog and Magog** by means of a verbal analogy. **It is written here,** with regard to Shabbat, **day. And it is written there,** with regard to the War of Gog and Magog, day: "And it shall be on that day, **on the day that Gog arrives** on the land of Israel" (Ezekiel 38:18).

אָמַר רַבִּי יוֹחָנָן מִשּׁוּם רַבִּי יוֹסֵי: כׇּל הַמְעַנֵּג אֶת הַשַּׁבָּת נוֹתְנִין לוֹ נַחֲלָה בְּלִי מְצָרִים, שֶׁנֶּאֱמַר: ״אָז תִּתְעַנַּג עַל ה׳ וְהִרְכַּבְתִּיךָ עַל בָּמֳתֵי אָרֶץ וְהַאֲכַלְתִּיךָ

Rabbi Yoḥanan said in the name of Rabbi Yosei: With regard to **anyone who delights in the Shabbat,** God **gives him a boundless portion,**[N] i.e., a very large reward, **as it is stated:** "If you keep your feet from violating Shabbat, from pursuing your affairs on My holy day, and you call Shabbat a delight, the Lord's holy day honored, and you honor it by not going your own way, or attending to your own matters or speaking idle words. **Then you shall delight in the Lord and I will cause you to ride on the heights of the world, and to feast**

HALAKHA

A poor person who is traveling from place to place – עָנִי הָעוֹבֵר מִמָּקוֹם לְמָקוֹם: One is obligated to provide a poor person who is traveling with a loaf of bread that costs at least a *pundeyon*, when the cost of grain is four *se'a* of wheat per *sela*. If the poor person stays overnight locally, one must provide him with bedding and a cushion. If the poor person is known in the community, he is provided with support commensurate with his standard of living prior to becoming impoverished (Rambam *Sefer Zera'im, Hilkhot Mattenot Aniyyim* 7:8; *Shulḥan Arukh, Yoreh De'a* 250:4).

Rinsing dishes on Shabbat – הֲדָחַת כֵּלִים בְּשַׁבָּת: It is only permitted to wash dishes on Shabbat for use on Shabbat. Therefore, the dishes used for the third and final meal of Shabbat may not be washed on Shabbat. Vessels used for drinking may be washed all day long because there are no fixed times for drinking (*Shulḥan Arukh, Oraḥ Ḥayyim* 323:6).

BACKGROUND

A loaf worth a *pundeyon* – כִּכָּר בְּפוּנְדְּיוֹן: According to the conclusion in the Gemara, the volume of this loaf of bread is between two-thirds and one ℓ of bread, which is sufficient for two meals.

Pundeyon from the time of the Talmud

LANGUAGE

***Pundeyon* – פּוּנְדְּיוֹן:** From the Latin dupondium, which means the sum of two pence. The *pundeyon* is a coin worth two *issar*. There are twelve *pundeyon* in a dinar or *zuz*, and forty-eight *pundeyon* in a *sela*.

NOTES

A loaf worth a *pundeyon* – כִּכָּר בְּפוּנְדְּיוֹן: It is explained in tractate *Eiruvin* that this refers to a loaf that was purchased from the storekeeper for a *pundeyon*. The profits of the baker and storeowner are factored into the price of the bread. Consequently, this loaf is actually only a quarter of a *kav*.

A boundless portion – נַחֲלָה בְּלִי מְצָרִים: The reward of a boundless portion is one that is measure for measure. Since one delights in Shabbat without limiting his expenditures, one is rewarded with a portion that is limitless (*Beit Yosef*). The Gemara proceeds to cite the verse from Isaiah, which speaks of one who delights in Shabbat as being rewarded with the portion of Jacob. Some commentaries explain that the portion of Abraham was shared with the descendants of Ishmael and Lot, and part of Isaac's portion was given to Esau. However, the portion of Jacob was complete, not shared with others, and therefore boundless (Maharsha; *Imrei Emet*).

HALAKHA

Delighting in Shabbat – עוֹנֶג שַׁבָּת: It is appropriate that one delight in and honor Shabbat. One should cook special food in deference to Shabbat, even if other people do not consider that dish to be important (Rambam *Sefer Zemanim, Hilkhot Shabbat* 30:7; *Shulḥan Arukh, Oraḥ Ḥayyim* 242).

NOTES

Idolatry as in the generation of Enosh – עֲבוֹדָה זָרָה כְּדוֹר אֱנוֹשׁ: The generation of Enosh was the first generation that believed that praying to intermediaries between man and God was effective (Rambam *Sefer HaMadda, Hilkhot Avoda Zara*).

נחלת יעקב אביך וגו׳״. לא כאברהם שכתוב בו: ״קום התהלך בארץ לארכה וגו׳״, ולא כיצחק שכתוב בו: ״כי לך ולזרעך אתן את כל הארצות האל״, אלא כיעקב שכתוב בו: ״ופרצת ימה וקדמה וצפונה ונגבה״.

on the inheritance of Jacob your father, as the mouth of God has spoken" (Isaiah 58:13–14). The reward for delighting in Shabbat is specifically the portion of Jacob. **Not that of Abraham, about whom it is written, "Rise, walk through the land through its length** and its width because I have given it to you" (Genesis 13:17), i.e., only this land alone in its borders. **And not that of Isaac, about whom it is written,** "Dwell in this land and I will be with you and I will bless you **because I will give all of these lands to you and your offspring"** (Genesis 26:3), meaning these lands and no others. **Rather, that of Jacob, about whom it is written,** "And your offspring will be like the dust of the earth, **and you will spread out to the west and to the east and to the north and to the south,** and all of the families of the land will be blessed through you and your offspring" (Genesis 28:14). There are no boundaries for Jacob's portion.

רב נחמן בר יצחק אמר: ניצול משעבוד גליות, כתיב הכא: ״והרכבתיך על במתי ארץ״, וכתיב התם: ״ואתה על במותימו תדרוך״. אמר רב יהודה אמר רב: כל המענג את השבת נותנין לו משאלות לבו, שנאמר: ״והתענג על ה׳ ויתן לך משאלות לבך״. עונג זה איני יודע מהו, כשהוא אומר: ״וקראת לשבת עונג״, הוי אומר: זה עונג שבת. במה מענגו? רב יהודה בריה דרב שמואל בר שילת משמיה דרב אמר: בתבשיל של תרדין, ודגים גדולים, וראשי שומין. רב חייא בר אשי אמר רב: אפילו דבר מועט, ולכבוד שבת עשאו – הרי זה עונג. מאי היא? אמר רב פפא: כסא דהרסנא.

Rav Naḥman bar Yitzḥak said: One who delights in Shabbat[H] is **rescued from the oppression of exile.** He derives it by means of a verbal analogy. **It is written here,** with regard to Shabbat: **"And I will cause you to ride on the heights [*bamotei*] of the world"** (Isaiah 58:14), **and it is written there:** "You are fortunate Israel, who is like you? A nation redeemed by God, the shield that aids you and the sword of your triumph. Your enemies will try to defeat you **and you will trample their high places [*bamoteimo*]"** (Deuteronomy 33:29). **Rav Yehuda said** that **Rav said:** With regard to **anyone who delights in the Shabbat,** God **grants him his heart's desires,** as **it is stated: "And you shall delight in God and He will grant you your heart's desires"** (Psalms 37:4). **This delight** in God, which is mentioned in the verse, **I do not know what it is. When it says: "And you shall call the Shabbat delight,"** one **must say: It is the delight of Shabbat.** The Gemara asks: **With what does one delight** in the day of Shabbat? **Rav Yehuda, son of Rav Shmuel bar Sheilat, said in the name of Rav: With a dish of beets, and large fish, and heads of garlic. Rav Ḥiyya bar Ashi** said that **Rav said: Even** with regard to **a small item and one prepared it in deference to Shabbat, it is a delight.** The Gemara asks: **What is** the small item mentioned? **Rav Pappa said: Small fried fish.**

אמר רבי חייא בר אבא אמר רבי יוחנן: כל המשמר שבת כהלכתו, אפילו עובד עבודה זרה [כדור] אנוש – מוחלין לו, שנאמר: ״אשרי אנוש יעשה זאת וגו׳ מחללו״, אל תקרי ׳מחללו׳ אלא ׳מחול לו׳.

Rabbi Ḥiyya bar Abba said that **Rabbi Yoḥanan said:** With regard to **anyone who observes Shabbat in accordance with its *halakhot*, even** if he **worships idolatry** as in **the generation of Enosh,**[N] God **forgives him** his sins, **as it is stated: "Fortunate is the man [enosh] who does this** and the person who holds strong to it, one who guards the Shabbat **from desecrating it [*meḥallelo*],** and guards his hand from doing any evil" (Isaiah 56:2). **Do not read** it as: **From desecrating it [*meḥallelo*], but rather: He is forgiven [*maḥul lo*].** With regard to the generation of Enosh it is written: "And to Seth, to him also there was born a son; and he called his name Enosh. Then they began [*huḥal*] to call upon the Name of God" (Genesis 4:26), meaning to desecrate [*leḥallel*] His name.

אמר רב יהודה אמר רב: אלמלי שמרו ישראל שבת ראשונה לא שלטה בהן אומה ולשון, שנאמר: ״ויהי ביום השביעי יצאו מן העם ללקוט״, וכתיב בתריה: ״ויבא עמלק״. אמר רבי יוחנן משום רבי שמעון בן יוחי: אלמלי משמרין ישראל שתי שבתות כהלכתן – מיד נגאלים, שנאמר: ״כה אמר ה׳ לסריסים אשר ישמרו את שבתותי״, וכתיב בתריה: ״והביאותים אל הר קדשי וגו׳״.

Rav Yehuda said that **Rav said: Had the Jewish people** properly **observed** the **first Shabbat** that was commanded them, **no nation or tongue would** have ever **ruled them, as it is stated: "And it happened on the seventh day, some people went out from the nation to collect** and they did not find" (Exodus 16:27). **And it is written after** they went out to collect manna: **"And Amalek came** and fought with Israel in Refidim" (Exodus 17:8). **Rabbi Yoḥanan said in the name of Rabbi Shimon ben Yoḥai: If only the Jewish people would keep two *Shabbatot* in accordance with their *halakhot*,** they would be **immediately redeemed, as it is stated: "So said God to the eunuchs who will keep My Shabbatot"** (Isaiah 56:4), **and it is written after** that: **"And I will bring them to My holy mountain** and will let them rejoice in My house of prayer" (Isaiah 56:7).

אָמַר רַבִּי יוֹסֵי: יְהֵא חֶלְקִי מֵאוֹכְלֵי שָׁלֹשׁ סְעוּדוֹת בַּשַּׁבָּת. אָמַר רַבִּי יוֹסֵי: יְהֵא חֶלְקִי מִגּוֹמְרֵי הַלֵּל בְּכׇל יוֹם. אִינִי?! וְהָאָמַר מָר: הַקּוֹרֵא הַלֵּל בְּכׇל יוֹם – הֲרֵי זֶה מְחָרֵף וּמְגַדֵּף! כִּי קָאָמְרִינַן – בִּפְסוּקֵי דְזִמְרָא.

Rabbi Yosei said: May my portion be among those who eat three meals on Shabbat. Apropos this statement of Rabbi Yosei, the Gemara cites additional declarations. **Rabbi Yosei said: May my portion be among those who complete hallel every day.** The Gemara is surprised at this: **Is that so? Didn't the Master say: One who reads *hallel* every day**[N] is tantamount to **one who curses and blasphemes** God. He displays contempt for *hallel* by not reserving it for days on which miracles occurred. The Gemara answers: **When we say** this statement of Rabbi Yosei, we are referring to **the verses of praise** [*pesukei dezimra*],[H] recited during the morning service, not to *hallel* (Psalms 113–118) recited on special days.

אָמַר רַבִּי יוֹסֵי: יְהֵא חֶלְקִי מִמִּתְפַּלְּלִים עִם דִּמְדּוּמֵי חַמָּה. אָמַר רַבִּי חִיָּיא בַּר אַבָּא אָמַר רַבִּי יוֹחָנָן: מִצְוָה לְהִתְפַּלֵּל עִם דִּמְדּוּמֵי חַמָּה. אָמַר רַבִּי זֵירָא: מַאי קְרָא – ״יִירָאוּךָ עִם שָׁמֶשׁ וְלִפְנֵי יָרֵחַ דּוֹר דּוֹרִים״.

And furthermore, **Rabbi Yosei said: May my portion be among those who pray** the morning and afternoon prayers **with the reddening of the sun,** i.e., the morning prayer at sunrise and the afternoon prayer adjacent to nightfall. **Rabbi Ḥiyya bar Abba said** that **Rabbi Yoḥanan said: It is a mitzva to pray with the reddening of the sun.**[H] **Rabbi Zeira said: What verse** alludes to this? **"They will fear You with the sun and before the moon, generation upon generation"** (Psalms 72:5). Fear of God, prayer, should be with the sun and before the moon.

וְאָמַר רַבִּי יוֹסֵי: יְהֵא חֶלְקִי מִמֵּתֵי בְּחוֹלִי מֵעַיִים. דְּאָמַר מָר: רוּבָּן שֶׁל צַדִּיקִים מֵתִים בְּחוֹלִי מֵעַיִים. וְאָמַר רַבִּי יוֹסֵי: יְהֵא חֶלְקִי מִמֵּתֵי בְּדֶרֶךְ מִצְוָה. וְאָמַר רַבִּי יוֹסֵי: יְהֵא חֶלְקִי מִמַּכְנִיסֵי שַׁבָּת בִּטְבֶרְיָא וּמִמּוֹצִיאֵי שַׁבָּת בְּצִפּוֹרִי. וְאָמַר רַבִּי יוֹסֵי: יְהֵא חֶלְקִי מִמּוֹשִׁיבֵי בֵּית הַמִּדְרָשׁ, וְלֹא מִמַּעֲמִידֵי בֵּית הַמִּדְרָשׁ.

And Rabbi Yosei said: May my portion be among those who die from intestinal disease, as the Master said: Most righteous people die of intestinal disease. It is a very harsh disease through which the sins of righteous people are cleansed before their death and also, as a result, they die with a clean body. **And Rabbi Yosei said: May my portion be among those who die on the path to** perform **a mitzva. And Rabbi Yosei said: May my portion be among those who accept Shabbat in Tiberias,**[NH] which is in a valley where day turns to evening earlier, **and among those who see Shabbat out in Tzippori,** which is located on a mountain top where the sun is visible for longer, and Shabbat ends later. **And Rabbi Yosei said: May my portion be among those who seat** others **in the study hall,** i.e., who cause others to come sit and study, **and not among those who cause** others **to stand in the study hall,** i.e., who announce that it is time to leave the study hall and go to eat.

וְאָמַר רַבִּי יוֹסֵי: יְהֵא חֶלְקִי מִגַּבָּאֵי צְדָקָה, וְלֹא מִמְחַלְּקֵי צְדָקָה. וְאָמַר רַבִּי יוֹסֵי: יְהֵא חֶלְקִי מִמִּי שֶׁחוֹשְׁדִין אוֹתוֹ וְאֵין בּוֹ. אָמַר רַב פַּפָּא: לְדִידִי חַשְׁדַן וְלָא הֲוָה בִּי.

And Rabbi Yosei said: May my portion be among the collectors of charity and not the distributors of charity. One who collects charity collects fixed amounts, whereas distributors may inadvertently fail to give the poor person enough to cover his needs. **And Rabbi Yosei said: May my portion be with one whom** others **suspect** of sin **and there is no** basis for suspecting **him. Rav Pappa said: They suspected me, and there was no** basis for suspecting **me.**

אָמַר רַבִּי יוֹסֵי: חָמֵשׁ בְּעִילוֹת בָּעַלְתִּי, וְנָטַעְתִּי חֲמִשָּׁה אֲרָזִים בְּיִשְׂרָאֵל. וּמַאן אִינּוּן – רַבִּי יִשְׁמָעֵאל בְּרַבִּי יוֹסֵי, וְרַבִּי אֶלְעָזָר בְּרַבִּי יוֹסֵי, וְרַבִּי חֲלַפְתָּא בְּרַבִּי יוֹסֵי, וְרַבִּי אַבְטִילָס בְּרַבִּי יוֹסֵי, וְרַבִּי מְנַחֵם בְּרַבִּי יוֹסֵי. וְהָאִיכָּא וַרְדִּימַס! הַיְינוּ וַרְדִּימַס הַיְינוּ מְנַחֵם. וְאַמַּאי קָרֵי לֵיהּ וַרְדִּימַס – שֶׁפָּנָיו דּוֹמִין לְוֶרֶד. לְמֵימְרָא דְּרַבִּי יוֹסֵי מִצְוַת עוֹנָה לֹא קִיֵּים?! אֶלָּא אֵימָא: חָמֵשׁ בְּעִילוֹת בָּעַלְתִּי וְשָׁנִיתִי.

Furthermore, **Rabbi Yosei said: I engaged in relations five times, and I planted five cedars in Eretz Yisrael. And who are these cedars?** The sons of Rabbi Yosei, who were great Sages of Israel: **Rabbi Yishmael, son of Rabbi Yosei, and Rabbi Elazar, son of Rabbi Yosei, and Rabbi Ḥalafta, son of Rabbi Yosei, and Rabbi Avtilas,**[L] **son of Rabbi Yosei, and Rabbi Menaḥem, son of Rabbi Yosei.** The Gemara asks: **Isn't there Vardimas,**[L] who was also Rabbi Yosei's son? The Gemara answers: **Vardimas is the same as Menaḥem. And why did they call him Vardimas?** Because **his face was as** beautiful as **a rose** [*vered*]. The Gemara asks: **Is that to say** based on this statement that **Rabbi Yosei did not fulfill the mitzva of** his wife's **conjugal rights,** but only had relations with her five times? **Rather, say** it this way: **I engaged in relations five times and I did so again,** and the Sages said that one who seeks to father male offspring should engage in relations and do so again.

NOTES

One who reads *hallel* every day – הַקּוֹרֵא הַלֵּל בְּכׇל יוֹם: Some commentaries explain that one who recites *hallel* daily demonstrates a lack of appreciation for the miracles that God performed throughout our history. He also fails to pray for future redemption (*Me'iri*).

Among those who accept Shabbat in Tiberias – מִמַּכְנִיסֵי שַׁבָּת בִּטְבֶרְיָא: One explanation of this statement is that the custom of the people of Tiberias was to perfume their clothing and homes at the start of Shabbat, while in Tzippori they did so when Shabbat ended. Therefore, Rabbi Yosei praised people who adopted both of these customs (*Tosefot Rabbi Yehuda HaḤasid*; *Aguda*).

HALAKHA

May my portion be among those who complete *hallel*…to verses of praise – יְהֵא חֶלְקִי מִגּוֹמְרֵי הַלֵּל...בִּפְסוּקֵי דְזִמְרָא: One should make certain to recite the verse of praise each morning, as Rabbi Yosei said: May my portion be among those who complete *hallel* every day (Rambam *Sefer Ahava*, *Hilkhot Tefilla* 7:12).

It is a mitzva to pray with the reddening of the sun – מִצְוָה לְהִתְפַּלֵּל עִם דִּמְדּוּמֵי חַמָּה: According to Rabbi Yosei and Rabbi Yoḥanan, one should rise early in the morning to recite the morning prayer at sunrise. The afternoon prayer should be recited as the sun is setting (Rambam *Sefer Ahava*, *Hilkhot Tefilla* 3:1; *Shulḥan Arukh*, *Oraḥ Ḥayyim* 89:1, 233:1).

May my portion be among those who accept Shabbat in Tiberias – יְהֵא חֶלְקִי מִמַּכְנִיסֵי שַׁבָּת בִּטְבֶרְיָא: Some authorities state that one is obligated to extend the sanctity of Shabbat into the week by beginning Shabbat early and ending it late. The *Magen Avraham* rules that this is a mitzva by Torah law. That is one explanation of Rabbi Yosei's statement. However, the primary source for the obligation to extend Shabbat is the interpretation of the verses cited in tractate *Yoma* (*Shulḥan Arukh*, *Oraḥ Ḥayyim* 261:2).

LANGUAGE

Avtilas – אַבְטִילָס: From the Greek εὔτολμος, *eutolmos*, meaning strong-hearted.

Vardimas – וַרְדִּימַס: From the Greek εὐρύδημος, *eurydēmos*. In this context, it relates to the Hebrew *vered*, or the Greek ῥόδον, *rhodon*, meaning rose.

אָמַר רַבִּי יוֹסֵי: מִיָּמַי לֹא קָרִיתִי לְאִשְׁתִּי ׳אִשְׁתִּי׳ וּלְשׁוֹרִי ׳שׁוֹרִי׳, אֶלָּא: לְאִשְׁתִּי ״בֵּיתִי״, וּלְשׁוֹרִי ״שָׂדִי״.

Furthermore, **Rabbi Yosei said** that he always spoke euphemistically: **In all my days, I did not call my wife, my wife,**[N] **nor my ox, my ox. Rather,** I called **my wife, my home,** because she is the essence of the home, **and my ox, my field,** because it is the primary force in the fields.

אָמַר רַבִּי יוֹסֵי: מִיָּמַי לֹא נִסְתַּכַּלְתִּי בְּמִילָה שֶׁלִּי. אִינִי?! וְהָאָמְרוּ לֵיהּ לְרַבִּי: מַאי טַעְמָא קָרְאוּ לָךְ ״רַבֵּינוּ הַקָּדוֹשׁ״? אֲמַר לְהוּ: מִיָּמַי לֹא נִסְתַּכַּלְתִּי בְּמִילָה שֶׁלִּי. בְּרַבִּי מִילְּתָא אַחֲרִיתִי הֲוָה בֵּיהּ – שֶׁלֹּא הִכְנִיס יָדוֹ תַּחַת אַבְנֵטוֹ. וְאָמַר רַבִּי יוֹסֵי: מִיָּמַי לֹא רָאוּ קוֹרוֹת בֵּיתִי אִימְרֵי חֲלוּקִי.

Rabbi Yosei said: In all my days, due to modesty, **I never looked at my circumcision.**[H] The Gemara asks: **Is that so? Didn't they say to Rabbi** Yehuda HaNasi: **Why did they call you our holy Rabbi? He said to them:** It is because **in all my days I never looked at my circumcision.** If so, why wasn't Rabbi Yosei also called our holy Rabbi? The Gemara replies: **In** the case of **Rabbi** Yehuda HaNasi, **another matter** of modesty **was** present **in him, as he did not insert his hand below his belt** due to his great modesty. **And Rabbi Yosei said: In all my days, the walls of my house never saw the seams of my robe**[H] due to modesty, as he would only undress under his bed sheets.

וְאָמַר רַבִּי יוֹסֵי: מִיָּמַי לֹא עָבַרְתִּי עַל דִּבְרֵי חֲבֵרַי. יוֹדֵעַ אֲנִי בְּעַצְמִי שֶׁאֵינִי כֹּהֵן, אִם אוֹמְרִים לִי חֲבֵירַי ״עֲלֵה לַדּוּכָן״ – אֲנִי עוֹלֶה. וְאָמַר רַבִּי יוֹסֵי: מִיָּמַי לֹא אָמַרְתִּי דָּבָר וְחָזַרְתִּי לַאֲחוֹרַי.

And Rabbi Yosei said: In all my days I never violated the words of my friends. I know about myself that I am not a priest, and nevertheless, **if my friends say to me: Go up to the platform**[N] with the priests, **I go up. And Rabbi Yosei said: In all my days I never said something and then retreated** from it.[N] Rabbi Yosei never said something positive or negative about a specific person and then denied it.

אָמַר רַב נַחְמָן: תֵּיתֵי לִי דְּקַיְּימִית שָׁלֹשׁ סְעוּדוֹת בַּשַּׁבָּת. אָמַר רַב יְהוּדָה: תֵּיתֵי לִי דְּקַיְּימִית עִיּוּן תְּפִלָּה. אָמַר רַב הוּנָא בְּרֵיהּ דְּרַב יְהוֹשֻׁעַ: תֵּיתֵי לִי דְּלָא סָגֵינָא אַרְבַּע אַמּוֹת בְּגִילּוּי הָרֹאשׁ. אָמַר רַב שֵׁשֶׁת: תֵּיתֵי לִי דְּקַיְּימִית מִצְוַת תְּפִילִּין. וְאָמַר רַב נַחְמָן: תֵּיתֵי לִי דְּקַיְּימִית מִצְוַת צִיצִית.

Rav Naḥman said: May I receive my reward[B] **because I fulfilled** the obligation to eat **three meals on Shabbat** magnificently. **Rav Yehuda said: May I receive** my reward **because I fulfilled** the obligation of **consideration** during **prayer. Rav Huna, son of Rav Yehoshua, said: May I receive** my reward because **I never walked four cubits with my head uncovered.**[H] **Rav Sheshet said: May I receive** my reward **because I fulfilled the mitzva of phylacteries** magnificently. **And Rav Naḥman said: May I receive** my reward **because I fulfilled the mitzva of ritual fringes** magnificently.

אֲמַר לֵיהּ רַב יוֹסֵף לְרַב יוֹסֵף בְּרֵיהּ דְּרַבָּה: אֲבוּךְ בְּמַאי זָהִיר טְפֵי? אֲמַר לֵיהּ: בְּצִיצִית. יוֹמָא חַד הֲוָה קָא סָלֵיק בְּדַרְגָּא, אִיפְּסִיק לֵיהּ חוּטָא – וְלָא נָחֵית וְאַתָא כַּמָּה דְּלָא רַמְיֵהּ. וְאָמַר אַבַּיֵי: תֵּיתֵי לִי, דְּכִי חָזֵינָא צוּרְבָא מֵרַבָּנַן דְּשַׁלֵּים מַסֶּכְתֵּיהּ

Rav Yosef said to Rav Yosef, son of Rabba: In what area **was your father,** Rabba, **especially vigilant? He said to him:** It was **in** the mitzva of **ritual fringes.** The Gemara relates: **One day he was climbing the stairs** when a **string** from his ritual fringes **was severed, and he would not descend until he placed** a new string **on** the garment. **And Abaye said: May I receive** my reward because **when I see a young Torah scholar who has completed a tractate** that **he** studied

NOTES

I did not called my wife, my wife – לֹא קָרִיתִי לְאִשְׁתִּי ׳אִשְׁתִּי׳: Some commentaries explain that Rabbi Yosei called his wife, my home, so she would realize that she was the essence of the home and would appreciate that responsibility for the home was incumbent upon her. Similarly, he called his ox, my field, so that his workers would appreciate the importance of caring properly for the ox (Maharsha).

Go up to the platform – עֲלֵה לַדּוּכָן: Many commentaries sought to clarify why people thought Rabbi Yosei was a priest and why he followed their instructions. There are two concerns with regard to this practice. First, by participating in the priestly blessing Rabbi Yosei was transgressing a positive commandment, as the mitzva to bless the people was restricted to priests. Second, doing so could create the mistaken impression that his descendants were priests, which would cause future pitfalls for the multitudes.

I never said something and then retreated from it [*ḥazarti la'aḥorai*] – לֹא אָמַרְתִּי דָּבָר וְחָזַרְתִּי לַאֲחוֹרַי: Rashi explained the term *ḥazarti la'aḥorai* in its literal sense, i.e., turned around. Rabbi Yosei never made a statement and then turned around to determine whether or not the person about whom he was speaking was standing behind him. Either because he believed that one who speaks the truth need not be concerned that he will be overheard, or because he was careful never to say anything offensive. Other commentaries explain that he meant that he never made a statement that he later retracted, as he was careful to say what he means the first time (*Me'iri*).

HALAKHA

In all my days I never looked at my circumcision – מִיָּמַי לֹא הִסְתַּכַּלְתִּי בְּמִילָה שֶׁלִּי: Rabbi Yehuda HaNasi, a member of one of the early generations of pious Sages and among the greatest of the Sages, took pride in the fact that he never looked at his circumcision, as per the statement of Rabbi Yosei (*Shulḥan Arukh, Even HaEzer* 23:7).

In all of my days the walls of my house never saw the seams of my robe – מִיָּמַי לֹא רָאוּ קוֹרוֹת בֵּיתִי אִימְרֵי חֲלוּקִי: A person should dress while covered in bed, so that he is not even briefly naked (*Shulḥan Arukh, Oraḥ Ḥayyim* 2:1).

I never walked four cubits with my head uncovered – דְּלָא סָגֵינָא אַרְבַּע אַמּוֹת בְּגִילּוּי הָרֹאשׁ: A man should not walk even four cubits his head uncovered. The *Magen Avraham* writes that it is meritorious to refrain from walking even less than four cubits with an uncovered head. This applies to walking indoors as well as to sitting or standing for the time it would take to walk four cubits (*Mishna Berura*). This worthwhile custom is learned from the greatest Sages. Even though there were authorities who argued that it is only a custom of piety and of extra scrupulousness (Maharshal; Vilna Gaon), the men of Israel have accepted the custom of covering their heads for a variety of reasons (*Shulḥan Arukh, Oraḥ Ḥayyim* 2:6).

BACKGROUND

May I receive my reward – תֵּיתֵי לִי: The *ge'onim* had a tradition that Rav was meticulous in observing ten measures of piety, but his students could not maintain all of them. Therefore, each student sought to uphold at least several of the practices. When doing so, each one prefaced it by saying: May I receive my reward. The ten degrees of piety are as follows: (1) Rav did not walk four cubits standing erect; (2) he always walked with his head covered; (3) he ate three meals on Shabbat; (4) he did not look to the sides as he walked; (5) he prayed with great concentration; (6) he walked around the congregation rather than into the congregation, so that the people would not have to stand up for him and would not be disturbed; (7) he never ate a meal that was not required; (8) he appeased those who provoked him; (9) he had a beautiful voice and served as the translator of the Torah reading in the synagogue; (10) he was meticulous in the performance of the mitzvot of ritual fringes and phylacteries.

עבידנא יומא טבא לרבנן. אמר רבא: תיתי לי דכי אתא צורבא מרבנן לקמאי לדינא, לא מזיגנא רישי אבי סדיא כמה דלא מהפיכנא בזכותיה. אמר מר בר רב אשי: פסילנא ליה לצורבא מרבנן לדינא. מאי טעמא – דחביב עלי כגופאי, ואין אדם רואה חובה לעצמו.

I make a feast for the Sages.[H] **Rava said: May I receive** my reward **because when a young Torah scholar comes before me for judgment, I do not put my head on the pillow**[H] **until** I seek as many of **his merits** as possible, based on conditions and his claims. **Mar bar Rav Ashi said: I am disqualified to** sit in **judgment of a young Torah scholar. What is the reason** that I am disqualified? It is **because** the Torah scholar **is as beloved to me as my** own **self, and a person does not find fault in himself.**

רבי חנינא מיעטף וקאי אפניא דמעלי שבתא, אמר: בואו ונצא לקראת שבת המלכה. רבי ינאי לביש מאניה מעלי שבת, ואמר: בואי כלה בואי כלה. רבה בר רב הונא איקלע לבי רבה בר רב נחמן, קריבו ליה תלת סאוי טחיי. אמר להו: מי הוה ידעיתון דאתינא? אמרו ליה: מי עדיפת לן מינה.

The Gemara now returns to the issue of delight in and deference to Shabbat. **Rabbi Ḥanina would wrap himself** in his garment **and stand at nightfall on Shabbat eve,** and **say: Come and we will go out to greet Shabbat the queen. Rabbi Yannai put on his garment on Shabbat eve and said: Enter, O bride. Enter, O bride.**[H] The Gemara relates: **Rabba bar Rav Huna happened** to come **to the house of Rabba bar Rav Naḥman. They brought** before **him three se'a of oiled biscuits. He said to them: Did you know I was coming** and prepared all of this in my honor? **They said to him: Are you** more **important to us than** Shabbat? The biscuits were prepared in deference to Shabbat.

רבי אבא זבן בתליסר אסתירי פשיטי בישרא מתליסר טבחי, ומשלים להו אצינורא דדשא, ואמר להו: אשור הייא, אשור הייא! רבי אבהו הוה יתיב אתכתקא דשינא ומושיף נורא. רב ענן לביש גונדא; דתנא דבי רבי ישמעאל: בגדים שבישל בהן קדירה לרבו – אל ימזוג בהן כוס לרבו.

Rabbi Abba bought thirteen plain staters [*astirei peshitei*][B] worth half a *zuz* **of meat from thirteen butchers** in deference to Shabbat, so that he would have various types of fine meat. **And he would place** the meats **at the door hinge** at the entrance to his house to hurry to bring another type of meat. **And** he **said to** the cooks, in order to rush them: **Hurry and prepare it, hurry and prepare it.** The Gemara also relates: **Rabbi Abbahu would sit on an ivory chair** [*takhteka*][LN] **and fan the fire** cooking the food for Shabbat, in order to play a role in preparations for Shabbat. **Rav Anan would don a** simple **black garment**[N] for the Shabbat preparations, **as the school of Rabbi Yishmael taught:** While wearing the **garments in which he** cooked **a pot** of food **for his master, one should not dilute a cup of wine for his Master.** One should wear a garment appropriate for the task at hand.

רב ספרא מחריך רישא – רבא מלח שיבוטא. רב הונא מדליק שרגי, רב פפא גדיל פתילתא. רב חסדא פרים סילקא. רבה ורב יוסף מצלחי ציבי. רבי זירא מצתת צתותי. רב נחמן בר יצחק מכתף ועייל מכתף ונפיק, אמר: אילו מקלעין לי רבי אמי ורבי אסי מי לא מכתיפנא קמייהו?! ואיכא דאמרי: רבי אמי ורבי אסי מכתפי ועיילי מכתפי ונפקי, אמרי: אילו איקלע לן רבי יוחנן, מי לא מכתפינן קמיה?!

Rav Safra would **roast the head** of an animal to prepare it for Shabbat. **Rava salted a** *shibuta* fish in deference to Shabbat. **Rav Huna kindled lamps** in deference to Shabbat. **Rav Pappa spun the wicks** for the Shabbat lamp. **Rav Ḥisda cut the beets** in preparation for Shabbat. **Rabba and Rav Yosef cut wood. Rabbi Zeira prepared thin sticks** for kindling. **Rav Naḥman bar Yitzḥak** would **load objects on his shoulder and enter,** load objects **on his shoulder and exit. He said: If Rabbi Ami and Rabbi Asi happened to visit me, would I not load** objects **on my shoulder before them?** So too, it is fitting to do so in deference to Shabbat. **And some say** that **Rabbi Ami and Rabbi Asi** would **load** objects **on their shoulders and enter,** load objects **on their shoulders and exit. They said: If Rabbi Yoḥanan happened** to come **to** visit **us, would we not load** objects **on our shoulders before him?**

NOTES

An ivory chair – תכתקא דשינא: This anecdote teaches that even a wealthy person, like Rabbi Abbahu, should participate in the Shabbat preparations. Indeed, Rabbi Abbahu showed deference to the mitzva by sitting on an expensive ivory chair.

Would don a simple black garment – לביש גונדא: Apparently, Rav Anan disagrees with Rabbi Abbahu and maintains that one should wear simple, not special, clothing for the preparations of Shabbat, as per the statement of Rabbi Yishmael (Rabbi Elazar Moshe Horovitz).

HALAKHA

A feast upon completing a tractate – סעודה לסיום מסכת: It is a mitzva to rejoice with a feast when one completes a tractate of Talmud. It is a mitzva feast based on Abaye's statement (*Shulḥan Arukh, Yoreh De'a* 246:26 and in the comment of the Rema).

I do not put my head on the pillow – לא מזיגנא רישי אבי סדיא: Following Rava's example, it is proper for a judge to seek the merits of a Torah scholar in judgment (*Shulḥan Arukh, Ḥoshen Mishpat* 15:1).

Accepting Shabbat – קבלת שבת: It is appropriate to put on special clothes to welcome Shabbat joyously. In addition, it is our custom to accept Shabbat by reciting: Come and we will go out to greet Shabbat the queen, as well as: Enter, O bride. Enter, O bride, in the framework of the *Lekha Dodi* poem (Rambam *Sefer Zemanim, Hilkhot Shabbat* 30:2; *Shulḥan Arukh, Oraḥ Ḥayyim* 262:3).

LANGUAGE

Chair [*takhteka*] – תכתקא: Related to the middle Persian *taxtag*, meaning a board or plank, which seems to connote a chair.

BACKGROUND

Plain staters [*astirei peshitei*] – אסתירי פשיטי: A stater is the name of a weight and of a common coin from the Greek **στατήρ**, *statèr*. The Talmud uses the term to refer to various coins of different value with this name and it is roughly parallel to the talmudic *sela*. Primarily, there was a stater equal to four dinars, a Tyrean *sela*, or the small stater equal to half a *dinar*, a state *sela*. The smaller stater is referred to as the plain [*pashit*] stater.

Corinthian stater

יוֹסֵף מוֹקִיר שַׁבֵּי, הֲוָה הַהוּא גּוֹי בְּשֵׁבָבוּתֵיהּ, דַּהֲוָה נְפִישֵׁי נִכְסֵיהּ טוּבָא. אָמְרִי לֵיהּ כַּלְדָּאֵי: כּוּלְּהוּ נִכְסֵי – יוֹסֵף מוֹקַר שַׁבֵּי אָכֵיל לְהוּ. אֲזַל זַבְּנִינְהוּ לְכוּלְּהוּ נִיכְסֵי, זְבַן בְּהוּ מַרְגָּנִיתָא, אוֹתְבָהּ בְּסַיְינֵיהּ. בַּהֲדֵי דְּקָא עָבַר מִבְרָא – אַפְרַחֵיהּ זִיקָא, שַׁדְיֵיהּ בְּמַיָּא, בַּלְעֵיהּ כַּוְורָא. אַסְקוּהָ אַיְיתוּהָ אַפַּנְיָא דְּמַעֲלֵי שַׁבְּתָא. אָמְרִי: מַאן זָבֵין כִּי הַשְׁתָּא? אָמְרִי לְהוּ: זִילוּ אַמְטִיוּהוּ לְגַבֵּי יוֹסֵף מוֹקַר שַׁבֵּי, דִּרְגִיל דְּזָבֵין. אַמְטִיוּהָ נִיהֲלֵיהּ, זַבְנֵיהּ. קַרְעֵיהּ, אַשְׁכַּח בֵּיהּ מַרְגָּנִיתָא, זַבְנֵיהּ בִּתְלֵיסַר עִילִיתָא דְּדִינָרֵי דְּדַהֲבָא. פְּגַע בֵּיהּ הַהוּא סָבָא, אֲמַר: מַאן דְּיָזֵיף שַׁבְּתָא – פָּרְעֵיהּ שַׁבְּתָא.

The Gemara relates with regard to **Yosef who cherishes Shabbat: There was a gentile in his neighborhood whose property was extremely plentiful. The astrologers said to** the gentile with regard to **all his property: Yosef who cherishes Shabbat will consume it.** The gentile **went and sold all of his property,** and with the money he received **he bought a pearl,** and he **placed it in his hat. When he was crossing a river** in **a ferry, the wind blew** his hat **and cast it into the water,** and **a fish swallowed it.** The fish **was** caught and **removed** from the water and **it was brought** to shore adjacent to **nightfall on Shabbat eve.** The fishermen **said: Who buys** fish at a time **like this?** The townspeople **said to** the fishermen: **Go bring it to Yosef who cherishes Shabbat, as he regularly purchases** delicacies in deference to Shabbat. **They brought it to him** and **he purchased it. He ripped** the fish open and **found a pearl inside it. He sold it for thirteen vessels filled with golden dinars** (*Tosafot*). **This elderly man** who **encountered him and said: One who lends** to **Shabbat, Shabbat repays him.**

בְּעָא מִינֵּיהּ רַבִּי מֵרַבִּי יִשְׁמָעֵאל בְּרַבִּי יוֹסֵי: עֲשִׁירִים שֶׁבְּאֶרֶץ יִשְׂרָאֵל בַּמָּה הֵן זוֹכִין? אָמַר לֵיהּ: בִּשְׁבִיל שֶׁמְּעַשְּׂרִין, שֶׁנֶּאֱמַר: ״עַשֵּׂר תְּעַשֵּׂר״ – עַשֵּׂר בִּשְׁבִיל שֶׁתִּתְעַשֵּׁר. שֶׁבְּבָבֶל בַּמָּה הֵן זוֹכִין? אָמַר לֵיהּ: בִּשְׁבִיל שֶׁמְּכַבְּדִין אֶת הַתּוֹרָה.

Rabbi Yehuda HaNasi **raised a dilemma before Rabbi Yishmael, son of Rabbi Yosei:** With regard to **the wealthy of Eretz Yisrael, by what** virtue **do they merit** their wealth? He **said to him: Because they tithe, as it is stated: "A tithe you shall tithe** [*asser te'asser*] from all the crops of your seed that come out of the field each year" (Deuteronomy 14:22). The Sages interpreted this homiletically: **Take a tithe** [*asser*] **so that you will become wealthy** [*titasher*]. He asked: With regard to **the wealthy of Babylonia,** who are not obligated to tithe, **by what** virtue **do they merit** their wealth? **He said to him: Because they honor the Torah** and the Sages in Babylonia.

וְשֶׁבִּשְׁאָר אֲרָצוֹת בַּמָּה הֵן זוֹכִין? אָמַר לֵיהּ: בִּשְׁבִיל שֶׁמְּכַבְּדִין אֶת הַשַּׁבָּת. דְּאָמַר רַבִּי חִיָּיא בַּר אַבָּא: פַּעַם אַחַת נִתְאָרַחְתִּי אֵצֶל בַּעַל הַבַּיִת בְּלוּדְקְיָא, וְהֵבִיאוּ לְפָנָיו שֻׁלְחָן שֶׁל זָהָב מַשּׂוֹי שִׁשָּׁה עָשָׂר בְּנֵי אָדָם, וְשֵׁשׁ עֶשְׂרֵה שַׁלְשְׁלָאוֹת שֶׁל כֶּסֶף קְבוּעוֹת בּוֹ, וּקְעָרוֹת וְכוֹסוֹת וְקִיתוֹנִיּוֹת וּצְלוֹחִיּוֹת קְבוּעוֹת בּוֹ, וְעָלָיו כׇּל מִינֵי מַאֲכָל וְכׇל מִינֵי מְגָדִים וּבְשָׂמִים, וּכְשֶׁמַּנִּיחִים אוֹתוֹ אוֹמְרִים: ״לַה׳ הָאָרֶץ וּמְלוֹאָהּ וגו׳״, וּכְשֶׁמְּסַלְּקִין אוֹתוֹ אוֹמְרִים: ״הַשָּׁמַיִם שָׁמַיִם לַה׳ וְהָאָרֶץ נָתַן לִבְנֵי אָדָם״. אָמַרְתִּי לוֹ: בְּנִי, בַּמֶּה זָכִיתָ לְכָךְ? אָמַר לִי: קַצָּב הָיִיתִי, וּמִכׇּל בְּהֵמָה שֶׁהָיְתָה נָאָה אָמַרְתִּי: זוֹ תְּהֵא לְשַׁבָּת. אָמַרְתִּי לוֹ [אַשְׁרֶיךָ שֶׁזָּכִיתָ], וּבָרוּךְ הַמָּקוֹם שֶׁזִּיכְּךָ לְכָךְ.

With regard to **the wealthy of other countries,** where there are no Sages, **by what** virtue **do they merit** their wealth? He **said to him: Because they honor Shabbat, as Rabbi Ḥiyya bar Abba said: One time I was hosted at** the home of **a homeowner in Laodicea and** they **brought before him a table of gold** that was so heavy it required **sixteen people to carry it, and** there were **sixteen chains of silver attached to it, and** there were **bowls and cups and pitchers and flasks attached to it, and** there were **all sorts of food, and delicacies, and fragrant spices on it. And when they placed it** there **they** would **say: "The earth and all that fills it is God's,** the world and all that inhabit it" (Psalms 24:1). **And when they removed it they** would **say: "The heavens are God's heavens, but the earth He gave to mankind"** (Psalms 115:16). **I said to him: My son, what did you** do to **merit this? He said to me: I was a slaughterer, and** when I would come across parts **from every animal** that I slaughtered that was **fine, I would say: This will be for Shabbat. I said to him: Happy are you that you merited** this, **and blessed is God, Who has afforded you this merit.**

אָמַר לוֹ קֵיסָר לְרַבִּי יְהוֹשֻׁעַ בֶּן חֲנַנְיָא: מִפְּנֵי מָה תַּבְשִׁיל שֶׁל שַׁבָּת רֵיחוֹ נוֹדֵף? אָמַר לוֹ: תַּבְלִין אֶחָד יֵשׁ לָנוּ, וְשֶׁבֶת שְׁמוֹ, שֶׁאָנוּ מַטִּילִין לְתוֹכוֹ – וְרֵיחוֹ נוֹדֵף. אָמַר לוֹ: תֵּן לָנוּ הֵימֶנּוּ! אָמַר לוֹ: כׇּל הַמְשַׁמֵּר אֶת הַשַּׁבָּת – מוֹעִיל לוֹ, וְשֶׁאֵינוֹ מְשַׁמֵּר אֶת הַשַּׁבָּת – אֵינוֹ מוֹעִיל לוֹ.

The Roman **emperor said to Rabbi Yehoshua ben Ḥananya: Why does the fragrance of a cooked Shabbat dish diffuse? He said to him: We have a certain spice called dill** [*shevet*],[BN] **which we place in** the cooked dishes **and its fragrance diffuses.** The emperor **said to him: Give us** some **of it. He said to him: For anyone who observes Shabbat,** the spice **is effective, and for one who does not observe Shabbat, it is not effective.**

BACKGROUND

Dill [***shevet***] **– שֶׁבֶת:** The aromatic *shevet*, *Anethum graveolens*, is an annual or biannual plant from the Apiaceae family. The plant reaches a height of 50–80 cm, with small flowers arranged like umbrellas. The plant has a particular fragrance. The leaves that support the lobes are string-like and are used in cooking or to spice cooked food. The seeds of the dill and the oil that is extracted from them are also eaten. During talmudic times, dill was an important spice, cultivated in vegetable gardens. In modern times, it is rarely cultivated; however, it grows wild.

Dill plant

NOTES

Shabbat…*shevet* – שַׁבָּת...שֶׁבֶת: Rabbi Yehoshua is referring to the sanctity of Shabbat, and not to the dill plant, *shevet*, which was used as a spice. Therefore, he had to explain that only one who observes Shabbat benefits from *shevet*, the spice (Maharsha).

אָמַר לֵיהּ רֵישׁ גָּלוּתָא לְרַב הַמְנוּנָא: מַאי דִּכְתִיב ״וְלִקְדוֹשׁ ה׳ מְכוּבָּד״? אָמַר לֵיהּ: זֶה יוֹם הַכִּפּוּרִים, שֶׁאֵין בּוֹ לֹא אֲכִילָה וְלֹא שְׁתִיָּה. אָמְרָה תּוֹרָה: כַּבְּדֵהוּ בִּכְסוּת נְקִיָּה. ׳וְכִבַּדְתּוֹ׳ רַב אָמַר: לְהַקְדִּים, וּשְׁמוּאֵל אָמַר: לְאַחֵר. אֲמַרוּ לֵיהּ בְּנֵי רַב פַּפָּא בַּר אַבָּא לְרַב פַּפָּא: כְּגוֹן אֲנַן דִּשְׁכִיחַ לָן בִּישְׂרָא וְחַמְרָא כָּל יוֹמָא, בְּמַאי נִישַׁנְּיֵיהּ? אֲמַר לְהוּ: אִי רְגִילִיתוּ לְאַקְדּוּמֵי – אַחֲרוּהּ, אִי רְגִילִיתוּ לְאַחֲרוּהּ – אַקְדְּמוּהּ. רַב שֵׁשֶׁת, בְּקַיְטָא מוֹתִיב לְהוּ לְרַבָּנַן הֵיכָא דְּמַטְיָא שִׁימְשָׁא, בְּסִיתְוָא מוֹתִיב לְהוּ לְרַבָּנַן הֵיכָא דְּמַטְיָא טוּלָּא, כִּי הֵיכִי דְּלֵיקוּמוּ הַיְּיא. רַבִּי זֵירָא

The Exilarch said to Rav Hamnuna: What is the meaning of that which is written, "The holy one of God is honored" (Isaiah 58:13)? Rav Hamnuna said to him: That is Yom Kippur, when there is no eating or drinking, and so the Torah said: Honor it with a clean garment.[H] And with regard to that which is stated about Shabbat, "And you shall honor it," Rav said: To honor Shabbat, make the Shabbat feast earlier than on other days, in order to show that one delights in eating it. And Shmuel said: To honor Shabbat, make the Shabbat feast later, so that one's appetite will be greater. The sons of Rav Pappa bar Abba said to Rav Pappa: People like us, for whom meat and wine is found on our table every day, in what manner can we change it on Shabbat? He said to them: If you are accustomed to eating your meal early, make it later on Shabbat; if you are accustomed to making it late, make it earlier on Shabbat.[H] This difference will underscore the uniqueness of Shabbat. The Gemara relates: In the summer, Rav Sheshet would seat the Sages[N] who attended his lecture in a place where the sun would reach; in the winter, he would seat the Sages in a place where the shade would reach. He did this so that they would stand quickly after the lecture ended and not engage in discussion, which would detract from the time devoted to delighting in Shabbat. Rabbi Zeira

HALAKHA

Honoring Yom Kippur – כְּבוֹד יוֹם הַכִּפּוּרִים: Even though there are no festive meals on Yom Kippur, it is a Festival and a sacred day and must be honored by wearing fine clothes (*Shulḥan Arukh, Oraḥ Ḥayyim* 610:4).

The time for eating the Shabbat meal – זְמַן אֲכִילַת סְעוּדַּת שַׁבָּת: The Shabbat meals should be distinguished from weekday meals in every respect. Indeed, if one eats a large meal during the week as one does on Shabbat, the time of the Shabbat meal should be changed (Rema, based on the *Tur*). One should adopt the custom of eating the meal earlier or later based on whatever will make the meal more pleasurable (Rambam *Sefer Zemanim, Hilkhot Shabbat* 30:8; *Shulḥan Arukh, Oraḥ Ḥayyim* 288:7).

NOTES

In the summer Rav Sheshet would seat the Sages – רַב שֵׁשֶׁת בְּקַיְטָא מוֹתִיב לְהוּ לְרַבָּנַן: Rashi's emphasis on the fact that Rav Sheshet was blind is not necessary to understand this statement. Rather, Rav Sheshet sat his students there so that they would not tarry there after the lesson, but would leave without prodding and proceed to delight in Shabbat (Maharsha).

מְהַדֵּר אַזּוּזֵי זוּזֵי דְּרַבָּנַן, אָמַר לֵיהּ: בְּמָטוּתָא מִינַּייכוּ, לָא תְּחַלְּלוּנֵיהּ.

would seek pairs of Sages engaged in conversation on Shabbat and said to them: Please do not desecrate Shabbat by failing to delight in Shabbat.

אָמַר רָבָא וְאִיתֵימָא רַבִּי יְהוֹשֻׁעַ בֶּן לֵוִי: אֲפִילּוּ יָחִיד הַמִּתְפַּלֵּל בְּעֶרֶב שַׁבָּת צָרִיךְ לוֹמַר ״וַיְכוּלּוּ״. דְּאָמַר רַב הַמְנוּנָא: כׇּל הַמִּתְפַּלֵּל בְּעֶרֶב שַׁבָּת וְאוֹמֵר ״וַיְכוּלּוּ״ – מַעֲלֶה עָלָיו הַכָּתוּב כְּאִילּוּ נַעֲשָׂה שׁוּתָּף לְהַקָּדוֹשׁ בָּרוּךְ הוּא בְּמַעֲשֵׂה בְרֵאשִׁית, שֶׁנֶּאֱמַר ״וַיְכוּלּוּ״, אַל תִּקְרֵי ״וַיְכוּלּוּ״ אֶלָּא וַיְכַלּוּ. אָמַר רַבִּי אֶלְעָזָר: מִנַּיִין שֶׁהַדִּיבּוּר כְּמַעֲשֶׂה – שֶׁנֶּאֱמַר: ״בִּדְבַר ה׳ שָׁמַיִם נַעֲשׂוּ״.

Rava said, and some say it was Rabbi Yehoshua ben Levi who said: Even an individual who prays on Shabbat evening must recite the passage: "And the heavens and the earth were finished [*vaykhullu*]" (Genesis 2:1–3),[H] as Rav Hamnuna said: Anyone who prays on Shabbat evening and recites the passage of vaykhullu, the verse ascribed him credit as if he became a partner with the Holy One, Blessed be He, in the act of Creation.[N] As it is stated: "And the heavens and the earth were finished [*vaykhullu*]." Do not read it as: Were finished [*vaykhullu*]; rather, as: They finished [*vaykhallu*]. It is considered as though the Holy One, Blessed be He, and the individual who says this become partners and completed the work together. Rabbi Elazar said: From where is it derived that speech is like action? As it is stated: "By the word of God the heavens were made, and all of their hosts by the breath of His mouth" (Psalms 33:6).

אָמַר רַב חִסְדָּא אָמַר מָר עוּקְבָא: כׇּל הַמִּתְפַּלֵּל בְּעֶרֶב שַׁבָּת וְאוֹמֵר ״וַיְכוּלּוּ״ שְׁנֵי מַלְאֲכֵי הַשָּׁרֵת הַמְלַוִּין לוֹ לָאָדָם מַנִּיחִין יְדֵיהֶן עַל רֹאשׁוֹ וְאוֹמְרִים לוֹ: ״וְסָר עֲוֹנֶךָ וְחַטָּאתְךָ תְּכֻפָּר״. תַּנְיָא, רַבִּי יוֹסֵי בַּר יְהוּדָה אוֹמֵר: שְׁנֵי מַלְאֲכֵי הַשָּׁרֵת מְלַוִּין לוֹ לָאָדָם בְּעֶרֶב שַׁבָּת מִבֵּית הַכְּנֶסֶת לְבֵיתוֹ, אֶחָד טוֹב וְאֶחָד רַע. וּכְשֶׁבָּא לְבֵיתוֹ וּמָצָא נֵר דָּלוּק וְשׁוּלְחָן עָרוּךְ וּמִטָּתוֹ מוּצַּעַת, מַלְאָךְ טוֹב אוֹמֵר: יְהִי רָצוֹן שֶׁתְּהֵא לְשַׁבָּת אַחֶרֶת כָּךְ. וּמַלְאָךְ רַע עוֹנֶה אָמֵן בְּעַל כׇּרְחוֹ. וְאִם לָאו, מַלְאָךְ רַע אוֹמֵר: יְהִי רָצוֹן שֶׁתְּהֵא לְשַׁבָּת אַחֶרֶת כָּךְ, וּמַלְאָךְ טוֹב עוֹנֶה אָמֵן בְּעַל כׇּרְחוֹ.

Rav Ḥisda said that Mar Ukva said: One who prays on Shabbat evening and recites *vaykhullu*, the two ministering angels who accompany the person at all times place their hands on his head and say to him: "And your iniquity has passed, and your sin has been atoned" (Isaiah 6:7). It was taught in a *baraita*: Rabbi Yosei bar Yehuda says: Two ministering angels accompany a person on Shabbat evening from the synagogue to his home, one good angel and one evil angel. And when he reaches his home and finds a lamp burning and a table set[H] and his bed made, the good angel says: May it be Your will that it shall be like this for another Shabbat. And the evil angel answers against his will: Amen. And if the person's home is not prepared for Shabbat in that manner, the evil angel says: May it be Your will that it shall be so for another Shabbat, and the good angel answers against his will: Amen.

HALAKHA

One must recite the passage: And the heavens and the earth were finished [*vaykhullu*] – צָרִיךְ לוֹמַר וַיְכוּלּוּ: An individual also recites: Then the heavens and the earth were finished [*vaykhullu*], during the evening prayer of Shabbat (*Shulḥan Arukh, Oraḥ Ḥayyim* 268:1).

A lamp burning and a table set – נֵר דָּלוּק וְשׁוּלְחָן עָרוּךְ: It is most appropriate to set the table, make the beds, and prepare other household matters before Shabbat begins, so the house will be ready for Shabbat when people return from the synagogue (Rambam *Sefer Zemanim, Hilkhot Shabbat* 30:5; *Shulḥan Arukh, Oraḥ Ḥayyim* 262:1).

NOTES

A partner with the Holy One, Blessed be He, in the act of Creation – שׁוּתָּף לְהַקָּדוֹשׁ בָּרוּךְ הוּא בְּמַעֲשֵׂה בְרֵאשִׁית: Since the purpose of Creation is for all to acknowledge the greatness of God and to serve Him, by proclaiming one's faith in the Creator one sustains the world (*Or HaḤayyim*).

LANGUAGE

Remedy [*melugma*] – מְלוּגְמָא: From the Greek μάλαγμα, *malagma*, meaning a bandage placed on a wound.

NOTES

God, faithful King [*el melekh ne'eman*] – אֵל מֶלֶךְ נֶאֱמָן: Rashi explains that the Gemara interprets the Hebrew word *amen* as an acronym for *el melekh ne'eman*, to underscore the importance of answering amen and to explain both why specifically amen is the word employed for this purpose and how it includes the acceptance of the yoke of the kingdom of Heaven.

אָמַר רַבִּי אֶלְעָזָר: לְעוֹלָם יְסַדֵּר אָדָם שֻׁלְחָנוֹ בְּעֶרֶב שַׁבָּת, אַף עַל פִּי שֶׁאֵינוֹ צָרִיךְ אֶלָּא לִכְזַיִת. וְאָמַר רַבִּי חֲנִינָא: לְעוֹלָם יְסַדֵּר אָדָם שֻׁלְחָנוֹ בְּמוֹצָאֵי שַׁבָּת, אַף עַל פִּי שֶׁאֵינוֹ צָרִיךְ אֶלָּא לִכְזַיִת. חַמִּין בְּמוֹצָאֵי שַׁבָּת – מְלוּגְמָא, פַּת חַמָּה בְּמוֹצָאֵי שַׁבָּת – מְלוּגְמָא. רַבִּי אַבָּהוּ הֲוָה עַבְדִין לֵיהּ בְּאַפּוֹקֵי שַׁבְּתָא עִיגְלָא תִּילְתָּא, הֲוָה אָכֵיל מִינֵּיהּ כּוּלְיָיתָא. כִּי גְּדַל אֲבִימִי בְּרֵיהּ, אָמַר לֵיהּ: לָמָּה לָךְ לְאַפְסוֹדֵי כּוּלֵּי הַאי? נִשְׁבּוֹק כּוּלְיָיתָא מִמַּעֲלֵי שַׁבְּתָא. שַׁבְקוּהוּ, וַאֲתָא אַרְיָא אַכְלֵיהּ.

Rabbi Elazar said: A person should always set his table[H] **on Shabbat eve** with all the preparations for an important feast, **even if he only needs** the table set for **an olive-bulk** of food. **And Rabbi Ḥanina said: A person should always set his table at the conclusion of Shabbat,**[H] Saturday night, for a feast in deference to the Shabbat that passed, **even if he only needs** the table set for **an olive-bulk** of food. And with regard to the meal at the conclusion of Shabbat, they said: **Hot water after Shabbat** is a **remedy** [*melugma*],[L] **warm bread at the conclusion of Shabbat** is a **remedy.** The Gemara relates: **They would prepare for Rabbi Abbahu at the conclusion of Shabbat a third-born calf,** and **he would eat** one **kidney from it. When his son Avimi grew up,** he **said to** his father: **Why do you waste so much? Let us leave a kidney over from Shabbat eve,** and you will not need to slaughter an entire calf for that purpose. Indeed, **they left** the calf and did not slaughter it, **and a lion came and ate it.** This teaches that one should not be miserly when it comes to honoring Shabbat.

אָמַר רַבִּי יְהוֹשֻׁעַ בֶּן לֵוִי: כׇּל הָעוֹנֶה ״אָמֵן יְהֵא שְׁמֵיהּ רַבָּא מְבָרַךְ״ בְּכׇל כֹּחוֹ – קוֹרְעִין לוֹ גְּזַר דִּינוֹ, שֶׁנֶּאֱמַר: ״בִּפְרוֹעַ פְּרָעוֹת בְּיִשְׂרָאֵל בְּהִתְנַדֵּב עָם בָּרְכוּ ה׳״. מַאי טַעְמָא ״בִּפְרוֹעַ פְּרָעוֹת״ – מִשּׁוּם דְּ״בָרְכוּ ה׳״. רַבִּי חִיָּיא בַּר אַבָּא אָמַר רַבִּי יוֹחָנָן: אֲפִילּוּ יֵשׁ בּוֹ שֶׁמֶץ שֶׁל עֲבוֹדָה זָרָה – מוֹחֲלִין לוֹ, כְּתִיב הָכָא ״בִּפְרוֹעַ פְּרָעוֹת״ וּכְתִיב הָתָם ״כִּי פָרוּעַ הוּא״. אָמַר רֵישׁ לָקִישׁ: כׇּל הָעוֹנֶה אָמֵן בְּכׇל כֹּחוֹ – פּוֹתְחִין לוֹ שַׁעֲרֵי גַן עֵדֶן, שֶׁנֶּאֱמַר: ״פִּתְחוּ שְׁעָרִים וְיָבֹא גּוֹי צַדִּיק שֹׁמֵר אֱמוּנִים״. אַל תִּיקְרֵי ׳שׁוֹמֵר אֱמוּנִים׳ אֶלָּא ׳שֶׁאוֹמְרִים אָמֵן׳. מַאי אָמֵן? אָמַר רַבִּי חֲנִינָא: אֵל מֶלֶךְ נֶאֱמָן.

Apropos the reward for honoring Shabbat, the Gemara cites statements about the reward for answering amen. **Rabbi Yehoshua ben Levi said** that **anyone who answers: Amen, may His great name be blessed,** wholeheartedly, **with all his might,** they **rip his sentence, as it is stated: "When punishments are annulled in Israel, when the people offer themselves, bless the Lord"** (Judges 5:2). **What is the reason for when punishments are annulled? Because** the Jewish people **blessed God.** When one recites: Amen, may His great name be blessed, and blesses God, his punishment is annulled. **Rabbi Ḥiyya bar Abba** said that **Rabbi Yoḥanan said: Even if one has within him a trace of idolatry,** when he answers amen **he is forgiven. It is written here,** in the verse above: **"When punishments** [*pera'ot*] **are annulled." And it is written there,** with regard to the sin of the Golden Calf: "And Moses saw **that** the nation **was wild** [*paru'a*], for Aaron had let them loose for anyone who might rise against them" (Exodus 32:25). Even one with the wildness of idolatry is forgiven. **Reish Lakish said: One who answers amen**[H] **with all his strength, they open the gates of the Garden of Eden before him, as it is stated: "Open the gates, and a righteous nation shall come who keeps the faith"** (Isaiah 26:2). **Do not read: Who keeps** [*shomer*] **the faith** [*emunim*], **but rather: Who say** [*she'omerim*] **amen. What** is the allusion of the word ***amen*****? Rabbi Ḥanina said:** It is an acronym of the words: **God, faithful King** [***El Melekh ne'eman***].[N]

אָמַר רַב יְהוּדָה בְּרֵיהּ דְּרַב שְׁמוּאֵל מִשְּׁמֵיהּ דְּרַב: אֵין הַדְּלֵיקָה מְצוּיָה אֶלָּא בְּמָקוֹם שֶׁיֵּשׁ חִילּוּל שַׁבָּת, שֶׁנֶּאֱמַר: ״וְאִם לֹא תִשְׁמְעוּ אֵלַי לְקַדֵּשׁ אֶת יוֹם הַשַּׁבָּת וּלְבִלְתִּי שְׂאֵת מַשָּׂא וגו׳ וְהִצַּתִּי אֵשׁ בִּשְׁעָרֶיהָ וְאָכְלָה אַרְמְנוֹת יְרוּשָׁלִַם וְלֹא תִכְבֶּה״. מַאי ״וְלֹא תִכְבֶּה״? אָמַר רַב נַחְמָן בַּר יִצְחָק: בְּשָׁעָה שֶׁאֵין בְּנֵי אָדָם מְצוּיִין לְכַבּוֹתָהּ. אָמַר אַבָּיֵי: לֹא חָרְבָה יְרוּשָׁלִַים אֶלָּא בִּשְׁבִיל שֶׁחִלְּלוּ בָּהּ אֶת הַשַּׁבָּת, שֶׁנֶּאֱמַר: ״וּמִשַּׁבְּתוֹתַי הֶעְלִימוּ עֵינֵיהֶם וָאֵחַל בְּתוֹכָם״.

Rav Yehuda, son of Rav Shmuel, said in the name of Rav: Fire is only found in a place where there is desecration of Shabbat, as it is stated: "And if you do not heed Me to sanctify the day of Shabbat, and to refrain from carrying burdens and come to the gates of Jerusalem on the day of Shabbat, **and I will light a fire in its gates and it will consume the palaces of Jerusalem and it will not be extinguished"** (Jeremiah 17:27). The Gemara asks: **What is the meaning of: And it will not be extinguished? Rav Naḥman bar Yitzḥak said:** Fire will break out **at a time when people are not found to extinguish it. Abaye said: Jerusalem was destroyed only because people desecrated the Shabbat in it, as it is stated: "And from My *Shabbatot* they averted their eyes, and I was profaned among them"** (Ezekiel 22:26). Several punishments were decreed to befall Jerusalem as punishment for this transgression.

HALAKHA

A person should always set his table – לְעוֹלָם יְסַדֵּר אָדָם שֻׁלְחָנוֹ: One should always set the table for the meal on Shabbat evening to honor the Shabbat, even if one will only eat an olive-bulk of food (Rambam *Sefer Zemanim, Hilkhot Shabbat* 30:5).

A person should always set his table at the conclusion of Shabbat – לְעוֹלָם יְסַדֵּר אָדָם שֻׁלְחָנוֹ בְּמוֹצָאֵי שַׁבָּת: One should set the table after Shabbat to honor the departure of Shabbat in a manner similar to the beginning of Shabbat, even if one will only eat an olive-bulk of food. This is the meal known as the meal accompanying the queen [*melaveh malka*] (Rambam *Sefer Zemanim, Hilkhot Shabbat* 30:5; *Shulḥan Arukh, Oraḥ Ḥayyim* 300).

One who answers amen – כׇּל הָעוֹנֶה אָמֵן: During the recitation of the *kaddish*, one should concentrate and answer amen aloud (Rambam *Sefer Ahava, Hilkhot Tefilla* 9:1; *Shulḥan Arukh, Oraḥ Ḥayyim* 56:1).

אָמַר רַבִּי אַבָּהוּ: לֹא חָרְבָה יְרוּשָׁלַיִם אֶלָּא בִּשְׁבִיל שֶׁבִּיטְּלוּ קְרִיאַת שְׁמַע שַׁחֲרִית וְעַרְבִית, שֶׁנֶּאֱמַר: "הוֹי מַשְׁכִּימֵי בַבֹּקֶר שֵׁכָר יִרְדֹּפוּ וגו'", וּכְתִיב: "וְהָיָה כִנּוֹר וָנֶבֶל תֹּף וְחָלִיל וָיַיִן מִשְׁתֵּיהֶם וְאֵת פֹּעַל ה' לֹא יַבִּיטוּ", וּכְתִיב: "לָכֵן גָּלָה עַמִּי מִבְּלִי דָעַת".

The Gemara suggests additional reasons for the destruction of Jerusalem. **Rabbi Abbahu said: Jerusalem was destroyed only because** its citizens intentionally **omitted recitation of *Shema* morning and evening, as it is stated: "Woe to those who rise early in the morning and pursue the drink** and are aflame from wine until late in the evening" (Isaiah 5:11). **And it is written** in the continuation of that passage: **"And their drinking parties have lyre and lute, drum and flute and wine, and they do not look upon the actions of God,** and they do not see His hands' creations" (Isaiah 5:12). This means that in the morning and evening, when the Jews should have been reciting *Shema*, they were drinking wine and liquor. **And it is written** in that passage: **"Therefore My nation is being exiled for its ignorance;** its honor will die of hunger and its multitudes will be parched with thirst" (Isaiah 5:13).

אָמַר רַב הַמְנוּנָא: לֹא חָרְבָה יְרוּשָׁלַיִם אֶלָּא בִּשְׁבִיל שֶׁבִּיטְּלוּ בָּהּ תִּינוֹקוֹת שֶׁל בֵּית רַבָּן, שֶׁנֶּאֱמַר: "שְׁפֹךְ עַל עוֹלָל בַּחוּץ וגו'" מַה טַּעַם 'שְׁפוֹךְ' – מִשּׁוּם דְּ'עוֹלָל בַּחוּץ'. אָמַר עוּלָּא: לֹא חָרְבָה יְרוּשָׁלַיִם אֶלָּא מִפְּנֵי שֶׁלֹּא הָיָה לָהֶם בּוֹשֶׁת פָּנִים זֶה מִזֶּה, שֶׁנֶּאֱמַר: "הוֹבִישׁוּ כִּי תוֹעֵבָה עָשׂוּ גַּם בּוֹשׁ לֹא יֵבוֹשׁוּ וגו'". אָמַר רַבִּי יִצְחָק: לֹא חָרְבָה יְרוּשָׁלַיִם אֶלָּא בִּשְׁבִיל שֶׁהוּשְׁווּ קָטָן וְגָדוֹל, שֶׁנֶּאֱמַר: "וְהָיָה כָעָם כַּכֹּהֵן", וּכְתִיב בַּתְרֵיהּ: "הִבּוֹק תִּבּוֹק הָאָרֶץ".

Rav Hamnuna said: Jerusalem was destroyed only because schoolchildren there were interrupted from studying Torah, **as it is stated:** "And I am filled with the wrath of God, I cannot contain it, **pour it onto the infants in the street** and onto the gathering of youths together, for men and women alike will be captured, the elderly along with those of advanced years" (Jeremiah 6:11). Rav Hamnuna explains: **What is the reason that** the wrath is **poured?** It is **because infants are outside** in the streets and are not studying Torah.

Ulla said: Jerusalem was destroyed only because people had no shame before each other, as it is stated: "They acted shamefully; they have performed abominations, yet they neither were ashamed nor did they know humiliation. Therefore, they will fall among the fallen, they will fail at the time that I punish them, said God" (Jeremiah 6:15).

Rabbi Yitzhak said: Jerusalem was destroyed only because its **small and** the **great** citizens **were equated.** They did not properly value the prominent leaders of their generation, **as it is stated: "And the common people were like the priest,** the slave like his master, the maidservant like her mistress, the buyer like the seller, the lender like the borrower, the creditor like the one indebted to him" (Isaiah 24:2). **And it is written afterward: "The land shall be utterly desolate** and completely plundered, for God has said this" (Isaiah 24:3).

אָמַר רַב עַמְרָם בְּרֵיהּ דְּרַבִּי שִׁמְעוֹן בַּר אַבָּא אָמַר רַבִּי שִׁמְעוֹן בַּר אַבָּא אָמַר רַבִּי חֲנִינָא: לֹא חָרְבָה יְרוּשָׁלַיִם אֶלָּא בִּשְׁבִיל שֶׁלֹּא הוֹכִיחוּ זֶה אֶת זֶה, שֶׁנֶּאֱמַר: "הָיוּ שָׂרֶיהָ כְּאַיָּלִים לֹא מָצְאוּ מִרְעֶה". מָה אַיָּל זֶה רֹאשׁוֹ שֶׁל זֶה בְּצַד זְנָבוֹ שֶׁל זֶה – אַף יִשְׂרָאֵל שֶׁבְּאוֹתוֹ הַדּוֹר, כָּבְשׁוּ פְּנֵיהֶם בַּקַּרְקַע וְלֹא הוֹכִיחוּ זֶה אֶת זֶה. אָמַר רַבִּי יְהוּדָה: לֹא חָרְבָה יְרוּשָׁלַיִם אֶלָּא בִּשְׁבִיל שֶׁבִּיזּוּ בָּהּ תַּלְמִידֵי חֲכָמִים, שֶׁנֶּאֱמַר: "וַיִּהְיוּ מַלְעִבִים בְּמַלְאֲכֵי הָאֱלֹהִים וּבוֹזִים דְּבָרָיו וּמִתַּעְתְּעִים בִּנְבִיאָיו עַד עֲלוֹת חֲמַת ה' בְּעַמּוֹ עַד [לְ]אֵין מַרְפֵּא". מַאי "עַד לְאֵין מַרְפֵּא"? אָמַר רַב יְהוּדָה אָמַר רַב: כׇּל הַמְבַזֶּה תַּלְמִידֵי חֲכָמִים אֵין לוֹ רְפוּאָה לְמַכָּתוֹ.

Rav Amram, son of Rabbi Shimon bar Abba, said that **Rabbi Shimon bar Abba said** that **Rabbi Hanina said: Jerusalem was destroyed only because the people did not rebuke one another, as it is stated: "Her ministers were like stags that found no pasture,** and they walked without strength before their pursuer" (Lamentations 1:6). **Just as this stag** turns **its head toward the other's tail** when it grazes, and each one feeds on its own, **so too, the Jewish people in that generation lowered their faces to the ground and did not rebuke one another.**

Rabbi Yehuda said: Jerusalem was destroyed only because they disparaged the Torah scholars in it, as it is stated: "And they mocked the messengers of God and disdained His words and taunted His prophets, until the wrath of God arose against His people, until it could not be healed" (II Chronicles 36:16). **What** is the meaning of: **Until it could not be healed? Rav Yehuda said** that **Rav said:** It means that **anyone who disparages Torah scholars**[H] **cannot be healed from his wound.**[N]

HALAKHA

Anyone who disparages Torah scholars – כׇּל הַמְבַזֶּה תַּלְמִידֵי חֲכָמִים: It is a great sin to disparage a Torah scholar, even with words alone and even if the scholar is not present. The court has the power to ostracize one who disparaged a Torah scholar until he is forgiven by the Sage whom he insulted (Rambam *Sefer HaMadda, Hilkhot Talmud Torah* 6:11; *Shulhan Arukh, Yoreh De'a* 243:7).

NOTES

Cannot be healed from his wound – אֵין לוֹ רְפוּאָה לְמַכָּתוֹ: This statement is supported by various verses (see I Kings 13) that indicate that God is forgiving with regard to His own honor but does not forgive the disparagement of His messengers and the righteous. Therefore, one who disparages Torah scholars will certainly be punished (*Havot Ya'ir*).

NOTES

Do not touch my anointed ones, these are the schoolchildren – אל תגעו במשיחי, אלו תינוקות של בית רבן: See Rashi, who cites a reason for this interpretation. Other commentaries explain that the children were called: My anointed ones, because the Gemara states that children's study of Torah sustains the world and brings redemption. Consequently, there is an aspect of Messiah in schoolchildren (*Iyyun Ya'akov*).

HALAKHA

One may not interrupt schoolchildren – אין מבטלין תינוקות של בית רבן: One may not interrupt the Torah study of schoolchildren for any reason, even for a great mitzva, e.g., building the Temple (Rambam *Sefer HaMadda, Hilkhot Talmud Torah* 2:2; *Shulḥan Arukh, Yoreh De'a* 245:13).

A city in which there are no schoolchildren – עיר שאין בה תינוקות של בית רבן: Every city is obligated to establish a school where children are taught Torah. If the children of a city do not study Torah, the inhabitants must rectify the situation. Severe measures, including excommunication, are aimed at residents of a city who fail to establish a school (Rambam *Sefer HaMadda, Hilkhot Talmud Torah* 2:1; *Shulḥan Arukh, Yoreh De'a* 245:7).

אמר רב יהודה אמר רב: מאי דכתיב ״אל תגעו במשיחי ובנביאי אל תרעו״? ״אל תגעו במשיחי״ – אלו תינוקות של בית רבן, ״ובנביאי אל תרעו״ – אלו תלמידי חכמים. אמר ריש לקיש משום רבי יהודה נשיאה: אין העולם מתקיים אלא בשביל הבל תינוקות של בית רבן. אמר ליה רב פפא לאביי: דידי ודידך מאי? אמר ליה: אינו דומה הבל שיש בו חטא, להבל שאין בו חטא. ואמר ריש לקיש משום רבי יהודה נשיאה: אין מבטלין תינוקות של בית רבן אפילו לבנין בית המקדש. ואמר ריש לקיש לרבי יהודה נשיאה: כך מקובלני מאבותי, ואמרי לה מאבותיך: כל עיר שאין בה תינוקות של בית רבן – מחריבין אותה. רבינא אמר: מחרימין אותה.

Rav Yehuda said that **Rav said: What** is the meaning of that **which is written: "Do not touch My anointed ones and do My prophets no harm"** (1 Chronicles 16:22)? **"Do not touch My anointed ones," these are the schoolchildren,**[N] who are as precious and important as kings and priests (Maharsha); **"and do not harm My prophets," these are Torah scholars. Reish Lakish said in the name of Rabbi Yehuda Nesia: The world only exists because of the breath,** i.e., reciting Torah, **of schoolchildren. Rav Pappa said to Abaye: My** Torah study **and yours, what** is its status? Why is the Torah study of adults worth less? He **said to him: The breath** of adults, **which is** tainted by **sin, is not similar to the breath** of children, **which is not** tainted by **sin. And Reish Lakish said in the name of Rabbi Yehuda Nesia: One may not interrupt schoolchildren**[H] from studying Torah, **even in order to build the Temple. And Reish Lakish said to Rabbi Yehuda Nesia: I have received from my ancestors, and some say** that he said to him: I have received **from your ancestors as follows: Any city in which there are no schoolchildren**[H] studying Torah, they **destroy it. Ravina said:** They leave **it desolate.**

ואמר רבא: לא חרבה ירושלים אלא בשביל שפסקו ממנה אנשי אמנה, שנאמר: ״שוטטו בחוצות ירושלים וראו נא [ודעו ובקשו ברחובותיה אם תמצאו איש] (אם יש איש) עושה משפט מבקש אמונה ואסלח לה״. איני?! והאמר רב קטינא: אפילו בשעת כשלונה של ירושלים לא פסקו ממנה אנשי אמנה, שנאמר: ״כי יתפש איש באחיו בית אביו (לאמר) שמלה לכה קצין תהיה לנו״ – דברים שבני אדם מתכסין בהן כשמלה ישנן בידיך, ״והמכשלה הזאת תחת ידך״,

And Rava said: Jerusalem was destroyed only because there were no more trustworthy people there, as it is stated: "Roam about the streets of Jerusalem and see, and search its plazas, if you can find a person, who acts justly, who seeks integrity, that I should forgive it" (Jeremiah 5:1). The Gemara asks: **Is that so? Didn't Rav Ketina say: Even at the time of Jerusalem's failure, trustworthy people did not cease there, as it is stated: "For a man will grab his brother of his father's house and say: You have a garment. Come be a chief over us** and let this ruin be under your care" (Isaiah 3:6)? **Things that people use to cover up like a garment,** secrets, **are in your hands** and you know about them. Therefore, you should be a leader of the community. And that which is stated: **"And let this ruin be under your care,"** meaning:

Perek **XVI**
Daf **120** Amud **a**

דברים שאין בני אדם עומדין עליהם אלא אם כן נכשלים בהן ישנן תחת ידיך ״קצין תהיה לנו״. ״ישא ביום ההוא לאמר לא אהיה חובש וגו׳״. אין ״ישא״ אלא לשון שבועה, וכן הוא אומר: ״לא תשא את שם ה׳״. ״לא אהיה חובש״ – לא אהיה מחובשי עצמן בבית המדרש, ״ובביתי אין לחם ואין שמלה״ – שאין בידי לא מקרא ולא משנה ולא גמרא. וממאי? דילמא שאני התם, דאי אמר להו ׳גמירנא׳, אמרו ליה: אימא לן! הוה ליה למימר: גמר ושכח. מאי ״לא אהיה חובש״ – כלל. לא קשיא, כאן – בדברי תורה, כאן – במשא ומתן.

Matters of Torah **that people do not ascertain unless they misunderstand them are in your hands;** therefore, **be a chief over us.** It is stated later on in that passage: **"He will rise [*yissa*] on that day, saying, I will not be a ruler** while in my house there is no bread and no garment, you shall not appoint me as chief of the people" (Isaiah 3:7). **The term rise [*yissa*] means nothing other than an oath, as it says: "Do not raise [*tissa*] the name of the Lord** your God in vain" (Exodus 20:17). **I will not be a ruler,** means: **I will not be one of those who close themselves up in the study hall,** as I do not regularly do so, **while in my house there is no bread and no garment, for I have neither Bible nor Mishna nor Gemara in my hands.** According to this explanation, there were people of faith who truthfully admitted that they did not study Torah, even during the time of the destruction of Jerusalem. The Gemara rejects this: **And from what** do you conclude that this admission was due to their faithfulness? **Perhaps it is different** in that case, **as had he told them: I studied** Torah, **they would have said to him: Tell us** what you studied. As he would not know to respond, he would have no choice other than to admit that he did not study. The Gemara rejects this: That is not difficult, as **he could have** at least **said he learned and forgot.** The Gemara asks: Therefore, **what is: I will not be a ruler?** It means that he is telling the truth and although he could have lied, he admits that he did **not** study Torah **at all.** The Gemara answers: This is **not difficult. Here,** where it was taught that they were faithful, that was **with regard to matters of Torah;** whereas **here,** where it was taught that there were no more people of faith in Jerusalem, that was **with regard to** matters of **business.**

מתני׳ מַצִּילִין סַל מָלֵא כִּכָּרוֹת – אַף עַל פִּי שֶׁיֵּשׁ בּוֹ מֵאָה סְעוּדוֹת, וְעִיגּוּל שֶׁל דְּבֵילָה, וְחָבִית שֶׁל יַיִן. וְאוֹמֵר לַאֲחֵרִים: בּוֹאוּ וְהַצִּילוּ לָכֶם. וְאִם הָיוּ פִּיקְחִין – עוֹשִׂין עִמּוֹ חֶשְׁבּוֹן אַחַר הַשַּׁבָּת.

MISHNA **One may rescue a basket**[H] **full of loaves** and the like from a fire on Shabbat, **even if there is** food for **one hundred meals in it. And** one may rescue **a round** cake **of dried figs,** even though it is very large, **and** one may rescue **a barrel** full **of wine. And one may** even **say to others: Come and rescue for yourselves.**[N] **And if** the people who rescue with him were **clever,**[N] **they make a calculation with him after Shabbat** in order to receive payment for the items that they rescued.

לְהֵיכָן מַצִּילִין אוֹתָן? לֶחָצֵר הַמְעוֹרֶבֶת. בֶּן בְּתֵירָה אוֹמֵר: אַף לְשֶׁאֵינָהּ מְעוֹרֶבֶת. וּלְשָׁם מוֹצִיא כָּל כְּלֵי תַשְׁמִישׁוֹ, וְלוֹבֵשׁ כָּל מַה שֶּׁיָּכוֹל לִלְבּוֹשׁ, וְעוֹטֵף כָּל מַה שֶּׁיָּכוֹל לַעֲטוֹף. רַבִּי יוֹסֵי אוֹמֵר: שְׁמֹנָה עָשָׂר כֵּלִים. וְחוֹזֵר וְלוֹבֵשׁ וּמוֹצִיא, וְאוֹמֵר לַאֲחֵרִים: בּוֹאוּ וְהַצִּילוּ עִמִּי.

To where may one rescue items moved from the fire?[H] One may do so **to a courtyard** where an ***eiruv*** was established, and it is permitted to carry. **Ben Beteira says:** One may do so **even to** a courtyard **where an** eiruv was **not** established. **And one may carry there all the utensils,**[H] **and put on all** the garments **that he can wear, and one may wrap all** the cloths **that he can wrap** around himself in order to rescue his property. **Rabbi Yosei says:** One may put on only **eighteen garments** at once, as people sometimes wear that number of garments, but not more. However, **one may again put on** that number of garments[H] **and carry** it **out. And he may say to others: Come and rescue with me.**

גמ׳ וְהָא תְּנָא לֵיהּ רֵישָׁא ״שָׁלֹשׁ סְעוּדוֹת״ וְתוּ לָא! אָמַר רַב הוּנָא: לָא קַשְׁיָא, כָּאן – בְּבָא לְהַצִּיל, כָּאן – בְּבָא לְקַפֵּל. וּבָא לְהַצִּיל – מַצִּיל אֶת כּוּלָּן, בָּא לְקַפֵּל – אֵינוֹ מְקַפֵּל אֶלָּא מְזוֹן שָׁלֹשׁ סְעוּדוֹת. רַבִּי אַבָּא בַּר זַבְדָּא אָמַר רַב: אִידִי וְאִידִי בְּבָא לְקַפֵּל, וְלָא קַשְׁיָא; כָּאן – לְאוֹתָהּ חָצֵר, כָּאן – לְחָצֵר אַחֶרֶת. בָּעֵי רַב הוּנָא בְּרֵיהּ דְּרַב יְהוֹשֻׁעַ: פֵּירֵשׁ טַלִּיתוֹ, וְקִיפֵּל וְהִנִּיחַ, וְקִיפֵּל וְהִנִּיחַ, מַאי? כְּבָא לְהַצִּיל דָּמֵי, אוֹ כְּבָא לְקַפֵּל דָּמֵי?

GEMARA The Gemara asks: **Wasn't it taught in the first clause,** i.e., the preceding mishna, that one may rescue **three meals and no more? Rav Huna said:** This is **not difficult. This** current mishna permitted rescuing a greater amount **when one comes to rescue** a basket or round cake of figs; **that** previous mishna permitted rescuing food for only three meals in a case where **one comes to collect**[N] the food. **When one comes to rescue, he may rescue everything; when one comes to collect, he may collect food for only three meals.** However, **Rabbi Abba bar Zavda said** that **Rav said: Both this and that** are referring to a case **where one comes to collect, and** this is **not difficult. This** current mishna permitted rescuing a greater amount when one moves the objects **to the same courtyard; that,** the previous mishna, permitted saving food for only three meals when one transfers it **to a different courtyard. Rav Huna, son of Rav Yehoshua, raised a dilemma:** If **one spread his cloak** on the ground **and collected and placed** objects in the cloak,[H] **and collected and placed** objects inside it, **what is the ruling?** Is he **considered as one who comes to rescue or** is he **like one who comes to collect?**

מִדַּאֲמַר רָבָא: אַטְעֵיהּ רַב שֵׁיזְבִי לְרַב חִסְדָּא, וּדְרַשׁ: וּבִלְבַד שֶׁלֹּא יָבִיא כְּלִי שֶׁהוּא מַחֲזִיק יוֹתֵר מִשָּׁלֹשׁ סְעוּדוֹת – שְׁמַע מִינַּהּ: כְּבָא לְהַצִּיל דָּמֵי, וְשַׁפִּיר דָּמֵי. אֲמַר לֵיהּ רַב נַחְמָן בַּר יִצְחָק לְרָבָא: מַאי טָעוּתָא? אֲמַר לֵיהּ, דְּקָתָנֵי: וּבִלְבַד שֶׁלֹּא יָבִיא כְּלִי אַחֵר וִיקְלוֹט, כְּלִי אַחֵר וִיצָרֵף. כְּלִי אַחֵר הוּא דְּלָא, אֲבָל בְּהַהוּא מָנָא – כַּמָּה דְּבָעֵי מַצִּיל.

The Gemara attempts to resolve the dilemma **from that which Rava said: Rav Sheizvi misled Rav Ḥisda, and** Rav Ḥisda **taught** (Rabbeinu Ḥananel) a *halakha* with regard to a barrel that breaks on a roof, and added: And it is permitted **provided that one does not bring a vessel that holds more than three meals. Conclude from** the fact that Rava said that Rav Ḥisda's restriction of the amount that can be rescued to food sufficient for three meals is mistaken, that one who takes a large amount all at once is **like one who comes to rescue, and** he may **well** do so. **Rav Naḥman bar Yitzḥak said to Rava: What is the error** in Rav Ḥisda's statement? Perhaps it is actually prohibited. He **said to him, as it is taught: Provided that he does not bring another vessel** and place it on the ground to **catch** the liquid, **another vessel and attach** the vessel next to the roof. Apparently **it is another vessel that one may not** bring, **but in that same vessel, one may rescue as much as he wants,** and the Sages did not establish a maximum size for the vessel.

NOTES

And one may say to others: Come and rescue for yourselves – וְאוֹמֵר לַאֲחֵרִים: בּוֹאוּ וְהַצִּילוּ לָכֶם: It is explained in the Jerusalem Talmud: Since one is permitted to invite guests and feed them and clothe them on Shabbat, one may also invite others to come and rescue food and clothes for themselves as they are potential guests. Some commentaries teach that the others may rescue items in any manner that they choose. Since it is not their property, there is no concern lest they extinguish the fire in their agitation (Rabbi Yeshaya of Terani as cited in the Ran).

And if the people were clever – וְאִם הָיוּ פִּיקְחִין: In the Jerusalem Talmud, it is asserted that the novel element in this statement is that if the rescuers return the objects to their owner on Shabbat and did not take ownership of them, they may receive direct payment after Shabbat and not merely take ownership of the ownerless property. This is the Rambam's interpretation in his Commentary on the Mishna.

One who comes to collect – בָּא לְקַפֵּל: Some commentaries explain that this refers to pouring the contents of a small vessel into a large vessel, and not to attaching two vessels together (Ramban).

HALAKHA

One may rescue a basket – מַצִּילִין סַל: It is permitted to rescue a single vessel from a fire, even if it contains enough food for a hundred meals (Rambam *Sefer Zemanim, Hilkhot Shabbat* 23:22–23; *Shulḥan Arukh, Oraḥ Ḥayyim* 334:6).

To where may one rescue items moved from the fire – לְהֵיכָן מַצִּילִין אוֹתָן: One may only rescue objects by moving them into a courtyard that is joined to the owner's courtyard by an *eiruv*, in accordance with the opinion of the first *tanna* in the mishna (Rambam *Sefer Zemanim, Hilkhot Shabbat* 23:20; *Shulḥan Arukh, Oraḥ Ḥayyim* 334:17).

One may carry there all the utensils – מוֹצִיא כָּל כְּלֵי תַשְׁמִישׁוֹ: It is permitted to rescue eating utensils needed for the entire day and carry them to a courtyard that is joined to the owner's courtyard by an *eiruv* (*Magen Avraham*; Rambam *Sefer Zemanim, Hilkhot Shabbat* 23:20; *Shulḥan Arukh, Oraḥ Ḥayyim* 334:7).

And put on garments… and one may again put on garments – וְלוֹבֵשׁ...וְחוֹזֵר וְלוֹבֵשׁ: One who wants to rescue clothing from a fire may put on garments, walk to a safe place, undress, return, and put on other garments, as stated in the mishna. There is an opinion that ascribes the phrase: One may again put on garments, in the mishna to Rabbi Yosei, indicating that repeated trips to save clothing are permitted. However, since the *halakha* is not in accordance with the opinion of Rabbi Yosei in a dispute with an unattributed mishna, it is permitted to return and put on garments only once (*Beit Yosef*, based on the Rambam). This approach was not accepted as the normative *halakha* (Vilna Gaon and others; Rambam *Sefer Zemanim, Hilkhot Shabbat* 23:25; *Shulḥan Arukh, Oraḥ Ḥayyim* 334:8).

One who comes to rescue in his cloak – הַבָּא לְהַצִּיל בְּטַלִּית: One who seeks to rescue objects from a fire on Shabbat may spread out a cloak and place many items in it, provided that they are removed all at once, in accordance with the opinion of Rava (Rambam *Sefer Zemanim, Hilkhot Shabbat* 23:23; *Shulḥan Arukh, Oraḥ Ḥayyim* 334:6).

״וְעִיגּוּל שֶׁל דְּבֵילָה כו׳״. חֶשְׁבּוֹן מַאי עֲבִידְתֵּיהּ? מֵהֶפְקֵירָא קָזָכוּ! אָמַר רַב חִסְדָּא: מִדַּת חֲסִידוּת שָׁנוּ כָּאן. אֲמַר רָבָא: חֲסִידֵי אַגְרָא דְּשַׁבְּתָא שָׁקְלִי?! אֶלָּא אֲמַר רָבָא: הָכָא בִּירֵא שָׁמַיִם עָסְקִינַן, וְלָא נִיחָא לֵיהּ דְּלִיתְהַנֵּי מֵאֲחֵרִים, וּבְחִנָּם נַמִּי לָא נִיחָא לֵיהּ דְּלִיטְרַח. וְהָכִי קָאָמַר: וְאִם הָיוּ פִּיקְחִין, דְּיָדְעִי דְּכְהַאי גַּוְונָא לָאו שְׂכַר שַׁבָּת הוּא – עוֹשִׂין עִמּוֹ חֶשְׁבּוֹן לְאַחַר הַשַּׁבָּת.

And we learned in the mishna that one is permitted to rescue **a round** cake **of dried figs** from a fire, and one may even say to others: Come and rescue for yourselves. And if the people who rescue with him are clever, they make a calculation with him after Shabbat. The Gemara is surprised at this: **What is** the mention of **a calculation doing** here? **Aren't they acquiring** food **from ownerless** property?[H] What calculation is necessary here? Whatever they rescue is theirs, and they do not need to return it to the original owner. **Rav Ḥisda said: They taught an attribute of piety here.** These are pious people. They want to return the objects to their owner even though they are not legally obligated to do so, and they were permitted to receive payment for their efforts. **Rava said:** And do **pious** people **take payment** for work they do on **Shabbat? Rather, Rava said: Here, we are dealing with one who is Heaven-fearing**[N] but not completely pious. **And** it is **uncomfortable for him to benefit from** the property of **others, and it is also uncomfortable for him to exert** himself **for free. And this is what** the mishna **is saying: And if they are clever and know that in a situation of this kind it is not** technically **payment for Shabbat** labor, and it is permitted because they are only receiving a small portion of the value of the objects that they rescued, **they** may **make a calculation with him after Shabbat.**

״וּלְהֵיכָן מַצִּילִין כו׳״. מַאי שְׁנָא הָכָא דְּקָתָנֵי ׳לָכֶם׳, וּמַאי שְׁנָא הָכָא דְּקָתָנֵי ׳עִמִּי׳? אָמְרִי: גַּבֵּי מְזוֹנוֹת קָתָנֵי ׳לָכֶם׳ – מִשּׁוּם דְּלָא קָא חֲזוּ אֶלָּא מְזוֹן שָׁלֹשׁ סְעוּדוֹת, אֲבָל גַּבֵּי לְבוּשִׁים קָתָנֵי ׳עִמִּי׳ – מִשּׁוּם דְּקָחֲזֵי לֵיהּ לְכוּלֵּי יוֹמָא.

We learned in the mishna that one may say to others: Come and rescue for yourselves. We also learned: **And to where may one rescue** the food? According to the first *tanna*, one may rescue to a courtyard in which an *eiruv* was established. According to ben Beteira, one may rescue even to a courtyard in which an *eiruv* was not established. The Gemara asks: **What is different here,** with regard to rescuing food, **that it is taught** that one may say to others: Come and rescue **for yourselves, and what is different here,** with regard to rescuing clothing, **that it is taught** that one may say to others: Come and rescue **with me?** The Gemara answers: **With regard to food, it taught: For yourselves, because only food for three meals is suited for him,** and only others can benefit from the rest. **However, with regard to** the **garments, it is taught: With me, because it is suited for him** to continue rescuing garments **all day,** since he is permitted to wear other clothes.

תָּנוּ רַבָּנַן: לוֹבֵשׁ מוֹצִיא וּפוֹשֵׁט, וְחוֹזֵר וְלוֹבֵשׁ וּמוֹצִיא וּפוֹשֵׁט, וַאֲפִילּוּ כָּל הַיּוֹם כּוּלּוֹ – דִּבְרֵי רַבִּי מֵאִיר. רַבִּי יוֹסֵי אוֹמֵר: שְׁמֹנָה עָשָׂר כֵּלִים, וְאֵלּוּ הֵם שְׁמֹנָה עָשָׂר כֵּלִים: מִקְטוֹרֶן, אוּנְקָלִי, וּפוּנְדָּא. קַלְבּוּס שֶׁל פִּשְׁתָּן, וְחָלוּק, וְאַפִּילְיוֹת, וּמַעֲפוֹרֶת, וּשְׁנֵי סְפַרְקִין, וּשְׁנֵי מִנְעָלִים, וּשְׁנֵי אַנְפִּילָאוֹת, וּשְׁנֵי פַּרְגּוֹד, וַחֲגוֹר שֶׁבְּמָתְנָיו, וְכוֹבַע שֶׁבְּרֹאשׁוֹ, וְסוּדָר שֶׁבְּצַוָּארוֹ.

The Sages taught in a *baraita*: If one wants to rescue objects from a fire and there are many garments there, he **may wear** them, and **take** them **out** to a safe place, **and remove** them there, **and return** to the fire, **and wear** other clothes, **and take** them **out and remove** them. **And** he may **even** do so **all day long;** this is **the statement of Rabbi Meir. Rabbi Yosei says:** One may wear only **eighteen garments, and these are** the **eighteen garments: A cloak** [*miktoren*],[L] **a cape** [*unkali*],[L] a broad garment worn on one's shoulders, **and a** large hollow **belt** worn over the clothes, **a wide linen garment** [*kalbus*],[L] **and a robe** worn against the skin, **a robe** wrapped above, **and a kerchief** on one's head, **and two straps,** i.e., belts, **and two shoes, and two socks** [*anpilaot*],[L] **and two** tall **boots** [*pargod*],[L] **and a belt around one's loins** over the robe, **and a hat on one's head, and a scarf around one's neck.**

מתני׳ רַבִּי שִׁמְעוֹן בֶּן נַנָּס אוֹמֵר: פּוֹרְסִין עוֹר שֶׁל גְּדִי עַל גַּבֵּי שִׁידָּה תֵּיבָה וּמִגְדָּל שֶׁאָחַז בָּהֶן אֶת הָאוּר, מִפְּנֵי שֶׁהוּא מְחָרֵךְ. וְעוֹשִׂין מְחִיצָּה בְּכָל הַכֵּלִים, בֵּין מְלֵאִין בֵּין רֵיקָנִים, בִּשְׁבִיל שֶׁלֹּא תַּעֲבוֹר הַדְּלֵיקָה. רַבִּי יוֹסֵי אוֹסֵר בִּכְלֵי חֶרֶס חֲדָשִׁים מְלֵאִין מַיִם, לְפִי שֶׁאֵין יְכוֹלִין לְקַבֵּל אֶת הָאוּר, וְהֵן מִתְבַּקְּעִין וּמְכַבִּין אֶת הַדְּלֵיקָה.

MISHNA **Rabbi Shimon ben Nannas says: One may spread** out a moist **goat's hide**[H] **over a box, a chest, or a closet that caught fire, because** the fire **singes** and does not burn it. The fire does not burn the wet goat's hide but merely singes it, and by doing so the wooden vessels are preserved. **And one may establish a barrier** against the fire **with all vessels,**[H] **both full and empty, so that the fire will not pass. Rabbi Yosei prohibits** using **new earthenware vessels full of water,** because **they cannot withstand** the heat of **the fire and they will burst and extinguish the fire,** and it is prohibited to cause the fire to be extinguished on Shabbat even indirectly.

NOTES

An attribute of piety…with one who is Heaven-fearing – מִדַּת חֲסִידוּת...בִּירֵא שָׁמַיִם: Judging from the Gemara here and elsewhere, one who is Heaven-fearing or sin-fearing is praiseworthy, but he has not reached the level of piety. That was only attributed to a limited number of people who were exemplary in Torah knowledge, virtuous character traits and interpersonal relations.

LANGUAGE

Cloak [*miktoren*] – מִקְטוֹרֶן: From the Latin amictorium, meaning a garment that one throws on one's shoulders or a light garment that does not directly touch the body, generally worn by women.

Cape [*unkali*] – אוּנְקְלִי: From the Greek **ἀνάκωλος**, *anakolos*, meaning a type of skirt or short robe.

Wide linen garment [*kalbus*] – קַלְבּוּס: From the Greek **κολόβιον**, *kolobiyon*, meaning a type of shirt without sleeves or with short sleeves.

Socks [*anpilaot*] – אַנְפִּילָאוֹת: From the Greek **ἐμπίλια**, *empiliya*, meaning a shoe made of felt.

Boots [*pargod*] – פַּרְגּוֹד: Apparently adapted from Persian to the Greek **παραγαύδιον**, *paragodiyon*, and then to the Latin paragauda. It means a garment with sleeves that is decorated with purple dye [*argaman*].

HALAKHA

Acquiring from ownerless property – מֵהֶפְקֵירָא קָזָכוּ: If one tells others: Come and rescue for yourselves, they can put on whatever clothes they want and are permitted to keep anything they rescue. It is as if they acquired ownerless property. If they want to return the objects later and be rewarded for their efforts, they may do so. That money would not be considered prohibited payment for labor on Shabbat (Rambam *Sefer Zemanim*, *Hilkhot Shabbat* 23:24; *Shulḥan Arukh*, *Oraḥ Ḥayyim* 334:9).

One may spread out a goat's hide – שֶׁל גְּדִי פּוֹרְסִין עוֹר: If a chest caught fire, it is permitted to spread a wet goat's hide or the like on the part of the chest that is not on fire, to prevent the entire chest from burning, in accordance with the opinion of Rabbi Shimon ben Nannas (Rambam *Sefer Zemanim*, *Hilkhot Shabbat* 12:5; *Shulḥan Arukh*, *Oraḥ Ḥayyim* 334:22).

And one may establish a barrier with all vessels – וְעוֹשִׂין מְחִיצָּה בְּכָל הַכֵּלִים: It is permitted to erect a barrier to stop a fire from spreading using any type of vessel, including new earthenware vessels filled with water, because it is permitted to indirectly extinguish a fire. Some authorities state that this is only permitted in a situation where otherwise one will suffer significant monetary loss (*Mordekhai*; Rambam *Sefer Zemanim*, *Hilkhot Shabbat* 12:4; *Shulḥan Arukh*, *Oraḥ Ḥayyim* 334:22 and the comments of the Rema).

גמ׳ אָמַר רַב יְהוּדָה אָמַר רַב: טַלִּית שֶׁאָחַז בָּהּ הָאוּר מִצַּד אֶחָד – נוֹתְנִין עָלֶיהָ מַיִם מִצַּד אַחֵר, וְאִם כָּבְתָה – כָּבְתָה. מֵיתִיבִי: טַלִּית שֶׁאָחַז בָּהּ הָאוּר מִצַּד אֶחָד – פּוֹשְׁטָהּ וּמִתְכַּסֶּה בָּהּ, וְאִם כָּבְתָה – כָּבְתָה. וְכֵן סֵפֶר תּוֹרָה שֶׁאָחַז בּוֹ הָאוּר – פּוֹשְׁטוֹ וְקוֹרֵא בּוֹ, וְאִם כָּבָה – כָּבָה!

GEMARA Rav Yehuda said that Rav said: If a garment caught fire on one side,[H] one may place water on its other side, and if as a result the fire is extinguished, it is extinguished. The Gemara raises an objection based on the following *Tosefta*: If a garment caught fire on one side, one may stretch it out and cover himself with it, and if the fire is extinguished, it is extinguished. And so too, if a Torah scroll caught fire, one may open it and read it, and if the fire is extinguished, it is extinguished. Apparently, it is prohibited to actually pour water, but one may perform a permitted act that will incidentally extinguish.

Perek **XVI**
Daf **120** Amud **b**

הוּא דְּאָמַר כְּרַבִּי שִׁמְעוֹן בֶּן נַנָּס.

The Gemara answers: It was Rav who said his statement in accordance with the opinion of Rabbi Shimon ben Nannas in the mishna.

אֵימַר דְּאָמַר רַבִּי שִׁמְעוֹן בֶּן נַנָּס – מִפְּנֵי שֶׁהוּא מְחָרֵךְ, גְּרָם כִּיבּוּי מִי אָמַר? אִין, מִדְּקָתָנֵי סֵיפָא: ״רַבִּי יוֹסֵי אוֹסֵר בִּכְלֵי חֶרֶס חֲדָשִׁים מְלֵאִים מַיִם שֶׁאֵינָן יְכוֹלִים לְקַבֵּל אֶת הָאוּר וְהֵן מִתְבַּקְּעִין וּמְכַבִּין אֶת הַדְּלֵיקָה״ – מִכְּלָל דְּתַנָּא קַמָּא שָׁרֵי.

The Gemara asks: Say that Rabbi Shimon ben Nannas said it is permitted to place the goat's hide on the burning item because it singes and does not burn; did he say it is permitted to indirectly cause the fire to extinguish? The Gemara answers: Yes, Rabbi Shimon ben Nannas permitted that as well, and we learn this from that which is taught in the latter clause in the mishna: Rabbi Yosei prohibits using new earthenware vessels that are full of water, because they cannot withstand the fire and will burst and extinguish the fire. This proves by inference that the first *tanna*, Rabbi Shimon ben Nannas, permits it.

תָּנוּ רַבָּנַן: נֵר שֶׁעַל גַּבֵּי טַבְלָא – מְנַעֵר אֶת הַטַּבְלָא וְהִיא נוֹפֶלֶת, וְאִם כָּבְתָה – כָּבְתָה. אָמְרִי דְּבֵי רַבִּי יַנַּאי: לֹא שָׁנוּ אֶלָּא בְּשׁוֹכֵחַ, אֲבָל בְּמַנִּיחַ – נַעֲשָׂה בָּסִיס לְדָבָר הָאָסוּר.

The Sages taught: With regard to a candle that is atop a board,[NH] one shakes the board and the candle falls, and if it is extinguished, it is extinguished. The Sages of the school of Rabbi Yannai said: They only taught that this is permitted in a case where one forgets the candle atop the board when Shabbat began. However, in a case where one places it there, the board becomes a base for a prohibited object and may not be moved.

תָּנָא: נֵר שֶׁאֲחוֹרֵי הַדֶּלֶת – פּוֹתֵחַ וְנוֹעֵל כְּדַרְכּוֹ. וְאִם כָּבְתָה – כָּבְתָה. לָיֵיט עֲלַהּ רַב. אֲמַר לֵיהּ רָבִינָא לְרַב אַחָא בְּרֵיהּ דְּרָבָא, וְאָמְרִי לַהּ רַב אַחָא בְּרֵיהּ דְּרָבָא לְרַב אַשִׁי: מַאי טַעְמָא לָיֵיט עֲלַהּ רַב? אִילֵּימָא מִשּׁוּם דְּרַב סָבַר לַהּ כְּרַבִּי יְהוּדָה, וְתַנָּא קָתָנֵי לַהּ כְּרַבִּי שִׁמְעוֹן – מִשּׁוּם דְּרַב סָבַר לַהּ כְּרַבִּי יְהוּדָה, כׇּל דְּתָנֵי כְּרַבִּי שִׁמְעוֹן מֵילַט לָיֵיט לֵיהּ?!

It was taught: With regard to a candle behind a door,[NH] one may open and shut the door in his usual manner, and if it is extinguished, it is extinguished. Rav would curse one who did so.[N] Ravina said to Rav Aḥa, son of Rava, and some say that Rav Aḥa, son of Rava, said to Rav Ashi: What is the reason that Rav cursed and reprimanded one who did so? If you say it is because Rav holds in accordance with the opinion of Rabbi Yehuda that it is prohibited to perform an unintentional act from which a prohibited labor could ensue, and the *tanna* taught in accordance with the opinion of Rabbi Shimon that it is permitted to perform an unintentional act in those circumstances; because Rav holds in accordance with the opinion of Rabbi Yehuda, he curses anyone who teaches the *halakha* in accordance with the opinion of Rabbi Shimon? They rely on the ruling of a *tanna*, whose opinion is legitimate.

HALAKHA

If a garment caught fire on one side – מִצַּד אֶחָד טַלִּית שֶׁאָחַז בָּהּ הָאוּר: If a garment began burning on one side, one may spread it out and cover himself in it without concern that the fire will be extinguished. Some authorities say that this applies only when he has no intention of extinguishing the fire (*Beit Yosef* based on the *Tur*). The *Magen Avraham* adds an additional stipulation: One may not perform an act that is likely to contribute to extinguishing the fire.

Some authorities prohibit pouring liquids onto the part of the garment that is not on fire, in accordance with the challenge posed in the Gemara (Rif and others). Others permit dousing the garment with water, in accordance with the opinion of Rav (Rambam). A third opinion permits using liquids other than water, due to the concern that by dousing the garment with water one performs the prohibited labor of laundering the garment (*Tosafot*; *Tur*). Later authorities ruled in accordance with the last opinion (Rambam *Sefer Zemanim, Hilkhot Shabbat* 12:6; *Shulḥan Arukh, Oraḥ Ḥayyim* 334:23–24).

HALAKHA

A candle that is atop a board – נֵר שֶׁעַל גַּבֵּי הַטַּבְלָה: If one forgot a candle atop a board before Shabbat, and he needs the board on Shabbat, he may shake the board so the candle falls. If the candle was burning, he is permitted to shake the board only provided that he does not intend to extinguish the candle. This rule applies only to a wax candle. However, an oil lamp that is burning may not be shaken off a board, since it will certainly decrease the flame (*Tosafot*; Rosh; Ran). Nevertheless, even with regard to a wax candle, it is preferable to have a non-Jew to shake it off the board (*Kol Bo*).

If one did not forget the candle on the board but left it there intentionally, it is prohibited to shake it off, since the board itself is a base for a prohibited object and may not be moved, in accordance with the opinion of the school of Rabbi Yanai (Rambam *Sefer Zemanim, Hilkhot Shabbat* 12:6; *Shulḥan Arukh, Oraḥ Ḥayyim* 277:3).

A candle behind a door – נֵר מֵאֲחוֹרֵי הַדֶּלֶת: If there is a kindled lamp behind a door, it is prohibited to open the door in the usual manner, because it might extinguish the flame. The same applies to a window as well. This is according to Rashi's interpretation of the opinion of Rav. If the lamp is set into the wall behind the door, and when opened the door will bang into the candle and extinguish it, one must open and close the door gently so that it does not touch the candle (Rosh, based on Rabbeinu Ḥananel and Rambam). If the candle is set into the door itself, it is prohibited to open and close the door (*Tosafot*; Rambam *Sefer Zemanim, Hilkhot Shabbat* 5:17; *Shulḥan Arukh, Oraḥ Ḥayyim* 277:1).

NOTES

A candle that is atop a board – נֵר שֶׁעַל גַּבֵּי הַטַּבְלָה: The great difficulty in understanding this *halakha* is that it is nearly impossible to shake an oil lamp off a board without extinguishing it or causing a conflagration. Therefore, commentaries explain that this ruling is referring to a wax candle. Some commentaries explain, however, based on the Ra'avad, that this applies even to an oil lamp. They assert that although Rabbi Shimon prohibits an unintentional action whose inevitable consequence is a prohibited labor, in a case where the inevitable consequence is undesirable the action is permitted. In this case, one neither wants to lose the remaining oil, nor does he want the lamp thrown to the floor. In the Jerusalem Talmud, this is explained as referring to a case where the candle is already extinguished.

A candle behind a door – נֵר שֶׁאֲחוֹרֵי הַדֶּלֶת: There are three interpretations of this statement. The first explanation is that it refers to a lamp that is permanently fixed in a wall behind the door, and the concern is that the wind may extinguish it. The second is that the lamp is fixed on the door itself. Opening and closing the door will bring the oil and the wick closer together or farther apart, which will cause the flame to burn brighter or to be extinguished, respectively (Rabbeinu Yitzḥak). The third opinion is that the lamp is right behind the door; opening the door will move the lamp and extinguish it (Rabbeinu Ḥananel).

He would curse one who did so – לָיֵיט עֲלַהּ: This expression is employed only when the action is not completely prohibited but can lead to transgression. Due to the danger of transgression it is improper to act in this manner, and the Sages reproached anyone who was lax in this matter (*Me'iri*).

אֲמַר לֵיהּ: בְּהָא – אֲפִילּוּ רַבִּי שִׁמְעוֹן מוֹדֶה, דְּהָא אַבַּיֵּי וְרָבָא דְּאָמְרִי תַּרְוַיְיהוּ: מוֹדֶה רַבִּי שִׁמְעוֹן בִּפְסִיק רֵישֵׁיהּ וְלֹא יָמוּת.

He said to him: **In this** case, **even Rabbi Shimon concedes** that it is prohibited, **as it was Abaye and Rava who both said** that **Rabbi Shimon concedes in a case of: Cut off its head, will it not die?** In an instance where the unintentional act leads to an inevitable prohibited consequence, even Rabbi Shimon agrees that the person who performs the unintentional act is liable.

אָמַר רַב יְהוּדָה: פּוֹתֵחַ אָדָם דֶּלֶת כְּנֶגֶד מְדוּרָה בְּשַׁבָּת. לָיֵיט עֲלַהּ אַבַּיֵּי. בְּמַאי עָסְקִינַן? אִילֵימָא בְּרוּחַ מְצוּיָה – מַאי טַעְמֵיהּ דְּמַאן דַּאֲסַר? אִי בְּרוּחַ שֶׁאֵינָהּ מְצוּיָה – מַאי טַעְמָא דְּמַאן דְּשָׁרֵי? לְעוֹלָם בְּרוּחַ מְצוּיָה, מָר סָבַר: גָּזְרִינַן, וּמָר סָבַר: לָא גָּזְרִינַן.

Rav Yehuda said: A person opens a door opposite a fire[H] **on Shabbat.** The Gemara relates that **Abaye would curse** anyone who did so. The Gemara clarifies: **With what are we dealing? If you say** this is referring to a case where **a typical wind** is blowing outside, **what is the reason of the one** who **prohibits** opening the door? A typical wind will neither fan nor extinguish the fire. And **if** it is referring to a case where **an atypical wind** is blowing outside, **what is the reason of the one who permits** opening the door? The Gemara answers: **Actually,** it is referring to the case of **a typical wind.** However, one **Sage,** Abaye, **holds** that **we issue a decree** prohibiting to open the door in the case of a typical wind due to a case of an atypical wind, **and** the other **Sage,** Rav Yehuda, **holds** that **we do not issue** that **decree.**

״עוֹשִׂין מְחִיצָּה כו׳״. לְמֵימְרָא דְּרַבָּנַן סָבְרִי: גְּרָם כִּבּוּי מוּתָּר, וְרַבִּי יוֹסֵי סָבַר: גְּרָם כִּבּוּי אָסוּר, וְהָא אִיפְּכָא שָׁמְעִינַן לְהוּ! דְּתַנְיָא: עוֹשִׂין מְחִיצָּה בְּכֵלִים רֵיקָנִין, וּבִמְלֵאִין שֶׁאֵין דַּרְכָּן לְהִשְׁתַּבֵּר. וְאֵלּוּ מְלֵאִין שֶׁאֵין דַּרְכָּן לְהִשְׁתַּבֵּר – כְּלֵי מַתָּכוֹת. רַבִּי יוֹסֵי אוֹמֵר: אַף כְּלֵי כְּפַר שִׁיחִין וּכְלֵי כְּפַר חֲנַנְיָה אֵין דַּרְכָּן לְהִשְׁתַּבֵּר! וְכִי תֵּימָא: אִיפּוּךְ מַתְנִיתִין, וְרַבִּי יוֹסֵי דִּבְרַיְיתָא – לְדִבְרֵיהֶם קָאָמַר. וּמִי מָצֵית אָפְכַתְּ לַהּ? וְהָאָמַר רַבָּה בַּר תַּחְלִיפָא מִשְּׁמֵיהּ דְּרַב: מַאן תְּנָא ״גְּרָם כִּבּוּי אָסוּר״ – רַבִּי יוֹסֵי!

We learned in the mishna that **one may establish a barrier** with all earthenware vessels, and Rabbi Yosei prohibits using new earthenware vessels. The Gemara asks: **Is that to say that the Rabbis hold** that **indirect extinguishing is permitted** on Shabbat, **and Rabbi Yosei holds** that **indirect extinguishing is prohibited? Didn't we hear them** state **the opposite, as it was taught** in a *baraita*: **One may establish a barrier with empty vessels, and with full ones that do not typically break. And these are full** vessels **that do not typically break; metal vessels. Rabbi Yosei says: Even** earthenware **vessels** from **the village of Shiḥin and vessels from the village of Ḥananya**[B] **do not typically break.** Apparently, Rabbi Yosei's opinion is more lenient than the opinions of the Rabbis. **And if you say: Reverse the** attribution of opinions in the **mishna** and attribute Rabbi Yosei's opinion to the Rabbis, and say that **Rabbi Yosei is saying** his statement in **the** ***baraita*** **in accordance with** the opinion of the Rabbis, although he himself disagrees and permits using all vessels. But **can you reverse** the mishna? **Didn't Rabba bar Taḥalifa say in the name of Rav: Who is** the *tanna* who **teaches** that **indirect extinguishing is prohibited?** It is **Rabbi Yosei.**

אֶלָּא, לְעוֹלָם לָא תֵּיפוֹךְ, וּבָרַיְיתָא כּוּלָּהּ רַבִּי יוֹסֵי הִיא, וְחַסּוֹרֵי מִחַסְּרָא וְהָכִי קָתָנֵי: עוֹשִׂין מְחִיצָּה בְּכֵלִים רֵיקָנִין, וּבִמְלֵאִים שֶׁאֵין דַּרְכָּן לְהִשְׁתַּבֵּר. וְאֵלּוּ הֵן כֵּלִים שֶׁאֵין דַּרְכָּן לְהִשְׁתַּבֵּר – כְּלֵי מַתָּכוֹת, וּכְלֵי כְּפַר שִׁיחִין וּכְלֵי כְּפַר חֲנַנְיָה נַמִי אֵין דַּרְכָּן לְהִשְׁתַּבֵּר, שֶׁרַבִּי יוֹסֵי אוֹמֵר: אַף כְּלֵי כְּפַר שִׁיחִין וּכְלֵי כְּפַר חֲנַנְיָה אֵין דַּרְכָּן לְהִשְׁתַּבֵּר.

Rather, actually, do **not reverse** the attribution of the opinions in the mishna, **and the entire** ***baraita*** **is** in accordance with the opinion of **Rabbi Yosei, and it is incomplete and is teaching the following: One may establish a barrier with empty vessels and full ones that do not typically break. And these are vessels that do not typically break: Metal vessels;** and **vessels** from **the village of Shiḥin and vessels** from **the village of Ḥananya also do not typically break, as Rabbi Yosei says: Even vessels** from **the village of Shiḥin and vessels** from **the village of Ḥananya do not typically break.**

וְרָמֵי דְּרַבָּנַן אַדְּרַבָּנַן, וְרָמֵי דְּרַבִּי יוֹסֵי אַדְּרַבִּי יוֹסֵי. דְּתַנְיָא: הֲרֵי שֶׁהָיָה שֵׁם כָּתוּב לוֹ עַל בְּשָׂרוֹ – הֲרֵי זֶה לֹא יִרְחוֹץ וְלֹא יָסוּךְ וְלֹא יַעֲמוֹד בִּמְקוֹם הַטִּינּוֹפֶת. נִזְדַּמְּנָה לוֹ טְבִילָה שֶׁל מִצְוָה – כּוֹרֵךְ עָלֶיהָ גֶּמִי וְיוֹרֵד וְטוֹבֵל. רַבִּי יוֹסֵי אוֹמֵר: לְעוֹלָם יוֹרֵד וְטוֹבֵל כְּדַרְכּוֹ, וּבִלְבַד שֶׁלֹּא יְשַׁפְשֵׁף!

The conclusion is that Rabbi Yosei prohibits indirect extinguishing, and the Rabbis permit it. The Gemara **raises a contradiction between** one statement of **the Rabbis** and a second statement of **the Rabbis; and it raises a contradiction between** one statement of **Rabbi Yosei** and a second statement of **Rabbi Yosei. As it was taught** in a *baraita*: **If** one **had a** sacred **name** of God **written on his skin**[H] **he may neither wash** it in water lest it be erased,[N] **nor may he smear** it with oil, **nor may he stand in a place of filth** because it is disrespectful of God's name. **If an immersion of mitzva happened to** present itself, **he wraps a reed over** God's name **and** then **descends and immerses. Rabbi Yosei says: Actually, he descends and immerses in his** usual **manner,** even if it is not an immersion of mitzva, **provided that he does not rub** the spot and erase the name. Apparently, Rabbi Yosei's opinion is more lenient than that of the Sages with regard to indirectly causing a prohibited outcome.

HALAKHA

A door opposite a fire – **דֶּלֶת כְּנֶגֶד מְדוּרָה**: If there is a fire burning in the hearth on Shabbat, it is prohibited to open a door opposite the hearth, even if there is only a typical wind blowing outside. This is in accordance with the view of Abaye (*Shulḥan Arukh, Oraḥ Ḥayyim* 277:2).

A sacred name written on his skin – **שֵׁם כָּתוּב לוֹ עַל בְּשָׂרוֹ**: One who has one of God's sacred names written on his skin may neither wash nor smear oil on himself. The person may not stand in a filthy place. When immersing in a ritual bath, he must wrap a reed around the name. This reed may not be attached so firmly that it interposes between the water and his skin. The rationale for wrapping the reed over the name is because it is prohibited to stand naked before the name of God. The *halakha* is in accordance with the opinion of the Rabbis (Rambam *Sefer HaMadda, Hilkhot Yesodei HaTorah* 6:6).

BACKGROUND

The village of Shiḥin and the village of Ḥananya – **כְּפַר שִׁיחִין וּכְפַר חֲנַנְיָה**: Shiḥin and Ḥananya were two large villages in the upper Galilee where various earthenware vessels were produced. The manufacturers of these items were skilled artisans. Their vessels were strongly reinforced and could withstand high temperatures.

NOTES

Erasure of the name of God – **מְחִיקַת הַשֵּׁם**: It is apparent from the conclusion of the discussion in the Gemara that all the Sages agree that the prohibition of erasing the name of God only applies when the erasure is performed directly and intentionally, while indirect erasure is not prohibited at all. Therefore, this case is not comparable to indirectly causing a fire to be extinguished on Shabbat, which may be prohibited by Torah law.

שָׁאנֵי הָתָם דְּאָמַר קְרָא: ״וְאִבַּדְתֶּם אֶת שְׁמָם מִן הַמָּקוֹם הַהוּא לֹא תַעֲשׂוּן כֵּן לַה׳ אֱלֹהֵיכֶם״, עֲשִׂיָּיה הוּא דְּאָסוּר, גְּרָמָא – שָׁרֵי.

The Gemara answers: **It is different there** because **the verse says:** "And you shall break down their altars, and you shall smash their pillars, and their sacred trees, and burn with fire, and the graven images of their gods you shall hew down **and you shall destroy their name from that place. You shall not do so to the Lord your God"** (Deuteronomy 12:3–4). From the prohibition: "You shall not do so," Rabbi Yosei derives that actually **doing so is that which is prohibited; indirectly causing** that result **is permitted.**

אִי הָכִי, הָכָא נַמִי: כְּתִיב ״לֹא תַעֲשֶׂה [כָל] מְלָאכָה״ – עֲשִׂיָּיה הוּא דְּאָסוּר, גְּרָמָא שָׁרֵי! מִתּוֹךְ שֶׁאָדָם בָּהוּל עַל מָמוֹנוֹ – אִי שָׁרֵית לֵיהּ אָתֵי לְכַבּוֹיֵי.

The Gemara asks: **If so, here too,** with regard to Shabbat, **it is written:** "And the seventh day is Shabbat for the Lord your God, **you shall not perform any labor"** (Exodus 20:9). And here, too, one could derive: **Performance is that which is prohibited; indirectly causing** a prohibited action **is permitted.** The Gemara answers: Actually, Rabbi Yosei maintains there is no prohibition in indirectly causing a fire to be extinguished; however, **since a person is agitated about his property, if you permit him** to indirectly extinguish the fire, **he will come to extinguish** it directly.

אִי הָכִי – קַשְׁיָא דְּרַבָּנַן אַדְּרַבָּנַן: וּמַה הָתָם דְּאָדָם בָּהוּל עַל מָמוֹנוֹ – שָׁרֵי, הָכָא לֹא כׇּל שֶׁכֵּן?!

The Gemara asks: **If so, there is a contradiction** between one statement **of the Rabbis** and another statement **of the Rabbis: If** in the case of a fire, **where a person is agitated about his property,** nevertheless, the Rabbis hold that indirect extinguishing **is permitted; here,** in the case of erasing God's name, **all the more so** it should be permitted to indirectly cause erasure of God's name. Why did the Rabbis in the *baraita* issue a stringent ruling in this matter?

וְתִסְבְּרָא, הַאי גֶּמִי הֵיכִי דָּמֵי? אִי דְּמִיהֲדָק – קָא הָוֵי חֲצִיצָה, אִי לָא מִיהֲדָק – עָיְילִי בֵּיהּ מַיָּא! חֲצִיצָה – תֵּיפוֹק לֵיהּ מִשּׁוּם דְּיוֹ! בְּלַחָה, דְּתַנְיָא: הַדָּם וְהַדְּיוֹ הַדְּבַשׁ וְהֶחָלָב יְבֵשִׁין – חוֹצְצִין, לַחִים – אֵין חוֹצְצִין. מִכׇּל מָקוֹם קַשְׁיָא!

The Gemara rejects this: **And** how can **you understand** it that way? **What are the circumstances** of **this reed** with which God's name is covered while immersing according to the Rabbis? **If** it is **firmly attached, it is an interposition; if it is not firmly attached, the water enters** and erases the name. The Gemara questions this: If the concern is with regard to an **interposition, derive** that **it** is an interposition in any case **due to** the **ink** on his skin. The Gemara answers: This is referring to **moist** ink that does not interpose, **as it was taught** in a *baraita*: With regard to **blood, and ink,** and **honey, and milk** on a person's skin, when they are **dry,** they **interpose** during immersion; when they are **moist,** they **do not interpose.**[H] The Gemara continues: **Nevertheless,** it is **difficult:** Why do the Rabbis require wrapping a reed around God's name?

אֶלָּא אָמַר רָבָא בַּר רַב שֵׁילָא: הַיְינוּ טַעְמַיְיהוּ דְּרַבָּנַן, דְּקָסָבְרִי: אָסוּר לַעֲמוֹד בִּפְנֵי הַשֵּׁם עָרוֹם. מִכְּלָל דְּרַבִּי יוֹסֵי סָבַר מוּתָּר לַעֲמוֹד בִּפְנֵי הַשֵּׁם עָרוֹם?! דְּמַנַּח יְדֵיהּ עִילָּוֵיהּ.

Rather, Rava bar Rav Sheila said that **this is the reasoning of the Rabbis: They hold** that **it is prohibited** for a person **to stand before the name** of God while **naked,** and therefore there must be a barrier between one's naked body and the name. The Gemara asks: Is that to say **by inference** that **Rabbi Yosei holds** that **it is permitted to stand before the name** while **naked?** The Gemara answers: No, he does not allow doing so; however, he does not require that the name be covered with a reed. It is sufficient for **one to place his hand over** the name.

לְרַבָּנַן נַמִי, דְּמַנַּח יְדֵיהּ עִילָּוֵיהּ! זִימְנִין דְּמִשְׁתְּלֵי, וְשָׁקֵיל לֵיהּ. לְרַבִּי יוֹסֵי נַמִי, זִימְנִין דְּמִשְׁתְּלֵי וְשָׁקֵיל לֵיהּ! אֶלָּא: אִי דְּאִיכָּא גֶּמִי – הָכִי נַמִי, הָכָא בְּמַאי עָסְקִינַן – לְאַהֲדוּרֵי אַגְּמִי. רַבָּנַן סָבְרִי:

The Gemara asks: If so, according **to the Rabbis** it should **also** be sufficient for **one to place his hand over it.** The Gemara explains: The Rabbis are concerned because **sometimes one** will **forget and remove** his hand. The Gemara asks: Shouldn't **Rabbi Yosei also** be concerned because **sometimes one** will **forget and remove** his hand? **Rather, if there is a reed** available, Rabbi Yosei **indeed** concedes that one covers God's name with it. However, **with what** situation **are we dealing here?** We are dealing with a case in which one would have **to seek a reed.** In that case, **the Rabbis hold**

HALAKHA

Interposition during immersion – **חֲצִיצָה בִּטְבִילָה**: When immersing in a ritual bath, blood, ink, honey, and milk, as well as fig and berry nectar, interpose when they are dry, but not when they are wet (Rambam *Sefer Tahara, Hilkhot Mikvaot* 2:2; *Shulḥan Arukh, Yoreh De'a* 198:15).

טְבִילָה בִּזְמַנָּהּ לָאו מִצְוָה – וּמְהַדְּרִינַן, וְרַבִּי יוֹסֵי סָבַר: טְבִילָה בִּזְמַנָּהּ מִצְוָה – וְלָא מְהַדְּרִינַן.

that performing **immersion at its** designated **time**[N] **is not a mitzva, and we seek** a reed to wrap around God's name even if it means postponing immersion to the next day, **and Rabbi Yosei holds** that **immersion at its** designated **time is a mitzva, and** therefore **we do not seek** a reed, since immersion cannot be postponed.

NOTES

Immersion at its designated time – **טְבִילָה בִּזְמַנָּהּ**: There are two essential issues at the basis of this *baraita*. The first is the opinion that it is a mitzva for a person to immerse at the designated time, as opposed to it being simply good advice. The second is that there was a custom in effect over the course of many generations that a man who experienced a seminal emission would not pray until he had immersed. Some commentaries explain that Rabbi Yosei does not merely hold that the people mentioned in the *baraita* do not have to immerse on Yom Kippur; rather, he is of the opinion that it is forbidden for them to do so. Still, Rabbi Yosei does hold that it is permitted for a man who has experienced a seminal emission to immerse on Yom Kippur if it will enable him to pray, i.e., if it is before the afternoon prayer (*Tosefot Rid*).

וְסָבַר רַבִּי יוֹסֵי טְבִילָה בִּזְמַנָּהּ מִצְוָה?! וְהָתַנְיָא: הַזָּב וְהַזָּבָה הַמְּצוֹרָע וְהַמְּצוֹרַעַת בּוֹעֵל נִדָּה וּטְמֵא מֵת – טְבִילָתָן בַּיּוֹם, נִדָּה וְיוֹלֶדֶת – טְבִילָתָן בַּלַּיְלָה. בַּעַל קֶרִי טוֹבֵל וְהוֹלֵךְ כָּל הַיּוֹם כּוּלּוֹ, רַבִּי יוֹסֵי אוֹמֵר: מִן הַמִּנְחָה וּלְמַעְלָה – אֵינוֹ צָרִיךְ לִטְבּוֹל! הַהִיא רַבִּי יוֹסֵי בְּרַבִּי יְהוּדָה הִיא, דְּאָמַר: דַּיָּהּ טְבִילָה בָּאַחֲרוֹנָה.

The Gemara asks: **And does Rabbi Yosei hold** that **immersion at its** designated **time is a mitzva? Wasn't it taught** in a *baraita*: With regard to **a** ***zav*** **and a** ***zava*****, a male and female leper, one who has relations with a menstruating woman, and a person impure** with impurity imparted by **a corpse, their immersion is during the day.**[H] They immerse at the designated time even on Yom Kippur, when bathing is prohibited.[H] **A menstruating woman and a woman after childbirth immerse at night. A man who has had a seminal emission immerses** at any point **during the entire day** after the emission. **Rabbi Yosei says: From** the time that he recited **the afternoon prayer**[N] **and on he does not immerse.** Since he already recited the afternoon prayer, he waits until after Yom Kippur to immerse, and then recites the evening prayer in a state of purity. Apparently, Rabbi Yosei holds that immersion at the designated time is not a mitzva. The Gemara rejects this: In **that** *baraita* the reference is not to the Rabbi Yosei most commonly cited in tannaitic literature without a patronymic, Rabbi Yosei ben Ḥalafta, but it **is** to **Rabbi Yosei, son of Rabbi Yehuda, who said: Her latest immersion is sufficient.**[N] A woman who is uncertain with regard to the correct time for her immersion need not immerse multiple times. She may postpone her immersion until a time when she will be certain to fulfill her obligation, even though it might not be immersion at the designated time.

מתני׳ גּוֹי שֶׁבָּא לְכַבּוֹת, אֵין אוֹמְרִים לוֹ ״כַּבֵּה״ וְ״אַל תְּכַבֶּה״ – מִפְּנֵי שֶׁאֵין שְׁבִיתָתוֹ עֲלֵיהֶן. אֲבָל קָטָן שֶׁבָּא לְכַבּוֹת אֵין שׁוֹמְעִין לוֹ, מִפְּנֵי שֶׁשְּׁבִיתָתוֹ עֲלֵיהֶן.

MISHNA If **a gentile comes to extinguish** a Jew's fire on Shabbat,[H] **one may not say to him: Extinguish, and: Do not extinguish, because** responsibility for **his rest is not** incumbent **upon** the Jew. **However,** if a Jewish **child comes to extinguish** a fire on Shabbat,[H] **they do not listen to him** and allow him to extinguish it, even though he is not yet obligated in mitzva observance, **because** responsibility for **his rest is** incumbent **upon** the Jew.

גמ׳ אָמַר רַבִּי אַמִי: בִּדְלֵיקָה הִתִּירוּ לוֹמַר ״כָּל הַמְכַבֶּה אֵינוֹ מַפְסִיד״. נֵימָא מְסַיַּיע לֵיהּ: גּוֹי שֶׁבָּא לְכַבּוֹת אֵין אוֹמְרִים לוֹ ״כַּבֵּה״ וְ״אַל תְּכַבֶּה״ – מִפְּנֵי שֶׁאֵין שְׁבִיתָתוֹ עֲלֵיהֶן. ״כַּבֵּה״ הוּא דְּלָא אָמְרִינַן לֵיהּ, הָא ״כָּל הַמְכַבֶּה אֵינוֹ מַפְסִיד״ – אָמְרִינַן לֵיהּ. אֵימָא סֵיפָא: ״אַל תְּכַבֶּה״ לָא אָמְרִינַן לֵיהּ, וְ״כָל הַמְכַבֶּה אֵינוֹ מַפְסִיד״ – נַמִי לָא אָמְרִינַן לֵיהּ! אֶלָּא: מֵהָא לֵיכָּא לְמִשְׁמַע מִינָּהּ.

GEMARA Rabbi Ami said: During **a fire, the** Sages **permitted to say** in the presence of gentiles: **Anyone who extinguishes** the fire **will not lose,**[NH] so that the gentiles will come and extinguish the fire; it is only prohibited to tell gentiles to do so explicitly. The Gemara suggests: **Let us say** that the mishna **supports his** statement: If **a gentile comes to extinguish** a Jew's fire on Shabbat, **one may not say to him: Extinguish, and: Do not extinguish, because** responsibility for **his rest is not** incumbent **upon** the Jew. It can be inferred from the language of the mishna: **It is** a direct command, e.g., **extinguish, that we may not say to him; however, anyone who extinguishes will not lose,** we may **tell him,** which supports Rabbi Ami's statement. The Gemara rejects this. **Say** the **latter** clause of the mishna: **Do not extinguish, we do not tell him.** It can be inferred that **neither do we say to him: Anyone who extinguishes will not lose. Rather, nothing can be inferred from this** mishna.

תָּנוּ רַבָּנַן: מַעֲשֶׂה וְנָפְלָה דְּלֵיקָה בַּחֲצֵירוֹ שֶׁל יוֹסֵף בֶּן סִימַאי בְּשִׁיחִין, וּבָאוּ אַנְשֵׁי גִיסְטְרָא שֶׁל צִיפּוֹרִי לְכַבּוֹת, מִפְּנֵי שֶׁאַפִּטְרוֹפּוֹס שֶׁל מֶלֶךְ הָיָה. וְלֹא הִנִּיחָן מִפְּנֵי כְּבוֹד הַשַּׁבָּת, וְנַעֲשָׂה לוֹ נֵס וְיָרְדוּ גְשָׁמִים וְכִיבּוּ. לָעֶרֶב שִׁיגֵּר לְכָל אֶחָד מֵהֶן שְׁתֵּי סְלָעִין, וְלָאִפַּרְכוֹס שֶׁבָּהֶן חֲמִשִּׁים. וּכְשֶׁשָּׁמְעוּ חֲכָמִים בַּדָּבָר אָמְרוּ: לֹא הָיָה צָרִיךְ לְכָךְ, שֶׁהֲרֵי שָׁנִינוּ: גּוֹי שֶׁבָּא לְכַבּוֹת אֵין אוֹמְרִים לוֹ ״כַּבֵּה״ וְ״אַל תְּכַבֶּה״.

The Sages taught in a *baraita*: **There was an incident that a fire ignited** on Shabbat **in the courtyard of Yosef ben Simai in** a place called **Shiḥin. And men came from the fortress** [*gistera*][L] **of Tzippori to extinguish** the fire, **because he was a steward** [*apotropos*][L] **of the king** and they wanted to help him. **However,** Yosef ben Simai **would not allow them** to extinguish the fire **in deference to Shabbat; and a miracle transpired for him and rain fell and extinguished** the fire. **That evening** after Shabbat **he sent two** ***sela*** **to each one of** the soldiers who came to his aid, **and fifty to their commander** [*iparkhos*].[L] **And when the Sages heard about this, they said: He need not** have prevented them from extinguishing the fire, **as we learned** in the mishna: If **a gentile comes to extinguish** a Jew's fire on Shabbat, **one may not say to him: Extinguish, and: Do not extinguish, because** responsibility for **his rest is not** incumbent **upon** the Jew; rather, the gentile may do as he pleases.

HALAKHA

Times for immersion – זְמַנֵּי הַטְּבִילָה: Everyone who is obligated to immerse in a ritual bath must do so during the day. The exceptions to the rule are a menstruating woman and a woman who has given birth, who immerse at night (Rambam *Sefer Tahara, Hilkhot Mikvaot* 1:6 and *Sefer Kedusha, Hilkhot Issurei Bia* 4:6; *Shulḥan Arukh, Oraḥ Ḥayyim* 554:8 and *Yoreh De'a* 197:3, 381:5).

Immersion on Yom Kippur – טְבִילָה בְּיוֹם הַכִּפּוּרִים: Since it is a mitzva to immerse oneself at the designated time, one may do so on Yom Kippur if that day is the designated time for immersion. In contemporary times, the *halakha* of immersing at a designated time does not apply in most cases. Therefore, anyone required to immerse, including a menstruating woman, does so after Yom Kippur (Rambam *Sefer Zemanim, Hilkhot Shevitat Asor* 3:2–3; *Shulḥan Arukh, Oraḥ Ḥayyim* 554:8, 613:11–12).

If a gentile comes to extinguish a Jew's fire on Shabbat – גּוֹי שֶׁבָּא לְכַבּוֹת: If a gentile comes to extinguish a fire on Shabbat, there is no requirement to prevent him from doing so (Rambam *Sefer Zemanim, Hilkhot Shabbat* 6:4; *Shulḥan Arukh, Oraḥ Ḥayyim* 334:25).

If a Jewish child comes to extinguish a fire on Shabbat – קָטָן שֶׁבָּא לְכַבּוֹת: A child, even one who has not reached the age of training to perform mitzvot (*Mishna Berura*), who comes to extinguish a fire on Shabbat must be prevented from doing so (Rambam *Sefer Zemanim, Hilkhot Shabbat* 12:7; *Shulḥan Arukh, Oraḥ Ḥayyim* 334:25).

Anyone who extinguishes the fire will not lose – כָּל הַמְכַבֶּה אֵינוֹ מַפְסִיד: On Shabbat, when a fire does not pose a threat to human life, it is prohibited to explicitly tell a gentile to extinguish it. Nevertheless, it is permitted to state in his presence: Anyone who extinguishes the fire will not lose. In life-threatening situations, early and later authorities permit anyone to extinguish the fire directly. One who hastens to do so is praised (Rema; Rambam *Sefer Zemanim, Hilkhot Shabbat* 12:7; *Shulḥan Arukh, Oraḥ Ḥayyim* 334:26).

NOTES

From the time that he recited the afternoon prayer – מִן הַמִּנְחָה: The *Me'iri* comments that one need not be concerned about the *ne'ila* prayer, the additional closing service on Yom Kippur, since this prayer may be recited at night, after immersion.

Her latest immersion is sufficient – דַּיָּהּ טְבִילָה בָּאַחֲרוֹנָה: In certain cases discussed in tractate *Nidda*, when a woman forgets or is uncertain with regard to when she is required to immerse in a ritual bath, some Sages rule that she should immerse herself each day that might be her designated time. Rabbi Yosei, son of Rabbi Yehuda, disagrees and maintains that it is sufficient for the woman to wait and immerse once at a time when she is certain that she may immerse.

Anyone who extinguishes the fire will not lose – כָּל הַמְכַבֶּה אֵינוֹ מַפְסִיד: Since the mishna stated that one need not say: Do not extinguish, one can infer that although one need not dissuade the gentile from extinguishing the fire, it is prohibited to encourage him to extinguish it. Otherwise, the mishna should have stated explicitly that one may say: One who extinguishes will not lose, and it would have been clear that one need not prevent the gentile from extinguishing the fire.

LANGUAGE

Fortress [*gistera*] – גִּיסְטְרָא: From the Latin castra, meaning a fortified encampment or a fortress. In talmudic sources, this word is often used to indicate a permanent encampment of Roman soldiers.

Steward [*apotropos*] – אַפּוֹטְרוֹפּוֹס: From the Greek ἐπίτροπος, *epitropos*, meaning appointee or supervisor. In this context, it means the person who managed the king's properties in a specific region.

Commander [*iparkhos*] – אִפַּרְכוֹס: From the Greek ἔπαρχος, *eparkos*, meaning commander or appointed official.

"אֲבָל קָטָן שֶׁבָּא לְכַבּוֹת אֵין שׁוֹמְעִין לוֹ מִפְּנֵי שֶׁשְּׁבִיתָתוֹ עֲלֵיהֶן". שְׁמַעַתְּ מִינַּהּ: קָטָן אוֹכֵל נְבֵלוֹת – בֵּית דִּין מְצוּוִּין עָלָיו לְהַפְרִישׁוֹ. אָמַר רַבִּי יוֹחָנָן: בְּקָטָן הָעוֹשֶׂה לְדַעַת אָבִיו. דִּכְוָותָהּ גַּבֵּי גּוֹי – דְּקָא עָבֵיד לְדַעְתֵּיהּ דְּיִשְׂרָאֵל, מִי שָׁרֵי?! גּוֹי לְדַעְתֵּיהּ דְּנַפְשֵׁיהּ עָבֵיד.

We learned in the mishna: **However,** if a Jewish **child comes to extinguish** a fire on Shabbat, **they do not listen to him** and allow him to extinguish it, even though he is not yet obligated in mitzva observance, **because** responsibility for **his rest is** incumbent **upon** the Jew. The Gemara seeks to conclude: **Learn** from **this** that a **child who eats** meat from **unslaughtered animals**[H] or violates other prohibitions, **the court is commanded to prevent him** from eating it. This mishna would resolve a dilemma that arose regarding that issue. The Gemara rejects this suggestion: **Rabbi Yoḥanan said:** This mishna is referring to **a child who is acting with** the intention of fulfilling **his father's will,** and therefore one is obligated to prevent him from doing so. However, if a child sins of his own volition, one is not obligated to prevent him from doing so. The Gemara asks: If so, the case **with regard to a gentile** in the mishna must be interpreted in a **similar** manner as referring to a case where **he is acting with** the intention to fulfill the **will of a Jew. Is** that **permitted?** It is prohibited to derive benefit from an action performed by a gentile for a Jew on Shabbat. The Gemara responds: This is not the case; **the gentile** is **acting of his own volition.**[N] Because he is paid for extinguishing the fire he is not doing so in order to help the Jew.

מתני׳ כּוֹפִין קְעָרָה עַל גַּבֵּי הַנֵּר בִּשְׁבִיל שֶׁלֹּא תֶּאֱחוֹז בַּקּוֹרָה, וְעַל צוֹאָה שֶׁל קָטָן, וְעַל עַקְרָב שֶׁלֹּא תִּישַּׁךְ. אָמַר רַבִּי יְהוּדָה: מַעֲשֶׂה בָּא לִפְנֵי רַבָּן יוֹחָנָן בֶּן זַכַּאי בַּעֲרָב, וְאָמַר: חוֹשְׁשַׁנִי לוֹ מֵחַטָּאת.

MISHNA **One may overturn a bowl on top of a lamp**[H] **so that fire will not take hold in the** ceiling **beam** on Shabbat. **And** similarly, one may overturn a bowl **on top of a child's feces** inside the house so he will not touch it and dirty himself, **and on top of a scorpion so that it will not bite. Rabbi Yehuda said: An incident came before Rabban Yoḥanan ben Zakkai in** his village of **Arav,**[B] where a person covered a scorpion on Shabbat, **and** Rabban Yoḥanan **said: I am concerned** that **he** is liable to bring **a sin-offering**[N] because he might have violated a Torah prohibition.

גמ׳ רַב יְהוּדָה וְרַב יִרְמְיָה בַּר אַבָּא וְרַב חָנָן בַּר רָבָא אִיקְלְעוּ לְבֵי אָבִין דְּמִן נְשִׁיקְיָא, לְרַב יְהוּדָה וְרַב יִרְמְיָה בַּר אַבָּא

GEMARA The Gemara relates: **Rav Yehuda and Rav Yirmeya bar Abba and Rav Ḥanan bar Rava happened to come to the house of Avin from** a place called **Nashikiya. For Rav Yehuda and Rav Yirmeya bar Abba,**

HALAKHA

A child who eats meat from unslaughtered animals – קָטָן אוֹכֵל נְבֵלוֹת: The rabbinical court is not obligated to prevent a child from violating even a Torah prohibition. However, the child's father, who is commanded to train his children in fulfillment of mitzvot, should reprimand the child and prevent him from violating Torah prohibitions. Some commentaries hold that if the child has reached the age of training, even the court is commanded to prevent the child from sinning (Rema; Rambam *Sefer Kedusha, Hilkhot Ma'akhalot Assurot* 17:27–28; *Shulḥan Arukh, Oraḥ Ḥayyim* 343).

One may overturn a bowl on top of a lamp – כּוֹפִין קְעָרָה עַל גַּבֵּי הַנֵּר: It is permitted to overturn an earthenware (*Mishna Berura*) bowl over a candle so that the fire will not spread to the ceiling. Similarly, one may cover a scorpion with a bowl to prevent it from stinging (Rambam *Sefer Zemanim, Hilkhot Shabbat* 12:4; *Shulḥan Arukh, Oraḥ Ḥayyim* 277:5).

NOTES

The gentile is acting of his own volition – גּוֹי לְדַעְתֵּיהּ דְּנַפְשֵׁיהּ עָבֵיד: Since a gentile is an independent and intelligent person, even if his intention is to benefit a Jew, he is considered to be acting independently. That is not the case with a child, who is not capable of making his own decisions and therefore acts based on his parents' will (Ritva).

I am concerned that he is liable to bring a sin-offering – חוֹשְׁשַׁנִי לוֹ מֵחַטָּאת: Rabban Yoḥanan did not consider the scorpion to have been potentially dangerous, otherwise he would surely have permitted it. He maintained that there was no danger and was uncertain whether or not this falls into the category of the prohibited labor of trapping (Rabbi Elazar Moshe Horovitz).

BACKGROUND

Arav – עֲרָב: Arav was a village close to Tzippori where Rabban Yoḥanan ben Zakkai lived for eighteen years. According to the Talmud it was not a place of Torah study, and during his entire time there he was asked only two halakhic questions, which are cited here and on 146a, p. 362.

Perek **XVI**
Daf **121** Amud **b**

אַיְיתוּ לְהוּ פּוּרְיָיתָא, לְרַב חָנָן בַּר רָבָא לָא אַיְיתוּ לֵיהּ. אַשְׁכְּחֵיהּ מַתְנֵי לֵיהּ לִבְרֵיהּ: "וְעַל צוֹאָה שֶׁל קָטָן מִפְּנֵי קָטָן". אָמַר לֵיהּ: אָבִין שַׁטְיָא מַתְנֵי שְׁטוּתָא לִבְנֵיהּ, וַהֲלֹא הִיא עַצְמָהּ מוּכֶנֶת לִכְלָבִים! וְכִי תֵּימָא דְּלָא חַזְיָא לֵיהּ מֵאֶתְמוֹל – וְהָתַנְיָא: נַהֲרוֹת הַמּוֹשְׁכִין וּמַעְיָינוֹת הַנּוֹבְעִין הֲרֵי הֵן כְּרַגְלֵי כָּל אָדָם.

they brought beds for them to sit on, whereas **for Rav Ḥanan bar Rava, they did not bring** one **for him.** Rav Ḥanan was insulted and got angry at his host. **He found** Rabbi Avin **teaching his son** the mishna and saying: **And** one may place a bowl **on top of the feces of a child**[N] **due to the child** so that he will not touch it and dirty himself. Rav Ḥanan **said to him: Avin the fool is teaching his son folly; aren't** the feces **themselves prepared** as food **for dogs?** An object that is fit for consumption by a dog may be carried, so why need one cover the feces if he can remove them? **And if you say** these feces **were not prepared for** that use **from yesterday,** that would not prohibit moving them. **Wasn't it taught** in a *baraita*: With regard to **rivers that flow**[H] **and springs that gush,** they do not have specific Shabbat boundaries, but **they** may be used anywhere and their boundaries **are like the feet of all people** who draw from them. Even though the water was not within the boundaries when Shabbat began, since the nature of flowing water is to move from place to place, it is as if they were prepared for this purpose. So too, here, since a child will relieve himself in any place, it is as if it was prepared from before Shabbat.

וְאֶלָּא הֵיכִי אַתְנְיֵיהּ? אֵימָא: עַל צוֹאָה שֶׁל תַּרְנְגוֹלִים מִפְּנֵי קָטָן.

Rabbi Avin asked: **And how, then, should I teach it to him?** Rav Ḥanan answered: **Say,** one may place a bowl **on top of chicken feces**[H] **due to a child.**

NOTES

Feces of a child – צוֹאָה שֶׁל קָטָן: Rav Ḥanan understood that this phrase should not be taken literally. Rather, it is referring to any feces that a child might touch and thereby become dirty. The interpretation in the Jerusalem Talmud is that this refers to soft feces, which will make a child dirty if he touches them, but which would otherwise be suitable as chickenfeed.

HALAKHA

Rivers that flow – נַהֲרוֹת הַמּוֹשְׁכִין: The flowing water in rivers and wells is considered to come from within the Shabbat boundaries of the people who draw water from them, even if their source is beyond the Shabbat boundaries. It is permitted to draw river and well water on Shabbat and on Festivals (Rambam *Sefer Zemanim, Hilkhot Yom Tov* 5:14; *Shulḥan Arukh, Oraḥ Ḥayyim* 397:15).

Chicken feces – צוֹאָה שֶׁל תַּרְנְגוֹלִים: Any disgusting object, such as a vessel containing human or animal feces, may be thrown in the garbage, whether the object is in a courtyard where people live or inside a house, and even if the disgusting object is not in a vessel. If it is in a courtyard where no one lives, one may not move it. If there is concern that a child might become soiled with it, it is permitted to cover the repulsive item with a vessel. This is in accordance with Rashi's interpretation of the conclusion of the Gemara (Rambam *Sefer Zemanim, Hilkhot Shabbat* 26:13; *Shulḥan Arukh, Oraḥ Ḥayyim* 308:34).

וְתֵיפּוֹק לֵיהּ דְּהָוֵי גְּרָף שֶׁל רְעִי. וְכִי תֵּימָא: גְּרָף שֶׁל רְעִי אַגַּב מָנָא – אִין, אִיהוּ גּוּפֵיהּ – לָא, וְהָא הַהוּא עַכְבָּר דְּאִישְׁתַּכַּח בְּאִיסְפַּרְמָקֵי דְּרַב אַשִׁי, וַאֲמַר לְהוּ: נְקוֹטוּ בְּצוּצִיתֵיהּ וְאַפְּקוּהּ! בְּאַשְׁפָּה. וְקָטָן בָּאַשְׁפָּה מַאי בָּעֵי לֵיהּ? בֶּחָצֵר. חָצֵר נַמִי, גְּרָף שֶׁל רְעִי הוּא! בְּאַשְׁפָּה שֶׁבֶּחָצֵר.

The Gemara asks: **And derive** that **it** is permitted to remove the feces **because it is** like **a chamber pot of feces,** which may be moved out of the room because it is disgusting. **And if you say** that **a chamber pot of feces together with the vessel, yes,** it may be moved; but feces **itself, no,** it may not be moved. What about **that mouse that was found among the spices** [***isperamaki***][L] **of Rav Ashi, and he said to** his servants: **Take it by its tail and remove it?** Apparently, a disgusting object may be moved even without a vessel. Rather, we must say that the feces were **in the garbage** dump, and since the feces were not before the household members it was only permitted to conceal them, not to move them. The Gemara asks: **And what is a child doing in the garbage** dump in the public domain? It is not adjacent to the house; how would the child get there? The Gemara answers that the feces were not in the garbage dump but were **in the courtyard.** The Gemara rejects this: **In the courtyard, it is also** considered **a chamber pot of feces** and may be moved. Rather, it is referring to **a garbage** dump **that is in the courtyard,** to which the child sometimes has access. Feces in a place designated for garbage are no more disgusting than their surroundings, and therefore it is prohibited to move the feces.

״וְעַל עַקְרָב שֶׁלֹּא תִּישַּׁךְ״. אָמַר רַבִּי יְהוֹשֻׁעַ בֶּן לֵוִי: כׇּל הַמַּזִּיקִין נֶהֱרָגִין בַּשַּׁבָּת. מְתִיב רַב יוֹסֵף: חֲמִשָּׁה נֶהֱרָגִין בַּשַּׁבָּת, וְאֵלּוּ הֵן: זְבוּב שֶׁבְּאֶרֶץ מִצְרַיִם, וְצִירְעָה שֶׁבְּנִינְוֵה, וְעַקְרָב שֶׁבְּחַדְיַיב, וְנָחָשׁ שֶׁבְּאֶרֶץ יִשְׂרָאֵל, וְכֶלֶב שׁוֹטֶה בְּכׇל מָקוֹם. מַנִּי? אִילֵימָא רַבִּי יְהוּדָה – הָא אָמַר: מְלָאכָה שֶׁאֵינָהּ צְרִיכָה לְגוּפָהּ חַיָּיב עָלֶיהָ! אֶלָּא לָאו – רַבִּי שִׁמְעוֹן, וְהָנֵי הוּא דְּשָׁרֵי, אַחֲרִינֵי – לָא!

And we also learned in the mishna that one may cover **a scorpion** with a bowl on Shabbat so **that it will not bite. Rabbi Yehoshua ben Levi said: All harmful creatures are killed on Shabbat. Rav Yosef raised an objection to this** from the following *baraita*: **Five** creatures **may be killed** even **on Shabbat,**[HB] **and they are: The** poisonous **fly that is in the land of Egypt,**[B] **and the hornet that is in Ninveh, and the scorpion that is in Ḥadyab, and the snake that is in Eretz Yisrael, and a mad dog in any place.** The Gemara clarifies this: In accordance with **whose** opinion is this *baraita*? **If you say** it is in accordance with the opinion of **Rabbi Yehuda, didn't he say** that **one is liable for a** prohibited **labor that is not needed for its own sake,** and it is therefore prohibited to kill even these creatures? **Rather, is it not** in accordance with the opinion of **Rabbi Shimon, and these are those** creatures **that it is permitted** to kill; **others, no,** it is **not** permitted to kill?

אָמַר רַבִּי יִרְמְיָה: וּמַאן נֵימָא לַן דְּהָא מְתַרְצְתָּא הִיא, דִּילְמָא מְשַׁבַּשְׁתָּא הִיא? אֲמַר רַב יוֹסֵף: אֲנָא מַתְנֵינָא לַהּ וְאוֹתִיבְנָא לַהּ, וַאֲנָא מְתָרֵיצְנָא לַהּ – בְּרָצוּ אַחֲרָיו וְדִבְרֵי הַכֹּל.

Rabbi Yirmeya said: And who will say to us that this *baraita* **is accurate? Perhaps it is corrupted,**[N] and an objection cannot be raised from it. **Rav Yosef said: I taught** the *baraita* **and raised an objection from it, and I will answer it** as follows: Rabbi Yehoshua ben Levi permitted killing all harmful creatures on Shabbat **when they are running after him;** as in that case the danger is real, **and** therefore it is permitted to kill them according to **all opinions.**

תָּנֵי תַּנָּא קַמֵּיהּ דְּרָבָא בַּר רַב הוּנָא: הַהוֹרֵג נְחָשִׁים וְעַקְרַבִּים בַּשַּׁבָּת אֵין רוּחַ חֲסִידִים נוֹחָה הֵימֶנּוּ. אֲמַר לֵיהּ: וְאוֹתָן חֲסִידִים – אֵין רוּחַ חֲכָמִים נוֹחָה מֵהֶם. וּפְלִיגָא דְּרַב הוּנָא, דְּרַב הוּנָא חַזְיֵיהּ לְהַהוּא גַּבְרָא דְּקָא קָטֵיל זִיבּוּרָא, אֲמַר לֵיהּ: שְׁלֵימְתִּינְהוּ לְכוּלְּהוּ?!

The *tanna* who recited tannaitic literature **before Rava bar Rav Huna taught** a *baraita*: **One who kills snakes and scorpions on Shabbat, the spirit of** the **pious is not pleased with him.** Rava bar Rav Huna **said to him: And** with regard to **those pious, the spirit of the Sages is not pleased with them,** as snakes and scorpions harm people. The Gemara comments: **And** this statement **disagrees** with the opinion of **Rav Huna,** for **Rav Huna saw a person killing a hornet** on Shabbat and **said to him: Have you finished killing all** the hornets? This indicates that he was not pleased with him.

תָּנוּ רַבָּנַן: נִזְדַּמְּנוּ לוֹ נְחָשִׁים וְעַקְרַבִּים, הֲרָגָן – בְּיָדוּעַ שֶׁנִּזְדַּמְּנוּ לוֹ לְהוֹרְגָן, לֹא הֲרָגָן – בְּיָדוּעַ שֶׁנִּזְדַּמְּנוּ לְהוֹרְגוֹ, וְנַעֲשָׂה לוֹ נֵס מִן הַשָּׁמַיִם. אֲמַר עוּלָּא וְאִיתֵימָא רַבָּה בַּר בַּר חָנָה אָמַר רַבִּי יוֹחָנָן: בְּנִישּׁוֹפִין בּוֹ.

The Sages taught in a *baraita*: One who **snakes and scorpions happened** before him, if he **killed them, it is clear that they happened** before **him** in order for him **to kill them.** If **he did not kill them it is clear that they happened** before **him** in order for them **to kill him, but a miracle from heaven transpired for him** and he was saved. **Ulla said, and some say** it was **Rabba bar bar Ḥana** who said that **Rabbi Yoḥanan said:** This is referring to **when they were touching** and brushing up against him (Rabbeinu Ḥananel), as in that case if they cause him no harm, it is surely a miracle that saved him.

LANGUAGE

Spices [*isperamaki*] – אִיסְפַּרְמָקֵי: From the Iranian isprahmak, meaning fragrant herbs.

HALAKHA

Five creatures may be killed on Shabbat – חֲמִשָּׁה נֶהֱרָגִין בַּשַּׁבָּת: Any animal or creeping animal whose bite or sting poses a definite threat to human life may be killed on Shabbat. The *Mishna Berura* adds that this applies even if the creature is not pursuing a person, or even if it is running away. As for other harmful creatures, it is permitted to trample them if it appears that one is doing so innocently. Otherwise, it is prohibited (Rambam *Sefer Zemanim, Hilkhot Shabbat* 11:4; *Shulḥan Arukh, Oraḥ Ḥayyim* 316:10).

BACKGROUND

Five creatures may be killed on Shabbat – חֲמִשָּׁה נֶהֱרָגִין בַּשַּׁבָּת: In this context, the hornet is the large hornet also found in Eretz Yisrael, the *Vespa orientalis*. This hornet lives in families within nests built in the ground. The hornet's sting causes tremendous pain, even though a single sting is not fatal. There have been many instances in which people and animals have died after being stung by a swarm of hornets. The scorpion mentioned here may be the common yellow scorpion, the *Ceiurus guinquestriatas*, whose sting is extremely poisonous and life threatening.

The poisonous fly that is in the land of Egypt – זְבוּב שֶׁבְּאֶרֶץ מִצְרַיִם: The fly found in Egypt seems to refer to the gadfly of the *Chrysops* and *Tabanus* types that bite people. This bite is quite painful and causes a rash and swelling.

Gadfly

NOTES

Perhaps it is corrupted – דִּילְמָא מְשַׁבַּשְׁתָּא הִיא: Questions regarding the accuracy of a text are sometimes raised about *baraitot*, but only rarely about *mishnayot* (see *Yad Malakhi*). When this question is posed, the Gemara must prove that the *baraita* text is corrupted. In this context, however, the *baraita* was not well known, and it was only Rav Yosef who introduced it to the study hall. Therefore, the suggestion was made that it be rejected, especially because it contradicted the statement of the great *amora*, Rabbi Yehoshua ben Levi.

אָמַר רַבִּי אַבָּא בַּר כָּהֲנָא: פַּעַם אַחַת נָפַל אֶחָד בְּבֵית הַמִּדְרָשׁ, וְעָמַד נִיוָתִי אֶחָד וַהֲרָגוֹ. אָמַר רַבִּי: פָּגַע בּוֹ כַּיּוֹצֵא בּוֹ.

Rabbi Abba bar Kahana said: One time, a snake **fell into the study hall** on Shabbat, **and a Nabatean** [*Nivati*][L] **stood and killed it. Rabbi Yehuda** HaNasi **said: One of its type killed it.**[N]

אִיבַּעְיָא לְהוּ: פָּגַע בּוֹ כַּיּוֹצֵא בּוֹ – דְּשַׁפִּיר עָבֵיד, אוֹ לָא? תָּא שְׁמַע: דְּרַבִּי אַבָּא בְּרֵיהּ דְּרַבִּי חִיָּיא בַּר אַבָּא וְרַבִּי זֵירָא הֲווּ יָתְבִי אַקִּילְעָא דְּבֵי רַבִּי יַנַּאי, נְפַק מִילְּתָא מִבֵּינַיְיהוּ, בְּעוֹ מִינֵּיהּ מֵרַבִּי יַנַּאי: מַהוּ לַהֲרוֹג נְחָשִׁים וְעַקְרַבִּים בַּשַּׁבָּת? אָמַר לְהוּ: צִירְעָה אֲנִי הוֹרֵג, נָחָשׁ וְעַקְרָב לֹא כׇּל שֶׁכֵּן?! דִּילְמָא לְפִי תוּמוֹ. דְּאָמַר רַב יְהוּדָה: רוֹק – דּוֹרְסוֹ לְפִי תוּמוֹ. וְאָמַר רַב שֵׁשֶׁת: נָחָשׁ – דּוֹרְסוֹ לְפִי תוּמוֹ. וְאָמַר רַב קְטִינָא: עַקְרָב – דּוֹרְסוֹ לְפִי תוּמוֹ.

A dilemma was raised before the Sages: When Rabbi Yehuda HaNasi said: **One of its type killed it,** did he mean that **he acted properly or not? Come** and **hear** a resolution to this dilemma from that which was related about **Rabbi Abba, son of Rabbi Ḥiyya bar Abba, and Rabbi Zeira,** who **were sitting in the courtyard of Rabbi Yannai's house. A matter emerged from among them,** and **they raised a dilemma before Rabbi Yannai: What is** the ruling with regard **to killing snakes and scorpions on Shabbat? He said to them: I would kill a hornet, all the more so** would I kill **a snake or a scorpion,** as they are more dangerous and it is permitted to kill them. The Gemara rejects this: There is no conclusive proof from this, as **perhaps** it is only permitted when one steps on it **innocently** as he is walking, so that it does not appear to others that he intended to step on it. **As Rav Yehuda said:** With regard to **spittle** on Shabbat, one may **trample it**[H] **innocently** and need not be concerned about the prohibitions of smoothing or leveling holes. **And Rav Sheshet said:** With regard to **a snake, one may trample it innocently. And Rav Ketina said:** With regard to **a scorpion, one may trample it innocently.**

אַבָּא בַּר מָרְתָא דְּהוּא אַבָּא בַּר מַנְיוֹמִי הֲוָה מַסְּקֵי בֵּיהּ דְּבֵי רֵישׁ גָּלוּתָא זוּזֵי, אַיְיתְיוּהוּ קָא מְצַעֲרָא לֵיהּ. הֲוָה שְׁדִי רוּקָא, אֲמַר לְהוּ רֵישׁ גָּלוּתָא: אַיְיתוּ מָאנָא סְחִיפוּ עִלָּוֵיהּ. אֲמַר לְהוּ: לָא צְרִיכְתּוּ, הָכִי אָמַר רַבִּי יְהוּדָה: רוֹק דּוֹרְסוֹ לְפִי תוּמוֹ. אֲמַר לְהוּ: צוּרְבָא מֵרַבָּנַן הוּא, שִׁבְקוּהוּ.

The Gemara relates: **Abba bar Marta,** who **is Abba bar Manyomi, owed money to** members of the **Exilarch's household. They brought him** to the house of the Exilarch on Shabbat and **they tormented him** to force him to pay. **There was spittle** there. **The Exilarch said to** the members of his household: **Bring me a vessel and place it over** the spittle so that people will not step on it. Abba bar Manyomi **said to them: You need not** do so, **as Rav Yehuda said** as follows: With regard to **spittle,** one may **trample it innocently.** The Exilarch **said to** the members of his household: **He is a Torah scholar,**[N] **leave him** alone.

אָמַר רַבִּי אַבָּא בַּר כָּהֲנָא אָמַר רַבִּי חֲנִינָא: פָּמוֹטוֹת שֶׁל בֵּית רַבִּי מוּתָּר לְטַלְטְלָן בַּשַּׁבָּת. אָמַר לֵיהּ רַבִּי זֵירָא: בְּנִיטָּלִין בְּיָדוֹ אַחַת, אוֹ בִּשְׁתֵּי יָדַיִם?

Apropos Rabbi Abba bar Kahana, the Gemara cites additional statements of his. **Rabbi Abba bar Kahana said** that **Rabbi Ḥanina said:** With regard to the **candlesticks**[NB] **of the house of Rabbi** Yehuda HaNasi,[H] **it is permitted to move them on Shabbat.** It was not clear what the nature of these candlesticks was, and **Rabbi Zeira said to him:** Is this referring **to** candlesticks that are small, which **are moved with one hand, or** even **to** those that are moved **with two hands?**

LANGUAGE

Nabatean [*Nivati*] – נִיוָתִי: Some linguists explain that the origin of this word is the Hebrew *naveh*, meaning oasis or beautiful place. A *Nivati*, then, is one who lives in a beautiful place. Alternatively, it could refer to who comes from the city of *Naveh* east of the Jordan River. According to the *Arukh*, the word *Nivati* means Nabatean, referring to a Jew who lives in the land of the Nabateans.

BACKGROUND

Candlestick – פָּמוֹט: Candlesticks from the mishnaic period, such as the one in the illustration below, were very large and heavy and could only be carried with both hands.

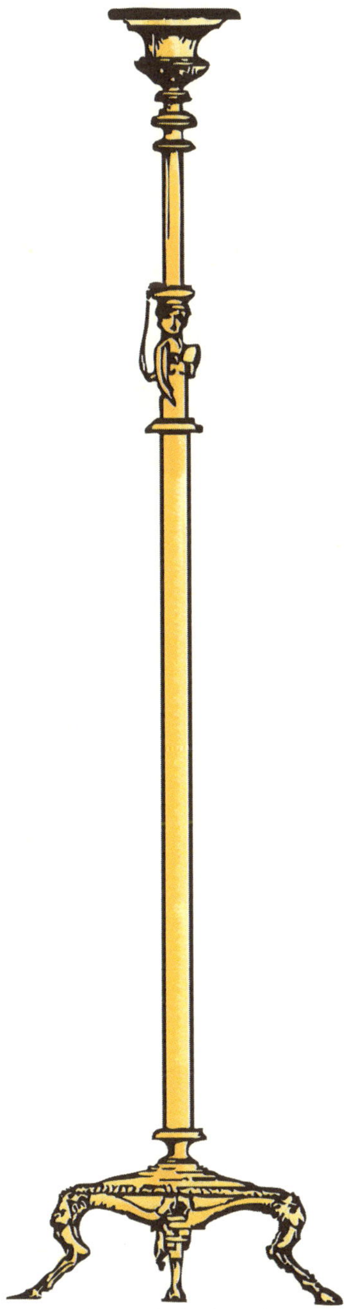

Large candlestick from Pompeii, from the mishnaic period

NOTES

One of its type killed it – פָּגַע בּוֹ כַּיּוֹצֵא בּוֹ: This can be understood as encouragement: The person killed the snake that sought to harm someone like himself. On the other hand, it can be interpreted as derision: The snake was killed by someone comparable to a snake.

A Torah scholar – צוּרְבָא מֵרַבָּנַן: Although the servants of the Exilarch were generally considered sinners, as a rule, they respected the Sages. At the very least, they would not have dared to torment a Torah scholar in the presence of the Exilarch himself.

Moving candlesticks – טִלְטוּל פָּמוֹטוֹת: The rationale for the prohibition against moving candlesticks on Shabbat is not due to the fact that they are set-aside. Rather, the concern is with regard to candelabra that are made with joints. If moved, these candelabra may break into their component parts and one might come to reassemble them, which is prohibited on Shabbat. This is also the reason for the rabbinic prohibition against moving candelabra that appear to be made of component parts.

HALAKHA

With regard to spittle one may trample it – רוֹק דּוֹרְסוֹ: One may not stomp on spittle that is on the ground, as it appears as though he is smoothing out the ground. However, it is permitted to tread on spittle while walking naturally. This ruling is in accordance with the opinion of Rabbi Yehuda (Rambam *Sefer Zemanim, Hilkhot Shabbat* 21:2; *Shulḥan Arukh, Oraḥ Ḥayyim* 316:11).

Candlesticks of the house of Rabbi Yehuda HaNasi – פָּמוֹטוֹת שֶׁל בֵּית רַבִּי: One may not carry a candelabrum with component parts on Shabbat, whether large or small. This prohibition includes candelabra that appear to have component parts. It is permitted to carry a lamp that does not come apart, like the candlesticks of Rabbi Yehuda HaNasi (Rambam *Sefer Zemanim, Hilkhot Shabbat* 26:11; *Shulḥan Arukh, Oraḥ Ḥayyim* 279:7).

אָמַר לֵיהּ: כְּאוֹתָן שֶׁל בֵּית אָבִיךָ.

Rabbi Abba bar Kahana **said to him:** They are **like those from your father's house,** which are large (*Tosafot*).[N]

וְאָמַר רַבִּי אַבָּא בַּר כָּהֲנָא אָמַר רַבִּי חֲנִינָא: קְרוֹנוֹת שֶׁל בֵּית רַבִּי מוּתָּר לְטַלְטְלָן בְּשַׁבָּת. אָמַר לֵיהּ רַבִּי זֵירָא: בְּנִיטָּלִין בְּאָדָם אֶחָד, אוֹ בִּשְׁנֵי בְּנֵי אָדָם? אָמַר לֵיהּ: כְּאוֹתָן שֶׁל בֵּית אָבִיךָ.

And Rabbi Abba bar Kahana said that **Rabbi Ḥanina said: The sedan chairs of the house of Rabbi** Yehuda HaNasi **may be moved on Shabbat. Rabbi Zeira said to** Rabbi Abba bar Kahana: Are you referring to sedan chairs **that can be moved by one person or** those that can be only moved **by two people? He said to him:** They are **like those from your father's house.**

וְאָמַר רַבִּי אַבָּא בַּר כָּהֲנָא: הִתִּיר לָהֶם רַבִּי חֲנִינָא לְבֵית רַבִּי לִשְׁתּוֹת יַיִן בִּקְרוֹנוֹת שֶׁל גּוֹי בְּחוֹתָם אֶחָד – וְלָא יָדַעְנָא אִי מִשּׁוּם דְּסָבַר לַהּ כְּרַבִּי אֱלִיעֶזֶר, אִי מִשּׁוּם אֵימְתָא דְּבֵי נְשִׂיאָה.

And Rabbi Abba bar Kahana said: Rabbi Ḥanina permitted the members **of the household of Rabbi** Yehuda HaNasi **to drink wine** transported **in a gentile's wagons** even though the wine was sealed only **with one seal.**[H] He was not concerned that perhaps the gentile may have opened the barrel and poured wine libations to idolatry from it or touched it, which would prohibit drinking it. Rabbi Abba bar Kahana adds: **And I do not know if** that is **because** Rabbi Ḥanina **holds in accordance with** the opinion of **Rabbi Eliezer,** who permits drinking wine from a gentile that was protected by a single seal, **or** if it was because the gentile would not dare to open these specific casks **due fear of the household of the** ***Nasi***, but in general Rabbi Ḥanina prohibited drinking wine protected by a single seal.

מתני׳ גּוֹי שֶׁהִדְלִיק אֶת הַנֵּר – מִשְׁתַּמֵּשׁ לְאוֹרוֹ יִשְׂרָאֵל, וְאִם בִּשְׁבִיל יִשְׂרָאֵל – אָסוּר. מִילֵּא מַיִם לְהַשְׁקוֹת בְּהֶמְתּוֹ – מַשְׁקֶה אַחֲרָיו יִשְׂרָאֵל, וְאִם בִּשְׁבִיל יִשְׂרָאֵל – אָסוּר. עָשָׂה גּוֹי כֶּבֶשׁ לֵירֵד בּוֹ – יוֹרֵד אַחֲרָיו יִשְׂרָאֵל, וְאִם בִּשְׁבִיל יִשְׂרָאֵל – אָסוּר. מַעֲשֶׂה בְּרַבָּן גַּמְלִיאֵל וּזְקֵנִים שֶׁהָיוּ בָּאִין בִּסְפִינָה, וְעָשָׂה גּוֹי כֶּבֶשׁ לֵירֵד בּוֹ, וְיָרְדוּ בּוֹ רַבָּן גַּמְלִיאֵל וּזְקֵנִים.

MISHNA If **a gentile kindled a lamp**[H] on Shabbat for his own purposes, **a Jew** also **uses its light; and if** the gentile kindled it **for a Jew,** the Sages **prohibited** to utilize its light. Similarly, if a gentile **drew water** from a well in the public domain **to give his animal to drink,**[N] **a Jew gives** his own animal **to drink after him** from the same water; **and if** he drew the water initially **for** the benefit of **a Jew, it is prohibited** for a Jew to give his animal to drink from that water. Similarly, if **a gentile made a ramp**[B] on Shabbat **to disembark** from a ship, **a Jew disembarks after him; and if** he made the ramp **for a Jew,** it is **prohibited.** There was **an incident** in which **Rabban Gamliel and the Elders were traveling on a ship and a gentile made a ramp** on Shabbat in order **to disembark** from the ship **on it; and Rabban Gamliel and the Elders disembarked on it** as well.

גמ׳ וּצְרִיכָא, דְּאִי אַשְׁמְעִינַן נֵר – מִשּׁוּם דְּנֵר לְאֶחָד נֵר לְמֵאָה, אֲבָל מַיִם – לִיגְזַר דִּילְמָא אָתֵי לְאַפּוֹשֵׁי בִּשְׁבִיל יִשְׂרָאֵל. וְכֶבֶשׁ לָמָּה לִי? מַעֲשֶׂה דְּרַבָּן גַּמְלִיאֵל וּזְקֵנִים קָא מַשְׁמַע לָן.

GEMARA The Gemara comments: **And it was necessary** to teach this *halakha* in all these cases. **As, had it taught us** only the *halakha* with regard to **a lamp,** I would have said that this is the *halakha* **because** the light of **a lamp for one is** the light of **a lamp for one hundred** people. There is no need to kindle multiple lamps for multiple people; the light of one candle suffices for many. Therefore, it is permitted to use the light of a lamp kindled by a gentile. **However,** with regard to **water,** there is room **to issue a decree** against benefitting from the gentile's efforts, **lest one come to increase** the amount of water he draws **for a Jew,** even without stating that intention. The Gemara asks: **And why do I need** the mishna to mention that it is permitted to use **the ramp?** The Gemara answers: **It taught us** the case of the ramp to cite **the incident** involving **Rabban Gamliel and the Elders** to indicate that they followed this ruling in practice.

תָּנוּ רַבָּנַן: גּוֹי שֶׁלִּיקֵּט עֲשָׂבִים – מַאֲכִיל אַחֲרָיו יִשְׂרָאֵל, וְאִם בִּשְׁבִיל יִשְׂרָאֵל – אָסוּר. מִילֵּא מַיִם לְהַשְׁקוֹת בְּהֶמְתּוֹ – מַשְׁקֶה אַחֲרָיו יִשְׂרָאֵל, וְאִם בִּשְׁבִיל יִשְׂרָאֵל – אָסוּר. בַּמֶּה דְּבָרִים אֲמוּרִים – שֶׁאֵין מַכִּירוֹ, אֲבָל מַכִּירוֹ – אָסוּר.

The Sages taught: If **a gentile collected grass**[H] on Shabbat for himself, in order to feed his animal, **a Jew may feed** his own animal **after him, and if** he collected it **for the benefit of a Jew,** it is **prohibited.** If he **drew water to give his animal to drink, a Jew may give** water to his own animal **to drink after him, and if** he drew it **for the benefit of a Jew** it is **prohibited. In what** case **is this statement,** that if the gentile acted for himself it is permitted for a Jew to benefit, **said?** When the gentile **does not know him; however,** if the gentile **knows him, it is prohibited,** as in that case, he certainly intended to benefit his Jewish acquaintance as well.

NOTES

Like those from your father's house – כְּאוֹתָן שֶׁל בֵּית אָבִיךָ: Most commentaries explain that the candlesticks belonging to Rabbi Zeira's father were large. They arrived at this conclusion because Rabbi Zeira's father was the king's executor and a wealthy man, who certainly owned large vessels. The uncertainty with regard to the household of Rabbi Yehuda HaNasi was whether or not Rabbi Abba bar Kahana was referring to the small candlesticks that were there (Ramban). The matter of the sedan chairs can be explained in a similar manner.

If a gentile drew water to give his animal to drink – מִילֵּא מַיִם לְהַשְׁקוֹת בְּהֶמְתּוֹ: Some commentaries explain that it is inconsequential whether the gentile actually draws the water for his own animal, and this example is used simply because there tend to be many people around when it is time to give the animals water to drink (Ran). Other commentaries explain that this example is cited because only in that case is there a concern that the gentile may draw extra water for other people's animals. However, if the gentile draws water to drink himself, there is no cause for concern (Rosh; see *Tosafot*).

HALAKHA

Wine with one seal – יַיִן בְּחוֹתָם אֶחָד: If a cask of wine in the hands of a gentile is closed with only one seal, one may not drink it. However, one may benefit from it. Some authorities permit consuming the wine in that case. The Rema writes that it is permitted after the fact (Rema based on Rabbeinu Tam). No proof can be cited from the case of Rabbi Yehuda HaNasi because the gentile feared the *Nasi* and dared not open the wine vessels (Rambam *Sefer Kedusha, Hilkhot Ma'akhalot Assurot* 13:10; *Shulḥan Arukh, Yoreh De'a* 130:2).

If a gentile kindled a lamp – גּוֹי שֶׁהִדְלִיק אֶת הַנֵּר: If a gentile kindled a lamp for a Jew on Shabbat, it is prohibited for the Jew to benefit from it. This applies to other Jews as well, even if the lamp was not kindled for them. If the gentile kindled the lamp for himself, a Jew may benefit from its light. This is also the *halakha* with regard to other actions prohibited on Shabbat (Rambam *Sefer Zemanim, Hilkhot Shabbat* 6:2; *Shulḥan Arukh, Oraḥ Ḥayyim* 276:1).

If a gentile collected grass – גּוֹי הַמְלַקֵּט עֲשָׂבִים: If a gentile collects grass or performs other actions that are prohibited for Jews on Shabbat, it is permitted for a Jew to benefit from the act, provided that the gentile does not know the Jew. The rationale is that in that case there is no concern that the gentile may perform additional labor for the Jew's benefit. However, if the gentile knows the Jew, benefit may be derived only after Shabbat, after the time that it takes to perform the action has passed (*Mishna Berura*; Rambam *Sefer Zemanim, Hilkhot Shabbat* 6:2; *Shulḥan Arukh, Oraḥ Ḥayyim* 325:11).

BACKGROUND

A ramp of a ship – כֶּבֶשׁ סְפִינָה:

Greek picture of a ship with a gangplank

אִינִי?! וְהָאָמַר רַב הוּנָא אָמַר רַבִּי חֲנִינָא: מַעֲמִיד אָדָם בְּהֶמְתּוֹ עַל גַּבֵּי עֲשָׂבִים בְּשַׁבָּת, אֲבָל לֹא עַל גַּבֵּי מוּקְצֶה בְּשַׁבָּת! דְּקָאֵים לָהּ בְּאַפָּהּ, וְאָזְלָא הִיא וְאָכְלָה.

The Gemara asks: **Is that so? Didn't Rav Huna say** that **Rabbi Ḥanina said: One may position his animal over grass on Shabbat,**[H] even grass that is growing in the ground, and there is no concern lest he detach the grass and feed the animal; **however,** he may **not** position the animal **over** an item that is **set aside**[N] **on Shabbat,** since there is concern lest one lift the item with his hand. The grass that the gentile collects for himself is certainly set aside, so why may the Jew feed it to his animal? The Gemara answers: Indeed, a Jew may not position his animal over the grass that a gentile picked; he may only **position it in before** the grass at a distance, **and** the animal **goes** on its own **and eats.**

אָמַר מָר: "בַּמֶּה דְּבָרִים אֲמוּרִים – שֶׁאֵין מַכִּירוֹ, אֲבָל מַכִּירוֹ – אָסוּר". הָא רַבָּן גַּמְלִיאֵל מַכִּירוֹ הֲוָה! אָמַר אַבַּיֵי: שֶׁלֹּא בְּפָנָיו הֲוָה. רָבָא אָמַר: אֲפִילּוּ תֵּימָא בְּפָנָיו, נֵר לְאֶחָד נֵר לְמֵאָה.

We learned above that **the Master said: In what** case **is this statement,** that if the gentile acted for himself it is permitted for a Jew to benefit, **said?** When the gentile **does not know him; however,** if the gentile **knows him, it is prohibited.** The Gemara asks: **However,** in the incident involving **Rabban Gamliel** and the ship, it is a case where the gentile **knows him** as they traveled together on the ship. **Abaye said:** The action was **not** performed **in** Rabban Gamliel's **presence,** and since the gentile had not seen him he intended to make it only for himself. **Rava said: Even if you say** that the gentile made the ramp **in his presence,** that is irrelevant because **a lamp for one is a lamp for one hundred;**[H] similarly, with regard to a ramp, once the gentile constructs it for his own use it can be used by others with no further adjustments.

מֵיתִיבִי, אָמַר לָהֶן רַבָּן גַּמְלִיאֵל: הוֹאִיל וְשֶׁלֹּא בְּפָנֵינוּ עֲשָׂאוֹ – נֵרֵד בּוֹ! אֵימָא: הוֹאִיל וַעֲשָׂאוֹ נֵרֵד בּוֹ.

The Gemara **raises an objection** to Rava's statement based on the *Tosefta*: **Rabban Gamliel said to them: Since he made it not in our presence, we will disembark on it.** Rabban Gamliel made use of the ramp only for this reason, contrary to Rava's explanation. The Gemara rejects this: **Say** the *Tosefta* in an emended form: Rabban Gamliel said to them: **Since he made it, we will disembark on it.**

תָּא שְׁמַע: עִיר שֶׁיִּשְׂרָאֵל וְגוֹיִם דָּרִין בְּתוֹכָהּ וְהָיְתָה בָּהּ מֶרְחָץ הַמַּרְחֶצֶת בְּשַׁבָּת, אִם רוֹב גּוֹיִם – מוּתָּר לִרְחוֹץ בָּהּ מִיָּד, אִם רוֹב יִשְׂרָאֵל – יַמְתִּין בִּכְדֵי שֶׁיֵּחַמּוּ חַמִּין! הָתָם, כִּי מְחַמְּמִי – אַדַּעְתָּא דְּרוּבָּא מְחַמְּמִי.

Come and **hear** proof from another *baraita* with regard to the dispute between Abaye and Rava: With regard to **a city where** both **Jews and gentiles live and there was a bathhouse in it**[H] in which **there is bathing on Shabbat, if the majority** of the city's residents are **gentiles, it is permitted to bathe in** the bathhouse **immediately** after Shabbat because the bathhouse was heated on Shabbat to serve the gentiles. However, **if** there is **a majority of Jews** in the city, **one waits** after Shabbat **for** a period of **time sufficient for them to heat the hot water** so as not to benefit from prohibited labor performed on Shabbat. Apparently, even when an action is not performed in the presence of a Jew, there is concern that it may have been performed for the benefit of Jews. The Gemara rejects this proof: **There,** in the case of the *baraita*, **when they heat** the water, **they heat it with the majority** of the city's inhabitants **in mind,** and the owner of the bathhouse sets the heating schedule to service the majority.

תָּא שְׁמַע: נֵר הַדָּלוּק בִּמְסִיבָּה, אִם רוֹב גּוֹיִם – מוּתָּר לְהִשְׁתַּמֵּשׁ לְאוֹרָהּ, אִם רוֹב יִשְׂרָאֵל – אָסוּר. מֶחֱצָה עַל מֶחֱצָה – אָסוּר. הָתָם נַמִי, כִּי מַדְלְקִי –

Come and **hear** a proof from the following *baraita*: With regard to **a lamp kindled at a banquet**[H] in which several people are participating, **if the majority** of those present are **gentiles it is permitted** for a Jew **to utilize its light,** and **if the majority** of those present are **Jews it is prohibited,** as in that case, the lamp was certainly lit for the Jews' benefit. If those present are **half** Jews **and half** gentiles, **it is prohibited.** Since they are participating in the same banquet, the gentile certainly knows the Jew. Why, then, is it permitted for a Jew to utilize the light of the lamp even when the majority of those present are gentiles? The Gemara rejects this proof: **There, too, when they kindle** the lamp,

HALAKHA

One may position his animal over grass on Shabbat – מַעֲמִיד אָדָם בְּהֶמְתּוֹ עַל גַּבֵּי עֲשָׂבִים בְּשַׁבָּת: A person may position his animal over grass growing in the ground without concern lest he pull out grass to feed the animal. However, it is prohibited to position an animal over an object that is set-aside. Nonetheless, it is permitted to position the animal near the set-aside item and allow the animal to approach the object by itself, in accordance with the opinion of Rav Huna (Rambam *Sefer Zemanim, Hilkhot Shabbat* 21:36; *Shulḥan Arukh, Oraḥ Ḥayyim* 324:13).

A lamp for one is a lamp for one hundred – נֵר לְאֶחָד נֵר לְמֵאָה: If a gentile performed a labor on Shabbat for himself, it is permitted for a Jew to benefit from it provided that no further effort is necessary for others to benefit from it. Examples of this are kindling a lamp and the lowering a ramp. This applies even if the gentile knows the Jew (Rambam *Sefer Zemanim, Hilkhot Shabbat* 6:4; *Shulḥan Arukh, Oraḥ Ḥayyim* 325:11).

A bathhouse in a city in which Jews and gentiles live – מֶרְחָץ בְּעִיר שֶׁיִּשְׂרָאֵל וְגוֹיִם דָּרִים בְּתוֹכָהּ: If there is a bathhouse that operates on Shabbat in a city where both Jews and gentiles reside, it may be used by Jews immediately after Shabbat if the majority of the city's inhabitants are gentiles. If the majority or half of the city's residents are Jews, one must wait after Shabbat for the period of time it would take to heat the bath before using it (Rambam *Sefer Zemanim, Hilkhot Shabbat* 6:7; *Shulḥan Arukh, Oraḥ Ḥayyim* 326:13).

A lamp kindled at a banquet – נֵר הַדָּלוּק בִּמְסִיבָּה: When Jews and gentiles are gathered together on Shabbat and a gentile kindles a lamp, the Jews are permitted to benefit from the light if the majority of people present are gentiles. If the majority or half of those in attendance are Jews, the Jews may not benefit from the light (Rambam *Sefer Zemanim, Hilkhot Shabbat* 6:4; *Shulḥan Arukh, Oraḥ Ḥayyim* 276:2).

NOTES

However, not over an item that is set aside – אֲבָל לֹא עַל גַּבֵּי מוּקְצֶה: The *ge'onim* explain that the reference here is not to an item that is set-aside but to a place, known as *muktze*, in one's courtyard designated for laying out fruits to dry. With regard to the Gemara's discussion, it is permitted to position one's animal over grass growing from the ground. Just as there is no problem with the animal severing grass from the ground (see *Tosafot*), there is also no concern lest one uproot the grass to feed the animal due to the severity of the category of prohibited labor of reaping. However, with regard to items that are set-aside, which is a rabbinic prohibition, the Sages were concerned lest one move the object because the prohibition of moving items that are set-aside is not as severe. Therefore, they prohibited positioning an animal directly over set-aside items.

אַדַּעְתָּא דְּרוּבָּא מַדְלְקִי.

they kindle it with the majority of the those present at the banquet **in mind.** When the majority of those present are gentiles, it is permitted.

שְׁמוּאֵל אִיקְלַע לְבֵי אָבִין תּוֹרָן, אֲתָא הַהוּא גּוֹי אַדְלִיק שְׁרָגָא. אַהַדְרִינְהוּ שְׁמוּאֵל לְאַפֵּיהּ. כֵּיוָן דַּחֲזָא דְּאַיְיתִי שְׁטָר וְקָא קָרֵי, אָמַר: אַדַּעְתָּא דְּנַפְשֵׁיהּ הוּא דְּאַדְלִיק. אַהַדְרִינְהוּ אִיהוּ לְאַפֵּיהּ גַּבֵּי שְׁרָגָא.

The Gemara relates that **Shmuel happened** to come **to the house of Avin Toran.**[N] **A certain gentile came** and **kindled a lamp. Shmuel turned his face back** away from the lamp in order to avoid benefitting from the light. **When** Shmuel **saw** that the gentile **brought a document and was reading** it, **he said: He kindled it with his** own benefit **in mind.**[H] **He turned his face back toward the lamp.**

הדרן עלך כל כתבי

NOTES

Shmuel happened to come to the house of Avin Toran – שְׁמוּאֵל אִיקְלַע לְבֵי אָבִין תּוֹרָן: According to the Jerusalem Talmud, Avin Toran was a Persian who hosted Shmuel. Therefore, Shmuel was concerned that the gentile kindled the lamp for him.

HALAKHA

A gentile who performs an act for himself – גּוֹי הָעוֹשֶׂה לְצוֹרֶךְ עַצְמוֹ: If a gentile kindles a lamp for his own use on Shabbat, a Jew is permitted to benefit from its light (*Shulḥan Arukh, Oraḥ Ḥayyim* 276:2).

Summary of **Perek XVI**

The halakhic principles presented in this chapter are based upon the idea that extinguishing a fire on Shabbat is biblically prohibited. In these circumstances, the fire poses no danger to human life. There are significant differences between the rules described in the Talmud and what is actual halakhic practice nowadays, for two main reasons. The risk to human life has increased, both because of the way houses are built and because of the prevalence of combustible materials in private homes. Also, most halakhic authorities have concluded that extinguishing a fire only involves a rabbinic prohibition.

At any rate, the conclusions reached in this chapter were as follows: One can rescue from a fire on Shabbat only those materials that are essential for human consumption or use on that Shabbat, that are not detectable by an observer as superfluous materials, and whose rescue constitutes no additional burden.

For many of the materials mentioned in this chapter, one can employ stratagems to rescue more than what would otherwise be permitted. This is because the core of the prohibition is based only upon rabbinic decree, and the Sages did not institute additional stringencies in these matters.

Since this chapter discussed the rescue of sacred writings and elucidated many laws concerning under what circumstances rescuing them is permissible, it also elucidated which texts are not included in the category of holy writings.

In connection with the subject of fire, various other problems arose, e.g., is it permissible to use objects gentiles produced on Shabbat, either while they were extinguishing a fire or through other means. Here too, an underlying principle was established that forms the basis of many laws. Essentially, anything produced through an act that was not performed directly at a Jew's behest or that was originally performed for the sole benefit of the gentile himself is permissible for a Jew to use, even if the act was performed on Shabbat. But it is prohibited for a Jew to use an item a gentile produced on Shabbat on the Jew's behalf, even if he did not explicitly request that the gentile do so. All the more so is this the case if the Jew instructed the gentile to perform labor on his behalf.

Requesting that a gentile perform labor on Shabbat constitutes a transgression of a *shevut*, a rabbinic prohibition.

Introduction to **Perek XVII**

This chapter is devoted to a thorough analysis of the prohibition against handling items that are *muktze*, set aside from use on Shabbat. This *halakha* has already been mentioned several times in tractate *Shabbat*, but it has not yet been addressed in a systematic and thorough fashion. The prohibition applies to items that one has mentally set aside from using on Shabbat for some reason, meaning that one assumes he will not use them over the course of Shabbat.

It is not entirely clear why handling items that have been set aside is prohibited. Some have explained that the decree against handling such items serves as a protective measure to ensure that one will not perform prohibited labors on Shabbat. If one may not handle the items used to perform prohibited labors, one will not perform the prohibited labors themselves. Others have suggested that the prohibition is meant to protect against violation of the prohibited labor of carrying from one domain to another. By limiting one's ability to handle a large number of items, the Sages sought to decrease the likelihood that one would carry items between domains.

Halakhic discussions generally focus on three types of set-aside [*muktze*] items: Items set aside because of repulsiveness, items set aside because of function, and items set aside because of monetary loss. The first group includes things that are not generally used or handled, either because they are dirty or because they are repulsive for some other reason. The second group includes objects whose primary function is for an activity that constitutes a prohibited labor on Shabbat. The third group includes items that are generally used only for a particular activity that is prohibited on Shabbat, and the owner of these items is careful not to use them for any other purpose, due to a concern that they will be damaged and he will suffer a financial loss.

This chapter cites the opinions of the *tanna'im* and a variety of different views with regard to the categories of items that are set-aside and that therefore are fully or partially forbidden to be handled on Shabbat. It also establishes the halakhic conclusions that are to be drawn based upon these opinions.

The laws and principles of the prohibition of set-aside form the primary subject matter of this chapter, but the topic is not exhausted here. Various aspects of this prohibition will be addressed in later chapters.

מתני׳ כָּל הַכֵּלִים נִיטָּלִין בְּשַׁבָּת וְדַלְתוֹתֵיהֶן עִמָּהֶן, אַף עַל פִּי שֶׁנִּתְפָּרְקוּ, בְּשַׁבָּת, שֶׁאֵינָן דּוֹמִין לְדַלְתוֹת הַבַּיִת, לְפִי שֶׁאֵינָן מִן הַמּוּכָן.

MISHNA **All vessels may be moved on Shabbat, and their doors,** which are part of these vessels, along **with them,**[H] **even if they were dismantled on Shabbat,**[N] as the doors of these vessels **are unlike the doors of the house.** It is prohibited to make use of the doors of a house on Shabbat, even if they were removed from the entrance, **because they are not prepared** from before Shabbat.

נוֹטֵל אָדָם קוּרְנָס לְפַצֵּעַ בּוֹ אֶת הָאֱגוֹזִין, קַרְדּוֹם – לַחְתּוֹךְ בּוֹ אֶת הַדְּבֵילָה, מְגֵירָה – לָגוֹר בָּהּ אֶת הַגְּבִינָה, מַגְרֵיפָה – לִגְרוֹף בָּהּ אֶת הַגְּרוֹגָרוֹת,

Likewise **a person may move a mallet,** which is generally used for labor prohibited on Shabbat,[H] **to crack nuts with it.** Likewise, one may move **an axe,** a tool generally used to chop wood, **to cut a cake of figs with it.** So too, one may move **a saw to cut cheese with it.** Similarly, one may move **a spade to scoop dried figs with it.**

אֶת הָרַחַת וְאֶת הַמַּלְגֵּז – לָתֵת עָלָיו לְקָטָן, אֶת הַכּוּשׁ וְאֶת הַכַּרְכָּר – לִתְחוֹב בּוֹ, מַחַט שֶׁל יָד – לִיטּוֹל בּוֹ אֶת הַקּוֹץ, וְשֶׁל סַקָּאִים – לִפְתּוֹחַ בּוֹ אֶת הַדֶּלֶת.

One may also move **a winnowing shovel and a pitchfork,** both of which are designated for use with crops in a barn, **to place** food **on it for a child.** One is likewise permitted to take **a reed or a shuttle** from a spindle, ordinarily used for weaving, in order **to insert it** into food like a fork. One is permitted to move an ordinary **hand needle** used for sewing clothes **to extract a thorn with it, and** one may move **a sack maker's** needle[B] **to open the door with it.**

גמ׳ ״כָּל הַכֵּלִים נִיטָּלִין וְאַף עַל פִּי שֶׁנִּתְפָּרְקוּ בְּשַׁבָּת״, וְלָא מִיבַּעְיָא בַּחוֹל?

GEMARA The mishna states: **All vessels may be moved, and even if they were dismantled on Shabbat.** Should we learn from here that there is only a question with regard to vessels which were dismantled on Shabbat, **and** that **there is no need** to mention vessels detached **during the week,** as it is certainly permitted to carry them on Shabbat?

אַדְּרַבָּה, בְּשַׁבָּת – מוּכָנִין עַל גַּבֵּי אֲבִיהֶן, בַּחוֹל – אֵין מוּכָנִין עַל גַּבֵּי אֲבִיהֶן.

On the contrary, if they were dismantled **on Shabbat** it can be said that the parts of the vessel **were prepared** for use at the onset of Shabbat, **due** to their being attached to **their original** vessels[N] from which they were removed. However, if they were detached **during the week,** at the onset of Shabbat they would **not** have been **prepared** for use, **due to** their being detached from **their original** vessels from which they were removed.

אָמַר אַבָּיֵי, הָכִי קָאָמַר: כָּל הַכֵּלִים נִיטָּלִין בְּשַׁבָּת וְדַלְתוֹתֵיהֶן עִמָּהֶן, אַף עַל פִּי שֶׁנִּתְפָּרְקוּ בַּחוֹל – נִיטָּלִין בְּשַׁבָּת.

Abaye said that **this is what** the mishna **is saying: All vessels may be moved on Shabbat along with their doors. And even if they came apart during the week, they may be moved on Shabbat.**

תָּנוּ רַבָּנַן: דֶּלֶת שֶׁל שִׁידָּה וְשֶׁל תֵּיבָה וְשֶׁל מִגְדָּל – נוֹטְלִין, אֲבָל לֹא מַחֲזִירִין. וְשֶׁל לוּל שֶׁל תַּרְנְגוֹלִים – לֹא נוֹטְלִין וְלֹא מַחֲזִירִין.

The Sages taught: With regard to **the door of a chest, or of a box, or of a closet,**[H] **one may remove** them from their hinges on Shabbat, **but** he **may not restore** them to their original places. **And** with regard to the door of **a chicken coop,** one may neither **move** it **nor restore** it to its place.

בִּשְׁלָמָא שֶׁל לוּל שֶׁל תַּרְנְגוֹלִים – קָסָבַר: כֵּיוָן דִּמְחַבְּרִי בְּאַרְעָא – יֵשׁ בִּנְיָן בְּקַרְקַע, יֵשׁ סְתִירָה בְּקַרְקַע. אֶלָּא שֶׁל שִׁידָּה וְשֶׁל תֵּיבָה וְשֶׁל מִגְדָּל מַאי קָסָבַר?

Granted, in the case of **a chicken coop** the *tanna* **holds: Since** the coop **is attached to the ground, there is** a prohibition against **building on the ground** and **there is** a prohibition against **dismantling on the ground.** Consequently when one dismantles or restores the door he has performed the prohibited labor of building. **However,** in the case of the door **of a chest,** or **a box,** or **a closet, what does he hold?**

אִי קָסָבַר ״יֵשׁ בִּנְיָן בְּכֵלִים״ – יֵשׁ סְתִירָה בְּכֵלִים, וְאִי ״אֵין סְתִירָה בְּכֵלִים״ – אֵין בִּנְיָן בְּכֵלִים.

If the tanna **holds** that **there is** a prohibition against **building with regard to vessels,** then **there is** also a prohibition against **dismantling with regard to vessels**[H] and it should be prohibited to remove the door. **And if there is no** prohibition against **dismantling with regard to vessels** and it is permitted to remove the door, then there should also be **no** prohibition against **building with regard to vessels.** Why, then, is it prohibited to restore a door to its original place?

אָמַר אַבָּיֵי: לְעוֹלָם קָסָבַר ״יֵשׁ בִּנְיָן בְּכֵלִים וְיֵשׁ סְתִירָה בְּכֵלִים״ – וְשֶׁנִּיטְּלוּ קָאָמַר.

Abaye said: Actually, he holds that there is a prohibition against **building with regard to vessels and there is** also a prohibition against **dismantling with regard to vessels.** To resolve the difficulty, emend the text. Rather than saying: One may remove them, **it is saying:** The doors of a chest, or a box, or a closet **that were** already **removed** may not be restored.

HALAKHA

All vessels may be moved on Shabbat, and their doors with them – כָּל הַכֵּלִים נִיטָּלִין בְּשַׁבָּת וְדַלְתוֹתֵיהֶן עִמָּהֶן: It is permitted to move doors that were removed from vessels that may be moved on Shabbat, whether the doors were removed during the week or on Shabbat (Rambam *Sefer Zemanim, Hilkhot Shabbat* 22:25; *Shulḥan Arukh, Oraḥ Ḥayyim* 308:8).

A utensil whose primary function is for a prohibited use – כְּלִי שֶׁמְּלַאכְתּוֹ לְאִיסּוּר: It is permitted to move a utensil whose primary function is for a prohibited use, e.g., a hammer, for the purpose of performing a labor permitted on Shabbat, e.g., cracking nuts, in accordance with the mishna and with Rava's explanation (Rambam *Sefer Zemanim, Hilkhot Shabbat* 22:7; *Shulḥan Arukh, Oraḥ Ḥayyim* 308:3).

The door of a chest, or of a box, or of a closet – דֶּלֶת שֶׁל שִׁידָּה וְשֶׁל תֵּיבָה וְשֶׁל מִגְדָּל: It is permitted to remove the doors from chests, boxes, and closets on Shabbat. However, it is forbidden by rabbinic decree to restore them, lest one fix them in place firmly, which is prohibited as the work of a craftsman. It is forbidden to remove or to replace the door of a chicken coop or other structures connected to the ground, due to the prohibitions against building and dismantling, as per Rava's explanation and the Tosefta (*Shulḥan Arukh, Oraḥ Ḥayyim* 308:9).

There is building with regard to vessels, there is dismantling with regard to vessels – יֵשׁ בִּנְיָן בְּכֵלִים יֵשׁ סְתִירָה בְּכֵלִים: There is no prohibition against building or dismantling vessels on Shabbat. It is permitted to dismantle and reassemble a vessel that comes apart, provided this requires no exertion or craftsmanship (Rambam *Sefer Zemanim, Hilkhot Shabbat* 22:26; *Shulḥan Arukh, Oraḥ Ḥayyim* 314:1).

NOTES

They were dismantled on Shabbat – שֶׁנִּתְפָּרְקוּ בְּשַׁבָּת: The commentaries dispute whether or not the phrase: On Shabbat, appears in the mishna. Most subscribe to the version that includes the phrase. Otherwise, it would be difficult to explain that the Gemara introduced the possibility that the vessels were dismantled on Shabbat, only to reject it (*Tosefot Rid*).

Due to their original vessels – מוּכָנִין עַל גַּבֵּי אֲבִיהֶן: *Tosafot* raise the suggestion that based on the Gemara below, the opposite is true. Specifically, when vessels break on Shabbat eve it should be permitted to carry the shards. The Me'iri explains that if the vessel is whole, the status of part of it can be defined by the whole. However, if the vessel is broken, the status of individual parts cannot be defined by the main part of the vessel.

BACKGROUND

A sack maker's needle – מַחַט סַקָּאִים:

Sack maker's needle from mishnaic era, Eretz Yisrael

NOTES

Lest one fix it firmly in place – שֶׁמָּא יִתְקַע: Some commentaries explain the meaning of this phrase as: Lest one insert a nail or stake to fix the door firmly in its place (Rabbeinu Ḥananel).

And a winnowing shovel or a pitchfork in order to place food for a child on it – וְאֶת הָרַחַת וְאֶת הַמַּלְגֵּז לָתֵת עָלָיו לְקָטָן: The father places the food on a winnowing shovel because he is impure and does not want to render the food that he is feeding his child impure by touching it with his hands (*Me'iri*).

אָמַר לֵיהּ רָבָא: [שְׁתֵּי תְּשׁוּבוֹת בַּדָּבָר] חֲדָא: דְּ״נִיטָּלִין״ קָתָנֵי, וְעוֹד: מַאי ״אֲבָל לֹא מַחֲזִירִין״? אֶלָּא אָמַר רָבָא: קָסָבַר אֵין בִּנְיָן בְּכֵלִים וְאֵין סְתִירָה בְּכֵלִים, וּגְזֵירָה שֶׁמָּא יִתְקַע.

Rava said to him: There are **two** possible **responses** with which your statement can be rejected. **One** is that **it is taught** in the *baraita*: **One may remove** them, *ab initio*. **And furthermore, what is** the meaning of: **But one may not restore** them? According to your emendation, what is the meaning of the word, but, in this context? **Rather, Rava said:** The *tanna* holds that **there is no** prohibition against **building with regard to vessels and there is no** prohibition against **dismantling with regard to vessels, and** so why did the *tanna* rule one may not restore the door? It is due to **a decree lest one fix** it firmly in place[N] in the manner of a full-fledged prohibited labor, completing the production process of a vessel.

״נוֹטֵל אָדָם קוּרְנָס כו׳״. אָמַר רַב יְהוּדָה: קוּרְנָס שֶׁל אֱגוֹזִין לְפַצֵּעַ בּוֹ אֶת הָאֱגוֹזִין, אֲבָל שֶׁל נַפָּחִין – לֹא.

The mishna states: **A person may take a mallet** on Shabbat in order to crack nuts with it. **Rav Yehuda said:** The type of hammer in this case is **a hammer** designated **for nuts to crack nuts with it, but blacksmiths'** hammers, **no,** they may not be used.

קָסָבַר: דָּבָר שֶׁמְּלַאכְתּוֹ לְאִיסּוּר – אֲפִילּוּ לְצוֹרֶךְ גּוּפוֹ אָסוּר.

That *tanna* **holds** that using **an object whose** primary **function** is **for a prohibited** use, **even for the purpose** of utilizing the object **itself** to perform a permitted action, is **prohibited.**

אָמַר לֵיהּ רַבָּה: אֶלָּא מֵעַתָּה, סֵיפָא דְּקָתָנֵי ״וְאֶת הָרַחַת וְאֶת הַמַּלְגֵּז לָתֵת עָלָיו לְקָטָן״ רַחַת וּמַלְגֵּז מִי מְיַיחֲדֵי לֵיהּ לְקָטָן?! אֶלָּא אָמַר רַבָּה: קוּרְנָס שֶׁל נַפָּחִין לְפַצֵּעַ בּוֹ הָאֱגוֹזִין.

Rabba said to him: But if what you say is so, how do you reconcile this with **the latter clause** of the mishna in which **it is taught: And a winnowing shovel or a pitchfork** in order **to place** food **for a child on it;**[N] are **a winnowing shovel and a pitchfork designated for** use by **a child? Rather, Rabba said:** The mishna should be interpreted as follows: One may use **a blacksmiths' hammer** on Shabbat **to crack nuts with it.**

קָסָבַר:

The *tanna* **holds:**

Perek **XVII**
Daf **123** Amud **a**

HALAKHA

Moving a pestle – טִלְטוּל עֱלִי: It is permitted to move a pestle designated for crushing groats, which is a prohibited labor on Shabbat, in order to use it for cutting meat. However, it is prohibited to move it for a different purpose (*Shulḥan Arukh*, *Oraḥ Ḥayyim* 499:5).

NOTES

One designates a place for them – מְיַיחֵד לְהוּ מָקוֹם: To designate a place means that one makes sure that the object remains in place and that no one touches it. Therefore, the object in question can be utilized only for a specific action, and is set aside from use for any other activity. This category of set-aside, which will be addressed at length, is referred to as: Set-aside due to monetary loss.

דָּבָר שֶׁמְּלַאכְתּוֹ לְאִיסּוּר לְצוֹרֶךְ גּוּפוֹ – מוּתָּר.

Using **an object whose** primary **function** is **for a prohibited** use, **for the purpose** of utilizing the object **itself** to perform a permitted action, is **permitted.**

אֵיתִיבֵיהּ אַבָּיֵי לְרַבָּה: מְדוֹכָה, אִם יֵשׁ בָּהּ שׁוּם – מְטַלְטְלִין אוֹתָהּ, וְאִם לָאו – אֵין מְטַלְטְלִין אוֹתָהּ!

Abaye raised an objection to the opinion of **Rabba** from the *Tosefta*: **A mortar, if it** still **has garlic in it, one may move it** on Shabbat, **and if not, one may not move it.** Apparently, under no circumstances may a mortar be used, even for an action that is generally permitted on Shabbat, because the mortar's primary function is prohibited.

אָמַר לֵיהּ: הָא מַנִּי – רַבִּי נְחֶמְיָה הִיא, דְּאָמַר: אֵין כְּלִי נִיטָּל אֶלָּא לְצוֹרֶךְ תַּשְׁמִישׁוֹ.

Abaye **said to him:** In accordance with **whose** opinion **is this** *baraita*? **It is** the opinion of **Rabbi Neḥemya, who says: A vessel may not be moved** on Shabbat **except for the purpose of its** designated **use.**

אֵיתִיבֵיהּ: (בֵּית שַׁמַּאי אוֹמְרִים: אֵין נוֹטְלִין אֶת הָעֱלִי לְקַצֵּב עָלָיו בָּשָׂר, וּבֵית הִלֵּל מַתִּירִין). וְשָׁוִין, שֶׁאִם קִצֵּב עָלָיו בָּשָׂר – שֶׁאָסוּר לְטַלְטְלוֹ!

Abaye **raised** another **objection** to Rabba's opinion. We learned in a mishna that **Beit Shammai say: One may not take a** large **pestle** from a mortar, which is typically used for a prohibited action, in order **to cut meat on it**[H] for the purpose of a Festival. **And Beit Hillel permit** doing so due to the mitzva of rejoicing on the Festival. **And everyone agrees** that **if one cut meat on it** for the purpose of the Festival, **that it is** then **prohibited to move it** because there is no further need for it on the Festival. Apparently, it is prohibited to use an object whose primary function is for a prohibited use, even to perform a permitted action.

סְבַר לְשַׁנּוֹיֵי לֵיהּ כְּרַבִּי נְחֶמְיָה, כֵּיוָן דִּשְׁמַעָהּ לְהָא דְּאָמַר רַב חִינְּנָא בַּר שְׁלֶמְיָא מִשְּׁמֵיהּ דְּרַב: הַכֹּל מוֹדִים בִּסִיכֵּי זִיֵּירֵי וּמְזוֹרֵי דְּכֵיוָן דְּקָפֵיד עֲלַיְיהוּ – מְיַיחֵד לְהוּ מָקוֹם, הָא נַמִּי: מְיַיחֵד לְהוּ מָקוֹם.

Initially, Rabba **thought to respond to** Abaye's objection by saying that this mishna, too, is **in accordance with** the opinion of **Rabbi Neḥemya,** that a vessel may only be moved on Shabbat for the purpose of its designated use. However, he changed his mind **once he heard that** which **Rav Ḥinana bar Shelemya said in the name of Rav: Everyone agrees in the case of launderers' pins, presses, and clothing rods** (*Arukh*), that **since** one **is particular about them** to ensure that they remain intact, he **designates a place for them** and does not move them for other purposes. Therefore, everyone agrees that it is prohibited to move them. **Here, too,** the mortar and pestle are specifically designated for a particular use and **one designates a place for them;**[N] therefore, it is prohibited to move them.

אִיתְּמַר, רַבִּי חִיָּיא בַּר אַבָּא אָמַר רַבִּי יוֹחָנָן: קוּרְנָס שֶׁל זֶהָבִים שָׁנִינוּ, רַב שֶׁמֶן בַּר אַבָּא אָמַר: קוּרְנָס שֶׁל בַּשָּׂמִים שָׁנִינוּ.

It was stated that there was another amoraic dispute on this topic. **Rabbi Ḥiyya bar Abba** said that **Rabbi Yoḥanan said:** It was with regard to **the hammer of goldsmiths**[HB] **that we learned** it may be used to crack nuts. Although the goldsmith is particular about ensuring that the hammer remains smooth and avoids using it for any purpose other than its particular use, nevertheless, it was allowed to be used for other permitted actions. **Rav Shemen bar Abba said:** It was with regard to **the hammer of spice merchants**[B] **that we learned** it may be used to crack nuts.

מַאן דְּאָמַר דְּבַשָּׂמִים – כָּל שֶׁכֵּן דְּזֶהָבִים. מַאן דְּאָמַר שֶׁל זֶהָבִים – אֲבָל דְּבַשָּׂמִים קָפֵיד עֲלַיְיהוּ.

The Gemara explains: **The one who said** it is permitted to crack nuts on Shabbat using **the hammer of spice merchants, all the more so** that it is permitted to use a hammer typically used by **goldsmiths.** However, **the one who said** that it is only permitted to use a hammer used by **goldsmiths, but** with regard to the hammer **of spice merchants,** the merchant **is particular about it** and would not allow it to be used for cracking nuts. Use for other purposes would cause the hammer to absorb foreign smells, which would ruin the spices.

״וְאֶת הַכּוּשׁ וְאֶת הַכַּרְכַּר כו׳״. תָּנוּ רַבָּנַן: פַּגָּה שֶׁטְּמָנָהּ בְּתֶבֶן, וַחֲרָרָה שֶׁטְּמָנָהּ בְּגֶחָלִים, אִם מְגוּלָּה מִקְצָתָהּ – מוּתָּר לְטַלְטְלָהּ. וְאִם לָאו – אָסוּר לְטַלְטְלָהּ.

And we learned in the mishna: one may move **a reed or a shuttle** [*karkar*][LB] in order to stick it into food. **The Sages taught** in a *baraita*: With regard to **an unripe fig that one buried in straw** to accelerate its ripening, **and** likewise with regard to **a cake that one buried in coals**[NH] in order to heat it, **if part of it is exposed, it is permitted to move it** on Shabbat. **And if not,** and it was completely covered, **it is prohibited to move it** lest one come to carry straw or coals, which are set-aside, along with it. It is prohibited for one to move set-aside objects or to cause them to be moved.

רַבִּי אֶלְעָזָר בֶּן תַּדַּאי אוֹמֵר: תּוֹחֲבִין בְּכוּשׁ אוֹ בְּכַרְכָּר וְהֵן מִנַּעֲרוֹת מֵאֵילֵיהֶם. אָמַר רַב נַחְמָן: הֲלָכָה כְּרַבִּי אֶלְעָזָר בֶּן תַּדַּאי.

Rabbi Elazar ben Tadai says: One may insert a reed or a shuttle into an unripe fig or a cake that is buried in coals to remove it from its place, **and** the straw and the coals **are shaken off on their own. Rav Naḥman says:**[N] **The *halakha* is in accordance with** the opinion of **Rabbi Elazar ben Tadai.**

לְמֵימְרָא דְּסָבַר רַב נַחְמָן ״טִלְטוּל מִן הַצַּד לָא שְׁמֵיהּ טִלְטוּל״? וְהָאָמַר רַב נַחְמָן: הַאי פּוּגְלָא, מִלְּמַעְלָה לְמַטָּה – שָׁרֵי, מִמַּטָּה לְמַעְלָה – אָסִיר! הֲדַר בֵּיהּ רַב נַחְמָן מֵהַהִיא.

The Gemara asks: **Is that to say that Rav Naḥman holds: Moving** an object **in an atypical manner is not** considered to be a bona fide act of **moving** and is permitted on Shabbat? **Didn't Rav Naḥman say: This radish** that was buried in the dirt to protect it, if it was inserted **from the top to bottom,** i.e., the wider part of the radish is closer to the surface and the narrower part is farther, it is **permitted** to remove it from the dirt. If it was inserted **from bottom to top,** and the wider part was farther from the surface, **it is prohibited** because he thereby moves the dirt. Apparently, Rav Naḥman prohibits moving set-aside items even if one does so in an atypical manner. The Gemara answers: **Rav Naḥman reversed** his opinion with regard to **that** *halakha* of the radish.

״מַחַט שֶׁל יָד לִיטּוֹל בָּהּ כו׳״. שְׁלַח לֵיהּ רָבָא בְּרֵיהּ דְּרַבָּה לְרַב יוֹסֵף: יְלַמְּדֵנוּ רַבֵּינוּ, מַחַט שֶׁנִּיטַּל חֲרִירָהּ אוֹ עוּקְצָהּ מַהוּ?

We learned in the mishna: One is permitted to take **an** ordinary **hand needle** used for sewing clothes **to extract** a thorn **with it. Rava, son of Rabba, sent** the following question **to Rav Yosef: Let our teacher teach us:** With regard to a **needle whose eye or point was removed, what is its** legal status, i.e., is moving it on Shabbat permitted?

אָמַר לֵיהּ: תְּנֵיתוּהָ, מַחַט שֶׁל יָד לִיטּוֹל בָּהּ אֶת הַקּוֹץ. וְכִי מָה אִיכְפַּת לֵיהּ לַקּוֹץ בֵּין נְקוּבָה לְבֵין שֶׁאֵינָהּ נְקוּבָה?

Rav Yosef **said to him: You** already **learned** the answer to that question in the mishna: One is permitted to take **an** ordinary **hand needle** used for sewing clothes **to extract a thorn with it. And what does the thorn** that is stuck in his flesh **care whether** the needle **has an eye or whether it does not have an eye?** Since the needle is suited for that purpose, it is permitted to move it.

HALAKHA

The hammer of goldsmiths – קוּרְנָס שֶׁל זֶהָבִים: It is permitted to carry a goldsmith's hammer on Shabbat to use for a permitted activity, when no permitted utensil is available (*Mishna Berura*; Rambam *Sefer Zemanim*, *Hilkhot Shabbat* 25:7; *Shulḥan Arukh*, *Oraḥ Ḥayyim* 308:3).

An unripe fig that one buried in straw and a cake that one buried in coals – פַּגָּה שֶׁטְּמָנָהּ בְּתֶבֶן, וַחֲרָרָה שֶׁטְּמָנָהּ בְּגֶחָלִים: It is permitted to skewer food items buried in a set-aside substance to remove the food, even though the set-aside substance moves along with it, because the set-aside substance is moved in an atypical manner (Rambam *Sefer Zemanim*, *Hilkhot Shabbat* 25:15; *Shulḥan Arukh*, *Oraḥ Ḥayyim* 311:9).

BACKGROUND

Hammer of goldsmiths – קוּרְנָס שֶׁל זֶהָבִים:

Goldsmith's hammer

Hammer of spice merchants – קוּרְנָס שֶׁל בַּשָּׂמִים:

Hammer used for spices

Shuttle – כַּרְכַּר:

Shuttle, which holds the woof threads, being thrown between the warp threads

LANGUAGE

Shuttle [*karkar*] – כַּרְכַּר: From the Greek **κερκίς**, *kerkis*, or **κερκίδος**, *kerkidos*, meaning shuttle or sharply pointed stick used for weaving, as well as any type of pointed rod.

NOTES

A cake that was buried in coals – וַחֲרָרָה שֶׁטְּמָנָהּ בְּגֶחָלִים: Rashi emphasizes that these coals were extinguished and the only remaining concern is the prohibition of set-aside. Others explain that even if the coals are smoldering, it is permitted to remove the cake, as the possibility that the coals will ignite or be extinguished is not inevitable (*Tosefot Rid*).

Rav Naḥman's opinion – שִׁיטַת רַב נַחְמָן: Some commentaries state that the question with regard to the opinion of Rav Naḥman does not emerge directly from the statement of Rabbi Elazar ben Tadai. Rather, since Rav Naḥman ruled in accordance with the opinion of Rabbi Elazar, he certainly also accepted that part of the opinion of the Rabbis which permits removing an object partially covered in a set-aside substance if part of the object is uncovered, and without distinguishing between which of the different parts of the object remains covered (*Tosefot Rid*).

אִיתִיבֵיהּ מַחַט שֶׁנִּיטַּל חֲרָרָהּ אוֹ עוּקְצָהּ – טְהוֹרָה!

Rava, son of Rabba, **raised an objection to** Rav Yosef from that which we learned in a mishna: A ritually impure **needle whose eye or point was removed** becomes **ritually pure,** because its status as a vessel is negated. Since it is no longer considered a vessel, why would it be permitted to move it?

אָמַר אַבָּיֵי: טוּמְאָה אַשַּׁבָּת קָרְמֵית?! טוּמְאָה – כְּלִי מַעֲשֶׂה בָּעֵינַן, לְעִנְיַן שַׁבָּת – מִידֵּי דַּחֲזֵי בָּעֵינַן, וְהָא נַמִי חֲזְיָא לְמִשְׁקְלָא בָּהּ קוֹץ.

Abaye said: Are you raising a contradiction from the *halakhot* of **ritual impurity to** the *halakhot* of **Shabbat?**[N] With regard to **ritual impurity, we require a functional utensil** for it to become ritually impure or to retain impurity, and anything which is not functional is ritually pure. However, **with regard to Shabbat we require something that is fit** for use, **and this too is fit to extract** a **thorn with it,** and therefore, its legal status is that of a utensil and moving it is permitted.

אָמַר רָבָא: מַאן דְּקָמוֹתִיב – שַׁפִּיר קָמוֹתִיב, מִדִּלְעִנְיַן טוּמְאָה לָאו מָנָא הוּא – לְעִנְיַן שַׁבָּת נַמִי לָאו מָנָא הוּא.

Rava said: The one **who raises the objection, raises the objection well. From** the fact that **with regard to ritual impurity it is not** considered **a utensil, with regard to Shabbat, it is also not** considered **a utensil,** and if it is not a utensil it may not be moved on Shabbat.

מֵיתִיבִי: מַחַט, בֵּין נְקוּבָה בֵּין שֶׁאֵינָהּ נְקוּבָה – מוּתָּר לְטַלְטְלָהּ בְּשַׁבָּת, וְלֹא אָמְרוּ ״נְקוּבָה״ אֶלָּא לְעִנְיַן טוּמְאָה בִּלְבַד!

The Gemara **raises an objection to** the opinion of Rava based on what was taught in a *baraita*: **A needle, whether it is perforated**[H] **or whether it is not perforated, it is permitted to move it on Shabbat. And they said** that the status of a **perforated** needle is different **only with regard to ritual impurity alone.**

תַּרְגְּמָא אַבָּיֵי אַלִּיבָּא דְּרָבָא: בְּגוֹלְמֵי עָסְקִינַן, זִימְנִין דְּמִימְּלֵךְ עֲלַיְיהוּ וּמְשַׁוֵּי לְהוּ מָנָא. אֲבָל הֵיכָא דְּנִיטַּל חֲרָרָהּ אוֹ עוּקְצָהּ – אָדָם זוֹרְקָהּ לְבֵין גְּרוּטָאוֹת.

Abaye interpreted it according to the opinion of Rava: In this mishna, **we are dealing with unfinished** needles. **Sometimes one decides** to **render them a utensil** for other purposes without perforating them. **However,** in a case **where its eye or its point was removed** from the finished needle, its status as a vessel was negated, since **a person throws it among the junk** [*gerutaot*].[L]

אִסּוּבֵי יְנוּקָא, רַב נַחְמָן אָסַר וְרַב שֵׁשֶׁת שָׁרֵי. אָמַר רַב נַחְמָן: מְנָא אָמֵינָא לַהּ – דִּתְנַן: ״אֵין עוֹשִׂין

With regard to the matter of **aligning the** limbs of an **infant**[NH] on Shabbat when it is necessary to do so, **Rav Naḥman prohibits** doing so on Shabbat, due to concern that it is similar to the prohibited labor of completing the production process of a vessel, **and Rav Sheshet permits** doing so. **Rav Naḥman says: From where do I say** that this is the *halakha*? **As we learned in a mishna: One may not make**

Perek **XVII**
Daf **123** Amud **b**

״אַפִּיקְטְוִיזִין בְּשַׁבָּת״. וְרַב שֵׁשֶׁת – הָתָם לָאו אוֹרְחֵיהּ, הָכָא – אוֹרְחֵיהּ.

afiktoizin, a drug to induce vomiting, **on Shabbat.** Apparently, actions associated with treating the body on Shabbat are prohibited. **And Rav Sheshet** explains: **There,** with regard to a drug to induce vomiting, drinking **it** for any reason other than medicinal purposes **is atypical. Here,** aligning the limbs of an infant is **typical** conduct not undertaken solely for medicinal purposes.

אָמַר רַב שֵׁשֶׁת: מְנָא אָמֵינָא לַהּ – דִּתְנַן: ״מַחַט שֶׁל יָד לִיטּוֹל בָּהּ אֶת הַקּוֹץ״. וְרַב נַחְמָן – הָתָם פְּקִיד, הָכָא – לָא פְּקִיד.

Rav Sheshet said: From where do I say that this is the *halakha*? **As we learned** in the mishna: One is permitted to take **an** ordinary **hand needle** used for sewing clothes **to extract a thorn with it.** Apparently, some curative actions are permitted and there is no concern that they are similar to completing the production process of a vessel. **And Rav Naḥman** objects: That is no proof, as **there,** the thorn **is** merely **deposited** in the skin and it is not an organic part of the body. Removing a foreign object from the body effects no fundamental change in the body. **Here,** in the case of aligning the limbs, **it is not** merely tending to a foreign object **deposited** in the body; rather it involves effecting a fundamental change in the body itself, which is both a curative act and one similar to completing the production process.

NOTES

The matter of ritual impurity and Shabbat – עִנְיַן טוּמְאָה וְשַׁבָּת: Although there are distinctions between the *halakhot* of Shabbat and the *halakhot* of ritual impurity, an item that is no longer considered a vessel with regard to ritual impurity is not considered a utensil with regard to Shabbat either. Indeed, the shard of a broken utensil is set-aside, unless it was designated for a use permitted on Shabbat.

Aligning the limbs of an infant – אִסּוּבֵי יְנוּקָא: Some commentaries explain that this term does indeed mean aligning an infant's limbs. However, it is not referring to a newborn infant, as aligning the limbs of a newborn is certainly permitted, due to the potential risk to its life if its limbs are not aligned. Consequently, it must be referring to a somewhat older infant (*Me'iri*). According to the *ge'onim*, this is referring to the epiglottis, which was dislocated and prevented the child from swallowing. That is the reason it was compared to *afiktoizin*, either because this too may cause vomiting (Rosh) or because the purpose of this procedure, like vomiting, is to restore digestive function (Rashba).

HALAKHA

A needle, whether it is perforated, etc. – מַחַט, בֵּין נְקוּבָה וכו׳: It is permitted to move an intact needle on Shabbat to remove a thorn. However, if the point or the eye of the needle was removed, it is prohibited to move it. It is permitted to move a new needle, which has not yet been perforated, to remove a thorn. The *halakha* is in accordance with the opinions of Rava and Abaye (Rambam *Sefer Zemanim*, *Hilkhot Shabbat* 31:8; *Shulḥan Arukh*, *Oraḥ Ḥayyim* 308:11).

Aligning the limbs of an infant – אִסּוּבֵי יְנוּקָא: It is permitted to align the limbs of an infant on Shabbat with one's hands (*Mishna Berura*), if the limbs were dislocated at birth. In the *Magen Avraham* it is explained that it is permitted specifically on the day of birth, but afterward it is prohibited. Many authorities disagree and permit aligning the infant's limbs up until the age of one month and beyond (see *Biur HaGra* and *Mishna Berura*). The *halakha* is in accordance with the opinion of Rav Sheshet in disputes with Rav Naḥman over ritual matters (Rashi; Rambam *Sefer Zemanim*, *Hilkhot Shabbat* 2:14; *Shulḥan Arukh*, *Oraḥ Ḥayyim* 330:9).

LANGUAGE

Junk [*gerutaot*] – גְּרוּטָאוֹת: From the Greek γρύτη, *grutè*, originally meaning haberdashery and what is sold in it, a collection of objects of little value, or a vessel to hold those objects.

מתני׳ קָנֶה שֶׁל זֵיתִים, אִם יֵשׁ קֶשֶׁר בְּרֹאשׁוֹ – מְקַבֵּל טוּמְאָה, וְאִם לָאו – אֵין מְקַבֵּל טוּמְאָה. בֵּין כָּךְ וּבֵין כָּךְ נִיטָּל בַּשַּׁבָּת.

MISHNA A reed that is used **for turning olives**[NH] in a bundle, **if there is** a cork-like **knot at the top of it,** it **can become ritually impure** as a vessel, **and if not,** it **cannot become ritually impure,** because it is not a vessel. **In either case, it may be moved on Shabbat** for use in a permitted action.

גמ׳ אַמַּאי? פְּשׁוּטֵי כְּלֵי עֵץ הוּא, וּפְשׁוּטֵי כְּלֵי עֵץ אֵינָן מְקַבְּלִין טוּמְאָה! מַאי טַעְמָא – דּוּמְיָא דְּשַׂק בָּעֵינַן. תָּנָא מִשְּׁמֵיהּ דְּרַבִּי נְחֶמְיָה: בְּשָׁעָה שֶׁמְּהַפֵּךְ בַּזֵּיתִים הוֹפְכוֹ וְרוֹאֶה בּוֹ.

GEMARA The Gemara asks: **Why** would this reed become impure? **It is** in the category of **flat wooden vessels** without a receptacle, **and** the governing principle in that case is: **Flat wooden vessels do not become ritually impure.**[H] **What is the reason** for this? **We require** an object **similar to a sack.** The *halakhot* of ritual impurity are derived from the sack mentioned in the Torah as an example of an item that can become ritually impure. If it lacks a receptacle, it is unlike that sack and it cannot become ritually impure. To explain this *halakha,* the Gemara cites that which was **taught** in a *baraita* **in the name of** Rabbi **Neḥemya: At the time that one turns over the olives**[H] with the reed, **he turns over** the reed **and sees inside it.** There is a small cavity at the end of the reed near the knot. He looks there to ascertain whether it has filled with oil, which would indicate that the olives are ready to be placed in the olive press. That cavity is a type of small receptacle, which renders the reed fit to become ritually impure.

מתני׳ רַבִּי יוֹסֵי אוֹמֵר: כׇּל הַכֵּלִים נִיטָּלִין, חוּץ מִן הַמַּסָּר הַגָּדוֹל וְיָתֵד שֶׁל מַחֲרֵישָׁה.

MISHNA **Rabbi Yosei says: All utensils may be moved** on Shabbat **except for a large saw**[H] **and the blade of a plow.** Since they must be sharp and ready for use and there is concern that they might be damaged, one sets them aside from his consciousness and they may not be used for any other purpose.

גמ׳ אָמַר רַב נַחְמָן: הַאי אוּכְלָא דְּקַצְרֵי כְּיָתֵד שֶׁל מַחֲרֵישָׁה דָּמְיָא.

GEMARA **Rav Naḥman says: A launderer's sprinkler**[B] is considered to be **like the blade of a plow.** Moving it is prohibited on Shabbat because one sets it aside from use out of concern that it might be damaged.

אָמַר אַבַּיֵי: חַרְבָּא דְּאוּשְׁכָּפֵי, וְסַכִּינָא דְּאַשְׁכַּבְתָּא, וַחֲצִינָא דְּנַגָּרֵי – כְּיָתֵד שֶׁל מַחֲרֵישָׁה דָּמֵי.

Abaye says: A shoemaker's knife, and a butcher's knife, and a carpenter's drawknife are considered to be **like the blade of a plow,** because their owners set them aside from use out of concern that they might be damaged.

תָּנוּ רַבָּנַן: בָּרִאשׁוֹנָה הָיוּ אוֹמְרִים, שְׁלֹשָׁה כֵּלִים נִיטָּלִין בַּשַּׁבָּת: מַקְצוּעַ שֶׁל דְּבֵילָה, וְזוּהֲמָא לִיסְטְרָן שֶׁל קְדֵרָה וְסַכִּין קְטַנָּה שֶׁעַל גַּבֵּי שֻׁלְחָן. הִתִּירוּ, וְחָזְרוּ וְהִתִּירוּ, וְחָזְרוּ וְהִתִּירוּ, עַד שֶׁאָמְרוּ: כׇּל הַכֵּלִים נִיטָּלִין בַּשַּׁבָּת חוּץ מִן מַסָּר הַגָּדוֹל וְיָתֵד שֶׁל מַחֲרֵישָׁה.

The Sages taught in the *Tosefta*: **Initially, they would say** that only **three utensils may be moved**[N] **on Shabbat: A knife for** cutting **a cake of dried figs, and a** combined **spoon and fork** (*ge'onim*) to clean the **filth** [*zuhama listeran*][LB] **of a pot, and a small knife that is on the table.** Each of these items is required for eating and may be used, and it had been prohibited to move any other utensil. However, over the generations, when the Rabbis saw that Jewish people were vigilant in observing the prohibitions of Shabbat, **they permitted, and then they permitted** again, **and then they permitted** again, **until they said** in the last mishna: **All utensils may be moved on Shabbat except for a large saw and the blade of a plow.**

מַאי ״הִתִּירוּ וְחָזְרוּ וְהִתִּירוּ וְחָזְרוּ וְהִתִּירוּ״?

The Gemara asks: **What** are the stages described in the *Tosefta*: **They permitted, and then they permitted, and then they permitted?**

NOTES

A reed for turning olives – קָנֶה שֶׁל זֵיתִים: In the Jerusalem Talmud, Shmuel explains that the reed for olives is referring to a reed with a small receptacle at one end used to lift olives from the pile. The receptacle is made by knotting the reed, thereby closing off a segment of it. Some commentaries explain that the reed was otherwise hollow and that therefore it could not become impure (*Shenot Eliyahu*).

Three utensils may be moved – שְׁלֹשָׁה כֵּלִים נִיטָּלִין: Apparently, these three utensils are permitted always and for any purpose, because they are used so frequently (Ritva).

BACKGROUND

A launderer's sprinkler – אוּכְלָא דְּקַצְרֵי: A launderer's sprinkler is a utensil full of holes, used to sprinkle water onto garments while they are being ironed or tailored.

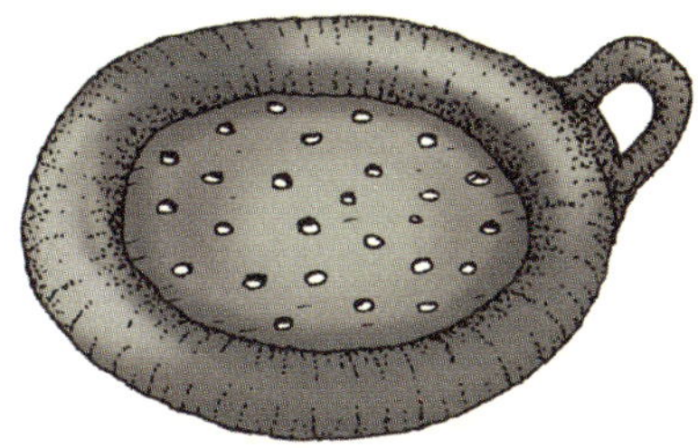

Talmudic era launderer's sprinkler

Spoon and fork to clean the filth [*zuhama listeran*] – זוּהֲמָא לִיסְטְרָן:

Zuhama listeran according to the interpretation of the *ge'onim*

LANGUAGE

Spoon and fork to clean the filth [*zuhama listeran*] – זוּהֲמָא לִיסְטְרָן: In the Jerusalem Talmud, the word appears as *zumei listeran,* which is closer to the original Greek **ζωμός**, *zomos,* meaning soup, and **λίστρον**, *listron,* meaning shovel or a spoon. These two words combined are almost identical to the talmudic expression and mean a large spoon used to ladle soup.

HALAKHA

A reed for turning olives – קָנֶה שֶׁל זֵיתִים: An olive reed that has the status of a utensil is an object whose primary function is for a prohibited use and may be moved for the purpose of utilizing the vessel itself and for utilizing its place (Rambam *Sefer Zemanim, Hilkhot Shabbat* 26:7).

The impurity of flat wooden utensils – טוּמְאַת פְּשׁוּטֵי כְּלֵי עֵץ: By Torah law, flat wooden vessels without a receptacle cannot become ritually impure with most impurities, with the exception of ritual impurity imparted by the treading of a *zav.* They do become impure with ritual impurity by rabbinic decree (Rambam *Sefer Tahara, Hilkhot Kelim* 1:10).

The impurity of reeds for turning olives – טוּמְאַת קָנֶה שֶׁל זֵיתִים: If a reed used to turn olives has a receptacle, the receptacle and the part of the reed supporting the receptacle can become ritually impure by Torah law, whereas the remainder of the reed can become impure with ritual impurity by rabbinic law, as per the opinion of Rabbi Neḥemya (Rambam *Sefer Tahara, Hilkhot Kelim* 2:2).

All utensils may be moved on Shabbat except for a large saw – כׇּל הַכֵּלִים נִיטָּלִין, חוּץ מִן הַמַּסָּר הַגָּדוֹל: All utensils may be moved on Shabbat except for those which are set aside due to monetary loss, i.e., utensils that one sets aside so they will not be damaged. Everyone agrees that these items are set-aside, and it is prohibited to move them even for the purpose of utilizing the vessel itself or for utilizing its place (Rambam *Sefer Zemanim, Hilkhot Shabbat* 25:9; *Shulḥan Arukh, Oraḥ Ḥayyim* 308:1).

HALAKHA

An object whose primary function is for a permitted use – דָּבָר שֶׁמְּלַאכְתּוֹ לְהֶיתֵּר: On Shabbat it is permitted to move an object whose primary function is for a permitted use. It is also permitted to move an object whose primary function is for both prohibited and permitted uses on Shabbat (*Magen Avraham*), even for the benefit of the object itself, e.g., moving it from the sun to the shade, as per the opinion of Rava (Rambam *Sefer Zemanim*, *Hilkhot Shabbat* 25:3; *Shulḥan Arukh*, *Oraḥ Ḥayyim* 308:4).

NOTES

The dispute between Abaye and Rava – מַחְלוֹקֶת אַבָּיֵי וְרָבָא: Ultimately, Abaye and Rava disagree whether or not it is also permitted to move vessels so large that a single person cannot carry them. A similar dispute appears explicitly in the Jerusalem Talmud: With regard to a vessel that is so large and heavy that one designates a place for it, is he considered to have set it aside from use on Shabbat?

This mishna was taught in the days of Nehemiah, son of Hacaliah – בִּימֵי נְחֶמְיָה בֶּן חֲכַלְיָה נִשְׁנֵית מִשְׁנָה זוֹ: Rabbeinu Tam explains that this mishna only applied to that specific generation. There was no intent to establish a *halakha* for all generations, but merely to address the situation extant at that time. Otherwise, the later courts could not abrogate a decree issued by its predecessors, as that would be in contravention of the principle: A court may not override a decree issued by a previous court, unless it is greater in wisdom and number.

BACKGROUND

Poles – מַקְלוֹת:

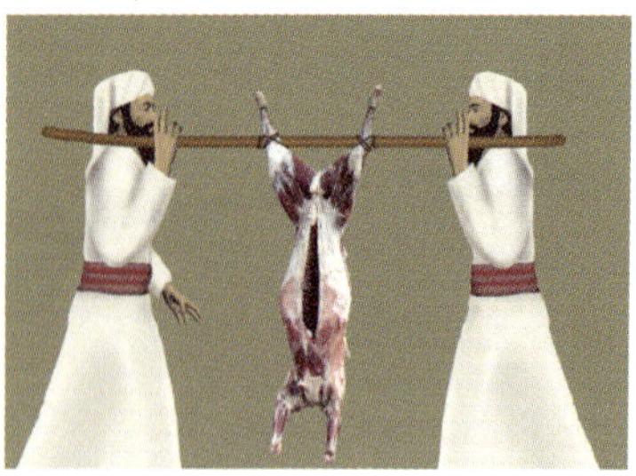

Paschal offering hanging from a pole

LANGUAGE

Thick end [*gelostera*] – גְּלוֹסְטְרָא: From the Greek κλεῖστρον, *kleistron*, or the Latin claustrum, meaning a bar used to lock a door.

אָמַר אַבָּיֵי: ״הִתִּירוּ״ דָּבָר שֶׁמְּלַאכְתּוֹ לְהֶיתֵּר לְצוֹרֶךְ גּוּפוֹ, ״וְחָזְרוּ וְהִתִּירוּ״ דָּבָר שֶׁמְּלַאכְתּוֹ לְהֶיתֵּר לְצוֹרֶךְ מְקוֹמוֹ, ״וְחָזְרוּ וְהִתִּירוּ״ דָּבָר שֶׁמְּלַאכְתּוֹ לְאִיסּוּר לְצוֹרֶךְ גּוּפוֹ – אִין, לְצוֹרֶךְ מְקוֹמוֹ – לָא. וַעֲדַיִין, בְּיָדוֹ אַחַת – אִין, בִּשְׁתֵּי יָדָיו – לָא. עַד שֶׁאָמְרוּ: כׇּל הַכֵּלִים נִיטָּלִין בְּשַׁבָּת, וַאֲפִילּוּ בִּשְׁתֵּי יָדַיִם.

Abaye says: Initially, **they permitted** moving **an object whose** primary **function** is **for a permitted** use,[H] **for the purpose of** utilizing the object **itself** to perform a permitted action. **And then they permitted** moving **an object whose** primary **function** is **for a permitted** use, **for the purpose of** sitting in or utilizing **its place. And then they permitted** moving **an object whose** primary **function** is for a **prohibited** use, **for the purpose of** utilizing the object **itself** to perform a permitted action, **yes;** however, **for the purpose of** utilizing **its place, no. And still,** utensils that can be held **in one of his hands, yes,** they may be moved; however, utensils that can only be held **in his two hands, no,** they may not be moved, in order to signify that there is a prohibition to move certain items. This prohibition remained intact **until they said: All utensils may be moved on Shabbat, and even** those that can only be held **in both hands.**

אָמַר לֵיהּ רָבָא: מִכְּדֵי ״הִתִּירוּ״ קָתָנֵי, מַה לִּי לְצוֹרֶךְ גּוּפוֹ מַה לִּי לְצוֹרֶךְ מְקוֹמוֹ? אֶלָּא אָמַר רָבָא: ״הִתִּירוּ״ דָּבָר שֶׁמְּלַאכְתּוֹ לְהֶיתֵּר בֵּין לְצוֹרֶךְ גּוּפוֹ וּבֵין לְצוֹרֶךְ מְקוֹמוֹ, ״וְחָזְרוּ וְהִתִּירוּ״ מֵחַמָּה לַצֵּל, ״וְחָזְרוּ וְהִתִּירוּ״ דָּבָר שֶׁמְּלַאכְתּוֹ לְאִיסּוּר לְצוֹרֶךְ גּוּפוֹ וּלְצוֹרֶךְ מְקוֹמוֹ – אִין, מֵחַמָּה לַצֵּל – לָא, וַעֲדַיִין, בְּאָדָם אֶחָד – אִין, בִּשְׁנֵי בְּנֵי אָדָם – לָא, עַד שֶׁאָמְרוּ: כׇּל הַכֵּלִים נִיטָּלִין בְּשַׁבָּת אֲפִילּוּ בִּשְׁנֵי בְּנֵי אָדָם.

Rava said to him: After all, it was taught in the *Tosefta*: **They permitted, what** difference is there **to me** if it is **for the purpose of** utilizing the object **itself,** and **what** difference is there **to me** if it is **for the purpose of** utilizing **its place;** why introduce distinctions that are not explicitly stated in the *Tosefta*? **Rather, Rava said** that it should be explained as follows: Initially, **they permitted** moving **an object whose** primary **function** is **for a permitted** use, **both for the purpose of** utilizing the object **itself and for the purpose of** sitting in or utilizing **its place. And then they permitted** moving that object **from the sun into the shade. And then they permitted** moving **an object whose** primary **function** is **for a prohibited** use, **both for the purpose of** utilizing the object **itself and for the purpose of** sitting in or utilizing **its place, yes;** however, moving that object **from the sun into the shade, no,** they did not permit it. **And still,** utensils that can be carried **by one person, yes,** they may be moved; however, utensils that can only be carried **by two people, no,** they may not be moved. This prohibition remained intact **until they said: All utensils may be moved on Shabbat, and even** those that can only be carried **by two people.**

אֵיתִיבֵיהּ אַבָּיֵי: מְדוֹכָה, אִם יֵשׁ בָּהּ שׁוּם – מְטַלְטְלִין אוֹתָהּ, וְאִם לָאו – אֵין מְטַלְטְלִין אוֹתָהּ! הָכָא בְּמַאי עָסְקִינַן – מֵחַמָּה לַצֵּל. אֵיתִיבֵיהּ: וְשָׁוִין שֶׁאִם קִצֵּב עָלָיו בָּשָׂר שֶׁאָסוּר לְטַלְטְלוֹ! הָכָא נַמִי, מֵחַמָּה לַצֵּל.

Abaye raised a challenge to Rava's opinion[N] from that which was taught: With regard to **a mortar, if it has garlic in it, one may move it** on Shabbat, **and if not, one may not move it** on Shabbat. According to Rava's opinion that all utensils may be moved, why is it prohibited to move the mortar? Rava responded: **With what we are dealing here?** We are dealing with a case of moving the mortar **from the sun to the shade.** Abaye **raised a challenge** to Rava's opinion from that which was taught: Beit Shammai and Beit Hillel **agree** that **if one cut meat on it** for the purpose of a Festival **that** it is then **prohibited to move it** because there is no further need for it on the Festival. According to Rava's opinion, all utensils may be moved. He answered him: **Here, too,** we are dealing with a case of moving the mortar **from the sun to the shade.**

אָמַר רַבִּי חֲנִינָא בִּימֵי נְחֶמְיָה בֶּן חֲכַלְיָה נִשְׁנֵית מִשְׁנָה זוֹ, דִּכְתִיב: ״בַּיָּמִים הָהֵמָּה רָאִיתִי בִיהוּדָה דוֹרְכִים גִּתּוֹת בַּשַּׁבָּת וּמְבִיאִים הָעֲרֵימוֹת״.

Rabbi Ḥanina said: This mishna was taught in the days of Nehemiah, son of Hacaliah,[N] a period when many stringent decrees were issued with regard to Shabbat prohibitions, **as it is written: "In those days I saw in Judea some treading winepresses on Shabbat and bringing in heaps** of grain and lading donkeys with them; as also wine, grapes, figs, and all manner of burdens which are brought into Jerusalem on the Shabbat day. I forewarned them on that day when they sold food" (Nehemiah 13:15). Since the people treated the sanctity of Shabbat with disdain, Nehemiah instituted many stringencies with regard to all the *halakhot* of Shabbat in order to educate the people to observe Shabbat.

אָמַר רַבִּי אֶלְעָזָר: קָנִין וּמַקְלוֹת גְּלוֹסְטְרָא וּמְדוֹכָה כּוּלָּן קוֹדֶם הַתָּרַת כֵּלִים נִשְׁנוּ.

Rabbi Elazar said: The *mishnayot* that deal with the topics of **rods, poles,**[B] **the thick end** [*gelostera*][L] of the bolt in a door lock, **and a mortar were all** taught **before permission** to move **utensils** on Shabbat was adopted. At that time, moving most utensils was still prohibited and only a small number of utensils whose primary function was for a permitted use were permitted to be moved. The Gemara cites the relevant *mishnayot*.

קָנִין – דִּתְנַן: לֹא סִידּוּר הַקָּנִין וְלֹא נְטִילָתָן דּוֹחֶה אֶת הַשַּׁבָּת.

Rods: Golden rods were placed between the loaves of showbread in the Temple to support the loaves and to aerate them. At that time, moving the rods was prohibited because they were considered to be set-aside, **as we learned** in a mishna: **Neither arranging the rods nor moving them**[H] **overrides** the prohibition of set-aside on **Shabbat.**

מַקְלוֹת – דִּתְנַן: מַקְלוֹת דַּקִּין חֲלָקִין הָיוּ שָׁם וּמַנִּיחוֹ עַל כְּתֵפוֹ וְעַל כֶּתֶף חֲבֵירוֹ וְתוֹלֶה וּמַפְשִׁיט. (אָמַר) רַבִּי אֶלְעָזָר: אַרְבָּעָה עָשָׂר שֶׁחָל לִהְיוֹת בְּשַׁבָּת מַנִּיחַ

And the source for the matter of **poles is as we learned** in a mishna: **There were thin, smooth poles** in the Temple, **and** every Passover eve **one places** the pole **on his shoulder and on the shoulder of another, and suspends** the Paschal lamb on it **and flays** its hide.[H] And **Rabbi Elazar said:** With regard to **the fourteenth** of Nisan, the day that the Paschal lamb is sacrificed, **that occurred on Shabbat,** they would not use the poles, as a conspicuous reminder that it was Shabbat. Instead, **one places**

HALAKHA

Arranging the rods…moving them – סִידּוּר הַקָּנִין...נְטִילָתָן: Arranging or removing the rods of the showbread does not override the prohibitions of Shabbat. They were removed on Shabbat eve and replaced between the loaves after Shabbat (Rambam *Sefer Avoda, Hilkhot Temidin UMusafin* 5:11).

Procedures for the Paschal lamb – סִדְרֵי קׇרְבַּן פֶּסַח: People would hang and flay their Paschal lambs on iron hooks that were fixed in the walls of the Temple. Those unable to find an available hook would place a thin, smooth staff on the shoulders of two people, hang the sacrifice on it, and flay it, as per the unattributed mishna (Rambam *Sefer Korbanot, Hilkhot Korban Pesaḥ* 1:14).

Perek **XVII**
Daf **124** Amud **a**

יָדוֹ עַל כֶּתֶף חֲבֵירוֹ, וְיַד חֲבֵירוֹ עַל כְּתֵיפוֹ, וְתוֹלֶה וּמַפְשִׁיט.

his hand on the shoulder of another, and the other's hand on his shoulder, and suspends the lamb **and flays** its hide.

גְּלוֹסְטְרָא – דִּתְנַן: נֶגֶר שֶׁיֵּשׁ בְּרֹאשׁוֹ גְּלוֹסְטְרָא, רַבִּי יְהוֹשֻׁעַ אוֹמֵר: שׁוֹמְטָהּ מִן פֶּתַח זֶה וְתוֹלֶה בַּחֲבֵירוֹ בְּשַׁבָּת, רַבִּי טַרְפוֹן אוֹמֵר: הֲרֵי הוּא כְּכׇל הַכֵּלִים וּמִיטַּלְטֵל בֶּחָצֵר.

The source for the **thick end** of a bolt is **as we learned** in a mishna: With regard to **a bolt** used in a door lock **which has a thick end at the head** of the bolt,[H] **Rabbi Yehoshua says: One may drag it from this doorway and hang it in another** doorway **on Shabbat,** but he may not move it with his hands, because it was considered to be set-aside. **Rabbi Tarfon says: It is like all the** other **utensils and may be moved in a courtyard.**

מְדוֹכָה – הָא דַּאֲמַרַן. אָמַר רַבָּה: מִמַּאי? דִּילְמָא לְעוֹלָם אֵימָא לָךְ – לְאַחַר הַתָּרַת כֵּלִים נִשְׁנוּ. קָנִים טַעְמָא מַאי – מִשּׁוּם אִיעַפּוּשֵׁי, בְּהַאי פּוּרְתָּא לָא מִיעַפַּשׁ. מַקְלוֹת – אֶפְשָׁר כְּרַבִּי אֶלְעָזָר.

The case of **a mortar** is **that which we said** above. **Rabba said: From what** does that conclusion ensue? **Perhaps, actually I** could **say to you** that these *mishnayot* **were taught after permission** to move **utensils** on Shabbat was adopted,[N] and nevertheless, the prohibitions can be understood. With regard to the **rods** for the showbread, **what is the reason** that they are used? They are used **due to concern** that the bread will **decay. In that brief** period until the conclusion of Shabbat **it will not decay.** With regard to **poles,** why may they not be used on Passover eve? It is prohibited because **it is possible** to flay the lamb **in accordance with** the opinion of **Rabbi Elazar.** Use of the pole is superfluous, and therefore it is set-aside.

גְּלוֹסְטְרָא – כְּדְרַבִּי יַנַּאי, דְּאָמַר רַבִּי יַנַּאי: בְּחָצֵר שֶׁאֵינָהּ מְעוּרֶבֶת עָסְקִינַן. רַבִּי יְהוֹשֻׁעַ סָבַר: תּוֹךְ הַפֶּתַח כְּלִפְנִים דָּמֵי, וְקָמְטַלְטֵל מָנָא דְּבָתִּים בְּחָצֵר. וְרַבִּי טַרְפוֹן סָבַר: תּוֹךְ הַפֶּתַח כְּלַחוּץ דָּמֵי, וּמָנָא דְּחָצֵר בְּחָצֵר קָא מְטַלְטֵל.

In the case of **the thick end** of the bolt in the door, why was it prohibited to move it by hand? It was prohibited **in accordance with** the opinion of **Rabbi Yanai, as Rabbi Yanai says: We are dealing with a courtyard** for which a joining of courtyards [*eiruv*] was not established. **Rabbi Yehoshua holds** that **inside the doorway is** considered to be **like inside** the house, **and** therefore, **he is moving utensils** of the **houses in the courtyard.** Since there is no joining of the courtyards, one may not move a vessel from the house to the courtyard. **And Rabbi Tarfon holds** that **inside the doorway is** considered to be **like outside** the house, **and therefore, he is moving utensils** of the **courtyard in the courtyard,** which is permitted.

מְדוֹכָה – רַבִּי נְחֶמְיָה הִיא.

With regard to **a mortar,** the *halakha* **is** in accordance with the opinion of **Rabbi Neḥemya,** who holds that a vessel may only be moved on Shabbat for the purpose of its designated use.

מַתְנִי׳ כׇּל הַכֵּלִים נִיטָּלִין לְצוֹרֶךְ וְשֶׁלֹּא לְצוֹרֶךְ, רַבִּי נְחֶמְיָה אוֹמֵר: אֵין נִיטָּלִין אֶלָּא לְצוֹרֶךְ.

MISHNA **All vessels may be moved**[H] **for a** specific **purpose and not for a** specific **purpose.**[N] **Rabbi Neḥemya says:** Vessels **may only be moved for a** specific **purpose.**

גְּמ׳ מַאי לְצוֹרֶךְ וּמַאי שֶׁלֹּא לְצוֹרֶךְ?

GEMARA The Gemara asks: **What** is the meaning of: **For a** specific **purpose, and what is** the meaning of: **Not for a** specific **purpose?**

HALAKHA

A bolt used in a door lock which has a thick end at the head of the bolt – נֶגֶר שֶׁיֵּשׁ בְּרֹאשׁוֹ גְּלוֹסְטְרָא: It is permitted to move a bolt with one thick end on Shabbat because it is a vessel (Rambam *Sefer Zemanim, Hilkhot Shabbat* 26:9; *Shulḥan Arukh, Oraḥ Ḥayyim* 313:1).

All vessels may be moved – כׇּל הַכֵּלִים נִיטָּלִין: Vessels whose primary function is for a permitted use may be moved for the benefit of the vessel itself, e.g., to move it from the sun into the shade, as per Rava's interpretation of the unattributed mishna. Some authorities rule that it is prohibited to move a vessel for this purpose (Rashba, citing the Rambam; Rambam *Sefer Zemanim, Hilkhot Shabbat* 25:3; *Shulḥan Arukh, Oraḥ Ḥayyim* 308:4).

NOTES

Perhaps…were taught after permission to move utensils on Shabbat was adopted – דִּילְמָא...לְאַחַר הַתָּרַת כֵּלִים נִשְׁנוּ: Rabba's statements on this matter correspond to his later statements. He holds that even according to the Rabbis, it was not permitted to move all types of vessels.

For a specific purpose and not for a specific purpose – לְצוֹרֶךְ וְשֶׁלֹּא לְצוֹרֶךְ: Rashi explains the mishna as referring to two different circumstances. All vessels may be moved; some may be moved only for a specific purpose and others may be moved even if not for a specific purpose. The tannaitic dispute is with regard to the definitions of for a purpose and not for a purpose.

אמר רבה: לצורך – דבר שמלאכתו להיתר לצורך גופו. שלא לצורך – דבר שמלאכתו להיתר לצורך מקומו. ודבר שמלאכתו לאיסור, לצורך גופו – אין, לצורך מקומו – לא. ואתא רבי נחמיה למימר: ואפילו דבר שמלאכתו להיתר, לצורך גופו – אין, לצורך מקומו – לא. אמר ליה רבא: לצורך מקומו שלא לצורך קרית ליה?!

Rabba said: For a specific **purpose** means: Moving **an object whose** primary **function** is **for a permitted** use **for the purpose of** utilizing the object **itself. Not for a** specific **purpose** means: Moving **an object whose** primary **function** is **for a permitted** use **for the purpose of** utilizing **its place. And** an object **whose** primary **function** is **for a prohibited** use, **for the purpose of** utilizing the object **itself, yes,** it is permitted; **for the purpose of** utilizing **its place, no,** it is prohibited. **And Rabbi Neḥemya came to say: And even an object whose** primary **function** is **for a permitted** use, moving it **for the purpose of** utilizing the object **itself, yes; for the purpose of** utilizing **its place, no. Rava said to him: Do you call for the purpose of** utilizing **its place, not for a** specific **purpose?** It is for a purpose.

אלא אמר רבא: לצורך – דבר שמלאכתו להיתר, בין לצורך גופו בין לצורך מקומו. שלא לצורך – ואפילו מחמה לצל. ודבר שמלאכתו לאיסור לצורך גופו ולצורך מקומו – אין, מחמה לצל – לא. ואתא רבי נחמיה למימר: ואפילו דבר שמלאכתו להיתר, לצורך גופו ולצורך מקומו – אין, מחמה לצל – לא.

Rather, Rava said: For a specific **purpose** means: Moving **an object whose** primary **function** is **for a permitted** use **both for the purpose of** utilizing the object **itself and for the purpose of** utilizing **its place. Not for a** specific **purpose** means: Moving it **even from the sun to the shade. And an object whose** primary **function** is **for a prohibited** use, **both for the purpose of** utilizing the object **itself and for the purpose of** utilizing **its place, yes,** it is permitted; moving it **from the sun to the shade, no,** it is prohibited. **And Rabbi Neḥemya came to say: Even an object whose** primary **function** is **for a permitted** use, moving it **for the purpose of** utilizing the object **itself and for the purpose of** utilizing **its place, yes,** it is permitted; moving it **from the sun to the shade, no,** it is prohibited.

יתיב רב ספרא ורב אחא בר הונא ורב הונא בר חנינא ויתבי וקאמרי: לרבה אליבא דרבי נחמיה, הני קערות היכי מטלטלינן? אמר להו רב ספרא: מידי דהוה אגרף של רעי.

It is told that **Rav Safra and Rav Aḥa bar Huna and Rav Huna bar Ḥanina sat** together **and they sat and they said: According to Rabba's** explanation **in accordance with** the opinion of **Rabbi Neḥemya**[N] that it is prohibited to move an object whose primary function is for a permitted use for the purpose of utilizing its place, **these** empty **bowls, how do we carry** them?[N] **Rav Safra said to them:** You may move them, **just as is** the case of a **chamber pot** containing waste that may be moved because it is disgusting.

אמר ליה אביי לרבה: למר, אליבא דרבי נחמיה הני קערות היכי מטלטלינן להו? אמר ליה: רב ספרא חברין תרגמה – מידי דהוה אגרף של רעי.

Abaye said this same matter **to Rabba: According to the Master's** explanation **in accordance with** the opinion of **Rabbi Neḥemya, these** empty **bowls, how do we carry** them? **He said to him: Our colleague Rav Safra interpreted it: Just as is** the case of a **chamber pot.**

איתיביה אביי: מדוכה, אם יש בה שום – מטלטלין אותה, ואם לאו – אין מטלטלין אותה! הכא במאי עסקינן – מחמה לצל. איתיביה: ושוין שאם קצב עליו בשר שאסור לטלטלו! הכא נמי, מחמה לצל.

Abaye raised an objection to Rava's opinion from that which was taught: With regard to **a mortar, if it has garlic in it, one may move it** on Shabbat, **and if not, one may not move it** on Shabbat. According to Rava's opinion that all utensils may be moved, why is it prohibited to move the mortar? Rava responded: **With what are we dealing here?** We are dealing with a case of moving the mortar **from the sun to the shade,** which Rava prohibited. **Abaye raised an objection** to Rava's opinion from that which was taught: Beit Shammai and Beit Hillel **agree** that **if one cut meat on it** for the purpose of the Festival **that** it is then **prohibited to move it** because there is no further need for it on the Festival. According to Rava's opinion, all utensils may be moved. He answered him: **Here, too,** we are dealing with a case of moving the mortar **from the sun to the shade.**

והא דתנן: אין סומכין את הקדירה בבקעת, וכן בדלת. והא בקעת דביום טוב – דבר שמלאכתו להיתר הוא, אלמא: דבר שמלאכתו להיתר, בין לצורך גופו בין לצורך מקומו אסור! התם מאי טעמא – כיון דבשבת דבר שמלאכתו לאיסור הוא, גזירה יום טוב אטו שבת.

And Abaye raised another objection with regard to **that which we learned** in a mishna: **One may not prop a pot with a piece of wood,**[H] **and so too,** one may not prop **a door** on a piece of wood. **Isn't a piece of wood on a Festival an object whose** primary **function** is **for a permitted** use, since it is permitted to move it to light an oven? **Apparently,** there is an opinion that moving **an object whose** primary **function** is **for a permitted** use, **both for the purpose of** utilizing the object **itself and for the purpose of** utilizing **its place** is **prohibited,** and according to Rabba, even Rabbi Neḥemya does not hold that this is so. Rava answers: **There, what is the reason** for the prohibition? It is **because on Shabbat it is an object whose** primary **function** is **for a prohibited** use. Since the wood is set aside from use on Shabbat, the Sages issued **a decree** prohibiting moving it **on a Festival, due to Shabbat.**

NOTES

Rabbi Neḥemya's opinion – שיטת רבי נחמיה: Rabbi Neḥemya's opinion was not completely explicated because the *halakha* is not in accordance with his opinion. The commentaries dispute its details. Rashi explains that when Rabbi Neḥemya permitted moving an object whose primary function is for a permitted use on Shabbat, he did so only for the purpose of using the object itself for its designated purpose. It follows that Rabbi Neḥemya prohibits moving an object whose primary function is for a prohibited use.

Others explain that Rabbi Neḥemya permitted moving an object whose primary function is for a prohibited use, for the purpose of using the vessel itself for a permitted purpose similar to its designated purpose. For example, Rabbi Neḥemya permits utilizing a smith's hammer to crack nuts, which is similar to the manner in which the smith uses the hammer (see Rashba).

In accordance with the opinion of Rabbi Neḥemya, these empty bowls, how do we carry them – אליבא דרבי נחמיה, הני קערות היכי מטלטלינן: This question is based on the interpretation that Rabbi Neḥemya even prohibits moving an object whose primary function is for a permitted use, for the purpose of utilizing its location. According to Rava, one may move the bowls for the purpose of utilizing their location. In the Jerusalem Talmud it is explained that it is certainly permitted to move the bowls if one seeks to refill them. The dispute is only with regard to moving empty bowls for the purpose of utilizing their location.

HALAKHA

One may not prop a pot with a piece of wood – אין סומכין את הקדירה בבקעת: It is prohibited to prop a pot or a door on a piece of wood on a Festival (Rambam *Sefer Zemanim*, *Hilkhot Yom Tov* 4:11; *Shulḥan Arukh*, *Oraḥ Ḥayyim* 502:3).

וְכִי תֵּימָא שַׁבָּת גּוּפֵיהּ תִּישְׁתְּרִי, דְּהָא דָּבָר שֶׁמְּלַאכְתּוֹ לְאִיסּוּר לְצוֹרֶךְ גּוּפוֹ וּלְצוֹרֶךְ מְקוֹמוֹ שָׁרֵי! הָנֵי מִילֵּי – הֵיכָא דְּאִיכָּא תּוֹרַת כְּלִי עָלָיו, הֵיכָא דְּלֵיכָּא תּוֹרַת כְּלִי עָלָיו – לָא.

And if you say: Moving the wood should be **permitted on Shabbat itself because an object whose** primary **function** is **for a prohibited** use **is permitted both for the purpose of** utilizing the object **itself and for the purpose of** utilizing **its place,** that assertion is rejected. **This** ruling, which permits moving an object whose primary use is prohibited, **applies** only in a case **where the status of a vessel**[H] **applies to it; in a case where the status of a vessel does not apply to it, no,** it is prohibited.

וּמִי גָּזְרִינַן? וְהָתְנַן: מַשִּׁילִין פֵּירוֹת דֶּרֶךְ אֲרוּבָּה בְּיוֹם טוֹב, אֲבָל לֹא בְּשַׁבָּת.

The Gemara asks: **And do we issue decrees** prohibiting actions on Festivals due to the fact that they are prohibited on Shabbat? **Didn't we learn** in a mishna: **One may drop fruits**[H] from the roof **through a skylight on a Festival, but not on Shabbat.** Apparently, the Sages do not prohibit on a Festival all of the actions that are prohibited on Shabbat.

וּמִי לָא גָּזְרִינַן? וְהָתְנַן: אֵין בֵּין יוֹם טוֹב לְשַׁבָּת אֶלָּא אוֹכֶל נֶפֶשׁ בִּלְבַד!

The Gemara asks on the contrary: **And do we not issue decrees** on a Festival due to Shabbat? **Didn't we learn** in a mishna: **The only** difference **between a Festival and Shabbat is** with regard to the preparation of **food alone.**[H] In all other matters the Sages established that the *halakhot* of Shabbat and Festivals are the same.

אָמַר רַב יוֹסֵף: לָא קַשְׁיָא. הָא – רַבִּי אֱלִיעֶזֶר, הָא – רַבִּי יְהוֹשֻׁעַ. דְּתַנְיָא: אוֹתוֹ וְאֶת בְּנוֹ שֶׁנָּפְלוּ לַבּוֹר, רַבִּי אֱלִיעֶזֶר אוֹמֵר: מַעֲלֶה אֶת הָרִאשׁוֹן עַל מְנָת לְשׁוֹחֲטוֹ וְשׁוֹחֲטוֹ, וְהַשֵּׁנִי עוֹשֶׂה לוֹ פַּרְנָסָה בִּמְקוֹמוֹ בִּשְׁבִיל שֶׁלֹּא יָמוּת. רַבִּי יְהוֹשֻׁעַ אוֹמֵר: מַעֲלֶה אֶת הָרִאשׁוֹן עַל מְנָת לְשׁוֹחֲטוֹ וְאֵינוֹ שׁוֹחֲטוֹ, וּמַעֲרִים וּמַעֲלֶה אֶת הַשֵּׁנִי. רָצָה – זֶה שׁוֹחֵט, רָצָה – זֶה שׁוֹחֵט.

Rav Yosef says: This is **not difficult. This** mishna, which rules that it is prohibited, is in accordance with the opinion of **Rabbi Eliezer; that** mishna, which rules that it is permitted, is in accordance with the opinion of **Rabbi Yehoshua. As it was taught** in a *baraita*: It is prohibited to slaughter a mother animal and its offspring on the same day, as it is stated: "You shall not slaughter it and its offspring both in one day" (Leviticus 22:28). With regard to **it and its offspring that fell into a pit** on a Festival, **Rabbi Eliezer says: One may raise the first in order to slaughter it, and** then **slaughter it; and** with regard to **the second one, one may provide it sustenance in its place** in the pit **so that it will not die. Rabbi Yehoshua says: One may raise the first in order to slaughter it, and** then reconsider and **not slaughter it, and** then **employ artifice** and say that he reconsidered and wants to slaughter the other, **and raise the second. If he** so **desires, he slaughters this** one; **if he** so **desires, he slaughters that** one. Apparently, Rabbi Yehoshua permits certain actions on a Festival due to financial considerations, and does not issue decrees in those cases.

מִמַּאי? דִּילְמָא עַד כָּאן לָא קָאָמַר רַבִּי אֱלִיעֶזֶר הָתָם – אֶלָּא דְּאֶפְשָׁר לְפַרְנָסָה, אֲבָל הֵיכָא דְּלָא אֶפְשָׁר לְפַרְנָסָה – לָא.

The Gemara rejects this: **From what** does that conclusion ensue? **Perhaps Rabbi Eliezer only stated** that he may not raise the second animal **there,** in a case **where it is possible to** save the animal by **feeding** it in the pit; **however,** in a case **where it is impossible to** save it by **feeding** it in the pit, **no,** he would permit raising the animal.

אִי נָמֵי; עַד כָּאן לָא קָאָמַר רַבִּי יְהוֹשֻׁעַ הָתָם – דְּאֶפְשָׁר בְּהַעֲרָמָה, אֲבָל הֵיכָא דְּלָא אֶפְשָׁר בְּהַעֲרָמָה – לָא.

Alternatively, Rabbi Yehoshua only said that he may raise the second animal in a case **where it is possible to employ artifice; however,** in a case **where it is not possible to employ artifice, no,** he would not permit doing so.

אֶלָּא אָמַר רַב פַּפָּא: לָא קַשְׁיָא, הָא – בֵּית שַׁמַּאי, הָא – בֵּית הִלֵּל. דְּתְנַן, בֵּית שַׁמַּאי אוֹמְרִים:

Rather Rav Pappa said: This is **not difficult. This** mishna is in accordance with the opinion of **Beit Shammai, and that** mishna is in accordance with the opinion of **Beit Hillel. As we learned** in a mishna **that Beit Shammai say:**

Perek **XVII**
Daf **124** Amud **b**

אֵין מוֹצִיאִין אֶת הַקָּטָן וְאֶת הַלּוּלָב וְאֶת סֵפֶר תּוֹרָה לִרְשׁוּת הָרַבִּים, וּבֵית הִלֵּל מַתִּירִין.

One may neither carry a child nor a *lulav* nor a Torah scroll out to the public domain on a Festival,[H] **and Beit Hillel permit** doing so. Beit Hillel permit carrying objects from one domain to another on a Festival for purposes other than preparing food.

HALAKHA

The status of a vessel – תּוֹרַת כְּלִי: It is prohibited to move an object that is not and never was a vessel and is nothing more than raw material, even for the purpose of utilizing it or utilizing its location (Rambam *Sefer Zemanim, Hilkhot Shabbat* 25:6; *Shulḥan Arukh, Oraḥ Ḥayyim* 308:7 and in the comment of the Rema).

One may drop fruits, etc. – מַשִּׁילִין פֵּירוֹת וכו׳: It is permitted to lower fruit from the roof into the house via a skylight on a Festival, if it will be ruined by rain. However, on Shabbat it is prohibited to do so, in accordance with the mishna in tractate *Beitza* (Rambam *Sefer Zemanim, Hilkhot Yom Tov* 5:5; *Shulḥan Arukh, Oraḥ Ḥayyim* 338:7, 521:1).

The only difference between a Festival and Shabbat is with regard to the preparation of food alone – אֵין בֵּין יוֹם טוֹב לַשַּׁבָּת אֶלָּא אוֹכֶל נֶפֶשׁ בִּלְבַד: It is prohibited to perform any labor on a Festival that is prohibited on Shabbat whether by Torah law or by rabbinic decree (*Mishna Berura*), with the exception of activities involved in the preparation of food. Such activities include igniting a fire and carrying items from one domain to another. Some authorities prohibit carrying or igniting a fire if these activities have no specific purpose (Rambam *Sefer Zemanim, Hilkhot Yom Tov* 1:1; *Shulḥan Arukh, Oraḥ Ḥayyim* 495:1).

HALAKHA

Carrying out objects on a Festival – הוֹצָאָה בְּיוֹם טוֹב: It is permitted to carry objects into the public domain for a specific purpose, even if they are not needed for the purpose of food preparation (Rema), in accordance with the opinion of Beit Hillel (Rambam *Sefer Zemanim, Hilkhot Yom Tov* 1:4; *Shulḥan Arukh, Oraḥ Ḥayyim* 518:1 and in the comment of the Rema).

אֵימַר דִּשְׁמַעַתְּ לְהוּ לְבֵית שַׁמַּאי הוֹצָאָה – טִלְטוּל מִי שְׁמַעַתְּ לְהוּ?! וְטִלְטוּל גּוּפֵיהּ, לָאו מִשּׁוּם הוֹצָאָה הִיא?!

The Gemara rejects this: **Say that you heard Beit Shammai** prohibit **carrying out** an object from one domain to another; **did you hear** that they prohibited **moving** an object? The Gemara rejects that distinction: **And isn't** the prohibition of **moving itself** a decree issued **due to** the prohibition of **carrying out?**[N] One who prohibits carrying out certainly prohibits moving an object as well.

וְאַף רַב סָבַר לַהּ לְהָא דְּרָבָא, דְּאָמַר רַב: מַר שֶׁלֹּא יִגָּנֵב – זֶהוּ טִלְטוּל שֶׁלֹּא לְצוֹרֶךְ, וְאָסוּר. טַעְמָא – שֶׁלֹּא יִגָּנֵב, אֲבָל לְצוֹרֶךְ גּוּפוֹ וּלְצוֹרֶךְ מְקוֹמוֹ – מוּתָּר.

The Gemara adds: **And even Rav holds** in accordance with **this** *halakha* of **Rava, as Rav said:** Moving **a hoe** so **that** it will **not be stolen; that is** an example of **moving** an object **not for a** specific **purpose,**[H] **and it is prohibited.** The Gemara infers: **The reason** that it is prohibited **is that** it is moved **so it will not be stolen; however, for the purpose of** utilizing the object **itself and for the purpose of** utilizing **its place,** it is **permitted.**

אִינִי?! וְהָא רַב כָּהֲנָא אִיקְּלַע לְבֵי רַב, וְאָמַר: אַיְיתוּ לֵיהּ שׁוּתָא לְכָהֲנָא לֵיתֵיב עֲלֵיהּ. לָאו לְמֵימְרָא דְּדָבָר שֶׁמְּלַאכְתּוֹ לְאִיסּוּר לְצוֹרֶךְ גּוּפוֹ – אִין, לְצוֹרֶךְ מְקוֹמוֹ – לָא?

The Gemara asks: **Is that so? Didn't Rav Kahana happen** to come **to the house of Rav, and** he **said: Bring a net for Kahana** so that he may **sit on** it? **Is that not to say that** with regard to **an object whose** primary **function is prohibited, for the purpose of** utilizing the object **itself, yes,** it is permitted to move it; and **for the purpose of** utilizing **its place, no,** it is prohibited?

הָכִי אָמַר לְהוּ: שְׁקוֹלוּ שׁוּתָא מִקַּמֵּי כָּהֲנָא. וְאִי בָּעֵית אֵימָא: הָתָם מֵחַמָּה לַצֵּל הֲוָה.

The Gemara answers that **this is what he said to them: Remove** the **net from before Kahana.** That is a case of moving for the purpose of utilizing its place. **And if you wish, say** instead: **There,** it was a case of moving the object **from the sun to the shade,** as it was in a place where it could have been damaged. One might have mistakenly concluded that this was the reason that they were moving the net. Rav specified that the net was being moved for the purpose of utilizing the object itself, not to indicate that moving it for the purpose of utilizing its place is prohibited, but to indicate that moving from the sun to the shade is prohibited.

רַב מָרִי בַּר רָחֵל הֲוָה לֵיהּ הָהִיא בֵּי סַדְיָותָא בְּשִׁמְשָׁא. אֲתָא לְקַמֵּיהּ דְּרָבָא. אֲמַר לֵיהּ: מַהוּ לְטַלְטוּלִינְהוּ? אֲמַר לֵיהּ: שָׁרֵי. אִית לִי אַחֲרִינָא. חֲזוּ לְאוֹרְחִין. אִית לִי נַמִּי לְאוֹרְחִים. אֲמַר לֵיהּ: גַּלִּית אַדַּעְתִּיךְ דִּכְרַבָּה סְבִירָא לָךְ, לְכוּלֵּי עָלְמָא – שָׁרֵי, לְדִידָךְ – אָסִיר.

The Gemara relates that **Rav Mari bar Raḥel, had felt cushions in the sun** on Shabbat. Rav Mari **came before Rava** and **said to him: What is** the ruling with regard **to carrying them?** Rava **said to him: It is permitted.** Rav Mari said to Rava: **I have others,** and I do not need these cushions specifically. Rava said to him: Even so, these cushions are **suitable for guests.** Rav Mari said to him: **I also have** others **for guests and therefore** would be moving the cushions so that they would not be ruined in the sun. Rava **said to him: You have revealed your opinion** that **you hold in accordance with** the opinion of **Rabba. For everyone** else, **it is permitted** to move the cushions in this situation; however, **for you, it is prohibited,**[N] as it is inappropriate to permit one to perform an action that he considers prohibited.

אָמַר רַבִּי אַבָּא אָמַר רַבִּי חִיָּיא בַּר אַשִׁי אָמַר רַב: מַכְבֵּדוֹת שֶׁל מֵילְתָא – מוּתָּר לְטַלְטְלָן בְּשַׁבָּת, אֲבָל שֶׁל תְּמָרָה – לָא.

Rabbi Abba said that **Rabbi Ḥiyya bar Ashi said** that **Rav said:** With regard to **brooms** made **of fine wool** garments,[NH] **it is permitted to move them on Shabbat** because it is permitted to use them. **However,** brooms made **of date-palm** fronds, **no,** they may not be moved. It is prohibited to fill holes in the ground.

רַבִּי אֶלְעָזָר אוֹמֵר: אַף שֶׁל תְּמָרָה. בְּמַאי עָסְקִינַן? אִילֵימָא לְצוֹרֶךְ גּוּפוֹ וּלְצוֹרֶךְ מְקוֹמוֹ – בְּהָא לֵימָא רַב "שֶׁל תְּמָרָה לָא"? וְהָא רַב כְּרָבָא סְבִירָא לֵיהּ! אֶלָּא מֵחַמָּה לַצֵּל, בְּהָא לֵימָא רַבִּי אֶלְעָזָר "אַף שֶׁל תְּמָרָה"?! לְעוֹלָם מֵחַמָּה לַצֵּל, אֵימָא: וְכֵן אָמַר רַבִּי אֶלְעָזָר.

Rabbi Elazar says: It is permitted to move **even** those made **of date-palm** fronds. The Gemara asks: **With what are we dealing? If you say** that this is referring to moving it **for the purpose of** utilizing the object **itself and for the purpose of** utilizing **its place, would Rav say** a broom made **of date-palm** fronds, **no,** it may not be moved? **Doesn't Rav hold in accordance with** the opinion of **Rava? Rather,** this is referring to moving the broom **from the sun to the shade,** and that these brooms are in a place where they can be damaged. However, it is still puzzling: **In this** case, **would Rabbi Elazar say** that **even** brooms made **from date-palm** fronds may be moved? The Gemara answers: **Actually,** this is referring to moving them **from the sun,** where they will be damaged, **to the shade.** Emend this and **say: And so too, Rabbi Elazar said,**[N] like Rav, that it is prohibited.

מתני׳ כָּל הַכֵּלִים הַנִּיטָּלִין בְּשַׁבָּת – שִׁבְרֵיהֶן נִיטָּלִין עִמָּהֶן, וּבִלְבַד שֶׁיְּהוּ עוֹשִׂין מֵעֵין מְלָאכָה.

MISHNA **All vessels that may be moved on Shabbat, their shards may be moved along with them,**[H] **as long as they are suited for some purpose.**

NOTES

And isn't the prohibition of moving itself a decree issued due to the prohibition of carrying out – וְטִלְטוּל גּוּפֵיהּ, לָאו מִשּׁוּם הוֹצָאָה הִיא: Rashi understands this statement to mean that the decree of set-aside was issued only to prevent carrying objects from one domain to another. It is permitted to move certain objects in order to facilitate delighting in Shabbat and to enable performing necessary activities on Shabbat.

For you, it is prohibited – לְדִידָךְ אָסִיר: This prohibition is based on the principle that one rendered it for himself a prohibited object. When one claims a particular item is prohibited, that item becomes prohibited for him, although his claim does not prohibit the item for others.

Brooms made of fine wool garments – מַכְבֵּדוֹת שֶׁל מֵילְתָא: The *ge'onim* explain this as referring to brushes used to clean fine wool garments. Clothes brushes are made out of other materials.

And so too, Rabbi Elazar said – וְכֵן אָמַר רַבִּי אֶלְעָזָר: *Ba'al Halakhot Gedolot* cites a variant reading of the *ge'onim*: Rabbi Elazar holds in accordance with the opinion of Rabbi Shimon. Rabbi Shimon, who holds that it is permitted to perform an unintentional act from which a prohibited labor might ensue, also permits sweeping the house with brooms made of palm fronds. Therefore, it is permitted to move them as well.

HALAKHA

Moving an object not for a specific purpose – טִלְטוּל שֶׁלֹּא לְצוֹרֶךְ: It is prohibited to move an object whose primary function is prohibited in order to protect it from theft or destruction, which is neither for the purpose of utilizing the object for itself nor for utilizing its location (Rambam *Sefer Zemanim, Hilkhot Shabbat* 25:3; *Shulḥan Arukh, Oraḥ Ḥayyim* 308:3).

Brooms made of fine wool garments – מַכְבֵּדוֹת שֶׁל מֵילְתָא: According to most authorities, it is permitted on Shabbat to move a broom and to use it to sweep the floor. Since it is permitted to sweep on Shabbat, a broom is considered to be an object whose primary function is permitted. The authorities who prohibit sweeping with brooms made of palm fronds (Rema and others) also prohibit moving them (*Magen Avraham*; Rambam *Sefer Zemanim, Hilkhot Shabbat* 26:2; *Shulḥan Arukh, Oraḥ Ḥayyim* 308:49).

All vessels that may be moved on Shabbat, their shards may be moved along with them – כָּל הַכֵּלִים הַנִּיטָּלִין בְּשַׁבָּת שִׁבְרֵיהֶן נִיטָּלִין עִמָּהֶן: It is permitted to move the shards of a utensil whose original function is permitted if the shards can be utilized for any purpose, even if the utensil broke on Shabbat, in accordance with the unattributed mishna. If the shards are not suitable for use, it is prohibited to move them unless they pose a potential hazard (*Kol Bo*; *Mordekhai*; and others). According to the opinion that it is prohibited to move objects that came into being on Shabbat, it is permitted to move the shards, provided they can be used for the original purpose of the utensil (Rambam *Sefer Zemanim, Hilkhot Shabbat* 26:3; *Shulḥan Arukh, Oraḥ Ḥayyim* 308:6).

שִׁבְרֵי עֲרֵיבָה – לְכַסּוֹת בָּהֶן אֶת פִּי הֶחָבִית, שִׁבְרֵי זְכוּכִית – לְכַסּוֹת בָּהֶן אֶת פִּי הַפַּךְ.

Shards of a large **bowl** may be used **to cover the mouth of a barrel. Shards of** a **glass** vessel[N] may be used **to cover the mouth of a cruse.**

רַבִּי יְהוּדָה אוֹמֵר: בִּלְבַד שֶׁיְּהוּ עוֹשִׂין מֵעֵין מְלַאכְתָּן; שִׁבְרֵי עֲרֵיבָה – לָצוּק לְתוֹכָן מִקְפָּה, וְשֶׁל זְכוּכִית – לָצוּק לְתוֹכָן שֶׁמֶן.

Rabbi Yehuda **says: As long as they are suited for a purpose similar to their** original **use. Shards of** a large **bowl** must be suited **to pour soup into them, and shards of a glass** vessel must be suited **to pour oil into them.**

גמ׳ אָמַר רַב יְהוּדָה אָמַר שְׁמוּאֵל: מַחֲלוֹקֶת שֶׁנִּשְׁבְּרוּ מֵעֶרֶב שַׁבָּת, דְּמָר סָבַר: מֵעֵין מְלַאכְתָּן – אִין, מֵעֵין מְלָאכָה אַחֶרֶת – לָא. וּמָר סָבַר: אֲפִילּוּ מֵעֵין מְלָאכָה אַחֶרֶת.

GEMARA Rav Yehuda said that **Shmuel said:** This **dispute** in the mishna is only with regard to a case **where** the vessels **broke on Shabbat eve, as this Sage,** Rabbi Yehuda, **holds** that if they are suited for a purpose **similar to their** original **use, yes,** it is permitted, and for **some other use, no,** it is prohibited. **And this Sage,** the Rabbis, **hold: Even** if they are suited **for some other use,** it is also permitted.

אֲבָל נִשְׁבְּרוּ בְּשַׁבָּת – דִּבְרֵי הַכֹּל מוּתָּרִין. הוֹאִיל וּמוּכָנִין עַל גַּבֵּי אֲבִיהֶן – מוּתָּר.

But if the vessels **broke on Shabbat, everyone agrees they are permitted.** The reason for this is **since they were** designated for Shabbat use and consequently considered **prepared** at the onset of Shabbat **due to their original** vessels, **it is permitted** to move the shards as well.

מוֹתִיב רַב זוּטְרַאי: מַסִּיקִין בְּכֵלִים וְאֵין מַסִּיקִין בְּשִׁבְרֵי כֵלִים.

Rav Zutrai raised an objection from a *baraita*: **One may kindle** a fire on a Festival **with whole vessels, but one may not kindle** a fire **with shards of vessels.**

דְּנִשְׁבְּרוּ אֵימַת? אִילֵימָא דְּנִשְׁבְּרוּ מֵעֶרֶב יוֹם טוֹב – עֵצִים בְּעָלְמָא נִינְהוּ! אֶלָּא לָאו – בְּיוֹם טוֹב, וְקָתָנֵי "מַסִּיקִין בְּכֵלִים וְאֵין מַסִּיקִים בְּשִׁבְרֵי כֵלִים"!

The Gemara seeks to clarify: Vessels **that were broken when? If you say** that **they were broken before the Festival,** why is it prohibited to light a fire with them? **They are** pieces of **ordinary wood. Isn't** this referring to a case where they broke **on the Festival, and it is taught: One may kindle** a fire on a Festival **with** whole **vessels, but one may not kindle** a fire **with shards of vessels.** The legal status of a vessel broken on a Festival, and all the more so one broken on Shabbat, is more stringent, not less.

אֶלָּא, אִי אִיתְּמַר הָכִי אִיתְּמַר, אָמַר רַב יְהוּדָה אָמַר שְׁמוּאֵל: מַחֲלוֹקֶת שֶׁנִּשְׁבְּרוּ בְּשַׁבָּת, דְּמָר סָבַר: מוּכָן הוּא, וּמָר סָבַר: נוֹלָד הוּא. אֲבָל מֵעֶרֶב שַׁבָּת – דִּבְרֵי הַכֹּל מוּתָּרִין הוֹאִיל וְהוּכְנוּ לִמְלָאכָה מִבְּעוֹד יוֹם.

Rather, if it was stated, it was stated as follows. Rav Yehuda said that **Shmuel said:** This **dispute** in the mishna is only with regard to a case **where** the vessels **broke on Shabbat, as this Sage,** the Rabbis, **holds it was prepared** before Shabbat as part of the original vessel, **and this Sage,** Rabbi Yehuda, **holds** that **it** is an item that **came into being** on Shabbat. Since they were not shards before Shabbat, they are a new entity and are set-aside. **However,** if they were broken **from before** the onset of **Shabbat everyone agrees** that it is **permitted** to move them, **since they were prepared to** serve some **function while it was still day,** before the onset of Shabbat.

וְתָנֵי חֲדָא: מַסִּיקִין בְּכֵלִים וְאֵין מַסִּיקִין בְּשִׁבְרֵי כֵלִים. וְתַנְיָא אִידָּךְ: כְּשֵׁם שֶׁמַּסִּיקִין בְּכֵלִים כָּךְ מַסִּיקִין בְּשִׁבְרֵי כֵלִים. וְתַנְיָא אִידָּךְ: אֵין מַסִּיקִין לֹא בְּכֵלִים וְלֹא בְּשִׁבְרֵי כֵלִים.

With regard to the *halakhot* of Festivals, **it was taught** in **one** *baraita*: **One may kindle** a fire **with** whole **vessels, but one may not kindle** a fire **with shards of vessels. And it was taught** in the **other** *baraita*: **Just as one may kindle** a fire **with vessels, so** too, **one may kindle** a fire **with shards of vessels. And it was taught** in yet **another** *baraita*: **One may neither kindle** a fire **with vessels nor with shards of vessels.**

הָא – רַבִּי יְהוּדָה, הָא – רַבִּי שִׁמְעוֹן, הָא – רַבִּי נְחֶמְיָה.

The Gemara resolves the apparent contradiction between the *baraitot*: **This** *baraita*, which distinguishes between vessels and broken vessels, **is** in accordance with the opinion of **Rabbi Yehuda,** who holds that there is a prohibition of set-aside on a Festival. **That** *baraita*, which permits kindling with both vessels and shards, **is** in accordance with the opinion of **Rabbi Shimon,** who holds that there is no prohibition of set-aside on a Festival. **This** third *baraita*, which prohibits kindling with both vessels and shards, **is** in accordance with the opinion of **Rabbi Neḥemya,** who prohibits moving a vessel for any purpose other than its designated function.

אָמַר רַב נַחְמָן: הָנֵי לִיבְנֵי דְּאִישְׁתַּיּוּר מִבִּנְיָינָא – שָׁרֵי לְטַלְטוּלִינְהוּ, דַּחֲזוּ לְמֵיזְגָּא עֲלַיְיהוּ. שַׂרְגִינְהוּ – וַדַּאי אַקְצִינְהוּ.

Rav Naḥman said: With regard to **these bricks that remained from the building**[H] after construction was completed, **it is permitted to move them** on Shabbat, because **they are suited** for one **to sit on them.** And if **one arranged them** in a pile, he **certainly** thereby **set them aside** from his consciousness, and it is prohibited to move them.

NOTES

Shards of a glass vessel – שִׁבְרֵי זְכוּכִית: The Sages of the Jerusalem Talmud asked: Why doesn't the Gemara state that a shard of glass can be utilized to cut something, just as is stated in the mishna, which deals with the laws of carrying from domain to domain? They offer two answers: The first is that the Gemara is discussing a shard of glass that is not sharp enough to cut something. The second is that there is a distinction in size between an object large enough to be considered significant with regard to the prohibited labor of carrying out on the one hand, and a smaller size which is sufficient to remove an object from the category of set-aside [*muktze*].

HALAKHA

These bricks that remained from the building – הָנֵי לִיבְנֵי דְּאִישְׁתַּיּוּר מִבִּנְיָינָא: It is permitted to move for one's own use bricks that remain from constructing a building because he no longer intends to build with them, but to use them for sitting and the like. If the bricks are arranged in a stack, which indicates that the builder intends to use them for building and they are therefore set-aside, it is prohibited to move them even for the purpose of utilizing the object for itself or for making use of its location (*Magen Avraham*; *Mishna Berura*). This is in accordance with the opinion of Rav Naḥman (Rambam *Sefer Zemanim*, *Hilkhot Shabbat* 26:2; *Shulḥan Arukh*, *Oraḥ Ḥayyim* 308:17).

HALAKHA

A small earthenware shard – חֶרֶס קְטַנָּה: It is permitted to move for a specific purpose an earthenware shard that broke off of a vessel either on Shabbat or during the week (*Magen Avraham*). This applies everywhere, including the public domain, in accordance with the opinion of Rava, who is a later *amora*, and in accordance with the action, which is greater as a halakhic source. However, one must be certain not to carry four cubits in the public domain because he would thereby violate a Torah prohibition (Rambam *Sefer Zemanim*, *Hilkhot Shabbat* 26:3; *Shulḥan Arukh*, *Oraḥ Ḥayyim* 308:7).

NOTES

And one may not break a shard – וְלֹא יִסְפּוֹת...שֶׁבֶר: Some commentaries explain that one may not cut, nor even merely smooth over, protrusions of shards to render them usable (Rashi and others). Others explain that this means that it is prohibited to attach two shards together (*Arukh*).

אָמַר רַב נַחְמָן אָמַר שְׁמוּאֵל: חֶרֶס קְטַנָּה מוּתָּר לְטַלְטֵל בֶּחָצֵר, אֲבָל בְּכַרְמְלִית – לֹא. וְרַב נַחְמָן דִּידֵיהּ אָמַר: אֲפִילּוּ בְּכַרְמְלִית, אֲבָל בִּרְשׁוּת הָרַבִּים – לֹא. וְרָבָא אָמַר: אֲפִילּוּ בִּרְשׁוּת הָרַבִּים.

Rav Naḥman said that **Shmuel said:** With regard to **a small earthenware shard,**[H] **it is permitted to move** it on Shabbat **in the courtyard,** because there are vessels there that need to be covered; **but in a** ***karmelit*****, no,** one may not move it, because typically there are no vessels there and there would be no use for the shard. **And Rav Naḥman himself said: Even in a** ***karmelit*** it is permitted, **but in the public domain, no,** it is prohibited. **And Rava said: Even in the public domain,** it is permitted.

וְאַזְדָּא רָבָא לְטַעְמֵיהּ; דְּרָבָא הֲוָה קָאָזֵיל בְּרִיתְקָא דִּמְחוֹזָא, אִתְוַוסַּאי מְסָאנֵיהּ טִינָא, אֲתָא שַׁמָּעֵיהּ שְׁקַל חַסְפָּא וְקָא מְכַפֵּר לֵיהּ, רָמוּ בֵּיהּ רַבָּנַן קָלָא. אֲמַר: לָא מִיסְתַּיָּיא דְּלָא גְּמִירִי, מִיגְמַר נַמִי מַגְמְרִי?! אִילּוּ בֶּחָצֵר הֲוָאי – מִי לָא הֲוָה חַזְיָא לְכַסּוּיֵי בֵּיהּ מָנָא? הָכָא נַמִי – חַזְיָא לְדִידִי.

And Rava follows his regular line of **reasoning, as Rava was walking in the street of Meḥoza and his shoes became dirty with clay. His servant came, took** a shard of **earthenware** from the street, **and wiped** the clay off. **The Sages raised** their **voice at him** to reprimand him. Rava **said: Is it not enough** for them that **they did not learn,** but **they are also teaching** others? **If** the shard **was in a courtyard, wouldn't it be suited to cover a vessel with it? Here too,** the shard **is also suited to me,** and moving it should not be prohibited.

אָמַר רַב יְהוּדָה אָמַר שְׁמוּאֵל: מְגוּפַת חָבִית שֶׁנִּכְתְּתָה – מוּתָּר לְטַלְטֵל בְּשַׁבָּת. תַּנְיָא נַמִי הָכִי: מְגוּפָה שֶׁנִּכְתְּתָה – הִיא וּשְׁבָרֶיהָ מוּתָּר לְטַלְטְלָהּ בְּשַׁבָּת, וְלֹא יִסְפּוֹת מִמֶּנָּה שֶׁבֶר לְכַסּוֹת בָּהּ אֶת הַכְּלִי וְלִסְמוֹךְ בָּהּ כַּרְעֵי הַמִּטָּה, וְאִם זְרָקָהּ בָּאַשְׁפָּה – אָסוּר.

Rav Yehuda said that **Shmuel said:** With regard to **the clay seal of a jug that was broken, it is permitted to move** it **on Shabbat. That was also taught** in a *baraita*: With regard to **the clay seal that was broken, it is permitted to move it, and its shards are permitted to be carried on Shabbat. And one may not break a shard**[N] **from it to cover a vessel with it or to support the legs of a bed with it. And if one threw it into the garbage dump, it is prohibited** to move it because he set it aside from his consciousness.

מַתְקִיף לָהּ רַב פַּפָּא: אֶלָּא מֵעַתָּה, זָרֵיק לֵיהּ לִגְלִימֵיהּ – הָכִי נַמִי דְּאָסוּר? אֶלָּא אָמַר רַב פַּפָּא:

Rav Pappa strongly objects to this: If that is **so,** if **one throws his cloak** into the garbage dump, would you **also** say that **it is prohibited** to move it because it is set-aside? Isn't the cloak still fit for use, and its status is not dependent on his intention? **Rather, Rav Pappa said:**

Perek **XVII**
Daf **125** Amud **a**

NOTES

Remains of cloaks – שְׁיָרֵי פְרוֹזְמִיּוֹת: The Ra'avad explains that this refers specifically to the remains of a prayer shawl, as it is indecent to use an object that was used for a mitzva for certain purposes. However, other small rags that are fit for use to wipe surfaces may be moved on Shabbat.

LANGUAGE

Cloaks [*perozemiyyot*] – פְּרוֹזְמִיּוֹת: From the Greek **περίζωμα**, *perizoma*, meaning hips, a girdle worn around the loins, or a garment placed over the thighs.

אִם זְרָקָהּ מִבְּעוֹד יוֹם לָאַשְׁפָּה – אֲסוּרָה.

If one threw the clay seal of a jug **into the garbage dump while it** is still **day,** before Shabbat, **it is prohibited** to move it on Shabbat because he indicated that he set it aside from use.

אָמַר בַּר הַמְדוּרִי אָמַר שְׁמוּאֵל: קְרוּמִיּוֹת שֶׁל מַחְצֶלֶת מוּתָּר לְטַלְטְלָם בְּשַׁבָּת. מַאי טַעְמָא? אָמַר רָבָא, בַּר הַמְדוּרִי אַסְבְּרָא לִי: מַחְצֶלֶת גּוּפָא לְמַאי חַזְיָא – לְכַסּוּיֵי בֵּיהּ עַפְרָא, הָנֵי נַמִי חַזְיָין לְכַסּוּיֵי בְּהוּ טִינּוֹפֶת.

Bar Hamduri said that **Shmuel said:** With regard to **shreds** of reeds that separated **from a mat,**[H] **it is permitted to move them on Shabbat.** The Gemara asks: **What is the reason** for this? **Rava said: Bar Hamduri explained** it **to me:** The **mat itself, for what** use is it **suited?** It is suited **to cover dirt with it. These** shreds, **too, are suited to cover filth with them.**

אָמַר רַבִּי זֵירָא אָמַר רַב: שְׁיָרֵי פְרוֹזְמִיּוֹת אָסוּר לְטַלְטְלָן בְּשַׁבָּת. אָמַר אַבַּיֵי: בִּמְטַלְנִיּוֹת שֶׁאֵין בָּהֶן שָׁלֹשׁ עַל שָׁלֹשׁ, דְּלָא חַזְיָין לֹא לַעֲנִיִּים וְלֹא לַעֲשִׁירִים.

Rabbi Zeira said that **Rav said:** With regard to **the remains of cloaks** [*perozemiyyot*],[NL] **it is prohibited to move them on Shabbat. Abaye said:** This is referring to **small rags that do not have** an area of **three by three** fingerbreadths,[H] **that are neither suited** for use **by the poor nor by the wealthy.**

HALAKHA

Shreds of reeds that separated from a mat – קְרוּמִיּוֹת שֶׁל מַחְצֶלֶת: It is permitted to move the remains of a mat on Shabbat, even from the sun into the shade, because they are suited for covering filth. This is the ruling even if the remains are each smaller than three by three fingerbreadths, the minimal size a rag must be in order for it to be permissible to move it on Shabbat. If they were thrown away before Shabbat, it is prohibited to move them because by throwing them away one has set them aside, thereby preventing their use on Shabbat (Rambam *Sefer Zemanim*, *Hilkhot Shabbat* 26:6; *Shulḥan Arukh*, *Oraḥ Ḥayyim* 308:12).

Small rags that do not have an area of three by three fingerbreadths – מְטַלְנִיּוֹת שֶׁאֵין בָּהֶן שָׁלֹשׁ עַל שָׁלֹשׁ: On Shabbat, it is prohibited to move rags that are smaller than three by three fingerbreadths in size, as per the opinion of Abaye. Some authorities permit moving rags even smaller than three by three fingerbreadths because they are usable (*Magen Avraham*). If the rags are the remains of an object used for a mitzva, e.g., a prayer shawl, it is prohibited to use them (Rambam *Sefer Zemanim*, *Hilkhot Shabbat* 26:6; *Shulḥan Arukh*, *Oraḥ Ḥayyim* 308:13).

תָּנוּ רַבָּנַן: שִׁבְרֵי תַּנּוּר יָשָׁן הֲרֵי הֵן כְּכָל הַכֵּלִים הַנִּיטָּלִין בֶּחָצֵר. דִּבְרֵי רַבִּי מֵאִיר. רַבִּי יְהוּדָה אוֹמֵר: אֵין נִיטָּלִין. הֵעִיד רַבִּי יוֹסֵי מִשּׁוּם רַבִּי אֱלִיעֶזֶר בֶּן יַעֲקֹב: עַל שִׁבְרֵי תַּנּוּר יָשָׁן שֶׁנִּיטָּלִין בַּשַּׁבָּת, וְעַל כִּיסּוּיוֹ שֶׁאֵינוֹ צָרִיךְ בֵּית יָד.

The Sages taught in the *Tosefta*: The **shards of an old oven**[H] may be moved in a courtyard on Shabbat **like all of the vessels that may be moved in a courtyard** on Shabbat; this is the **statement of Rabbi Meir. Rabbi Yehuda says: They may not be moved. Rabbi Yosei testified in the name of Rabbi Eliezer ben Ya'akov about shards of an old oven that may be moved on Shabbat, and about its cover,**[H] **which does not require a handle.**

בְּמַאי קָמִיפַּלְגִי? אָמַר אַבָּיֵי: בְּעוֹשִׂין מֵעֵין מְלָאכָה, וְאֵין עוֹשִׂין מֵעֵין מְלַאכְתָּן קָמִיפַּלְגִי, וְאַזְדָּא רַבִּי יְהוּדָה לְטַעְמֵיהּ, וְרַבִּי מֵאִיר לְטַעְמֵיהּ.

The Gemara asks: **With regard to what do they disagree? Abaye said:** It is with regard to shards **when they serve some function but do not serve a function similar to their own** original function that **they disagree. And Rabbi Yehuda follows his** own line of **reasoning, and Rabbi Meir follows his** own line of **reasoning,** as they differed in the mishna.

מַתְקִיף לַהּ רָבָא: אִי הָכִי, אַדְּמִיפַּלְגִי בְּשִׁבְרֵי תַּנּוּר – לִיפַּלְגוּ בְּשִׁבְרֵי כֵּלִים בְּעָלְמָא!

Rava strongly objects to this: If so, instead **of disagreeing with regard to shards of an oven, let them disagree with regard to ordinary shards.** Why is the dispute specifically with regard to an oven?[N]

אֶלָּא אָמַר רָבָא: בְּשִׁבְרֵי דְּהַאי תַּנּוּר קָמִיפַּלְגִי, דִּתְנַן: נְתָנוֹ עַל פִּי הַבּוֹר אוֹ עַל פִּי הַדּוּת וְנָתַן שָׁם אֶבֶן, רַבִּי יְהוּדָה אוֹמֵר: אִם מַסִּיק מִלְּמַטָּה וְהוּא נִסּוֹק מִלְמַעְלָה – טָמֵא, וְאִם לָאו – טָהוֹר. וַחֲכָמִים אוֹמְרִים: הוֹאִיל וְהוּסַּק מִכָּל מָקוֹם טָמֵא.

Rather, Rava said: It is **with regard to shards of this** particular **oven that they disagree, as we learned** in a mishna: With regard to a clay oven that is not attached to the ground with mortar in the standard manner, but rather, **one placed it over the mouth of a pit**[NB] **or over the mouth of a cistern, and he placed a stone there** between the wall of the pit and the oven to secure the oven in place, **Rabbi Yehuda says: If one heats** the oven **from beneath** the oven, inside the pit, **and** the oven **is** thereby **heated at the top,** the oven serves its standard function; it is a full-fledged utensil and it can become **ritually impure. And if** it is **not** attached so tightly that it is heated at the top, it is **ritually pure,** because it is not a full-fledged vessel. **And the Rabbis say: Since it can be heated in some manner,** it can become **ritually impure,** because it serves its standard purpose.

וּבְמַאי קָמִיפַּלְגִי – בְּהַאי קְרָא: ״תַּנּוּר וְכִירַיִם יוּתָּץ טְמֵאִים הֵם וּטְמֵאִים יִהְיוּ לָכֶם״. רַבִּי יְהוּדָה סָבַר: מְחוּסַּר נְתִיצָה – טָמֵא, שֶׁאֵין מְחוּסַּר נְתִיצָה – טָהוֹר. וְרַבָּנַן סָבְרִי: ״טְמֵאִים יִהְיוּ לָכֶם״ – מִכָּל מָקוֹם.

And with regard to what do they disagree? It is **with regard to this verse:** "And everything upon which any part of their carcass falls shall be impure; **whether oven, or stove, it shall be broken in pieces; they are impure, and they shall be impure to you"** (Leviticus 11:35). **Rabbi Yehuda holds:** An oven that **lacks smashing,** i.e., it is whole and can be broken, can become **impure.** One **that does not lack smashing,** but it is situated in a place where it is not completely effective, is considered broken and is **pure,** i.e., it cannot become ritually impure. **And the Rabbis hold** that the verse comes to add: **"They shall be impure to you," in any case,** under any circumstances.

וְרַבָּנַן נַמִי, הָכְתִיב ״יוּתָּץ״! הַהוּא לְאִידָךְ גִּיסָא. דְּסָלְקָא דַּעְתָּךְ אָמִינָא: כֵּיוָן דְּחַבְּרֵיהּ בְּאַרְעָא – כְּגוּפָא דְּאַרְעָא דָּמֵי, קָא מַשְׁמַע לַן.

The Gemara asks: **And** according to **the Rabbis, too, isn't it written: "They shall be broken into pieces,"** and why don't they interpret the verse in the same way that Rabbi Yehuda does? The Gemara explains: The Rabbis understand **this verse from another direction, as it could have entered your mind to say: Since he attached it to the ground,** its legal status is **like that of the ground itself,** and anything attached to the ground cannot become impure. Therefore, **it teaches us** that since it is possible to detach it from the ground, it is indeed impure.

וְאִידָךְ נַמִי, הָכְתִיב: ״טְמֵאִים יִהְיוּ לָכֶם״! הַהִיא כִּדְרַב יְהוּדָה אָמַר שְׁמוּאֵל, דְּאָמַר רַב יְהוּדָה אָמַר שְׁמוּאֵל: מַחֲלוֹקֶת בְּהֶיסֵּק רִאשׁוֹן, אֲבָל בְּהֶיסֵּק שֵׁנִי – אֲפִילּוּ תָּלוּי בְּצַוַּאר גָּמָל.

The Gemara asks: **And** according to **the other** *tanna*, Rabbi Yehuda, **too, isn't it written: "They shall be impure to you"?** The Gemara answers: He understood **that** verse **in accordance with** that which **Rav Yehuda** said that **Shmuel said, as Rav Yehuda said** that **Shmuel said:** The **dispute** between Rabbi Yehuda and the Rabbis **is** specifically **with regard to the first lighting.** The first lighting transforms an earthenware oven that did not yet completely dry into a vessel. **However, with regard to the second lighting** they do not disagree, **even** if it was **hanging around a camel's neck;**[H] since it had already been fired up once, it is impure.

HALAKHA

Shards of an old oven – שִׁבְרֵי תַּנּוּר יָשָׁן: It is permitted to move shards of an oven on Shabbat if they can still be used in a manner similar to the way the oven is used (*Maggid Mishne*). This is in accordance with the opinion of Rabbi Meir, to whom unattributed *mishnayot* are generally attributed, and the opinions of Rabbi Yosei and Rabbi Eliezer ben Ya'akov (Rambam *Sefer Zemanim*, *Hilkhot Shabbat* 26:6).

About its cover – עַל כִּיסּוּיוֹ: It is permitted to move vessel covers on Shabbat, even those without a handle. This applies only to objects that were already used to cover vessels, as per the opinion of Rabbi Eliezer ben Ya'akov (Rambam *Sefer Zemanim*, *Hilkhot Shabbat* 25:13; *Shulḥan Arukh*, *Oraḥ Ḥayyim* 308:10).

Even if it was hanging around a camel's neck – אֲפִילּוּ תָּלוּי בְּצַוַּאר גָּמָל: An oven that is not connected to the ground, even one hanging around the neck of a camel, can still become ritually impure like any other oven, as per the opinion of the Rabbis in the mishna in tractate *Kelim* (Rambam *Sefer Tahara*, *Hilkhot Kelim* 15:8).

NOTES

Rava's opinion in explaining the *Tosefta* – שִׁיטַת רָבָא בְּבֵיאוּר הַתּוֹסֶפְתָּא: The early commentaries wondered about the connection between the ritual impurity of an oven and whether or not it may be moved as a vessel on Shabbat. According to Rava, an object that is not considered a vessel with regard to impurity is not considered a vessel with regard to Shabbat. Therefore, it is prohibited to move its shards (see Ramban; Rashba; *Tosefot Rid*).

Placed it over the mouth of a pit – נְתָנוֹ עַל פִּי הַבּוֹר: In ancient times, people generally attached their ovens to the ground with mortar, lit a fire inside the oven, and baked. An oven suspended in the airspace of a pit is not considered a full-fledged oven and is not complete. In addition, there is a Torah edict in the verse in Leviticus (11:35) that states that detaching an oven from the ground renders the oven incomplete. According to Shmuel, even if the oven was fired for the first time, and was thereby rendered a vessel in an unusual manner, its status is not that of a full-fledged vessel.

BACKGROUND

Oven over the mouth of a pit – תַּנּוּר עַל פִּי בּוֹר: The oven over the mouth of a pit is supported by stones alongside the pit. The oven is heated by igniting a fire inside the pit.

Oven over the mouth of a pit

אָמַר עוּלָּא: וְהֶיסֵּק רִאשׁוֹן לְרַבָּנַן – אֲפִילּוּ תָּלוּי בְּצַוַּאר גָּמָל.

Ulla says: And with regard to **the first lighting** according **to the Rabbis, even** if it was **hanging around a camel's neck,** since it had already been fired up once it is a full-fledged oven and is impure.

מַתְקִיף לַהּ רַב אַשִׁי: אִי הָכִי, אַדְּמִיפַּלְגִי בִּשְׁבָרֵי תַנּוּר – לִיפַּלְגוּ בְּתַנּוּר גּוּפֵהּ! הַשְׁתָּא תַּנּוּר גּוּפֵהּ – לְרַבִּי יְהוּדָה לָא הָוֵי מָנָא, שְׁבָרָיו מִיבַּעְיָא?!

Rav Ashi strongly objects to this line of reasoning: **If so, instead of disagreeing with regard to the shards of an oven, let them disagree with regard to the oven itself. Now the oven itself, according to Rabbi Yehuda, is not** considered **a vessel;** therefore, to say that **its broken pieces** are not vessels, **is it necessary?**

אֶלָּא אָמַר רַב אַשִׁי: לְעוֹלָם כִּדְאָמְרַן מֵעִיקָּרָא, וּבְעוֹשֶׂה מַעֲשֵׂה טַפְקָא; וְרַבִּי מֵאִיר לִדְבָרָיו דְּרַבִּי יְהוּדָה קָאָמַר: לְדִידִי – אֲפִילּוּ בְּעוֹשִׂין מֵעֵין מְלָאכָה, אֶלָּא לְדִידָךְ – אוֹדִי לִי מִיהָא דְּכְהַאי גַּוְונָא מְלַאכְתּוֹ הוּא.

Rather, Rav Ashi said: Actually, it is as we said initially, that it is referring to shards of any oven, **and** with which **he crafts a ceramic board** [*tapka*],[NL] **and Rabbi Meir is speaking in accordance with the statement of Rabbi Yehuda:** According **to my** opinion, it is permitted to move **even** shards that **serve** any **purpose. However, according to your** opinion, **agree with me at least that in a case of this sort, it is a function** similar to their own original function. The shards can be used for baking.

וְרַבִּי יְהוּדָה – לָא דָּמֵי, הָתָם – הֶסֵּקוֹ מִבִּפְנִים, הָכָא – הֶסֵּקוֹ מִבַּחוּץ, הָתָם – מְעוּמָּד, הָכָא – לָאו מְעוּמָּד.

And Rabbi Yehuda says: It is **not similar. There,** in the case of an intact oven, **its firing is from within. Here,** with regard to the shard, **its firing is from without. There,** in the case of an intact oven, it bakes **standing; here,** it does **not** bake **standing.** Therefore, its function is not similar to its original function.

"הֵעִיד רַבִּי יוֹסֵי מִשּׁוּם רַבִּי אֱלִיעֶזֶר בֶּן יַעֲקֹב עַל שִׁבְרֵי תַנּוּר יָשָׁן שֶׁנִּיטָּלִין בַּשַּׁבָּת וְעַל כִּיסּוּיוֹ שֶׁאֵינוֹ צָרִיךְ בֵּית יָד". אָמַר רָבִינָא: כְּמַאן מְטַלְטְלִינַן הָאִידָּנָא כִּיסּוּי דְּתַנּוּרֵי דְּמָתָא מְחַסְיָא דְּאֵין לָהֶם בֵּית אֲחִיזָה, כְּמַאן – כְּרַבִּי אֱלִיעֶזֶר בֶּן יַעֲקֹב.

In that same *Tosefta* where **Rabbi Yosei testified in the name of Rabbi Eliezer ben Ya'akov about shards of an old oven that may be moved on Shabbat, and about its cover, which does not require a handle,** and which is considered a vessel and may be moved as is, **Ravina says: In accordance with whose** opinion **do we now move the oven covers** in **the city of Meḥasya that do not have handles? In accordance with whose** opinion is it? It is **in accordance with** the opinion of **Rabbi Eliezer ben Ya'akov.**

מתני׳ הָאֶבֶן שֶׁבַּקֵּירוּיָה, אִם מְמַלְּאִין בָּהּ וְאֵינָהּ נוֹפֶלֶת – מְמַלְּאִין בָּהּ, וְאִם לָאו – אֵין מְמַלְּאִין בָּהּ.

MISHNA A stone that is in a gourd used to draw water [*kiruya*],[NHB] **if they fill** it with water **and** the stone **does not fall, one may fill with it** on Shabbat, **and if not,** and the stone does fall, **one may not fill with it.**

וְמוֹרָה שֶׁהִיא קְשׁוּרָה בְּטָפִיחַ – מְמַלְּאִין בָּהּ בַּשַּׁבָּת.

With regard to a vine **branch that is tied to a pitcher, one may fill** water **with it on Shabbat** because the branch became part of the vessel.

NOTES

Ceramic board – טַפְקָא: According to Rabbi Yehuda, food is roasted, not baked, on a ceramic board. Therefore, the earthenware shard is not comparable to a complete oven used for baking.

Gourd used to draw water – קֵירוּיָה: According to the Rambam, this is a small, light ceramic vessel used to draw water.

LANGUAGE

Ceramic board [*tapka*] – טַפְקָא: From the Iranian root tap-, meaning to warm up or to heat. The Persian tābag refers to a frying pan.

HALAKHA

A stone that is in a gourd used to draw water – הָאֶבֶן שֶׁבַּקֵּירוּיָה: It is permitted to use a gourd to draw water from a well if the stone inside it to weigh it down is firmly attached and will not fall out when filling the gourd with water. If the stone will fall out, it is prohibited to use the gourd, because the stone is set-aside (Rambam *Sefer Zemanim, Hilkhot Shabbat* 25:18; *Shulḥan Arukh, Oraḥ Ḥayyim* 309:2).

BACKGROUND

A gourd used to draw water – קֵירוּיָה: Different vessels are fashioned from various kinds of gourds, especially from the species *Lagenaria vulgaris*. These vessels include jugs, buckets for drawing water, and dishes. Since these vessels are particularly lightweight and float on water, it is necessary to place a rock inside the gourd to draw water from a well or a stream.

Jugs fashioned from gourds

פְּקַק הַחַלּוֹן, רַבִּי אֱלִיעֶזֶר אוֹמֵר: בִּזְמַן שֶׁהוּא קָשׁוּר וְתָלוּי – פּוֹקְקִין בּוֹ, וְאִם לָאו – אֵין פּוֹקְקִין בּוֹ. וַחֲכָמִים אוֹמְרִים: בֵּין כָּךְ וּבֵין כָּךְ פּוֹקְקִין בּוֹ.

With regard to **a window shutter,**[B] **Rabbi Eliezer says: When it is tied** to **and hanging** from the window, i.e., it is not touching the ground, **one may shutter** the window **with it,** because it is not considered building; **and if not,** i.e., it is touching the ground, **one may not shutter** the window **with it. And the Rabbis say: Both in this** case **and in that** case **one may shutter with it.**

גמ׳ תְּנַן הָתָם: אֶבֶן שֶׁעַל פִּי הֶחָבִית מַטָּה עַל צִידָּהּ וְהִיא נוֹפֶלֶת. אָמַר רַבָּה אָמַר רַבִּי אַמִי אָמַר רַבִּי יוֹחָנָן: לֹא שָׁנוּ אֶלָּא בְּשׁוֹכֵחַ, אֲבָל בְּמַנִּיחַ – נַעֲשָׂה בָּסִיס לְדָבָר הָאָסוּר. וְרַב יוֹסֵף אָמַר רַבִּי אַסִי אָמַר רַבִּי יוֹחָנָן: לֹא שָׁנוּ אֶלָּא בְּשׁוֹכֵחַ, אֲבָל בְּמַנִּיחַ – נַעֲשָׂה כִּיסּוּי לֶחָבִית.

GEMARA We learned in a mishna **there:** In the case of **a stone that is atop a barrel** and one wants to open the barrel, **he tilts** the barrel **on its side and** the stone **falls. Rabba said** that **Rabbi Ami said** that **Rabbi Yoḥanan said: They only taught** this in a case **where one forgets** the stone atop the barrel; **however,** in a case **where one places**[H] the stone atop the barrel intentionally, the barrel **becomes a base for a prohibited object,** and it is therefore prohibited to move the barrel. **And Rav Yosef** said that **Rabbi Asi said** that **Rabbi Yoḥanan said: They only taught** this in a case **where one forgets** it; **however,** in a case **where one places** it there, the stone **becomes a cover for the barrel** and it is permitted to use it like other barrel covers.

אָמַר רַבָּה: מוֹתְבִינַן אַשְׁמַעְתִּין ״הָאֶבֶן שֶׁבַּקֵּירוּיָה אִם מְמַלְּאִין בָּהּ וְאֵינָהּ נוֹפֶלֶת מְמַלְּאִין בָּהּ״! וְלָא הִיא, הָתָם כֵּיוָן דְּהִדְקָהּ – שַׁוְיַא דּוֹפֶן.

Rabba said: We raise an objection to our ***halakha*** from the mishna: With regard to **a stone that is in a gourd** used to draw water, **if they fill it** with water **and** the stone **does not fall, one may fill with it** on Shabbat. Apparently, if the stone is designated for a purpose, it is no longer set-aside. He rejects the proof: **And that is not so,** as these cases are not comparable. **There,** in the case of the stone in the gourd, **since one attached** it to the gourd, **he rendered** the stone **a wall** of the gourd and part of the vessel, unlike in the case of the stone atop the barrel.

אָמַר רַב יוֹסֵף: וּמוֹתְבִינַן אַשְׁמַעְתִּין ״אִם לָאו אֵין מְמַלְּאִין בָּהּ״! וְלָא הִיא, הָתָם כֵּיוָן דְּלָא הִדְקָהּ – בַּטּוֹלֵי בַּטְלָהּ.

Rav Yosef said: And we raise an objection to our ***halakha*** from the mishna: **And if not,** and the stone does fall, **one may not fill with it.** A stone that is not attached is not considered to be part of the vessel and is therefore set-aside. He rejects the proof. **And that is not so,** as these cases are not comparable. **There, since he did not attach** the stone to the gourd, **he negates its** status as a part of the vessel and it remains set-aside.

בְּמַאי קָמִיפַּלְגִי? מָר סָבַר: בָּעֵינַן מַעֲשֶׂה, וּמָר סָבַר: לָא בָּעֵינַן מַעֲשֶׂה.

The Gemara explains: **With regard to what do they disagree? One Sage,** Rabba, **holds** that **we require an action** to change the status of a stone or another set-aside object into a vessel, **and one Sage,** Rav Yosef, **holds** that **we do not require an action.**

וְאָזְדוּ לְטַעֲמַיְיהוּ; דְּכִי אֲתָא רַב דִּימִי אָמַר רַבִּי חֲנִינָא וְאָמְרִי לַהּ אָמַר רַבִּי זֵירָא אָמַר רַבִּי חֲנִינָא: פַּעַם אַחַת הָלַךְ רַבִּי לְמָקוֹם אֶחָד וּמָצָא נִדְבָּךְ שֶׁל אֲבָנִים, וְאָמַר לְתַלְמִידָיו: צְאוּ וְחַשְּׁבוּ כְּדֵי שֶׁנֵּשֵׁב עֲלֵיהֶן לְמָחָר, וְלֹא הִצְרִיכָן רַבִּי לְמַעֲשֶׂה.

And they, Rabbi Ami and Rabbi Asi, **follow their** regular line of **reasoning, as when Rav Dimi came** from Eretz Yisrael to Babylonia he said that **Rabbi Ḥanina said, and some say that** it was **Rabbi Zeira** who **said** that **Rabbi Ḥanina said: Once Rabbi** Yehuda HaNasi **went to one place and found a course of** building **stones,**[H] **and he said to his students: Go out and think** that you are designating these stones for Shabbat **so that we may sit on them tomorrow** on Shabbat, **and Rabbi** Yehuda HaNasi **did not require them** to perform **an action** with those stones. Thought alone was sufficient.

רַבִּי יוֹחָנָן אָמַר: הִצְרִיכָן רַבִּי לְמַעֲשֶׂה. מַאי אָמַר לְהוּ? רַבִּי אַמִי אָמַר: צְאוּ וְלַמְּדוּם אָמַר לְהוּ. רַבִּי אַסִי אָמַר: צְאוּ וְשַׁפְשְׁפוּם אָמַר לְהוּ.

Rabbi Yoḥanan said: That is not what happened. **Rabbi** Yehuda HaNasi **required them** to perform **an action** to designate the stones. The Gemara asks: **What** action **did he say to them** to perform? **Rabbi Ami said** that Rabbi Yehuda HaNasi **said to them: Go out and arrange** the stones.[N] **Rabbi Asi said** that **he said to them: Go out and rub** the mortar off of **them.** Rabbi Ami requires a more significant action to render the stones a vessel.

אִיתְּמַר, רַבִּי יוֹסֵי בֶּן שָׁאוּל אָמַר: סוֹאָר שֶׁל קוֹרוֹת הֲוָה, וְרַבִּי יוֹחָנָן בֶּן שָׁאוּל אָמַר: גְּשׁוֹשׁ שֶׁל סְפִינָה הֲוָה. מַאן דְּאָמַר גְּשׁוֹשׁ – כׇּל שֶׁכֵּן סוֹאָר, וּמַאן דְּאָמַר סוֹאָר, אֲבָל גְּשׁוֹשׁ – קָפֵיד עֲלֵיהּ.

It was stated that there was a dispute with regard to this matter. **Rabbi Yosei ben Shaul said: It was a** new **stack of beams,** not stones. **And Rabbi Yoḥanan ben Shaul said: It was the sounding pole of a ship** used to determine the depth of the water. **The one who said** that Rabbi Yehuda HaNasi permitted sitting on a ship's **sounding pole, all the more so** he permitted doing so in the case of **beams. And** with regard to **the one who said** that Rabbi Yehuda HaNasi permitted sitting on a stack of **beams, but** in the case of the **sounding pole** he would prohibit doing so because it is set-aside due to monetary loss, as he is **particular about it** that it will not become warped and damaged.

BACKGROUND

Window shutter – פְּקַק הַחַלּוֹן: In talmudic times, the window shutter was typically tied to and hanging from the window. At times, wood that was not attached to the window was placed in the window as a shutter. When not in use, it was placed alongside the window and utilized for other purposes as well.

Window shutters resembling those used in talmudic times

HALAKHA

Where one forgets…where one places – בְּשׁוֹכֵחַ...בְּמַנִּיחַ: If one forgets a set-aside item upon a vessel, e.g., a stone atop a barrel, prior to Shabbat, and then wants to take wine from the barrel on Shabbat, it is permitted to tilt the vessel so that the set-aside item will fall. If one placed the set-aside item on the vessel with the intention that it remain there after the start of Shabbat, it is prohibited to tilt or to shake the vessel because the vessel became a base for a prohibited object, in accordance with the opinion of Rabbi Yoḥanan. Some authorities permit tilting the vessel even if one placed the set-aside item on the vessel with the intention that it remain there after the start of Shabbat, if his intention was to remove it on Shabbat. If he intended that it remain in place for the duration of Shabbat, then the vessel becomes a base for a prohibited object (Rambam *Sefer Zemanim, Hilkhot Shabbat* 25:17; *Shulḥan Arukh, Oraḥ Ḥayyim* 309:4).

A course of building stones – נִדְבָּךְ שֶׁל אֲבָנִים: One may not sit on stones designated for construction, even if before Shabbat he thought to utilize them. However, if one arranged the stones before Shabbat, it is permitted to sit on them, in accordance with Rabbi Yoḥanan and the explanation of Rabbi Ami. Some authorities permitted one to use them even if he merely thought to use them before Shabbat, which is the *halakha* in the case of palm fronds (Rema based on the *Maggid Mishne* in the name of the Rif, Ran, and Rosh; Rambam *Sefer Zemanim, Hilkhot Shabbat* 25:21; *Shulḥan Arukh, Oraḥ Ḥayyim* 308:21 and in the comment of the Rema).

NOTES

Go out and arrange the stones – צְאוּ וְלַמְּדוּם: Some commentaries explain this phrase to mean learn to identify them. Each student was instructed to choose a specific stone and identify it. That is sufficient to prepare the stone for use on Shabbat, and no action is necessary (*ge'onim*).

״זְמוֹרָה שֶׁהִיא קְשׁוּרָה כו׳״. קְשׁוּרָה – אִין, לֹא קְשׁוּרָה – לָא, לֵימָא מַתְנִיתִין דְּלָא כְּרַבָּן שִׁמְעוֹן בֶּן גַּמְלִיאֵל,

We learned in the mishna: With regard to a vine **branch that is tied** to a pitcher, one may fill water with it on Shabbat. The Gemara infers: If it is **tied, yes,** it is permitted; if it is **not tied, no,** it is prohibited. **Let us say that the mishna is in accordance with** the opinion of **Rabban Shimon ben Gamliel.**

דְּתַנְיָא: חֲרָיוֹת שֶׁל דֶּקֶל שֶׁגְּדָרָן לְעֵצִים וְנִמְלַךְ עֲלֵיהֶן לִישִׁיבָה – צָרִיךְ לִקְשׁוֹר, רַבָּן שִׁמְעוֹן בֶּן גַּמְלִיאֵל אוֹמֵר: אֵין צָרִיךְ לִקְשׁוֹר.

As it was taught in a *baraita*: With regard to **hard branches of a palm tree**[N] **that one cut for** firewood or for construction, **and** then **he reconsidered their** designation and decided to use them **for sitting, he must tie** the branches together on Shabbat eve so that they will not be set-aside. **Rabban Shimon ben Gamliel says: He need not tie** them together, and nevertheless, it is permitted to move them. According to Rabban Shimon ben Gamliel, cut wood need not be specially prepared to be used on Shabbat.

אָמַר רַב שֵׁשֶׁת: אֲפִילּוּ תֵּימָא רַבָּן שִׁמְעוֹן בֶּן גַּמְלִיאֵל, הָכָא בְּמַאי עָסְקִינַן – בִּמְחוּבֶּרֶת בְּאָבִיהָ. אִי הָכִי קָא מִשְׁתַּמֵּשׁ בִּמְחוּבָּר לַקַּרְקַע! לְמַטָּה מִשְּׁלֹשָׁה. רַב אַשִׁי אָמַר: אֲפִילּוּ תֵּימָא בִּתְלוּשָׁה, גְּזֵירָה שֶׁמָּא יִקְטוֹם.

Rav Sheshet says: Even if **you say** that the mishna is in accordance with the opinion of **Rabban Shimon ben Gamliel, with what are we dealing here? With** a case where the shoot is still **connected to its origin,** the vine.[NH] The Gemara asks: **If so, he is making use** of an item that **is attached to the ground,** and the Sages issued a decree prohibiting the use of any plant attached to the ground. The Gemara answers: This is referring to a branch attached to the vine **below three** handbreadths off the ground. A vine attached to the ground below three handbreadths off the ground was not prohibited in that decree, just as it is permitted to make use of tree roots adjacent to the ground. **Rav Ashi said: Even** if **you say** that it is referring **to a** branch that **is detached,** nevertheless, its use is prohibited due to the **decree lest one cut** and straighten the branch to prepare it for use with the bucket. Therefore, Rabban Shimon ben Gamliel teaches that there is no need for concern.

״פְּקָק הַחַלּוֹן כו׳״. אָמַר רַבָּה בַּר בַּר חָנָה אָמַר רַבִּי יוֹחָנָן: הַכֹּל מוֹדִים שֶׁאֵין עוֹשִׂין אֹהֶל עֲרַאי בַּתְּחִלָּה בְּיוֹם טוֹב, וְאֵין צָרִיךְ לוֹמַר בַּשַּׁבָּת. לֹא נֶחְלְקוּ אֶלָּא לְהוֹסִיף, שֶׁרַבִּי אֱלִיעֶזֶר אוֹמֵר: אֵין מוֹסִיפִין בְּיוֹם טוֹב, וְאֵין צָרִיךְ לוֹמַר בַּשַּׁבָּת. וַחֲכָמִים אוֹמְרִים: מוֹסִיפִין בַּשַּׁבָּת, וְאֵין צָרִיךְ לוֹמַר בְּיוֹם טוֹב. ״וַחֲכָמִים אוֹמְרִים בֵּין כָּךְ וּבֵין כָּךְ פּוֹקְקִין בּוֹ״.

We learned in the mishna that Rabbi Eliezer and the Rabbis dispute the case of **a window shutter**[N] and in what manner one is permitted to shutter a window on Shabbat. **Rabba bar bar Ḥana said** that **Rabbi Yoḥanan said: Everyone agrees that one may not construct a temporary tent**[H] **on a Festival** for the **first time, and needless to say,** one may not do so **on Shabbat.** The *tanna'im* **disagree only** with regard to **adding** to an existing tent,[H] **as Rabbi Eliezer says: One may not add** to an existing structure **on a Festival, and needless to say,** one may not do so **on Shabbat. And the Rabbis say: One may add** to a temporary structure **on Shabbat, and needless to say,** one may do so **on a Festival.**

מַאי ״בֵּין כָּךְ וּבֵין כָּךְ״? אָמַר רַבִּי אַבָּא אָמַר רַב כָּהֲנָא:

We learned in the mishna that the Rabbis say: Both in this case and in that case one may shutter with it. The Gemara asks: **What** is the meaning of: **Both in this** case **and in that** case, in this context? **Rabbi Abba said** that **Rav Kahana said:**

Perek **XVII**
Daf **126** Amud **a**

בֵּין קָשׁוּר בֵּין שֶׁאֵינוֹ קָשׁוּר, וְהוּא שֶׁמְּתוּקָּן.

Both if it is **tied**[H] **and** if it is **not** tied it is permitted, **and that** is only **if it is prepared** for this purpose beforehand.

NOTES

Stones…hard branches of a palm tree – אֲבָנִים...חֲרָיוֹת שֶׁל דֶּקֶל: Some commentaries are of the opinion that since people use these objects in different ways, one cannot make a clear halakhic distinction between stones and branches and therefore thought alone is sufficient to allow them to be moved on Shabbat. Other commentaries explain that there is in fact a difference between these two objects, with regard to the way they are generally used, in one of the following ways: (1) Palm fronds are more suitable for sitting (*Tosafot*); (2) stones are not particularly suitable for sitting because they are hard and cold; (3) stones are expensive and are only prepared for use in construction (*Me'iri*).

A shoot that is still connected – זְמוֹרָה מְחוּבֶּרֶת: The law permitting the use of a shoot connected to the ground within three handbreadths of the ground is based on the principle that objects separated by less than three handbreadths are considered connected. Therefore, a shoot within three handbreadths of the ground is considered to be part of the ground. Therefore, the rabbinic decree prohibiting use of a tree does not apply in that case.

A window shutter – פְּקַק הַחַלּוֹן: There are various opinions among the commentaries with regard to a window shutter. Rashi holds that the prohibition of building temporary structures applies only to a roof and not to walls. Therefore, the window here is a skylight in the roof. That opinion was rejected in *Tosafot*. With regard to the shutter, some say that it is referring to a piece of wood that is neither connected to the window by a hinge nor by a rope (*Me'iri*). Other commentaries state that this is referring to a cloth curtain that slides open and closed (Rav Natan Av HaYeshiva; Rambam's Commentary on the Mishna).

HALAKHA

A shoot that is still connected – זְמוֹרָה מְחוּבֶּרֶת: If a shoot is tied to a bucket, one may utilize the bucket to draw water. However, if the shoot is not tied to the bucket, then it is prohibited to use it, lest the person sever the shoot and attach it to the bucket (Rambam *Sefer Zemanim*, *Hilkhot Shabbat* 23:7).

A temporary tent – אֹהֶל עֲרַאי: It is prohibited to build a tent on Shabbat or on a Festival, even if it is temporary. The definition of a temporary tent in this context is a structure with a roof. Constructing permanent, significant partitions, e.g., the walls of a *sukka*, is also prohibited. However, it is permitted to build temporary or insignificant partitions, e.g., a partition established for privacy (Rambam *Sefer Zemanim*, *Hilkhot Shabbat* 22:27; *Shulḥan Arukh*, *Oraḥ Ḥayyim* 315:1).

Adding to a temporary tent – הוֹסָפָה לְאֹהֶל עֲרַאי: It is permitted to add to a temporary tent. For example, one who partially spread at least one handbreadth of a tent-like covering before Shabbat is permitted to extend it (Rambam *Sefer Zemanim*, *Hilkhot Shabbat* 22:27; *Shulḥan Arukh*, *Oraḥ Ḥayyim* 315:2).

HALAKHA

Tied – קָשׁוּר: It is permitted to move a bolt attached to a door and utilize it to lock any other door, in accordance with the opinion of Rabbi Yehuda (Rambam *Sefer Zemanim*, *Hilkhot Shabbat* 26:10; *Shulḥan Arukh*, *Oraḥ Ḥayyim* 313:1).

אָמַר לֵיהּ רַבִּי יִרְמְיָה: וְלֵימָא מָר ״בֵּין תָּלוּי וּבֵין שֶׁאֵינוֹ תָּלוּי וְהוּא שֶׁקָּשׁוּר״ – דְּאָמַר רַבָּה בַּר בַּר חָנָה אָמַר רַבִּי יוֹחָנָן: כְּמַחֲלוֹקֶת כָּאן כָּךְ מַחֲלוֹקֶת בְּנֶגֶר הַנִּגְרָר. דִּתְנַן: נֶגֶר הַנִּגְרָר – נוֹעֲלִין בּוֹ בַּמִּקְדָּשׁ אֲבָל לֹא בַּמְּדִינָה, וְהַמּוּנָּח – כָּאן וְכָאן אָסוּר. רַבִּי יְהוּדָה אוֹמֵר: הַמּוּנָּח – בַּמִּקְדָּשׁ, וְהַנִּגְרָר – בַּמְּדִינָה.

Rabbi Yirmeya said to Rabbi Abba: **And let the Master say** it in this way: **Both if it is hanging and if it is not hanging, and that** is only **if it is tied, as Rabba bar bar Ḥana said** that **Rabbi Yoḥanan said: Like the dispute here** with regard to the window shutter, **so too is the dispute with regard to a bolt**[N] **that was dragged,** which refers to a pole that was stuck through a hole in the door and into the ground in order to hold the door in place. **As we learned** in a mishna: With regard to **a bolt that is dragged,** which is not a part of the door itself but is attached to it and is dragged on the ground, **one locks with it in the Temple** on Shabbat, because the rabbinic decrees are not in effect in the Temple, **but not in the** rest of the **country** outside the Temple. **And** a bolt **that is placed** alongside the door and not attached, **here,** in the Temple, **and there,** outside the Temple, it is **prohibited** to lock with it on Shabbat. **Rabbi Yehuda says: One that was placed** is permitted **in the Temple and one that is dragged** is permitted even **in the** rest of the **country.**[N]

וְתַנְיָא: אֵיזֶהוּ נֶגֶר הַנִּגְרָר שֶׁנּוֹעֲלִין בּוֹ בַּמִּקְדָּשׁ אֲבָל לֹא בַּמְּדִינָה – כֹּל שֶׁקָּשׁוּר וְתָלוּי וְרֹאשׁוֹ מַגִּיעַ לָאָרֶץ. רַבִּי יְהוּדָה אוֹמֵר: זֶה – אַף בַּמְּדִינָה מוּתָּר, אֶלָּא אֵיזֶהוּ שֶׁבַּמְּדִינָה אָסוּר – כֹּל שֶׁאֵינוֹ לֹא קָשׁוּר וְלֹא תָּלוּי, וְשׁוֹמְטוֹ וּמַנִּיחוֹ בְּקֶרֶן זָוִית.

And it was taught in a *baraita*: **What is a bolt that is dragged that one locks with it in the Temple but not in the** rest of the **country?** Any bolt **that is tied and hangs** from the door **and** one of **its edges reaches the ground. Rabbi Yehuda says: That is permitted even in the** rest of the **country. Rather, what is prohibited in the** rest of the **country?** Any bolt **that is neither tied nor hung, and** one **removes it** from the door **and places it in a corner.**

וְאָמַר רַבִּי יְהוֹשֻׁעַ בַּר אַבָּא מִשְּׁמֵיהּ דְּעוּלָּא: מַאן תְּנָא נֶגֶר הַנִּגְרָר – רַבִּי אֱלִיעֶזֶר הִיא!

And Rabbi Yehoshua bar Abba said in the name of Ulla: Who is the *tanna* **who taught** the *halakha* of **a bolt that is dragged?** The *tanna* **is Rabbi Eliezer,** whose opinion in this case is identical to his opinion in the mishna with regard to the window shutter. It is certainly referring to a shutter that is attached. If it is not attached, Rabbi Eliezer holds that it is prohibited for use even in the Temple.

אָמַר לֵיהּ: אֲנָא דַּאֲמַרִי – כִּי הַאי תַּנָּא, דְּתַנְיָא: קָנֶה שֶׁהִתְקִינוֹ בַּעַל הַבַּיִת לִהְיוֹת פּוֹתֵחַ וְנוֹעֵל בּוֹ, בִּזְמַן שֶׁקָּשׁוּר וְתָלוּי בַּפֶּתַח – פּוֹתֵחַ וְנוֹעֵל בּוֹ, אֵין קָשׁוּר וְתָלוּי – אֵין פּוֹתֵחַ וְנוֹעֵל בּוֹ. רַבָּן שִׁמְעוֹן בֶּן גַּמְלִיאֵל אוֹמֵר: מְתוּקָּן, אַף עַל פִּי שֶׁאֵינוֹ קָשׁוּר.

Rabbi Abba **said to** Rabbi Yirmeya: **It is I who say** that this case is **in accordance with** the opinion of **this** *tanna*, **as it was taught** in the *Tosefta*: With regard to **a reed that the homeowner installed to open and lock** the door **with it** like a bolt, **when it is tied and hanging in the entrance, one may open and lock** the door **with it** on Shabbat, and when it is **not tied and hanging, one may not open and lock** the door **with it. Rabban Shimon ben Gamliel says:** If it was **prepared**[N] for that use, it is permitted to use it **even if it is not tied.** There is an opinion that holds that a bolt need not be attached, and preparation is sufficient to permit its use.[H]

אָמַר רַב יְהוּדָה בַּר שֵׁילַת אָמַר רַב אַסִּי אָמַר רַבִּי יוֹחָנָן: הֲלָכָה כְּרַבָּן שִׁמְעוֹן בֶּן גַּמְלִיאֵל.

Rav Yehuda bar Sheilat said that **Rav Asi said** that **Rabbi Yoḥanan said:** The *halakha* in this case **is in accordance with** the opinion of **Rabban Shimon ben Gamliel.**

וּמִי אָמַר רַבִּי יוֹחָנָן הָכִי? וְהָתְנַן: כָּל כִּסּוּיֵי הַכֵּלִים

The Gemara asks: **Did Rabbi Yoḥanan** really **say this? Didn't we learn** in the mishna: **All covers of vessels**

Perek **XVII**
Daf **126** Amud **b**

שֶׁיֵּשׁ לָהֶם בֵּית אֲחִיזָה – נִיטָּלִין בַּשַּׁבָּת. וְאָמַר רַב יְהוּדָה בַּר שֵׁילָא אָמַר רַב אַסִּי אָמַר רַבִּי יוֹחָנָן: וְהוּא שֶׁיֵּשׁ תּוֹרַת כְּלִי עֲלֵיהֶן!

that have a handle may be moved on Shabbat. And Rav Yehuda bar Sheila said that **Rav Asi said** that **Rabbi Yoḥanan said: And that is** specifically when **the status of a vessel applies to them,** i.e., when the cover itself is suited for use as a vessel. This is contrary to the opinion of Rabban Shimon ben Gamliel, who holds that preparation alone is sufficient.

NOTES

A bolt and a shutter – **נֶגֶר וּפְקָק**: There are a variety of approaches among the commentaries, both in terms of interpreting the Gemara and in terms of drawing the halakhic conclusion. The simple understanding is that the problem in the cases of the bolt and the shutter is the same, i.e., concern about the prohibited labor of building on Shabbat (Rashi). Others explain that the cases are similar only superficially (*Tosafot* and others). In fact, in the case of the bolt, there is an element of prohibition due to the fact that it is set-aside, because if the bolt is not attached to the door it does not have the status of a vessel and may not be moved. The window shutter is prohibited due to the prohibition against constructing a tent. In the Jerusalem Talmud, Rabbi Yoḥanan did not rule in accordance with the opinion of Rabban Shimon ben Gamliel with regard to the bolt. He ruled in accordance with the opinion of Rabbi Yehuda. There is an anecdote cited in the Jerusalem Talmud that in the house of Rabbi Yehuda HaNasi, they would lock the door with a bolt that was tied to the door even if it was not hanging. This ruling is in accordance with the opinion of Rabbi Yehuda.

In the Temple…in the rest of the country – **בַּמִּקְדָּשׁ...בַּמְּדִינָה**: Rabbinic decrees prohibiting labor on Shabbat were not in effect in the Temple, because the priests are vigilant in their performance of mitzvot and there is no concern that they will come to violate a Torah prohibition. Therefore, there is no need to institute preventative measures. The same is true in other areas of *halakha*. For example, with regard to ritual impurity, decrees issued by the Sages were not in effect in the Temple.

Prepared – **מְתוּקָּן**: Some commentaries explain that according to the Gemara, a prepared bolt means there that the reed underwent a physical change that transformed it into a vessel that may be moved even if it is not attached to the door (*Me'iri*).

HALAKHA

The *halakhot* of a bolt – **דִּינֵי נֶגֶר**: If it is evident that a bolt was fashioned for the express purpose of locking a door, e.g., if it has a thick end, it need not be attached to the door or to the doorframe to permit it to be moved, in accordance with the opinion of Rabban Shimon ben Gamliel and the ruling of Rabbi Yoḥanan (see *Hagahot Maimoniyot*; Rambam *Sefer Zemanim*, *Hilkhot Shabbat* 26:10).

וְכִי תֵּימָא: הָכָא נַמִי דְּאִיכָּא תּוֹרַת כְּלִי עָלָיו. וּמִי בָּעֵי רַבָּן שִׁמְעוֹן בֶּן גַּמְלִיאֵל תּוֹרַת כְּלִי עָלָיו?! וְהָתַנְיָא: חֲרָיוֹת שֶׁל דֶּקֶל שֶׁגְּדָרָן לְשֵׁם עֵצִים וְנִמְלַךְ עֲלֵיהֶן לִישִׁיבָה – צָרִיךְ לִקְשׁוֹר, רַבָּן שִׁמְעוֹן בֶּן גַּמְלִיאֵל אוֹמֵר: אֵין צָרִיךְ לִקְשׁוֹר.

And if you say: Here, too, Rabban Shimon ben Gamliel is referring to a case where **the status of a vessel applies to** the reed, **does Rabban Shimon ben Gamliel require** that **the status of a vessel apply** to it? **Wasn't it taught** in a *baraita*: With regard to **hard branches of a palm** tree **that one cut for** firewood or for construction **and** then **he reconsidered their** designation and decided to use them **for sitting, he must tie** the branches together on Shabbat eve so that they will not be set-aside. **Rabban Shimon ben Gamliel says: He need not tie** them together, and nevertheless, it is permitted to move them. Rabban Shimon ben Gamliel does not require that one render it a vessel. Thought is sufficient.

רַבִּי יוֹחָנָן סְבִירָא לֵיהּ כְּוָותֵיהּ בַּחֲדָא, וּפְלִיג עֲלֵיהּ בַּחֲדָא.

The Gemara answers: **Rabbi Yoḥanan holds in accordance with** the opinion of Rabban Shimon ben Gamliel **in one** matter **and disagrees with him in one** matter.[N]

דָּרַשׁ רַבִּי יִצְחָק נַפָּחָא אַפִּתְחָא דְּבֵי רֵישׁ גָּלוּתָא: הֲלָכָה כְּרַבִּי אֱלִיעֶזֶר. מְתִיב רַב עַמְרָם: ״וּמִדִּבְרֵיהֶם לָמַדְנוּ שֶׁפּוֹקְקִין וּמוֹדְדִין וְקוֹשְׁרִין בְּשַׁבָּת״!

Rabbi Yitzḥak taught at the entrance of the house **of the Exilarch:** The ***halakha* is in accordance with** the opinion of **Rabbi Eliezer** in the matter of a window shutter. **Rav Amram raised an objection** from that we learned explicitly in a mishna: **And from their statements** and their actions, **we derived that one may seal** a window, **and measure, and tie** a knot **on Shabbat.** Apparently, one may shutter the window under any circumstances, not only when the shutter was prepared for use, as Rabbi Eliezer said.

אָמַר לֵיהּ [אַבַּיֵי]: מַאי דַּעְתִּיךְ – מִשּׁוּם דְּקָתָנֵי סְתָמָא – ״נֶגֶר הַנִּגְרָר״ נַמִי סְתָמָא הִיא! וַאֲפִילּוּ הָכִי – מַעֲשֶׂה רַב.

Abaye said to Rav Amram: **What is your opinion,** that the proof is decisive because it **was taught** in the mishna **unattributed** and the *halakha* is in accordance with an unattributed mishna? The mishna with regard to **a bolt that is dragged is also** an **unattributed** mishna. The *halakha* should be in accordance with that mishna as well. The Gemara concludes: **And even so, an action is greater.**[N] Even though the two *mishnayot* are of equal weight, since one of them not only cites an unattributed opinion but also relates an incident where the Sages shuttered a window, that source is decisive.

מתני׳ (כָּל) כִּיסּוּי הַכֵּלִים שֶׁיֵּשׁ לָהֶם בֵּית אֲחִיזָה – נִיטָּלִין בְּשַׁבָּת. אָמַר רַבִּי יוֹסֵי: בַּמֶּה דְּבָרִים אֲמוּרִים – בְּכִיסּוּי קַרְקָעוֹת, אֲבָל בְּכִיסּוּי הַכֵּלִים – בֵּין כָּךְ וּבֵין כָּךְ נִיטָּלִין בְּשַׁבָּת.

MISHNA All covers of vessels that have a handle may be moved[H] **on Shabbat. Rabbi Yosei said: In what** case **is this statement said?** In the case of **a cover for the ground,** i.e., the cover of a pit; **however, with regard to covers of vessels, both** in **this** case **and** in **that** case, even if they do not have handles, **they may be moved on Shabbat.**

גמ׳ אָמַר רַב יְהוּדָה בַּר שֵׁילָא אָמַר רַבִּי אַסִי אָמַר רַבִּי יוֹחָנָן: וְהוּא שֶׁיֵּשׁ תּוֹרַת כְּלִי עֲלֵיהֶן. דְּכוּלֵּי עָלְמָא, כִּסּוּי קַרְקָעוֹת אִם יֵשׁ לָהֶן בֵּית אֲחִיזָה – אִין, אִי לָא – לָא. כִּסּוּי הַכֵּלִים, אַף עַל גַּב דְּאֵין לָהֶם בֵּית אֲחִיזָה.

GEMARA Rav Yehuda bar Sheila said that **Rabbi Asi said** that **Rabbi Yoḥanan said: And this applies** specifically when **the status of a vessel applies to them** and they are suited for some use. The Gemara adds: **Everyone holds** that with regard to **a cover for the ground, if it has a handle, yes,** it is permitted to move it, and **if not, no,** it is prohibited to move it; with regard to **a cover of a vessel, even if it does not have a handle,** it is permitted to move it.

כִּי פְּלִיגִי – בְּכֵלִים דְּחַבְּרִינְהוּ בְּאַרְעָא, מָר סָבַר: גָּזְרִינַן, וּמָר סָבַר: לָא גָּזְרִינַן.

When they disagree in the mishna, it is with regard to **vessels that one attached to the ground. This Sage,** the first *tanna*, **holds** that **we issue a decree** according to which it is prohibited to move the cover of a vessel attached to the ground due to the concern that one will move a cover for the ground itself, **and that Sage,** Rabbi Yosei, **holds** that **we do not issue a decree.**

לִישָּׁנָא אַחֲרִינָא: כִּי פְּלִיגִי – בְּכִיסּוּי תַּנּוּר, מָר מְדַמֵּי לֵיהּ לְכִיסּוּי קַרְקַע, וּמָר מְדַמֵּי לֵיהּ לְכִיסּוּי כֵּלִים.

Another version of this statement: **When they disagree** in the mishna, it is with regard to **the cover of an oven; this Sage likens it to a cover for the ground, and this Sage likens it to a cover of a vessel.**

הדרן עלך כל הכלים

NOTES

Rabbi Yoḥanan holds in accordance with the opinion of Rabban Shimon ben Gamliel in one matter and disagrees with him in one matter – רַבִּי יוֹחָנָן סְבִירָא לֵיהּ כְּוָותֵיהּ בַּחֲדָא וּפְלִיג עֲלֵיהּ בַּחֲדָא: Even though it is inappropriate for an *amora* to disagree with a *tanna*, he may adopt a compromise between two conflicting tannaitic opinions. Therefore, an *amora* can partially accept the opinion of one of the *tanna'im* (see *Yad Malakhi*).

An action is greater – מַעֲשֶׂה רַב: Since there is a contradiction between two unattributed *mishnayot*, the action is significant in determining the *halakha*. However, the Gemara employs the actions of the Sages in determining the *halakha* in other cases as well.

In the Jerusalem Talmud, this is phrased: There is an individual opinion in accordance with the unattributed mishna there, and there is an individual opinion in accordance with the unattributed mishna here.

HALAKHA

Moving the covers of vessels – טִלְטוּל כִּסּוּיֵי הַכֵּלִים: It is prohibited to move the cover of a pit on Shabbat, unless it has a handle, which renders it a vessel. It is permitted to move a vessel cover, even if the vessel is attached to the ground, and even if it does not have a handle. This latter ruling applies if one designated the covers for this purpose before Shabbat or if one performed an action indicating that that is their designation, in accordance with the opinion of Rabbi Yosei, which is usually the basis for the *halakha*, and which in this case is Rabbi Yoḥanan's second version of the dispute (Rambam *Sefer Zemanim*, *Hilkhot Shabbat* 25:13; *Shulḥan Arukh*, *Oraḥ Ḥayyim* 308:10).

Summary of **Perek XVII**

The *halakhot* of items that are set aside from use on Shabbat, as explained in this chapter, are unique in that earlier generations at the beginning of the Second Temple era were especially stringent with regard to these laws and forbade handling practically all utensils. Over the course of time, as the Sages saw that the nation as a whole was more meticulous in observing Shabbat, they became progressively more lenient with regard to this prohibition.

In the final halakhic conclusions in these matters, the lenient opinions of Rabbi Shimon and Rabbi Yosei were accepted. In their view, items that are set-aside [*muktze*] because of monetary loss are entirely forbidden from being handled, while utensils whose function is prohibited on Shabbat may be handled in order to use them for a permitted purpose or if one needs the place on which they are located. Items that are repulsive are not prohibited to be handled.

Nonetheless, there are still several aspects of this area of *halakha* for which no leniencies apply. According to all opinions, anything that does not have the status of a utensil, such as raw materials and money, is set-aside. Additionally, according to most opinions, any item that was set aside at the beginning of Shabbat remains set-aside for the duration of Shabbat. It should also be emphasized that the decision to be lenient with the laws pertaining to items that are set-aside applies specifically to Shabbat. On Festivals, the *halakha* follows the stringent view with regard to this prohibition. This is based upon the assumption that the sanctity of Shabbat had been internalized by the nation to the point that it did not need further strengthening and safeguarding. Concerning the Festivals, however, since certain prohibited labors are permitted for the sake of food preparation, it was necessary to impose additional decrees and safeguards in order to ensure that the sanctity of the Festivals would not be disregarded.

Introduction to
Perek XVIII

This chapter addresses three different *halakhot* that are only slightly related to one another. One topic continues the discussion of some of the laws of items that have been set aside from Shabbat use; see Chapter Seventeen for the major principles. The second topic addresses caring for and handling animals on Shabbat. The third topic examines the situation of a woman who has given birth on Shabbat, and caring for her in ways that could constitute prohibited labors. These *halakhot* do not seem to be related, but they are all included in the category of *shevut*, prohibitions that are not from the Torah like the categories of prohibited labor, but which were instituted by the Sages on Shabbat and the Festivals in order to prevent the violation of Torah prohibitions or to enhance the sanctity of the day.

There are *shevut* decrees that apply to many different areas, and this chapter addresses only some of them. However, we can derive from these examples the scope of *shevut* restrictions in many areas, remembering that each one is based upon rabbinic decree.

The *halakhot* discussed in this chapter are further related. Since the Sages themselves instituted these prohibitions as protective measures to prevent violation of Torah law, they could also be lenient in certain cases. This is possible only with regard to rabbinic decrees, but not with regard to prohibitions that stem from Torah law; as the Sages expressed it: They said [it is prohibited] and they said [it is permitted in particular circumstances]. For example, in cases of significant need, such as for the honor of guests or to facilitate Torah study, the Sages permitted several actions that would otherwise have been prohibited due to *muktze*. Such leniencies also exist with regard to other *shevut* restrictions, such as caring for animals on Shabbat. Although there are restrictions due to several relevant rabbinic decrees and concerns, since these are not Torah prohibitions, the Sages were lenient when necessary in order to prevent significant monetary loss or to prevent animals from experiencing pain.

After addressing the permitted methods of caring for birthing animals on Shabbat, the chapter discusses how to care for a woman who gives birth on Shabbat. Here the Gemara even addresses activities that are prohibited by Torah law as well as those prohibited by rabbinic decree, as both are permitted in order to save a life. The *halakha* is very lenient in such cases, to the point that it is permissible to perform any prohibited labor in the event of even a small concern for danger to human life.

Perek **XVIII**
Daf **126** Amud **b**

מתני׳ מְפַנִּין אֲפִילּוּ אַרְבַּע וְחָמֵשׁ קוּפּוֹת שֶׁל תֶּבֶן וְשֶׁל תְּבוּאָה מִפְּנֵי הָאוֹרְחִים, וּמִפְּנֵי בִּטּוּל בֵּית הַמִּדְרָשׁ, אֲבָל לֹא אֶת הָאוֹצָר.

MISHNA On Shabbat, **one** may **move even four or five baskets**[H] **of straw and** baskets **of produce, due to the guests,** who require that place to sit, **and due to suspension** of Torah study in **the study hall,** where space is required to seat the students. **However,** one may **not** move these items to create space in **the storeroom.**

מְפַנִּין תְּרוּמָה טְהוֹרָה, וּדְמַאי, וּמַעֲשֵׂר רִאשׁוֹן שֶׁנִּיטְּלָה תְּרוּמָתוֹ, וּמַעֲשֵׂר שֵׁנִי וְהֶקְדֵּשׁ שֶׁנִּפְדּוּ, וְהַתּוּרְמוּס הַיָּבֵשׁ – מִפְּנֵי שֶׁהוּא מַאֲכָל לָעִזִּים.

One may **move ritually pure** ***teruma,***[N] although it may only be eaten by a priest; **and doubtfully tithed produce** [***demai***], which may not be eaten until tithes are separated from it due to concern that an *am ha'aretz* did not separate its tithes; and **first tithe whose** ***teruma*** of the tithe **has** already **been taken** and given to priests; **and second tithe and consecrated items that were redeemed; and** even **dry lupine,** which is not fit for consumption by a person, **because it is goat food.**

אֲבָל לֹא אֶת הַטֶּבֶל, וְלֹא אֶת מַעֲשֵׂר [רִאשׁוֹן] שֶׁלֹּא נִטְּלָה תְּרוּמָתוֹ, וְלֹא אֶת מַעֲשֵׂר שֵׁנִי וְהֶקְדֵּשׁ שֶׁלֹּא נִפְדּוּ, וְלֹא אֶת הַלּוּף וְלֹא אֶת הַחַרְדָּל. רַבִּי שִׁמְעוֹן בֶּן גַּמְלִיאֵל מַתִּיר בְּלוּף מִפְּנֵי שֶׁהוּא מַאֲכַל עוֹרְבִין.

However, one may **neither** move **untithed produce, nor first tithe whose** ***teruma*** **has not been taken, nor second tithe and consecrated items that were not redeemed, nor** raw **arum and** raw **mustard,** as all of these items are not fit for consumption and are therefore set aside. **Rabban Shimon ben Gamliel permits** moving in the case of **arum**[B] **because it is food** for **ravens.**[N]

חֲבִילֵי קַשׁ וַחֲבִילֵי עֵצִים וַחֲבִילֵי זְרָדִים, אִם הִתְקִינָן לְמַאֲכַל בְּהֵמָה – מְטַלְטְלִין אוֹתָן, וְאִם לָאו – אֵין מְטַלְטְלִין אוֹתָן.

With regard to **bundles of straw, and bundles of wood, and bundles of twigs, if one prepared them** on Shabbat eve **for animal food, one may move them. And if not, one may not move them.**

גמ׳ הָשְׁתָּא חָמֵשׁ מְפַנִּין, אַרְבַּע מִיבַּעְיָא?!

GEMARA The Gemara asks: **Now** that the mishna stated that **one** may **move five** baskets, **is** mentioning **four** baskets **necessary?**

אָמַר רַב חִסְדָּא: אַרְבַּע מֵחָמֵשׁ. (אִיכָּא דְּאָמְרִי: אַרְבַּע מֵאוֹצָר קָטָן) וְחָמֵשׁ מֵאוֹצָר גָּדוֹל.

Rav Ḥisda said: The mishna means that one may move **four** out **of five**[N] baskets, but not all of them. **Some say:** It is permitted to move **four** baskets **from a small storeroom and five** baskets **from a large storeroom.**

וּמַאי ״אֲבָל לֹא אֶת הָאוֹצָר״– שֶׁלֹּא יַתְחִיל בָּאוֹצָר תְּחִלָּה. וּמַנִּי – רַבִּי יְהוּדָה הִיא, דְּאִית לֵיהּ מוּקְצֶה.

The Gemara asks: **And what** then is the meaning of: **However,** one may **not** move these items to create space in **the storeroom?** It means that **one may not** use **the storeroom** for the **first time.** If he has never taken supplies from this storeroom, he may not begin moving baskets from it. **And whose** opinion is cited in this mishna? It is the opinion of **Rabbi Yehuda, who is** of the opinion that this constitutes a prohibition of **set-aside.** The contents of a storeroom that was never used are set-aside.

וּשְׁמוּאֵל אָמַר: אַרְבַּע וְחָמֵשׁ.

And Shmuel says: The difficulty in the mishna should be explained as a figure of speech: **Four and five,**

Perek **XVIII**
Daf **127** Amud **a**

כִּדְאָמְרִי אֱינָשֵׁי, וְאִי בָּעֵי – אֲפִילּוּ טוּבָא נַמִי מְפַנִּין. וּמַאי ״אֲבָל לֹא אֶת הָאוֹצָר״– שֶׁלֹּא יִגְמוֹר כּוּלּוֹ דִּילְמָא אָתֵי לְאַשְׁוּוֹיֵי גּוּמּוֹת, אֲבָל אַתְחוּלֵי מַתְחִיל. וּמַנִּי – רַבִּי שִׁמְעוֹן הִיא, דְּלֵית לֵיהּ מוּקְצֶה.

as people who are not so precise in their formulation **say:** Four or five. **And if one so desires, he may clear even more. And what** then is the meaning of: **However,** one may **not** move these items to create space in **the storeroom?** It means **that one may not finish** moving the baskets out of the **entire** storeroom, **lest he come to level** the floor by filling the **holes. However, one may begin** removing baskets from the storeroom. **And whose** opinion is cited in this mishna? It is the opinion of **Rabbi Shimon, who is not** of the opinion that there is a prohibition of **set-aside.**

HALAKHA

One may move even four or five baskets – מְפַנִּין אֲפִילּוּ אַרְבַּע וְחָמֵשׁ קוּפּוֹת: Moving some of the contents of a storehouse to make room for guests is permitted. This is done in the following manner: If the storehouse is large, one moves five baskets, each with a capacity of three *se'a* (*Mordekhai*; Ran), to make room for guests. And if the warehouse is small and there are only five baskets in it, one may move only four out of the five. Although the ruling is fundamentally in accordance with the opinion of Rabbi Shimon, the number of baskets was restricted to prevent exertion, as per the opinion of Rav Ḥisda. Also, the simple understanding of the mishna and the Gemara is in accordance with Rav Ḥisda's opinion (Rabbeinu Ḥananel; Rambam *Sefer Zemanim, Hilkhot Shabbat* 21:2, 26:15; *Shulḥan Arukh, Oraḥ Ḥayyim* 333:1).

NOTES

One may move ritually pure ***teruma*** **– מְפַנִּין תְּרוּמָה טְהוֹרָה:** It is prohibited to move ritually impure teruma on Shabbat because it must be burned, and the only way one may benefit from it is through burning it. Since it is prohibited to kindle a fire on Shabbat, that teruma is set-aside (see Ramban).

Ravens – עוֹרְבִין: Ravens are raised for beauty and sport (Rashi). Although this is a pastime limited to the wealthy people, Rabban Shimon ben Gamliel maintains that all Jewish people are worthy of high status (see p. 158).

Four out of five – אַרְבַּע מֵחָמֵשׁ: The same applies to three out of four. The concept is that one may not move all of the baskets; he must leave some in place (*Korban Netanel*).

BACKGROUND

Arum – לוּף: This plant is generally identified as the arum of Eretz Yisrael, *Arum palaestinum*, from the Araceae family. This plant has a bulb in the ground from which large leaves sprout. The arum inflorescence has a unique structure and is covered with a special type of leaf called a spathe. All parts of the plant contain calcium oxalate, $Ca(COO)_2$, which is poisonous and causes extreme itching to any skin that comes in contact with it. Consequently, arum is not eaten by people in its raw state, and few animals draw sustenance from it. The bulb and leaves are cooked or roasted to make them edible for people. The plant grows in the wild in all regions of Eretz Yisrael.

Arum plant

תנו רבנן: אין מתחילין באוצר תחילה, אבל עושה בו שביל כדי שיכנס ויצא. עושה בו שביל?! והא אמרת "אין מתחילין"! הכי קאמר: עושה בו שביל ברגליו בכניסתו וביציאתו.

The Sages taught in a *baraita*: **One may not** use **the storeroom** for the **first time.**[H] If one has never taken supplies from this storeroom, he may not begin moving baskets from it. **However, he makes a path in it, so that he will** be able to **enter and exit.** The Gemara asks: He **makes a path in it? Did you not say: One may not** use **the storeroom** for the **first time?** The Gemara answers that the *baraita* **is saying as follows: He makes a path in it** by moving baskets **with his feet, as he enters** the storehouse **and as he exits.** He may not move the basket with his hand.

תנו רבנן: תבואה צבורה, בזמן שהתחיל בה מערב שבת – מותר להסתפק ממנה בשבת, ואם לאו – אסור להסתפק ממנה בשבת, דברי רבי שמעון. רבי אחא מתיר. כלפי לייא?! אלא אימא: דברי רבי אחא, ורבי שמעון מתיר.

The Sages taught in a *baraita*: With regard to **piled grain,**[N] **if one had started** to take grain from the pile **on Shabbat eve, it is permitted to satisfy his needs from it on Shabbat, and if not, it is prohibited to satisfy his needs from it on Shabbat;** this is **the statement of Rabbi Shimon. Rabbi Aḥa permits** doing so in any case. The Gemara raises a difficulty: **On the contrary;** it is Rabbi Shimon who is lenient with regard to the *halakhot* of set-aside. **Rather,** emend the *baraita* and **say:** This is **the statement of Rabbi Aḥa. Rabbi Shimon permits** doing so in any case.

תנא: כמה שיעור תבואה צבורה – לתך. בעא מיניה רב נחומי בר זכריה מאביי: שיעור תבואה צבורה בכמה? אמר ליה: הרי אמרו "שיעור תבואה צבורה – לתך".

It was taught: How much is the **measure of piled grain** needed to confer the legal status of a storeroom? **A half-kor. Rav Naḥumi bar Zekharya raised a dilemma before Abaye:** The **measure of piled grain, how much** is it? Abaye **said to him** that **they said: The measure of piled grain is a half-*kor*.**

איבעיא להו: הני ארבע וחמש קופות דקאמר, בארבע וחמש קופות – אין, טפי – לא, אלמא: למעוטי בהילוכא עדיף. או דילמא: למעוטי משוי עדיף?

A dilemma was raised before the Sages: **These four or five baskets, which** the *tanna* **stated** in the mishna, is he saying the following: **Four or five baskets, yes,** one may move them, **more** baskets, **no,** one may not move them? This would indicate **that it is preferable to minimize** the **walking** distance[H] because fewer baskets results in less walking in and out of the storeroom. **Or perhaps it is preferable to minimize** the size of the **burden** by carrying smaller baskets, as long as the total measure of all that one carries does not exceed the capacity of five large baskets?

תא שמע, דתני חדא: מפנין אפילו ארבע וחמש קופות של כדי שמן ושל כדי יין. ותניא אידך: בעשר ובחמש עשרה. מאי לאו בהא קמיפלגי – דמר סבר: מעוטי בהילוכא עדיף, ומר סבר: מעוטי במשוי עדיף?

Come and **hear** a resolution to this dilemma, **as one** *baraita* **taught: One** may **move even four or five baskets** containing **jugs of oil and jugs of wine. And it was taught** in **another** *baraita*: One may move them even **in ten and in fifteen** baskets. **What, is it not that** the two *baraitot* **disagree** concerning **the following** matter, **as this Sage** in the first *baraita* **holds** that **it is preferable to minimize** the **walking** distance by moving fewer, heavier baskets, **and this Sage** in the second *baraita* **holds** that **it is preferable to minimize** the size of the **burden** by moving lighter baskets over the course of several trips.

לא, דכולי עלמא מעוטי בהילוכא עדיף. ומי סברת "בעשר ובחמש עשרה" אקופות קאי?! אכדין קאי. ולא קשיא, הא – דמשתקלי חד חד בקופה, והא – דמישתקלי תרי תרי, והא – דמשתקלי תלתא תלתא, ובדקורי דהרפניא.

The Gemara rejects this: **No, everyone agrees that it is preferable to minimize** the **walking** distance. **And do you hold** that: **In ten and in fifteen, is referring to baskets? It is referring to jugs,** and there is no dispute between the *baraitot*. **And** this is **not difficult: This** *baraita*, which spoke of moving five, is referring to a case **in which** the jugs **are taken one by one in** each **basket. And that** *baraita*, which speaks of moving ten, is referring to a case **in which** the jugs **are taken two by two** in each basket. **And that** *baraita*, which speaks of moving fifteen, is referring to a case **in which** the jugs **are taken three by three,** e.g., in the case of **the small jugs of Harpanya.**

איבעיא להו: הני ארבע וחמש דקאמר – אף על גב דאית ליה אורחין טובא, או דילמא, הכל לפי האורחין, ואם תמצי לומר: הכל לפי האורחין, חד גברא מפני לכולהו, או דילמא, גברא גברא מפני לנפשיה?

A dilemma was raised before the Sages: **These four or five baskets, which** the *tanna* **stated** in the mishna, is he saying that one may move only four or five baskets **even though he has many guests? Or perhaps, it is all according to** the number **of guests,**[H] and if there are more guests one may move more baskets. **And if you say it is all according to the** number of **guests,** does **one man move** the baskets to make room **for all of them, or perhaps each and every man moves** a basket to make room **for himself?**

תא שמע: דאמר רבה אמר רבי חייא: פעם אחת הלך רבי למקום אחד וראה מקום דחוק לתלמידים, ויצא לשדה ומצא שדה מלאה עומרים ועימר רבי כל השדה כולה (שמע מינה: הכל לפי האורחין).

Come and **hear** a resolution to this dilemma from that which **Rabba said** that **Rav Ḥiyya said: Once Rabbi** Yehuda HaNasi **went to a certain place and saw** that the **place was** too **crowded for the students. And he went to the field and found a field full of bundles** of grain, **and Rabbi** Yehuda HaNasi **cleared the bundles** from **the whole field in its entirety.**[N] **Conclude from it** that the quantity that can be moved **is all according to the** number of **guests.**

HALAKHA

One may not use the storeroom for the first time – אין מתחילין באוצר תחילה: If a storehouse is filled with produce or jugs of wine, it is permitted to avail oneself of its contents on Shabbat. Nevertheless, it may only be emptied for the purpose of a mitzva, e.g., receiving guests or setting up a study hall. It is permitted to forge a path through the contents of the storehouse with one's feet while entering and exiting (Rambam *Sefer Zemanim, Hilkhot Shabbat* 26:15).

To minimize the walking distance – למעוטי בהילוכא: When clearing baskets from a storehouse on Shabbat, one should not divide the contents of the larger baskets into smaller baskets, thereby increasing the number of trips and making one's exertion more conspicuous. The dilemma pertaining to this issue remained unresolved, and therefore the ruling is stringent (*Shulḥan Arukh, Oraḥ Ḥayyim* 333:2).

It is all according to the number of guests – הכל לפי האורחין: The allowance to move four or five baskets means that a basket may be moved for each guest. This ruling is in accordance with the conclusion of the Gemara (Rambam *Sefer Zemanim, Hilkhot Shabbat* 26:15; *Shulḥan Arukh, Oraḥ Ḥayyim* 333:3).

NOTES

Piled grain – תבואה צבורה: Some authorities explain that this *halakha* with regard to piled grain is only according to Rav Ḥisda, who holds that the *halakha* is in accordance with the opinion of Rabbi Yehuda. However, according to Shmuel, who holds that the *halakha* is in accordance with the opinion of Rabbi Shimon, there is no prohibition of set-aside, and piled grain is not prohibited (see *Me'iri*).

Several *ge'onim* cited this *halakha* as proof for Rav Ḥisda's opinion. The *ge'onim* added that the measurement mentioned in the Gemara corresponds to the measurement mentioned in the Jerusalem Talmud. The Jerusalem Talmud states that each basket may weigh three *se'a*, which means that five baskets equal fifteen *se'a*, which is half of a *kor*, or a *letekh*.

And Rabbi Yehuda HaNasi cleared the bundles from the whole field in its entirety – ועימר רבי כל השדה כולה: It is important to note that Rabbi Yehuda HaNasi neither gathered the bundles nor ordered them to be gathered in one place, as that would involve performance of the prohibited labor of gathering. Rather, each bundle was moved to a separate place.

וְרַב יוֹסֵף אָמַר רַבִּי הוֹשַׁעְיָא: פַּעַם אַחַת הָלַךְ רַבִּי חִיָּיא לְמָקוֹם אֶחָד וְרָאָה מָקוֹם דָּחוּק לְתַלְמִידִים, וְיָצָא לַשָּׂדֶה וּמָצָא שָׂדֶה מְלֵאָה עוֹמָרִים וְעִימֵּר רַבִּי חִיָּיא כׇּל הַשָּׂדֶה כּוּלָּהּ. שְׁמַע מִינַּהּ: הַכֹּל לְפִי הָאוֹרְחִין.

And Rav Yosef said that **Rav Hoshaya said: Once Rabbi Ḥiyya went to a certain place and saw** that the **place was too crowded for the students. And he went to the field and found a field full of bundles** of grain, **and Rabbi Ḥiyya cleared the bundles** from **the whole field in its entirety. Conclude from it** that the quantity that can be moved **is all according to the** number of **guests.**

וַעֲדַיִין תִּבְּעֵי לָךְ: חַד גַּבְרָא מְפַנֵּי לֵיהּ לְכוּלָּא, אוֹ דִילְמָא כׇּל גַּבְרָא וְגַבְרָא מְפַנֵּי לְנַפְשֵׁיהּ?

The Gemara continues: **And still you have a dilemma.** Does **one man move** the baskets to make room **for all of them, or perhaps each and every man moves** baskets to make room **for himself?**

תָּא שְׁמַע: "וְעִימֵּר רַבִּי". וּלְטַעְמִיךְ, רַבִּי בְּדְנַפְשֵׁיהּ עִימֵּר?! אֶלָּא: צִוָּה וְעִימֵּר, וּלְעוֹלָם כׇּל חַד וְחַד מְפַנֵּי לְנַפְשֵׁיהּ.

Come and **hear** a resolution to this question. We learned: **And Rabbi** Yehuda HaNasi **cleared the bundles.** Apparently, one person moved the bundles to make room for the others. The Gemara rejects the proof: **And according to your reasoning,** your opinion, do you think **Rabbi** Yehuda HaNasi, the spiritual leader of his generation, **cleared the bundles himself? Rather, he ordered** others to do so, **and** he thereby **cleared the bundles. And actually, each and every one moves** a bundle to make room **for himself.**[H]

"מִפְּנֵי הָאוֹרְחִין וכו'". אָמַר רַבִּי יוֹחָנָן: גְּדוֹלָה הַכְנָסַת אוֹרְחִין כְּהַשְׁכָּמַת בֵּית הַמִּדְרָשׁ, דְּקָתָנֵי: "מִפְּנֵי הָאוֹרְחִין וּמִפְּנֵי בִּטּוּל בֵּית הַמִּדְרָשׁ". וְרַב דִּימִי מִנְּהַרְדְּעָא אָמַר: יוֹתֵר מֵהַשְׁכָּמַת בֵּית הַמִּדְרָשׁ, דְּקָתָנֵי: "מִפְּנֵי הָאוֹרְחִין", וַהֲדַר: "וּמִפְּנֵי בִּטּוּל בֵּית הַמִּדְרָשׁ". אָמַר רַב יְהוּדָה אָמַר רַב: גְּדוֹלָה הַכְנָסַת אוֹרְחִין מֵהַקְבָּלַת פְּנֵי שְׁכִינָה, דִּכְתִיב: "וַיֹּאמַר (ה') אִם נָא מָצָאתִי חֵן בְּעֵינֶיךָ אַל נָא תַעֲבֹר וגו'". אָמַר רַבִּי אֶלְעָזָר: בֹּא וּרְאֵה, שֶׁלֹּא כְּמִדַּת הַקָּדוֹשׁ בָּרוּךְ הוּא מִדַּת בָּשָׂר וָדָם; מִדַּת בָּשָׂר וָדָם – אֵין קָטָן יָכוֹל לוֹמַר לְגָדוֹל "הַמְתֵּן עַד שֶׁאָבֹא אֶצְלְךָ", וְאִילּוּ בְּהַקָּדוֹשׁ בָּרוּךְ הוּא כְּתִיב: "וַיֹּאמַר (ה') אִם נָא מָצָאתִי וגו'".

We learned in the mishna: One may move baskets of produce **due to the guests** and in order to prevent the suspension of Torah study in the study hall. **Rabbi Yoḥanan said: Hospitality** toward **guests is as great**[H] **as rising** early to go **to the study hall,**[N] as the mishna equates them **and teaches: Due to the guests and due to suspension of** Torah study in **the study hall. And Rav Dimi from Neharde'a says:** Hospitality toward guests is **greater than rising early to the study hall, as it teaches: Due to the guests, and** only **afterward: And due to suspension of** Torah study in **the study hall. Rav Yehuda said** that **Rav said** on a related note: **Hospitality** toward **guests is greater than receiving the Divine Presence, as** when Abraham invited his guests **it is written: "And he said: Lord, if now I have found favor in Your sight, please pass not** from Your servant" (Genesis 18:3). Abraham requested that God, the Divine Presence, wait for him while he tended to his guests appropriately.[N] **Rabbi Elazar said: Come and see that the attribute of the Holy One, Blessed be He, is not like that of flesh and blood. The attribute of flesh and blood** people is such that **a less significant** person **is unable to say to a more significant** person: **Wait until I come to you, while with regard to the Holy One, Blessed be He, it is written: "And he said: Lord, if now I have found favor** in Your sight, please pass not from Your servant." Abraham requested that God wait for him due to his guests.

אָמַר רַב יְהוּדָה בַּר שֵׁילָא אָמַר רַבִּי אַסִּי אָמַר רַבִּי יוֹחָנָן: שִׁשָּׁה דְּבָרִים אָדָם אוֹכֵל פֵּירוֹתֵיהֶן בָּעוֹלָם הַזֶּה, וְהַקֶּרֶן קַיֶּימֶת לוֹ לָעוֹלָם הַבָּא. וְאֵלּוּ הֵן: הַכְנָסַת אוֹרְחִין, וּבִיקּוּר חוֹלִים, וְעִיּוּן תְּפִלָּה, וְהַשְׁכָּמַת בֵּית הַמִּדְרָשׁ, וְהַמְגַדֵּל בָּנָיו לְתַלְמוּד תּוֹרָה, וְהַדָּן אֶת חֲבֵרוֹ לְכַף זְכוּת.

Rav Yehuda bar Sheila said that **Rabbi Asi said** that **Rabbi Yoḥanan said:** There are **six matters a person enjoys** the **profits of in this world,**[N] and nevertheless **the principal exists for him for the World-to-Come, and they are: Hospitality** toward **guests, and visiting** the **sick, and consideration** during **prayer,** and **rising early to the study hall, and one who raises his sons to** engage **in Torah study, and one who judges another favorably,**[H] giving him the benefit of the doubt.

אִינִי?! וְהָא אֲנַן תְּנַן: אֵלּוּ דְּבָרִים שֶׁאָדָם עוֹשֶׂה אוֹתָם וְאוֹכֵל פֵּירוֹתֵיהֶן בָּעוֹלָם הַזֶּה וְהַקֶּרֶן קַיֶּימֶת לוֹ לָעוֹלָם הַבָּא, וְאֵלּוּ הֵן: כִּיבּוּד אָב וָאֵם וּגְמִילוּת חֲסָדִים וַהֲבָאַת שָׁלוֹם שֶׁבֵּין אָדָם לַחֲבֵרוֹ וְתַלְמוּד תּוֹרָה כְּנֶגֶד כּוּלָּם [הָנֵי – אִין, מִידֵּי אַחֲרִינָא – לָא]!

The Gemara asks: **Is that so? And did we not learn** in a mishna: **These** are the **matters that a person does them and enjoys their profits in this world, and** nevertheless **the principal exists for him for the World-to-Come, and they are: Honoring one's father and mother, and acts of loving kindness, and bringing peace between a person and another, and Torah study is equal to all of them.**[H] By inference: **These** matters, **yes,** one enjoys their profits in this world and the principal exists for him in the World-to-Come; **other matters, no.**

HALAKHA

Each and every one moves a bundle to make room for himself – **כׇּל חַד וְחַד מְפַנֵּי לְנַפְשֵׁיהּ:** It is prohibited to clear numerous objects for many guests because of the extra exertions. Therefore, each guest should clear for himself or one other person. Since the question with regard to this issue was not resolved in the Gemara, the authorities ruled stringently (Rambam *Sefer Zemanim, Hilkhot Shabbat* 26:15; *Shulḥan Arukh, Oraḥ Ḥayyim* 333:3).

Hospitality toward guests is as great – **גְּדוֹלָה הַכְנָסַת אוֹרְחִין:** The mitzva to display hospitality toward guests is greater than that of receiving the Divine Presence (Rambam *Sefer Shofetim, Hilkhot Evel* 14:2).

One who judges another favorably – **הַדָּן אֶת חֲבֵרוֹ לְכַף זְכוּת:** Even after a judge renders a decision and it is accepted by all the parties involved, the judge must make a concerted effort to judge the guilty party favorably. One must judge favorably especially in cases where there is no ruling (Rambam *Sefer Shofetim, Hilkhot Sanhedrin* 23:10 and *Sefer HaMadda, Hilkhot Deot* 5:7; *Shulḥan Arukh, Ḥoshen Mishpat* 17:10).

And Torah study is equal to all of them – **וְתַלְמוּד תּוֹרָה כְּנֶגֶד כּוּלָּם:** The mitzva to study Torah is greater than all other mitzvot. If there is a mitzva that can be performed by others, one should not be derelict in his Torah study to fulfill that mitzva (Rambam *Sefer HaMadda, Hilkhot Talmud Torah* 3:3; *Shulḥan Arukh, Yoreh De'a* 246:18).

NOTES

Rising early to the study hall – **הַשְׁכָּמַת בֵּית הַמִּדְרָשׁ:** Rising early to the study hall is not referring exclusively to students. Those who bring others to the study hall are equally praiseworthy (Rav Ya'akov Emden).

Abraham and the angels – **אַבְרָהָם וְהַמַּלְאָכִים:** The verse states: "And he said: Adonai, if now I have found favor in Your sight, please pass not from Your servant" (Genesis 18:3). The commentaries dispute the interpretation of the term: Adonai. Most interpret it as a sacred reference to God. Abraham asks God to wait for him until he finishes hosting his guests. Other commentaries explain it as a non-sacred plural form of the word master [*adon*]. Abraham addressed his guests using this honorific.

The profits of in this world – **פֵּירוֹתֵיהֶן בָּעוֹלָם הַזֶּה:** The Rambam explains: Reward for observing mitzvot between man and God is received in the World to Come. However, some of the reward for fulfilling mitzvot between man and man is received in this world because their fulfillment is enjoyed by others. Some of the reward for Torah study is also received in this world because Torah study facilitates fulfillment of all the mitzvot (Rambam's Commentary on the Mishna).

NOTES

And there was an incident involving a certain person who…was hired to work for a certain homeowner – וּמַעֲשֶׂה בְּאָדָם אֶחָד...וְנִשְׂכַּר אֵצֶל בַּעַל הַבַּיִת: In the *She'iltot*, Rav Aḥai Gaon cited this incident and identified the homeowner as Rabbi Eliezer ben Hyrcanus and the worker that he hired as Rabbi Akiva.

They dissolved all my vows – הִתִּירוּ לִי כׇּל נְדָרַי: Some explained that the Sages dissolved the homeowner's vows because they assumed that he only vowed to threaten his son. Otherwise, they would not have dissolved a vow of consecration.

LANGUAGE

Merchandise [*perakmatya*] – פְּרַקְמַטְיָא: From the Greek πραγματεία, *pragmateia*, meaning business or merchandise.

הָנֵי נַמִי (בִּגְמִילוּת חֲסָדִים שָׁיְיכִי. לִישָּׁנָא אַחֲרִינָא: הָנֵי) בְּהָנֵי שָׁיְיכִי.

The Gemara answers: **These too,** hospitality toward guests and visiting the sick, **are in the category of acts of loving-kindness. A different version** of that answer: **These** matters on the longer list **are attributable to those,** the matters on the shorter list.

תָּנוּ רַבָּנַן: הַדָּן חֲבֵירוֹ לְכַף זְכוּת דָּנִין אוֹתוֹ לִזְכוּת. וּמַעֲשֶׂה בְּאָדָם אֶחָד שֶׁיָּרַד מִגָּלִיל הָעֶלְיוֹן וְנִשְׂכַּר אֵצֶל בַּעַל הַבַּיִת אֶחָד בַּדָּרוֹם שָׁלֹשׁ שָׁנִים. עֶרֶב יוֹם הַכִּפּוּרִים אָמַר לוֹ: תֵּן לִי שְׂכָרִי, וְאֵלֵךְ וְאָזוּן אֶת אִשְׁתִּי וּבָנַי. אָמַר לוֹ: אֵין לִי מָעוֹת. אָמַר לוֹ: תֵּן לִי פֵּירוֹת. אָמַר לוֹ: אֵין לִי. תֵּן לִי קַרְקַע. אֵין לִי. תֵּן לִי בְּהֵמָה. אֵין לִי. תֵּן לִי כָּרִים וּכְסָתוֹת. אֵין לִי. הִפְשִׁיל כֵּלָיו לַאֲחוֹרָיו, וְהָלַךְ לְבֵיתוֹ בְּפַחֵי נֶפֶשׁ.

The Sages taught in a *baraita*: **One who judges another favorably is himself judged favorably. And there was an incident** involving **a certain person who descended from the Upper Galilee and was hired** to work **for a certain homeowner**[N] **in the South** for **three years. On the eve of the Day of Atonement, he said to** the homeowner: **Give me my wages, and I will go and feed my wife and children.** The homeowner **said to him: I have no money. He said to him:** In that case, **give me** my wages in the form of **produce. He said to him: I have none.** The worker said to him: **Give me** my wages in the form of **land.** The homeowner said to him: **I have none.** The worker said to him: **Give me** my wages in the form of **animals. He said to him: I have none.** The worker said to him: **Give me cushions and blankets.** He said to him: **I have none.** The worker **slung his tools** over his shoulder **behind him and went to his home in anguish.**

לְאַחַר הָרֶגֶל נָטַל בַּעַל הַבַּיִת שְׂכָרוֹ בְּיָדוֹ, וְעִמּוֹ מַשּׂוֹי שְׁלֹשָׁה חֲמוֹרִים, אֶחָד שֶׁל מַאֲכָל וְאֶחָד שֶׁל מִשְׁתֶּה וְאֶחָד שֶׁל מִינֵי מְגָדִים, וְהָלַךְ לוֹ לְבֵיתוֹ. אַחַר שֶׁאָכְלוּ וְשָׁתוּ נָתַן לוֹ שְׂכָרוֹ.

After the festival of *Sukkot*, **the homeowner took** the worker's **wages in his hand, along with a burden** that required **three donkeys, one** laden **with food, one** laden **with drink, and one** laden **with types of sweets, and went to the** worker's **home. After they ate and drank,** the homeowner **gave him his wages.**

אָמַר לוֹ: בְּשָׁעָה שֶׁאָמַרְתָּ לִי ״תֵּן לִי שְׂכָרִי״ וְאָמַרְתִּי ״אֵין לִי מָעוֹת״ בַּמֶּה חֲשַׁדְתַּנִי? אָמַרְתִּי: שֶׁמָּא פְּרַקְמַטְיָא בְּזוֹל נִזְדַּמְּנָה לְךָ, וְלָקַחְתָּ בָּהֶן. וּבְשָׁעָה שֶׁאָמַרְתָּ לִי ״תֵּן לִי בְּהֵמָה״ וְאָמַרְתִּי ״אֵין לִי בְּהֵמָה״ בַּמֶּה חֲשַׁדְתַּנִי? אָמַרְתִּי: שֶׁמָּא מוּשְׂכֶּרֶת בְּיַד אֲחֵרִים. בְּשָׁעָה שֶׁאָמַרְתָּ לִי ״תֵּן לִי קַרְקַע״ וְאָמַרְתִּי לְךָ ״אֵין לִי קַרְקַע״ בַּמֶּה חֲשַׁדְתַּנִי? אָמַרְתִּי: שֶׁמָּא מוּחְכֶּרֶת בְּיַד אֲחֵרִים הִיא. וּבְשָׁעָה שֶׁאָמַרְתִּי לְךָ ״אֵין לִי פֵּירוֹת״ בַּמֶּה חֲשַׁדְתַּנִי? אָמַרְתִּי ״שֶׁמָּא אֵינָן מְעוּשָּׂרוֹת״. וּבְשָׁעָה שֶׁאָמַרְתִּי לְךָ ״אֵין לִי כָּרִים וּכְסָתוֹת״ בַּמֶּה חֲשַׁדְתַּנִי? אָמַרְתִּי: שֶׁמָּא הִקְדִּישׁ כׇּל נְכָסָיו לַשָּׁמַיִם.

The homeowner **said to him: When you said to me: Give me my wages, and I said: I have no money, of what did you suspect me?** Why did you not suspect me of trying to avoid paying you? The worker answered, **I said: Perhaps the opportunity to purchase merchandise [*perakmatya*]**[L] **inexpensively presented itself, and you purchased** it **with** the money that you owed me, and therefore you had no money available. The homeowner asked: **And when you said to me: Give me animals, and I said: I have no animals, of what did you suspect me?** The worker answered: **I said: Perhaps** the animals **are hired to others.** The homeowner asked: **When you said to me: Give me land, and I said: I have no land, of what did you suspect me?** The worker answered: **I said: Perhaps** the land **is leased to others,** and you cannot take the land from the lessees. The homeowner asked: **And when** you said to me: Give me produce, and **I said: I have no produce, of what did you suspect me?** The worker answered: **I said: Perhaps they are not tithed,** and that was why you could not give them to me. The homeowner asked: **And when I said: I have no cushions or blankets, of what did you suspect me?** The worker answered: **I said: Perhaps he consecrated all his property to Heaven** and therefore has nothing available at present.

אָמַר לֵיהּ: הָעֲבוֹדָה, כָּךְ הָיָה! הִדַּרְתִּי כׇּל נְכָסַי בִּשְׁבִיל הוֹרְקְנוֹס בְּנִי שֶׁלֹּא עָסַק בַּתּוֹרָה, וּכְשֶׁבָּאתִי אֵצֶל חֲבֵירַי בַּדָּרוֹם הִתִּירוּ לִי כׇּל נְדָרַי. וְאַתָּה, כְּשֵׁם שֶׁדַּנְתַּנִי לִזְכוּת – הַמָּקוֹם יָדִין אוֹתְךָ לִזְכוּת.

The homeowner **said to him:** I swear by **the** Temple **service** that **it was so.** I had no money available at the time because I **vowed** and consecrated **all my property on account of Hyrcanus, my son, who did not engage in Torah study.** The homeowner sought to avoid leaving an inheritance for his son. **And when I came to my fellow** residents **in the South,** the Sages of that generation, **they dissolved all my vows.**[N] At that point, the homeowner had immediately gone to pay his worker. Now the homeowner said: **And you, just as you judged favorably, so may God judge you favorably.**

BACKGROUND

Matron– מַטְרוֹנִיתָא: During the time of Rabbi Yehoshua and his colleagues, in the years preceding and following the destruction of the Temple, many women from the Roman upper classes expressed strong interest in Judaism. Several actually converted. Those who remained gentiles attempted to provide assistance to the Jewish Sages. It is related on several occasions that the Sages took advantage of the counsel of these women and of their ability to serve as intermediaries between them and the Roman authorities.

תָּנוּ רַבָּנַן: מַעֲשֶׂה בְּחָסִיד אֶחָד שֶׁפָּדָה רִיבָה אַחַת בַּת יִשְׂרָאֵל, וְלַמָּלוֹן הִשְׁכִּיבָהּ תַּחַת מַרְגְּלוֹתָיו, לְמָחָר יָרַד וְטָבַל וְשָׁנָה לְתַלְמִידָיו.

On a similar note, the Gemara relates that **the Sages taught** in a *baraita*: There was **an incident involving a certain pious man who redeemed a young Jewish woman** from captivity. When they arrived **at the inn he had her lie beneath his feet. The next day, he descended, and immersed** in a ritual bath to purify himself before Torah study and prayer, **and taught his students.** This conduct could arouse suspicion that the pious man kept the maiden for himself, as immersion in the morning is customary for men who have experienced a seminal emission by engaging in sexual relations.

וְאָמַר (לְהֶן): בְּשָׁעָה שֶׁהִשְׁכַּבְתִּיהָ תַּחַת מַרְגְּלוֹתַי בַּמֶּה חֲשַׁדְתּוּנִי? אָמְרוּ: שֶׁמָּא יֵשׁ בָּנוּ תַּלְמִיד שֶׁאֵינוֹ בָּדוּק לְרַבִּי.

And the pious man **said to** his students: **When I had her lie beneath my feet, of what did you suspect me?** They said to him: **We said: Perhaps there is a student among us whose** conduct **is not established** before **the rabbi,** and he wanted to make certain that this student would not inappropriately accost the young woman. Therefore, the rabbi kept the woman close by.

בְּשָׁעָה שֶׁיָּרַדְתִּי וְטָבַלְתִּי בַּמֶּה חֲשַׁדְתּוּנִי? אָמְרוּ: שֶׁמָּא מִפְּנֵי טוֹרַח הַדֶּרֶךְ אֵירַע קֶרִי לְרַבִּי. אָמַר לָהֶם: הָעֲבוֹדָה, כָּךְ הָיָה. וְאַתֶּם, כְּשֵׁם שֶׁדַּנְתּוּנִי לְכַף זְכוּת – הַמָּקוֹם יָדִין אֶתְכֶם לְכַף זְכוּת.

He said to them: **When I descended and immersed, of what did you suspect me?** They answered: **Perhaps due to the exertion of travel,** a seminal **emission befell the rabbi. He said to them:** I swear **by the** Temple **service** that **it was so. And you, just as you judged** me **favorably,** so **may God judge you favorably.**

תָּנוּ רַבָּנַן: פַּעַם אַחַת הוּצְרַךְ דָּבָר אֶחָד לְתַלְמִידֵי חֲכָמִים אֵצֶל מַטְרוֹנִיתָא אַחַת, שֶׁכָּל גְּדוֹלֵי רוֹמִי מְצוּיִין אֶצְלָהּ. אָמְרוּ: מִי יֵלֵךְ? אָמַר לָהֶם רַבִּי יְהוֹשֻׁעַ: אֲנִי אֵלֵךְ.

The Sages taught a similar *baraita*: **Once** there was **a certain matter needed by Torah scholars.** They wanted to discuss an issue **with a certain matron**[B] **whose** company was kept **by all the prominent** people **of Rome.** The Torah scholars wanted to address the government on behalf of the Jewish people, and they sought the matron's advice. **They said: Who will go? Rabbi Yehoshua said to them: I shall go.**

הָלַךְ רַבִּי יְהוֹשֻׁעַ וְתַלְמִידָיו, כֵּיוָן שֶׁהִגִּיעַ לְפֶתַח בֵּיתָהּ חָלַץ תְּפִילָּיו בְּרִחוּק אַרְבַּע אַמּוֹת, וְנִכְנַס וְנָעַל הַדֶּלֶת בִּפְנֵיהֶן. אַחַר שֶׁיָּצָא יָרַד וְטָבַל, וְשָׁנָה לְתַלְמִידָיו.

Rabbi Yehoshua and his students went to her. **When he arrived** with his students **at the entrance of her house, he removed his phylacteries at a distance of four cubits** from the door, **and entered, and locked the door before them. After he emerged, he descended and immersed** in a ritual bath, **and taught his students.** Here too, this was conduct that could arouse suspicion that something improper transpired.

וְאָמַר (לְהֶן): בְּשָׁעָה שֶׁחָלַצְתִּי תְּפִילִּין בַּמֶּה חֲשַׁדְתּוּנִי? אָמְרוּ: כְּסָבוּר רַבִּי "לֹא יִכָּנְסוּ דִּבְרֵי קְדוּשָּׁה בִּמְקוֹם טוּמְאָה".

And he said to his students: **When I removed the phylacteries, of what did you suspect me?** They said to him, **we said: The rabbi must hold** that **sacred items may not enter a place of impurity.** Therefore, it would have been inappropriate to enter the house with phylacteries.

בְּשָׁעָה שֶׁנָּעַלְתִּי בַּמֶּה חֲשַׁדְתּוּנִי? אָמְרוּ: שֶׁמָּא דְּבַר מַלְכוּת יֵשׁ בֵּינוֹ לְבֵינָהּ.

He asked: **When I locked** the door, **of what did you suspect me?** They said to him: **We said: Perhaps there is a** discreet **royal matter** that must be discussed **between him and her** and should not be revealed.

בְּשָׁעָה שֶׁיָּרַדְתִּי וְטָבַלְתִּי בַּמֶּה חֲשַׁדְתּוּנִי? אָמְרוּ: שֶׁמָּא נִיתְּזָה צִינּוֹרָא מִפִּיהָ עַל בְּגָדָיו שֶׁל רַבִּי. אָמַר לָהֶם: הָעֲבוֹדָה, כָּךְ הָיָה. וְאַתֶּם, כְּשֵׁם שֶׁדַּנְתּוּנִי לִזְכוּת – הַמָּקוֹם יָדִין אֶתְכֶם לִזְכוּת.

Rabbi Yehoshua asked: **When I descended and immersed, of what did you suspect me?** They said to him, **we said: Perhaps a bit of spittle sprayed from her mouth onto the rabbi's clothes.** The Sages decreed that the legal status of a gentile is like that of a *zav*; their bodily fluids transmit ritual impurity. Rabbi Yehoshua **said to them:** I swear **by the** Temple **service** that **it was so. And you, just as you judged favorably,** so **may God judge you favorably.**

"מְפַנִּין תְּרוּמָה טְהוֹרָה וכו'". פְּשִׁיטָא! לָא צְרִיכָא, דְּמַנְּחָה בְּיַד יִשְׂרָאֵל. מַהוּ דְּתֵימָא: כֵּיוָן דְּלָא חֲזֵיָא לֵיהּ – אָסוּר, קָא מַשְׁמַע לָן: כֵּיוָן דַּחֲזֵיָא לְכֹהֵן – שַׁפִּיר דָּמֵי.

We learned in the mishna: **One** may **move ritually pure *teruma***[H] on Shabbat. The Gemara objects: That is **obvious.** The Gemara answers: **It is necessary** to teach this **only** in a case **in which it is placed in Israelite hands. Lest you say: Since it is not suitable for** the Israelite to eat, he is **prohibited** to move it on Shabbat; therefore, **it teaches us** that **since it is suitable for** a **priest** to eat, one may **well** move it on Shabbat.

HALAKHA

One may move ritually pure *teruma* – מְפַנִּין תְּרוּמָה טְהוֹרָה: An Israelite is permitted to move ritually pure *teruma* on Shabbat, even though only a priest may eat it (Rambam *Sefer Zemanim, Hilkhot Shabbat* 25:20).

״וּדְמַאי (וכו׳)״. דְּמַאי, הָא לָא חֲזֵי לֵיהּ?! כֵּיוָן דְּאִי בָּעֵי, מַפְקַר לֵיהּ לְנִכְסֵיהּ וַהֲוָה עָנִי, וְחַזְיָא לֵיהּ – הַשְׁתָּא נַמִי חֲזֵי לֵיהּ. דִּתְנַן: מַאֲכִילִין אֶת הָעֲנִיִּים דְּמַאי וְאֶת הָאַכְסַנְיָא דְּמַאי. וְאָמַר רַב הוּנָא; תָּנָא, בֵּית שַׁמַּאי אוֹמְרִים: אֵין מַאֲכִילִין אֶת הָעֲנִיִּים דְּמַאי וְאֶת הָאַכְסַנְיָא דְּמַאי, וּבֵית הִלֵּל אוֹמְרִים: מַאֲכִילִין אֶת הָעֲנִיִּים דְּמַאי וְאֶת הָאַכְסַנְיָא דְּמַאי.

And we also learned in the mishna: One may move **doubtfully tithed produce.**[H] The Gemara asks: With regard to **doubtfully tithed produce,** why may one move it? **It is not suitable for him** to eat. The Gemara answers: **Since if he** so **desires,** he may **renounce** all **his property,**[N] declaring it ownerless, **and he** would then **be poor, and** the doubtfully tithed produce would be **suitable for him, now too it is suitable for him.** A pauper may eat doubtfully tithed produce, **as we learned** in a mishna: **One** may **feed the poor doubtfully tithed produce and soldiers** [***akhsanya***][L] **doubtfully tithed produce.**[N] **And Rav Huna said** that **it was taught: Beit Shammai say: One** may **neither feed the poor doubtfully tithed produce nor** feed **soldiers doubtfully tithed produce. And Beit Hillel say: One** may **feed the poor doubtfully tithed produce and** feed **soldiers doubtfully tithed produce.** The *halakha* is in accordance with the opinion of Beit Hillel.

״וּמַעֲשֵׂר רִאשׁוֹן שֶׁנִּיטְּלָה תְּרוּמָתוֹ וכו׳״. פְּשִׁיטָא! לָא צְרִיכָא שֶׁהִקְדִּימוֹ בַּשִּׁבּוֹלִים, וְנִטְּלָה הֵימֶנּוּ תְּרוּמַת מַעֲשֵׂר, וְלֹא נִטְּלָה הֵימֶנּוּ תְּרוּמָה גְּדוֹלָה.

We learned in the mishna: And one may move **first tithe whose** teruma of the tithe **has** already **been taken.** The Gemara poses a question: **It is obvious** that if the *teruma* was already tithed it is non-sacred produce in every sense. The Gemara explains: **It was necessary** to teach this ***halakha*** **only in** the following case: A Levite **preceded** the priest while the grain was still **on the stalks**[HN] **and brought it to the threshing floor, and before the grain was threshed, the *teruma* of the tithes was taken and the *teruma gedola* was not taken.**

וְכִי הָא דְּאָמַר רַבִּי אַבָּהוּ אָמַר רֵישׁ לָקִישׁ: מַעֲשֵׂר רִאשׁוֹן שֶׁהִקְדִּימוֹ בַּשִּׁבּוֹלִין – פָּטוּר מִתְּרוּמָה גְּדוֹלָה, שֶׁנֶּאֱמַר: ״וַהֲרֵמוֹתֶם מִמֶּנּוּ תְּרוּמַת ה׳ מַעֲשֵׂר מִן הַמַּעֲשֵׂר״ מַעֲשֵׂר מִן הַמַּעֲשֵׂר אָמַרְתִּי לְךָ, וְלֹא תְּרוּמָה גְּדוֹלָה וּתְרוּמַת מַעֲשֵׂר מִן הַמַּעֲשֵׂר.

And the above mentioned *halakha* is **in accordance with** the opinion of **Rabbi Abbahu, as Rabbi Abbahu said** that **Reish Lakish said:** With regard to **first tithe, in a case in which** the Levite **preceded** the priest while the grain was still **on the stalks, one is exempt from separating *teruma gedola from it,* as it is stated: "And you shall set apart from it a gift for the Lord, even a tenth part of the tithe"** (Numbers 18:26). By inference: **A tenth part of the tithe,** i.e., the *teruma* of the tithe, **I,** God, **said to you** that you must take, **and not both *teruma gedola* and the *teruma* of the tithe.**

אָמַר לֵיהּ רַב פַּפָּא לְאַבַּיֵּי: אִי הָכִי אֲפִילּוּ הִקְדִּימוֹ בַּכְּרִי נַמִי לִיפָּטֵר! אָמַר לֵיהּ, עָלֶיךָ אָמַר קְרָא: ״מִכֹּל מַתְּנוֹתֵיכֶם תָּרִימוּ וגו׳״.

Rav Pappa said to Abaye: If so, even if the Levite **preceded** the priest after the kernels of grain were removed from the stalks and placed **in a pile,** the Levite should **also be exempt** from taking *teruma gedola.* Abaye **said to him: With regard to your** claim, **the verse states: "From all that is given to you, you shall set apart** that which is the Lord's ***teruma***" (Numbers 18:29). God's *teruma,* i.e., *teruma gedola,* must be taken from all the Levites' gifts.

וּמָה רָאִיתָ?! הַאי אִידְּגַן, וְהַאי לָא אִידְּגַן.

The Gemara asks: **What did you see** that led you to require *teruma gedola* from first tithe that was taken from grain in piles, and not from first tithe that was taken from grain on stalks? Abaye answers: **This,** stalks that were threshed and placed into piles, are completely processed and **have become grain, and that,** grains that have remained on the stalk, **have not** yet **become grain.** The verse states the following with regard to *teruma gedola*: "The first of your grain" (Deuteronomy 18:4) is given to the priest. Once it is considered grain, the rights of the priest take effect and the Levite is required to separate *teruma gedola.*

״וּמַעֲשֵׂר שֵׁנִי וכו׳״. פְּשִׁיטָא! לָא צְרִיכָא, שֶׁנָּתַן אֶת הַקֶּרֶן וְלֹא נָתַן אֶת הַחוֹמֶשׁ, הָא קָא מַשְׁמַע לָן – דְּאֵין חוֹמֶשׁ מְעַכֵּב.

We learned in the mishna: One may move second tithe that was redeemed. The Gemara asks: This is obvious. The Gemara answers: **It was necessary** to teach this *halakha* **only in** a case where the consecrated property was not completely redeemed, i.e., **where one gave** payment for **the principal,** the value of the tithe, **but he did not give** payment for **the fifth** that he must add when redeeming items that he consecrated. **And** the mishna **teaches us** that failure to add **the fifth does not invalidate** the redemption, and the second tithe assumes non-sacred status from the moment that one pays the principal.

HALAKHA

Doubtfully tithed produce and tithes – דְּמַאי וּמַעֲשֵׂר: On Shabbat, it is permitted to move doubtfully tithed produce, even though it is prohibited to eat it, because it may be eaten by the poor. Similarly, it is permitted to move the fruit of the second tithe and consecrated items that have been redeemed, even though the fifth was not added (Rambam *Sefer Zemanim, Hilkhot Shabbat* 25:19).

First tithe…a Levite preceded the priest while the grain was still on the stalks – מַעֲשֵׂר רִאשׁוֹן...שֶׁהִקְדִּימוֹ בְּשִׁבּוֹלִין: An Israelite who separates tithes from the grain before *teruma gedola* is separated does not violate Torah law. There is no need to compensate the priest for his somewhat smaller portion (Rambam *Sefer Zera'im, Hilkhot Terumot* 3:13; *Tur, Yoreh De'a* 331).

NOTES

Doubtfully tithed produce…if he so desires he may renounce all his property – דְּמַאי...דְּאִי בָּעֵי, מַפְקַר לֵיהּ לְנִכְסֵיהּ: The early commentaries ask (see *Tosafot*): Why is the possibility of a person renouncing his property necessary in order to explain the reason that it is permitted to move doubtfully tithed produce? It is sufficient to establish that it may be eaten by the poor. Some explain that the explanation involving the renouncing of property is indeed extraneous in this context, but that this discussion appears elsewhere in the Talmud where this rationale is required. Therefore, it is cited here in passing. Others explain that only if something is totally unfit for someone, is the rationale employed that it may be fit for others. Since doubtfully tithed produce will be fit for a person after Shabbat after he tithes it, one sets it aside from use until then. Therefore, the Gemara cited the fact that he could renounce his property (Rashba).

One may feed the poor doubtfully tithed produce and soldiers doubtfully tithed produce – מַאֲכִילִין אֶת הָעֲנִיִּים דְּמַאי וְאֶת הָאַכְסַנְיָא דְּמַאי: Various explanations were suggested for these *halakhot*, which are subject to dispute in the Jerusalem Talmud. Some explain that these *halakhot* apply to all poor people and all guests, even those who are meticulous and separate tithes from doubtfully tithed produce. The Sages exempted doubtfully tithed produce given as charity from the obligation to separate tithes, in order to increase the funds available for charity (Rambam). Others rule that one must inform his guests and the poor that the food is doubtfully tithed produce, and anyone who wishes may separate the tithe (see Rosh).

Rashi explains that *akhsanya* refers to the king's army, while others state that it refers to Jewish soldiers, who, like the poor, are exempt from tithing doubtfully tithed produce. Others say that a gentile army may be fed with doubtfully tithed produce, and they are not considered to have benefitted from the portion of the priest.

The Levite preceded the priest while the grain was still on the stalks – שֶׁהִקְדִּימוֹ בְּשִׁבּוֹלִין: The proper way to separate *teruma* is as follows: The owner of the grain first separates *teruma gedola* from the produce. Typically the amount of the *teruma gedola* is one-fiftieth, or 2%, of the crop, which would be given to a priest. The owner then tithes the remaining produce, separating 9.8% of the original crop and giving it to the Levite. The Levite separates the *teruma* of the tithe, one-tenth of what he received, or 0.98% of the original crop, which he gives to the priest.

However, if the Levite arrives at the granary before the priest, he receives a full 10% of the grain, which he retains even after the *teruma gedola* is separated. In that case, the priest receives a total of only 2.8% instead of 2.98%. The Levite need not separate *teruma gedola* from the tithe.

LANGUAGE

Soldiers [*akhsanya*] – אַכְסַנְיָא: From the Greek **ξενία**, *xenia*, meaning a domicile for foreigners as well as food for foreigners and guests. Some understood the word in this context as related to the Greek **ὀψωνία**, *opsonia*, meaning provision of food for the army. There are variant readings that support this interpretation.

״וְהַתּוּרְמוֹס הַיָּבֵשׁ כו׳״. דַּוְקָא יָבֵשׁ, אֲבָל לַח – לֹא. מַאי טַעְמָא? כֵּיוָן דְּמָרִיר – לֹא אָכְלָה.

And we learned in the mishna: One may move even **dry lupine,** which is not fit for consumption by a person, because it is goat food. The Gemara comments: This applies **only** when lupine is **dry. However,** when it is **moist, no** it is prohibited to move it. **What is the reason** for this prohibition? **Since** lupine **is** extremely **bitter** when wet, an animal **will not eat** it.

״אֲבָל לֹא אֶת הַטֶּבֶל וכו׳״. פְּשִׁיטָא! לָא צְרִיכָא, בְּטֶבֶל טָבוּל מִדְּרַבָּנַן – שֶׁזְּרָעוֹ בְּעָצִיץ שֶׁאֵינוֹ נָקוּב.

We learned in the mishna: **However,** one may **not** move **untithed produce**[H] on Shabbat. The Gemara asks: This is **obvious.** The Gemara answers: **It was only necessary** to teach this *halakha* with regard to a case in which the produce is permitted by Torah law, but is considered **untithed produce** only **by rabbinic law. What are the circumstances?** It is referring to a case where the produce grew **in an unperforated flowerpot. The legal status of produce that grows in an unperforated flowerpot** is not like that of produce that grows in the ground.

״וְלֹא מַעֲשֵׂר רִאשׁוֹן וכו׳״. פְּשִׁיטָא! לָא צְרִיכָא, שֶׁהִקְדִּימוֹ בַּכְּרִי שֶׁנִּטַּל מִמֶּנּוּ מַעֲשֵׂר וְלֹא נִטְּלָה מִמֶּנּוּ תְּרוּמָה גְּדוֹלָה. מַהוּ דְּתֵימָא כְּדַאֲמַר לֵיהּ רַב פָּפָּא לְאַבַּיֵּי – קָא מַשְׁמַע לָן כִּדְשַׁנֵּי לֵיהּ אַבַּיֵּי.

We learned in the mishna: **Nor** may one move **first tithe**[H] from which *teruma* has not been taken. The Gemara asks: This is **obvious.** The Gemara answers: **It was only necessary** for the mishna to teach this *halakha* for a case **in which** the Levite **preceded** the priest after the kernels of grain were placed **in a pile, where first tithe was taken and *teruma gedola* was not taken. Lest you say concerning this case, as Rav Pappa said to Abaye,** here too, the produce should be exempt from the obligation to separate *teruma gedola,* the *tanna* of the mishna **teaches us as** Abaye **responded** to Rav Pappa: There is a difference between the case in which the grain was on the stalks and the case in which the grain was in a pile.

״וְלֹא אֶת מַעֲשֵׂר שֵׁנִי וכו׳״. פְּשִׁיטָא! לָא צְרִיכָא דְּנִפְדּוּ, וְלֹא נִפְדּוּ כְּהִלְכָתָן. מַעֲשֵׂר – שֶׁפְּדָאוֹ עַל גַּבֵּי אֲסִימוֹן, דְּרַחֲמָנָא אָמַר: ״וְצַרְתָּ הַכֶּסֶף בְּיָדְךָ״– דָּבָר שֶׁיֵּשׁ בּוֹ צוּרָה. הֶקְדֵּשׁ – שֶׁחִילְּלוֹ עַל גַּבֵּי קַרְקַע, דְּרַחֲמָנָא אָמַר: ״וְנָתַן הַכֶּסֶף וְקָם לוֹ״.

We learned in the mishna: **Nor** may one move **second tithe**[H] and consecrated items that were not redeemed. The Gemara asks: This **is obvious. It was only necessary** for the mishna to teach this *halakha* with regard to a case **where they were redeemed but not redeemed properly.** When the mishna lists the **second tithe,** it is referring to **that which was redeemed with an unminted coin** [*asimon*],[L] i.e., a silver bullion that had not been engraved. **And God,** in the Torah, **states** in the case of second tithe: **"And bind up** [*vetzarta*] **the money in your hand"** (Deuteronomy 14:25). The Sages interpreted this as follows: *Vetzarta* is **money that has a form** [*tzura*] engraved **upon it.** When the mishna lists **consecrated property,** it is referring to **that which was redeemed** by exchanging it **for land instead of money. And God,** in the Torah, **states** with regard to this: **He will give the money "and it will be assured to him"** (Leviticus 27:19). Money and not land may be used in redeeming consecrated property.

״וְלֹא אֶת הַלּוּף״. תָּנוּ רַבָּנַן: מְטַלְטְלִין אֶת הֶחָצָב – מִפְּנֵי שֶׁהוּא מַאֲכָל לַצְּבָיִים, וְאֶת הַחַרְדָּל – מִפְּנֵי שֶׁהוּא מַאֲכָל לַיּוֹנִים, רַבָּן שִׁמְעוֹן בֶּן גַּמְלִיאֵל אוֹמֵר: אַף מְטַלְטְלִין שִׁבְרֵי זְכוּכִית, מִפְּנֵי שֶׁהוּא מַאֲכָל לַנַּעֲמִיּוֹת.

We learned in the mishna: **Nor** may one move **arum** on Shabbat. **The Sages taught** in a *Tosefta:* **One may move squill** on Shabbat **because it is food for deer and mustard because it is food for doves. Rabban Shimon ben Gamliel says: One may even move glass shards because they are food for ostriches.**[HN]

אָמַר לֵיהּ רַבִּי נָתָן: אֶלָּא מֵעַתָּה חֲבִילֵי זְמוֹרוֹת יְטַלְטְלוּ – מִפְּנֵי שֶׁהוּא מַאֲכָל לַפִּילִין! וְרַבָּן שִׁמְעוֹן בֶּן גַּמְלִיאֵל: נַעֲמִיּוֹת – שְׁכִיחִי, פִּילִין – לָא שְׁכִיחִי.

Rabbi Natan said to Rabban Shimon ben Gamliel: **If** that is so, even **bundles of grapevines one should** be permitted to **move because** they are **food for elephants.** The Gemara answers that **Rabban Shimon ben Gamliel** responded: **Ostriches are common,** whereas **elephants are not common.**

HALAKHA

However, one may not move untithed produce – אֲבָל לֹא אֶת הַטֶּבֶל: It is prohibited to move untithed produce on Shabbat, even if its status is only by rabbinic law (Rambam *Sefer Zemanim, Hilkhot Shabbat* 25:19).

Nor may one move first tithe – וְלֹא מַעֲשֵׂר רִאשׁוֹן: It is prohibited to move the first tithe from which *teruma* of the tithe has not been separated (Rambam *Sefer Zemanim, Hilkhot Shabbat* 25:19).

Nor may one move second tithe – וְלֹא אֶת מַעֲשֵׂר שֵׁנִי: It is prohibited to move second tithe that has not been properly redeemed (Rambam *Sefer Zemanim, Hilkhot Shabbat* 25:19).

Carrying food for animals – טִלְטוּל מַאַכְלֵי בַּעֲלֵי חַיִּים: Anything fit for consumption by common, domesticated animals may be moved on Shabbat, even by one who does not own these animals. If one owns rare animals, he is permitted to move food suited for them. However, others are prohibited to do so. This ruling is in accordance with the opinion of the Rabbis (Rambam *Sefer Zemanim, Hilkhot Shabbat* 26:16–17; *Shulḥan Arukh, Oraḥ Ḥayyim* 308:29).

LANGUAGE

Unminted coin [*asimon*] – אֲסִימוֹן: From the Greek **ἄσημον**, *asèmon*, meaning an unstamped coin.

Unminted coin

NOTES

Food for ostriches – מַאֲכָל לַנַּעֲמִיּוֹת: In the Jerusalem Talmud, Ameimar's statement is accepted and Rav Ashi's objection is rejected. If a particular species is unavailable for purchase, one may not move items for its benefit on Shabbat, even if one owns an animal from that species.

אָמַר אֲמֵימָר: וְהוּא דְּאִית לֵיהּ נַעֲמִיּוֹת. אָמַר רַב אַשִׁי לְאַמֵימָר: אֶלָּא דְּקָאָמַר לֵיהּ רַבִּי נָתָן לְרַבָּן שִׁמְעוֹן בֶּן גַּמְלִיאֵל: ״חֲבִילֵי זְמוֹרוֹת יְטַלְטֵל מִפְּנֵי שֶׁהוּא מַאֲכָל לַפִּילִין״. אִי אִית לֵיהּ פִּילִין – אַמַּאי לָא?! אֶלָּא – רָאוּי, הָכָא נַמִּי – רָאוּי.

Ameimar said: And Rabban Shimon ben Gamliel permits moving glass shards **only** in a case **where one has ostriches. Rav Ashi said to Ameimar: However, with regard to** that **which Rabbi Natan said to Rabban Shimon ben Gamliel:** If that is so, even **bundles of grapevines one should** be permitted to **move because** they are **food for elephants. If one has elephants, why** would he **not** feed them? The relevant criterion to permit moving the animal food is not whether or not one owns an elephant, but **rather** whether or not the food is **suitable** as food for elephants. **Here too,** in the case of glass shards, the criterion is whether or not they are **suitable** as food for ostriches, not whether or not one owns an ostrich.[H]

אָמַר אַבַּיֵי: רַבָּן שִׁמְעוֹן בֶּן גַּמְלִיאֵל וְרַבִּי שִׁמְעוֹן וְרַבִּי יִשְׁמָעֵאל וְרַבִּי עֲקִיבָא כּוּלְּהוּ סְבִירָא לְהוּ, כׇּל יִשְׂרָאֵל בְּנֵי מְלָכִים הֵם.

Abaye said: Rabban Shimon ben Gamliel, Rabbi Shimon, Rabbi Yishmael, and Rabbi Akiva all hold that **all Jewish people are princes.** There is nothing that is unsuitable for them due to its extravagance. How do we know that all of them hold this position?

רַבָּן שִׁמְעוֹן בֶּן גַּמְלִיאֵל – הָא דַּאֲמַרַן,

Rabban Shimon ben Gamliel: From that which we said in the mishna, that it is permitted to move arum, this is because arum is food for ravens, and it is as if every Jew owns ravens.

רַבִּי שִׁמְעוֹן – דִּתְנַן: בְּנֵי מְלָכִים סָכִין עַל גַּבֵּי מַכּוֹתֵיהֶן שֶׁמֶן וֶורֶד, שֶׁכֵּן דַּרְכָּן שֶׁל בְּנֵי מְלָכִים לָסוּךְ בַּחוֹל. רַבִּי שִׁמְעוֹן אוֹמֵר: כׇּל יִשְׂרָאֵל בְּנֵי מְלָכִים הֵם.

Rabbi Shimon: As we learned in a mishna: **Princes may smear rose oil on their wounds** on Shabbat, **as it is the way of princes to smear** it on **during the week,** even without the purpose of healing a wound. **Rabbi Shimon says: All the Jewish people are princes,** and it is permitted for them to smear themselves with rose oil on Shabbat.

רַבִּי יִשְׁמָעֵאל וְרַבִּי עֲקִיבָא – דְּתַנְיָא: הֲרֵי שֶׁהָיוּ נוֹשִׁין בּוֹ אֶלֶף מָנֶה וְלָבוּשׁ אִיצְטְלָא בַּת מֵאָה מָנֶה – מַפְשִׁיטִין אוֹתוֹ וּמַלְבִּישִׁין אוֹתוֹ אִיצְטְלָא הָרְאוּיָה לוֹ. תָּנָא מִשּׁוּם רַבִּי יִשְׁמָעֵאל, וְתָנָא מִשּׁוּם רַבִּי עֲקִיבָא: כׇּל יִשְׂרָאֵל רְאוּיִן לְאוֹתָהּ אִיצְטְלָא.

Rabbi Yishmael and Rabbi Akiva: From that which was taught in a *baraita*: **One from whom** his creditors **were demanding repayment** of a debt **of a thousand** times **one hundred** dinar **[*maneh*]**[NH] **and he was wearing a cloak [*itztela*]**[L] **worth one hundred** times **one hundred** dinar,[B] **they strip him** of that cloak and sell it, **and dress him with a cloak worthy of him** based on his wealth. **It was taught in the name of Rabbi Yishmael, and it was taught in the name of Rabbi Akiva: All the Jewish people are worthy of that** more expensive **cloak,** and it cannot be said that one is unworthy of it. Rather, the coat is treated like any other vital garment. The principle that one need not sell his vital garments to pay off a debt applies to it.

״חֲבִילֵי קַשׁ וַחֲבִילֵי כו׳״. תָּנוּ רַבָּנַן: חֲבִילֵי קַשׁ וַחֲבִילֵי עֵצִים וַחֲבִילֵי זְרָדִים, אִם הִתְקִינָן לְמַאֲכַל בְּהֵמָה – מְטַלְטְלִין אוֹתָן, וְאִם לָאו – אֵין מְטַלְטְלִין אוֹתָן. רַבָּן שִׁמְעוֹן בֶּן גַּמְלִיאֵל אוֹמֵר: חֲבִילִין הַנִּיטָּלִין בְּיָד אֶחָד – מוּתָּר לְטַלְטְלָן, בִּשְׁתֵּי יָדַיִם – אָסוּר לְטַלְטְלָן.

We learned in the mishna: With regard to **bundles of straw, and bundles** of wood,[H] and bundles of twigs, if one prepared them on Shabbat eve for animal food, one may move them. If not, one may not move them. **The Sages taught** in a *Tosefta*: With regard to **bundles of straw, and bundles of wood, and bundles of twigs, if one prepared them** on Shabbat eve **for animal food, one may move them. And if not, one may not move them. Rabban Shimon ben Gamliel says: Bundles that are taken in one hand,** it is **permitted to move them,** as no exertion is involved. However, if they can only be taken **in two hands,** it **is prohibited to move them.**

חֲבִילֵי סִיאָה אֵזוֹב וְקוֹרָנִית, הִכְנִיסָן לְעֵצִים – אֵין מִסְתַּפֵּק מֵהֶן בְּשַׁבָּת, לְמַאֲכַל בְּהֵמָה – מִסְתַּפֵּק מֵהֶן בְּשַׁבָּת.

With regard to **bundles of savory, hyssop, and thyme,**[HB] fragrant plants suitable as food for people, **if one brought them in for** use as **firewood, he may not supply himself from them on Shabbat** for food. If he brought them in **for** use as **food for animals,** he too **may supply himself from them on Shabbat.**

NOTES

One from whom his creditors were demanding repayment of a debt of a thousand times one hundred dinar – הֲרֵי שֶׁהָיוּ נוֹשִׁין בּוֹ אֶלֶף מָנֶה: There is a halakhic principle that the court makes an arrangement for a debtor. Even though one committed to pay his entire debt and designated all of his property as collateral, the court does not collect everything that he owns. Instead, the court leaves certain necessary items, including clothing, in the debtor's possession. The only dispute in this matter concerns one who grew accustomed to using certain expensive belongings when he was wealthy. There is a question as to whether or not he may keep those items in his possession.

LANGUAGE

Cloak [*itztela*] – אִיצְטְלָא: From the Greek **στολίς**, *stolis*, meaning garment or cloak.

BACKGROUND

One hundred times one hundred dinar [*maneh*] – מֵאָה מָנֶה: The *maneh* is a coin worth one hundred dinar. To evaluate the purchasing power of one hundred *maneh*, it should be kept in mind that a worker's daily wages amounted to roughly four dinar. One hundred *maneh* were worth approximately seven years of the average worker's wages.

Maneh coin, from the end of the talmudic period

Thyme – קוֹרָנִית: *Koranit*, according to various identifications in the Talmud, probably refers to the plant called conehead thyme, *Coridothymus capitatus* L. It is a branched shrub 10–50 cm in height, with small, short branches 5 mm long. Its leaves are pink and emit a fragrance. Conehead thyme grows wild in most areas of Israel.

Conehead thyme

HALAKHA

One from whom his creditors were demanding repayment of a debt of a thousand times one hundred dinar – הֲרֵי שֶׁהָיוּ נוֹשִׁים בּוֹ אֶלֶף מָנֶה: The court does not collect a debtor's clothes and essential household items in payment of a debt. However, if the debtor dresses in very expensive garments, the court may sell those garments to repay the debt and provide the debtor with other garments (Rambam *Sefer Mishpatim, Hilkhot Malve VeLoveh* 1:7 and *Sefer Hafla'a, Hilkhot Arakhin VaHaramim* 3:16; *Shulḥan Arukh, Ḥoshen Mishpat* 97:28).

Bundles of straw and bundles of wood – חֲבִילֵי קַשׁ וַחֲבִילֵי עֵצִים: It is permitted to move bundles of straw and wood that were prepared as food for one's animals on Shabbat, even if the bundles are very large (Rambam *Sefer Zemanim, Hilkhot Shabbat* 26:18; *Shulḥan Arukh, Oraḥ Ḥayyim* 308:28).

Bundles of savory, hyssop, and thyme – חֲבִילֵי סִיאָה אֵזוֹב וְקוֹרָנִית: It is prohibited to make use of plants that are not designated specifically for people to eat, if one stored them with the firewood. However, if he stored them as animal feed, he may pick them by hand and eat them. He may not pick them with a utensil in the manner that he does during the week. It is permitted to crush the herbs with his fingertips, but not with his entire hand as he would during the week (Rambam *Sefer Zemanim, Hilkhot Shabbat* 26:18; *Shulḥan Arukh, Oraḥ Ḥayyim* 321:1).

וְקוֹטֵם בַּיָּד וְאוֹכֵל, וּבִלְבַד שֶׁלֹּא יִקְטוֹם בִּכְלִי. וּמוֹלֵל וְאוֹכֵל, וּבִלְבַד שֶׁלֹּא יָמְלוֹל בִּכְלִי הַרְבֵּה, דִּבְרֵי רַבִּי יְהוּדָה. וַחֲכָמִים אוֹמְרִים: מוֹלֵל בְּרָאשֵׁי אֶצְבְּעוֹתָיו וְאוֹכֵל, וּבִלְבַד שֶׁלֹּא יָמְלוֹל בְּיָדוֹ הַרְבֵּה כְּדֶרֶךְ שֶׁהוּא עוֹשֶׂה בַּחוֹל.

And one may pick them **with** his **hand and eat, as long as he does not pick** them **with a vessel. And one may crush** and remove the seeds with his hand **and eat** them, **as long as he does not crush a lot with a vessel;** this is **the statement of Rabbi Yehuda. And the Rabbis say: One may crush** them only **with the ends of his fingers,** in an atypical manner, **as long as he does not crush a lot with his hand in the manner that he does during the week.**

וְכֵן בְּאָמִיתָא, וְכֵן בְּפֵיגָם, וְכֵן בִּשְׁאָר מִינֵי תַבְלִין. מַאי אָמִיתָא? נִינְיָא. "סִיאָה". אָמַר רַב יְהוּדָה: (סִיאָה) – צַתְרֵי. "אֵזוֹב" – אַבְרָתָא. "קוֹרָנִית" – קוֹרָנִיתָא שְׁמָהּ.

And that **too** is the *halakha* **with regard to** *amita*, **and with regard to rue** [*peigam*],[L] **and with regard to all the other types of spices.** The Sages asked: **What is** *amita*? They answered: It is **mint** [*ninya*].[L] What is *sia*? **Rav Yehuda says:** *Sia* **is savory.** *Ezov* **is hyssop.** *Koranit* **is called** *koranita*, i.e., it is not known to us by any other name.

וְהָא הַהוּא דַּאֲמַר לְהוּ: "מַאן בָּעֵי קוֹרָנִיתָא", וְאִישְׁתַּכַּח "חַשֵּׁי"! אֶלָּא: סִיאָה – צַתְרֵי, אֵזוֹב – אַבְרָתָא, קוֹרָנִיתָא – חַשֵּׁי.

The Gemara asks: **The one who came** to sell **and said to them: Who wants** *koranita*? **And he was found** to be selling **thyme.** Therefore, we see that *koranita* is in fact a plant that is known to us. **Rather,** it should be explained: *Sia* **is savory,** *ezov* **is hyssop,** and *koranita* **is thyme.**

אִיתְּמַר: בָּשָׂר מָלִיחַ מוּתָּר לְטַלְטְלוֹ בְּשַׁבָּת; בָּשָׂר תָּפֵל, רַב הוּנָא אָמַר: מוּתָּר לְטַלְטְלוֹ, רַב חִסְדָּא אָמַר: אָסוּר לְטַלְטְלוֹ.

It was stated: It is permitted to move salted meat on Shabbat, as it is fit for consumption. With regard to **unsalted meat, Rav Huna said: It is permitted to move it. Rav Ḥisda said: It is prohibited to move it.**

רַב הוּנָא אָמַר: מוּתָּר לְטַלְטְלוֹ? וְהָא רַב הוּנָא תַּלְמִיד דְּרַב הֲוָה, וְרַב כְּרַבִּי יְהוּדָה סְבִירָא לֵיהּ, דְּאִית לֵיהּ מוּקְצֶה!

The Gemara asks: Did **Rav Huna say** that **it is permitted to move it? Wasn't Rav Huna a student of Rav, and Rav holds in accordance with** the opinion of **Rabbi Yehuda, who is** of the opinion that there is a prohibition of **set-aside** for salted meat? How could Rav Huna disagree with the opinion of his teacher?

בְּמוּקְצֶה לַאֲכִילָה – סָבַר לַהּ כְּרַבִּי יְהוּדָה, בְּמוּקְצֶה לְטַלְטֵל – סָבַר לַהּ כְּרַבִּי שִׁמְעוֹן.

The Gemara answers: **With regard to** a food item **set aside from eating,** Rav **holds in accordance with** the opinion of **Rabbi Yehuda,** that it may not be eaten. With regard to an item **set aside from moving, he holds in accordance with** the opinion of **Rabbi Shimon,**[N] who is not of the opinion that there is a prohibition of set-aside, and moving it is permitted.

רַב חִסְדָּא אָמַר: אָסוּר לְטַלְטְלוֹ. וְהָא רַב יִצְחָק בַּר אַמֵּי אִיקְּלַע לְבֵי רַב חִסְדָּא, וַחֲזָא הַהוּא בַּר אַוָּוזָא דַּהֲווּ קָא מְטַלְטְלוּ לֵיהּ מִשִּׁמְשָׁא לְטוּלָּא. וְאָמַר רַב חִסְדָּא: חֶסְרוֹן כִּיס קָא חָזֵינַן הָכָא! שָׁאנֵי בַּר אַוָּוזָא דַּחֲזֵי לְאוּמְצָא.

Rav Ḥisda said: It is prohibited to move unsalted meat on Shabbat. The Gemara asks: **Didn't Rav Yitzḥak bar Ami happen** to come **to Rav Ḥisda's house, and he saw** the meat **of that duck?** He saw **that they were moving it from the sun to the shade** so that it would not spoil. **And Rav Ḥisda said** to the members of his household: **We see** a case of **monetary loss here.** One must make certain that the meat does not stay in the sun and spoil. Apparently, Rav Ḥisda holds that it is permitted to move inedible meat. The Gemara answers: The meat of a **duck is different, as it is fit to** be eaten as **raw meat.**

תָּנוּ רַבָּנַן: דָּג מָלִיחַ – מוּתָּר לְטַלְטְלוֹ, דָּג תָּפֵל – אָסוּר לְטַלְטְלוֹ. בָּשָׂר, בֵּין תָּפֵל וּבֵין מָלִיחַ – מוּתָּר לְטַלְטְלוֹ, (וּסְתָמָא כְּרַבִּי שִׁמְעוֹן).

The Sages taught in a *baraita*: With regard to **salted fish,**[H] **it is permitted to move it** on Shabbat. With regard to **unsalted fish, it is prohibited to move it. Meat, both unsalted** meat[H] **and salted** meat, **it is permitted to carry it. And this unattributed** *baraita* **is in accordance with** the opinion of **Rabbi Shimon.**

תָּנוּ רַבָּנַן: מְטַלְטְלִין אֶת הָעֲצָמוֹת מִפְּנֵי שֶׁהוּא מַאֲכָל לִכְלָבִים,

The Sages taught: One may move bones[H] on Shabbat, **because** they are **food for dogs.**

LANGUAGE

Rue [*peigam*] – פֵּיגָם: From the Greek πήγανον, *pèganon*, a plant from the ruta family.

Mint [*ninya*] – נִינְיָא: From the Akkadian *nīnû*, referring to a medicinal plant.

NOTES

With regard to an item set aside from moving, he holds in accordance with the opinion of Rabbi Shimon – בְּמוּקְצֶה לְטַלְטֵל סָבַר לַהּ כְּרַבִּי שִׁמְעוֹן: Fundamentally, Rav holds in accordance with the opinion of Rabbi Yehuda with regard to the prohibition of set-aside that objects set aside due to prohibition may not be moved. However, Rav ruled that if a food item may not be eaten because it is set-aside, there is no reason to prohibit moving it (Rashba).

HALAKHA

Salted fish – דָּג מָלִיחַ: It is permitted to move salted fish on Shabbat. However, it is prohibited to move unsalted, raw, uncooked fish, as per the *baraita* (Rambam *Sefer Zemanim, Hilkhot Shabbat* 26:18; *Shulḥan Arukh, Oraḥ Ḥayyim* 308:32).

Unsalted meat – בָּשָׂר תָּפֵל: It is permitted to move raw meat even if it unsalted because it is edible, as per the *baraita* (Rambam *Sefer Zemanim, Hilkhot Shabbat* 26:18; *Shulḥan Arukh, Oraḥ Ḥayyim* 321:31).

One may move bones – מְטַלְטְלִין אֶת הָעֲצָמוֹת: On Shabbat, it is permitted to move bones whose meat was removed on Shabbat eve. It is all the more so permitted if the meat was removed on Shabbat, because the bones are dog food. This ruling is according to the *Beit Yosef*, in accordance with the *baraita* (Rambam *Sefer Zemanim, Hilkhot Shabbat* 26:18; *Shulḥan Arukh, Oraḥ Ḥayyim* 308:29 and in the comment of the Rema).

Perek **XVIII**
Daf **128** Amud **b**

בָּשָׂר תָּפוּחַ – מִפְּנֵי שֶׁהוּא מַאֲכָל לְחַיָּה, מַיִם מְגוּלִּין – מִפְּנֵי שֶׁהֵן רְאוּיִין לְחָתוּל. רַבָּן שִׁמְעוֹן בֶּן גַּמְלִיאֵל אוֹמֵר: כׇּל עִצְמָן אָסוּר לְשַׁהוֹתָן, מִפְּנֵי הַסַּכָּנָה.

With regard to **swollen meat**[N] that began to putrefy, it is permitted to move it **because it is food for non-domesticated animals.** With regard to **exposed water,** from which a snake might have drunk and into which it injected its venom, it is permitted to move it **because it is suitable for a cat,** which is somewhat immune to snake venom. **Rabban Shimon ben Gamliel says:** Exposed water **itself may not be kept due to the danger** that one may inadvertently drink it.

NOTES

Swollen meat – בָּשָׂר תָּפוּחַ: Some commentaries explain that swollen meat is meat so putrefied that it is not fit for consumption even by a dog. Others explain that it is swollen due to venom and can only be eaten by certain animals (*Korban Netanel*).

מתני׳ כּוֹפִין אֶת הַסַּל לִפְנֵי הָאֶפְרוֹחִים כְּדֵי שֶׁיַּעֲלוּ וְיֵרְדוּ. תַּרְנְגוֹלֶת שֶׁבָּרְחָה דּוֹחִין אוֹתָהּ עַד שֶׁתִּכָּנֵס.

MISHNA One may overturn a basket in front of the chicks[H] so that **they can climb on and climb off** of it. Likewise, with regard to **a hen that fled** that one seeks to retrieve, **one may push it** even with his hands **until it reenters** the house.

מְדַדִּין עֲגָלִין וּסְיָיחִין. אִשָּׁה מְדַדָּה אֶת בְּנָהּ. אָמַר רַבִּי יְהוּדָה: אֵימָתַי – בִּזְמַן שֶׁהוּא נוֹטֵל אַחַת וּמַנִּיחַ אַחַת! אֲבָל אִם הָיָה גּוֹרֵר – אָסוּר.

One may help calves and foals to walk,[N] and likewise **a woman may help her son to walk.**[H] **Rabbi Yehuda said: When** is it permitted? **When** her son **picks one** foot **up and puts one** foot **down** by himself. **However, if** her son **were dragging** both his feet, **it would be prohibited** because it would be like carrying him in the public domain.

גמ׳ אָמַר רַב יְהוּדָה אָמַר רַב: בְּהֵמָה שֶׁנָּפְלָה לְאַמַּת הַמַּיִם – מֵבִיא כָּרִים וּכְסָתוֹת וּמַנִּיחַ תַּחְתֶּיהָ, וְאִם עָלְתָה – עָלְתָה.

GEMARA Rav Yehuda said that **Rav said:** With regard **to an animal that fell into an aqueduct,**[H] **one brings cushions and blankets,** and throws them into the water ditch, **and places them beneath** the animal in the aqueduct. **And if** the animal thereby **emerges, it emerges.**

מֵיתִיבִי: בְּהֵמָה שֶׁנָּפְלָה לְאַמַּת הַמַּיִם – עוֹשֶׂה לָהּ פַּרְנָסָה בִּמְקוֹמָהּ בִּשְׁבִיל שֶׁלֹּא תָּמוּת. פַּרְנָסָה – אִין, כָּרִים וּכְסָתוֹת – לָא!

The Gemara **raises an objection** from a *Tosefta*: With regard to **an animal that fell into an aqueduct** on Shabbat, **one provides it with sustenance in its place so that it will not die.** This implies that providing it with **sustenance, yes,** that is permitted, providing it with **cushions and blankets, no,** that it is prohibited.

לָא קַשְׁיָא; הָא – דְּאֶפְשָׁר בְּפַרְנָסָה, הָא – דְּאִי אֶפְשָׁר בְּפַרְנָסָה. אֶפְשָׁר בְּפַרְנָסָה – אִין, וְאִי לָא – מֵבִיא כָּרִים וּכְסָתוֹת וּמַנִּיחַ תַּחְתֶּיהָ,

The Gemara answers: This is **not difficult,** as there is room to distinguish between the cases. **This,** the *Tosefta* in which it was taught that one provides the animal with sustenance, is referring to a case where **it is possible to provide** it with **sustenance. That,** the mishna in which Rav said that one brings cushions and blankets, is referring to a case where **it is impossible to provide** it with **sustenance.** Where **it is possible to provide** it with **sustenance, yes,** he does so. **And if** it is **not** possible to provide it with sustenance, **he brings cushions and blankets and places them beneath** the animal.

וְהָא קָא מְבַטֵּל כְּלִי מֵהֵיכָנוֹ! סָבַר, מְבַטֵּל כְּלִי מֵהֵיכָנוֹ – דְּרַבָּנַן, צַעַר בַּעֲלֵי חַיִּים – דְּאוֹרַיְיתָא, וְאָתֵי דְּאוֹרַיְיתָא וְדָחֵי דְּרַבָּנַן.

The Gemara asks: **Does he not,** by placing the cushions and blankets, **negate a vessel's preparedness?** The cushions and blankets are no longer fit for their designated use on Shabbat, and this negation of their designated use is similar to the prohibited labor of dismantling. The Gemara answers: Rav **holds** that **negating a vessel's preparedness** is prohibited **by rabbinic law. Causing a living creature to suffer** is a **Torah** prohibition.[H] **And** a matter prohibited by **Torah law comes and overrides** a matter prohibited **by rabbinic law.**

״תַּרְנְגוֹלֶת שֶׁבָּרְחָה וכו׳״. דּוֹחִין – אִין, מְדַדִּין – לָא. תְּנֵינָא לְהָא, דְּתָנוּ רַבָּנַן: מְדַדִּין בְּהֵמָה חַיָּה וְעוֹף בֶּחָצֵר, אֲבָל לֹא אֶת הַתַּרְנְגוֹלֶת.

We learned in the mishna: With regard to **a hen that fled** that one seeks to retrieve, he may push it back to its place. By inference: **Push** the hen, **yes,** it is permitted, **help** it **to walk, no,** it is prohibited. The Gemara comments: **We** already **learned this, as the Sages taught: One may help domesticated animals, non-domesticated animals, and fowl walk**[H] **in the courtyard** on Shabbat, **but not hens.**

תַּרְנְגוֹלֶת מַאי טַעְמָא לָא? אָמַר אַבַּיֵי: מִשּׁוּם דְּמַקְפְּיָא נַפְשָׁהּ.

The Gemara asks: With regard to **a hen, what** is the **reason** that one may **not** help it walk? **Abaye says:** It is prohibited **because** the hen **lifts itself** off the ground. As a result, one actually carries it.

תָּנֵי חֲדָא: מְדַדִּין בְּהֵמָה וְחַיָּה וְעוֹף בֶּחָצֵר, אֲבָל לֹא בִּרְשׁוּת הָרַבִּים. וְהָאִשָּׁה מְדַדָּה אֶת בְּנָהּ בִּרְשׁוּת הָרַבִּים, וְאֵין צָרִיךְ לוֹמַר בֶּחָצֵר. וְתַנְיָא אִידָךְ: אֵין עוֹקְרִין בְּהֵמָה וְחַיָּה וְעוֹף בֶּחָצֵר, אֲבָל דּוֹחִין בָּהֶן שֶׁיִּכָּנְסוּ.

It was taught in **one** *baraita*: **One may help domesticated animals, non-domesticated animals, and fowl walk in the courtyard, but not in the public domain. And a woman may help her son walk in the public domain, and, needless to say,** it is permitted **in the courtyard. And it was taught** in **another** *baraita*: **One may not lift domesticated animals, non-domesticated animals, and fowl** off the ground **in the courtyard, but one may push them so that they will enter.**

הָא גּוּפָא קַשְׁיָא, אָמְרַתְּ: ״אֵין עוֹקְרִין״ אֲבָל דַּדּוֹיֵי – מְדַדִּינַן. הֲדַר אָמְרַתְּ: דּוֹחִין – אִין, מְדַדִּין – לָא! אָמַר אַבַּיֵי: סֵיפָא אֲתָאן לְתַרְנְגוֹלֶת.

The Gemara first seeks to clarify the second *baraita*. **This** *baraita* **itself is difficult.** On the one hand, **you said** that **one may not lift,** from which it may be inferred, **however,** that **one may help it walk. Then you said: Push, yes,** it is permitted, **help walk, no,** it is prohibited. **Abaye said: The latter clause,** which states that one may not help it walk, **we came to** the *halakha* of a **hen,** which, as mentioned above, one may not help it walk.

HALAKHA

One may overturn a basket in front of the chicks – כּוֹפִין אֶת הַסַּל לִפְנֵי הָאֶפְרוֹחִים: On Shabbat, it is permitted to overturn a basket so chicks may climb on and climb off it. However, it is prohibited to move the basket while the chicks are on it (Rambam *Sefer Zemanim, Hilkhot Shabbat* 25:25; *Shulḥan Arukh, Oraḥ Ḥayyim* 308:39).

A woman may help her son to walk – אִשָּׁה מְדַדָּה אֶת בְּנָהּ: It is permitted to help a child walk on Shabbat, even in the public domain, provided that the child takes each step by himself and that one does not drag the child. This ruling is based on the principle that when Rabbi Yehuda asks in the mishna the rhetorical question: When, he is explaining the opinion of the Rabbis, and that opinion is the *halakha* (Rambam *Sefer Zemanim, Hilkhot Shabbat* 18:16, 25:25; *Shulḥan Arukh, Oraḥ Ḥayyim* 308:41).

An animal that fell into an aqueduct – בְּהֵמָה שֶׁנָּפְלָה לְאַמַּת הַמַּיִם: If an animal falls into an aqueduct on Shabbat, it is preferable to feed it there. However, if the water in the aqueduct is deep, and feeding the animal there is impossible, it is permitted to bring cushions or blankets and place them beneath the animal so it can climb out (Rambam *Sefer Zemanim, Hilkhot Shabbat* 25:26; *Shulḥan Arukh, Oraḥ Ḥayyim* 305:19).

Causing a living creature to suffer is a Torah prohibition – צַעַר בַּעֲלֵי חַיִּים דְּאוֹרַיְיתָא: Causing a living creature to suffer is prohibited by Torah law. Indeed, one must make every effort to ease the pain of living creatures (Rambam *Sefer Nezikin, Hilkhot Rotze'aḥ UShemirat HaNefesh* 13:13; *Shulḥan Arukh, Ḥoshen Mishpat* 272:9 and in the comment of the Rema).

One may help domesticated animals…walk, etc. – מְדַדִּין בְּהֵמָה וכו׳: It is permitted to help young animals and fowl of all kinds walk in a courtyard, so long as they require the assistance and provided that one does not lift them off of the ground. Assisting hens is prohibited because a hen lifts itself off of the ground. Therefore, assisting it entails carrying it. However, it is permitted to gently nudge a hen with one's hand to encourage it to walk, as per the mishna and in accordance with the opinion of Abaye (Rambam *Sefer Zemanim, Hilkhot Shabbat* 25:26; *Shulḥan Arukh, Oraḥ Ḥayyim* 308:40).

NOTES

Help…walk – מְדַדִּין: The rationale for helping young animals to walk is to prevent a living creature from suffering. However, it is only permitted to help the animal when it needs help (Ran).

אָמַר אַבָּיֵי: הַאי מַאן דְּשָׁחֵיט תַּרְנְגוֹלֶת – לִכְבְשִׁינְהוּ לְכַרְעֵיהּ בְּאַרְעָא, אִי נַמִי – נִידַל לְהוּ מִידָל. דְּדִילְמָא מַנַּח לְהוּ לְטוּפְרֵיהּ בְּאַרְעָא, וְעָקַר לְהוּ לְסִימָנִים.

Having mentioned moving the hen, the Gemara cites that which **Abaye said: One who slaughters a hen**[H] **should force its legs into the ground, or alternatively lift it** entirely into the air. Failure to do so leads to the concern **lest** the hen **place its claws into the ground** and convulse during the slaughter **and dislocate the signs,**[N] the trachea and gullet. This would invalidate the slaughter and render the hen an unslaughtered animal carcass.

מתני׳ אֵין מְיַלְּדִין אֶת הַבְּהֵמָה בְּיוֹם טוֹב! אֲבָל מְסַעֲדִין. וּמְיַלְּדִין אֶת הָאִשָּׁה בְּשַׁבָּת, וְקוֹרִין לָהּ חֲכָמָה מִמָּקוֹם לְמָקוֹם, וּמְחַלְּלִין עָלֶיהָ אֶת הַשַּׁבָּת, וְקוֹשְׁרִין אֶת הַטִּיבּוּר. רַבִּי יוֹסֵי אוֹמֵר: אַף חוֹתְכִין. וְכָל צָרְכֵי מִילָה עוֹשִׂין בְּשַׁבָּת.

MISHNA **One may not birth an animal**[NH] **on a Festival,** and all the more one may not birth it on Shabbat. **However, one may assist it** to give birth. **And one may birth a woman**[H] even **on Shabbat, and call a midwife for her** to travel **from place to place,** even when the midwife's travel involves the desecration of Shabbat. **And one may desecrate Shabbat for** a woman giving birth. **And one may tie the umbilical cord** of a child born on Shabbat. **Rabbi Yosei says: One may even cut** the umbilical cord. **And all the requirements of circumcision may be performed** for a baby whose eighth day of life occurs **on Shabbat.**

גמ׳ כֵּיצַד מְסַעֲדִין? רַב יְהוּדָה אָמַר: אוֹחֵז אֶת הַוָּלָד שֶׁלֹּא יִפּוֹל לָאָרֶץ. רַב נַחְמָן אָמַר: דּוֹחֵק בַּבָּשָׂר כְּדֵי שֶׁיֵּצֵא הַוָּלָד.

GEMARA The Gemara asks: **How may one assist** in the birth of an animal? **Rav Yehuda said: One holds the newborn so that it will not fall to the ground. Rav Naḥman says: One presses the flesh** around the womb **so that the newborn will emerge.**

תַּנְיָא כְּוָותֵיהּ דְּרַב יְהוּדָה: כֵּיצַד מְסַעֲדִין – אוֹחֲזִין אֶת הַוָּלָד שֶׁלֹּא יִפּוֹל לָאָרֶץ, וְנוֹפֵחַ לוֹ בְּחוֹטְמוֹ, וְנוֹתֵן לוֹ דַּד לְתוֹךְ פִּיו כְּדֵי שֶׁיִּינַק.

It was taught in a *baraita* **in accordance with** the opinion of **Rav Yehuda: How may one assist** in the birth of an animal? **One holds the newborn so that it will not fall to the ground, and he blows into its nostrils** to remove mucus obstructing the air passages, enabling the offspring to breathe, **and he places** the mother's **teat into its mouth so that it will suckle.**

אָמַר רַבָּן שִׁמְעוֹן בֶּן גַּמְלִיאֵל: מְרַחֲמִין הָיִינוּ עַל בְּהֵמָה טְהוֹרָה בְּיוֹם טוֹב. הֵיכִי עָבֵיד? אָמַר אַבָּיֵי: מֵבִיא בּוּל שֶׁל מֶלַח וּמַנִּיחַ לָהּ בְּתוֹךְ הָרֶחֶם, כְּדֵי שֶׁתִּזְכּוֹר צַעֲרָהּ וּתְרַחֵם עָלָיו. וּמְזַלְּפִין מֵי שִׁלְיָא עַל גַּבֵּי וָלָד כְּדֵי שֶׁתָּרִיחַ רֵיחוֹ וּתְרַחֵם עָלָיו. וְדַוְקָא טְהוֹרָה, אֲבָל טְמֵאָה – לֹא.

Rabban Shimon ben Gamliel says: We would have mercy on kosher animals[H] **on a Festival,** to help the offspring. The Gemara asks: **How does** one have mercy? **Abaye said:** If the mother does not draw her offspring near and tend to it, **one may bring a lump of salt and place** it **in the** animal's **womb, so that** it will suffer, **remember its suffering** while giving birth, **and have mercy on** the offspring. And **one may pour fluids of the afterbirth on** the offspring **so that** the mother **will smell it and have mercy on it,** her offspring. **And** this may be done **specifically** for a **kosher** animal, **but** for a **non-kosher** animal, **no,** it may not be done.

מַאי טַעְמָא? טְמֵאָה לָא מְרַחֲקָא וְלָדָא, וְאִי מְרַחֲקָא וְלָדָא – לָא מְקָרְבָא.

The Gemara asks: **What is the reason** one may not do so for **a non-kosher** animal? The Gemara answers: **A non-kosher** animal **does not distance its offspring, and if it does distance its offspring, it will not draw** it **near** again. No purpose is served by taking these steps with a non-kosher animal.

״מְיַלְּדִין אֶת הָאִשָּׁה וכו׳״. מִכְּדֵי תְּנָא לֵיהּ ״מְיַלְּדִין אֶת הָאִשָּׁה וְקוֹרִין לָהּ חֲכָמָה מִמָּקוֹם לְמָקוֹם״, ״וּמְחַלְּלִין עָלֶיהָ אֶת הַשַּׁבָּת״ לְאֵתוֹיֵי מַאי?

We learned in the mishna: **And one may birth a woman** even when that involves the desecration of Shabbat. The Gemara asks: **After all, it was taught** explicitly in the mishna: **And one may birth a woman** even **on Shabbat, and call a midwife for her** to travel **from place to place.** The phrase: **And one may desecrate Shabbat for** a woman giving birth, **what** does it come **to include?** All the possible acts of desecrating Shabbat for the birthing woman were already listed.

NOTES

Dislocate the signs – עָקַר לְהוּ לְסִימָנִים: When slaughtering an animal, dislocating the trachea and the gullet instead of cutting them renders the animal an unslaughtered carcass.

One may not birth an animal – אֵין מְיַלְּדִין אֶת הַבְּהֵמָה: According to Rashi, birthing an animal is prohibited because it involves exertion, and it is prohibited by rabbinic decree. Others maintain that delivering an animal on Shabbat is a violation of a prohibition by Torah law.

HALAKHA

One who slaughters a hen – הַאי מַאן דְּשָׁחֵיט תַּרְנְגוֹלֶת: One who slaughters hens must make certain to force their legs into the ground or lift them completely off of the ground, so as not to invalidate the kosher slaughter. This ruling is as per the opinion of Abaye (Rambam *Sefer Kedusha, Hilkhot Sheḥita* 3:14; *Shulḥan Arukh, Yoreh De'a* 24:20).

One may not birth an animal – אֵין מְיַלְּדִין אֶת הַבְּהֵמָה: It is prohibited to birth an animal on Shabbat or on a Festival; however, it is permitted to assist in the birth, even on Shabbat. The manners in which it is permitted to assist the birth are the following: Holding the newborn so it does not fall, blowing into its nostrils, and placing a teat into its mouth. This ruling is as per the mishna, and in accordance with the statements of all the *amora'im*. The *amora'im* do not disagree on this matter, they merely cite different examples (Rambam *Sefer Zemanim, Hilkhot Yom Tov* 4:16; *Shulḥan Arukh, Oraḥ Ḥayyim* 332:1, 523:3).

And one may birth a woman – וּמְיַלְּדִין אֶת הָאִשָּׁה: The legal status of a woman in childbirth is that of a dangerously sick person, and all her needs may be performed on Shabbat. A lamp may be kindled for her even if she is blind, as it calms her. Any labors that can be performed in an atypical manner should be performed that way (Rambam *Sefer Zemanim, Hilkhot Shabbat* 2:11; *Shulḥan Arukh, Oraḥ Ḥayyim* 330:1).

We would have mercy on kosher animals – מְרַחֲמִין הָיִינוּ עַל בְּהֵמָה טְהוֹרָה: When a kosher animal pushes away its newborn, it is permitted to splash fluid from the placenta onto the newborn. It is also permitted to place a lump of salt into the mother's womb to cause it pain, so that it will have pity on the child and draw it near. This procedure may not be performed on a non-kosher animal because it is ineffective (Rambam *Sefer Zemanim, Hilkhot Yom Tov* 4:16; *Shulḥan Arukh, Oraḥ Ḥayyim* 523:4).

NOTES

Womb [*kever*] – קֶבֶר: Although the Talmud does not shy away from discussing any issue, as all aspects of life require talmudic study, the Sages consistently employ euphemisms. In this case, the word *kever*, literally grave, is a euphemism for the womb. This particular euphemism was influenced by the verse in which these two items are listed together among things that are never satisfied: "The grave and the barren womb" (Proverbs 30:16).

לְאַתּוֹיֵי הָא דְּתָנוּ רַבָּנַן: אִם הָיְתָה צְרִיכָה לְנֵר – חֲבֶירְתָּהּ מַדְלֶקֶת לָהּ אֶת הַנֵּר, וְאִם הָיְתָה צְרִיכָה לְשֶׁמֶן – חֲבֶירְתָּהּ מְבִיאָה לָהּ שֶׁמֶן בַּיָּד, וְאִם אֵינוֹ סִפֵּק בַּיָּד – מְבִיאָה בִּשְׂעָרָהּ, וְאִם אֵינוֹ סִפֵּק בִּשְׂעָרָהּ – מְבִיאָה לָהּ בַּכְּלִי.

The Gemara answers: It comes **to include that which the Sages taught** with regard to this issue: **If a** woman giving birth **were to need a lamp, her friend lights the lamp for her** on Shabbat. **And if she were to need oil, her friend brings her oil** via the public domain in an atypical manner, carrying it **in** the palm of her **hand** but not in a vessel. **And if** the oil that her friend brings **in** her **hand is not enough, she brings** oil **in her hair. And if** oil that she brings **in** her **hair is not enough, she brings** oil **for her** in the typical manner, **in a vessel.**

אָמַר מָר: אִם הָיְתָה צְרִיכָה לְנֵר – חֲבֶירְתָּהּ מַדְלֶקֶת לָהּ אֶת הַנֵּר. פְּשִׁיטָא! לָא צְרִיכָא בְּסוּמָא. מַהוּ דְּתֵימָא: כֵּיוָן דְּלָא חָזְיָא – אָסוּר, קָא מַשְׁמַע לָן: אִיתּוֹבֵי מִיתְבָא דַּעְתָּהּ, סָבְרָא: אִי אִיכָּא מִידֵּי – חָזְיָא חֲבֶירְתָּהּ וְעָבְדָה לִי.

The Master said in the *baraita*: **If** a woman giving birth **were to need a lamp, her friend** would **light the lamp for her** on Shabbat. The Gemara asks: This is **obvious.** The Gemara answers: It is **necessary** to teach this *halakha* **only in the case of a blind** woman giving birth. **Lest you say: Since she cannot see** even with the light **it is prohibited** to bring a lamp for her, **it teaches us** that lighting the lamp is permitted to **settle her mind.** The blind woman **thinks: If there is something** that needs to be done in the course of childbirth, the lamp will enable my **friend to see and she will do** it **for me.**

"אִם הָיְתָה צְרִיכָה לְשֶׁמֶן וכו׳". תֵּיפוֹק לֵיהּ מִשּׁוּם סְחִיטָה!

We learned in the mishna: **And if she needed oil,** her friend brings her oil in her hair. The Gemara asks: What good is this advice? **Derive** that **it** is prohibited **due to** the prohibited labor of **wringing.** The friend will need to wring her hair in order to extract the oil for the birthing woman.

רַבָּה וְרַב יוֹסֵף דְּאָמְרִי תַּרְוַויְיהוּ: אֵין סְחִיטָה בַּשֵּׂיעָר. רַב אַשִׁי אָמַר: אֲפִילּוּ תֵּימָא "יֵשׁ סְחִיטָה בַּשֵּׂיעָר" – מְבִיאָה לָהּ בִּכְלִי דֶּרֶךְ שְׂעָרָהּ. דְּכַמָּה דְּאֶפְשָׁר לְשַׁנּוֹיֵי – מְשַׁנֵּינַן.

It was **Rabba and Rav Yosef who both said: There is no** prohibition of **wringing with regard to hair,** since hair does not absorb liquids like other materials. **Rav Ashi said: Even if you say** that **there is** a prohibition of **wringing with regard to hair,** here the friend does not actually bring the oil in her hair. Rather, **she brings it in a vessel** tied **through her hair.** She does this because **as much** as **it is possible to change** the manner in which one performs a labor that is being done to save a life, **we change it.**

אָמַר רַב יְהוּדָה אָמַר שְׁמוּאֵל: חַיָּה, כָּל זְמַן שֶׁהַקֶּבֶר פָּתוּחַ, בֵּין אָמְרָה "צְרִיכָה אֲנִי" בֵּין לֹא אָמְרָה "צְרִיכָה אֲנִי" – מְחַלְּלִין עָלֶיהָ אֶת הַשַּׁבָּת.

Rav Yehuda said that **Shmuel said:** With regard to **a woman in childbirth, as long as the womb**[N] **is open, whether she said: I need** Shabbat to be desecrated, or **whether she did not say: I need** Shabbat to be desecrated, **one desecrates Shabbat for her.** Generally, a woman in childbirth is in danger, and prohibited labors may be performed in life-threatening circumstances.

נִסְתַּם הַקֶּבֶר, בֵּין אָמְרָה

Once **the womb closed** after birth, **whether** the woman who gave birth **said:**

Perek **XVIII**
Daf **129** Amud **a**

NOTES

Said I need…did not say I need – אָמְרָה צְרִיכָה אֲנִי...לֹא אָמְרָה צְרִיכָה אֲנִי: The Ramban writes that this discussion is referring to a situation in which there is no doctor present. However, if a doctor is present, and he determines that the woman requires care that involves desecrating Shabbat, then her protestations to the contrary are ignored. Perhaps her ability to make a rational decision is compromised due to her pain and suffering. Halakhic rulings are always lenient in cases of uncertainty with regard to a life-threatening situation.

In cases of uncertainty concerning a life-threatening situation, the *halakha* is lenient – סָפֵק נְפָשׁוֹת לְהָקֵל: According to Rashi, the source for this law is the instruction to the court: "And the congregation shall deliver" (Numbers 35:25). It is the duty of the court to tend towards leniency whenever there is uncertainty whether or not the situation is a life-threatening one.

"צְרִיכָה אֲנִי" בֵּין לֹא אָמְרָה "צְרִיכָה אֲנִי" – אֵין מְחַלְּלִין עָלֶיהָ אֶת הַשַּׁבָּת,

I need Shabbat to be desecrated, or **whether she did not say: I need**[N] Shabbat to be desecrated, **one does not desecrate Shabbat for her.**

רַב אַשִׁי מַתְנֵי הָכִי. מָר זוּטְרָא מַתְנֵי הָכִי: אָמַר רַב יְהוּדָה אָמַר שְׁמוּאֵל: חַיָּה כָּל זְמַן שֶׁהַקֶּבֶר פָּתוּחַ, בֵּין אָמְרָה "צְרִיכָה אֲנִי" וּבֵין אָמְרָה "אֵין צְרִיכָה אֲנִי" – מְחַלְּלִין עָלֶיהָ אֶת הַשַּׁבָּת. נִסְתַּם הַקֶּבֶר, אָמְרָה "צְרִיכָה אֲנִי" – מְחַלְּלִין עָלֶיהָ אֶת הַשַּׁבָּת, לֹא אָמְרָה "צְרִיכָה אֲנִי" – אֵין מְחַלְּלִין עָלֶיהָ אֶת הַשַּׁבָּת.

That is how **Rav Ashi taught it. This is** how **Mar Zutra taught it: Rav Yehuda said** that **Shmuel said:** With regard to **a woman in childbirth, as long as the womb is open, whether she said: I need** Shabbat to be desecrated, or **whether she did not say: I need** Shabbat to be desecrated, **one desecrates Shabbat for her.** Once **the womb closed** after birth, if **she said: I need** Shabbat to be desecrated, **one desecrates Shabbat for her.** If **she did not say: I need** Shabbat to be desecrated, and all the more so if she said: I do not need Shabbat to be desecrated, **one does not desecrate Shabbat for her.**

אָמַר לֵיהּ רָבִינָא לְמָרֵימָר: מָר זוּטְרָא מַתְנֵי לְקוּלָּא, וְרַב אַשִׁי מַתְנֵי לְחוּמְרָא, הִלְכְתָא כְּמַאן? אָמַר לֵיהּ: הֲלָכָה כְּמָר זוּטְרָא, סָפֵק נְפָשׁוֹת לְהָקֵל.

Ravina said to Mareimar: Since **Mar Zutra teaches leniently, and Rav Ashi teaches stringently, in accordance with whose** opinion **is the *halakha*?** Mareimar **said to him: The *halakha* is in accordance** with the opinion **of Mar Zutra,** based on the following principle: In cases of **uncertainty** concerning **a life-threatening** situation, the *halakha* **is lenient.**[N]

מֵאֵימָתַי פְּתִיחַת הַקֶּבֶר? אָמַר אַבַּיֵי: מִשָּׁעָה שֶׁתֵּשֵׁב עַל הַמַּשְׁבֵּר. רַב הוּנָא בְּרֵיהּ דְּרַב יְהוֹשֻׁעַ אָמַר: מִשָּׁעָה שֶׁהַדָּם שׁוֹתֵת וְיוֹרֵד. וְאָמְרִי לָהּ: מִשָּׁעָה שֶׁחַבְרוֹתֶיהָ נוֹשְׂאוֹת אוֹתָהּ בַּאֲגַפֶּיהָ.

With regard to the matter of the open womb, the Gemara asks: **From when is** it considered that **the opening of the womb** has begun?[HB] **Abaye says:** It begins **from when** the woman **sits on the travailing chair. Rav Huna, son of Rav Yehoshua, said:** It begins **from when the blood flows and descends; and others say when her friends** need to **carry her by her arms,** as she can no longer walk on her own.

עַד מָתַי פְּתִיחַת הַקֶּבֶר? אָמַר אַבַּיֵי: שְׁלֹשָׁה יָמִים. רָבָא אָמַר מִשְּׁמֵיהּ דְּרַב יְהוּדָה: שִׁבְעָה, וְאָמְרִי לָהּ: שְׁלֹשִׁים.

The Gemara asks: **Until when** does **the opening of the womb** continue? **Abaye said:** It lasts **three days. Rava said in the name of Rav Yehuda:** It lasts **seven** days. **And others say:** It lasts **thirty** days.

אָמְרִי נְהַרְדְּעֵי: חַיָּה שְׁלֹשָׁה, שִׁבְעָה וּשְׁלֹשִׁים. שְׁלֹשָׁה, בֵּין אָמְרָה ״צְרִיכָה אֲנִי״ וּבֵין אָמְרָה ״לֹא צְרִיכָה אֲנִי״ – מְחַלְּלִין עָלֶיהָ אֶת הַשַּׁבָּת. שִׁבְעָה, אָמְרָה ״צְרִיכָה אֲנִי״ – מְחַלְּלִין עָלֶיהָ אֶת הַשַּׁבָּת, אָמְרָה ״לֹא צְרִיכָה אֲנִי״ – אֵין מְחַלְּלִין עָלֶיהָ אֶת הַשַּׁבָּת. שְׁלֹשִׁים, אֲפִילּוּ אָמְרָה ״צְרִיכָה אֲנִי״ – אֵין מְחַלְּלִין עָלֶיהָ אֶת הַשַּׁבָּת, אֲבָל עוֹשִׂין עַל יְדֵי אַרְמַאי.

The Sages of **Neharde'a say:** For **a woman in childbirth,** there are halakhic distinctions between **three, seven, and thirty** days after she gives birth.[H] The Gemara elaborates: During the first **three** days after birth, **whether she said: I need** Shabbat to be desecrated, or **whether she did not say: I need** Shabbat to be desecrated, **one desecrates Shabbat for her.** Between three and **seven** days after birth, if **she said: I need** Shabbat to be desecrated, **one desecrates Shabbat for her.** If **she did not say: I need** Shabbat to be desecrated, **one does not desecrate Shabbat for her.** Between seven and **thirty** days after birth, **even** if **she said: I need** Shabbat to be desecrated, **one does not desecrate Shabbat for her; however, we perform** all necessary prohibited labors **by means of a gentile.**

כִּדְרַב עוּלָּא בְּרֵיהּ דְּרַב עִילַּאי, דְּאָמַר: כׇּל צׇרְכֵי חוֹלֶה נַעֲשִׂין עַל יְדֵי אַרְמַאי בַּשַּׁבָּת. וְכִדְרַב הַמְנוּנָא, דְּאָמַר רַב הַמְנוּנָא: דָּבָר שֶׁאֵין בּוֹ סַכָּנָה – אוֹמֵר לַגּוֹי וְעוֹשֶׂה.

This ruling is **in accordance with** the statement of **Rav Ulla, son of Rav Ilai,** who **said: All needs** of a sick person whose life is not in danger **are performed by means of a gentile on Shabbat. And** this ruling is **in accordance with** the opinion of **Rav Hamnuna, as Rav Hamnuna says:** With regard to **a matter in which there is no danger,**[H] but only potential illness, **one says to the gentile** to perform the act, **and the gentile performs** the act.

אָמַר רַב יְהוּדָה אָמַר שְׁמוּאֵל: לְחַיָּה שְׁלֹשִׁים יוֹם. לְמַאי הִלְכְתָא? אָמְרִי נְהַרְדְּעֵי: לִטְבִילָה.

Rav Yehuda said that **Shmuel said:** For **a woman in childbirth,** there is a *halakha* of **thirty days.** The Gemara asks: **With regard to what *halakha*** was this stated? The Sages of **Neharde'a say:** It was stated **with regard to** the *halakha* of **immersion.** A woman does not purify herself through ritual immersion within thirty days of giving birth because she is in a weakened state and susceptible to catching cold.

אָמַר רָבָא: לָא אֲמַרַן אֶלָּא שֶׁאֵין בַּעְלָהּ עִמָּהּ, אֲבָל בַּעְלָהּ עִמָּהּ – בַּעְלָהּ מְחַמְּמָהּ. כִּי הָא דִּבְרַתֵּיהּ דְּרַב חִסְדָּא טְבַלָה תּוֹךְ תְּלָתִין יוֹמִין שֶׁלֹּא בִּפְנֵי בַּעְלָהּ וְאִצְטְנִיאַת, וְאַמְטוּהָ לְעַרְסָהּ בָּתְרֵיהּ דְּרָבָא לְפוּמְבְּדִיתָא.

Rava said: We say that the ruling that she does not immerse during that period applies **only when her husband is not with her. However,** if **her husband is with her, her husband warms her** by engaging in relations with her, and she is not susceptible to catching cold, **as** is illustrated **in this** incident involving **the daughter of Rav Ḥisda,** Rava's wife. She **immersed within thirty days** of giving birth, **not in the presence of her husband, and caught cold, and** afterward **they brought her** funeral **bier after Rava to Pumbedita.**

אָמַר רַב יְהוּדָה אָמַר שְׁמוּאֵל: עוֹשִׂין מְדוּרָה לְחַיָּה בַּשַּׁבָּת (בִּימוֹת הַגְּשָׁמִים). סָבוּר מִינָּהּ: לְחַיָּה – אִין, לְחוֹלֶה – לָא. בִּימוֹת הַגְּשָׁמִים – אִין, בִּימוֹת הַחַמָּה – לָא. (וְלָא הִיא, לָא שְׁנָא חַיָּה וְלָא שְׁנָא חוֹלֶה, לָא שְׁנָא בִּימוֹת הַגְּשָׁמִים וְלָא שְׁנָא בִּימוֹת הַחַמָּה – מִדְּאִתְּמַר) אָמַר רַב חִיָּיא בַּר אָבִין אָמַר שְׁמוּאֵל: הִקִּיז דָּם וְנִצְטַנֵּן – עוֹשִׂין לוֹ מְדוּרָה אֲפִילּוּ בִּתְקוּפַת תַּמּוּז.

Rav Yehuda said that **Shmuel said: One builds a fire for a woman in childbirth**[B] **on Shabbat during the rainy season.** The Sages **thought** to infer **from here** the following: **For a woman in childbirth, yes,** one builds a fire; **for sick people, no, he** does not build a fire. **In the rainy season, yes,** one builds a fire; **in the summer, no, he** does not build a fire. **And** the Gemara concludes: **That is not** the case. **There is no difference** between **a woman in childbirth and a sick person, and there is no difference between the rainy season and the summer.** In all of these cases one may build a fire on Shabbat. This conclusion emerges **from that which was stated: Rav Ḥiyya bar Avin said** that **Shmuel said:** With regard to one who **let blood and caught cold, one makes a fire for him even during the season of Tammuz,** i.e., the summer. Failure to do so could result in serious illness.

HALAKHA

From when is it considered that the opening of the womb has begun – מֵאֵימָתַי פְּתִיחַת הַקֶּבֶר: A woman is considered in childbirth when she sits on the travailing chair, when the blood begins to flow from the womb, or when her friends carry her. If any one of these instances occurs on Shabbat, Shabbat may be violated to assist her. This ruling is in accordance with all the lenient opinions cited in the Gemara (Ramban; Rambam *Sefer Zemanim, Hilkhot Shabbat* 2:13; *Shulḥan Arukh, Oraḥ Ḥayyim* 330:3).

Until when is she considered in childbirth – עַד מָתַי נִקְרֵאת יוֹלֶדֶת: During the first three days after birth, even if the mother says: I do not need Shabbat to be desecrated for me, Shabbat is desecrated for her. From the fourth to the seventh day after giving birth, if she says: I don't need Shabbat to be desecrated for me, Shabbat may not be desecrated for her. From the eighth to the thirtieth days, she is considered a sick person not in danger, and Shabbat may not be desecrated for her (Rambam *Sefer Zemanim, Hilkhot Shabbat* 2:10; *Shulḥan Arukh, Oraḥ Ḥayyim* 330:4).

A matter in which there is no danger – דָּבָר שֶׁאֵין בּוֹ סַכָּנָה: When one is ill and there is no threat to his life, or if one experiences a pain that affects the entire body, he is permitted to instruct a gentile to cure him (Rambam *Sefer Zemanim, Hilkhot Shabbat* 2:10; *Shulḥan Arukh, Oraḥ Ḥayyim* 328:17).

BACKGROUND

The beginning of birth – תְּחִילַּת לֵידָה: The accepted modern medical opinion is that birth begins the moment the womb is open.

One builds a fire for a woman in childbirth – עוֹשִׂין מְדוּרָה לְחַיָּה: The commentaries wondered why this specific example of desecrating Shabbat was mentioned. Perhaps the fire was for the benefit of the newborn to avert the danger of the condition called cold injury.

LANGUAGE

Teak [*shaga*] – שָׁאגָא: From the Sanskrit *saka*, which entered the Persian as saj, meaning teak tree. Aramaic may have borrowed the word from Persian.

Ebony [*yavna*] – יַוְנָה: Apparently from the Greek ἔβενος, *ebenos*, meaning a tree of the *Diospyros* genus with dark wood. Conceivably, the original source of this word is the Hebrew word *huvanim*, meaning ebony trees.

שְׁמוּאֵל צְלַחוּ לֵיהּ תַּכְתַּקָא דְּשָׁאגָא, רַב יְהוּדָה צְלַחוּ לֵיהּ פְּתוֹרָא דְּיַוְנָה, לְרַבָּה צְלַחוּ לֵיהּ שַׁרְשִׁיפָא.

The Gemara relates that after **Shmuel** underwent bloodletting, **they broke for him a** wooden **armchair** made **of teak** [*shaga*][L] to build a fire. Similarly, for the sake of **Rav Yehuda they broke** a wooden **table** made **of ebony** [*yavna*],[L] **and for Rabba they broke a bench.** They needed to build a fire due to the potential danger to Rabba. Since they could not find firewood, they kindled the fire with the furniture.

וְאָמַר לֵיהּ אַבַּיֵי לְרַבָּה: וְהָא קָעָבַר מָר מִשּׁוּם ״בַּל תַּשְׁחִית״! אָמַר לֵיהּ בַּל תַּשְׁחִית דְּגוּפַאי – עֲדִיף לִי.

And Abaye said to Rabba: In breaking the bench, **didn't the Master violate** the prohibition, **"Do not destroy"** (Deuteronomy 20:19)? It is prohibited to destroy objects of value. Rabba **said to him: Do not destroy** also with regard to destruction **of my body.** Preventing illness and danger **is preferable to me.**

אָמַר רַב יְהוּדָה אָמַר רַב: לְעוֹלָם יִמְכּוֹר אָדָם קוֹרוֹת בֵּיתוֹ וְיִקַּח מִנְעָלִים לְרַגְלָיו, הִקִּיז דָּם וְאֵין לוֹ מַה יֹּאכַל – יִמְכּוֹר מִנְעָלִים שֶׁבְּרַגְלָיו וְיַסְפִּיק מֵהֶן צָרְכֵי סְעוּדָה.

With regard to the danger of bloodletting, the Gemara cites that which **Rav Yehuda said** that **Rav said: One should always sell the beams of his house and purchase shoes for his feet** with the proceeds, as shoes protect him from stepping on obstacles and from catching cold. **If he let blood and has nothing to eat** after the bloodletting, **he should** even **sell the shoes on his feet, and from** the proceeds **provide the needs of a meal.** After bloodletting, a meal is more crucial to one's well-being than shoes are.

מַאי צָרְכֵי סְעוּדָה? רַב אָמַר: בָּשָׂר, וּשְׁמוּאֵל אָמַר: יַיִן. רַב אָמַר: בָּשָׂר, נַפְשָׁא חֲלַף נַפְשָׁא. וּשְׁמוּאֵל אָמַר: יַיִן, סוּמָּקָא חֲלַף סוּמָּקָא.

The Gemara asks: **What are** these special **needs of a meal? Rav said:** It is referring to **meat. And Shmuel said:** It is referring to **wine.** The Gemara explains: **Rav says:** It is referring to **meat** because **the soul replaces the soul,** i.e., the meat replenishes the person's strength. **And Shmuel said:** It is referring to **wine** because **the red replaces the red,** i.e., red wine substitutes for red blood.

(סִימָן שֶׁנִּמְסַר)

A mnemonic for the names of the Sages cited in the following discussion is the word ***shenimsar***; *shin* for Shmuel, *nun* for Rabbi Yoḥanan, *mem* for Rav Naḥman, *samekh* for Rav Yosef, *reish* for Rava.

שְׁמוּאֵל בְּיוֹמָא דַּעֲבַד מִילְּתָא עָבְדִי לֵיהּ תַּבְשִׁילָא דְּטַחְלֵי. רַבִּי יוֹחָנָן שָׁתֵי עַד דְּנָפֵיק תִּיהְיָא מֵאוּנֵיהּ. וְרַב נַחְמָן שָׁתֵי עַד דְּקָפֵי טַחְלֵיהּ. רַב יוֹסֵף שָׁתֵי עַד דְּנָפֵיק מֵרִיבְדָּא דְּכוּסִילְתָּא. רָבָא מְהַדַּר אַחַמְרָא בַּר תְּלָתָא טַרְפֵי.

The Gemara relates the following about bloodletting and drinking wine. **Shmuel, on the day** on which he **would perform the practice** of bloodletting,[B] **they** would **prepare for him** a dish of **cooked spleen. Rabbi Yoḥanan** would **drink** wine after bloodletting **until the odor emerged from his ears. And Rav Naḥman** would **drink until his spleen floated** in wine. **Rav Yosef** would **drink until** the wine **would emerge from the bloodletting incision. Rava would search** for **wine** that was sufficiently aged such **that three leaves** had already grown over three years on the vine from which the grapes were picked (Rashash).

אֲמַר לְהוּ רַב נַחְמָן בַּר יִצְחָק לְרַבָּנַן: בְּמָטוּתָא מִינַּיְיכוּ, בְּיוֹמָא דְּהַקָּזָה אִמְרוּ לְבֵיתַיְיכוּ: נַחְמָן אִקְלַע לְגַבַּן.

Rav Naḥman bar Yitzhak said to the Sages: I beg of you, on the day that you undergo **bloodletting, tell your households,** your wives: **Naḥman** bar Yitzhak **happened** to come **to** visit **us.** Due to the visit of the important guest, the women will prepare a large meal. The husbands will eat well, recover from the lost blood, and avoid endangering themselves.

וְכוּלְּהוּ אַעֲרוּמֵי אַסִּירֵי, בַּר מֵהַאי עָרְמָה דְּשָׁרֵי: מַאן דְּעָבֵיד מִילְּתָא וְלָא אֶפְשַׁר לֵיהּ, לִישְׁקוֹל זוּזָא מַכָּא וְלֵיזִיל לְשַׁב חַנְוָתָא, עַד דְּטָעֵים שִׁיעוּר רְבִיעֲתָא. וְאִי לָא – לֵיכוּל שַׁב תַּמְרֵי אוּכְמָתָא, וְלֵישׁוּף מִשְׁחָא בְּצִידְעֵיהּ, וְנִיגְנֵי בְּשִׁמְשָׁא.

And Rav Naḥman bar Yitzhak said: **All types of artifice** that come at the expense of others **are prohibited except for this artifice,**[N] **which is permitted. One who performed the practice** of bloodletting **and it is not possible for him** to purchase food due to lack of means, **let him take a worn *zuz* coin**[B] **and go to seven stores.** In each store, he tastes the wine as one who seeks to buy wine would. After tasting, he hands the *zuz* to the storekeeper, who will not accept it because it is worn. He then proceeds to do the same in all the stores **until he has tasted the measure of a quarter** of a *log* of wine. **And if** doing so **is not** possible, **let him eat seven black dates and smear oil on his temple and lie in the sun.**

BACKGROUND

On the day he would perform…bloodletting – בְּיוֹמָא דַּעֲבַד מִילְּתָא עָבְדִי: There is an element of danger involved in all bloodletting, and there were several methods undertaken to reinforce the body afterward. Eating meat in general, and eating organs from the circulatory system in particular, e.g., the spleen, is useful in restoring lost blood and replenishing hemoglobin after bloodletting. Wine accelerates circulation, as does warming oneself by a fire.

A worn *zuz* coin – זוּזָא מַכָּא: Although the primary value of a coin in ancient times was determined by the precious metal it contained, the value of a minted coin was slightly greater in civilized states. Consequently, merchants would refuse to accept coins whose image was worn. Moreover, a worn coin weighed less.

Roman dinar whose image eroded

NOTES

All types of artifice are prohibited except for this artifice – וְכוּלְּהוּ אַעֲרוּמֵי אַסִּירֵי, בַּר מֵהַאי עָרְמָה: In fact, Rav Naḥman bar Yitzḥak advised deviating from the truth both when he instructed that one should tell his wife that Rav Naḥman bar Yitzḥak would be visiting and when he recommended that a poor person use a worn-out *zuz* to procure wine. Both situations involve serious health issues. However, only the latter deception is called artifice because it comes at the expense of another. Indeed, it is stated in the midrash that this type of behavior is characteristic of Sodom.

אַבְלַט אַשְׁכַּחֵיהּ לִשְׁמוּאֵל דְּגָנֵי בְּשִׁמְשָׁא. אָמַר לֵיהּ: חַכִּימָא דִּיהוּדָאֵי! בִּישָׁא מִי הָוֵי טָבָא? אָמַר לֵיהּ: יוֹמָא דְּהַקָּזָה הוּא.

The Gemara relates: The gentile scholar, **Ablat, found Shmuel lying in the sun.** Ablat **said to** Shmuel: **Wise man of the Jews,** a matter that is **evil, can it become good?** Are there any circumstances in which the heat of the sun, which is harmful, can be beneficial? Shmuel **said to him: It** happens on **a day of bloodletting,** for which the heat of the sun is beneficial.

וְלָא הִיא, אֶלָּא: אִיכָּא יוֹמָא דְּמַעֲלֵי בָּהּ שִׁמְשָׁא בְּכוּלֵּיהּ שַׁתָּא – יוֹמָא דְּנָפְלָה בֵּיהּ תְּקוּפַת תַּמּוּז, וְסָבַר: לָא אִיגְלֵי לֵיהּ.

The Gemara comments: **And** actually, **that is not** what occurred. **Rather, there is a day on which the sun is beneficial** more than **the entire year,** and that is **the day on which the Tammuz solstice,** the longest day of the year, occurs. **And Shmuel thought: I will not reveal** this remedy **to him.**[N]

(הֵיקֵיל בְּרוּחַ טַעְמָא שָׁהָה סִימָן) רַב וּשְׁמוּאֵל דְּאָמְרִי תַּרְוַיְיהוּ: כׇּל הַמֵּקִיל בִּסְעוּדַּת הַקָּזַת דָּם – מְקִילִין לוֹ מְזוֹנוֹתָיו מִן הַשָּׁמַיִם. וְאוֹמְרִים: הוּא עַל חַיָּיו לֹא חָס, אֲנִי אָחוּס עָלָיו?!

Indifferent, in wind, taste, waited are a **mnemonic** for the following matters. It was **Rav and Shmuel who both said: Anyone who is indifferent** and not vigilant with regard to **the meal** eaten after **bloodletting, they are indifferent** with regard to providing **his food from the Heavens. And they say** in the name of Heaven: **He took no pity on his life, will I take pity on him?**

רַב וּשְׁמוּאֵל דְּאָמְרִי תַּרְוַיְיהוּ: הַאי מַאן דְּעָבֵיד מִילְּתָא לָא לֵיתֵיב הֵיכָא דְּכָרֵיךְ זִיקָא, דִּילְמָא שָׁפֵי לֵיהּ אוּמָּנָא וּמוֹקִים לֵיהּ אַרְבִיעָתָא, וְאָתֵי זִיקָא וְשָׁאֵיף מִינֵּיהּ – וְאָתֵי לִידֵי סַכָּנָה.

Similarly, it was **Rav and Shmuel who both said: One who performs the practice** of bloodletting **should not sit where the wind is blowing,** due to the concern that **perhaps the blood letter let** too much blood from **him and established** the amount of remaining blood **at a quarter** of a *log*. **And** there is concern **the wind will come and draw out** a little more blood **from him, and he will be endangered.**

שְׁמוּאֵל הֲוָה רָגִיל וְעָבֵד מִילְּתָא בְּבֵיתָא דְּשַׁב לְבֵינַיָּא וַאֲרִיחָא. יוֹמָא חֲדָא עֲבַד, וְאַרְגֵּישׁ בְּנַפְשֵׁיהּ. בְּדַק, וַחֲסַר חַד אֲרִיחָא,

The Gemara relates: **Shmuel would customarily perform the practice** of bloodletting **in a house** whose walls were **seven and a half bricks** thick. **One day he performed** bloodletting **and felt himself** weakened. **He examined** and discovered that **one half-brick was lacking** from the thickness of the walls. The resultant chill caused his weakness.

רַב וּשְׁמוּאֵל דְּאָמְרִי תַּרְוַיְיהוּ: הַאי מַאן דְּעָבֵיד מִילְּתָא – לִיטְעוֹם מִידֵּי וַהֲדַר לֵיפּוֹק, דְּאִי לָא טָעֵים מִידֵּי, אִי פָּגַע בְּשַׁכְבָא – יָרְקָא אַפֵּיהּ, אִי פָּגַע בְּמַאן דְּקָטַל נַפְשָׁא – מָיֵית, אִי פָּגַע

It was **Rav and Shmuel who both said: One who performs the practice of bloodletting should taste something and then go outside, since if he does not taste anything, if he encounters a corpse, his face will turn green. If he encounters one who killed a person, he will die. If he encounters**

Perek **XVIII**
Daf **129** Amud **b**

בְּדָבָר אַחֵר – קָשֶׁה לְדָבָר אַחֵר.

something else, a euphemism for a pig, **it is harmful with regard to something else,** a euphemism for leprosy.

רַב וּשְׁמוּאֵל דְּאָמְרִי תַּרְוַיְיהוּ: הַאי מַאן דְּעָבֵיד מִילְּתָא – לִישְׁהֵי פּוּרְתָּא וַהֲדַר לֵיקוּם. דְּאָמַר מָר: חֲמִשָּׁה דְּבָרִים קְרוֹבִין לְמִיתָה יוֹתֵר מִן הַחַיִּים, וְאֵלּוּ הֵן: אָכַל וְעָמַד, שָׁתָה וְעָמַד, יָשֵׁן וְעָמַד, הִקִּיז דָּם וְעָמַד, שִׁימֵּשׁ מִטָּתוֹ וְעָמַד.

It was **Rav and Shmuel who both said:** With regard to **one who performs the practice** of bloodletting, **let him wait a bit and then let him rise,**[H] **as the Master said:** There are **five matters** that render one **closer to death than life, and they are these:** If **one ate and** immediately **rose,**[H] if **one drank and rose,** if **one slept and** immediately **rose,** if **one let blood and rose,** if **one engaged in** conjugal **relations and rose.**[H]

אָמַר שְׁמוּאֵל: פּוּרְסָא דִּדְמָא – כָּל תְּלָתִין יוֹמִין. וּבֵין הַפְּרָקִים – יְמַעֵט, וּבֵין הַפְּרָקִים – יַחֲזוֹר וִימַעֵט.

Shmuel said: The interval for bloodletting[N] is **every thirty days. And during the** middle **periods** of one's life, **he should decrease** the frequency of bloodletting; **and during the** later **periods, he should decrease** its frequency **again.**

וְאָמַר שְׁמוּאֵל: פּוּרְסָא דִּדְמָא – חַד בְּשַׁבְּתָא, אַרְבָּעָה וּמַעֲלֵי שַׁבְּתָא. אֲבָל שֵׁנִי וַחֲמִישִׁי – לֹא, דְּאָמַר מָר: מִי שֶׁיֵּשׁ לוֹ זְכוּת אָבוֹת – יַקִּיז דָּם בְּשֵׁנִי וּבַחֲמִישִׁי, שֶׁבֵּית דִּין שֶׁל מַעְלָה וְשֶׁל מַטָּה שָׁוִין כְּאֶחָד.

And Shmuel said: The times for bloodletting are **the first** day **of the week, the fourth** day of the week **and Shabbat eve. However,** on the **second and the fifth** days of the week, **no,** one should not let blood, **as the Master said:** Only **one who has the merit of** his **ancestors** and relies on it **should let blood on** the **second and on the fifth** days of the week, **as the court on High,** in the heavens, **and the court below are equal.** The courts in the cities convene on Mondays and Thursdays, as does the heavenly court. Letting blood on a day of judgment is dangerous. If one is judged unfavorably all his blood could flow out.

NOTES

I will not reveal this remedy to him – לָא אִיגְלֵי לֵיהּ: There is an opinion that Shmuel did not want to suggest a supernatural cure, so he gave a reason based on contemporary medical science. Rather than explain only the supernatural curing power of the sun during the summer solstice, Shmuel also cited contemporary medical science and mentioned the benefit of sunlight to one whose blood has been let.

HALAKHA

Precautions in bloodletting – זְהִירוּת בְּהַקָּזָה: One must make certain after bloodletting not to enter a bathhouse and to eat and keep warm (Rambam *Sefer HaMadda, Hilkhot Deot* 4:18).

Closer to death…ate and rose – קְרוֹבִין לְמִיתָה...אָכַל וְעָמַד: One should refrain from exertion immediately after eating because exertion could make him ill (Rambam *Sefer HaMadda, Hilkhot Deot* 4:3).

Engaged in conjugal relations and rose – שִׁימֵּשׁ מִטָּתוֹ וְעָמַד: A person should not engage in conjugal relations after bloodletting, nor engage in any other strenuous activity, as per the *baraita* (Rambam *Sefer HaMadda, Hilkhot Deot* 4:19; *Shulḥan Arukh, Oraḥ Ḥayyim* 240:15).

NOTES

The interval for bloodletting – פּוּרְסָא דִּדְמָא: In accordance with an ancient tradition, Rabbeinu Ḥananel explains the phrase: During the periods, as follows: When one turns fifty, he should minimize bloodletting to once every two or three months. When he grows older, he should let blood only once every six months or every year.

בְּתְלָתָא בְּשַׁבְּתָא מַאי טַעְמָא לָא – מִשּׁוּם דְּקַיְימָא לֵיהּ מַאְדִּים בְּזָוֵוי, מַעֲלֵי שַׁבְּתָא נַמִי קַיְימָא בְּזָוֵוי! כֵּיוָן דְּדָשׁוּ בֵּיהּ רַבִּים – ״שׁוֹמֵר פְּתָאִים ה׳״.

The Gemara explains: **On the third day of the week, what is the reason** that one does **not** let blood? It is **because** the planet **Mars is dominant during the even** hours.[N] Since it is a planet of blood, and the even hours are a bad omen, that combination gives cause for concern. The Gemara asks: On **Shabbat eve,** Mars **also dominates during the even** hours. The Gemara answers: **Since** the **multitudes have** already become **accustomed to** letting blood on Shabbat eve, the verse: **"The Lord protects the simple-hearted"** (Psalms 116:6) applies in this case.

אָמַר שְׁמוּאֵל: אַרְבָּעָה דְּהוּא אַרְבָּעָה, אַרְבָּעָה דְּהוּא אַרְבֵּיסַר, אַרְבָּעָה דְּהוּא עֶשְׂרִים וְאַרְבָּעָה, אַרְבָּעָה דְּלֵיכָּא אַרְבַּע בַּתְרֵיהּ – סַכַּנְתָּא.

Similarly, **Shmuel says:** On **the fourth** day of the week that **is the fourth day** of the month; on **the fourth** day of the week that **is the fourteenth** of the month; on **the fourth** day of the week that **is the twenty-fourth** of the month; and on **the fourth** day of the week after which **there are not four** days remaining in the month **it is dangerous** to let blood.[B]

רֹאשׁ חוֹדֶשׁ וְשֵׁנִי לוֹ – חוּלְשָׁא, שְׁלִישִׁי לוֹ – סַכָּנָה; מַעֲלֵי יוֹמָא טָבָא – חוּלְשָׁא, מַעֲלֵי יוֹמָא דַּעֲצַרְתָּא – סַכַּנְתָּא. וְגָזְרוּ רַבָּנַן אַכּוּלְּהוּ מַעֲלֵי יוֹמָא טָבָא מִשּׁוּם יוֹמָא טָבָא דַּעֲצֶרֶת. דְּנָפֵיק בֵּיהּ זִיקָא וּשְׁמֵיהּ טִבוֹחַ – דְּאִי לֹא קִבְּלוּ יִשְׂרָאֵל תּוֹרָה – הֲוָה טָבַח לְהוּ לְבִשְׂרַיְיהוּ וּלְדָמַיְיהוּ.

Bloodletting on **the New Moon and** on the **second** day of the month causes **weakness;** bloodletting on the **third** day of the month leads to **danger.** Bloodletting on **the eve of a Festival** causes **weakness;** bloodletting on **the eve of the festival of** ***Shavuot*** leads to **danger. And the Sages issued a decree** prohibiting bloodletting **on the eve of every Festival due to the festival** of ***Shavuot.***[H] **On** ***Shavuot,*** **an evil spirit named** ***Tibbuah,*** from the Hebrew word meaning slaughter, **emerges, as had the Jewish people not accepted the Torah** on the festival of *Shavuot, Tibbuah* **would have slaughtered their flesh and their blood.** Consequently, it remains a dangerous day.

אָמַר שְׁמוּאֵל: אָכַל חִטָּה וְהִקִּיז דָּם לֹא הִקִּיז אֶלָּא לְאוֹתָהּ חִטָּה וְהָנֵי מִילֵּי – לִרְפוּאָה, אֲבָל לְאוֹקוּלֵי – מֵיקַל.

Shmuel said: If **one ate wheat and** afterward **let blood, he only let that wheat.** The bloodletting was ineffective as the wheat replaced any blood that was let. **And this** ineffectiveness **applies** only if he let blood **to cure** an illness; **however, to relieve** discomfort, bloodletting after eating wheat **relieves** one's discomfort.

הַמַּקִּיז דָּם, שְׁתִיָּה – לְאַלְתַּר, אֲכִילָה – עַד חֲצִי מִיל.

One who lets blood should engage in **drinking immediately;** he should not engage in **eating until** the time that it takes to walk **half a** ***mil*** has elapsed.

אִיבַּעְיָא לְהוּ: ״שְׁתִיָּה לְאַלְתַּר״ מַעֲלֵי, אֲבָל בָּתַר הָכִי – קָשֵׁי, אוֹ דִּילְמָא: לָא קָשֵׁי וְלָא מַעֲלֵי? תֵּיקוּ.

A dilemma was raised before the Sages: When they said that one should engage in **drinking immediately,** does that mean that drinking immediately is **beneficial; however, thereafter, it is injurious? Or perhaps,** thereafter **it is neither injurious nor beneficial.** No resolution is found for this dilemma, therefore **it stands** unresolved.

אִיבַּעְיָא לְהוּ: ״אֲכִילָה עַד חֲצִי מִיל״ הוּא דְּקָמַעֲלֵי, הָא בָּתַר הָכִי וּמִקַּמֵּי הָכִי – קָשֵׁי, אוֹ דִּילְמָא: לָא קָשֵׁי וְלָא מַעֲלֵי? תֵּיקוּ.

Similarly, **a dilemma was raised before** the Sages: When they said one should not engage in **eating until** the time that it takes to walk **half a** ***mil*** has elapsed, does that mean **that** only at that time **it is beneficial,** however, **after that** time **or before that** time **it is injurious? Or perhaps,** before and after that time **it is neither injurious nor beneficial.** No resolution is found for this dilemma, therefore **it** too **stands** unresolved.

מַכְרִיז רַב: מְאָה קָרֵי – בְּזוּזָא, מְאָה רֵישֵׁי – בְּזוּזָא, מְאָה שְׂפָמֵי – וְלֹא כְּלוּם. אָמַר רַב יוֹסֵף: כִּי הֲוֵינַן בֵּי רַב הוּנָא, יוֹמָא דְּמִפַּגְּרִי בֵּיהּ רַבָּנַן אָמְרִי ״הָאִידָּנָא יוֹמָא דִּשְׂפָמֵי הוּא״ וְלָא יָדַעְנָא מַאי קָאָמְרִי.

Rav would **announce: One hundred bloodlettings for a** ***zuz;***[N] cutting the hair on **one hundred heads for a** ***zuz;*** grooming **one hundred moustaches** does **not** cost **anything** (*ge'onim*). Blood letters typically served as barbers as well and did not charge for grooming a moustache. If one hundred men happened to arrive one day to have their moustaches groomed, the barber would work all day without receiving any pay. **Rav Yosef said: When we were** students **in Rav Huna's school,** on **a day when the Sages were sluggish** in their studies, **they would say: Today is the day of the moustaches, and I did not know what they were saying.** Now that I heard Rav's statement, I understand that they meant that it was a day without purpose.

״וְקוֹשְׁרִין הַטַּבּוּר״. תָּנוּ רַבָּנַן: קוֹשְׁרִין הַטַּבּוּר, רַבִּי יוֹסֵי אוֹמֵר: אַף חוֹתְכִין, וְטוֹמְנִין הַשִּׁלְיָא כְּדֵי שֶׁיֵּחַם הַוָּלָד. אָמַר רַבָּן שִׁמְעוֹן בֶּן גַּמְלִיאֵל: בְּנוֹת מְלָכִים טוֹמְנוֹת בִּסְפָלִים שֶׁל שֶׁמֶן, בְּנוֹת עֲשִׁירִים בִּסְפוֹגִים שֶׁל צֶמֶר, בְּנוֹת עֲנִיִּים בְּמוֹכִין.

We learned in the mishna: **And one may tie the umbilical cord** of a child born on Shabbat.[B] **The Sages taught** similarly in the *Tosefta* and even added to it: **One may tie the umbilical cord** of a child born on Shabbat. **Rabbi Yosei said: One may even cut** the umbilical cord. **And one may insulate the placenta**[N] as a healing remedy **so as to warm the newborn. Rabban Shimon ben Gamliel said: Princesses insulate** the placenta **in mugs of oil; the daughters of the wealthy** do so **in combed wool; the daughters of the poor in** soft **rags.**

NOTES

Mars is dominant during the even hours – מַאְדִּים בְּזָוֵוי: Since the planet Mars is a symbol of calamity and bloodshed and even numbers are also considered dangerous, the Sages warned that a person should not let blood at a time when those two factors coincide. See the table on p. 420, which indicates the concern is only about hours when bloodletting is regularly performed, not at night.

One hundred bloodlettings [*karei*] for a *zuz* – מְאָה קָרֵי בְּזוּזָא: Rashi offers a different explanation, by which *karei* means gourds. This is connected to the previous statement that certain foods enhance one's strength and increase one's blood supply. The Gemara teaches that there is little benefit from eating gourds, animal heads, and animal lips.

Insulate the placenta – טוֹמְנִין הַשִּׁלְיָא: In the Jerusalem Talmud, the explanation is that they would bury the placenta as a talisman, to reassure the earth that all those born will ultimately return. Since it is prohibited to dig on Shabbat, they would temporarily insulate it in something else.

BACKGROUND

The intervals for bloodletting – זְמַנֵּי הַקָּזַת דָּם: Throughout history bloodletting was a significant medical procedure, eliminating harmful materials from the body, as well as draining superfluous blood to treat high blood pressure. However, there is an inherent danger in bloodletting, especially when blood is let from elderly people, whose blood does not replenish quickly. Therefore, Shmuel established the times for bloodletting.

And one may tie the umbilical cord of a child born on Shabbat – וְקוֹשְׁרִין הַטַּבּוּר: The umbilical cord is tied after it is cut to prevent additional bleeding and the spread of infection through the open wound. Apparently, the Sages permitted tying a cut umbilical cord, and they only disagreed in a case where, for some reason, the cord remained intact.

HALAKHA

Times for bloodletting – זְמַנֵּי הַקָּזָה: It is customary to refrain from bloodletting on a Festival eve (*Shulḥan Arukh, Oraḥ Ḥayyim* 468:10 in the comment of the Rema).

אָמַר רַב נַחְמָן אָמַר רַבָּה בַּר אֲבוּהּ אָמַר רַב: הֲלָכָה כְּרַבִּי יוֹסֵי.

Rav Naḥman said that **Rabba bar Avuh said** that **Rav said: The *halakha* is in accordance with** the opinion of **Rabbi Yosei** that it is even permitted to cut the umbilical cord on Shabbat.

וְאָמַר רַב נַחְמָן אָמַר רַבָּה בַּר אֲבוּהּ אָמַר רַב: מוֹדִים חֲכָמִים לְרַבִּי יוֹסֵי בְּטַבּוּר שֶׁל שְׁנֵי תִינוֹקוֹת שֶׁחוֹתְכִין, מַאי טַעְמָא – דִּמְנַתְּחִי אַהֲדָדֵי.

And Rav Naḥman said that **Rabba bar Avuh said** that **Rav said: The Rabbis concede to Rabbi Yosei with regard to the umbilical cord** attached to **twin babies that one may cut** it on Shabbat. **What is the reason** for this? In that case, leaving the cord attached is dangerous. **Since** the attached twins will try to **disengage from each other,** they could potentially rip each other's cords.

וְאָמַר רַב נַחְמָן אָמַר רַבָּה בַּר אֲבוּהּ אָמַר רַב: כָּל הָאָמוּר בְּפָרָשַׁת תּוֹכֵחָה עוֹשִׂין לְחַיָּה בַּשַּׁבָּת, שֶׁנֶּאֱמַר: ״וּמוֹלְדוֹתַיִךְ בְּיוֹם הוּלֶּדֶת אוֹתָךְ לֹא כָרַּת שָׁרֵּךְ וּבְמַיִם לֹא רֻחַצְתְּ לְמִשְׁעִי וְהָמְלֵחַ לֹא הֻמְלַחַתְּ וְהָחְתֵּל לֹא חֻתָּלְתְּ״.

And Rav Naḥman said that **Rabba bar Avuh said** that **Rav said: Everything stated in the passage of rebuke** (Ezekiel 16) **one may perform for a woman in childbirth on Shabbat.**[H] Since that chapter speaks of the dangerous birth of an abandoned child, for all other children, these issues should be addressed. **As it is stated** there: **"And as for your birth, on the day you were born, your navel was not cut, and you were not washed in water for cleansing, and you were not salted, nor were you swaddled"** (Ezekiel 16:4).

״וּמוֹלְדוֹתַיִךְ בְּיוֹם הוּלֶּדֶת״ – מִכָּאן שֶׁמְּיַילְּדִים אֶת הַוָּלָד בַּשַּׁבָּת, ״לֹא כָרַּת שָׁרֵּךְ״ – מִכָּאן שֶׁחוֹתְכִין הַטַּבּוּר בַּשַּׁבָּת, ״וּבְמַיִם לֹא רֻחַצְתְּ לְמִשְׁעִי״ – מִכָּאן שֶׁרוֹחֲצִין הַוָּלָד בַּשַּׁבָּת, ״וְהָמְלֵחַ לֹא הֻמְלַחַתְּ״ – מִכָּאן שֶׁמּוֹלְחִין הַוָּלָד בַּשַּׁבָּת, ״וְהָחְתֵּל לֹא חֻתָּלְתְּ״ – מִכָּאן שֶׁמְּלַפְּפִין הַוָּלָד בַּשַּׁבָּת.

The Gemara explains: **"And as for your birth, on the day you were born"; from here** it is derived **that one delivers the newborn on Shabbat. "Your navel was not cut"; from here** it is derived **that one cuts the umbilical cord on Shabbat. "And you were not washed in water for cleansing"; from here** it is derived **that one washes the newborn on Shabbat. "And you were not salted"; from here** it is derived **that one salts the newborn on Shabbat. "Nor were you swaddled"; from here** it is derived **that one swaddles the newborn on Shabbat.**

הדרן עלך מפנין

HALAKHA

Everything stated in the passage of rebuke one may perform for a woman in childbirth on Shabbat – כָּל הָאָמוּר בְּפָרָשַׁת תּוֹכֵחָה עוֹשִׂין לְחַיָּה בַּשַּׁבָּת: All the needs of a child born on Shabbat are met: The umbilical cord is cut and the child is washed and rubbed with salt, in accordance with the statement of Rav (Rambam *Sefer Zemanim, Hilkhot Shabbat* 2:11; *Shulḥan Arukh, Oraḥ Ḥayyim* 330:7).

Summary of **Perek XVIII**

This chapter continued the discussion of the *halakhot* of items that have been set aside from Shabbat use. Until this chapter, the Gemara primarily addressed the laws of utensils that have been set aside from Shabbat use, whereas this chapter addressed the quite different laws of raw materials and other items that are not utensils. Since utensils by definition are made to be used, it is necessary to decide explicitly or implicitly not to use them in order to remove them from the category of items designated for use on Shabbat. In contrast, raw materials are not inherently considered ready for use, and one must explicitly designate them for use to ensure that they are not set-aside [*muktze*]. In this chapter, we saw how the Sages acted with regard to this issue and how they determined which items are permitted or forbidden to be handled.

The Gemara also established guidelines with regard to the application of the laws of *muktze* to the care of animals on Shabbat. When an animal is likely to suffer pain due to a prohibition of rabbinic origin, that prohibition is overridden in order to care for the animal, as cruelty to animals is itself a Torah prohibition. In this area, loss of money to the animal's owner is not a significant factor.

Finally, this chapter discussed the permissible methods of attending to the sick on Shabbat. First it addressed the case of a woman after childbirth, and then it proceeded to address the laws of treating people with other ailments. The *halakha* distinguishes between different levels of illness. Whenever there is a danger to life, no distinction is made between Torah law and rabbinic law; it is permitted to do whatever is necessary to save a person's life. However, the *halakha* is somewhat more stringent when there is only a concern for possible danger, or when the patient feels that his life is in danger but the expert doctors testify otherwise.

It is important to note that the *halakha* also takes into account the patient's feelings. The Sages were concerned that the patient's anxiety could cause his condition to deteriorate and become life-threatening. They therefore permitted preparing things for a patient in order to calm him, and under certain conditions they even permitted the performance of labors prohibited by Torah law.

The Sages agreed in this chapter that a newborn and a woman after childbirth are included in the category of the dangerously ill for the first few days after birth. Any medical attention they need immediately after childbirth is considered to be a medical procedure undertaken in order to save a life, and those caring for them may take all necessary measures without concern for any prohibitions that would otherwise apply.

Introduction to **Perek XIX**

And God said to Abraham: And as for you, you shall keep My covenant; you, and your seed after you throughout their generations. This is My covenant which you shall keep, between Me and you and your seed after you: every male among you shall be circumcised. And you shall be circumcised in the flesh of your foreskin; and it shall be a token of a covenant between Me and you. And he that is eight days old shall be circumcised among you, every male throughout your generations, he that is born in the house, or bought with money of any foreigner, that is not of your seed. He that is born in your house, and he that is bought with your money, must be circumcised; and My covenant shall be in your flesh for an everlasting covenant. And the uncircumcised male who is not circumcised in the flesh of his foreskin, that soul shall be cut off from his people; he has broken My covenant.

(Genesis 17:9–14)

Speak to the children of Israel, saying: If a woman bears seed and gives birth to a male, she shall be unclean seven days; as in the days of the impurity of her sickness shall she be unclean. And on the eighth day the flesh of his foreskin shall be circumcised.

(Leviticus 12:2–3)

The Sages received an oral tradition that the mitzva of circumcision overrides Shabbat when it is performed at its proper time, on the eighth day after birth. Although all the Sages accepted this tradition, they disputed many details of its application. Such details include the handling of borderline cases, the precise definitions of the act of circumcision, and the actions necessary for its performance.

Several issues arise with regard to circumcision on Shabbat. The first question pertains to situations in which it is not entirely clear whether there is a mitzva to circumcise the child or whether the proper time for circumcision has arrived. Some Sages are of the opinion that circumcision overrides Shabbat only if there is absolutely no doubt as to its obligation. Others hold that in some circumstances an uncertain obligation to circumcise does override Shabbat, and these Sages debate which conditions are required.

Another issue is whether the preparations for circumcision override Shabbat. The medical attention the baby will require immediately after the circumcision does override Shabbat, as his life could be endangered if he does not receive it. The Sages consider whether actions to prepare for the circumcision, such as bringing the knife and preparing it for use, also override Shabbat, and if so, which preparations are considered essential in this regard.

A more fundamental question that arises is whether circumcision is the only mitzva that overrides Shabbat prohibitions or whether all mitzvot override Shabbat if the optimal time for their performance occurs on Shabbat. If there are distinctions between different mitzvot, what are the reasons for these distinctions?

Another essential issue pertains to how broadly circumcision overrides Shabbat. Does circumcision override Shabbat at every stage of the operation no matter how it is performed, and is anyone involved in circumcision exempt from Shabbat prohibitions? Or perhaps circumcision overrides Shabbat only when one completes the mitzva properly and in its entirety? To address these questions it becomes necessary to clarify the scope of the mitzva and to identify its obligatory components.

מתני׳ רַבִּי אֱלִיעֶזֶר אוֹמֵר: אִם לֹא הֵבִיא כְּלִי מֵעֶרֶב שַׁבָּת – מְבִיאוֹ בַּשַּׁבָּת מְגוּלֶּה. וּבַסַּכָּנָה מְכַסֵּהוּ עַל פִּי עֵדִים.

MISHNA As a continuation to the discussion at the end of the previous chapter, which mentioned circumcision in the context of a discussion of the *halakhot* of childbirth on Shabbat, the mishna continues to address the *halakhot* of circumcision. **Rabbi Eliezer says: If he did not bring an implement** for circumcising the child **on Shabbat eve, he brings it on Shabbat** itself **uncovered** so that it will be clear to all that he is bringing a circumcision scalpel. **And in** times of **danger,** when decrees of persecution prohibit Jews from circumcising their children, **one covers it in the presence of witnesses** who can testify that he transported the scalpel to perform a mitzva.

וְעוֹד אָמַר רַבִּי אֱלִיעֶזֶר: כּוֹרְתִים עֵצִים לַעֲשׂוֹת פֶּחָמִין לַעֲשׂוֹת (כְּלִי) בַּרְזֶל.

And furthermore, Rabbi Eliezer said with regard to this issue: **One** may even **cut down trees to prepare charcoal** in order **to fashion iron tools** for the purpose of circumcision.

כְּלָל אָמַר רַבִּי עֲקִיבָא: כׇּל מְלָאכָה שֶׁאֶפְשָׁר לַעֲשׂוֹתָהּ מֵעֶרֶב שַׁבָּת – אֵינָהּ דּוֹחָה אֶת הַשַּׁבָּת, (וּמִילָה) שֶׁאִי אֶפְשָׁר לַעֲשׂוֹתָהּ מֵעֶרֶב שַׁבָּת – דּוֹחָה אֶת הַשַּׁבָּת.

Rabbi Eliezer's approach was not universally accepted, and **a principle was stated by Rabbi Akiva: Any prohibited labor that can be performed on Shabbat eve**[H] **does not override Shabbat,** including transporting the circumcision scalpel. However, any prohibited labor involved in the mitzva of **circumcision** itself **that cannot be performed on Shabbat eve overrides Shabbat.**

גמ׳ אִיבַּעְיָא לְהוּ: טַעְמָא דְּרַבִּי אֱלִיעֶזֶר מִשּׁוּם חִבּוּבֵי מִצְוָה, אוֹ דִּילְמָא מִשּׁוּם חֲשָׁדָא? לְמַאי נָפְקָא מִינַּהּ? לְאַתּוֹיֵי מְכוּסֶּה עַל פִּי עֵדִים. אִי אָמְרַתְּ מִשּׁוּם חִבּוּבֵי מִצְוָה, מְגוּלֶּה – אִין, מְכוּסֶּה – לָא. אֶלָּא אִי אָמְרַתְּ מִשּׁוּם חֲשָׁדָא – אֲפִילּוּ מְכוּסֶּה שַׁפִּיר דָּמֵי. מַאי?

GEMARA **A dilemma was raised before** the Sages: Is **the reason for Rabbi Eliezer's** opinion that the scalpel must be uncovered **due to affection for the mitzva** and the desire to publicize it, **or perhaps** it is **due to** avoiding **suspicion?** The Gemara asks: **What** practical **difference is there** between the two reasons suggested for Rabbi Eliezer's opinion? The Gemara answers: The difference is with regard to the question of whether or not it is permitted **to bring** the scalpel **covered in the presence of witnesses** who are aware that one is bringing the scalpel for the purpose of circumcision. **If you say** the reason is **due to affection for the mitzva,** then if it is **uncovered, yes,** there is a display of affection for the mitzva. If it is **covered, no,** there is no display of affection. **However, if you say** the reason for this ruling is **due to** avoiding **suspicion, even** if it is **covered** he may **well** do so, because the witnesses are aware that a circumcision will be performed. **What** is the resolution of this dilemma?

אִיתְּמַר, אָמַר רַבִּי לֵוִי: לֹא אֲמָרָהּ רַבִּי אֱלִיעֶזֶר אֶלָּא לְחִבּוּבֵי מִצְוָה. תַּנְיָא נַמִי הָכִי: מְבִיאוֹ מְגוּלֶּה, וְאֵין מְבִיאוֹ מְכוּסֶּה, דִּבְרֵי רַבִּי אֱלִיעֶזֶר. אָמַר רַב אַשִׁי: מַתְנִיתִין נַמִי דַּיְקָא, דְּקָתָנֵי: וּבִשְׁעַת הַסַּכָּנָה מְכַסֵּהוּ עַל פִּי עֵדִים, בְּסַכָּנָה – אִין, שֶׁלֹּא בְּסַכָּנָה – לָא. שְׁמַע מִינַּהּ: מִשּׁוּם חִבּוּבֵי מִצְוָה: שְׁמַע מִינַּהּ.

It was stated that Rabbi Levi said: Rabbi Eliezer only stated this ruling **to express affection for the mitzva. That** opinion **was also taught** in a *baraita*: If a child is to be circumcised on Shabbat and they failed to bring the scalpel on Shabbat eve, **one brings it** on Shabbat **uncovered,** but **he does not bring it covered;** this is **the statement of Rabbi Eliezer. Rav Ashi said:** The language of **the mishna is also precise** in support of this opinion, **as it teaches: And in a time of danger he covers it in the presence of witnesses.** By inference, **in** a time of **danger, yes,** he covers it; when it is **not** a time of **danger, no,** he does not cover it. **Conclude from this** that the scalpel is uncovered **due to affection for the mitzva.** The Gemara states: Indeed, **conclude from this.**

תַּנְיָא אִידָּךְ: מְבִיאוֹ מְגוּלֶּה וְאֵין מְבִיאוֹ מְכוּסֶּה, דִּבְרֵי רַבִּי אֱלִיעֶזֶר. רַבִּי יְהוּדָה אוֹמֵר מִשּׁוּם רַבִּי אֱלִיעֶזֶר: נוֹהֲגִין הָיוּ בִּשְׁעַת הַסַּכָּנָה שֶׁהָיוּ מְבִיאִין מְכוּסֶּה עַל פִּי עֵדִים.

It was taught in **another** *baraita*: **He brings** the scalpel **uncovered, and he does not bring it covered;** this is **the statement of Rabbi Eliezer. Rabbi Yehuda says in the name of Rabbi Eliezer: In a time of danger they would customarily bring** the scalpel **covered in the presence of witnesses.**

אִיבַּעְיָא לְהוּ: עֵדִים דְּקָאָמַר – אִיהוּ וְחַד, אוֹ דִּילְמָא: הוּא וּתְרֵי?

With regard to these witnesses, **a dilemma was raised before** the Sages: **The** necessary **witnesses that he is saying,** do they include **he** who is bringing the scalpel **and one** other witness? **Or perhaps** they include **he** who brought the scalpel **and two** other witnesses to testify on his behalf.

HALAKHA

Any prohibited labor that can be performed on Shabbat eve, etc. – מְלָאכָה שֶׁאֶפְשָׁר לַעֲשׂוֹתָהּ מֵעֶרֶב שַׁבָּת וכו׳: Preparations for a circumcision that can be performed before Shabbat do not override Shabbat prohibitions. This includes prohibitions instituted by the Sages. Consequently, if a scalpel for circumcision was not brought before Shabbat, it is prohibited to carry it from one domain to another, and the circumcision is not performed. It is even prohibited to transport the knife in a manner prohibited by rabbinic decree, as the Sages instituted their ordinances to parallel Torah law. It is permitted to ask a gentile to bring the knife if he can transport it in a manner prohibited by rabbinic decree but not one that violates Torah law, in accordance with the opinion of Rabbi Akiva (Rambam *Sefer Ahava, Hilkhot Mila* 2:6, 9; *Shulḥan Arukh, Oraḥ Ḥayyim* 331:6 and *Yoreh De'a* 266:2, 5).

LANGUAGE

Peacock [*tavsa*] – טַוְוסָא: From the Greek ταώς, *taos*, referring to the bird known in Modern Hebrew as *tavas*. The Hebrew word is a cognate of the Aramaic *tavsa*, which is a peacock.

תָּא שְׁמַע: וּבְסַכָּנָה מְכַסֵּהוּ עַל פִּי עֵדִים, אִי אָמְרַתְּ בִּשְׁלָמָא הוּא וּתְרֵי – שַׁפִּיר, אֶלָּא אִי אָמְרַתְּ הוּא וְחַד – מַאי עֵדִים? שֶׁרְאוּיִם לְהָעִיד בְּמָקוֹם אַחֵר.

Come and **hear** a resolution to this dilemma from the language of the mishna, which stated: **And in times of danger he covers it in the presence of witnesses. Granted, if you say** it is referring to **him and two** other witnesses, **it** works out **well;** the wording is appropriate. **However, if you say** it is referring to **him and one** other witness, **what** is to be made of the use of the term **witnesses** in the plural when there is only one other witness? The Gemara refutes this proof: They may still be called witnesses, in the plural, because **they,** i.e., he and the other witness, **are fit to testify elsewhere.**[N]

״וְעוֹד אָמַר רַבִּי אֱלִיעֶזֶר״. תָּנוּ רַבָּנַן: בִּמְקוֹמוֹ שֶׁל רַבִּי אֱלִיעֶזֶר הָיוּ כּוֹרְתִין עֵצִים לַעֲשׂוֹת פֶּחָמִין לַעֲשׂוֹת בַּרְזֶל בַּשַּׁבָּת. בִּמְקוֹמוֹ שֶׁל רַבִּי יוֹסֵי הַגְּלִילִי הָיוּ אוֹכְלִין בְּשַׂר עוֹף בְּחָלָב.

We learned in our mishna: **And furthermore, Rabbi Eliezer said:** One may even cut down trees to prepare charcoal for the purpose of circumcision on Shabbat. With regard to this issue, **the Sages taught** in a *baraita*: **In the locale of Rabbi Eliezer,**[N] where they would follow his ruling, **they would** even **cut down trees** on Shabbat **to prepare charcoal** from it in order **to fashion iron** tools with which to circumcise a child **on Shabbat.** On a related note, the *baraita* relates: **In the locale of Rabbi Yosei HaGelili they would eat poultry meat in milk,** as Rabbi Yosei HaGelili held that the prohibition of meat in milk does not include poultry.

לֵוִי אִיקְּלַע לְבֵי יוֹסֵף רִישְׁבָּא קְרִיבוּ לֵיהּ רֵישָׁא דְּטַוְוסָא בְּחַלְבָּא לָא אֲכַל כִּי אֲתָא לְקַמֵּיהּ דְּרַבִּי אָמַר לֵיהּ: אַמַּאי לָא תְּשַׁמְּתִינְהוּ? אָמַר לֵיהּ: אַתְרֵיהּ דְּרַבִּי יְהוּדָה בֶּן בְּתֵירָה הֲוָה, וְאָמִינָא: דִּילְמָא דָּרַשׁ לְהוּ כְּרַבִּי יוֹסֵי הַגְּלִילִי.

The Gemara relates: **Levi happened** to come **to the house of Yosef the hunter. They served him the head of a peacock** [*tavsa*][L] **in milk** and **he did not eat. When** Levi **came before Rabbi** Yehuda HaNasi, the latter **said to him: Why did you not excommunicate** these people who eat poultry in milk, contrary to the decree of the Sages? Levi **said to him: It was** in **the locale** of **Rabbi Yehuda ben Beteira, and I said: Perhaps he taught them** that the *halakha* is **in accordance with** the opinion of **Rabbi Yosei HaGelili,** who permits the eating of poultry meat in milk. Given the possibility that their rabbi rules that it is permitted, I cannot come and prohibit it, and I certainly cannot excommunicate them for it.

דִּתְנַן, רַבִּי יוֹסֵי הַגְּלִילִי אוֹמֵר: נֶאֱמַר ״לֹא תֹאכְלוּ כָל נְבֵלָה״ וְנֶאֱמַר ״לֹא תְבַשֵּׁל גְּדִי בַּחֲלֵב אִמּוֹ״ אֶת שֶׁאָסוּר מִשּׁוּם נְבֵלָה – אָסוּר לְבַשֵּׁל בְּחָלָב, עוֹף שֶׁאָסוּר מִשּׁוּם נְבֵלָה יָכוֹל יְהֵא אָסוּר לְבַשֵּׁל בְּחָלָב – תַּלְמוּד לוֹמַר ״בַּחֲלֵב אִמּוֹ״ – יָצָא עוֹף שֶׁאֵין לוֹ חֲלֵב אֵם.

As we learned in a mishna, **Rabbi Yosei HaGelili says: It is stated** in the verse: **"You shall not eat anything that dies of itself;** to the stranger at your gates you may give it, that he may eat it; or you may sell it to a foreigner; for you are a holy people to the Lord your God" (Deuteronomy 14:21), **and it is stated** later in the same verse: **"You shall not cook a kid in its mother's milk."** From the juxtaposition of the two issues it is derived: **That which is prohibited due to** the prohibition against eating an **unslaughtered animal, it is prohibited to cook** it **in milk.** The prohibition against cooking a creature in milk is not limited to only a kid. If so, with regard to **poultry, which is prohibited due to** the prohibition against eating an **unslaughtered animal,** I **might** have thought **it should be prohibited to cook** it **in milk; therefore, the verse states: "In its mother's milk."** This **excludes poultry, which does not have mother's milk** and is therefore not included in the prohibition.[N]

אָמַר רַבִּי יִצְחָק: עִיר אַחַת הָיְתָה בְּאֶרֶץ יִשְׂרָאֵל שֶׁהָיוּ עוֹשִׂין כְּרַבִּי אֱלִיעֶזֶר, וְהָיוּ מֵתִים בִּזְמַנָּן. וְלֹא עוֹד אֶלָּא שֶׁפַּעַם אַחַת גָּזְרָה מַלְכוּת הָרְשָׁעָה גְּזֵרָה עַל יִשְׂרָאֵל עַל הַמִּילָה, וְעַל אוֹתָהּ הָעִיר לֹא גָּזְרָה.

Rabbi Yitzḥak said: There was one city in Eretz Yisrael where they would act in accordance with the opinion of **Rabbi Eliezer** with regard to circumcision, **and they would die at their appointed time** and not earlier, as a reward for their affection for this mitzva. **And not only that, but on one occasion the wicked empire,** Rome, **issued a decree against the Jewish people** prohibiting **circumcision; but against that city it did not** issue the **decree.**

NOTES

Because they are fit to testify elsewhere – שֶׁרְאוּיִם לְהָעִיד בְּמָקוֹם אַחֵר: The Gemara teaches here that, even according to the opinion that one other witness is sufficient, the person who brings the scalpel and the witness must both be valid witnesses. The second person must not be a disqualified witness or a relative of the person who brings the scalpel, as relatives cannot testify together (Rashash; Rabbi Eliezer Moshe Horowitz).

In the locale of Rabbi Eliezer – בִּמְקוֹמוֹ שֶׁל רַבִּי אֱלִיעֶזֶר: *Tosafot* explain that in Rabbi Eliezer's locale people would deliberately place themselves in situations where they were required to cut wood on Shabbat to display their affection for the mitzva of circumcision. Although this ruling was not accepted as normative, the Sages praised the people of that locale, who were rewarded for their meticulousness in observing this mitzva.

Meat in milk – בָּשָׂר בְּחָלָב: The basic details of this *halakha* appear in tractate *Ḥullin*, where a variety of derivations are cited in order to establish the parameters of this prohibition, which includes cooking meat and milk together as well as eating and benefiting from that combination. The halakhic conclusion is that the Torah does not prohibit cooking poultry in milk. Nevertheless, the Sages issued a decree prohibiting it, lest one come to confuse poultry meat with meat of an animal.

תַּנְיָא, רַבָּן שִׁמְעוֹן בֶּן גַּמְלִיאֵל אוֹמֵר: כׇּל מִצְוָה שֶׁקִּיבְּלוּ עֲלֵיהֶם בְּשִׂמְחָה כְּגוֹן מִילָה, דִּכְתִיב ״שָׂשׂ אָנֹכִי עַל אִמְרָתֶךָ כְּמוֹצֵא שָׁלָל רָב״ – עֲדַיִין עוֹשִׂין אוֹתָהּ בְּשִׂמְחָה, וְכׇל מִצְוָה שֶׁקִּבְּלוּ עֲלֵיהֶם בִּקְטָטָה, כְּגוֹן עֲרָיוֹת – דִּכְתִיב ״וַיִּשְׁמַע מֹשֶׁה אֶת הָעָם בֹּכֶה לְמִשְׁפְּחוֹתָיו״ עַל עִסְקֵי מִשְׁפְּחוֹתָיו – עֲדַיִין עוֹשִׂין אוֹתָהּ בִּקְטָטָה, דְּלֵיכָּא כְּתוּבָּה דְּלָא רָמוּ בַּהּ תִּיגְרָא.

Apropos affection for the mitzva of circumcision, the Gemara cites a *baraita* in which **it was taught** that **Rabban Shimon ben Gamliel says: Every mitzva that** the Jews initially **accepted upon themselves with joy, such as circumcision,**[H] **as it is written: "I rejoice at Your word**[N] **as one who finds great spoil"** (Psalms 119:162), and as the Sages explained, this "word" refers to the mitzva of circumcision, over which they rejoiced, **they still perform it with joy. And every mitzva that** the Jews initially **accepted upon themselves with contentiousness** and regret, **such as** the prohibition against **incestuous relations, as it is written: "And Moses heard the people weeping, family by family"** (Numbers 11:10), and as the Sages interpreted homiletically: They wept **over matters** pertaining to **their families,** as they were prohibited at that time from marrying family members, **they still perform with contentiousness.** The fact is **that there is no marriage contract** and wedding **in which contentiousness does not arise,** as there is inevitably some conflict between the parties. The *baraita* asserts that this is because, initially, the Jews did not accept the laws governing marriage and family relationships willingly.

תַּנְיָא, רַבִּי שִׁמְעוֹן בֶּן אֶלְעָזָר אוֹמֵר: כׇּל מִצְוָה שֶׁמָּסְרוּ יִשְׂרָאֵל עַצְמָן עֲלֵיהֶם לְמִיתָה בִּשְׁעַת גְּזֵרַת הַמַּלְכוּת, כְּגוֹן עֲבוֹדָה זָרָה וּמִילָה – עֲדַיִין הִיא מוּחְזֶקֶת בְּיָדָם, וְכׇל מִצְוָה שֶׁלֹּא מָסְרוּ יִשְׂרָאֵל עַצְמָן עָלֶיהָ לְמִיתָה בִּשְׁעַת גְּזֵרַת הַמַּלְכוּת, כְּגוֹן תְּפִילִּין – עֲדַיִין הִיא מְרוּפָּה בְּיָדָם.

It was taught in a *baraita* that **Rabbi Shimon ben Elazar says** in praise of the observance of the mitzva of circumcision: **Any mitzva for which the Jews sacrificed their lives at the time of the decrees of the** wicked **empire, such as** the prohibition of **idolatry and** the mitzva of **circumcision, is still steadfastly observed. And any mitzva for which the Jews did not sacrifice their lives at the time of the decrees of the** wicked **empire, such as phylacteries, is still casually observed,** meaning that they are not as careful in its fulfillment as they should be.

דְּאָמַר רַבִּי יַנַּאי: תְּפִילִּין צְרִיכִין גּוּף נָקִי כֶּאֱלִישָׁע בַּעַל כְּנָפַיִם. מַאי הִיא? אָמַר אַבַּיֵי: שֶׁלֹּא יָפִיחַ בָּהֶם, רָבָא אָמַר: שֶׁלֹּא יִישַׁן בָּהֶם.

The Gemara cites proof that the mitzva of phylacteries was not fulfilled properly at the time of the decrees, based upon an incident related to the following *halakha*. **As Rabbi Yannai said:** Donning **phylacteries requires a clean body like** that of **Elisha, Man of Wings. What is** included in the requirement to have a clean body? **Abaye said: That one may not pass wind in them. Rava said: That one may not sleep in them.**

וְאַמַּאי קָרוּ לֵיהּ ״אֱלִישָׁע בַּעַל כְּנָפַיִם״? שֶׁפַּעַם אַחַת גָּזְרָה מַלְכוּת הָרְשָׁעָה גְּזֵירָה עַל יִשְׂרָאֵל, שֶׁכׇּל הַמַּנִּיחַ תְּפִילִּין עַל רֹאשׁוֹ – יִקְּרוּ אֶת מוֹחוֹ. וְהָיָה אֱלִישָׁע מַנִּיחַ תְּפִילִּין וְיָצָא לַשּׁוּק. וְרָאָהוּ קַסְדּוֹר אֶחָד, רָץ מִלְּפָנָיו וְרָץ אַחֲרָיו. כֵּיוָן שֶׁהִגִּיעַ אֶצְלוֹ – נְטָלָן מֵרֹאשׁוֹ וַאֲחָזָן בְּיָדוֹ. אָמַר לֵיהּ: מַה בְּיָדְךָ? אָמַר לוֹ: כַּנְפֵי יוֹנָה. פָּשַׁט אֶת יָדוֹ וְנִמְצְאוּ בָּהּ כַּנְפֵי יוֹנָה. לְפִיכָךְ הָיוּ קוֹרִאין אוֹתוֹ ״בַּעַל כְּנָפַיִם״.

The Gemara asks: **And why did they call him Elisha, Man of Wings? Because on one occasion the wicked empire** of Rome **issued a decree against the Jewish people that,** as punishment, **they would pierce the brain of anyone who dons phylacteries on his head.** Nevertheless, **Elisha would don them and** defiantly **go out to the marketplace.** One day, **an official** who was appointed to enforce the decree **saw him.** Elisha **ran away from him, and** the official **ran after him. When** the official **reached him,** Elisha **removed** the phylacteries **from his head and held them in his hand.** The officer **asked him: What is in your hand?** Elisha **said to him:** It is merely **a dove's wings.** A miracle took place: **He opened his hand, and,** indeed, **it was found** to be **a dove's wings. Therefore,** in commemoration of this miracle, **they** would **call him** Elisha, **Man of Wings.**

מַאי שְׁנָא כַּנְפֵי יוֹנָה דְּאָמַר לֵיהּ, וְלֹא אָמַר לֵיהּ שְׁאָר עוֹפוֹת? מִשּׁוּם דְּדָמְיָא כְּנֶסֶת יִשְׂרָאֵל לְיוֹנָה, שֶׁנֶּאֱמַר ״כַּנְפֵי יוֹנָה נֶחְפָּה בַכֶּסֶף וְאֶבְרוֹתֶיהָ בִּירַקְרַק חָרוּץ״, מַה יּוֹנָה זוֹ כְּנָפֶיהָ מְגִינּוֹת עָלֶיהָ, אַף יִשְׂרָאֵל – מִצְוֹת מְגִינּוֹת עֲלֵיהֶן.

The Gemara asks: **And what is different** about **a dove's wings,** that Elisha specifically **told him** that he was holding the wings of a dove **and he did not tell him** he was holding the wings of **other birds?** The Gemara answers: **Because the congregation of Israel is likened to a dove, as it is stated:** "You shall shine as **the wings of a dove covered with silver and her pinions with yellow gold"** (Psalms 68:14). **Just as a dove** has only **its wings to protect it, so too, the Jewish people** have only **mitzvot to protect them.** Apparently, Elisha Man of Wings was vigilant in fulfilling the mitzva of phylacteries in the face of the decree, whereas the rest of the people were not.

אָמַר רַבִּי אַבָּא בַּר רַב אַדָּא אָמַר רַבִּי יִצְחָק: פַּעַם אַחַת שָׁכְחוּ וְלֹא הֵבִיאוּ אִיזְמֵל מֵעֶרֶב שַׁבָּת, וֶהֱבִיאוּהוּ בַּשַּׁבָּת [דֶּרֶךְ גַּגּוֹת וְדֶרֶךְ חֲצֵירוֹת]

Rabbi Abba bar Rav Adda said that **Rabbi Yitzḥak said** as follows: **On one occasion** they were supposed to circumcise a baby on Shabbat, and **they forgot and did not bring a scalpel** with which to circumcise him **on Shabbat eve, and they brought it on Shabbat via roofs and via courtyards,**

HALAKHA

Every mitzva that the Jews accepted upon themselves with joy, such as circumcision, etc. – כׇּל מִצְוָה שֶׁקִּיבְּלוּ עֲלֵיהֶם בְּשִׂמְחָה כְּגוֹן מִילָה וכו׳: It is customary to mark a circumcision with a celebratory meal. This custom is mentioned in several midrashic sources, and one can glean support for this notion from the Gemara here, which comments that the mitzva is performed with joy (*Shulḥan Arukh, Yoreh De'a* 265:12).

NOTES

Such as circumcision, as it is written: "I rejoice at Your word" – כְּגוֹן מִילָה, דִּכְתִיב ״שָׂשׂ אָנֹכִי עַל אִמְרָתֶךָ״: Both Rashi and *Tosafot* explain how this verse is interpreted as referring to circumcision. Rav Hai Gaon explains that it is derived by means of a verbal analogy: This verse reads: "I rejoice at Your word" (Psalms 119:162), while another verse states: "For they have observed Your word and kept Your covenant" (Deuteronomy 33:9). The parallel formulation of these two verses indicates that the subject of the verse in Psalms is also a covenant, the covenant of circumcision.

HALAKHA

Carrying a circumcision scalpel on Shabbat from one domain to another – **טִילְטוּל סַכִּין שֶׁל מִילָה בְּשַׁבָּת מֵרְשׁוּת לִרְשׁוּת**: If the circumcision scalpel were not brought to the place where the circumcision was to be performed on Shabbat, it is prohibited to carry it from one domain to another, including from a public domain or a *karmelit* into a private domain, and from one courtyard to another or to an alleyway, if they were not joined together through an *eiruv*, in accordance with the opinion of the Rabbis (Rambam *Sefer Ahava, Hilkhot Mila* 2:6; *Shulḥan Arukh, Oraḥ Ḥayyim* 331:6 and *Yoreh De'a* 266:2).

Roofs, enclosures, and courtyards – **גַּגּוֹת קַרְפֵּיפוֹת וַחֲצֵירוֹת**: Roofs, enclosures, and courtyards are considered a single domain with regard to the vessels found there at the beginning of Shabbat. Consequently, it is permitted to carry from one to another, even if the individual areas belong to different owners and they were not joined by an *eiruv*. However, if the vessels were in the house at the beginning of Shabbat, it is prohibited to carry them out of the courtyard area of that house, in accordance with the opinion of Rabbi Shimon (Rambam *Sefer Zemanim, Hilkhot Eiruvin* 3:18; *Shulḥan Arukh, Oraḥ Ḥayyim* 372:1).

שֶׁלֹּא בִּרְצוֹן רַבִּי אֱלִיעֶזֶר.

contrary to the wishes of Rabbi Eliezer. Even though the roofs and courtyards were not halakhically joined in a manner where it would be permitted to carry from one to the other, the Rabbis permitted carrying the scalpel in this manner.

מַתְקִיף לַהּ רַב יוֹסֵף: "שֶׁלֹּא בִּרְצוֹן רַבִּי אֱלִיעֶזֶר"?! אַדְּרַבָּה, רַבִּי אֱלִיעֶזֶר הוּא דְּשָׁרֵי! וְכִי תֵּימָא שֶׁלֹּא בִּרְצוֹן רַבִּי אֱלִיעֶזֶר – דְּשָׁרֵי אֲפִילּוּ בִּרְשׁוּת הָרַבִּים, אֶלָּא בִּרְצוֹן רַבָּנַן – דְּאָסְרוּ דֶּרֶךְ רְשׁוּת הָרַבִּים, וְשָׁרוּ דֶּרֶךְ גַּגּוֹת דֶּרֶךְ חֲצֵירוֹת וְקַרְפֵּיפוֹת. וּמִי שָׁרֵי?! וְהָתַנְיָא: כְּשֵׁם שֶׁאֵין מְבִיאִין אוֹתוֹ דֶּרֶךְ רְשׁוּת הָרַבִּים – כָּךְ אֵין מְבִיאִין אוֹתוֹ לֹא דֶּרֶךְ גַּגּוֹת וְלֹא דֶּרֶךְ קַרְפֵּיפוֹת וְלֹא דֶּרֶךְ חֲצֵירוֹת.

Rav Yosef strongly objects to this: Contrary to the wishes of Rabbi Eliezer? On the contrary, it is Rabbi Eliezer who permits this, as he permits carrying the scalpel even through the public domain.[H] **And if you say** that it means **contrary to the wishes of Rabbi Eliezer, who permits** carrying **even in the public domain, but in accordance with the wishes of the Rabbis,** who **prohibited** carrying **via the public domain and** only **permitted** carrying **via roofs, via courtyards and enclosures,** that is also difficult. **And is it permitted** according to the opinion of the Rabbis? **Wasn't it taught** in a *baraita*: **Just as one may not bring** the circumcision knife **via the public domain, so too, one may not bring it via roofs, via enclosures, or via courtyards?**

אֶלָּא אָמַר רַב אָשֵׁי: שֶׁלֹּא בִּרְצוֹן רַבִּי אֱלִיעֶזֶר וּמַחְלוֹקְתּוֹ, אֶלָּא בִּרְצוֹן רַבִּי שִׁמְעוֹן. דִּתְנַן, רַבִּי שִׁמְעוֹן אוֹמֵר: אֶחָד גַּגּוֹת וְאֶחָד קַרְפֵּיפוֹת וְאֶחָד חֲצֵירוֹת – כּוּלָּן רְשׁוּת אַחַת הֵן לְכֵלִים שֶׁשָּׁבְתוּ בְּתוֹכָן, וְלֹא לְכֵלִים שֶׁשָּׁבְתוּ בְּתוֹךְ הַבַּיִת.

Rather, Rav Ashi said: It means **contrary to the wishes of Rabbi Eliezer and his disputants,**[N] **but in accordance with the wishes of Rabbi Shimon. As we learned** in a mishna that **Rabbi Shimon says: Roofs, enclosures, and courtyards**[H] **are all** considered as **one domain with regard to vessels that rested inside them** at the beginning of Shabbat. Therefore, it is permitted to carry vessels that rested inside one to another. However, they are **not** considered the same domain **with regard to vessels that rested inside the house** at the beginning of Shabbat. If the homeowners did not join the courtyard by means of an *eiruv*, it is prohibited to carry vessels from their houses to the courtyard. Even if the houses in a courtyard were joined, it is prohibited to carry from the courtyard to an enclosure unless they were joined by means of an *eiruv*. In any case, there are circumstances in which Rabbi Shimon allows carrying via roofs, courtyards, and enclosures.

בְּעָא מִינֵּיהּ רַבִּי זֵירָא מֵרַבִּי אַסִּי: מָבוֹי שֶׁלֹּא נִשְׁתַּתְּפוּ בּוֹ, מַהוּ לְטַלְטֵל בְּכוּלּוֹ? מִי אָמְרִינַן כְּחָצֵר דָּמֵי, מָה חָצֵר – אַף עַל גַּב דְּלֹא עָרְבוּ מוּתָּר לְטַלְטֵל בְּכוּלּוֹ, הַאי נָמֵי – אַף עַל גַּב דְּלֹא נִשְׁתַּתְּפוּ בּוֹ מוּתָּר לְטַלְטֵל בְּכוּלּוֹ. אוֹ דִּילְמָא: לָא דָּמֵי לְחָצֵר, דְּחָצֵר אִית לֵיהּ אַרְבַּע מְחִיצוֹת, הַאי – לֵית לֵיהּ אַרְבַּע מְחִיצוֹת. אִי נָמֵי, חָצֵר – אִית לֵיהּ דִּיּוּרִין, הַאי – לֵית בֵּיהּ דִּיּוּרִין. שָׁתֵיק וְלָא אֲמַר לֵיהּ וְלָא מִידֵּי.

Rabbi Zeira raised a dilemma before Rabbi Asi: An alleyway whose residents **did not merge** together, **what is** its legal status with regard **to carrying** items **in all of it** according to Rabbi Shimon? Rabbi Zeira explains the dilemma: **Do we say** that **it is like a courtyard,** and **just as** with regard to **a courtyard, even though they did not join** the houses in it together and despite the fact that it is prohibited to carry out items from the houses to the courtyard, **it is** nonetheless **permitted to carry in all of it?** Therefore, in **this** alleyway **too, even though they did not merge** together, **it is permitted to carry in all of it** despite the fact that it is prohibited to carry items into the alleyway. **Or, perhaps** an alleyway is **not similar** in this regard **to a courtyard,** as a **courtyard has four partitions,** whereas **this,** the alleyway, **does not have four partitions,** but only three. **Alternatively,** there may be a different reason for the inferior status of an alleyway in this regard: **A courtyard has residents** and can therefore be considered like a house, which would allow carrying within it, whereas **this** alleyway **does not have residents.** Rabbi Asi **was silent and did not say anything to him,** as he was unable to provide a satisfactory response.[N]

NOTES

Contrary to the wishes of Rabbi Eliezer and his disputants – **שֶׁלֹּא בִּרְצוֹן רַבִּי אֱלִיעֶזֶר וּמַחְלוֹקְתּוֹ**: This statement appears in several contexts involving similar cases where the Gemara associates an entire discussion with the name of a particular Sage who took part in the discussion. It refers not only to the opinion of that Sage but also to that of his disputants, whose names are not mentioned.

Carrying in courtyards and alleyways – **טִלְטוּל בַּחֲצֵירוֹת וּמְבוֹאוֹת**: The laws of alleyways and courtyards are addressed at great length in tractate *Eiruvin*. The discussion here is based on several principles. All the areas referred to here, i.e., courtyards, roofs, enclosures, and alleyways, have the legal status of a private domain by Torah law, since they are surrounded by halakhically satisfactory partitions. Nevertheless, for various reasons, the Sages decreed that it is prohibited to carry within them. They also prohibited carrying from houses located in a common courtyard to the courtyard. The rationale is that each house is a private domain, while the common courtyard is similar to a domain frequented by the public, as it is used jointly by many people. To permit carrying in the courtyard, the residents of all the houses must join together and create a partnership [*eiruv*] that accords them the legal status of members of one family living in a single house. This also applies to an alleyway shared by numerous courtyards.

A different *halakha* applies to enclosures and roofs. Since people do not live there, the Sages were stringent and accorded them *karmelit* status, even though they are actually private domains. Rabbi Shimon, however, distinguishes between carrying from houses to roofs and courtyards and carrying between roofs and courtyards themselves. He prohibits carrying items from houses to any area of the courtyard, including roofs. However, he considers the roofs and courtyards themselves to be private domains in which it is permitted to carry. The question that arose in the Gemara sought to clarify which of those models applies to an alleyway.

זִימְנִין אַשְׁכַּחֵיהּ דְּיָתֵיב וְקָא אָמַר: אָמַר רַבִּי שִׁמְעוֹן בֶּן לָקִישׁ מִשּׁוּם רַבִּי יְהוּדָה הַנָּשִׂיא: פַּעַם אַחַת שָׁכְחוּ וְלֹא הֵבִיאוּ אִיזְמֵל מֵעֶרֶב שַׁבָּת, וֶהֱבִיאוּהוּ בַּשַּׁבָּת, וְהָיָה הַדָּבָר קָשֶׁה לַחֲכָמִים: הֵיאַךְ מַנִּיחִין דִּבְרֵי חֲכָמִים וְעוֹשִׂין כְּרַבִּי אֱלִיעֶזֶר. חֲדָא – דְּרַבִּי אֱלִיעֶזֶר שַׁמּוּתִי הוּא, וְעוֹד – יָחִיד וְרַבִּים הֲלָכָה כְּרַבִּים.

On another occasion Rabbi Zeira **found** Rabbi Asi **sitting and saying: Rabbi Shimon ben Lakish said in the name of Rabbi Yehuda HaNasi: One time they forgot and did not bring a scalpel on Shabbat eve** for the purpose of circumcising a child on Shabbat, **and they brought it on Shabbat, and the matter was difficult** in the eyes of **the Rabbis: How can they abandon the words of the Rabbis,** who prohibit doing so, **and act in accordance with** the opinion of **Rabbi Eliezer?** Why did they find this difficult? **One** reason was **that Rabbi Eliezer was a** ***Shammuti***, i.e., a follower of the views of Beit Shammai (Jerusalem Talmud), and the *halakha* is generally in accordance with the opinion of Beit Hillel in their disputes with Beit Shammai. **And furthermore,** there is a general rule that in a dispute between **an individual and the many,** the ***halakha*** **is in accordance with** the opinion of **the many.** Here too, the *halakha* should certainly be in accordance with the opinion of the Rabbis, who disagree with Rabbi Eliezer.

וְאָמַר רַבִּי אוֹשַׁעְיָא: שְׁאֵילִית אֶת רַבִּי יְהוּדָה הַגּוֹזֵר, וְאָמַר לִי: מָבוֹי שֶׁלֹּא נִשְׁתַּתְּפוּ בּוֹ הֲוָה, וְאַיְיתוּהוּ מֵהַאי רֵישָׁא לְהַאי רֵישָׁא. אָמַר לֵיהּ: סְבִירָא לֵיהּ לְמָר מָבוֹי שֶׁלֹּא נִשְׁתַּתְּפוּ מוּתָּר לְטַלְטֵל בְּכוּלּוֹ? וְאָמַר לֵיהּ: אִין. אֲמַר לֵיהּ: וְהָא זִימְנִין בְּעַאי מִינָּךְ וְלָא אֲמַרְתְּ לִי הָכִי! דִּילְמָא אַגַּב שִׁיטְפָךְ רְהִיט לָךְ גְּמָרָךְ? אָמַר לֵיהּ: אִין, אַגַּב שִׁיטְפָא רְהִיטָא לִי גְּמָרִי.

And Rabbi Oshaya said: I asked Rabbi Yehuda the Cutter, i.e., the circumcisor, **and he told me** that this incident occurred in **an alleyway** whose residents **did not merge** together, **and they brought** the scalpel **from this end** of the alleyway **to that end,** where the baby was. That concludes Rabbi Asi's account of the event. Rabbi Zeira **said to** Rabbi Asi: Since you related that story without expressing any reservations, it appears that **the Master** must **hold** that with regard to **an alleyway** whose residents **did not merge** together, **it is permitted to carry in all of it. And** Rabbi Asi **said to him: Yes,** that is the *halakha*. Rabbi Zeira **said to him: But on a** different **occasion I raised a dilemma** on this matter **before you and you did not say so to me. Perhaps in the course** of your studies **your knowledge was restored to you?**[N] **He said to him: Yes, in the course** of my studies **my knowledge was restored to me,** and I remembered this *halakha*.

אִיתְּמַר, אָמַר רַבִּי זֵירָא אָמַר רַב: מָבוֹי שֶׁלֹּא נִשְׁתַּתְּפוּ בּוֹ – אֵין מְטַלְטְלִין בּוֹ אֶלָּא בְּאַרְבַּע אַמּוֹת.

With regard to the very same *halakha*, **it was stated** as a principle that **Rabbi Zeira said** that **Rav said: An alleyway that was not merged** by the residents of the courtyards that open into it, **it is only permitted to carry in it** within **four cubits.**

אֲמַר אַבָּיֵי: הָא מִילְּתָא אֲמָרָהּ רַבִּי זֵירָא וְלָא פֵּירְשָׁהּ, עַד דַּאֲתָא רַבָּה בַּר אֲבוּהּ וּפֵירְשָׁהּ, דְּאָמַר רַב נַחְמָן אָמַר רַבָּה בַּר אֲבוּהּ אָמַר רַב: מָבוֹי שֶׁלֹּא נִשְׁתַּתְּפוּ בּוֹ, עֵירְבוּ חֲצֵירוֹת עִם בָּתִּים – אֵין מְטַלְטְלִין בּוֹ אֶלָּא בְּאַרְבַּע אַמּוֹת, לֹא עֵירְבוּ חֲצֵירוֹת עִם בָּתִּים – מוּתָּר לְטַלְטֵל בְּכוּלּוֹ.

Abaye said: This halakhic **matter was stated by Rabbi Zeira, and he did not explain it.** It remained enigmatic **until Rabba bar Avuh came and explained it. As Rav Naḥman said** that **Rabba bar Avuh said** that **Rav said:** With regard to **an alleyway that was not merged**[H] by the residents of the courtyards that open into it, if they **joined the courtyards with the houses,** i.e., the homeowners within each courtyard joined together and are therefore permitted to carry within the courtyards themselves, **it is only permitted to carry in it within four cubits,** as in an intermediate domain [*karmelit*]. However, if they **did not join the courtyards with the houses** and it is prohibited to carry within the courtyards, **it is permitted to carry in the entire** alleyway.

אֲמַר לֵיהּ רַב חֲנִינָא חוֹזָאָה לְרַבָּה: מַאי שְׁנָא כִּי עֵירְבוּ חֲצֵירוֹת עִם בָּתִּים – דְּנִיתְּקוּ חֲצֵירוֹת וְנַעֲשׂוּ בָּתִּים, וְרַב לְטַעְמֵיהּ, דְּאָמַר רַב: אֵין הַמָּבוֹי נִיתָּר בְּלֶחִי וְקוֹרָה עַד שֶׁיְּהוּ

Rav Ḥanina Ḥoza'a said to Rabba: What is different about a case **where** they **joined the courtyards with the houses?** Is it **because** the **courtyards were detached and became** like **houses? And Rav follows his** regular line of **reasoning, for Rav said: An alleyway** can only be made into **a permitted** area for carrying **by means of a sidepole and a crossbeam,** which is the standard *halakha* in a closed alleyway, **if there are**

Perek **XIX**
Daf **131** Amud **a**

בָּתִּים וַחֲצֵרוֹת פְּתוּחִין לְתוֹכוֹ. וְהָכָא, בָּתִּים – אִיכָּא, חֲצֵרוֹת – לֵיכָּא. כִּי לָא עֵירְבוּ נַמִי, לֶיחֱזִינְהוּ לְהָנֵי בָּתִּים כְּמַאן דִּסְתִימִי דָּמוּ, וַחֲצֵרוֹת – אִיכָּא, וּבָתִּים – לֵיכָּא!

houses and courtyards open to it, and each courtyard contains at least two houses, and there are at least two courtyards. **And here, there are houses** but **there are no courtyards,** and therefore the standard *halakhot* of a closed alleyway do not apply. However, if that is the case, **when they did not join** the courtyards with the houses **too, let us consider these houses as though they were sealed,** because their residents may not carry from their houses into the courtyards, and the houses should be considered irrelevant. Therefore, in that case too, **there are courtyards** but **there are no houses.**

NOTES

In the course of your studies your knowledge was restored to you – אַגַּב שִׁיטְפָךְ רְהִיט לָךְ גְּמָרָךְ: The Rashash explains this phrase to mean the opposite: Through your preoccupation with your studies you forgot what you had learned through oral tradition.

HALAKHA

An alleyway that was not merged – מָבוֹי שֶׁלֹּא נִשְׁתַּתְּפוּ בּוֹ: Vessels that were located in a closed alleyway from the beginning of Shabbat may be moved anywhere within that alleyway, whether or not the courtyards were merged together or the houses within the courtyards were joined together. The *halakha* in this matter is not in accordance with the opinion Rav but in accordance with the opinion of Rabbi Yoḥanan cited in tractate *Eiruvin*, as Rabbi Shimon's ruling with regard to the *halakhot* of roofs and courtyards is accepted (*Beit Yosef*). According to the Rambam, if the houses in the courtyards were joined together but the various courtyards in the alleyway did not merge, it is permitted to carry only four cubits in the alleyway (Rambam *Sefer Zemanim*, *Hilkhot Eiruvin* 5:15; *Shulḥan Arukh*, *Oraḥ Ḥayyim* 388).

אֶפְשָׁר דִּמְבַטְּלִי לֵיהּ רְשׁוּתָא דְּכוּלְּהוּ לְגַבֵּי חַד. סוֹף סוֹף, בַּיִת – אִיכָּא, בָּתִּים – לֵיכָּא!

The Gemara answers: In that case **it is possible for them to renounce all of their property rights** and transfer them **to one** person.[N] Just as the residents of a courtyard can join together, thereby rendering it permitted to carry in the courtyard, they can also relinquish their property rights to a single resident. In that way, it is considered as though there is only one inhabited house in the courtyard, and it is therefore permitted to carry within the courtyard as well as between that particular house and the courtyard. The Gemara rejects this answer: **Ultimately,** even in that case, **there is** one **house,** yet **there are not** multiple **houses,** as it is possible to relinquish one's privileges to only one homeowner and not to two. This would fail to meet the minimum requirement of two houses for the area to be considered a courtyard.

אֶפְשָׁר דְּמִצַּפְרָא וְעַד פַּלְגָא דְּיוֹמָא לְגַבֵּי חַד, מִפַּלְגֵיהּ דְּיוֹמָא וּלְפַנְיָא לְגַבֵּי חַד. סוֹף סוֹף, בְּעִידָּנָא דְּאִיתֵיהּ לְהַאי – לֵיתֵיהּ לְהַאי! אֶלָּא אָמַר רַב אַשִׁי: מִי גָּרַם לַחֲצֵרוֹת שֶׁיֵּאָסְרוּ – בָּתִּים, וְלֵיכָּא.

The Gemara answers: **It is possible** to resolve this: **From morning until midday** they can relinquish their rights **to one,** and **from midday until evening** they can relinquish their rights **to another,** and as a result there will be two houses. The Gemara rejects this answer: **Ultimately, at the time when this** house **has** the ownership rights, **that** house **does not have** them, as at any point in time there is only one house from which it is permitted to carry into the courtyard. **Rather, Rav Ashi said:** The explanation that there are no houses and courtyards here is rejected, and the explanation is: **What caused the courtyards to be prohibited?** It is the presence of the **houses.** Had there been no houses, it would have been permitted to carry from the courtyards into the alleyway, since they are one domain according to Rabbi Shimon. **And** here, it is considered as though **there are no** houses. Therefore, it is permitted to carry in the alleyway.

אָמַר רַבִּי חִיָּיא בַּר אַבָּא אָמַר רַבִּי יוֹחָנָן: לֹא לַכֹּל אָמַר רַבִּי אֱלִיעֶזֶר מַכְשִׁירֵי מִצְוָה דּוֹחִין אֶת הַשַּׁבָּת, שֶׁהֲרֵי שְׁתֵּי הַלֶּחֶם חוֹבַת הַיּוֹם הֵן וְלֹא לְמָדָן רַבִּי אֱלִיעֶזֶר אֶלָּא מִגְּזֵירָה שָׁוָה. דְּתַנְיָא, רַבִּי אֱלִיעֶזֶר אוֹמֵר: מִנַּיִין לְמַכְשִׁירֵי שְׁתֵּי הַלֶּחֶם שֶׁדּוֹחִין אֶת הַשַּׁבָּת – נֶאֶמְרָה הֲבָאָה בָּעוֹמֶר, וְנֶאֶמְרָה הֲבָאָה בִּשְׁתֵּי הַלֶּחֶם. מָה הֲבָאָה הָאֲמוּרָה בָּעוֹמֶר – מַכְשִׁירִין דּוֹחִין אֶת הַשַּׁבָּת, אַף הֲבָאָה הָאֲמוּרָה בִּשְׁתֵּי הַלֶּחֶם – מַכְשִׁירִין דּוֹחִין אֶת הַשַּׁבָּת.

Rabbi Ḥiyya bar Abba said that **Rabbi Yoḥanan said: Rabbi Eliezer did not say** with regard **to all** mitzvot that **actions that facilitate** performance of **a mitzva override Shabbat.** This is not a fixed principle with regard to preparations for all mitzvot. Rather, each case must be considered on its own merits, and proof must be cited that this principle applies to a specific mitzva. **As the two loaves** offered on the festival of *Shavuot* **are an obligation of** that **day, and Rabbi Eliezer only learned** that the activities that facilitate **their** sacrifice override Shabbat **from a** special **verbal analogy. As it was taught** in a *baraita,* **Rabbi Eliezer says: From where** is it derived **that the actions that facilitate** the offering of **the two loaves override Shabbat?** The term **bringing is stated** in the verse **with regard to the *omer*** offering, **and** the term **bringing is stated with regard to the two loaves. Just as** in the case of **the bringing stated with regard to the *omer*,** all the **actions that facilitate** its offering **override Shabbat,** as the reaping of the *omer*, which facilitates its offering, overrides Shabbat, **so too,** in the case of **the bringing stated with regard to the two loaves, actions that facilitate** its offering **override Shabbat.**

מוּפְנֵי, דְּאִי לָא מוּפְנֵי – אִיכָּא לְמִיפְרַךְ: מַה לָּעוֹמֶר – שֶׁכֵּן אִם מָצָא קָצוּר – קוֹצֵר, תֹּאמַר בִּשְׁתֵּי הַלֶּחֶם שֶׁאִם מָצָא קָצוּר – אֵינוֹ קוֹצֵר. לָאֵי, אַפְנוּיֵי מוּפְנֵי. מִכְּדֵי כְּתִיב "וַהֲבֵאתֶם אֶת עוֹמֶר רֵאשִׁית קְצִירְכֶם אֶל הַכֹּהֵן", "בְּיוֹם הֲבִיאֲכֶם" לָמָּה לִי? שְׁמַע מִינָּהּ – לְאַפְנוּיֵי.

With regard to this verbal analogy the Gemara comments: It must be that those terms are **free,** i.e., they are superfluous in their context and therefore available for the purpose of establishing a verbal analogy. **As, if they are not free,** the verbal analogy **can be** logically **refuted,** as it is possible to say: **What** is unique **to the *omer*? That if one found reaped** barley **one must** nevertheless **reap** more barley for the sake of the mitzva. Can **you say** the same with regard to the *halakhot* of **the two loaves,** where it is taught that **if one found reaped** grain **one need not reap** additional grain for the sacrifice? Apparently, the *halakhot* of the offering of the two loaves are not parallel to those of the *omer*. The same might be true with regard to actions that facilitate the performance of the mitzva. **In truth,** the verse **is free** for establishing the verbal analogy. The Gemara explains: **Since the verse** already **states:** "When you come to the land that I am giving to you, and you reap its harvest, **then you shall bring the sheaf [*omer*], the first of your harvest to the priest**" (Leviticus 23:10), when the verse restates, "And you shall count for yourselves from the morrow after the day of rest, **from the day you have brought** the sheaf of the waving, seven whole weeks they shall be" (Leviticus 23:15), **why do I** need this repetition? **Conclude from this** that the additional statement is there **to** render the term "bringing" **free** for establishing a verbal analogy.

NOTES

It is possible for them to renounce all of their property rights and transfer them to one person – אֶפְשָׁר דִּמְבַטְּלִי לֵיהּ רְשׁוּתָא דְּכוּלְּהוּ לְגַבֵּי חַד: Inhabitants of different houses located in the same courtyard would typically participate in the joining of courtyards for Shabbat. The joining of courtyards is accomplished in the following manner: Each of the families places a piece of bread or some other food in one location. Consequently, all the households in the courtyard are considered one extended household, and they may carry items on Shabbat from their houses to the courtyard and within the courtyard itself. However, in cases where there is no joining of courtyards, or where the *halakha* prohibits joining the courtyards, a different option is available. All the homeowners may relinquish authority over their shares of the courtyard to one homeowner. In that case, it is permitted to carry within the courtyard and between the courtyard and the house of the resident to whom all the other residents ceded control of their shares of the courtyard. However, it is prohibited to carry between the courtyard and any of the other houses. According to one opinion, upon which the Gemara here is based, not only is it permitted to renounce authority in favor of one resident; it is even permitted for all the homeowners to then relinquish authority over their shares of the courtyard to a different resident on Shabbat itself.

וְאַכַּתִּי, מוּפְנֶה מִצַּד אֶחָד הוּא, וְשָׁמְעִינַן לֵיהּ לְרַבִּי אֱלִיעֶזֶר דְּאָמַר: מוּפְנֶה מִצַּד אֶחָד – לְמֵידִין וּמְשִׁיבִין! ׳תָּבִיאוּ׳ רִבּוּיָא הוּא.

And yet there is **still** a difficulty: The verbal analogy **is free** only **from one side,** as only the verse that mentions bringing in the context of the *omer* offering is superfluous in its context, **and we heard Rabbi Eliezer, who said** with regard to a verbal analogy that it is only **free from one side,** that **one** can **derive** from it, **and one** can also **refute**[N] it logically. The Gemara answers: There is a superfluous usage of the term with regard to the two loaves as well, as in the verse: "From your dwelling places you shall bring the loaves of waving of two tenth parts of an ephah; they shall be of fine flour, they shall be baked with leaven for first-fruits unto the Lord" (Leviticus 23:17) the phrase: **"You shall bring" is an amplification.** Since it was mentioned in the previous verse it is superfluous in its context. Consequently, the verbal analogy is available from both sides.

לְמַעוּטֵי מַאי? אִילֵימָא לְמַעוּטֵי לוּלָב – וְהָתַנְיָא: לוּלָב וְכָל מַכְשִׁירָיו דּוֹחִין אֶת הַשַּׁבָּת, דִּבְרֵי רַבִּי אֱלִיעֶזֶר! וְאֶלָּא לְמַעוּטֵי סוּכָּה – וְהָתַנְיָא: סוּכָּה וְכָל מַכְשִׁירֶיהָ דּוֹחִין אֶת הַשַּׁבָּת, דִּבְרֵי רַבִּי אֱלִיעֶזֶר! וְאֶלָּא לְמַעוּטֵי מַצָּה – וְהָתַנְיָא: מַצָּה וְכָל מַכְשִׁירֶיהָ דּוֹחִין אֶת הַשַּׁבָּת, דִּבְרֵי רַבִּי אֱלִיעֶזֶר! וְאֶלָּא לְמַעוּטֵי שׁוֹפָר – וְהָתַנְיָא: שׁוֹפָר וְכָל מַכְשִׁירָיו דּוֹחִין אֶת הַשַּׁבָּת, דִּבְרֵי רַבִּי אֱלִיעֶזֶר!

The Gemara poses a question with regard to Rabbi Yoḥanan's statement: Rabbi Eliezer did not say with regard to all mitzvot that actions that facilitate performance of a mitzva override Shabbat; **to exclude** actions that facilitate the performance of **what** mitzva was he referring?

If you say that it was **to exclude** actions that facilitate the performance of the mitzva of taking the **palm branch** [*lulav*] and the other three species on the festival of *Sukkot*, **wasn't it taught** in a *baraita*: The mitzva of ***lulav* and all its facilitators override Shabbat; this is the statement of Rabbi Eliezer?**

Rather, say that it comes **to exclude** the mitzva to dwell in a ***sukka*** on *Sukkot*. **Wasn't it taught** in a *baraita*: The mitzva of ***sukka* and all its facilitators override Shabbat; this is the statement of Rabbi Eliezer?**

Rather, say that it comes **to exclude** the mitzva to eat ***matza*** on Passover. **Wasn't it taught** in a *baraita*: The mitzva of ***matza* and all its facilitators override Shabbat;** this is **the statement of Rabbi Eliezer?**

Rather, say that it comes **to exclude** the mitzva to sound the ***shofar*** on Rosh HaShana. **But wasn't it taught** in a *baraita*: The mitzva of ***shofar* and all its facilitators override Shabbat;** this is **the statement of Rabbi Eliezer?**

אָמַר רַב אַדָּא בַּר אַהֲבָה: לְמַעוּטֵי צִיצִית לְטַלִּיתוֹ, וּמְזוּזָה לְפִתְחוֹ. תַּנְיָא נַמִי הָכִי: וְשָׁוִין, שֶׁאִם צִיֵּיץ טַלִּיתוֹ וְעָשָׂה מְזוּזָה לְפִתְחוֹ – שֶׁהוּא חַיָּיב.

Rav Adda bar Ahava said: The statement of Rabbi Yoḥanan comes **to exclude** attaching **ritual fringes to his garment and** affixing **a *mezuza* to the doorway,**[N] which do not override Shabbat. The Gemara notes that **that was also taught** in a *baraita*: **And they,** Rabbi Eliezer and the Rabbis, **agree that if one attached ritual fringes to his garment** on Shabbat, **and** similarly, if **one affixed a *mezuza* to his doorway** on Shabbat, **that he is liable.**

מַאי טַעְמָא? אָמַר רַב יוֹסֵף: לְפִי שֶׁאֵין קָבוּעַ לָהֶם זְמַן. אָמַר לֵיהּ אַבַּיֵי: אַדְּרַבָּה, מִדְּאֵין קָבוּעַ לָהֶם זְמַן –

The Gemara asks: **What is the reason** that Rabbi Eliezer concedes that actions that facilitate the performance of these mitzvot do not override Shabbat? **Rav Yosef said: Because they have no fixed time** and these mitzvot need not be performed on Shabbat. **Abaye said to him: On the contrary, from** the fact **that they have no fixed time,**

NOTES

One can derive and one can also refute – לְמֵידִין וּמְשִׁיבִין: According to Rabbi Eliezer and several other *tanna'im*, only a verbal analogy based upon words that are superfluous in both contexts is considered to be incontrovertible. However, if the words of a verbal analogy are free only on one side, it is considered an analogy that can be refuted by distinguishing between the subjects under discussion.

The exclusion of ritual fringes and *mezuza* – מִיעוּט צִיצִית וּמְזוּזָה: The Gemara's question as to why ritual fringes and *mezuza* are not included among the mitzvot whose facilitating actions override Shabbat law was puzzling to the early commentaries. Rabbi Yoḥanan had already stated that even according to Rabbi Eliezer, there is no one principle that governs all the mitzvot. Therefore, a separate proof is necessary to include each mitzva on the list of mitzvot whose facilitating actions override Shabbat, and there should be no question as to why the mitzvot of ritual fringes and *mezuza* are not included on this list. *Tosafot* answer that unless another reason was found, it might have been possible to derive that ritual fringes and *mezuza* are included based upon the *halakha* with regard to *sukka*. The Ramban explains that the question refers to the Torah's own rationale for this *halakha*: Why did the Torah not permit the overriding of Shabbat law in preparing for these mitzvot?

Perek **XIX**
Daf **131** Amud **b**

כָּל שַׁעְתָּא וְשַׁעְתָּא זְמַנֵּיהּ הוּא! אֶלָּא אָמַר רַב נַחְמָן אָמַר רַבִּי יִצְחָק, וְאִיתֵּימָא רַב הוּנָא בְּרֵיהּ דְּרַב יְהוֹשֻׁעַ: הוֹאִיל וּבְיָדוֹ לְהַפְקִירָן.

it can be said that **each and every moment is its** proper **time.** The obligation to fulfill the mitzva is perpetual and one may not neglect it. Why should it be prohibited for him to perform actions that facilitate the performance of the mitzva on Shabbat? **Rather, Rav Naḥman said** that **Rav Yitzḥak said, and some say** that he said that **Rav Huna, son of Rav Yehoshua, said:** The actions that facilitate the performance of these mitzvot do not override Shabbat, **since one can render** the relevant objects **ownerless.**[N] One is only required to perform these mitzvot if the objects, i.e., the garment and the house, belong to him. If he renders them ownerless, he is no longer obligated to perform these mitzvot.

NOTES

Since one can render the relevant objects ownerless – הוֹאִיל וּבְיָדוֹ לְהַפְקִירָן: According to Rashi, who is of the opinion that there is an obligation to affix ritual fringes even to a garment not currently in use, rendering one's garment ownerless is the only way to exempt oneself from the mitzva to affix ritual fringes to its corners. According to other authorities, who rule that a garment which is not being worn is exempt from ritual fringes, either the Gemara chose one rationale from a number of possible explanations (Rashba), or this reason was chosen because it applies to both ritual fringes and *mezuza* (Ramban).

NOTES

The derivation with regard to *sukka* – הַלִּימּוּד לְעִנְיַן סוּכָּה: The early commentaries (see *Tosafot*) point out that some of the verbal analogies cited with regard to Rabbi Eliezer's position do not meet his own criteria for an incontrovertible verbal analogy, since the words are not superfluous in both verses. The Rashba explains that in fact Rabbi Eliezer is of the opinion that logic dictates that mitzvot, along with their facilitators, should override Shabbat. Consequently, a full-fledged verbal analogy is not necessary.

And with regard to what *halakha* – וּלְמַאי הִלְכְתָא: There is a general and obvious rule that the Torah does not permit actions that it never prohibited. It also does not revoke decrees it never issued. Consequently, if the Torah emphasizes that something is permitted, this emphasis cannot allude to the rabbinic decrees issued with regard to that action.

אָמַר מָר: לוּלָב וְכָל מַכְשִׁירָיו דּוֹחִין אֶת הַשַּׁבָּת, דִּבְרֵי רַבִּי אֱלִיעֶזֶר. מְנָא לֵיהּ לְרַבִּי אֱלִיעֶזֶר הָא? אִי מֵעוֹמֶר וּשְׁתֵּי הַלֶּחֶם – שֶׁכֵּן צוֹרֶךְ גָּבוֹהַּ! אֶלָּא אָמַר קְרָא: ״בַּיּוֹם״, ״בַּיּוֹם״ – אֲפִילּוּ בְּשַׁבָּת.

It was taught that **the Master said** in a *baraita*: The mitzva of *lulav* **and all its facilitators override Shabbat;** this is **the statement of Rabbi Eliezer.** The Gemara poses a question: **From where does** Rabbi Eliezer derive **this** *halakha*?[N] **If** you say he derives it **from** the mitzvot of the ***omer* and the two loaves,** whose facilitators override Shabbat, this can be refuted by saying that the performance of facilitating actions is permitted on Shabbat in these cases **because they are for the necessities of** Temple service to God on **High,** as they are connected to the sacrificial service, which proceeds even on Shabbat. **Rather,** we can say that he derives it from the fact that **the verse states:** "And you shall take for yourselves **on the** first **day,** the fruit of goodly trees, branches of palm trees, boughs of thick-leaved trees, and willows of the river, and you shall rejoice before the Lord your God seven days" (Leviticus 23:40), from which he infers: **"On the** first **day,"** meaning that one is obligated to take it on the first day **even** if it occurs **on Shabbat.**

וּלְמַאי הִלְכְתָא? אִילֵּימָא לְטַלְטוּל – אִיצְטְרִיךְ קְרָא לְמִישְׁרֵי טִלְטוּל?! אֶלָּא לְמַכְשִׁירָיו.

The Gemara clarifies: **And with regard to what *halakha***[N] is this emphasis stated? In what way would the laws of Shabbat have prohibited fulfilling the mitzva of *lulav*? **If you say** that it comes **to** permit **moving** the *lulav* despite the prohibition against moving set-aside items, **is a verse required in order to permit moving** the *lulav*? The prohibition to move items that are set-aside is not a Torah prohibition. The Torah would not come to permit an action prohibited by the Sages. **Rather,** it must be that the verse is coming to permit violation of Shabbat prohibitions **for** the **facilitators of** the *lulav*.

וְרַבָּנַן – הַהוּא מִיבְּעֵי לֵיהּ: ״בַּיּוֹם״ וְלֹא בַּלַּיְלָה.

The Gemara asks: **And** how do **the Rabbis** who disagree with Rabbi Eliezer understand the verse's emphasis that the mitzva must be performed on that day? The Gemara answers: According to the Rabbis, **that** expression in the verse **is necessary** to teach that this mitzva must be performed **by day and not by night.**

וְרַבִּי אֱלִיעֶזֶר, בַּיּוֹם וְלֹא בַּלַּיְלָה מְנָא לֵיהּ? נָפְקָא לֵיהּ מִ״וּשְׂמַחְתֶּם לִפְנֵי ה׳ אֱלֹהֵיכֶם שִׁבְעַת יָמִים״, יָמִים וְלֹא לֵילוֹת.

The Gemara asks: **And from where does Rabbi Eliezer** derive that this mitzva must be performed **by day and not by night?** The Gemara answers: **He derives** this *halakha* **from** the phrase: **"And you shall rejoice before the Lord your God seven days,"** as this indicates that the mitzva applies during **the days and not the nights.**

וְרַבָּנַן – אִיצְטְרִיךְ, סָלְקָא דַּעְתָּךְ אָמֵינָא: נֵילַף שִׁבְעַת יָמִים מִסּוּכָּה, מָה לְהַלָּן – יָמִים וַאֲפִילּוּ לֵילוֹת, אַף כָּאן – יָמִים וַאֲפִילּוּ לֵילוֹת, קָא מַשְׁמַע לַן.

The Gemara asks: **And** how do **the Rabbis** respond to this? The Gemara answers: The previous derivation **was necessary** because **it might have entered your mind to say** that **we should derive** the **seven days** stated here **from** the seven days stated with regard to ***sukka***, and say: **Just as there,** the mitzva of *sukka* applies not only during **the days** but **even the nights, so too here,** the mitzva of *lulav* applies not only during **the days** but **even the nights.** Therefore, the derivation **teaches us** that the mitzva only applies during the day based upon the original expression: "On the first day."

וְלִיכְתּוֹב רַחֲמָנָא בְּלוּלָב וְנֵיתוּ הָנָךְ וְנֵילְפוּ מִינֵּיהּ! מִשּׁוּם דְּאִיכָּא לְמִיפְרַךְ: מָה לְלוּלָב שֶׁכֵּן טָעוּן אַרְבָּעָה מִינִים.

The Gemara asks: **And** according to Rabbi Eliezer's approach, **let the Torah write** this principle only **with regard to *lulav*, and let these,** the mitzva of the *omer* and similar cases, **be derived from it.** The Gemara answers: **Because** the analogy **can be refuted. What** is unique **about *lulav*? That it requires four species,** as the Torah demands that three other species be taken along with the *lulav*. Therefore, *lulav* cannot serve as a paradigm for other mitzvot that do not share this characteristic.

״סוּכָּה וְכָל מַכְשִׁירֶיהָ דּוֹחִין אֶת הַשַּׁבָּת דִּבְרֵי רַבִּי אֱלִיעֶזֶר״. מְנָא לֵיהּ לְרַבִּי אֱלִיעֶזֶר הָא? אִי מֵעוֹמֶר וּשְׁתֵּי הַלֶּחֶם – שֶׁכֵּן צוֹרֶךְ גָּבוֹהַּ הוּא! אִי מִלּוּלָב – שֶׁכֵּן טָעוּן אַרְבָּעָה מִינִים!

Earlier, it was taught in a *baraita*: The mitzva of ***sukka* and all its facilitators override Shabbat;** this is **the statement of Rabbi Eliezer.** The Gemara asks: **From where does Rabbi Eliezer** derive **this** matter? **If** you say he derives it **from** the *halakha* with regard to the ***omer* and the two loaves,** this can be refuted by saying that the performance of facilitators is permitted on Shabbat in these cases **as** these are **the necessities of** Temple service to God on **High. If** you say he derives it **from the** *halakha* with regard to ***lulav***, this too can be refuted, **as *lulav* requires four species** and therefore has special significance.

אֶלָּא: גָּמַר שִׁבְעַת יָמִים מִלּוּלָב, מָה לְהַלָּן – מַכְשִׁירָיו דּוֹחִין אֶת הַשַּׁבָּת, אַף כָּאן נַמִי – מַכְשִׁירָיו דּוֹחִין אֶת הַשַּׁבָּת.

Rather, he **derived** it through the following verbal analogy based upon the expression **"seven days,"** which is stated with regard to both the mitzva of *sukka* and the mitzva of *lulav*. **Just as below,** with regard to the mitzva of *lulav*, **its facilitators override Shabbat, so too here,** with regard to the mitzva of *sukka*, **its facilitators override Shabbat.**

וְלִיכְתּוֹב רַחֲמָנָא בְּסוּכָּה, וְנֵיתֵי הָנָךְ וְנִגְמוֹר מִינֵּיהּ! מִשּׁוּם דְּאִיכָּא לְמִיפְרַךְ: מָה לְסוּכָּה – שֶׁכֵּן נוֹהֶגֶת בַּלֵּילוֹת כְּבַיָּמִים.

The Gemara asks: **And let the Torah write only** that actions that facilitate the performance of the mitzva override the *halakhot* of Shabbat, **and let us bring these** other mitzvot **and derive** their *halakhot* **from** *sukka*. The Gemara answers: **Because** this suggestion **can be refuted: What** is unique about the mitzva of ***sukka*****? That it applies during the nights** just **as** it applies **during the days,** whereas the others apply only during the day.

"מַצָּה וְכָל מַכְשִׁירֶיהָ דּוֹחִין אֶת הַשַּׁבָּת, דִּבְרֵי רַבִּי אֱלִיעֶזֶר". מְנָא לֵיהּ לְרַבִּי אֱלִיעֶזֶר הָא? אִי מֵעוֹמֶר וּשְׁתֵּי הַלֶּחֶם – שֶׁכֵּן צוֹרֶךְ גָּבוֹהַּ! אִי מִלּוּלָב – שֶׁכֵּן טָעוּן אַרְבָּעָה מִינִים! אִי מִסּוּכָּה – שֶׁכֵּן נוֹהֶגֶת בַּלֵּילוֹת כְּבַיָּמִים!

Earlier it was taught in a *baraita*: The mitzva of ***matza*** **and all its facilitators override Shabbat;** this is **the statement of Rabbi Eliezer.** The Gemara asks: **From where does Rabbi Eliezer** derive **this** matter? **If** you say he derives it **from** the *halakha* with regard to the ***omer*** **and the two loaves,** this can be refuted, **as** these are **the necessities of** Temple service to God on **High. If** you say he derives it **from** the *halakha* with regard to ***lulav*****,** this too can be refuted, **as it requires four species. If** you say he derives it **from** the precedent of ***sukka*****,** this too can be refuted, **as it applies during the nights** just **as** it applies **during the days.**

אֶלָּא: גָּמַר 'חֲמִשָּׁה עָשָׂר', 'חֲמִשָּׁה עָשָׂר' מֵחַג הַסּוּכּוֹת, מָה לְהַלָּן – מַכְשִׁירֶיהָ דּוֹחִין אֶת הַשַּׁבָּת, אַף כָּאן – מַכְשִׁירֶיהָ דּוֹחִין אֶת הַשַּׁבָּת.

Rather, Rabbi Eliezer **derived** it by means of a verbal analogy based upon the word **fifteenth** stated with regard to the mitzva of *matza*, and the word **fifteenth** stated with regard to **the festival of *Sukkot*: Just as below,** with regard to the mitzva to dwell in a *sukka* on the festival of *Sukkot*, which is on the fifteenth of the month, **its facilitators override Shabbat, so too here,** with regard to the mitzva to eat *matza* on the fifteenth of the month, **its facilitators override Shabbat.**

וְלִיכְתּוֹב רַחֲמָנָא בְּמַצָּה וְנֵיתוּ הָנָךְ וְלִיגְמוֹר מִינֵּיהּ! מִשּׁוּם דְּאִיכָּא לְמִיפְרַךְ: מָה לְמַצָּה – שֶׁכֵּן נוֹהֶגֶת בְּנָשִׁים כִּבַאֲנָשִׁים.

The Gemara asks: **And let the Torah write** this principle **with regard to *matza*, and and let us bring these** other mitzvot **and derive** their *halakhot* **from** *matza*. The Gemara answers: **Because** this suggestion **can be refuted: What** is unique about the mitzva of ***matza*****? That it applies to women as it does to men.** It is therefore different from the other mitzvot under discussion, which only apply to men.

"שׁוֹפָר וְכָל מַכְשִׁירָיו דּוֹחִין אֶת הַשַּׁבָּת, דִּבְרֵי רַבִּי אֱלִיעֶזֶר". מְנָא לֵיהּ לְרַבִּי אֱלִיעֶזֶר הָא? אִי מֵעוֹמֶר וּשְׁתֵּי הַלֶּחֶם – שֶׁכֵּן צוֹרֶךְ גָּבוֹהַּ, אִי מִלּוּלָב – שֶׁכֵּן טָעוּן אַרְבָּעָה מִינִים! אִי מִסּוּכָּה – שֶׁכֵּן נוֹהֶגֶת בַּלֵּילוֹת כְּבַיָּמִים! אִי מִמַּצָּה – שֶׁכֵּן נוֹהֶגֶת בְּנָשִׁים כִּבַאֲנָשִׁים! אֶלָּא: אָמַר קְרָא "יוֹם תְּרוּעָה יִהְיֶה לָכֶם" – בַּיּוֹם, אֲפִילּוּ בְּשַׁבָּת.

It was also taught in the *baraita*: The mitzva of ***shofar*** **and all its facilitators override Shabbat;** this is **the statement of Rabbi Eliezer.** The Gemara asks: **From where does Rabbi Eliezer** derive **this** matter? **If** you say he derives it **from** the *halakha* with regard to **the *omer*** **and the two loaves,** this can be refuted, **as** these are **the necessities of** Temple service to God on **High. If** you say he derives it **from** the *halakha* with regard to ***lulav*****,** this too can be refuted, **as it requires four species. If** you say he derives it **from** the precedent of ***sukka*****,** this too can be refuted, **as it applies during the nights** just **as** it applies **during the days. If** you say he derives it **from *matza*****,** this too can be refuted, **as it applies to women** just **as** it applies **to men. Rather,** Rabbi Eliezer derives it from the fact that **the verse stated:** "And in the seventh month, on the first of the month, a holy calling it shall be to you; any prohibited labor of work you shall not perform; **a day of sounding the *shofar* it shall be for you"** (Numbers 29:1). The verse's emphasis that the *shofar* must be sounded **on that day** teaches us that it applies **even on Shabbat.**

וּלְמַאי? אִילֵימָא לִתְקִיעָה – הָא תָּנָא דְּבֵי שְׁמוּאֵל: "כָּל מְלֶאכֶת עֲבוֹדָה לֹא תַעֲשׂוּ" – יָצְתָה תְּקִיעַת שׁוֹפָר וּרְדִיַּית הַפַּת, שֶׁהִיא חָכְמָה וְאֵינָהּ מְלָאכָה, אֶלָּא לְמַכְשִׁירִין.

And for what purpose was this emphasized? **If you say** it is in order **to** permit **sounding** the *shofar*, this **has** already **been taught** by one of the Sages **of the school of Shmuel** with regard to the verse that prohibits performing prohibited labor on Festivals: **"Any prohibited labor of work you shall not perform"** (Numbers 29:1), which comes **to exclude** from the category of prohibited labors **the sounding of the *shofar* and the removal of bread** from the oven, **which are skills and not labors. Rather,** it is necessary **to** teach with regard to **actions that facilitate** the performance of the mitzva.

NOTES

It introduces the remembrances of the Jewish people – מַכְנֶסֶת זִכְרוֹנוֹת שֶׁל יִשְׂרָאֵל: The Torah states with regard to the sounding of the *shofar* on Rosh HaShana: "A memorial proclaimed with the blast of horns, a holy convocation" (Leviticus 23:24); and a significant section of the Rosh HaShana prayers, Remembrances, emphasizes the aspect of remembrance on Rosh HaShana, whereby the remembrances of the Jewish people are brought before their Father in Heaven.

וְרַבָּנַן – הַהוּא מִיבָּעֵי לֵיהּ: בַּיּוֹם וְלֹא בַּלַּיְלָה. וְרַבִּי אֱלִיעֶזֶר, בַּיּוֹם וְלֹא בַּלַּיְלָה מְנָא לֵיהּ? נָפְקָא לֵיהּ מִ״בְּיוֹם הַכִּפּוּרִים תַּעֲבִירוּ שׁוֹפָר בְּכָל אַרְצְכֶם״ וְגָמְרִי מֵהֲדָדֵי.

The Gemara asks: **And** how do **the Rabbis** understand the verse's emphasis that the mitzva must be performed on that day? The Gemara answers: **That** expression in the verse **is necessary** according to the Rabbis in order to teach that this mitzva must be performed **by day and not by night.** The Gemara asks: **And from where does Rabbi Eliezer** derive that this mitzva must be performed **by day and not by night?** The Gemara answers: **He derives** this *halakha* **from** the verse with regard to the laws of the Jubilee Year: "And you shall pass a *shofar* of sounding in the seventh month, on the tenth of the month, **on the Day of Atonement you shall pass a *shofar* throughout your land"** (Leviticus 25:9), **and** the laws of all instances of sounding the *shofar* during the seventh month **are derived from each other.** Therefore, just as on Yom Kippur the *shofar* is sounded during the day, as emphasized by the fact that the verse uses the phrase Day of Atonement, the same applies on Rosh HaShana.

וְלִיכְתּוֹב רַחֲמָנָא בְּשׁוֹפָר, וְלֵיתוּ הָנָךְ וְלִיגְמְרוּ מִינֵּיהּ! מִתְּקִיעַת שׁוֹפָר דְּרֹאשׁ הַשָּׁנָה לֵיכָּא לְמִיגְמַר – שֶׁכֵּן מַכְנֶסֶת זִכְרוֹנוֹת שֶׁל יִשְׂרָאֵל לַאֲבִיהֶן שֶׁבַּשָּׁמַיִם, מִתְּקִיעוֹת [שׁוֹפָר] דְּיוֹם הַכִּפּוּרִים לֵיכָּא לְמִיגְמַר – דְּאָמַר מָר: תָּקְעוּ בֵּית דִּין שׁוֹפָר נִפְטְרוּ עֲבָדִים לְבָתֵּיהֶם וְשָׂדוֹת חוֹזְרוֹת לְבַעֲלֵיהֶן.

The Gemara asks: **And** according to Rabbi Eliezer's approach, **let the Torah write** this principle only **with regard to *shofar*, and let us bring these** other mitzvot **and derive** their *halakhot* **from** *shofar*. The Gemara answers: **From the sounding of the *shofar* of Rosh HaShana,** the principle that actions that facilitate the performance of a mitzva override Shabbat **cannot be derived,** because it has special significance in that **it introduces the remembrances of the Jewish people**[N] **before their Father in heaven. From the sounding of the *shofar* of Yom Kippur,** the principle that actions that facilitate the performance of a mitzva override Shabbat **cannot be derived,** as this *shofar* sounding also has special significance, as **the Master said: Once the court sounds the *shofar*** on Yom Kippur in the Jubilee Year, the declaration of freedom applies at once. **Slaves** may **take leave** of their masters and go **to their homes, and fields** that had been sold **return to their** ancestral **owners.** Therefore, other mitzvot cannot be derived from the sounding of the *shofar* of Yom Kippur.

(אָמַר מָר) ״מִילָה וְכָל מַכְשִׁירֶיהָ דּוֹחִין אֶת הַשַּׁבָּת, דִּבְרֵי רַבִּי אֱלִיעֶזֶר״ מְנָא לֵיהּ לְרַבִּי אֱלִיעֶזֶר הָא? אִי מִכּוּלְּהוּ גָּמַר – כִּדְאָמְרִינַן. וְעוֹד: מָה לְהָנָךְ –

Earlier it was taught that **the Master said** in the *baraita*: The mitzva of **circumcision and all its facilitators override Shabbat;** this is **the statement of Rabbi Eliezer.** The Gemara asks: **From where does Rabbi Eliezer** derive **this** *halakha*? **If he derives it from all of** the other mitzvot cited above, we can refute it, **as we have** already **said** that each one of them includes a unique aspect of severity or significance. **And furthermore,** there is another difficulty: **What** is unique about **these** mitzvot

Perek **XIX**
Daf **132** Amud **a**

NOTES

If its time passed, it is void – אִם עָבַר זְמַנָּהּ בְּטֵלָה: While it is true that if one failed to fulfill the mitzva of *sukka* on the first day of the Festival he may still fulfill the mitzva on the intermediate days, there is no way to compensate for the failure to fulfill the mitzva on the first day as well. It is especially true that the mitzva is void according to Rabbi Eliezer's own view, that it is prohibited build a *sukka* during the intermediate days (Rashba).

שֶׁכֵּן אִם עָבַר זְמַנָּהּ בְּטֵלָה. אֶלָּא, הַיְינוּ טַעְמָא דְּרַבִּי אֱלִיעֶזֶר: דְּאָמַר קְרָא ״וּבַיּוֹם הַשְּׁמִינִי יִמּוֹל בְּשַׂר עָרְלָתוֹ״ – וַאֲפִילּוּ בַּשַּׁבָּת.

in each, **as if its time passed, it is void,**[N] unlike the mitzva of circumcision, which can be fulfilled at a later date if the child is not circumcised on the eighth day. **Rather, this is the reason** for the opinion **of Rabbi Eliezer, as the verse says: "And on the eighth day the flesh of his foreskin shall be circumcised"** (Leviticus 12:3), indicating that he is circumcised on the eighth day **even** if it falls **on Shabbat.**

וְלִיכְתּוֹב רַחֲמָנָא בְּמִילָה, וְלֵיתוּ הָנָךְ וְלִיגְמוֹר מִינֵּיהּ! מִשּׁוּם דְּאִיכָּא לְמִיפְרַךְ: מַה לְּמִילָה שֶׁכֵּן נִכְרְתוּ עָלֶיהָ שְׁלֹשׁ עֶשְׂרֵה בְּרִיתוֹת.

The Gemara asks: **And let the Torah write** this principle only **with regard to** the mitzva of **circumcision, and let these** other mitzvot **come and derive** their *halakhot* **from it.** The Gemara answers: **Because** this suggestion **can be refuted: What** is unique about the mitzva of **circumcision? That thirteen covenants were established over it,** as the word covenant is mentioned thirteen times in the passage dealing with the circumcision of Abraham (Genesis 17). Owing to its great significance, other mitzvot cannot be derived from it.

עַד כָּאן לָא פְּלִיגִי רַבָּנַן עֲלֵיהּ אֶלָּא בְּמַכְשִׁירֵי מִילָה, אֲבָל מִילָה גּוּפָהּ – דִּבְרֵי הַכֹּל דּוֹחָה שַׁבָּת. מְנָלַן? אָמַר עוּלָּא: הֲלָכָה. וְכֵן אָמַר רַבִּי יִצְחָק: הֲלָכָה.

The Gemara departs from the facilitators of circumcision to the *halakha* of circumcision itself and asks: **The Rabbis only disagree with** Rabbi Eliezer **with regard to actions that facilitate circumcision,** which, in their view, do not override Shabbat; **however,** with regard to **circumcision itself, everyone agrees** that it **overrides Shabbat. From where do we** derive this *halakha*? **Ulla said:** This is **a *halakha*** transmitted to Moses from Sinai, but there is no biblical basis for it. **And so too, Rabbi Yitzhak said:** It is **a *halakha*** transmitted to Moses from Sinai.

מֵיתִיבִי: מִנַּיִין לְפִיקּוּחַ נֶפֶשׁ שֶׁדּוֹחֶה אֶת הַשַּׁבָּת – רַבִּי אֶלְעָזָר בֶּן עֲזַרְיָה אוֹמֵר: מָה מִילָה שֶׁהִיא אַחַת מֵאֵיבָרָיו שֶׁל אָדָם – דּוֹחָה אֶת הַשַּׁבָּת, קַל וָחוֹמֶר לְפִיקּוּחַ נֶפֶשׁ שֶׁדּוֹחֶה אֶת הַשַּׁבָּת.

The Gemara **raises an objection** from that which was taught in the *Tosefta*: **From where** is it derived **that saving a life overrides Shabbat? Rabbi Elazar ben Azarya says** it is derived from the mitzva of circumcision: **Just as circumcision, which** pertains to only **one of a person's limbs, overrides Shabbat,** all the more so it is an ***a fortiori*** inference that **saving a life,** which is a mitzva that pertains to the entire person, **overrides Shabbat.**[N]

וְאִי סָלְקָא דַּעְתָּךְ הֲלָכָה, קַל וָחוֹמֶר מֵהֲלָכָה מִי אָתֵי?! וְהָתַנְיָא, אָמַר לוֹ רַבִּי אֶלְעָזָר (בֶּן עֲזַרְיָה): עֲקִיבָא, עֶצֶם כִּשְׂעוֹרָה מְטַמֵּא הֲלָכָה, וּרְבִיעִית דָּם – קַל וָחוֹמֶר, וְאֵין דָּנִין קַל וָחוֹמֶר מֵהֲלָכָה!

And if it should enter your mind to say that circumcision may be performed on Shabbat based on a ***halakha*** transmitted to Moses from Sinai, **is an *a fortiori* inference derived from a *halakha*** transmitted to Moses from Sinai? **Wasn't it taught** explicitly in a *baraita* that an *a fortiori* inference cannot be derived from a *halakha* transmitted to Moses from Sinai? Rabbi Akiva sought to derive that a nazirite who comes into contact with a quarter *log* of blood from a corpse becomes ritually impure[N] and is required to shave his hair. He sought to do this based on an *a fortiori* inference from the *halakha* of the bone from a dead person the size of a grain of barley, as he had a received tradition that a nazirite is required to shave his hair due to that contact. **Rabbi Elazar ben Azarya said to him: Akiva,** the *halakha* that **a bone the size of a** grain of **barley transmits ritual impurity is a *halakha*** transmitted to Moses from Sinai, **and** you would derive from it that **a quarter** of a *log* **of blood** transmits ritual impurity based upon **an *a fortiori* inference, and one does not derive an *a fortiori* inference from a *halakha*** transmitted to Moses from Sinai. The *Tosefta* explicitly states that Rabbi Elazar ben Azarya himself derived an *a fortiori* inference from the *halakha* of circumcision on Shabbat. Clearly, then, it is derived from the Torah itself and not from a *halakha* transmitted to Moses from Sinai.

אֶלָּא אָמַר רַבִּי אֶלְעָזָר: אָתְיָא 'אוֹת' 'אוֹת'.

Rather, Rabbi Elazar said: This *halakha* is **derived** by means of a verbal analogy between the word **sign** that appears with regard to circumcision: "And you shall be circumcised in the flesh of your foreskin; and it shall be a sign of the covenant between Me and you" (Genesis 17:11), and **sign** that appears with regard to Shabbat: "However, you shall keep My *Shabbatot*, for it is a sign between Me and you throughout your generations" (Exodus 31:13). From this verbal analogy, it is derived that circumcision, which is a sign, may be performed even on Shabbat, which is itself a sign.

אֶלָּא מֵעַתָּה, תְּפִילִּין דִּכְתִיב בְּהֶן אוֹת – לִידְחִי שַׁבָּת!

The Gemara asks: **But if** what you say is **so, phylacteries, with regard to which** the term **sign** is also **written:** "And it shall be for a sign on your hand and for frontlets between your eyes" (Exodus 13:16), **should** also **override Shabbat,** and they should be donned on that day.

אֶלָּא אָתְיָא 'בְּרִית' 'בְּרִית'.

Rather, this principle is **derived** by means of a different verbal analogy from the word **covenant** that appears with regard to circumcision: "And you shall be circumcised in the flesh of your foreskin; and it shall be a sign of the covenant between Me and you" (Genesis 17:11), and the word **covenant** that appears with regard to Shabbat: "The children of Israel shall keep the Shabbat, to observe the Shabbat throughout their generations for a perpetual covenant" (Exodus 31:16).

גָּדוֹל, דִּכְתִיב בֵּיהּ בְּרִית – לִידְחֵי שַׁבָּת!

The Gemara raises a difficulty: If this is so, then the circumcision of **an adult** should also be permitted on Shabbat and it should not be limited to a child on the eighth day, **as the term covenant is written with regard to him** as well, as it applies to any Jewish male not yet circumcised. Therefore, **let** his circumcision **override Shabbat.** The *halakha*, however, is that only circumcision at its proper time on the eighth day overrides Shabbat.

NOTES

Just as circumcision, which pertains to only one of a person's limbs, overrides Shabbat…it is an *a fortiori* inference that saving a life overrides Shabbat – מָה מִילָה שֶׁהִיא אַחַת מֵאֵיבָרָיו שֶׁל אָדָם דּוֹחָה אֶת הַשַּׁבָּת...קַל וָחוֹמֶר לְפִיקּוּחַ נֶפֶשׁ שֶׁדּוֹחֶה אֶת הַשַּׁבָּת: This should be understood as follows: Just as circumcision, through which one fulfills only one mitzva with just one of his limbs, overrides Shabbat, all the more so should saving a life, which ensures that a person will be able to fulfill the entire Torah with all of his limbs, override Shabbat (*Tosafot*).

The ritual impurity of a nazirite – טוּמְאַת נָזִיר: The *halakhot* of a nazirite are articulated in the Torah (Numbers 6) and explained at great length in tractate *Nazir*, which is devoted entirely to these *halakhot*. A nazirite must refrain from cutting his hair and drinking wine, and avoid ritual impurity imparted by a corpse. If the nazirite becomes impure, all the previous days of his nazariteship are nullified, and he must shave his hair, bring a special offering, and restart his naziriteship. A large portion of tractate *Nazir* deals with clarifying various details of impurity imparted by a corpse, and explaining when that nullifies one's naziriteship and obligates the nazirite to shave his hair.

אֶלָּא: אָתְיָא ׳דּוֹרוֹת׳ ׳דּוֹרוֹת׳.

Rather, this *halakha* **is derived** by means of a verbal analogy between the word **generations** that appears with regard to Shabbat: "Throughout their generations for a perpetual covenant" (Exodus 31:16), and the word **generations** that appears with regard to circumcision: "And I shall establish My covenant between Me and you, and between your seed after you throughout their generations, for an everlasting covenant" (Genesis 17:7).

צִיצִית דִּכְתִיב בֵּיהּ דּוֹרוֹת לִידְחֵי שַׁבָּת!

The Gemara asks: If so, **let ritual fringes** too, **with regard to which** the term **generations is** also **written, override Shabbat,** and it should be permitted to affix ritual fringes to a garment on Shabbat.[N]

אֶלָּא אָמַר רַב נַחְמָן בַּר יִצְחָק: דָּנִין ׳אוֹת׳ ׳בְּרִית׳ וְ׳דוֹרוֹת׳ מֵ׳אוֹת׳ ׳בְּרִית׳ וְ׳דוֹרוֹת׳ – לְאַפּוֹקֵי הָנָךְ דְּחַד חַד הוּא דִּכְתִיב בָּהֶן.

Rather, Rav Naḥman bar Yitzḥak said: This *halakha* is derived not from one common word alone, but **one derives** it based upon the three words **sign, covenant, and generations** that appear with regard to circumcision, **from sign, covenant, and generations** that appear with regard to Shabbat, **to the exclusion of these,** i.e., ritual fringes and phylacteries, **that with regard to each of them, one** of these **is written** but not all three words together.

וְרַבִּי יוֹחָנָן אָמַר: אָמַר קְרָא ׳בַּיּוֹם׳ – בַּיּוֹם אֲפִילּוּ בְּשַׁבָּת.

And Rabbi Yoḥanan said: The verse says: "And **on the** eighth day… shall be circumcised" (Leviticus 12:3), which means that the child is circumcised **on the** eighth **day** whenever it occurs, **even on Shabbat.**

אֲמַר לֵיהּ רֵישׁ לָקִישׁ לְרַבִּי יוֹחָנָן: אֶלָּא מֵעַתָּה, מְחוּסְּרֵי כַּפָּרָה דִּכְתִיב בְּהוּ ׳בַּיּוֹם׳ – הָכִי נַמִי דְּדָחוּ שַׁבָּת! הַהוּא מִיבְּעֵי לֵיהּ: ׳בַּיּוֹם׳ – וְלֹא בַּלַּיְלָה.

Reish Lakish said to Rabbi Yoḥanan: But if what you say is **so,** then, with regard to **those lacking atonement,** such as a *zav* or a healed leper, who must after their immersion still bring an atonement offering in order to complete their purification process, **with regard to whom** the term **on the day is** also **written,** as in the verse: "And on the eighth day he shall take two he-lambs without blemish, and one ewe-lamb of the first year without blemish" (Leviticus 14:10), sacrificing their atonement offerings **should also override Shabbat.** Rabbi Yoḥanan responded: **That** verse **is necessary** to teach that the sacrifice must be brought **during the day and not at night.**

הַאי נַמִי מִיבְּעֵי לֵיהּ ׳בַּיּוֹם׳ וְלֹא בַּלַּיְלָה! הַהוּא מִ״בֶּן שְׁמֹנַת יָמִים״ נָפְקָא.

Reish Lakish asked: **This** verse with regard to the mitzva of circumcision **is also necessary** to teach that circumcision must be performed **during the day and not at night.** Rabbi Yoḥanan replied: **That** is derived **from** a different verse, which states: "And **he that is eight days old** shall be circumcised among you throughout your generations" (Genesis 17:12). That circumcision must take place during the day is derived from that verse.

הַאי נַמִי מִ׳בְּיוֹם צַוּוֹתוֹ׳ נָפְקָא!

Reish Lakish says: **That** matter, that the atonement offering must be sacrificed during the day, can **also** be derived **from** a different verse, as it is stated: "This is the law of the burnt-offering, of the meal-offering, and of the sin-offering, and of the guilt-offering, and of the consecration-offering, and of the sacrifice of the peace-offerings; which the Lord commanded Moses at Mount Sinai **on the day He commanded** the children of Israel to present their offerings to the Lord in the wilderness of Sinai" (Leviticus 7:37–38), and from here **it is derived** that all offerings are sacrificed by day and not at night.

אַף עַל גַּב דְּנָפְקָא מִ׳בְּיוֹם צַוּוֹתוֹ׳ אִצְטְרִיכָא, סָלְקָא דַּעְתָּךְ אָמִינָא: הוֹאִיל וְחָס רַחֲמָנָא עֲלֵיהּ לְאַתּוֹיֵי בְּדַלּוּת, בַּלַּיְלָה נַמִי לֵיתֵי – קָא מַשְׁמַע לָן.

The Gemara answers: **Although** this *halakha* **is derived from: "On the day He commanded,"** an additional source **is necessary** for those lacking atonement. **It might have entered your mind to say** that **since the Torah shows him mercy** by allowing him **to bring** an offering **of poverty,** as if one cannot afford to sacrifice the regular atonement offering, the Torah enables him to sacrifice a less costly one, **let him also bring it at night,** as perhaps the Torah shows him mercy and allows him to hasten his atonement. Therefore, **it teaches us** that he too must bring his offering only by day and not at night.

מַתְקִיף לָהּ רָבִינָא: אֶלָּא מֵעַתָּה – יְהֵא זָר כָּשֵׁר בָּהֶן, וִיהֵא אוֹנֵן כָּשֵׁר בָּהֶן! הָא אַהַדְרֵיהּ קְרָא.

Ravina strongly objects to this reasoning: **But if** what you say is **so,** that the Torah has compassion on a person lacking atonement and is lenient with regard to the *halakhot* of the atonement offering, **a non-priest should be fit** to sacrifice **them,**[N] **and** similarly, a priest who is **an acute mourner,** i.e., one whose relative died that same day and has not yet been buried, **should be fit to** sacrifice **them.** The Gemara answers: **The verse has restored this.**[N] The additional verse that teaches that even one lacking atonement must sacrifice during the day, also teaches that the Torah was lenient with regard to this offering only in the ways explicitly stated in the Torah.

NOTES

Ritual fringes and phylacteries overriding Shabbat – צִיצִית וּתְפִילִּין שֶׁיִּדְחוּ שַׁבָּת: Obviously, this discussion does not refer to wearing ritual fringes, which is a mitzva on Shabbat as it is on every other day, or to donning phylacteries, which does not involve a desecration of Shabbat. Rather, the issue is whether or not one may prepare the fringes and phylacteries for the observance of the mitzva on Shabbat.

A non-priest should be fit to sacrifice them – יְהֵא זָר כָּשֵׁר בָּהֶן: A question is raised in *Tosafot*: How can the Gemara suggest that these sacrifices could be offered by anyone other than a priest when the Torah itself states clearly that these offerings must be sacrificed by a priest? The Rashba answers that the question with regard to the non-priest is not meant literally. The non-priest was mentioned as a prelude to the main question regarding the acute mourner. According to the Ramban, the question presumes that the word priest in the verse does not prove that offering sacrifices is limited to a priest. Rather, the Torah may have been teaching that although a priest should offer the sacrifices *ab initio*, if a non-priest offered them, they are valid after the fact.

The verse has restored this – הָא אַהַדְרֵיהּ קְרָא: This is an example of one of the thirteen hermeneutical principles by which the Torah is expounded: When a particular case, though included in the general statement, is explicitly mentioned with a new provision, the terms of the general statement no longer apply to it unless the Torah explicitly indicates that they do apply. If a *halakha* diverges from some general principle, one would assume that it was excluded entirely from that principle and that the guidelines of the general principle do not apply to it. Only if it is determined that the Torah explicitly restored the specific case to that principle can the conclusion be drawn that the exception was only with regard to the stated issue.

רַב אַחָא בַּר יַעֲקֹב אָמַר: אָמַר קְרָא ׳שְׁמִינִי׳, שְׁמִינִי אֲפִילּוּ בְּשַׁבָּת.

Rav Aḥa bar Ya'akov said: There is a different proof from the Torah that circumcision is performed even on Shabbat, for **the verse said:** "On the **eighth** day," underscoring that circumcision is performed specifically on the **eighth** day and indicating that it is performed **even on Shabbat.**

הַאי שְׁמִינִי מִיבָּעֵי לֵיהּ לְמַעוֹטֵי שְׁבִיעִי! שְׁבִיעִי – מִבֶּן שְׁמֹנַת יָמִים נָפְקָא.

The Gemara raises a difficulty: **This** usage of the term **eighth is necessary to exclude** the **seventh** day, i.e., a child may not be circumcised before the eighth day. The Gemara answers: The fact that one may not circumcise on the **seventh** day **is derived** from a different verse, as it is stated: "And **he that is eight days old** shall be circumcised among you throughout your generations" (Genesis 17:12).

וְאַכַּתִּי מִיבָּעֵי לֵיהּ, חַד – לְמַעוֹטֵי שְׁבִיעִי, וְחַד – לְמַעוֹטֵי תְּשִׁיעִי; דְּאִי מֵחַד הֲוָה אָמִינָא: שְׁבִיעִי הוּא – דְּלָא מְטָא זִמְנֵיהּ, אֲבָל מִשְּׁמִינִי וְאֵילָךְ – זִמְנֵיהּ הוּא! אֶלָּא מְחַוַּורְתָּא כִּדְרַבִּי יוֹחָנָן.

The Gemara raises a further difficulty: Both verses are **still necessary, one to exclude** the **seventh** day **and one to exclude** the **ninth** day. **As if** it were derived **from one** verse alone, **I would have said: It is** on the **seventh** day that one may not circumcise, since **the time** to circumcise this child **has not** yet **arrived** and the obligation of circumcision is not yet in effect; **however, from** the **eighth** day **and onward is its time,** and therefore it is permissible to postpone a circumcision until the ninth day. No answer was found to this question, and the Gemara concludes: **Rather,** the derivation **is clear according to Rabbi Yoḥanan.**

תַּנְיָא כְּוָותֵיהּ דְּרַבִּי יוֹחָנָן, וּדְלָא כְּרַב אַחָא בַּר יַעֲקֹב: ׳שְׁמִינִי יִמּוֹל׳ – אֲפִילּוּ בְּשַׁבָּת. וּמָה אֲנִי מְקַיֵּים ״מְחַלְלֶיהָ מוֹת יוּמָת״ – בִּשְׁאָר מְלָאכוֹת חוּץ מִמִּילָה, אוֹ אֵינוֹ אֶלָּא אֲפִילּוּ מִילָה, וּמָה אֲנִי מְקַיֵּים ׳שְׁמִינִי יִמּוֹל׳ – חוּץ מִשַּׁבָּת – תַּלְמוּד לוֹמַר ׳בַּיּוֹם׳ – אֲפִילּוּ בְּשַׁבָּת.

It was taught in a *baraita* **in accordance with** the opinion of **Rabbi Yoḥanan and not in accordance with** the opinion of **Rav Aḥa bar Ya'akov,** as the *tanna* interprets the phrase: "On the **eighth** day **he shall be circumcised"** to mean that the circumcision must be performed **even on Shabbat. And how do I fulfill** the prohibition against performing prohibited labor explicit in the Torah in the verse: "And you shall guard the Shabbat, for it is holy to you; **he who desecrates it shall surely die"** (Exodus 31:14)? That is referring **to other prohibited labors besides circumcision.** The *tanna* questions his previous statement: **Or perhaps that is not** the case, and the prohibition of performing prohibited labor on Shabbat includes **even circumcision, and,** on the contrary, **how do I fulfill** the verse: "On the **eighth** day **he shall be circumcised"?** It applies when the eighth day is any day **other than Shabbat. The verse states: "On the day,"** meaning on that very day when he turns eight days old, **even on Shabbat.** The *tanna* of this *baraita* rejects Rav Aḥa bar Ya'akov's proof and accepts Rabbi Yoḥanan's assertion that the phrase "On the day" conclusively establishes that circumcision is performed even on Shabbat.

אָמַר רָבָא: הַאי תַּנָּא, מֵעִיקָּרָא מַאי קָא נִיחָא לֵיהּ, וּלְבַסּוֹף מַאי קָא קַשְׁיָא לֵיהּ?

With regard to this *baraita,* **Rava said: Initially, what** did **this** *tanna* find **acceptable, and ultimately, what** did **he** find **difficult?** Initially he suggested that: "On the eighth day he shall be circumcised" is a valid source for the fact that circumcision overrides Shabbat, but ultimately, he deemed that difficult and turned to an alternative source, yet provided no reason, neither for his initial statement nor for his second statement.

הָכִי קָאָמַר: ׳שְׁמִינִי יִמּוֹל׳ אֲפִילּוּ בְּשַׁבָּת, וּמָה אֲנִי מְקַיֵּים ״מְחַלְלֶיהָ מוֹת יוּמָת״ – בִּשְׁאָר מְלָאכוֹת חוּץ מִמִּילָה, אֲבָל מִילָה דָּחְיָא.

Rather, we can explain that **this is what he is saying:** "On the **eighth** day **he shall be circumcised"** applies **even on Shabbat. And how do I fulfill: "He who desecrates it shall surely die"?** That is referring to the **other prohibited labors besides circumcision; however, circumcision overrides** Shabbat.

מַאי טַעְמָא – קַל וָחוֹמֶר הוּא וּמַה צָּרַעַת שֶׁדּוֹחָה אֶת הָעֲבוֹדָה,

What is the reason for this? **It is** derived by means of **an** ***a fortiori*** **inference: Just as leprosy, which overrides the** Temple **service,** as a priest who is a leper may not serve in the Temple and it is prohibited to cut off the symptoms of leprosy,

וַעֲבוֹדָה דּוֹחָה אֶת הַשַּׁבָּת – מִילָה דּוֹחָה אוֹתָהּ. שַׁבָּת שֶׁנִּדְחֵית מִפְּנֵי הָעֲבוֹדָה – אֵינוֹ דִּין שֶׁתְּהֵא מִילָה דּוֹחָה אוֹתָהּ?

and the Temple **service overrides Shabbat,** as Shabbat offerings are sacrificed at their appointed time, and nevertheless **circumcision overrides** leprosy, i.e., if there were symptoms of leprosy on the foreskin of the baby, one circumcises the child even though he thereby violates the prohibition to cut off symptoms of leprosy; therefore, with regard to **Shabbat, which is overridden by the** Temple **service, is it not logical that circumcision,** which is so stringent that it overrides leprosy, **overrides** Shabbat as well? This was the *tanna's* reasoning at the outset.

וּמַאי ׳אוֹ אֵינוֹ׳ דְּקָאָמַר – הֲדַר אָמַר: וּמִמַּאי דְּצָרַעַת חֲמוּרָה? דִּילְמָא שַׁבָּת חֲמוּרָה, שֶׁכֵּן יֵשׁ בָּהּ עוֹנָשִׁין וְאַזְהָרוֹת הַרְבֵּה. (אִי נַמִי) וּמִמַּאי מִשּׁוּם דַּחֲמִירָא צָרַעַת הִיא – דִּילְמָא מִשּׁוּם גַּבְרָא הוּא דְּלָא חֲזֵי? וּמָה אֲנִי מְקַיֵּים ׳שְׁמִינִי יִמּוֹל׳ – חוּץ מִשַּׁבָּת, תַּלְמוּד לוֹמַר ׳בַּיּוֹם׳ – אֲפִילּוּ בַּשַּׁבָּת.

And what was the reason the *tanna* **said: Or perhaps,** and questioned his previous statement? **He reconsidered** and **said: And from where** do we know **that leprosy is** more **stringent** than Shabbat? **Perhaps Shabbat is** more **stringent, as it includes** the severe **punishments** of *karet* and execution by stoning, **and numerous warnings** pertaining to it throughout the Torah. **Alternatively, and from where** do we know[N] that the reason the Temple service does not override the prohibition of leprosy is specifically **because leprosy is** more **stringent** than the Temple service? **Perhaps** the Temple service does not override the prohibition of leprosy **because a man** afflicted with leprosy **is unfit**[N] to perform the Temple service and not due to the stringency of the prohibition to remove symptoms of leprosy from one's body. **And** if so, **how do I establish** the verse: "And on the **eighth** day the flesh of his foreskin **shall be circumcised**" (Leviticus 12:3)? That it applies to days **other than Shabbat.** Consequently, the *tanna* cited additional proof from that which **the Torah states: "On the day,"** indicating that circumcision is performed **even on Shabbat.**

תָּנוּ רַבָּנַן: מִילָה דּוֹחָה אֶת הַצָּרַעַת בֵּין בִּזְמַנָּהּ בֵּין שֶׁלֹּא בִּזְמַנָּהּ. יוֹם טוֹב אֵינָהּ דּוֹחָה אֶלָּא בִּזְמַנָּהּ בִּלְבַד.

The Sages taught: Circumcision overrides leprosy.[H] The foreskin is cut even if it has symptoms of leprosy on it, despite the fact that there is a Torah prohibition to cut off symptoms of leprosy. This is the *halakha* **both** when the circumcision takes place **at its** appointed **time,** on the eighth day, **or when it is not** performed **at its** appointed **time** but after the eighth day. However, circumcision **overrides a Festival only** when performed **at its** appointed **time.**[H]

מְנָהָנֵי מִילֵּי? דְּתָנוּ רַבָּנַן: ״יִמּוֹל בְּשַׂר עָרְלָתוֹ״ – וְאַף עַל פִּי שֶׁיֵּשׁ שָׁם בַּהֶרֶת יָקוֹץ. וּמָה אֲנִי מְקַיֵּים ״הִשָּׁמֶר בְּנֶגַע הַצָּרַעַת״ – בִּשְׁאָר מְקוֹמוֹת חוּץ מִמִּילָה.

The Gemara asks: **From where are these matters** derived? **As the Sages taught** in a *baraita* with regard to the verse: "And on the eighth day **the flesh of his foreskin shall be circumcised**" (Leviticus 12:3), since this verse is stated in general terms, it teaches that **even though there is a bright white** leprous **spot there, he should cut it. And how do I establish** the verse: **"Take care with regard to the plague of leprosy** to take great care and to perform in accordance with all that the priests, the Levites, instruct you; as I commanded them you shall take care to perform" (Deuteronomy 24:8)? Does usage of the term "take care" indicate that there is a negative mitzva that prohibits cutting off symptoms of leprosy? We establish this prohibition as applying **in other places, other than** the place of a **circumcision.**

אוֹ אֵינוֹ אֶלָּא אֲפִילּוּ מִילָה, וּמָה אֲנִי מְקַיֵּים ״יִמּוֹל בְּשַׂר עָרְלָתוֹ״ – בִּזְמַן שֶׁאֵין בָּהּ בַּהֶרֶת? תַּלְמוּד לוֹמַר: ׳בָּשָׂר׳ – וְאַף עַל פִּי שֶׁיֵּשׁ שָׁם בַּהֶרֶת.

The *tanna* asks: **Or** perhaps **that is not** the case; **rather,** this prohibition applies **even** in the place of **circumcision, and how do I validate** the verse: **"The flesh of his foreskin shall be circumcised"**? It applies **when there is no bright white** leprous **spot** on the foreskin. So that we will not interpret the verse that way, **the verse states** the superfluous word **flesh.** It would have been sufficient to state: His foreskin shall be circumcised, but instead the verse stated: "The flesh of his foreskin shall be circumcised," indicating that the foreskin must be removed **even though there is a bright white spot there.**

אָמַר רָבָא: הַאי תַּנָּא, מֵעִיקָּרָא מַאי נִיחָא לֵיהּ וּלְבַסּוֹף מַאי קַשְׁיָא לֵיהּ?

Rava said: Initially, what did **this** *tanna* find **acceptable, and ultimately, what** did he find **difficult?** At first he assumed that the mitzva of circumcision is more stringent, but he ultimately rejected this assumption with no explanation.

NOTES

Alternatively, and from where do we know, etc. – אִי נַמִי וּמִמַּאי וכו׳: According to the Maharshal, the words translated as alternatively should be erased, and only the following argument is offered: Perhaps Shabbat is stringent and leprosy is less stringent. However, according to the existing version of the text, two points are being raised, one relating to the great stringency of the mitzva of Shabbat, the second, that perhaps everything raised with regard to the *a fortiori* inference from the fact that leprosy overrides the Temple service is of no relevance to this argument.

A man afflicted with leprosy is unfit – גַּבְרָא הוּא דְּלָא חֲזֵי: This explanation should be understood as follows: It is not the stringency of the prohibition against cutting a bright white leprous spot that overrides the Temple service. Rather, the Temple service cannot be performed in this case, because the person is not fit to perform it at that time. In other words, the prohibition against a leper being involved with the Temple service should be seen as merely a delay that prevents the priest from serving, similar to any other delay that might occur when he comes to serve. Consequently, one cannot conclude that the cause of the delay is more important than the service itself.

HALAKHA

Circumcision overrides leprosy – מִילָה דּוֹחָה אֶת הַצָּרַעַת: Circumcision overrides leprosy. If there is a bright white leprous spot on the foreskin, the child is circumcised, even though cutting the bright spot is a violation of a negative mitzva (Rambam *Sefer Ahava, Hilkhot Mila* 1:9 and *Sefer Tahara, Hilkhot Tumat Tzara'at* 10:5; *Shulḥan Arukh, Yoreh De'a* 266:1).

Overrides a Festival only when performed at its appointed time – יוֹם טוֹב אֵינָהּ דּוֹחָה אֶלָּא בִּזְמַנָּהּ בִּלְבַד: Performing a circumcision, on the eighth day overrides Shabbat and, all the more so, a Festival. However, performing a circumcision at any time after the eighth day does not override Shabbat or a Festival (Rambam *Sefer Ahava, Hilkhot Mila* 1:9 and *Sefer Tahara, Hilkhot Tumat Tzara'at* 10:5; *Shulḥan Arukh, Yoreh De'a* 266:2).

הָכִי קָאָמַר: ״יִמּוֹל בְּשַׂר עָרְלָתוֹ״ – וְאַף עַל פִּי שֶׁיֵּשׁ בַּהֶרֶת, וּמָה אֲנִי מְקַיֵּים ״הִשָּׁמֶר בְּנֶגַע הַצָּרַעַת״ – בִּשְׁאָר מְקוֹמוֹת חוּץ מִמִּילָה, אֲבָל מִילָה דּוֹחָה אֶת הַצָּרַעַת. מַאי טַעְמָא? דְּאַתְיָא מִקַּל וָחוֹמֶר; וּמַה שַּׁבָּת חֲמוּרָה – מִילָה דּוֹחָה אוֹתָהּ, צָרַעַת לֹא כׇּל שֶׁכֵּן?

Rather, **this is what he is saying:** Initially he held that the phrase: **The flesh of his foreskin shall be circumcised** teaches that it is permitted to remove the foreskin **even though there is a bright white spot** there. **And how do I validate** the following verse: **Take care with regard to the plague of leprosy?** It applies **in other places, aside from** the place of **circumcision, but circumcision overrides leprosy. What is the reason** for this? **It is derived by** means of an ***a fortiori*** **inference: Just as Shabbat is stringent** and nevertheless **circumcision overrides it, all the more so** that circumcision overrides **leprosy,** which is less stringent than Shabbat.

וּמַאי ״אוֹ אֵינוֹ״ דְּקָאָמַר – הֲדַר קָאָמַר: מִמַּאי דְּשַׁבָּת חֲמִירָא, דִּילְמָא צָרַעַת חֲמִירָא? שֶׁכֵּן דּוֹחָה אֶת הָעֲבוֹדָה, וַעֲבוֹדָה דּוֹחָה אֶת הַשַּׁבָּת! תַּלְמוּד לוֹמַר: ׳בְּשַׂר׳ – וְאַף עַל פִּי שֶׁיֵּשׁ שָׁם בַּהֶרֶת.

And what was the reason for the term **or perhaps that** the *tanna* **is saying** to question his previous statement? **He reconsidered** and **said: From where** do we know **that Shabbat** is more **stringent? Perhaps leprosy is** more **stringent, as** leprosy **overrides the** Temple **service,** as stated earlier, **and the** Temple **service overrides Shabbat.** Therefore, **the verse states** the additional word **flesh,** to teach that the foreskin is removed **even though there is a bright white** leprous **spot there.**

לִישָּׁנָא אַחֲרִינָא: מִילָה דּוֹחָה אֶת הַצָּרַעַת מַאי טַעְמָא – דְּאָתֵי עֲשֵׂה וְדָחֵי לֹא תַעֲשֶׂה, וּמַאי ״אוֹ אֵינוֹ״ דְּקָאָמַר – הֲדַר קָאָמַר: אֵימַר דְּאָמְרִינַן דְּאָתֵי עֲשֵׂה וְדָחֵי אֶת לֹא תַעֲשֶׂה – לֹא תַעֲשֶׂה גְּרֵידָא, הַאי עֲשֵׂה וְלֹא תַעֲשֶׂה הוּא. וּמָה אֲנִי מְקַיֵּים ״יִמּוֹל בְּשַׂר עָרְלָתוֹ״ – בִּזְמַן שֶׁאֵין בָּהּ בַּהֶרֶת! תַּלְמוּד לוֹמַר: ׳בְּשַׂר׳ – וְאַף עַל פִּי שֶׁיֵּשׁ שָׁם בַּהֶרֶת.

The Gemara cites **another version** of Rava's comments. Initially the *tanna* thought that **circumcision overrides leprosy. What is the reason** for this? He relied on the principle **that a positive** mitzva **comes and overrides a negative** mitzva. **And what** was the reason the *tanna* **is saying: Or perhaps** to question his previous statement? **He reconsidered** and **said: Say that we say that a positive** mitzva **comes and overrides a negative** mitzva when there is **a negative** mitzva **alone.** However, **this** cutting off leprosy is prohibited by both **a positive** mitzva **and a negative** mitzva. **And how do I establish** the verse: **The flesh of his foreskin shall be circumcised?** It applies only **when there is no bright white spot on** the foreskin. Therefore, **the verse states** the additional word **flesh** in order to emphasize that the foreskin is removed, **even though there is a bright white spot there.**

תִּינַח גָּדוֹל דִּכְתִיב בְּהוּ ׳בְּשַׂר׳, קָטָן נַמִי כְּתִיב בֵּיהּ ׳בְּשַׂר׳, בֵּינוֹנִי מְנָלַן?

The Gemara questions the derivation from the word flesh: This **works out well** with regard to the circumcision of **an adult** who has not yet been circumcised, **as** the word **flesh is written with regard to** adults in the verse: "And an uncircumcised male who will not circumcise the flesh of his foreskin, that soul shall be cut off from its people; My covenant he has broken" (Genesis 17:14). Similarly, it works out well with regard to **a minor** who is circumcised on the eighth day, as the superfluous word **flesh is also written** with regard to him. However, with regard to a person at an **intermediate** stage of life, i.e., a child who was not circumcised on the eighth day but has not yet reached majority, **from where do we derive** that his circumcision overrides leprosy? The Torah explicitly mandates his circumcision: "Circumcise for yourselves every male" (Genesis 17:10). However, that verse does not employ the term flesh.

אָמַר אַבַּיֵי: אָתְיָא מִבֵּינַיָּא; מִגָּדוֹל לָא אָתְיָא – שֶׁכֵּן עָנוּשׁ כָּרֵת, מִקָּטָן לָא אָתְיָא – שֶׁכֵּן מִילָה בִּזְמַנָּהּ, הַצַּד הַשָּׁוֶה שֶׁבָּהֶן – שֶׁכֵּן נִימּוֹלִין וְדוֹחִין אֶת הַצָּרַעַת, אַף כׇּל שֶׁנִּימּוֹלִין דּוֹחִין אֶת הַצָּרַעַת.

Abaye said: It is derived from a combination[N] of the two sources about the status of a child at the intermediate stage, from the common denominator between an eight-day-old and one who reached majority. **From an adult** alone, the *halakha* with regard to an intermediate child **cannot be derived, as** an adult **is punishable by** ***karet*** if he fails to circumcise himself, but an intermediate child is not punishable by *karet*. Likewise, **from** the case of **an** eight-day-old **child,** the case of an intermediate child **cannot be derived; since** the **circumcision at its time** overrides Shabbat it may also override leprosy. However, the **common denominator** between an eight-day-old and an adult **is that they are circumcised and** their circumcision **overrides leprosy. So too, all who are circumcised,** including those in the intermediate stage, **override leprosy.**

רָבָא אָמַר: מִילָה בִּזְמַנָּהּ דּוֹחָה לָא צְרִיכָא קְרָא, מִקַּל וָחוֹמֶר אָתְיָא: וּמַה שַּׁבָּת דַּחֲמִירָא – דּוֹחָה, צָרַעַת לֹא כׇּל שֶׁכֵּן!

Rava said: No verse is required to teach that **circumcision at its** appointed **time overrides** leprosy, as it **is derived by means of an** ***a fortiori*** **inference: Just as** circumcision **overrides Shabbat, which is more stringent than** leprosy, **all the more so** that circumcision overrides **leprosy.**

NOTES

It is derived from a combination – אָתְיָא מִבֵּינַיָּא: Deriving a new *halakha* based on a common denominator is an accepted method. While it was impossible to derive the new *halakha* from one existing *halakha*, it was possible to derive the new *halakha* from the common denominator of two existing *halakhot*.

NOTES

Pure symptoms of leprosy – נְגָעִים טְהוֹרִים: Some commentators explain that the expression pure symptoms of leprosy refers to various intermediate stages of leprosy, e.g., when the priest commands that the afflicted person be quarantined until it can be determined conclusively whether or not the leprosy has spread. Even though this person is not yet impure or considered a leper, it is nevertheless prohibited to remove the symptoms, because it is possible that impure signs might develop from them (*Tosafot*). The phrase pure leprosy is a rabbinic term. The Torah only recognizes impure leprosy. If it is pure, the Torah does not refer to it as leprosy but in some other way (Rabbi Betzalel Regensburg).

Ritual fringes and diverse kinds – צִיצִית וְכִלְאַיִם: The cases cited here are not classic examples of positive mitzvot overriding negative mitzvot, because both cases mentioned here are derived from a particular source. The *halakha* in the case of leprosy and circumcision is derived from an *a fortiori* inference, and the *halakha* in the case of ritual fringes and diverse kinds is based on a juxtaposition of verses. Nevertheless, the following principle learned from these cases applies to other laws: The positive commandment overrides the negative commandment only when the fulfillment of the positive commandment is simultaneous with the violation of the negative commandment (Ramban; see *Me'iri*).

אֲמַר לֵיהּ רַב סָפְרָא לְרָבָא: מִמַּאי דְּשַׁבָּת חֲמִירָא? דִּילְמָא צָרַעַת חֲמִירָא, שֶׁכֵּן דּוֹחָה אֶת הָעֲבוֹדָה, וַעֲבוֹדָה דּוֹחָה אֶת הַשַּׁבָּת! הָתָם, לָאו מִשּׁוּם דַּחֲמִירָא צָרַעַת, אֶלָּא מִשּׁוּם דְּגַבְרָא הוּא דְּלָא חֲזֵי. אַמַּאי? וְיָקוֹץ בַּהַרְתּוֹ וְיַעֲבוֹד! מְחוּסַּר טְבִילָה הוּא.

Rav Safra said to Rava: From where do we know that **Shabbat** is more **stringent? Perhaps leprosy** is more **stringent, as** leprosy **overrides the** Temple **service, and the** Temple **service overrides Shabbat.** Rava answered: **There,** when leprosy overrides the Temple service, **it is not because leprosy is** more **stringent; rather,** it is **because the man** afflicted with leprosy **is unfit** for the Temple service. Rav Safra asked: **Why** is he unfit? **Let him cut off his bright white** leprous **spot and serve.** Rava answered: He would remain unfit to serve, as **he is lacking immersion.** In order to purify himself for service in the Temple, he must immerse himself and wait until the following day. In the meantime he is unfit.

תֵּינַח – נְגָעִים טְמֵאִים, נְגָעִים טְהוֹרִים – מַאי אִיכָּא לְמֵימַר?

Rav Safra raised a difficulty: **It works out well** if we are referring to **impure** symptoms of **leprosy,** as even one who removes them must immerse afterward. However, with regard to **pure** symptoms of **leprosy,**[N] there is a prohibition to cut off the symptoms even though there is no impurity. They have the legal status of blemishes that invalidate a priest from serving until it is cured. Once the bright white spot is removed, he may immediately serve in the Temple without immersion. **What is there to say** in that case?

אֶלָּא אָמַר רַב אַשִׁי: הֵיכָא אָמְרִינַן דְּאָתֵי עֲשֵׂה וְדָחֵי לֹא תַעֲשֶׂה – כְּגוֹן מִילָה בְּצָרַעַת, אִי נַמִי צִיצִית וְכִלְאַיִם, דִּבְעִידָּנָא דְּמִתְעַקֵּר לָאו – קָא מוֹקִים עֲשֵׂה. הָכָא, בְּעִידָּנָא דְּמִתְעַקֵּר לְלָאו – לָא קָא מוֹקִים עֲשֵׂה.

Rather, Rav Ashi said that this is the reason that leprosy overrides the Temple service: **Where do we say that a positive** mitzva **overrides a negative** mitzva? It is in cases **like circumcision in** a case of **leprosy,** or **alternatively, ritual fringes and diverse kinds**[N] of wool and linen, **as at the time the negative** mitzva **is uprooted,** the **positive** mitzva **is fulfilled** in the very same action, e.g., when the ritual fringes are woolen and will be attached to a linen garment, a prohibited mixture is created. However, **here,** in the case of a person afflicted with pure symptoms of leprosy cutting off his symptoms to enable his involvement in the Temple service, it is different, **at the time the negative** mitzva **is uprooted,** the **positive** mitzva **is not** yet **fulfilled,** as cutting off the symptoms is only a preliminary action that enables him to serve. In that case, the positive mitzva does not override the negative one.

וְהָא דְּרָבָא וְרַב סָפְרָא

The Gemara points out that **this** disagreement between **Rava and Rav Safra**

Perek **XIX**
Daf **133** Amud **a**

תַּנָּאֵי הִיא; דְּתַנְיָא: 'בְּשַׂר' וְאַף עַל פִּי שֶׁיֵּשׁ שָׁם בַּהֶרֶת יִמּוֹל, דִּבְרֵי רַבִּי יֹאשִׁיָּה. רַבִּי יוֹנָתָן אוֹמֵר: אֵינוֹ צָרִיךְ, שַׁבָּת חֲמוּרָה – דּוֹחָה, צָרַעַת – לֹא כָּל שֶׁכֵּן?!

is a dispute of *tanna'im*, **as it was taught** in a *baraita*: The term **flesh** comes to teach that **even though there is a bright white spot there, one should circumcise;** this is **the statement of Rabbi Yoshiya. Rabbi Yonatan says: There is no need** for this derivation from the word flesh in the verse. Rather, the same law can be derived by means of an *a fortiori* inference: If circumcision **overrides Shabbat,** which is **stringent, all the more so** that it overrides **leprosy.**

אָמַר מָר: 'בְּשַׂר' אַף עַל פִּי שֶׁיֵּשׁ שָׁם בַּהֶרֶת יִמּוֹל דִּבְרֵי רַבִּי יֹאשִׁיָּה. הָא לָמָּה לִי קְרָא? דָּבָר שֶׁאֵין מִתְכַּוֵּין הוּא, וְדָבָר שֶׁאֵין מִתְכַּוֵּין – מוּתָּר!

We earlier learned that **the Master said:** When the verse states the term **flesh,** it comes to teach that **even though there is a bright white spot there, one should circumcise;** this is **the statement of Rabbi Yoshiya.** Rabbi Yonatan agrees with this *halakha*, albeit for a different reason. The Gemara addresses the fundamental question: **Why do I need a verse** to derive **this?** The removal of leprous skin **is an unintentional act.** One does not intend to cut the symptom of leprosy; he intended to circumcise the baby. **And** the general rule is that **an unintentional act is permitted.** Consequently, there is no need for a special derivation in this case.

אָמַר אַבַּיֵי: לָא נִצְרְכָא אֶלָּא לְרַבִּי יְהוּדָה, דְּאָמַר: דָּבָר שֶׁאֵין מִתְכַּוֵּין אָסוּר. רָבָא אָמַר: אֲפִילּוּ תֵּימָא רַבִּי שִׁמְעוֹן, מוֹדֶה רַבִּי שִׁמְעוֹן בִּפְסִיק רֵישֵׁיהּ וְלָא יְמוּת. וְאַבַּיֵי לֵית לֵיהּ הַאי סְבָרָא?! וְהָא אַבַּיֵי וְרָבָא דְּאָמְרִי תַּרְוַויְיהוּ: מוֹדֶה רַבִּי שִׁמְעוֹן בִּפְסִיק רֵישֵׁיהּ וְלָא יְמוּת! בָּתַר דִּשְׁמַעָהּ מֵרָבָא סְבָרָהּ.

Abaye said: This derivation **is only necessary according to** the opinion **of Rabbi Yehuda, who said** that **an unintentional act is prohibited. Rava said: Even if you say** that it is according to the opinion of **Rabbi Shimon,** who holds that an unintentional act is permitted, as **Rabbi Shimon concedes** to Rabbi Yehuda in the case of: **Cut off its head and will it not die,** i.e., an unintentional act from which a prohibited labor ensued as an inevitable consequence. In that case, the one who performs the action cannot claim that the outcome was unintended. In the case of circumcising a leprous foreskin, the removal of leprosy is an inevitable consequence of the circumcision. The Gemara asks: And **does Abaye not accept this reasoning? Wasn't** it **Abaye and Rava who both say** that **Rabbi Shimon concedes** to Rabbi Yehuda that in the case of: **If you cut off its head will it not die?** The Gemara answers: **After** Abaye **heard** this principle **from Rava, he accepted it.**

אִיכָּא דְּמַתְנֵי לְהָא דְּאַבַּיֵי וְרָבָא אַהָא: ״הִשָּׁמֶר בְּנֶגַע הַצָּרַעַת לִשְׁמֹר מְאֹד וְלַעֲשׂוֹת״, לַעֲשׂוֹת – אִי אַתָּה עוֹשֶׂה, אֲבָל עוֹשֶׂה אַתָּה בְּסִיב שֶׁעַל גַּבֵּי רַגְלוֹ וּבְמוֹט שֶׁעַל גַּבֵּי כְּתֵיפוֹ. וְאִם עָבְרָה – עָבְרָה.

Some teach that which Abaye and Rava said as referring **to this** *baraita*. The verse states: **"Take heed with regard to the plague of leprosy that you observe diligently and do** in accordance with all that the priests, the Levites, instruct you; as I commanded them you shall take care to do" (Deuteronomy 24:8). The Sages derived from here that **to do** something in order to remove leprosy directly, **you may not do;**[N] **but you may do** something that will indirectly remove one's symptom, such as tying **a thick rope on his foot,**[H] **and** placing **a rod on his shoulder.** This is permitted even though there is a bright white spot present, **and if** the bright white spot **is** thereby **removed, it is removed.**

וְהָא לָמָּה לִי קְרָא? דָּבָר שֶׁאֵין מִתְכַּוֵּין הוּא, וְדָבָר שֶׁאֵין מִתְכַּוֵּין מוּתָּר! אָמַר אַבַּיֵי: לָא נִצְרְכָא אֶלָּא לְרַבִּי יְהוּדָה, דְּאָמַר: דָּבָר שֶׁאֵין מִתְכַּוֵּין אָסוּר. וְרָבָא אָמַר: אֲפִילּוּ תֵּימָא רַבִּי שִׁמְעוֹן, וּמוֹדֶה רַבִּי שִׁמְעוֹן בִּפְסִיק רֵישֵׁיהּ וְלָא יְמוּת. וְאַבַּיֵי לֵית לֵיהּ הַאי סְבָרָא?! וְהָא אַבַּיֵי וְרָבָא דְּאָמְרִי תַּרְוַויְיהוּ: מוֹדֶה רַבִּי שִׁמְעוֹן בִּפְסִיק רֵישֵׁיהּ וְלָא יְמוּת! לְבָתַר דִּשְׁמַעֵיהּ מֵרָבָא – סְבָרָהּ.

The Gemara asks: **Why do I** need **a verse** to address **this?**[N] **It is an unintentional act, and an unintentional act is permitted. Abaye said:** This derivation **is only necessary according to** the opinion **of Rabbi Yehuda, who said** that **an unintentional act is prohibited. Rava said: Even if you say** that it is according to the opinion of **Rabbi Shimon,** who holds that an unintentional act is permitted, as **Rabbi Shimon concedes** to Rabbi Yehuda in the case of: **If you cut off its head will it not die?** The Gemara asks: And **does Abaye not accept this reasoning? Wasn't** it **Abaye and Rava who both say** that **Rabbi Shimon concedes** to Rabbi Yehuda that in the case of: **Cut off its head and will it not die?** The Gemara answers: **After** Abaye **heard** this principle **from Rava, he accepted it.**

וְאַבַּיֵי אַלִּיבָּא דְּרַבִּי שִׁמְעוֹן, הַאי ׳בָּשָׂר׳ מַאי עָבֵיד לֵיהּ? אָמַר רַב עַמְרָם: בְּאוֹמֵר: לָקוֹץ בַּהַרְתּוֹ הוּא מִתְכַּוֵּין.

The Gemara clarifies: According to **Abaye's** initial understanding of the *halakha* **in accordance with** the opinion of **Rabbi Shimon,** i.e., even the inevitable consequence of an unintended act is permitted, **what does** he **do with this** term **flesh,** which appears in the verse with regard to circumcision? **Rav Amram said:** This term teaches that even **in a** case where the person who is circumcising himself **says** explicitly that **his intention is** also **to cut off the bright white spot,** the circumcision nonetheless overrides the prohibition to remove symptoms of leprosy.

תֵּינַח גָּדוֹל, קָטָן מַאי אִיכָּא לְמֵימַר? אָמַר רַב מְשַׁרְשְׁיָא: בְּאוֹמֵר אֲבִי הַבֵּן לָקוֹץ בַּהֶרֶת דִּבְנוֹ הוּא קָא מִתְכַּוֵּין.

The Gemara asks: This **works out well** in the case of **an adult** who intends to perform the prohibited act. With regard to the circumcision of **a minor,** who has no intention at all, **what is there to say,** i.e., how does this teaching apply? **Rav Mesharshiya said:** The teaching applies in a case **where the father of the** circumcised **child says** that **his intention is to cut off his son's bright white** leprous **spot.**

וְאִי אִיכָּא אַחֵר – לִיעֲבֵיד אַחֵר, דְּאָמַר רַבִּי שִׁמְעוֹן בֶּן לָקִישׁ: כׇּל מָקוֹם שֶׁאַתָּה מוֹצֵא עֲשֵׂה וְלֹא תַעֲשֶׂה, אִם אַתָּה יָכוֹל לְקַיֵּים שְׁנֵיהֶם – מוּטָב, וְאִם לָאו – יָבֹא עֲשֵׂה וְיִדְחֶה לֹא תַעֲשֶׂה! דְּלֵיכָּא אַחֵר.

The Gemara asks: In that case, **if there is another** person present who can circumcise the child, **let the other** person **perform** the circumcision. Presumably the other person will not intend to excise the bright white spot but rather will intend to fulfill the mitzva of circumcision, and no transgression will be committed, **as Rabbi Shimon ben Lakish said: Any place that you find positive and negative mitzvot**[H] that clash with one another, **if you can** find some way to **fulfill both,** that is **preferable; and if that is not** possible, **the positive** mitzva **will come and override the negative** mitzva.[N] Here it is possible to fulfill both the positive and negative mitzvot by having another person perform the circumcision. The Gemara answers: This is a case **where there is no other** person to perform circumcision; only the boy's father can circumcise him. Therefore, a particular verse is needed to teach us that the mitzva of circumcision overrides the prohibition to cut off symptoms of leprosy.

NOTES

You may not do – אִי אַתָּה עוֹשֶׂה: The Rashba questions the version in the Gemara because the phrase you may not do implies that there is a prohibition to perform an action that removes the symptoms of leprosy, in which case there are both negative and positive mitzvot pertaining to leprosy. Therefore, the Rashba accepts Rashi's version of the text, which reads as follows: You may do. This means that the mitzva to take care with regard to leprosy does not prevent a person from performing other tasks in their usual manner, even if the result will be the removal of the symptoms.

Why do I need a verse to address this, etc. – וְהָא לָמָּה לִי קְרָא וכו׳: If the removal of a leprous symptom is permitted when there is no performance of a mitzva, as in the case of a thick rope, why is it necessary to derive from a verse that it is permitted to remove a leprous symptom when performing a mitzva? Some commentaries explain that the verse teaches that even if one intends to remove the leprous symptoms and does not do so in an unusual manner, he may still perform a circumcision (Rashba).

The positive mitzva will come and override the negative mitzva – יָבֹא עֲשֵׂה וְיִדְחֶה לֹא תַעֲשֶׂה: Rav Nissim Gaon explains this issue at length. In his view, the reason that positive mitzvot override negative mitzvot is not because the former are more stringent or more significant. Rather, the positive mitzva is seen as limiting the scope of the prohibition. The Sages taught that the verses: "He who desecrates it [Shabbat] shall surely die" (Exodus 31:14) and "On the Shabbat day two sheep [shall be offered]" (Numbers 28:9) were stated in a single utterance. This teaching should be understood along similar lines. Indeed, the verses are not contradictory. Rather, the positive mitzva to offer sacrifices on Shabbat limits the scope of the prohibition against performing labor on Shabbat. The same principle can be said to apply to other mitzvot. However, when both a positive and a negative commandment pertain to the same mitzva, it cannot be said that a separate positive mitzva comes and limits its scope, since this act already includes a positive mitzva.

HALAKHA

But you may do so by tying a thick rope, etc. – אֲבָל עוֹשֶׂה אַתָּה בְּסִיב וכו׳: The Torah prohibits the removal of the symptoms of leprosy. It is permissible, however, for the leper to act in a usual manner and carry a rod on his shoulder or tie a thick rope around his leg, even if there is a bright white spot there. If the signs of impurity are thereby removed, there is no violation of the Torah prohibition as long as the leper did not intend to remove them (Rambam *Sefer Tahara, Hilkhot Tumat Tzara'at* 10:1).

Any place that you find positive and negative mitzvot, etc. – כׇּל מָקוֹם שֶׁאַתָּה מוֹצֵא עֲשֵׂה וְלֹא תַעֲשֶׂה וכו׳: Whenever a positive and a negative mitzva clash, it is preferable if one can fulfill both. However, if this is not possible, the positive mitzva overrides the negative one (Rambam *Sefer Ahava, Hilkhot Tzitzit* 3:6).

NOTES

Circumcision on a Festival could have been derived through an *a fortiori* inference – מִילָה בְּיוֹם טוֹב מִקַּל וָחוֹמֶר: In some editions, the Gemara delineates the *a fortiori* inference in the following manner: Just as one's own needs override the prohibition of labor on a Festival, all the more so circumcision, which is a mitzva, overrides the prohibition of labor on a Festival (Rabbeinu Zeraḥya HaLevi). According to Rashi and others, this is not a valid *a fortiori* inference because eating and drinking on a Festival are included among the mitzvot of the day, and they are not considered the exclusive needs of the individual. Rather, the *a fortiori* inference that can be applied here is the one used in the case of circumcision on Shabbat, i.e., the derivation from the Temple service and leprosy (Rashba).

אָמַר מָר: יוֹם טוֹב אֵינָהּ דּוֹחָה אֶלָּא בִּזְמַנָּהּ בִּלְבַד. מְנָא הָנֵי מִילֵּי?

We learned earlier that **the Master said** that circumcision **only overrides a Festival when** the circumcision takes place **at its** proper **time,** on the eighth day after birth. The Gemara asks: **From where are these matters** derived?

אָמַר חִזְקִיָּה, וְכֵן תָּנָא דְּבֵי חִזְקִיָּה: אָמַר קְרָא ״לֹא תוֹתִירוּ מִמֶּנּוּ עַד בֹּקֶר״ שֶׁאֵין תַּלְמוּד לוֹמַר ׳עַד בֹּקֶר׳. מָה תַּלְמוּד לוֹמַר ׳עַד בֹּקֶר׳ – בָּא הַכָּתוּב לִיתֵּן לוֹ בֹּקֶר שֵׁנִי לִשְׂרֵיפָתוֹ.

Ḥizkiya said, and likewise one of the Sages **of the school of Ḥizkiya taught: The verse states** with regard to the Paschal lamb: "And **you shall not leave any of it until morning;** but that which remains of it until morning you shall burn with fire" (Exodus 12:10). This verse contains a superfluous phrase, **as the Torah did not need to state until morning** the second time; it would have been sufficient to state: But that which remains of it you shall burn with fire. Rather, **why does the Torah state until morning? The verse comes to provide him** with **the second morning for burning.** Leftover meat of the Paschal lamb is not burned on the following morning, which is a Festival, but rather on the following day, the first of the intermediate days of the Festival. Even though the labor of kindling a fire is not entirely prohibited on a Festival, as one may cook and bake, it is derived from here that kindling a fire is permitted only for the purpose of preparing food for the immediate needs of the day and not for purposes that can be postponed until the intermediate days. Similarly, since circumcision involves a prohibited labor, it is permitted on the eighth day only when there is no option of postponing it. Otherwise, doing so is prohibited.

אַבַּיֵי אָמַר: אָמַר קְרָא ״עוֹלַת שַׁבָּת בְּשַׁבַּתּוֹ״ – וְלֹא עוֹלַת חוֹל בְּשַׁבָּת, וְלֹא עוֹלַת חוֹל בְּיוֹם טוֹב.

Abaye said there is a different source for the fact that only circumcision on the eighth day overrides the Festival, as **the verse stated: "The burnt-offering of each Shabbat on its Shabbat** in addition to the continual burnt-offering and its libation" (Numbers 28:10). This verse teaches that one may **not** sacrifice **the burnt-offering of a weekday on Shabbat, and** one may **not** sacrifice **the burnt-offering of a weekday on a Festival.** Although slaughtering is permitted on a Festival for sustenance, it is nevertheless prohibited to slaughter animals for sacrifices other than those specifically mandated on the Festival. Temple service only overrides prohibited labor in the case of Temple service that is an essential obligation of that day. Similarly, circumcision only overrides the prohibition of labor when it is an essential obligation of that day, which is the case only on the eighth day; it is not the case after the eighth day.

רָבָא אָמַר: אָמַר קְרָא ״הוּא לְבַדּוֹ יֵעָשֶׂה לָכֶם״, ׳הוּא׳ – וְלֹא מַכְשִׁירִין, ׳לְבַדּוֹ׳ – וְלֹא מִילָה שֶׁלֹּא בִּזְמַנָּהּ, דְּאָתְיָא מִקַּל וָחוֹמֶר.

Rava said there is a different proof, as **the verse states** with regard to Festivals: "And in the first day there shall be to you a holy convocation, and in the seventh day a holy convocation; no manner of work shall be done in them, save that which every man must eat; **that alone may be done for you**" (Exodus 12:16). The superfluous term **"that"** in the verse teaches the following: That which is necessary for food preparation itself is permitted **and not** actions that **facilitate** food preparation or which prepare utensils necessary for eating. Similarly, "that **alone** may be done" teaches: Only food preparation may be performed **and not circumcision that is not at its** appointed **time, which** could have been **derived through an *a fortiori* inference.**[N] Therefore, the verse emphasizes that "that alone" may be performed, to teach that prohibited labors are permitted for sustenance on a Festival, and are not permitted for other mitzvot.

רַב אַשִׁי אָמַר: ׳שַׁבָּתוֹן׳ עֲשֵׂה הוּא, וַהֲוָה לֵיהּ יוֹם טוֹב עֲשֵׂה וְלֹא תַעֲשֶׂה, וְאֵין עֲשֵׂה דּוֹחֶה אֶת לֹא תַעֲשֶׂה וַעֲשֵׂה.

Rav Ashi said: The mitzvot of a Festival include not only a negative mitzva but also a positive one. There is a prohibition of labor as well as ***Shabbaton,*** an obligation to engage in solemn rest, which **is a positive mitzva, and** therefore the observance of a **Festival** constitutes both **a positive mitzva and a negative mitzva. And** there is a principle that **a positive mitzva does not override** both **a negative mitzva and a positive mitzva.**

״כְּלָל אָמַר רַבִּי עֲקִיבָא וכו׳״. אָמַר רַב יְהוּדָה אָמַר רַב: הֲלָכָה כְּרַבִּי עֲקִיבָא.

We learned in the mishna: **A principle was stated by Rabbi Akiva:** Any prohibited labor that can be performed on Shabbat eve does not override Shabbat; however, any prohibited labor that cannot be performed on Shabbat eve overrides Shabbat. **Rav Yehuda said** that **Rav said:** The ***halakha*** **is in accordance with** the opinion of **Rabbi Akiva** in this matter.

וּתְנַן נַמִי גַּבֵּי פֶּסַח כִּי הַאי גַּוְונָא: כְּלָל אָמַר רַבִּי עֲקִיבָא: כׇּל מְלָאכָה שֶׁאֶפְשָׁר לָהּ לַעֲשׂוֹתָהּ מֵעֶרֶב שַׁבָּת – אֵינָהּ דּוֹחָה אֶת הַשַּׁבָּת, שְׁחִיטָה שֶׁאִי אֶפְשָׁר לַעֲשׂוֹתָהּ מֵעֶרֶב שַׁבָּת – דּוֹחָה אֶת הַשַּׁבָּת. וְאָמַר רַב יְהוּדָה אָמַר רַב: הֲלָכָה כְּרַבִּי עֲקִיבָא.

And we also learned in a mishna **pertaining to the Paschal lamb, in a similar vein: A principle was stated by Rabbi Akiva: Any prohibited labor that can be performed on Shabbat eve does not override Shabbat.** By contrast, the **slaughtering** of the Paschal lamb, **which cannot be performed on Shabbat eve,** as it has a fixed time from the Torah, **overrides Shabbat.**[H] **And Rav Yehuda said** that **Rav said:** The ***halakha* is in accordance with Rabbi Akiva.**

וּצְרִיכָא, דְּאִי אַשְׁמְעִינַן גַּבֵּי מִילָה – הָתָם הוּא דְּמַכְשִׁירִין אֶפְשָׁר לַעֲשׂוֹת מֵאֶתְמוֹל לֹא דָּחוּ שַׁבָּת, דְּלֵיכָּא כָּרֵת. אֲבָל פֶּסַח דְּאִיכָּא כָּרֵת – אֵימָא לִידְחוּ שַׁבָּת.

The Gemara comments: **And** both statements that the *halakha* is in accordance with Rabbi Akiva **were necessary. As had** Rav **taught us** that the *halakha* is in accordance with Rabbi Akiva only **with regard to circumcision,** the conclusion would have been: **It is** specifically **there** that **facilitators** that **can be performed the day before do not override Shabbat,** as **there is no** punishment of ***karet*** if the circumcision is delayed, as liability for *karet* only applies when the child becomes obligated in mitzvot and chooses not to circumcise himself. **However,** with regard to **the Paschal lamb, where there is** ***karet*** for one who fails to offer the sacrifice at its proper time, one would **say** that those facilitators **should override Shabbat.** Therefore, it was necessary for Rav to state that the *halakha* is in accordance with the opinion of Rabbi Akiva with regard to the Paschal lamb.

וְאִי אַשְׁמְעִינַן גַּבֵּי פֶּסַח – מִשּׁוּם דְּלֹא נִכְרְתוּ עָלֶיהָ שְׁלֹשׁ עֶשְׂרֵה בְּרִיתוֹת, אֲבָל מִילָה דְּנִכְרְתוּ עָלֶיהָ שְׁלֹשׁ עֶשְׂרֵה בְּרִיתוֹת – אֵימָא לִידְחוּ שַׁבָּת, צְרִיכָא.

And if Rav **had taught us** that the *halakha* is in accordance with Rabbi Akiva only **with regard to the Paschal lamb,** the conclusion would have been that the reason that facilitators that can be performed on the eve of the Festival do not override the Festival is **because thirteen covenants** were **not established upon** the Paschal lamb, and it is therefore not so significant. **However,** with regard to **circumcision, upon which thirteen covenants** were **established,** the conclusion would have been that even actions that facilitate the mitzva that could have been performed on Shabbat eve **should override Shabbat.** It was therefore **necessary** to teach that the *halakha* is in accordance with Rabbi Akiva in both cases.

מתני׳ עוֹשִׂין כׇּל צׇרְכֵי מִילָה [בַּשַּׁבָּת]; מוֹהֲלִין וּפוֹרְעִין וּמוֹצְצִין, וְנוֹתְנִין עָלֶיהָ אִיסְפְּלָנִית וְכַמּוֹן.

MISHNA When the eighth day of a baby's life occurs on Shabbat, he must be circumcised on that day. Therefore, **one performs all the necessities of** the **circumcision,** even **on Shabbat:**[H] **One circumcises** the foreskin, **and uncovers** the skin by removing the thin membrane beneath the foreskin, **and sucks** the blood from the wound, **and places on it** both **a bandage** [***ispelanit***][L] **and cumin** as a salve.

אִם לֹא שָׁחַק מֵעֶרֶב שַׁבָּת – לוֹעֵס בְּשִׁינָּיו וְנוֹתֵן, אִם לֹא יָרַף יַיִן וָשֶׁמֶן מֵעֶרֶב שַׁבָּת – יִנָּתֵן זֶה בְּעַצְמוֹ וְזֶה בְּעַצְמוֹ.

If one did not grind the cumin **from Shabbat eve, he chews** it **with his teeth and places** it on the place of circumcision as a salve. **If he did not mix wine and oil on Shabbat eve,** a mixture designed to heal and strengthen the child, **this,** the wine, **is placed** on the wound **by itself and that,** the oil, is placed **by itself.**[H]

וְאֵין עוֹשִׂין לָהּ חָלוּק לְכַתְּחִילָּה, אֲבָל כּוֹרֵךְ עָלֶיהָ סְמַרְטוּט. אִם לֹא הִתְקִין מֵעֶרֶב שַׁבָּת – כּוֹרֵךְ עַל אֶצְבָּעוֹ וּמֵבִיא, וַאֲפִילּוּ מֵחָצֵר אַחֶרֶת.

And on Shabbat **one may not make a pouch** to place over the circumcision as a bandage ***ab initio*****, but he may wrap a rag over it** as a dressing. **If he did not prepare** the bandage **on Shabbat eve** by bringing it to the place where the circumcision was performed, **he wraps** the bandage **on his finger and brings** it on Shabbat, **even from a different courtyard.** While the Sages permitted it to be brought, they required that it be performed in an unusual fashion, by wearing it in the manner of a garment.

Perek **XIX**
Daf **133** Amud **b**

גמ׳ מִכְּדִי קָתָנֵי כּוּלְּהוּ, ׳כׇּל צוֹרְכֵי מִילָה׳ לְאֵתוֹיֵי מַאי?

GEMARA The Gemara asks: **Since** the mishna **is teaching all of them,** i.e., enumerated all the requirements of circumcision, when the mishna added: One performs **all the requirements of circumcision** even on Shabbat, **what** did it come **to include?**

HALAKHA

Slaughtering the Paschal lamb on Shabbat – שְׁחִיטַת פֶּסַח בַּשַּׁבָּת: The slaughtering of the Paschal lamb, the sprinkling of its blood, and all the other necessary requirements of the sacrifice override Shabbat, because their time is fixed by the Torah and they cannot be performed before Shabbat. However, preparations that can be performed the day before do not override Shabbat, in accordance with the opinion of Rabbi Akiva (Rambam *Sefer Korbanot, Hilkhot Korban Pesaḥ* 1:18).

Preparing the necessities of circumcision on Shabbat – הֲכָנַת צׇרְכֵי מִילָה בַּשַּׁבָּת: Every aspect of the circumcision may be performed on Shabbat; however, preparations for the circumcision do not override Shabbat (Rambam *Sefer Ahava, Hilkhot Mila* 2:6; *Shulḥan Arukh, Oraḥ Ḥayyim* 331:1, 6 and *Yoreh De'a* 266:2).

Preparing medicine on Shabbat for the sake of circumcision – הֲכָנַת סַמְמָנִים בַּשַּׁבָּת לְצוֹרֶךְ מִילָה: With regard to grinding cumin and mixing wine and oil to use as medications after the circumcision, if one failed to prepare them before Shabbat, one may prepare them on Shabbat in an unusual manner (Rambam *Sefer Ahava, Hilkhot Mila* 2:7; *Shulḥan Arukh, Oraḥ Ḥayyim* 331:7 and *Yoreh De'a* 266:3).

LANGUAGE

Bandage [*ispelanit*] – אִיסְפְּלָנִית: From the Greek, **σπληνίον**, *splènion*, meaning bandage or piece of cloth placed on a wound.

לְאַתּוֹיֵי הָא, דְּתָנוּ רַבָּנַן: הַמָּל, כׇּל זְמַן שֶׁהוּא עוֹסֵק בְּמִילָה – חוֹזֵר בֵּין עַל הַצִּיצִין הַמְעַכְּבִין אֶת הַמִּילָה בֵּין עַל הַצִּיצִין שֶׁאֵין מְעַכְּבִין אֶת הַמִּילָה. פֵּירֵשׁ, עַל צִיצִין הַמְעַכְּבִין אֶת הַמִּילָה – חוֹזֵר, עַל צִיצִין שֶׁאֵין מְעַכְּבִין אֶת הַמִּילָה – אֵינוֹ חוֹזֵר.

The Gemara answers: It comes **to include that which the Sages taught** in a *baraita*: **One who circumcises** on Shabbat, **as long as he is engaged in the circumcision, he may return** and remove shreds of skin that were not cut properly. This is the ruling **both for shreds** of skin[NH] and flesh **that invalidate the circumcision** if they are not cut, i.e., the child is not considered circumcised if they remain, **and for shreds that do not invalidate the circumcision** if they are not cut. But if the circumcisor has **withdrawn** from engaging in the mitzva of circumcision, **he may return for shreds that invalidate the circumcision** if they were not cut, as the mitzva has not yet been properly performed, but **he may not return for shreds that do not invalidate the circumcision** if they are not cut. Consequently, when the mishna refers to all the requirements of circumcision, it means that as long as one is still involved in the act of circumcision, one may go back and remove even pieces of skin that do not invalidate the circumcision.

מַאן תַּנָּא ״פֵּירֵשׁ אֵינוֹ חוֹזֵר״? אָמַר רַבָּה בַּר בַּר חָנָה אָמַר רַבִּי יוֹחָנָן: רַבִּי יִשְׁמָעֵאל בְּנוֹ שֶׁל רַבִּי יוֹחָנָן בֶּן בְּרוֹקָה הִיא. דְּתַנְיָא: אַרְבָּעָה עָשָׂר שֶׁחָל לִהְיוֹת בַּשַּׁבָּת – מַפְשִׁיט (אָדָם) הַפֶּסַח עַד הֶחָזֶה, דִּבְרֵי רַבִּי יִשְׁמָעֵאל בְּנוֹ שֶׁל רַבִּי יוֹחָנָן בֶּן בְּרוֹקָה. וַחֲכָמִים אוֹמְרִים: מַפְשִׁיטִין אֶת כּוּלּוֹ.

With regard to this law, the Gemara asks: **Who is the *tanna*** who holds that if one has already **withdrawn** from a mitzva **he may not return** to engage in its performance? Which *tanna* asserts that as long as a person is involved in a mitzva whose performance overrides Shabbat, he may complete it; however, if he is no longer involved in the mitzva, he may not exceed the minimum requirements if doing so would desecrate Shabbat? **Rabba bar bar Ḥanna said** that **Rabbi Yoḥanan said: It is Rabbi Yishmael, son of Rabbi Yoḥanan ben Beroka, as it was taught** in a *baraita*: In a case of **the fourteenth of Nisan,** the day the Paschal lamb is sacrificed, **that occurs on Shabbat, one flays the Paschal lamb until** he exposes **the breast,** in order to remove the portions that are offered on the altar, but one does not flay anymore, as it is not necessary for the mitzva of the day; this is the statement of **Rabbi Yishmael, son of Rabbi Yoḥanan ben Beroka. And the Rabbis say: One may** even **flay** the **entire** hide.

מִמַּאי?! עַד כָּאן לָא קָאָמַר רַבִּי יִשְׁמָעֵאל בְּנוֹ שֶׁל רַבִּי יוֹחָנָן בֶּן בְּרוֹקָה הָתָם – מִשּׁוּם דְּלָא בָּעֵינַן ״זֶה אֵלִי וְאַנְוֵהוּ״, אֲבָל הָכָא דְּבָעֵינַן ״זֶה אֵלִי וְאַנְוֵהוּ״ – הָכִי נַמִי,

The Gemara raises a difficulty: **From where** do you draw this comparison? Perhaps **Rabbi Yishmael, son of Rabbi Yoḥanan ben Beroka, only stated** his opinion that one may do no more than the minimum requirement **there,** with regard to the Paschal lamb, **because we do not need** to fulfill the mitzva of: **"This is my God and I will glorify Him"** (Exodus 15:2). The manner in which the animal is flayed does not impact the mitzva of the sacrifice. **However, here,** with regard to circumcision, **where we need** to fulfill the mitzva of: **"This is my God and I will glorify Him,"** which requires performing the circumcision in a beautiful manner, **indeed,** Rabbi Yishmael would agree that the mitzva must be performed as aesthetically as possible.[N]

דְּתַנְיָא: ״זֶה אֵלִי, וְאַנְוֵהוּ״ – הִתְנָאֵה לְפָנָיו בְּמִצְוֹת; עֲשֵׂה לְפָנָיו סוּכָּה נָאָה, וְלוּלָב נָאֶה, וְשׁוֹפָר נָאֶה, צִיצִית נָאָה, סֵפֶר תּוֹרָה נָאֶה וּכְתוֹב בּוֹ לִשְׁמוֹ בִּדְיוֹ נָאָה, בְּקוּלְמוֹס נָאֶה, בְּלַבְלָר אוּמָּן וְכוֹרְכוֹ בְּשִׁירָאִין נָאִין.

What is the source for the requirement of: "This is my God and I will glorify Him"? **As it was taught** in a *baraita* with regard to the verse: **"This is my God and I will glorify Him** [*anveihu*], the Lord of my father and I will raise Him up." The Sages interpreted *anveihu* homiletically as linguistically related to *noi*, beauty, and interpreted the verse: **Beautify yourself before Him in mitzvot.**[H] Even if one fulfills the mitzva by performing it simply, it is nonetheless proper to perform the mitzva as beautifully as possible. **Make before Him a beautiful *sukka*, a beautiful *lulav*, a beautiful *shofar*, beautiful ritual fringes, beautiful** parchment for a **Torah scroll, and write in it in His name in beautiful ink, with a beautiful quill by an expert scribe, and wrap** the scroll **in beautiful silk fabric.**

אַבָּא שָׁאוּל אוֹמֵר: ״וְאַנְוֵהוּ״ – הֲוֵי דּוֹמֶה לוֹ: מָה הוּא חַנּוּן וְרַחוּם – אַף אַתָּה הֱיֵה חַנּוּן וְרַחוּם.

Abba Shaul says: *Ve'anveihu* should be interpreted as if it were written in two words: *Ani vaHu*, me and Him [God]. **Be similar,** as it were, **to Him,** the Almighty: **Just as He is compassionate and merciful, so too should you be compassionate and merciful.**[H] In any case, there is no proof from Rabbi Yishmael's statement with regard to the Paschal lamb that he would say the same with regard to circumcision, as in that case, he might agree that fulfilling the mitzva beautifully justifies overriding Shabbat.

NOTES

As long as he is engaged in the circumcision, he may return, both for shreds of skin, etc. – כׇּל זְמַן שֶׁהוּא עוֹסֵק בְּמִילָה חוֹזֵר בֵּין עַל הַצִּיצִין וכו׳: In the Jerusalem Talmud, two opinions are cited as the source of the obligation to remove shreds of skin. According to Rabbi Akiva, it is derived from the double Hebrew expression *himmol yimmol*, which is translated as: "He shall surely circumcise" (Genesis 17:13). Usage of the double expression implies that both the foreskin and the relevant shreds of skin must be removed. According to Rabbi Yishmael, who does not derive laws from double expressions of this kind, the source for this *halakha* is the term: "A bridegroom of blood for circumcisions" (Exodus 4:26) used in a verse pertaining to the circumcision of the son of Moses. The plural form, circumcisions, indicates that there are two elements to circumcision.

Beautifying a mitzva on Shabbat – הִידּוּר מִצְוָה בְּשַׁבָּת: In an attempt to identify the opinion of the *tanna* who deals with the removal of the shreds of skin, the Gemara searches for the sources of the two underlying foundations of his view. The first is the distinction between the basic obligation of the mitzva and its beautification. The second is the principle that when the performance of a mitzva is interrupted in the middle, its subsequent continuation is not considered part of the same action. Each attempt to find a precedent focuses on identifying one of these foundations.

HALAKHA

As long as he is engaged in the circumcision, he may return, both for shreds of skin, etc. – כׇּל זְמַן שֶׁהוּא עוֹסֵק בְּמִילָה חוֹזֵר בֵּין עַל הַצִּיצִין וכו׳: On Shabbat, one who circumcises a child may remove shreds of skin and flesh even if they do not invalidate the circumcision, as long as he is still engaged in the circumcision. However, if he has already withdrawn his hand, he may only return to remove the shreds of skin that invalidate the circumcision (Rambam *Sefer Ahava, Hilkhot Mila* 2:4, 6; *Shulḥan Arukh, Oraḥ Ḥayyim* 331:2 and *Yoreh De'a* 266:2).

Beautify yourself before Him in mitzvot – הִתְנָאֵה לְפָנָיו בְּמִצְוֹת: One should make an effort to ensure that the objects he uses in the performance of a mitzva are beautiful. The Sages taught that for the purpose of beautifying mitzvot, one should be willing to spend up to an additional one-third of the price of an object with which he could fulfill the mitzva in a valid, less beautiful manner (Rambam *Sefer Ahava, Hilkhot Tefillin Umezuza VeSefer Torah* 7:4; *Sefer Zemanim, Hilkhot Shofar VeSukka VeLulav* 7:6; *Shulḥan Arukh, Oraḥ Ḥayyim* 656).

Just as He is compassionate and merciful, so too should you be compassionate and merciful – מָה הוּא חַנּוּן וְרַחוּם אַף אַתָּה הֱיֵה חַנּוּן וְרַחוּם: The Prophets used descriptive praises of God's attributes and thereby taught us that these attributes are laudable virtues. One should seek to emulate them and become compassionate, merciful, and holy like the Creator, as per the statement of Abba Shaul (Rambam *Sefer HaMadda, Hilkhot Deot* 1:6).

אֶלָּא אָמַר רַב אַשִׁי: הָא מַנִּי – רַבִּי יוֹסֵי הִיא, דִּתְנַן: בֵּין שֶׁנִּרְאָה בַּעֲלִיל וּבֵין שֶׁלֹּא נִרְאָה בַּעֲלִיל – מְחַלְּלִין עָלָיו אֶת הַשַּׁבָּת, רַבִּי יוֹסֵי אוֹמֵר: נִרְאָה בַּעֲלִיל – אֵין מְחַלְּלִין עָלָיו אֶת הַשַּׁבָּת.

Rather, Rav Ashi said: This should be understood differently. In accordance with **whose** opinion **is this** *baraita* with regard to circumcision? **It is** in accordance with the opinion of **Rabbi Yosei. As we learned** in a mishna: **Whether** the new moon **was clearly seen** by everyone **or whether it was not clearly seen, one may desecrate Shabbat** in order to sanctify the New Moon.[H] Eyewitnesses who saw the appearance of the moon may desecrate Shabbat in order to go to court and testify. **Rabbi Yosei says:** If the moon **was clearly seen, they may not desecrate Shabbat for it,** since other witnesses, located nearer to the court, will certainly testify. If these distant witnesses go to court to testify, they will desecrate Shabbat unnecessarily. Apparently, Rabbi Yosei holds that if the basic requirements of a mitzva have already been fulfilled, one may no longer desecrate Shabbat in its performance.

מִמַּאי?! דִּילְמָא עַד כָּאן לָא קָאָמַר רַבִּי יוֹסֵי הָתָם – דְּלֹא נִיתְּנָה שַׁבָּת לִידָּחוֹת, אֲבָל הָכָא דְּנִיתְּנָה שַׁבָּת לִידָּחוֹת – הָכִי נָמֵי!

The Gemara rejects this: **From where** do you draw this comparison? **Perhaps Rabbi Yosei only stated** his opinion **there,** in the case of sanctification of the New Moon, because there **no allowance was made for Shabbat to be overridden.** Given that the moon was clearly seen and testimony to that effect could have been delivered easily, there was no need for additional witnesses to come and desecrate Shabbat, and the prohibition to desecrate Shabbat remained in place. **However, here,** in the case of circumcision, where **allowance was made for Shabbat desecration,** as it is permitted and required to perform circumcision on Shabbat at its appointed time, **indeed,** it would be permitted to complete the circumcision even according to Rabbi Yosei.

אֶלָּא אָמְרִי נְהַרְדְּעֵי: רַבָּנַן דִּפְלִיגִי עֲלֵיהּ דְּרַבִּי יוֹסֵי הִיא, דִּתְנַן: אַרְבָּעָה כֹּהֲנִים נִכְנָסִין, שְׁנַיִם בְּיָדָם שְׁנֵי סְדָרִים, וּשְׁנַיִם בְּיָדָם שְׁנֵי בָזִיכִין. וְאַרְבָּעָה מַקְדִּימִין לִפְנֵיהֶם, שְׁנַיִם – לִיטּוֹל שְׁנֵי סְדָרִים, וּשְׁנַיִם – לִיטּוֹל שְׁנֵי בָזִיכִין. הַמַּכְנִיסִין עוֹמְדִים בַּצָּפוֹן וּפְנֵיהֶם לַדָּרוֹם, וְהַמּוֹצִיאִין עוֹמְדִים בַּדָּרוֹם וּפְנֵיהֶם לַצָּפוֹן. אֵלּוּ מוֹשְׁכִים וְאֵלּוּ מַנִּיחִין, טִפְחוֹ שֶׁל זֶה בְּצַד טִפְחוֹ שֶׁל זֶה, מִשּׁוּם שֶׁנֶּאֱמַר ״לְפָנַי (ה׳) תָּמִיד״.

Rather, the Sages of **Neharde'a say:** This ruling is in accordance with the opinion of **the Rabbis, who disagree** with **Rabbi Yosei. As we learned** in a mishna: **Four priests would enter** the Sanctuary every Shabbat to arrange the showbread,[NB] **two** of whom **had two orders** of six loaves each **in their hands, and two had two bowls** of frankincense **in their hands. And four** priests **would precede them; two** came **to take** the **two orders** of bread left on the table from the previous week, **and two** came **to take** the **two bowls** of frankincense. Next, **those bringing** the loaves and bowls **into** the Sanctuary **would stand in the north** of the Sanctuary, **facing south, while those carrying** the loaves and bowls **out would stand in the south** of the Sanctuary, **facing north. These slide** the old bread along the table, **and these place** the new bread on the table, and as a result, **the handbreadth of this one would be alongside the handbreadth of that one,** so that the requisite amount of bread would always be present on the table, **as it is stated:** "And you shall place on the table showbread **before Me continuously**" (Exodus 25:30).[H]

רַבִּי יוֹסֵי אוֹמֵר: אֲפִילּוּ אֵלּוּ נוֹטְלִין וְאֵלּוּ מַנִּיחִין – אַף זֶה הָיָה תָּמִיד.

Rabbi Yosei said: Even if these priests **were** first **to take** the old bread off the table entirely, **and** only afterward **were these** priests **to place** the new ones on the table, **this too would** fulfill the requirement that the showbread be on the table **continuously.** It is unnecessary to ensure the uninterrupted presence of the showbread on the table. Apparently, the Rabbis hold that even a moment's break in the performance of a mitzva is deemed an interruption. The same principle applies to circumcision. Once one withdrew and is no longer engaged in its performance, it is as though he completed the mitzva and he may no longer return to it.

תָּנוּ רַבָּנַן: מְהַלְּקְטִין אֶת הַמִּילָה, וְאִם לֹא הִילְּקֵט עָנוּשׁ – כָּרֵת. מַנִּי? אָמַר רַב כָּהֲנָא: אוּמָּן.

The Sages taught: We complete the cutting[N] **of the foreskin, and if he did not complete the cutting he is punishable by** ***karet.*** The Gemara asks: **Who** is punishable by *karet*? **Rav Kahana said: The craftsman,** i.e., the circumcisor. If he failed to complete the circumcision properly on Shabbat he is punishable by *karet*, as he wounded the baby on Shabbat without fulfilling the mitzva circumcision.

HALAKHA

Shabbat and the sanctification of the New Moon – שַׁבָּת וְקִידּוּשׁ הַחֹדֶשׁ: In ancient times, when new months were sanctified based on the sighting of the moon, witnesses who saw the moon would rush to the rabbinical court to testify. The witnesses were permitted to desecrate Shabbat to expedite their arrival. If the moon was clearly visible, and it was safe to assume that it had been seen by others who live closer to the court, it was unnecessary for them to rush to the court and desecrate Shabbat. Nevertheless, the witnesses were encouraged to proceed to the court even at the expense of Shabbat, in accordance with the unattributed mishna (Rambam *Sefer Zemanim, Hilkhot Kiddush HaḤodesh* 3:4).

The arrangement of the showbread – סִידּוּר לֶחֶם הַפָּנִים: The arrangement of the showbread was carried out in the following manner: Eight priests entered the Sanctuary, four carrying the new bread and bowls of frankincense, and four to remove the old bread and frankincense. The priests removed the old bread by sliding it off the table very slowly. The priests inserting the new bread immediately placed the loaves in the vacated spot, in accordance with the unattributed mishna (Rambam *Sefer Avoda, Hilkhot Temidin UMusafin* 5:4).

BACKGROUND

The showbread table – שׁוּלְחַן לֶחֶם הַפָּנִים: The loaves are arranged on the showbread table in two stacks. Between the two arrangements, or, according to some, on them, the priests would place the bowls of frankincense.

Showbread table with loaves

NOTES

The showbread – לֶחֶם הַפָּנִים: The showbread, which was placed on the sacred table in the Sanctuary (Exodus 25:23–30), was comprised of twelve loaves arranged on wooden slats in two stacks of six loaves each. Atop each stack or, according to another opinion, between them, were two bowls of frankincense. The showbread remained on the table from one Shabbat to the next. Every Shabbat the priests would remove the old bread and replace it with new bread. The old bread was divided among the priests and eaten. The dispute between Rabbi Yosei and the Sages is with regard to the proper interpretation of the word "always" (Exodus 25:30) with regard to the transition from the old loaves to the new ones.

Complete the cutting [*mehalketin*] – מְהַלְּקְטִין: Most commentators explain that this term is related to the word *likkut*, gathering. It refers to the act of taking and cutting. Some of the *ge'onim* explain that the foreskin is similar to a *yalkut*, a sack or covering. Consequently, the word *mehalketin* means the removal of this covering.

מַתְקִיף לָהּ רַב פַּפָּא: אוּמָּן לֵימָא לְהוּ ״אֲנָא עֲבַדִי פַּלְגָא דְּמִצְוָה – אַתּוּן עֲבַדִיתוּ פַּלְגָא דְּמִצְוָה״! אֶלָּא אָמַר רַב פַּפָּא: גָּדוֹל.

Rav Pappa strongly objects to this: Why should the **craftsman** be liable? **Let him say to** those present: **I performed half** the **mitzva;** now **you perform** the other **half** of the **mitzva.** I am not liable, as I was engaged in performance of a mitzva, even though I did not complete it. **Rather, Rav Pappa said:** The reference here is not to circumcision on Shabbat, but rather to the mitzva of circumcision in general. The one liable for *karet* is **an adult** whose circumcision was not completed. He is not considered to have been circumcised according to *halakha*. Therefore, he is punishable by *karet*, like one who was not circumcised at all.

מַתְקִיף לָהּ רַב אַשִׁי: גָּדוֹל בְּהֶדְיָא כְּתִיב בֵּיהּ ״וְעָרֵל זָכָר אֲשֶׁר לֹא יִמּוֹל״! אֶלָּא אָמַר רַב אַשִׁי: לְעוֹלָם אוּמָּן, וּכְגוֹן דַּאֲתָא בֵּין הַשְּׁמָשׁוֹת דְּשַׁבָּת, וַאֲמַרוּ לֵיהּ: לָא מַסְפְּקַתְּ, וַאֲמַר לְהוּ: מַסְפְּקִינָא. וַעֲבַד וְלָא אִיסְתַּפֵּק, וְאִישְׁתַּכַּח דְּחַבּוּרָה הוּא דַּעֲבַד, וְעָנוּשׁ כָּרֵת.

Rav Ashi strongly objects to this: This cannot be, as if so what is the *baraita* teaching? The fact that **an adult** is liable for *karet* is **explicitly written** in the verse: **"And an uncircumcised male who will not circumcise** the flesh of his foreskin, that soul shall be cut off from its people; My covenant he has broken" (Genesis 17:14). **Rather, Rav Ashi said: Actually,** it refers to the **craftsman** who performed the partial circumcision on Shabbat, **and** it is a case **where he came** to perform the circumcision **at twilight**[N] on **Shabbat** day, just before the conclusion of Shabbat, **and** those present **said to him: You will not manage**[H] to complete the circumcision before the conclusion of Shabbat, **and he said to them: I will manage. And he performed** the circumcision **and did not manage** to complete the mitzva before Shabbat ended. **It turns out that he made a wound** in the child but did not fulfill the mitzva. **And** since he was forewarned not to do so, he is therefore **punishable by *karet*** like anyone who violates Shabbat not for the purpose of performing a mitzva.

״מוֹצְצִין וכו׳״. אָמַר רַב פַּפָּא: הַאי אוּמָּנָא דְּלָא מָיֵיץ – סַכָּנָה הוּא, וְעָבְרִינַן לֵיהּ.

We learned in the mishna that **one sucks** blood from the wound after the circumcision was performed on Shabbat. **Rav Pappa said: A craftsman who does not suck**[HB] the blood after every circumcision **is a danger** to the child undergoing circumcision, **and we remove him** from his position as circumcisor.

פְּשִׁיטָא, מִדְּקָא מְחַלְּלִי עֲלֵיהּ שַׁבְּתָא – סַכָּנָה הוּא! מַהוּ דְּתֵימָא: הַאי דָּם מִיפְקָד פָּקִיד, קָא מַשְׁמַע לָן: חַבּוּרֵי מִיחַבַּר.

The Gemara comments: This is **obvious. Given that one desecrates Shabbat** to suck the blood, which involves performance of a prohibited labor, obviously, failure to do so poses **a danger.** Desecration of Shabbat would not be permitted if it was not a life-threatening situation. The Gemara answers: This is not an absolute proof. **Lest you say** that **this blood is collected and contained** in place, and one who removes that which is pooled in its place does not perform the subcategory of the prohibited labor of threshing on Shabbat, i.e., drawing blood; that is the reason sucking the blood is permitted, not due to any danger involved in failing to do so. Therefore, the mishna **teaches us** that this blood **is attached** and flowing and not merely pooled. One who draws it out performs an act that is generally prohibited by Torah law on Shabbat, and it is nonetheless permitted due to danger to the child.

וְדוּמְיָא דְּאִיסְפְּלָנִית וְכַמּוֹן, מָה אִיסְפְּלָנִית וְכַמּוֹן – כִּי לָא עָבֵיד סַכָּנָה הוּא, אַף הָכָא נַמִי – כִּי לָא עָבֵיד – סַכָּנָה הוּא.

And **it is similar** to the *halakhot* of **a bandage and cumin** stated in the mishna. **Just as** in the case of **a bandage and cumin, failure to do** what is necessary with these items poses **a danger** to the child, **here too, if he does not perform** the sucking after circumcision, **it poses a danger** to the child; Shabbat is overridden in cases of danger.

״וְנוֹתְנִין עָלֶיהָ אִיסְפְּלָנִית״. אָמַר אַבַּיֵי, אָמְרָה לִי אֵם: אִיסְפְּלָנִיתָא דְּכוּלְּהוֹן כִּיבֵי – שַׁב מִינָּאי תַּרְבָּא וַחֲדָא קִירָא. רָבָא אֲמַר: קִירָא וְקַלְבָּא רִישִׁינָא.

We learned in the mishna: **And** on Shabbat **one places on** the wound from the circumcision **a bandage. Abaye said: My nurse said to me: A bandage for all wounds** should be made from **seven parts fat**[N] **and one part wax. Rava said:** A bandage should be made from **wax and sap** of a tree.

דְּרָשָׁהּ רָבָא בִּמְחוֹזָא, קַרְעִינְהוּ בְּנֵי מַנְיוֹמֵי אַסְיָא לְמָנַיְיהוּ. אֲמַר לְהוּ: שְׁבַקִי לְכוּ חֲדָא, דַּאֲמַר שְׁמוּאֵל: הַאי מַאן דְּמַשִׁי אַפֵּיהּ וְלָא נַגֵּיב טוּבָא – נִקְטְרוּ לֵיהּ

When **Rava taught** this cure **in Meḥoza, the sons of Manyomei the doctor tore their clothes** in misery, as he taught everyone how to make a bandage, and their services would no longer be required. Rava **said to them: I left you one** cure that I did not reveal, with which you can make a profit, **for Shmuel said: One who washes his face and does not wipe it a lot will develop**

NOTES

Actually, it refers to a craftsman…where he came to perform the circumcision at twilight, etc. – לְעוֹלָם אוּמָּן וּכְגוֹן דַּאֲתָא בֵּין הַשְּׁמָשׁוֹת וכו׳: Some commentaries explain that the Gemara had to resort to the unlikely scenario of one who was warned not to perform the circumcision, ignored the warning, and became liable for *karet* because the unwitting sinner is liable for a sin-offering, not *karet*. We accept the principle that one who erred while engaged in performance of a mitzva, yet performed some aspect of the mitzva, is exempt from a sin-offering. However, if one sinned wittingly in a similar case, he is punishable by *karet* (Rabbi Elazar Moshe Horowitz).

Seven parts fat – שַׁב מִינָּאי תַּרְבָּא: Some commentaries explain that this means seven types of fat from seven different kinds of animals (Rabbi Ya'akov Emden).

HALAKHA

If he came at twilight on Shabbat, and those present said to him: You will not manage, etc. – דַּאֲתָא בֵּין הַשְּׁמָשׁוֹת דְּשַׁבָּת וַאֲמַרוּ לֵיהּ: לָא מַסְפְּקַתְּ וכו׳: If the conclusion of Shabbat is nearing, and a child who is supposed to be circumcised on Shabbat has not yet been circumcised, and people warn the circumcisor that he will not manage to complete the circumcision in time, and he proceeds to circumcise the child on the assumption that he will complete it on time, but he fails to do so, he is liable to bring a sin-offering. He is not punishable with *karet*. Even though he was warned, he did not willfully intend to commit a transgression (Rambam *Sefer Korbanot, Hilkhot Shegagot* 2:9 and in the *Kesef Mishne*).

A craftsman who does not suck – הַאי אוּמָּנָא דְּלָא מָיֵיץ: After removing the foreskin, the person performing the circumcision sucks blood from the wound so that the child does not become dangerously ill. If the circumcisor does not suck the blood, he is removed from his position. Whether or not this procedure can be performed utilizing implements available in modern times is disputed by the later authorities (Rambam *Sefer Ahava, Hilkhot Mila* 2:2; *Shulḥan Arukh, Yoreh De'a* 264:3).

BACKGROUND

Sucking in circumcision – מְצִיצָה בִּבְרִית מִילָה: The purpose of sucking is to prevent the closing of the blood vessels as well as to remove any infection that might have entered the wound by means of the circumcision scalpel.

חַסְפַּנִיתָא. מַאי תַּקַּנְתֵּיהּ? לִימְשֵׁי טוּבָא בְּמַיָּא דְסִילְקָא.

sores on his flesh. **What is his remedy? Let him wash extensively in beet water,** in which beets have been boiled.

״לֹא שָׁחַק מֵעֶרֶב שַׁבָּת״. תָּנוּ רַבָּנַן דְּבָרִים שֶׁאֵין עוֹשִׂין לַמִּילָה בְּשַׁבָּת עוֹשִׂין לָהּ בְּיוֹם טוֹב: שׁוֹחֲקִין לָהּ כַּמּוֹן, וְטוֹרְפִין לָהּ יַיִן וְשֶׁמֶן.

We learned in the mishna: **If one did not grind** the cumin **from Shabbat eve,** he chews it with his teeth and places it on the place of circumcision as a salve. **The Sages taught:** There are **actions that may not be performed** in preparation **for a circumcision on Shabbat** but **may be performed** in preparation **for it on a Festival.** For example: **One grinds cumin for it, and one mixes wine and oil for it.**[NH]

אָמַר לֵיהּ אַבַּיֵי לְרַב יוֹסֵף: מַאי שְׁנָא כַּמּוֹן בְּיוֹם טוֹב – דַּחֲזֵי לִקְדֵרָה, יַיִן וְשֶׁמֶן חֲזֵי נָמֵי בְּשַׁבָּת לְחוֹלֶה! דְּתַנְיָא: אֵין טוֹרְפִין יַיִן וְשֶׁמֶן לְחוֹלֶה בְּשַׁבָּת. אָמַר רַבִּי שִׁמְעוֹן בֶּן אֶלְעָזָר מִשּׁוּם רַבִּי מֵאִיר: אַף טוֹרְפִין יַיִן וְשֶׁמֶן.

Abaye said to Rav Yosef: What is different about cumin that makes it permissible to grind it **on a Festival?** The fact **that it is suitable** for use **to** spice **a pot,** in cooking. Based on that explanation, mixed **wine and oil are also suitable** for use **on Shabbat for a sick person, as it was taught** in a *baraita*: **One may not mix wine and oil for a sick person on Shabbat. Rabbi Shimon ben Elazar said in the name of Rabbi Meir: One may even mix wine and oil** on Shabbat.

אָמַר רַבִּי שִׁמְעוֹן בֶּן אֶלְעָזָר: פַּעַם אַחַת חָשׁ רַבִּי מֵאִיר בְּמֵעָיו, וּבִקַּשְׁנוּ לִטְרוֹף לוֹ יַיִן וְשֶׁמֶן, וְלֹא הִנִּיחָנוּ. אָמַרְנוּ לוֹ: דְּבָרֶיךָ יִבָּטְלוּ בְּחַיֶּיךָ?! אָמַר לָנוּ: אַף עַל פִּי שֶׁאֲנִי אוֹמֵר כָּךְ, וַחֲבֵירַי אוֹמְרִים כָּךְ – מִיָּמַי לֹא מְלָאַנִי לִבִּי לַעֲבוֹר עַל דִּבְרֵי חֲבֵירַי. הוּא נִיהוּ דְּמַחְמִיר אַנַּפְשֵׁיהּ, אֲבָל לְכוּלֵּי עָלְמָא – שָׁרֵי!

Rabbi Shimon ben Elazar said: It happened **on one occasion** that **Rabbi Meir had intestinal pain** on Shabbat, **and we sought to mix wine and oil for him** as treatment **and he did not let us** do so. **We said to him:** Will **your statement be negated in your lifetime?** You permit mixing these ingredients for a sick person. **He said to us: Even though I say this and my colleagues say that,** and I do not retract my statement, still, **in all my days I have never been so presumptuous as to violate the statements of my colleagues** and act in accordance with my opinion. Apparently, **it was he who was stringent** with regard to **himself, but for everyone it is permitted.**[N]

הָתָם לָא בָּעֵי לִיכָּא, הָכָא בָּעֵי לִיכָּא. הָכָא נָמֵי, נִיעָבֵיד וְלָא לִילַךְ! הַיְינוּ דְּקָתָנֵי: נוֹתֵן זֶה בִּפְנֵי עַצְמוֹ וְזֶה בִּפְנֵי עַצְמוֹ.

The Gemara answers that there is a distinction between the cases: **There,** for medicinal purposes, **it need not be beaten,** whereas **here,** for circumcision, **it must be beaten.** The Gemara asks: **Here too, let us prepare** the mixture **but not beat** it.. The Gemara answers: That is in fact the custom, and **that is what** the mishna **teaches: He places this by itself and that by itself,** meaning that he may mix the wine and oil, but he may not beat them.

תָּנוּ רַבָּנַן: אֵין מְסַנְּנִין אֶת הַחַרְדָּל בִּמְסַנֶּנֶת שֶׁלּוֹ וְאֵין מְמַתְּקִין אוֹתוֹ בְּגַחֶלֶת. אָמַר לֵיהּ אַבַּיֵי לְרַב יוֹסֵף: מַאי שְׁנָא מֵהָא דִּתְנַן: נוֹתְנִים בֵּיצָה בִּמְסַנֶּנֶת שֶׁל חַרְדָּל?

The Sages taught with regard to labor on a Festival: **One may not strain mustard in its strainer, and one may not sweeten it with coal. Abaye said to Rav Yosef:** In **what** way **is this different from that which we learned** in a mishna: **One may place an egg in a mustard strainer** on Shabbat?

אָמַר לֵיהּ: הָתָם – לָא מִיחְזֵי כְּבוֹרֵר, הָכָא – מִיחְזֵי כְּבוֹרֵר.

Rav Yosef **said to him:** There is a distinction between the cases, that **there,** in the case of the egg, the act **does not appear like selecting,** whereas **here,** in the case of the mustard, the act **appears like selecting.** Straining an egg does not actually separate it into its component parts. Straining mustard does.

וְאֵין מְמַתְּקִין אוֹתוֹ בְּגַחֶלֶת. וְהָתַנְיָא: מְמַתְּקִין אוֹתוֹ בְּגַחֶלֶת! לָא קַשְׁיָא: כָּאן בְּגַחֶלֶת שֶׁל מַתֶּכֶת כָּאן בְּגַחֶלֶת שֶׁל עֵץ.

We learned that **one may not sweeten** the mustard **with coal.**[H] The Gemara asks: **Wasn't it taught** in a *baraita*: **One may sweeten it with coal.** The Gemara answers: This is **not difficult,** as there is a distinction: **There,** where it is permitted, it is referring to the case **of a metal coal,** as extinguishing metal coals is not prohibited by Torah law, whereas **here,** where it is prohibited, it is referring to the case **of a wooden coal.**

NOTES

And one mixes wine and oil for it – וְטוֹרְפִין לָהּ יַיִן וְשֶׁמֶן: Some authorities explain that the prohibition against using medicine on Shabbat involves two issues: First, preparing the medication for use may involve violation of the Torah prohibition against grinding, and second, there is a rabbinic decree prohibiting use of medicine already prepared. The Rabbis did not prohibit the use of medication on Festivals. Therefore, one may mix wine and oil. According to Rabbi Meir, the mixture is considered food and not medicine; therefore, it may be mixed on Shabbat. However, grinding cumin violates the Torah prohibition against grinding. Therefore, it is prohibited on Shabbat. It is permitted on a Festival only because it can be used for cooking (Rabbi Elazar Moshe Horowitz).

It was he who was stringent with regard to himself, but for everyone it is permitted – הוּא נִיהוּ דְּמַחְמִיר אַנַּפְשֵׁיהּ, אֲבָל לְכוּלֵּי עָלְמָא שָׁרֵי: Among the Sages, it was a common practice that a Sage who issued a lenient ruling in a dispute would not rely on his own ruling because he did not wish to violate the ruling of his colleagues. Nevertheless, he would allow the general public to act in accordance with his more lenient ruling.

HALAKHA

Preparations for circumcision on a Festival – תִּיקּוּנֵי מִילָה בְּיוֹם טוֹב: Any activity that is not actually a component of the mitzva of circumcision per se does not override Shabbat or Festival prohibitions. The exception to this rule is grinding cumin and mixing wine and oil, which may be performed on a Festival (Rambam *Sefer Ahava, Hilkhot Mila* 2:10; *Shulḥan Arukh, Yoreh De'a* 266:6).

Preparing mustard on a Festival – טִיפּוּל בְּחַרְדָּל בְּיוֹם טוֹב: It is prohibited to strain mustard in a strainer on a Festival. One may not sweeten it by extinguishing wooden coals with it. However, it is permitted to sweeten it by extinguishing metal coals with it (Rambam *Sefer Zemanim, Hilkhot Yom Tov* 3:17; *Shulḥan Arukh, Oraḥ Ḥayyim* 510:3).

אָמַר לֵיהּ אַבַּיֵי לְרַב יוֹסֵף: מַאי שְׁנָא מִבִּישְׂרָא אַגּוּמְרֵי? אָמַר לֵיהּ: הָתָם – לָא אֶפְשָׁר, הָכָא – אֶפְשָׁר.

Abaye said to Rav Yosef: In **what** way **is** mustard placed on coals, which is prohibited, **different from meat** placed **on coals,**[N] which is permitted even if the coals are extinguished by the blood dripping from the meat? Rav Yosef **said to** Abaye: The two cases are not similar, as **there,** with regard to meat, **it is not possible** to accomplish this in any other way, but **here,** with regard to mustard, **it is possible** to accomplish this in another way.

אָמַר לֵיהּ אַבַּיֵי לְרַב יוֹסֵף: מַהוּ לְגַבֵּן? אָמַר לֵיהּ: אָסוּר. מַאי שְׁנָא מִלִּישָׁה? אָמַר לֵיהּ: הָתָם – לָא אֶפְשָׁר, הָכָא – אֶפְשָׁר.

Abaye said to Rav Yosef: What is the *halakha* with regard to whether it is permissible **to curdle** cheese on a Festival?[HN] **He said to him: It is prohibited.** Abaye asked: In **what** way **is** this **different from kneading** dough, which is permitted on a Festival? Rav Yosef **said to him: There,** with regard to dough, **it is not possible** to bake bread before a Festival, as day-old bread is inferior to fresh bread. Therefore, kneading dough to bake bread on a Festival is permitted. **Here,** with regard to cheese, **it is possible** to curdle cheese before a Festival and it will not deteriorate in any way.

וְהָא אָמְרִי נְהַרְדְּעֵי: גְּבִינָה בַּת יוֹמָא מַעַלְיָא! הָכִי קָאָמְרִי: דַּאֲפִילּוּ גְּבִינָה בַּת יוֹמָא מַעַלְיָא.

Abaye challenged this distinction: **Didn't** the Sages of **Neharde'a say** that **one-day-old cheese** is **excellent?** Curdling cheese on a Festival should be permitted? Rav Yosef responded: **This is what they are saying: Even one-day-old cheese** is **excellent;** however, cheese that aged longer is better. Therefore, they did not permit curdling cheese on a Festival, as it is not necessary for the Festival.

״אֵין עוֹשִׂין לָהּ חָלוּק כו׳״. אָמַר אַבַּיֵי, אָמְרָה לִי אֵם: הַאי חָלוּק דִּינוּקָא – לְפַנְיֵיהּ לְסִיטְרָא לְעִילָּאֵי, דִּילְמָא מִידְּבִיק גַּרְדָּא מִינֵּיהּ וְאָתֵי לִידֵי כְּרוּת שָׁפְכָה. אִימֵּיהּ דְּאַבַּיֵי עָבְדָא כִּיסְתָּתָא לְפַלְגָא. אָמַר אַבַּיֵי: הַאי יְנוּקָא דְּלֵית לֵיהּ חָלוּק – לַיְיתֵי בְּלִיתָא דְּאִית לֵיהּ שִׂיפְתָּא, וְלִיכַּרְכֵיהּ לְשִׂיפְתָּא לְתַתַּאי, וְעָיֵיף לֵיהּ לְעִילָּאֵי.

We learned in the mishna: **And** on Shabbat **one may not make a pouch** to place over the circumcision as a bandage *ab initio.* **Abaye said: My mother,** actually his foster mother who was the nursemaid who raised him, **told me:** With regard to **that pouch,** placed as a bandage over the circumcision **of a baby, let one place it on the upper side** with the threads below, **lest a thread from it stick to** the place of circumcision and cause the baby **to become** one with **a severed urethra.** The Gemara relates that **Abaye's mother would make a pouch** that covered **half** the place of circumcision so that it would not be damaged through contact with the threads emerging from the edge of the pouch. **Abaye said:** If **this baby does not have a pouch** to put on the place of the circumcision, **let one bring a worn-out garment with a hem, and wrap the hem under, and fold** the garment **over,** so that the threads from the worn-out garment will not adhere to the wound.

וַאֲמַר אַבַּיֵי אָמְרָה לִי אֵם: הַאי יְנוּקָא דְּלָא יְדִיעַ מַפַּקְתֵּיהּ – לְשַׁיְיפֵיהּ מִישְׁחָא, וְלוּקְמֵיהּ לַהֲדֵי יוֹמָא, וְהֵיכָא דְּזִיג לִיקַרְעֵיהּ בִּשְׂעַרְתָּא שְׁתִי וָעֵרֶב. אֲבָל בִּכְלִי מַתָּכוֹת – לָא, מִשּׁוּם דְּזָרֵיף. וַאֲמַר אַבַּיֵי, אָמְרָה לִי אֵם: הַאי יְנוּקָא דְּלָא מָיֵיץ – מֵיקַר דְּקָר פּוּמֵּיהּ, מַאי תַּקַּנְתֵּיהּ – לַיְתוּ כָּסָא גּוּמְרֵי, וְלִינַקְטֵיהּ לֵיהּ לַהֲדֵי פּוּמֵּיהּ, דְּחָיֵים פּוּמֵּיהּ וּמָיֵיץ. וַאֲמַר אַבַּיֵי אָמְרָה לִי אֵם: הַאי יְנוּקָא דְּלָא מְנַשְׁתֵּיהּ – לִינַפְּפֵיהּ בְּנַפְוָותָא וּמְנַשְׁתֵּיהּ.

And Abaye also **said: My mother told me:** In the case **of a baby** the location of **whose exit,** i.e., anus, **is unknown,**[B] as it is obscured by skin, **let one rub it with oil and stand it before** the light **of the day. And where** it appears **transparent, let one tear it with a barley grain widthwise and lengthwise. However,** one may **not** tear it **with a metal implement because it causes infection and swelling. And Abaye said** that **my mother told me:** If **a baby refuses to nurse,**[B] that is because **its mouth is cold** and it is unable to nurse. **What is his remedy? They should bring a cup** of **coals and place it near his mouth, so that his mouth will warm and he will nurse. And Abaye said** that **my mother told me:** A **baby that does not urinate, let one place him in a sieve** and shake him, **and he will urinate.**

HALAKHA

What is the *halakha* with regard to whether it is permissible to curdle cheese on a Festival – מַהוּ לְגַבֵּן: One may not prepare cheese on a Festival, even to be eaten on the Festival, because it can be done the day before (*Shulḥan Arukh, Oraḥ Ḥayyim* 510:5).

BACKGROUND

A baby whose exit is unknown – יְנוּקָא דְּלָא יְדִיעַ מַפַּקְתֵּיהּ: The Gemara refers to a congenital defect known as *atresia ani*, the obstruction of the anal cavity. This defect can be surgically corrected.

A baby that refuses to nurse – תִּינוֹק שֶׁאֵינוֹ יוֹנֵק: Occasionally, cold temperatures can suppress muscular activity, including in the mouth. Consequently, the baby is unable to nurse. Warming the child helps in those cases.

NOTES

Meat on coals – בִּישְׂרָא אַגּוּמְרֵי: Some commentaries explain that placing meat on top of hot coals on a Festival is not a direct violation of the labor of extinguishing, because the fire ultimately burns stronger. The Sages permitted roasting meat in this manner, as no Torah prohibition is violated. According to this approach, there is a variant reading of the Gemara: There, there is no extinguishing; here, there is extinguishing (Rif).

Others authorities state that the labor of extinguishing is also permitted on a Festival if extinguishing is required for food preparation, with the following caveat: If the food could have been prepared beforehand, it may not be prepared on a Festival. However, if preparing the food prior to the Festival would produce food not as tasty as food prepared on the Festival, it is even permitted to extinguish a fire in its preparation (Rabbeinu Zeraḥya HaLevi).

What is the *halakha* with regard to whether it is permissible to curdle cheese on a Festival – מַהוּ לְגַבֵּן: Some explain the statement that kneading is not possible, whereas curdling is possible as follows: Flour itself is inedible in its current form, whereas the raw material of cheese, i.e., milk, can be legitimately consumed in its present state (Rabbeinu Zeraḥya HaLevi).

ואמר אביי אמרה לי אם: האי ינוקא דלא מעוי – ליתו סליתא דאימיה, ולישרקיה עילויה ומעוי. ואמר אביי, אמרה לי אם: האי ינוקא דקטין – לייתו לסילתא דאימיה, ולישרקיה עילויה מקוטנא לאולמא. ואי אלים – מאולמא לקוטנא. ואמר אביי, אמרה לי אם: האי ינוקא דסומק – דאכתי לא איבלע ביה דמא, ליתרחו ליה עד דאיבלע ביה דמא ולימהלוה. דירוק ואכתי לא נפל ביה דמיה – ליתרחו עד דנפל ביה דמיה, ולימהלוה.

And Abaye said: My nurse told me: If a baby is not breathing, let them bring his mother's placenta and place the placenta **on him, and** the baby **will breathe. And Abaye said** that **my mother told me: If a baby is too small, let them bring his mother's placenta and rub** the baby **with it from the narrow** end **to the wide** end of the placenta. **And if** the baby **is strong,** i.e., too large, let them rub the baby **from the wide** end of the placenta **to the narrow** end. **And Abaye said** that **my mother told me: If a baby is red,** that is because **the blood has not yet been absorbed in him.** In that case, **let them wait until his blood is absorbed and then circumcise him.** Likewise, if a baby is **pale and his blood has not yet entered him, let them wait until his blood enters him and then circumcise him.**

דתניא, אמר רבי נתן: פעם אחת הלכתי לכרכי הים ובאת אשה אחת לפני, שמלה בנה ראשון ומת, שני ומת, שלישי הביאתו לפני. ראיתיו שהוא אדום. אמרתי לה: המתיני לו עד שיבלע בו דמו. המתינה לו עד שנבלע בו דמו, ומלה אותו וחיה. והיו קורין אותו "נתן הבבלי" על שמי.

As it was taught in a *baraita*, **Rabbi Natan said: On one occasion, I went to the coastal cities, and one woman came before me who circumcised her first son and he died,** and she circumcised her **second** son **and he died,** and since she feared circumcising the **third** due to concern that he might die as well, **she brought him before me. I saw that he was red. I said to her: Wait until his blood is absorbed into him. She waited until his blood was absorbed into him and then circumcised him, and he lived. And they would call him Natan the Babylonian after my name.**

שוב פעם אחת הלכתי למדינת קפוטקיא, ובאת אשה אחת לפני, שמלה בנה ראשון ומת, שני ומת, שלישי הביאתו לפני. ראיתיו שהוא ירוק. הצצתי בו ולא ראיתי בו דם ברית. אמרתי לה: המתיני לו עד שיפול בו דמו. והמתינה לו, ומלה אותו וחיה, והיו קורין שמו "נתן הבבלי" על שמי.

Rabbi Natan further related: **On another occasion I went to the state of Cappadocia, and a woman came before me** who **circumcised her first son and he died,** and she circumcised her **second** son **and he died.** Since she feared circumcising the **third** due to concern that he might die as well, **she brought him before me. I saw that he was pale.**[B] **I looked at him and I could not see in him the blood of the covenant,** i.e., he had a blood deficiency. **I said to her: Wait until blood enters him. And she waited and then circumcised him,**[H] **and he lived. And they would call his name Natan the Babylonian after my name.**

BACKGROUND

The red and pale child – הילד האדום והירוק: Several medical explanations were proposed to identify the diseases from which the babies seen by Rabbi Natan were suffering. With regard to the child who was red, some presume that the children of that family suffered from a rare hereditary blood disease known as purple disease, *purpura hemorrhagica*. The child who was pale was probably sick with hemolytic jaundice of the newborn, which is also hereditary.

HALAKHA

The circumcision of a sick baby – מילת תינוק חולה: If a baby displays signs of possible illness, and the circumcision might be dangerous, the baby is not circumcised at the appointed time. For example, if the baby is too pale or too red, the circumcision is postponed until he is healthy enough to be circumcised. This ruling is in accordance with Abaye's statement in the name of his nursemaid and the incidents involving Rabbi Natan (Rambam *Sefer Ahava, Hilkhot Mila* 1:17; *Shulḥan Arukh, Yoreh De'a* 263:1).

Perek **XIX**
Daf **134** Amud **b**

מתני׳ מרחיצין את הקטן, בין לפני המילה ובין לאחר המילה. ומזלפין עליו ביד, אבל לא בכלי. רבי אלעזר בן עזריה אומר: מרחיצין את הקטן ביום השלישי שחל להיות בשבת, שנאמר "ויהי ביום השלישי בהיותם כואבים".

MISHNA **One may wash the baby** on Shabbat, **both before the circumcision and after the circumcision.**[H] **And one may sprinkle** hot water **on him by hand but not with a vessel,** in order to depart from the usual manner in which this is done. **Rabbi Elazar ben Azarya says: One may wash the baby on the third day** following his circumcision, even if **that** third day **occurs on Shabbat.** On the third day following circumcision, the baby is considered to be in danger, **as it is stated** with regard to the men of Shekhem, who were circumcised: **"And it came to pass on the third day, when they were in pain"** (Genesis 34:25). This teaches us that on the third day the pain of circumcision poses a danger.[N]

ספק ואנדרוגינוס – אין מחללין עליו את השבת. ורבי יהודה מתיר באנדרוגינוס.

If there is **uncertainty** whether or not to circumcise a baby, **and** likewise in the case of **a hermaphrodite** [*androginos*][L] baby, who possesses both male and female genitals, **one does not desecrate Shabbat** to perform the circumcision, since it is not certain that the circumcision is required. **And Rabbi Yehuda permits** doing so **for a hermaphrodite** baby.

HALAKHA

Washing the circumcised baby – הרחצת התינוק הנימול: During the talmudic era, failure to wash a baby in hot water both before and after the circumcision, as well as on the third day following the circumcision, was deemed life-threatening. Nowadays, this practice is no longer followed. Therefore, if one wishes to wash the child on Shabbat, the standard restrictions that apply to washing any other person apply to the child as well. The Rema writes: In our countries, the custom is to wash him before the circumcision in hot water prepared the day before. After the circumcision, the custom is to wait and wash him after Shabbat has ended. If the third day after his circumcision occurs on Shabbat and it will be necessary to wash him, hot water is prepared the day before and the child is washed on Shabbat. The Rema adds that in a case where there is potential danger if he is not washed, it is permitted to heat water for him on Shabbat. The same applies with regard to any sick person whose life is in danger (Rambam *Sefer Ahava, Hilkhot Mila* 2:8 and *Sefer Zemanim, Hilkhot Shabbat* 2:14; *Shulḥan Arukh, Oraḥ Ḥayyim* 331:9 and in the comment of the Rema).

NOTES

On the third day – ביום השלישי: The commentaries and halakhic authorities disagree over the significance of the third day after circumcision. According to Rashi, Rabbeinu Ḥananel, and most other commentaries, the baby remains in danger on the third day, and Shabbat prohibitions should be overridden so that he can be washed. This certainly applies on the first and second days as well, as the child has had even less time to recuperate. Others authorities, including the Rambam, state that this law refers specifically to the third day, not to the second, because the pain of the wound increases on the third day. There is support for this explanation in *Pirkei DeRabbi Eliezer* and elsewhere.

LANGUAGE

Hermaphrodite [*androginos*] – אנדרוגינוס: From the Greek ἀνδρόγυνος, *androgynos*, meaning a man-woman, i.e., a creature with attributes of both genders.

גמ׳ וְהָא אָמְרַתְּ רֵישָׁא ׳מַרְחִיצִין׳!

GEMARA The Gemara questions the mishna's statement that one may sprinkle hot water on the baby only by hand: **Didn't you say** in the **first clause** of the mishna that **one may wash** him? If it is permissible to wash the baby, it is certainly permitted to sprinkle water on him with a vessel.

רַב יְהוּדָה וְרַבָּה בַּר אֲבוּהּ דְּאָמְרִי תַּרְוַיְיהוּ: ״כֵּיצַד״ תָּנֵי; מַרְחִיצִין אֶת הַקָּטָן בֵּין לִפְנֵי מִילָה בֵּין לְאַחַר מִילָה, כֵּיצַד – מְזַלְּפִין עָלָיו בַּיָּד, אֲבָל לֹא בַּכְּלִי.

It was **Rav Yehuda and Rabba bar Avuh who both said** that this mishna **is taught** employing the style known as: **How.** In this style, the latter clause clarifies the former. It should be understood as follows: **One may wash the baby both before circumcision and after circumcision. How** may one wash him? **One sprinkles** water **on him by hand, but not with a vessel.**

אֲמַר רָבָא: וְהָא ׳מַרְחִיצִין׳ קָתָנֵי! אֶלָּא אָמַר רָבָא, הָכִי קָתָנֵי: מַרְחִיצִין אֶת הַקָּטָן בֵּין מִלִּפְנֵי מִילָה בֵּין לְאַחַר הַמִּילָה, בַּיּוֹם הָרִאשׁוֹן – כְּדַרְכּוֹ, וּבַיּוֹם הַשְּׁלִישִׁי שֶׁחָל לִהְיוֹת בַּשַּׁבָּת – מְזַלְּפִין עָלָיו בַּיָּד, אֲבָל לֹא בַּכְּלִי. רַבִּי אֶלְעָזָר בֶּן עֲזַרְיָה אוֹמֵר: מַרְחִיצִין אֶת הַקָּטָן בַּיּוֹם הַשְּׁלִישִׁי שֶׁחָל לִהְיוֹת בַּשַּׁבָּת, שֶׁנֶּאֱמַר ״וַיְהִי בַיּוֹם הַשְּׁלִישִׁי בִּהְיוֹתָם כּוֹאֲבִים״.

Rava said: Doesn't it teach the phrase **one may wash,** and washing is not sprinkling. **Rather, Rava said that this is** what the mishna **is teaching: One may wash the baby, both before circumcision and after circumcision. On the first day,** one may wash him **in his** usual **manner. However, on the third day** following his circumcision, if **that** third day **occurs on Shabbat, one may sprinkle** water **on him** only **by hand, but not with a vessel,** and one may certainly not wash him. **Rabbi Elazar ben Azarya says: One may** even **wash the baby on the third day** following his circumcision, if **that** third day **occurs on Shabbat,** because the baby is considered to be in a state of danger, as **it is stated: "And it came to pass on the third day, when they were in pain."**

תַּנְיָא כְּוָותֵיהּ דְּרָבָא: מַרְחִיצִין הַקָּטָן בֵּין לִפְנֵי מִילָה בֵּין לְאַחַר מִילָה, בְּיוֹם רִאשׁוֹן – כְּדַרְכּוֹ, וּבַיּוֹם הַשְּׁלִישִׁי שֶׁחָל לִהְיוֹת בַּשַּׁבָּת – מְזַלְּפִין עָלָיו בַּיָּד, רַבִּי אֶלְעָזָר בֶּן עֲזַרְיָה אוֹמֵר: מַרְחִיצִין אֶת הַקָּטָן בַּיּוֹם הַשְּׁלִישִׁי שֶׁחָל לִהְיוֹת בַּשַּׁבָּת, וְאַף עַל פִּי שֶׁאֵין רְאָיָה לַדָּבָר – זֵכֶר לַדָּבָר, שֶׁנֶּאֱמַר ״וַיְהִי בַיּוֹם הַשְּׁלִישִׁי בִּהְיוֹתָם כּוֹאֲבִים״.

A *baraita* **was taught in accordance with** the opinion of **Rava: One may wash the baby, both before circumcision** and **after circumcision. On the first day,** the baby is washed **in its** usual **manner; and on the third day that occurs on Shabbat, one sprinkles** water **on him by hand but not with a vessel,** and one may not wash him. **Rabbi Elazar ben Azarya says: One may** even **wash the baby on the third day that occurs on Shabbat. And although there is no** absolute **proof for** this **matter,** there is **an allusion to** this **matter,** as **it is stated: "And it came to pass on the third day, when they were in pain."**

וּכְשֶׁהֵן מְזַלְּפִין – אֵין מְזַלְּפִין לֹא בְּכוֹס וְלֹא בִּקְעָרָה וְלֹא בִּכְלִי, אֶלָּא בַּיָּד. אֲתָאן לְתַנָּא קַמָּא.

The *baraita* continues: **And when one sprinkles** water, **he may not sprinkle** it **with a cup or with a bowl or with** any other **vessel; rather,** he does so **by hand.** The Gemara comments: **We have arrived at** the opinion of the **first *tanna*,** as this clarification of how the sprinkling was performed is not in accordance with the opinion of Rabbi Elazar ben Azarya. Rather, it is an elaboration of the statement of the first *tanna*.

מַאי ״אַף עַל פִּי שֶׁאֵין רְאָיָה לַדָּבָר זֵכֶר לַדָּבָר״? מִשּׁוּם דְּגָדוֹל – לָא סָלֵיק בִּישְׂרָא הַיָּיא, קָטָן – סָלֵיק בֵּיהּ בִּישְׂרָא הַיָּיא.

The Gemara comments: **What** is the meaning of the *baraita's* statement: **And although there is no** absolute **proof for** this **matter,** there is **an allusion to** this **matter?** Why does the *baraita* refer to it as a mere allusion when it appears to offer absolute proof that the pain of circumcision is significant on the third day? The Gemara answers: Indeed, it is not a complete proof, **because an adult's flesh does not heal immediately,** but **a child's flesh heals immediately.** Perhaps a baby is not considered to be in danger on the third day.

הַהוּא דַּאֲתָא לְקַמֵּיהּ דְּרָבָא, אוֹרֵי לֵיהּ כִּשְׁמַעְתֵּיהּ. אִיחֲלַשׁ רָבָא. אֲמַר אֲנָא בַּהֲדֵי תַּרְגִּימְנָא דְּסָבֵי לָמָּה לִי?

The Gemara relates: **A certain** person **came before Rava** to ask a question with regard to washing a baby after circumcision. **Rava ruled in accordance with its halakhic** ruling, that everyone agrees that it is permitted to wash the baby on the first day. Afterward, **Rava became ill.** He **said: Why** did **I** involve myself **in the opinions of the Elders?** The Sages of the previous generation, Rav Yehuda and Rabba bar Avuh, articulated the *halakha* in a different, more stringent manner. Rava felt that his illness was divine punishment for taking their opinions lightly.

אֲמַרוּ לֵיהּ רַבָּנַן לְרָבָא: וְהַתַנְיָא כְּוָותֵיהּ דְּמָר! אֲמַר לְהוּ מַתְנִיתִין כְּוָותַיְיהוּ דַּיְקָא.

The Sages said to Rava: Wasn't it taught in the *baraita* **in accordance with the** opinion of the **Master,** so why are you concerned with regard to your ruling, which is correct? Rava **said to them: The** language of the **mishna is precise according to their** opinion.

ממאי – מדקאמר "רבי אלעזר בן עזריה אומר: מרחיצין את הקטן ביום השלישי שחל להיות בשבת". אי אמרת בשלמא תנא קמא מזלפין קאמר – היינו דקאמר ליה רבי אלעזר בן עזריה מרחיצין, אלא אי אמרת תנא קמא מרחיצין ביום הראשון קאמר, ומזלפין ביום השלישי – האי "רבי אלעזר בן עזריה אומר מרחיצין?" "אף מרחיצין" מיבעי ליה.

From where can this be concluded? **From the fact that it is stated: Rabbi Elazar ben Azarya says: One may wash the baby on the third day that occurs on Shabbat. Granted, if you say** that the **first *tanna* is saying** only that **one may sprinkle,** but prohibited washing the baby even on the first day, **that** explains **what Rabbi Elazar ben Azarya said to him** in response: **One may wash. However, if you say** that the **first *tanna* is saying one may wash on the first day and one may sprinkle on the third day, this** statement: **Rabbi Elazar ben Azarya says** that **one may wash,** is imprecise. Rather, **he should have** said that **one may even wash**[N] on the third day. Rabbi Elazar ben Azarya is not disputing whether it is ever permitted to wash the baby, as the first *tanna* also agrees that it is permitted on the first day; the dispute is whether or not that leniency extends to the third day as well. Since a precise reading of the mishna supports the opinion of Rav Yehuda and Rabba bar Avuh, the *baraita* supporting Rava's opinion is not sufficiently authoritative to supplant that understanding.

כי אתא רב דימי אמר רבי אלעזר: הלכה כרבי אלעזר בן עזריה.

When Rav Dimi came from Eretz Yisrael to Babylonia, he said that **Rabbi Elazar said: The *halakha* is in accordance with** the opinion of **Rabbi Elazar ben Azarya.**

הוו בה במערבא: הרחצת כל גופו או הרחצת מילה?

They discussed the following question **in the West,** in Eretz Yisrael:[N] Is this referring to **washing the entire body** of the baby, **or** to **washing the** place of **the circumcision?**

אמר להו ההוא מרבנן, ורבי יעקב שמיה: מסתברא, הרחצת כל גופו. דאי סלקא דעתך הרחצת מילה – מי גרע מחמין על גבי מכה, דאמר רב: אין מונעין חמין ושמן מעל גבי מכה בשבת.

One of the Sages, named Rabbi Ya'akov, said to them: It stands to reason that it is referring to **washing his entire body, as if it should enter your mind** that the dispute is with regard to **washing** the place of **the circumcision, is this** washing any **worse than** placing **hot water on a wound? Rav said: One does not prevent** placing **hot water and oil on a wound on Shabbat.** Therefore, it should certainly be permissible to wash the place of the circumcision.

מתקיף לה רב יוסף: ולא שני לך בין חמין שהוחמו בשבת לחמין שהוחמו מערב שבת?!

Rav Yosef strongly objects to this proof: **And is there no difference for you between hot water heated on Shabbat and hot water heated on Shabbat eve?** Placing hot water heated on Shabbat eve on a wound violates only the rabbinic decree prohibiting healing; whereas heating hot water on Shabbat violates a Torah prohibition.

מתקיף לה רב דימי: וממאי דהכא בחמין שהוחמו בשבת פליגי, דילמא בחמין שהוחמו בערב שבת פליגי?! אמר אביי: אנא בעאי דאישני ליה, וקדם ושני ליה רב יוסף: מפני שסכנה הוא לו.

Rav Dimi strongly objects to Rav Yosef's point: **And from where** do you know **that here** it is **with regard to hot water heated on Shabbat** that **they disagree? Perhaps** it is **with regard to hot water heated on Shabbat eve** that **they disagree. Abaye said: I wanted to answer him, but Rav Yosef answered him first:** The dispute is certainly with regard to heating water on Shabbat, **because** failure to do so poses **a danger for** the baby.

איתמר נמי, כי אתא רבין אמר רבי אבהו אמר רבי אלעזר, ואמרי לה אמר רבי אבהו אמר רבי יוחנן: הלכה כרבי אלעזר בן עזריה, בין בחמין שהוחמו בשבת בין בחמין שהוחמו מערב שבת, בין הרחצת כל גופו, בין הרחצת מילה – מפני שסכנה היא לו.

It was also stated that **when Ravin came** to Babylonia from Eretz Yisrael, he said that **Rabbi Abbahu said** that **Rabbi Elazar said, and others say** that **Rabbi Abbahu said** that **Rabbi Yoḥanan said: The *halakha* is in accordance** with the opinion of **Rabbi Elazar ben Azarya, both with regard to hot water heated on Shabbat and with regard to hot water heated on Shabbat eve; both** with regard to **washing the entire body and** with regard to **washing** the place of the **circumcision** alone, **because** failure to do so poses **a danger for** the baby.[N]

גופא, אמר רב: אין מונעין חמין ושמן מעל גבי מכה בשבת. ושמואל אמר: נותן חוץ למכה, ושותת ויורד למכה.

Rav's statement with regard to the treatment of a wound on Shabbat was mentioned in passing. The Gemara proceeds to discuss the **matter itself. Rav said: One does not prevent** placing **hot water and oil on a wound on Shabbat. And Shmuel said:** It is prohibited to place hot water or oil directly onto the wound, because it appears to be medical treatment. Rather, **one places** the hot water or the oil **outside the wound,** above it, **and it flows and descends to the wound** itself.

מיתיבי: אין נותנין שמן וחמין על גבי מוך ליתן על גבי מכה בשבת! התם משום סחיטה.

The Gemara **raises an objection** from that which was taught in a *baraita*: **One may not place oil or hot water on soft material to place** it **on a wound**[H] **on Shabbat.** This supports the opinion of Shmuel, who prohibits performing actions that appear to be medical treatment. However, that ruling contradicts the opinion of Rav. The Gemara answers: **There,** the *baraita* prohibited placing oil or hot water on a rag, not because it appears to be medical treatment; **rather,** it is prohibited **due to** concern that one might perform the prohibited labor of **squeezing.**

NOTES

One may even wash – אף מרחיצין: The *baraita* cited above states explicitly: One may wash, which is in accordance with the opinion of Rava. That should serve as indication that the inference from the mishna is invalid. Some explain that based on the inference in the mishna, Rava arrived at a variant reading of the entire *baraita*, which conforms to the inference from the mishna (Rashba and others). Alternately, the wording of the *baraita* is not as authoritative and reliable as that of the mishna.

They discussed the following question in the West – הוו בה במערבא: Indeed, this dilemma is raised in the Jerusalem Talmud, where a dispute is cited between two *amora'im* who had different opinions with regard to this matter.

Washing the baby in hot water – רחיצת התינוק בחמין: At least one question was disputed by halakhic authorities from the times of the *ge'onim* and onward without resolution: Is it permissible to heat water on Shabbat in order to wash the child before circumcision? Some of the *ge'onim* were inclined to permit heating water before circumcision, and all the more so after the circumcision. However, most subsequent authorities raised doubts about these rulings, even the allowance to heat water after the circumcision, unless there was clear danger to the life of the baby. They certainly did not permit heating water before the circumcision. See the *Halakha* notes; this matter resolved itself over time as the practice to wash the baby before and after circumcision was no longer customary.

HALAKHA

Oil and hot water on a wound – שמן וחמין מעל גבי המכה: On Shabbat, one may not place a mixture of oil and hot water on top of a wound, but he may place it near a wound so it flows and descends into the wound, in accordance with the opinion of Shmuel, since the *baraita* supports him (Rambam *Sefer Zemanim*, *Hilkhot Shabbat* 21:26; *Shulḥan Arukh*, *Oraḥ Ḥayyim* 328:22).

HALAKHA

One may place a dry compress…on a wound, etc. – נוֹתְנִין עַל גַּבֵּי הַמַּכָּה מוֹךְ יָבֵשׁ וכו׳: Contrary to Rashi's explanation that appears in the Gemara, it is permitted to wrap a wound with swatches of new fabric on Shabbat, since they do not heal but only protect the wound. However, old rags may not be used, because they have a medicinal effect. If they have already been used to dress a wound, it is permitted to reuse them, because they no longer have a medicinal effect (Rambam *Sefer Zemanim, Hilkhot Shabbat* 21:26; *Shulḥan Arukh, Oraḥ Ḥayyim* 328:23).

תָּא שְׁמַע: אֵין נוֹתְנִין חַמִּין וָשֶׁמֶן עַל גַּבֵּי מוֹךְ שֶׁעַל גַּבֵּי מַכָּה בַּשַּׁבָּת! הָתָם נַמִי מִשּׁוּם סְחִיטָה.

The Gemara cites an additional proof. **Come** and **hear** that which was taught in a similar *baraita*: **One may not place oil or hot water on soft material that is on a wound on Shabbat.** This *baraita* supports the opinion of Shmuel. The Gemara answers: **There too,** it is prohibited **due to** concern for **squeezing.**

תַּנְיָא כְּוָותֵיהּ דִּשְׁמוּאֵל: אֵין נוֹתְנִין חַמִּין וָשֶׁמֶן עַל גַּבֵּי מַכָּה בַּשַּׁבָּת, אֲבָל נוֹתְנִין חוּץ לַמַּכָּה, וְשׁוֹתֵת וְיוֹרֵד לַמַּכָּה.

A *baraita* **was taught** explicitly **in accordance with** the opinion of **Shmuel: One may not place oil or hot water on a wound on Shabbat; however, one may place it outside the wound so it flows and descends to the wound.**

תָּנוּ רַבָּנַן: נוֹתְנִין עַל גַּבֵּי הַמַּכָּה מוֹךְ יָבֵשׁ וּסְפוֹג יָבֵשׁ, אֲבָל לֹא גֶּמִי יָבֵשׁ וְלֹא כְּתִיתִין יְבֵשִׁין. קַשְׁיָא כְּתִיתִין אַכְּתִיתִין! לֹא קַשְׁיָא, הָא – בַּחֲדָתֵי, הָא – בְּעַתִּיקֵי, אָמַר אַבָּיֵי: שְׁמַע מִינַּהּ – הָנֵי כְּתִיתִין מָסוּ.

The Sages taught another *baraita*: **One may place a dry compress and a dry sponge on a wound,**[H] **but not a dry reed and not dry rags.** The Gemara comments: This is **difficult,** as the first statement with regard to **rags,** i.e, a dry compress which is a type of rag, contradicts the second statement with regard to **rags,** as the *baraita* first permitted placing rags on a wound and then prohibited doing so. The Gemara answers: This is **not difficult. This** statement, which prohibits placing rags on a wound, is referring **to new** rags, which heal the wound; **that** statement, which permits placing rags on a wound, is referring **to old** rags, which are not effective in healing. **Abaye said: Conclude from this** that **these rags heal,** which is useful information with regard to the treatment of wounds.

״סָפֵק וְאַנְדְּרוֹגִינוֹס כו׳״. תָּנוּ רַבָּנַן: ׳עָרְלָתוֹ׳ – עָרְלָתוֹ וַדַּאי דּוֹחָה אֶת הַשַּׁבָּת,

We learned in the mishna: If there is **uncertainty** whether or not to circumcise a baby, **and** likewise in the case of **a hermaphrodite** baby, one does not desecrate Shabbat to perform the circumcision of **a hermaphrodite,** even on the eighth day following the birth. **The Sages taught** in a *baraita*: The verse states: "And on the eighth day the flesh of his foreskin shall be circumcised" (Leviticus 12:3), and they interpreted the verse: **"His foreskin"** indicates that only the circumcision of **his** halakhically **certain foreskin overrides Shabbat,**

Perek **XIX**
Daf **135** Amud **a**

BACKGROUND

Born circumcised – נוֹלַד מָהוּל: Occasionally, a baby is born without a foreskin. This is caused by the degeneration of the foreskin, and in this respect, the medical assessment would agree with the view expressed in the Gemara that one born circumcised has a type of concealed foreskin.

וְלֹא סָפֵק דּוֹחֶה אֶת הַשַּׁבָּת. עָרְלָתוֹ וַדַּאי דּוֹחָה אֶת הַשַּׁבָּת, וְלֹא אַנְדְּרוֹגִינוֹס דּוֹחֶה אֶת הַשַּׁבָּת.

and the circumcision of a halakhically **uncertain** foreskin **does not override Shabbat.** And by means of the same inference from the term his foreskin, derive that circumcision of **his definite foreskin overrides Shabbat, and** circumcising the foreskin of **a hermaphrodite** baby,[H] with regard to whom there is uncertainty whether or not circumcision is required, **does not override Shabbat.**

רַבִּי יְהוּדָה אוֹמֵר: אַנְדְּרוֹגִינוֹס דּוֹחֶה אֶת הַשַּׁבָּת וְעָנוּשׁ כָּרֵת. עָרְלָתוֹ וַדַּאי דּוֹחָה אֶת הַשַּׁבָּת, וְלֹא נוֹלַד בֵּין הַשְּׁמָשׁוֹת דּוֹחֶה אֶת הַשַּׁבָּת. עָרְלָתוֹ וַדַּאי דּוֹחָה אֶת הַשַּׁבָּת, וְלֹא נוֹלַד כְּשֶׁהוּא מָהוּל דּוֹחֶה אֶת הַשַּׁבָּת. שֶׁבֵּית שַׁמַּאי אוֹמְרִים: צָרִיךְ לְהַטִּיף מִמֶּנּוּ דַּם בְּרִית, וּבֵית הִלֵּל אוֹמְרִים: אֵינוֹ צָרִיךְ.

Rabbi Yehuda says: The circumcision of **a hermaphrodite overrides Shabbat, and** if he is not circumcised, when he reaches majority **he is punishable by *karet*.** Rabbi Yehuda interprets the verse in the following manner: **His definite foreskin overrides Shabbat; however,** the circumcision of one **born at twilight**[H] **does not override Shabbat.** And likewise, **his definite foreskin overrides Shabbat; however,** the circumcision of one **who was born circumcised,**[H] i.e., without a foreskin,[B] **does not override Shabbat.** With regard to a child in that condition, there is a dispute between Beit Shammai and Beit Hillel, **as Beit Shammai say: It is necessary to drip covenantal blood from him,** in lieu of circumcision of the foreskin, **and Beit Hillel say: It is not necessary,** as he is already circumcised.

HALAKHA

Circumcising a hermaphrodite baby – מִילַת אַנְדְּרוֹגִינוֹס: The circumcision of a hermaphrodite does not override Shabbat, in accordance with the opinion of the Rabbis (Rambam *Sefer Ahava, Hilkhot Mila* 1:11; *Shulḥan Arukh, Oraḥ Ḥayyim* 331:5 and *Yoreh De'a* 266:10).

Born at twilight – נוֹלַד בֵּין הַשְּׁמָשׁוֹת: When a child is born at twilight, the eight days for his circumcision begin the night following twilight. However, this later date does not override Shabbat or a Festival, or even the second day of the Festival in the exile (Rosh; Rambam *Sefer Ahava, Hilkhot Mila* 1:12; *Shulḥan Arukh, Oraḥ Ḥayyim* 331:5 and *Yoreh De'a* 266:8).

Born circumcised – נוֹלַד כְּשֶׁהוּא מָהוּל: If a child was born circumcised, even though he is circumcised at the age of eight days, his circumcision does not override Shabbat (Rambam *Sefer Ahava, Hilkhot Mila* 1:11; *Shulḥan Arukh, Oraḥ Ḥayyim* 331:5 and *Yoreh De'a* 266:10).

אָמַר רַבִּי שִׁמְעוֹן בֶּן אֶלְעָזָר: לֹא נֶחְלְקוּ בֵּית שַׁמַּאי וּבֵית הִלֵּל עַל נוֹלָד כְּשֶׁהוּא מָהוּל שֶׁצָּרִיךְ לְהַטִּיף מִמֶּנּוּ דַּם בְּרִית, מִפְּנֵי שֶׁעׇרְלָה כְּבוּשָׁה הִיא. עַל מָה נֶחְלְקוּ – עַל גֵּר שֶׁנִּתְגַּיֵּיר כְּשֶׁהוּא מָהוּל, שֶׁבֵּית שַׁמַּאי אוֹמְרִים: צָרִיךְ לְהַטִּיף מִמֶּנּוּ דַּם בְּרִית, וּבֵית הִלֵּל אוֹמְרִים: אֵין צָרִיךְ לְהַטִּיף מִמֶּנּוּ דַּם בְּרִית.

Rabbi Shimon ben Elazar said: That was not the subject of their dispute, as **Beit Shammai and Beit Hillel did not disagree over** the fact that **from one who was born circumcised, it is necessary to drip covenantal blood,**[NH] **because** they agree that **it is** a case of a **concealed foreskin.** The child is not actually circumcised; it is just that his foreskin is not visible. **With regard to what did they disagree? With regard to a convert who** for some reason was circumcised when he was a gentile and **converted when he was** already **circumcised,**[H] **as Beit Shammai say: Dripping covenantal blood from him is necessary, and Beit Hillel say: Dripping covenantal blood from him is not necessary,** and he needs only a ritual immersion to complete his conversion.

אָמַר מָר ״וְלֹא סָפֵק דּוֹחֶה אֶת הַשַּׁבָּת״. לְאֵתוֹיֵי מַאי? לְאֵתוֹיֵי הָא דְּתָנוּ רַבָּנַן: בֶּן שִׁבְעָה מְחַלְּלִין עָלָיו אֶת הַשַּׁבָּת, וּבֶן שְׁמוֹנָה אֵין מְחַלְּלִין עָלָיו אֶת הַשַּׁבָּת. סָפֵק בֶּן שִׁבְעָה סָפֵק בֶּן שְׁמוֹנָה – אֵין מְחַלְּלִין עָלָיו אֶת הַשַּׁבָּת.

The Gemara cited above that **the Master said:** The circumcision of a halakhically **uncertain** foreskin **does not override Shabbat.** The Gemara asks: **What** case of uncertainty does this statement come **to include?** The Gemara answers: It comes **to include that which the Sages taught:** To circumcise a **child** born after **seven** months of pregnancy, **one desecrates Shabbat,** as it will likely live. **However,** to circumcise a **child** born after **eight** months[HBN] of pregnancy, with regard to whom the presumption was that he would not survive, **one may not desecrate Shabbat.** And even **for** the circumcision of a child with regard to whom there is **uncertainty** whether the **child** was born after **seven** months and **uncertainty** whether the **child** was born after **eight** months, **one may not desecrate Shabbat.**

בֶּן שְׁמוֹנָה הֲרֵי הוּא כְּאֶבֶן, וְאָסוּר לְטַלְטְלוֹ. אֲבָל אִמּוֹ שׁוֹחָה וּמְנִיקַתּוֹ מִפְּנֵי הַסַּכָּנָה.

And the Sages taught: **A child** born after **eight** months **is like a stone** with regard to the *halakhot* of set-aside [*muktze*], **and it is prohibited to move him. However, his mother may bend over** the child **and nurse him due to the danger** that failure to nurse will cause her to fall ill.

אִיתְּמַר, רַב אָמַר: הֲלָכָה כְּתַנָּא קַמָּא, וּשְׁמוּאֵל אָמַר: הֲלָכָה כְּרַבִּי שִׁמְעוֹן בֶּן אֶלְעָזָר.

With regard to the halakhic ruling in the case of a child born circumcised, **it is stated** that the Sages disagree. **Rav said: The *halakha* is in accordance with** the explanation of the **first *tanna*,** i.e., in accordance with Rabbi Yehuda's explanation of the dispute between Beit Shammai and Beit Hillel, that they disagree with regard to one born circumcised. Since we rule in accordance with the opinion of Beit Hillel, it is not necessary to drip covenantal blood from a child born circumcised. **And Shmuel said: The *halakha* is in accordance with** the explanation of **Rabbi Shimon ben Elazar,** that Beit Shammai and Beit Hillel do not disagree with regard to one born circumcised, and that everyone agrees that it is necessary to drip covenantal blood from him.

רַב אַדָּא בַּר אַהֲבָה אִתְיְלִיד לֵיהּ הָהוּא יָנוֹקָא כְּשֶׁהוּא מָהוּל, אַהַדְרֵיהּ אַתְּלֵיסַר מְהוֹלָאֵי עַד דְּשַׁוְיֵיהּ כְּרוּת שׇׁפְכָה. אֲמַר: תֵּיתֵי לִי דַּעֲבַרִי אַדְּרַב.

The Gemara relates that **to Rav Adda bar Ahava** there was **this child that was born circumcised,** and the time for his circumcision was on Shabbat. **He inquired after thirteen** ritual **circumcisors,** but they refused to circumcise him, **until** ultimately, he circumcised his son himself and **rendered him** one with a **severed urethra.** He did not know how to perform a circumcision and made too deep an incision.[N] Rav Adda bar Ahava **said: I have it coming to me,** i.e., I deserve to be punished, **as I violated the** ruling **of Rav,** who ruled that one born circumcised does not even need covenantal blood drawn.

NOTES

It is necessary to drip covenantal blood – צָרִיךְ לְהַטִּיף...דַּם בְּרִית: The primary discussion of the *halakhot* of circumcision appears in tractate *Yevamot*, including a discussion concerning the *halakhot* of circumcision of a convert. The early and late commentaries debated whether the essence of the mitzva of circumcision is for the person to remain without a foreskin or whether the essence of the mitzva is to perform the act of circumcision itself. Apparently, dripping blood from a child without a foreskin is a form of circumcision and fulfills the mitzva. Nevertheless, the authorities dispute whether or not a blessing is recited over this act. With regard to converts, however, the consensus appears to be that the central act of conversion is the immersion in a ritual bath for the sake of conversion.

Born after eight months – בֶּן שְׁמוֹנָה: The Sages of the Gemara cited sources that allude to the notion that a child born after eight months of pregnancy cannot survive. Nevertheless, they provided clear physical signs that indicate whether or not a child was fully developed. In later generations, the authorities ruled that the *halakhot* with regard to a child born after eight months apply only if there is absolute certainty that the child was indeed born after eight months. Some authorities state that since we lack the expertise to identify the physical signs described by the Sages, these *halakhot* cannot be applied. Rather, every newborn is treated equally: He is circumcised even on Shabbat, all of his needs are met, and Shabbat is desecrated to save his life (see *Me'iri*).

The incident of Rav Adda bar Ahava – מַעֲשֶׂה רַב אַדָּא בַּר אַהֲבָה: This incident is related in somewhat greater detail in the Jerusalem Talmud, which cites divergent traditions with regard to the details of the incident. Some say that, in his ignorance, Rav Adda fatally wounded the child, while others say that after he saw what he had done to him, knowing that a male whose tubes have been severed cannot have children and is even prohibited to marry a Jew (Deuteronomy 23:2), Rav Adda prayed for mercy that the child should die of his own accord.

HALAKHA

From one who was born circumcised it is necessary to drip covenantal blood – נוֹלָד כְּשֶׁהוּא מָהוּל שֶׁצָּרִיךְ לְהַטִּיף מִמֶּנּוּ דַּם בְּרִית: When a baby is born circumcised, his circumcision involves dripping covenantal blood from him. This must be performed very carefully to avoid endangering him, based on the incident involving Rav Adda bar Ahava and the statements of Rabbi Shimon ben Elazar and Rabbi Eliezer HaKappar (Rambam *Sefer Ahava, Hilkhot Mila* 1:7; *Shulḥan Arukh, Yoreh De'a* 263:4).

A gentile who converted when he was already circumcised – גֵּר שֶׁנִּתְגַּיֵּיר כְּשֶׁהוּא מָהוּל: When a circumcised gentile converts to Judaism, a drop of covenantal blood is drawn from him. Then he immerses in a ritual bath, as ruled by the *ge'onim*, the *Ba'al Halakhot Gedolot*, the Rif, and the Rambam. Some dispute this ruling (Rabbeinu Ḥananel). There are many opinions with regard to the rationale for this ruling. Some commentaries explain that based on the ruling of the later authorities, the *halakha* is in accordance with the opinion of Rabbi Eliezer HaKappar, that one must drip covenantal blood from a circumcised convert. Other authorities explain that it is based on the ruling in tractate *Yevamot* that a drop of covenantal blood is drawn from a circumcised convert (see *Kesef Mishne*; Rambam *Sefer Ahava, Hilkhot Mila* 1:7 and *Sefer Kedusha, Hilkhot Issurei Bia* 14:5; *Shulḥan Arukh, Yoreh De'a* 268:1).

Born after seven months…after eight months – בֶּן שִׁבְעָה...בֶּן שְׁמוֹנָה וכו׳: One may desecrate Shabbat to save the life of a baby born after seven months of pregnancy. If the eighth day after his birth occurs on Shabbat, he is circumcised on Shabbat. However, it is assumed that a baby born after eight months cannot survive. Therefore, one may not move the baby on Shabbat; one may not desecrate Shabbat to save its life; and if the eighth day after his birth occurs on Shabbat, he is not circumcised on Shabbat. This rule refers to a baby whose hair and nails are not fully developed. If the baby is fully developed, then Shabbat is desecrated on his behalf, as it is for any other child (Rambam *Sefer Ahava, Hilkhot Mila*, 1:13–14; *Shulḥan Arukh, Oraḥ Ḥayyim* 330:7–8 and *Yoreh De'a* 266:11 and in the comment of the Rema).

BACKGROUND

Born after seven or eight months of pregnancy – בֶּן שִׁבְעָה וּבֶן שְׁמוֹנָה: During talmudic times, conventional wisdom was that a child born after eight months of pregnancy had no chance of survival, while a child born after seven months was more likely to survive. In modern medicine, there is no support for this distinction. Yet in practice, the Sages ruled that the determination is not based on the counting of the months of pregnancy. Rather, the physical signs of development, i.e., the nails and hair, are used to determine whether or not a child is potentially viable.

אָמַר לֵיהּ רַב נַחְמָן: וְאַדִּשְׁמוּאֵל לָא עֲבַר?! אֵימַר דַּאֲמַר שְׁמוּאֵל בַּחוֹל, בַּשַּׁבָּת מִי אֲמַר? הוּא סָבַר: וַדַּאי עָרְלָה כְּבוּשָׁה הִיא. דְּאִיתְּמַר, רַבָּה אָמַר: חָיְישִׁינַן שֶׁמָּא עָרְלָה כְּבוּשָׁה הִיא, רַב יוֹסֵף אָמַר: וַדַּאי עָרְלָה כְּבוּשָׁה הִיא.

Rav Naḥman said to him: And did he not violate the ruling of **Shmuel? Say that Shmuel said** that one is required to drip covenantal blood **during the week, on Shabbat, did he say** so? Certainly one does not desecrate Shabbat in that case. The Gemara explains that Rav Adda bar Ahava **held** differently, that in that case there is not merely a concern that perhaps there is a concealed foreskin. In that case, that **there is definitely a concealed foreskin.** Therefore, a form of circumcision must be performed on the child, and it overrides Shabbat. **As it was stated** that there is an amoraic dispute as to whether or not it is permitted to drip covenantal blood on Shabbat from a child born circumcised. **Rabba said: We are concerned lest there is a concealed foreskin,** and therefore there is uncertainty whether or not he is considered uncircumcised, and therefore it is prohibited to circumcise him on Shabbat. **Rav Yosef said:** In that case, **there is certainly a concealed foreskin** and therefore, it is permitted to circumcise him even on Shabbat.[N]

אֲמַר רַב יוֹסֵף: מְנָא אָמִינָא לָהּ – דְּתַנְיָא, רַבִּי אֱלִיעֶזֶר הַקַּפָּר אוֹמֵר: לֹא נֶחְלְקוּ בֵּית שַׁמַּאי וּבֵית הִלֵּל עַל נוֹלָד כְּשֶׁהוּא מָהוּל – שֶׁצָּרִיךְ לְהַטִּיף מִמֶּנּוּ דַּם בְּרִית, עַל מַה נֶּחְלְקוּ – לְחַלֵּל עָלָיו אֶת הַשַּׁבָּת. בֵּית שַׁמַּאי אוֹמְרִים: מְחַלְּלִין עָלָיו אֶת הַשַּׁבָּת, וּבֵית הִלֵּל אוֹמְרִים: אֵין מְחַלְּלִין עָלָיו אֶת הַשַּׁבָּת. לָאו מִכְּלָל דְּתַנָּא קַמָּא סָבַר "מְחַלְּלִין עָלָיו אֶת הַשַּׁבָּת"?

Rav Yosef said: From where do I say this line of reasoning? **As it was taught** in a *baraita*: **Rabbi Eliezer HaKappar says:** There is a tradition that **Beit Shammai and Beit Hillel did not disagree with regard to** a child who **was born circumcised, that one is required to drip covenantal blood from him. With regard to what did they disagree?** With regard to whether or not **to desecrate Shabbat on his** behalf. **Beit Shammai say: One desecrates Shabbat** in order to circumcise **him, and Beit Hillel say: One does not desecrate Shabbat** in order to circumcise **him.** Rav Yosef concludes: **Does this not** prove **by inference that the first *tanna*,** whose opinion Rabbi Eliezer HaKappar disputes, **holds** that everyone agrees that **one desecrates Shabbat on his** behalf, and Rabbi Eliezer HaKappar disagrees and states that Beit Shammai and Beit Hillel dispute that very matter?

וְדִילְמָא: תַּנָּא קַמָּא דִּבְרֵי הַכֹּל אֵין מְחַלְּלִין קָאָמַר? אִם כֵּן, רַבִּי אֱלִיעֶזֶר הַקַּפָּר טַעְמָא דְּבֵית שַׁמַּאי אֲתָא לְאַשְׁמַעִינַן?! דִּילְמָא הָכִי קָאָמַר: לֹא נֶחְלְקוּ בֵּית שַׁמַּאי וּבֵית הִלֵּל בְּדָבָר זֶה.

The Gemara refutes this: **And perhaps** the **first *tanna* is saying** that **everyone agrees** that **one may not desecrate** Shabbat in that case, and Rabbi Eliezer HaKappar disagrees and holds that there is a dispute in this regard. The Gemara immediately rejects this assertion: **If** that is **so,** that Rabbi Eliezer HaKappar is coming to introduce an opinion that allows desecrating Shabbat to perform circumcision in this case, that is the opinion of Beit Shammai; did **Rabbi Eliezer HaKappar come to teach us the reasoning** of **Beit Shammai?**[N] Their opinion is rejected as *halakha*, and there would be no purpose in making a statement simply to explain the opinion of Beit Shammai. The Gemara answers that proof is not absolute; **perhaps this is what he is saying: Beit Shammai and Beit Hillel did not disagree with regard to this matter** of circumcision of a baby born circumcised on Shabbat. They disagree with regard to the requirement to drip covenantal blood on a weekday.

אָמַר רַבִּי אַסִי: כֹּל שֶׁאִמּוֹ טְמֵאָה לֵידָה – נִימּוֹל לִשְׁמוֹנָה, וְכֹל שֶׁאֵין אִמּוֹ טְמֵאָה לֵידָה – אֵין נִימּוֹל לִשְׁמֹנָה, שֶׁנֶּאֱמַר "אִשָּׁה כִּי תַזְרִיעַ וְיָלְדָה זָכָר וְטָמְאָה וגו׳ וּבַיּוֹם הַשְּׁמִינִי יִמּוֹל בְּשַׂר עָרְלָתוֹ".

Rabbi Asi stated a principle: **Any** child **whose** birth renders his **mother ritually impure** due to **childbirth is circumcised at eight** days; **and any** child **whose** birth does **not** render **his mother ritually impure** due to **childbirth,** e.g., the birth was not natural, but by caesarean section, is **not** necessarily **circumcised at eight** days. **As it is stated: "If a woman bears seed and gives birth to a male, she shall be impure** seven days… **and on the eighth day the flesh of his foreskin shall be circumcised"** (Leviticus 12:2–3). This verse draws a parallel between the two issues, indicating that only a child whose birth renders his mother impure is circumcised on the eighth day.

אֲמַר לֵיהּ אַבַּיֵי: דּוֹרוֹת הָרִאשׁוֹנִים יוֹכִיחוּ, שֶׁאֵין אִמּוֹ טְמֵאָה לֵידָה – וְנִימּוֹל לִשְׁמֹנָה!

Abaye said to him: The early generations, from Abraham through the revelation at Sinai, **will prove** that the principle is not valid, **as** the birth of a male during that era did **not** render **his mother ritually impure** due to **childbirth,** as the *halakhot* of the impurity of childbirth were commanded at Sinai, **and** nevertheless, the child **was circumcised at eight** days, as stated in the Torah, in the book of Genesis.

אֲמַר לֵיהּ: נִתְּנָה תּוֹרָה

Rabbi Asi **said to him:** There is no proof from here, as when **the Torah** was later **given,**

NOTES

The dispute between Rabba and Rav Yosef – מַחְלוֹקֶת רַבָּה וְרַב יוֹסֵף: The version in the Gemara corresponds with Rashi's version of the text: Rav Yosef sought to cite proof for his opinion by approximating what the first *tanna*, whose opinion Rabbi Eliezer HaKappar disputes, might have said, even though only part of that *baraita* remains extant and there is no way to ascertain with certainty what the first *tanna* said. According to the *ge'onim*, this first *tanna* is Rabbi Shimon ben Elazar, and Rabbi Eliezer HaKappar's statement constitutes a continuation of the *baraita* that cited the dispute between Rabbi Yehuda and Rabbi Shimon. However, according to the variant reading of the majority of the *ge'onim*, it is not Rav Yosef who cites a proof from this source, but Rabba, who seeks to infer that the first *tanna*, Rabbi Shimon ben Elazar, is of the opinion that everyone agrees that one may not desecrate Shabbat for a child of that sort. Therefore, the entire discussion proceeds in a slightly different manner, as Rabbi Shimon ben Elazar did not explain his statement in this matter. Many commentaries considered this version and its rationale clearer (see Rashba and Ran).

Come to teach us the reasoning of Beit Shammai – טַעְמָא דְּבֵית שַׁמַּאי אֲתָא לְאַשְׁמְעִינַן: There are exceptions to this principle, where the Gemara analyzes the opinion of Beit Shammai or reveals their opinion. However, there is typically a reason for the discussion, e.g., so that if this opinion appears unattributed, it would be identified and rejected (see *Yad Malakhi*).

וְנִתְחַדְּשָׁה הֲלָכָה.

halakha **was introduced.** No proof can be cited from the observance of mitzvot prior to the revelation at Sinai.

אִינִי?! וְהָא אִיתְּמַר: יוֹצֵא דוֹפֶן וּמִי שֶׁיֵּשׁ לוֹ שְׁתֵּי עָרְלוֹת, רַב הוּנָא וְרַב חִיָּיא בַּר רַב. חַד אָמַר: מְחַלְּלִין עָלָיו אֶת הַשַּׁבָּת; וְחַד אָמַר: אֵין מְחַלְּלִין. עַד כָּאן לָא פְּלִיגִי – אֶלָּא לְחַלֵּל עָלָיו אֶת הַשַּׁבָּת, אֲבָל לִשְׁמֹנָה – וַדַּאי מְהַלִּינַן לֵיהּ! הָא בְּהָא תַּלְיָא.

The Gemara asks: **Is that so? Wasn't it stated** that there is a dispute with regard to this *halakha*? As it was taught with regard to **a child born by caesarean section**[B] **and one who has two foreskins,**[H] **Rav Huna and Rav Ḥiyya bar Rav** disputed their status. **One said: One desecrates Shabbat on his** behalf and performs the circumcision; **and one said: One does not desecrate** Shabbat on his behalf. **They only disagree with regard to** whether or not it is permissible **to desecrate Shabbat on his** behalf; **however, with regard to** circumcising him **at eight** days, in principle, **we certainly circumcise him,** even though the birth of a child by caesarean section does not render his mother ritually impure due to childbirth. The Gemara answers: The two disputes **are interdependent.** The one who holds that one desecrates Shabbat for this child's circumcision also holds that one must circumcise him on the eighth day. The one who holds that one may not desecrate Shabbat for this child's circumcision holds that one need not circumcise him on the eighth day.

כְּתַנָּאֵי: יֵשׁ יְלִיד בַּיִת שֶׁנִּימּוֹל לְאֶחָד וְיֵשׁ יְלִיד בַּיִת שֶׁנִּימּוֹל לִשְׁמֹנָה, יֵשׁ מִקְנַת כֶּסֶף שֶׁנִּימּוֹל לְאֶחָד, וְיֵשׁ מִקְנַת כֶּסֶף שֶׁנִּימּוֹל לִשְׁמֹנָה. יֵשׁ מִקְנַת כֶּסֶף שֶׁנִּימּוֹל לְאֶחָד, וְיֵשׁ מִקְנַת כֶּסֶף שֶׁנִּימּוֹל לִשְׁמוֹנָה.

The Gemara comments: The issue of Rabbi Asi's statement that the obligation to circumcise after eight days depends upon whether or not his birth renders his mother ritually impure due to childbirth is **parallel to** a **tannaitic** dispute, as we learned: **There is a home-born child** of a Canaanite maidservant born in a Jewish home, who has the legal status of a Canaanite slave and his Jewish owner is obligated to circumcise him, **who is circumcised at** the age of **one** day, i.e., immediately after birth; **and there is a home-born child circumcised at eight** days. **And there is a** slave **purchased** in a **money** transaction **who is circumcised at one** day, **and there is** a slave **purchased** in a **money** transaction **who is circumcised at eight** days.

כֵּיצַד? לָקַח שִׁפְחָה מְעוּבֶּרֶת וְאַחַר כָּךְ יָלְדָה – זֶהוּ מִקְנַת כֶּסֶף הַנִּימּוֹל לִשְׁמוֹנָה, לָקַח שִׁפְחָה וּוְלָדָהּ עִמָּהּ – זוֹ הִיא מִקְנַת כֶּסֶף שֶׁנִּימּוֹל לְאֶחָד.

The *baraita* explains: **How so?** If a Jew **purchased a pregnant maidservant and she then gave birth** to a child while in his possession; **that is** a slave **purchased** in a **money** transaction **who is circumcised at eight** days, as the fetus was purchased along with the maidservant. If **he purchased a maidservant** who had already given birth **and** purchased **her child** along **with her,** he is obligated to circumcise the child as soon as the child enters his possession; **this is** a slave **purchased** in a **money** transaction, **who is circumcised at one** day.

וְיֵשׁ יְלִיד בַּיִת שֶׁנִּימּוֹל לִשְׁמֹנָה, כֵּיצַד? לָקַח שִׁפְחָה וְנִתְעַבְּרָה אֶצְלוֹ וְיָלְדָה – זֶהוּ יְלִיד בַּיִת הַנִּימּוֹל לִשְׁמֹנָה. רַב חָמָא אוֹמֵר: יָלְדָה וְאַחַר כָּךְ הִטְבִּילָהּ – זֶהוּ יְלִיד בַּיִת שֶׁנִּימּוֹל לְאֶחָד, הִטְבִּילָהּ וְאַחַר כָּךְ יָלְדָה – זֶהוּ יְלִיד בַּיִת הַנִּימּוֹל לִשְׁמֹנָה.

And likewise, **there is a home-born child circumcised at eight** days. **How so?** If he **bought a maidservant and she became pregnant in his possession and gave birth; that is a home-born child circumcised at eight** days. **Rav Ḥama says** there is a distinction: If the maidservant **gave birth and he subsequently** had **her immerse** for the purpose of becoming a maidservant, **that is a home-born child circumcised at one** day. But if **he** had **her immerse and she then gave birth; that is a home-born child circumcised at eight** days.

וְתַנָּא קַמָּא לָא שָׁנֵי לֵיהּ בֵּין הִטְבִּילָהּ וְאַחַר כָּךְ יָלְדָה, בֵּין יָלְדָה וְאַחַר כָּךְ הִטְבִּילָהּ, דְּאַף עַל גַּב דְּאֵין אִמּוֹ טְמֵאָה לֵידָה – נִימּוֹל לִשְׁמֹנָה.

And the first *tanna* **does not distinguish between whether he** had **her immerse and she then gave birth, or whether she gave birth and he then** had **her immerse.** Apparently, **even though** the child's birth does **not** render **his mother ritually impure** due to **childbirth,** as she is not obligated in mitzvot before immersing and she is not susceptible to ritual impurity of childbirth, **he is circumcised at eight** days. The dispute between Rabbi Ḥama and the first *tanna* revolves around the *halakha* stated by Rabbi Asi.

BACKGROUND

A child born by caesarean section – יוֹצֵא דוֹפֶן: In the time of the Gemara, these operations were not commonly performed on humans, but were occasionally performed to save a baby whose mother was about to die in childbirth. From the perspective of the *halakha*, a child who does not emerge through the opening of the womb has a somewhat different status, which affects certain *halakhot* pertaining to the date and time of birth.

HALAKHA

A child born by caesarean section and one who has two foreskins – יוֹצֵא דוֹפֶן וּמִי שֶׁיֵּשׁ לוֹ שְׁתֵּי עָרְלוֹת: Both a child born by caesarean section and one who has two foreskins are circumcised on the eighth day. However, one does not desecrate Shabbat for their circumcision; the circumcision is postponed until Sunday. The reason for this ruling is that the *amora'im* disputed the matter and no definitive conclusion was reached. Therefore, the ruling is stringent (Rif; Rambam *Sefer Ahava, Hilkhot Mila* 1:7, 11; *Shulḥan Arukh, Yoreh De'a* 262:3, 266:10).

(אֲמַר רָבָא): בִּשְׁלָמָא לְרַבִּי חָמָא – מַשְׁכַּחַת לָהּ יְלִיד בַּיִת נִימּוֹל לְאֶחָד, יְלִיד בַּיִת נִימּוֹל לִשְׁמוֹנָה. מִקְנַת כֶּסֶף נִימּוֹל לְאֶחָד, וּמִקְנַת כֶּסֶף נִימּוֹל לִשְׁמוֹנָה. יָלְדָה וְאַחַר כָּךְ הִטְבִּילָהּ – זֶהוּ יְלִיד בַּיִת שֶׁנִּימּוֹל לְאֶחָד, הִטְבִּילָהּ וְאַחַר כָּךְ יָלְדָה – זֶהוּ יְלִיד בַּיִת שֶׁנִּימּוֹל לִשְׁמוֹנָה.

With regard to the dispute between the *tanna'im*, **Rava said: Granted,** according **to** the opinion of **Rabbi Ḥama,** cases **can be found** of **a home-born child circumcised at one** day, **a home-born child circumcised at eight** days, a slave **purchased** in a **money** transaction **circumcised at one** day, **and** a slave **purchased** in a **money** transaction **circumcised at eight** days, in the following manner: If a maidservant **gave birth and he subsequently** had **her immerse, that is** the case of **a home-born child circumcised at one** day. If **he** had **her immerse and she then gave birth, that is** the case of **a home-born child circumcised at eight** days.

מִקְנַת כֶּסֶף נִימּוֹל לִשְׁמוֹנָה – כְּגוֹן שֶׁלָּקַח שִׁפְחָה מְעוּבֶּרֶת וְהִטְבִּילָהּ וְאַחַר כָּךְ יָלְדָה, מִקְנַת כֶּסֶף נִימּוֹל לְאֶחָד – כְּגוֹן שֶׁלָּקַח זֶה שִׁפְחָה וְזֶה עוּבָּרָהּ.

A slave **purchased** in a **money** transaction **is circumcised at eight** days in a case **where** a Jew **purchased a pregnant maidservant** and thereby paid for and purchased the fetus as well, **and** then had **her immerse, and she then gave birth.** A slave **purchased** in a **money** transaction **is circumcised at one** day in a case **where that** person **purchased a maidservant, and that** person, i.e., someone else, bought **her fetus;** since the owner of the fetus has no share in its mother, the child may be circumcised immediately after birth.

אֶלָּא לְתַנָּא קַמָּא בִּשְׁלָמָא כּוּלְּהוּ מַשְׁכַּחַת לְהוּ, אֶלָּא יְלִיד בַּיִת נִימּוֹל לְאֶחָד הֵיכִי מַשְׁכַּחַת לָהּ?

However, according to the opinion of the **first *tanna*, granted** that **all** the cases **can be found; however, how** can the case of **a home-born child circumcised at one** day **be found?**

אֲמַר רַבִּי יִרְמְיָה: בְּלוֹקֵחַ שִׁפְחָה לְעוּבָּרָהּ.

Rabbi Yirmeya said: It can be found **in the** case of **one who purchases a maidservant for** the purpose of purchasing rights to **her fetus** without purchasing the maidservant herself.

הָנִיחָא לְמַאן דַּאֲמַר קִנְיַן פֵּירוֹת לָאו כְּקִנְיַן הַגּוּף דָּמֵי, אֶלָּא לְמַאן דַּאֲמַר קִנְיַן פֵּירוֹת כְּקִנְיַן הַגּוּף דָּמֵי – מַאי אִיכָּא לְמֵימַר?

The Gemara asks: This **works out well according to** the opinion of **the one who said** that **a transaction** to purchase an item for its **product is not a transaction** to purchase **the item itself,** i.e., one who purchased a field for its fruit did not purchase the field itself. **However, according to** the opinion of **the one who said** that **a transaction** to purchase an item for its **product is a transaction** to purchase **the item itself, what can be said,** as he does not distinguish between the purchase of the maidservant herself and the purchase of the children that she bears?

אֲמַר רַב מְשַׁרְשְׁיָא: בְּלוֹקֵחַ שִׁפְחָה עַל מְנַת שֶׁלֹּא לְהַטְבִּילָהּ.

Rav Mesharshiya said: According to this opinion, it must explained as referring **to** one who **purchases a maidservant on condition that he will not** have **her immerse.** They can stipulate that he will not have her immerse as a maidservant and that she will remain a gentile. In that case, the child is a slave born to a Jew, and the mitzva of circumcision is in effect immediately upon birth.[H]

תַּנְיָא, רַבָּן שִׁמְעוֹן בֶּן גַּמְלִיאֵל אוֹמֵר: כֹּל שֶׁשָּׁהָה שְׁלֹשִׁים יוֹם בָּאָדָם – אֵינוֹ נֵפֶל, שֶׁנֶּאֱמַר ״וּפְדוּיָו מִבֶּן חֹדֶשׁ תִּפְדֶּה״. שְׁמוֹנַת יָמִים בַּבְּהֵמָה אֵינוֹ נֵפֶל, שֶׁנֶּאֱמַר ״וּמִיּוֹם הַשְּׁמִינִי וָהָלְאָה יֵרָצֶה לְקָרְבַּן״ וגו׳.

The Gemara cites a related *baraita* where **it was taught** that **Rabban Shimon ben Gamliel says: With regard to people, any** child **that remains** alive **thirty days** after birth[H] **is no** longer suspected of being a **stillborn,** and is assumed to be a regular child who will go on living. Proof is cited from that which **is stated** with regard to the laws of redemption and valuations: **"And their redemption, from a month old you shall redeem** according to your valuation, five shekels of silver, according to the shekel of the Sanctuary; it is twenty *gera*" (Numbers 18:16), indicating that no value is ascribed to an infant less than a month old, as its viability is uncertain. Likewise, a newborn **animal** that survives for **eight days**[H] **is no** longer suspected of being a **stillborn, as it is stated:** "When a bullock or a sheep or a goat is born, it shall be seven days under its mother; **and from the eighth day and onward it may be accepted for an offering** made by fire to the Lord" (Leviticus 22:27).

הָא לֹא שָׁהָה – סְפֵיקָא הָוֵי

The Gemara asks: Is that to say by inference: If the child **did not** yet **remain** alive for thirty days, **it is** considered an **uncertainty** whether or not it is a stillborn with regard to several *halakhot*?

HALAKHA

Home-born and purchased in a money transaction – יְלִיד בַּיִת וּמִקְנַת כֶּסֶף: If one purchased a pregnant maidservant, and she accepted upon herself the obligations of a maidservant belonging to a Jew, when she gives birth, her child is circumcised at eight days. However, if one purchased a maidservant on the condition that he would not immerse her as a maidservant, or if one only purchased the fetus, the child is considered to have been purchased in a money transaction. Therefore, the child is circumcised on the first possible day after the transaction is completed, even if it is the day of his birth, as stated in the *baraita* according to the explanations of Rabbi Yirmeya and Rav Mesharshiya (Rambam *Sefer Ahava, Hilkhot Mila* 1:4–5; *Shulḥan Arukh, Yoreh De'a* 267:1).

Any child that remains alive thirty days after birth – כֹּל שֶׁשָּׁהָה שְׁלֹשִׁים יוֹם בָּאָדָם: When it is unclear if a child was born after a full-term pregnancy, the child loses the possible status of a stillborn after it lives for thirty days. If the infant then dies, the child is mourned by his family members. If the child's father is a priest, he is permitted to attend the funeral, in accordance with the opinion of Rabban Shimon ben Gamliel (Rambam *Sefer Ahava, Hilkhot Mila* 1:13; *Sefer Nashim, Hilkhot Yibbum VaḤalitza* 1:22; *Sefer Nezikin, Hilkhot Rotze'aḥ UShmirat HaNefesh* 2:6; and *Sefer Shofetim, Hilkhot Evel* 1:6; *Shulḥan Arukh, Yoreh De'a* 340:30, 373:4 and *Even HaEzer* 156:4).

A newborn animal that survives for eight days – שְׁמוֹנַת יָמִים בַּבְּהֵמָה: A newborn animal that has not yet lived for eight days is still considered potentially non-viable. Therefore, it is prohibited to partake of its flesh, due to concern for the prohibition to eat an unslaughtered animal, in accordance with the opinion of Rabban Shimon ben Gamliel (Rambam *Sefer Kedusha, Hilkhot Ma'akhalot Assurot* 4:4).

HALAKHA

The circumcision of a child born after seven months – מִילַת בֶּן שִׁבְעָה: A baby born after seven months of pregnancy is circumcised even on Shabbat; the same is true of a baby with regard to whom there is uncertainty whether it was born after seven or after eight months (Rambam *Sefer Ahava, Hilkhot Mila* 1:14; *Shulḥan Arukh, Yoreh De'a* 266:11 in the comment of the Rema).

The slaughtering of a stillborn – שְׁחִיטַת נֵפֶל: Slaughtering a stillborn or any animal fetus whose gestation was not full term does not prevent it from causing ritual impurity as an unslaughtered animal (Rambam *Sefer Tahara, Hilkhot She'ar Avot HaTumot* 2:6).

מִימְהַל הֵיכִי מָהֲלִינַן לֵיהּ?

If so, with regard to **circumcision, how can we circumcise him?** Perhaps he is a stillborn and one may not desecrate Shabbat for his circumcision.

אָמַר רַב אַדָּא בַּר אַהֲבָה: מָלִין אוֹתוֹ מִמָּה נַפְשָׁךְ; אִם חַי הוּא – שַׁפִּיר קָא מָהֵיל, וְאִם לָאו – מְחַתֵּךְ בְּבָשָׂר הוּא.

Rav Adda bar Ahava said: One may circumcise him whichever way you look at it, based on the following calculation: **If he is** a child who will **live,** the circumcisor **may well circumcise** the child, **and if not,** if the child is a stillborn and the circumcisor **is** merely **cutting flesh,** one who cuts the flesh of a corpse or the flesh of one with the legal status of a corpse is not considered to have made a wound, and therefore has not performed a prohibited labor.

וְאֶלָּא הָא דְּתַנְיָא: סָפֵק בֶּן שִׁבְעָה סָפֵק בֶּן שְׁמוֹנָה – אֵין מְחַלְּלִין עָלָיו אֶת הַשַּׁבָּת, אַמַּאי? נִימְהֲלֵיהּ מִמָּה נַפְשָׁךְ! אִם חַי הוּא – שַׁפִּיר קָא מָהֵיל, וְאִם לָאו – מְחַתֵּךְ בְּבָשָׂר הוּא!

The Gemara raises a difficulty: **And however,** with regard to **that which was taught** in a *baraita*: If there is **uncertainty** whether he was **born after seven** months of pregnancy,[H] and **uncertainty** whether he was **born after eight** months, **one does not desecrate Shabbat on his** behalf and circumcise him. The Gemara asks: **Why? Let us circumcise him** on Shabbat, as **whichever way you look at it,** that is appropriate. **If he is** a child that will **live,** the circumcisor **may well circumcise** the child, **and if not, he is** merely **cutting** the **flesh** of a corpse, which does not violate any Shabbat prohibitions.

אָמַר מָר בְּרֵיהּ דְּרָבִינָא; אֲנָא וְרַב נַחוּמֵי בַּר זְכַרְיָה תַּרְגִּימְנָא: מִימְהַל – הָכִי נַמִי מָהֲלִינַן לֵיהּ, לֹא נִצְרְכָה אֶלָּא לְמַכְשִׁירֵי מִילָה, וְאַלִּיבָּא דְּרַבִּי אֱלִיעֶזֶר.

Mar, son of Ravina, said: Rav Naḥumei bar Zekharya and I interpreted this as follows: Indeed, as for **circumcision** itself, **we do indeed circumcise** that child even on Shabbat. It **was only necessary** to say that one does not desecrate Shabbat on his behalf **with regard to** the issue of preparing **facilitators of circumcision** on Shabbat, **in accordance with** the opinion of **Rabbi Eliezer** that actions that facilitate circumcision at its appointed time override Shabbat.

אָמַר אַבַּיֵי: כְּתַנָּאֵי ״וְכִי יָמוּת מִן הַבְּהֵמָה אֲשֶׁר הִיא לָכֶם לְאָכְלָה״ לְהָבִיא בֶּן שְׁמֹנָה שֶׁאֵין שְׁחִיטָתוֹ מְטַהַרְתּוֹ, רַבִּי יוֹסֵי בְּרַבִּי יְהוּדָה וְרַבִּי אֶלְעָזָר בְּרַבִּי שִׁמְעוֹן אוֹמְרִים: שְׁחִיטָתוֹ מְטַהַרְתּוֹ.

Abaye said: The issue of whether a child who has not yet survived thirty days from his birth is considered viable is **parallel to** a dispute between **the** ***tanna'im***[N] with regard to the interpretation of the verse: **"And if any animal of which you may eat shall die,** one who touches its carcass shall be impure until the evening" (Leviticus 11:39). The verse is interpreted as coming **to include offspring of eight** months. Large domesticated animals typically give birth after a gestation period of nine months. If an animal of that sort gives birth after eight months, its offspring is deemed to be not viable and **its slaughter does not purify it.**[H] Rather, it assumes the status of an unslaughtered animal, which is not only prohibited to be eaten, but also transmits ritual impurity to those who touch or move it. **Rabbi Yosei, son of Rabbi Yehuda, and Rabbi Elazar, son of Rabbi Shimon, say: Its slaughter purifies it,** and it does not assume unslaughtered animal status.

מַאי לָאו בְּהָא קָא מִיפַּלְגִי, דְּמָר סָבַר: חַי הוּא, וּמָר סָבַר: מֵת הוּא.

What, is it not that this is the matter with regard to which **they disagree? That** this **Master holds** that the animal **is** considered **alive** and therefore its slaughter is effective, as is the case with regard to all pure animals, **while** this **Master,** the first *tanna*, **holds** that it **is** considered **dead.**

אָמַר רָבָא: אִי הָכִי, אַדְּמִיפַּלְגִי לְעִנְיַן טוּמְאָה וְטָהֳרָה – לִיפַּלְגִי לְעִנְיַן אֲכִילָה!

Rava said: If so, instead of disagreeing over the issue of **impurity and purity, let them disagree over** the issue of **eating,** i.e., whether it is permitted to eat this offspring after it is slaughtered. Since they did not dispute this point, their disagreement must revolve around a different factor.

NOTES

Parallel to a dispute between the ***tanna'im*** **– כְּתַנָּאֵי:** According to Rashi and the majority of the commentaries, Abaye applies the dispute between *tanna'im* to Rav Adda bar Ahava's statement. According to this interpretation, the *tanna'im* dispute whether the legal status of one who will not survive is that of a living person in certain respects or whether it is that of a dead person, in the sense that cutting his flesh would be tantamount to cutting meat. Other commetaries explain that the dispute between the *tanna'im* is cited with regard to the statement of Rabban Shimon ben Gamliel, as they dispute whether the legal status of an animal less than eight days old or a human child less than a month old is that of a living or a or dead person(see Rashba).

אֶלָּא, דְּכוּלֵּי עָלְמָא מֵת הוּא, וְרַבִּי יוֹסֵי בְּרַבִּי יְהוּדָה וְרַבִּי אֶלְעָזָר בְּרַבִּי שִׁמְעוֹן סָבְרִי: כִּטְרֵפָה; טְרֵפָה, לָאו אַף עַל גַּב דְּמֵתָה הִיא – שְׁחִיטָתָהּ מְטַהַרְתָּהּ, הָכָא נַמִּי – לָא שְׁנָא. וְרַבָּנַן: לָא דָּמֵי לִטְרֵפָה, טְרֵפָה – הָיְתָה לָהּ שְׁעַת הַכּוֹשֶׁר, הַאי – לֹא הָיְתָה לָהּ שְׁעַת הַכּוֹשֶׁר.

Rather, it must be that **everyone agrees** that **it is** considered **dead,** yet **Rabbi Yosei, son of Rabbi Yehuda, and Rabbi Elazar, son of Rabbi Shimon, hold** that it has the legal status **like** that of **a** ***tereifa***, an animal with a condition that will cause it to die within twelve months. With regard to a ***tereifa***, **is it not that even though it is** considered **dead** from the perspective of *halakha* because there is no possibility of long-term survival, nevertheless, if it is slaughtered, **its slaughter purifies it?**[H] It does not cause ritual impurity like an unslaughtered animal, even though it may not be eaten. **Here too, it is no different. And the Rabbis,** who do not accept this claim, say: **It is not similar to a** ***tereifa***, since **a** ***tereifa*** **had a period of fitness** before it became a *tereifa*. However, **this** animal that was born after eight months of pregnancy **did not** ever **have a period of fitness.**[N]

וְכִי תֵּימָא טְרֵפָה מִבֶּטֶן מַאי אִיכָּא לְמֵימַר? הָתָם, יֵשׁ בְּמִינָהּ שְׁחִיטָה, הָכָא – אֵין בְּמִינָהּ שְׁחִיטָה.

And if you say: With regard to an animal that was a ***tereifa*** **from the womb** and was born in that condition, **what is there to say?** It too never had a period of fitness. There is a distinction between the cases. **There,** with regard to a *tereifa*, **there is slaughter in its type; here,** with regard to a stillborn, **there is no slaughter in its type,** as there is no circumstance where slaughter of a stillborn animal is appropriate.

אִיבַּעְיָא לְהוּ: מִי פְּלִיגִי רַבָּנַן עֲלֵיהּ דְּרַבָּן שִׁמְעוֹן בֶּן גַּמְלִיאֵל אוֹ לֹא? אִם תִּמְצֵי לוֹמַר ״פְּלִיגִי״ – הֲלָכָה כְּמוֹתוֹ אוֹ אֵין הֲלָכָה כְּמוֹתוֹ?

A dilemma was raised before the Sages: **Do the Rabbis disagree with Rabban Shimon ben Gamliel,** who holds that any animal that survived for eight days after birth is presumed viable, **or not? If you say** that they **disagree,** the dilemma is: **Is the** ***halakha*** **in accordance with his** opinion, **or is the** ***halakha*** **not in accordance with his** opinion?

תָּא שְׁמַע: עֵגֶל שֶׁנּוֹלַד בְּיוֹם טוֹב – שׁוֹחֲטִין אוֹתוֹ בְּיוֹם טוֹב. הָכָא בְּמַאי עָסְקִינַן – דְּקִים לֵיהּ בְּגַוֵּיהּ שֶׁכָּלוּ לוֹ חֳדָשָׁיו.

Come and **hear** proof from that which we learned: With regard to a **calf that was born on a Festival,**[H] **one may slaughter** it **on** the **Festival.** Apparently, Rabban Shimon ben Gamliel's opinion is not accepted, and one need not wait eight days after the animal is born. The Gemara refutes this: **With what are we dealing here?** It is a case in **which one is certain that its months** of gestation **were completed,** and therefore, it is certainly not stillborn.

תָּא שְׁמַע: וְשָׁוִין, שֶׁאִם נוֹלַד הוּא וּמוּמוֹ עִמּוֹ – שֶׁזֶּה מִן הַמּוּכָן. הָכָא נַמִּי: שֶׁכָּלוּ לוֹ חֳדָשָׁיו.

Come and **hear** another proof from that which we learned: Rabbi Yehuda and Rabbi Shimon, who disagreed with regard to whether or not it is permitted to inspect firstborn animals for blemishes on a Festival, **agree that if** a firstborn animal **was born with its blemish,**[H] **it is** considered **prepared** for use on the Festival. It is not deemed set-aside and an expert may examine it to determine whether or not it is a permanent blemish. Apparently, a firstborn animal may be slaughtered on the day of its birth. The Gemara refutes this proof as well: It is a case in **which one is certain that its months** of gestation **were completed,** and it is certainly not stillborn.

תָּא שְׁמַע, דְּאָמַר רַב יְהוּדָה אָמַר שְׁמוּאֵל: הֲלָכָה כְּרַבָּן שִׁמְעוֹן בֶּן גַּמְלִיאֵל. הֲלָכָה – מִכְּלָל דִּפְלִיגִי, שְׁמַע מִינָּהּ.

Come and **hear** a solution to the dilemma, **as Rav Yehuda said** that **Shmuel said:** The ***halakha*** in this matter **is in accordance with** the opinion of **Rabban Shimon ben Gamliel.** Nonetheless, from the fact that the ***halakha*** was ruled in accordance with Rabban Shimon ben Gamliel, **by inference,** the Sages **disagree** with his ruling. The Gemara concludes: Indeed, **conclude from this** the resolution to both dilemmas raised above.

אָמַר אַבַּיֵי: נָפַל מִן הַגַּג אוֹ אֲכָלוֹ אֲרִי – דִּבְרֵי הַכֹּל חַי הוּא, כִּי פְּלִיגִי – שֶׁפִּיהֵק וָמֵת. מָר סָבַר: חַי הוּא, וּמָר סָבַר: מֵת הוּא.

Abaye said: With regard to a baby less than thirty days old that **fell off a roof or was eaten by a lion, everyone agrees** that **he is** considered to have been **alive;** it was a viable baby that died in the accident. **Where they disagree is** in a case where the baby **yawned,** i.e., breathed momentarily after birth, **and** then immediately **died.**[N] This **Master,** the Rabbis, **hold:** The baby **is** considered to have been **living,** since it was born alive; **and** this **Master holds: It is** considered to have been born **dead** until it lives a month after its birth.

לְמַאי נָפְקָא מִינֵּיהּ – לִפְטוֹר מִן הַיִּיבּוּם.

What practical **difference is there** whether or not the baby is considered to have been alive? The difference is **to exempt** the child's mother **from levirate marriage.** If a man died with no children, and his wife was pregnant and a viable child was born, the woman is exempt from levirate marriage; however, if the child was born dead, the man is considered to have died childless, and his widow is obligated in levirate marriage.[H]

HALAKHA

The slaughtering of a ***tereifa*** **– שְׁחִיטַת טְרֵיפָה:** When one slaughters an animal that will die within twelve months [*tereifa*], the slaughter is valid; although the animal may not be eaten, it does not cause the ritual impurity of an unslaughtered animal [*neveila*] (Rambam *Sefer Tahara, Hilkhot She'ar Avot HaTumot* 2:6).

A calf that was born on a Festival – עֵגֶל שֶׁנּוֹלַד בְּיוֹם טוֹב: A calf born on a Festival to an animal that was designated for eating may be slaughtered on that day if it is clear that its gestation was full term (Rambam *Sefer Zemanim, Hilkhot Yom Tov* 2:1; *Shulḥan Arukh, Oraḥ Ḥayyim* 498:5).

A firstborn born blemished – בְּכוֹר שֶׁנּוֹלַד בַּעַל מוּם: Since the destruction of the Temple, the firstborn of a kosher animal may not be eaten unless it is blemished. A Sage may not examine it on a Festival to determine if it has a blemish that would permit it to be slaughtered. However, if the firstborn was born blemished, and the Sage violated the *halakha* and examined the blemish on a Festival and determined that it was permanent, the animal may be slaughtered and eaten on the Festival (Rambam *Sefer Zemanim, Hilkhot Yom Tov* 2:4; *Shulḥan Arukh, Oraḥ Ḥayyim* 498:9).

A baby that died within thirty days with regard to levirate marriage and ***ḥalitza*** **– תִּינוֹק שֶׁמֵּת לִפְנֵי שְׁלוֹשִׁים לְעִנְיַן חוֹבַת יִיבּוּם וַחֲלִיצָה:** If a man died childless while his wife was pregnant, and she then gave birth to a child that lived for thirty days, the child exempts its mother and its father's other wives from *ḥalitza* and levirate marriage. However, if the infant died within thirty days, even if it died through an accident, it was not clearly demonstrated to have been viable. Therefore, although its mother may not be married in a levirate marriage, she must perform *ḥalitza* due to the uncertainty, in accordance with the Gemara's final understanding of Abaye's statement (Rambam *Sefer Nashim, Hilkhot Yibbum VaḤalitza* 1:5; *Shulḥan Arukh, Even HaEzer* 156:4).

NOTES

Have a period of fitness – הָיְתָה לָהּ שְׁעַת הַכּוֹשֶׁר: One rationale for this statement is that an animal that was once fit has a presumption of fitness, and a substantial reason is required to undermine that presumption. This is not true of a stillborn, with regard to whom no presumption of fitness was established and who is considered unfit from the outset.

It yawned and died – פִּיהֵק וָמֵת: Rabbeinu Zeraḥya HaLevi explains that the phrase yawned and died refers specifically to a case where the baby breathed a bit and immediately died. However, if it died as a result of illness, the baby is considered like one that fell from a roof and died accidentally. Other commentaries state that the phrase yawned and died is only a figure of speech, and if the baby died as a result of illness, we assume that its naturally weak constitution was the cause of its death (Rabbeinu Yona; see *Me'iri*).

נָפַל מִן הַגַּג אוֹ אֲכָלוֹ אֲרִי דִּבְרֵי הַכֹּל חַי הוּא?! וְהָא רַב פָּפָּא וְרַב הוּנָא בְּרֵיהּ דְּרַב יְהוֹשֻׁעַ אִיקְּלְעוּ לְבֵי בְּרֵיהּ דְּרַב אִידִי בַּר אָבִין, וַעֲבִיד לְהוּ עִיגְלָא תִּילְתָּא בְּיוֹמָא דְּשִׁבְעָה. וְאָמְרִי לֵיהּ: אִי אִיתְרַחִיתוּ לֵיהּ עַד לְאוּרְתָּא – הֲוָה אָכְלִינַן מִינֵּיהּ, הַשְׁתָּא – לָא אָכְלִינַן מִינֵּיהּ!

The Gemara raises a difficulty: Is that to say that if the child **fell off a roof or was eaten by a lion, everyone agrees** that **it is** considered to have been **alive? Didn't Rav Pappa and Rav Huna, son of Rav Yehoshua, happen** to come **to the house of the son of Rav Idi bar Avin, and he prepared for them a third-born calf**[N] **on the seventh day** after its birth. **And they said to him: Had you waited** to slaughter **it until the evening, we would have eaten from it. Now** that you did not wait, **we shall not eat from it.**[H] Apparently, if a calf is slaughtered before it was alive for eight days and definitely viable, suspicion that it is stillborn remains; the same is true of a child who dies from an accident within thirty days of birth.

אֶלָּא, כְּשֶׁפִּיהֵק וָמֵת – דִּבְרֵי הַכֹּל מֵת הוּא, כִּי פְּלִיגִי – בְּנָפַל מִן הַגַּג וַאֲכָלוֹ אֲרִי. מָר סָבַר: מֵת הוּא, וּמָר סָבַר: חַי הוּא.

Rather, Abaye's statement must be reformulated: **When** the baby **yawned and died, everyone agrees** that **it is** considered to have been **dead** from the outset. **Where they disagree is in** a case **when it fell off a roof or was eaten by a lion:** This **Master,** Rabban Shimon ben Gamliel, **holds: It is** considered to have been **dead;** and this **Master holds** that since it did not die on its own, **it is** considered to have been **alive.**

בְּרֵיהּ דְּרַב דִּימִי בַּר יוֹסֵף אִתְיְלִיד לֵיהּ הַהוּא יְנוּקָא, בְּגוֹ תְּלָתִין יוֹמִין שְׁכִיב. יָתֵיב קָמִתְאַבֵּיל עִילָּוֵיהּ. אֲמַר לֵיהּ אֲבוּהּ: צְוּוֹרוֹנִיתָא קָבָעֵית לְמֵיכַל?! אֲמַר לֵיהּ: קִים לִי בֵּיהּ שֶׁכָּלוּ לוֹ חֳדָשָׁיו.

The Gemara relates: **A baby was born to the son of Rav Dimi bar Yosef. Within thirty days** the baby **died. He sat** and **mourned over him.**[H] **His father,** Rav Dimi bar Yosef, **said to him:** Are you mourning because **you wish to partake of the delicacies fed to mourners?** The *halakha* deems a child that dies before thirty days stillborn, and one does not mourn over it. **He said to him: I am certain that its months** of gestation **were completed.**

רַב אָשֵׁי אִיקְּלַע בֵּי רַב כָּהֲנָא, אִיתְרַע בֵּיהּ מִילְּתָא בְּגוֹ תְּלָתִין יוֹמִין. חַזְיֵיהּ דְּיָתֵיב וְקָא מִתְאַבֵּל עִילָּוֵיהּ, אֲמַר לֵיהּ: לָא סָבַר לַיהּ מָר לְהָא דַּאֲמַר רַב יְהוּדָה אָמַר שְׁמוּאֵל ״הֲלָכָה כְּרַבָּן שִׁמְעוֹן בֶּן גַּמְלִיאֵל״? אֲמַר לֵיהּ: קִים לִי בְּגַוֵּיהּ שֶׁכָּלוּ לוֹ חֳדָשָׁיו.

The Gemara similarly relates that **Rav Ashi happened** to come **to Rav Kahana's house. A matter befell him,** i.e., his child died **within thirty days** of its birth. Rav Ashi **saw him** and observed **that he was sitting and mourning over him. He said to him: Doesn't the Master hold** in accordance with **that which Rav Yehuda said** that **Shmuel said: The *halakha* is in accordance with Rabban Shimon ben Gamliel,** that only a child who lived for thirty days is not considered stillborn? **He said to him: I am certain that its months** of gestation **were completed** and he is not to be considered a stillborn.

אִיתְּמַר, מֵת בְּתוֹךְ שְׁלֹשִׁים, וְעָמְדָה וְנִתְקַדְּשָׁה. אָמַר רָבִינָא מִשְּׁמֵיהּ דְּרָבָא:

It was stated that the Sages discussed the following question: What is the ruling in a case where a baby **died within thirty days** after birth, leaving its mother a childless widow, **and** before they decided whether or not she was obligated in levirate marriage, **she stood and was betrothed** to another? **Ravina said in the name of Rava:**

NOTES

A third-born calf – עִיגְלָא תִּילְתָּא: A calf that is the third born to its mother is considered to be of choice quality, because its mother is fully matured, and the birth is less difficult and the calf is not injured during birth. Even calves born thereafter are not considered to be of comparable quality, because the mother has already begun to age. Consequently, the third calf is the choicest (*ge'onim*).

HALAKHA

Eating a newborn animal – אֲכִילַת וְלַד בְּהֵמָה: A newborn animal that is known to have been carried to full term may be slaughtered immediately upon birth. If it not known whether the gestation was full term, it may be slaughtered from the night of the eighth day after its birth (Rambam *Sefer Kedusha, Hilkhot Ma'akhalot Assurot* 4:4; *Shulḥan Arukh, Yoreh De'a* 15:2).

Mourning for a newborn baby – אֲבֵילוּת עַל תִּינוֹק: There is no halakhic obligation to mourn a baby that died within thirty days after its birth, because it has the status of a potential stillborn. However, if it can be established that the mother carried the child to full term, one mourns the baby, as indicated by the incidents related in the Gemara (Rambam *Sefer Shofetim, Hilkhot Evel* 1:6–7; *Shulḥan Arukh, Yoreh De'a* 374:8).

Perek **XIX**
Daf **136** Amud **b**

אִם אֵשֶׁת יִשְׂרָאֵל הִיא – חוֹלֶצֶת, אִם אֵשֶׁת כֹּהֵן הִיא – אֵינָהּ חוֹלֶצֶת.

If she is the wife of an Israelite,[H] meaning she became betrothed to an Israelite, who may marry a woman who has undergone *ḥalitza*, **she performs *ḥalitza*** due to uncertainty. Given that the child may have been stillborn and therefore never considered alive, in which case she would be obligated to undergo levirate marriage or perform *ḥalitza*, by performing *ḥalitza*, she removes any doubt and can remain with her new husband. However, **if she is the wife of a priest, she does not perform *ḥalitza*,** as if she were to perform *ḥalitza* she would be prohibited to her husband the priest.[N] Since there are those who hold that that the baby is considered alive from the moment of its birth, based on that opinion, she is exempt from performing *ḥalitza*, after the fact.

HALAKHA

If she is the wife of an Israelite, etc. – אִם אֵשֶׁת יִשְׂרָאֵל וכו׳: If a man passed away without children and his wife was pregnant, and she gave birth to a child who died within thirty days, and it was not clear whether or not the child was carried full term, the widow is rabbinically obligated to perform *ḥalitza*. This is due to the possibility that the child was not viable. If she becomes betrothed to another man who is an Israelite, the brother of her late husband performs *ḥalitza* with her, and she marries the man to whom she was betrothed. However, if she became betrothed to a priest, she does not perform *ḥalitza*. This is in accordance with Ravina's statement that Rava exempted a woman in that case from *ḥalitza* (Rambam *Sefer Nashim, Hilkhot Yibbum VaḤalitza* 2:21; *Shulḥan Arukh, Even HaEzer* 164:7).

NOTES

Levirate marriage and *ḥalitza* – יִבּוּם וַחֲלִיצָה: The laws of levirate marriage and *ḥalitza* appear in the Torah (Deuteronomy 28:5–10) and are articulated at length in tractate *Yevamot*, which is devoted to this topic. The basic concept is that if a man dies with no living descendants, his wife is obligated by a levirate bond to her husband's brother. The brother must either take her as a wife through levirate marriage, or sever the bond by means of the ceremony of *ḥalitza*. As long as the levirate bond is intact, it is prohibited for her to marry a different man, and if she does so, as long as her marriage continues she is performing an ongoing transgression. Although the *halakhot* of levirate marriage and *ḥalitza* are not like those of a regular marriage, and a woman who has undergone *ḥalitza* is not prohibited to marry a priest by Torah law, the Sages decreed that the legal status of a woman who undergoes *ḥalitza* is that of a divorcée, in the sense that it is prohibited for a priest to marry her.

וְרַב שֵׁרֵבְיָא מִשְּׁמֵיהּ דְּרָבָא אָמַר: אַחַת זוֹ וְאַחַת זוֹ – חוֹלֶצֶת.

Rav Sherevya said in the name of Rava: **Both this,** the woman married to an Israelite, **and that,** the woman married to a priest, **perform *ḥalitza*,** as the prohibition against marrying a woman not released from her bond of levirate marriage is a stringent one, and the fact that her husband is a priest is not taken into consideration.

אֲמַר לֵיהּ רָבִינָא לְרַב שֵׁרֵבְיָא: בְּאוּרְתָּא אֲמַר רָבָא הָכִי, לְצַפְרָא הֲדַר בֵּיהּ. אֲמַר לֵיהּ: שְׁרִיתוּהָ? יְהֵא רַעֲוָא דְּתִשְׁרוּ תַּרְבָּא.

Ravina said to Rav Sherevya: In the evening Rava indeed **said so,** as you said; however, **in the morning he retracted** his statement, and that is what I cited. Rav Sherevya, however, did not accept this explanation, and said: **Did you permit** the wife of a priest without *ḥalitza*, despite the fact that Rabban Shimon ben Gamliel deems the baby stillborn unless he survives to the age of thirty days? Since you have violated his ruling, **may it be** God's **will that you** continue along this path and **permit** the eating of **forbidden fat.**

״רַבִּי יְהוּדָה מַתִּיר וכו׳״. אָמַר רַב שֵׁיזְבִי אָמַר רַב חִסְדָּא: לֹא לַכֹּל אָמַר רַבִּי יְהוּדָה אַנְדְּרוֹגִינוֹס זָכָר הוּא, שֶׁאִם אַתָּה אוֹמֵר כֵּן – בַּעֲרָכִין יֵעָרֵךְ!

We learned in the mishna that **Rabbi Yehuda permits** circumcising a hermaphrodite on Shabbat. **Rav Sheizvi said** that **Rav Ḥisda said: Not with regard to all** matters **did Rabbi Yehuda say** that **a hermaphrodite is** considered **a male;** it was only with regard to circumcision, **as if you say so,** that the legal status of a hermaphrodite is that of a male in every sense, then even **with regard to** vows of **valuation,**[N] **he should be valuated.**

וּמְנָלַן דְּלָא מִיעֲרַךְ – דְּתַנְיָא: ״הַזָּכָר״ – וְלֹא טוּמְטוּם וְאַנְדְּרוֹגִינוֹס. יָכוֹל לֹא יְהֵא בְּעֶרֶךְ אִישׁ, אֲבָל יְהֵא בְּעֶרֶךְ אִשָּׁה – תַּלְמוּד לוֹמַר: ״הַזָּכָר וְאִם נְקֵבָה הִיא״. זָכָר וַדַּאי, נְקֵבָה וַדָּאִית, וְלֹא טוּמְטוּם וְאַנְדְּרוֹגִינוֹס.

And from where do we derive **that he is not valuated? As it was taught** in the *Sifra*, the halakhic midrash on Leviticus, with regard to the verse: "Then your valuation shall be for **the male** from the age of twenty years until the age of sixty years, your valuation shall be fifty shekel of silver, after the shekel of the Sanctuary" (Leviticus 27:3). The Sages inferred: "The male" means the definite male **but not a *tumtum*[B] or a hermaphrodite.**[N] I **might** have thought that these **shall not be** valuated according to **the valuation of a man, but shall be** valuated according to **the valuation of a woman.** Therefore, **the verse states: "The male,"** and in the following verse: **"And if she is a female,** then your valuation shall be thirty shekels" (Leviticus 27:4), indicating: Only **a definite male** or a **definite female, but not a *tumtum* or a hermaphrodite,**[H] which are categorized as neither male nor female.

Perek **XIX**
Daf **137** Amud **a**

וּסְתָם סִפְרָא רַבִּי יְהוּדָה.

And an unattributed *halakha* cited in the ***Sifra*** generally reflects the opinion of **Rabbi Yehuda.**[N]

אָמַר רַב נַחְמָן בַּר יִצְחָק: אַף אֲנַן נַמִּי תָּנֵינָא ״הַכֹּל כְּשֵׁרִים לְקַדֵּשׁ, חוּץ מֵחֵרֵשׁ שׁוֹטֶה וְקָטָן. רַבִּי יְהוּדָה מַכְשִׁיר בְּקָטָן, וּפוֹסֵל בְּאִשָּׁה וְאַנְדְּרוֹגִינוֹס״ – שְׁמַע מִינָּהּ.

Rav Naḥman bar Yitzḥak said: We too also learned in a mishna that Rabbi Yehuda does not consider a hermaphrodite to be a male in every sense. The Sages disagreed over sanctification of the waters of a purification offering, i.e., the placing of the ashes of the red heifer in potable, running spring water: **Everyone is fit to sanctify** the waters of a purification offering,[H] **except for a deaf-mute, an imbecile, and a minor. Rabbi Yehuda deems a minor fit, but deems a woman and a hermaphrodite unfit.** Apparently, Rabbi Yehuda does not consider the legal status of a hermaphrodite to be like that of a male. The Gemara concludes: **Conclude from this.**

NOTES

Vows of valuation – עֲרָכִין: The laws of valuations appear in the Torah (Leviticus 27:1–8), and are detailed in tractate *Arakhin*. The basic concept of valuation refers to a situation where one donates his value to the Temple treasury. The Torah fixes certain values for each gender and age group. The consensus is that one who is not categorized as belonging to a particular gender has no specific, Torah-determined value, and the value of that person cannot be calculated by other means. Therefore, valuation to the Temple would be meaningless.

A *tumtum* or a hermaphrodite – טוּמְטוּם וְאַנְדְּרוֹגִינוֹס: A *tumtum* and a hermaphrodite are classified together in regard to many issues, since they are neither male nor female. There is, however, a fundamental difference between them: A *tumtum* is a case of unresolved uncertainty, which can sometimes be resolved either way. A hermaphrodite, by contrast, might be an entity in and of itself, constituting a third, unique gender.

BACKGROUND

Tumtum – טוּמְטוּם: A *tumtum* is one whose external sexual organs are indeterminate, and it is unclear whether the person is male or female. In certain cases, the gender of the *tumtum* is later established, which is described in the language of the *halakha* as: A *tumtum* who was torn, revealing his gender, at which point this person is considered a full-fledged member of that gender.

HALAKHA

The valuations of a *tumtum* and a hermaphrodite – עֶרְכֵּי טוּמְטוּם וְאַנְדְּרוֹגִינוֹס: The Torah established fixed amounts for the valuations of males and females, but there is no valuation whatsoever given for a *tumtum* or a hermaphrodite. When that type of person donates his value, no obligation is incurred (Rambam *Sefer Hafla'a, Hilkhot Arakhin* 1:5).

NOTES

An unattributed *Sifra* generally reflects the opinion of Rabbi Yehuda – סְתָם סִפְרָא רַבִּי יְהוּדָה: There is a talmudic tradition that unattributed *mishnayot* were formulated by and reflect the views of Rabbi Meir. Similar traditions exist with regard to other tannaitic works. The *Sifra*, also known as *Torat Kohanim*, the halakhic midrash on Leviticus, generally reflects the opinion of Rabbi Yehuda.

HALAKHA

The sanctification of the waters of a purification offering – קִידּוּשׁ מֵי חַטָּאת: The sanctification of the waters of a purification offering, i.e., the placing of the ashes of the red heifer in potable, running spring water, is valid if performed by any Jew, including a woman, apart from a deaf-mute, an imbecile, and a minor, in accordance with the view of the Rabbis (Rambam *Sefer Tahara, Hilkhot Para Aduma* 6:2).

וּמַאי שְׁנָא מִילָה – מִשּׁוּם דִּכְתִיב ״הִמּוֹל לָכֶם כׇּל זָכָר״.

The Gemara asks: **What is different** about the *halakhot* of **circumcision,** with regard to which Rabbi Yehuda categorizes a hermaphrodite as a male in regard to its laws? The Gemara answers that it is **due to** the fact **that it is written:** "This is My covenant which you shall keep, between Me and you and your seed after you: **Circumcise for yourselves every male**" (Genesis 17:10), and he interprets the phrase "every male" as an amplification including anyone who could possibly be included in the category of a male.[N]

מתני׳ מִי שֶׁהָיוּ לוֹ שְׁנֵי תִּינוֹקוֹת, אֶחָד לָמוּל אַחַר הַשַּׁבָּת וְאֶחָד לָמוּל בַּשַּׁבָּת. וְשָׁכַח, וּמָל אֶת שֶׁל אַחַר הַשַּׁבָּת בַּשַּׁבָּת – חַיָּיב.

MISHNA **One who had two babies** to circumcise, **one** of whom he needed **to circumcise** on the day **after Shabbat, and one** of whom he needed **to circumcise on Shabbat, and he forgot and circumcised the one** that should have been circumcised **after Shabbat on Shabbat, he is liable** to bring a sin-offering, because he performed the prohibited labor of causing a wound not in the framework of performing a mitzva, as no obligation yet exists to circumcise the child.

אֶחָד לָמוּל בְּעֶרֶב שַׁבָּת, וְאֶחָד לָמוּל בַּשַּׁבָּת, וְשָׁכַח וּמָל אֶת שֶׁל עֶרֶב שַׁבָּת בַּשַּׁבָּת, רַבִּי אֱלִיעֶזֶר מְחַיֵּיב חַטָּאת, וְרַבִּי יְהוֹשֻׁעַ פּוֹטֵר.

If there were two babies, **one to circumcise on Shabbat eve, and one to circumcise on Shabbat, and he forgot and circumcised the one** that he should have circumcised on **Shabbat eve on Shabbat, Rabbi Eliezer deems him liable** to bring **a sin-offering,** as circumcision after its appointed time does not override Shabbat. **And Rabbi Yehoshua exempts** him; since he intended to perform a mitzva, and despite his error in fact performed a mitzva, he is exempt from bringing a sin-offering.

גמ׳ רַב הוּנָא מַתְנֵי ״חַיָּיב״ רַב יְהוּדָה מַתְנֵי פָּטוּר.

GEMARA There is a dispute among the *amora'im* with regard to the correct version of our mishna, based on an early dispute of the *tanna'im*: **Rav Huna teaches** the first clause of the mishna as stating: **Liable,** whereas **Rav Yehuda teaches** the first clause as stating: **Exempt.**

רַב הוּנָא מַתְנֵי ״חַיָּיב״ – דְּתַנְיָא, אָמַר רַבִּי שִׁמְעוֹן בֶּן אֶלְעָזָר: לֹא נֶחְלְקוּ רַבִּי אֱלִיעֶזֶר וְרַבִּי יְהוֹשֻׁעַ עַל מִי שֶׁהָיוּ לוֹ שְׁנֵי תִּינוֹקוֹת, אֶחָד לָמוּל בַּשַּׁבָּת וְאֶחָד לָמוּל אַחַר הַשַּׁבָּת, וְשָׁכַח וּמָל אֶת שֶׁל אַחַר הַשַּׁבָּת בַּשַּׁבָּת – שֶׁהוּא חַיָּיב.

The Gemara explains: **Rav Huna taught** the first clause as stating: **Liable,** based on that which **was taught** in a *baraita* that **Rabbi Shimon ben Elazar said: Rabbi Eliezer and Rabbi Yehoshua did not disagree with regard to one who had two babies, one to circumcise on Shabbat and one to circumcise after Shabbat, and he forgot and circumcised the one** who should have been circumcised **after Shabbat on Shabbat;** in that case, everyone agrees **that he is liable** to bring a sin-offering.

עַל מָה נֶחְלְקוּ – עַל מִי שֶׁהָיוּ לוֹ שְׁנֵי תִּינוֹקוֹת, אֶחָד לָמוּל בְּעֶרֶב שַׁבָּת וְאֶחָד לָמוּל בַּשַּׁבָּת, וְשָׁכַח וּמָל אֶת שֶׁל עֶרֶב שַׁבָּת בַּשַּׁבָּת. שֶׁרַבִּי אֱלִיעֶזֶר מְחַיֵּיב חַטָּאת, וְרַבִּי יְהוֹשֻׁעַ פּוֹטֵר.

With regard to what did they disagree? With regard to one who had two babies, one to circumcise on Shabbat eve and one to circumcise on Shabbat, and he forgot and circumcised the one who should have been circumcised on **Shabbat eve on Shabbat, as Rabbi Eliezer renders him liable** to bring **a sin-offering** for this unwitting transgression, **and Rabbi Yehoshua exempts** him

וּשְׁנֵיהֶם לֹא לְמָדוּהָ אֶלָּא מֵעֲבוֹדָה זָרָה. רַבִּי אֱלִיעֶזֶר סָבַר: כַּעֲבוֹדָה זָרָה, מָה עֲבוֹדָה זָרָה אָמַר רַחֲמָנָא ״לֹא תַעֲבִיד״ וְכִי עָבֵיד – מִיחַיֵּיב, הָכָא נַמִי – לָא שְׁנָא.

And both of them only derived it from idolatry,[N] where the Torah details the *halakhot* of bringing a sin-offering for an unwitting transgression. **Rabbi Eliezer holds:** The law of every unwitting transgression is **like** that of **idolatry. Just as** with regard to **idolatry the Torah stated: Do not perform** certain activities, **and when one performs** them unwittingly, he is **liable** to bring a sin-offering, **here too it is no different,** and since he transgressed the prohibition, he is liable to bring a sin-offering.

וְרַבִּי יְהוֹשֻׁעַ: הָתָם – דְּלָאו מִצְוָה, הָכָא – מִצְוָה.

And Rabbi Yehoshua holds: **There,** where the unwitting transgression was **not** performed in order to fulfill **a mitzva,** one is liable to bring a sin-offering. **Here,** his intention was to perform **a mitzva,** and one who unwittingly violates a prohibition in the course of attempting to fulfill a mitzva is exempt from bringing a sin-offering. This is according to the opinion of Rav Huna, based on the opinion of Rabbi Shimon ben Elazar.

רַב יְהוּדָה מַתְנֵי. ״פָּטוּר״ – דְּתַנְיָא, אָמַר רַבִּי מֵאִיר: לֹא נֶחְלְקוּ רַבִּי אֱלִיעֶזֶר וְרַבִּי יְהוֹשֻׁעַ עַל מִי שֶׁהָיוּ לוֹ שְׁנֵי תִּינוֹקוֹת אֶחָד לָמוּל בְּעֶרֶב שַׁבָּת וְאֶחָד לָמוּל בַּשַּׁבָּת, וְשָׁכַח וּמָל אֶת שֶׁל עֶרֶב שַׁבָּת בַּשַּׁבָּת – שֶׁהוּא פָּטוּר.

Rav Yehuda taught the first clause as stating: **Exempt,** based on that which **was taught** in a *baraita* that **Rabbi Meir said: Rabbi Eliezer and Rabbi Yehoshua did not disagree**[H] **over one who had two babies** to circumcise, **one to circumcise on Shabbat eve and one to circumcise on Shabbat, and he forgot and circumcised the one** who should have been circumcised on **Shabbat eve on Shabbat;** in that case, everyone agrees **that he is exempt** from bringing a sin-offering, as that circumcision fulfilled a mitzva.

NOTES

The meaning of male according to Rabbi Yehuda – מַשְׁמָעוּת זָכָר לְרַבִּי יְהוּדָה: In the Jerusalem Talmud as well, Rabbi Yehuda considers a hermaphrodite to be male only with regard to circumcision. The explanation given there is that Rabbi Yehuda and the Rabbis disagree over the implication of the phrase "uncircumcised male" that appears in a different verse. The Rabbis understood that the superfluous word "male" indicates that circumcision only applies to one who is indisputably male. Rabbi Yehuda understood that the word "uncircumcised" indicates that the mitzva applies to anyone who is uncircumcised.

And both of them only derived it from idolatry – וּשְׁנֵיהֶם לֹא לְמָדוּהָ אֶלָּא מֵעֲבוֹדָה זָרָה: The Sages had a tradition that the verses in Numbers (15:22–31) refer to the *halakhot* of the special sin-offering for unwitting idolatry. Nevertheless, that passage is the source for many of the general *halakhot* of sin-offerings, and therefore analogies are made between other transgressions of Torah law and idolatry.

HALAKHA

Rabbi Yehuda taught the first clause as stating exempt…Rabbi Eliezer and Rabbi Yehoshua did not disagree, etc. – רַב יְהוּדָה מַתְנֵי פָּטוּר...לֹא נֶחְלְקוּ רַבִּי אֱלִיעֶזֶר וְרַבִּי יְהוֹשֻׁעַ וכו׳: If one had two babies to circumcise, one to circumcise on Shabbat, and one on Shabbat eve or after Shabbat, and he mistakenly circumcised them both on Shabbat, he is exempt from bringing a sin-offering. Since he is permitted, and even required, to override Shabbat in order to circumcise one of them, his mistake is attributed to his preoccupation with the performance of the mitzva, and therefore he is exempt. The *halakha* is in accordance with the version of Rav Yehuda, since the *baraita* of the school of Rabbi Ḥiyya supports him, and Rabbi Yannai's statement also explains this opinion (*Kesef Mishne*; Rambam *Sefer Korbanot*, *Hilkhot Shegagot* 2:8).

עַל מַה נֶּחְלְקוּ – עַל מִי שֶׁהָיוּ לוֹ שְׁנֵי תִּינוֹקוֹת, אֶחָד לָמוּל אַחַר הַשַּׁבָּת וְאֶחָד לָמוּל בַּשַּׁבָּת, וְשָׁכַח וּמָל אֶת שֶׁל אַחַר הַשַּׁבָּת בַּשַּׁבָּת. שֶׁרַבִּי אֱלִיעֶזֶר מְחַיֵּיב חַטָּאת, וְרַבִּי יְהוֹשֻׁעַ פּוֹטֵר.

With regard to what did they disagree? With regard to one who had two babies, one to circumcise after Shabbat and one to circumcise on Shabbat, and he forgot and circumcised the one who should have been circumcised **after Shabbat on Shabbat, as Rabbi Eliezer deems him liable** to bring **a sin-offering, and Rabbi Yehoshua exempts** him.

וּשְׁנֵיהֶם לֹא לְמָדוּהָ אֶלָּא מֵעֲבוֹדָה זָרָה. רַבִּי אֱלִיעֶזֶר סָבַר: כַּעֲבוֹדָה זָרָה, מָה עֲבוֹדָה זָרָה אָמַר רַחֲמָנָא "לָא תַּעֲבֵיד", וְכִי עָבֵיד – מִיחַיַּיב, הָכָא נַמִי – לָא שְׁנָא.

And the Gemara notes here too that **both of them only derived it from idolatry. Rabbi Eliezer holds:** The *halakha* of every unwitting transgression sin **is like** that of **idolatry: Just as** with regard to **idolatry the Torah stated: Do not perform** certain activities, **and when one performs** them unwittingly he is **liable** to bring a sin-offering, **here too it is no different,** and since he violated the prohibition, he is liable to bring a sin-offering.

וְרַבִּי יְהוֹשֻׁעַ: הָתָם – לָא טָרֵיד מִצְוָה, הָכָא – טָרֵיד מִצְוָה.

And Rabbi Yehoshua holds: **There,** with regard to idolatry, one is liable to bring a sin-offering when he performs the transgression, because **he is not preoccupied** with the performance of a **mitzva. Here, he is preoccupied** with the performance of a **mitzva,** and anyone who unwittingly transgresses a prohibition while preoccupied with a mitzva is exempt from bringing a sin-offering.

תָּנֵי רַבִּי חִיָּיא, אוֹמֵר הָיָה רַבִּי מֵאִיר: לֹא נֶחְלְקוּ רַבִּי אֱלְעָזָר וְרַבִּי יְהוֹשֻׁעַ עַל מִי שֶׁהָיוּ לוֹ שְׁנֵי תִּינוֹקוֹת אֶחָד לָמוּל בְּעֶרֶב שַׁבָּת וְאֶחָד לָמוּל בַּשַּׁבָּת, וְשָׁכַח וּמָל אֶת שֶׁל עֶרֶב שַׁבָּת בַּשַּׁבָּת – שֶׁהוּא חַיָּיב.

Rabbi Ḥiyya taught another version of the same dispute between the *tanna'im*: **Rabbi Meir would say** that **Rabbi Eliezer and Rabbi Yehoshua did not disagree over one who had two babies, one to circumcise on Shabbat eve and one to circumcise on Shabbat, and he forgot and circumcised the one** who should have been circumcised **on Shabbat eve on Shabbat;** in that case, everyone agrees **that he is liable** to bring a sin-offering.

עַל מַה נֶּחְלְקוּ – עַל מִי שֶׁהָיוּ לוֹ שְׁנֵי תִּינוֹקוֹת, אֶחָד לָמוּל אַחַר הַשַּׁבָּת וְאֶחָד לָמוּל בַּשַּׁבָּת. וְשָׁכַח וּמָל שֶׁל אַחַר הַשַּׁבָּת בַּשַּׁבָּת, שֶׁרַבִּי אֱלִיעֶזֶר מְחַיֵּיב חַטָּאת וְרַבִּי יְהוֹשֻׁעַ פּוֹטֵר.

With regard to what did they disagree? With regard to one who had two babies to circumcise, **one to circumcise after Shabbat and one to circumcise on Shabbat, and he forgot and circumcised the one** who should have been circumcised **after Shabbat on Shabbat, Rabbi Eliezer deems him liable** to bring **a sin-offering, and Rabbi Yehoshua exempts** him.

הַשְׁתָּא, רַבִּי יְהוֹשֻׁעַ סֵיפָא דְּלָא קָא עָבֵיד מִצְוָה – פּוֹטֵר, רֵישָׁא דְּקָא עָבֵיד מִצְוָה מְחַיֵּיב?!

The Gemara expresses surprise at this last version: **Now,** after all, in **the latter clause, where he did not perform a mitzva, Rabbi Yehoshua exempts** him; **in the first clause, where he performed a mitzva, does Rabbi Yehoshua deem him liable?**

אָמְרִי דְּבֵי רַבִּי יַנַּאי: רֵישָׁא – כְּגוֹן שֶׁקָּדַם וּמָל שֶׁל שַׁבָּת בְּעֶרֶב שַׁבָּת, דְּלֹא נִיתְּנָה שַׁבָּת לִידָּחוֹת. סֵיפָא – נִיתְּנָה שַׁבָּת לִידָּחוֹת.

In the school of Rabbi Yannai they say: The first clause of the *baraita* is referring to a unique situation, **where** the circumcisor **first** unwittingly **circumcised** the baby who should have been circumcised **on Shabbat on Shabbat eve.** In that case, **Shabbat** is **not given to be overridden** at all, since the baby who was supposed to be circumcised on Shabbat was already circumcised. In the **latter clause,** however, the circumcision was performed in a situation where **Shabbat** is **given to be overridden.**

אֲמַר לֵיהּ רַב אַשִׁי לְרַב כָּהֲנָא: רֵישָׁא נַמִי, נִיתְּנָה שַׁבָּת לִידָּחוֹת לְגַבֵּי תִּינוֹקוֹת דְּעָלְמָא! לְהַאי גַּבְרָא מִיהָא לָא אִיתְיְהֵיב.

Rav Ashi said to Rav Kahana that this explanation is difficult: **In the first clause too, Shabbat** is **given to be overridden with regard to babies in general,** as it is permitted to circumcise a baby whose eighth day occurs on Shabbat. He replied: That is indeed so; **however, with regard to this person,** Shabbat is **not given** to be overriden, as there is no longer any child who is supposed to be circumcised on Shabbat. Therefore, if he unwittingly performed a circumcision on Shabbat, he is not considered to have unwittingly performed a transgression while preoccupied with the performance of a mitzva.

מתני׳ קָטָן נִימּוֹל לִשְׁמוֹנָה לְתִשְׁעָה וְלַעֲשָׂרָה וּלְאַחַד עָשָׂר וְלִשְׁנֵים עָשָׂר, לֹא פָּחוֹת וְלֹא יוֹתֵר.

MISHNA Although **a child is** generally **circumcised at eight** days, as the verse states: "And on the eighth day, the flesh of his foreskin shall be circumcised" (Leviticus 12:3), nevertheless, at times he is circumcised **at nine** days, at times **at ten** days, **at eleven** days, **and at twelve** days, **no earlier and no later.**

הָא כֵּיצַד: כְּדַרְכּוֹ – לִשְׁמוֹנָה, נוֹלַד לְבֵין הַשְּׁמָשׁוֹת – נִימּוֹל לְתִשְׁעָה, בֵּין הַשְּׁמָשׁוֹת שֶׁל עֶרֶב שַׁבָּת – נִימּוֹל לַעֲשָׂרָה.

How so? In his usual manner, a child is circumcised at eight days. If he was born at twilight[N] and it is therefore uncertain on which day he was born, he is circumcised at nine days,[H] as his circumcision is postponed due to that uncertainty, as perhaps the eighth day from his birth has not yet arrived. If he was born at twilight on Shabbat eve, he is not circumcised on the following Shabbat, due to the uncertainty whether it is the eighth or ninth day since his birth, and only a circumcision definitely performed at the appointed time overrides Shabbat. Rather, he is circumcised on Sunday, and the result is that he is circumcised at ten days.

יוֹם טוֹב לְאַחַר הַשַּׁבָּת – נִימּוֹל לְאַחַד עָשָׂר, שְׁנֵי יָמִים שֶׁל רֹאשׁ הַשָּׁנָה – נִימּוֹל לִשְׁנֵים עָשָׂר.

If there was a Festival after that Shabbat, he is not circumcised on the Festival either, and he is circumcised at eleven days. And if that Shabbat was followed by two days of Rosh HaShana, the result is that he is circumcised at twelve days.

קָטָן הַחוֹלֶה – אֵין מוֹהֲלִין אוֹתוֹ עַד שֶׁיַּבְרִיא.

The mishna states another *halakha*: With regard to a sick child, one does not circumcise him until he becomes healthy.

גמ׳ אָמַר שְׁמוּאֵל: חֲלָצַתּוּ חַמָּה – נוֹתְנִין לוֹ כָּל שִׁבְעָה לְהַבְרוֹתוֹ.

GEMARA We learned in the mishna that one does not circumcise a sick baby until he becomes healthy. Shmuel said: A baby that was sick and had a high fever, and subsequently the fever left him,[H] one gives him a full seven days to heal before circumcising him.

אִיבַּעְיָא לְהוּ: מִי בָּעֵינַן מֵעֵת לְעֵת?

With regard to this issue, a dilemma was raised before the Sages: Do we require, during the recovery period, to wait from the time the seven days begin to the exact same time seven days later, i.e., seven complete, twenty-four-hour periods, or is it enough to wait seven days without taking into account the time of day?

תָּא שְׁמַע: דְּתָנֵי לוּדָא ״יוֹם הַבְרָאָתוֹ כְּיוֹם הוּלַּדְתּוֹ״. מַאי לָאו, מָה יוֹם הוּלַּדְתּוֹ – לָא בָּעֵינַן מֵעֵת לְעֵת, אַף יוֹם הַבְרָאָתוֹ לָא בָּעֵינַן מֵעֵת לְעֵת.

The Gemara suggests: Come and hear a solution to this from that which the Sage Luda taught: The day of his healing is like the day of his birth. What, is it not that just as from the day of his birth we need not wait from the time he is born to the same time on the eighth day to circumcise him, so too, with regard to the day of his healing, we need not wait from the time he heals to the same time seven days later?

לָא, עָדִיף יוֹם הַבְרָאָתוֹ מִיּוֹם הוּלַּדְתּוֹ. דְּאִילּוּ יוֹם הוּלַּדְתּוֹ – לָא בָּעֵינַן מֵעֵת לְעֵת, וְאִילּוּ יוֹם הַבְרָאָתוֹ – בָּעֵינַן מֵעֵת לְעֵת.

The Gemara refutes this: No, the day of his healing is superior to the day of his birth. While from the day of his birth until circumcision we need not wait from time to time, from the day of his healing we need to wait seven complete days from time to time.

מתני׳ אֵלּוּ הֵן צִיצִין הַמְעַכְּבִין אֶת הַמִּילָה: בָּשָׂר הַחוֹפֶה אֶת רוֹב הָעֲטָרָה, וְאֵינוֹ אוֹכֵל בִּתְרוּמָה.

MISHNA These are the shreds of flesh that invalidate the circumcision[N] if they are not cut. The essential element of circumcision is the removal of the flesh that covers most of the corona, and a child that was not circumcised in this manner is considered uncircumcised, and he does not eat *teruma*.

וְאִם הָיָה בַּעַל בָּשָׂר – מְתַקְּנוֹ מִפְּנֵי מַרְאִית הָעַיִן.

And if he was properly circumcised but he was fleshy,[H] and it appears as though he has not been properly circumcised, the circumcisor should correct it by circumcising more than necessary, to avoid the appearance of transgression, so he will not appear uncircumcised.

NOTES

Born at twilight – נוֹלַד לְבֵין הַשְּׁמָשׁוֹת: It is explained in the Jerusalem Talmud that a baby born at twilight cannot be circumcised eight days later at twilight, since it is impossible to approximate the same exact moment as the birth, as there is uncertainty with regard to each moment of twilight as to whether it is considered day or night. Therefore, the circumcision must be postponed until the following day.

HALAKHA

A child is circumcised at eight days…at nine days, etc. – קָטָן נִימּוֹל לִשְׁמוֹנָה לְתִשְׁעָה וכו׳: The circumcision of a baby born at twilight might be postponed due to the sanctity of Shabbat and Festivals in the exile or the sanctity of Rosh HaShana for as many as twelve days after his birth (Rambam *Sefer Ahava*, *Hilkhot Mila* 1:12; *Shulḥan Arukh*, *Yoreh De'a* 266:8).

The fever left him – חֲלָצַתּוּ חַמָּה: A baby that became physically ill is not circumcised until he regains his health. His circumcision is postponed seven complete days from the time he recovered from his illness (Rambam *Sefer Ahava*, *Hilkhot Mila* 1:16; *Shulḥan Arukh*, *Yoreh De'a* 262:2).

Shreds of flesh that invalidate the circumcision – צִיצִין הַמְעַכְּבִין אֶת הַמִּילָה: After a circumcision, if skin remains that covers most of the height of the corona, even in a single place, the circumcision is invalid. However, if only a small amount of skin is left and it does not cover most of the corona, it does not invalidate the circumcision after the fact. Nevertheless, *ab initio*, it is fitting to circumcise the infant completely (Rambam *Sefer Ahava*, *Hilkhot Mila* 2:3; *Shulḥan Arukh*, *Yoreh De'a* 264:5).

A fleshy baby – תִּינוֹק בַּעַל בָּשָׂר: A fleshy baby that looks as though he has not been circumcised is examined. If he appears circumcised when his penis is erect, there is no need to circumcise him again, but his skin is pulled back and held in place. However, if he does not appear to be circumcised when his penis is erect, the infant is circumcised a second time in order to avoid the appearance of being uncircumcised (Rambam *Sefer Ahava*, *Hilkhot Mila* 2:5; *Shulḥan Arukh*, *Yoreh De'a* 264:6).

Perek **XIX**
Daf **137** Amud **b**

מָל וְלֹא פָּרַע אֶת הַמִּילָה – כְּאִילּוּ לֹא מָל.

If one circumcised but did not uncover[H] the flesh at the area of the circumcision by folding back the thin membrane beneath the foreskin, it is as if he had not circumcised.

גמ׳ אָמַר רַבִּי אָבִינָא אָמַר רַבִּי יִרְמְיָה בַּר אַבָּא אָמַר רַב: בָּשָׂר הַחוֹפֶה אֶת רוֹב גּוֹבְהָהּ שֶׁל עֲטָרָה.

GEMARA Rabbi Avina said that Rabbi Yirmeya bar Abba said that Rav said: When the mishna said most of the corona, they meant the flesh that covers most of the height of the corona, as well as most of its circumference.

HALAKHA

Circumcised but did not uncover – מָל וְלֹא פָּרַע: After the foreskin is removed, the area must be uncovered by removing the membrane under the foreskin. If this was not done, the circumcision is invalid (*Shulḥan Arukh*, *Yoreh De'a* 264:4).

״וְאִם הָיָה בַּעַל בָּשָׂר וכו׳״. אָמַר שְׁמוּאֵל: קָטָן הַמְסוּרְבָּל בְּבָשָׂר, רוֹאִין אוֹתוֹ, כָּל זְמַן שֶׁמִּתְקַשֶּׁה וְנִרְאֶה מָהוּל – אֵינוֹ צָרִיךְ לָמוּל, וְאִם לָאו – צָרִיךְ לָמוּל.

We learned in the mishna: **If** the baby **was fleshy,** the circumcisor corrects the circumcision so that it will not appear uncircumcised. **Shmuel said: A child who is encumbered with flesh, one examines him,** and **as long as when** his limb **hardens he looks circumcised, one need not circumcise** him again. **And if not,** meaning he does not appear circumcised even then, **one must circumcise** him again.

בְּמַתְנִיתָא תְּנָא, רַבָּן שִׁמְעוֹן בֶּן גַּמְלִיאֵל אוֹמֵר: קָטָן הַמְסוּרְבָּל בְּבָשָׂר רוֹאִין אוֹתוֹ, כָּל זְמַן שֶׁמִּתְקַשֶּׁה וְאֵינוֹ נִרְאֶה מָהוּל – צָרִיךְ לְמוּלוֹ, וְאִם לָאו – אֵינוֹ צָרִיךְ לְמוּלוֹ.

It was taught in a *baraita* that Rabban Shimon ben Gamliel says: A child who is encumbered with flesh, one examines him, and **as long as when it hardens it does not appear circumcised, one needs to circumcise him** again, **and if not, one need not circumcise him** again.

מַאי בֵּינַיְיהוּ? אִיכָּא בֵּינַיְיהוּ: נִרְאֶה וְאֵינוֹ נִרְאֶה.

The Gemara asks: **What is** the practical difference **between these** two formulations? The Gemara answers: **There is** a practical difference **between them** in a case where he **appears** circumcised but **does not appear** fully circumcised.[N] According to Shmuel, in order to avoid an additional circumcision, one must appear fully circumcised, and this state is insufficient. According to Rabban Shimon ben Gamliel, only one who appears uncircumcised requires further circumcision; this partial circumcision is adequate.

״מָל וְלֹא פָּרַע״. תָּנוּ רַבָּנַן: הַמָּל אוֹמֵר: ״אֲשֶׁר קִדְּשָׁנוּ בְּמִצְוֹתָיו וְצִוָּנוּ עַל הַמִּילָה״. אֲבִי הַבֵּן אוֹמֵר: ״אֲשֶׁר קִדְּשָׁנוּ בְּמִצְוֹתָיו וְצִוָּנוּ לְהַכְנִיסוֹ בִּבְרִיתוֹ שֶׁל אַבְרָהָם אָבִינוּ״. הָעוֹמְדִים אוֹמְרִים: ״כְּשֵׁם שֶׁנִּכְנַס לַבְּרִית כָּךְ יִכָּנֵס לַתּוֹרָה לְחוּפָּה וּלְמַעֲשִׂים טוֹבִים״.

We learned in the mishna: If **he circumcised** a child **but did not uncover** the area of the circumcision, it is as if he did not circumcise him. **The Sages taught** in a *Tosefta* that **one who circumcises** a child **recites: Who has made us holy through His commandments, and commanded us concerning circumcision. The father of the** circumcised **child recites: Who has made us holy through His commandments, and commanded us to bring him into the covenant of Abraham, our father. Those standing** there **recite: Just as he has entered into the covenant, so may he enter into Torah, marriage, and good deeds.**

וְהַמְבָרֵךְ אוֹמֵר: ״אֲשֶׁר קִידֵּשׁ יְדִיד מִבֶּטֶן, חוֹק בִּשְׁאֵרוֹ שָׂם, וְצֶאֱצָאָיו חָתַם בְּאוֹת בְּרִית קֹדֶשׁ. עַל כֵּן בִּשְׂכַר זֹאת, אֵל חַי חֶלְקֵנוּ, צִוָּה לְהַצִּיל יְדִידוּת שְׁאֵרֵינוּ מִשַּׁחַת, לְמַעַן בְּרִיתוֹ אֲשֶׁר שָׂם בִּבְשָׂרֵנוּ בָּרוּךְ אַתָּה ה׳ כּוֹרֵת הַבְּרִית״.

And the one who recites the additional **blessing says:**[N] **Who made the beloved one holy from the womb,**[N] **marked the decree in his flesh, and gave his descendants the seal and the sign of the holy covenant. Therefore, as a reward for this, the living God, our Portion, commanded to deliver the beloved of our flesh from destruction, for the sake of His covenant that He set in our flesh. Blessed are You, Lord, Who establishes the covenant.**[H]

הַמָּל אֶת הַגֵּרִים אוֹמֵר: ״בָּרוּךְ אַתָּה ה׳ אֱלֹהֵינוּ מֶלֶךְ הָעוֹלָם אֲשֶׁר קִדְּשָׁנוּ בְּמִצְוֹתָיו וְצִוָּנוּ עַל הַמִּילָה״. וְהַמְבָרֵךְ אוֹמֵר ״אֲשֶׁר קִדְּשָׁנוּ בְּמִצְוֹתָיו וְצִוָּנוּ לָמוּל אֶת הַגֵּרִים וּלְהַטִּיף מֵהֶם דַּם בְּרִית, שֶׁאִילְמָלֵא דַּם בְּרִית לֹא נִתְקַיְּימוּ שָׁמַיִם וָאָרֶץ שֶׁנֶּאֱמַר ״אִם לֹא בְרִיתִי יוֹמָם וָלָיְלָה חוּקוֹת שָׁמַיִם וָאָרֶץ לֹא שָׂמְתִּי״ בָּרוּךְ אַתָּה ה׳ כּוֹרֵת הַבְּרִית״.

One who circumcises converts[H] **says: Blessed are You, Lord, our God, King of the universe, Who made us holy with His commandments, and commanded us concerning circumcision. And the one who recites the** additional **blessing recites: Who has made us holy with His commandments, and commanded us to circumcise converts, and to drip from them covenantal blood,**[N] **as were it not for the blood of the covenant, the heaven and earth would not be sustained, as it is stated: "If My covenant would not be with day and night, the ordinances of heaven and earth I would not have placed"** (Jeremiah 33:25), which is interpreted to mean that were it not for the covenant of circumcision that is manifest both day and night, the world would cease to exist. He concludes the blessing with the phrase: **Blessed are You, Lord, Who establishes the covenant.**

הַמָּל אֶת הָעֲבָדִים אוֹמֵר: ״אֲשֶׁר קִדְּשָׁנוּ בְּמִצְוֹתָיו וְצִוָּנוּ עַל הַמִּילָה״, וְהַמְבָרֵךְ אוֹמֵר ״אֲשֶׁר קִדְּשָׁנוּ בְּמִצְוֹתָיו וְצִוָּנוּ לָמוּל אֶת הָעֲבָדִים וּלְהַטִּיף מֵהֶם דַּם בְּרִית שֶׁאִילְמָלֵא דַּם בְּרִית חוּקוֹת שָׁמַיִם וָאָרֶץ לֹא נִתְקַיְּימוּ, שֶׁנֶּאֱמַר ״אִם לֹא בְרִיתִי יוֹמָם וָלָיְלָה חוּקוֹת שָׁמַיִם וָאָרֶץ לֹא שָׂמְתִּי״ בָּרוּךְ אַתָּה ה׳ כּוֹרֵת הַבְּרִית״.

When a Jew buys a Canaanite slave, he is obligated to circumcise the slave,[H] as the slave is partially entering the covenant of the Jewish people. **One who circumcises slaves recites** a blessing similar to those mentioned above: **Who made us holy with His commandments, and commanded us to circumcise slaves, and to drip from them covenantal blood, as were it not for the blood of the covenant the heaven and earth would not be sustained, as it is stated: "If My covenant would not be with day and night, the ordinances of heaven and earth I would not have placed"** (Jeremiah 33:25). **Blessed are You, Lord, Who establishes the covenant.**

הדרך עלך רבי אליעזר דמילה

NOTES

He appears circumcised but does not appear fully circumcised – נִרְאֶה וְאֵינוֹ נִרְאֶה: In other words, the difference between the mishna and the *baraita* is not simply a matter of formulation. Rather, there is a practical difference: Is it necessary to examine the child to make certain that he is clearly circumcised, or is it enough to ascertain that he does not appear uncircumcised? Although there is no difference between the two opinions in ordinary cases, there are ramifications in borderline cases.

The one who recites the additional blessing says – הַמְבָרֵךְ אוֹמֵר: The one who recites the blessing is a designated individual, whether the person who performed the circumcision or any other person, who holds a cup of wine in his hand and recites an additional blessing over the circumcision. Some authorities explain that the rationale for the second blessing is that since this mitzva was already fulfilled by the Patriarchs, the Sages instituted a special blessing in their honor (*Tosefot Rid*).

Made the beloved one holy from the womb – קִידֵּשׁ יְדִיד מִבֶּטֶן: See *Tosafot*, who explain that this blessing alludes to all of the Patriarchs. Some commentaries understand that Rashi says this entire blessing refers only to Isaac, because he was the first to be circumcised at eight days. Isaac is described as beloved in the verse "Your son…whom you love" (Genesis 22:2; *Me'iri*). There is also a dispute over the word *tzadi, vav, heh* that appears in this blessing: Some commentaries explain that it should be pronounced *tzavei*, and it is a request that God save us from the punishments of Gehenna. That reading appeared in many prayer books. The *ge'onim* and others, however, read it as *tziva*, past tense in praise for an event that already took place.

To circumcise and drip covenantal blood – לָמוּל וּלְהַטִּיף דַּם בְּרִית: Some commentaries explain that dripping blood is mentioned in the blessing because there are converts who enter the covenant already circumcised. Other authorities suggest that it comes to remind the convert, a mature adult, of the value and significance of the covenant as he sees his blood dripping (Rabbeinu Zeraḥya HaLevi). Alternatively, while the sanctity of the Jewish people begins in the womb, the sanctity of a convert begins with the drip of the blood of the covenant (see *Me'iri*).

HALAKHA

The blessings upon circumcision – בִּרְכוֹת הַמִּילָה: The person performing the circumcision recites the blessing: Concerning circumcision, and the father of the circumcised child recites the blessing: To bring him into the covenant of Abraham, our father. If the father is absent or is unable to recite the blessing, the custom is for the one who holds the baby to do so. The custom is to recite a blessing over the wine and then to recite: Who made the beloved one holy… who establishes the covenant (*Shulḥan Arukh, Yoreh De'a* 265:1).

Circumcision of converts – מִילַת גֵּרִים: One who circumcises converts recites the blessing: To circumcise converts, and then recites the blessing: Who has made us holy…to circumcise…were it not for the blood of the covenant…Who establishes the covenant (*Shulḥan Arukh, Yoreh De'a* 268:5).

Circumcision of slaves – מִילַת עֲבָדִים: One who circumcises a slave recites the blessing: Who has made us holy…to circumcise slaves, and then adds the blessing: Who has made us holy…to circumcise slaves…Who establishes the covenant, as stated by the Gemara, in accordance with the reading of the Rif (*Shulḥan Arukh, Yoreh De'a* 267:12).

Summary of **Perek XIX**

This chapter thoroughly examined all topics related to circumcision on Shabbat or a festival. Most of the remaining laws of circumcision are discussed in tractate *Yevamot*.

The Sages established that only the mitzvot of circumcision and the concomitant obligatory sacrifices override Shabbat. They also decided that only the mitzva of circumcision itself overrides Shabbat, whereas preparations and acts that facilitate its performance do not, even if this means that the circumcision will have to be delayed to another day. Similarly, they determined that circumcision must be delayed until after Shabbat in any case of doubt, such as uncertainty as to the baby's sex or as to whether the baby was born during the day or at night. A different kind of uncertainty arises in the unusual case of one who is born circumcised; the Sages agreed that drawing a drop of blood is part of the mitzva of circumcision and it therefore overrides Shabbat.

In contrast to the limitations regarding the circumstances in which circumcision overrides Shabbat, we also saw in this chapter how broadly circumcision overrides Shabbat once it is permitted. First, the *mohel* may perform the mitzva with all its components, and he is not limited to those components which are absolutely essential for fulfilling the mitzva by Torah law. Furthermore, even if a person intended to fulfill the mitzva of circumcision on Shabbat, and he unwittingly performed a prohibited labor without ultimately fulfilling the mitzva, he is not treated as others who unwittingly transgress. He is considered a person who unwittingly transgressed due to preoccupation with a mitzva, and he is therefore exempt from the punishments which generally apply to others who unwittingly transgress on Shabbat.

Image **Credits**

All images are copyright © Koren Publishers Jerusalem Ltd., except:

p186 1st image © Leszek Jańczuk; **p186** 2nd image © Nenya Aleks; **p186** 3rd image © Pula'imenes; **188** © Eliahu Misgav; **p203** © Jastrow; **p218** © suwa; **p225** © Clara Amit, Yoram Lehman, Yael Yolovitch, Miki Koren, and Mariana Salzberger, courtesy of the Israel Antiquities Authority; **p247** © Eitan f; **p254** 2nd image © Denis Barthel; **p260** © Magnus Manske; **p289** © HaRav Menachem Makover, courtesy of *Harenu Bevinyano*.

Page numbers refer to the original Koren Talmud edition.

תלמוד בבלי

מהדורת נאה

שבת · חלק ו

Steinsaltz Center

KOREN

Please note that the number ranges that appear at the bottom of each daf of the Vilna pages indicate the corresponding pages of the Koren Talmud Bavli translation and commentary.

תלמוד בבלי

הוצאת קורן ירושלים

מהדורת נאה

מסכת שבת
דף קטו. עד דף קלז:

COMMENTARY BY

Rabbi Adin Even-Israel Steinsaltz

EDITOR-IN-CHIEF

Rabbi Dr Tzvi Hersh Weinreb

EXECUTIVE EDITOR

Rabbi Joshua Schreier

STEINSALTZ CENTER

KOREN PUBLISHERS JERUSALEM

מוּתָּר בְּקְנִיבַת יָרָק. *(וְאָמַר רַבִּי חִיָּיא בַּר אַבָּא אָמַר רַבִּי יוֹחָנָן: יוֹם כִּפּוּרִים שֶׁחָל לִהְיוֹת בַּחוֹל) – מְפַצְּעִין בָּאֱגוֹזִים, וּמְפַרְכְּסִין בְּרִימּוֹנִים מִן הַמִּנְחָה וּלְמַעְלָה מִפְּנֵי *עָגְמַת נֶפֶשׁ. דְּבֵי רַב יְהוּדָה מְקַנְּבֵי כְּרָבָא, דְּבֵי רַבָּה גָּרְדֵי קָארֵי. כֵּיוָן דַּחֲזָא דַּהֲווּ קָא מַחְרְפֵי, אֲמַר לְהוּ: אֲתָא אִיגַּרְתָּא מִמַּעְרְבָא מִשְּׁמֵיהּ דְּר' יוֹחָנָן דַּאֲסִיר.§

הדרן עלך ואלו קשרים

כָּל כִּתְבֵי הַקֹּדֶשׁ מַצִּילִין אוֹתָן מִפְּנֵי הַדְּלֵיקָה, בֵּין שֶׁקּוֹרִין בָּהֶן וּבֵין שֶׁאֵין קוֹרִין בָּהֶן. (א)אע"פ שֶׁכְּתוּבִים בְּכָל לָשׁוֹן [א]טְעוּנִים גְּנִיזָה. וּמִפְּנֵי מָה אֵין קוֹרִין בָּהֶם – מִפְּנֵי בִּיטּוּל בֵּית הַמִּדְרָשׁ.§ **גמ'** אִיתְּמַר: [ב]הָיוּ כְּתוּבִים תַּרְגּוּם אוֹ בְּכָל לָשׁוֹן, רַב הוּנָא אָמַר: אֵין מַצִּילִין אוֹתָן מִפְּנֵי הַדְּלֵיקָה, וְרַב חִסְדָּא אָמַר: מַצִּילִין אוֹתָן מִפְּנֵי הַדְּלֵיקָה. אַלִּיבָּא דְּמַאן דְּאָמַר "נִיתְּנוּ לִקְרוֹת בָּהֶן" – דְּכוּלֵּי עָלְמָא לָא פְּלִיגֵי דְּמַצִּילִין. כִּי פְּלִיגֵי – אַלִּיבָּא דְּמַאן דְּאָמַר "לֹא נִיתְּנוּ לִקְרוֹת בָּהֶן". רַב הוּנָא אָמַר: אֵין מַצִּילִין – דְּהָא לֹא נִיתְּנוּ לִקְרוֹת בָּהֶן, רַב חִסְדָּא אָמַר: מַצִּילִין – מִשּׁוּם בִּזְיוֹן כִּתְבֵי הַקֹּדֶשׁ. תְּנַן: כָּל כִּתְבֵי הַקֹּדֶשׁ מַצִּילִין אוֹתָן מִפְּנֵי הַדְּלֵיקָה, בֵּין שֶׁקּוֹרִין בָּהֶן בֵּין שֶׁאֵין קוֹרִין בָּהֶן, (ב)אע"פ שֶׁכְּתוּבִין בְּכָל לָשׁוֹן. מַאי לָאו "שֶׁקּוֹרִין בָּהֶן" – נְבִיאִים, וְ"שֶׁאֵין קוֹרִין בָּהֶן" – כְּתוּבִים, אע"פ שֶׁכְּתוּבִין בְּכָל לָשׁוֹן, דְּלָא נִיתְּנוּ לִקְרוֹת בָּהֶן, וְקָתָנֵי "מַצִּילִין", וּתְיוּבְתָּא דְּרַב הוּנָא! אָמַר לָךְ רַב הוּנָא: וְתִסְבְּרָא?! אֵימָא סֵיפָא: טְעוּנִין גְּנִיזָה. הַשְׁתָּא אַצּוֹלֵי מַצִּילִינַן, גְּנִיזָה מִיבַּעְיָא?! אֶלָּא, רַב הוּנָא מְתָרֵץ לְטַעְמֵיהּ, וְרַב חִסְדָּא מְתָרֵץ לְטַעְמֵיהּ. רַב הוּנָא מְתָרֵץ לְטַעְמֵיהּ: בֵּין שֶׁקּוֹרִין בָּהֶם – נְבִיאִים, וּבֵין שֶׁאֵין קוֹרִין בָּהֶם – כְּתוּבִים, בַּמֶּה דְּבָרִים אֲמוּרִים – שֶׁכְּתוּבִין בִּלְשׁוֹן הַקֹּדֶשׁ, אֲבָל בְּכָל לָשׁוֹן – אֵין מַצִּילִין, וַאֲפִילּוּ הָכִי – גְּנִיזָה בָּעוּ. רַב חִסְדָּא מְתָרֵץ לְטַעְמֵיהּ: בֵּין שֶׁקּוֹרִין בָּהֶן – נְבִיאִים, וּבֵין שֶׁאֵין קוֹרִין בָּהֶן – כְּתוּבִים, אע"פ שֶׁכְּתוּבִין בְּכָל לָשׁוֹן – נַמִּי מַצִּילִין, וְהָכִי קָאָמַר: וּמֶקֶק שֶׁלָּהֶן טְעוּנִין גְּנִיזָה. מֵיתִיבִי: הָיוּ כְּתוּבִים תַּרְגּוּם(ג) וְכָל לָשׁוֹן מַצִּילִין אוֹתָן מִפְּנֵי הַדְּלֵיקָה, תְּיוּבְתָּא דְּרַב הוּנָא! אָמַר לָךְ רַב הוּנָא: הַאי תַּנָּא סָבַר נִיתְּנוּ לִקְרוֹת בָּהֶן. ת"ש: הָיוּ כְּתוּבִין גִּיפְטִית, מָדִית, עִיבְרִית, עֵילָמִית, יְוָונִית, אע"פ שֶׁלֹּא נִיתְּנוּ לִקְרוֹת בָּהֶן – מַצִּילִין אוֹתָן מִפְּנֵי הַדְּלֵיקָה, תְּיוּבְתָּא דְּרַב הוּנָא! אָמַר לָךְ רַב הוּנָא: תַּנָּאֵי הִיא; דְּתַנְיָא: *הָיוּ כְּתוּבִין תַּרְגּוּם וּבְכָל לָשׁוֹן – מַצִּילִין אוֹתָן מִפְּנֵי הַדְּלֵיקָה, ר' יוֹסֵי אוֹמֵר: אֵין מַצִּילִין אוֹתָן מִפְּנֵי הַדְּלֵיקָה, אָמַר ר' יוֹסֵי: *מַעֲשֶׂה בְּאַבָּא חֲלַפְתָּא שֶׁהָלַךְ אֵצֶל רַבָּן גַּמְלִיאֵל בְּרִיבִּי לְטִבֶרְיָא, וּמְצָאוֹ שֶׁהָיָה יוֹשֵׁב עַל שֻׁלְחָנוֹ שֶׁל (*יוֹחָנָן הַנָּזוֹף) וּבְיָדוֹ סֵפֶר אִיּוֹב תַּרְגּוּם וְהוּא קוֹרֵא בּוֹ. אָמַר לוֹ: זָכוּר אֲנִי בְּרַבָּן גַּמְלִיאֵל אֲבִי אָבִיךָ שֶׁהָיָה עוֹמֵד ע"ג מַעֲלָה בְּהַר הַבַּיִת, וְהֵבִיאוּ לְפָנָיו סֵפֶר אִיּוֹב תַּרְגּוּם, וְאָמַר לַבַּנַּאי: שַׁקְּעֵהוּ תַּחַת הַנִּדְבָּךְ! אַף הוּא צִוָּה עָלָיו וּגְנָזוֹ. ר' יוֹסֵי בְּרַבִּי יְהוּדָה אוֹמֵר: עֲרֵיבָה שֶׁל טִיט כָּפוּ עָלָיו. אָמַר רַבִּי: שְׁתֵּי תְשׁוּבוֹת בַּדָּבָר, חֲדָא – וְכִי טִיט בְּהַר הַבַּיִת מְנַיִן?! וְעוֹד: וְכִי מוּתָּר לְאַבְּדָן בַּיָּד?! אֶלָּא: מַנִּיחָן בִּמְקוֹם הַתּוֹרְפָּה, וְהֵן *מַרְקִיבִין מֵאֲלֵיהֶן. מַאן תַּנָּאֵי? אִילֵימָא

רש"י

מוּתָּר בִּקְנִיבַת יָרָק. דְּשְׁבוּת לָאו אִיסּוּרָא דְּאוֹרַיְיתָא הוּא, אֶלָּא דְּרַבָּנַן. וְהָכָא מִשּׁוּם עָגְמַת נֶפֶשׁ, שֶׁמְּתַקֵּן וְאֵינוֹ אוֹכֵל, וְהָוֵי קָרוֹב לְעִינּוּי – שָׁרֵי. וְדַוְקָא מִן הַמִּנְחָה וּלְמַעְלָה, שֶׁהוּא שׁוֹאֵף וּמְצַפֶּה לְעֵת אֲכִילָה, וְאִיכָּא עָגְמַת נֶפֶשׁ טְפֵי: כֵּיוָן דַּחֲזֵי דַּהֲוֵי קָא מַחְרְפֵי. מַקְדִּימִין לִפְנֵי הַמִּנְחָה, דְּהַשְׁתָּא לָאו עָגְמַת נֶפֶשׁ הוּא: אֲמַר לְהוּ. לְאֵינָשֵׁי בֵּיתֵיהּ: אֲתָא אִיגַּרְתָּא מִמַּעְרְבָא כו'. כִּי הֵיכִי דְּלִקַבְּלוּ מִינֵּיהּ:

הדרן עלך ואלו קשרים

כָּל כִּתְבֵי הַקֹּדֶשׁ. כְּגוֹן תּוֹרָה נְבִיאִים וּכְתוּבִים. וְלָא תֵּימָא תּוֹרָה לְחוּד הוּא דְּשָׁרֵי לְמִיטְרַח וּלְאַצּוֹלֵי, וְלֹא שְׁאָר סְפָרִים: מַצִּילִין אוֹתָן. כִּדְקָתָנֵי לְקַמָּן: לְמָבוֹי שֶׁאֵינוֹ מְפוּלָּשׁ, וְטִירְחָא בְּעָלְמָא הוּא דְּשָׁרֵי(ד) בֵּיהּ, וְחֶסְרוֹן עֵירוּב, כִּדְמְפָרֵשׁ בַּגְּמָרָא: בֵּין שֶׁקּוֹרִין בָּהֶן. כְּגוֹן נְבִיאִים שֶׁמַּפְטִירִין בָּהֶן בְּשַׁבָּת בְּבֵית הַכְּנֶסֶת: בֵּין שֶׁאֵין קוֹרִין בָּהֶן. כְּגוֹן כְּתוּבִים. וְרַבֵּינוּ הַלֵּוִי אָמַר: דַּאֲפִי' יְחִידִים אֵין קוֹרִין בָּהֶן, כִּדְקָתָנֵי טַעְמָא מִשּׁוּם בִּיטּוּל בֵּית הַמִּדְרָשׁ, דְּמָשְׁכֵי לְבָא, וּבַשַּׁבָּת הָיוּ דּוֹרְשִׁין דְּרָשָׁה לְבַעֲלֵי בָתִּים שֶׁעֲסוּקִין בִּמְלָאכָה כָּל יְמוֹת הַחוֹל, וּבְתוֹךְ הַדְּרָשָׁה הָיוּ מוֹרִין לָהֶן הִלְכוֹת אִיסּוּר וְהֶיתֵּר. וְטוֹב לָהֶן לִשְׁמוֹעַ מִלִּקְרוֹת בַּכְּתוּבִים: וְאע"פ שֶׁכְּתוּבִין בְּכָל לָשׁוֹן. וְאִיכָּא לְמַאן דְּאָמַר לְקַמָּן לֹא נִיתְּנוּ לִקְרוֹת בָּהֶן, מַצִּילִין אוֹתָן: טְעוּנִין גְּנִיזָה. אָסוּר לְהַנִּיחָן בִּמְקוֹם הֶפְקֵר. וּבַגְּמָרָא מְתָרֵץ לָהּ. וְרַבּוֹתַי פֵּירְשׁוּ, דְּהַאי בְּכָל לָשׁוֹן דְּקָאָמַר – אַכְּתוּבִים קָאֵי, וְלֹא אַנְּבִיאִים. וּמְדוּמֶּה אֲנִי, מִפְּנֵי שֶׁמָּצִינוּ דְּיוֹנָתָן בֶּן עוּזִּיאֵל שֶׁאָמְרוּ תַּרְגּוּם הֵן מְפָרְשִׁין כָּךְ. וַאֲנִי אוֹמֵר: אַף בִּנְבִיאִים, אִם אָמַר יוֹנָתָן – לֹא כְּתָבוֹ, וְלֹא נִיתְּנוּ לִיכָּתֵב. וְהָכִי מְפָרֵשׁ בְּמַסֶּכֶת מְגִילָּה (דף ט.) וּמַאן דְּאָסַר בְּכוּלְּהוּ אָסַר בַּר מִס"ת יְוָונִית, מִשּׁוּם מַעֲשֶׂה דְּתַלְמַי הַמֶּלֶךְ, וְלֹא מַפְלִיג הָתָם בֵּין נְבִיאִים לִכְתוּבִים: מִפְּנֵי בִּטּוּל בֵּית הַמִּדְרָשׁ. שֶׁהָיָה קָבוּעַ בְּשַׁבָּת, כִּדְפָרֵישִׁית לְעֵיל: **גמ'** אִיתְּמַר הָיוּ כְּתוּבִין תַּרְגּוּם. אַכְּתוּבִים קָאָמַר. וְל"נ: אַכָּל כִּתְבֵי הַקֹּדֶשׁ קָאֵי: אַלִּיבָּא דְּמַאן דְּאָמַר נִיתְּנוּ לִקְרוֹת בָּהֶן. מוּתָּר לִקְרוֹת בְּכִתְבֵי הַקֹּדֶשׁ הַכְּתוּבִין בְּכָל לָשׁוֹן, בְּמַסֶּכֶת מְגִילָּה (דף ח:). וְאֵין בֵּין סְפָרִי' וּתְפִילִּין וּמְזוּזוֹת, אֶלָּא שֶׁהַסְּפָרִים נִכְתָּבִין בְּכָל לָשׁוֹן: לֹא נִיתְּנוּ. (*רַבָּן גַּמְלִיאֵל) פָּלֵיג עֲלָהּ, וְאָמַר: אַף סְפָרִים לֹא הִתִּירוּ שֶׁיִּכָּתְבוּ אֶלָּא יְוָונִית: וְאע"פ שֶׁכְּתוּבִין בְּכָל לָשׁוֹן. וְלֹא נִיתְּנוּ לִקְרוֹת, דְּמִדְּקָאָמַר "אַף עַל פִּי" – מִכְּלָל דְּלֹא נִיתְּנוּ לִקְרוֹת בָּהֶן. דְּאִי נִיתְּנוּ – מַאי גְּרִיעוּתַיְיהוּ? אֵימָא סֵיפָא. לְדִידָךְ דְּאָמְרַתְּ "אע"פ שֶׁכְּתוּבִין בְּכָל לָשׁוֹן" אַמַּצִּילִין קָאֵי, אֵימָא סֵיפָא; עַל כָּרְחִיךְ מִילְּתָא בְּאַנְפֵּיהּ נַפְשֵׁיהּ הוּא, וּטְעוּנִין גְּנִיזָה בְּחוֹל. פְּשִׁיטָא! הַשְׁתָּא בְּשַׁבָּת מַצִּילִין לְהוּ, גְּנִיזָה בְּחוֹל מִיבַּעְיָא?! וַאֲפִילּוּ הָכִי בָּעוּ גְּנִיזָה. וּדְקָתָנֵי: "וְאע"פ שֶׁכְּתוּבִין בְּכָל לָשׁוֹן" – לָאו אַהַצָּלָה קָאֵי, אֶלָּא אַטְּעוּנִין גְּנִיזָה. וְהָכִי קָאָמַר: אַף עַל פִּי שֶׁכְּתוּבִים בְּכָל לָשׁוֹן, וּבְשַׁבָּת אֵין מַצִּילִין אוֹתָן – בְּחוֹל מִיהָא טְעוּנִין גְּנִיזָה: וּמֶקֶק שֶׁלָּהֶם. אִם בָּלוּ וְנַעֲשׂוּ רְקָבוֹן, אַף הַמֶּקֶק – רִקְבוּבִית(ה) שֶׁל אֲכִילַת הַתּוֹלָעִים – טְעוּנִין גְּנִיזָה: עִבְרִית. כְּתָב שֶׁל עֵבֶר הַנָּהָר: אַבָּא חֲלַפְתָּא. אַבָּא שֶׁל רַבִּי יוֹסֵי, חֲלַפְתָּא שְׁמוֹ: רַבָּן גַּמְלִיאֵל בְּרִיבִּי. לֹא שֶׁהָיָה בְּנוֹ שֶׁל רַבִּי, אֶלָּא אָדָם גָּדוֹל קָרֵי בְּרִיבִּי: רַבָּן גַּמְלִיאֵל אֲבִי אָבִיךָ. הוּא רַבָּן גַּמְלִיאֵל הַזָּקֵן. וְרַבָּן גַּמְלִיאֵל שֶׁהָיָה בְּדוֹרוֹ שֶׁל חֲלַפְתָּא הוּא אֲבִי אָבִיו שֶׁל רַבֵּינוּ הַקָּדוֹשׁ: גַּב מַעֲלָה בְּהַר הַבַּיִת. שֶׁבְּהַר הַבַּיִת הָיוּ מַעֲלוֹת כְּשֶׁהוּא הוֹלֵךְ וְגָבוֹהַּ, כִּדְתְנַן בְּמַסֶּכֶת מִדּוֹת (פ"ב מ"ג): נִדְבָּךְ. שׁוּרַת אַבְנֵי הַבִּנְיָן: טִיט בְּהַר הַבַּיִת מְנַיִן. וְכִי בְּטִיט הָיוּ בּוֹנִין? וַהֲלֹא בְּטַרְכְּסִיד הָיוּ בּוֹנִים, חוֹל וְסִיד מְעוֹרָבִין. וְטִיט לָא הָוֵי אֶלָּא עָפָר וּמַיִם: הַתּוֹרְפָּה. גָּלוּי וְהֶפְקֵר: מַאן תַּנָּאֵי. דְּקָאָמַר רַב הוּנָא לְעֵיל תַּנָּאֵי הִיא, מַאן מֵהָנֵי תַּנָּאֵי קָאֵי כְּרַב חִסְדָּא, וּמַאן כְּרַב הוּנָא: אִילֵימָא

תוספות

כל כתבי הקדש מצילין אותן מפני הדליקה כו'. אומר ר"ת: דכולא האי פירקא איירי כשנפלה דליקה באותו בית או באותו חצר, דכיון שהאש שם – ודאי בהול הוא, ואי שרית ליה – אתי לכבויי, כדמפרש בגמרא. אבל נפלה דליקה בבית אחר – מותר להציל הכל:

אליבא דמ"ד ניתנו לקרות בהן כ"ע לא פליגי דמצילין. והשתא ספרים שלנו מצילין, דנתנו לקרות בהן, משום "עת לעשות לה' הפרו תורתך" כדאמרינן ב"הניזקין" (גיטין ס.): **לא** ניתנו לקרות בהן. פירש רש"י: דהיינו רבן שמעון בן גמליאל דפליג במתניתין בפ"ק דמגילה (דף ח:) דאף ספרים לא התירו שיכתבו אלא יוונית. ופירש הרב פור"ת: דהיינו טעמא – כיון דלא ניתנו ליכתב אסור לקרות בהן, משום דדברים שבכתב אסור לאומרן בעל פה. וקשה: דאין זה "אי אתה רשאי לאומרו בעל פה", כיון שאינו אומרו בלשון הקדש אלא באותו לשון כשהן כתובין, דהא שרי למימר בעל פה תרגום כדמתרגם רב יוסף:

עילמית יוונית. אומר ר"י: דאתיא כרבי יהודה דאסר שאר ספרים לכתוב יוונית, ולא התיר אלא בס"ת בלבד. אבל רבנן שרו אף בשאר ספרים כדאמר בפ"ק דמגילה (דף ט.):

ובידו ספר איוב תרגום. משמע שבימי התנאים כבר נעשה תרגום כתובים, וכן תניא במגילה (דף כא:): (ו)במגילה ובהלל אפילו עשרה קורין ועשרה מתרגמין, מה שאין כן בתורה. אע"פ שיונתן לא עשאו – מ"מ שוב נעשה בימי התנאים, ודלא(ז) כאומרים דתרגום של כתובים רב יוסף עשאו*:

עין משפט נר מצוה

א א מיי' פ"י מהלכות ס"ת הלכה ג טוש"ע יו"ד סימן רפב סעיף ה:

ב ב מיי' פכ"ג מהלכות שבת הלכה כו סמג לאוין סה טוש"ע או"ח סימן שלד סעיף יב:

רבינו חננאל

מהתם. דגרסי' התם א"ר ישמעאל אחוי דר' ברכיה ויבדיל שכן הוא מותר להדיח כבשים ושלקות, כלומר דברים שאסורי' בשבת ומותרי' ביוה"כ ומשני לא מן המנחה ולמעלה מותר להדיח דאלמא שבת דחוקה היא ויבדיל מן המנחה ולמעלה. ושנינן מה נפשך כום אין כאן נר אין כאן במה מבדילין א"ר אבין בתפלה: וראינו שפירש בה רבינו האי הגאון נר ישראל יחיה ויפרה לעד. האי קושטא קושיא היא מיהו מחויא מילתא דבערב יוה"כ נמי הוות תקיעה להבטיל העם מן המלאכה ולהבדיל בין קודש לחול ולערבי יו"ט נמי איכא טובא אלא מיהו כד הוי ערב יוה"כ ועיו"ט חול. אלא כד הוי קודש לא תקעינן. ואע"ג דלא מיפרשא בתקיעות שהיו במקדש. דייקינן מהא דתנן בפ' קמא דשחיטת חולין (דף כו:) כל מקום שיש הבדלה אין תקיעה וכל מקום שיש תקיעה אין הבדלה כיצד יו"ט שחל להיות ערב שבת תוקעין אבל לא מבדילין מבלל דבמו"ם שאינו ע"ש היו מבדילין אבל לא תוקעין) מבלל דאי הוה יו"ט בתר חול היו תוקעין וראוי לדעת דהני כולהו שמעתתא אליבא דאחרים. אבל לדילן לא מיתרמי לן יוה"כ סמוך לשבת לא מלפניה ולא מאחריה. ומפרש בגמרא דחליל. דבר מיקלע כפורים בחד בשבא מדחינן ליה, ומקשינן ומי דחינן והתנן חלבי שבת קריבן ביוה"כ. וא"ר זירא כי הוינא בבבל אמרי' הא דתניא יוה"כ שחל להיות ע"ש לא היו תוקעין ובמוצ"ש לא היו מבדילין דברי הכל היא. ופרקי' ההיא מתניתא אחרים היא דתניא אחרים אומרים אין בין עצרת לעצרת אין בין ר"ה לר"ה אלא ד' ימים. ואם היתה שנה מעוברת חמשה. וגרסינן בירושל' בתחלת מגילה. א"ר יוסי לית כאן חל להיות בשני חל להיות בשבת דאם חל להיות י"ד בשני צומא רבא בחד בשבא. ואם חל בשבת צומא רבא בעירובתא שמעינן מינה דאע"ג דסתם משנה היא דהויה היא ומשנה יחיד היא ולאו דסמכא היא. וכן כל משנה והלכה שהיא כיוצא בה. יכולין בדין ואוהן בה תלוין שהלכה למשה מסיני שלא לקבוע יו"כ סמוך לשבת בין מלפניה בין מאחריה. ולענין קניבת ירק הלכתא יוה"כ שחל להיות בשבת אסור בקניבת ירק ואפילו מן המנחה ולמעלה. ואם חל להיות בחול מפצעין באגוזים ומפרכין ברמונים ומותר בקניבת ירק מן המנחה ולמעלה אבל [משום] מינדר [מלתא אסרוהו]: הדרן עלך ואלו קשרים

פרק טז כל כתבי הקודש מצילין אותן מפני הדליקה בין שקורין בהן בין שאין קורין בהן. פירוש קורין בהן בצבור. תורה הפרשה בתורה ואפטרתא בנביאים ושאין קורין בהן בצבור כתובים. איתמר היו כתובין תרגום ובכל לשון רב הונא אמר אין מצילין אותן מפני הדליקה. רב חסדא אמר מצילין ובכתבי הקדש שמתורגמין בלשון אחר בין בכתב עברי בין בכתב אחר. ר' יוסי אמר לא ניתנו לקרות בהן דא"ר יוסי מעשה באבא חלפתא שהלך אצל רבן גמליאל לטבריא ומצאו יושב על שולחנו של יוחנן בן הנזוף ובידו ספר איוב תרגום א"ל רבי זכור אני את רבן גמליאל אבי אביך שהיה עומד ע"ג מעלה בהר הבית והביאו לפניו ספר איוב תרגום ואמר לבנאי שקעהו תחת הנדבך. אף הוא צוה עליו וגנזו ור' נמי הכי קאמר מניחו במקום התורפה והן כלין מאליהן. ולפום הכי תנא ר' יוסי אין מצילין אותן.

מסורת הש"ס

[פי' שלא יהא טורח במוצאי היום בקניבה והכא נקטו עגומה עליו וכן מפלעין באגוז' ומפרכין ברמונים ודוקא מן המנחה ולמעלה שמאחר שהוא קרוב לעת האוכל דומה למי שיש לו פת בסלו ולא אתי למיכל מיניה אבל קודם המנחה אסור גזרינן דילמא אתי למיכל מיניה ורש"י פי' בזה שאמרו משום עגמת נפש כענין אחר ולא ישר בעיני עכ"ל בעל המאור]

ר"ה ל: | מ"ז | [תוספ' פי"ד] | [מס' סופרים פ"ה הט"ו] | [בתוספתא אי' ר' יוחנן בן ניזוף] | ס"א מתאבדין

הגהות הגר"א

[א] גמ' מותר. נ"ל אסור: [ב] שם (ואמר רחב"א אר"י) תא"מ: [ג] שם בחול. נ"ב מותר כן הוא גירסת הרמב"ם ומ"מ (ועמ"ש רבינו בא"ח סימן תרי"א סק"ד):

גליון הש"ס

תום' ד"ה לא ניתנו. כדמתרגם ר"י. עיין בב"ק דף ג ע"ב בתוס' ד"ה כדמתרגם:

הגהות הב"ח

(א) במשנה ואע"פ שכתובין: (ב) גמ' ואע"פ כו' ואע"פ כו' ולא ניתנו: (ג) שם תרגום ובכל לשון: (ד) רש"י ד"ה מצילין וכו' דשרי בהו וחסרון: (ה) ד"ה ומקק שלהן וכו' רקבובית. נ"ב עי' לעיל דף ל ע"א: (ו) תוס' ד"ה ובידו וכו' ובהלל ובמגילה אפילו עשרה: (ז) בא"ד ולא כאומרים. נ"ב כלומר אבל קודם זה לא נעשה בימי התנאים ולא גרסי' ועשרה מתרגמין וכמו שפירש"י במגילה אלא בכבר נעשה בימי התנאים כמו שמוכח הכל:

*) תוס' וכו' ותתקן יו"ט שחל במו"ש תבדילין ולא תוקעין.

ג א מיי' שם הלכה כז סמג שם טוש"ע שם:
ד ב מיי' וסמג שם טור שו"ע שם סעיף יז:
ה ג מיי' שם טוש"ע שם סעיף יב:
ו ד מיי' פ"ב מהלכות מגילה הלכה ט סמג עשין ד טוש"ע או"ח סימן תרצא סעיף א:
ז ה ו ז ח מיי' פרק כג מהלכות שבת הלכה כח סמג לאוין סה טור שו"ע או"ח סימן שלד סעיף יב:

אילימא תנא קמא *דרבי יוסי – ודילמא בהא קמיפלגי, מר סבר: ניתנו לקרות בהן, ומר סבר: לא ניתנו לקרות בהן. אלא: רבי יוסי ותנא דגיפטית. *ת"ר: אהברכות בוהקמיעין אע"פ שיש בהן אותיות של שם, ומעניינות הרבה שבתורה – אין מצילין אותן מפני הדליקה, אלא נשרפים במקומן [הן ואזכרותיהן]. מכאן אמרו: כותבי ברכות כשורפי תורה. מעשה באחד שהיה כותב בצידן, באו והודיעו את רבי ישמעאל, והלך רבי ישמעאל לבודקו. כשהיה עולה בסולם הרגיש בו, נטל טומוס של ברכות ושקען בספל של מים. ובלשון הזה אמר לו רבי ישמעאל: גדול עונש האחרון מן הראשון. בעא מיניה ריש גלותא מרבה בר רב הונא: גהיו כתובין בסם ובסיקרא בקומוס ובקנקנתום בלשון הקדש, מצילין אותן מפני הדליקה או אין מצילין? תיבעי למ"ד "מצילין", תיבעי למ"ד "אין מצילין". תיבעי למ"ד "אין מצילין"; הני מילי – היכא דכתיבי תרגום ובכל לשון, אבל הכא דכתיבי בלשון הקדש – מצילין. או דילמא: אפי' למ"ד "מצילין" – ה"מ – היכא דכתיבי בדיו, דמיקיים. אבל הכא, כיון דלא מיקיים – לא? א"ל: אין מצילין. והא רב המנונא תנא "מצילין"! א"ל: *אי תניא – תניא. מאי תניא? אמר רב אשי, כדתניא: *אין בין ספרים למגילה אלא שהספרים נכתבים בכל לשון, דומגילה עד שתהא כתובה אשורית, על הספר ובדיו. [מגילה ח:] בעא מיניה רב הונא בר חלוב מרב נחמן: ס"ת שאין בו ללקט שמונים וחמש אותיות, כגון פרשת "ויהי בנסוע הארון" מצילין אותה מפני הדליקה, או אין מצילין? א"ל: ותיבעי לך פרשת "ויהי בנסוע הארון" גופה! ההיכא דחסר פרשת "ויהי בנסוע" – לא קמיבעיא לי, דכיון דאית ביה הזכרות, אע"ג דלית ביה שמונים וחמש אותיות – מצילין. כי קא מיבעיא לי – ס"ת שאין בו ללקט, מאי? א"ל: ואין מצילין. איתיביה: זתרגום שכתבו מקרא, ומקרא שכתבו תרגום. וכתב עברית – מצילין מפני הדליקה; ואצ"ל תרגום שבעזרא ושבדניאל ושבתורה. תרגום שבתורה מאי ניהו – °"יגר שהדותא" – ואף על גב דלית בה שמונים וחמש אותיות, כי תניא ההיא – להשלים. איבעיא להו: הני שמונים וחמש אותיות, מכונסות או מפוזרות? רב הונא אמר: מכונסות. רב חסדא אמר: אפילו מפוזרות. מיתיבי: ס"ת שבלה, אם יש בו ללקט שמונים וחמש אותיות, כגון פרשת "ויהי בנסוע הארון" – מצילין, ואם לאו – אין מצילין. [לעיל קטו:] תיובתא דרב הונא! *תרגמה רב חסדא אליבא דרב הונא – חבתיבות. ת"ר: °"ויהי בנסוע הארון ויאמר משה" פרשה זו עשה לה הקב"ה סימניות מלמעלה ולמטה, לומר שאין

בראשית לא
במדבר י

אילימא ת"ק. כרב חסדא, ור' יוסי כרב הונא: דילמא. טעמא דת"ק משום דקסבר ניתנו לקרות בהן. ונהי דר' יוסי קאי כרב הונא, מיהו כרב חסדא לא קאי ולא חד. דהא רב חסדא אפילו למ"ד לא ניתנו, קאמר מצילין: הברכות. מטבע ברכות שטבעו חכמים, כגון תורה אור י"ח ושאר ברכות: ומעניינות הרבה. מפרשיות, שהיו כותבין בקמיעין פסוקים ללחש, כגון "כל המחלה", וכגון "לא תירא מפחד לילה": נשרפין במקומן. אם נפלה דליקה בשבת: כשורפי תורה. שהרי לא יצילם בשבת: לבודקו. אם אמת היה הדבר: טומוס. קבוצות קונטרסים: היו כתובין. תורה נביאים וכתובים: תיבעי למ"ד. בנכתבים בכל לשון מצילין, תיבעי למ"ד אין מצילין: דלא מיקיימי. אין מתקיים כדיו: הא רב המנונא תנא. מצילין: מאי תניא. היכא תניא: מדקאמר מגילה בדיו. וקתני דהוא מן הדברים שבין ספרים למגילה, ש"מ שאר ספרים נכתבים בסם ובסיקרא: בר חלוב. שם אדם: פ"ה אותיות. זהו שיעור לספר תורה שנמחק או בלה, להיות עומד בקדושתו: כגון פרשת ויהי בנסוע הארון. שהוא ספר לעצמו, כדלקמן, ויש בה פ"ה אותיות: ללקט. שנשארת כאן תיבה, ובמקום אחר תיבה: מהו. להצילן: ותיבעי לך לפרשת ויהי בנסוע הארון גופה. שנכתבה לבדה, וחסרה אות, מהו להצילה: שאין בו כדי ללקוט. ובאותו ליקוט עצמו ליכא אזכרות: תרגום שבתורה. "יגר שהדותא", ושבנביאים כגון: "כדנא תימרון להום" (ירמיהו י) שכתבו מקרא. [א"נ], התרגום שבעזרא כתבו מקרא: כתב עברית. אותיות גדולות הן, ואין דומות לכתב אשורית. אף ע"פ שכתובין בלשון הקדש, אלא שכתב האותיות משונות: ואין צריך לומר תרגום שבעזרא ושבדניאל ושבתורה. שכתבו תרגום כהלכתו: להשלים. אם היה בו כדי ללקט, ותרגום זו משלימו, מצטרף ומצילין בשבילו: תיובתא דרב הונא. דמדקתני ללקט – מכלל דמפוזרות נינהו: בתיבות. הא דקתני ללקט, דמשמע מפוזרות – לא ללקט אות ואות לבד, אלא ללקט תיבה שלימה, תיבה כאן ותיבה כאן, עד פ"ה אותיות. וכי פלגינן – באותיות המפוזרות: עשה לה סימניות מלמעלה ומלמטה. להבדיל' מן הסמוכות לה: למעלה ולמטה. בתחלה ובסוף "ויהי בנסוע הארון":

ג"ל ור' יוסי

לעיל סא: ע"ש [תוספתא פי"ד מ"ש טו הלכה ד]

[חגיגה יט: מו"ק ד. יומא לא: יבמות קיב: נדרים יט: זבחים כה: מנחות קז. בכורות ז. חולין נג. תמורה לג. נדה כב: וע"ש פרש"י]

היו כתובים בסם ובסיקרא כו'. משמע דפשיטא ליה שאין קורין בהן, דאי קורין בהן – פשיטא דמצילין, כדאמר לעיל. וקשה לרשב"א: דבסמוך משמע דפשיטא ליה לריש גלותא גופיה דקורין בהן, דקאמר: והתניא מצילין. והיינו ההוא ברייתא דמייתי, שהספרים נכתבים בכל לשון, ומגילה עד שתהא כתובה אשורית על הספר ובדיו, אבל שאר ספרים נכתבין שלא בדיו. ולפי מה שאפרש בסמוך, דהך ברייתא איירי לענין הצלה – אתי שפיר, ולעולם אין קורין בהן:

אבל הכא כיון דלא מקיים לא. אע"ג דבפ"ב דגיטין (דף יט.) קרי להו דבר שמתקיים, דתנן: בכל כותבין, בסם ובדיו ובסקרא ובקומוס ובקנקנתוס, ובכל דבר שמתקיים. אומר ר"י: דהתם קרי ליה מתקיים טפי ממשקין ומי פירות, דקתני התם בסיפא דאין כותבין בהן. אבל אין מתקיימין כמו דיו. אבל קשה לר"י: דתנן בפ"ב דסוטה (דף יז:) גבי מגילת סוטה: אין כותבין לא בקומוס ולא בקנקנתוס, שנאמר: "ומחה" כתב שיכול למחוק, אלמא קומוס וקנקנתוס מתקיימין יותר מדיו! ואומר ר"י: דלעולם אין מתקיימין כמו דיו, ואין יכול למחות כמו דיו, לפי שנבלעין בקלף: **מגילה** עד שתהא כתובה אשורית על הספר ובדיו. משמע דשאר ספרים לא בעי ספר ודיו, וקשה: דבפ' "המוציא יין" (לעיל דף עט:) משמע דספר תורה בעי ספר, דתני': על הנייר ועל המטלית – פסולה, ומוקי לה בס"ת וה"ה על הדיפתרא. אע"ג דלא חשיב ליה לענין פסול – ה"נ לא חשיב ליה לענין כשרות. דקתני: על הקלף ועל הדוכסוסטוס – כשירה. ולא קתני דיפתרא. ועוד, תנן במסכת סופרים (פ"א): אין כותבין לא ע"ג דיפתרא ולא ע"ג נייר מחוק. ועוד: דמגילה פסולה אדיפתרא, כדתנן פ"ב דמגילה (דף יז.): וכן מגילת סוטה פסולה אדיפתרא, כדאמר בפ"ב דסוטה (דף יז:) משום דבעיא ספר. וכ"ש ס"ת, דנקראת כמה פעמים ספר. ודיו נמי צריך, כדאמר בפרק "הבונה" (לעיל קג:): כתבה שלא בדיו, או שכתב האזכרות בזהב – הרי אלו יגנזו! ותירץ הרב יוסף: דס"ת ודאי בעי ספר ודיו. והכא איירי דווקא בשאר ספרים, והא דלא קתני: אין בין ספרים לס"ת ומגילה – משום דס"ת נכתבים בכל לשון, להכי לא עריב לה. ואכתי קשה לר"י, דתנן בפ"ק דמגילה (דף ח:): אין בין ספרים לתפילין ומזוזות אלא שהספרים נכתבין בכל לשון כו'. ופריך בגמרא: וספרים נכתבין בכל לשון? ורמינהו: מקרא שכתבו תרגום ותרגום שכתבו מקרא וכתב עברי אינו מטמא את הידים עד שיכתבנו בכתב אשורית על הספר ובדיו! ומשני: כאן בספרים, כאן במגילה. ורב אשי משני: כי תניא ההיא – בשאר ספרים, ורבי יהודה היא. אלמא: בשאר ספרים נמי בעי רבי יהודה ספר ודיו, והוא הדין לרבנן. דלא אשכחן דפליגי רבנן עליה אלא בכתב אשורית, אבל בספר ודיו – לא אשכחן דפליגי. ועוד קשה, דשביק רב אשי התם שינויא קמא דמוקי לה במגילה, ומסייע ליה ברייתא דהכא, דקתני בהדיא דמגילה בעי שתהא כתובה אשורית וספר ודיו, ורב אשי גופיה מייתי לה הכא. ונראה לר"י: דדוקא לענין הצלה מיתניא הך ברייתא, דאין בין ספרים למגילה אלא שהספרים נכתבין בכל לשון, ואפי' בלא ספר ודיו חשיבו לענין דמצילין אותו מפני הדליקה, אע"ג דלא חזו לקריאה, משום דיש בהו אזכרות. אבל במגילה אין מצילין אלא א"כ ראויה לקריאה, שתהא כתובה אשורית על הספר ובדיו, לפי שאין בה הזכרה, וא"ת: א"כ תקשה מברייתא דהכא, דאמר לעיל: כל היכא דלא ניתנו לקרות בהן אין מצילין! וי"ל: דהא מסיק לעיל תנאי היא: **מיתיבי** ס"ת שבלה אם יש בה כדי ללקט כו'. השתא משמע דמלשון ללקט קא פריך, דמשמע אפי' מפוזרות. ותימה: א"כ אמאי קא בעי מעיקרא מכונסות או אפי' מפוזרות? פשיטא דאפי' מפוזרות, מדבעא רב הונא ס"ת שאין בו ללקט, משמע: הא יש בו ללקט – מצילין, אע"פ שהן מפוזרות:

רבינו חננאל

ושאר תנאי*) [דאמרי] (דתנן) מצילין לא מסיים מן מינהון סבר ניתנו לקרות בהן. ומאן מנהון סבר לא ניתנו לקרות בהן אלא האי תנא דגפטית. דתני אע"פ שלא ניתנו לקרות בהן מצילין אותן. ות"ק דר' יוסי בניתנו לקרות בהן פליג. וקי"ל כרב הונא דרב חסדא לגביה תלמיד הוא. והא דתנינן כל כתבי הקדש מוקים לה רב הונא בתרי בבי. כל כתבי הקדש מצילין אותן מפני הדליקה בין נביא' שקורין בהן בין כתובים שאין קורין בהן. בר"א בכתבי הקדש הכתובים בלשה"ק [אבל אי הוי] אינון כתבי הקדש כתובי' בכל לשון אין מצילין אותן מפני הדליקה ואפי' הכי טעונין גניזה והא ברייתא דתניא הברכות והקמיעות אע"פ שיש בהן כו' של שם ומעניינות של תורה הרבה אין מצילין אותן מפני הדליקה ונגנזין במקומן הלכה היא. והלכה כדתנא רב המנונא שאם היו כתובים בסם ובסיקרא מצילין אותן אע"פ שאינו דבר של קיימא. ולענין בעיא דרב הונא בר חלוב מרב נחמן סוגיא דשמעתא. כל ס"ת דאית ביה פיסקא דאית ביה שם אע"ג דאין בו ללקט פ"ה אותיות מצילין אותו. והאי דתניא יגר שהדותא מצילין אותו להשלים דאי איכא פ"ה אותיות אע"ג שמהן יגר שהדותא מצילין אותו. והלכתא כרב הונא דהני פ"ה אותיות מכונסות ולא מפוזרות. ופי' מכונסות כדתרגמא רב חסדא אליבא דרב הונא בתיבות' אי יכול ללקט פ"ה אותיות מס"ת [illegible] מצילין אותו כגון דמשכחת בראשית והיא מנויה לששה. ויצא מנויה לארבע. ואלה מנויה לארבע. ויקרא מנויה לחמשה כולן תיבות שלימות עשרים (וא"ו) [או] פחות או יתר שמנין אותיותיהן פ"ה. אבל אותיות שמתוך תיבות שאינן שלימות אין מצילין כגון ויאמר מכלל ויאמר. אבר מכלל אברם או אברהם וכיוצא בהן. כל שנמצאת תיבה שלימה מונין אותיותיה להעלות לפ"ה אותיות וכל תיבה מקצתה מטושטשת אין אותיותיה המנוהות עולות למנין פ"ה. ומשו"ה אמרו ללקט ואע"פ שהתיבות מפוזר' במקומו' רחוקין זה מזה: גליונים של ס"ת. איבעיא אם מצילין אותן ולא איפשטא.

פורענות

ס"ת שנמחק מקום המחק אין בו קדושה דאמרינן כי קדוש היכא דאיכא כתב. ליכא כתב לא קדוש. ומשום דאית טעותא בנוסחאות בהא שמעתא כתבנא כולה. ת"ש ס"ת שבלה אם יש בו ללקט פ"ה אותיות מצילין אותו ואם לאו אין מצילין אותו. וליפוק ליה משום גליון. בלה שאני כלומר אם מצילין מפני הגליונים לא הוה צריך לדקדוקי בתר פ"ה אותיות. ושנינן בלה שאני מכלל כי אם לא בלה מצילין אותו מפני הגליונין אע"פ שאין בו ללקט פ"ה אותיות. ת"ש ס"ת שנמחק אם יש בו כדי ללקט פ"ה אותיות מצילין אותו ואם לאו אין מצילין אותו. ושנינן נמחק לא קא מיבעיא לן דכי קדוש כי איכא כתב. ליכא כתב לא קדוש. כי קא מיבעיא לי גליונות של מעלה ושל מטה ושבין דף לדף ושבין פרשה לפרשה שבתחילת הספר ושבסופו (מ"מ) [מאי]. ת"ש גליונין של מעלה ושל מטה שבין דף לדף שבין פרשה לפרשה שבתחלת הספר ושבסופו מטמאין את הידים. ומשנינן דילמא כי חשיבי אגב ס"ת. אבל גליונים דלא מטמו את הידים לאו כוותיה אינון. וכיון דבעיא זו לא איפשיטא מחמרינן בבזיון כתבי קדש. ומצילין אותן מפני הדליקה בשבת ותוב מהא דתניא הגליונין וספרי המינין אין מצילין אותן מפני הדליקה. מיגו דדחינן ומוקמינן לה גליונין של ספרי מינין. ואקשינן מכלל דספרי מינין גופיהן מצילין. ושנינן הגליונין הרי הן כבנין. כלומר כשם שהגליונין שאין כתיבה עליהן אין להן כבוד ואין מצילין אותן. כך ספרי מינין אין מצילין אותן. והני ספרי מינין. ספרי תורה שכתבן מין אינון דקי"ל כר"ג דאמר נקטינן ס"ת שכתבו מין ישרף. כתבו נכרי יגנז. נמצא ביד מין יגנז. ביד נכרי אמרי לה יגנו ואמרי לה קורין בו. אבל הספרים שחיברו אותן המינין דברי הכל ישרפו. דהא כתבי קדש שכתובין תרגום אפילו בהן אם

*) נראה מזה דלרבינו היה גורס אילימא ת"ק דר"י ודילמא בהא קמיפלגי רק היה לו גי' אחרת בזה וצ"ע.

שאין זה מקומה. ר' אומר: לא מן השם הוא זה, אלא מפני שספר חשוב הוא בפני עצמו. כמאן אזלא הא דא"ר שמואל בר *נחמן א"ר יונתן: (משלי ט) °"חצבה עמודיה שבעה" — אלו שבעה ספרי תורה. כמאן — כר'. מאן תנא דפליג עליה דר' — רשב"ג הוא, דתניא, רשב"ג אומר: עתידה פרשה זו שתיעקר מכאן ותכתב במקומה. ולמה כתבה כאן — כדי להפסיק בין פורענות ראשונה לפורענות שנייה. פורענות שנייה מאי היא? (במדבר יא) °"ויהי העם כמתאוננים". פורענות ראשונה — (שם י) °"ויסעו מהר ה'"; וא"ר *חמא בר' חנינא: שסרו מאחרי ה'. והיכן מקומה? אמר רב אשי: בדגלים. איבעיא להו: הגליונין של ס"ת מצילין אותן מפני הדליקה, או אין מצילין אותן מפני הדליקה? ת"ש: ס"ת שבלה, אם יש בו ללקט שמונים וחמש אותיות, כגון פרשת "ויהי בנסוע הארון" — מצילין, ואם לאו — אין מצילין. ואמאי? תיפוק ליה משום גיליון דידיה! בלה שאני. ת"ש: ס"ת שנמחק, אם יש בו ללקט שמונים וחמש אותיות, כגון פרשת "ויהי בנסוע הארון" — מצילין, ואם לאו — אין מצילין. ואמאי?! תיפוק ליה משום גיליון דידיה! מקום הכתב לא קמיבעיא לי, דכי קדוש — אגב כתב הוא דקדוש, אזל כתב — אזלא לה קדושתיה. כי קמיבעיא לי — של מעלה ושל מטה, שבין פרשה לפרשה, שבין דף לדף, שבתחלת הספר שבסוף הספר. ותיפוק ליה משום ההוא! דגייז ושדי. ת"ש: *הגליונין של מעלה ושל מטה, שבין פרשה לפרשה, שבין דף לדף, שבתחלת הספר שבסוף הספר — מטמאין את הידים. דילמא — אגב ס"ת שאני. ת"ש: הגיליונין וספרי מינין אין מצילין אותן מפני הדליקה, אלא נשרפין במקומן הן ואזכרותיהן. מאי לאו — גליונין דספר תורה? לא, גליונין דספרי מינין. (א)השתא ספרי מינין גופייהו אין מצילין, גליונין מבעיא?! הכי קאמר: וספרי מינין הרי הן כגליונים. גופא: *הגליונים וספרי מינין אין מצילין אותם מפני הדליקה, רבי יוסי אומר: בחול קודר את האזכרות שבהן וגונזן, והשאר שורפן. א"ר טרפון: *אקפח את בני, שאם יבאו לידי שאני אשרוף אותם ואת האזכרות שבהן, שאפי' אדם רודף אחריו להורגו, ונחש רץ להכישו — נכנס לבית ע"ז, ואין נכנס לבתיהן של אלו. שהללו מכירין וכופרין, והללו — אין מכירין וכופרין. ועליהן הכתוב אומר (ישעיהו נז) °"[ו]אחר הדלת והמזוזה שמת זכרונך". א"ר ישמעאל: ק"ו, *ומה לעשות שלום בין איש לאשתו אמרה תורה: שמי שנכתב בקדושה ימחה על המים. הללו שמטילין קנאה ואיבה ותחרות בין ישראל לאביהן שבשמים — על אחת כמה וכמה, ועליהם אמר דוד (תהלים קלט) °"הלא משנאיך ה' אשנא ובתקוממיך אתקוטט תכלית שנאה שנאתים לאויבים היו לי". וכשם שאין מצילין אותן מפני הדליקה, כך אין מצילין אותן לא מן המפולת ולא מן המים ולא מדבר המאבדן. בעי מיניה(ב) יוסף בר חנין מר' אבהו: הני ספרי דבי אבידן, מצילין אותן מפני הדליקה או אין מצילין? *אין ולאו ורפיא בידיה. רב לא אזיל לבי אבידן, וכ"ש לבי נצרפי. שמואל, לבי נצרפי — לא אזיל, לבי אבידן — אזיל. אמרו ליה לרבא: מ"ט לא אתית לבי אבידן? אמר להו: דיקלא פלניא איכא באורחא, וקשי לי. ניעקריה! דוכתיה קשי לי. מר בר יוסף אמר: אנא מינייהו אנא, ולא מסתפינא מינייהו. זימנא חדא אזיל, בעו לסכוניה. רבי מאיר הוה קרי ליה און גליון, ר' יוחנן הוה קרי ליה עוון גליון. אימא שלום דביתהו דרבי אליעזר אחתיה דרבן גמליאל הואי. הוה ההוא *פילוסופא בשבבותיה דהוה

רש"י

שאין זה מקומה. שאינה ראויה לכאן, דלאו בהליכות מסעות משתעי לעיל מינה, אלא בדגלים היתה ראויה ליכתב, בפרשת במדבר סיני: לא מן השם הוא זה. לא זה הטעם של טעמי הסימניות, דמקומה הוא, דפרשה זו בתחלת מסע שנסעו מהר סיני *איירי, כדכתיב לעיל מיניה:(ג) "ויהי בחדש השני בשנה השנית בעשרים לחדש נעלה הענן" וגו': ז' ספרי תורה. דפרשה זו ספר לעצמו, נמצא שלמעלה ספר לעצמו [ושלמטה ספר לעצמו], הואיל וזה מקומה, נמצא ספר "וידבר" נחלק לג' ספרים: עתידה פרשה זו. לעתיד, שיהו כל הפורעניות בטלין, ולא ידחגו לפורענות, ויצר הרע בטל: מאחרי ה'. בתוך ג' ימים למסעם התאוו האספסוף תאוה להתרעם על הבשר כדי למרוד בהקב"ה: הגליונין. קלפים חלקים. וקס"ד השתא דבכל לדדין שיהו חלקים קמיבעיא ליה, כגון חלק שלמעלה ושלמטה, ושנמחק כתבו ונעשה חלק: בלה שאני. דכיון שבלה — אף הגליון בטל, וכי מיבעיא ליה — שהגליונין קיימים, אלא שהכתב הלך: ותיפוק ליה משום גליון דידיה. דהיינו כל הספר תורה: מקום הכתב. שנמחק: לא מבעיא לי. דודאי מיגרע גרע, דכי קדיש מעיקרא — לאו לשם גליון חלק קדיש, אלא אדעתא דכתב. וכיון דאזל ליה כתב — פקע מקדושתיה: של מעלה ומטה. דמתחלה לשם חלק קדיש, והשתא כשנמחק כתב הספר — נמי חלק הוא: ה"ג: ותיפוק ליה משום ההוא דגייז ושדי. והכי פירושא: ותיפוק לי', דאע"ג דאין בו כדי ללקט פ"ה אותיות הוה ליה למיתני בברייתא "מצילין" — משום ההוא ריוח של מעלה ומטה, אלא לאו פשוט מיניה — דאין מצילין! ומשני: דגייז ושדי — שנחתכו הגליונים, ולא נשתייר בו אלא מקום הכתב: שבתחלת הספר ושבסוף הספר. שכולן היו כתובין כמגילה כס"ת, ואמרי' בב"ב בפ"ק (דף יג:): ראשו כדי לגול עמוד, סופו כדי לגול היקף, להקיף כל הספר: מטמא את הידים. אם נגע בו ונגע בתרומה פוסלה, דמגזירת י"ח דבר היא (לעיל דף יד.): דילמא אגב ס"ת. שלא נמחק כתב הספר, אלא כולו קיים, וזה נגע בגליונים. וכי מבעיא לן — בנמחק הספר, ואין כאן קדושה אלא משום גליון שמשמשו בעודו קיים: ספרי מינין. משרתים לע"ז, וכתבו להן תורה נביאים כתובים כתב אשורית ולשון הקודש: וספרי המינין גופייהו מצילין. בתמיה: ספרי המינין הרי הן כגליונים. כקלפים חלקים, שלא נכתב בהם מעולם: קודר. חותך חתיכות הקלף, מקום השם: שאפי' רודף אדם להורגו. על עצמו קאמר: שהללו. גוים העובדים ע"ז אינן מכירין, שהרי בכך גדלו, וכך למדום אבותם: ואחר הדלת והמזוזה שמת זכרונך. זכרון הוא בידך ואינה שכחה לך, אלא שהשלכת אותי אחרי הדלת: כך אין מצילין אותן. אפי' בחול: דבי אבידן. ספרים שכתבו להם המינין להתווכח עם ישראל. ומקום שמתווכחים שם קרי ליה בי אבידן: אין ולא. זימנין אמר ליה אין, זימנין א"ל לא: לבי נצרפי. ע"ז, וכך שמה: וקשה לי. ששורשן נעשו גבשושית. ולדחותם בקש בא: אמרי ליה ניעקריה קשה לי דוכתיה. שתהא שם גומא. אי נמי: נסיתיו, וקשה לי ריחו. וכל זה שהיו מתייראין רב ורבא מלכת לבי אבידן, שמא מתוך שיתווכחו יעמדו עליהם ויהרגום: מינייהו אנא. מכירי הם: פילוסופא. *מין: דהוה

תוספות

פורענות ראשונה ויסעו וא"ר חנינא שסרו מאחרי השם. פי' בקונטרס: שמאז התחילו לשאול בשר. ואומר ר"י: דאין נ"ל כן, אלא פורענות ראשונה כדאמר במדרש (ילמדנו) "ויסעו" — שנסעו מהר סיני דרך שלשת ימים, כתינוק היוצא מבית הספר שבורח לו והולך לו. כך היו בורחים מהר סיני דרך שלשת ימים לפי שלמדו הרבה תורה בסיני אמר הקב"ה(ד) נסמוך פורענות לפורענות, לאו, אלא נפסוק פרשת ויהי בנסוע הארון*: ספרי מינין כו' א"ר טרפון כו'. אומר ר"י: דמיירי בנמצאו ביד מינין. דאי כתבן מין — הא אמר בפרק "השולח" (גיטין דף מה:): נמצא ביד מין — יגנז, כתבו מין — ישרף. ודוחק לומר דאתי כר"ט, ודלא כרבנן ורבי יוסי:

כך אין מצילין אותן לא מן המים כו'. דלא תימא: דוקא מן הדליקה אין מצילין, משום דאי שרית ליה אתי לכבויי, אלא: אפילו היכא דליכא למיגזר מידי — אסור לטלטלן ולהוציאן. והך סיפא כרבנן, דלרבי טרפון לא איצטריך:

פילוסופא. מין כדפי' בקונטרס. ורבינו שמע [מיהודי אחד שבא מארץ יון ואמר] דבלשון יון פלוספוס הוא דוד החכמה. ואית דגרסי פילא סבא, והוא לשון לצון שחוק כדאמר באיכה רבתי "דפלי ביהודאי" פירוש: שחק ונתלוצץ:

ושמואל

עין משפט נר מצוה

ח א מיי' פכ"ג מהלכות שבת הלכה כז טוש"ע או"ח סימן שלד סעיף כ:

ט ב מיי' פ"ט מהלכות שאר אבות הטומאות הלכה ו:

י ג ד מיי' פ"ו מהלכות יסודי התורה הלכה ח ופ"א מהלכות תפילין הלכה יג טור שו"ע או"ח סימן שלד סעיף כא וטור שו"ע יו"ד סימן רפא סעיף א:

[עי' תוי"ט פ"ה דאבות משנה ד]

יא ה טוש"ע יו"ד סימן קנז סעיף ג:

מסורת הש"ס

כס"י דאיירי לעיל מיניה; [נ"ל נחמני]; [תענית כט.]; ידים פ"ג מ"ד ע"ש; [תוספת' פי"ד]; [לעיל יז.] [זבחים יג.]; [סוכה נג: נדרים סו: מכות יא. חולין קמא.]; [לעיל קיג. וש"נ]; [פירוש חוזה בכוכבי' ערוך]; [ובע"ז דף נד: פירש רש"י פילוסופין חכמי האומות]

רבינו חננאל

אם מצילין אותן מפני הדליקה אי לא. ספרי מינין מיבעיא. ואלו פ"ה אותיו' כנגד פרשת ויהי בנסוע הארון. ופרשת ויהי בנסוע הארון ספר בפני עצמו הוא. ומקומו בדגלים ולמה נכתב כאן. להפסיק בין פורענו' ראשונה שהיא ויסעו מהר ה' וגו' לפורענות שנייה. שהיא ויהי העם כמתאוננים וגו': ספרי דבי אבידן. חצר ידועה ויש בה ספרי חכמות מכל אומה ויש בה ספרי תור' קדש ונביאים וכתובי' כתובי' בלשה"ק. ומפני שאינו ידוע מי כתבו או ישראל או זולתן. אמרו על ר' אבהו שהיה הדבר רפיא בידיה להורות עליהן להצילן או לא. וזה [בי] אבידן היו מתקבצין שם חכמי' ונבונים מכל אומה ונושאין ונותנין בדברי חכמה. וכן בי נצרפי. מהו בבי נצרפי היתה שם ע"ז. דגרסי' בע"ז איזו היא אשירה סתם. אמר שמואל כגון דאמרי הני תמרי נהווינן לשכרא דבי נצרפי ושתו ליה ביום אידם. אמר אמימר אמרו לי סבי (דשם בריתא) [דפומבדיתא] הלכתא כשמואל והני מילי אלה שהיו באותו זמן (הן) שעד אותה שעה לא טוכסין להן הטוכסוסין שהן עכשיו בידיהן אלא כתועין היו יש מהן שומרין התורה ויש מהן שאינן שומרין וכולן קוראין אותה ויש מי שהיה קוראה בלשה"ק כיון דאסיקנא קוראין בהן בתורה ובנביאים. אבל בכתובים אין קוראין בהן.

רב נסים גאון

פט"ז כמאן אזל הא דא"ר שמואל בר נחמני חצבה עמודיה שבעה אלו ז' חומשי תורה כמאן כר'. דר' סבר ויהי בנסוע הארון ספר בפני עצמו א"כ על דעת ר' מתחילת ספר וידבר עד ויהי בנסוע הארון ספר בפני עצמו ופרש' ויהי בנסוע הארון ספר בפני עצמו ומן שם עד סוף ספר וידבר ספר בפני עצמו נחלק ספר וידבר לג' ספרים הרי ג' ספרי וידבר עם ד' ספרים הנשארים יהיו הכל ז' ובבראשי' דר' אושעיא בפרשת אלה תולדות יצחק (פרשה סד) תניא כוותיה ויקרא אותה שבעה כנגד ספר וידבר שהוא משלים ז' ספרי תורה והלא ה' הם אלא בר קפרא עבד מן ספר וידבר עד ויהי בנסוע הארן ספר בפני עצמו ויהי בנסוע הארן ספר בפני עצמו מן תמן ועד סיפיה דספרא ספר בפני עצמו: **בי** נצרפי מן בתי ע"ז ומשכחת במסכת עירובין בפרק חלון (דף פ) ובמסכת ע"ז בפרק כל הצלמין (דף מח) אי זו היא אשירה סתם אמר רב כל שכומרין משמרין אותה ואין טועמין מפירותיה ושמואל אמר כגון דאמרי הני תמרי נינהו לשיכרא דבי ניצרופי ושתו ליה ביום אידם:

הגהות הב"ח

(א) גמ' דספרי מינין (השתא ספרי וכו' מבעיא תא"מ) ונ"ב גי' רש"י וספרי מינין גופייהו מצילין: (ב) שם בעי מיניה רב יוסף: (ג) רש"י ד"ה לא מן השם וכו' כדכתיב לעיל מיניה ויהי בשנה השנית בחדש השני בעשרים בחדש: (ד) תוס' ד"ה פורעניות וכו' אמר הקב"ה לא נסמוך פורענות לפורענות אלא:

גליון הש"ס

גמ' איבעיא להו הגליונין. עי' מגילה דף לב ע"א תוס' ד"ה הלוחות: שם דגייז ושדי. עי' תשובות זכרון יוסף סימן יא ויב: שם אקפח את בני. לעיל דף יז ע"א זבחים דף יג ע"ב: שם לא אזיל לבי אבידן עי' ע"ז דף יז ע"א תוס' ד"ה הרחק: רש"י בד"ה פילוסופא מין. עי' מס' ד"א רבה פ"ה: תוס' ד"ה פורענות פי' בקונטרס. עי' תוי"ט פ"ה מ"ד לאבות:

דהוה שקיל שמא דלא מקבל שוחדא. בעו לאחוכי ביה; אעיילא ליה שרגא דדהבא, ואזול לקמיה, אמרה ליה: בעינא דניפלגי לי בנכסי דבי נשי. אמר להו: פלוגו. א"ל: כתיב לן, במקום ברא ברתא לא תירות. א"ל: מן יומא דגליתון מארעכון איתנטלית אורייתא דמשה, ואיתיהיבת עוון גליון, וכתיב ביה: ברא וברתא כחדא ירתון. למחר הדר עייל ליה איהו חמרא לובא. אמר להו: שפילית לסיפיה דעוון גליון וכתב ביה: אנא לא למיפחת מן אורייתא דמשה אתיתי [*ולא לאוספי על אורייתא דמשה אתיתי. וכתיב ביה: במקום ברא ברתא לא תירות. אמרה ליה: נהור נהוריך כשרגא! א"ל רבן גמליאל: אתא חמרא ובטש לשרגא.§ "ומפני מה אין קורין כו".§ אמר רב: לא שנו אאלא בזמן בית המדרש, אבל שלא בזמן בהמ"ד - קורין. ושמואל אמר: אפילו שלא בזמן בית המדרש אין קורין. איני?! והא נהרדעא אתריה דשמואל הוה, ובנהרדעא *פסקי סידרא בכתובים במנחתא דשבתא! אלא, אי איתמר הכי איתמר; אמר רב: לא שנו אלא במקום בהמ"ד, אבל שלא במקום בהמ"ד - קורין. ושמואל אמר: בין במקום בהמ"ד בין שלא במקום בהמ"ד, בזמן בהמ"ד - אין קורין, שלא בזמן בית המדרש - קורין. ואזדא שמואל לטעמיה, דבנהרדעא פסקי סידרא דכתובים במנחתא דשבתא. רב אשי אמר: לעולם כדאמרן מעיקרא, ושמואל כרבי נחמיה. דתניא: *אע"פ שאמרו כתבי הקדש אין קורין בהן - אבל שונין בהן ודורשין בהן, נצרך לפסוק - מביא ורואה בו. א"ר נחמיה: מפני מה אמרו, כתבי הקדש אין קורין בהן - כדי שיאמרו: בכתבי הקדש אין קורין, וכ"ש בשטרי הדיוטות.§ **מתני'** במצילין תיק הספר עם הספר. ותיק התפילין עם התפילין, ואע"פ שיש בתוכן מעות. גולהיכן מצילין אותן? למבוי שאינו מפולש, בן בתירא אומר: אף למפולש.§ **גמ'** *ת"ר: ארבעה עשר שחל להיות בשבת מפשיטין את הפסח עד החזה, דברי רבי ישמעאל בנו של רבי יוחנן בן ברוקה, וחכ"א: דמפשיטין את כולו. בשלמא לרבי ישמעאל בנו של ר' יוחנן בן ברוקה - דהא איתעביד ליה צורך גבוה. אלא לרבנן - מ"ט? אמר רבה בר בר חנה א"ר יוחנן: דאמר קרא °"כל פעל ה' למענהו" (משלי טז). והכא, מאי 'למענהו' איכא? רב יוסף אמר: שלא יסריח. רבא אמר: *שלא יהו קדשי שמים מוטלין כנבלה. מאי בינייהו? איכא בינייהו: דמנח אפתורא דדהבא, אי נמי - יומא דאסתנא. ורבי ישמעאל בנו של רבי יוחנן בן ברוקה, האי *"פעל ה' למענהו" מאי עביד ליה? שלא יוציא את האימורין קודם הפשטת העור. מ"ט? אמר רב הונא בריה דרב נתן: משום נימין. אמר רב חסדא אמר מר עוקבא: מאי אהדרו ליה חברייא לרבי ישמעאל בנו של רבי יוחנן בן ברוקה - הכי קאמרי ליה: אם מצילין תיק הספר עם הספר - לא נפשיט את הפסח מעורו? מי דמי? התם - טלטול, הכא - מלאכה! אמר רב אשי: בתרתי פליגי; פליגי בטלטול, ופליגי במלאכה. והכי קאמרי ליה: אם מצילין תיק הספר עם הספר - לא נטלטל עור אגב בשר?! מי

רש"י

דהוה שקיל שמא דלא מקבל שוחדא. היה מוציא עליו שם שאינו מקבל שוחד מבעלי דינין הבאין לפניו, והיה מקבלו בסתר: א"ל. פילוסופא לר"ג מיומא דגליתון כו': שפילית. כל סוף הדבר הוא תחתית שלו, ושייך למימר "שפילית לסיפיה": נהור נהורך כשרגא. תורה אור הנהר אורך כשרגא, רמזה שנתנה לו מנורה בשוחד: אמר לו ר"ג אתא חמרא ובטשא. דחפתו לארץ, כלומר: אני נצחתי בשוחד*. [והכל כדי שישמעו המתחספים שם נבלותו, ומי הוא]: בזמן בית המדרש. קודם אכילה היו דורשים: שלא בזמן בית המדרש. לאחר אכילה לא דרשו, משום שכרות: פסקי סדרא בכתובים. *[היו רגילים לקרא בבהמ"ד פרשה בכתובים]: במקום בהמ"ד. שהחכם דורש. דהיינו בבהמ"ד, אבל בעלמא - קורין: בין במקום בהמ"ד כו' בזמן בהמ"ד אין קורין. לפי שמבטלו מלילך אצל הדורש. אבל שלא בזמן בהמ"ד, כגון לאחר אכילה - קורין: ושמואל. דאמר לעיל, אפילו לאחר אכילה אין קורין: כר' נחמיה. אמרה למילתיה, דלית ליה טעמא דאין קורין משום בטול, אלא כדי שיאמרו קל וחומר לשטרי הדיוטות. ומיהו, שמואל הנהיג במקומו כדברי חכמים דמתניתין, דאמרי טעמא (דמתני') משום ביטול תורה. הלכך: לאחר אכילה דליכא דרשה - קורין: שונין בהן. כגון מדרש שה"ש וקהלת: שטרי הדיוטות. כגון של חשבונות, או איגרות השלוחות למלא חפץ: גמ' עד החזה. מתחיל מרגליו האחרונים עד החזה, שיוכל להוציא אימורים, שהקטר חלביו דוחין שבת, ותו לא מפשיט מידי עד אורתא, דצורך הדיוט הוא: למענהו. לכבודו: שלא יסריח. שהעור מחממו ומסריחו, ואין זה כבודו להיות פרס אוכלי שולחנו מגואל: אפתורי דדהבא. שאינו מוטל בבזיון, אבל לשמא יסריח חייש רב יוסף. ורבא לא חייש עד אורתא: יומא דאסתנא. רוח צפונית, שהיא בינונית, לא חמה ולא צנה, כדאמרינן ביבמות בפרק "הערל" (דף עב.). ואיזו רוח המסרחת - רוח מזרחית בשעת החום, כדאמרינן בגיטין (דף לא:): אפילו שכבת זרע שבמעי אשה מסרחת בו, דכתיב (הושע יג): "יבא קדים רוח ה' ממדבר עולה" וגו'. ויש מפרשין: יומא דאסתנא - רוח דרומית, שהיא לוננת. אמת שרוח דרומית לוננת, אבל אסתנא על כרחיך צפונית היא, ונוחה, כדאמר בעלמא (עירובין ד' סה.): צריכא שמעתא צילותא כיומא דאסתנא. ורוח דרומית היא בלשון ארמי "יומא דשותא": קודם הפשטת העור. עד החזה: מ"ט. עור לאימורין מאי קא עביד: משום נימין. של צמר, הנדבקין באימורין: חברייא. בני מחלוקתו: אם מצילין. בשבת: תיק עם הספר. ואע"פ שיש בתוכו מעות, ומשום כבוד הספר שהוא צורך גבוה עבדינן בהדיה הצלת מעות שהן צורך הדיוט: לא נפשיט את הפסח. בתמיה. משום צורך גבוה לא שרי צורך הדיוט בהדיה: התם. תיק ומעות דקמייתי ראיה מיניה - טלטול בעלמא הוא: הכא. גבי פלוגתייהו דפסח, דאיירי בה השתא - מלאכה גמורה, דהפשטה מאבות מלאכות היא: בתרתי פליגי. גבי פסח פליגי בטלטולו, דאסר רבי ישמעאל לטלטל [הפסח] אחר שהוציא אימוריו אפי' מחמה לצל, משום עור, דלאו בר טלטול הוא(א). ולא דמי לשלחין, דאמרן ב"במה טומנין" (לעיל מט.) שמטלטלין אותן. דהתם עור בהמה גסה, דחזי למשכביה ולמיזגא עליה: והכי קאמרי ליה. תשובה לענין טלטול: לא נטלטל עור אגב בשר. דהוי נמי כבוד שמים, דבשר דומיא דספר, ומותר לטלטלו מחמה לצל, ואגב בשר יטלטלו עור המחובר בו: מי

תוספות

ושמואל דאמר כר' נחמיה. ולא פליג אדרב, דשפיר מודה למתני' דמפרש טעמא מפני ביטול בית המדרש קורין שלא בזמן בית המדרש. אלא בא לומר דר' נחמיה פליג עלה דמתני': וכ"ש בשטרי הדיוטות. פירש בקונטרס: איגרות. ותימה; דנהגו העולם לקרות בכתב ואיגרות השלוחים ממקום למקום, ולטלטלן ודאי שרי דהא ראויין לצור ע"פ צלוחית. ונראה לר"י: דלא קרי שטרי הדיוטות אלא שטרי חובות וכיוצא בהן, אבל איגרות - שרי, דפעמים שיש בהן פקוח נפש. ואפי' יודע שאין בו פקוח נפש מתיר ר"ת, דלא הוי שטרי הדיוטות - כיון שאין צריך למה שכתוב בה, לפי שיודע מה שבאיגרות. ואם אינו יודע - שמא יש בו צורך גדול, או פקוח נפש - ושרי. וכ"מ בירושלמי, דקאמר: מפני מה אין קורין בכתבי הקדש - מפני שטרי הדיוטות. שאם אתה אומר לו שהוא מותר, אף הוא אומר: מה בכך אם אתעסק בשטרותי. משמע דווקא כעין חובות ושטרות קאמר. וכן פי' רש"י לקמן, *גבי גזירה שלא יקרא בשטרי הדיוטות. דבשטרי מקח וממכר קאמר. וכן הגיה בפי' כתב ידו. ומיהו, אותן מלחמות הכתובין בלע"ז - נראה לרבינו יהודה דאסור לעיין בהן, דלא גרע מהא דתניא בפ' "שואל" (לקמן קמט.): כתב שתחת הצורה והדיוקנאות אסור לקרות בהן בשבת. ואפי' בחול לא ידע ר"י מי התיר, דהו"ל כמושב לצים: פליגי בטלטול כו'. פי': אחר שנפשט כל העור פליגי, דרבנן שרו לטלטל - שעדיין צריך לבשר שלא יתלכלך, ור' ישמעאל אסר. אבל כשאינו מופשט אלא עד החזה - שרי לכ"ע לטלטל, כדמוכח בסמוך. ואע"ג דר' ישמעאל לא שרי להפשיט אלא עד החזה, מ"מ פליגי במופשט כולו, כגון שעבר והפשיט. אי נמי: בתמידים ומוספים, דמותר להפשיטן הכל:

עין משפט נר מצוה

יב א מיי' פכ"ג מהל' שבת הלכה יט סמג לאוין סה:
יג ב מיי' שם הלכה כח סמג שם טוש"ע או"ח סימן שלז סעיף טו טז:
יד ג מיי' שם הלכה כו טור שו"ע שם סעיף יז יח:
טו ד מיי' פ"א מהלכות ק"פ הלכה טז:

רבינו חננאל

חזר ופירש מפני מה אין קוראין בכתובים מפני ביטול בהמ"ד ומסייעא לה הא דתני העוסק במקרא מדה שאינה מדה כו'. ובית תלמוד טפי עדיף [מהעוסק] במקרא. אמר רב לא שנו שאין קורין בהן אלא בזמן בית המדרש. פי' בשעה שהחכמים יושבי' במדר' ומתעסקין בתלמוד. אבל שלא בזמן בהמ"ד כגון שכבר עמדו בעלי מדרש ונכנסו לבתיהן קורין. ושמואל [אמר] במקום שיש מדרש קבוע כו'. ואסקה רב אשי הכי לעולם כדקאמרינן מעיקרא. אמר רב אין קורין בזמן בהמ"ד כדאמרן אבל בזמן שלא בהמ"ד קורין. ושמואל אמר בין בזמן בהמ"ד בין שלא בזמן בהמ"ד אין קורין. דסבירא ליה כר' נחמיה וגזירה היא משום שטרי הדיוטות והלכתא כלישנא קמא בזמן בית המדרש אין קורין שלא בזמן בית המדרש קורין: ירושלמי (ה"א) אמר ר' יהושע בן לוי הדא אגדתא הכותבה אין לו חלק. הדורשה מתחרך. השומעה אינו מקבל שכר. מיומוי לא איסתכלית בה אלא חד זמן. ואשכחית כתוב בה קע"ה פרשיו' דיבור אמירה צווי שכתוב בתורה כנגד שנות [של] אהע"ה. שנא' לקחת מתנות באדם. וכתיב האדם הגדול בענקים. קמ"ז מזמורי' דכתיב בתילים כנגד שנות יעקב אבינו ללמד שכל קילוסין שישראל (עושין הללויה) מקלסין להקב"ה כנגד שנותיו של יעקב שנא' ואתה קדוש יושב תהלות ישראל קכ"ג פעמים שישראל עונין הללויה כנגד שני אהרן שנאמר הללויה הללו אל בקדשו לקדושו לאהרן קדוש ה' אפילו כן הוינא מיבעיא בליליא: מצילין תיק הספר עם הספר. אמרי רבנן דהאי תיק קאי לחודיה. ונוטלין ממקו' שהוא עם הספר וכן תיק [של] תפילין: י"ד שחל להיות בשבת ר' ישמעאל בנו של ר' יוחנן בן ברוקא אומר מפשיטין את הפסח עד החזה. סבר כיון דאיתעביד ליה צורך גבוה שיכול להוציא החלבים לא יפשוט יותר מזה. ורבנן סבר מפשיט כולו. וטעמא כל פעל ה' למענהו. מאי למענהו לעשות כבוד לקדשים: פי' יומא דאסתנא יום שמנשבת רוח צפון שאין הבשר מסריח בו. רבא אמר שלא יהו קדשים מוטלין בעורותיהן כנבילה. אבל אם הוא מוטל בשלחן של זהב שהוא דרך כבוד לא יפשיט יותר למטה מן החזה וכו'. וגרסי' בפסחים בפרק תמיד [נשחט] שהיו מפשיטין. דתנן י"ד שחל להיות בשבת מניח ידו על כתף חבירו כו'. ואמרינן עלה. תנא כל אחד נוטל פסחו בעורו ומפשילו לאחוריו. אמר רב עיליש טייע. פי' שהערביים מפשילין כליהן לאחוריהן. ור' ישמעאל בנו של ר' יוחנן בן ברוקא מוקים למענהו שלא יוצא האמורין קודם הפשטת העור כדי שלא ידבק שיער העור בחלבים: אמרו ליה רבנן (אין) [אי] מצילין תיק הספר עם הספר לא נפשוט (עור עם החזה) [את הפסח מעורו]. אמר להן מי דמי. הצלת תיק טלטול בעלמא הפשטת עור מלאכה דקא בעי ליה לעור. אמר רב אשי בתרי פליגי עליה במלאכה ובטלטול. והכי קאמרי ליה תינח הפשטה שהיא מלאכה טלטול מאי דאינון

מסורת הש"ס

גי' רש"ל
גי' רש"ל
בספרים ישנים ליתא אלא
[והיינו הפטרה עי' תוס' לעיל כג. ד"ה שאלמלא וכו' וכ"כ תוספות להדיא במגילה כח. ד"ה ואין מפטירין]
[תוספ' פי"ד מ"ס פט"ו הלכה ג ע"ש]
לקמן קלג: מנחות סג: [וגוש' לעמוד' פ"ד]
[זבחים פה:]
[נ"ל כל פעל]

גליון הש"ס

גמ' דבנהרדעא פסקי סדרי. ע"ל דף כד ע"א תוס' ד"ה שאלמלא:

הגהות הב"ח

(א) רש"י ד"ה בתרתי פליגי וכו' דלאו בר טלטול הוא הס"ד ואחר כך מ"ה והכי קאמרי ואח"כ ד"ה לא נטלטל וכו' המחובר בו ולא דמי לשלחין וכו'. נ"ב הך קושיא היא אף לחברייא וע"ל בתוס' פ' במה טומנין דף מט בד"ה טומנין בשלחין:

מי דמי? התם – נעשה בסים לדבר המותר, הכא – נעשה בסים לדבר האסור. אלא, הכי קאמרי ליה: אם מצילין תיק של ספר עם הספר, ואע"פ שיש בתוכו מעות, לא נטלטל עור אגב בשר? מי דמי?! התם – נעשה בסים לדבר האסור ולדבר המותר, הכא – כולו נעשה בסים לדבר האסור! אלא, הכי קאמרי ליה: אם מביאין תיק שיש בתוכו מעות מעלמא להציל בו ספר תורה, לא נטלטל עור אגב בשר?! והיא גופה מנלן? אילימא דמדהיכא דאית ביה לא שדי להו – איתויי נמי מייתינן, מי דמי?! התם – אדהכי והכי נפלה דליקה, הכא – אדהכא והכי לישדינן! אלא אמר מר בר רב אשי: לעולם כדאמרינן מעיקרא, ודקא קשיא לך *"הכא טלטול והכא מלאכה" – כגון דלא קבעי ליה לעור. והא *אביי ורבא דאמרי תרוייהו: מודה ר"ש בפסיק רישיה ולא ימות! דשקיל ליה *בברזי. § "ולהיכן מצילין אותן וכו'". § היכי דמי מפולש, היכי דמי שאינו מפולש? אמר רב חסדא: שלש מחיצות ושני לחיין – זהו מבוי שאינו מפולש, ג' מחיצות ולחי אחד – זהו מבוי המפולש. ותרווייהו אליבא דרבי אליעזר, דתנן: *הכשר מבוי, ב"ש אומרים: לחי וקורה, וב"ה [א]אומרים: או לחי או קורה, ר' אליעזר אומר: שני לחיים. א"ל רבה: ג' מחיצות ולחי אחד מפולש קרית ליה?! ועוד, לרבנן נציל לתוכו אוכלין ומשקין! אלא אמר רבה: שתי מחיצות ושני לחיין – זהו מבוי שאינו מפולש, שתי מחיצות ולחי אחד – זהו מבוי המפולש. ותרווייהו אליבא דרבי יהודה, *דתניא: יתר על כן אמר ר' יהודה: מי שיש לו שני בתים בשני צדי ר"ה עושה לחי מיכן ולחי מיכן, או קורה מיכן וקורה מיכן – ונושא ונותן באמצע. אמרו לו: אין מערבין רה"ר בכך. א"ל אביי: לדידך נמי, לרבנן נציל לתוכו אוכלין ומשקין! אלא

רש"י

(א) מי דמי. תיק הספר נעשה בסים לדבר המותר לטלטלו בלא שום דליקה, דספר בר טלטול הוא. ולדבר האסור, כגון מעות: הכא. האי עור נעשה בסיס לדבר שכולו אסור בטלטול, שהבשר אסור לטלטלו, דלא חזי לאכילה עד אורתא. דפסח אינו נאכל אלא בלילה, ורבי ישמעאל לית ליה כבוד שמים בנאכל להדיוט. ואפילו הוי עור תורת כלי עליו – מיתסר משום דהוי בסים לאיסור, וכ"ש דהוא גופיה לאו בר טלטול הוא: אם מביאין תיק שבתוכו מעות. דהוי בסים לדבר שכולו אסור, ומניח בו ספר להצילו ואינו צריך להשליך המעות, כדמפרש ואזיל – לא נטלטל עור אגב הבשר: אי נימא דמדהיכא דאית ביה. מעות עם הספר לא שדי להו, לא מצריך ליה תנא דידן למשדינהו, כדקתני: "ואע"פ שיש בתוכו מעות": איתויי נמי מייתינן. מעלמא, מאחת זוית הבית תיק ובתוכו מעות, להניח בתוכו ספר ולהציל: מי דמי. היכא דספר מונח עם המעות, להיכא דהוא בא עכשיו להביאו עם המעות ולתת בו ספר: התם. דספר ומעות בתוכו – להכי לא מצרכינן ליה למשדינהו: דילמא אדהכי והכי נפלה דליקה. על הספר: הכא. אדמייתי ליה – נישדינהו דרך ביאתו: כדאמרינן מעיקרא. דלא פליגי אלא בהפשטה, ומייתי רבנן ראיה מתיק הספר דמתניתין דמצילין מעות אגב ספר, צרכי הדיוט אגב צרכי גבוה, הואיל ולכך שהות למשדינהו. וה"נ: אגב צרכי גבוה ד"כל פעל ה' למענהו" – יפשיט: ודקשיא לך כו' דלא בעי ליה לעור. אינו צריך לו לעור, ואינו מתכוין להפשיטו משום עור, ולא דמי להפשט אילים ותחשים דמשכן: והא ר"ש מודה בפסיק רישיה ולא ימות. והכא, אע"ג דלא מיכוין – מיפשיט הוא: דשקיל ליה בברזי. בחתיכות דקות. מפשיט וחותך, דאין דרך הפשטה בכך, ולאו מלאכה הוא אלא שבות: שני לחיים. לפתח שאין לו מחיצה: זהו מבוי שאינו מפולש. כלומר: מבוי המותר בכל הלכותיו, בין בעירוב בין בשאר דברים, וכל היתר שאר מבואות יש לו, כגון שיתופי מבואות: ותרווייהו. רבנן ובן בתירה להוי כר"א דאמר: אין מבוי, ואפילו סתום, ניתר בלחי א'. ולשמעינן בן בתירה דבהצלת כתבי הקדש לא בעינן לחיים כרבי אליעזר: מפולש קרית ליה. נהי נמי דבעי ר' אליעזר לחיים, מיהו מפולש לא מיקרי: ועוד לרבנן. דאמרי לשאינו מפולש, וקאמרת דהיינו מבוי המותר בכל הלכותיו: נציל לתוכן אף אוכלין ומשקין. כמו לחצר המעורבת, ואמאי פלגינהו מהדדי דגבי ספר קתני "למבוי שאינו מפולש", וגבי אוכלין קתני "להיכן מצילין אותן – לחצר המעורבת, דמשמע: אבל למבוי – לא: שתי מחיצות. מכאן ומכאן – לחי לכל פתח ופתח: אליבא דרבי יהודה. דאמר בשתי מחיצות סגי ושני לחיים. ואתא בן בתירה למימר, דלגבי ספר מודה ר' יהודה דסגי בחד, דג' מחיצות הוו לדידך נמי. איכא למיפרך כדמתקפתא דלעיל: לרבנן. כיון דאמרת דתרוייהו כר' יהודה, לרבנן דאמרי דשאינו מפולש, ומפרשי ליה לשאינו חסר כלום כר' יהודה, דלא בעי אלא שתי מחיצות ושני לחיים – אי הכי לרבנן נציל לתוכו אוכלין ומשקין, כמו לחצר המעורבת. אלא

תוספות

הכא נעשה בסים לדבר האסור. פי' בקונטרס: שהבשר אסור לטלטל, שהרי אינו ראוי לאכילה עד הלילה. ואינו נראה, דא"כ – היכי קאמר "לא נטלטל עור אגב בשר" כיון דבשר אסור לטלטל: ונראה, דלכ"ע בשר מותר לטלטל. אע"ג דמאן דשרי *בשר תפל בעלמא לטלטל, היינו משום דחזי לכלבים, והכא לא חזי לכלבים – מ"מ משום דזיון קדשי שמים שרי לכ"ע. ובטלטול עור אגב בשר הוא דפליגי. והא דקאמר הכא דהוי בסים לדבר האסור – היינו קודם שנשחטה היה בסים לדבר האסור, שכל הבהמה מוקצה היא מטלטול:

מי דמי התם אדהכי והכי נפלה דליקה. וא"ת, אמאי לא קאמר: התם נעשה בסים לדבר המותר ולדבר האסור, הכא נעשה בסים לדבר האסור גרידא? וי"ל: דאין נראה לו לחלק, כיון דהשתא סבור שיכול לנער מעות מן הכיס, ואפילו הכי א"ל לנער ושרי כל שהוא עושה להצלת ס"ת – ה"ה דשרי להביא תיק שיש בו מעות גרידא:

אדהכי והכי לשדינהו. משמע דאי לא מצי למשדי המעות הוה מצי להביא התיק עם המעות להביא בו ס"ת. וא"כ, כשאינו מופשט אלא עד החזה – מותר לכ"ע לטלטל הואיל ולא מצי שדי ליה. ולא פליגי אלא כשהופשט לגמרי, כדפי' לעיל:

דשקיל ליה בברזי. פירש בקונט': דאיכא שבות בכה"ג. וקשה: דהוה ליה למיתני בפסחים בפרק "אלו דברים" (דף סה:) הפשט דדחי שבת בהדי הנהו שבות דקתני התם, דלדחו שבת! ונראה לר"י: דליכא אפילו שבות, דאינו מפשיט כשיעור תשיבות עור יחד. ולא דמי למפיס מורסא – דהתם פתח קעביד, אף שא"צ לו. וכן לר מזיקין – מ"מ לך הוא. אבל הכא, דלא קא עביד הפשט – אפי' שבות ליכא:

ועוד לרבנן נציל לתוכו אוכלין ומשקין. (ואמאי נקט חצר מעורבת), ולאמפלגי בין חצר מעורבת למבוי – הוה לן לפלוגי בין מבוי משותף למבוי שאינו משותף, דבמשותף יהא מותר להציל לתוכו אוכלין ומשקין, ואמאי נקט חצר מעורבת?

שלש מחיצות ושני לחיים כו'. השתא האי דמפרש לה הכי, ומוקי תרוייהו אליבא דר"א, ולא בעי למימר שלש מחיצות ולחי א' – אינו מפולש, ובלא לחי – זהו מפולש, והוה מפרש אליבא דהלכתא – היינו משום דסבר דבלא לחי כלל לא הוה שרי בן בתירה, דהוי כרמלית, ולא דמי לחצר שאינה מעורבת דפיסלא:

פלוגתא ילפינן דהזאה אינה דוחה, להכי קתני לה: *ארבעה עשר שחל בשבת! ואיכא למימר: דלא קאי אשבת, א"נ: נוטלו בעורו שנפשט עד החזה. ועוד אומר ר"י: דאיכא למימר דרבנן לדברי רבי ישמעאל קאמרי, לדידן – מותר להפשיט לגמרי – אודי לן מיהא דמותר להפשיט בברזי. וא"ת: לפי זה ה"ל למיחשב התם דחיית הפשט! וי"ל: דבפלוגתא לא קא מיירי, דלר' ישמעאל לא דחי ליה הפשט כלל. ואע"ג דחשיב הרכבה והבאתו מחוץ לתחום, דפליגי בה ר"ע ור' אליעזר – לא חשיב לה בפלוגתא דר"א דשמותי הוא. ועוד: דמההיא

אלא אמר רבה כו'. תימה: מה תירץ רבה מקושיא דנציל לתוכו אוכלין ומשקין, ולמה ר"ש: דרבה רוצה לומר דרבנן סברי כרבי יהודה, דוקא לצורך הצלת כתבי הקדש, ולא לצורך אחר. ואביי פריך משום דלאינו נראה לו סברא שיסברו כר' יהודה לתלאין. ומשני אביי ג' מחיצות כו'. ולאביי לא סברי רבנן כר"א לתלאין, דר"א להצלת כתבי הקדש סגי בלחי אחד, דלמסיים ואזיל ואפילו לרבי אליעזר כו':

הא

מסורת הש"ס

[נ"ל התם]

לעיל עה: קג. קיח: לקמן קכ: קלג. קמג. סוכה לג: [בילה לו.] כתובות ו. כריתות כ.

עירובין יא:

לעיל ו. עירובין ו: יב: כב: נט: ע.

עין משפט נר מצוה

טז א מיי' פי"ג מהלכות שבת הל' ב סמג עשין א טוש"ע או"ח סימן שסג סעיף ג וסעיף יד:

[לקמן קכח.]

[ועיין פי' ברזא נקבים והכי קאמר מאן דבעי לי' לעור כשהוא מפשטו מוכחא מילתא דלא בעי לעור ואין לו הנאה ממנו ולא דמי לפסיק רישיה עכ"ל ולפי זה יתיישב קושית התוס' ד"ה דשקיל הא דתניא בתמיד נשחט תנא חשבה וכו']

רש"ל מ"ז

(*דשקיל ליה בברזי). וא"ת: דתני בסוף "תמיד נשחט" (פסחים סה:) תנא: *חשבה, כל אחד ואחד נוטל פסחו בעורו. אם כן, לאו בברזי היה מופשט. ומשמע דבשבת איירי, דאמתני' דהתם קאי, דקתני:

[מגלת תענית ליתא שם ע"ש]

רבינו חננאל

דאינון סברי מטלטלין העור אע"ג בשר מקום שחיטתו כל חד לדוכתיה והוא אסר. ואהדרו ליה אם מטלטלין להציל תיק של ספר אנו לא נטלטל עור אגב בשר ואהדר להו מי דמי תיק נעשה בסים לס"ת שמותר לטלטלו. עור נעשה בסים לבשר אסור לטלטלו. אלא הכי קאמרו ליה כו' ודחה ר' ישמעאל מי דמי. התם תיק נעשה בסים לס"ת שהוא מותר. ולמעות שהן אסורין הכא בבשר כולן אסור. והדר רב אשי ואמר הכי אהדרו ליה אם מביאין מעלמא תיק שיש בו מעות להציל לו ס"ת אנו לא נטלטל עור אגב בשר. והא מנ"ל אי נימא דדייקינן מינה מה התיק שיש בו מעות וס"ת אינך מסיר המעות מתוך התיק ומציל הס"ת

הגהות הב"ח

(א) רש"י ד"ה (מי דמי) וכו' כגון מעות הכא האי וכו' אסור בטלטול) תא"מ ונ"ב ס"א ועיקר מי דמי תיק הספר נעשה בסים לדבר המותר לטלטלו בלא שום דליקה דספר בר טלטול הוא והאי עור נעשה בסים לדבר האסור בטלטול כו':

לבדו אלא אתה מציל אפי' המעות כך אם יש מעות בתיק והצרכת להביאו להציל ס"ת אינך מסיר המעות מתוכו דילמא שני התם במקום שכבר הגיעה הדליקה עד הספר ואם יתעסק בהשלכת המעות תאכלם הלהבה. אבל במקום דהדליקה לא הגיעה [עדיין] והולכין להביא תיק להציל הספר. אם יש בתיק מעות אסור מטלטלן עד שישליכם. ושני רב אשי לעולם כדאמרינן מעיקרא. ודקא אמרת התם בתיק טלטול הבא בעור מלאכה כגון דמתכוין לגלות הבשר ואין כוונתו לעור. ואקשינן והא אביי ורבא דאמרי תרוייהו מודה ר"ש דסבר דבר שאינו מתכוין שרי בפסיק רישיה ולא ימות כגון זה אמרינן באומר המפשיט דאינו מתכוין לעור דומה לאומר הנני מחתך ראש זה העוף ואין כוונתו לשוחטו כגון זה אפי' לר' שמעון שוחט הוא. ואסקי' דשקיל ליה בברזי. פי' ברזי נקבים והכי קאמר מאן דמבעי ליה כשהוא מפשטו מוכחא מילתא דלא בעי ליה לעור ולא דמי לפסיק רישיה ולא ימות. ולהיכן מצילין אותו למבוי שאינו מפולש וכן הלכה. ולית הלכתא כבן בתירא דאמר אפילו למבוי המפולש והיכי דמי מפולש. שמצילין בו כתבי הקדש:
אסקה

יז א מיי' פי"ז מהל' שבת הלכה ב ופכ"ג הלכ"ו סמג לאוין סה ועשין א טור שו"ע או"ח סימן שלב סעיף יז וסימן שסג סעיף א ג יד:
יח ב מיי' פכ"ג שם הלכ"א וסמג שם טור ושו"ע או"ח סימן שלד סעיף א:
יט ג מיי' פרק כ"ב שם הלכה טז סמג שם טוש"ע או"ח סימן שלה סעיף ב:
כ ד מיי' שם טור שו"ע שם סעיף ג:
כא ה מיי' פ"ב מהלכות יו"ט הלכה ד טור שו"ע או"ח סימן תלא סעיף י:
כב ו מיי' פכ"ג מהלכות שבת הלכה כה טור שו"ע או"ח סימן שלד סעיף ג:
כג ז מיי' שם טור שו"ע שם סעיף ד:
כד ח מיי' פכ"ב שם הל"א סמג שם טור ושו"ע או"ח סימן רנד סעיף ה:
כה ט טוש"ע או"ח סי' רנ סעיף א:
כו י כ מיי' פ"ל שם הלכה ט סמג עשין ל טור שו"ע או"ח סימן רעד סעיף א ב וסימן רפט סעיף א:
כז ל טוש"ע או"ח סימן שלד סעיף ב בהג"ה:
כח מ מיי' וסמג שם טוש"ע או"ח סימן רלא סעיף א:

הא דתניא נשברה לו חבית בראש גגו. הקשה הרב פורת: אמאי לא פריך ממתניתין דריש "חבית" (לקמן קמג:), דתנן: חבית שנשברה – מצילין ממנה מזון שלש סעודות, ואומר לאחרים: בואו והצילו לכם, ובלבד שלא יספוג! ותירץ: דהתם איכא למימר כגון שהחבית בכרמלית, דחיישינן שמא יעביר כלי ד' אמות בכרמלית. אבל בהך ברייתא קתני בהדיא בראש גגו. ור"י תירץ: דהתם מיירי כשנשפך היין לארץ, דחיישינן שמא יספוג. אומר ה"ר שמואל בשם ר"ת: דדוקא נשברה לו חבית, אבל נסדקה ועושה טיף טיף – מותר להביא כלים לקלוט ולצרף, דאינו בהול כל כך להביא כלים דרך רה"ר כמו כשנשברה:

כלי אחר ויקלוט כלי אחר ויצרף. אומר ר"י: דזו אף זו קתני; לא מבעי לקלוט – דמינכר שמציל, דאסור. אלא אפילו לצרף, דלא מינכר כולי האי שהוא מציל – אסור: **הציל** פת נקיה לא יציל פת הדראה. אומר ר"י: כשאפו בי"ט של פסח מצות מסולת נקיה, שיש לו די לצורך י"ט – אין אופין אחריהן פת של הדראה. אלא מתחילה יעשה של הדראה, ואחרי כן יעשה הנקיה:

אבל לא משבת ליום הכפורים. פירש בקונטרס: למוצאי יוה"כ. וא"ת: פשיטא, דחול גמור הוא, ומ"ש משבת למוצאי שבת? וי"ל: דמלוה לאכול במוצאי יוה"כ כדפי' לעיל(ב) (דף קיד:). ועוד: לפי שהתענו מותר יותר. אי נמי: ליום הכפורים עצמו קאמר ולהאכיל התינוקות:

והתנא דבי רבי ישמעאל כל מלאכת עבודה לא תעשו. וא"ת: ואמאי מייתי קרא ד"כל מלאכת עבודה" דכתיב גבי י"ט, הא אפי' בשבת דכתיב: "לא תעשה מלאכה" סתם ולא כתיב עבודה – שרי לתקוע ולרדות מן התורה, כדמשמע הכא דאשבת מייתי לה. ופירש רבינו שמואל: דגרס *"כל מלאכה לא תעשו" ורשב"א מפרש: דלעולם מ"כל מלאכת עבודה" אימעיט תקיעה ורדייה. ושבת ילפינן מי"ט, דאין בין י"ט לשבת אלא אוכל נפש בלבד, כדכתיב: "אך אשר יאכל לכל נפש" (שמות יב):

שהיא חכמה ואינה מלאכה. וכיון דמדאורייתא שריא, אע"ג דמדרבנן אסירא, כדאמר בראש השנה (דף לג.): אין מעכבין את התינוקות מלתקוע, הא נשים – מעכבין הכא הוה לן למישרי, משום ג' סעודות:

אלא אמר רב אשי: [א]שלש מחיצות ולחי אחד – זה מבוי שאינו מפולש, ג' מחיצות בלא לחי – זהו מבוי המפולש. ואפילו לרבי אליעזר דאמר "בעינן לחיים", הני מילי – לאוכלין ומשקין, אבל לספר תורה – בחד לחי סגי.§

מתני' [ב]מצילין *מזון ג' סעודות, הראוי לאדם – לאדם, הראוי לבהמה – לבהמה. כיצד: נפלה דליקה בלילי שבת – מצילין מזון ג' סעודות, בשחרית – מצילין מזון ב' סעודות, במנחה – מזון סעודה אחת. ר' יוסי אומר: לעולם מצילין מזון שלש סעודות.§

גמ' מכדי בהיתרא קטרח, נציל טפי! אמר רבא: *מתוך שאדם בהול על ממונו, אי שרית ליה – אתי לכבויי. א"ל אביי: אלא הא דתניא, *נשברה לו חבית בראש גגו – מביא כלי ומניח תחתיה, *ובלבד שלא יביא כלי אחר ויקלוט, כלי אחר ויצרף. התם מאי גזירה איכא? ה"נ, גזירה שמא יביא כלי דרך רה"ר. גופא, [ג]נשברה לו חבית בראש גגו – מביא כלי ומניח תחתיה, ובלבד שלא יביא כלי אחר ויקלוט, כלי אחר ויצרף. [ד]נזדמן לו אורחין – מביא כלי אחר וקולט, כלי אחר ומצרף. ולא יקלוט ואחר כך יזמין, אלא יזמין ואח"כ יקלוט, ואין מערימין בכך. משום רבי יוסי בר יהודה אמרו: מערימין. לימא בפלוגתא דרבי אליעזר ור' יהושע קמיפלגי; דתניא, *אותו ואת בנו שנפלו לבור, רבי אליעזר אומר: מעלה את הראשון על מנת לשוחטו, והשני עושה לו פרנסה במקומו, בשביל שלא ימות. רבי יהושע אומר: [ה]מעלין את הראשון על מנת לשוחטו, ואינו שוחטו, ומערים ומעלה את השני. רצה – זה שוחט, רצה – זה שוחט. ממאי? דילמא עד כאן לא קאמר רבי אליעזר התם – דאפשר בפרנסה, אבל הכא דלא אפשר – לא. ועד כאן לא קאמר רבי יהושע התם – משום דאיכא צער בעלי חיים, אבל הכא דליכא צער בעלי חיים – לא! ת"ר: *[ו]הציל פת נקיה אין מציל פת *הדראה. פת הדראה – מציל פת נקיה. [ז]ומצילין מיום הכפורים לשבת – אבל לא משבת ליום הכפורים, ואין צריך לומר משבת ליום טוב, ולא משבת לשבת הבאה. ת"ר*: [ח]שכח פת בתנור וקידש עליו היום – מצילין מזון שלש סעודות, ואומר לאחרים: בואו והצילו לכם. וכשהוא רודה – לא ירדה במרדה אלא בסכין. איני?! והא *תנא דבי רבי ישמעאל(א): °"לא תעשה כל מלאכה" – יצא תקיעת שופר ורדיית הפת, שהיא חכמה ואינה מלאכה! *כמה דאפשר לשנויי משנינן. א"ר חסדא: [ט]לעולם ישכים אדם להוצאת שבת, שנאמר: °"והיה ביום הששי והכינו את אשר יביאו" – לאלתר. *[י]אמר ר' אבא: בשבת חייב אדם לבצוע על שתי ככרות, דכתיב: "לחם משנה". *אמר רב אשי: חזינא ליה לרב כהנא דנקט תרתי ובצע חדא, אמר "לקטו" כתיב. רבי זירא [כ]הוה בצע אכולה שירותיה. אמר ליה רבינא לרב אשי: והא מיחזי כרעבתנותא! אמר ליה: כיון דכל יומא לא עביד, והאידנא הוא דקעביד – לא מיחזי כרעבתנותא. רבי אמי ורבי אסי [ל]כי מיקלע להו ריפתא דעירובא – שרו עילויה, אמרי: הואיל ואיתעביד בה חדא מצוה – ליתעביד בה מצוה אחרינא.§ "כיצד, נפלה דליקה כו'".§ *ת"ר: כמה סעודות חייב אדם לאכול בשבת? [מ]שלש, רבי חידקא אומר: ארבע. א"ר יוחנן: ושניהם מקרא אחד דרשו, °"ויאמר משה אכלוהו היום כי שבת היום לה' היום לא תמצאהו בשדה". רבי חידקא סבר: הני תלתא "היום" – לבר מאורתא, ורבנן סברי: בהדי דאורתא. תנן: נפלה דליקה בלילי שבת – מצילין

אלא אמר רב אשי כו'. בין רבנן ובין בן בתירא כר' אליעזר סבירא להו, דבעי ג' מחיצות וב' לחיים בעלמא. והכא לגבי ספר אמרי רבנן מודה ר' אליעזר בלחי אחד, ובן בתירא אמר דמודה ר' אליעזר אף בלא לחי: בחד לחי סגי ליה. מילתא דרבנן קא מפרשי:

מתני' נפלה דליקה בלילי שבת. קודם אכילה: שחרית. קודם סעודה: לעולם הוא מציל. הואיל ויומא בר הכי הוא, ובהיתרא טרח, דהא בני טלטול נינהו. ולחצר המעורבת ואפי' טובא הוה שרי ליה, אי לאו משום גזירה, וכדמפרש בגמרא: **גמ'** מכדי בהיתרא קטרח. חזו לטלטול, ולחצר המעורבת: ואי שרית ליה. לאתחולי בהצלה כולי האי, מתוך שהוא בהול – מינשי ליה שבת, ואתי נמי לכבויי: ויקלוט. קילוח הנופל מן האויר: ויצרף. סמוך לגג כעין שאיבה. אלא שאינו ראוי לשאוב, שהגג חלק והיין אינו בגומא, מצרף כלי לגג שיזוב מן הגג לכלי, והוא אוחז הכלי בידו: התם מאי גזירה איכא. כיון דמידי דהתירא הוא, אמאי לא יקלוט ויצרף? שמא יביא כלי כו'. מתוך שהוא מחזר על כלים הרבה, ישכח ויביא: ולא יקלוט ואחר כך יזמין. אורחים, דבשעת קליטה לא מיבעיא ליה: אין מערימין בכך. לזמן אורחים שאינן צריכין לאכול ויותירו: שנפלו לבור. ביו"ט, ואין שניהם ראוים לשחיטה ביום אחד: ואינו שוחטו. שמוצא לו עלילה, שמא חברו שמן ממנו: עד כאן לא קאמר ר' אליעזר. דאין מערימין: הציל פת נקיה. לשלש סעודות: לא יציל פת הדראה. פת קיבר, שניטל הדרה. לפי שאין ערמה כשרה לומר: פת הדראה נוחה לי: אבל לא משבת ליום הכפורים. כגון אם חל יוה"כ באחד בשבת, דהא לא אכיל עד לאורתא, ולאורתא ליטרח וליתי: ואין צריך לומר משבת לי"ט. דיכול להכין בו ביום: מרדה. כלי שרודין בו הפת, ומפרידין אותו מכותל התנור שנדבק בה – לא ירדה אותו במרדה, שהוא דרך חול: ישכים אדם. בע"ש לטרוח ולזמן הוצאת שבת: והכינו את אשר יביאו לאלתר. בשעת הבאה. הכנה והבאה בהשכמה היא, דכתיב: "וילקטו אותו בבקר בבקר" (שמות טז): לבצוע. ברכת המוציא: נקיט תרתי. אוחזן בידו: לקטו כתיב. דמשמע אחיזה, אבל בציעה לא כתיב "משנה": בצע לכוליה שירותיה. פרוסה גדולה, ודי לו בה לאותה סעודה ולכבוד שבת. ונראה כמחבב סעודת שבת להתחזק ולאכול הרבה: כי מקלע להו. פעמים שהעירוב בביתם ופעמים בבית אחד משאר בני אדם: שרו ביה. היינו ברכת המוציא שהיא התחלת אכילה. שרו = מתחילין: תלתא היום. למנין שלש סעודות בא לעולם

(לקמן קמג:) (לקמן קכ:) (לקמן קכ:) (ביצה לז. ותוספתא דביצה פ"ג) [לקמן קכ.] (ויקרא כג) [נ"ל לא תעשה כל מלאכה שמות כ] (שמות טז) (שם טז) (ברכות לט:) (כתובות סד:) (שמות טז) [תוס' פי"ד] [גי' הערוך בערך רד הדראה פי' לחם עב ובלע"ז ארד"י] [שם] (לקמן קלא: ע"ש ר"ה כט: ע"ש ולקמן קכח: וש"נ)

הגהות הב"ח
(א) גמ' והא תנא דבי ר' ישמעאל לא תעשו. נ"ב עי' בפ' ר"א דמילה דף קלא ע"ב דנקט קרא דכל מלאכת עבודה לא תעשו: (ב) תוס' ד"ה אבל וכו' כדפי' לעיל. נ"ב בס"פ אלו קשרים ממש וכ"כ התוס' סוף יומא דף פב ד"ה והאמר רב:

גליון הש"ס
גמ' ואין מערימין בכך. עי' מו"ק דף יב ע"ב:

רבינו חננאל
אסקה רב אשי ג' מחיצות ולחי אחד זהו מבוי שאינו מפולש שאין בו שיתוף ולא עירוב וזה להציל כתבי הקדש אבל אוכלין ומשקין אין מצילין אלא לחצר המעורבת דהלכת' כת"ק. והא דאמר רבה ב' מחיצות ולחי אחד זהו מפולש. ב' מחיצות וב' לחיים זהו שאינו מפולש. ואליבא דר' יהודה דאמר מי שיש לו ב' בתים בב' צדי רה"ר עושה לחי מכאן ולחי מכאן או קורה מיכן וקורה מיכן ונושא ונותן באמצע והכי פי' דכד פסיק לה לרה"ר לרחבה מב' צדיה ב' בתים עושה לחי מיכן ולחי מיכן ומערב ונושא ונותן באמצע. והתם איכא פלוגתא דת"ק (וחנינא) [וחנניה] ורב אמר הלכה כת"ק. ושמואל אמר הלכה (כחנינא) [כחנניה]. וקאי במבוי שיש בו ב' מחיצו' בלבד כנגד זו וב' פתחים יש לו זה כנגד זה והאי איכא עליה לחי או קורה מיכן ולחי או קורה מיכן. לר' יהודה דלא מצריך דלת יכול לערב אותו. א"ל אביי א"כ למר נמי כיון שמתערב יצילו לתוכן אוכלין ומשקין. ובא רב אשי ופירק. וסלקא כותיה: **מצילין** מזון ג' סעודות. ואקשינן מכדי בהיתרא קא טרח דקתני להיכן מצילין לחצר המעורבת נציל טפי. ופרקי' אמר רבה מתוך שאדם בהול על ממונו דאי שרית ליה להציל כל מאי דבעי אתי לכבויי. א"ל אביי ואלא הא דתניא נשברה לו חבית בראש גגו מביא כלי ומניח תחתיה ובלבד שלא יביא כלי אחר ויקלוט כלי אחר ויצרף. התם מ"ט לא יביא כלי אחר ויקלוט כלי אחר ויצרף והא בהיתרא קא טרח. אהדר ליה רבה התם נמי גזרו עליה דאי שרית לאתויי כלי [אחר יביא כלי] דרך רה"ר וכיון שנאסר מלהביא כלי אחר הרי זה מייאש ולא פשיט באיסורא. והא דמי שנשברה לו חבית בראש גגו. סלקא דלאו בפלוגתא דר' אליעזר ור' יהושע היא. ולענין פת בתנור הלכתא כי הא דתניא שכח פת בתנור וקדש עליה היום מציל מזון ג' סעודות. ואומר לאחרים בואו והצילו לכם. ולא ירדה במרדה אלא בסכין. ואע"ג דתנא דבי שמואל כל מלאכת עבודה לא תעשו. יצא תקיעת שופר ורדיית הפת שהיא חכמה ואינה מלאכה. כמה שאפשר לשנויי משנינן: **אמר** רב חסדא לעולם ישכים אדם להוצאת שבת שנאמר והיה ביום הששי והכינו לאלתר. והלכתא כר' אבא דאמר חייב אדם לבצוע על ב' ככרות בשבת.
ואיתא

תורה אור

מַצִּילִין מְזוֹן ג' סְעוּדוֹת, מַאי לָאו – דְּלָא אֲכַל? לָא, דַּאֲכַל. "שַׁחֲרִית מַצִּילִין מְזוֹן שְׁתֵּי סְעוּדוֹת", מַאי לָאו דְּלָא אֲכַל? לָא, דַּאֲכַל. "בְּמִנְחָה, מַצִּילִין מְזוֹן סְעוּדָה אַחַת", מַאי לָאו דְּלָא אֲכַל? לָא, דַּאֲכַל. וְהָא מִדְּקָתָנֵי סֵיפָא "רַבִּי יוֹסֵי אוֹמֵר: לְעוֹלָם מַצִּילִין מְזוֹן ג' סְעוּדוֹת" מִכְּלָל דְּתַנָּא קַמָּא ג' סְבִירָא לֵיהּ! אֶלָּא מַחְוַורְתָּא, מַתְנִי' דְּלָא כְּרַבִּי חִידְקָא. וְהָא *דִּתְנַן: מִי [א]שֶׁיֵּשׁ לוֹ מְזוֹן שְׁתֵּי סְעוּדוֹת – לֹא יִטּוֹל מִן הַתַּמְחוּי, מְזוֹן אַרְבַּע עֶשְׂרֵה – לֹא יִטּוֹל מִן הַקּוּפָּה. מַנִּי? לָא רַבָּנַן וְלָא רַבִּי חִידְקָא! אִי רַבָּנַן – חַמְסְרֵי הָוְיָין, אִי רַבִּי חִידְקָא – שִׁית סְרֵי הָוְיָין! לְעוֹלָם רַבָּנַן, דְּאָמְרִינַן לֵיהּ: מַאי דְּבָעֵית לְמֵיכַל בְּאַפּוֹקֵי שַׁבְּתָא – אַכְלֵיהּ בְּשַׁבְּתָא. לֵימָא רַבָּנַן הִיא וְלָא ר' חִידְקָא? אֲפִי' תֵּימָא ר' חִידְקָא, דְּאָמְרִינַן לֵיהּ: מַאי דְּבָעֵית לְמֵיכַל בְּמַעֲלֵי שַׁבְּתָא – אַכְלֵיהּ לְאוּרְתָּא. וְכוּלֵּי יוֹמָא דְּמַעֲלֵי שַׁבְּתָא בְּתַעֲנִיתָא מוֹתְבִינַן לֵיהּ?! אֶלָּא, הָא מַנִּי – רַבִּי עֲקִיבָא הִיא, דְּאָמַר: *[ב]עֲשֵׂה שַׁבַּתְּךָ חוֹל, וְאַל תִּצְטָרֵךְ לַבְּרִיּוֹת. *וְהָא דִּתְנַן: [ג]אֵין פּוֹחֲתִין לֶעָנִי הָעוֹבֵר מִמָּקוֹם לְמָקוֹם מִכִּכָּר בְּפוּנְדְּיוֹן מִד' סְאִין בְּסֶלַע. לָן – נוֹתְנִין לוֹ פַּרְנָסַת לִינָה, וְאִם שָׁבַת – נוֹתְנִין לוֹ מְזוֹן ג' סְעוּדוֹת. לֵימָא רַבָּנַן הִיא וְלָא ר' חִידְקָא! לְעוֹלָם ר' חִידְקָא, כְּגוֹן דְּאִיכָּא סְעוּדָה בַּהֲדֵיהּ, דְּאָמְרִינַן לֵיהּ: הָא דְּאִיכָּא בַּהֲדָךְ – אַכְלֵיהּ. וְכִי אָזֵיל בְּרֵיקָן אָזֵיל?! דְּמַלְוִוינַן לֵיהּ סְעוּדָה בַּהֲדֵיהּ. מַאי "פַּרְנָסַת לִינָה"? אָמַר רַב פָּפָּא: פּוּרְיָא וּבֵי סַדְיָא.§ ת"ר: [ד]קְעָרוֹת שֶׁאָכַל בָּהֶן עַרְבִית מְדִיחָן לֶאֱכוֹל בָּהֶן שַׁחֲרִית, שַׁחֲרִית – מְדִיחָן לֶאֱכוֹל בָּהֶן בַּצׇּהֳרַיִם, בַּצׇּהֳרַיִם – מְדִיחָן לֶאֱכוֹל בָּהֶן בַּמִּנְחָה. מִן הַמִּנְחָה וְאֵילָךְ שׁוּב אֵינוֹ מֵדִיחַ, אֲבָל כּוֹסוֹת וְקִיתוֹנִיּוֹת וּצְלוֹחִיּוֹת – מֵדִיחַ וְהוֹלֵךְ כׇּל הַיּוֹם כּוּלּוֹ, לְפִי שֶׁאֵין קֶבַע לִשְׁתִיָּה. א"ר שִׁמְעוֹן בֶּן פָּזִי א"ר יְהוֹשֻׁעַ בֶּן לֵוִי מִשּׁוּם בַּר קַפָּרָא: [ה]כׇּל הַמְקַיֵּים שָׁלֹשׁ סְעוּדוֹת בַּשַּׁבָּת נִיצּוֹל מִשָּׁלֹשׁ פּוּרְעָנִיּוֹת: מֵחֶבְלוֹ שֶׁל מָשִׁיחַ, וּמִדִּינָהּ שֶׁל גֵּיהִנָּם, וּמִמִּלְחֶמֶת גּוֹג וּמָגוֹג. מֵחֶבְלוֹ שֶׁל מָשִׁיחַ – כְּתִיב הָכָא 'יוֹם' וּכְתִיב הָתָם °"הִנֵּה אָנֹכִי שׁוֹלֵחַ לָכֶם אֵת אֵלִיָּה הַנָּבִיא לִפְנֵי בּוֹא יוֹם וגו'". מִדִּינָהּ שֶׁל גֵּיהִנָּם – כְּתִיב הָכָא 'יוֹם' וּכְתִיב הָתָם °"יוֹם עֶבְרָה הַיּוֹם הַהוּא". מִמִּלְחֶמֶת גּוֹג וּמָגוֹג – כְּתִיב הָכָא 'יוֹם' וּכְתִיב הָתָם °"בְּיוֹם בֹּא גוֹג". א"ר יוֹחָנָן מִשּׁוּם רַבִּי יוֹסֵי: כׇּל הַמְעַנֵּג אֶת הַשַּׁבָּת נוֹתְנִין לוֹ נַחֲלָה בְּלִי מְצָרִים, שֶׁנֶּאֱמַר: °"אָז תִּתְעַנַּג עַל ה' וְהִרְכַּבְתִּיךָ עַל בָּמֳתֵי אָרֶץ וְהַאֲכַלְתִּיךָ נַחֲלַת

מלאכי ג
צפניה א
יחזקאל לח
ישעיהו נח

לְעוֹלָם מַצִּילִין מְזוֹן ג' סְעוּדוֹת. מִדְּלָא קָאָמַר אַרְבַּע – לֵית לֵיהּ דְּרַבִּי חִידְקָא: מִכְּלָל דְּתַנָּא קַמָּא שָׁלֹשׁ סְעוּדוֹת סְבִירָא לֵיהּ. דִּבְהָא לָא אִיפְלִיגוּ, אֶלָּא דְּת"ק סָבַר מַה שֶּׁעָבַר כְּבָר לֹא יַצִּיל, וּלְרַבִּי יוֹסֵי יַצִּיל: תַּמְחוּי. קְעָרָה גְּדוֹלָה הִיא, וְגוֹבִין בָּהּ גַּבָּאִים מַאֲכָל מִבַּעֲלֵי בָּתִּים, וּמְחַלְּקִין לָעֲנִיִּים ב' סְעוּדוֹת לְיוֹם מִיּוֹם לְיוֹם: לֹא יִטּוֹל. כֵּיוָן דְּיֵשׁ לוֹ – נִמְצָא גּוֹזֵל לָעֲנִיִּים: קוּפָּה. מָעוֹת הֵן לְפַרְנֵס עֲנִיִּים בְּנֵי טוֹבִים דְּזִיל לְהוּ מִילְּתָא דְּתַמְחוּי, וּמִתְחַלְּקִין מֵע"ש לְע"ש: י"ד סְעוּדוֹת לֹא יִטּוֹל מִן הַקּוּפָּה. שֶׁהֲרֵי יָכוֹל לְהַמְתִּין לְע"ש הַבָּאָה. אֲבָל כְּשֶׁיֵּשׁ לוֹ מְזוֹן י"ג – יִטּוֹל, שֶׁהֲרֵי לֹא תֵּחָלֵק עוֹד עַד שֶׁיַּגִּיעַ ע"ש, וַהֲרֵי לְשִׁבְעָה יְמֵי שַׁבָּת צְרִיכִין י"ד סְעוּדוֹת: אַכְלֵיהּ בְּשַׁבְּתָא. שֶׁהֲרֵי תֹּאכְלֶנָּה סָמוּךְ לָעֶרֶב, וְלֹא תִּצְטָרֵךְ לֶאֱכוֹל בַּלַּיְלָה. וְאַף עַל גַּב דְּאָמְרִינַן לְקַמָּן: לְעוֹלָם יְסַדֵּר אָדָם שֻׁלְחָנוֹ בְּמוֹצָאֵי שַׁבָּת – ה"מ לְמַאן דְּאֶפְשָׁר לֵיהּ: בְּתַעֲנִיתָא מוֹתְבִינַן לֵיהּ. בִּתְמִיָּה: אֶלָּא הָא מַנִּי ר' עֲקִיבָא הִיא. וּלְעִנְיַן סְעוּדַת שַׁבָּת בְּמַאן דְּאֶפְשָׁר לֵיהּ – אִיכָּא לְמֵימַר כְּרַבָּנַן, וְאִיכָּא לְמֵימַר כְּרַבִּי חִידְקָא. וּמִיהוּ, הַאי דְּצָרִיךְ לַבְּרִיּוֹת – יַעֲשֶׂה שַׁבָּתוֹ חוֹל, וְלֹא יַטִּיל עַל אֲחֵרִים כְּבוֹד שַׁבְּתוֹתָיו: אֵין פּוֹחֲתִין לֶעָנִי הָעוֹבֵר מִמָּקוֹם לְמָקוֹם. שֶׁאֵינוֹ לָן בַּלַּיְלָה אֶלָּא: מִכִּכָּר. הַלָּקוּחַ בְּפוּנְדְּיוֹן, כְּשֶׁהַשַּׁעַר ד' סְאִין בְּסֶלַע, וְהַפּוּנְדְּיוֹן אֶחָד מִי"ב בַּדִּינָר, דְּהוּא אֶחָד מִמ"ח בַּסֶּלַע, וְשִׁיעֲרוּ לוֹ חֲכָמִים כִּכָּר זוֹ לִשְׁתֵּי סְעוּדוֹת הַיּוֹם וְהַלַּיְלָה: לָן נוֹתְנִין לוֹ פַּרְנָסַת לִינָה. לְקַמָּן מְפָרֵשׁ מַאי הִיא, שֶׁהֲרֵי סְעוּדָה שֶׁל לַיְלָה בִּכְלַל כִּכָּר הִיא. וְכִכָּר זוֹ מְשַׁעֲרִינַן בְּעֵירוּבִין (דף פב:) לִמְזוֹן שְׁתֵּי סְעוּדוֹת, לְעֵירוּבֵי תְּחוּמִין: וְאִם שָׁבַת. אֶצְלָם בַּשַּׁבָּת: מַאי פַּרְנָסַת לִינָה. הָא קִבֵּל לֵיהּ סְעוּדַת הַלַּיְלָה: בֵּי סַדְיָא. לְבָדִין, פולטר"א, לְהַנִּיחַ תַּחַת מְרַאֲשׁוֹתָיו: שׁוּב אֵינוֹ מְדִיחָן. דְּאֵין הֲדָחָה זוֹ אֶלָּא לַחוֹל: חֶבְלוֹ שֶׁל מָשִׁיחַ. כִּדְאָמְרִי' בִּכְתוּבּוֹת (דף קיג:): דּוֹר שֶׁבֶּן דָּוִד בָּא בּוֹ, קַטֵּיגוֹרְיָא בְּתַלְמִידֵי חֲכָמִים, שֶׁנֶּאֱמַר: "וְעוֹד בָּהּ עֲשִׂירִיָּה" וגו'. חֶבְלֵי לְשׁוֹן "חֶבְלֵי יוֹלֵדָה" (הושע יג): בְּלִי מְצָרִים. כְּלוֹמַר: אֵין לָהּ קֵץ: אָז תִּתְעַנַּג. בָּתַר "וְקָרָאתָ לַשַּׁבָּת עוֹנֶג" כְּתִיב: נַחֲלַת

פאה פ"ח מ"ז
פסחי' קיב. קיג.
פאה פ"ח מ"ז ב"ב ט.

במנחה מצילין מזון סעודה אחת. מכאן משמע דזמן אכילה שלישית בשבת היא מן המנחה ולמעלה, דלא כאותם שמחלקין סעודת שחרית ומברכין בינתים. ומיהו, מהא דאמרינן בפסחים בפ"ק (דף יג.): י"ד שחל להיות בשבת, משייר מזון שתי סעודות – אין ראיה מדאין משיירין מזון ג' סעודות, שאין לעשות ב' סעודות שחרית, דהא כיון שאוכל הכל שחרית חשיב כסעודה אחת. ועוד אומר ר"י: שיש כאן איסור ברכה שאינה צריכה, כדאי' בפ' "בא לו" (יומא דף ע.) גבי "ובעשור שבחומש הפקודים" דקאמר: וניתי ס"ת אחרינא ונקרי! א"ר שמעון בן לקיש: מפני ברכה שאינה צריכה: **מככר** בפונדיון כו'. היינו כר' יוחנן בן ברוקא, דחשיב ככר בפונדיון מד' סאין בסלע שתי סעודות דעירוב. ופליג התם (עירובין דף פב:) ארבי מאיר ורבי יהודה שאומרים התם שיעור אחר:

והא דתנן אין פוחתין כו' נימא רבנן היא ולא רבי חידקא. אומר ר"י, דאין לפרש: שבת נותנין לו מזון ג' סעודות, דהיינו כשבא שם בע"ש לעת האוכל, דמסתמא ישבות שם שאין רגילות כל כך ללכת ערב שבת, ובשביל שבת נותנים לו סעודה אחת יותר ממה שנותנין לו בשאר ימים. דא"כ – היכי ניחא לרבנן? והלא מן הכל אין לו כי אם ד' סעודות, אחת שהביא עמו דמלוינן בהדיה, ושלשה שנתנו לו. וכשיאכל אחת בערב שבת – לא ישארו בידו רק ג' סעודות, ואותן יאכל בשבת. וא"כ תיקשי נמי לרבנן: וכי אזיל ריקן אזיל, כדפריך בסמוך. ומיהו, איכא למימר דבסמוך לרבנן נמי פריך. אבל קשה: דכי משני דמלוינן ליה סעודה בהדיה – לא תירץ כלום לר' חידקא, דאין לו לשבת כ"א שלש סעודות, ולר' חידקא צריך ד'! ונראה לר"י: דכשבא בע"ש, לעת האוכל נותנין לו מזון ב' סעודות כמו בשאר ימים. ואם בא לשבות שם – מוסיפין לו עוד ג' סעודות. וקאמר: לימא רבנן היא ולא רבי חידקא, דלרבנן ניחא שיש בידו ה' סעודות בתחילת שבת, ואותה שהביא עמו יאכל בע"ש, ומאותן ה' סעודות יאכל ג' בשבת ואחת במוצאי שבת. ואחת יוליך עמו. אלא לרבי חידקא, כשיאכל ד' בשבת ואחת להוליך עמו למחר – א"כ מה יאכל במוצאי שבת? וליכא למימר דאמרינן ליה מה דהוה לך למיכל באפוקי שבתא אכול בשבתא, כדאמרי' לעיל – דהתם אמרינן ליה כדי שלא יהא ניזון מן הצדקה, אבל הכא כבר הוא ניזון, ולהכי נוטל כל צרכו! ומשני: דאיכא סעודה בהדיה. המתרץ היה סבור שהיה פשוט למקשה שהסעודה שיוליך עמו נותנין לו באחד בשבת, אע"פ שבשאר ימים נותנין לו סעודה שיוליך עמו עם אחרות – בע"ש אין נותנין לו אותה עד שילך, לפי שאינו הולך מיד עד אחר השבת. ולכך היה סבור שהמקשה לא היה יודע שהביא סעודה עמו, ואין לו בתחלת השבת אלא ד', להכי משני ליה: דאיכא סעודה בהדיה. והמקשה משיב: דפשיטא ליה דאיכא סעודה בהדיה. אך קשה ליה: כיון דמתרלת דאכיל לכולהו, וכי אזיל בריקן אזיל שכמו שהביא עמו לכאן כן ישאנה עמו בצאתו מכאן? ומשני: דמלוינן ליה כו':

דמלוינן סעודה בהדיה. וא"ת: א"כ אמאי נותנים לו ב' סעודות? כיון שמביא אחת עמו – יתנו לו אחת, ויאכל אחת, והאחת יוליך עמו. וי"ל: דאין מחלקין תמחוי בלילה אלא ביום, בזמן הסעודה. ולכך נותנין לו שנים, שיאכל אחת מיד ואחת בלילה במקום שיהיה, ואחת להוליך עמו למחר: **לפי** שאין קבע לשתיה. מכאן יש ללמוד: בלילה, כשרוצה להתענות למחר לאחר אכילה, אע"פ שאינו יכול לאכול אם לא התנה, לפי שמסתמא כשבירך סילק דעתו מלאכול – מלשתות ודאי לא סילק דעתו. כדאמר הכא דאין קבע לשתיה. והיכא דלא שכיח יין, אע"ג דסילק דעתו מן היין – מ"מ ממים לא סילק דעתו. ומיהו, אומר ר"י: דשמא דוקא בימיהם שהיו קובעין עצמן לשתיה אחר אכילה אמרו דאין קבע לשתיה, אבל לדידן – לא. וריב"א פירש במסכת תענית (דף יב.): שאף לאחר שישן מותר לשתות, על פי הירושלמי. ואין ר"י רוצה להקל כל כך, כיון שלא נזכר בהדיא בתלמוד שלנו [עיין תוספות תענית יב: ד"ה נים]:
רוצם

ל א מיי' פ"ט מהלכות מתנות עניים הלכה יג סמג עשין קסב טור שו"ע יו"ד סימן רנג סעיף א ב:
לא ב מיי' פ"ל מהלכות שבת הלכה ז סמג עשין ל טוש"ע או"ח סי' רמב:
לב ג מיי' פ"ז מהלכות מ"ע הלכה ח סמג עשין קסב טוש"ע יו"ד סימן רנ סעיף ד:
לג ד מיי' פכ"ג מהלכות שבת הלכה ז סמג לאוין סה טוש"ע או"ח סימן שכג סעיף ו:
לד ה מיי' פ"ל שם הלכה ט סמג עשין ל טוש"ע או"ח סימן רצא סעיף א:

רבינו חננאל

ואיתא בפ' ביצד מברכין. ת"ר כמה סעודות חייב אדם לוכל בשבת ג'. פי' א' בלילה וב' ביום. וכן הלכה. ולפיכך שנינו שמציל מזון ג' סעודו' ומתני' מחוורתא דלא כר' חידקא: **בלי** מאכל אינו מדיח אלא מה שצריך לוכל בו בשבת. לפי זמן סעודותיו אבל כלי שתיה כל היום. שאין קבע לשתיה:

עין משפט נר מצוה

[בראשית רבה פרשה פב]

לה א מיי' פ"ל מהל' שבת הלכה ז סמג עשין ל טור שו"ע או"ח סימן רמב:

לו ב מיי' פ"ז מהלכות תפלה הלכה יב טור שו"ע או"ח סימן נא סעיף ח:

לז ג מיי' פ"ג מהלכות תפילה הלכה א' סמג עשין יט טוש"ע או"ח סימן פט סעיף א וסימן רלג סעיף א [ברי"ף כאן ובפ"ה דברכות דף כו. וכן ברא"ש כאן ושם סי' ה']:

לח ד טור שו"ע או"ח סימן רסא סעיף ב וסימן רלג סעיף א:

לט ה מיי' פכ"א מהל' איסורי ביאה הלכה כג טוש"ע אה"ע סימן כג סעיף ז בהגה:

מ ו ז טוש"ע או"ח סימן ב סעיף א ו:

[ברכות נה.]

מא ח טוש"ע יו"ד סי' רמו סעיף כו בהג"ה:

[פרק היה קורא הלכה י]

[ועי' תוס' ברכות לב: ד"ה כל]

רובם של צדיקים מתים בחולי מעיים. פי' בקונטרס: למרק עונותיהם. ור"י אומר: כי יש במדרש *למרק אכילה מן המעיים, להיות נקיים וטהורים כמלאכי השרת: **אימא** ה' בעילות בעלתי ושניתי. ובירושלמי משני: דיבמות היו, ולא רצה לקיים בהן מצות עונה, אלא רק כדי לקיים מצות יבום, דהיינו ביאה ראשונה: **אילו** היו אומרים לי חברי עלה לדוכן. לא ידע ר"י מה איסור יש בזר העולה לדוכן אם לא משום ברכה לבטלה, של כהנים אמרה תורה לברך את ישראל: **עיון** תפלה. פי': בכוונת הלב. וכן ההיא ד"אלו דברים שאוכל מפירותיהן בעולם הזה" (לקמן דף קכז.) דחשיב עיון תפלה. אבל הא דאמר בברכות (דף לב: ונה.): המעיין בתפלתו סוף בא לידי כאב לב – ההוא עיון דמצפה מתי יעשה הקב"ה בקשתו, שסבור שתפלתו מקובלת. כדמייתי עלה: "תוחלת ממושכה מחלה לב". וכן ההיא *דאמר ר"י: שלשה דברים מזכירין עוונותיו של אדם; קיר נטוי, ועיון תפלה, [ומוסר דין לשמים על חבירו]. והא דאמר בפרק "גט פשוט" (ב"ב קסד:): שלשה דברים אין אדם ניצול מהם בכל יום: לשון הרע, והרהור עבירה, ועיון תפלה. אין לפרש שמצפה מתי תיעשה בקשתו – שהרבה בני אדם ניצולים מזה. אלא הוה כי ההוא דשמעתין, כלומר: שאינו מתכוין בתפלה, שאי אפשר ליזהר. כדאמרינן בירושלמי*: מחזיקנא טיבו לרישא, דכי מטא למודים, מנפשיה כרע*: בתליסר

נחלת יעקב. ולא נחלת אברהם ויצחק: לארבה ולרחבה. ארץ זו ולא יותר: הארצות האל. ותו לא: תבשיל של תרדין. חשוב הוא: ראשי שומין. חשובים היו להן: כסא דהרסנא. דגים קטנים מטוגנים בשמן קרביהן ובקמח: דור אנוש. התחילו לעבוד ע"ז, דכתיב (בראשית ד): "אז הוחל לקרוא" וגו': בתריה. בתר ההיא פרשתא: הרי זה מחרף ומגדף. שנביאים הראשונים תיקנו לומר בפרקים לשבח ולהודיה, כדאמרינן ב"ערבי פסחים" (דף קיח.). וזה הקורא תמיד בלא עתה, אינו אלא כמזמר שיר ומתלוצץ: פסוקי דזמרא. שני מזמורים של הילולים – "הללו את ה' מן השמים", "הללו אל בקדשו": דמדומי חמה. כשהיא אדומה. שחרית אחרי הנצה מיד היא אדומה, וערבית סמוך לשקיעתה: עם שמש. עם זריחתה: ולפני ירח. קודם אור הירח, בעוד השמש לא שקעה: ממתי מחולי בני מעיים. שמתייסרין ביסורין ומתמרקין עונותיהן: ממכניסי שבת בטבריא. מפני שהיא עמוקה, ומחשכת מבעוד יום, ומכניסין שחשכה. וממוציאי שבת בצפורי – שיושבת בראש ההר, ובעוד כשהחמה שוקעת נראית שם אור גדול, ומאחרין לצאת: ממושיבי בית המדרש. חזנים מאספי תלמידים בכל יום לצאת: ממעמידי. ממונים לעת האוכל, לומר: הגיע עת לעמוד ולאכול: ממחלקי. לעניים צדקה, דאמרינן בבבא בתרא פ"ק (דף ח:): צדקה נגבית בשנים ומתחלקת בשלשה. והמחלקים אותה, עליהם לדקדק לפי הצריך לכל אחד ואחד, ופעמים שקרובין דעתם לרחם על זה ולחלוק יותר מן הצורך, שאומדין אותו בהרווחה ואומדין את חברו בצמצום: בעלתי ושניתי. כדי שיהיו זכרים. דאמר מר: הרוצה שיהיו בניו זכרים, יבעול וישנה (עירובין דף ק:): לא קריתי לאשתי אשתי. שאף שיחת חולין שלי יש ללמוד הימנה חכמה: אשתי ביתי. שהיא עיקר של בית: ולשורי שדי. שהוא עיקר של שדה, דכתיב: "ורב תבואות בכח שור" (משלי יד): לא נסתכלתי בו'. מרוב צניעות: והא אמרו לו כו'. וא"כ לרבי יוסי נמי הוה ליה למיקרייה "רבינו הקדוש": תחת אבנטו. מן האבנט ולמטה: לא ראו קורות בו'.(ב) כשפושט חלוקו [פושטו] כמו שהוא לובשו דרך ראשו, ומכסה את עצמו תחלה משום צניעות בסדינו מתחת, ויושב במטתו: לא אמרתי דבר וחזרתי לאחורי. שאם בא מי שאמרתי עליו דבר ושאל אם אמרתי כן עליו – לא חזרתי בי לאמר אינו כדבריו, לפי שמתחלה אמת אמרתי. וקסבר: כל מילתא דמתאמרא באפי מרה – לית בה משום לישנא בישא. וכן מפרש במסכת ערכין (דף טו:): דקיימתי מצות תפילין. שלא הלך ארבע אמות בלא תפילין, וכן לענין ציצית: עד דרמיה. שתקנה. וזה לשון תליית ציצית, כדאמרינן בעלמא (תענית ד' כב.): לא רמי חוטי: דשלים מסכתיה. שגרסה: עבידנא

תורה אור

נחלת יעקב אביך וגו'". לא כאברהם שכתוב בו: °"קום התהלך בארץ לארכה וגו'", ולא כיצחק שכתוב בו: °"כי לך ולזרעך אתן את כל הארצות האל", אלא כיעקב שכתוב בו: °"ופרצת ימה וקדמה וצפונה ונגבה". ר"נ בר יצחק אמר: ניצול משעבוד גליות, כתיב הכא: "והרכבתיך על במתי ארץ", וכתיב התם: °"ואתה על במותימו תדרוך". אמר רב יהודה אמר רב: כל המענג את השבת נותנין לו משאלות לבו, שנאמר: °"והתענג על ה' ויתן לך משאלות לבך". עונג זה איני יודע מהו, כשהוא אומר: "וקראת לשבת עונג", [א]הוי אומר: זה עונג שבת. במה מענגו? רב יהודה בריה דרב שמואל בר שילת משמי' דרב אמר: בתבשיל של תרדין(א), ודגים גדולים, וראשי שומין. רב חייא בר אשי אמר רב: אפי' דבר מועט, ולכבוד שבת עשאו – הרי זה עונג. מאי היא? א"ר פפא: כסא דהרסנא. אמר ר' חייא בר אבא א"ר יוחנן: כל המשמר שבת כהלכתו, אפי' עובד ע"ז [כדור] אנוש – מוחלין לו, שנאמר: °"אשרי אנוש יעשה זאת וגו' מחללו", אל תקרי 'מחללו' אלא 'מחול לו'. אמר רב יהודה אמר רב: אלמלי שמרו ישראל שבת *ראשונה לא שלטה בהן אומה ולשון, שנאמר: °"ויהי ביום השביעי יצאו מן העם ללקוט", וכתיב בתריה: "ויבא עמלק". אמר רבי יוחנן משום רבי שמעון בן יוחי: *אלמלי משמרין ישראל שתי שבתות כהלכתן – מיד נגאלים, שנא': °"כה אמר ה' לסריסים אשר ישמרו את שבתותי", וכתיב בתריה: "והביאותים אל הר קדשי וגו'". אמר ר' יוסי: *יהא חלקי מאוכלי שלש סעודות בשבת. א"ר יוסי: [ב]יהא חלקי מגומרי הלל בכל יום. איני?! והאמר מר: הקורא הלל בכל יום – הרי זה מחרף ומגדף! כי קאמרינן – בפסוקי דזמרא. א"ר יוסי: יהא חלקי ממתפללים עם דמדומי חמה. *א"ר חייא בר אבא א"ר יוחנן: [ג]מצוה להתפלל עם דמדומי חמה. א"ר זירא: מאי קרא – °"ייראוך עם שמש ולפני ירח דור דורים". וא"ר יוסי: יהא חלקי ממתי בחולי מעיים. דאמר מר: *רובן של צדיקים מתים בחולי מעיים. וא"ר יוסי: יהא חלקי ממתי בדרך מצוה. וא"ר יוסי: [ד]יהא חלקי ממכניסי שבת בטבריא וממוציאי שבת בצפורי. וא"ר יוסי: יהא חלקי ממושיבי בהמ"ד, ולא ממעמידי בהמ"ד. וא"ר יוסי: יהא חלקי מגבאי צדקה, ולא ממחלקי צדקה. *וא"ר יוסי: יהא חלקי ממי שחושדין אותו ואין בו. אמר רב פפא: לדידי חשדן ולא הוה בי. א"ר יוסי: חמש בעילות בעלתי, ונטעתי חמשה ארזים בישראל. ומאן אינון – ר' ישמעאל ברבי יוסי, ור' *אלעזר בר"י, ור' חלפתא בר"י, ור' אבטילס בר"י, ורבי מנחם בר' יוסי. והאיכא ורדימס! היינו ורדימס היינו מנחם. ואמאי קרי ליה ורדימס – *שפניו דומין לורד. למימרא דרבי יוסי מצות עונה לא קיים?! אלא אימא: חמש בעילות בעלתי ושניתי. *אמר רבי יוסי: מימי לא קריתי לאשתי 'אשתי' ולשורי 'שורי', אלא: לאשתי "ביתי", ולשורי "שדי". אמר ר' יוסי: [ה]מימי לא נסתכלתי במילה שלי. איני?! והאמרו ליה לרבי: מאי טעמא קראו לך "רבינו הקדוש"? אמר להו: מימי לא נסתכלתי במילה שלי. ברבי מילתא אחריתי הוה ביה – שלא הכניס ידו תחת אבנטו. וא"ר יוסי: [ו]מימי לא ראו קורות ביתי אימרי חלוקי. וא"ר יוסי: מימי לא עברתי על דברי חברי. יודע אני בעצמי שאיני כהן, אם אומרים לי חבירי "עלה לדוכן" – אני עולה. *וא"ר יוסי: מימי לא אמרתי דבר וחזרתי לאחורי. אמר רב נחמן: *)תיתי לי דקיימית ג' סעודות בשבת. אמר רב יהודה: תיתי לי דקיימית עיון תפלה. אמר רב הונא בריה דרב יהושע: [ז]תיתי לי דלא סגינא ד' אמות בגילוי הראש. אמר רב ששת: תיתי לי דקיימית מצות תפילין. ואמר ר"נ: תיתי לי דקיימית מצות ציצית. אמר ליה רב יוסף לרב יוסף בריה דרבה: אבוך במאי זהיר טפי? אמר ליה: בציצית. יומא חד הוה קא סליק בדרגא, איפסיק ליה חוטא – ולא נחית ואתא כמה דלא רמייה. ואמר אביי: תיתי לי, דכי [ח]חזינא צורבא מרבנן דשלים מסכתיה עבידנא

*) [לקמן ריש קיט. ז"ל רש"י תיתי לי ישולם שכרי ובבכורות ל. ז"ל רש"י תיתי לי שכר טוב ועי' תוס' בבכורות ב: ד"ה שמא].

מסורת הש"ס

[ע"ל פ"ז ע"ב תוס' ד"ה כאשר]

[עי' תוס' נדה יג: ד"ה עד שיכלו]

[עי' תוס' בכורות כ: ד"ה שמא וכו']

ברכות כד:

[כתובות קג:]

מו"ק יח:

בדפו"י אליעזר

[סוטה לו:]

גיטין נב:

ערכין טו: [ע"ש כרש"י]

רב נסים גאון

אמר ר' יוסי יהא חלקי עם מכניסי שבת בטבריא ועם מוציאי שבתות בציפורי. לפי שטבריא היתה נמוכה והחמה שוקעת שם בעוד יומם והיו יושביה מקבלין עליהן השבת משקיעת החמה אצלם ושקיעתה לשם קודם שקיעתה במקומות הגבוהין ומי שמקבל עליו הכנסת השבת מוותח חשעה חרי עשה סייג לעצמו והוא משובח ומעולה מן היושבים במקומות הגבוהין ובהרים וכנגדן מוציאי שבת בציפורי שהיא גבוהה טפי ומאחרין לשם פני המזרח להכסיף ושוהין ומאדימין והיו מקבלין עליהן שימור השבת עד שמכסיפין פני המזרח התחתון והעליון ולפיכך הן משובחים בזה הענין יותר מאנשי טבריא ובמסכת ראש השנה בפרק יו"ט של ראש השנה (דף לא) משכחת וטבריא עמוקה מכולן שנאמר (ישעיה כט) ושפלת מארץ תדברי ובמסכת מגילה בפרק מגילה נקראת (דף ו) ולמה נקראת שמה ציפורי אמר רב פפא שיושבת בראש ההר כצפור והרי נתברר לך מיכן כי טבריא נמוכה וציפורי גבוהה:

גליון הש"ס

גמ' יהא חלקי ממכניסי שבת בטבריא. ברבינו יונה פ"ח דברכות דף מג ע"א כתב די"מ שבטבריא היו מגמרים הכלים בע"ש מפני כבוד שבת שיריתו ריח טוב ובציפורי היו מגמרים במ"ש והיו עושין כן לכבוד שבת שהיו מראין הצער שיש להם מהנפש יתירה שהיה להם בשבת ועתה בפרידת השבת צריכין למוגמר להריח ריח טוב עיין שם. וכעין זה כ' באגודה. והר"י מיגאש בתשובה סימן מ"ה כ' יהא חלקי וכו' היינו עם אותם שבתחלת שבת המה בטבריא ובמפוקי יומא הם בציפורי כי טבריא וציפורי תוך תחום אחד ומקדמי ומאחרי שבת: תוס' ד"ה אילו וכו' לא ידע ר"י וכזה לקמן קלא ע"ב תוס' ד"ה קמ"ל. וקלח ע"א תוס' ד"ה מי סברת ובכתובות דף נג ע"א תוס' ד"ה תימא:

הגהות הב"ח

(א) גמ' בתבשיל של תרדין. נ"ב בעירובין ראש ד' ס"ט אמר רב חסדא תבשיל של תרדין יפה ללב וטוב לעינים וכל שכן לבני מעים ואמר אביי והוא דיתיב אבי תפי וכו' ובס"פ מרובה דף פ"ב ע"א חמשה דברים נאמרו בשום משביע ומשחין ומצהיל פנים ומרבה הזרע והורג כנים שבבני מעים ומכניס אהבה ומוציא קנאה ובפ' כיצד מעברין ריש דף נ"ו פירש"י לשבח ולא לגנאי וע"ש: (ב) רש"י ד"ה לא ראו קורות כו' כשפושט חלוקו. נ"ב ס"א לא היה הופכו מרוב צניעות שכשפושטו כו':

עֲבֵידְנָא יוֹמָא טָבָא לְרַבָּנַן. אָמַר רָבָא: תֵּיתֵי לִי דְּכִי אֲתָא צוּרְבָא מֵרַבָּנַן לְקַמַּאי לְדִינָא, לָא מָזֵיגְנָא (א) רֵישַׁי אַבֵּי סַדְיָא כַּמָּה דְּלָא מְהַפֵּיכְנָא בִּזְכוּתֵיהּ. אָמַר מָר בַּר רַב אַשִׁי: פְּסִילְנָא לֵיהּ לְצוּרְבָא מֵרַבָּנַן לְדִינָא. מ"ט – דַּחֲבִיב עֲלַי כְּגוּפַאי, וְאֵין אָדָם רוֹאֶה חוֹבָה לְעַצְמוֹ. *רַבִּי חֲנִינָא מִיעֲטַף וְקָאֵי אַפַּנְיָא דְּמַעֲלֵי שַׁבְּתָא, אָמַר: בּוֹאוּ וְנֵצֵא לִקְרַאת שַׁבָּת הַמַּלְכָּה. רַבִּי יַנַּאי לָבֵישׁ מָאנֵיהּ *(ב) מַעֲלֵי שַׁבָּת, וְאָמַר: בּוֹאִי כַלָּה בּוֹאִי כַלָּה. רַבָּה *בַּר רַב הוּנָא אִיקְלַע לְבֵי רַבָּה בַּר רַב נַחְמָן, קְרִיבוּ לֵיהּ תְּלָת סָאוֵי טַחֲיֵי. א"ל: מִי הֲוָה יָדְעִיתוּן דְּאָתֵינָא? אֲמַרוּ לֵיהּ: מִי עֲדִיפַתְּ לָן מִינַּהּ. *רַבִּי אַבָּא זָבֵן בִּתְלֵיסַר אַסְתֵּירֵי פְּשִׁיטֵי בִּישְׂרָא מִתְּלֵיסַר טַבָּחֵי, וּמַשְׁלֵים לְהוּ אַצִּינוֹרָא דְּדַשָּׁא, וְאָמַר לְהוּ: אַשּׁוּר *הַיָּיא, אַשּׁוּר הַיָּיא! ר' אַבָּהוּ הֲוָה יָתֵיב אַתַּכְתַּקָא דְּשִׁינָּא וּמוֹשֵׁיף נוּרָא. רַב עָנָן לָבֵישׁ גּוּנְדָּא; *דְּתָנָא דְּבֵי רַבִּי יִשְׁמָעֵאל: בְּגָדִים שֶׁבִּישֵּׁל בָּהֶן קְדֵירָה לְרַבּוֹ – אַל יִמְזוֹג בָּהֶן כּוֹס לְרַבּוֹ. *רַב סָפְרָא מְחָרֵיךְ רֵישָׁא – רָבָא מָלַח שִׁיבּוּטָא. רַב הוּנָא מַדְלִיק שְׁרָגֵי, רַב פָּפָּא גָּדֵיל פְּתִילָתָא. רַב חִסְדָּא פָּרֵים סִילְקָא. רַבָּה וְרַב יוֹסֵף מְצַלְחֵי צִיבֵי. ר' זֵירָא מְצַתַּת צִתּוּתֵי. רַב נַחְמָן בַּר יִצְחָק מְכַתֵּף וְעָיֵיל מְכַתֵּף וְנָפֵיק, אָמַר: אִילּוּ מִקַּלְעִין לִי ר' אַמִי וְר' אַסִי מִי לָא מְכַתֵּיפְנָא קַמַּיְיהוּ?! וְאִיכָּא דְּאָמְרִי: ר' אַמִי וְרַבִּי אַסִי מְכַתְּפִי וְעָיְילִי מְכַתְּפִי וְנָפְקִי, אָמְרִי: אִילּוּ אִיקְלַע לָן רַבִּי יוֹחָנָן, מִי לָא מְכַתְּפִינַן קַמֵּיהּ?! יוֹסֵף מוֹקִיר שַׁבֵּי, הֲוָה הָהוּא גּוֹי בְּשִׁיבָבוּתֵיהּ, דַּהֲוָה נְפִישִׁי נִכְסֵיהּ טוּבָא. אָמְרִי לֵיהּ כַּלְדָּאֵי: כּוּלְּהוּ נִכְסֵי – יוֹסֵף מוֹקַר שַׁבֵּי אָכֵיל לְהוּ. אֲזַל זַבְּנִינְהוּ לְכוּלְּהוּ נִיכְסֵי, זְבַן בְּהוּ מַרְגָּנִיתָא, אוֹתְבַהּ בְּסַיְינֵיהּ. בַּהֲדֵי דְּקָא עָבַר מַבְרָא – אַפְרַחֵיהּ זִיקָא, שַׁדְיֵיהּ בְּמַיָּא, בַּלְעֵיהּ כַּוְורָא. אַסְקוּהּ אַיְיתוּהּ אַפַּנְיָא דְּמַעֲלֵי שַׁבְּתָא. אָמְרִי: מַאן זָבֵין כִּי הַשְׁתָּא? אָמְרִי לְהוּ: זִילוּ אַמְטְיוּהוּ לְגַבֵּי יוֹסֵף מוֹקַר שַׁבֵּי, דְּרָגִיל דְּזָבֵין. אַמְטְיוּהּ נִיהֲלֵיהּ, זַבְנֵיהּ. קַרְעֵיהּ, אַשְׁכַּח בֵּיהּ מַרְגָּנִיתָא, זַבְנֵיהּ בִּתְלֵיסַר עִילִּיתָא דְּדִינָרֵי דְּדַהֲבָא. פְּגַע בֵּיהּ הָהוּא סָבָא, אֲמַר: מַאן דְּיָזֵיף שַׁבְּתָא – פָּרְעֵיהּ שַׁבְּתָא. בְּעָא מִינֵּיהּ רַבִּי מֵר' יִשְׁמָעֵאל בְּרַבִּי יוֹסֵי: עֲשִׁירִים שֶׁבא"י בַּמֶּה הֵן זוֹכִין? א"ל: בִּשְׁבִיל שֶׁמְּעַשְּׂרִין, שֶׁנֶּאֱמַר: °"עַשֵּׂר תְּעַשֵּׂר" – *עַשֵּׂר בִּשְׁבִיל שֶׁתִּתְעַשֵּׁר. שֶׁבְּבָבֶל בַּמֶּה הֵן זוֹכִין? א"ל: בִּשְׁבִיל שֶׁמְּכַבְּדִין אֶת הַתּוֹרָה. וְשֶׁבִּשְׁאָר אֲרָצוֹת בַּמֶּה הֵן זוֹכִין? א"ל: בִּשְׁבִיל שֶׁמְּכַבְּדִין אֶת הַשַּׁבָּת. דְּאָמַר רַבִּי חִיָּיא בַּר אַבָּא: פַּעַם אַחַת נִתְאָרַחְתִּי אֵצֶל בַּעַל הַבַּיִת בְּלוּדְקִיָא, וְהֵבִיאוּ לְפָנָיו שֻׁלְחָן שֶׁל זָהָב מַשּׂוֹי שִׁשָּׁה עָשָׂר בְּנֵי אָדָם, וְשֵׁשׁ עֶשְׂרֵה שַׁלְשְׁלָאוֹת שֶׁל כֶּסֶף קְבוּעוֹת בּוֹ, וּקְעָרוֹת וְכוֹסוֹת וְקִיתוֹנִיּוֹת וּצְלוֹחִיּוֹת קְבוּעוֹת בּוֹ, וְעָלָיו כָּל מִינֵי מַאֲכָל וְכָל מִינֵי מְגָדִים וּבְשָׂמִים, *וּכְשֶׁמַּנִּיחִים אוֹתוֹ אוֹמְרִים: °"לַה' הָאָרֶץ וּמְלוֹאָהּ וגו'", *וּכְשֶׁמְּסַלְּקִין אוֹתוֹ אוֹמְרִים: °"הַשָּׁמַיִם שָׁמַיִם לַה' וְהָאָרֶץ נָתַן לִבְנֵי אָדָם". אָמַרְתִּי לוֹ: בְּנִי, בַּמֶּה זָכִיתָ לְכָךְ? אָמַר לִי: קַצָּב הָיִיתִי, וּמִכָּל בְּהֵמָה שֶׁהָיְתָה נָאָה אָמַרְתִּי: זוֹ תְּהֵא לְשַׁבָּת. אָמַרְתִּי לוֹ [אַשְׁרֶיךָ שֶׁזָּכִיתָ], וּבָרוּךְ הַמָּקוֹם שֶׁזִּיכְּךָ לְכָךְ. א"ל קֵיסָר לְרַבִּי יְהוֹשֻׁעַ בֶּן חֲנַנְיָא: מִפְּנֵי מָה תַּבְשִׁיל שֶׁל שַׁבָּת רֵיחוֹ נוֹדֵף? אָמַר לוֹ: תַּבְלִין אֶחָד יֵשׁ לָנוּ, וְשַׁבָּת שְׁמוֹ, שֶׁאָנוּ מַטִּילִין לְתוֹכוֹ – וְרֵיחוֹ נוֹדֵף. אָמַר לוֹ: תֵּן לָנוּ הֵימֶנּוּ! אָמַר לוֹ: כָּל הַמְשַׁמֵּר אֶת הַשַּׁבָּת – מוֹעִיל לוֹ, וְשֶׁאֵינוֹ מְשַׁמֵּר אֶת הַשַּׁבָּת – אֵינוֹ מוֹעִיל לוֹ. א"ל רֵישׁ גָּלוּתָא לְרַב הַמְנוּנָא: מַאי דִּכְתִיב °"וְלִקְדוֹשׁ ה' מְכוּבָּד"? א"ל: זֶה יוה"כ, שֶׁאֵין בּוֹ לֹא אֲכִילָה וְלֹא שְׁתִיָּה. אָמְרָה תּוֹרָה: כַּבְּדֵהוּ בִּכְסוּת נְקִיָּה. ה' "וְכִבַּדְתּוֹ" רַב אָמַר: לְהַקְדִּים, וּשְׁמוּאֵל אָמַר: לְאַחֵר. אָמְרוּ לֵיהּ בְּנֵי רַב פָּפָּא בַּר אַבָּא לְרַב פָּפָּא: כְּגוֹן אֲנַן דְּשְׁכִיחַ לָן בִּישְׂרָא וְחַמְרָא כָּל יוֹמָא, בְּמַאי נִישַׁנְּיֵיהּ? אָמַר לְהוּ: אִי רְגִילִיתוּ לְאַקְדּוֹמֵי – אַחֲרוּהּ, אִי רְגִילִיתוּ לְאַחֲרוּהּ – אַקְדְּמוּהּ. רַב שֵׁשֶׁת, בְּקַיְטָא מוֹתִיב לְהוּ לְרַבָּנַן הֵיכָא דְּמָטְיָא שִׁמְשָׁא, בְּסִיתְוָא מוֹתִיב לְהוּ לְרַבָּנַן הֵיכָא דְּמָטְיָא טוּלָּא, כִּי הֵיכִי דְּלֵיקוּמוּ הַיָּיא. ר' זֵירָא מְהַדֵּר

רש"י

עֲבֵידְנָא יוֹמָא טָבָא לְרַבָּנַן. לַתַּלְמִידִים. רֹאשׁ יְשִׁיבָה הָיָה: תֵּיתֵי לִי. יְשׁוּלַּם שְׂכָרִי: דְּכִי אָתֵי צוּרְבָא מֵרַבָּנַן כו'. שֶׁחִיבַּת תַּלְמִידֵי חֲכָמִים עָלַי: דְּלָא מָזֵיגְנָא רֵישָׁא אַבֵּי סַדְיָא. אֵינִי מַנִּיחַ רֹאשִׁי עַל הַכַּר: כַּמָּה דְּלָא מְהַפֵּיכְנָא לֵיהּ בִּזְכוּתֵיהּ. עַד שֶׁאֶרְאֶה אִם יֵשׁ בִּדְבָרָיו לְזַכּוֹתוֹ: מִתְעַטֵּף. בִּבְגָדִים נָאִים: בּוֹאִי כַלָּה. הָכִי קָרֵי לֵיהּ לִשְׁבִיתַת שַׁבָּת, מִתּוֹךְ חֲבִיבוּת: טַחֲיֵי. רְקִיקִין, טָחִין פְּנֵיהֶן בְּשׁוּמָּן אַלְיָה אוֹ בְּשֶׁמֶן: מִי עֲדִיפַתְּ לָן מִינַּהּ. כְּלוּם אַתָּה חָשׁוּב לָנוּ מִן הַשַּׁבָּת? לִכְבוֹד שַׁבָּת הֵכַנּוּס, וְלֹא הָיִינוּ יוֹדְעִים שֶׁתָּבֹא: מִתְּלֵיסַר טַבָּחֵי. לִטְעוֹם בְּשַׁבָּת מִן הַמּוּבְחָר: אִיסְתֵּירֵי. סְלָעִים. אִיסְתֵּירֵי פְּשִׁיטֵי – סְלָעִים מְדִינָה, וְהֵן א' מח' בְּסֶלַע צוֹרִי, וְהַיְינוּ חֲצִי דִּינָר: וּמַשְׁלֵים לְהוּ אַצִּינוֹרָא דְּדַשָּׁא. לִפְנֵי בּוֹאָם לְהָבִיא לוֹ הַבָּשָׂר הָיָה מְזַמֵּן לָהֶן מְעוֹתֵיהֶן עַל פִּתְחָן, וְאוֹמֵר לָהֶן: "אַשּׁוּר הַיָּיא" – הִתְאַשְּׁרוּ וְהִתְחַזְּקוּ מַהֵר בְּאוּמָּנוּתֵיכֶם, לְמַהֵר וְלַחֲזוֹר וְלִמְכּוֹר וּלְהִתְעַסֵּק בְּצָרְכֵי שַׁבָּת. וְלִי נִרְאֶה: וּמַשְׁלֵים לְהוּ אַצִּינוֹרָא דְּדַשָּׁא – כְּשֶׁהָיָה מֵבִיא רִאשׁוֹנָה הָיָה נוֹתְנָהּ לַשַּׁמָּשִׁין הַמְּכִינִים סְעוּדָתוֹ עַל פֶּתַח בֵּיתוֹ, וְלֹא הָיָה נִכְנָס אֶלָּא מְמַהֵר לַחֲזוֹר וּלְהָבִיא אַחֶרֶת, וְאָמַר לָהֶן לַשַּׁמָּשִׁין: אַשּׁוּר הַיָּיא – הִתְאַשְּׁרוּ מַהֵר לְהָכִין אֶת זוֹ, בְּעוֹד שֶׁאֵלֵךְ לְהָבִיא אֶת זוֹ: אַתַּכְתַּקָא דְּשִׁינָּא. פסטדו"ל שֶׁל שֵׁן, שֶׁחָשׁוּב הָיָה וְעָשִׁיר: וּמוֹשֵׁיף נוּרָא. נוֹפֵחַ מִשָּׁם נוּרָא לִכְבוֹד הַשַּׁבָּת. וְרַבֵּינוּ לֵוִי גָּרַס: אַתַּכְתַּקָא דְּשָׁאגָא – תִּדְהָר: לָבֵישׁ גּוּנְדָּא. כְּלִי שָׁחוֹר. לְהוֹדִיעַ שֶׁהַיּוֹם אֵינוֹ כְּדַי לְהִתְנַהֵג בַּחֲשִׁיבוּת מִלְּהִתְעַסֵּק בְּתַבְשִׁילֵי שַׁבָּת, וְלֹא יְטַנֵּף בְּגָדָיו בְּבִישּׁוּל קְדֵירוֹת: דְּתָנָא דְּבֵי רַבִּי יִשְׁמָעֵאל כו'. דְּבִישּׁוּל קְדֵירָה מְטַנֵּף בְּגָדִים: מְחָרֵיךְ רֵישָׁא. אִם הָיָה שָׁם רֹאשׁ בְּהֵמָה לַחֲרוֹךְ, מְחָרְכוֹ הוּא בְּעַצְמוֹ: פָּרֵים. לְשׁוֹן פְּרוּמִים, מְחַתֵּךְ: מְצַתַּת צִתּוּתֵי. מַצִּית הָאוּר בְּעֵצִים דַּקִּים: מְכַתֵּף וְעָיֵיל מְכַתֵּף וְנָפֵיק. בְּעֶרֶב שַׁבָּת יוֹצֵא וְנִכְנָס לְהָבִיא תָּמִיד מַשּׂוּאוֹת כְּלֵי תַּשְׁמִישׁ וּבִגְדֵי חוֹפֶשׁ וּמְגָדִים, כְּאָדָם שֶׁמְּקַבֵּל אֶת רַבּוֹ בְּבֵיתוֹ, וּמַרְאֶה לוֹ שֶׁהוּא חָשׁוּב עָלָיו וְחָרֵד לִכְבוֹדוֹ לִטְרוֹחַ וּלְהַרְבּוֹת בִּשְׁבִילוֹ: מוֹקַר שַׁבֵּי. מְכַבֵּד שַׁבָּתוֹת: אָמְרִי לֵיהּ כַּלְדָּאֵי. לְהַאי גּוֹי: כַּלְדָּאֵי. חוֹזִים בַּכּוֹכָבִים: אָכֵיל לְהוּ. סוֹפָךְ לִיפּוֹל בְּיָדוֹ: אוֹתְבַהּ בְּסַיְינֵיהּ. עָשָׂה לוֹ כּוֹבַע שֶׁל לֶבֶד, וְשִׁבְּצוֹ בְּמִשְׁבְּצוֹת שֶׁל זָהָב, וְקָבַע בּוֹ מַרְגָּלִיּוֹת, וְקָבַע אֶת זוֹ עִמָּהֶם: סַיְינֵיהּ. כּוֹבַע. וְרַבֵּינוּ הַלֵּוִי גָּרַס: בְּסַדִּינֵיהּ – בְּסוּדָרוֹ. וְרִאשׁוֹן הָגוּן לִי, וְהוּא לְשׁוֹן ר' יִצְחָק ב"ר יְהוּדָה: תְּלֵיסַר עִילִיתֵי דְּדִינָרֵי. עֲלִיּוֹת מְלֵאוֹת דִּינָרֵי זָהָב. וְגוּזְמָא בְּעָלְמָא הוּא, כְּלוֹמַר: הוֹן עָתֵק מְאֹד. כָּךְ פֵּירֵשׁ רַבֵּינוּ הַלֵּוִי. וְכֵן בְּכָל מָקוֹם, כְּגוֹן תְּלֵיסַר גַּמְלֵי סְפִיקֵי טְרֵיפְתָּא (חולין דף נה:), וְכֵן תְּלֵיסַר טַבָּחֵי דִּלְעֵיל: בַּמֶּה הֵן זוֹכִין. לְעוֹשֶׁר גָּדוֹל כָּזֶה: לַה' הָאָרֶץ. דְּאֵין אָנוּ רַשָּׁאִין לֵיהָנוֹת עַד שֶׁנְּבָרֵךְ שְׁמוֹ בְּבִרְכַּת הַלֶּחֶם: וְהָאָרֶץ נָתַן לִבְנֵי אָדָם. ע"י מַתְּנָתוֹ נֶהֱנֵינוּ הַטּוֹבָה הַזֹּאת: מַאי דִּכְתִיב וְלִקְדוֹשׁ ה' מְכוּבָּד. מִדִּכְתִיב: "וְקָרָאתָ לַשַּׁבָּת עוֹנֶג", מִכְּלָל דְּ"לִקְדוֹשׁ ה'" לָאו אַשַּׁבָּת קָאֵי: וְכִבַּדְתּוֹ. אַשַּׁבָּת מְהַדַּר. דְּאִי בְּיוה"כ – הָא כְּתִיב בֵּיהּ מְכוּבָּד: לְהַקְדִּים. זְמַן סְעוּדַּת שַׁבָּת לִזְמַן סְעוּדַּת חוֹל, וְזֶהוּ כְּבוֹדוֹ: לְאַחֵר. וְזֶהוּ כְּבוֹדוֹ, שֶׁהוּא מִתְאַוֶּה לֶאֱכוֹל: בְּמַאי נִשַׁנְּיֵיהּ. בַּמָּה נְשַׁנֵּיהוּ מִשְּׁאָר יָמִים? אִי רְגִילִיתוּ לְאַקְדּוֹמֵי. סְעוּדַּתְכֶם בַּבֹּקֶר – אַחֲרוּהָ: רַב שֵׁשֶׁת. סַגִּי נְהוֹר הָיָה, וְאֵינוֹ רוֹאֶה עֵת הָאֲכִילָה. וּכְשֶׁהָיָה דּוֹרֵשׁ בְּשַׁבָּת, מוֹשִׁיב הַתַּלְמִידִים בַּמָּקוֹם שֶׁתַּגִּיעַ שָׁם הַחַמָּה לְעֵת הָאוֹכֶל, כְּדֵי שֶׁיִּצְטַעֲרוּ וִימַהֲרוּ לָקוּם: דְּמָטֵי טוּלָּא. שֶׁיִּצְטַנְּנוּ: הַיָּיא. מַהֵר: מְהַדֵּר

תוספות

בתליסר עיליתא דדינרי. אומר ר"ת: דעיליתא שם כלי הוא, כדאמרינן בריש "כיצד מעברין" (עירובין דף נג:) עלת נקפת בכדה*: רב אמר להקדים ושמואל אמר לאחר. ולא פליגי, אלא רב איירי בדרכו לאחר, ושמואל איירי בדרכו להקדים, כדאמרינן בסמוך: ומלא

עין משפט נר מצוה

מב א טוש"ע חו"מ סי' טו סעיף א:
מג ב מיי' פ"ל מהלכות שבת הלכה ב סמג עשין ל טוש"ע או"ח סי' רסב סעיף ג:
מד ג מיי' שם הלכה ו סמג שם טור שו"ע או"ח סימן ר"נ סעיף א:
מה ד טוש"ע או"ח סי' תרי סעיף ד:
[וע"ע תוס' ב"ב קלג: ד"ה עיליתא]
מו ה מיי' פ"ל שם הל"ח וסמג שם טוש"ע או"ח סימן רפח סעיף ז:

[חולין קיח.]
פי' מהר וכ"כ בכסף עמוד זה
קדושין מח.
עי' תוס' שם

רבינו חננאל

ורבנן הני דעבדי צרכי שבת בנפשייהו. כגון ר' אבהו דהוה [יתיב] (הציבי) אתכתקא דשינא ומשייף נורא. ורב חנן דשגר תנורא ורב הונא גדיל פתילתא. ורב חסדא מדליק שרגי ורב פפא פרים סילקי. רבה ורב יוסף צלחי ציבי כולהו כדמפרש בגמרא בריש האיש מקדש. שקיום המצוה באדם עצמו טפי עדיף יתר מבשלוחו: **וכבדתו** שמשנה זמן סעודתו בהקדמה או באיחור. ויחיד המתפלל בעצמו אומר ויכולו:

מסורת הש"ס

[כתובות קה:]
ב"ק לב. ע"ש
נ"א מעילי ולמכבי
[נ"ל דכתיב וקראת לשבת עונג רבי אבא וכו' וכ"א בחולין קיח.]
לעיל קיד. [יומא כג:]
תענית ט.
[עי' תוספות ברכות לה: ד"ה כאן]
דברים יד
תהלים כד
שם קטו
ישעיהו נח

הגהות הב"ח

(א) גמ' לא מזיגנא רישא אבי: (ב) שם לביש מאני במעלי:

גליון הש"ס

גמ' אשור הייא. גיטין דף לד ע"א: רש"י ד"ה תליסר עיליתא לדינרי וכו' וגוזמא בעלמא. עי' ברכות דף כ ע"א בתוס' ד"ה תליסר מתיבתא:

עין משפט נר מצוה

מז א מיי' פכ"ט מהל' שבת הלכה ז סמג עשין ל טוש"ע או"ח סי' רסח סעיף א:

מח ב מיי' פ"ל שם הל' ה סמג שם טור שו"ע או"ח סימן רסב סעיף א:

מט ג מיי' שם הלכה ה וסמג שם:

נ ד מיי' וסמג שם טור שו"ע או"ח סימן ש:

נא ה מיי' פ"ט מהלכות תפלה הלכה א טוש"ע או"ח סימן נו סעיף א [וברב אלפס ברכות פג דף ט"ו: וברא"ש שם סימן יט]:

[פרשת יתרו סימן נד]

[וע"ע תוס' פסחים ק: ד"ה שאין]

נב ו מיי' פ"ו מהלכות ת"ת הלכה יא טור שו"ע יו"ד סימן רמג סעיף ז:

נג ז מיי' פ"ב שם הל"ב טוש"ע יו"ד סי' רמה סעיף יג [וברב אלפס פ"ב דב"ב דף קסג: וברא"ש פ"ג דמו"ק סי' ס"א]:

נד ח מיי' שם הלכה א טוש"ע שם סעיף ז [וברב אלפס שם]:

מסורת הש"ס

מהדר אזוזי דרבנן, א"ל: במטותא מינייכו, לא תחללוניה. אמר *רבא ואיתימא ר' יהושע בן לוי: אאפי' יחיד המתפלל בע"ש צריך לומר "ויכולו". דאמר רב המנונא: כל המתפלל בע"ש ואומר "ויכולו" – מעלה עליו הכתוב כאילו נעשה שותף להקב"ה במעשה בראשית, שנאמר "ויכולו", אל תקרי "ויכולו"(א) אלא ויכלו. אמר רבי אלעזר: מנין שהדיבור כמעשה – שנאמר: °"בדבר ה' שמים נעשו". (תהלים לג) אמר רב חסדא אמר מר עוקבא: כל המתפלל בע"ש ואומר "ויכולו" שני מלאכי השרת המלוין לו לאדם מניחין ידיהן על ראשו ואומרים לו: °"וסר עונך וחטאתך תכפר". (ישעיהו ו) תניא, ר' יוסי בר יהודה אומר: שני מלאכי השרת מלוין לו לאדם בע"ש מבית הכנסת לביתו, אחד טוב ואחד רע. בוכשבא לביתו ומצא נר דלוק ושלחן ערוך ומטתו מוצעת, מלאך טוב אומר: יהי רצון שתהא לשבת אחרת כך. ומלאך רע עונה אמן בעל כרחו. ואם לאו, מלאך רע אומר: יהי רצון שתהא לשבת אחרת כך, ומלאך טוב עונה אמן בעל כרחו. אמר ר' אלעזר: גלעולם יסדר אדם שלחנו בע"ש, אע"פ שאינו צריך אלא לכזית. ואמר ר' חנינא: דלעולם יסדר אדם שלחנו במוצאי שבת, אע"פ שאינו צריך אלא לכזית. חמין במוצאי שבת – מלוגמא, פת חמה במוצאי שבת – מלוגמא. ר' אבהו הוה עבדין ליה באפוקי שבתא עיגלא תילתא, הוה אכיל מיניה כולייתא. כי גדל אבימי בריה, א"ל: למה לך לאפסודי כולי האי? נשבוק כולייתא ממעלי שבתא. שבקוהו, ואתא אריא אכליה. אריב"ל: הכל העונה "אמן יהא שמיה רבא מברך" בכל כחו – קורעין לו גזר דינו, שנאמר: °"בפרוע פרעות בישראל בהתנדב עם ברכו ה'". (שופטים ה) מ"ט "בפרוע פרעות" – משום ד"ברכו ה'". רבי חייא בר אבא א"ר יוחנן: אפילו יש בו שמץ של עבודה זרה – מוחלין לו, כתיב הכא "בפרוע פרעות" וכתיב התם °"כי פרוע הוא"(ב). (שמות לב) אמר ריש לקיש: כל העונה אמן בכל כחו – פותחין לו שערי ג"ע, שנאמר: °"פתחו שערים ויבא גוי צדיק שומר אמונים". (ישעיהו כו) *אל תיקרי 'שומר אמונים' אלא 'שאומרים אמן'. (סנהדרין קי:) *מאי אמן? – א"ר חנינא: אל מלך נאמן. [סנהדרין קיא.] א"ר יהודה בריה דרב שמואל משמיה דרב: אין הדליקה מצויה אלא במקום שיש חילול שבת, שנאמר: °"ואם לא תשמעו אלי לקדש את יום השבת ולבלתי שאת משא וגו' והצתי אש בשעריה ואכלה ארמנות ירושלים ולא תכבה". (ירמיהו יז) מאי "ולא תכבה"? אמר רב נחמן בר יצחק: בשעה שאין בני אדם מצויין לכבותה. אמר אביי: לא חרבה ירושלים אלא בשביל שחללו בה את השבת, שנאמר: °"ומשבתותי העלימו עיניהם ואחל בתוכם". (יחזקאל כב) אמר ר' אבהו: לא חרבה ירושלים אלא בשביל שביטלו ק"ש שחרית וערבית, שנאמר: °"הוי משכימי בבקר שכר ירדפו וגו'", (ישעיהו ה) וכתיב: °"והיה כנור ונבל תוף וחליל ויין משתיהם ואת פועל ה' לא יביטו", (שם) וכתיב: °"לכן גלה עמי מבלי דעת". (שם) אמר רב המנונא: לא חרבה ירושלים אלא בשביל שביטלו בה תינוקות של בית רבן, שנאמר: °"שפוך על עולל בחוץ וגו'" (ירמיהו ו) מה טעם 'שפוך' – משום ד'עולל בחוץ'. אמר עולא: לא חרבה ירושלים אלא מפני שלא היה להם בושת פנים זה מזה, שנאמר: °"הובישו כי תועבה עשו גם בוש לא יבושו וגו'". (שם) אמר ר' יצחק: לא חרבה ירושלים אלא בשביל שהושוו קטן וגדול, שנאמר: °"והיה כעם ככהן", (ישעיהו כד) וכתיב בתריה: *"הבוק תבוק הארץ". [פי' תתרוקן] אמר רב עמרם בריה דר"ש בר אבא א"ר שמעון בר אבא א"ר חנינא: לא חרבה ירושלים אלא בשביל שלא הוכיחו זה את זה, שנאמר: °"היו שריה כאילים לא מצאו מרעה". (איכה א) מה איל זה ראשו של זה בצד זנבו של זה – אף ישראל שבאותו הדור, כבשו פניהם בקרקע ולא הוכיחו זה את זה. א"ר יהודה: לא חרבה ירושלים אלא בשביל שביזו בה ת"ח, שנאמר: °"ויהיו מלעיבים במלאכי האלהים ובוזים דבריו ומתעתעים בנביאיו עד עלות חמת ה' בעמו עד [ל]אין מרפא". (דה"ב לו) מאי "עד לאין מרפא"? אמר רב יהודה אמר רב: וכל המבזה ת"ח אין לו רפואה למכתו. אמר רב יהודה אמר רב: מאי דכתיב °"אל תגעו במשיחי ובנביאי אל תרעו"? (דה"א טז) "אל תגעו במשיחי" – אלו תינוקות של בית רבן, "ובנביאי אל תרעו" – אלו ת"ח. אמר ריש לקיש משום רבי יהודה נשיאה: אין העולם מתקיים אלא בשביל הבל תינוקות של בית רבן. א"ל רב פפא לאביי: דידי ודידך מאי? א"ל: אינו דומה הבל שיש בו חטא, להבל שאין בו חטא. ואמר ריש לקיש משום ר"י נשיאה: זאין מבטלין תינוקות של בית רבן אפי' לבנין בית המקדש. ואמר ר"ל לר"י נשיאה: כך מקובלני מאבותי, ואמרי לה מאבותיך: חכל עיר שאין בה תינוקות של בית רבן – מחריבין אותה. רבינא אמר: מחרימין אותה. *ואמר רבא: לא חרבה ירושלים אלא בשביל שפסקו ממנה אנשי אמנה, (חגיגה יד.) שנאמר: °"שוטטו בחוצות ירושלים וראו נא [ודעו ובקשו ברחובותיה אם תמצאו איש] (אם יש איש) עושה משפט מבקש אמונה ואסלח לה". (ירמיהו ה) איני?! והאמר רב קטינא: *אפי' בשעת כשלונה של ירושלים לא פסקו ממנה אנשי אמנה, [חגיגה שם. גיטין מג.] שנאמר: °"כי יתפש איש באחיו בית אביו (לאמר) שמלה לכה קצין תהיה לנו" – (ישעיהו ג) דברים שבני אדם מתכסין בהן כשמלה ישנן בידיך, *"והמכשלה הזאת תחת ידך" [חגיגה יד.]

דברים

מהדר אזוזי דרבנן. כשהיה רואה אותן זוגות זוגות ומדברין בתורה – מחזר אחריהם ואומר להם: במטותא מנכון, לכו והתעסקו בעונג שבת, ולא תחללוניה לבטל תענוגים: ויכלו. הקב"ה וזה שמספר בשבחו של מקום ובשבח של שבת: יסדר אדם שלחנו בע"ש. ללילי שבת: במוצ"ש. נמי כבוד שבת ללוות ביציאתו דרך כבוד, כאדם המלוה את המלך בצאתו מן העיר: חמין. לשתות ולרחוץ: מלוגמא. רפואה: אכליה אריא. לעגל הראוי לשחוט: בכל כחו. בכל כוונתו: בפרוע פרעות. ביטול פורעניות. כגון "פרוע" דמתרגמין "בטל": בהתנדב עם ברכו. כשמתנדבין ישראל לברך את בוראן: כי פרוע. "כי פרעו אהרן" – ע"ז. והכי קאמר: בהבטל פריעות ע"ז, שתשתקע ותשתכח שלא יזכר עונש – משום "התנדב עם" הוא: אל מלך נאמן. כך מעיד על בוראו, שהוא אל מלך נאמן: שאין בני אדם מצויין לכבותה. בשבת: בבקר. בזמן ק"ש, וכן מאחרי בנשף: והיה כנור ונבל. בסיפיה דקרא "ואת פועל ה' לא יביטו" – לא שמו לב ליחד שמו על בריותיו: שפוך על עולל. רישא דקרא "ואת חמת ה' נלאיתי הכיל שפוך" וגו'. שפוך החמה בנקמה, בשביל שעולל לחוץ ובטלין מבית רבן: הובישו כי תועבה עשו וגו'. סיפיה דקרא: "גם בוש לא יבושו וגם הכלם לא" כו': במשיחי אלו תינוקות של בית רבן. שדרך תינוקות למושחן בשמן*: ובנביאי אלו תלמידי חכמים. שנאמר: "ונביא לבב חכמה" (תהלים צ): מחריבין. איכא שיור: מחרימין. ליכא שיור: מתכסין בהן כשמלה. כששואלין אותן טעמי תורה הללו, עושין עצמן כמעלימין את דבריהם, מפני שאינן יודעים להשיב: ישנן בידך. אתה בקי – לפיכך קצין תהיה לנו ותלמדנו חכמה:

דברים

ומצא נר דלוק ושולחן ערוך. וא"ת: דאמר בריש ערבי פסחים (דף ק:): ושוין שאין מביאין את השולחן אא"כ קידש! וי"ל: דערוך הוא במקום אחר, אלא שאין מביאין אותו עד אחר הקידוש, כי היכי דתיתי סעודתא ביקרא דשבת, כדאיתא בשאלתות דרב אחאי. *ודוקא בימיהם שהיו להם שלחנות קטנים לפני כל אחד ואחד, אבל שלנו גדולים הם, וקשה לטלטלם*(ג): כל העונה אמן יהא שמיה רבא בכל כחו. פי': בכל כוונתו, וכן פירש רש"י. ור"י אומר: דיש בפסיקתא במעשה דר' ישמעאל בן אלישע, דקאמר התם: כשישראל נכנסים לבתי כנסיות ואומרים יהא שמיה רבא מברך בקול רם – מבטלים גזירות קשות: א"ר חנינא אל מלך נאמן. צריך להרהר בו בשעה שאומר אמן:

אידי

[בהרא"ש וטור סי' רסח איתא אמר רב וכו' ואמר רב המנונא כל המתפלל וכו' וכ"ה בשאלתות בראשית סי' א]

[כדאיתא לעיל יב:]

הגהות הב"ח

(א) גמ' אל תיקרי ויכלו אלא ויכלו: (ב) שם כי פרוע הוא כי פרעו אהרן אמר ריש לקיש: (ג) תוס' ד"ה ומצא וכו' וקשה לטלטלם. נ"ב פי' אחר קידוש שלא להפסיק כל כך בין קידוש לסעודה אנו רגילין לפרוס מפה ולקדש:

גליון הש"ס

גמ' שנא' ויהיו מלעיבים במלאכי האלהים. ע"ד שאחז"ל נדרים דף כ ע"ב מאן מה"ש רבנן: שם כך מקובלני מאבותי. עיין ב"מ דף פד ע"א ד"ה אי הדרת.

דְּבָרִים שֶׁאֵין אָדָם עוֹמֵד בָּהֶן. עַל בּוּרְיָין, לְאוֹמְרָן כְּהִלְכָתָן: אֶלָּא אִם כֵּן נִכְשָׁל בָּהֶן. עַד שֶׁאוֹמְרָן ג׳ וְד׳ פְּעָמִים בְּשִׁיבּוּשׁ, דְּהַיְינוּ טַעֲמֵי תּוֹרָה הַמְסוּתָּרִין: לֹא אֶהְיֶה חוֹבֵשׁ. אֵינִי רָגִיל לִהְיוֹת חוֹבֵשׁ – חָבוּשׁ בְּבֵהמ״ד. ״אֶהְיֶה״ – הוּרְגַּלְתִּי, כְּמוֹ ״שְׂחוֹק לְרֵעֵהוּ אֶהְיֶה״ (איוב יב) – אֲנִי הוֹוֶה: וּמִמַּאי. דְּמִשּׁוּם דְּיֵשׁ בָּהֶן אֲמָנָה הוּא, דִּילְמָא עַל כָּרְחָךְ צְרִיכִים שֶׁיָּשִׁיבוּ הָאֱמֶת: דְּאִי אֲמַר לְהוּ גְּמִירְנָא. אוֹתָן טַעֲמֵי תּוֹרָה: אָמְרֵי לֵיהּ. שׁוֹאֲלִים: אֵימָא לָן: וּמְשַׁנֵּי הֲוָה לֵיהּ לְמֵימַר גָּמַר וְשָׁכַח, מַאי לֹא אֶהְיֶה חוֹבֵשׁ. מוֹדֶה הוּא עַל הָאֱמֶת שֶׁלֹּא יָגַע בַּתּוֹרָה: בְּדִבְרֵי תוֹרָה. הָיוּ נֶאֱמָנִין, וְאֵין מִתְהַלְּלִים עַל שֶׁקֶר:

תורה אור

דְּבָרִים שֶׁאֵין בְּנֵי אָדָם עוֹמְדִין עֲלֵיהֶם אֶלָּא אִם כֵּן נִכְשָׁלִים בָּהֶן יֶשְׁנָן תַּחַת יָדֶיךָ ״קָצִין תִּהְיֶה לָּנוּ״. (ישעיהו ג) °״יִשָּׂא בַיּוֹם הַהוּא לֵאמֹר לֹא אֶהְיֶה חוֹבֵשׁ וגו׳״. אֵין ״יִשָּׂא״ אֶלָּא לְשׁוֹן שְׁבוּעָה, וְכֵן הוּא אוֹמֵר: ״לֹא תִשָּׂא אֶת שֵׁם ה׳״. ״לֹא אֶהְיֶה חוֹבֵשׁ״ – לֹא אֶהְיֶה מֵחוֹבְשֵׁי עַצְמָן בְּבֵית הַמִּדְרָשׁ, ״וּבְבֵיתִי אֵין לֶחֶם וְאֵין שִׂמְלָה״ – שֶׁאֵין בְּיָדִי לֹא *מִקְרָא וְלֹא מִשְׁנָה וְלֹא גְּמָרָא. וּמִמַּאי? דִּילְמָא שָׁאנֵי הָתָם, דְּאִי אֲמַר לְהוּ ׳גְּמִירְנָא׳, אָמְרוּ לֵיהּ: אֵימָא לָן! הֲוָה לֵיהּ לְמֵימַר: גָּמַר וְשָׁכַח. מַאי ״לֹא אֶהְיֶה חוֹבֵשׁ״ – כְּלָל. לָא קַשְׁיָא, כָּאן – בְּדִבְרֵי תוֹרָה, כָּאן – בְּמַשָּׂא וּמַתָּן.§ **מתני׳** אמַצִּילִין סַל מָלֵא כִּכָּרוֹת – אע״פ שֶׁיֵּשׁ בּוֹ מֵאָה סְעוּדוֹת, וְעִיגּוּל שֶׁל דְּבֵילָה, וְחָבִית שֶׁל יַיִן. וְאוֹמֵר לַאֲחֵרִים: בּוֹאוּ וְהַצִּילוּ לָכֶם. וְאִם הָיוּ פִּיקְחִין – עוֹשִׂין עִמּוֹ חֶשְׁבּוֹן אַחַר הַשַּׁבָּת. לְהֵיכָן מַצִּילִין אוֹתָן? בלְחָצֵר הַמְעוֹרֶבֶת, בֶּן בְּתֵירָה אוֹמֵר: אַף לְשֶׁאֵינָהּ מְעוֹרֶבֶת. *גוּלְשָׁם מוֹצִיא כָּל כְּלֵי תַשְׁמִישׁוֹ, דוְלוֹבֵשׁ כָּל מַה שֶּׁיָּכוֹל לִלְבּוֹשׁ, וְעוֹטֵף כָּל מַה שֶּׁיָּכוֹל לַעֲטוֹף. ר׳ יוֹסֵי אוֹמֵר: י״ח כֵּלִים. הוְחוֹזֵר וְלוֹבֵשׁ וּמוֹצִיא, וְאוֹמֵר לַאֲחֵרִים: בּוֹאוּ וְהַצִּילוּ עִמִּי.§ **גמ׳** וְהָא תְּנָא לֵיהּ *״רֵישָׁא ג׳ סְעוּדוֹת״ וְתוּ לָא! אָמַר רַב הוּנָא: לָא קַשְׁיָא, כָּאן – בְּבָא לְהַצִּיל, כָּאן – בְּבָא לְקַפֵּל. וּבָא לְהַצִּיל – מַצִּיל אֶת כּוּלָּן, בָּא לְקַפֵּל – אֵינוֹ מְקַפֵּל אֶלָּא מְזוֹן ג׳ סְעוּדוֹת. *ר׳ אַבָּא בַּר זַבְדָּא אָמַר רַב: אִידִי וְאִידִי בְּבָא לְקַפֵּל, וְלָא קַשְׁיָא; כָּאן – לְאוֹתָהּ חָצֵר, כָּאן – לְחָצֵר אַחֶרֶת. בָּעֵי רַב הוּנָא בְּרֵיהּ דְּרַב יְהוֹשֻׁעַ: פֵּירֵשׁ טַלִּיתוֹ, וְקִיפֵּל וְהִנִּיחַ, וְקִיפֵּל וְהִנִּיחַ, מַאי? כְּבָא לְהַצִּיל דָּמֵי, אוֹ כְּבָא לְקַפֵּל דָּמֵי?(א) מִדַּאֲמַר רָבָא: אַטְעְיֵיהּ רַב שֵׁיזְבִי לְרַב חִסְדָּא, וּדְרַשׁ: וּבִלְבַד שֶׁלֹּא יָבִיא כְּלִי שֶׁהוּא מַחֲזִיק יוֹתֵר מִג׳ סְעוּדוֹת – ש״מ: כְּבָא לְהַצִּיל דָּמֵי, וְשַׁפִּיר דָּמֵי. א״ל רַב נַחְמָן בַּר יִצְחָק לְרָבָא: מַאי טָעוּתָא? אָמַר לֵיהּ, דְּקָתָנֵי: *וּבִלְבַד שֶׁלֹּא יָבִיא כְּלִי אַחֵר וְיִקְלוֹט, כְּלִי אַחֵר וְיִצָרֵף. כְּלִי אַחֵר הוּא דְּלָא, אֲבָל בְּהַהוּא מָנָא – כַּמָּה דְּבָעֵי מַצִּיל.§ ״וְעִיגּוּל שֶׁל דְּבֵילָה כו׳״.§ חחֶשְׁבּוֹן מַאי עֲבִידְתֵּיהּ? מֵהֶפְקֵירָא קָזָכוּ! אָמַר רַב חִסְדָּא: מִדַּת חֲסִידוּת שָׁנוּ כָּאן. אָמַר רָבָא: חֲסִידֵי אַגְרָא דְשַׁבְּתָא שָׁקְלִי?! אֶלָּא אָמַר רָבָא: הָכָא בִּירֵא שָׁמַיִם עָסְקִינַן(ב), טוְלָא נִיחָא לֵיהּ דְּלִיתְהַנֵּי מֵאֲחֵרִים, וּבְחִנָּם נַמִי לָא נִיחָא לֵיהּ דְּלִיטְרַח. וְהָכִי קָאָמַר: וְאִם הָיוּ פִּיקְחִין, דְּיָדְעֵי דְּכה״ג לָאו שְׂכַר שַׁבָּת הוּא – עוֹשִׂין עִמּוֹ חֶשְׁבּוֹן לְאַחַר הַשַּׁבָּת.§ ״וּלְהֵיכָן מַצִּילִין כו׳״.§ מ״ש הָכָא דְּקָתָנֵי ׳לָכֶם׳, וּמ״ש הָכָא דְּקָתָנֵי ׳עִמִּי׳? אָמְרִי: גַּבֵּי מְזוֹנוֹת קָתָנֵי ׳לָכֶם׳ – מִשּׁוּם דְּלָא קָא חָזוּ(ג) אֶלָּא מְזוֹן ג׳ סְעוּדוֹת, אֲבָל גַּבֵּי לְבוּשִׁים קָתָנֵי ׳עִמִּי׳ – מִשּׁוּם דְּקָחֲזֵי לֵיהּ לְכוּלֵּי יוֹמָא.§ ת״ר: לוֹבֵשׁ(ד) מוֹצִיא וּפוֹשֵׁט, וְחוֹזֵר וְלוֹבֵשׁ וּמוֹצִיא וּפוֹשֵׁט, וַאֲפִילּוּ כָּל הַיּוֹם כּוּלּוֹ – דִּבְרֵי רַבִּי מֵאִיר. רַבִּי יוֹסֵי אוֹמֵר: [ע״ב] שְׁמֹנָה עָשָׂר כֵּלִים, וְאֵלּוּ הֵם שְׁמֹנָה עָשָׂר כֵּלִים: °מִקְטוֹרֶן, *אוּנְקְלִי, וּפוּנְדָּא. קַלְבּוּס שֶׁל פִּשְׁתָּן, וְחָלוּק, *וְאַפִּילְיוֹת, וּמַעֲפוֹרֶת, °וּשְׁנֵי סְפַרְקִין, וּשְׁנֵי מִנְעָלִים, וּשְׁנֵי אַנְפִּילָאוֹת, וּב׳ פַּרְגּוֹד, וַחֲגוֹר שֶׁבְּמָתְנָיו, וְכוֹבַע שֶׁבְּרֹאשׁוֹ, וְסוּדָר שֶׁבְּצַוָּארוֹ.§ **מתני׳** ר׳ שִׁמְעוֹן בֶּן נַנָּס אוֹמֵר: יפּוֹרְסִין °עוֹר שֶׁל גְּדִי עַל גַּבֵּי שִׁידָּה תֵּיבָה וּמִגְדָּל שֶׁאָחַז בָּהֶן אֶת הָאוּר, מִפְּנֵי שֶׁהוּא מְחָרֵךְ. כוְעוֹשִׂין מְחִיצָה בְּכָל הַכֵּלִים, בֵּין מְלֵאִין בֵּין רֵיקָנִים, בִּשְׁבִיל שֶׁלֹּא תַּעֲבוֹר הַדְּלֵיקָה. רַבִּי יוֹסֵי אוֹסֵר בִּכְלֵי חֶרֶס חֲדָשִׁים מְלֵאִין מַיִם, לְפִי שֶׁאֵין יְכוֹלִין לְקַבֵּל אֶת הָאוּר, וְהֵן מִתְבַּקְּעִין וּמְכַבִּין אֶת הַדְּלֵיקָה.§ **גמ׳** אָמַר רַב יְהוּדָה אָמַר רַב: טַלִּית שֶׁאָחַז בָּהּ הָאוּר מִצַּד אֶחָד – נוֹתְנִין עָלֶיהָ מַיִם מִצַּד אַחֵר, וְאִם כָּבְתָה – כָּבְתָה. מֵיתִיבִי: *לטַלִּית שֶׁאָחַז בָּהּ הָאוּר מִצַּד אֶחָד – פּוֹשְׁטָהּ וּמִתְכַּסֶּה בָּהּ, וְאִם כָּבְתָה – כָּבְתָה. וְכֵן סֵפֶר תּוֹרָה שֶׁאָחַז בּוֹ הָאוּר – פּוֹשְׁטוֹ וְקוֹרֵא בּוֹ, וְאִם כָּבָה – כָּבָה! הוּא

רש״י

מתני׳ וְעִיגּוּל שֶׁל דְּבֵילָה. שֶׁהוּא גָּדוֹל, וְיֵשׁ בּוֹ סְעוּדוֹת הַרְבֵּה: וְאִם הָיוּ פִּקְחִין. לִישָּׁאֵל שְׂכָרָן כְּפוֹעֲלִים: כָּל כְּלֵי תַשְׁמִישׁוֹ. שֶׁצְּרִיכִין לוֹ לְאוֹתוֹ הַיּוֹם, כְּגוֹן כּוֹסוֹת וְקִיתוֹנִיּוֹת: י״ח כֵּלִים. מְפָרֵשׁ לְהוּ בַּגְּמָרָא, שֶׁכֵּן דֶּרֶךְ לְלוֹבְשָׁן בְּחוֹל יַחַד. אֲבָל טְפֵי מֵהָכִי – לָא. וְאֵינוֹ פּוֹשְׁטָן לַחֲזוֹר וְלִלְבּוֹשׁ וּלְהַצִּיל אֲחֵרִים: (ס״א טעם) **גמ׳** כְּבָא לְהַצִּיל. [שֶׁהִצִּיל] בְּסַל [אֶחָד], כִּדְקָתָנֵי: סַל מָלֵא כִּכָּרוֹת. וְאֵינוֹ טוֹרֵחַ אֶלָּא לְהַצִּילָן מִתּוֹךְ הַדְּלֵיקָה, בְּבַת אַחַת מַצִּיל כָּל מַה שֶּׁבַּסַּל, דְּהָא חֲדָא זִימְנָא הוּא, מַה לִּי פּוּרְתָּא מַה לִּי טוּבָא: כְּבָא לְקַפֵּל. סַלִּים הַרְבֵּה זֶה עִם זֶה, לִטְרוֹחַ [וּלְאוֹסְפָם] וְלַחֲזוֹר וּלְהוֹצִיא – מְזוֹן ג׳ סְעוּדוֹת הוּא דְּיָכוֹל לְהַצִּיל בְּסַלִּים הַרְבֵּה, וְתוּ לָא. שֶׁכָּל א׳ טוֹרֵחַ בְּעַצְמוֹ הוּא: (עירובין לה:) פֵּירֵשׁ טַלִּיתוֹ וְקִיפֵּל וְהִנִּיחַ. הֵבִיא אוֹכָלִין וְהִנִּיחַ, וְחָזַר וְהֵבִיא וְהִנִּיחַ, מַהוּ? (לעיל קיז:) כְּבָא לְהַצִּיל דָּמֵי. הוֹאִיל וְאֵין כָּאן אֶלָּא כְּלִי אֶחָד, וּבְפַעַם אַחַת הוּא מוֹצִיאָם: [לעיל יט:] אוֹ כְּבָא לְקַפֵּל דָּמֵי. הוֹאִיל וְטוֹרֵחַ לֶאֱסוֹף וְלִכְנוֹס: אַטְעְיֵיהּ רַב שֵׁיזְבִי לְרַב חִסְדָּא. (ס״י) *[עַד] שֶׁדָּרַשׁ לְפָנָיו, וְהוֹדָה לוֹ רַב חִסְדָּא. וְאַהָא מַתְנִי׳ דַּאֲמַרַן לְעֵיל (דף קיז:): נִשְׁבְּרָה לוֹ חָבִית בְּרֹאשׁ גַּגּוֹ, מֵבִיא כְּלִי וּמַנִּיחַ תַּחְתֶּיהָ. וְדָרַשׁ רַב שֵׁיזְבִי לְרַב חִסְדָּא: (עירובין לט:) וּבִלְבַד שֶׁלֹּא(ה) יִתֵּן כְּלִי הַמַּחֲזִיק יוֹתֵר מִשָּׁלֹשׁ סְעוּדוֹת. וְהוֹדָה לוֹ רַב חִסְדָּא. וּמִדְּאָמַר רָבָא: ״אַטְעְיֵיהּ״ – שְׁמַע מִינַּהּ טָעוּתָא הוּא, דַּאֲפִילּוּ מַחֲזִיק סְעוּדוֹת הַרְבֵּה – מוּתָּר, כֵּיוָן דְּחַד מָנָא הוּא. וְהַאי כִּמְקַפֵּל וְנוֹתֵן בִּכְלִי אֶחָד דָּמֵי, דְּהָא מְעַט מְעַט הוּא נוֹפֵל *וּמְטַפְטֵף בּוֹ, ש״מ: כְּחַד מָנָא כְּבָא לְהַצִּיל דָּמֵי: ([נ״ל ומטלטל עי׳ רש״א]) מַאי טָעוּתָא. מְנָא לָךְ דְּטָעוּתָא הוּא בִּידֵיהּ: אָמַר לֵיהּ. מִדְּקָתָנֵי בָּהּ בְּבָרַיְיתָא: וּבִלְבַד שֶׁלֹּא יָבִיא כְּלִי אַחֵר וכו׳. ש״מ כֵּלִים טוּבָא הוּא דַּאֲסִירִי, אֲבָל בְּחַד – שַׁפִּיר דָּמֵי: ([פי׳ בגד רקוק שלובש אדם על בשרו ערוך]) מֵהֶפְקֵירָא וכו׳. דְּהָא ״הַצִּילוּ לָכֶם״ קָאָמַר לְהוּ, לְצָרְכֵיהֶם. וְאִם פִּקְחִים הֵם – ״יַעַכְבוּ הַכֹּל״ הֲוָה לֵיהּ לְמִיתְנֵי: מִדַּת חֲסִידוּת. שֶׁמַּחֲזִירִין לוֹ: חֲסִידֵי אַגְרָא דְּשַׁבְּתָא שָׁקְלִי. בִּתְמִיָּה: אִם חֲסִידִים הֵם – יֵשׁ לָהֶם לְוַותֵּר מִשֶּׁלָּהֶם בְּכָל דָּבָר שֶׁיֵּשׁ בּוֹ נִדְנוּד עֲבֵירָה. וְאע״ג דְּלָאו שְׂכַר שַׁבָּת גָּמוּר הוּא, שֶׁהֲרֵי לֹא הִתְנָה, וּמֵהֶפְקֵירָא קָא זָכוּ – מִיהוּ חָסִיד לָא מִיקְרֵי אא״כ מְוַותֵּר מִשֶּׁלּוֹ: ([תוספתא׳ פי״ד]) הָכָא בִּירֵא שָׁמַיִם עָסְקִינַן. הַמַּצִּיל הַזֶּה יְרֵא שָׁמַיִם הוּא וְלֹא חָסִיד לְוַותֵּר מִשֶּׁלּוֹ: דְּלָא נִיחָא לֵיהּ דְּלִיתְהַנֵּי מֵאֲחֵרֵינֵי. בִּזְכִיָּה דְּהֶפְקֵירָא, דְּיָדַע דְּלָא מֵרְצוֹנוֹ הִפְקִירוֹ: וּבְחִנָּם נַמִי לָא נִיחָא לֵיהּ דְּלִיטְרַח. דְּלָאו חָסִיד הוּא(ו) וְלִמְחוֹל עַל שֶׁלּוֹ: וְהָכִי קָאָמַר כו׳. כְּלוֹמַר: דְּהַאי ״אִם הָיוּ פִּקְחִין״ דְּמַתְנִי׳ – לָאו פִּקְחִין בְּדִין קָאָמַר, לִיטּוֹל אֶת הָרָאוּי לָהֶם – דְּאִם כֵּן ״יַעַכְבוּ הַכֹּל״ הֲוָה לֵיהּ לְמִתְנֵי. אֶלָּא לָאו, הָכִי קָאָמַר: הָנֵי יִרְאֵי שָׁמַיִם, אִם פִּקְחִין הֵן בְּהִלְכוֹת שַׁבָּת, דְּיָדְעֵי דְּכה״ג לָאו שְׂכַר שַׁבָּת הוּא, דְּמֵעִיקָּרָא לָאו אַדַּעְתָּא דְּשָׂכָר פְּעוּלָּה נְחִית – ([שייך לעיל במשנה]) עוֹשִׂין עִמּוֹ חֶשְׁבּוֹן. וְהָכִי קָאָמַר: אַדְּרַב חִסְדָּא נַמִי קָאֵי, אֶלָּא לָא שַׁבְקִינֵיהּ לְרַב חִסְדָּא לְסַיְּימֵיהּ לְמִלְּתֵיהּ: ״לְחָצֵר הַמְעוֹרֶבֶת״. אַפְּשָׁר הָכִי טוּבָא לָא לֵיזוֹל, כִּדְאָמַר לְעֵיל (דף קיז:): מִתּוֹךְ שֶׁבָּהוּל, אִי שָׁרֵי לְאִיעֲסוּקֵי בְּהַצָּלָה כּוּלֵּי הַאי – אָתֵי לְכַבּוֹיֵי: מִקְטוֹרֶן. מנטו״ל: אוּנְקְלִי. לְבוּשׁ רָחָב כְּעֵין סרבל״א. וּבִלְשׁוֹן עַרְבִי מחסיא״ה: פּוּנְדָּא. אֵזוֹר חָלוּל מֵעַל לְמַדָּיו: קַלְבּוּס. נביי״ש: וְאַפִּילְיוֹת. סָדִין לְהִתְעַטֵּף בּוֹ כּוּלּוֹ: מַעֲפוֹרֶת. לַעֲטוֹף רֹאשׁוֹ: וּשְׁנֵי סְפַרְקִין. פיישול״ש: אַנְפִּילְיָאוֹת. קלצו״ש: פַּרְגּוֹד. גנולי״ש וּבִלְשׁוֹן אַשְׁכְּנַז קניהו״ן: חָגוּר. עַל חֲלוּקוֹ מִבִּפְנִים: וְסוּדָר שֶׁבְּצַוָּארוֹ. וּתְלוּיִין רָאשָׁיו לְפָנָיו, לְקַנֵּחַ בּוֹ פִּיו וְעֵינָיו: **מתני׳** עוֹר שֶׁל גְּדִי. לַח: מִפְּנֵי שֶׁהוּא מְחָרֵךְ. מִן הָאוּר, וּבְלַעַ״ז רטרי״ט. וְאֵינוֹ נִשְׂרָף, וּמִתּוֹךְ כָּךְ הוּא מֵגֵן עַל הַתֵּיבָה: בֵּין מְלֵאִים. מַיִם: שֶׁאֵין יְכוֹלִין לְקַבֵּל. כָּל סָאוּר הַמְחַדָּשִׁים הֵם:

תוספות

אידי ואידי בבא לקפל. פירש הר״ב פורת: דלקפל היינו אפי׳ בא לקפל, דלר׳ אבא אין חילוק בין לקפל בין להציל. דאפילו להציל בחצר אחרת לא שרי אלא מזון ג׳ סעודות. אבל אין נראה לומר דלהציל שרי אפילו מאה סעודות בחצר אחרת גם לרבי אבא, דאם כן – הוה ליה לאוקומי מתני׳ אידי ואידי בחצר אחרת. וכאן – בבא לקפל, וכאן – בבא להציל:

נותן מים מצד זה. פירש רשב״ס: לאו דוקא על הטלית, דהא קי״ל בפ׳ ״דם חטאת״ (זבחים לד:) דכבגד – שרייתו זהו כיבוסו. ולעיל, בסוף פרק ״שמנה שרצים״ (דף קיא.) פירשתי:

עין משפט נר מצוה

נה א מיי׳ פכ״ג מהל׳ שבת הל׳ כב כג סמג לאוין סה טור שו״ע או״ח סימן שלד סעיף ו [וסימן שא סעיף מד]:

נו ב מיי׳ שם הלכה כ טוש״ע שם סעיף יז:

נז ג מיי׳ שם טור שו״ע שם סעיף ז:

נח ד ה מיי׳ שם הלכה כה טור שו״ע שם סעיף ח:

נט ו ז מיי׳ שם הלכה כב כג טור שו״ע שם סעיף ו:

ס ח ט מיי׳ שם הלכה כד טור שו״ע שם סעיף ט:

סא י כ מיי׳ פרק יב שם הלכה ד ה סמג שם טוש״ע שם סעיף כב:

סב ל מיי׳ שם הלכה ו טור שו״ע שם סעיף כג כד:

רבינו חננאל

מצילין סל מלא ככרות ואע״ג שיש בו ק׳ סעודות. אקשינן איני והא תני רישא מצילין מזון ג׳ סעודות ותו לא ושני רב הונא לא קשיא רישא בבא לקפל. פי׳ כגון שמקבץ מתוך הבית ממקומות [הרבה] ונותן בכמה כלים שאין לו להציל אלא מזון של ג׳ סעודות בלבד. סיפא במציל כולו בכלי אחד כמות שהוא. ואע״פ שאין זה הטעם כאשר פירשנו. כי רישא במקפל ונותן בכלים שנים ושלשה. וסיפא במציל סל אחד כמות שהוא מפורש (היכנוהו מז׳). בעי רב הונא בריה דר׳ יהושע פירש טליתו וקיפל והניח וקיפל והניח מהו. כבא לקפל דמי או כבא להציל דמי. דמגלג לן שאם קיפל בכלי אחד ונטלו וחזר וקיפל בכלי אחר ונטלו זהו לקפל פשיטא שאינו מציל אלא מזון ג׳ סעודות. וכי קא מבעיא שקיפל והניח בתוך טליתו וחזר וקיפל והניח בתוך טליתו מי אמרינן כיון שמקפל ומביא במקפל דמי ואסור. או דילמא כיון שהוא מניח בתוך טלית אחד ונוטלו כאחד כבא להציל דמי ושרי. ומיפרשא נמי הא בגמ׳ בסוף יציאות השבת. הנהו תרי תלמידי. מר מציל בחד מנא ומר מציל בתרי מני קמפלגי בפלוגתא דר׳ אבא בר זבדא ורב הונא. הכין גמרא ומיגמר מינה דלקפל בתרי תלתא מני כדפרישנא לעילא דאסור לרב הונא ושרי לר׳ אבא בר זבדא ומסתייע נמי בתלמוד א״י דאמרי על מצילין סל מלא ככרות מכיון שבוללה גוף אחד כמין שבולה סעודה אחת היא והאי במימרא דרב הונא ובא ר׳ אבא בר זבדא ופירק פירוק אחר. ואמר רישא דמתני׳ במציל לחצר אחרת שאין לו להציל אלא מזון ג׳ סעודות בלבד בין בכלי א׳ בין בב׳ בין בג׳ כלים. וסיפא במציל באותו חצר שיש לו להציל אפילו ק׳ סעודות בין בכלי בין בכמה כלים. ולענין בעיא דרב הונא בריה דר׳ יהושע פשט גמ׳

[illegible]

הגהות הב״ח

(א) גמ׳ לקפל דמי תא שמע מדאמר רבא: (ב) שם בירא שמים עסקינן דלא: (ג) שם דלא קא חזי ליה אלא: (ד) שם תנו רבנן לובש ומוציא: (ה) רש״י ד״ה אטעייה וכו׳ ובלבד שלא יביא כלי: (ו) ד״ה ובחנם וכו׳ דלאו חסיד הוא ולמחול:

גליון הש״ס

מתני׳ ולובש כל מה שיכול ללבוש. ע״ל דף סה ע״ב: גמ׳ מקטורן אונקלי ופונדא. עי׳ לעיל דף נט ע״ב תוס׳ ד״ה תרי המייני: שם ושני ספרקין. נזכר במתני׳ פרק כ״ט משנה ב דכלים: מתני׳ עור של גדי. עיין לעיל דף מט ע״א תוס׳ ד״ה טומנין:

הוא דאמר כר' שמעון בן ננס. אימר דאמר רבי שמעון בן ננס – מפני שהוא מחרך, גרם כיבוי מי אמר? אין, מדקתני סיפא: "רבי יוסי אוסר בכלי חרס חדשים מלאים מים שאינן יכולים לקבל את האור והן מתבקעין ומכבין את הדליקה" – מכלל דתנא קמא שרי. ת"ר: [א]נר שעל גבי טבלא – מנער את הטבלא והיא נופלת, ואם כבתה – כבתה. אמרי דבי רבי ינאי: [ב]לא *שנו אלא בשוכח, אבל במניח – נעשה בסיס לדבר האסור. תנא: נר שאחורי הדלת – פותח ונועל כדרכו. ואם כבתה – כבתה. [ג]לייט עלה רב. אמר ליה רבינא לרב אחא בריה דרבא, ואמרי לה רב אחא בריה דרבא לרב אשי: מאי טעמא לייט עלה רב? *אילימא משום דרב סבר לה כרבי יהודה, ותנא קתני לה כר' שמעון – משום דרב סבר לה כר' יהודה, כל דתני כר' שמעון מילט לייט ליה?! אמר ליה: בהא – אפילו ר' שמעון מודה, *דהא אביי ורבא דאמרי תרוייהו: מודה רבי שמעון בפסיק רישיה ולא ימות. אמר רב יהודה: פותח אדם דלת כנגד(א) מדורה בשבת. *[ד]לייט עלה אביי. במאי עסקינן? אילימא ברוח מצויה – מאי טעמיה דמאן דאסר? אי ברוח שאינה מצויה – מאי טעמא דמאן דשרי? לעולם ברוח מצויה, מר סבר: גזרינן, ומר סבר: לא גזרינן.§ "עושין מחיצה כו'".§ למימרא דרבנן סברי: גרם כבוי מותר, ור' יוסי סבר: גרם כבוי אסור, והא איפכא שמעינן להו! דתניא: עושין מחיצה בכלים ריקנין, ובמלאין שאין דרכן להשתבר. ואלו מלאין שאין דרכן להשתבר – כלי מתכות. רבי יוסי אומר: אף כלי כפר שיחין וכלי כפר חנניה אין דרכן להשתבר! וכי תימא: איפוך מתני', ורבי יוסי דברייתא – לדבריהם קאמר. ומי מצית אפכת לה? והאמר רבה בר תחליפא משמיה דרב: מאן תנא "גרם כבוי אסור" – ר' יוסי! אלא, לעולם לא תיפוך, וברייתא כולה ר' יוסי היא, וחסורי מחסרא והכי קתני: עושין מחיצה בכלים ריקנין, ובמלאים שאין דרכן להשתבר. ואלו הן כלים שאין דרכן להשתבר – כלי מתכות, וכלי כפר שיחין וכלי כפר חנניה נמי אין דרכן להשתבר, שר' יוסי אומר: אף כלי כפר שיחין וכלי כפר חנניה אין דרכן להשתבר. ורמי דרבנן אדרבנן, ורמי דרבי יוסי אדרבי יוסי. *דתניא: [ה]"הרי שהיה שם כתוב לו על בשרו – הרי זה לא ירחוץ ולא יסוך ולא יעמוד במקום הטינופת. [ו]נזדמנה לו טבילה של מצוה – כורך עליה גמי ויורד וטובל. רבי יוסי אומר: לעולם יורד וטובל כדרכו, ובלבד שלא ישפשף! שאני התם דאמר קרא: ○"ואבדתם את שמם מן המקום ההוא לא תעשון כן לה' אלהיכם", עשייה הוא דאסור, גרמא – שרי. אי הכי, הכא נמי: כתיב ○"לא תעשה [כל] מלאכה" – עשייה הוא דאסור, גרמא שרי! *מתוך שאדם בהול על ממונו – אי שרית ליה אתי לכבויי. אי הכי – קשיא דרבנן אדרבנן: ומה התם דאדם בהול על ממונו – שרי, הכא לא כל שכן?! ותסברא, האי גמי היכי דמי? אי דמיהדק – קא הוי חציצה, אי לא מיהדק – עיילי ביה מיא! חציצה – תיפוק ליה משום דיו! בלחה, *דתניא: [ז]"הדם והדיו הדבש והחלב יבשין – חוצצין, לחים – אין חוצצין". מכל מקום קשיא! אלא אמר רבא בר רב שילא: [ח]היינו טעמייהו דרבנן, דקסברי: אסור לעמוד בפני השם ערום. מכלל דר"י סבר מותר לעמוד בפני השם ערום?! דמנח ידיה עילויה. לרבנן נמי, דמנח ידיה עילויה! זימנין דמשתלי, ושקיל ליה. לר' יוסי נמי, זימנין דמשתלי ושקיל ליה! אלא: אי דאיכא גמי – ה"נ, הב"ע – לאהדורי אגמי. רבנן סברי:

טבילה

[חולין קז:]

רש"י

גמ' הוא דאמר כר"ש. דשרי לעכובי דליקה בעור גדי: גרם כיבוי. כי האי גוונא, כשמגיע למים הוא כבה: מי אמר. דילמא הא דקתני במתני': "ועושין מחיצה בכל הכלים" – לאו בחדשים המתבקעים קאמר: נר. דולק, קרוסיי"ל: אלא בשכח. דשכחו מבעוד יום על הטבלא שלא מדעת: אבל מניח נעשית. טבלא בסיס לדבר האסור, ואסור לטלטלה כדי לנערה: לייט עליה. על כל המורין כן: כר' יהודה. דאמר: דבר שאין מתכוין – אסור: בפסיק רישיה. והכא נמי, הרוח מכבהו: כנגד המדורה. ואע"פ שרוח מנשבת ומבעיר האור: מאי טעמא דמאן דאסר. אין דרך להבעיר ברוח מצויה, ולא "פסיק רישיה ולא ימות" הוא: אף כלי כפר שיחין. חרס העשוי מאותו עפר – חזק הוא, ואין משתבר. אלמא: לר' יוסי בגרם כבוי טפי מיקל מדרבנן: וכי תימא איפוך מתני'. ותני ברישא "דברי ר' יוסי" וחכמים אוסרין בכלי חרס חדשים כו': ור' יוסי דברייתא. דמשמע דבהנהו דפקעי מודה, דהא כפר שיחין וכפר חנניה הוא דקשרי: לדבריהם קאמר להו. לדידי כל הכלים שרו, דגרם כבוי מותר. אלא לדידכו, נהי דאסריתו גרם כבוי – אודו לי מיהת דבהני אפילו גרם ליכא: כורך עליו גמי. קס"ד השתא: כדי שלא ימחק את השם במים, אלמא: לרבנן גרם מחק אסור, ולר' יוסי שרי: ובלבד שלא ישפשף. דהוי מוחק בידים: ותסברא. דהכא נמי דמצרכו רבנן משום שלא ימחק הוא: האי גמי היכי דמי. להגין עליו: אי דמיהדק. שלא יכנסו בו מים וימחק – הוי חציצה: ואי דלא מיהדק. לבשרו: עיילי ביה מיא. ואינו מגין מלמחוק: תיפוק ליה דמשום דיו. בלא גמי נמי, חייץ דיו. ומשני: בלחה: מכל מקום קשיא. גמי לרבנן למה להו? מכלל דלר' יוסי כו'. בתמיה; והא כתיב: "לא יראה בך ערות דבר" (דברים כג): אלא אי איכא גמי הכי נמי. דמודה ר' יוסי דצריך לכרוך עליו גמי, ולא סגי ליה לאנוחי ידיו עליו, דילמא מישתלי ושקיל ליה לידיה:

תוספות

גרם כיבוי מי אמר. וא"ת, הא קתני מתני': "בין מלאים בין ריקנים" ומאי רבותא איכא טפי במלאים מבריקנים אי לאו דמיירי בדרכן להשתבר? וי"ל: דס"ד דמיירי בכלים שאין דרכן להשתבר, וקמ"ל דלא גזרינן אטו כלים שדרכן להשתבר:

מנער את הטבלא והיא נופלת ואם כבתה כבתה. אומר ר"י: דמיירי דליכא שמן בנר. דאי איכא שמן בנר – חייב, שהרי שופך ממנו והוי כמסתפק ממנו, דחייב משום מכבה, כדאמר בפ"ב דביצה (דף כב:), ובירושלמי מוקי לה בנר שכבה, ולא קתני בהך ברייתא: "ואם כבתה כבתה". ואתא לאשמעינן היתר טלטול ע"י ניעור לר' יהודה דאסר טלטול בנר שכבה. אי נמי: אפילו לר"ש, ובנר גדול – כגון קערה ועששית, דמודה ר"ש כדאמר בפרק ["כירה"] (דף מד.) או כשיש אפר וגחלת, אלא שכבה השלהבת: פותח ונועל כדרכו. אע"פ שע"י כן מתנדנד הנר ומתרחק השמן מן השלהבת, או מתקרב והוי מכבה או מבעיר. אבל אין לפרש משום כיבוי דרוח – דאחורי הדלת ליכא רוח. ועוד, דא"כ הוה ליה למימר: פותח אדם דלת כנגד הנר, כדקאמר בסמוך כנגד המדורה. ועוד: דתינח פותח, נועל מאי איסורא איכא? אלא כדפרישית. ואי לאו משום כיבוי והבערה – משום טלטול אין לאסור, דבנעילת דלת לא חשיב טלטול, וגם לא הוי בסיס לדבר האסור, דבית חשוב הוא, ובטל אגב בית. אי נמי: בשכח, דלא הוי בסיס: מר סבר גזרינן. הלכך צריך ליזהר שלא לפתוח הדלת לפני המדורה, אפילו ברוח מצויה, דהא לייט עלה אביי דהוי בתרלה. והנ"מ – כשהמדורה קצת קרובה אצל הדלת: והא איפכא שמעינן להו. לאו דווקא איפכא, דר' יוסי דברייתא הוי כמו מתני', דאסר דרכו להשתבר. אלא היינו איפכא: דבמתניתין מחמיר ר' יוסי טפי מדרבנן, ובברייתא מיקל טפי: וכי תימא איפוך מתני' כו'. וא"ת: מ"מ תקשה, דבמתני' לא אסרי רבנן אלא חרס חדש, ובברייתא אסרי אפי' ישן, מדנקט כלי מתכות! וי"ל: דנקט בברייתא כלי מתכות – משום דאין חילוק בהם בין חדשים לישנים, וה"ה כלי חרס ישן: והאמר רבה כו'. ואם תאמר: ואמאי לא מפיך ברייתא? דטפי אית לן לאפוכה ממתני', ושוי אתי נמי שפיר הא דרבה בר תחליפא וניחא דרבנן לדברי ר' יוסי קאמרי ואינהו שרי אף בכלי חרס חדש! וי"ל: דהתלמוד לא קאמר אלא דאפילו מפיך מתני' – לא אתי שפיר, אלא על כרחיך – ברייתא אית לן לתרוצי – וכיון דאתינא להכי – לא צריך להפוכה, אלא למימר חסורי מיחסרא: אי הכי קשה דרבנן אדרבנן. בלאו הכי הוה קשיא דרבנן אדרבנן. אלא, משום דהשתא פריך מכ"ש קאמר: אי הכי*):

*) [ועי' תוס' עירובין כג: ובכילה ח: וכתובות ג: וב"מ לג. שבועות מה: ד"ה אי הכי].

עין משפט נר מצוה

סג א ב מיי' פי"ב מהל' שבת הלכה ו סמג לאוין סה טוש"ע או"ח סימן רעז סעיף ג:

סד ג מיי' שם פ"ה הל' יז טוש"ע שם ס"א:

סה ד מיי' שם טוש"ע שם סעיף ב:

סו ה ו מיי' פ"ו מהל' יסודי התורה הל' ו סמג עשין ג:

סז ז מיי' פ"ב מהלכות מקואות הלכה ב סמג לאוין קיא טוש"ע יו"ד סימן קצח סעיף טו:

סח ח מיי' פ"ו מהל' יסודי התורה הל"ו:

רבינו חננאל

אמרינן בגמרא דפורפת על האבן ועל האגוז כו' תיבעי למאן דאמר מערימין תיבעי למ"ד אין מערימין. ואמר לאחרים בואו והצילו עמי שכן דרך בני אדם להשאיל כליו בשבת. פי' י"ח כלים דקא"ר יוסי [מקטורין] כמו מעיל. ובלשון ישמעאל כרכום שיש לו בית ראש ועוטה לו הלובשו ויש לו לולאות וקרסים (שהוא הווה) [שמחברן והוא] כמו מלבוש: אונקלי. בגד דקיקי שנקרא מערקה שלובש אדם על בשרו וחולם כל גופו וכן שנינו (מגילה כ"ד) בענין תפלין של יד ציפהו זהב ונתנו על בית יד של אונקלי שלו הרי זה דרך החיצונים: פונדא. גם היא מגעת עד למטה מטבורו של אדם וקורין לו בלשון פרסי פֶשֶׁת. ונקשר כחשב אפודה והיא אפוד האמורה בתורה ויש בה כסים כסים כנגד הלב ותחת הידים: קנבום של פשתן. חלוק התחתון שלובשין אותו ונקרא גלאלה. חלוק הוא המלובש העליון וקורין לו ורבנן: שני. ספרקים*) ויש שגורם סובריקין והם בלשון יון המכנסים ושמענו שאמר הגאון נט' דח' דם תפנקי שמלבישין בהן הידים עד האציל ויש בהן בתי אצבעות שני מנעלים כמשמען: שני פרגוד. בלשון ישמעאל גודאבי: אנפליאות. גם הם מנעלים לשוקים עליון האנין שעל השוקים מן העור. ומעפורת וחגור שבמתנים וכובע הרי י"ח כלים: ר' שמעון בן ננס אומר פורשין עור של גדי כו'. אמר רב יהודה טלית שאחז בה האור מצד אחד נותן עליה מים מצד אחר ואם כבתה כבתה. והא ודאי גרם כיבוי הוא. ואקשינן עליה ממתנית' דקתני פושטה ומתכסה בה אבל מים שהן גרם כיבוי לא קתני ואתנינן לאוקמיה לרב יהודה כ"ר שמעון בן ננס ולא קם. דר' שמעון בן ננס לא קאמר אלא מפני שהוא מחרך הא גרמא בידים לא קאמר אלא קם רב יהודה כרבנן. דתנן עושין מחיצה בכל הכלים בין מלאים בין ריקנין דשרו גרם כיבוי ור' יוסי אוסר גרם כיבוי והלכה כרבנן וכרב יהודה: נר שעל גבי טבלא איתא דאוקמה דבי ר' ינאי בשכח נר שעל גבי טבלא. אבל המניח נר על טבלא נעשה טבלא בסיס לנר שהיא מוקצה מחמת איסור ואסור לטלטוליה. ודתנא תנא קמיה דרב ולייט עלה רב. היכא דידע שבודאי כשפותח ונועל יכבה הנר מפני שהדלת נוגעת בו ומכבתו שאסור דבהא אפי' ר"ש מודה דהוי פסוק רישיה ולא ימות. אבל אי גרם בעלמא שרי: אמר רב יהודה אמר שמואל פותח אדם דלת כנגד המדורה בשבת ואינו חושש. ואע"פ שהרוח מלבה את האש לייט עלה אביי דחשיב ליה כמבעיר את האש ואי רוח שאינה מצויה היא והוא שמניף ומושבה לא פליגי דאסיר. כי פליגי ברוח מצויה. (רב) [אביי] סבר גזרינן ברוח מצויה אטו רוח שאינה מצויה. ומר סבר לא גזרינן והלכתא כאביי וקאמרינן בגמרא דהכונס צאן לדיר בנזיקין המלבה ואין בליבויו כדי ללבותה פטור. ואקשינן אמאי פטור. ליהוי כי זורה ורוח מסייעתו. ואמרינן בה כמה טעמי. סימן ברו"ש. אמר אביי כגון שליבה מצד זה וליבתה הרוח מצד אחר רבא אמר כגון שליבה ברוח מצויה וליבתו הרוח שאינה מצויה. רב זירא אמר דצמדא צמידי. רב אשי אמר היכא אמרינן זורה ורוח מסייעתו לענין שבת דמלאכת מחשבת אסרה תורה. אבל הכא גרמא בעלמא היא וגרמא בנזקין פטור. ש"מ דכיון דמשוי אורחא אפי' לרוח מצויה ללבות ומחשב לכן אסור בשבת דהיינו מלאכת מחשבת: סוגיא דשמעתא דר' יוסי מתיר בכלים מלאין מים כגון כלי מתכות וכלי כפר חנניה וכפר שיחין שחרש שלהן חזק ואינן מתבקעין באור. ואע"פ שאין גרם כיבוי אסור כגון הני שקי. ור' יוסי דשרי

*) עיין ערוך ערך ספרק.

מסורת הש"ס

לקמן קכה: ודף קמב:

לעיל עח. קג. קיא: קיז. קלג. [קמג.] ביצה לו. סוכה לג: כתובות ז. בכורות כה.

יומא ח. כח. [מס' סופרים פ"ה הל"י]

דברים יב

לעיל קיז:

שמות כ

פסחים סה: מנחות כא. זבחים לה.

הגהות הב"ח

(א) גמ' כנגד המדורה:

גליון הש"ס

גמ' הרי זה לא ירחוץ. עי' נדה דף סו ע"ב תוס' ד"ה אם סמוך: שם דמנח ידיה עלויה. עי' בתרומת הדשן סימן י:

רב נסים גאון

מאי טעמא לייט עלה רב אי נימא דרב סבר לה כר' יהודה תמצא בירורו בפ' במה מדליקין (לעיל דף כג) רב אמר אין הלכה כר' שמעון בגרירה מכלל דכר' יהודה סבירא ליה דפליג על ר' שמעון ואסר דבר שאינו מתכוין ובסוף פ' שמונה שרצים (לעיל דף קיא) ובפרק בתולה נשאת (כתובות דף ו) הלכה אמרו אמר רב הלכה כר' יהודה ורב חייא בר אבין מתני לה בלא גברי רב אמר הלכה כר' יהודה ושמואל אמר הלכה כר' שמעון ותניא כוותיה בבכורות בפרק כל פסולי המוקדשין (דף לד) הרי מיכן למדנו שרב סבר דבר שאין מתכוין אסור כר' יהודה:

ההיא

טבילה בזמנה לאו מצוה – ומהדרינן, ור' יוסי סבר: טבילה בזמנה מצוה – ולא מהדרינן. וסבר ר' יוסי טבילה בזמנה מצוה?! *והתניא: אהזב והזבה המצורע והמצורעת בועל נדה וטמא מת – טבילתן ביום, נדה ויולדת – טבילתן בלילה. בעל קרי טובל והולך כל היום כולו, ר' יוסי אומר: מן המנחה ולמעלה – אינו *צריך לטבול! ההיא ר' יוסי בר' יהודה היא, *דאמר: דייה טבילה באחרונה.§ [נדה כט:]

מתני' *בגוי שבא לכבות, אין אומרים לו "כבה" ו"אל תכבה" – מפני שאין שביתתו עליהן. אבל קטן שבא לכבות אין שומעין לו, מפני ששביתתו עליהן.§ [ויקרא ל. יומא פח.]

גמ' *א"ר אמי: גבדליקה התירו לומר "כל המכבה אינו מפסיד". נימא מסייע ליה: גוי שבא לכבות אין אומרים לו "כבה" ו"אל תכבה" – מפני שאין שביתתו עליהן. "כבה" הוא דלא אמרינן ליה, הא "כל המכבה אינו מפסיד" – אמרינן ליה. אימא סיפא: "אל תכבה" לא אמרינן ליה, ו"כל המכבה אינו מפסיד" – נמי לא אמרינן ליה! אלא: *מהא ליכא למשמע מינה. ת"ר: *מעשה ונפלה דליקה בחצירו של יוסף בן סימאי בשיחין, ובאו אנשי גיסטרא של ציפורי לכבות, מפני שאפטרופוס של מלך היה. ולא הניחן מפני כבוד השבת, ונעשה לו נס וירדו גשמים וכיבו. לערב שיגר לכל אחד מהן שתי סלעין, ולאפרכוס שבהן חמשים. וכששמעו חכמים בדבר אמרו: לא היה צריך לכך, שהרי שנינו: גוי שבא לכבות אין אומרים לו "כבה" ו"אל תכבה".§ "אבל דקטן שבא לכבות אין שומעין לו מפני ששביתתו עליהן".§ שמעת מינה: *קטן אוכל נבלות – ב"ד מצווין עליו להפרישו. אמר רבי יוחנן: הבקטן העושה לדעת אביו. דכוותה גבי גוי – דקא עביד לדעתיה דישראל, מי שרי?! גוי לדעתיה דנפשיה עביד.§ [תוספ' פי"ד]

מתני' *וכופין קערה על גבי הנר בשביל שלא תאחוז בקורה, ועל צואה של קטן, ועל עקרב שלא תישך. *א"ר יהודה: מעשה בא לפני רבן יוחנן בן זכאי בערב, ואמר: חוששני לו מחטאת.§ **גמ'** רב יהודה ורב ירמיה בר אבא ורב חנן בר רבא איקלעו לבי אבין דמן נשיקיא, לרב יהודה ורב ירמיה בר אבא אייתו

רש"י

טבילה בזמנה מצוה. דכתיב: "והיה לפנות ערב ירחץ במים" (דברים כג): לאו מצוה. ואי לא מטבל בשמי האידנא – לישתהי עד למחר, ולמ"ד לאו מצוה – קרא עצה טובה קמ"ל, כדי שיעריב שמשו ביום לאחר טבילה, שאם ימתין לטבול עד הלילה – לא יהא לו הערב שמש עד ליל המחרת: הזב והזבה כו'. בברייתא זו אגב יוה"כ שנויה, בתוספתא דיומא (פ"ד): הזב והזבה והמצורע והמצורעת ובועל נדה וטמא מת טובלין ביום. משאחר המזרח ביום השביעי שלהם. וטעמא(א) בפ"ב דמגילה (דף כ.) מקרא ד"ביום השביעי", מקצת שביעי ספירה. ואם חל שביעי שלהם ביוה"כ – טובלין כדרכן לאכול תרומה לערב: נדה ויולדת. טובלות כדרכן בליל יוה"כ, אם חל שביעי שלהם בערב יוה"כ. שאינה יכולה לטבול ביום ז', דכתיב בה: "תהיה בנדתה" – כהווייתה תהא כל ז' (פסחים דף צ:): בעל קרי. שצריך טבילה לדברי תורה ולדברי סופרים, ואפי' אין(ב) אוכל טהרות לאו ביום: טובל כל היום כולו. ואע"פ שראה קרי מן המנחה ולמעלה, לאחר שהתפלל תפלת המנחה, שהרי הוא יכול להמתין עד שתחשך ויטבול לתפלת ערבית – אפ"ה טובל ביוה"כ מבעוד יום, אע"פ שאסור ברחיצת הרשות, דטבילה בזמנה מצוה: ר' יוסי אומר מן המנחה ולמעלה. אם ראה קרי לאחר שהתפלל תפלת מנחה, שהרי הוא יכול להמתין עד שתחשך ויטבול, ויתפלל תפלת ערבית, ותפלת נעילה נמי ס"ל שיכול להתפלל בלילה כרב, דאמר (יומא דף פז:): תפלת נעילה פוטרת של ערבית: אין צריך לטבול. בו ביום משום זמן טבילה, דלאו מצוה לטבילה בזמנה: דייה לטבילה שתהא באחרונה. במסכת נדה בפרק "המפלת", גבי אשה שילדה מלאה וטפה ריקנית, ואינה יודעת מתי ילדה, דמצרכינן לה ל"ה טבילות לספק ד' טבילות שעליה: טבילת זכר לז', או טבילת נקבה לשבועיים, ובלילה. או שמא יולדת זכר בזוב, וצריכה אף טבילת זבה ביום שבעה לספוריס שלה, או יולדת נקבה בזוב היתה. ומשום דלא ידעינן מתי ילדה ואימתי מטי זמן טבילה דידה, מצרכינן לה טבילה כל לילה וכל יום שיש לספוקי בזמן טבילתה. ופליג ר' יוסי ברבי יהודה עלה, ואמר: דייה לטבילה שתהא באחרונה – לסוף ספורים של נקבה, דהיינו לסוף שלש שבועים. שאם ילדה נקבה בזוב, טמאה שבועיים לנדתה וז' נקיים בשביל הזיבה, ולא אמרינן טבילה בזמנה מצוה:

מתני' אין אומרים לו כבה. רבנן גזור על אמירה לגוי משום שבות: ולא תכבה. אין צריך למחות בידו, אלא יניחנו ויכבה: שאין שביתתו. של גוי עליהן, דישראל אינו מוזהר על שביתתו של גוי שאינו עבדו: גמ' כבה הוא דלא אמרינן ליה. שעושהו שלוחו ממש: הא כל המכבה אינו מפסיד כו'. וגלוי מלתא בעלמא הוא אמרינן ליה: אל תכבה הוא דלא אמרינן ליה. שאינו צריך למחות בידו. ומיהו, גילוי דעתא דלא יפסיד בדבר – נמי לא משתרי, דאי גילוי דעתא שרי – למה ליה למיתני סיפא אין צריך למחות? אלא מהא ליכא למשמע מינה. דודאי מתניתין לאו כולה דוקא, אלא חדא מינייהו דוקא, או רישא או סיפא, ותנא אידך אטו הכי, ולא ידעינן הי מינייהו דוקא דנגמר מינה: גיסטרא. שלטון: אפטרופוס. ממונה על ממונו: שמעת מינה קטן אוכל נבלות בית דין מצווין להפרישו. ותקשי לר' יוחנן דאמר ביבמות (דף קיד.) לרבה בר בר חנה דאפלגסו ליה מפתחות של בית המדרש ברשות הרבים בשבת, דאי מפקדי להו מייתי להו לאיטלוי התם, דבר טלי וטליתא ליטיילי התם, דאי משכחי להו מייתי להו: על דעת אביו. בקטן שיודע להבחין שכבודו זה כותל לאביו, ועושה בשבילו: גוי אדעתיה דנפשיה עביד. ואפילו יודע שעושה לו לישראל – הוא להצלת עצמו מתכוין, שיודע שאם יכבה – יטול שכרו: מתני' כופין קערה. של חרס: על גבי הנר. ואע"פ שמבטל כלי להצלת קורה שאינה ניטלת בשבת – הא אוקימנא מינה (דף מג.) לר' יצחק דאמר אין כלי ניטל אלא לדבר הניטל, ושאין צריך למקומו: מעשה בא. כפיית כלי על עקרב: בערב. מקום: חוששני לו מחטאת. כיון דלא היה עקרב רץ אחריו, איני יודע אם חייב משום צידה אם לאו, וחוששני לומר חייב חטאת הוא:

תוספות

הכי גרסי' ר' יוסי אומר מן המנחה ולמעלה אינו צריך לטבול. וכן גירסת רש"י ור"ת. אבל לא גרסי': אינו יכול לטבול. דלפי מאן דסבר טבילה בזמנה לאו מצוה – "שרי לטבול, כדמשמע בסוף מסכת יומא (דף פז:), דפריך לרב דאמר תפלת נעילה פוטרת של ערבית משום דקסבר דתפלת נעילה בלילה, והתניא: אור יוה"כ כו' נעילה מתפלל שבע ומתודה בערבית כו'! ומשני: תנאי היא, דתניא: כל חייבי טבילות טובלין כדרכן ביום, נדה ויולדת טובלין בלילה, בעל קרי טובל והולך עד המנחה, דסבר תפלת נעילה בלילה, וטבילה בזמנה לאו מצוה. ר' יוסי אומר: כל היום כולו טובל, דתפלת נעילה ביום. אלמא: אע"ג דת"ק סבר דטבילה בזמנה לאו מצוה, אפ"ה קתני כל חייבי טבילות טובלין ביום, אפילו טמא מת וטמא שרץ שאין צריכין טבילה לתפלה יכולין לטבול. והא דפירש בקונטרס דר' יוסי כרב, דאמר תפלת נעילה בלילה – לא דק, דבשלהי יומא (דף פח.) פריך מהך ברייתא דר' יוסי אדר' יוסי: דהכא קאמר מן המנחה ולמעלה א"צ לטבול, ובהסיא קאמר כל היום! ומשני: דהכא איירי דבדלי כבר תפלת נעילה, והתם דבלא לא. ובכולהו רבי יוסי דלא כרב:

רבי יוסי בר' יהודה היא. וא"ת: א"כ בשלהי יומא (דף פח.) מנא ליה לרב דההוא ת"ק דברייתא קמייתא, דקאמר דבעל קרי טובל עד המנחה, אתי כותיה דתפלת נעילה בלילה? דילמא איירי בדלא, וטבילה בזמנה לאו מצוה, ור' יוסי סבר מצוה, ותנא קמא דהכא הוא ר' יוסי דהתם! ויש לומר: דסבר דר' יוסי דהכא ודהתם מסתמא חד תנא הוא, ותרוייהו רבי יוסי ברבי יהודה דאיירי בטבילת בעל קרי ביו"כ, וא"כ קשיא ר' יוסי בר' יהודה אדר' יוסי בר' יהודה, וע"כ איח לן לשנויי: הא – דבדלי, והא – דלא בדלי:

אין אומרים לו כבה. אפי' באיסור דרבנן אמירה לגוי שבות, כדאמרינן לקמן בפרק "שואל" (דף קנ.): לא יאמר אדם לחבירו שכור לי פועלים כו' דמוקי לה בחבירו גוי. וכן מוכח בפרק "הדר" (דף סו:) גבי נייתי חמימי מגו ביתא:

אלא מהא ליכא למישמע מינה. מ"מ קי"ל כר' אמי. ובירושלמי אמר שעשה ר' אמי מעשה כזה:

שמע מינה קטן אוכל נבלות בית דין מצווין עליו להפרישו. נ"ל דמוקי מתניתין כרבי יהודה, דאמר: מלאכה שאינה צריכה לגופה חייב עליה, או כר"ש וכשצריך לאותו כיבוי, כגון לעשות פחמין. דבאיסורא דרבנן מוכח בפרק "חרש" (יבמות קיד.) דאין ב"ד מצווין להפרישו. ונראה דמיירי בקטן שלא הגיע לחינוך. דבהגיע לחינוך, כיון שחייב לחנכו – כ"ש דצריך להפרישו שלא יעשה עבירה. וכל הנהו דפריך ביבמות – הוה מצי לשנויי כשהגיע לחינוך, אלא דניחא ליה לאוקמי בכל ענין. והא דבעי לאיתויי התם דאין ב"ד מצווין להפרישו, מדקתני: תינוק יונק והולך, וקתני ובגדול אסור – משמע דוקא גדול, אבל קטן אפי' בהגיע לחינוך שרי – התם ע"כ גדול לאו דוקא בר עונשין, דהא במסקנא מפרש טעמא משום דסתם תינוק מסוכן הוא אצל חלב, והאי טעמא לא שייך אלא בבן שתים או שלש שנים:

כל

עין משפט נר מצוה

סט א מיי' פ"א מהלכות מקואות הלכה ו וע"ש מהלכות שביתת עשור הלכה ב ג ופ"ד מהלכות איסורי ביאה הלכה ו סמג עשין רמג טוש"ע או"ח סימן תקנד סעיף ח וסי' תריג סעיף יא יב וטוש"ע יו"ד סימן קצז סעיף ג וסימן שפא סעיף ה ובריף פ"ב דשבועות דף לב ובכולה בהלכות מקואות סי' לו:

ע ב מיי' פ"ו מהלכות שבת הלכה ז ופי"ב הלכה ז סמג לאוין סה טוש"ע או"ח סימן שלד סעיף כה:

עא ג מיי' פי"ב שם וסמג שם טוש"ע שם סעיף כו:

עב ד ה מיי' פי"ב שם ופכ"ד הל"א ופי"ז מהל' מאכלות אסורות הל' כו כח ופ"ב מהלכות אבל הלכה יב סמג שם ולאוין קמח טוש"ע שם סעיף כה וסימן שמג וטוש"ע יו"ד סימן שעג סעיף א בהגה"ה:

עג ו מיי' פכ"ה מהלכות שבת הלכה ד סמג לאוין סה טוש"ע או"ח סימן רעג סעיף ה וסימן שלד סעיף כב בהגה"ה:

רבינו חננאל

גרם מחיקת שם משום דאמר לך התם עשייה אסור גרמא שרי רבנן בשבת גרמא כמו מלאכת מחשבת היא ואסור. ואע"ג דכתיב לא תעשה כל מלאכה. (כל מלאכה) מדאורייתא עשייה אסורה מיהו גזרו רבנן אפי' גרמא משום דק"ל אדם בהול על ממונו אי שרית ליה אתי לכבויי. תוב אקשינן דרבנן אדרבנן. התם בגרם מחיקת השם מצריכי ליה גמי לה. והכא שרו בגרם כיבוי. ואקשינן עלה האי גמי לה היכי דמי אי דקטור ומיהדק הוא גופיה חייץ בטבילה. ואי לא מיהדק עייל ביה מיא ומסקי לשם ולא מהני גמי לה לשם שכתוב על בשרו מידי ולא איפרקא הא קושיא. תוב אקשינן עליה ותיפוק ליה דהוי גופיה שהשם כתוב בו שחוצץ. ופרקינן הב"ע ברו לחה שאינו חוצצת. דתניא הדם והדיו והדבש והחלב יבישין חוצצין לחים אין חוצצין. ופרק' על קושיא הראשונה רבנן דאסרי לטבול עד דכרך על השם גמי לא לאו משום דסבירא להו גרם מחיקת השם אסור דכל גרמא שרי. והכא משום דאסור לעמוד בפני השם ערום מצריכי גמי לה. וכיון דלא צריך אלא לכסויי השם וממילא ידעינן שאין מהדק הגמי לה ולא איכפת ליה אי עייל מיא דלא חייש לגרם מחיקה. ואקשינן וכי לר' יוסי מותר לעמוד בפני השם. ושנינן לר' יוסי מכסהו לשם בידו וטובל. אי הכי לרבנן נמי נכסיה בידיה ונדחה זה הפירוק. ופרקינן לדברי הכל אסור לעמוד בפני השם ערום. ואי איכא גמי וכיוצא בו לכרוך על השם ולטבול בזמנה הב"ע בדרכך. כי פליגי היכא דליכא מידי

מצוה וצריך להדורי ולאתויי. ר' יוסי אומר טבילה בזמנה מצוה ואתיא מצוה זו ודחה לעמידת ערום בפני השם. ורבנן סברי טבילה בזמנה לאו מצוה הלכך לא הדרי. ואקשינן איני דר' יוסי סבר טבילה בזמנה מצוה והתנן בעל קרי טובל כל היום כולו. ר' יוסי אומר מן המנחה ולמעלה אינו צריך לטבול וטובל בדלא מיכסי*). ורבנן סברי טבילה בזמנה מצוה והחזן בעל קרי מ"ט דרבנן דמחייבי ליה למיטבל ביומא **) ברבלה. ואמרינן אי צלי ליה מנחה מקמי דליחוי

*) נראה דצ"ל ולא בעי לאהדורי ואגמי ורבנן סברי טבילה בזמנה לאו מצוה הלכך בעי להדורי. **) לפנינו בגמ' ליתא להך אוקימתא אולי כוונתו להסוגיא ביומא דף פח ע"ש.

מסורת הש"ס

פסחים ג: יומא ו. פח. ע"ש [תוספתא יומא פ"ד ע"ש]

[נ"ל יכול וכ"ה ביומא פח.]

יבמות קיד.

כתובות ע:

[ברכות כה. וש"נ]

יבמות קיד. נדה מו: [גיטין נה.]

לעיל מג. קז.

[לקמן קמו.]

גליון הש"ס

רש"י ד"ה אין אומרים לו וכו' אמירה לנכרי משום שבות. עי' ע"ל דף קנ ע"ב ברש"י ד"ה נהי דלכתובה: תוס' ד"ה אין וכו' שרי לטבול כדמשמע. ע"ל דף קיא ע"א תוס' ד"ה לא ס"ל:

הגהות הב"ח

(א) רש"י ד"ה הזב והזבה והמצורע וכו' וטעמא בפ"ב דמגילה: (ב) ד"ה בעל קרי וכו' אוכל טהרות הס"ד ואח"כ מ"ה טובל כל היום כולו נמחק:

רב נסים גאון

ההיא ר' יוסי בר' יהודה היא דתניא ר' יוסי בר' יהודה אומר דייה לטבילה באחרונה משכחת לה במס' נדה (דף כט) בפרק המפלת: שמעת מינה קטן אוכל נבלות בית דין מצווין עליו

גמ' אייתו להו פורייתא, לרב חנן בר רבא לא אייתו ליה. אשכחיה מתני ליה לבריה: "ועל צואה של קטן מפני קטן". א"ל: אבין שטיא מתני שטותא לבניה, והלא היא עצמה מוכנת לכלבים! וכ"ת דלא חזיא ליה מאתמול – *והתניא: [א] נהרות המושכין ומעיינות הנובעין הרי הן כרגלי כל אדם. ואלא היכי אתנייה? אימא: [ב] על צואה של תרנגולים מפני קטן. ותיפוק ליה דהוי גרף של רעי. וכ"ת: גרף של רעי אגב מנא – אין, איהו גופיה – לא, [ג] והא *ההוא עכבר דאישתכח באיספרמקי דרב אשי, ואמר להו: נקוטו בצוציתיה ואפקוה! באשפה. וקטן באשפה מאי בעי ליה? בחצר. חצר נמי, גרף של רעי הוא! [א] באשפה שבחצר. § "ועל עקרב שלא תישך". § א"ר יהושע בן לוי: כל המזיקין נהרגין בשבת. מתיב רב יוסף: [ד] חמשה נהרגין בשבת, ואלו הן: זבוב שבארץ מצרים, וצירעה שבנינוה, ועקרב שבחדייב, ונחש שבא"י, וכלב שוטה בכל מקום. מני? אילימא *ר' יהודה – הא אמר: מלאכה שאינה צריכה לגופה חייב עליה! אלא לאו – ר"ש, והני הוא דשרי, אחריני – לא! אמר ר' ירמיה: *ומאן נימא לן דהא מתרצתא היא, דילמא משבשתא היא? אמר רב יוסף: אנא מתנינא לה ואותיבנא לה, ואנא מתריצנא לה – [ה] ברצו אחריו ודברי הכל. תני תנא קמיה דרבא בר רב הונא: ההורג נחשים ועקרבים בשבת אין רוח חסידים נוחה הימנו. א"ל: ואותן חסידים – אין רוח חכמים נוחה מהם. ופליגא דרב הונא, דרב הונא חזייה לההוא גברא דקא קטיל זיבורא, א"ל: שלימתינהו לכולהו?! ת"ר: נזדמנו לו נחשים ועקרבים, *הרגן – בידוע שנזדמנו לו להורגן, לא הרגן – בידוע שנזדמנו להורגו, ונעשה לו נס מן השמים. אמר עולא ואיתימא רבה בר בר חנה א"ר יוחנן: בנישופין בו. א"ר אבא בר כהנא: פעם אחת נפל אחד בבהמ"ד, ועמד ניותי אחד והרגו. אמר רבי: פגע בו כיוצא בו. איבעיא להו: פגע בו כיוצא בו – דשפיר עביד, או לא? ת"ש: דר' אבא בריה דר' חייא בר אבא ור' זירא הוו יתבי אקילעא דבי ר' ינאי, נפק מילתא מביניהו, בעו מיניה מר' ינאי: מהו להרוג נחשים ועקרבים בשבת? אמר להו: צירעה אני הורג, נחש ועקרב לא כ"ש?! דילמא לפי תומו. דאמר רב יהודה: [ו] רוק – דורסו לפי תומו. ואמר רב ששת: [ז] נחש – דורסו לפי תומו. ואמר רב קטינא: [ח] עקרב – דורסו לפי תומו. *אבא בר מרתא דהוא אבא בר מניומי הוה מסקי ביה דבי ריש גלותא זוזי, אייתיוהו קא מצערא ליה. הוה שדי רוקא, אמר להו ריש גלותא: אייתו מאנא סחיפו עלויה. אמר להו: לא צריכתו, הכי א"ר יהודה: רוק דורסו לפי תומו. אמר להו: צורבא מרבנן הוא, שבקוהו. *אמר ר' אבא בר כהנא א"ר חנינא: [ט] פמוטות של בית רבי מותר לטלטלן בשבת. א"ל ר' זירא: בניטלין בידו אחת, או בשתי ידים? א"ל

רש"י

גמ' אייתו להו פורייתא. מטות לישב עליהן: **לא אייתו ליה.** והושיבוהו לארץ: **מפני קטן.** שלא יטפח בו ויתלכלך: **א"ל.** רב חנן, שהיה כעוס, ומתכוין להקניטו לר' אבין: **והלא מוכנת לכלבים.** ולמה לי לכפות כלי? יפנוה משם, שהרי ראויה לטלטל: **דלא חזיא מאתמול.** שהיום נולדה: **נהרות המושכים ברגלי כל אדם.** משום דמידי דנייד הוא, ולא קני שביתה, ואע"פ שבא מחוץ לתחום – כל אדם מוליכן למקום שעירב לו לילך. מיהו, שמעינן מינה דמותרין בטלטול, ואע"ג דמאתמול לא הוי הני הכא, כיון דאורחייהו בהכי – דעתיה עלייהו. ה"נ: כיון דאורחיה דקטן בהכי – דעתיה עליה, דלכי תיתי – יאכילנה לכלבים: **א"ל ר' אבין. ואלא היכי אתנייה: צואה של תרנגולים.** דלא חזיא לכלבים. ושל קטן דקתני מתניתין – שמטפח בה קטן קאמר, ובשביל הקטן אמר כופין: **תיפוק ליה דגרף של רעי הוא.** דמאיס, ולפנייה, דהא קי"ל במסכת ביצה: גרף של רעי מותר להוציאו לאשפה: **וכי תימא גרף של רעי דמותר אגב מנא אין.** הא דקי"ל מותר להוציאו – משום דרמי במנא. דגרף היינו כלי חרס העשוי לכך, ואגב מנא הוא דשרי לטלטולי, אבל בפני עצמו לא, והכא לאו במנא רמי: **באיספרמקי.** בשמים: **בצוציתיה.** בזנבו. אלמא: בלאו מנא נמי מטלטלי ליה: **ומשני: באשפה.** דלא רמי קמייהו, ולא גרף של רעי הוא: **קטן באשפה מאי בעי.** סתם אשפה ברה"ר הוא, ומאי בעי קטן התם, דקא מיכסי ליה בשביל קטן? **ומשני: בחצר.** דשכיח קטן התם. קס"ד בחצר דלאו אשפה, וקפריך: סוף סוף גרף של רעי הוא! ומשני: באשפה שבחצר: **כל המזיקין.** ההורגין: **נהרגין בשבת.** וקס"ד: אפי' אין רצין אחריו, ומשום דס"ל כר"ש דמלאכה שאינה צריכה לגופה מדרבנן היא דאסירא, והכא לא גזור: (**נהרגין בשבת.** אפי' אין רצין אחריו) משום דס"ל דסתמן הורגין הן: **האמר חייב עליה.** והיכי שרי במלאכה גמורה כשאין רצין אחריו, דליכא פקוח נפש? **ומאן לימא לן כו'.** דרב יוסף הוא מתני ליה כדלקמן, ולא בדבי ר' חייא ור' אושעיא מיתנייא, וכל מתניתא דלא מתנייא בתוספתא דר' חייא ור' אושעיא – איכא לספוקי במשבשתא, ולא מותבינן מינה: **אנא תנינא לה.** במתניתא דידי, ואנא אותבינא בבי מדרשא אדר' יהושע בן לוי: **ואנא מתרצנא לה.** דלא תיקשי. כי אמר ר' יהושע בן לוי כל המזיקין נהרגין – ברצין אחריו קאמר, דפקוח נפש הוא: **ודברי הכל.** ואפי' לר' יהודה. והא דחמשה נהרגין – כשאין רצין אחריו, ור' שמעון: **אין רוח חסידים נוחה הימנו.** דעתן של חסידים אינה מעורבת עמו, שאינו הגון בעיניהם על מה שעשה: **נוחה.** עריבה, אין מתרצין במעשיו: **אמר ליה.** רבה לתנא: **ואותן חסידים.** השונאין אותו על כך – אין רוח חכמים עריבה עמהם, להיות נוחה ומיושבת במה שרואין במדת חסידים הללו, דשפיר עביד, דאי לא מזיקין השתא – סופן להזיק בשעת כעסן: **שלימתינהו לכולהו.** הרגת את כולן?! כלומר: מה הנאה בהא? הא כתי טובא איכא. אלמא: לאו שפיר עבד. והא דרבה פליג אדאביי: **שנזדמנו לו להורגן.** לכך באו לידו, שזימן לו המקום לאבדן, לפי שהיו עתידות להזיק ומגלגלו זכות על ידי זכאי: **לא הרגן בידוע שנזדמנו לו להרוג אותו.** והראה לו הקב"ה שחטא, אלא שנעשה לו נס: **בנישופין בו.** בכה"ג קתני בידוע שנזדמנו להורגו. נישופין – כך דרך הנחש, עושה כעין שריקה כשהוא רואה שונאו וכועס: **ניותי.** על שם מקומו, וישראל היה: **דשפיר עביד.** וכיוצא בו דקאמר – לאו לנגחי הוא, אלא הנחש רודף, ונעשה זה כיוצא בו: **או לא.** וכיוצא בו דקאמר – לנגחי הוא: **צרעה אני הורג.** בשבת, לכולות מזיקין, ואף על פי שאינה מועדת כאלו: **לא כל שכן.** אלמא: שפיר עביד: **דילמא לפי תומו.** לא שיעמוד עליו ויהרגנו להדיא, אלא כשהוא הולך לתומו, ונחש או עקרב בפניו – אין צריך לישמט ממנו, אלא דורכו והולך, ואם מת בדריכתו – ימות, הואיל ולא נתכוין. דדבר שאין מתכוין לר' יהודה מדרבנן הוא, ולענין מזיקין לא גזור: **רוק דורסו לפי תומו.** שאין מתכוין למרח ולאשווי גומות. דאף על גב דממילא ממרח הוא, כי לא מיכוין – שרי, משום מאיסותא: **הוה שדי רוקא.** היה רוק מוטל לפניהם, ושבת היתה: **פמוטות.** מנורות, ולא של חוליות היו: של

תוספות

כל המזיקין נהרגין בשבת. אף על גב דתנן במתניתין: ועל עקרב שלא ישוך – איצטריך לאשמעינן דהריגה נמי שרינן. דסלקא דעתך דאסירא משום דמיפרסמא מילתא טפי מצלידה. ומהאי טעמא נמי פליג רב הונא בסמוך ואסר הריגה:

ברצין אחריו וד"ה. פי' בקונט': דרבי יהושע בן לוי ברצין אחריו, והוי פקוח נפש, וברייתא באין רצין, וכר"ש. וקשה דא"כ תקשה מהך ברייתא לרבא בר רב הונא דשרי להרוג נחשים ועקרבים בשבת, דע"כ באין רצין אחריו מיירי. דאי ברצין אחריו, אמאי אין רוח חסידים נוחה הימנו, לפירוש הקונטרס דברצין אחריו איכא פקוח נפש? ועוד: בניותי שהרג נחש, ומיבעיא לן אי שפיר עבד – תיפשוט מהכא דלא שרינן לר"ש באין רצין אלא ה' בלבד! ועוד קשה לר"י: דלישנא דאנא מתרצנא לה משמע לברייתא עצמה. ונראה לר"י לפרש: דברייתא ברצין אחריו, וד"ה – פירוש אפילו ר' יהודה מודה דחמשה שרי להרוג ברצין אחריו, אבל שאר – אסור להורגן אפילו רצין אחריו לר' יהודה. ור' יהושע בן לוי כר"ש, דשרי שאר(א) אפילו באין רצין אחריו. ורב הונא דאסר בסמוך לא סבר כרבי יהושע בן לוי. ונראה לר"י, וכן פירש ר"ח: שאין להקל כרבי יהושע בן לוי אלא כהנהו אמוראי דלקמן, דלא שרו אלא בדריסה לפי תומו:

עין משפט נר מצוה

עד א מיי' פ"ה מהלכות י"ט הלכה יד וטוש"ע א"ח סימן שכה סעיף טו:

עה ב ג מיי' פכ"ו מהל' שבת הלכה יג סמג לאוין סה טוש"ע א"ח סימן שח סעיף לד:

עו ד ה מיי' פי"א שם הלכה ד סמג שם טור שו"ע א"ח סימן שטז סעיף י:

עז ו מיי' פי"א שם הלכה ב ופכ"ב הלכה יג סמג שם טור שו"ע א"ח שם סעיף יא:

עח ז ח מיי' פי"א מהלכות שבת הל"ד סמג שם טור שו"ע שם סעיף יא:

עט ט מיי' פכ"ו מהל' שבת הלכה יא טור שו"ע א"ח סימן רעט סעיף ז:

מסורת הש"ס

ביצה לג. עירובין מו. מח. [תוספתא ביצה פ"ד]

ביצה לו:

[לעיל נג: וש"נ]

[פסחים נט:]

[יומא פד. יבמות קכ.]

[נ"ל ואמר]

הגהות הב"ח

(א) תוס' ד"ה ברצין וכו' כר"ש דשרי שאר מזיקין אפילו:

הגהות הגר"א

[א] גמ' באשפה שבחצר כו'. נ"ב גירסת הרי"ף בחצר אחרת:

גליון הש"ס

גמ' והלא היא עצמה מוכנת לכלבים. ע"ל דף קכב ע"ב תוס' ד"ה שמן: רש"י ד"ה דלמא לפי תומו וכו' לדבר שאין מתכוין לר"י מדרבנן. ע"ל דף קג ע"ב תוס' ד"ה מיחס:

רבינו חננאל

ביומא ליתעקב עד לאורתא ולטבול. ומסקינן משום דסברי רבנן אע"ג דצלי ליה טבילה בזמנה מצוה ור' יוסי סבר טבילה בזמנה לאו מצוה היא האי ר' יוסי בר' יהודה דגרסינן בנדה פרק המפלת בענין טועה. ר' יוסי בר"י ווומר דייה לטבול באחרונה דקסבר טבילה בזמנה לאו מצוה היא. וזה רבי יוסי דהיה (אומר) שם כתוב על בשרו. אסיקנא בגמרא דשבעת ימים (ביומא דף ז') דטבילה בזמנה מצוה פליגי ונתבררה בסוף יום הכפורים דהא לר' יוסי בר"י יהודה היא ואיכא אחריתי התם לר' יוסי דאמר כל היום כולו כשר לטבילה. דאלמא סבר טבילה בזמנה מצוה] היא: **א"ר** אמי בדליקה התירו לומר כל המכבה אינו מפסיד. וכן הלכה: **נכרי** שבא לכבות אין אומרים לו כבה ואל תכבה אלא מניחין אותו. ואין אומרים לו כבה וגם אין מונעין אותו מלכבות. אבל קטן העושה לדעת אין מניחין אותו לכבות: **אריב"ל** כל המזיקין נהרגין. אסיקנא כשהן רצין אחריו. אבל אין רצין אחריו אין נהרגין אלא אלו בלבד. זבוב שבארץ מצרים. וצירעה שבנינוה ועקרב שבחדייב ונחש שבא"י וכלב שוטה בכ"מ. פי' נישופין כדכתיב הוא ישופך ראש ואתה תשופנו עקב: רוק וכן נחש וכן עקרב אם דורסן לפי תומן שפיר דמי ושרי: **א"ר** חנינא פמוטות של בית רבי מותר לטלטלן בשבת. א"ל ר' זירא בניטלין בידו אחת

רב נסים גאון

להפרישו מאי דשקלינן וטרינן בהא מילתא איתא במס' יבמות (דף קיד) בפרק חרש שנשא פיקחת: **סוף** גרף של רעי הוא ונפקיה כבר פירשנו בפרק כירה כי עיקר השמועה שיש בה התרת זה הדבר

בפרק משילין פירות (ביצה דף לו): **ר'** יהודה אומר כל מלאכה שאינה צריכה לגופה חייב עליה כבר פירשנוה בפרק יציאות השבת ואמרנו כי עיקרה הן דברי ר' יהודה שאמרים כאן בזו המשנה מעשה בא: לפני

א"ל: כְּאוֹתָן שֶׁל בֵּית אָבִיךָ. וְאָמַר ר' אַבָּא בַּר כָּהֲנָא אָמַר ר' חֲנִינָא: קְרוֹנוֹת שֶׁל בֵּית רַבִּי מוּתָּר לְטַלְטְלָן בְּשַׁבָּת. א"ל ר' זֵירָא: בְּנִיטָּלִין בְּאָדָם אֶחָד, אוֹ בִּשְׁנֵי בְּנֵי אָדָם? א"ל: כְּאוֹתָן שֶׁל בֵּית אָבִיךָ. וְאָמַר ר' אַבָּא בַּר כָּהֲנָא: הִתִּיר לָהֶם ר' חֲנִינָא לְבֵית רַבִּי לִשְׁתּוֹת יַיִן בִּקְרוֹנוֹת שֶׁל גּוֹי [א]בְּחוֹתָם אֶחָד – וְלָא יָדַעְנָא אִי מִשּׁוּם דְּסָבַר לָהּ *כְּר' אֱלִיעֶזֶר, אִי מִשּׁוּם אֵימָתָא דְּבֵי נְשִׂיאָה.§ **מתני'** [ב]גּוֹי שֶׁהִדְלִיק אֶת הַנֵּר – מִשְׁתַּמֵּשׁ לְאוֹרוֹ יִשְׂרָאֵל, וְאִם בִּשְׁבִיל יִשְׂרָאֵל – אָסוּר. מִילֵּא מַיִם לְהַשְׁקוֹת בְּהֶמְתּוֹ – מַשְׁקֶה אַחֲרָיו יִשְׂרָאֵל, וְאִם בִּשְׁבִיל יִשְׂרָאֵל – אָסוּר. עָשָׂה גּוֹי כֶּבֶשׁ לֵירֵד בּוֹ – יוֹרֵד אַחֲרָיו יִשְׂרָאֵל, וְאִם בִּשְׁבִיל יִשְׂרָאֵל – אָסוּר. מַעֲשֶׂה בְּרַבָּן גַּמְלִיאֵל וּזְקֵנִים שֶׁהָיוּ בָּאִין בִּסְפִינָה, וְעָשָׂה גּוֹי כֶּבֶשׁ לֵירֵד בּוֹ, וְיָרְדוּ בּוֹ ר"ג וּזְקֵנִים.§ **גמ'** וּצְרִיכָא, דְּאִי אַשְׁמְעִינַן נֵר – מִשּׁוּם דְּנֵר לְאֶחָד נֵר לְמֵאָה, אֲבָל מַיִם – לִיגְזַר דִּילְמָא אָתֵי לְאַפּוּשֵׁי בִּשְׁבִיל יִשְׂרָאֵל. וְכֶבֶשׁ ל"ל? מַעֲשֶׂה דְּרַבָּן גַּמְלִיאֵל וּזְקֵנִים קמ"ל. ת"ר: [ג]גּוֹי שֶׁלִּיקֵּט עֲשָׂבִים – מַאֲכִיל אַחֲרָיו יִשְׂרָאֵל, וְאִם בִּשְׁבִיל יִשְׂרָאֵל – אָסוּר. מִילֵּא מַיִם לְהַשְׁקוֹת בְּהֶמְתּוֹ – מַשְׁקֶה אַחֲרָיו יִשְׂרָאֵל, וְאִם בִּשְׁבִיל יִשְׂרָאֵל – אָסוּר. [ד]בד"א – שֶׁאֵין מַכִּירוֹ, אֲבָל מַכִּירוֹ – אָסוּר. אִינִי?! *וְהָאָמַר רַב הוּנָא אָמַר רַבִּי חֲנִינָא: [ה]מַעֲמִיד אָדָם בְּהֶמְתּוֹ עַל גַּבֵּי עֲשָׂבִים בְּשַׁבָּת, אֲבָל לֹא עַל גַּבֵּי מוּקְצֶה בְּשַׁבָּת! [ו]דְּקָאֵים לָהּ בְּאַפַּהּ, וְאָזְלָא הִיא וְאָכְלָה. אָמַר מָר: "בד"א – שֶׁאֵין מַכִּירוֹ, אֲבָל מַכִּירוֹ – אָסוּר". הָא רַבָּן גַּמְלִיאֵל מַכִּירוֹ הֲוָה! אָמַר אַבָּיֵי: שֶׁלֹּא בְּפָנָיו הֲוָה. רָבָא אָמַר: [ז]אֲפִי' תֵּימָא בְּפָנָיו, נֵר לְאֶחָד נֵר לְמֵאָה. מֵיתִיבִי, *אָמַר לָהֶן רַבָּן גַּמְלִיאֵל: הוֹאִיל וְשֶׁלֹּא בְּפָנֵינוּ עֲשָׂאוֹ – נֵרֵד בּוֹ! אֵימָא: הוֹאִיל וַעֲשָׂאוֹ – נֵרֵד בּוֹ. תָּא שְׁמַע: *[ח]עִיר שֶׁיִּשְׂרָאֵל וְגוֹיִם דָּרִין בְּתוֹכָהּ וְהָיְתָה בָּהּ מֶרְחָץ הַמַּרְחֶצֶת בְּשַׁבָּת, אִם רוֹב גּוֹיִם – מוּתָּר לִרְחוֹץ בָּהּ מִיָּד, אִם רוֹב יִשְׂרָאֵל – יַמְתִּין בִּכְדֵי שֶׁיֵּחַמּוּ חַמִּין! הָתָם, כִּי מְחַמְּמִי – אַדַּעְתָּא דְּרוּבָּא מְחַמְּמִי. תָּא שְׁמַע: [ט]נֵר הַדָּלוּק בִּמְסִיבָּה, אִם רוֹב גּוֹיִם – מוּתָּר לְהִשְׁתַּמֵּשׁ לְאוֹרָהּ, אִם רוֹב יִשְׂרָאֵל – אָסוּר. מֶחֱצָה עַל מֶחֱצָה – אָסוּר. הָתָם נַמִי, כִּי מַדְלְקִי – אַדַּעְתָּא

רש"י

שֶׁל בֵּית אָבִיךָ. דִּקְטַנּוֹת הָיוּ, אֲבָל גְּדוֹלוֹת – אָדָם קוֹנֵעַ לָהֶם מָקוֹם: קְרוֹנוֹת. עֲשׂוּיוֹת לִבְנֵי אָדָם: אִי מִשּׁוּם דְּסָבַר כְּרַבִּי אֱלִיעֶזֶר. דְּאָמַר בְּמַסֶּכֶת ע"ז (דף לא.): יַיִן מוּתָּר בְּחוֹתָם אֶחָד: אִי מִשּׁוּם אֵימְתָא דְּבֵי נְשִׂיאָה. שֶׁהָיָה הַגּוֹי הַמְּבִיאוֹ יָרֵא מִן הַנָּשִׂיא שֶׁהָיָה שַׁלִּיט עַל פִּי הַמַּלְכוּת. וּמִשּׁוּם דְּאַיְירֵי ר' אַבָּא בַּר כָּהֲנָא לְעֵיל גַּבֵּי נָחָשׁ, נָקַט כָּל הָנֵי בִּשְׁמֵיהּ: **מתני'** אִם בִּשְׁבִיל יִשְׂרָאֵל אָסוּר. מִדְּרַבָּנַן: מִילֵּא מַיִם. מִבּוֹר בִּרה"ר: כֶּבֶשׁ. עוֹשִׂין בִּסְפִינָה גְּדוֹלָה, לֵירֵד בּוֹ מִסְּפִינָה לַיַּבָּשָׁה: **גמ'** נֵר לְאֶחָד נֵר לְמֵאָה. כֵּיוָן דְּגוֹי לְצָרְכּוֹ הִדְלִיקוֹ, לֵיכָּא לְמֵימַר דְּבִשְׁבִיל יִשְׂרָאֵל אַפֵּישׁ: כֶּבֶשׁ לָמָּה לִי. הָא דּוּמְיָא דְּנֵר הוּא, כֶּבֶשׁ לְאֶחָד כֶּבֶשׁ לְמֵאָה: מַאֲכִיל אַחֲרָיו יִשְׂרָאֵל. אֶת בְּהֶמְתּוֹ. וְאַחֲרָיו דַּוְקָא נָקַט בְּכוּלְּהוּ, דְּגוֹי לְצוֹרֶךְ עַצְמוֹ עָבֵיד: אֲבָל מַכִּירוֹ אָסוּר. דְּחַיְישִׁינַן דְּעָבֵיד נַמִי אַדַּעְתָּא דִּידֵיהּ: מַעֲמִיד אָדָם בְּהֶמְתּוֹ עַל גַּבֵּי עֲשָׂבִים. מְחוּבָּרִים: בְּשַׁבָּת. לִרְעוֹת, וְלֵיכָּא לְמִיגְזַר שֶׁמָּא יִתְלוֹשׁ וְיַאֲכִיל: וְאֵינוֹ מַעֲמִידָהּ ע"ג מוּקְצֶה. שֶׁמָּא יִטּוֹל בְּיָדוֹ וְיַאֲכִיל. וְהָא נַמִי מוּקְצִין נִינְהוּ לְגַבֵּי טִלְטוּל, דְּאֶתְמוֹל הֲווּ מְחוּבָּרִין: דְּקָאֵים לֵיהּ בְּאַפַּהּ. שֶׁלֹּא תִּפְנֶה לְמָקוֹם אַחֵר: וְאָזְלָא וְאָכְלָה. אֲבָל הוּא אֵינוֹ עוֹמֵד עַל הָעֲשָׂבִים קָרוֹב לָהֶם, דְּנֵיחוּשׁ לְשֶׁמָּא יִטּוֹל וְיַאֲכִיל: מַכִּירוֹ הֲוָה. שֶׁהֲרֵי בִּסְפִינָה הָיָה בָּא עִמּוֹ: שֶׁלֹּא בְּפָנָיו הֲוָה. כְּשֶׁעֲשָׂאוֹ לֹא הָיָה רַבָּן גַּמְלִיאֵל שָׁם, דְּנִיכַּוֵּין לֵיהּ: נֵר לְאֶחָד נֵר לְמֵאָה. כֶּבֶשׁ לְאֶחָד כֶּבֶשׁ לְמֵאָה. אֲבָל גַּבֵּי עֲשָׂבִים, כְּשֶׁהוּא מַכִּירוֹ – מַרְבֶּה בִּשְׁבִילוֹ: הוֹאִיל וְשֶׁלֹּא בְּפָנֵינוּ כו'. קַשְׁיָא לְרָבָא, דְּשָׁמְעִינַן מִינָּהּ דִּבְפָנָיו אָסוּר, וְאַע"פ שֶׁאֵין כָּאן מַרְבֶּה בִּשְׁבִילוֹ: אֵימָא הוֹאִיל וַעֲשָׂאוֹ נֵרֵד בּוֹ. וְטַעְמָא לָאו מִשּׁוּם שֶׁלֹּא בְּפָנָיו הוּא, אֶלָּא הָכִי הֲוָה מַעֲשֶׂה: מוּתָּר לִרְחוֹץ בָּהּ מִיָּד. לְמוֹצָאֵי שַׁבָּת: בִּכְדֵי שֶׁיֵּחַמּוּ חַמִּין. שֶׁלֹּא יֵהָנֶה בְּמַה שֶּׁהִקְדִּימוּ לְהָחֵם בְּשַׁבָּת. וְכֵן בְּכָל מַעֲשֵׂה שַׁבָּת נָתְנוּ חֲכָמִים שִׁיעוּר לְהַמְתִּין לָעֶרֶב בִּכְדֵי שֶׁיֵּעָשׂוּ. וְהָא הָכָא דְּחִימּוּם לְאֶחָד חִימּוּם לְמֵאָה, דִּבְבַת אַחַת מְחַמְּמִין, וְקָתָנֵי: אִם רוֹב יִשְׂרָאֵל דְּהָוֵי דּוּמְיָא דְּמַכִּירוֹ, דְּמַסֵּיק אַדַּעְתֵּיהּ לַעֲשׂוֹת אַף בִּשְׁבִילוֹ – אָסוּר, וְאַע"ג דְּשֶׁלֹּא בְּפָנָיו, וְקַשְׁיָא בֵּין לְאַבַּיֵי בֵּין לְרָבָא: אַדַּעְתָּא דְּרוּבָּא מְחַמְּמִי. וְעִיקַּר חִילּוּל הַשַּׁבָּת בִּשְׁבִילָם. אֲבָל גּוֹי וְיִשְׂרָאֵל, דְּגוֹי אַדַּעְתָּא דְּנַפְשֵׁיהּ הוּא דְּעָבֵיד – שָׁרֵי, לְאַבַּיֵי שֶׁלֹּא בְּפָנָיו, וּלְרָבָא אֲפִילּוּ בְּפָנָיו: נֵר הַדָּלוּק בִּמְסִיבָּה. שֶׁל בְּנֵי אָדָם: אִם רוֹב יִשְׂרָאֵל אָסוּר. וְהָא הָכָא, דְּהָוֵי דּוּמְיָא דְּמַכִּירוֹ, הוֹאִיל וְרוּבָּא נִינְהוּ – אַסֵּיק דַּעְתֵּיהּ לְהַדְלִיק אַף בִּשְׁבִילָם, וְקָתָנֵי "אָסוּר": אַדַּעְתָּא

תוספות

אמר ליה כאותן של בית אביך. פי': שהם גדולים, או קטנים דאית להו חידקי, כמו שפירשתי לעיל (דף לה.*): **משתמש** ישראל לאורה. ולא גזרינן שמא ידליק, כדגזרינן בפ"ק דביצה (דף ג.) פירות הנושרין – שמא יעלה ויתלוש, ובמשקין שזבו – שמא יסחוט. משום דסחיטה ותלישה הם קלים לעשות, ואדם להוט אחריהם לפי שהן דבר אכילה. אבל בכל הני דהכא – אינן קלין לעשות כל כך, ואין אדם להוט אחריהן: **ואם** בשביל ישראל אסור. נראה דאסור לכל ישראל דדוקא בחוץ לתחום דרבנן אמר בפרק "בכל מערבין" (עירובין דף מ.) וב"אין לדין" (ביצה דף כה.) הבא בשביל ישראל זה – מותר לישראל אחר. אבל באיסורא דאורייתא כי הכא – לא. ואע"ג דישראל המבשל בשבת בשוגג יאכל – התם לא חיישינן אי שרית ליה לאכול דילמא אתי לבשולי במזיד – דהא איכא איסור סקילה, וחמיר עליה. אבל בגוי העושה לצורך ישראל, אי שרית ליה – אתי למימר לגוי לעשות בשבילו, ולא דמי להא דאמר לעיל:* גוי שבא לכבות אין אומרים לו 'כבה' ו'אל תכבה', והכא אסור כשעושה בשביל ישראל. דכי אמרינן דגוי אדעתא דנפשיה קא עביד – הנ"מ בכיבוי וכיוצא בו, שאין ישראל נהנה במעשה הגוי. אבל הכא שגוף ישראל נהנה במעשה של גוי – לא אמרינן אדעתא דנפשיה קעביד, הואיל והגוי מתכוין להנאתו. כך פירש רבינו שמשון הזקן: **משקה** אחריו ישראל ואם בשביל ישראל אסור. אומר ר"ת: מדנקט בהמתו ולא נקט מילא מים לעצמו – דווקא להשקות בהמתו אסור, משום שלא היה יכול להביאה לתוך הבור. אבל הוא עצמו שרי, דמטפס ועולה מטפס ויורד. וכיון שיכול ליכנס לתוך הבור ולשתות – לא אסרו לו בשביל שמילא אותם גוי. והא דאסרינן בגמרא גוי שליקט עשבים לצורך ישראל, אע"ג דישראל יכול להעמיד בהמתו על גבי העשבים במחובר – אומר ר"ת: דהתם נמי איירי בתרי עברי דנהרא, שלא היה יכול *להביא הבהמה לשם. ואע"ג דהך בבא דמילא מים משום חידוש דהיתרא קתני לה, כדמוכח בגמרא – מיהא בהמתו משום איסורא נקט לה. וה"ר אליהו הביא ראיה להתיר מפירות שיצאו חוץ לתחום וחזרו, שלא הפסידו היתירן הראשון, כדאמר בפרק "מי שהוציאוהו" (עירובין דף מא:), ה"ה המים, שמתחילה היה יכול(א) לבא שם והביאו דרך רה"ר – דשרו. ולא דמי, דהתם לא אתעבידא בהו איסורא דאורייתא. מיהו, לענין אותו ישראל עצמו לא מצינו חילוק. ור"י אומר: דה"ה לישראל עצמו אסור, והאי דנקט בהמתו – לאשמעינן רבותא, דלא גזרינן דילמא אתי לאפושי בשביל ישראל, שבהמה רגילה לשתות הרבה. אבל ישראל עצמו – פשיטא דשותה אחריו, דליכא למיחש כולי האי דילמא אתי לאפושי, דבדלייה אחת מושך הרבה לצורכו ולצורך ישראל. ולפי זה, אם נמשכו המים לצורך ישראל זה – אסור לכל ישראל אי איכא איסורא דאורייתא, כגון שמביאם דרך רה"ר, או מרה"י לרה"ר. אבל בכרמלית שרי לישראל אחר. ויש שרצו לומר דדוקא שתיה אסורה, אבל לרחוץ ידיו ורגליו ושאר תשמישין – שרי, כדאמר בפרק "חרש" (יבמות דף קיד.): רבי יצחק אירכסו ליה מפתחות דבי מדרשא כו', אמר ליה: דבר טליא וטליתא ליטיילו התם, דאי משכח להו מייתי להו. אלמא: יכולין ליהנות ממפתחות להשתמש בהם בשבת. ואין נראה לר"י כלל, דהתם אין עושין לדעת ישראל. ועוד: דהרי כבש ונר וכמה דברים דאסור להשתמש בהם בשבת כשנעשין לצורך ישראל, ה"נ לא שנא שתיה לא שנא שאר תשמישין אסירי: **איני** והאמר רב הונא אמר רב חנינא מעמיד אדם כו' אבל לא על גבי מוקצה. והני עשבים נמי מוקצין נינהו, שנלקטו היום מן המחובר. וא"ת: ולימא דהך ברייתא רבי שמעון היא, דלית ליה מוקצה! וי"ל: דמשני לה אפילו כר' יהודה. א"נ: מודה ר"ש במוקצה דמחובר, כדפי' בקונטרס בפרק "אין לדין" (ביצה דף כד:). מדלא ליקטן מאתמול אקצינהו, והוי כגרוגרות וצימוקים. ובריש ביצה (דף ג.) דאסר פירות הנושרים משום גזירה שמא יעלה ויתלוש, ולא אסר להו משום מוקצה – משום דמוכנים לעורבים, כי ההיא ד"מקום שנהגו" (פסחים דף נו:). והכא איירי כשאין הבהמה יכולה לבא ולאכול מן המחובר, ולהכי הוי מוקצה. א"נ: עשבים מוקצין הם אפילו לר"ש, לפי שאינו יושב ומצפה שילקטום. אבל בנר – יושב ומצפה מתי יכבה, כדאמרינן לעיל (דף מו:). וכן פירות הנושרין יושב ומצפה מתי יפלו. ולהכי, אי לאו טעמא דשמא יעלה ויתלוש – הוו שרו: **מעמיד** אדם בהמתו ע"ג עשבים בשבת. כדדרשי' במכילתין: "למען ינוח שורך וחמורך וגו'", יכול לא יניחנו תולש, לא יניחנו עוקר – ת"ל: "למען ינוח" ואין זה נוח אלא צער. ר"ת: **אמר** אביי שלא בפניו הוה. נראה לר"י: דמודה אביי דנר לאחד נר למאה, אלא דסבר דהכא אם היה בפניו – עיקר היה נעשה לצורך ר"ג, שהיה נשיא ושר וראש בספינה: אהדרינהו

מסורת הש"ס

[ע"ז לא.]

[עירובין עט.]

[תוספת' פי"ד]

לקמן קנא. מכשירין פ"ב מ"ה

הגהות הב"ח

(א) תוס' ד"ה משקה וכו' שמתחלה היה יכול לילך ולשתות שם והביאו נכרי לדרך רה"ר:

עין משפט נר מצוה

[ד"ה ואפילו]

פ א מיי' פי"ג מהלכות מאכלות אסורות הל"י סמג לאוין קלח טור שו"ע יו"ד סימן קיח סעיף א וסימן קל סעיף ב:

פא ב מיי' פ"ו מהלכות שבת הלכה ב ג סמג לאוין סה טוש"ע או"ח סימן רעו סעיף א וסימן שכה סעיף יא ויב:

פב ג ד מיי' וסמג שם טוש"ע או"ח סימן שכה סעיף י יא:

פג ה ו מיי' פכ"א מהל' שבת הלכה לו סמג שם טוש"ע או"ח סימן שכד סעיף יג וסימן שכה סעיף יא:

פד ז מיי' פ"ו שם הל"ד וסמג שם טור שו"ע שם:

פה ח מיי' שם הלכה ז סמג שם טוש"ע או"ח סימן שכו סעיף יג:

[דף קכא.]

פו ט מיי' שם הלכה ד סמג שם טוש"ע שם סימן רעו סעיף ב:

רבינו חננאל

או בב' ידים. אמר ליה כאותן של בית אביך ש"מ דניטלת בידו אחת שרי. ניטלת בב' ידים לא איתברירא לן בהדיא. וכן קרונות של בית רבי הניטלין בב' בני אדם לא איפשיטא. והתיר ר' חנינא לשתות יין הבא בקרונות של גוים בחותם אחת ולא ידענא אי משום דסבר לה כר' אליעזר אי משום אימתא דבי נשיאה: **גוי** שהדליק את הנר. ת"ר גוי שליקט עשבים מאכיל אחריו ישראל ואם בשביל ישראל אסור. וכן מילא מים להשקות בהמתו וכו'. בד"א

להביא הבהמה לשם ואין זה דוחק דלומיא דמתני' איירי האי בתרי עברי דנהרא שאין הבהמה יכולה לירד לבור ואע"ג דהך בבא וכו' כצ"ל רש"ל

רב נסים גאון

לפני רבן יוחנן בן זכאי בערב ואמר חושש אני לו מחטאת: **אי** משום דסבר לה כר' אליעזר דלא חייש לזיופא ומימרא דר' אליעזר במס' ע"ז אין מעמידין בהמה (דף לא) דתניא אחד הלוקח וא' השוכר בית כו' ר' אליעזר מתיר בשתייה ואמרו מר סבר כי פליגי רבנן עליה דר' אליעזר בחותם אחד כו' ובפ' השוכר את הפועלין (שם דף סט) אמרו וכי מאחר דקיימא לן כוותיה דרשב"ג וכוותיה דר' אליעזר דלא חייש לזיופא:

סליק פרק כל כתבי הקודש

פז א טור ש"ע שם:
א ב מיי' פכ"ב מהלכות שבת הלכה כה ופכ"ה הלכה יב סמג לאוין סה טוש"ע או"ח סימן שח סעיף ח:
ב ג מיי' שם הלכה ז טוש"ע שם סעיף ג:
ג ד מיי' שם הלכה ח טוש"ע שם סעיף יא:
ד ה מיי' פכ"ב שם הלכה כה טור ש"ע שם סעיף ט:
ה ו מיי' שם הלכה כו סמג שם טוש"ע או"ח סימן שיד סעיף א:

אהדרינהו שמואל לאפיה. איירי שהיה לכל הפתות מחלה על מחלה, דמשום נר לאחד נר למאה לא משתריא אלא היכא שהוא ניכר שהוא עושה לצרכו, דתו לא גזרינן אפילו במכירו שמא ירבה בשבילו: **הדרן עלך כל כתבי**

כל הכלים הניטלין בשבת דלתותיהן עמהם גרסינן ול"ג: כל הכלים ניטלין – דטובא איכא דאין ניטלין, כגון מסר הגדול ויתד של מחרישה, דאפילו ר"ש מודה כדאיתא בשילהי מכילתין. (דף קנז.) וכגון אלתא* בת תרי כורי, דאסר רבה בשילהי "במה מדליקין" (דף לה.) וכן אצוצרות לרבי יהודה* ונר ישן*. מ"ר: **אדרבה** בשבת מוכנין אגב אביהן. אע"ג דלקמן בפירקין (דף קכד:) אמר איפכא גבי שברי כלי חרס, דשרי לטלטל יותר כשנשברו בע"ש משנשברו בשבת – לא דמיא: דהכא אכתי כלי הוא, שעדיין עומד למלאכה ראשונה, וראוי להתחבר הכיסוי עם הכלי. אבל לקמן לא חשיב כלי אלא מחמת שעומד למלאכה אחרת, הלכך כשנשבר בשבת – אסור טפי, דהוי נולד: **לעולם** קסבר יש בנין בכלים כו'. וכשניטלו מטלטלין קאמר. וה"פ הברייתא: דלת של שידה תיבה ומגדל ניטלין, פירוש: מטלטלין כשניטלין. ולא כפירוש הקונטרס דמפרש שניטלין דקתני – היינו שניטלו קאמר, כלומר: כשניטל אין מחזירין אותן. דלא יתכן לפרש כן "ניטלין" דסיפא. אלא לשון טלטול הוא, כדפרשתי. ופריך: והא(א) נמי ניטלין קתני, ועוד: מאי "אבל לא מחזירין" דלא שייך למיתני אמילתיה דלא (דמיא) [שייך] כלל למאי דאיירי בה, דמעיקרא קאמר ניטלין – שמותר לטלטל ואין בו איסור מוקצה, והדר קאמר "אבל לא מחזירין" – שהוא משום איסור בנין, מאי ענין זה אצל זה? לא שייך כה"ג למיתני "אבל" כלל: **רחת** ומלגז מי מייחדי ליה לקטן. ורב יהודה ידע ליה לסיפא, אלא דילמא הוה מוקי לה בשיחדה לכך ככל הנך דמתניתין. ואם תאמר: והאמר רב יהודה אמר שמואל בפרק "אלו קשרים" (לעיל דף קיג.): כלי קיואי מותר לטלטל בשבת, דהיינו לצורך גופו, אע"פ שמלאכתו לאיסור. ואין לומר (דמתניתו) דשמואל קאמר ליה וליה לא סבירא ליה, מדבעי מיניה מרב יהודה: כובד עליון וכובד התחתון מהו? אין ולאו ורפיא בידיה. משמע דס"ל הכי. ועוד: דרב יהודה גופיה בסוף "כירה" (לעיל ד' מו.) קאמר: שרגא דמישחא שרי לטלטולי. ואין לומר דמיירי כשייחדו להיתר, כדמוקי רב יהודה הנך דמתני' – דהא כלי קיואי לא משמע שייחדו, דאם כן – אפילו כובד העליון וכובד תחתון נמי. ויש לומר: דלא אסר רב יהודה אלא דומיא דפילוע אגוזים, שהיא מלאכה גרועה לגבי קורנס שמיוחד למלאכה חשובה. וכן כל הנך דמתניתין הוה אסור בלא ייחוד, דמלאכת היתר שלהן מלאכה גרועה היא לגבי הנך כלים שמיוחדין למלאכה חשובה. אבל כלי קיואי ושרגא דמישחא – מותר לטלטל לצורך גופן, דמלאכה שלהן חשובה יותר מפילוע אגוזים:

בסיכי

אַדַעֲתָא דְרוּבָּא מַדְלְקִי. שְׁמוּאֵל אִיקְלַע לְבֵי אָבִין תּוֹרָן, אֲתָא הַהוּא גּוֹי אַדְלִיק שְׁרָגָא. אַהַדְרִינְהוּ שְׁמוּאֵל לְאַפֵּיהּ. כֵּיוָן דַּחֲזָא דְּאַיְיתִי שְׁטָר וְקָא קָרֵי, אֲמַר: א אַדַּעֲתָא דְנַפְשֵׁיהּ הוּא דְּאַדְלִיק. אַהַדְרִינְהוּ אִיהוּ לְאַפֵּיהּ גַּבֵּי שְׁרָגָא.§

הדרן עלך כל כתבי

כָּל ב הַכֵּלִים נִיטָּלִין בַּשַּׁבָּת וְדַלְתוֹתֵיהֶן עִמָּהֶן, אע"פ שֶׁנִּתְפָּרְקוּ (בַּשַּׁבָּת) שֶׁאֵינָן דּוֹמִין לְדַלְתוֹת הַבַּיִת, לְפִי שֶׁאֵינָן מִן הַמּוּכָן. ג נוֹטֵל אָדָם קוּרְנָס לְפַצֵּעַ בּוֹ אֶת הָאֱגוֹזִין, קַרְדּוֹם – לַחְתּוֹךְ בּוֹ אֶת הַדְּבֵילָה, מְגֵירָה – לָגוֹר בָּהּ אֶת הַגְּבִינָה, מַגְרֵיפָה – לִגְרוֹף בָּהּ אֶת הַגְּרוֹגְרוֹת, אֶת הָרַחַת וְאֶת *הַמַּלְגֵּז – לָתֵת עָלָיו לַקָּטָן, אֶת הַכּוּשׁ וְאֶת הַכַּרְכַּר – לִתְחוֹב בּוֹ, * ד מַחַט שֶׁל יָד – לִיטּוֹל בּוֹ אֶת הַקּוֹץ, וְשֶׁל סַקָּאִים – לִפְתּוֹחַ בּוֹ אֶת הַדֶּלֶת.§ **גמ'** "כָּל הַכֵּלִים נִיטָּלִין וְאע"פ שֶׁנִּתְפָּרְקוּ בַּשַּׁבָּת", וְלָא מִיבַּעְיָא בַּחוֹל? אַדְּרַבָּה, בַּשַּׁבָּת – מוּכָנִין עַל גַּבֵּי אֲבִיהֶן, בַּחוֹל – אֵין מוּכָנִין עַל גַּבֵּי אֲבִיהֶן! אָמַר אַבַּיֵי, הָכִי קָאָמַר: כָּל הַכֵּלִים נִיטָּלִין בַּשַּׁבָּת וְדַלְתוֹתֵיהֶן עִמָּהֶן, אע"פ שֶׁנִּתְפָּרְקוּ בַּחוֹל – נִיטָּלִין בַּשַּׁבָּת. ת"ר: * ה דֶּלֶת שֶׁל שִׁידָּה וְשֶׁל תֵּיבָה וְשֶׁל מִגְדָּל – נוֹטְלִין, אֲבָל לֹא מַחֲזִירִין. וְשֶׁל לוּל שֶׁל תַּרְנְגוֹלִים – לֹא נוֹטְלִין וְלֹא מַחֲזִירִין. בִּשְׁלָמָא שֶׁל לוּל שֶׁל תַּרְנְגוֹלִים – קָסָבַר: כֵּיוָן דִּמְחַבְּרִי בְּאַרְעָא – יֵשׁ בִּנְיָן בְּקַרְקַע, יֵשׁ סְתִירָה בְּקַרְקַע. אֶלָּא שֶׁל שִׁידָּה וְשֶׁל תֵּיבָה וְשֶׁל מִגְדָּל מַאי קָסָבַר? אִי קָסָבַר "יֵשׁ בִּנְיָן בְּכֵלִים" – יֵשׁ סְתִירָה בְּכֵלִים, וְאִי "אֵין סְתִירָה בְּכֵלִים" – אֵין בִּנְיָן בְּכֵלִים! אָמַר אַבַּיֵי: לְעוֹלָם קָסָבַר "יֵשׁ בִּנְיָן בְּכֵלִים וְיֵשׁ סְתִירָה בְּכֵלִים" – וְשֶׁנִּיטְּלוּ קָאָמַר. א"ל רָבָא: [שְׁתֵּי תְּשׁוּבוֹת בַּדָּבָר], חֲדָא: ד'נִיטָּלִין' קָתָנֵי, וְעוֹד: מַאי "אֲבָל לֹא מַחֲזִירִין"? אֶלָּא אָמַר רָבָא: קָסָבַר * ו אֵין בִּנְיָן בְּכֵלִים וְאֵין סְתִירָה בְּכֵלִים, וּגְזֵירָה שֶׁמָּא יִתְקַע.§ "נוֹטֵל אָדָם קוּרְנָס כו'".§ אָמַר רַב יְהוּדָה: קוּרְנָס שֶׁל אֱגוֹזִין לְפַצֵּעַ בּוֹ אֶת הָאֱגוֹזִין, אֲבָל שֶׁל נַפָּחִין – לֹא. קָסָבַר: דָּבָר שֶׁמְּלַאכְתּוֹ לְאִיסּוּר – אֲפִילּוּ לְצוֹרֶךְ גּוּפוֹ אָסוּר. א"ל רַבָּה: אֶלָּא מֵעַתָּה, סֵיפָא דְּקָתָנֵי "וְאֶת הָרַחַת וְאֶת הַמַּלְגֵּז לָתֵת עָלָיו לַקָּטָן" רַחַת וּמַלְגֵּז מִי מְיַיחֲדִי לֵיהּ לַקָּטָן?! אֶלָּא אָמַר רַבָּה: קוּרְנָס שֶׁל נַפָּחִין לְפַצֵּעַ בּוֹ הָאֱגוֹזִין. קָסָבַר:

דָּבָר

[ל"א דמטמיה]

אַדַּעֲתָא דְּרוּבָּא. הִלְכָּךְ יִשְׂרָאֵל עִיקָּר. וּמֶחֱצָה עַל מֶחֱצָה נַמִי לֵיכָּא לְמֵיקַם עֲלָהּ דְּמִלְּתָא, דְּאִיכָּא לְמֵימַר עִיקַּר דַּעְתֵּיהּ דְּמַדְלִיק בִּשְׁבִיל יִשְׂרָאֵל, וְאִיכָּא לְמֵימַר עִיקַּר דַּעְתֵּיהּ דְּמַדְלִיק בִּשְׁבִיל גּוֹי, אֲבָל גּוֹי וְיִשְׂרָאֵל וְהַמַּדְלִיק עַצְמוֹ מִשְׁתַּמֵּשׁ לְאוֹרָהּ – וַדַּאי עִיקַּר אַדַּעְתָּא דִּידֵיהּ עָבֵיד, וְכֵיוָן דְּנֵר לְאֶחָד נֵר לְמֵאָה – שָׁרֵי: תּוֹרָן. מָקוֹם: דְּאַיְיתִי שְׁטָר. הַהוּא דְּאַדְלְקָהּ:

הדרן עלך כל כתבי

כָּל הַכֵּלִים נִיטָּלִין בַּשַּׁבָּת וְדַלְתוֹתֵיהֶן עִמָּהֶם. כָּל הַכֵּלִים שֶׁיֵּשׁ לָהֶם דְּלָתוֹת, כְּגוֹן שִׁידָּה תֵּיבָה וּמִגְדָּל – נִיטָּלִין בַּשַּׁבָּת, וּדְלָתוֹת שֶׁיֵּשׁ לָהֶם בִּלְבַד עִמָּהֶן, נִיטָּלִין עִמָּהֶן: וְאע"פ שֶׁנִּתְפָּרְקוּ. הַדְּלָתוֹת מִן הַכֵּלִים – נִיטָּלִין, וְאֵין דּוֹמִין לְדַלְתוֹת הַבַּיִת שֶׁאֵין נִיטָּלִין. לְפִי שֶׁדַּלְתוֹת הַבַּיִת אֵינָן מִן הַמּוּכָן לְטַלְטֵל, שֶׁאֵינָן כְּלִי, אֲבָל אֵלּוּ הֵן כְּלִי אַגַּב אֲבִיהֶן: קוּרְנָס. מרטי"ל: דְּבֵילָה. מֵאַחַר שֶׁעֲשָׂאָהּ עִיגּוּל עָבָה הִיא מְאֹד, וְקָשָׁה כִּגְבִינָה, וְצָרִיךְ קוֹרְדּוֹס לְחוֹתְכָהּ: וּמְגֵירָה. כְּעֵין סַכִּין, וְיֵשׁ בּוֹ פְּגִימוֹת הַרְבֵּה: לָגוֹר בָּהּ אֶת הַגְּבִינָה. לְחָתְכוֹ וּלְחַלְּקוֹ, לְפִי שֶׁמְּמַהֶרֶת לַחְתּוֹךְ דָּבָר עָב: מַגְרֵיפָה. וודי"ל: לִגְרוֹף בָּהּ אֶת הַגְּרוֹגְרוֹת. מִן הֶחָבִיּוֹת: רַחַת. פאל"א: מַלְגֵּז. כְּמִין עֶתֶר, שֶׁקּוֹרִין פורק"א, שֶׁל בַּרְזֶל, וְלוֹ ג' שִׁינַּיִים, וּמְהַפְּכִין בּוֹ קַשׁ בַּגּוֹרֶן: לָתֵת עָלָיו לַקָּטָן. מְזוֹנוֹת: כּוּשׁ. פֶּלֶךְ, פוסי"ל: כַּרְכַּר. רא"י"ל: לִתְחוֹב בּוֹ. לֶאֱכוֹל בּוֹ תּוּתִים וְכָל פְּרִי רַךְ: מַחַט שֶׁל יָד. מַחַט קָטָן שֶׁתּוֹפֵר בּוֹ בְּגָדִים: וְשֶׁל סַקָּאִים. מַחַט גְּדוֹלָה שֶׁתּוֹפְרִים בָּהּ שַׂקִּים: לִפְתּוֹחַ בּוֹ אֶת הַדֶּלֶת. מִי שֶׁאָבַד מַפְתְּחוֹ: **גמ'** וְלָא מִיבַּעְיָא בַּחוֹל. קָא סָלְקָא דַּעְתָּךְ "וְאע"פ שֶׁנִּתְפָּרְקוּ" – אַשַּׁבָּת דְּקָתָנֵי רֵישָׁא קָאֵי, וּמַשְׁמַע אע"פ שֶׁנִּתְפָּרְקוּ הַיּוֹם מוּתָּרִים, וְלָא מִיבַּעְיָא אִם נִתְפָּרְקוּ מֵאֶמֶשׁ: אַדְּרַבָּה. מַאי "אע"פ" שַׁיָּיךְ לְמִתְנֵי, הָא וַדַּאי נִתְפָּרְקוּ בַּשַּׁבָּת אִיכָּא לְמִישְׁרֵי, מִשּׁוּם דְּכִי קָדֵישׁ יוֹמָא הָווּ מוּכָנִין לְטַלְטֵל אַגַּב אֲבִיהֶן: הָכִי קָאָמַר כו'. וְ"אע"פ" לָאו אַרְבוּתָא דְּנִתְפָּרְקוּ בַּשַּׁבָּת קָאֵי, אֶלָּא אַרְבוּתָא דְּנִתְחַבְּרוּ אוֹ בַּחוֹל אוֹ בַּשַּׁבָּת קָאֵי, וְלָא מִיבַּעְיָא כְּשֶׁהֵן מְחוּבָּרִין: נוֹטְלִין. מַשְׁמַע מְסַלְּקִין אוֹתָן בַּשַּׁבָּת *[מֵהֵיכָּר] צִיר שֶׁלָּהֶן: לוּל. בִּנְיָן הֶעָשׂוּי לְתַרְנְגוֹלִין: לֹא נוֹטְלִין וְלֹא מַחֲזִירִין. כִּדְמְפָרֵשׁ וְאָזֵיל, חֲזָרָתוֹ בִּנְיָן מַמָּשׁ הוּא, וְסִילּוּקוֹ סְתִירָה גְּמוּרָה הִיא: מַאי קָסָבַר. שֶׁמַּתִּיר סִילּוּקוֹ וְאוֹסֵר חֲזָרָתוֹ: אִי קָסָבַר יֵשׁ בִּנְיָן בְּכֵלִים. וַחֲזָרָתוֹ בִּנְיָן, עַל כָּרְחֵיךְ אִם יֵשׁ בִּנְיָן – יֵשׁ סְתִירָה, וְאַמַּאי נוֹטְלִין: וְשֶׁנִּיטְּלוּ קָאָמַר. וְה"ק: דֶּלֶת שֶׁל תֵּיבָה שִׁידָּה וּמִגְדָּל שֶׁנִּיטְּלוּ – אֵין מַחֲזִירִין: מַאי אֲבָל. כֵּיוָן דְּלָא תָּנָא נוֹטְלִין, לָא שַׁיָּיךְ לְמִיתְנֵי אֲבָל: לְעוֹלָם קָסָבַר אֵין סְתִירָה וְאֵין בִּנְיָן. הִלְכָּךְ נוֹטְלִין, וּמִיהוּ אֵין מַחֲזִירִין – מִדְּרַבָּנַן: גְּזֵירָה שֶׁמָּא יִתְקַע. בְּחָזְקָה בְּסַכִּין וִיתֵדוֹת, וְהָוֵה לֵיהּ גְּמַר מְלָאכָה, וְחַיָּיב מִשּׁוּם מַכֶּה בַּפַּטִּישׁ: קוּרְנָס שֶׁל אֱגוֹזִים. הַמְיוּחָד לִפְלִיעַת אֱגוֹזִים, הוּא דְּקָתָנֵי מַתְנִיתִין דְּנוֹטְלִין אוֹתוֹ לִמְלַאכְתּוֹ, מִשּׁוּם דְּעִיקָּרוֹ לִמְלֶאכֶת הֵיתֵּר: אֲבָל שֶׁל נַפָּחִים. דְּעִיקָּרוֹ לִמְלֶאכֶת אִיסּוּר – לֹא: לְצוֹרֶךְ גּוּפוֹ. שֶׁגּוּפוֹ צָרִיךְ עוֹד לִמְלָאכָה אַחֶרֶת שֶׁל הֵיתֵּר – אֵין מְטַלְטְלִין אוֹתוֹ לְאוֹתָהּ מְלָאכָה, וְכ"שׁ אִם אֵין צָרִיךְ לְגוּפוֹ אֶלָּא לְפַנּוֹת מְקוֹמוֹ, דְּאֵין מְטַלְטְלִין: מִי מְיַיחֲדִי לַקָּטָן. בִּשְׁלָמָא כּוּלְּהוּ הָנֵי דְּמַתְנִי' אִיכָּא לְאוֹקְמָא בַּעֲשׂוּיִין וּמְיוּחָדִין לְכָךְ, בַּר מֵהָנֵי דְּלֵיכָּא דְּעָבֵיד לְהוּ לְהָכִי:

דָּבָר

רבינו חננאל

בגוי שאינו מכירו אבל אם מכירו אסור. ת"ש עיר של ישראל וגוים דרין כו'. הדרן עלך כל כתבי הקודש

פי"ז כל הכלים ניטלין בשבת כו'. באנו לפרש מתי נפרקו בשבת או אפי' בחול. ואוקמה אביי להא מתני' אע"פ שנתפרקו בחול ניטלין בשבת לפי שאינן דומין דלתות הכלים לדלתות הבית. כי דלתות הבית קבועין בקרקע ולא הוכנו להיטלטל. אבל הכלים הוכנו לטלטול וכ"ש דלתותיהן. ופשוטה היא. ומפרקינן* גזירה שמא יתקע. פי' שמא יתקע בה מסמר או יתד וכדומה להן: **נוטל** אדם קורנס לפצוע בו אגוזים וכו'. בא רב יהודה להעמיד משנתנו זו בקורנס המוכן לפצוע אגוזים. ולא כל קורנס מותר. אלא זה בלבד. אבל קורנס של נפחים וכדומה להן אפילו לצורך גופו אסור. ואקשי' עלה רבה אלא מעתה סיפא דקתני ואת הרחת ואת המלגז לתת עליו לקטן. פי' לתת עליו מאכל לקטן כגון תבשיל. רחת ומלגז [מי] מכינין בנ"א לתבשיל

*) נראה דחסר בדברי רבינו וצ"ל דלת של שידה ושל תיבה ושל מגדל נוטלין אבל לא מחזירין.

[עי' לעיל לה. תוס' ד"ה ואפילו]
[לעיל לו.]
[לעיל מד.]
פירשו מזלג [ובמשנה שבמשניות איתא המזלג]
לעיל קז. סנהדרין פד:
[תוספתא פ"ט]
[עירובין לה. ביצה י. יא: נג.]
*רש"ל וכס"י איתא מהיכר וכן איתא ברא"ש בד"ה לעולם

הגהות הב"ח

(א) תוס' ד"ה לעולם וכו' ופריך והא ניטלין קתני ולא תני נמי נתפרקו כו' ועוד מאי אבל:

גמרא

דבר שמלאכתו לאיסור לצורך גופו – מותר. איתיביה אביי לרבה: *מדוכה, אם יש בה שום – מטלטלין אותה, ואם לאו – אין מטלטלין אותה! א"ל: הא מני – ר' נחמיה היא, דאמר: *אין כלי ניטל אלא לצורך תשמישו. איתיביה: (*ב"ש אומרים: אין נוטלין את העלי לקצב עליו בשר, א ובה"ה מתירין). *ושוין, שאם קצב עליו בשר – שאסור לטלטלו! סבר לשנויי ליה כר' נחמיה, כיון דשמעה להא דאמר רב חיננא בר שלמיא משמיה דרב: הכל מודים בסיכי זיירי ומזורי דכיון דקפיד עלייהו – מייחד להו מקום, ה"נ: מייחד להו מקום. איתמר, ר' חייא בר אבא אמר ר' יוחנן: ב קורנס של זהבים שנינו, רב שמן בר אבא אמר: קורנס של בשמים שנינו. מאן דאמר דבשמים – כ"ש דזהבים. מאן דאמר של זהבים – אבל דבשמים קפיד עלייהו. § "ואת הכוש ואת הכרכר כו'". *ת"ר: פגה שטמנה בתבן, וחררה שטמנה(א) בגחלים, אם מגולה מקצתה – מותר לטלטלה. ואם לאו – אסור לטלטלה. ר"א בן תדאי אומר: ג תוחבין בכוש או בכרכר והן מנערות מאיליהם. אמר רב נחמן: הלכה כר"א בן תדאי. למימרא דסבר רב נחמן *"טלטול מן הצד לא שמיה טלטול"? *והאמר רב נחמן: האי פוגלא, מלמעל' למטה – שרי, ממטה למעלה – אסיר! הדר ביה רב נחמן מההיא. § "מחט של יד ליטול בה כו'". § שלח ליה רבא בריה דרבה לרב יוסף: ילמדנו רבינו, מחט שניטל חררה או עוקצה מהו? א"ל: תניתוה, מחט של יד ליטול בה את הקוץ. וכי מה איכפת ליה לקוץ בין נקובה לבין שאינה נקובה? איתיביה: *מחט שניטל חררה או עוקצה – טהורה! אמר אביי: טומאה אשבת קרמית?! *טומאה – כלי מעשה בעינן, לענין שבת – מידי דחזי בעינן, והא נמי חזיא למשקלא בה קוץ. אמר רבא: מאן דקמותיב – שפיר קמותיב, *מדלענין טומאה לאו מנא הוא – לענין שבת נמי לאו מנא הוא. מיתיבי: *ד מחט, בין נקובה בין שאינה נקובה – מותר לטלטלה בשבת, ולא אמרו "נקובה" אלא לענין טומאה בלבד! *תרגמא אביי אליבא דרבא: בגולמי עסקינן, זימנין דמימלך עלייהו ומשוי להו מנא. ה אבל היכא דניטל חררה או עוקצה – אדם זורקה לבין גרוטאות. *אסובי ינוקא, רב נחמן *אסיר ורב ששת ו שרי. אמר רב נחמן: מנא אמינא לה – דתנן: *"אין עושין אפיקטויזין

רש"י

דבר שמלאכתו לאיסור. אם צריך בשבת לגופו(ב) של מלאכה אחרת של היתר – מותר: מדוכה. שדוכין בה שום: אם יש בה שום מטלטלין אותה. אגב השום: ואם לאו אין מטלטלין. כגון ליישב עליה. כיון דעיקר מלאכתו לשחיקה, דהיא מלאכת איסור משום טוחן: תשמישו. תשמיש המיוחד לו: ושוין. ב"ש וב"ה שאחלקו בנוטלין את העלי לקצב עליו בשר ביו"ט: שאם קצב עליו בשר. שעשה לצורך שמחת יו"ט: שאסור לטלטלו. דהאי דקשרו ב"ה – משום שמחת יו"ט קשרו, אלמא משום דעלי מלאכתו לאיסור לכתישת טרגים וטיסני וקליפת עלים לעבד בהן עורות – אסור: הכל מודים. רבנן דאיפלגו אדר' נחמיה: בסיכי זיירי ומזורי. כלי צבעין הן. ורבינו הלוי פירש: כלי אורגין; סיכי הן עמודין, זיארי הן קנים שבשתי, ומזורי – כובד עליון ותחתון. ולאשון נראה לי, דזיארי לשון עוצרים הן, כמו מעצרתא זיירא (ע"ז דף ס.): דקפיד עלייהו. האומן, שלא יתקלקלו ושלא יתעקמו: מייחד להם מקום. מקלה להן בידים: הני נמי. עלי ומדוכה: קורנס של זהבים. אע"פ דקפיד עליה קצת, שצריך שיהא חלק לרדד טסין, אפ"ה כיון שמתקן על ידי הכאה שמכה על הסדן – לא מקלי ליה, וכ"ש של אחר נפחים כרבה: בשמים. לשחוק בו: קפיד עליה. שלא ימאס: פגה. תאנה שלא בשלה כל צרכה, וטומנין בתבן להתבשל. ותבן מוקצה הוי לטיט: אם מגולה מקצתה. שיכול לאוחזה במקום המגולה, דאפי' טלטול מן הצד ליכא, שאין צריך להגביה התבן, אלא מגביה מקום המגולה, והתבן נשמט ונופל: פוגלא. צנון תלוש שהטמינו בארץ ונתגלה ראשו: מלמעלה למטה שרי. אם היה העליון שלה למעלה והקצר למטה, וכשהוא שולפה אוחזה מעליון שלה לתחתון שלה, ורוחב הצנון למעלה – מותר, דליכא טלטול לעפר כלל, שהרי נתגלה ראשו: ממטה למעלה אסור. שמזיז עפר, לפי שהגומא קצרה מלמעלה, ורוחב הצנון מלמטה. ואע"ג דטלטול עפר מן הצד הוא, שאינו אוחזו ממש בידו: חררה. חור שלה: עוקצה. פויינט"א: מהו. לטלטלה. מי בטל תורת כלי מינה, או לא: כלי מעשה. שמעשה שלו קיים: ולא אמרו נקובה. להיות תורת כלי עליה יותר משאין נקובה אלא לענין טומאה, וקס"ד דבנטל חור שלה קאמר, דלענין טומאה בטל שם כלי מינה, ולטלטול שרי: בגולמי. גולמי מחטין העומדות לינקב, דנקובה נגמרה מלאכתה, ושאינה נקובה אינה נגמרה מלאכתה. הלכך, לענין טומאה הוא דלא הוי כלי, אבל בטלטול – שריא, דחזי לקוץ: דמימליך. ולא נקיב לה: ומשוי לה מנא. כמות שהיא, ולנטילת קוץ: גרוטאות. שברי מתכות אדם זורק, לבין גרוטאו', ובטל שם כלי מינה: אסובי ינוקא. להחליק סדר אבריו, כשהוא נולד אבריו מתפרקין, וצריך ליישבן: אסיר. דדמי למתקן:

תוספות

בסיכי זיירי ומזורי. פי' סיכי – הם יתדות המוכנין לנעץ בהן משי וכיוצא בה תרגום יתדות סיכי. זיירי – כלי עץ, כמו קרשים שכובשין בהן בגדים, דתנן (לקמן דף קמא.): מכבש של בעלי בתים. מזורי כלי עץ שהכובס מכה בו הבגדים על האבן שמלבנו ואלו כלים מקפיד עליהם שלא יתעקמו ולא יתפגמו שלא יתקלקלו הבגדים והמשי ומסיח דעתו מלטלטלן. וכן מפרש בירושלמי: זיירי – דין עצר ביה, מזורא – דין חביט ביה. ולפי' הקונט' דמפרש מזורי כובד עליון וכובד תחתון נ"ל דסבירא ליה כמאן דאסר בפרק "אלו קשרים" (לעיל דף קיג.): **הא** נמי מייחד לה מקום. מ"מ משום שמחת יו"ט מותר לטלטלו לקצב עליו בשר: *) **הדר** ביה רב נחמן מההיא. מסתברא דמההיא הדר ביה, מדאמר בפרק "תולין" (לקמן דף קמא.): אמרי בי רב, תנינא דלא כרב נחמן: **פגה** שהטמינה כו'. מיירי שהניחה שם ע"מ ליטלה, אבל אם הניחה שם לכל השבת – הוי בסיס לדבר האסור, כדאמר לקמן בפרק "נוטל" (ד' קמב:) גבי אבן שעל פי החבית: לא שנו אלא בשוכח, אבל במניח – נעשה בסיס לדבר האסור: **האי** פוגלא. וא"ת: האי פוגלא היכי דמי, אי במניח – מ"ט דמאן דשרי מלמטה למעלה? הא אפילו ניעור לא שרי, כ"ש טלטול מן הצד! ואי בשכח – מ"ט דמאן דאסר? אפי' טלטול גמור שרי לצורך, לטלטל אגב היתר, לקמן בפרק "נוטל" (קמא. וד' קמב:) במעות שעל גבי הכר בצריך למקומו, דמטלטלו בעודן עליו. ואבן שעל פי החבית, כשהוא בין החביות – מגביה ומטה, כ"ש טלטול מן הצד! וי"ל: דמניח על מנת ליטלה איירי, אע"ג דכשכח דמי, כמו טמן וכיסה בדבר שאינו ניטל בסוף "במה טומנין" (לעיל דף נא.) דשרי לנער משום דאין מניח לכל השבת. ובעצמות וקליפין דריש ביצה (ד' ב.) דשרי ב"ה לסלק את הטבלא ולנער, מ"מ לא היה לו להניח באותו ענין שיצטרך טלטול מן הצד. ועצמות וקליפין לא מסתייה דלא לינח בהן על גבי השלחן. וטמן וכיסה דפרק "במה טומנין" (לעיל ד' נא.) אין לחוש, כיון דאפשר בניעור, דאפילו טלטול מן הצד אינו א): **מדלענין** טומאה לאו מנא לענין שבת נמי לאו מנא. תימה, הא תנן לקמן: *כל הכלים הניטלין שבריהן ניטלין. אע"ג דלענין טומאה לא הוי מנא כשנשבר אלא על ידי ייחוד לפי' הקונטרס דסוף "המצניע" (לעיל דף צה:)! י"ל; דה"פ: מדלענין טומאה לאו מנא, אפי' על ידי ייחוד, דכיון דניטל חררה או עוקצה לא מהני ביה ייחוד – לענין שבת נמי לאו מנא היא. אבל היכא דהוה מנא לענין טומאה ע"י ייחוד – איכא למימר דהוי מנא לענין שבת אפי' בלא ייחוד כיון דיכול להיות כלי לענין טומאה. וכן משמע בסמוך, דתרגמא אביי אליבא דרבא בגולמי, דזימנין דמימלך עלייהו ומשוי להו מנא. משמע דלהכי מותר לטלטל אע"ג דטהורה היא – דלאכתי לא מימלך עלה, כיון שראוי ליחדה להיות כלי: **אסובי** ינוקא. לאו היינו לפופי ינוקא דשרי בפרק "במה אשה" (לעיל דף סו:) ולקמן בסוף "חבית" (דף קמז:) – דהיינו שכורכין אותו בבגדים וקושרים בחגורה רחבה. וכן פירש בקונטרס בסוף "מפנין", ג) כי היכי דלא תקשי דרב נחמן אדרב נחמן דשרי התם לפופי, והכא אסר אסובי. והא דתנן בפ' "חבית" (שם): אין מעצבין את הקטן. פירש לה התם דהיינו לפופי, ומוקי לה בחומרי שדרה, דמיחזי כבונה. וקשה! דמייתי לה מאין עושין אפיקטויזין, שהוא תיקוני גברא, כדפירש בקונטרס. הוה ליה לאתויי מסיפא דאין מעצבין את הקטן, דהוי נמי תקוני ינוקא ודמי טפי, שהכל בקטן מענין אסובי! ופירש רבינו תם: דהכי נמי מייתי, ונקט רישא "אין עושין אפיקטויזין כו'" עד "אין מעצבין" וסכינה

*) שייך לקמן קודם ד"ה מדלענין.

עין משפט נר מצוה

[ערך זיירי]

ו א טוש"ע או"ח סימן תלט סעיף ה:

ז ב מיי' פכ"ה מהלכות שבת הלכה ז סמג לאוין סה טוש"ע או"ח סימן שח סעיף ג [ועי' בכ"י]:

ח ג מיי' שם הלכה טו סמג שם טוש"ע או"ח סימן שיא סעיף ט:

ט ד ה מיי' שם הלכה ח סמג שם טוש"ע או"ח סימן שח סעיף יא:

י ו מיי' פ"ב מהלכות שבת הלכה יד ופכ"א הלכה לא טור שו"ע או"ח סימן של סעיף ט:

רבינו חננאל

לתבשיל וכדומה לו. ולא מצא רב יהודה פירוקי והעמיד רבה משנתנו בקורנס של נפחים וה"ה לכל קורנס. ושמעינן מינה דכל דבר שמלאכתו אפי' לאיסור כגון מלאכת הקורנס של נפחים שהן עושי מלאכת כלי נחשת וברזל. ומלאכתם [זו] שהוכנו לכך אסורה בשבת. אם הוצרכו (לומר) [לדבר] שהוא מותר בשבת. כגון פיצוע האגוזים שהן הכנת מאכל ואינה מלאכה מותר. ואקשינן עליה והא מדוכה אם יש בה שום מטלטלין [אותה] ואם לאו אין מטלטלין אותה. דכיון שמלאכתה לאיסור היא אפי' לצורך גופה אין מטלטלין אותה. ופריק ליה מני מתניתא ר' נחמיה היא דאמר אין כלי ניטל אלא לצורך תשמישו. פי' מצאנו ר' נחמיה שאמר בפי' אפי' טלית ואפי' [תרווד] אין ניטלין אלא לצורך והיא טלית ללבישה. ותרווד לאכל בו ומתני' דקתני נוטל אדם קורנס לפצוע בו [וקרדום] (ומדוכה) דלא כר' נחמיה. ותוב אקשי' עליה ושוין שאם קצב עליו בשר ופשוטה היא. ומוקמינן להני מתניתא לדברי הכל ואפילו לרבנן ומודו רבנן במדוכה ובעלי דכיון דקפיד עליה מכין עליה מקום וגמר בדעתו שלא לטלטלן מאותו מקום. לפיכך אסור לטלטלן מן המקום המוכן להם. ודין אלו כדין סיכי זיירי ומזורי. פי' סיכי הן יתדות המכונין לנער בהן משי וכדומה לו. והן תרגום של יתדות סיכי. זיירי. כלי עץ כגון קרשים שכובשין בהן הבגדים. כדתנן מכבש של בעלי בתים. מזורי כלי עץ שהכובס מכה בו הבגדים על אבן בעת שמלבנן. ואלו כולן קפיד עליהן שלא יתעוותו או יפגמו. שאם יפגמו יקרעו הבגדים והמשי. לפיכך מסיח דעתו מטלטולן ונעשו מוקצים ועל כן אסור לטלטלן. וכך זה מפורשין בתלמוד א"י. בזייר די [במכונה] עצר ביה. במזורה. די חבוט ביה (בכיבאנא) די כתיש ביה. ונתבררו דברי משנתנו כי כל הקורנס מותר לפצוע בו אגוזין ואפי' קורנס של זהבים. ובקורנס של בשמים חלקו בו ר' חייא בר אבא ורב שמן בר אבא משמיה דרבי יוחנן. ר' חייא אוסר. ורב שמן מתיר. ומסתברא כר' חייא חדא דכיון דקפיד עליה דלא ליפגום כזיירי דמי. ותוב דהוא אשכחן דהוה תדיר קמי ר' יוחנן דהוה גריס ודייק. והוה מהדר תלמודיה עליה כל תלתין יומין: **ת"ר** פגה שטמנה בתבן וחררה שטמנה בגחלים אם מגולה מקצתה מותר לטלטלה ואם לאו אסור. אלעזר בן תדאי [אומר] תוחבן בכוש או בכרכר והן נגררות מאליהן. פי' פגה בדכתיב התאנה חנטה פגיה והן פירות שלא נתבשלו באילן וטומנן בתבן להתבשל בחמות התבן להוכשר לאכילה. ותרוה ע"ג גחלים טמנה בהן ליאפות מבעו"י ובא בשבת לנוטלן ת"ק סבר אסור להסיר הגחלים או התבן מעליהן ולינטלן. אלא אם מקצתן מגולין אוחז בידו המקום המגולה ושומטן ואם אין בהם מקום מגולה בחררה בלא גחלים, ובפגה בלא תבן אסור לטלטלן. ואלעזר בן תדאי סבר אע"ג שאין בהן מקום מגולה תוחבן בכוש או בכרכר. פי' נועץ בהן כוש והוא דתנן כוש שבלע את הצינורא או כרכר שהוא וכו'. ומגביהן ונופלין התבן או הגחלים מאליהן וא"ח נוטלן בידו שלא נמצא טלטל הגחלים והתבן כדרכן אלא מן הצד. ואמר רב נחמן הלכה כאלעזר בן תדאי. ומקשינן וכי רב נחמן סבר דטלטול מן הצד לאו שמיה טלטול. והא רב נחמן בפרק "ר' אליעזר אומר תולין". בסופו בגמרא הקש שע"ג המטה לא יגענו בידו כו'. אמר רב נחמן האי פוגלא מלמעלה למטה שרי. ממטה

רב נסים גאון

הכל מודים בסיכי זיארי ומזורי. בגמרא דבני מערבא גרסי זירה די עצר בה מזורי די חבט בה וסיכי הן יתדות וגלוי הוא הדבר וידוע לכל:

הגהות הב"ח

(א) גמ' וחררה שטמנה. נ"ב לשון רש"י בעירובין דף עז וחררה שטמונה אתמול בגחלים ועכשיו כבו ומ"מ מוקצין הן אבל לא כבו לא דמתוך שנהפכו מכבה את התחתונות ומבעיר את העליונות כדאמרינן בכריתות: (ב) רש"י ד"ה דבר שמלאכתו וכו' לגופו למלאכה כצ"ל ותיבת של נמחק:

גליון הש"ס

רש"י ד"ה הני נמי עלי ומדוכה. ע"ל פא ע"א ברש"י ד"ה מדוכה קטנה:

מסורת הש"ס

[לקמן קכה. תוספתא פי"ד] | [לעיל לו. וש"נ] | ביצה יא. | רס"ל מ"ז | [לקמן קכד. ביצה יא.] | עירובין מו. | [לעיל מג: לקמן קמא.] | שם | לעיל נב: כלים פי"ג מ"ה | [לעיל ס.] | [לעיל קיב.] | לעיל נב: [תוספ' כלים ב"מ פ"ב] | [לעיל נב: וש"נ] | לקמן קמז. | נ"ל אוסר | [בערוך פירש כשנפלה ערלת הגרון של תינוק משימה היתה אלבטא בפיו ומסלקת אותה הערלה ופעמים שמקיף התינוק ע"י הקאה או ראה שאין עושין אפיקטויזין עכ"ל ועיין בהרא"ש שם על הגליון]

הערות

א) ועי' תוס' לעיל דף נא. ד"ה לא שמטתן. ב) וע"ע תוס' חולין דף נב. ד"ה שיטולו. ג) דף קכט:

תוס' ד"ה פגה שהטמינה וכו' מיירי שהניחה. עיין לעיל דף נא ע"א תוס' ד"ה לא שמטתן. תוס' ד"ה מדלענין וכו' ע"ש יחוד. ע"ל דף פ ע"א תוס' ד"ה לא אמרו. תוס' ד"ה אסובי ינוקא וכו' אין עושין אפיקטויזין. וכזה כתבו תוס' בכסא ד"ה כדאמר

יא א מיי' פכ"ו מהל' שבת הלכה ז:
יב ב מיי' פ"א מהלכות כלים הלכה י:
יג ג מיי' שם פ"ב הל"ב:
יד ד ה מיי' פכ"ה מהל' שבת הלכה ט סמג לאוין סה טור ושו"ע או"ח סימן שח סעיף א:
טו ו מיי' שם הלכה ג טוש"ע שם סעיף ג ד:
טז ז מיי' פ"ה מהלכות תמידין ומוספין הלכה יא:
יז ח מיי' פ"א מהלכות ק"פ הלכה יד:

[במשנה שבמשניות ליתא ר' יוסי אומר וכן מוכח מסוגיא דלקמן קנז. ע"ש אבל בעירובין לה. איתא סבר לה כר' יוסי דאמר כל הכלים ניטלין וכו' [illegible]]

[וע"ע תוס' מנחות נו. ד"ה לא סידור ותוספות עירובין דף קב: ד"ה והעליון]

אַפִּיקְטְוִיזִין בַּשַּׁבָּת". וְרַב שֵׁשֶׁת – הָתָם לָאו אוֹרְחֵיהּ, הָכָא – אוֹרְחֵיהּ. אָמַר רַב שֵׁשֶׁת: מְנָא אָמִינָא לָהּ – דִּתְנַן: "מַחַט שֶׁל יָד לִיטּוֹל בָּהּ אֶת הַקּוֹץ". וְרַב נַחְמָן – הָתָם פְּקִיד, הָכָא – לָא פְּקִיד.§ **מתני'** קָנֶה שֶׁל זֵיתִים, אִם יֵשׁ קֶשֶׁר בְּרֹאשׁוֹ – מְקַבֵּל טוּמְאָה, וְאִם לָאו – אֵין מְקַבֵּל טוּמְאָה. [א]בֵּין כָּךְ וּבֵין כָּךְ נִיטָּל בַּשַּׁבָּת.§ **גמ'** אַמַּאי? פְּשׁוּטֵי כְּלֵי עֵץ הוּא, *[ב]וּפְשׁוּטֵי כְּלֵי עֵץ אֵינָן מְקַבְּלִין טוּמְאָה! מ"ט – *דּוּמְיָא דְּשַׂק בָּעֵינַן. תָּנָא מִשְּׁמֵיהּ דְּר' נְחֶמְיָה: [ג]בְּשָׁעָה שֶׁמְּהַפֵּךְ בַּזֵּיתִים הוֹפְכוֹ וְרוֹאֶה בּוֹ.§ **מתני'** *ר' יוֹסֵי אוֹמֵר: *כָּל הַכֵּלִים נִיטָּלִין, [ד]חוּץ מִן הַמַּסָּר הַגָּדוֹל וְיָתֵד שֶׁל מַחֲרֵישָׁה.§ **גמ'** אָמַר ר"נ: *הַאי *אוּכְלָא דְּקַצְרֵי כְּיָתֵד שֶׁל מַחֲרֵישָׁה דָּמְיָא. אָמַר אַבַּיֵי: [ה]חַרְבָּא דְּאוּשְׁכָּפֵי, וְסַכִּינָא דְּאַשְׁכַּבְתָּא, וַחֲצִינָא דְּנַגָּרֵי – כְּיָתֵד שֶׁל מַחֲרֵישָׁה דָּמֵי. ת"ר: *בָּרִאשׁוֹנָה הָיוּ אוֹמְרִים, שְׁלֹשָׁה כֵּלִים נִיטָּלִין בַּשַּׁבָּת: מַקְצוּעַ שֶׁל דְּבֵילָה, וְזוּהֲמָא לִיסְטְרָן שֶׁל קְדֵרָה וְסַכִּין קְטַנָּה שֶׁעַל גַּבֵּי שֻׁלְחָן. הִתִּירוּ, וְחָזְרוּ וְהִתִּירוּ, וְחָזְרוּ וְהִתִּירוּ, עַד שֶׁאָמְרוּ: כָּל הַכֵּלִים נִיטָּלִין בַּשַּׁבָּת חוּץ מִן מַסָּר הַגָּדוֹל וְיָתֵד שֶׁל מַחֲרֵישָׁה. מַאי "הִתִּירוּ וְחָזְרוּ וְהִתִּירוּ וְחָזְרוּ וְהִתִּירוּ"? אָמַר אַבַּיֵי: "הִתִּירוּ" דָּבָר שֶׁמְּלַאכְתּוֹ לְהֶיתֵּר לְצוֹרֶךְ גּוּפוֹ, "וְחָזְרוּ וְהִתִּירוּ" דָּבָר שֶׁמְּלַאכְתּוֹ לְהֶיתֵּר לְצוֹרֶךְ מְקוֹמוֹ, "וְחָזְרוּ וְהִתִּירוּ" דָּבָר שֶׁמְּלַאכְתּוֹ לְאִיסּוּר לְצוֹרֶךְ גּוּפוֹ – אִין, לְצוֹרֶךְ מְקוֹמוֹ – לָא. וַעֲדַיִין, בְּיָדוֹ אַחַת – אִין, בִּשְׁתֵּי יָדָיו – לָא. עַד שֶׁאָמְרוּ: כָּל הַכֵּלִים נִיטָּלִין בַּשַּׁבָּת, וַאֲפִי' בִּשְׁתֵּי יָדַיִם. א"ל רָבָא: מִכְּדֵי 'הִתִּירוּ' קָתָנֵי, מָה לִי לְצוֹרֶךְ גּוּפוֹ מָה לִי לְצוֹרֶךְ מְקוֹמוֹ? אֶלָּא אָמַר רָבָא: [ו]"הִתִּירוּ" דָּבָר שֶׁמְּלַאכְתּוֹ לְהֶיתֵּר בֵּין לְצוֹרֶךְ גּוּפוֹ וּבֵין לְצוֹרֶךְ מְקוֹמוֹ, "וְחָזְרוּ וְהִתִּירוּ" מֵחַמָּה לַצֵּל, "וְחָזְרוּ וְהִתִּירוּ" דָּבָר שֶׁמְּלַאכְתּוֹ לְאִיסּוּר לְצוֹרֶךְ גּוּפוֹ וּלְצוֹרֶךְ מְקוֹמוֹ – אִין, מֵחַמָּה לַצֵּל – לָא, וַעֲדַיִין, בְּאָדָם אֶחָד – אִין, בִּשְׁנֵי בְּנֵי אָדָם – לָא, עַד שֶׁאָמְרוּ: כָּל הַכֵּלִים נִיטָּלִין בַּשַּׁבָּת אֲפִילּוּ בִּשְׁנֵי בְּנֵי אָדָם. *אֵיתִיבֵיהּ אַבַּיֵי: מְדוֹכָה, אִם יֵשׁ בָּהּ שׁוּם – מְטַלְטְלִין אוֹתָהּ, וְאִם לָאו – אֵין מְטַלְטְלִין אוֹתָהּ! הָכָא בְּמַאי עָסְקִינַן – מֵחַמָּה לַצֵּל. אֵיתִיבֵיהּ: *וְשָׁוִין שֶׁאִם קָצַב עָלָיו בָּשָׂר שֶׁאָסוּר לְטַלְטְלוֹ! הָכָא נַמִי, מֵחַמָּה לַצֵּל. אָמַר ר' חֲנִינָא *)בִּימֵי נְחֶמְיָה בֶּן חֲכַלְיָה נִשְׁנֵית מִשְׁנָה זוֹ, דִּכְתִיב: °"בַּיָּמִים הָהֵמָּה רָאִיתִי בִיהוּדָה דּוֹרְכִים גִּתּוֹת בַּשַּׁבָּת וּמְבִיאִים הָעֲרֵימוֹת". אָמַר ר' אֶלְעָזָר: קָנִין וּמַקְלוֹת גְּלוֹסְטְרָא וּמְדוֹכָה כּוּלָּן קוֹדֶם הַתָּרַת כֵּלִים נִשְׁנוּ. קָנִין – דִּתְנַן: *[ז]לֹא סִידּוּר הַקָּנִין וְלֹא נְטִילָתָן דּוֹחֶה אֶת הַשַּׁבָּת. מַקְלוֹת – דִּתְנַן: *[ח]מַקְלוֹת דַּקִּין חֲלָקִין הָיוּ שָׁם וּמַנִּיחוֹ עַל כְּתֵפוֹ וְעַל כֶּתֶף חֲבֵירוֹ וְתוֹלֶה וּמַפְשִׁיט. (*אָמַר) רַבִּי אֶלְעָזָר: אַרְבָּעָה עָשָׂר שֶׁחָל לִהְיוֹת בַּשַּׁבָּת מַנִּיחַ יָדוֹ

נחמיה יג

*) [עי' תוס' ב"ק לג. ד"ה בימי].

תורה אור

רש"י

אַפִּיקְטְוִיזִין. לְהָקִיא. שׁוֹתֶה מַשְׁקִים וּמֵקִיא, וְלֹא לִרְפוּאָה, אֶלָּא לְהָרִיק אֶת מֵעָיו, שֶׁיּוּכַל לֶאֱכוֹל וְלִשְׁתּוֹת [הַיּוֹם] הַרְבֵּה, כִּדְאָמְרִי' בְּפֶרֶק "חָבִית". וְאַע"ג דְּלָא גְּזוּר בָּהּ מִשּׁוּם שְׁחִיקַת סַמְמָנִין, דְּהָא לָאו לִרְפוּאָה הִיא – אָסוּר מִשּׁוּם דִּמְתַקֵּן גַּבְרָא: הָכָא אוֹרְחֵיהּ. וַהֲרֵי הוּא כְּמִי שֶׁמַּאֲכִילוֹ וּמַשְׁקֵהוּ: לִיטּוֹל בָּהּ אֶת הַקּוֹץ. אַלְמָא: תַּקּוּנֵי גַּבְרָא בְּמִידֵי דְּלָאו לִרְפוּאָה, דְּלֵיכָּא מִשּׁוּם שְׁחִיקַת סַמְמָנִין – שָׁרֵי: פָּקִיד. הַקּוֹץ הַזֶּה אֵינוֹ מְחוּבָּר בּוֹ, אֶלָּא מוּפְקָד וְנָתוּן שָׁם, וְהוֹצָאָה זוֹ אֵינוֹ תִּיקּוּן: הָכָא לָא פָּקִיד. וְדָמֵי לִמְלָאכָה, שֶׁמְּסַדְּרָן וּמַכְנִיסָן לִמְקוֹם חִבּוּר: **מתני'** קָנֶה שֶׁל זֵיתִים. לְאַחַר מְסִיקָתָן נוֹתֵן בַּמַּעֲטָן, וְשַׁמְנָן מִתְאַסֵּף בְּתוֹכָן וְנוֹחַ לָצֵאת, וְיֵשׁ לוֹ קָנֶה לְהָפְכָן בּוֹ וְלִבְדּוֹק אִם גָּמְרוּ כָּל צָרְכָּן, וּמַגִּיעָן לְבֵית הַבַּד: אִם יֵשׁ קֶשֶׁר בְּרֹאשׁוֹ. כְּעֵין פְּקָק שֶׁל קָנֶה קוּלְמוֹס: מְקַבֵּל טוּמְאָה. דִּכְלִי הוּא, לְפִי שֶׁעָב בְּרֹאשׁוֹ קְצָת: וְאִם לָאו. לָא דָּמֵי לִכְלִי, וּבַגְּמָ' מְפָרֵשׁ לָהּ: **גמ'** וְאַמַּאי. כִּי יֵשׁ בּוֹ קֶשֶׁר בְּרֹאשׁוֹ, נְהִי נַמִי דְּקֶשֶׁר מְשַׁוֵּי לֵיהּ מָנָא – מֵיהוּ פְּשׁוּטֵי כְּלֵי עֵץ הוּא, שֶׁאֲפִילּוּ חָלוּל הוּא – אֵין חֲלָלוֹ עָשׂוּי לְקַבֵּל כְּלוּם: הוֹפְכוֹ וְרוֹאֶה. בַּחֲלַל רֹאשׁוֹ, שֶׁמִּשְׁתַּיֵּיר שָׁם ע"י שֶׁהוּא פָּקוּק בְּקֶשֶׁר מִן הַשֶּׁמֶן הַזָּב מִן הַזֵּיתִים, וּבוֹדֵק בּוֹ אִם הִגִּיעוּ לַעֲצוֹר, וְזוֹ הִיא לוֹ קַבָּלָה בַּחֲלָל שֶׁלּוֹ. וְאִם לָאו – שֶׁאֵין קֶשֶׁר בְּרֹאשׁוֹ – אֵין הַשֶּׁמֶן נִרְאֵית שָׁם, מִפְּנֵי שֶׁאֵינוֹ פָּקוּק וְכוּלּוֹ חָלָל, הִלְכָּךְ לָאו לְקַבֵּל הוּא עָשׂוּי, וְהָוֵי פְּשׁוּטֵי כְּלֵי עֵץ. וּבֵין כָּךְ וּבֵין כָּךְ – נִיטָּל בְּשַׁבָּת, דְּהָא כְּלִי הוּא לַהֲפוֹךְ בּוֹ זֵיתִים: **מתני'** מַסָּר הַגָּדוֹל. מְגֵירָה גְּדוֹלָה שֶׁעֲשׂוּיָה לִקְצוֹץ קוֹרוֹת: וְיָתֵד שֶׁל מַחֲרֵישָׁה. הוּא כְּלִי גָּדוֹל הֶעָשׂוּי כְּסַכִּין שֶׁבּוֹ עוֹשִׂין חָרִיץ שֶׁל תֶּלֶם הַמַּעֲנָה, קולטר"א בְּלַע"ז, דְּהָנָךְ קָפֵיד עֲלַיְיהוּ, וּמְיַיחֵד לָהֶם מָקוֹם, דְּלָא חֲזוּ לִמְלָאכָה אַחֶרֶת: **גמ'** אוּכְלָא דְּקַצְרֵי. כְּלִי נְחוֹשֶׁת הֶעָשׂוּי כְּנָפָה נְקָבִים נְקָבִים, וְהוּא שֶׁל כּוֹבְסִים, וְנוֹתְנוֹ עַל הַבְּגָדִים, וּמְזַלֵּף בּוֹ הַמַּיִם עֲלֵיהֶן. וְי"מ: שֶׁמְּגַמְּרִין מוּגְמָר מִתַּחְתָּיו, וְהַבְּגָדִים מוּנָּחִין עָלָיו וּמִתְגַּמְּרִין דֶּרֶךְ הַנְּקָבִים: חַרְבָּא דְּאוּשְׁכָּפֵי. סַכִּין שֶׁל רַצְעָנִין: וְסַכִּינָא דְּאַשְׁכַּבְתָּא. סַכִּין שֶׁל בֵּית הַמַּקּוּלִין שֶׁהַקַּצָּבִין מְקַצְּבִין בּוֹ בָּשָׂר: חֲצִינָא. דולויר"א. כָּל הָנֵי קָפְדִי עֲלַיְיהוּ מִשּׁוּם דְּמִפַּגְמִי, וּמַקְלֵי לְהוּ בְּיָדַיִם: ג' כֵּלִים. וְתוּ לָא. וּלְקַמָּן אָמְרִינַן דְּבִימֵי נְחֶמְיָה בֶּן חֲכַלְיָה בְּבַיִת שֵׁנִי גָּזְרוּ עַל טִלְטוּל כָּל הַכֵּלִים, כְּדֵי לְגוֹדוֹר גָּדֵר לְהַחְמִיר בְּאִיסּוּרֵי שַׁבָּת, חוֹפְגֵי שֶׁהָיוּ מְקִילִין בָּהּ: מַקְצוּעַ. אִיזְמֵל שֶׁמְּחַתְּכִין בּוֹ דְּבֵלָה. "יַעֲשֵׂהוּ בַּמַּקְצוּעוֹת" מְתַרְגְּמִינַן: בְּאִיזְמֵלַיָּא (ישעיהו מד): זוּהֲמָא לִסְטְרוֹן. כַּף גְּדוֹלָה שֶׁמְּסַלְּקִין בּוֹ זוּהֲמָא שֶׁל קְדֵרָה: וְסַכִּין קָטָן. שֶׁחוֹתְכִין בּוֹ לֶחֶם וּבָשָׂר וִירָקוֹת. דְּהָנֵי תְּדִירִין בְּתַשְׁמִישׁ: הִתִּירוּ. עוֹד, כְּשֶׁרָאוּ שֶׁחָזְרוּ לְהִזָּהֵר קְצָת בְּאִיסּוּר שַׁבָּת. וְחָזְרוּ וְהִתִּירוּ כְּשֶׁנִּזְהֲרוּ יוֹתֵר, וְחָזְרוּ וְהִתִּירוּ. וּלְקַמֵּיהּ מְפָרֵשׁ מַאי כּוּלְּהוּ הָנָךְ "הִתִּירוּ": עַד שֶׁאָמְרוּ. עוֹד חָזְרוּ וְהִתִּירוּ אֶת הַכֹּל, עַד שֶׁאָמְרוּ: "הַכֹּל נִיטָּלִין חוּץ מִן הַמַּסָּר הַגָּדוֹל" כו': הִתִּירוּ. לְטַלְטֵל דָּבָר שֶׁעִיקַּר מְלַאכְתּוֹ בְּחוֹל לְהֶיתֵּר, לְדָבָר הַמּוּתָּר בְּשַׁבָּת הִתִּירוּ לְטַלְטֵל לְצוֹרֶךְ גּוּפוֹ, אִם הוּצְרַךְ לְהִשְׁתַּמֵּשׁ בְּגוּף הַכְּלִי, אֲבָל לֹא מִשּׁוּם שֶׁהוּצְרַךְ לִמְקוֹמוֹ: וְחָזְרוּ וְהִתִּירוּ. אֶת אֵלּוּ לְצוֹרֶךְ מְקוֹמוֹ: וְחָזְרוּ וְהִתִּירוּ אַף מִי שֶׁמְּלַאכְתּוֹ לְאִיסּוּר. וְהוּצְרַךְ לוֹ בַּשַּׁבָּת לְגוּפוֹ לִמְלֶאכֶת הֶיתֵּר, וּמֵיהוּ לֹא הוּתְּרוּ אֵלּוּ לְצוֹרֶךְ מְקוֹמוֹ: כָּל הַכֵּלִים. חַלָּלוּ שֶׁאָמַרְנוּ חוּץ מִן הַמַּסָּר הַגָּדוֹל, דְּלָא שָׁרֵי לָא לְצוֹרֶךְ גּוּפוֹ וְלָא לְצוֹרֶךְ מְקוֹמוֹ. וְאַבַּיֵי דִּמְתָרֵץ הָכִי הֲדַר בֵּיהּ לְגַבֵּי רַבָּה, דְּאָמַר לְעֵיל: קוּרְנָס שֶׁל נַפָּחִים שָׁנִינוּ, דְּדָבָר שֶׁמְּלַאכְתּוֹ לְאִיסּוּר – שָׁרֵי לְצוֹרֶךְ גּוּפוֹ: א"ל רָבָא מִכְּדֵי. לְצוֹרֶךְ הִתִּירוּ בְּפַעַם רִאשׁוֹנָה: מַה לִּי גּוּפוֹ מַה לִּי מְקוֹמוֹ. תַּרְוַויְיהוּ לְצוֹרֶךְ נִינְהוּ: מֵחַמָּה לַצֵּל. [illegible] עַד שֶׁאָמְרוּ. [illegible] כָּל הַכֵּלִים אֲפִילּוּ גְּדוֹלִים. [illegible] וגו': קָנִים וּמַקְלוֹת כו'. מִשְׁנָיוֹת הֵן, כִּדְמְפָרֵשׁ וְאָזֵיל: קוֹדֶם הַתָּרַת כֵּלִים. מִנְיָן הָאַחֲרוֹן, שֶׁהוּתְּרוּ כּוּלָּן לְצוֹרֶךְ גּוּפָן לְאַבַּיֵי, וּלְרָבָא אַף לְצוֹרֶךְ מְקוֹמוֹ: לֹא סִידּוּר הַקָּנִים. שֶׁהָיוּ נוֹתְנִין בַּמַּעֲרֶכֶת לֶחֶם הַפָּנִים בֵּין חַלָּה לְחַלָּה, לְהַפְרִידָן לִיכָּנֵס הָרוּחַ בֵּינֵיהֶן שֶׁלֹּא יִתְעַפְּשׁוּ: וְלֹא נְטִילָתָן. מִן הַמַּעֲרָכָה יְשָׁנָה: דּוֹחֶה אֶת הַשַּׁבָּת. אֶלָּא נִכְנָס בְּע"ש וְנוֹטֵל הַקָּנִים, וּלְמָחָר מְסַלֵּק הַמַּעֲרָכָה הַיְשָׁנָה וּמְסַדֵּר הַחֲדָשָׁה בְּלֹא קָנִים, וּלְמוֹצָאֵי שַׁבָּת נִכְנָס וְנוֹתֵן הַקָּנִים בֵּינֵיהֶן – זוֹ נִשְׁנֵית קוֹדֶם הֶיתֵּר מִנְיָן הָרִאשׁוֹן, דְּהָא מְלַאכְתָּן לְהֶיתֵּר, וְקָאָסַר לְהוּ לְצוֹרֶךְ גּוּפָן: מַקְלוֹת דַּקִּין וַחֲלָקִין הָיוּ. בָּעֲזָרָה, בְּפֶסַח שֶׁחָל לִהְיוֹת י"ד בְּחוֹל:

תוספות

וסכינא דאשכבתא. פירש בקונטרס: סכין שהקצבים מקצבין בה בשר. וי"מ: סכין ששוחטין בה, שמקפיד שלא תיפגם. ויש ליזהר שלא לטלטלו אפי' לצורך גופו, דהוי כיתד של מחרישה, דאפי' ר"ש מודה כדאמרינן בסוף מכילתין (דף קנז.):

מקצוע של דבילה. לא חשיב אלא כלים דלאו בני קיבול, דהא פשיטא דכוסות וקערות וצלוחיות היו מטלטלין:

איתיביה אביי מדוכה. בשלמא לדידי מוקמינן לצורך מקומו. וה"מ לשנויי כר' נחמיה כדשני לעיל. ואביי נמי הוה ידע, דהא משני ליה רבה הכי לעיל, אלא פריך לרבא – אולי יאמר תירוץ אחר. ורבא לא בעי לשנויי כר' נחמיה, דלית הלכתא כוותיה. ורבה דמשני ליה כר' נחמיה – משום דמשמע ליה אין מטלטלין אותה בשום ענין: **הכא** נמי מחמה לצל. והא דנקט לקצב עליו בשר – אע"ג דלצורך גופו ומקומו נמי שרי – לאשמעינן דאפילו בהא פליגי ב"ש, דלא שרו מחמת שמחת יו"ט:

לא סידור קנים. אע"ג דאין שבות[א] במקדש, כמה שבותים אשכחן במקדש *שגזרו פעמים לצורך כי הכא בקנים ומקלות, לפי שהיו מחללים את השבת: *הרי היא ככל הכלים. אע"ג דקודם התרת כלים נשנית, איכא למימ' ככל הכלים – כעין כוסות וקערות: הא

גליון הש"ס: תוס' ד"ה לא וכו' אשכחן במקדש. ע"ל קנט ע"א תוס' ד"ה המוציא.

הגהות הב"ח: (א) תוס' ד"ה לא סידור וכו' דאין שבות. נ"ב ע"ל פרק המצניע דף צב ע"ב בתוס' ד"ה שרא זולתו. [illegible]

[חולין כה.] [לעיל פג: חגיגה כו: מנחות נו:] [בכורות לח.] לקמן קנז. עירובין לה. [גי' הערוך בערך אבל אובלא וע"ש פירוש בשני אופנים] [תוספ' פט"ו] [לקמן קכד.] ביצה יא. [תוספ' ביצה פ"א] מנחות צו. פסחים סד. [נ"ל ר' אלעזר אומר]

רבינו חננאל

ממטן למעלן אסיר. פי' אם יש לאדם פוגלא טמונה בתבן או אפילו בעפר תחתיו עומדת כעין נטועה ראשה טמונה ועליה מגולין עכשיו כשבא לנוטלה אם אוחזו בעלים ומושך הראש [illegible] זהו ממעלה למטה. אע"פ שנתבבה התבן והעפר משתרבב במקומו ויורד שרי אבל לאחוז קצה הראש הטמונה ולהגביה ממטה למעלה לא. אלמא שטלטול מן הצד שמיה טלטול. ומפרקינן הדר ביה מהאי. מחט [illegible] חדירה חרורה או עוקצה. פי' חדירה הנקב שלה. עוקצה ראשה הוא. [illegible]

אמר [illegible] אוכלא דקצרי [illegible] ואסור לטלטלה. אוכלא. אבן גדולה שנותן [illegible] ללבנה והיא שרויה במים ומכה עליו במזורי. מכה ומהפך ומכה. ועוד שורה ומכה. ואחרי שישלים שוטחה ומייבשה. ועוד חוזר ושורה אותה פעם אחר פעם עד שתתלבן היטב. וי"א [illegible] אותו ע"ג גחלים ומקטרן בגפרית הכלים ללבנן. אמר אביי חרבא דאושכפא. וסכינא דאשכבתא וחצינא דנגרי כיתד של מחרישה דמו ואסור לטלטלם. חרבא דאושכפי. איזמל של שכף [illegible] צורים. איזמלין חריפין. סכינא דאשכבתא. סכין המיוחדת לשחיטה בלבד. חצינא דנגרי הוא גרזן. והוא המעצד של חרש כיון דקפדי אפגמיהו קבע ליה מקום ומסיח דעתו [illegible] הללו וכיוצא בהן שהן מוקצה מחמת חסרון כיס אסור לטלטלן בשבת. והרי מפורש בסוף פרק מי שהחשיך דכולהו הני היינו טעמא דאסירי משום דמוקצה מחמת חסרון כיס נינהו. ואפילו [illegible] לדברי הכל כל הכלים ניטלין בשבת חוץ מן המסר הגדול ויתד של מחרישה. מקצוע של דבילה כלי ברזל שחותכין בו דבילה. זומליסטרון תרווד שמהפך בו הקדירה. כדתנן זומליס[illegible] המזלג וכו'. א"ר חנינא בימי נחמיה בן חכליה נשנית משנה זו דכתיב בימים ההמה ראיתי ביהודה דורכים גיתות בשבת. כיון שראום כך שהקילו בשבת אסרו להן כל הכלים ושרי להן [illegible]

רב נסים גאון

בשעה שמהפך בו זיתים הופכו ורואה בו. בגמ' דבני מערבא גרסי רבי ר' ינאי אמרי קנה שהתקינו להפך בו זיתים כיצד הוא יודע אם היה מלוכלך במשקה בידוע שנגמר מלאכת המעטן ואם לאו בידוע שלא נגמרה מלאכת המעטן אמר לון ר' לא תני שמואל אלא להיות שולה בו את הזיתים ומשום הכי אמרי דמקבל טומאה והואיל ובכלי קיבול דמי. אמר רב נחמן האי אוכלא דקצרי כיתד של מחרישה דמי אוכלא דקצרי הוא כלי שדומה לדלעת ומנוקב הוא כולו נקבין ובו מולפין מים להכובסים על הבגדים ומשכחת לה בפ' כל ישראל יש להם חלק (סנהדרין דף קג) אמרו אותו מנקבין אותו ככברה אמר אביי כאוכלא דקצרי:

ידו על כתף חברו. דלא מטלטלי מקלות: גלוסטרא. דתנן, רבי יהושע אמר: נגר שיש בראשו גלוסטרא שראשה עב וראוי לדוך בו שום ונועלין בו דלת: שומטה מפתח זה ותולה בחברו. ואע"ג דצריך לגופו, לתלותו בחברו ולנועלה בו – שומטו ע"י גרירה. אבל טלטול גמור לא, ואע"פ שמלאכתו להיתר לא שרי ליה לצורך גופו: מדוכה הא דאמרן. לעיל, אע"ג דשנייה רבה לעיל מחמה לצל ואביי שנייה לצורך מקומו, שינויי דחיקי נינהו, אלא קודם התרת כלים נשנו: קנים טעמא מאי. מסדרין אותם במערכה: משום איעפושי. דלא סמכינן אניסא, ומשום ההוא פורתא שהישנה מתעכבת בלא קנים מלילי שבת לשבת, והחדשה משבת למוצ"ש – לא מיעפשי: כדר"א. מניח ידו על כתף חבירו: שאינה מעורבת. שהרבה בתים פתוחים לה ולא עירבו. דכלים ששבתו בבתים אסור להוציאן לחצר, וששבתו בחצר מותר לטלטלן בחצר, שהחצר כולו רשות לעצמו הוא, והבתים מיוחדים לכל איש ביתו: תוך הפתח. שנטל הנגר משם: וקא מטלטל מנא דבית בחצר. הלכך שומטה אין, דטלטול מן הצד היא, אבל טלטול גמור – לא: מדוכה רבי נחמיה היא. דאמר* בעירובין (דף לה.): אפילו טלית ואפי' תרווד – אין ניטלין אלא לצורך תשמיש המיוחד: מתני' ה"ג במתניתין: כל הכלים ניטלין לצורך כו': גמ' מאי לצורך ומאי שלא לצורך אמר רבה כו'. לצורך דשרי תנא קמא – היינו דבר שמלאכתו להיתר, ומטלטלו לצורך גופו: שלא לצורך דבר שמלאכתו להיתר. ומטלטלו שלא לצורך גופו, אבל צריך למקומו: ודבר שמלאכתו לאיסור לצורך גופו. הוא דאישתראי אם צריך לו למלאכת היתר. אבל שלא לצורך גופו, ואע"ג דצריך למקומו – לא. ורבה לטעמיה, דאמר לעיל (דף קכג:) גבי קורנס של נפחים נמי מותר לצורך גופו: א"ל רבא כו' אלא אמר כו'. ולרבא דמוקי אליבא דרבי נחמיה, דלצורך גופו ולצורך מקומו מותר – ע"כ האי לצורך גופו כגון שזה התשמיש מיוחד לו, דתניא לקמן בפרק "חבית" (דף קמו.), רבי נחמיה אומר: אפילו תרווד ואפילו טלית אין ניטלין אלא לצורך תשמישן, וצורך מקומו נמי לרבא כצורך גופו ותשמישו דמי, ולרבה צורך גופו הוא דשרי רבי נחמיה, ודוקא לתשמיש המיוחד לו. ובין לרבה ובין לרבא דוקא דבר שמלאכתו להיתר, אבל דבר שמלאכתו לאיסור – אפילו לצורך גופו לא שרי רבי נחמיה. דהאי צורך גופו לאו תשמיש המיוחד לו הוא, דהא מיוחד למלאכת איסור: לרבה אליבא דרבי נחמיה. דאמר דבר שמלאכתו להיתר לצורך מקומו לא: הני קערות. לאחר אכילה, היכי מטלטלי להו לסלקן מלפניו? ואם לאו אין מטלטלין אותה. בשלמא לרבה – כגון דאין צריך לגופה [אלא למקומה], אלא לדידך אמאי? וכן בדלת. אוקימנא במסכת ביצה: וכן הדלת אין סומכין בבקעת, וביו"ט קיימי: והא בקעת ביו"ט מלאכתה להיתר היא. דלהסקה חזי וקיימא, וקאסר לטלטלה לצורך גופו למלאכה אחרת, וכל שכן לצורך מקומה: ומשני התם(ג): טעמא כיון דבשבת. אסור, דהא בקעת בשבת מלאכתה לאיסור היא, ביום טוב נמי אסור, גזירה י"ט אטו שבת: משילין פירות דרך ארובה ביום טוב. בהדיא תנן: "אבל לא בשבת". פירות השטוחים על הגג לייבשן, וראה גשמים ממשמשים ובאין – משילן לארץ דרך ארובת הגג, דלא טריחא מילתא, דנופלין מאליהן. אלמא דלא גזרינן. ופרכינן: ומי לא גזרינן, והתנן אין בין כו': לא קשיא הא. דתנן משילין, דשרי טירחא ביו"ט משום איבוד ממון – רבי יהושע היא, שהתיר להעלות בהמה בהערמה מן הבור: והא. דתנן אין בין כו' – ר"א היא: דאפשר בהערמה. דמיחזי כמאן דעביד לצורך יו"ט. אבל גבי משילין, דליכא הערמה לדמויי להתירא – לא:

אין

ידו על כתף חבירו, ויד חבירו על כתיפו, ותולה ומפשיט. גלוסטרא – דתנן*: [א]נגר שיש בראשו גלוסטרא, ר' יהושע אומר: שומטה מן פתח זה ותולה בחבירו בשבת, ר' טרפון אומר: הרי הוא ככל הכלים ומיטלטל בחצר. מדוכה – הא דאמרן. אמר רבה: ממאי? דילמא לעולם אימא לך – לאחר התרת כלים נשנו. קנים טעמא מאי – משום איעפושי, בהאי פורתא לא מיעפש. מקלות – אפשר כר' אלעזר. גלוסטרא – כדרבי ינאי, דאמר רבי ינאי: בחצר שאינה מעורבת עסקינן. רבי יהושע סבר: תוך הפתח כלפנים דמי, וקמטלטל מנא דבתים בחצר. ור' טרפון סבר: תוך הפתח כלחוץ דמי, ומנא דחצר בחצר קא מטלטל. מדוכה – ר' נחמיה היא.§ **מתני'** [ב]כל הכלים ניטלין לצורך ושלא לצורך, *ר' נחמיה אומר: אין ניטלין אלא לצורך.§ **גמ'** מאי לצורך ומאי שלא לצורך? אמר *רבה: לצורך – דבר שמלאכתו להיתר לצורך גופו. שלא לצורך – דבר שמלאכתו להיתר לצורך מקומו. ודבר שמלאכתו לאיסור, לצורך גופו – אין, לצורך מקומו – לא. ואתא רבי נחמיה למימר: ואפילו דבר שמלאכתו להיתר, לצורך גופו – אין, לצורך מקומו – לא. אמר ליה רבא: לצורך מקומו שלא לצורך קרית ליה?! אלא אמר רבא: [ג]לצורך – דבר שמלאכתו להיתר, בין לצורך גופו בין לצורך מקומו. שלא לצורך – ואפי' מחמה לצל. [ד]ודבר שמלאכתו לאיסור לצורך גופו ולצורך מקומו – אין, מחמה לצל – לא. ואתא רבי נחמיה למימר: ואפילו דבר שמלאכתו להיתר, לצורך גופו ולצורך מקומו – אין, מחמה לצל – לא. יתיב רב ספרא ורב אחא בר הונא ורב הונא בר חנינא ויתבי וקאמרי: לרבה אליבא דרבי נחמיה, הני קערות היכי מטלטלינן? אמר להו רב ספרא: מידי דהוה אגרף של רעי. אמר ליה אביי לרבה: למר, אליבא דרבי נחמיה הני קערות היכי מטלטלינן להו? אמר ליה: רב ספרא חברין תרגמה – מידי דהוה אגרף של רעי. איתיביה אביי לרבא*: מדוכה, אם יש בה שום – מטלטלין אותה, ואם לאו – אין מטלטלין אותה! הכא במאי עסקינן – מחמה לצל. איתיביה: *ושוין שאם קיצב עליו בשר שאסור לטלטלו! הכא נמי מחמה לצל. והא דתנן: *[ה]אין סומכין את הקדירה בבקעת, וכן בדלת. והא בקעת דביום טוב – דבר שמלאכתו להיתר הוא, אלמא: דבר שמלאכתו להיתר, בין לצורך גופו בין לצורך מקומו אסור! התם(א) מאי טעמא – כיון דבשבת דבר שמלאכתו לאיסור הוא, גזירה יו"ט אטו שבת. וכי תימא שבת גופיה תישתרי, דהא דבר שמלאכתו לאיסור לצורך גופו ולצורך מקומו שרי! [ו]הני מילי – היכא דאיכא תורת כלי עליו, היכא דליכא תורת כלי עליו – לא. [ז]ומי גזרינן? והתנן*: [ח]משילין פירות דרך ארובה ביום טוב, אבל לא בשבת. ומי לא גזרינן? והתנן*: [ט]אין בין יו"ט לשבת אלא אוכל נפש בלבד! אמר רב יוסף: לא קשיא. הא – ר' אליעזר, הא – רבי יהושע. *דתניא: אותו ואת בנו שנפלו לבור, ר' אליעזר אומר: מעלה את הראשון על מנת לשוחטו, ושוחטו, והשני עושה לו פרנסה במקומו בשביל שלא ימות. ר' יהושע אומר: מעלה את הראשון על מנת לשוחטו ואינו שוחטו, ומערים ומעלה את השני. רצה – זה שוחט, רצה – זה שוחט. *ממאי? דילמא עד כאן לא קאמר ר' אליעזר התם – אלא דאפשר לפרנסה, אבל היכא דלא אפשר לפרנסה – לא. אי נמי; עד כאן לא קאמר רבי יהושע התם – דאפשר בהערמה, אבל היכא דלא אפשר בהערמה – לא. אלא אמר רב פפא: לא קשיא, הא – בית שמאי, הא – בית הלל. דתנן, בית שמאי אומרים:

אין

הא ר"א. ההיא ד"אין בין" אע"ג דבפ"ק דמגילה (דף ז:) דייקינן עלה: הא לענין מכשירי אוכל נפש זה וזה שוין. וקאמר: מתני' דלא כרבי יהודה. ור"א סבירא ליה כר"י ועדיפא מדרבי יהודה, כדאמר בריש "תולין" (לקמן דף קלז:). איכא למימר דההוא תנא סבר לה כוותיה בחדא – דגזרינן י"ט אטו שבת, ופליג עליה במכשירין. ועוד יש לומר, ד"אין בין" דפ"ק דמגילה – מיירי במילי דאורייתא, ו"אין בין" דהכא – היינו דתנן ב"משילין" (ביצה ד' לז:) דמיירי במילי דשבות, ואינו מענין אחד. תדע, דהכי פריך עלה בפ' "משילין" כדפריך הכא בשמעתא, ולא פריך בפ"ק דמגילה. והא דדייק התם: "הא לענין מכשירין זה וזה שוין" – לא דייק בפרק משילין:

הא

מסורת הש"ס: כלים פי"א מ"ד [וכס ליתא להגך תיבות נגר שיש בראשו] | [לקמן קמו.] | [לעיל לו. וש"נ] | [לעיל קכג.] | [שם: ביצה יח.] | ביצה לב: | ביצה לה: לז. | ביצה לז. [תוספתא ביצה פ"ג] | [ביצה לז. ע"ש] | [גי' הרי"ף והרא"ש אביי] | לקמן קמז: ביצה לו: מגילה ז: [תוספתא דמגילה פ"א]

עין משפט נר מצוה

יח א מיי' פכ"ו מהלכות שבת הלכה ט סמג לאוין סה טוש"ע או"ח סימן שיג סעיף א:

יט ב ג מיי' פכ"ה שם הלכה ג סמג שם טוש"ע או"ח סימן שח סעיף ד:

כ ד מיי' שם טוש"ע שם סעיף ג:

כא ה מיי' פ"ד מהלכות יו"ט הלכה יא טור שו"ע או"ח סימן תקב סעיף ג:

כב ו מיי' פכ"ה מהל' שבת הלכה ו טוש"ע או"ח סימן שח סעיף ז:

כג ז מיי' פ"ה מהלכות יו"ט הלכה ה טור שו"ע או"ח סימן תקכא סעיף א:

כד ח טוש"ע או"ח סימן שלא סעיף ז:

כה ט מיי' פ"א מהלכות יו"ט הלכה א סמג לאוין עה טוש"ע או"ח סימן תצה סעיף א:

הגהות הב"ח

(א) גמ' התם היינו טעמא כיון דבשבת: (ב) רש"י ד"ה ומשני התם היינו טעמא:

גליון הש"ס

גמ' ומי גזרינן והתנן משילין. ע"ל דף כג ע"ב תוספות ד"ה גזירה:

רבינו חננאל

שאסור בשבת סידורן ונטולתן מתוך לחם הפנים. מקלות מפורש במס' פסחים. בזמן שחל י"ד להיות בשבת אסר ר' אלעזר לטלטל מקל ולהניחו על כתיפו ועל כתף חבירו לתלות הפסח בו ולהפשיטו. וכן גלוסטרא. היא משנה בכלים פ' י"א שאסר ר' יהושע לטלטלה בשבת. תוספתא דכלים בתחלת בב"מ קלוסטרא ר' טרפון מטמא וחכמים מטהרין. ברוריה אומר שומטה מפתח זה ותולה בחבירו בשבת. כשנאמרו דברים לפני ר' יהושע אמר יפה אמר ברוריה. והוא בענין הזה בעירובין בסופו. מדוכה זו שאמרנו למעלה אלו כולן כלים הן וקודם התרת כלים נשנו שאסור לטלטלן בשבת. *) אבל אחר התרת כלים מותרין הן וחלק רבא על רבי אלעזר ואמר דלמא אחר התרת כלים נשנו ואסורין הן לעולם. ודבריו פשוטין הן: **מתני'** כל הכלים הניטלין לצורך ניטלין לצורך ושלא לצורך כו'. פירש רבא משנה זו לצורך דבר שמלאכתו להיתר כגון קערות וכוסות וכדומה להן. שמותר לכתחלה לטלטלן לאכול ולשתות בהן הללו מותרין לטלטלן בין לצורך גופו לאכול בהן בין לצורך מקומו לפנותן כדי לישב במקומן. דבר שמלאכתו לאיסור כגון קורנס של נפחים וכדומה לו לצורך גופו לאכול בהן (מותר) [כגון] לפצוע בו אגוזין מותר. אבל לצורך מקומן אסור. ורבי נחמיה אמר אפילו דבר שמלאכתו להיתר כגון קערות וכדומה להן לצורך גופו לאכול בהן מותר. אבל אחר שיאכל בהן אסור לטלטלן [לצורך] מקומן. ועל זה הקשה ליה אביי לרבה למר אליבא דר' נחמי' הני קערות כלומר שאינו מטלטלן אלא לצורך אכילה בהן אחר שיאכל אדם היאך מטלטלן ומסלקן מן השולחן. והשיבו לו כבר נתקשה זה לרב ספרא חברין. ופירק מידי דהוה אגרף של רעי שמותר לטלטל לדברי הכל. דתניא בתוספתא גרף של רעי ושל מימי רגלים נוטלן ושופכן וכו'. ובזמן שאמר רבה דברים הללו השיבו רבא לצורך מקומו שלא לצורך קרית ליה. אלא אמר לצורך דבר שמלאכתו להיתר בין לצורך גופו בין לצורך מקומו. שלא לצורך אפילו מחמה לצל. ודבר שמלאכתו לאיסור לצורך גופו ולצורך מקומו אין. מחמה לצל לא. ואתא ר' נחמיה למימר דאפילו דבר שמלאכתו להיתר לצורך גופו ולצורך מקומו אין. מחמה לצל לא. מותיב אביי (לרבה) [לרבא] לדידך דאמרת דבר שמלאכתו לאיסור אפילו לצורך מקומו מטלטל והרי מדוכה שאינה מטלטלת אלא לצורך גופה אם יש בה שום. אבל אין בה שום לצורך מקומה אסור לטלטלו ופירק ליה הכא במאי עסקינן בשצריך לטלטלה להסירה מן החמה שלא תיבקע ולהניחה בצל. וכן שאר השמועה כולה פשוטה

היא

*) דברי רבינו כמות שהם אין להם הבנה ונראה דצ"ל אבל רבה אמר דלאחר התרת כלים וכו'.

כו א מיי' פ"א מהלכות יו"ט הלכה ד סמג לאוין עה טוש"ע או"ח סימן תקית סעיף ח:
כז ב מיי' פכ"ה מהלכו' שבת הלכה ג סמג לאוין סה טוש"ע או"ח סימן שח סעיף ג:
כח ג מיי' פכ"ו שם הלכה ב סמג שם טוש"ע שם סעיף מט:
[ביצה לב. ע"ש וכפרש"י שם]
כט ד מיי' פכ"ה מהלכו' שבת הלכה יב סמג שם טוש"ע או"ח סימן שח סעיף ו:
ל ה מיי' פכ"ו שם הלכה ב טוש"ע או"ח סימן שח סעיף יז:
לא ו ז ח מיי' שם הל' ג טוש"ע שם סעיף ז:
[גי' הרי"ף והרא"ש דבאביי]

*אין מוציאין את הקטן ואת הלולב ואת ספר תורה לרה"ר, ובית הלל [א]מתירין. אימר דשמעת להו לבית שמאי הוצאה – טלטול מי שמעת להו?! *ומלטול *גופיה, לאו משום הוצאה היא?! ואף רב סבר לה להא דרבא, דאמר רב: [ב]מר שלא יגנב – זהו טלטול שלא לצורך, ואסור. טעמא – שלא יגנב, אבל לצורך גופו ולצורך מקומו – מותר. איני?! והא רב כהנא איקלע לבי רב, ואמר: אייתו ליה שותא לכהנא ליתיב עליה. לאו למימרא דדבר שמלאכתו לאיסור לצורך גופו – אין, לצורך מקומו – לא? הכי אמר להו: שקולו שותא מקמי כהנא, ואי בעית אימא: התם מחמה לצל הוה. רב מרי בר רחל הוה ליה ההיא בי סדיותא בשמשא. אתא לקמיה דרבא. אמר ליה: מהו לטלטולינהו? אמר ליה: שרי. אית לי אחרינא. חזו לאורחין. אית לי נמי לאורחים. אמר ליה: גלית אדעתיך *דכרבה סבירא לך, *לכולי עלמא – שרי, לדידך – אסיר. אמר רבי אבא אמר רבי חייא בר אשי [ג]אמר רב: מכבדות של מילתא – מותר לטלטלן בשבת, אבל של תמרה – לא. רבי אלעזר אומר: אף של תמרה. במאי עסקינן? אילימא לצורך גופו ולצורך מקומו – בהא לימא רב "של תמרה לא"? והא רב כרבא סבירא ליה! אלא מחמה לצל, בהא לימא ר' אלעזר "אף של תמרה"?! [א]לעולם מחמה לצל, אימא: וכן אמר רבי אלעזר.§ **מתני'** *[ד]כל הכלים הניטלין בשבת – שבריהן ניטלין עמהן, ובלבד שיהו עושין מעין מלאכה. שברי עריבה – לכסות בהן את פי החבית, שברי זכוכית – לכסות בהן את פי הפך. רבי יהודה אומר: בלבד שיהו עושין מעין מלאכתן; שברי עריבה – לצוק לתוכן מקפה, ושל זכוכית – לצוק לתוכן שמן.§ **גמ'** אמר רב יהודה אמר שמואל: מחלוקת שנשברו מערב שבת, דמר סבר: מעין מלאכתן – אין, מעין מלאכה אחרת – לא. ומר סבר: אפילו מעין מלאכה אחרת. אבל נשברו בשבת – דברי הכל מותרין. הואיל ומוכנין על גבי אביהן – מותר. מותיב רב זוטראי: *מסיקין בכלים ואין מסיקין בשברי כלים. דנשברו אימת? אילימא דנשברו מערב יום טוב – עצים בעלמא נינהו! אלא לאו – ביום טוב, וקתני "מסיקין בכלים ואין מסיקים בשברי כלים"! אלא, אי איתמר הכי איתמר, אמר רב יהודה אמר שמואל: מחלוקת שנשברו בשבת, דמר סבר: מוכן הוא, ומר סבר: נולד הוא. אבל מערב שבת – דברי הכל מותרין הואיל והוכנו למלאכה מבעוד יום. תני חדא: מסיקין בכלים ואין מסיקין בשברי כלים. ותניא אידך: *כשם שמסיקין בכלים כך מסיקין בשברי כלים. ותניא אידך: אין מסיקין לא בכלים ולא בשברי כלים. הא – רבי יהודה, הא – רבי שמעון, הא – רבי נחמיה. *אמר רב נחמן: [ה]הני ליבני דאישתיור מבנייגא – שרי לטלטולינהו, דחזו למיזגא עלייהו. שרגינהו – ודאי אקצינהו. אמר רב נחמן אמר שמואל: [ו]חרס קטנה מותר לטלטל בחצר, אבל בכרמלית – לא. ורב נחמן דידיה אמר: אפילו בכרמלית, אבל ברה"ר – לא. ורבא אמר: [ז]אפילו ברה"ר. ואזדא רבא לטעמיה; דרבא הוה קאזיל בריתקא דמחוזא, אתווסאי מסאניה טינא, אתא שמעיה שקל חספא וקא מכפר ליה, רמו ביה רבנן קלא. אמר: לא מיסתייא דלא גמירי, מיגמר נמי מגמרי?! אילו בחצר הואי – מי לא הוה חזיא לכסויי ביה מנא? הכא נמי – חזיא לדידי. אמר רב יהודה אמר שמואל: מגופת חבית שנכתתה(א) – מותר לטלטל בשבת. תניא נמי הכי: *מגופה שנכתתה – היא ושבריה מותר לטלטלה בשבת, ולא *יספות ממנה שבר לכסות בה את הכלי ולסמוך בה כרעי המטה, ואם זרקה באשפה – אסור. מתקיף לה רב פפא: אלא מעתה, זריק ליה לגלימיה – ה"נ דאסור? [ח]אלא אמר רב פפא:
אם

רש"י

אין מוציאין. הוצאה שלא לצורך, דלא אישתרי לכתחילה ביו"ט טפי מדשבת אלא אוכל נפש, והך דמשלין – ב"ה: טלטול מי שמעת להו. דמשוי יו"ט לשבת: טלטול לאו לצורך הוצאה. בתמיה. הלכך: אי מזלזלת בטלטול – מזלזלת בהוצאה: להא דרבא. דאמר: לצורך מקומו כלצורך גופו: מר. פוסו"ר: שלא יגנב. דומיא דמחמה לצל, ואסור בדבר שמלאכתו לאיסור: שותא.(ב) מגודה: לאו למימרא כו'. למה לי לפרושי בהדיא דליתיב עלה – לאו משום למימרא דהאי דשרי לטלטולי משום דצורך גופו הוא? שקילו שותא מקמיה כהנא. דניתוב על מקומה קאמר, ולצורך מקומה הוא דהוה: מחמה לצל הוה. במקום הרע לה היתה, ואי לאו דפריש בהדיא ליתיב עלה – מאן דחזי סבר דמחמה לצל שרי, ולמקומה לא היה צריך, דלימא שיישב במקומה: בי סדיותא. כרים של בגד, שקורין פילטר"א: בי שמשי. בחמה: אמר ליה שרי. רבא לטעמיה, דאמר: דבר שמלאכתו להיתר – אף מחמה לצל מותר: אית לי אחריני. איני צריך לגופו: דכרבה סבירא לך. דאמר: מחמה לצל אסור, והלכה כרבא דאמר דבר שמלאכתו להיתר שרי לגמרי, ודבר שמלאכתו לאיסור – לצורך גופו ומקומו מותר, מחמה לצל ושלא יגנב אסור: מכבדות. איסקוב"א, שמכבדים בהן את השולחן: של מילתא.(ג) בגדים לכבד שולחן, שמלאכתו להיתר: של תמרה. כעין שלנו, לכבד את הבית, דאסור משום אשוויי גומות, דמודה רבי שמעון בפסיק רישיה ולא ימות: לצורך גופו. למלאכת היתר: אלא מחמה לצל בהא לימא רבי אלעזר אף של תמרה. דבר שמלאכתו לאיסור, ליכא מאן דשרי מחמה לצל: וכן אמר ר' אלעזר. של מילתא מותר, של תמרה אסור מחמה לצל: **מתני'** מעין מלאכה. שום מלאכה, ואפילו אינה מעין הראשונה: לצוק לתוכה מקפה. עבה, דומיא דעיסה מעורבת במים: **גמ'** הואיל ומוכנין על גבי אביהן. כשקדש היום: מסיקין בכלים. ביו"ט, שהרי ראוין לטלטל, ויטלטל ויתנס לתוך האור: ואין מסיקין בשברי כלים. דהוו להו מוקצין, ולא חזו לטלטול: עצים בעלמא נינהו. דהא מאתמול להסקה קיימי: וקתני אין מסיקין. ולא אמרינן מוכנין היו אגב אביהן, אלא אמרינן: נולד נינהו, ואסירי: מר סבר מוכן הוא. כיון דראוי לשום מלאכה. ומר סבר: נולד הוה, דמאתמול לאו להאי מלאכה הוה קאי. הלכך: מעין מלאכתו בעינן: הא רבי יהודה. "מסיקין בכלים ואין מסיקין בשברי כלים", דאית ליה מוקצה ונולד, כלים – לאו מוקצה נינהו, שברים – נולד נינהו: והא. דתני מסיקין בשניהם: רבי שמעון. דלית ליה מוקצה ולית ליה נולד: והא. דתניא אף בכלים אין מסיקין: רבי נחמיה היא. דאמר: אין כלי ניטל אלא לצורך תשמישו המיוחד לו, והאי לאו מיוחד הוא לו, דלאו להסקה קאי: דאישתיור. שהשלים בניינו וניתותר, ומהשתא לא קיימי לבנין אלא לישב עליהם, ותורת כלי עליהם: שרגינהו. אי סדרן זו על זו, ודאי אקצינהו לצורך בנין אחר: בחצר. דשכיחי בה כלים, שהחרס הזה ראוי להם לכיסוי, ותורת כלי עליו: אבל לא בכרמלית. אפי' בתוך ד' אמות, דלא שכיחי ביה מאני, ולא חזי לכסויי: אפילו בכרמלית. הואיל ולאו רה"ר הוא, שכיחי דאזלי ויתבי התם, וחזי לכסות בו רוק: ורבא אמר אף ברה"ר. כיון דמעיקר כלי הוא – בעלמא נמי לא פקע שם כלי מיניה: בריתקא. שם רה"ר: איתווסאי מסאניה טינא. נתלכלך מנעלו בטיט: כפר ליה. מקנחו: אמר רבא לא מסתייה דלא גמירי. מה אסור מה מותר: אלא מיגמר נמי מגמרי. מלמדין שיבוש שבידם לאחרים: לדידי. לקינוח, ואע"ג דלא שכיח – הרי שם כלי עליו מעיקר: שנתכתתה. החבית:(ד) מגופה. של חבית, שנתכתתה החבית: היא. המגופה: ושבריה. של חבית, ניטלין בשבת, דחזו לכיסוי מנא: לא יספות.(ה) יתקן, להסיר בליטותיו ועוקציו בשבת, דעביד כלי, והוי מכה בפטיש: ואם זרק. מגופה זו לאשפה – בטלה מתורת כלי: זרקיה לגלימיה. בשבת לאשפה, ה"נ דאסור לטלטולי?!
מבעוד

תוספות

הא רבי נחמיה. דסבירא ליה דאין כלי ניטל אלא לצורך תשמישו הרגיל בחול, כדמפרש בפרק "במה מדליקין", (לעיל דף לו.) והאי נמי – אין רגיל בחול לשרוף אותו: **ורבא** אמר אפילו ברה"ר. והני דנשברו בע"ש קאמר, דאי בנשברו בשבת האמר בפרק נוטל (לקמן דף קמג:) דרבא אית ליה מוקצה וכל שכן נולד:
אם

ביצה יב. לז.
ס"א אטו טלטול לאו צורך הוצאה היא
[ע"ז כח:]
חולין יד:
לעיל כח: כט. לקמן קמג. ביצה לב.
ביצה שם
ביצה לג.
[תוספ' פט"ו]
[ערוך בערך ספת פי' לא יתחוך. פי' אחר לא יתחבר]

רבינו חננאל

היא והלכתא כרבנן וכדמוקים לה רבה. דהכין סוגיא דשמעתא כולה. וזה שאמר רב שקולו שיתא מקמי כהנא. פי' שיתא שריתא והיא קורה כדמתרגמינן בצל קורתי בטלל שירותי. וי"א חבילה. וי"א רשת כדכתיב ויפרשו עליו גוים בשחתם נתפש. ושיתא היא שחתא. פי' מכבדת מטאטא שמכבדין הבית בהן. הנהו בי סדוותא. פי' כסתות והוא כגון כרים וכסתות: **מתני'** כל הכלים הניטלין בשבת שבריהן ניטלין [עמהן] ובלבד שיהו עושין מעין מלאכה וכו'. ר' יהודה אומר ובלבד שיהו עושין מעין מלאכתן כו'. פי' מקפה. מרק. בא רב יהודה משמיה דשמואל להעמיד מחלוקת ר' יהודה ות"ק כשנשברו מע"ש. ולא עמד אלא כשנשברו בשבת. דת"ק סבר מוכן הוא. ור' יהודה סבר מעין מלאכה או[ת]ו כנולד הוא כדמפרש בגמרא דהכל שוחטין. אבל מע"ש דברי הכל מותרין. ואפילו לר' יהודה הואיל והוכנו למלאכה אחרת מבעו"י ואינו כנולד בשבת וקיי"ל כרבנן. וכלישנא בתרא דשמואל בין נשברו בשבת בין נשברו מע"ש. מעין מלאכה סגיא. תני חדא מסיקין בכלים ואין מסיקין בשברי כלים. פירוש בקעת שברי עצים שמסיקין בהן כדכתיב ויבקע עצי עולה. ותניא אידך כשם שמסיקין בכלים כך מסיקין בשברי כלים. ותניא אידך אין מסיקין לא בכלים ולא בשברי כלים לא קשיא הא ר' יהודה הא ר"ש הא ר' נחמיה. הא דתני אין מסיקין בשברי כלים ר' יהודה דמתניתין היא דחשיב בשברי כלים בנולד. והא דתני מסיקין בזה ובזה ר"ש היא דלית ליה מוקצה. ומיפרשא בגמ' דבמה מדליקין. והא דתני אין מסיקין לא בזה ולא בזה ר' נחמיה היא דאמר אין כלי ניטל אלא לצורך תשמישו. ומפורש במס' יו"ט פרק המביא כדי יין. והא דאמר רב נחמן אמר שמואל לענין ליבני דאישתייר מבניינא שרגינהו אקצינהו אפילו לר' שמעון דהני כגרוגרות וכצמוקים דמו. דאית ליה מוקצה. וזה שאמר חרס קטנה מותר לטלטלה בחצר. הואיל וראוי לכסות בו כלי שבחצר. אבל בכרמלית שאין בו כלי לא ורב נחמן סבר כיון שהמוציא מרשות הרבים לכרמלית או המכנים אינו חייב זמנין דעייל ליה לחצר וחזי ליה. ורבא סבר אפילו ברה"ר חזי לכפורי ביה טינא ושרי לטלטולי בטעמיה. וזה שאמר רב יהודה אמר שמואל מגופת חבית שנכתתה מותר לטלטלה. פי' מגופת כסוי שסותם פי החבית מלשון יגיפו הדלתות [ולא יספות]. פי' לא יתחתך הוא. כדתנן סופת באבטיח. ותניא נמי הכי כולן פשוטות הן.

הגהות הגר"א

[א] גמ' לעולם מחמה לצל. נ"ב גי' הגאונים והרא"ש כר"ש סבירא ליה דדבר שאין מתכוין מותר:

הגהות הב"ח

(א) גמ' אמר שמואל מגופת חבית שנכתתה היא ושבריה מותר וכו' מגופת חבית שנכתתה: (ב) רש"י ד"ה שותא מגודה. נ"ב וכן פי' בעל המאור על הסוגא שותא דהוו מגנו עלה בי תרי דפ' הגוזל ומאכיל דף קיז א' אבל הכא פי' כמו שריתא דהיינו קורה כמו הסוגא שריתא דבי ר' פדת דפ' המוצא תפילין דף קב ע"א: (ג) ד"ה של מילתא של בגדים הס"ד ואח"כ מ"ה מותר לכבד בהן השלחן: (ד) ד"ה שנתכתתה החבית (מגופה וכו' החבית) תא"מ ונ"ב ס"א אין זה: (ה) ד"ה לא יספות לא יתקן להסיר:

רב נסים גאון

הא ר' יהודה והא ר' שמעון והא ר' נחמיה. דברי ר' יהודה ור"ש בפרק במה מדליקין (דף כט) אמר רב יהודה אמר רב מסיקין בכלים ואין מסיקין בשברי כלים דברי ר' יהודה ור' שמעון מתיר ודברי ר' נחמיה הן שנאמרו כן במשנה ר' נחמיה אומר אין ניטלין אלא לצורך וכמו שתירץ רבא ואמר ואתא ר' נחמיה למימר אפילו דבר שמלאכתו להיתר לצורך גופו ולצורך מקומו אין אבל מחמה לצל לא ובתוספתא (פט"ו) ר' נחמיה אומר אפילו טליתו ואפילו תרווד אין ניטלין אלא לצורך בברייתא שנאמר בה אין מסיקין לא בכלים ולא בשברי כלים הן דברי ר' נחמיה ובמס' יו"ט בפרק המביא כדי יין (דף לג) הזכירו עוד זה הדבר ואמרו תרי תנאי ואליבא דר' נחמיה כלומר קצת התנאים סוברין כי ר' (יהודה) [נחמיה] שאני ליה בין שבות שבת לשבות יום טוב:

דתנן

עין משפט נר מצוה

לב א מיי' פכ"ו מהל' שבת הלכה ח טור שו"ע או"ח סימן שח סעיף יב:
לג ב מיי' שם טוש"ע שם סעיף יג:
לד ג מיי' שם הל' יד:
לה ד מיי' פכ"ה מהל' שבת הלכה יג טור שו"ע או"ח סימן שח סעיף י:
לו ה מיי' פט"ו מהלכות כלים הלכה ח:
לז ו מיי' פכ"ה מהלכות שבת הלכה יח טוש"ע או"ח סימן שט סעיף ב:

גמרא

אִם זְרָקָהּ מִבְּעוֹד יוֹם לְאַשְׁפָּה – אֲסוּרָה. אָמַר בַּר הַמְּדוֹרִי אָמַר שְׁמוּאֵל: [א]קְרוּמִיּוֹת שֶׁל מַחְצֶלֶת מוּתָּר לְטַלְטְלָם בְּשַׁבָּת. מ"ט? אָמַר רָבָא, בַּר הַמְּדוֹרִי אַסְבְּרָא לִי: מַחְצֶלֶת גּוּפָא לְמַאי חַזְיָא – לְכַסּוּיֵי בֵּיהּ עַפְרָא, הָנֵי נַמִי חַזְיָין לְכַסּוּיֵי בְּהוּ טִינּוּפֶת. א"ר זֵירָא אָמַר רַב: *שְׁיָרֵי פְּרוֹזְמִיּוֹת אָסוּר לְטַלְטְלָן בְּשַׁבָּת. *אָמַר אַבַּיֵי: [ב]בִּמְטַלְּנִיּוֹת שֶׁאֵין בָּהֶן ג' עַל ג', דְּלָא חַזְיָין לֹא לַעֲנִיִּים וְלֹא לַעֲשִׁירִים.§ ת"ר: *[ג]שִׁבְרֵי תַּנּוּר יָשָׁן הֲרֵי הֵן כְּכָל הַכֵּלִים הַנִּיטָּלִין בֶּחָצֵר. דִּבְרֵי ר"מ. ר' יְהוּדָה אוֹמֵר: אֵין נִיטָּלִין. הֵעִיד ר' יוֹסֵי מִשּׁוּם ר"א בֶּן יַעֲקֹב: עַל שִׁבְרֵי תַּנּוּר יָשָׁן שֶׁנִּיטָּלִין בַּשַּׁבָּת, וְעַל [ד]כִּיסּוּיוֹ שֶׁאֵינוֹ צָרִיךְ בֵּית יָד. בְּמַאי קָמִיפַּלְגִי? אָמַר אַבַּיֵי: בְּעוֹשִׂין מֵעֵין מְלָאכָה, וְאֵין עוֹשִׂין מֵעֵין מְלַאכְתָּן קָמִיפַּלְגִי, וְאַזְדָּא ר' יְהוּדָה לְטַעְמֵיהּ, וְר"מ לְטַעְמֵיהּ. מַתְקִיף לַהּ רָבָא: אִי הָכִי, אַדְּמִיפַּלְגִי בְּשִׁבְרֵי תַנּוּר – לִיפַּלְגוּ בְּשִׁבְרֵי כֵלִים בְּעָלְמָא! אֶלָּא אָמַר רָבָא: בְּשִׁבְרֵי דְּהַאי תַּנּוּר קָמִיפַּלְגִי, דִּתְנַן: *[ה]נְתָנוֹ עַל פִּי הַבּוֹר אוֹ עַל פִּי הַדּוּת וְנָתַן שָׁם אֶבֶן, רַבִּי יְהוּדָה אוֹמֵר: אִם מַסִּיק מִלְּמַטָּה וְהוּא נִסּוֹק מִלְּמַעְלָה – טָמֵא, וְאִם לָאו – טָהוֹר. וַחֲכָמִים אוֹמְרִים: הוֹאִיל וְהוּסַּק מ"מ טָמֵא. וּבְמַאי קָמִיפַּלְגִי – בְּהַאי קְרָא: °"תַּנּוּר וְכִירַיִם יוּתָּץ טְמֵאִים הֵם וּטְמֵאִים יִהְיוּ לָכֶם". רַבִּי יְהוּדָה סָבַר: מְחוּסַּר נְתִיצָה – טָמֵא, שֶׁאֵין מְחוּסַּר נְתִיצָה – טָהוֹר. וְרַבָּנַן סָבְרִי: "טְמֵאִים יִהְיוּ לָכֶם" – מ"מ. וְרַבָּנַן נַמִי, הָכְתִיב "יוּתָּץ"! הַהוּא לְאִידָךְ גִּיסָא. דְּסָלְקָא דַּעְתָּךְ אָמִינָא: כֵּיוָן דְּחַבְּרֵיהּ בְּאַרְעָא – כְּגוּפָא דְאַרְעָא דָּמֵי, קמ"ל. וְאִידָךְ נַמִי, הָכְתִיב: "טְמֵאִים יִהְיוּ לָכֶם"! הַהִיא כִּדְרַב יְהוּדָה אָמַר שְׁמוּאֵל, דְּאָמַר רַב יְהוּדָה אָמַר שְׁמוּאֵל: מַחֲלוֹקֶת בְּהֶיסֵּק רִאשׁוֹן, אֲבָל בְּהֶיסֵּק שֵׁנִי – אֲפִילּוּ תָּלוּי בְּצַוַּאר גָּמָל. אָמַר עוּלָּא: וְהֶיסֵּק רִאשׁוֹן לְרַבָּנַן – אֲפִילּוּ תָּלוּי בְּצַוַּאר גָּמָל. מַתְקִיף לַהּ רַב אַשִׁי: אִי הָכִי, אַדְּמִיפַּלְגִי בְּשִׁבְרֵי תַנּוּר – לִיפַּלְגוּ בְּתַנּוּר גּוּפֵהּ! הַשְׁתָּא תַּנּוּר גּוּפֵהּ – לְרַבִּי יְהוּדָה לָא הָוֵי מָנָא, שְׁבָרָיו מִיבַּעְיָא?! אֶלָּא אָמַר רַב אַשִׁי: לְעוֹלָם כִּדַאֲמַרַן מֵעִיקָּרָא, וּבְעוֹשֶׂה מַעֲשֵׂה טַפְקָא; וְרַבִּי מֵאִיר לְדִבְרָיו דְּרַבִּי יְהוּדָה קָאָמַר: לְדִידִי – אֲפִילּוּ בְּעוֹשִׂין מֵעֵין מְלָאכָה, אֶלָּא לְדִידָךְ – אוֹדִי לִי מִיהָא דְּכְהַאי גַּוְונָא מְלַאכְתּוֹ הוּא. וְרַבִּי יְהוּדָה – לָא דָּמֵי, הָתָם – הֶסֵּקוֹ מִבִּפְנִים, הָכָא – הֶסֵּקוֹ מִבַּחוּץ, הָתָם – מְעוּמָּד, הָכָא – לָאו מְעוּמָּד.§ "הֵעִיד ר' יוֹסֵי מִשּׁוּם רַבִּי אֱלִיעֶזֶר בֶּן יַעֲקֹב עַל שִׁבְרֵי תַנּוּר יָשָׁן שֶׁנִּיטָּלִין בַּשַּׁבָּת וְעַל כִּיסּוּיוֹ שֶׁאֵינוֹ צָרִיךְ בֵּית יָד".§ אָמַר רָבִינָא: כְּמַאן מְטַלְטְלִינַן הָאִידָּנָא כִּיסּוּי דְּתַנּוּרֵי דְּמָתָא מְחַסְיָא דְּאֵין לָהֶם בֵּית אֲחִיזָה, כְּמַאן – כר"א בֶּן יַעֲקֹב.§

מתני' [ו]הָאֶבֶן שֶׁבַּקֵּירוּיָה, אִם מְמַלְּאִין בָּהּ וְאֵינָהּ נוֹפֶלֶת – מְמַלְּאִין בָּהּ, וְאִם לָאו – אֵין מְמַלְּאִין בָּהּ. זְמוֹרָה

(ויקרא יא)

רש"י

מִבְּעוֹד יוֹם. גַּלֵּי דַּעְתֵּיהּ מֵאֶתְמוֹל דְּלָאו מָנָא הוּא: קְרוּמִיּוֹת שֶׁל מַחְצֶלֶת. שֶׁנִּפְרְדוּ מִן מַחֲצֶלֶת יְשָׁנָה: בַּר הַמְּדוֹרִי פֵּירֵשׁ לִי טַעְמוֹ שֶׁל דָּבָר: לְכַסּוֹת בּוֹ צוֹאָה. א"נ: שֶׁלֹּא יַעֲלֶה הָאָבָק: שְׁיָרֵי פְּרוֹזְמִיּוֹת. טַלִּיתוֹת, כִּדְאָמַר בְּסוּכָּה (דף יח.): רָמָא תְּכֶלְתָּא בְּפִירְזְמָא דְּאֶינָשֵׁי בֵּיתֵיהּ: תַּנּוּר יָשָׁן. שֶׁכְּבָר הוּסַּק, וַחֲרָסָיו קָשִׁים וַחֲזוּ לִמְלָאכָה: הֲרֵי הֵן כְּכָל הַכֵּלִים. לְקַמֵּיהּ מְפָרֵשׁ פְּלוּגְתַּיְיהוּ וְטַעְמַיְיהוּ: וְעַל כִּיסּוּיוֹ. שֶׁל תַּנּוּר, שֶׁאֵינוֹ צָרִיךְ בֵּית יָד, דִּדְלָאו בֵּית אֲחִיזָה מְטַלְטְלִין לֵיהּ. וּפְלוּגְתָּא הִיא בְּמַתְנִיתִין, דְּאִיכָּא לְמ"ד בָּעֵינַן בֵּית אֲחִיזָה: מֵעֵין מְלָאכָה. כְּגוֹן לְכַסּוֹת בָּהֵן פִּי חָבִית: וְאֵין עוֹשִׂין מֵעֵין מְלַאכְתָּן. לֶאֱפוֹת: וְאַזְדָּא ר"מ לְטַעְמֵיהּ. דְּאָמַר בְּמַתְנִי' לָא בָּעֵינַן מֵעֵין מְלַאכְתָּן: דְּהַאי תַּנּוּר. הֶעָשׂוּי כְּעֵין זֶה שֶׁשָּׁנוּי בְּמִשְׁנָה זוֹ שֶׁאֲנִי מֵבִיא לְךָ, שֶׁלֹּא נִתְקַן כָּל צָרְכּוֹ מִתְּחִילָּתוֹ וְנִשְׁבַּר, קָמִיפַּלְגִי: נְתָנוֹ עַל פִּי הַבּוֹר. תַּנּוּרִים שֶׁלָּהֶם עֲשׂוּיִן כִּקְדֵירוֹת גְּדוֹלוֹת וְאֵין לָהֶם שׁוּלַיִם, וּמוֹשִׁיבוֹ לָאָרֶץ וּמַדְבִּיק טִיט סְבִיבוֹתָיו לַעֲשׂוֹתוֹ עָב שֶׁיַּחֲזִיק חוּמּוֹ, וְהִיא קְרוּיָה טְפֵילָה, וְהִיא מַגַּעַת לָאָרֶץ – וּמִתּוֹךְ כָּךְ הֶבֶל שֶׁלּוֹ קַיָּים. וְאִם נְתָנוֹ עַל פִּי הַבּוֹר אוֹ עַל פִּי הַדּוּת, שֶׁהִיא כְּעֵין בּוֹר, אֶלָּא שֶׁהַבּוֹר בַּחֲפִירָה וְהַדּוּת בְּבִנְיָן, וְנָתַן שָׁם אֶבֶן בֵּינוֹ לְבֵין דּוֹפֶן הַבּוֹר לְדוֹחֲקוֹ שֶׁלֹּא יִפּוֹל, וְהִיא עוֹמֵד בָּאֲוִיר: רַבִּי יְהוּדָה אוֹמֵר. אִם דּוֹפְנוֹתָיו לְמַעְלָה קְרוֹבִים לְדוֹפְנֵי הַבּוֹר, שֶׁלֹּא הוּצְרַךְ לָתֵת בֵּינְתַיִם אֶלָּא אֶבֶן דַּקָּה, וְאֵין אֲוִיר נִיכָּר בֵּין דּוֹפְנֵי הַתַּנּוּר לְדוֹפְנֵי הַבּוֹר שֶׁיְּעַכֵּב אֶת הֶיסֵּק הַתַּנּוּר, אֶלָּא יוֹעִילוּ לוֹ דּוֹפְנֵי הַבּוֹר לְהַחֲזִיק אֶת חוּמּוֹ. וְשׁוּלָיו קְרוֹבִים לְשׁוּלֵי הַבּוֹר, שֶׁאִם מַסִּיקִין אוֹתוֹ מִלְּמַטָּה שֶׁעוֹשִׂין הָאוּר בַּבּוֹר וְהַתַּנּוּר נִיסּוֹק (א) מִלְמַעְלָה בְּתוֹכוֹ מֵאוּר דֶּרֶךְ שׁוּלָיו. אוֹ שֶׁהַתַּנּוּר בְּתוֹךְ חֲלַל הַבּוֹר בָּאֲוִיר, וְהַהֶיסֵּק עוֹלֶה סְבִיב דּוֹפְנוֹתָיו וְנִיסּוֹק, כְּגוֹן שֶׁקָּצָר מִלְּמַטָּה וְרָחָב מִלְמַעְלָה, אוֹ הַבּוֹר רָחָב מִלְּמַטָּה וּפִיו קָצָר טָמֵא: וְאִם לָאו. אֶלָּא נִסּוֹק כִּשְׁאָר תַּנּוּרִים מִתּוֹכָן – טָהוֹר. כִּדְמְפָרֵשׁ טַעְמָא, דְּבָעֵינַן מְחוּסַּר נְתִיצָה, שֶׁיְּהֵא קָרוֹב לִהְיוֹת מְחוּבָּר. וְכִי אֵינוֹ קָרוֹב לָאָרֶץ – אֵין לְךָ תַּנּוּר נָתוּץ מִזֶּה, וְאֵין לְךָ לְקַיֵּים בּוֹ "תַּנּוּר וְכִירַיִים יוּתָּץ" – דִּנְתִיצָה לֹא שַׁיְּיכָא אֶלָּא בְּבִנְיָן מְחוּבָּר, וּכְשֶׁאֵין מְחוּבָּר, שְׁבִירָה שַׁיְּיכָא בֵּיהּ: טְמֵאִים הֵם וּטְמֵאִים יִהְיוּ לָכֶם. דְּכָפַל בֵּיהּ קְרָא – רִבּוּיָא הוּא, שֶׁאַעַ"פ שֶׁאֵינוֹ מְתוּקָּן כָּל צָרְכּוֹ: הַהוּא לְאִידָךְ גִּיסָא. הַאי "יוּתָּץ" לָאו לְאַגְמוּרֵי קוּלָּא אָתָא, וּלְמֵימַר דְּאִי לֵיכָּא לְקִיּוּמֵי בֵּיהּ נְתִיצָה, כְּגוֹן זֶה שֶׁאֵינוֹ בָּנוּי וּמְחוּבָּר וּמֵאֵילָיו הוּא נָתוּץ, דְּלֶיהֱוֵי טָהוֹר. דְּהָדַר תָּנָא בֵּיהּ קְרָא: "וּטְמֵאִים יִהְיוּ לָכֶם" – לְרַבּוּיֵי. אֶלָּא לְאַגְמוּרֵי חוּמְרָא אָתָא, דְּלָא תֵּימָא כָּל הַתַּנּוּרִים הָעֲשׂוּיִים כְּהִלְכָתָן וּמְחוּבָּרִים לָאָרֶץ הֲרֵי הֵן כִּשְׁאָר בָּתִּים, וּכְקַרְקַע דָּמֵי, הוֹאִיל וְחִבְּרָן וְלֹא לְקַבֵּל טוּמְאָה, קמ"ל "יוּתָּץ", דְּאַע"ג דְּשַׁיְּיכָא בֵּיהּ לְשׁוֹן נְתִיצָה, כְּלוֹמַר דִּמְחוּבָּר הוּא – טָמֵא. וְכ"שׁ (א) דִּמְחוּסַּר נְתִיצָה: בְּהֶיסֵּק רִאשׁוֹן. שֶׁלֹּא הוּסַּק מֵעוֹלָם. וְהֶיסֵּק רִאשׁוֹן שֶׁנֶּחְלְקוּ בּוֹ – דְּהַהוּא מְשַׁוֵּי לֵיהּ כְּלִי, כִּדְתַנְיָא בְּמַסֶּ' כֵּלִים (פ"ה): אֵיזֶהוּ גְּמַר מְלַאכְתּוֹ – מִשֶּׁיַּסִּיקֶנּוּ לֶאֱפוֹת בּוֹ סוּפְגָּנִין. בְּהַהִיא פָּלֵיג ר' יְהוּדָה, וְאָמַר דְּאֵינוֹ רָאוּי לֵיעָשׂוֹת כְּלִי: אֲבָל בְּהֶיסֵּק שֵׁנִי. שֶׁמִּתְּחִלָּה נַעֲשָׂה כִּשְׁאָר תַּנּוּרִים מְחוּבָּר לָאָרֶץ אוֹ לְאֶבֶן עָב, וְהוּסַּק שָׁם וְנַעֲשָׂה כְּלִי, וְסוֹף נְטָלוֹ מִשָּׁם וּנְתָנוֹ עַל פִּי הַבּוֹר וְכָאן נִטְמָא – מוֹדֶה ר' יְהוּדָה דְּאִיתְרַבַּאי מִ"וּטְמֵאִים יִהְיוּ לָכֶם": וַאֲפִילּוּ תָּלוּי בְּצַוַּאר גָּמָל. אא"כ חִלְּקוֹ כְּדִין טָהֳרַת תַּנּוּר, שֶׁצָּרִיךְ לִשְׁבּוֹר אַף אֶת חַרְסוֹ, וְאֵינוֹ נִטְהָר בִּנְטִילָתוֹ שָׁלֵם מִמְּקוֹמוֹ: אָמַר עוּלָּא הֶיסֵּק רִאשׁוֹן לְרַבָּנַן. דְּאָמְרֵי מֵרִיבּוּיָא דִּקְרָא, וְאַע"ג דְּאֵין הֶבֶל שֶׁלּוֹ מִתְקַיֵּים יָפֶה – מְקַבֵּל טוּמְאָה. לָא תֵּימָא "נְתָנוֹ ע"פ הַבּוֹר" דַּוְקָא, אֶלָּא אֲפִילּוּ תְּלָאוֹ בְּצַוַּאר גָּמָל וְהוּסַּק שָׁם הֶיסֵּק רִאשׁוֹן – טָמֵא: מַתְקִיף לַהּ רַב אַשִׁי. אַדְּרַבָּה, דְּאוֹקֵי פְּלוּגְתָּא דְּטִלְטוּל שִׁבְרֵי תַנּוּר יָשָׁן דִּלְעֵיל בִּשְׁבָרִים דְּכִי הַאי תַּנּוּר(ב) דְּהוּא גּוּפֵיהּ לְר' יְהוּדָה לָאו מָנָא הוּא: כִּדַאֲמַרַן מֵעִיקָּרָא. בְּעוֹשִׂין מֵעֵין מְלָאכָה וְלֹא מֵעֵין מְלַאכְתָּן, וְשִׁבְרֵי תַנּוּר מְעַלְיָא קָאָמַר. וּדְקַשְׁיָא לָךְ: אַמַּאי נָקַט תַּנּוּר, לִיפְלוֹג בְּשִׁבְרֵי כְלִי, בְּהַאי אִיצְטְרִיכָא לֵיהּ, דְּבְעוֹשִׂין קְצָת מֵעֵין מְלֶאכֶת אֲפִיָּיה, כְּגוֹן מַעֲשֵׂה טַפְקָא = רְעָפִים שֶׁקּוֹרִין טויל"ש, שֶׁמַּסִּיקִין אוֹתָם וְאוֹפִין בָּהֶן. כָּךְ שְׁבָרִים אֵלּוּ רְחָבִים. וּמִיהוּ, אֵין לָהֶן תּוֹךְ לְהַסִּיקָם מִבִּפְנִים אֶלָּא מִבַּחוּץ כִּרְעָפִים. וְלָאו מִשּׁוּם דְּבָעֵי ר' מֵאִיר מֵעֵין מְלַאכְתָּן, אֶלָּא מִשּׁוּם דְּרַבִּי יְהוּדָה נָקַט לַהּ: וְר"מ לִדְבָרָיו דְּר' יְהוּדָה. נָקַט תַּנּוּר, וְקָאָמַר: לְדִידִי אֲפִילּוּ עוֹשִׂין מֵעֵין מְלָאכָה, כִּדְאָמַר בְּמַתְנִיתִין: מְעוּמָּד. בְּתַנּוּר אוֹפִין מְעוּמָּד, שֶׁהַפַּת דְּבוּקָה בְּדוֹפְנֵי הַתַּנּוּר וְעוֹמֶדֶת וְאֵינָהּ מוּטֶּלֶת בִּשְׁכִיבָה ע"ג שׁוּלָיו, כִּרְעָפִים שֶׁהֵן שׁוֹכְבוֹת עַל רָחְבָּן: כִּיסּוּי דְּתַנּוּרֵי דְּמָתָא מְחַסְיָא. כִּיסּוּי תַּנּוּר שֶׁל אוֹתוֹ מָקוֹם לֹא הָיָה לָהֶן בֵּית אֲחִיזָה. תַּנּוּר, מִפְּנֵי שֶׁפִּיו לְמַעְלָה יֵשׁ לוֹ כִּסּוּי, שֶׁלֹּא יֵצֵא הֶבֶל שֶׁלּוֹ. לְאַחַר שֶׁהִדְבִּיק בּוֹ הַפַּת מְכַסֵּהוּ: מַתְנִי' הָאֶבֶן שֶׁבַּקֵּירוּיָה. דְּלַעַת יְבֵשָׁה חֲלוּלָה, וּמְמַלְּאִין בָּהּ מַיִם. וּמִתּוֹךְ שֶׁהִיא קַלָּה – אֵינָהּ שׁוֹקַעַת, אֶלָּא צָפָה, וְנוֹתְנִין בָּהּ אֶבֶן לְהַכְבִּידָהּ: אִם מְמַלְּאִין בָּהּ וְאֵינָהּ נוֹפֶלֶת. שֶׁקְּשׁוּרָה יָפֶה לְפִי הַקֵּירוּיָה – שַׁוְיָא כְּלִי: וְאִם לָאו. הֲרֵי הִיא כִּשְׁאָר אֲבָנִים, וְאֵין מְטַלְטֵל אֶת הַקֵּירוּיָה, דְּשַׁוְיָא בָּסִיס לָאֶבֶן שֶׁעֲשָׂאָהּ: זְמוֹרָה

א) בתוס' יו"ט פכ"ה דכלים משנה ו העתיק לשון רש"י וכ"ש שאינו מחוסר נתילה וכל"ל.

תוספות

אם זרקה מבעוד יום. הש"ס לא פריך אלא מעתה זרק לגלימא מבעוד יום, דכיון דלא היה מוכן מבעו"י – ליכא לדמויי לגלימי: מחצלת גופה למאי חזיא. לרווחא דמילתא מפרש הכי, אע"ג דלא בעי מעין מלאכה ראשונה, כדאמר רב נחמן לעיל: חרס קטנה מותר לטלטלה בחצר, משום דחזיא לכסויי בה מנא: הרי הן ככל הכלים הניטלין בחצר. לאו דוקא בחצר, לרב נחמן ולרבא דשרו בכרמלית ור"ה: בשעושין מעין מלאכה ואין עושין מעין מלאכתן. והא דנקט תנור ישן – דשברי תנור חדש אין ראוין לכלום: בשברי דהאי תנור קמיפלגי. לפי תירוץ זה תימה הא דנקט תנור ישן, דבהיסק ראשון פליגי: כמאן כר' אליעזר בן יעקב. ה"ה דה"מ למימר כרבי יוסי, דשרי לקמן* לטלטל כיסוי כלים שאין להם בית אחיזה בכלי דחברינהו בארעא אלא משום דמשנת ר' אליעזר בן יעקב קב ונקי: ואזדו

[עי' תוספות לקמן קכז: ד"ה כיון וכו'] [תוספ' פט"ו] כלים פ"ה מ"ו [סוכה טז.] [דף קכו:]

רבינו חננאל

אתווסאי מסאני טינא. נטנפו מנעלין בטיט. פי' קרומיות. שירי מחצלאות שבלו. וזה שאמר ר' זירא אמר רב שירי פרוזמיות אסור לטלטלן בשבת. פרוזמיות. פירושו טליתות. כדאמרינן התם. רב יהודה רמי תכלתא בפריזמא דאינשי ביתיה. פי' תלא ציצית בטלית של אשתו. ופשוטה היא: ת"ר שברי תנור ישן. ס"א שירי תנור ישן הרי הן ככל הכלים וניטלין בחצר דברי ר' מאיר ר' יהודה אומר אין ניטלין. העיד ר' יוסי וכו'. ואמרינן במאי קא מיפלגי בעושין מלאכה ואין עושין מעין מלאכתן. ור"מ לטעמיה דהוא ת"ק דמתני'. וקיי"ל סתם משנה ר"מ דשרי. אע"פ שאין עושין מעין מלאכתן. ור' יהודה לטעמיה דאסר ולא קא שרי אלא בעושין מעין מלאכתן. ואתקף עליה רבא ולא מצא פירוק. ואוקים רבא פלוגתיהן בשברין דהאי תנור. דכיון דתנינן בפ' המביא כדי יין ת"ר תנור וכירים חדשים הרי הן ככל הכלים הניטלין בחצר. אבל אין סכין אותן שמן וכו' הוצרכו להודיע כי תנור חדש הראוי לאפות בו ניטל בחצר ושבריו כיוצא בו. ומצאנו חלוקה בתנור חדש לענין טומאה והאומר מקבל טומאה סבר הואיל ויתכן לאפות בו כלי גמור הוא. ושבריו כיוצא בו. והואיל וככלים חשובין ניטלין. ופירשו חלוקתן לענין טומאה וה"ה לטלטול. דתנן נתנו ע"פ הבור או ע"פ הדות ונתן שם אבן. ר' יהודה אומר אם מסיק מלמטה והוא ניסוק מלמעלה טמא ואם לאו טהור. וחכ"א הואיל והוסק מ"מ טמא. וכך פירושו תנור שנתנו ע"פ הבור או ע"פ הדות ונתן שם אבן בפי הבור או בפי הדות. סבר ר' יהודה אם מסיק מלמטה בבור או בדות וניסק מלמעלה התנור הרי הוא כבנוי בקרקע ונגמרה מלאכתו ונעשה כלי לאפות בו ומקבל טומאה ואם לאו לא נגמרה מלאכתו וחשוב הוא כקדירה שלא *) בפת' לה פת או לתת לתוכה תבשיל. שאין דרך התנור לאפות בו והוא תלוי. וחכ"א כיון שנתן בפי הבור אבן ויכול להסיקו על האבן הרי הוא יכול לאפות בו. והיא כלי לקבל טומאה. וחלוקתן בזה הפסוק תנור וכירים יותץ. ר' יהודה סבר מדאמר קרא יותץ מכלל שצריך להיות בנוי ואם [לאו] אינו כלי. ורבנן סברי טמאים מ"מ ואפילו אינו בנוי: **תוספתא** ומודה ר' יהודה בתנור שנתנו ע"פ הבור או ע"פ הדות ונתן שם אבן ומירחו בטיט מן הצדדים שהוא טמא. וחכ"א בין כך ובין כך טמא. ועל זו הדרך סוגיא דהא שמעתא. ואתקיף לה רב אשי לרבא על זה שאמר ולא מצא פירוקי והעמיד רב אשי דברי אביי וחיזק דבריו ולא בטעמו. אלא העמיד חלוקתם בשברי תנור שאופין עליהם מעשה טפקא. ופירושו שנותנין זה השבר ע"ג אבנים ומסיקין אש מלמטה ומרתיחין אותן השברין ומדבקין הפת מלמעלה וקיי"ל כר' אליעזר ור"מ דהא רבינא פירש דמטלטלין כיסוי דתנורי כר' אליעזר: **מתני'** האבן שבקירויה וכו'. פי' מביאין קרא יבשה ומוציאין בני מעיה ועושה אותה חללה. ועושין אותה כגון זרנוקא לדלות בה מים מן הבור והיא קלה ואינה שוקעת במים אלא היא צפה ע"פ המים ואין יכולין למלאות בה מים וכשרוצין להכבידה נותנין בתוכה אבן מהודקת שלא תהיה מתנדנדת וממלאין בה מים מן הבורות. וזה פי' האבן שבקרוי':

הגהות הב"ח

(א) רש"י ד"ה ר' יהודה וכו' והתנור ניסוק בתוכו מלמעלה לאויר: (ב) ד"ה מתקיף וכו' האי תנור הס"ד ואח"כ מ"ה בתנור גופיה:

רב נסים גאון

דתנן נתנו על פי הבור או על פי הדות וכו'. זו המשנה במס' כלים בפרק ה' (משנה ו) תנור שנתן בו עפר עד חציו מעפר ולמטה מטמא במגע מעפר ולמעלה מטמא באויר נתנו על פי הבור או על פי הדות וכו' ועיקר זה הוא מה שנאמר בתורת כהנים (פ' שמיני פ"ט) [אי] מה כלי חרש בשמו אף תנור בשמו תנור שלא הוסק [תנור] שמו ת"ל אך מאימתי מקבל טומאה משיסיקנו כדי לאפות בו סופגנין יותץ טמאים הם את

לח א מיי' פכ"ה מהל' שבת הלכה יז סמג לאוין סה טוש"ע או"ח סימן שח סעיף כב וסימן שטו סעיף ד:
לט ב מיי' שם הל' כח סמג שם טור שו"ע או"ח סימן שח סעיף כח:
מ ג מיי' פכ"ג מהלכות שבת הלכה ז:
מא ד ה מיי' פכ"ב מהל' שבת הלכה כז סמג לאוין סה טוש"ע או"ח סימן שטו סעיף א:
מב ו מיי' שם טוש"ע שם סעיף ב:

זְמוֹרָה שֶׁהִיא קְשׁוּרָה בַּטְּפִיחַ – מְמַלְּאִין בָּהּ בַּשַּׁבָּת. *פְּקָק הַחַלּוֹן, ר"א אוֹמֵר: בִּזְמַן שֶׁהוּא קָשׁוּר וְתָלוּי – פּוֹקְקִין בּוֹ, וְאִם לָאו – אֵין פּוֹקְקִין בּוֹ. וַחכ"א: בֵּין כָּךְ וּבֵין כָּךְ פּוֹקְקִין בּוֹ.§

גמ' *תְּנַן הָתָם: אֶבֶן שֶׁעַל פִּי הֶחָבִית מַטָּהּ עַל צִידָּהּ וְהִיא נוֹפֶלֶת. אָמַר רַבָּה א"ר אַמִי א"ר יוֹחָנָן: *א לֹא שָׁנוּ אֶלָּא בְּשׁוֹכֵחַ, אֲבָל בְּמַנִּיחַ – נַעֲשָׂה בָּסִיס לְדָבָר הָאָסוּר. וְרַב יוֹסֵף א"ר אַסִי א"ר יוֹחָנָן: לֹא שָׁנוּ אֶלָּא בְּשׁוֹכֵחַ, אֲבָל בְּמַנִּיחַ – נַעֲשָׂה כִּיסּוּי לְהֶחָבִית. אָמַר רַבָּה: *מוֹתְבִינַן אַשְׁמַעְתִּין "הָאֶבֶן שֶׁבַּקֵּירוּיָה אִם מְמַלְּאִין בָּהּ וְאֵינָהּ נוֹפֶלֶת מְמַלְּאִין בָּהּ"! וְלֹא הִיא, הָתָם כֵּיוָן דְּהַדְקַהּ – שַׁוְיַא דּוֹפֶן. אָמַר רַב יוֹסֵף: וּמוֹתְבִינַן אַשְׁמַעְתִּין "אִם לָאו אֵין מְמַלְּאִין בָּהּ"! וְלֹא הִיא, הָתָם כֵּיוָן דְּלָא הַדְקַהּ – בַּטּוֹלֵי בַּטְּלָהּ. בְּמַאי קָמִיפַּלְגִי? מָר סָבַר: בָּעֵינַן מַעֲשֶׂה, וּמָר סָבַר: לָא בָּעֵינַן מַעֲשֶׂה. וְאָזְדוּ לְטַעֲמַיְיהוּ; דְּכִי אֲתָא רַב דִּימִי א"ר חֲנִינָא וְאָמְרִי לַהּ א"ר זֵירָא א"ר חֲנִינָא: פַּעַם אַחַת הָלַךְ רַבִּי לְמָקוֹם אֶחָד וּמָצָא נִדְבָּךְ שֶׁל אֲבָנִים, וְאָמַר לְתַלְמִידָיו: צְאוּ וְחַשְּׁבוּ כְּדֵי שֶׁנֵּשֵׁב עֲלֵיהֶן לְמָחָר, וְלֹא הִצְרִיכָן רַבִּי לְמַעֲשֶׂה. וְר' יוֹחָנָן אָמַר: הִצְרִיכָן רַבִּי לְמַעֲשֶׂה. מַאי אָמַר לְהוּ? ב רַבִּי אַמִי אָמַר: צְאוּ וְלַמְּדוּם אָמַר לְהוּ. רַבִּי אַסִי אָמַר: צְאוּ וְשַׁפְשְׁפוּם אָמַר לְהוּ. אִיתְּמַר, ר' יוֹסֵי בֶּן שָׁאוּל אָמַר: סְוָאר שֶׁל קוֹרוֹת הֲוָה, וְר' יוֹחָנָן בֶּן שָׁאוּל אָמַר: גָּשׁוֹשׁ שֶׁל סְפִינָה הֲוָה. מ"ד גָּשׁוֹשׁ – כ"ש סְוָאר, וּמ"ד סְוָאר, אֲבָל גָּשׁוֹשׁ – קָפֵיד עֲלֵיהּ.§ "זְמוֹרָה שֶׁהִיא קְשׁוּרָה כו'".§ ג קְשׁוּרָה – אִין, לֹא קְשׁוּרָה – לָא, לֵימָא מַתְנִיתִין דְּלָא כְּרשב"ג, דְּתַנְיָא: *חֲרָיוֹת שֶׁל דֶּקֶל שֶׁגְּדָרָן לְעֵצִים וְנִמְלַךְ עֲלֵיהֶן לִישִׁיבָה – צָרִיךְ לִקְשׁוֹר, רַבָּן שִׁמְעוֹן בֶּן גַּמְלִיאֵל אוֹמֵר: אֵין צָרִיךְ לִקְשׁוֹר. אָמַר רַב שֵׁשֶׁת: אֲפִי' תֵּימָא רשב"ג, הָכָא בְּמַאי עָסְקִינַן – בִּמְחוּבֶּרֶת בְּאָבִיהָ. אִי הָכִי קָא מִשְׁתַּמֵּשׁ בִּמְחוּבָּר לַקַּרְקַע! לְמַטָּה מִג'. רַב אַשִׁי אָמַר: ד אֲפִי' תֵּימָא בִּתְלוּשָׁה, גְּזֵירָה שֶׁמָּא יִקְטוֹם.§ "פְּקָק הַחַלּוֹן כו'".§ *אָמַר רַבָּה בַּר בַּר חָנָה א"ר יוֹחָנָן: *ה הַכֹּל מוֹדִים שֶׁאֵין עוֹשִׂין אֹהֶל עֲרַאי בַּתְּחִלָּה בְּיו"ט, וְא"צ לוֹמַר בַּשַּׁבָּת. לֹא נֶחְלְקוּ אֶלָּא לְהוֹסִיף, שֶׁר"א אוֹמֵר: אֵין מוֹסִיפִין בְּיו"ט, וְא"צ לוֹמַר בַּשַּׁבָּת. ו וַחכ"א: מוֹסִיפִין בַּשַּׁבָּת, וְא"צ לוֹמַר בְּיו"ט.§ "וַחכ"א בֵּין כָּךְ וּבֵין כָּךְ פּוֹקְקִין בּוֹ".§ מַאי "בֵּין כָּךְ וּבֵין כָּךְ"? אָמַר ר' אַבָּא אָמַר רַב כָּהֲנָא:
בֵּין

רש"י

זְמוֹרָה. שֶׁל גֶּפֶן: שֶׁהִיא קְשׁוּרָה בַּטְּפִיחַ. פַּךְ שֶׁשּׁוֹאֲבִין בּוֹ מִן הַבּוֹר אוֹ מִן הַמַּעְיָן: מְמַלְּאִין בָּהּ. דְּשַׁוְיָא כְּלִי לְהָךְ זְמוֹרָה: וְתָלוּי. שֶׁאֵינוֹ נִגְרָר בָּאָרֶץ, שֶׁהַחֶבֶל שֶׁהוּא קָשׁוּר בּוֹ אֵינוֹ מַגִּיעַ לָאָרֶץ: אֵין פּוֹקְקִין בּוֹ. דְּמֶיחֱזֵי כְּמוֹסִיף עַל הַבִּנְיָן: בֵּין כָּךְ וּבֵין כָּךְ. בַּגְּמָרָא מְפָרֵשׁ לָהּ: **גמ'** תְּנַן הָתָם. לְקַמָּן בְּהַאי מַסֶּכְתָּא: הָאֶבֶן שֶׁעַל פִּי הֶחָבִית. וְהוּלְרַךְ לִיטּוֹל מִן הַיַּיִן שֶׁבְּתוֹכָהּ: מַטָּהּ. הֶחָבִית עַל צִדָּהּ, וְהִיא נוֹפֶלֶת: לֹא שָׁנוּ. דְּמוּתָּר לְטַלְטֵל הֶחָבִית וְהָאֶבֶן עָלֶיהָ, דְּקָתָנֵי: וְאִם הָיְתָה בֵּין חָבִיּוֹת, שֶׁיָּרֵא לְהַטּוֹתָהּ שָׁם שֶׁלֹּא תִּפּוֹל הָאֶבֶן עַל הֶחָבִית שֶׁבְּצִדָּהּ – מַגְבִּיהַּ וּמַטָּהּ עַל צִדָּהּ וְהִיא נוֹפֶלֶת: בְּשׁוֹכֵחַ. הָאֶבֶן עָלֶיהָ שֶׁלֹּא בְּמִתְכַּוֵּין: אֲבָל בְּמַנִּיחַ נַעֲשֵׂית. הֶחָבִית בָּסִיס לָאֶבֶן, שֶׁהִיא דְּבַר הָאִיסּוּר, וְאֵין מְטַלְטֵל אֶת הֶחָבִית: וְרַב יוֹסֵף א"ר אַסִי. לְקוּלָּא אָמַר ר' יוֹחָנָן: לֹא שָׁנוּ דְּהוּלְרַךְ לְהַטּוֹת אֶת הֶחָבִית וְלֹא נִיתָּן לְטַלְטֵל הָאֶבֶן לְהֶדְיָא: אֶלָּא בְּשׁוֹכֵחַ. דְּלֹא נִתְכַּוֵּין לַעֲשׂוֹתָהּ כְּלִי: אֲבָל בְּמַנִּיחַ נַעֲשָׂה. הָאֶבֶן כִּיסּוּי לֶחָבִית, וּמְגַלֶּה אוֹתָהּ כְּדַרְכָּהּ: אַשְׁמַעְתִּין. עַל שְׁמוּעָה שֶׁלִּי, שֶׁאָמַרְתִּי בְּמַנִּיחַ אֵין הָאֶבֶן נַעֲשָׂה כְּלִי: מְמַלְּאִין בָּהּ. אַלְמָא אֶבֶן נַעֲשֶׂה כְּלִי: דְּהַדְקַהּ. שֶׁקְּשָׁרָהּ יָפֶה: וְאִם לָאו אֵין מְמַלְּאִין. וְלָא אָמְרִינַן נַעֲשֶׂה כְּלִי בְּהַנָּחָה בְּעָלְמָא. וְקַשְׁיָא לְדִידִי, דְּאָמְרִי לְעֵיל בְּמַנִּיחַ נַעֲשָׂה כִּיסּוּי לֶחָבִית: וְלֹא הִיא. לָא קַשְׁיָא לִי; דְּהָתָם הוֹאִיל וּבְלֹא קְשִׁירָה לָא חַזְיָא לְמַלְאכוֹת, דְּהָא נָפְלָה, וְהַאי לָאו הַדְקַהּ – בַּטּוֹלֵי בַּטְּלָהּ מִתּוֹרַת כְּלִי, גַּלֵּי דַּעְתֵּיהּ דְּלָא חָשִׁיב לֵיהּ. אֲבָל כִּיסּוּי חָבִית – הַנָּחָה מְשַׁוְיָא לֵיהּ כְּלִי: וְאָזְדוּ לְטַעְמַיְיהוּ. ר' אַמִי וְר' אַסִי: נִדְבָּךְ שֶׁל אֲבָנִים. אֲבָנִים סְדוּרוֹת וּמוּקְצוֹת לְבִנְיָן: מַאי אֲמַר לְהוּ. מַאי מַעֲשֶׂה הִצְרִיכָן לְרַבִּי יוֹחָנָן: צְאוּ וְלַמְּדוּם. סַדְּרוּ אוֹתָם וְהַשִּׁיבוּם, כְּדֵי שֶׁלֹּא נִצְטָרֵךְ לִיגַּע בָּהֶם לְמָחָר, לְפִי שֶׁאֵין הַזְמָנָה בְּמַעֲשֶׂה [*כָּל דְּהוּ] מוֹעֶלֶת לָאֶבֶן לַעֲשׂוֹתָהּ כְּלִי. וְר' אַמִי לְטַעְמֵיהּ, דְּאָמַר לְעֵיל: אֵין אֶבֶן נַעֲשֵׂית כְּלִי בְּהַנָּחָה: לַמְּדוּם. כִּדְאָמְרִי' בְּמו"ק (דף יב.): עוֹשֶׂה לָהֶם לִמּוּדִים, לְסַדֵּר נְסָרִים עַל פִּי הַבּוֹר: וְשַׁפְשְׁפוּם. מִן הַטִּיט, שֶׁיְּהוּ נָאוֹת לֵישֵׁב, וּלְמָחָר תְּלַמְּדוּם. דְּבְמַעֲשֶׂה כָּל דְּהוּ נַעֲשֶׂה כְּלִי: סְוָאר שֶׁל קוֹרוֹת. הֲוָה, וְלֹא אֲבָנִים: סְוָאר. סֵדֶר שֶׁל קוֹרוֹת חֲדָשׁוֹת שֶׁמְּנַסְּרִין אוֹתָן לְבִנְיָן כְּדֵי שֶׁלֹּא יִתְעַקְּמוּ: גָּשׁוֹשׁ. עֵץ אָרוֹךְ שֶׁמְּגַשְּׁשִׁים בּוֹ הַמַּיִם לִפְנֵי הַסְּפִינָה, לֵידַע שֶׁהוּא דִּמְוּתְקוֹ, שֶׁתּוּכַל סְפִינָה לְהַלֵּךְ בָּהֶן: קָפֵיד עֲלֵיהּ. שֶׁלֹּא יִתְעַקֵּם, וּמְיַיחֵד לֵיהּ מָקוֹם וּמַקְצֶה לֵיהּ בְּיָדַיִם, וַאֲפִי' לְר"ש אָסוּר לְטַלְטְלוֹ, דְּמוּקְצֶה מֵחֲמַת חֶסְרוֹן כִּיס הוּא, אֲפִי' ר"ש מוֹדֶה: שֶׁאֵינָהּ קְשׁוּרָה לָא. וַאֲפִי' יֵשׁ עַקְמוּמִית בְּרֹאשָׁהּ כְּעֵין מַזְלֵג, שֶׁרָאוּי לִתְלוֹת בָּהּ טָפִיחַ וּלְמַלְאכוֹת וְחִישֵּׁב עָלֶיהָ: שֶׁגְּדָרָן לְעֵצִים. שֶׁחֲתָכָן לְהֶסֵּק: צָרִיךְ לִקְשׁוֹר. מֵעֶ"שׁ: בְּאָבִיהָ. בַּגֶּפֶן: וְהָא קָא מִשְׁתַּמֵּשׁ בִּמְחוּבָּר. וַאֲפִילּוּ קְשׁוּרָה מִבְּעוֹד יוֹם לִיתְּסַר: לְמַטָּה מִג'. סָמוּךְ לַקַּרְקַע, וּכְגוֹן לִשְׁאוֹב מִן הַמַּעְיָן שֶׁאֵינוֹ עָמוֹק. וּמוּתָּר לְהִשְׁתַּמֵּשׁ בְּאִילָן לְמַטָּה מִג', כִּדְאָמְרִי' בְּפֶרֶק בַּתְרָא דְּעֵירוּבִין (דף לג:): הָיוּ שָׁרָשָׁיו גְּבוֹהִין מִן הָאָרֶץ ג' – לֹא יֵשֵׁב עֲלֵיהֶם: גְּזֵירָה שֶׁמָּא יִקְטוֹם. שֶׁמָּא לְמָחָר תִּהְיֶה לוֹ אֲרוּכָּה וְיִקְטְמֶנָּה, מִתּוֹךְ שֶׁהִיא רַכָּה וְנוֹחָה לִקְטוֹם, וְנִמְצָא עוֹשֶׂה כְּלִי, וְחַיָּיב מִשּׁוּם מַכֶּה בְּפַטִּישׁ. אֲבָל בַּחֲרָיוֹת לִישִׁיבָה לֵיכָּא לְמִיגְזַר הָכִי, הִלְכָּךְ בְּמַחֲשָׁבָה סַגִּי: שֶׁאֵין עוֹשִׂין אֹהֶל עֲרַאי. לִפְרוֹס מַחְצֶלֶת עַל ד' מְחִיצּוֹת אוֹ עַל ד' קוּנְדָּסִים לִהְיוֹת צֵל לָאֹהֶל מִן הַחַמָּה. וְדַוְקָא גַּג, אֲבָל מְחִיצָּה – לָאו אֹהֶל הוּא, וְשָׁרֵי לְפוֹרְסָהּ לִצְנִיעוּת, כִּדְאָמְרִי' בְּעֵירוּבִין (ד' מד.) בְּעוּבְדָּא דִּשְׁמוּאֵל. וּפְקַק הַחַלּוֹן דְּמַתְנִי' *) – מִשּׁוּם דְּבִנְיָן קָבוּעַ הוּא, וּמֶיחֱזֵי כְּמוֹסִיף עַל הַבִּנְיָן: לְהוֹסִיף. כְּגוֹן שֶׁהָיָה מַחְצֶלֶת פְּרוּסָה עֲלֵיהֶן וּכְרוּכָה, וְנִשְׁאַר בָּהּ אֲוִיר, וּלְמָחָר פּוֹשְׁטָהּ. דּוּמְיָא דִּפְקָק, דְּמוֹסִיף בְּעָלְמָא הוּא: בֵּין

*) גי' רש"ל הוי למעלה בגג ולא מן הצד אבל הר"ן מקיים פי' רש"י דהכא.

תוספות

ואזדו לטעמייהו. תימה: היכי הוה רבי אסי פליגי, דהכא קאמר ר' אסי: נעשה כיסוי לחבית בהנחה גרידא, בלא שום מעשה. וגבי נדבך אמר ר' אסי: לאו ושפשפום אמר להן, דהיינו מעשה שהצריכן רבי. ועוד קשה: גבי נדבך קאמר דסגי בשפשוף, ולקמן גבי כיסוי כלים א"ר אסי א"ר יוחנן: והוא שיש בהם תורת כלי! ויש לומר: דכיסוי חבית סגי לה בהנחה, שדרכו לעשותו כל דהו, דלא בעי תיקון ומעשה גמור כשאר כיסוי כלים. ונדבך של אבן מסותת ומרובע לבנין – סגי להו בשפשוף שאין צריך עוד תיקון. ומ"מ הוי ר' אסי לטעמיה, דכי היכי דמיקל רבי אסי גבי נדבך – ה"נ הכא. והא דקאמר ר' אסי בפרק "במה טומנין" (לעיל דף נ.): חריות של דקל – ישב אע"פ שלא קשר! התם רב אשי גרסינן. אי נמי: ראויין הם לישיבה טפי מאבנים:

הכל מודים שאין עושין אהל עראי בתחלה. פי' בקונ': דלא אסיר אהל אלא למעלה בגג, אבל בדפנות לא, כדמוכח בעובדא דשמואל ב"כל גגות" (עירובין דף מד.) דאיתמר: חצר כותל שנפרצה, רב אמר: אין מטלטלין אלא בד' אמות, ושמואל אמר: זה מטלטל עד עיקר המחיצה וזה מטלטל עד עיקר המחיצה. והא דרב לאו בפירוש איתמר אלא מכללא. דשמואל הוה יתיב בההוא חצר, נפל גודא דביני ביני. אמר להו שמואל: שקולו גלימא נגודי ליה, אהדרינהו רב לאפיה כו'. ושמואל למה ליה למיעבד הכי? הא אמר: זה מטלטל עד עיקר המחיצה כו' – שמואל לצניעותא בעלמא הוא דעבד. אלמא משמע דאהל דדפנות שרי למיעבד הכי. ורב שהיה מקפיד – לאו משום עשיית אהל דשרי, כדפרישית, אלא הוה קפיד אמאי דהוו מטלטלין גלימא ד' אמות בחצר. וקשה: דע"כ שייך איסור אהל אפילו בדפנות, כדאיתא בעירובין בפרק "מי שהוציאוהו" (דף מד. ושם) גבי עשיית דופן סוכה, דפריך התם: והאמר רבה בר בר חנה אמר רבי יוחנן הכל מודים שאין עושין אהל עראי בתחילה! ומשני: הא בדופן שלישית, והא בדופן רביעית. אלא נראה לר"ת: דשפיר שייך בדפנות אהל היכא דמחילה מועלת להיתר, ולהכי הדוחן שלישית דהויא מחילה ומכשר ליה לסוכה – חשיב עשיית אהל בתחלה. אבל דופן רביעית – אינה אלא תוספת בעלמא, הואיל וכבר הסוכה היתה כשרה. ועיקר פלוגתין דר"א ורבנן איתא באהל כבעשיית דופן. דפקק החלון משמע בחלון שבכותל. דאי בגג מיירי – הוה ליה למימר ארובה, כמו ששנינו: משילין פירות דרך ארובה (ביצה דף לה:). ומיהו, באהל שבגג נמי פליגי, כדמוכח לקמן בפרק "תולין" (דף קלז:), דמייתי הך גבי תליית משמרת שהיא כעין גג. וכן משמע בפרק בתרא דעירובין (דף קב.), דאמר: הנהו דיכרי דהוו בי רב הונא דביממא בעו טולא, ובליליא בעו אוירא. אתא לקמיה דרב, אמר ליה: כרוך בודיא ושייר בה טפח, דלמחר הוא מוסיף על אהל עראי ומותר. ומשמע דהיינו נמי תוספת אהל עראי דפליגי רבי אליעזר ורבנן. ועובדא דשמואל דכל

רבינו חננאל

וזה שאמר רבי צאו ולמדום עשו להם לימודים. יש מי שאומר עייני בהן. כלומר לימוד בעינן בלא מעשה וי"א לימודים כגון זה ששנינו במסכת משקין. ר' יהודה אומר עושה לו לימודים בשביל שלא יחמיץ. והן כיסויי עצים ועליהם טיט (שרוצים מעשים) [שהצריכן למעשה] וראייתן הא דגרסינן בבמה טומנין תני רבה בר רב הונא קמי דרב חריות של דקל שגרדום לעצים ונמלך עליהם לישיבה צריך לקשר רשב"ג אומר אין צריך לקשר. ואמרינן מאן תנא דפליג עליה דרשב"ג. ר' חנניה בן עקביא היא שהלך למקום א' ומצא חריות של דקל שגררום לעצים כו': **פיסקא** זמורה שהיא קשורה בטפיח כו'. זמורה היא כגון אמיר והיא זמורה של כרם ארוכה כמו חבל וטפיח הוא כלי בדלי. ואמרה המשנ' אם זמורה זו היתה קשורה בזה הכלי ממלאין בה בשבת שעשאה מאתמול במקום חבל ועשה בה מעשה ואם לאו אסור לחשב עליו בשבת להיותו בחבל. ואמרינן לימא מתניתין דלא כרשב"ג. דהא רשבג"א בחריות שגרדן לעצים ונמלך עליהן לישיבה אין צריך לקשר. ופירק רב ששת זמורה זו מחוברת באביה. כלומר מחוברת בקרקע. ואם לא קשרה מאתמול לאו בישלה. ואינה דומה לחריות של דקל שהן גרודין. ואקשינן אי הכי היכי משתמש במחובר ופרקינן למטה משלשה. כדתנן היו שרשין גבוהין מן הארץ שלשה טפחים לא ישב עליהן. אם גבוהין ג' טפחים הוא דאסירו. הא בפחות מותר לישב עליהן. מיהא שמעינן דפחות מג' במחובר לקרקע בקרקע דמי ומותר להשתמש בו. ויש שאומרים כי המים הם קרובים בפחות משלש' ולא אתי למחתך. רב אשי אמר אפילו תימא בתלושה גזירה שמא יקטום: **מתני'** פקק החלון. כגון מסך העשוי לסתום החלון בין אם הוא מבגד בין מזולתו בזמן שקשור ותלוי פוקקין בו. ואם לאו אין פוקקין בו. אמר (רבא) [רבה] בר בר חנה א"ר יוחנן הכל מודין שאין עושין אהל עראי בתחלה ביו"ט. ואין צ"ל בשבת. לא נחלקו אלא להוסיף. פי' שאם היה בו פקק פוקק במקצת החלון. ר' אליעזר אוסר למושכו כנגד כל החלון. וחכמים מתירים (וזהו) להוסיף כיוצא בו בסוף המוצא תפילין הנהו דכרי דהוו לרב הונא דביממא בעו טולא ובליליא בעו אוירא. ואמר ליה רב כרוך בודיא עלייהו ושייר בה טפח ולמחר פרסיה

מסורת הש"ס

לקמן קלז: עירובין מד. סוכה כז:
[לקמן קמב: ע"ש]
[לעיל קכ: לקמן קמב: ע"ש]
[קידושין נ: וש"נ]
לעיל נ: ולקמן קסו:
גי' רש"א
לקמן קלז: עירו' מד. פו:
[תוספתא סוכה פ"א]

רב נסים גאון

את שיש לו נתיצה ואת שאין לו נתיצה אין לו טומאה: **אי** הכי קא משתמש במחובר למטה מג' מכלל כי מה שיהיה מדבר המחובר לקרקע קרוב מהארץ פחות מג' טפחים מותר להשתמש בו ואין איסור משום שבות [רק] מה שהוא גבוה מן הארץ ג' טפחים ותמצא עיקר זה במשנה במס' עירובין בפרק המוצא תפילין (דף לג) אילן שהוא מיסך על הארץ אם אין נופו גבוה מן הארץ ג' טפחים לא ישב עליהן ודבר זה אין בו חלוקה אבל חלקו רבא ורב ששת באילן הבאים מלמעלה מג' לתוך ג' ובפ' בכל מערבין (שם דף לג) תניא נתנו באילן בתוך ג' מותר לטלטל: **סליק פרק כל הכלים**

אבֵּין קָשׁוּר בֵּין שֶׁאֵינוֹ קָשׁוּר, וְהוּא שֶׁמְּתוּקָּן. א"ל ר' יִרְמְיָה: וְלֵימָא מָר "בֵּין תָּלוּי וּבֵין שֶׁאֵינוֹ תָּלוּי וְהוּא שֶׁקָּשׁוּר" – דְּאָמַר רַבָּה בַּר בַּר חָנָה א"ר יוֹחָנָן: כְּמַחֲלוֹקֶת כָּאן כָּךְ מַחֲלוֹקֶת בְּנֶגֶר הַנִּגְרָר. *דִּתְנַן: נֶגֶר הַנִּגְרָר – נוֹעֲלִין בּוֹ בַּמִּקְדָּשׁ אֲבָל לֹא בַּמְּדִינָה, וְהַמּוּנָּח – כָּאן וְכָאן אָסוּר. ר' יְהוּדָה אוֹמֵר: הַמּוּנָּח – *בַּמִּקְדָּשׁ, וְהַנִּגְרָר – בַּמְּדִינָה. וְתַנְיָא: אֵיזֶהוּ נֶגֶר הַנִּגְרָר שֶׁנּוֹעֲלִין בּוֹ בַּמִּקְדָּשׁ אֲבָל לֹא בַּמְּדִינָה – כֹּל שֶׁקָּשׁוּר וְתָלוּי וְרֹאשׁוֹ מַגִּיעַ לָאָרֶץ. ר' יְהוּדָה אוֹמֵר: בזֶה – אַף בַּמְּדִינָה מוּתָּר, אֶלָּא אֵיזֶהוּ שֶׁבַּמְּדִינָה אָסוּר – כֹּל שֶׁאֵינוֹ לֹא קָשׁוּר וְלֹא תָלוּי, וְשׁוֹמְטוֹ וּמַנִּיחוֹ בְּקֶרֶן זָוִית. וְאָמַר רַבִּי יְהוֹשֻׁעַ בַּר אַבָּא מִשְּׁמֵיהּ דְּעוּלָּא: מַאן תְּנָא נֶגֶר הַנִּגְרָר – ר"א הִיא! א"ל: אֲנָא דַּאֲמַרִי – כִּי הַאי תַּנָּא, דְּתַנְיָא: *קָנֶה שֶׁהִתְקִינוֹ בעה"ב לִהְיוֹת פּוֹתֵחַ וְנוֹעֵל בּוֹ, בִּזְמַן שֶׁקָּשׁוּר וְתָלוּי בַּפֶּתַח – פּוֹתֵחַ וְנוֹעֵל בּוֹ, אֵין קָשׁוּר וְתָלוּי – אֵין פּוֹתֵחַ וְנוֹעֵל בּוֹ. רשב"ג אוֹמֵר: מְתוּקָּן, אע"פ שֶׁאֵינוֹ קָשׁוּר. אָמַר רַב יְהוּדָה בַּר שֵׁילַת אָמַר רַב אַסִּי א"ר יוֹחָנָן: גהֲלָכָה כְּרשב"ג. וּמִי אָמַר רַבִּי יוֹחָנָן הָכִי? וְהָתְנַן: כָּל כִּסּוּיֵי הַכֵּלִים

שֶׁיֵּשׁ

רש"י

בֵּין קָשׁוּר כו'. כְּלוֹמַר: אֲפִילּוּ קְשִׁירָה לֹא צָרִיךְ: וְהוּא שֶׁמְּתוּקָּן. מוּכָן מֵאֶתְמוֹל לְכָךְ: א"ל רַבִּי יִרְמְיָה. אַמַּאי פָּשֵׁיט לֵיהּ מָר לְקוּלָּא: לֵימָא מָר. דְּלָא פְּלִיגִי רַבָּנַן אֶלָּא אַתְּלוּיָה, דְּרַבִּי אֱלִיעֶזֶר בָּעֵי קָשׁוּר וְתָלוּי. וַאֲפִילּוּ קָשׁוּר, אִם רֹאשׁוֹ נִגְרָר לָאָרֶץ, חָשֵׁיב לֵיהּ רַבִּי אֱלִיעֶזֶר כְּשׁוֹמְטוֹ מִן הַקַּרְקַע וּבוֹנֶה בּוֹ לְכַתְּחִלָּה. וְרַבָּנַן אָמְרִי לֵיהּ: בֵּין תָּלוּי בֵּין נִגְרָר פּוֹקְקִין בּוֹ וּבִלְבַד שֶׁיְּהֵא קָשׁוּר: דְּאָמַר רַבָּה בַּר בַּר חָנָה. בִּתְלִיָּיה הוּא דִּפְלִיגִי וְלֹא בִּקְשִׁירָה, דִּמְדַמֵּי לָהּ לִפְלוּגְתָּא דְּנֶגֶר הַנִּגְרָר, וְהָתָם לְדִבְרֵי הַכֹּל קָשׁוּר בָּעֵינַן: נֶגֶר. יָתֵד שֶׁתּוֹקְעִין בַּחוֹר שֶׁבַּמִּפְתָּן וְנוֹעֲלִין בּוֹ אֶת הַדֶּלֶת: הַנִּגְרָר. כִּדְמְפָרֵשׁ: שֶׁקָּשׁוּר בַּדֶּלֶת, אֶלָּא שֶׁרֹאשׁוֹ נִגְרָר לָאָרֶץ: נוֹעֲלִין בּוֹ בַּמִּקְדָּשׁ. דְּכֵיוָן דְּקָשׁוּר בּוֹ – מְיוּחָד וְעוֹמֵד הוּא לְכָךְ, וּכְבָר נִבְנָה בִּנְיָן זֶה מִבְּעוֹד יוֹם, וְאֵין בּוֹ אֶלָּא גְּזֵירַת שְׁבוּת מִדִּבְרֵיהֶם – וְאֵין שְׁבוּת בַּמִּקְדָּשׁ: וְהַמּוּנָּח. שֶׁאֵינוֹ קָשׁוּר כְּלָל, אֶלָּא כְּשֶׁהוּא שׁוֹמְטוֹ מִן הַחוֹר מַנִּיחוֹ ע"ג קַרְקַע. הִלְכָּךְ, כְּשֶׁתּוֹקְעוֹ בְּשַׁבָּת – בּוֹנֶה הוּא, וְאִיסּוּרָא דְּאוֹרַיְיתָא הוּא אַף בַּמִּקְדָּשׁ: הַמּוּנָּח מוּתָּר בַּמִּקְדָּשׁ. דְּכֵיוָן דִּמְתוּקָּן מֵאֶתְמוֹל לְהָכִי, לָאו בּוֹנֶה הוּא: שֶׁקָּשׁוּר וְתָלוּי. רֹאשׁוֹ הָעֶלְיוֹן, אֲבָל רֹאשׁוֹ הַתַּחְתּוֹן מַגִּיעַ לָאָרֶץ: מַאן תַּנָּא נֶגֶר הַנִּגְרָר. אָסוּר, דְּבָעֵי תַּרְתֵּי: ר"א הִיא. דְּאָמַר גַּבֵּי פְּקָק הַחַלּוֹן תַּרְתֵּי בָּעֵינַן, מִכְּלָל דְּר' יְהוּדָה כְּרַבָּנַן, אַלְמָא רַבָּנַן קְשִׁירָה בָּעוּ: כִּי הַאי תַּנָּא. דַּאֲפִי' קְשִׁירָה לָא בָּעֵי, כְּרַבָּן שִׁמְעוֹן בֶּן גַּמְלִיאֵל דְּאָמַר מְתוּקָּן בְּהַזְמָנָה בְּעָלְמָא וְאע"פ שֶׁאֵינוֹ קָשׁוּר: שֶׁהִתְקִינוֹ. שֶׁהִזְמִינוֹ: אָמַר רַב יְהוּדָה. גָּרְסִינַן וְלָא גָּרְסִינַן וְאָמַר:

שֶׁיֵּשׁ

תוספות

ד"כל גגות" (עירובין לז.) דפריך: ושמואל למה ליה למיעבד הכי? וקאמר: זה מטלטל כו' – לאו משום דאי הוה אמר אין מטלטלין בו אלא בד' אמות דאז הוה ניחא ליה, אלא אז נמי היה קשה היכי עביד הכי, כיון דמחילה מתרת לטלטל בחצר – הוה כעשיית אהל עראי בתחלה, ואסור כדפרישית לעיל. ומהאי טעמא היה מקפיד רב, דס"ל שאין מטלטלין אלא בד'. אלא משום דהתלמוד ידע דסבר שמואל דזה מטלטל עד עיקר המחילה – ניחא למיפרך למה הוצרך לעשות מחילה:

בין קשור בין שאינו קשור והוא שמתוקן. נראה לר"ת דלאו בתיקון של מעשה, אלא במחשבה בעלמא. כדמוכח לקמן, דאמר כרשב"ג ס"ל דאמר: מתוקן אע"פ שאינו קשור. דהיינו במחשבה, ומשמע דלגמרי ס"ל כוותיה. דגבי ר' יוחנן דוקא הוא דאמר בסמוך סבר לה כוותיה בחדא ופליג עליה בחדא. ופריך: ולימא מר בין תלוי בין שאינו תלוי, והוא שקשור – כרבי יהודה דבעי קשירה. וטעמא משום טלטול ולא משום בנין. דאי משום בנין – מאי ראיה מנגר שצריך קשירה לפקק? והא בפקק לא שייך בנין אלא תוספת אהל עראי, ותוספת אהל עראי שרו רבנן בלא שום קשירה, כדמוכח ב"מי שהוציאוהו" (שם מד.):

והמונח כאן וכאן אסור. פי' רש"י: שכשתוקעו בשבת – בונה הוא, ואיסורא דאורייתא איכא. ואינו משמע שיהא בו איסורא דאורייתא, כיון שאינו מבטלו שם, אלא נראה לר"ת: דכולה מילתא בנגר הנגרר ליכא איסורא אלא משום טלטול, וכי ההיא דקנה שהתקינו בעה"ב להיות פותח ונועל בו, דמיירי משום טלטול. ואפ"ה בעי ר"א קשור ותלוי, יותר משאר כלי תשמיש שדי להם בתיקונם, לפי שהם תשמיש בית. מידי דהוי אכיסוי קרקעות שהחמירו בהם להצריכם בית אחיזה, אע"ג דהני משום שבות נאסר טלטולם במקדש כקנים וכמקלות דלעיל. אבל בשום בנין ליכא איסורא כלל, אפילו מדרבנן. וקשה לר"ת: מנלן דאפליגו רבי אליעזר ורבנן בתוספת אהל עראי? כיון דאפליגו בטלטול, דילמא בחד הוא דאיפליגו? ותירץ ר"ת בספר הישר: דא"כ הוה ליה למנקט פלוגתייהו במילתא דלא שייכא ביה תוספת אהל, כי ההיא דנגר הנגרר. ומדנקט פלוגתא בפקק החלון, דשייך ביה תוספת אהל – ש"מ דפליגי באהל. וליכא למימר דדוקא באהל פליגי, ולא בטלטול – דהא בההיא דנגר לא שייך אלא איסור טלטול – אפ"ה איפלוג בה ר"א ורבנן. דע"כ איבעי לן למימר דת"ק דנגר היינו ר"א, דרבנן שרו אפילו בפקק החלון כ"ש בנגר, דלא שייך איסור אהל אלא איסור טלטול. אלא ודאי בתרתי פליגי, דר"א אסר בפקק החלון ומשום טלטול, בשאין תורת כלי גמור עליו. ואפי' יש עליו תורת כלי גמור, כגון שיש לו בית יד – אסור מ"מ משום תוספת אהל עראי, כיון דבטלי' בפקק, ורבנן דשרו – אפי' אין עליו תורת כלי, דלית להו לא משום טלטול ולא משום אהל:

רבי יהודה אומר כו'. ובעירובין מסקינן: אמר רב יהודה אמר שמואל הלכה כרבי יהודה. וקשה לר"י: דהא שמואל גופיה סבר לעיל בפרק "במה טומנין" (דף נ.) גבי חריות של דקל שגדרן לעצים, דבמחשבה בעלמא סגי, דאיתמר: רב (יהודה) אומר קושר, ושמואל אמר חושב. וקאמר התם דשמואל ס"ל כרשב"ג, דאמר: חריות של דקל שגדרן לעצים ונמלך עליהן לישיבה – א"צ לקשר. וא"כ, היכי קאמר הלכה כרבי יהודה דבעי קשירה משום איסור טלטול? דהא לא שייך איסור בנין בההיא דנגר הנגרר, אלא איסור טלטול, ומשום איסור טלטול בעי רבי יהודה קשירה, כדפירשתי. וליכא לפרושי דבנגר הנגרר דהכא, לאפוקי מאיסור בנין הוא דבעי קישור, אבל משום איסור טלטול לא הוה בעי קישור אלא במחשבה בעלמא, כרשב"ג. א"כ, מאי קא מהדר ליה ר' אבא בר כהנא לר' ירמיה: אנא דאמרי – כי האי תנא כו'. דילמא מאי דלא בעי התם רשב"ג אלא מתוקן אע"פ שאינו קשור – היינו משום דהתם ליכא אלא איסור טלטול. דהתם ודאי לא מיירי מידי בבנין, דקאמר: קנה שהתקינו בעה"ב להיות פותח ונועל[א]. ומדקתני פותח ונועל – משמע שאינו נועל באותו קנה עצמו, דהוה ליה למיתני שהתקינו לנעול בו. אלא משמע שהוא כעין מפתחות שלנו, שיש מהם שמושכין המנעול שבדלת לכאן ולכאן – כך הקנה מושך המנעול. אבל הקנה עצמו אינו במקום המנעול. א"כ פשיטא דכה"ג לא שייך בנין בהאי קנה, אלא משום איסור טלטול הוא. ומיהו, אין ראיה מזה, דבהאי קנה מיירי כדפרישית, מדקתני פותח ונועל – דהא כה"ג קתני בתוספתא: חבילי עצים וסוכה של קוצים שעשאן דלת לפירצה ולחצר, אם היו קשורות ותלויות – פותחין ונועלין בהן, אם לאו כו'. מיהו, אומר ר"י: דאפילו הוה מפרש ההיא דקנה שהתקינו כו' דשייך ביה בנין, ובמקום מנעול הוה, ולהכי פשיט מיניה רבי אבא בר כהנא דס"ל כרשב"ג, דאמר דכי הוי מתוקן אע"פ שאינו קשור – נפיק מתורת איסור בנין – לא הוי אתי שפיר. (דה"א) מדקאמר התלמוד בסמוך: וכ"ת הכא נמי דאיכא תורת כלי עליהן, והתניא: חריות של דקל כו'. והיכי מוכח מההיא דחריות של דקל דהא דאמר מתוקן אע"פ שאינו קשור היינו בלא תורת כלי, אלא במחשבה בעלמא? דלמא באיסור טלטול הוא, דלא מצריך רשב"ג אלא מחשבה, אבל באיסור בנין – הוה בעי שיתקנוהו ויכינוהו ויעשו בו מעשה, שיהא תורת כלי עליו! על כן נראה לר"י: דבהכי פליגי רבי אבא בר כהנא ורבי יוחנן ורב יהודה דעירובין (דף קב.), דאינהו סבירא להו דבההיא דנגר לא שייך אלא איסור טלטול, ואיהו ס"ל דשייך בנין בנגר הנגרר. ולהכי בעי קישור – לאפוקי מאיסור בנין. והשתא אתיא שמעתין שפיר, דלא מיירי מידי באיסור בנין לא בההוא דנגר ולא בההיא דקנה, והשתא נמי ההיא דקנה משום טלטול. מ"ר:

שקשור ותלוי וראשו מגיע לארץ. פירוש: ראשו העליון תלוי, וראשו התחתון מגיע לארץ, כדפירש בקונטרס. ונראה לרשב"א: דאפילו שני הראשים מונחים לארץ, אלא שקשור – דשרי במקדש. והאי דנקט כהאי גוונא – לאשמעינן דאפ"ה אסור במדינה. והשתא אתי שפיר הא דתנן במשנה: והמונח – כאן וכאן אסור. היינו שאינו קשור ולא תלוי כלל. דאי אמרת דוקא נקט ראשו מגיע לארץ, אבל שני הראשים מונחין בארץ – אסור במקדש אע"פ שקשור. אם כן, השתא לא הוי מונח דרבי יהודה – כמונח דתנא קמא, דמונח דרבי יהודה על כרחיך היינו שאינו לא קשור ולא תלוי, ושומטו ומניחו בקרן זוית. דאי אמרת כמו מונח דת"ק, ששני ראשים מונחים בארץ אלא שקשורין – היכי קאמר המונח במקדש? ההוא אפילו במדינה שרי, דלא אסר רבי יהודה אפילו במדינה. אלא דוקא שאינו קשור כלל:

וכ"ת

עין משפט נר מצוה

מג א ב מיי' פכ"ב מהלכות שבת הלכה ל ופכ"ו הלכה י סמג לאוין סה טוש"ע או"ח סימן שיג סעיף א:

מד ג מיי' פכ"ו שם הלכה י:

רבינו חננאל

עליהן מוסיף על אהלי עראי הוא ושפיר דמי. וחכ"א בין כך ובין כך פוקקין בו. ומיבעיא לן מאי בין כך ובין כך אמר רבה בר כהנא בין קשור בין שאינו קשור אותו פקק פוקקין בו. והוא שמתוקן. כלומר שהתקינו לפקק בו. היכי דמי תיקון זה כדאמרינן בסוף המוצא תפילין: ת"ר סיכי קמצים וחבילי עצים שהתקינן לפירצה שבחצר. בזמן שקשורין ותלוין נועלין בשבת ואין צ"ל ביו"ט. א"ל ר' ירמיה ולימא מר בין תלוי בין שאינו תלוי והוא שקשור כלומר כבר נעשה בו מעשה לשום כלי. דאמר רבה ב"ב חנה א"ר יוחנן כמחלוקת כאן בפקק החלון כך חלוקתן בנגר הנגרר בקשור ותלוי בלבד. אבל לא לענין מקדש ומדינה. ותניא בסוף עירובין. איזהו נגר הנגרר שנועלין בו במקדש אבל לא במדינה: שומטו ומניחו בקרן זוית. דייקינן מינה מדקתני ושומטו ומניחו מכלל שאם הוא קשור שאם אינו יכול לשומטו ולהניחו בקרן זוית שפיר דמי. ואמרינן מאן תנא נגר הנגרר צריך להיות קשור ותלוי ר' אליעזר והא ר' יוחנן סבר כי חכמים חלוקין על ר' אליעזר סבירא להו כר' יהודה דאסר בשאינו קשור ולא תלוי ולא בתלוי אבל אם הוא קשור אע"פ שאינו תלוי שרי. וא"ל ר' אבא לר' ירמיה אנא דאמרי והוא שמתוקן אע"פ שאינו לא קשור ולא תלוי כי הא מתניתא דתני בקנה שהתקינו בעה"ב להיות פותח ונועל בו. ואמר רשב"ג מתוקן אע"פ שאינו קשור ואמר משמיה דר' יוחנן הלכה כרשב"ג דקאי רשב"ג כחכמים. ואקשינן היכי אמר ר' יוחנן הלכה

מסורת הש"ס

עירובין קב.

[נ"ל מותר במקדש]

[תוספ' פט"ו]

הגהות הב"ח

(א) תוס' ד"ה ר' יהודה וכו' פותח ונועל בו מלקתני פותח ונועל בו משמע:

גליון הש"ס

גמ' שנועלין בו במקדש אבל לא במדינה. עיין פי"א מ"ד דכלים:

שֶׁיֵּשׁ לָהֶם בֵּית אֲחִיזָה – נִיטָּלִין בַּשַּׁבָּת. וְאָמַר רַב יְהוּדָה בַּר שֵׁילָא אָמַר רַב אַסִּי אָמַר רַבִּי יוֹחָנָן: וְהוּא שֶׁיֵּשׁ תּוֹרַת כְּלִי עֲלֵיהֶן! וְכִי תֵּימָא: הָכָא נַמִּי דְּאִיכָּא תּוֹרַת כְּלִי עָלָיו. וּמִי בָּעֵי רשב״ג תּוֹרַת כְּלִי עָלָיו?! וְהָתַנְיָא: *חֲרָיוֹת שֶׁל דֶּקֶל שֶׁגְּדָרָן לְשֵׁם עֵצִים וְנִמְלַךְ עֲלֵיהֶן לִישִׁיבָה – צָרִיךְ לִקְשׁוֹר, רשב״ג אוֹמֵר: אֵין צָרִיךְ לִקְשׁוֹר. רַבִּי יוֹחָנָן סְבִירָא לֵיהּ כְּוָותֵיהּ בַּחֲדָא, וּפָלֵיג עֲלֵיהּ בַּחֲדָא. דָּרַשׁ רַבִּי יִצְחָק נַפָּחָא אַפִּתְחָא דְּרֵישׁ גָּלוּתָא: הֲלָכָה כְּרַבִּי אֱלִיעֶזֶר. מְתִיב רַב עַמְרָם: *"וּמִדִּבְרֵיהֶם לָמַדְנוּ שֶׁפּוֹקְקִין וּמוֹדְדִין וְקוֹשְׁרִין בַּשַּׁבָּת"! א״ל [אַבַּיֵי]: מַאי דַּעְתִּיךְ – מִשּׁוּם דְּקָתָנֵי סְתָמָא – "נֶגֶר הַנִּגְרָר" נַמִּי סְתָמָא הִיא! וַאֲפִ׳ הָכִי – *מַעֲשֶׂה רַב.§ **מתני׳** (*כָּל) כִּיסּוּי הַכֵּלִים שֶׁיֵּשׁ לָהֶם בֵּית אֲחִיזָה – נִיטָּלִין בַּשַּׁבָּת. א״ר יוֹסֵי: בד״א – [א]בְּכִיסּוּי קַרְקָעוֹת, אֲבָל בְּכִיסּוּי הַכֵּלִים – בֵּין כָּךְ וּבֵין כָּךְ נִיטָּלִין בַּשַּׁבָּת.§ **גמ׳** אָמַר רַב יְהוּדָה בַּר שֵׁילָא א״ר אַסִּי א״ר יוֹחָנָן: [ב]וְהוּא שֶׁיֵּשׁ תּוֹרַת כְּלִי עֲלֵיהֶן. דְּכ״ע, כִּסּוּי קַרְקָעוֹת אִם יֵשׁ לָהֶן בֵּית אֲחִיזָה – אִין, אִי לָא – לָא. כִּסּוּי הַכֵּלִים, אע״ג דְּאֵין לָהֶם בֵּית אֲחִיזָה. כִּי פְּלִיגִי – בְּכֵלִים דְּחַבְּרִינְהוּ בְּאַרְעָא, מ״ס: גָּזְרִינַן, [ג]וּמ״ס: לָא גָּזְרִינַן. לִישָּׁנָא אַחֲרִינָא: כִּי פְּלִיגִי – בְּכִיסּוּי תַּנּוּר, מָר מְדַמֵּי לֵיהּ לְכִיסּוּי קַרְקַע, וּמָר מְדַמֵּי לֵיהּ לְכִיסּוּי כֵּלִים.§

הדרן עלך כל הכלים

מְפַנִּין *[ד]אֲפִילּוּ אַרְבַּע וְחָמֵשׁ קוּפּוֹת שֶׁל תֶּבֶן וְשֶׁל תְּבוּאָה מִפְּנֵי הָאוֹרְחִים, וּמִפְּנֵי בִּטּוּל בהמ״ד, *אֲבָל לֹא אֶת הָאוֹצָר. מְפַנִּין תְּרוּמָה טְהוֹרָה, וּדְמַאי, וּמַעֲשֵׂר רִאשׁוֹן שֶׁנִּטְּלָה תְּרוּמָתוֹ, וּמַעֲשֵׂר שֵׁנִי וְהֶקְדֵּשׁ שֶׁנִּפְדּוּ, וְהַתּוּרְמוֹס הַיָּבֵשׁ – מִפְּנֵי שֶׁהוּא מַאֲכָל *לָעִזִּים. *אֲבָל לֹא אֶת הַטֶּבֶל, וְלֹא אֶת מַעֲשֵׂר [רִאשׁוֹן] שֶׁלֹּא נִטְּלָה תְּרוּמָתוֹ, וְלֹא אֶת מַעֲשֵׂר שֵׁנִי וְהֶקְדֵּשׁ שֶׁלֹּא נִפְדּוּ, וְלֹא *אֶת הַלּוּף וְלֹא אֶת הַחַרְדָּל. ר׳ שִׁמְעוֹן בֶּן גַּמְלִיאֵל *מַתִּיר בַּלּוּף מִפְּנֵי שֶׁהוּא מַאֲכָל עוֹרְבִין. חֲבִילֵי קַשׁ וַחֲבִילֵי עֵצִים וַחֲבִילֵי זְרָדִים, אִם הִתְקִינָן לְמַאֲכַל בְּהֵמָה – מְטַלְטְלִין אוֹתָן, וְאִם לָאו – אֵין מְטַלְטְלִין אוֹתָן.§ **גמ׳** הַשְׁתָּא חָמֵשׁ מְפַנִּין, אַרְבַּע מִיבַּעְיָא?! *אָמַר רַב חִסְדָּא: אַרְבַּע מֵחָמֵשׁ. (*אִיכָּא דְּאָמְרִי: [ה]אַרְבַּע מֵאוֹצָר קָטָן) וְחָמֵשׁ מֵאוֹצָר גָּדוֹל. וּמַאי "אֲבָל לֹא אֶת הָאוֹצָר" – שֶׁלֹּא יַתְחִיל בָּאוֹצָר תְּחִלָּה. וּמַנִּי – רַבִּי יְהוּדָה הִיא, דְּאִית לֵיהּ מוּקְצֶה. וּשְׁמוּאֵל אָמַר: אַרְבַּע וְחָמֵשׁ. כִּדְאָמְרִי

רש״י

שֶׁיֵּשׁ לָהֶן בֵּית אֲחִיזָה. בֵּית יָד: ה״ג: וְאָמַר רַב יְהוּדָה וְהוּא שֶׁיֵּשׁ תּוֹרַת כְּלִי עֲלֵיהֶן. שֶׁהַכִּיסּוּי רָאוּי לְתַשְׁמִישׁ[א] עַצְמוֹ – הוּא דְּנִיטָּלִין בַּשַּׁבָּת, וְאִם אֵין תּוֹרַת כְּלִי עָלָיו – לָא אָמְרִינַן כִּיסּוּי כְּלִי הֲוֵה כְּלִי. וְדַלְתוֹת שִׁידָּה תֵּיבָה וּמִגְדָּל דְּתָנָא מַתְנִי׳ נוֹטְלִין – יֵשׁ תּוֹרַת כְּלִי עֲלֵיהֶן, דִּרְאוּיִין לֵישֵׁב עֲלֵיהֶן וְלָתֵת עֲלֵיהֶן מְזוֹנוֹת לְקָטָן. וּלְקַמָּן מְפָרֵשׁ אַמַּאי בָּעֵינַן בֵּית אֲחִיזָה, הוֹאִיל וְתוֹרַת כְּלִי עֲלֵיהֶן. אַלְמָא לְרַבִּי יוֹחָנָן מִידֵי דְּלֵיכָּא תּוֹרַת כְּלִי עָלָיו – לֹא מְטַלְטְלִין. וְהַאי קָנֶה מַאי תּוֹרַת כְּלִי עָלָיו אִיכָּא? אִי מִשּׁוּם דְּפוֹתֵחַ וְנוֹעֵל בּוֹ – אֵין זוֹ תּוֹרַת כְּלִי עָלָיו, אֶלָּא תּוֹרַת בִּנְיָן: וְכ״ת הָכָא נַמִּי דְּאִיכָּא תּוֹרַת כְּלִי עָלָיו. שֶׁרָאוּי לְהַפֵּךְ בּוֹ זֵיתִים אוֹ לְפַצֵּעַ בּוֹ אֱגוֹזִים[ב]: (*תּוֹרַת כְּלִי עָלָיו. אֲפִי׳ אֵינוֹ רָאוּי לְדָבָר אַחֵר): סְבִירָא לֵיהּ כְּוָותֵיהּ בַּחֲדָא. דִּמְתוּקָּן, וְאע״פ שֶׁאֵינוֹ קָשׁוּר: וּפָלֵיג עֲלֵיהּ בַּחֲדָא. דְּבָעֵי תּוֹרַת כְּלִי: הֲלָכָה כְּרַבִּי אֱלִיעֶזֶר. דְּבָעֵינַן קָשׁוּר וְתָלוּי: מִדִּבְרֵיהֶם לָמַדְנוּ. בְּפֶ׳ בַּתְרָא, בִּימֵי אָבִיו שֶׁל ר׳ צָדוֹק וּבִימֵי אַבָּא שָׁאוּל בֶּן בָּטְנִית שֶׁפָּקְקוּ אֶת הַמָּאוֹר בְּטָפִיחַ, וְקָשְׁרוּ אֶת הַמְקֵידָה בְּגֶמִי לֵידַע אִם יֵשׁ בַּגִּיגִית פּוֹתֵחַ טֶפַח. וְהָתָם מְפָרֵשׁ לָהּ, וְקָתָנֵי: מִדִּבְרֵיהֶם לָמַדְנוּ: שֶׁפּוֹקְקִין. אֶת הַמָּאוֹר בְּדָבָר שֶׁאֵינוֹ קָשׁוּר וְתָלוּי: וְקוֹשְׁרִין. קֶשֶׁר שֶׁאֵינוֹ שֶׁל קַיָּימָא לְכַתְּחִלָּה: וּמוֹדְדִין. מִקְוֶה וּמַטְלָנִיּוֹת: מַאי דַּעְתִּיךְ. דְּמוֹתְבַתְּ לְרַבִּי יִצְחָק נַפָּחָא מֵהָא – מָצֵי לְשַׁנּוּיֵי לָךְ: הָא מַנִּי – רַבָּנַן הִיא. וְאִי מִשּׁוּם דְּקָתָנֵי לָהּ סְתָמָא מוֹתְבַתְּ לֵיהּ, דְּמִדְּסָתַם לָן כְּרַבָּנַן הִלְכְתָא כְּוָתַיְיהוּ: נֶגֶר הַנִּגְרָר נַמִּי סְתָמָא. קָתָנֵי לָהּ, וְסָתַם לָן בְּהָא כְּרַבִּי אֱלִיעֶזֶר דְּאָסוּר: מַעֲשֶׂה רַב. לְמֵילַף מִינֵּיהּ, דְּכֵיוָן דְּסָמִיךְ לְמֶיעֱבַד עוּבְדָּא לְקוּלָּא – ש״מ הִלְכְתָא הִיא: **מתני׳** בְּכִיסּוּי קַרְקַע. כְּגוֹן כִּיסּוּי בּוֹר וְדוּת דַּהֲוֵי כְּבוּנֶה, אִי לָאו דְּמוֹכְחָא בֵּית אֲחִיזָה דִּילָהּ דִּלְמִשְׁקַל וְאַהֲדוּרֵי עֲבִיד: **גמ׳** א״ר יוֹחָנָן וְהוּא שֶׁיֵּשׁ תּוֹרַת כְּלִי עֲלֵיהֶם. דְּכִיסּוּיִין הַלָּלוּ חֲזוּ לְתַשְׁמִישׁ דְּעָלְמָא. אֲבָל כִּיסּוּי כְּלִי – לָא אָמְרִינַן כְּלִי הוּא: וּדְכ״ע. מִשּׁוּם דְּאוֹקְמָא ר׳ יוֹחָנָן בְּשֶׁיֵּשׁ תּוֹרַת כְּלִי עֲלֵיהֶן – אִיצְטְרִיכָא לֵיהּ לְמֵימַר, דְּכִי פְּלִיגִי רַבָּנַן – בְּכֵלִים דְּחַבְּרִינְהוּ בְּאַרְעָא פְּלִיגִי. דְּאִילּוּ כֵּלִים דְּעָלְמָא, אע״ג דְּלֵית לְהוּ לְכִיסּוּיֵיהֶן בֵּית אֲחִיזָה – מִיטַּלְטְלֵי, דְּכֵיוָן דְּאִיכָּא תּוֹרַת כְּלִי עֲלֵיהֶן קַיְימִי, מַה לִּי אִיכָּא בֵּית אֲחִיזָה מַה לִּי לֵיכָּא בֵּית אֲחִיזָה. אֶלָּא בְּכִיסּוּי כֵּלִים הַמְחוּבָּרִ׳ לַקַּרְקַע, כְּגוֹן תַּנּוּר וְכִירַיִם הוּא דִּפְלִיגִי, מִשּׁוּם דְּדָמוּ קְצָת לְכִיסּוּי בּוֹר וְדוּת, וְגָזְרִינַן הָנֵי אַטּוּ הָנֵי:

הדרן עלך כל הכלים

מְפַנִּין. אִם צָרִיךְ לִמְקוֹמָן לְהוֹשִׁיב שָׁם אוֹרְחִים לְהָסֵב בִּסְעוּדָ׳, אוֹ תַּלְמִידִים לִדְרָשָׁה, וְלֹא חָיְישִׁינַן לְטִרְחָא דְּשַׁבָּת: אֲבָל לֹא אֶת הָאוֹצָר. מְפָרֵשׁ בַּגְּמָרָא: מְפַנִּין תְּרוּמָה טְהוֹרָה. כְּלוֹמַר: וּמַהוּ מְפַנִּין? – דָּבָר הָרָאוּי, כְּגוֹן אֵלּוּ: תְּרוּמָה טְהוֹרָה, דַּחֲזֵי לְבֶהֱמַת כֹּהֵן. אֲבָל תְּרוּמָה טְמֵאָה – לֹא, דַּאֲפִילּוּ לְבֶהֱמַת כֹּהֵן לָא חַזְיָא בַּשַּׁבָּת. דְּאע״ג דְּבְחוֹל חַזְיָא, כִּדְתַנְיָא בְּ"כָל שָׁעָה" בִּפְסָחִים (דף לג.), שֶׁאִם רָצָה כֹּהֵן מַרִילָהּ לִפְנֵי הַכֶּלֶב – בְּשַׁבָּת וּבְיוֹם טוֹב לָא חַזְיָא, דְּזוֹ הִיא בִּיעוּרָהּ מִן הָעוֹלָם, אוֹ לְהַסִּיק אוֹ לִבְהֵמָה, וְאֵין מְבַעֲרִין תְּרוּמָה טְמֵאָה וְקָדָשִׁים טְמֵאִין בְּיוֹם טוֹב, כִּדְתְנַן (לעיל דף כג:): וְאֵין מַדְלִיקִין בְּשֶׁמֶן שְׂרֵיפָה בְּיוֹם טוֹב. וְאוֹקִימְנָא *טַעְמָא מִשּׁוּם דְּאֵין שׂוֹרְפִין קָדָשִׁים בְּיוֹם טוֹב: [ג]לוּף. מִין קִטְנִיּוֹת, שֶׁאֵינוֹ רָאוּי חַי אֲפִילּוּ לִבְהֵמָה: לָעוֹרְבִין. כְּגוֹן עֲשִׁירִים שֶׁמְּגַדְּלִין עוֹרְבִין לִגְדוּלָּה: זְרָדִים. מִין קָנִים הֵם, שֶׁמְּזָרְדִים כְּשֶׁהֵן רַכִּים וְאוֹכְלִים אוֹתָם: **גמ׳** אַרְבַּע מֵחָמֵשׁ. אִם לֹא הָיָה שָׁם אֶלָּא כְּשִׁיעוּר ה׳ קוּפּוֹת לֹא יְפַנֶּה אֶלָּא ד׳ מֵהֶם, שֶׁאָסוּר לִגְמוֹר אֶת הָאוֹצָר, דִּילְמָא חָזֵי גּוּמּוֹת בְּקַרְקָעִיתוֹ וּמַשְׁוֵי לְהוּ: מֵאוֹצָר גָּדוֹל. וְאִם יֵשׁ הַרְבֵּה – אֵין מְפַנִּין אֶלָּא חָמֵשׁ, דְּחָיְישִׁינַן לְטִירְחָא: מַאי אֲבָל לֹא אֶת הָאוֹצָר. שֶׁלֹּא יִגְמוֹר אֶת הָאוֹצָר לָא מָצֵית אָמְרַתְּ, דְּהָא מֵרֵישָׁא שָׁמְעִינַן אַרְבַּע וְחָמֵשׁ: תְּחִלָּה. אִם לֹא הִתְחִיל בּוֹ לְהִסְתַּפֵּק מִמֶּנּוּ כְּבָר לְמַאֲכָלוֹ אוֹ לְמַאֲכַל בְּהֶמְתּוֹ, דְּאִם כֵּן – הֲוָה לֵיהּ מוּקְצֶה, וּמַתְנִיתִין רַבִּי יְהוּדָה הִיא: כִּדְאָמְרִי

*) ס״א ל״ג ומ״כ שלפני רש״י היה הגירסא בגמרא אחר ברייתא דחריות אלמא לא בעי רשב״ג תורת כלי עליו ומציין רש״י בזה.

תוספות

וכי תימא הכא נמי דאיכא תורת כלי עליו. פי׳ בקונטרס: שיהא ראוי לעשות שום תשמיש אחר. ואין נראה לר״ת; כי למה יש לנו להצריך שלדבר אחר יהא ראוי, כיון שראוי לדבר זה? אלא נראה לר״ת דה״פ: דאיכא תורת כלי עליו – שתיקנו ועשה בו מעשה והכינו לכך. שמאחר שלכך תיקנו והכינו לכך – יש תורת כלי עליו, אפילו אינו ראוי לדבר אחר. כמו חריות של דקל, שאינן ראוין לשום תשמיש אלא לישיבה – אף על פי כן[ד] יכול להכינם ולטלטלם בשבת. ואבנים נמי, אמרינן לעיל: לאו ושיפשפו. ועוד: אי תורת כלי עליהם ממש נריכא למימר דכלי ניטל לצורך גופו?! והא דאמרי׳ בעירובין (ד׳ קב.): נגר הנגרר עשה לו בית יד מהו? א״ל: בוכנא קאמרת. פירוש: ושרי. לאו משום דאי לא הוה כבוכנא ע״י הבית יד הזה הוה אסור, דאפילו לא חזי למילתא אחריתי, כיון שתקנוהו בידים לכך – היה מותר אפי׳ בלא בית יד. אלא נראה לר״י: דההיא מיירי בנקמז, דאסור לעיל מיני׳ בסמוך, משום דמיחזי כבונה. פי׳: שנועץ הנגר בתוך הנקב שבמפתן עד[ה] בתוך הארץ, כדפירש בקונטרס התם. ועלה קאי: הא עשה לו בית יד, באותו נגר שנקמז. אי נמי: שמואל לטעמיה, דסבר דטעמא דרבי יהודה משום בנין, אפילו בלא נעילת נגר בארץ. וכן נראה יותר, כי נקמז אין פתרונו נעילה בארץ אלא דומה שהוא מעין נשמט, רק שאינו נשמט ממש, כדמוכח בברייתא שהביא למעלה. דקתני: נגר, אם נשמט כולו – אסור, נקמז – מותר, רבי יהודה אומר: נקמז אע״פ שאינו נשמט. ולא נודע פירוש נקמז היטב. ובירושלמי גרסינן: נגר דר׳ אליעזר הוה קטיר בגמי, נשמט – אסור, נקמז – רבי יעקב בר אחא מורה בראשי אצבעותיו[ו]:

ומדבריהן למדנו שפוקקין ומודדין. ואע״ג דטפיח לא מבטל ליה כמו פקק, כדאמרי׳ בפרק "הישן" (סוכה דף כח.) גבי סדין – איכא למימר דמבטל ליה טפי מסדין. ולא מצי למימר נמי פקק דמלוה שאני, כדאמרי׳ בשילהי מכילתין (ד׳ קנז:) גבי מדידה. דהתם לא הוי איסור כל כך, אלא משום דהוי כעובדא דחול. אבל פקק דמשום תוספת אהל, דדמי לבנין – ליכא למישרי משום מלוה:

הדרן עלך כל הכלים

מפנין ארבע וחמש קופות. בירושלמי מפרש: כמה שיעור קופות – כההוא דתנינן* "שלשה קופות של שלשה סאין":
[בשקלים פ״ג מ״ב]

רב נסים גאון

פי״ז ר׳ יהודה היא דאמר מוקצה ור׳ שמעון לית ליה מוקצה אצל כל פחמא (פי׳ עיקר הדברים) בפרק במה יודליקין וכבר פירשנו זה בפרק יציאות השבת:

רבינו חננאל

כרשב״ג ורשב״ג שרי אע״פ דליכא תורת כלי עליו. ור׳ יוחנן שמעי׳ ליה דבעי תורת כלי. ואוקימנא בקנה שהתקינו להיות נועל ופותח בו בדאיכא תורת כלי עליו ובהא א״ר יוחנן הלכתא כרשב״ג. אבל בחריות של דקל שגדרן לעצים דשרי רשב״ג בלא קישור לא סבר לזה ר׳ יוחנן כוותיה. ועליהן [אמר דר׳] יוחנן סבר לה כוותיה בחדא ופליג עליה בחדא: **דרש** ר׳ יצחק נפחא אפתחא דבי ריש גלותא הלכתא כר׳ אלעזר שאין פוקקין (עליו) [בו] אם [לא שהוא] קשור ותלוי. ואותבה ר׳ (עולא) [רב עמרם] מהא דתנן בסוף שבת מדבריהן למדנו שפוקקין ומודדין וקושרין בשבת. א״ל אביי לרב (עזרא) [עמרם] למה אותיבתיה מהא מפני שהיא שנויה סתם. וקיי״ל הלכה כסתם משנה. נגר הנגרר נמי סתמא היא. והיא שנויה סתם אליבא דר׳ אלעזר. ושני ליה אע״פ דהא סתמא והא סתמא. הא סתמא דפוקקין ומודדין וקושרין בשבת עבדו בה עובדא ומעשה רב וזו הלכה למעשה והלכתא כחכמים ונדחה דרישא דר׳ יצחק נפחא. ואמרינן בתלמוד א״י. א״ר יוחנן אתיא יחידאה דהכא סתמא דתמן. ויחידאה דתמן כסתמא דהכא. פי׳ יחידאה דהכא דהוא ר׳ אלעזר דפקק החלון בסתמא דנגר נגרר [ויחידאי דנגר הנגרר] (דהוא ר׳ יהודה כסתמא) [דפקק החלון דחכ״א] בין כך ובין כך פוקקין בו: **כל** כסויי הכלים שיש להן בית אחיזה ניטלין בשבת. א״ר יוסי בד״א בכסויי קרקעות וכו׳. א״ר יהודה בר שילא א״ר אסי א״ר יוחנן והוא שיש תורת כלי עליהן. ואמרינן כולי עלמא בכסוי קרקעות אם יש להן בית אחיזה שרי ואי לא אסיר לטלטל. כגון כסויי הבארות וכסויי הדות וכיוצא בהן. כסויי כלים כגון כדות ופיטסים וכיוצא בהן אע״פ (שהן) [שאין] להן בית אחיזה מותר לטלטלן לגלותם ולכסותם. כי פליגי בכסויי כלים וחיברו בקרקע. ר׳ יוסי לא גזר ות״ק סבר גזרינן והלכתא כוותיה: **הדרן עלך פרק כל הכלים**

פי״ח מפנין אפילו ד׳ וה׳ קופות של תבן. פי׳ מפנין מעתיקין התבואה ממקום למקום מלשון וצוה הכהן ופנו את הבית. אקשינן על משנתנו. השתא ה׳ מפנין ד׳ מיבעיא ופריק רב חסדא ארבע מחמש וה׳ מאוצר גדול. ומאי אבל לא את האוצר שלא יתחיל באוצר תחלה ומני ר״י היא דאית ליה מוקצה ובא שמואל ופריק פירוק אחר ודברים פשוטין הן. אבל סוגיא דשמעתא כרב חסדא דמתניתא סתמא תנן כוותיה. שאין מתחילין

עין משפט נר מצוה

מה א ב ג מיי׳ פכ״ה מהלכות שבת הלכ״ג טוש״ע או״ח סימן שח סעיף ז:
א ד ה מיי׳ פכ״א מהל׳ שבת הלכה ב ופכ״ו הלכה טו סמג לאוין סה טוש״ע או״ח סימן שלג סעיף א:

מסורת הש״ס

[לעיל ג. וד״ה קכה:] [לקמן קנז.] [לעיל כח. וש״נ] [ביצה לג:] [שם לו.] [ס״א לעניים] [ב״מ קיג:] [ועי׳ תוס׳ לקמן קכח. ד״ה רשב״ג] [ועי׳ תוס׳ לעיל מ: ד״ה השתא] [שם כג:] [ועי׳ תוס׳ לקמן קכח. ד״ה אבל]

הגהות הב״ח

(א) רש״י ד״ה ה״ג וכו׳ לתשמיש עצמו הוא: (ב) ד״ה וכ״ת הכא וכו׳ אגוזים הס״ד ואח״כ מ״ה אין נריך לקשר אלמא דאיכא תורת כלי עליו: (ג) רש״י ד״ה לוף וכו׳ חי. וכ״ב ס״א תורמוס: (ד) תוס׳ ד״ה וכי תימא וכו׳ אלא לישיבה אעפ״כ. נ״ב ועי׳ בהשר: (ה) בא״ד עד לתוך הארץ: (ו) בא״ד מורה בראשי אצבעותיו כזה V:

כדאמרי אינשי, ואי בעי – אפילו טובא נמי מפנין. א ומאי *"אבל לא את האוצר" – שלא יגמור כולו(א) דילמא אתי לאשוויי גומות, אבל אתחולי מתחיל. ומני – ר"ש היא, דלית ליה מוקצה. ת"ר: ב אין מתחילין באוצר תחילה, אבל עושה בו שביל כדי שיכנס ויצא. עושה בו שביל?! והא אמרת "אין מתחילין"! הכי קאמר: עושה בו שביל ברגליו בכניסתו וביציאתו. תנו רבנן: תבואה *צבורה, בזמן שהתחיל בה מע"ש – מותר להסתפק ממנה בשבת, ואם לאו – אסור להסתפק ממנה בשבת, דברי ר"ש. ר' אחא מתיר. כלפי לייא?! אלא אימא: דברי ר' אחא, ג ורבי שמעון מתיר. תנא: כמה שיעור תבואה *צבורה – לתך. בעא מיניה רב נחומי בר זכריה מאביי: שיעור תבואה *צבורה בכמה? אמר ליה: הרי אמרו "שיעור תבואה צבורה – לתך". איבעיא להו: הני ארבע וחמש קופות דקאמר, בארבע וחמש קופות – אין, טפי – לא, אלמא: למעוטי בהילוכא עדיף. או דילמא: למעוטי משוי עדיף? ת"ש, דתני חדא: מפנין אפילו ארבע וחמש קופות של כדי שמן ושל כדי יין. ותניא אידך: בעשר ובחמש עשרה. מאי לאו בהא קמיפלגי – דמר סבר: מעוטי בהילוכא עדיף, ומר סבר: מעוטי במשוי עדיף? לא, ד דכ"ע מעוטי בהילוכא עדיף. ומי סברת "בעשר ובחמש עשרה" אקופות קאי?! אכדין קאי. ולא קשיא, הא – דמשתקלי חד חד בקופה, והא – דמישתקלי תרי תרי, והא – דמשתקלי תלתא תלתא, ובדקורי דהרפניא. איבעיא להו: הני ארבע וחמש דקאמר – אע"ג דאית ליה אורחין טובא, או דילמא, הכל לפי האורחין, ואת"ל: הכל לפי האורחין, חד גברא מפני לכולהו, או דילמא, גברא(ב) גברא מפני לנפשיה? ת"ש: דאמר רבה אמר רבי חייא: פעם אחת הלך רבי למקום אחד וראה מקום דחוק לתלמידים, ויצא לשדה ומצא שדה מלאה עומרים ועימר רבי כל השדה כולה (שמע מינה: הכל לפי האורחין). ורב יוסף א"ר הושעיא: פעם אחת הלך ר' חייא למקום אחד וראה מקום דחוק לתלמידים, ויצא לשדה ומצא שדה מלאה עומרים ועימר ר' חייא כל השדה כולה. ה שמע מינה: הכל לפי האורחין. ועדיין תבעי לך: חד גברא מפני ליה לכולא, או דילמא כל גברא וגברא מפני לנפשיה? ת"ש: "ועימר רבי". ולטעמיך, רבי בדנפשיה עימר?! ו אלא: צוה ועימר, ולעולם כל חד וחד מפני לנפשיה.§ "מפני האורחין וכו'".§ א"ר יוחנן: ז גדולה הכנסת אורחין כהשכמת בית המדרש, דקתני: "מפני האורחין ומפני בטול בית המדרש". ורב דימי מנהרדעא אמר: יותר מהשכמת בית המדרש, דקתני: "מפני האורחין", והדר: "ומפני בטול בית המדרש". *אמר רב יהודה אמר רב: ז גדולה הכנסת אורחין מהקבלת פני שכינה, דכתיב: °"ויאמר *(ה') אם נא מצאתי חן בעיניך אל נא תעבור וגו'". א"ר אלעזר: בא וראה, שלא כמדת הקב"ה מדת בשר ודם; מדת ב"ו – אין קטן יכול לומר לגדול "המתן עד שאבא אצלך", ואילו בהקדוש ברוך הוא כתיב: "ויאמר *(ה') אם נא מצאתי וגו'". אמר רב יהודה בר שילא א"ר אסי א"ר יוחנן: ח ששה דברים אדם אוכל פירותיהן בעולם הזה, והקרן קיימת לו לעולם הבא. ואלו הן: הכנסת אורחין, וביקור חולים, *ועיון תפלה, והשכמת בית המדרש, והמגדל בניו לתלמוד תורה, ט והדן את חברו לכף זכות. איני?! והא אנן *)תנן: אלו דברים שאדם עושה אותם ואוכל פירותיהן בעולם הזה והקרן קיימת לו לעולם הבא, ואלו הן: כיבוד אב ואם וגמילות חסדים והבאת שלום שבין אדם לחברו י ות"ת כנגד כולם **)[הני – אין, מידי אחרינא – לא]!
הני

*) פאה פ"ק מ"א קדושין לט: ע"ש **) ס"א

רש"י

כדאמרי אינשי. חשבון קטן תחילה, ואם יצטרך ליותר – יפנה יותר. משום הכי נקט ד' ברישא והדר חמשה, וה"ה אפילו טובא: שלא יגמור. משום אשוויי גומות: ברגלו. מפנה ברגלו לכאן ולכאן דרך הליכתו, דלא הוי טלטול: תבואה צבורה. מוכחא מילתא דהוקצה לאוצר: להסתפק. להאכיל לבהמתו: אסור דברי ר"ש ורבי אחא כו': כלפי לייא. כנגד היכן פונה הדבר הזה האמור להיפך? ר"ש מתיר מוקצה בכל מקום, וכאן הוא מחמיר: לייא. היכן. כגון: חלבי לנהרא, כגגי לייא דברכות (דף נח.): לתך. אבל בליר מהכי – לאו אוצר הוא: לתך. חצי כור הוא, ט"ו סאין: בד' וה' קופות אין טפי לא. בקופות עצמן הוא יפנה וימלאם אם ירצה, או שק בכתפו שיעור קופה בפעם אחת. אבל טפי, להלך יותר מה' פעמים, כגון לפנות בכלים קטנים וירבה בהילוך – לא: למעוטי בהילוכא עדיף. ואע"ג דאפושי משוי הוא: או דילמא מעוטי משוי עדיף. ואם בא לפנות בכלים קטנים כשיעור ה' קופות – מותר. ולרב חסדא קבעי לה, דאמר ה' דוקא: בי' וט"ו. קס"ד: אקופות קאי, לומר שמפנה בקופות קטנות, וירבה בהילוך: אכדין קאי. ולא פליגי, והכי קאמר: בי' בט"ו יפנה באותן ה' קופות: הא דמשתקלי חדא חדא בקופה. הך דתניא ד' וה' – ולא נחת למניינא דכדין, איירי בכדין גדולים דמשתקלי חדא בקופה. והך דתנא בי' וט"ו – איירי בכדים בינונים ובכדין קטנים, עשר כדמשתקלי תרי תרי בקופה, ט"ו כדמשתקלי תלתא תלתא בקופה דקטנים: כי דקורי דהרפניא. *כדין של הרפניא: איבעיא להו. אליבא דרב חסדא: דחוק לתלמידים. שאין מקום לתלמידים להושיב: ועימר. פנה את העומרים. וכרמלית הואי, ובפחות פחות מד' אמות: ת"ש ועימר רבי. אלמא: חד גברא פנינהו: רבי בנפשיה עימר. בתמיה: וכי אורחיה דנשיא בהכי?! כהשכמת ביהמ"ד. מדשוי להו במתני' כי הדדי: מהשכמת בית המדרש. דתנא דידן אקדמיה ברישא: אל נא תעבור. והניחו והלך לקבל האורחים: ועיון תפלה. לכוין בתפלתו:
הכי

תוספות

של כדי שמן ושל כדי יין. והא דתנן בפ' "המביא" (ביצה דף כט:): כדי יין לא יביאם בסל ובקופה – היינו ממקום רחוק, דמיחזי כעובדין דחול, אבל הכא בביתו:

דכולי עלמא למעוטי בהלוכא עדיף. לא מצי למימר למעוטי במשוי עדיף, דההיא דקתני ד' וה' קופות לא מצי סבר הכי, דא"כ הוה ליה למיתני בעשר וט"ו כשיעור ה' קופות. וא"ת: והא תנן בפרק "אין צדין" (שם דף כה.): שחטה בשדה – לא יביאנה במוט ובמוטה, אלא מביאה לאיברים, אף על גב דמפיש בהילוכא! התם שאני, דאיכא טירחא יותר מדאי להביאה שלימה. א"נ: משום דמיחזי כמוליכה למכור בשוק. והא דאמרינן בריש "שואל" (לקמן דף קמח.): היכי ליעבד, דמליא בחצבא רבא תימלי בחצבא זוטא – קא מפשא בהילוכא, דמליא בחצבא זוטא תמלא בחצבא רבא – קא מפשא במשוי! התם, כיון שנהגו למלאות המים בחצבא רבא או בחצבא זוטא – קשה להם לשנות מכמות שנהגו:

אע"ג דאית ליה אורחין טובא או דילמא הכל לפי האורחין. מכאן יש להוכיח דהא דתנן במתניתין ד' וה' קופות הוי אפי' בשביל אדם אחד. דאי הוי נמי לפי האורחין, אמאי נקט ד' וה'? ועוד: מדלא מספקא ליה אי חד מפני כולהו, או כל חד לנפשיה. אלא באת"ל הכל לפי האורחין, משמע הא אם אמר אף על גב דאיתרמו ליה אורחין טובא – ליכא לאיסתפוקי. ואי אמרינן דד' וה' קופות הוי לפי האורחין – אכתי איכא לספוקי אי חד גברא מפני לכולהו, או כל חד מפני לנפשיה, אלא משמע דפשיטא דד' וה' אינן לפי האורחין, אלא אפילו לצורך אדם אחד:

ולטעמיך רבי בנפשיה עימר. פי': כל השדה כולה:

דכתיב ויאמר ה' אם נא מצאתי חן וגו'. קסבר כמאן דאמר בשבועות (דף לה:): דהאי השם קדש, דאיכא מאן דאמר התם שהוא חול שלמלאכים היה מדבר, שהיו מזומנים:

אוכל מפירותיהן בעולם הזה. בפ"ק דקדושין (דף לט:) מפ': דהיינו אם היתה *שקולה – מכרעת, דשכר מצות בהאי עלמא ליכא:
כיון

עין משפט נר מצוה

ב א מיי' פכ"ו מהל' שבת הלכה טו טוש"ע שם:
ג ב ג מיי' שם הלכה יד וטו:
ד ד טוש"ע שם סעיף ב:
ה ה ו מיי' וסמג שם טוש"ע שם ס"ג:
ו ז מיי' פי"ד מהלכות אבל הלכה ב:
ז ח סמג עשין יב:
ח ט מיי' פ"ה מהלכות דעות הלכה ז ופכ"ג מהלכות סנהדרין הלכה י טוש"ע ח"מ סימן יז סעיף י:
ט י מיי' פ"ג מהלכות ת"ת הלכה ג סמג שם טוש"ע י"ד סימן רמו סעיף יח:

והך משנה דהכא פליגא אר' יעקב דס"ל בסוף פרק קמא דקדושין דשכר מצוה כו' רש"ל. ואפשר לפרש כוונת התוספות בלא הגה"ה שרוצים ליישב שם למאי דלא תירצו התם הקושיא באופן אחר דהני מצות הקרן כולה קיימת לעוה"ב לאפוקי שאר מצות ומתרצי תוס' דא"א לפרש כן דשכר מצוה בהאי עלמא ליכא אליבא דכ"ע ולא פליגי התם אר"י אלא בפירות ודוק כ"מ ומהרש"א גרס דשכר מצוה בהאי עלמא איכא:

מסורת הש"ס

תורה אור
[ביצה לו.]
[מלת צבורה ליתא בשאלתות פרשת ויגש סי' לח]
[ג"י ליתא שם]
[ג"י ליתא שם]
[ועי' כפרש"י ב"מ פד. ותוס' חולין ד. ד"ה דקורה]
רש"ל מ"ז
[שבועות לה:]
בראשית יח
[נ"ל אדני]
[נ"ל אדני]
[עי' תוספות לעיל קיח: ד"ה עיון ותוספות ברכות לב: ד"ה כל ותוס' ב"ב קסד: ד"ה עיון]

הגהות הב"ח

(א) גמ' שלא יגמור כולו (דילמא וכו' גומות) תא"מ ונ"ב ס"א מתחק: (ב) שם או דילמא גברא וגברא:

גליון הש"ס

גמרא גדולה הכנסת אורחים. עי' ב"מ דף פו ע"א ובתוספות שם ד"ה חזייה:

רבינו חננאל

מתחילין באוצר תחלה ולא בתבואה צבורה. ומדבעא רב נחומי כמה שיעורי תבואה צבורה. ותנא כמה שיעור תבואה צבורה לתך ש"מ דהלכתא כהני מתניתא מדקט[ר]חינן לפרושי טעמייהו ויש מי שאומר הלכתא כשמואל דמוקים למתניתין כרבי שמעון דלית ליה מוקצה והלכתא כוותיה. ולתך זה האמור כאן הוא שיעור הקופות ששנינו במשנתנו. ואע"ג דלא איתאמרא בהדיא בגמרא דילן הא איתפרש בתלמוד א"י. ר' זעירא שאל לר' יאשיה כמה שעור הקופות. א"ל נלמד סתום מן המפורש דתנינן תמן בג' קופות של ג' ג' סאין תורמין את הלשכה. ושיעור לתך חצי כור והוא ט"ו סאין. נמצא שעור המשנה והברייתא שיעור אחד. וכדאוקמה רב חסדא למתני' ד' מה'. והכין שמעתא דא סלקא ועלה קמבעיא לן מעוטי בהלוכא עדיף או מעוטי במשוי עדיף. ואמרי' ת"ש דתני חדא מפנין אפילו ד' וה' קופות של כדי יין וכדי שמן. ותניא אידך בעשר ובחמש עשרה. ואוקימנא להו דכ"ע מעוטי בהילוכא עדיף. ושיעורם אחד הם. ואכדין קאי ולא אקופות והא מתניתא דקתני חמש הכין פירושא. חמש כדות גדולות שאין מכילה הקופה יותר מכדה אחת. והא מתניתא דקתני בעשר ובחמש עשרה בעשר כדות בחמש קופות והן בינוניות שנמצאו ב' כדות בכל קופה והא דתני ט"ו ג' כדות בכל קופה והא דמשתקלי תלת כדי בכל קופה כגון דקורי הרפניא פי' כדות שעושין בהרפניא והן קטנות ונוטלות ג' ג' בקופה שנמצא שיעור משקל כל כדה קטנה סאה והבינונית סאה וחצי. והגדולה ג' סאין. ותוב איבעיא לן הני דקא מפנינן ד' או ה' קופות מפני האורחין אע"פ דאית ליה אורחין הרבה אין לו רשות לפנות יותר מזה השיעור או דילמא הכל לפי האורחין ועוד בעיא אחרת כשמפנין אחד מפנה לכולן או כל אחד מפנה לעצמו ואיפשיטא שמעתא הכל לפי האורחין אם יש לו אורחין הרבה מפנין להן כל צרכן. ובאנו לדקדק מדקתני ועימר רבי את כל השדה שאחד מפנה לכולן (ולא עמר) [ודחינן וליטעמיך] וכי ר' בעצמו עימר אלא צוה ועימרו. ולעולם כל חד וחד לנפשיה וכיון דלא איפשיט בהדיא חד מפנהו לכולהו מחמרינן לפנויי כל דחד וחד לנפשיה דאיסורא הוא. וסתמא לחומרא. זה נכון לפנות כל אחד לעצמו ומסתייעא הא מילתא מהא (לעיל דף קכ"ה ע"ב) דא"ר חנינה פעם אחד הלך למקום אחד ומצא נדבך של אבנים ואמר לתלמידיו צאו וחשבו כדי שנשב עליהן למחר ולא סמך במחשבתו שלו אלא הצריך כל אחד לעצמו וכדר' אסי ור' אמי אליבא דר' יוחנן כל אחד כטעמיה. פי' נדבך של אבנים אבנים סדורות זו ע"ג זו. ושפשפום לפשפשם ברגליהם. סואר של קורות קורות נתונות זו ע"ג זו. גשוש בלשון ישמעאל עירים ספינות. נגדר בלשון ישמעאל מתרו ופינוי לבית המדרש ולאורחים והכנת מקום לישיבתם שניהם שוין בדבר מצוה ושאר השמועה פשוטה היא. והא דתנן מפנין ד' ה' קופות. ה"מ לדבר מצוה מדקתני מפני האורחין

רב נסים גאון

כמה שיעור תבואה לתך. הלתך הוא חצי כור והוא ט"ו כי הכור הוא ל' סאה והכור והחומר מדה אחת כי תרגום חומר כמו שאתה מוצא ביחזקאל (מה) האיפה והבת תוכן אחד להם ואמר התרגום מכילתא וביתא טוקם חד יהי לכון סכום תלת סאין למיסב מעשר כורא הרי נתברר לו מכאן כי החומר הוא כור וכי הבת היא ג' סאין ואמר אחר כך כי עשרת הבתים חומר נמצא שיעור הכור ל' סאין ושם אמר (הושע ג) וחומר שעורים ולתך שעורים ואמרו חכמים בפרק גיד הנשה (חולין דף צב) אלו ארבעים וחמשה צדיקים החומר ל' ולתך ט"ו הכל מ"ה נתקיים לך כי הכור הוא שני לתכים:

שמא

הני נמי *(בגמילות חסדים שייכי. ל"א: הני) בהני שייכי. ת"ר: הדן חבירו לכף זכות דנין אותו לזכות. ומעשה באדם אחד שירד מגליל העליון ונשכר אצל בעה"ב אחד בדרום שלש שנים. ערב *יוה"כ אמר לו: תן לי שכרי, ואלך ואזון את אשתי ובני. אמר לו: אין לי מעות. אמר לו: תן לי פירות. אמר לו: אין לי. תן לי קרקע. אין לי. תן לי בהמה. אין לי. תן לי כרים וכסתות. אין לי. הפשיל כליו לאחוריו, והלך לביתו בפחי נפש. לאחר הרגל נטל בעה"ב שכרו בידו, ועמו משוי ג' חמורים, אחד של מאכל ואחד של משתה ואחד של מיני מגדים, והלך לו לביתו. אחר שאכלו ושתו נתן לו שכרו. אמר לו: בשעה שאמרת לי "תן לי שכרי" ואמרתי "אין לי מעות" במה חשדתני? אמרתי: שמא פרקמטיא בזול נזדמנה לך, ולקחת בהן. ובשעה שאמרת לי "תן לי בהמה" ואמרתי "אין לי בהמה" במה חשדתני? אמרתי: שמא מושכרת ביד אחרים. בשעה שאמרת לי "תן לי קרקע" ואמרתי לך "אין לי קרקע" במה חשדתני? אמרתי: שמא מוחכרת ביד אחרים(א) היא. ובשעה שאמרתי לך "אין לי פירות" במה חשדתני? אמרתי "שמא אינן מעושרות". ובשעה שאמרתי לך "אין לי כרים וכסתות" במה חשדתני? אמרתי: שמא הקדיש כל נכסיו לשמים. א"ל: העבודה, כך היה! הדרתי כל נכסי בשביל הורקנוס בני שלא עסק בתורה, וכשבאתי אצל חבירי בדרום התירו לי כל נדרי. ואתה, כשם שדנתני לזכות – המקום ידין אותך לזכות. ת"ר: *מעשה בחסיד אחד שפדה ריבה אחת בת ישראל, ולמלון השכיבה תחת מרגלותיו, למחר ירד וטבל ושנה לתלמידיו. ואמר (*להן): בשעה שהשכבתיה תחת מרגלותי במה חשדתוני? אמרנו: שמא יש בנו תלמיד שאינו בדוק לרבי. בשעה שירדתי וטבלתי במה חשדתוני? אמרנו: שמא מפני טורח הדרך אירע קרי לרבי. אמר להם: העבודה, כך היה. ואתם, כשם שדנתוני לכף זכות – המקום ידין אתכם לכף זכות. תנו רבנן: פעם אחת הוצרך דבר אחד לתלמידי חכמים אצל מטרוניתא אחת, שכל גדולי רומי מצויין אצלה. אמרו: מי ילך? אמר להם ר' יהושע: אני אלך. הלך רבי יהושע ותלמידיו, כיון שהגיע לפתח ביתה חלץ תפיליו ברחוק ארבע אמות, ונכנס ונעל הדלת בפניהן. אחר שיצא ירד וטבל, ושנה לתלמידיו. ואמר *(להן): בשעה שחלצתי תפילין במה חשדתוני? אמרנו: כסבור רבי "לא יכנסו דברי קדושה במקום טומאה". בשעה שנעלתי במה חשדתוני? אמרנו: שמא דבר מלכות יש בינו לבינה. בשעה שירדתי וטבלתי במה חשדתוני? אמרנו: שמא ויתזה צינורא מפיה על בגדיו של רבי. אמר להם: העבודה, כך היה. ואתם, כשם שדנתוני לזכות – המקום ידין אתכם לזכות.§ "מפנין תרומה טהורה וכו'".§ פשיטא! לא צריכא, אדמנחה ביד ישראל. מהו דתימא: כיון דלא חזיא ליה – אסור, קמ"ל: כיון דחזיא לכהן – שפיר דמי.§ ב"ודמאי (וכו')".§ דמאי, הא לא חזי ליה?! *כיון דאי בעי, מפקר ליה לנכסיה והוה עני, וחזיא ליה – השתא נמי חזי ליה. *דתנן: גמאכילין את העניים דמאי ואת האכסניא דמאי. ואמר רב הונא; תנא, ב"ש אומרים: אין מאכילין את העניים דמאי ואת האכסניא דמאי, וב"ה אומרים: מאכילין את העניים דמאי ואת האכסניא דמאי.§ "ומעשר ראשון שניטלה תרומתו וכו'".§ פשיטא! לא צריכא שהקדימו בשבולים, ונטלה הימנו תרומת מעשר, ולא נטלה הימנו תרומה גדולה. וכי הא *)דא"ר אבהו אר"ל: דמעשר ראשון שהקדימו בשבולין – פטור מתרומה גדולה, שנא': °"והרמותם ממנו תרומת ה' מעשר מן המעשר" מעשר מן המעשר אמרתי לך, ולא תרומה גדולה ותרומת מעשר מן המעשר. *א"ל רב פפא לאביי: א"ה אפי' הקדימו בכרי נמי ליפטר! א"ל, עליך אמר קרא: °"מכל מתנותיכם תרימו וגו'". ומה ראית?! האי אידגן, והאי לא אידגן.§ "ומעשר שני וכו'".§ פשיטא! הלא צריכא, שנתן את הקרן ולא נתן את החומש, הא קמ"ל – דאין חומש מעכב.§ "והתורמס היבש כו'".§ דווקא יבש, אבל לח – לא. מ"ט? כיון דמריר – לא אכלה.§ אבל

*) ברכות שם עירובין לא: פסחים לה: ביצה יג:

תוספות

כיון דחזיא לכהן שפיר דמי. אע"ג דאמר בשילהי כירה (לעיל דף מז.) דבגדי עניים לעשירים לא – הכא לכ"ע חזיא, אלא איסורא הוא דרביע עליה. אבל התם – לא חזו מחמת גריעותא. ומהאי טעמא נמי לא אמרינן התם טעמא דבסמוך דאי בעי מפקר לנכסיה. והא דאמר בפרק "כל הכלים" (לעיל ד' קכה.): שירי פרוזמיות שאין בהן ג' על ג' – אין מטלטלין אותן. משמע: הא יש בהן שלש על שלש – מטלטלים, היינו לעניים. א"נ: אפילו לעשירים בבית עניים: דאי בעי מפקר לנכסיה. הוה מצי למימר כדלעיל: כיון דחזי. אלא, כיון דמשכח טעמא דאפי' לדידיה מצי חזי – אמר. ובפרק "כל שעה" (פסחים דף לה:) ובפרק "שלשה שאכלו" (ברכות ד' מז.) איצטריך להאי טעמא*: האי אידגן. מדנקט אידגן – משמע אפי' לא ראה פני הבית. תימה: אכתי, אפילו הקדימו בכרי נמי לא לחייב אלא באידגן וראה פני הבית! וי"ל: דאי לא כתב "והרמותם" ה"א דכולם חייבין, אפילו לא אידגן. השתא דכתי' קרא – מוקמי ליה במסתבר, דהיינו לא אידגן. שאפילו ראה פני הבית לא היה חייב. א"נ, י"ל: הא דנקט אידגן – היינו ככל דינו, שראה פני הבית, אלא דמילתא דפסיקא נקט. דאיכא למאן דאמר בבא מציעא (ד' פח:) דלא בעינן ראיית פני הבית אלא בזיתים וענבים דלאו בני גורן נינהו: הא קמ"ל דאין חומש מעכב. ואף על גב דמבעיא לן בפרק "הזהב" (שם דף נד.) אי מעכב אי לא, ולא פשיט מהכא – משום דהוה מצי למידחי דאגב אחרינא תנייה: אבל

רש"י

ה"ג הני נמי בהני שייכי. הכנסת אורחים וביקור חולים היינו גמילות חסדים, ועיון תפלה היינו בכלל גמילות חסדים, דכתיב (משלי יא): "גומל נפשו איש חסד". *השכמת בית המדרש וגידול בנים לתלמוד תורה – היינו תלמוד תורה. דן את חבירו לכף זכות – בכלל הבאת שלום, דמתוך שהוא מכריעו לזכות, ואמר: לא חטא לי בזאת, אנוס היה, או לטובה נתכוון – יש שלום ביניהן. ורבי יוחנן לפרש לך אתא, דבכלל ג' דמתניתין איתנהו להנך ו'. ואיכא נמי לכבוד אב ואם, ורבי יוחנן לא פליג עליה: בפחי נפש. בדאבון נפש: מוחכרת. שנותנה לחבירו בכך וכך כורין לשנה: כל היכא דאמרינן* מעשה בחסיד אחד או רבי יהודה בן בבא, או רבי יהודה ברבי אלעאי: ריבה. נערה: שאינו בדוק לרבי. שאינו מכיר במדותיו, לסמוך עליו ולהניחה אצלנו: מטרוניתא. גויה: דבר מלכות. וצריך להעלימו: צינורא. רוק, וגזרו על הגוים שיהיו כזבים לכל דבריהם: מאכילין לעניים דמאי. לא אסרוהו עליהם, מפני שצריכים לחזור על פתח ע"ה, וסמכו על שרוב עמי הארץ מעשרין: אכסניא. (ב)חיל של מלך ישראל, ומטילו על בני העיר לפרנסן*: שניטלה תרומתו. קס"ד: תרומת מעשר שהלוי נותן לכהן, וכ"ש תרומה גדולה שיש על ישראל להפריש, והפרישו קודם שנתן המעשר ללוי: שהקדימו בשבולין. לתרומה. ישראל היה לו להפריש תרומה גדולה תחילה, דכתיב (שמות כב): "מלאתך ודמעך לא תאחר", מלאתך – אלו בכורים מכאן שהמקדים תרומה לבכורים לוקה. "ודמעך" – זו תרומה. שאם הקדים מעשר לתרומה – לוקה. והנ"מ – משנתמרח בכרי לוקה אם הקדים מעשר לתרומה. אבל הקדים למעשר קודם לתרומה בשבלים – אינו לוקה: והרמותם ממנו. בלוים כתיב, גבי תרומת מעשר: מכל מתנותיכם וגו'. נמי בלוים כתיב, גבי תרומת מעשר, וקאמר: "את כל תרומת ה'", כל – משמע כל לד תרומה שבו: האי. דנתמרח: אידגן. וחלה עליו חובת תרומה, כדכתיב (דברים יח): "ראשית דגנך". הלכך, כי שקלה לוי – בעי אהדורי לכהן תרי ממאה שבו בראשא, והדר חד מעשרה: דמריר. שהוא מר: שלא

עין משפט נר מצוה

י א מיי' פכ"ה מהלכות שבת הלכה כ:
יא ב שם הלכה יט:
יב ג מיי' פ"י מהלכות מעשר הלכה יא:
יג ד מיי' פ"ג מהלכות תרומות הלכה יג טוש"ע יו"ד סימן שלא:
יד ה מיי' פכ"ה מהל' שבת הלכה יט:

[ברי"ף וברא"ש איתא ערב הרגל]

[ועי' תוס' עירובין לא. ד"ה דמאי ותוס' סוכה לה. ד"ה דלאו כגון]

רבינו חננאל

ומפני ביטול בהמ"ד שהן מצות כדרב יהודה אמר שמואל דאמר גדול הכנסת אורחין. וכדר' יוחנן דאמר אחד משלשה דברים שאדם אוכל מפירותיהן בעוה"ז והקרן קיימת לו לעולם הבא: מפנין תרומה טהורה אע"פ שהיא בביתו של ישראל הואיל וראויה לכהן היום מטלטלין אותה ושפיר דמי וכן דמאי והדמאי כיון דאילו הפקיר כל נכסיו ויהיה עני מותר לאוכלו אע"פ שעכשיו לא הפקיר נכסיו מותר לטלטלו. והוא הלוקח תבואה מעם הארץ שאינו יודע אם הוציא מעשר ממנה אם לאו כי התרומה לא נחשדו עמי הארץ עליה (ודאי) והיו מפרישין אחד מחמשים והוא בבינונית ונתנו לכהן אבל המעשר הוי הרבה ע"ה שלא היו מפרישין אותו ונותנין ללוי. וחייבו חכמים הקונה מעם הארץ שאינו יודע אם הוציא מעשר ממנה אם לאו להפריש מזו התבואה חלק אחד ממאה שהיא תרומת מעשר שהוא א' מי' בתרומה והוא עון מיתה. וזה פירושו ישראל שיש לו מאה סאין תבואה חייב לתת לכהן ב' סאין מהן והוא תרומה גדולה וחייב לתת עשרה מהן פחות מעט והוא נקרא מעשר ראשון וחייב הלוי לתת מן העשרה סאה שנתנו לו ישראל סאה אחת לכהן והוא שאמר הכתוב והרמותם ממנו תרומת ה' מעשר מן המעשר. נמצא הסאה שביד כהן שהוא תרומת מעשר שנתן לו הלוי אחר מאה מן התבואה שביד ישראל שע"ה לא היו מפרישין מעשר ללוי [לכן] חייבו בן מיתה [לכן] חייבוהו להפריש [אבל] המעשר שתבואה בלאו אינו חייבוהו מספק. וזה מפורש בגמרא יומא(*) הודיית המעשר בסוף מס' סוטה ודמאי זה כיון שהוא ספק מעושר ספק אינו מעושר התירוהו מפני חיי נפש לאכסניא ולעניים (בפירושו). וזה שאמר ר"ל מעשר ראשון שהקדימו בשבלין פטור מתרומה גדולה פי' חייבה התורה להפריש תרומה ומעשר מן הדגן שכבר נעשה גורן כדכתיב ראשית דגנך תירושך ויצהרך כו' ואינו נקרא דגן אלא אחרי דישתו בגורן והעמדתו כרי והתורה אמרה להפריש מן הדגן ראשון תרומה גדולה ואחריו מעשר ראשון. ואחריו שנה ראשונה ושניה מעשר שני. ושנה שלישית אינו מפריש מעשר [שני] אלא מעשר עני. ואינו חייב להפריש כל אלו אלא אחרי שיקצור ויגדוש ויזרה ויעמיד כרי בגורן לפיכך אמר ר"ל אם בא ישראל מי שהיו לו עשרה עומרין שבלין וקודם שיכניסן לגורן לדוש נתן מהן עומר אחד מעשר ללוי הלוי אינו חייב לתת ממנו אלא תרומת מעשר לכהן שהשבלין לא נתחייבו אלא בתרומה ולא במעשר והביא טעם לדבריו מן המקרא הזה והקשה עליו רב פפא למה הוצרכת לדחוק הדבר בשבולין אפילו בכרי הקדים והפריש המעשר קודם שיפרוש התרומה ליפטר ולא יהא חייב הלוי להפריש ממנו אלא תרומת מעשר. ופירק לו כיון שהעמידו כרי אידגן וקרינא ביה מכל מתנותיכם תרימו שכולל הכל. ומעשר שני והקדש שנפדו הוצרך להזכירו התנא להודיע שאם לא נתן החומש מעכב

*) בסוף סוטה במשנת דיוחנן כ"ג העביר הודיית המעשר ובגמ' שם כל"ל.

מסורת הש"ס

כאן חסר ונפש כו' היינו תפלה דכתי' גבי חנה ואשפוך את נפשי לפני ה' ש"א א' ע' רש"י ברכות ל: ד"ה טורף נפשו וכו' פ"א מ"ט

[וכ"ק קג:]

[וי"ל להם]

[נ"ל להם]

ברכו' מז. וש"נ

ברכות מז. דמאי פ"ג מ"א עירובין יז: לא. פסחים לה: סוכה לה:

במדבר יח

תמורה ה: במדבר יח

אבות דר"נ פ"ח ופי"ב

הגהות הב"ח

(א) גמ' שמא מוחכרת ביד אחרים וכשעה כו' נמחק: (ב) רש"י ד"ה אכסניא חיל של מלך ישראל. נ"ב וכו'

גליון הש"ס

רש"י ד"ה כל היכא דאמרינן מעשה וכו'. עיין דבר נחמד כזה בברכות הזבח תמורה דף טו ע"ב:

רב נסים גאון

שמא ויתזה צינורא מפיה על רבי. פי' צינורא שינתז מפי האדם כשהוא מדבר למטרונית והיא גוית וצריך לטבול כי רוקן של גוים גזרו עליו חכמים טומאה ועיקר זה הוא מה שאמר הקב"ה בענין הזב (ויקרא טו) וכי ירוק הזב בטהור יכול אפילו רקק ולא נגע יהא טמא ת"ל בטהור ובתוספתא זבין בפרק חמישי אמרו ורירו וכיחו ומימי האף שלו הרי הן כרוקו דמעת עינו ודם מגפתו וחלב האשה משקה זובו ורוקו ומימי רגליו מטמאים טומאה חמורה וזאת התורה מיוחדת בישראל בלבד אבל לא בגוים והחכמים הם שגזרו עליהם שיהו כזבין לכל דבריהם ותמצא כיוצא בזה במס' נדה בפרק בנות כותים (דף לד) כשאמר בית שמי דם הגוית טהור הקשה להם מזו הברייתא ולא חלקו בית שמאי אלא ברמה בלבד אבל רוקה אין מי שחולק בו כי הוא טמא ושורפין עליו את התרומה וכבר פירשו טעמם של בית שמי שטיהרו דמה (וטיהרו) [וטמאו] רוקה ומימי רגליה דשכיחי גזרו בהו רבנן דמה דלא שכיחא לא גזרו בה רבנן ובית הלל הכל אצלם טמא ושם במסכת שקלים (פ"ח מ"א) שנינו כל הרוקין הנמצאים בירושלים טהורין חוץ משל שוק העליון וגרסי בתלמוד בני מערבא ר' אבון בשם ר' יהושע קצרין של גוים היה שם ובמשנת טהרות בפרק ה' (משנה ח) שנינו שוטה אחד בעיר או גוית או כותית כל הרוקין שבעיר טמאין וקודם לכן בפרק ד' אמרו על ו' ספיקות שורפין את התרומה אחד מהן ספק רוקין כבר נתבאר לך עכשיו ונתקיים מכל מה שהקדמנו כי רוק הגוים טמא וכי גזירה דרבנן היא ובפ' יציאות השבת (דף טו) אמרו ספיקות באושא גזור עליהן ולפיכך הוצרך ר' יהושע בן חנניא טבילה ותמצא במס' יומא בפרק הוציאו לו את הכף (דף מז) אמרו עליו על רבי ישמעאל בן קימחית שיצא ודבר עם ערבי אחד בשוק וניתזה צינורא מפיו על בגדו ונכנס ישבאב אחיו ושימש תחתיו ובחומר בקודש (חגיגה דף כג) תמצא גזירת צינורא דעם הארץ וזה בענין הקודש: **מפנין** תרומה טהורה ודמאי. כבר פירשנו דמאי בפ'

שֶׁלֹּא נִיטְּלָה תְּרוּמָתוֹ. קָא סָלְקָא דַּעְתָּךְ שֶׁלֹּא נִיטְּלָה תְּרוּמַת מַעֲשֵׂר שֶׁלּוֹ: אסימון. שֶׁאֵין עָלָיו צוּרָה: חָצָב. עֵשֶׂב שֶׁמַּשְׁרִישׁ בְּעוֹמֶק כְּנֶגְדּוֹ וְאֵין שָׁרָשָׁיו מִתְפַּשְּׁטִין, *וּבוֹ תִּיחֵם יְהוֹשֻׁעַ אֶת הָאָרֶץ לְיִשְׂרָאֵל: נַעֲמִיּוֹת. בְּנוֹת הַיַּעֲנָה: יְטַלְטְלוּ. רָאוּי הוּא לִהְיוֹת לוֹ פִּילִין וּלְהַאֲכִילָן: עַל מַכּוֹתֵיהֶן. בְּשַׁבָּת, וְלֹא גָּזַר מִשּׁוּם שְׁחִיקַת סַמְמָנִין: שֶׁכֵּן דַּרְכָּן לָסוּךְ. בְּלֹא מַכָּה, הִלְכָּךְ לָאו מוֹכְחָא מִילְּתָא דִּלְרְפוּאָה: הִתְקִינָן. הִזְמִינָן: אָסוּר לְטַלְטְלָן. וַאֲפִילּוּ הִזְמִינָם לְמַאֲכַל בְּהֵמָה, דִּטְירְחָא הִיא: סִיאָה אֵזוֹב וְקוֹרָנִית. לְקַמֵּיהּ מְפָרֵשׁ לְהוּ: הִכְנִיסָן לְעֵצִים. לְיַבְּשָׁן: שֶׁלֹּא יִקְטוֹם בִּכְלִי. כְּדֶרֶךְ חוֹל, כִּדְאָמְרַן (לעיל דף עד:): הַאי מַאן דְּפָרֵיס סִילְקָא – דָּמֵי לְטוֹחֵן. בְּמִילְּתֵיהּ דְּרַבִּי יְהוּדָה גָּרְסִינַן: "מוֹלֵל וְאוֹכֵל, וּבִלְבַד שֶׁלֹּא יִמְלוֹל בִּכְלִי הַרְבֵּה. וַחֲכָמִים אוֹמְרִים: מוֹלֵל בְּרָאשֵׁי אֶצְבְּעוֹתָיו, וּבִלְבַד שֶׁלֹּא יִמְלוֹל בְּיָדוֹ הַרְבֵּה כְּדֶרֶךְ חוֹל". כָּךְ מָצָאתִי בְּתוֹסֶפְתָּא דְּרַבָּנַן מַחְמְרִי, דִּבְכוּלֵּי יָדָא אָסוּר אֶלָּא בְּרָאשֵׁי אֶצְבְּעוֹתָיו. וּמַהוּ מוֹלֵל – כְּגוֹן אִם בָּא לֶאֱכוֹל הַזֶּרַע, מוֹלֵל הַשַּׁרְבִיטִין שֶׁהַזֶּרַע בְּתוֹכָם: וְכֵן בְּאַמִיתָא. לְקַמֵּיהּ מְפָרֵשׁ מַאי אֲמִיתָא: נִינְיָא. מינטא"ה: פֵּיגָם. רוד"א: צַתְרֵי. סדריא"ה לוי"ה, ל"א: פוליאו"ל: אַבְרָתָא. איסני"א: חַשֵׁי. סדריא"ה, וְלָשׁוֹן רִאשׁוֹן לֹא פּוֹרַשׁ: בָּשָׂר תָּפֵל. שֶׁאֵינוֹ מָלוּחַ. וּמַאן דְּגָרֵיס תָּפוּחַ – הִיא הִיא: מוּתָּר לְטַלְטְלוֹ. דְּלֵית לֵיהּ מוּקְצֶה בְּטִלְטוּל: בְּמוּקְצֶה לַאֲכִילָה סָבַר לָהּ כְּרַבִּי יְהוּדָה. כְּלוֹמַר: בְּאִיסּוּר מוּקְצֶה לְעִנְיַן אֲכִילָה – סָבַר לָהּ כְּרַבִּי יְהוּדָה דְּאָסַר לְאוֹכְלוֹ(ג), וּבְאִיסּוּר מוּקְצֶה לְטִלְטוּל – סָבַר לָהּ כְּרַבִּי שִׁמְעוֹן: בַּר אַוְּזָא. שָׁחוּט: מְשַׁמְשָׁא לְטוּלָא. שֶׁלֹּא יַסְרִיחַ: וְאָמַר לְהוּ רַב חִסְדָּא חֶסְרוֹן כִּיס קָא חָזֵינָא הָכָא. שֶׁאַתֶּם מַנִּיחִים אוֹתָהּ בַּשֶּׁמֶשׁ וּמִתְחַמֶּמֶת, וְסַלְּקוּהוּ עַל פִּיו מֵחַמָּה לְצֵל: בְּאוּמְצָא. כְּשֶׁהוּא חַי, אוֹכְלִין אוֹתוֹ בְּלֹא מֶלַח: דָּג תָּפֵל אָסוּר לְטַלְטְלוֹ. דְּאֵינוֹ רָאוּי לִכְלוֹס, וְלִכְלָבִים לָאו דַּעְתֵּיהּ לְמִישְׁדְּיֵיהּ. אֲבָל מָלִיחַ – נֶאֱכָל חַי עַל יְדֵי מִלְחוֹ: בָּשָׂר

---

*אבל לא את הטבל. והא דאמר(ד) רבה בפרק "כירה" (לעיל דף מג.): טבל מוכן הוא אצל שבת, שאם עבר ותיקנו – מתוקן, ה"מ לענין ביטול כלי מהיכנו, שלא החמירו כמו לענין טלטול בידים: שפדאו אגב אסימון. הא דנקט אסימון – היינו דלא כרבי דוסא דפרק "הזהב" (ב"מ דף מז:), והוה מצי למימר: "מעות הניתנות סימן לבית המרחץ" לד"ה, אלא משום דאם כן – מאי קמ"ל, אבל השתא – קמ"ל כרבנן: ונתן הכסף וקם לו. אין הפסוק כן אלא "ויסף חמישית כסף ערכך עליו וקם לו" (ויקרא כז) ודרך התלמוד לקצר ולומר בלשון אחר קצר, כי ההיא דפרק "הדר" (עירובין דף סה.): רבי חנינא ביומא דרתח לא מצלי, שנאמר: "בצר אל יורה", ובפרק "הרואה" (ברכות דף נה:) שנאמר: "כל החלומות הולכים אחר הפה". וקשה לר"י: נימא כסף דוקא! וכ"ת דשוה כסף ככסף, חדא: דגבי נזקין מצרכינן קרא "ישיב" – לרבות שוה כסף, ועוד: דאם כן – אפילו קרקע נמי, ומנלן למעוטי קרקע? ואומר ר"י: דמכלל ופרט נפקא, כדתנן בבכורות בפרק "יש בכור לנחלה" (דף נא.): אין פודין לא בעבדים ולא בקרקעות ולא בהקדשות, ומפרש בגמרא דבעי למימר: ולא הקדשות בכל אלו. לענין פדיון בכור דרשינן התם כלל ופרט "ופדויו מבן חדש", כלל "כסף", פרט, "תפדה" – חזר וכלל. מה הפרט מפורש דבר המיטלטל כו'. ה"נ איכא למימר בפדיון הקדשות: "ונתן" ,כלל, "כסף", פרט, "וקם לו", חזר וכלל כו'. מיהו, בת"כ דריש ליה מקרא אחרינא: "וכל ערכך יהיה בשקל הקדש" מה ת"ל? לפי שנאמר(ה) "תפדה" יכול בעבדים ושטרות וקרקעו' – ת"ל: "בשקל הקדש". אין לי אלא סלעים, מניין לרבות כל דבר המיטלטל? ת"ל: "ופדה בערכך". א"כ למה נאמר "בשקל" פרט לעבדים ושטרות וקרקעות. אלא כן דרך התלמוד שאינו מביא עיקר הדרשה. כמו שרגיל להביא *] (כתובות דף מו:) "בנעוריה בית אביה" – כל שבח נעורים לאביה, אע"ג דההוא בהפרת נדרים הוא דכתיב. וכן הרבה: רשב"ג אומר אף מטלטלין שברי זכוכית. משמע דמודה לת"ק דמתיר חרדל. והא דתנן: "רשב"ג מתיר בלוף" – וכל שכן דמתיר בחרדל: הכניסן לעצים אין מסתפק. איכא למימר דה"ק: הא סתמא – נעשה כמי שהכניסן למאכל בהמה, כי היכי דלא תקשה רישא לסיפא: דחזי לאומצא. מכאן ראיה דדם האברים שלא פירש מותר, דקאמר: דחזי לאומצא, אע"ג דלא מליח*: דג תפל אסור לטלטלו. תימה: מדשרי בשר תפל – אלמא כר"ש אתיא, אם כן דג תפל נמי לישרי כמו בשר תפל! וי"ל: דדג תפל אינו ראוי לכלבים. אי נמי: כר' יהודה אתיא, ודג תפל אע"פ שראוי לכלבים – אסור לטלטלו, דכל מידי דחזי לאינש לא מקצה לכלבים. בשר תפל – מותר לטלטלו לרבי יהודה, מפני שהוא מאכל לחיה: מטלטלין את העצמות. לר' יהודה דאית לי' מוקצה – מיירי כגון שלא הי' עליה' בשר מאתמול: בשר

"אֲבָל לֹא אֶת הַטֶּבֶל וכו'". פְּשִׁיטָא! לָא צְרִיכָא, בְּטֶבֶל טָבוּל מִדְּרַבָּנַן(א) – שֶׁזְּרָעוֹ בְּעָצִיץ שֶׁאֵינוֹ נָקוּב. "וְלֹא מַעֲשֵׂר רִאשׁוֹן וכו'". פְּשִׁיטָא! לָא צְרִיכָא, שֶׁהִקְדִּימוֹ בַּכְּרִי שֶׁנִּטַּל מִמֶּנּוּ מַעֲשֵׂר וְלֹא נִטְּלָה מִמֶּנּוּ תְּרוּמָה גְּדוֹלָה. מַהוּ דְּתֵימָא כְּדַאֲמַר לֵיהּ רַב פַּפָּא לְאַבַּיֵי – קמ"ל כְּדְשַׁנֵּי לֵיהּ אַבַּיֵי. "וְלֹא אֶת מַעֲשֵׂר שֵׁנִי וכו'". פְּשִׁיטָא! לָא צְרִיכָא דְּנִפְדּוּ, וְלֹא נִפְדּוּ כְּהִלְכָתָן. מַעֲשֵׂר – שֶׁפְּדָאוֹ עַל גַּבֵּי אֲסִימוֹן, דְּרַחֲמָנָא אָמַר: "וְצַרְתָּ הַכֶּסֶף בְּיָדְךָ" – דָּבָר שֶׁיֵּשׁ בּוֹ צוּרָה. הֶקְדֵּשׁ – שֶׁחִילְּלוֹ עַל גַּבֵּי קַרְקַע, דְּרַחֲמָנָא אָמַר: "וְנָתַן הַכֶּסֶף וְקָם לוֹ". "וְלֹא אֶת הַלּוּף". ת"ר: מְטַלְטְלִין אֶת הֶחָצָב – מִפְּנֵי שֶׁהוּא מַאֲכָל לִצְבָיִים, וְאֶת הַחַרְדָּל – מִפְּנֵי שֶׁהוּא מַאֲכָל לְיוֹנִים, רשב"ג אוֹמֵר: אַף מְטַלְטְלִין שִׁבְרֵי זְכוּכִית, מִפְּנֵי שֶׁהוּא מַאֲכָל לַנַּעֲמִיּוֹת. אֲמַר לֵיהּ רַבִּי נָתָן: אִם כֵּן יְטַלְטְלוּ חֲבִילֵי זְמוֹרוֹת – מִפְּנֵי שֶׁהוּא מַאֲכָל לַפִּילִין! וְרשב"ג: נַעֲמִיּוֹת – שְׁכִיחִי, פִּילִין – לָא שְׁכִיחִי. אָמַר אַמֵּימַר: וְהוּא דְּאִית לֵיהּ נַעֲמִיּוֹת. אָמַר רַב אַשִׁי לְאַמֵּימַר: אֶלָּא דְּקָאָמַר לֵיהּ ר' נָתָן לרשב"ג: "חֲבִילֵי זְמוֹרוֹת יְטַלְטֵל מִפְּנֵי שֶׁהוּא מַאֲכָל לַפִּילִין". אִי אִית לֵיהּ פִּילִין – אַמַּאי לָא?! אֶלָּא – רָאוּי, ה"נ – רָאוּי. *אָמַר אַבַּיֵי: רשב"ג וְרַבִּי שִׁמְעוֹן וְרַבִּי יִשְׁמָעֵאל וְרַבִּי עֲקִיבָא כּוּלְּהוּ סְבִירָא לְהוּ, כָּל יִשְׂרָאֵל בְּנֵי מְלָכִים הֵם. רשב"ג – הָא דַּאֲמַרַן, ר' שִׁמְעוֹן – *דִּתְנַן: בְּנֵי מְלָכִים סָכִין עַל גַּבֵּי מַכּוֹתֵיהֶן שֶׁמֶן וֶורֶד, שֶׁכֵּן דַּרְכָּן שֶׁל בְּנֵי מְלָכִים לָסוּךְ בַּחוֹל. *ר"ש אוֹמֵר: כָּל יִשְׂרָאֵל בְּנֵי מְלָכִים הֵם. ר' יִשְׁמָעֵאל וְר' עֲקִיבָא – דְּתַנְיָא: הֲרֵי שֶׁהָיוּ נוֹשִׁין בּוֹ אֶלֶף מָנֶה וְלָבוּשׁ *אִיצְטְלָא בַּת ק' מָנֶה – מַפְשִׁיטִין אוֹתוֹ וּמַלְבִּישִׁין אוֹתוֹ אִיצְטְלָא הָרְאוּיָה לוֹ. תָּנָא מִשּׁוּם רַבִּי יִשְׁמָעֵאל, וְתָנָא מִשּׁוּם רַבִּי עֲקִיבָא: כָּל יִשְׂרָאֵל רְאוּיִן לְאוֹתָהּ אִיצְטְלָא.

"חֲבִילֵי כו'". תָּנוּ רַבָּנַן: *חֲבִילֵי קַשׁ וַחֲבִילֵי עֵצִים(ב) וַחֲבִילֵי זְרָדִים, אִם הִתְקִינָן לְמַאֲכַל בְּהֵמָה – מְטַלְטְלִין אוֹתָן, וְאִם לָאו – אֵין מְטַלְטְלִין אוֹתָן. רשב"ג אוֹמֵר: חֲבִילִין הַנִּיטָּלִין בְּיָד אֶחָד – מוּתָּר לְטַלְטְלָן, בִּשְׁתֵּי יָדַיִם – אָסוּר לְטַלְטְלָן. *חֲבִילֵי *סִיאָה אֵזוֹב וְקוֹרָנִית, הִכְנִיסָן לְעֵצִים – אֵין [א] מִסְתַּפֵּק מֵהֶן בַּשַּׁבָּת, לְמַאֲכַל בְּהֵמָה – מִסְתַּפֵּק מֵהֶן בַּשַּׁבָּת. וְקוֹטֵם בַּיָּד וְאוֹכֵל, וּבִלְבַד שֶׁלֹּא יִקְטוֹם בִּכְלִי. וּמוֹלֵל וְאוֹכֵל, וּבִלְבַד שֶׁלֹּא יִמְלוֹל בִּכְלִי הַרְבֵּה, דִּבְרֵי רַבִּי יְהוּדָה. וַחֲכָמִים אוֹמְרִים: מוֹלֵל בְּרָאשֵׁי אֶצְבְּעוֹתָיו וְאוֹכֵל, וּבִלְבַד שֶׁלֹּא יִמְלוֹל בְּיָדוֹ הַרְבֵּה כְּדֶרֶךְ שֶׁהוּא עוֹשֶׂה בַּחוֹל. וְכֵן בְּאַמִיתָא, וְכֵן בְּפֵיגָם, וְכֵן בִּשְׁאָר מִינֵי תַבְלִין. *מַאי אֲמִיתָא? נִינְיָא. "סִיאָה". אָמַר רַב יְהוּדָה: (סִיאָה) – צַתְרֵי. "אֵזוֹב" – אַבְרָתָא. "קוֹרָנִית" – קוֹרָנִיתָא שְׁמָהּ. וְהָא הַהוּא דַּאֲמַר לְהוּ: "מַאן בָּעֵי קוֹרָנִיתָא", וְאִישְׁתַּכַּח "חָשֵׁי"! אֶלָּא: סִיאָה – צַתְרֵי, אֵזוֹב – אַבְרָתָא, קוֹרָנִיתָא – חָשֵׁי. *אִיתְּמַר: בָּשָׂר מָלִיחַ מוּתָּר לְטַלְטְלוֹ בְּשַׁבָּת; בָּשָׂר [ב] תָּפֵל, רַב הוּנָא אָמַר: מוּתָּר לְטַלְטְלוֹ, רַב חִסְדָּא אָמַר: אָסוּר לְטַלְטְלוֹ. רַב הוּנָא אָמַר: מוּתָּר לְטַלְטְלוֹ? וְהָא *רַב הוּנָא תַּלְמִיד דְּרַב הֲוָה, וְרַב כְּר' יְהוּדָה סְבִירָא לֵיהּ, דְּאִית לֵיהּ מוּקְצֶה! בְּמוּקְצֶה לַאֲכִילָה – סָבַר לָהּ כְּרַבִּי יְהוּדָה, בְּמוּקְצֶה לְטַלְטֵל – סָבַר לָהּ כְּרַבִּי שִׁמְעוֹן. רַב חִסְדָּא אָמַר: אָסוּר לְטַלְטְלוֹ. וְהָא רַב יִצְחָק בַּר אַמֵּי אִיקְלַע לְבֵי רַב חִסְדָּא, וַחֲזָא הַהוּא בַּר אַוְּזָא דַּהֲווֹ קָא מְטַלְטְלוּ לֵיהּ מִשִּׁמְשָׁא לְטוּלָא. וְאָמַר רַב חִסְדָּא: חֶסְרוֹן כִּיס קָא חָזֵינָא הָכָא! שָׁאנֵי בַּר אַוְּזָא דַּחֲזֵי לְאוּמְצָא. ת"ר: דָּג מָלִיחַ – מוּתָּר לְטַלְטְלוֹ, דָּג תָּפֵל – אָסוּר לְטַלְטְלוֹ. בָּשָׂר, בֵּין תָּפֵל וּבֵין מָלִיחַ – מוּתָּר לְטַלְטְלוֹ, (*וּסְתָמָא כְּרַבִּי שִׁמְעוֹן). תָּנוּ רַבָּנַן: מְטַלְטְלִין אֶת הָעֲצָמוֹת מִפְּנֵי שֶׁהוּא מַאֲכָל לִכְלָבִים, בָּשָׂר

רבינו חננאל

מעבב: אסימון מטבע שאין עליו צורה...

רב נסים גאון

בפרק שלשה שאכלו באחת כי הוא הדבר הנדמה דמי מתוקן ומי אינו מתוקן...

גליון הש"ס...

בשר תפוח מפני שהוא מאכל לחיה. תימה: לימא מפני שהוא מאכל לכלבים! וי"ל: דכרבי יהודה אתיא, ואינו מסריח כפירוש הקונטרס אלא חזי ליה. וכל מידי דחזי ליה לאינש – לא מקלה לכלבים. אבל מפני שהוא מאכל לחיה – מותר לטלטלו, דכל ישראל בני מלכים הם. ורב חסדא דלא שרי בשר תפל מהאי טעמא – לית ליה כל ישראל בני מלכים:

אין עוקרין בהמה חיה ועוף. לספרים דגרסי רה"ר – הך ברייתא פליגא אקמייתא בתרתי, דדייקינן: הא דדויי מדדינן אפילו ברה"ר. ולעיל קתני: דווקא בחצר. ותו: סיפא דמוקמת לתרנגולת דאין מדדין ברה"ר, ולעיל קתני: דאפי' בחצר לא. ולספרים דגרסי: "אין עוקרין בהמה חיה ועוף בחצר" – אתי שפיר: **קמ"ל** איתובי מיתבא דעתה. אע"ג דבפרק בתרא דיומא (דף פג.) אמר: חולה אין מאכילין אותו ביוה"כ אלא ע"פ מומחה, והכא(ה) שריא משום יתובי דעתא – היינו שיותר יכולה היולדת להסתכן על ידי פחד שתתפחד שמא אין עושין יפה מה שהיא צריכה, ממה שיסתכן החולה ברעב:
רבה

בשר תפוח – מפני שהוא מאכל לחיה, מים מגולין – מפני שהן ראויין לחתול. רשב"ג אומר: כל עצמן אסור לשהותן, מפני הסכנה.§ **מתני'** *א כופין את הסל לפני האפרוחים כדי שיעלו וירדו. תרנגולת שברחה דוחין אותה עד שתכנס. מדדין עגלין וסייחין.* (א)אשה מדדה את בנה, אמר רבי יהודה: ב אימתי – בזמן שהוא נוטל אחת ומניח אחת! אבל אם היה גורר – אסור.§ **גמ'** אמר רב יהודה אמר רב: בהמה שנפלה לאמת המים – מביא כרים וכסתות ומניח תחתיה, ואם עלתה – עלתה. מיתיבי: *בהמה שנפלה לאמת המים – עושה לה פרנסה במקומה בשביל שלא תמות. פרנסה – אין, כרים וכסתות – לא! לא קשיא; ג הא – דאפשר בפרנסה, הא – דאי אפשר בפרנסה. אפשר בפרנסה – אין, ואי לא – מביא כרים וכסתות ומניח תחתיה, והא *קא מבטל כלי מהיכנו! סבר, מבטל כלי מהיכנו – דרבנן, *ד צער בעלי חיים – דאורייתא, ואתי דאורייתא ודחי דרבנן.§ ה"תרנגולת שברחה וכו'".§ דוחין – אין, מדדין – לא. תנינא להא, דת"ר: ו מדדין בהמה חיה ועוף בחצר, אבל לא את התרנגולת. תרנגולת מאי טעמא לא? אמר אביי: משום דמקפיא נפשה. תני חדא: מדדין בהמה וחיה ועוף בחצר, אבל לא ברה"ר. והאשה מדדה את בנה ז ברה"ר, ואצ"ל בחצר. ותניא אידך: אין עוקרין בהמה וחיה ועוף בחצר, אבל דוחין בהן שיכנסו. הא גופא קשיא, אמרת: "אין עוקרין" אבל דדויי – מדדינן. (ב)הדר אמרת: דוחין – אין, מדדין – לא! אמר אביי: סיפא אתאן לתרנגולת. אמר אביי: ח האי מאן דשחיט תרנגולת – לכבשינהו לכרעיה בארעא, אי נמי – נידל להו מידל. דדילמא מנח להו לטופריה בארעא, ועקר להו לסימנים.§ **מתני'** ט אין מילדין את הבהמה ביום טוב! אבל מסעדין. ומילדין את האשה בשבת, וקורין לה חכמה ממקום למקום, ומחללין עליה את השבת, וקושרין את הטיבור. רבי יוסי אומר: *אף חותכין. *וכל צרכי מילה עושין בשבת.§ **גמ'** כיצד מסעדין? רב יהודה אמר: אוחז את הולד שלא יפול לארץ. רב נחמן אמר: דוחק בבשר כדי שיצא הולד. תניא כוותיה דרב יהודה: *כיצד מסעדין – י אוחזין את הולד שלא יפול לארץ, ונופח לו בחוטמו, ונותן לו דד לתוך פיו כדי שינק. אמר רשב"ג: כ מרחמין היינו על בהמה טהורה ביו"ט. היכי עביד? אמר אביי: מביא בול של מלח ומניח לה בתוך הרחם, כדי שתזכור צערה ותרחם עליו. ומזלפין מי שליא על גבי ולד כדי שתריח ריחו ותרחם עליו. ודוקא טהורה, אבל טמאה – לא. מ"ט? טמאה לא מרחקא ולדא, ואי מרחקא ולדא – לא מקרבא.§ ל "מילדין את האשה וכו'".§ מכדי תנא ליה "מילדין את האשה וקורין לה חכמה ממקום למקום", "ומחללין עליה את השבת" לאתויי מאי? לאתויי הא דתנו רבנן: מ אם היתה צריכה לנר – חבירתה מדלקת לה את הנר, ואם היתה צריכה לשמן – חבירתה מביאה לה שמן בידה, ואם אינו ספק בידה – מביאה בשערה, ואם אינו ספק בשערה – מביאה לה בכלי. אמר מר: אם היתה צריכה לנר – חבירתה מדלקת לה את הנר. פשיטא! נ לא צריכא בסומא. מהו דתימא: כיון דלא חזיא – אסור, קא משמע לן: איתובי מיתבא דעתה, סברא: אי איכא מידי – חזיא חבירתה ועבדה לי.§ "אם היתה צריכה לשמן וכו'".§ תיפוק ליה משום סחיטה! רבה ורב יוסף דאמרי תרווייהו: אין סחיטה בשיער. רב אשי אמר: אפי' תימא "יש סחיטה בשיער" – מביאה לה בכלי דרך שערה. *דכמה דאפשר לשנויי – משנינן. אמר רב יהודה אמר שמואל: חיה, כל זמן שהקבר פתוח, בין אמרה "צריכה אני" *)בין לא אמרה "צריכה אני" – מחללין עליה את השבת. נסתם הקבר, בין אמרה
צריכה

*) ס"א בין אמרה איני צריכה.

בשר תפוח. מסריח: לחתול. לא מזיק ליה ארס דנחש, שאף הנחשים היא אוכלת: מפני הסכנה. שמא ישתה אדם מהם: **מתני'** כופין סל בפני האפרוחים. אשמעינן דכלי ניטל לדבר שאינו ניטל בשבת. ורבי יצחק משני לה* בפ"ג – בצריך למקומו: שברחה. מן הבית: דוחין. בידים: מדדין עגלים. אוחז בצוארו ובצדדין וגוררו ומסייעו(ג), ומנענע לו ברגליו: אשה מדדה את בנה. אוחזתו בזרועותיו מאחוריו ומסייעתו, והוא מניע רגליו והולך: שנוטל אחת ומניח אחת. שהתינוק מניע את רגליו, כשמניח אחת מגביה אחת: אבל גורר אסור. מפני שנושאתו: **גמ'** ואי לא. כגון שהמים עמוקין: והא קמבטל כלי מהיכנו. דמשהכניסם תחתיה אין יכול לטלטלן, דדומה לסותר בנין(ד) מדרבנן: צער בעלי חיים דאורייתא. שנאמר: "עזוב תעזוב עמו", ואיכא מאן דדריש טעמא דקרא משום צער בעלי חיים ב"אלו מציאות" (ב"מ דף לב:): מדדין לא. שלא יהא אוחזה בגפיה ורגליה נוגעין לארץ ומוליכה: דמקפיא נפשה. מגבהת עצמה מן הארץ, ונמצא זה מטלטל. אבל אווזים – כשאוחזים בגפיהן, הן מהלכין ברגליהן. ומיהו, ברה"ר לא, משום שמא יגביה מן הארץ ונמצא נושאן. דסתמא כרבנן דפליגי עליה דרבי נתן ב"המצניע" (לעיל דף צד.) גבי המוציא חיה ועוף בין חיין בין שחוטין חייב. והאשה מדדה את בנה אפילו ברה"ר, דאי נמי מגביה ליה – חי נושא את עצמו, דהכי מוקמינן התם דבאדם מודו רבנן לרבי נתן: מקפיא. כגון "אקפו ידייכו" דחגיגה (דף טז:): אין עוקרין. רגליה לגמרי מן הארץ, דמוקצה היא לטלטלה: דדויי מדדינן. אוחזה בשני לדדיה בידו ומדדה, והוה טלטול טפי מדחייה שדוחפה מאחריה: סיפא. דקתני: "דוחין אבל לא מדדין": אתאן לתרנגולת. ורישא בשאר עופות: לכבשינהו לכרעיה בארעא. כדי שיתכפלו, ולא יוכל להתחזק עליהן: אי נמי לידלינהו. יגביהנו, שלא יהו רגליו נוגעות לארץ: **מתני'** מסעדין. מפרש בגמרא: חכמה. מילדת: אין מילדין את הבהמה ביום טוב. דאיכא טרחא יתירה: אבל מסעדין. אותה בי"ט: ומיילדין אשה בשבת. ואין צריך לומר שמסעדין, וכל שכן ביום טוב: וקושרין הטיבור. של ולד שהוא ארוך, שאם לא יתקשר ויכרך בשום דבר – יצאו מעיו אם יגביהו התינוק: **גמ'** דוחק. בבשר של בהמה לפנים, שיהא הולד בולט לחוץ: ונופח לו בחוטמו. שנחיריו סתומין לו בריר: ונותן דד. של אמו בתוך פיו: מרחמין. מאהבין את ולדה עליה: בול של מלח. מלא אגרוף, דכייב לה וזוכרת צער לידה, ומרחמה את הולד אם רחקתו: מי שליא. שורין את השליא במים: לא מרחקה. אין דרכה לרחק: מביאה לה שמן. דרך רה"ר: בידה. בכפה ולא בכלי, דכמה דאפשר משנינן: בשערה. סכה שערה שמן, וכשבאה אצלה מקנחתו. ואין כאן חילול שבת, כיון שאין דרך הוצאה בכך: פשיטא. דהא פקוח נפש דוחה שבת: תיפוק ליה משום סחיטה. למה לא הביאה לה בכלי – שלא תחלל שבת בהוצאה, הכא נמי הא קמחללה בסחיטה! אין סחיטה בשיער. שהוא קשה, ואין בולע: דרך שערה. כורכת הכלי בראשה, בשערה: חיה. יולדת: קבר. בית הרחם:
צריכה

עין משפט נר מצוה

בג א מיי' פכ"ה מהל' שבת הלכה כה סמג לאוין סה טוש"ע א"ח סימן שח סעיף לט:
בד ב מיי' פ"כ שם הלכה יז סמג שם טוש"ע שם סעיף מא:
בה ג מיי' פכ"ה שם הלכה כו וסמג שם טוש"ע א"ח סימן שה סעיף יט:
בו ד מיי' פי"ג מהלכות רוצח ושמירת הנפש הלכה יג סמג עשין פ ולאוין קסט טוש"ע ח"מ סימן רעב סעיף ט:
בז ה ו מיי' פכ"ה מהל' שבת הלכה כו סמג לאוין סה טוש"ע א"ח סימן שח סעיף מ:
בח ז שם סעיף מא:
בט ח [מיי' פ"ג מהל' שחיטה הל' יד] סמג עשין סג טוש"ע י"ד סי' כד סעיף ז:
ל ט מיי' פ"ד מהל' יו"ט הלכה טז סמג לאוין עה טוש"ע א"ח סימן תקכג סעיף ג:
לא א מיי' שם טוש"ע שם סע' ה:
לב ב ג מיי' פ"ב מהלכות שבת הלכה יא סמג לאוין סה טוש"ע א"ח סי' של סעיף א:

[וכש"ע א"ח סימן ש"ל סעיף ז פסק הלכתא כרבי יוסי וכן דעת הרמב"ם]

הגהות הב"ח

(א) במשנה ואשה מדדה: (ב) גמ' והדר אמרת: (ג) רש"י ד"ה מדדין וכו' ומסייעו ליכך ומנענע: (ד) ד"ה והא קא מבטל כלי וכו' לסתור בנין מבטל כלי מהיכנו מדרבנן צער בעלי חיים: (ה) תוס' ד"ה קמ"ל וכו' והכא שרינן משום וכו' היינו לפי שיותר:

גליון הש"ס

גמרא תיפוק ליה משום סחיטה. עיין לקמן דף קמה ע"א תוספות ד"ה כבשים:

מסורת הש"ס

[נ"ל לעיל כפ"ג מג:] [לעיל מג. וש"נ ועי"ש תוספות ד"ה דמבטל] [כ"מ לב:] לקמן קלב. [תוספ' פט"ו] [לעיל קז: לקמן קמח. ביצה ל.]

רבינו חננאל

לטלטלו: דג תפל אסור לטלטלו בשר בין חי ובין מליח מותר לטלטלו. ת"ר מטלטלין את העצמות מפני שהן מאכל לכלבים בשר תפוח מפני שהוא מאכל לחיה וזו היא דחויא כוותיה דרב הונא מים מגולין מפני שהן ראוין לחתול. ומתניתא אלין הלכתא אינון דליכא דהליו ואליבא דב"ה נשנו דתנן ב"ה אומרים מגביהין מעל השלחן עצמות וקליפין: **כופין** את הסל לפני האפרוחים שיעלו ושירדו. בהמה שנפלה לאמת המים אם אפשר לה בפרנסה עושין לה פרנסה במקומה. ואם אי אפשר לה בפרנסה מביא כרים וכסתות ומניח תחתיה ואם עלתה עלתה ואף על גב דמבטל כלי מהיכנו. מדרבנן היא. וצער ב"ח דאורייתא ואתא דאורייתא ודחה דרבנן. תרנגולת שברחה דוחין אותה עד שתכנס אבל אין מדדין אותה אפי' בחצר משום דמקפיא נפשה ואע"פ ששאר בהמה חיה ועוף מדדין בחצר אבל לא ברה"ר תרנגולת אפילו בחצר לא אלא אסור לדדותה אפילו בחצר. האשה מדדה את בנה ברה"ר וכ"ש בחצר והא דאמר ר' יהודה אימתי בזמן שנוטל אחת ומניח אחת [היינו] ברה"ר בלבד שאם נוטל התינוק רגלו אחת ונשען על רגלו האחרת נמצא כמטלטל אבל אם אינו נשען על רגליו אלא כשמדדדת נישאתו ברה"ר ואסור אבל בחצר מותר לטלטלו ולשאת אותו והא דאמר אביי מאן דשחיט תרנגולת ליכבשינהו לכרעיה בארעא אי נמי תדלינהו דילמא מנח להון לטופריה בארעא ועקרה להו לסימנים הלכתא היא: **מתני'** אין מילדין את הבהמה ביו"ט אבל מסעדין. רב יהודה אמר אוחז בולד שלא יפול לארץ והלכתא כמותיה. דתניא כוותיה. כיצד מסעדין אוחז בולד שלא יפול לארץ ונופח לו בחוטמו ונותן לו דד לתוך פיו כדי שיינק כו'. וקיי"ל דמסעדין ומרחמין דתנינן בה בו"ט אבל לא בשבת ומילדין את האשה בשבת וקורין לה חכמה ממקום למקום ומחללין עליה את השבת. ואסיקנא שמדלקת לה חברתה את הנר ואפילו היא סומא מותר להדליק לה נר בשבת דקי"ל יתובי מיתבא דעתה סברא אי איכא מידי חזיא חברתאי ועבדה לי. ואם היתה צריכה לשמן מביאה לה חברתה בידה [והא] הוצאה ביד בדרך המוציאו ומסקנא כמה דאיכא לשנויי משנינן. מר זוטרא מתני אמר רב יהודה אמר שמואל חיה כל זמן שהקבר פתוח. פירוש הקבר בית הרחם. בין אמרה צריכה אני ובין אמרה איני צריכה מחללין עליה את השבת. נסתם (הכלי) [הקבר] אמרה צריכה

רב נסים גאון

כדי שיתפרשו תחומין אחד מחבירו ואמינו בכך לענין עירובין של תחומין ושיתופים כי השרשים שהוא משלח בקרקע מוכיחים על הגבולים ועל פי זה אמרו שם במסכת יום טוב (פרק אין צדין דף כה) חצובא מקטע רגליהון דרשיעיא שהוא דבר שאין בו רוח חיים וכצמיחתו משלח שרשיו בארץ במשפט והרשעים מעקמין דרכיהם ואין הולכין בדרכיו של הקב"ה כמו שראוי להם לכן דרכם באפילה: **צער** בעלי חיים דאורייתא מה שאמר הקב"ה (שמות כג) כי תראה חמור שונאך רובץ תחת משאו ואמרו בבא מציעא בפרק אלו מציאות (דף לג) מצוה מן התורה לפרוק דקסבר תנא דידן צער בעלי חיים דאורייתא ורבי יוסי הגלילי סבר צער בעלי חיים דרבנן וסבר (אביי) [רב יהודה] בכאן כתנא קמא דצער בעלי חיים דאורייתא וביטול כלי מהיכנו דרבנן משכחת לה בפרק כירה (לעיל דף מג) דתנן אין נותנין כלי תחת הנר לקבל בו את השמן ואמר רב חסדא אין נותנין כלי תחת התרנגולת לקבל ביצתה כו' ופירש רב יוסף טעמא בכך ואמר היינו טעמא דרב חסדא דקא מבטל כלי מהיכנו והא מדרבנן הוא:

סליק פרק מפנין

"צְרִיכָה אֲנִי" בֵּין לֹא אָמְרָה "צְרִיכָה אֲנִי" – אֵין מְחַלְּלִין עָלֶיהָ אֶת הַשַּׁבָּת, רַב אַשִׁי מַתְנֵי הָכִי. מָר זוּטְרָא מַתְנֵי הָכִי: אָמַר רַב יְהוּדָה אָמַר שְׁמוּאֵל: חַיָּה כָּל זְמַן שֶׁהַקֶּבֶר פָּתוּחַ, בֵּין אָמְרָה "צְרִיכָה אֲנִי" וּבֵין אָמְרָה "אֵין צְרִיכָה אֲנִי" – מְחַלְּלִין עָלֶיהָ אֶת הַשַּׁבָּת. נִסְתַּם הַקֶּבֶר, אָמְרָה *"צְרִיכָה אֲנִי" – מְחַלְּלִין עָלֶיהָ אֶת הַשַּׁבָּת, לֹא אָמְרָה "צְרִיכָה אֲנִי" – אֵין מְחַלְּלִין עָלֶיהָ אֶת הַשַּׁבָּת. א"ל רָבִינָא לְמָרֵימָר: מָר זוּטְרָא מַתְנֵי לְקוּלָּא, וְרַב אַשִׁי מַתְנֵי לְחוּמְרָא, הִלְכְתָא כְּמַאן? א"ל: הֲלָכָה כְּמָר זוּטְרָא, *סָפֵק נְפָשׁוֹת לְהָקֵל. מֵאֵימָתַי פְּתִיחַת הַקֶּבֶר? אָמַר אַבַּיֵי: *[א]מִשָּׁעָה שֶׁתֵּשֵׁב עַל הַמַּשְׁבֵּר. רַב הוּנָא בְּרֵיהּ דְּרַב יְהוֹשֻׁעַ אָמַר: [ב]מִשָּׁעָה שֶׁהַדָּם שׁוֹתֵת וְיוֹרֵד. וְאָמְרִי לָהּ: [ג]מִשָּׁעָה שֶׁחֲבֵרוֹתֶיהָ נוֹשְׂאוֹת אוֹתָהּ בְּאַגַּפֶּיהָ. עַד מָתַי פְּתִיחַת הַקֶּבֶר? אָמַר אַבַּיֵי: שְׁלֹשָׁה יָמִים. רָבָא אָמַר מִשְּׁמֵיהּ דְּרַב יְהוּדָה: שִׁבְעָה, וְאָמְרִי לָהּ: שְׁלֹשִׁים. אָמְרִי נְהַרְדְּעֵי: [ד]חַיָּה ג', ז' וְל'. ג', בֵּין אָמְרָה "צְרִיכָה אֲנִי" וּבֵין *אָמְרָה "לֹא צְרִיכָה אֲנִי" – מְחַלְּלִין עָלֶיהָ אֶת הַשַּׁבָּת. ז', אָמְרָה "צְרִיכָה אֲנִי" – מְחַלְּלִין עָלֶיהָ אֶת הַשַּׁבָּת, אָמְרָה "לֹא צְרִיכָה אֲנִי" – אֵין מְחַלְּלִין עָלֶיהָ אֶת הַשַּׁבָּת. ל', אֲפִי' אָמְרָה "צְרִיכָה אֲנִי" – אֵין מְחַלְּלִין עָלֶיהָ אֶת הַשַּׁבָּת, אֲבָל עוֹשִׂין ע"י אֲרַמַּאי. *כִּדְרַב עוּלָּא בְּרֵיהּ דְּרַב עִילַּאי, דְּאָמַר: כָּל צָרְכֵי חוֹלֶה נַעֲשִׂין ע"י אֲרַמַּאי בְּשַׁבָּת. *וּכִדְרַב הַמְנוּנָא, דְּאָמַר רַב הַמְנוּנָא: *[ה]דָּבָר שֶׁאֵין בּוֹ סַכָּנָה – *אוֹמֵר לְגוֹי וְעוֹשֶׂה. אָמַר רַב יְהוּדָה אָמַר שְׁמוּאֵל: לְחַיָּה ל' יוֹם. לְמַאי הִלְכְתָא? אָמְרִי נְהַרְדְּעֵי: לִטְבִילָה. אָמַר רָבָא: לָא אֲמַרַן אֶלָּא שֶׁאֵין בַּעְלָהּ עִמָּהּ, אֲבָל בַּעְלָהּ עִמָּהּ – בַּעְלָהּ מְחַמְּמָהּ. כִּי הָא דִּבְרַתֵּיהּ דְּרַב חִסְדָּא טְבַלָה בְּגוֹ תְּלָתִין יוֹמִין שֶׁלֹּא בִּפְנֵי בַעְלָהּ וְאִצְטְנִיאַת, וְאַמְטוּי לְעַרְסָה בָּתְרֵיהּ דְּרָבָא לְפוּמְבְּדִיתָא. *אָמַר רַב יְהוּדָה אָמַר שְׁמוּאֵל: [ו]עוֹשִׂין מְדוּרָה לְחַיָּה בְּשַׁבָּת (בִּימוֹת הַגְּשָׁמִים). סְבוּר מִינָּהּ: לְחַיָּה – אִין, לְחוֹלֶה – לָא. בִּימוֹת הַגְּשָׁמִים – אִין, בִּימוֹת הַחַמָּה – לָא. (*וְלָא הִיא, ל"ש חַיָּה וְל"ש חוֹלֶה, ל"ש בִּימוֹת הַגְּשָׁמִים וְל"ש בִּימוֹת הַחַמָּה – מִדְּאִתְּמַר) אָמַר רַב חִיָּיא בַּר אָבִין אָמַר שְׁמוּאֵל: [ז]הִקִּיז דָּם וְנִצְטַנֵּן – עוֹשִׂין לוֹ מְדוּרָה אֲפִי' בִּתְקוּפַת תַּמּוּז. שְׁמוּאֵל צְלַחוּ לֵיהּ תַּכְתְּקָא דְּשָׁאגָא, רַב יְהוּדָה צְלַחוּ לֵיהּ פְּתוֹרָא דְּיוֹנָה, לְרַבָּה צְלַחוּ לֵיהּ שַׁרְשִׁיפָא. וְא"ל אַבַּיֵי לְרַבָּה: וְהָא קָעָבַר מָר מִשּׁוּם °"בַּל תַּשְׁחִית"! *א"ל: בַּל תַּשְׁחִית דְּגוּפַאי – עֲדִיף לִי. אָמַר רַב יְהוּדָה אָמַר רַב: לְעוֹלָם יִמְכּוֹר אָדָם קוֹרוֹת בֵּיתוֹ וְיִקַּח *מִנְעָלִים לְרַגְלָיו, הִקִּיז דָּם וְאֵין לוֹ מַה יֹּאכַל – יִמְכּוֹר מִנְעָלִים שֶׁבְּרַגְלָיו וְיַסְפִּיק מֵהֶן צָרְכֵי סְעוּדָה. מַאי צָרְכֵי סְעוּדָה? רַב אָמַר: בָּשָׂר, וּשְׁמוּאֵל אָמַר: יַיִן. רַב אָמַר: בָּשָׂר, נַפְשָׁא חֲלַף נַפְשָׁא. וּשְׁמוּאֵל אָמַר: יַיִן, סוּמָּקָא חֲלַף סוּמָּקָא.§ (סִימָן שֶׁנִּמְסַר) *שְׁמוּאֵל בְּיוֹמָא דַּעֲבַד מִילְּתָא עָבְדִי לֵיהּ תַּבְשִׁילָא דְּטַחְלֵי. ר' יוֹחָנָן שָׁתֵי עַד דְּנָפֵיק תִּיהְיָא מֵאוּנֵיהּ. וְרַב נַחְמָן שָׁתֵי עַד דְּקָפֵי טַחְלֵיהּ. רַב יוֹסֵף שָׁתֵי עַד דְּנָפֵיק מֵרִיבְדָּא דְּכוּסִילְתָּא. רָבָא מְהַדַּר אַחַמְרָא בַּר תְּלָתָא טַרְפֵי. אֲמַר לְהוּ רַב נַחְמָן בַּר יִצְחָק לְרַבָּנַן: בְּמָטוּתָא מִינַּייכוּ, בְּיוֹמָא דְּהַקָּזָה אִמְרוּ לְבֵיתַייכוּ: נַחְמָן אִקְלַע לְגַבַּן. וְכוּלְּהוּ אַעֲרוּמֵי אֲסִירֵי, בַּר מֵהַאי עָרְמָה דְּשָׁרֵי: מַאן דַּעֲבֵיד מִילְּתָא וְלָא אֶפְשָׁר לֵיהּ, לִישְׁקוֹל זוּזָא מַכָּא וְלֵיזִיל לְשַׁב חֲנוָתָא, עַד דְּטָעֵים שִׁיעוּר רְבִיעָתָא. וְאִי לָא – לֵיכוּל שַׁב תַּמְרֵי אוּכָּמָתָא, וְלֵישׁוּף מִשְׁחָא בְּצִידְעֵיהּ, וְנִיגְנֵי בְּשִׁמְשָׁא. אַבְלַט אַשְׁכְּחֵיהּ לִשְׁמוּאֵל דְּגָנֵי בְּשִׁמְשָׁא. א"ל: חַכִּימָא דִּיהוּדָאֵי! בִּישָׁא מִי הָוֵי טָבָא? א"ל: יוֹמָא דְּהַקָּזָה הוּא. וְלָא הִיא, אֶלָּא: אִיכָּא יוֹמָא דְּמַעֲלֵי בַּהּ שִׁמְשָׁא בְּכוּלֵּיהּ שַׁתָּא – יוֹמָא דְּנָפְלָה בֵּיהּ תְּקוּפַת *תַּמּוּז, וְסָבַר: לָא אִיגַּלֵּי לֵיהּ.§ (הֵיקִיל בְּרוּחַ טַעְמָא שָׁהָה סִימָן) רַב וּשְׁמוּאֵל דְּאָמְרִי תַּרְוַיְיהוּ: כֹּל הַמֵּקֵיל בִּסְעוּדַּת הַקָּזַת דָּם – מְקִילִין לוֹ מְזוֹנוֹתָיו מִן הַשָּׁמַיִם. וְאוֹמְרִים: הוּא עַל חַיָּיו לֹא חָס, אֲנִי אָחוּס עָלָיו?! רַב וּשְׁמוּאֵל דְּאָמְרִי תַּרְוַיְיהוּ: הַאי מַאן דַּעֲבֵיד מִילְּתָא לָא לֵיתֵיב הֵיכָא דְּכָרֵיךְ זִיקָא, דִּילְמָא שָׁפֵי לֵיהּ אוּמָּנָא וּמוֹקִים לֵיהּ אַרְבִּיעָתָא, וְאָתֵי זִיקָא וְשָׁאֵיף מִינֵּיהּ – וְאָתֵי לִידֵי סַכָּנָה. שְׁמוּאֵל הֲוָה רָגִיל וְעָבַד מִילְּתָא בְּבֵיתָא דְּשַׁב לְבֵינַיָּא וַאֲרִיחָא. יוֹמָא חֲדָא עֲבַד, וְאַרְגִּישׁ בְּנַפְשֵׁיהּ. בְּדַק, וַחֲסַר חַד אֲרִיחָא, רַב וּשְׁמוּאֵל דְּאָמְרִי תַּרְוַיְיהוּ: הַאי מַאן דַּעֲבֵיד מִילְּתָא – לִיטְעוֹם מִידֵּי וַהֲדַר לֵיפּוֹק, דְּאִי לָא טָעֵים מִידֵּי, אִי פָּגַע בְּשַׁכְבָּא – יַרְקָא אַפֵּיהּ, אִי פָּגַע בְּמַאן דִּקְטַל נַפְשָׁא – מִית, אִי פָּגַע בְּדָבָר

רש"י

צְרִיכָה אֲנִי. לְחִילּוּל: בֵּין שֶׁאָמְרָה אֵין צְרִיכָה אֲנִי. וַחֲבֵרוֹתֶיהָ אוֹמְרוֹת שֶׁהִיא צְרִיכָה – מְחַלְּלִין: בְּאַגַּפֶּיהָ. בִּזְרוֹעוֹתֶיהָ, שֶׁאֵינָהּ יְכוֹלָה לְהַלֵּךְ: חַיָּה ג' יָמִים וְז' יָמִים וְל' יוֹם. הוּזְכְּרוּ כָּאן לְחִילּוּק הִלְכוֹת חִילּוּל שַׁבָּת. ל' – מִז' עַד הַשְׁלָמַת ל', וְכֵן ז' – מִג' עַד הַשְׁלָמַת ז': כָּל צָרְכֵי חוֹלֶה. וְהָא חַיָּה עַד ל' יוֹם סְתָמָא חוֹלָה הִיא: דָּבָר שֶׁאֵין בּוֹ סַכָּנָה. חוֹלֶה שֶׁאִם לֹא יַעֲשׂוּ לוֹ רְפוּאָה זוֹ אֵין מְסוּכָּן לָמוּת, וּמ"מ צָרִיךְ הוּא לָהּ: אוֹמֵר לַאֲרַמַּאי וְעוֹשֶׂה. אֲבָל דָּבָר שֶׁיֵּשׁ בּוֹ סַכָּנָה – יִשְׂרָאֵל עַצְמוֹ עוֹשֶׂה לוֹ: לִטְבִילָה. עַד ל' יוֹם לֹא תִּטְבּוֹל מִפְּנֵי הַצִּינָּה: שֶׁאֵין בַּעְלָהּ עִמָּהּ. וְהִיא טוֹבֶלֶת לְטָהֳרוֹת: בַּעְלָהּ מְחַמְּמָהּ. לְאַחַר טְבִילָה בְּתַשְׁמִישׁ, וְהַגּוּף מִתְחַמֵּם מִן הַגּוּף: מְדוּרָה. הֶיסֵּק גָּדוֹל: הִקִּיז דָּם. וְכ"ש חוֹלֶה: צְלַחוּ לֵיהּ תַּכְתְּקָא דְּשָׁאגָא. לֹא מָצְאוּ עֵצִים מוּכָנִים לְהֶיסֵּק בְּיוֹם הַקָּזָה, וְנָזְיוּ וּבִקְעוּ כִּסֵּא שֶׁל תִּדְהָר, שֶׁהוּא מְעוּלֶּה בְּדָמִים: פְּתוֹרָא דְּיַוְנָה. מִין אֶרֶז הוּא. וְרַבֵּינוּ הַלֵּוִי אָמַר[(א)]: בוּי"ש: *רָבָא צְלַחוּ לֵיהּ שַׁרְשִׁיפָא. סַפְסָל: וְיִקַּח מִנְעָלִים. שֶׁאֵין לְךָ בִּיזּוּי מִן הַמְהַלֵּךְ יָחֵף בַּשּׁוּק: (מַאי) צָרְכֵי סְעוּדָה. (צָרְכֵי) סְעוּדַּת הַקָּזָה: בְּיוֹמָא דְּמִילְּתָא. דְּהַקָּזָה: דְּטַחְלֵי. טְחוֹל, סוּמָּקָא חֲלַף סוּמָּקָא: עַד דְּנָפֵיק תִּיהְיָא. הָרֵיחַ: מֵאוּנֵיהּ. מֵאָזְנָיו מְרִיחִין הַיַּיִן: מֵרִיבְדָּא דְּכוּסִילְתָּא. נִקְבֵי כְּלִי הָאוּמָּן שֶׁבִּבְשָׂרוֹ, פלימ"א: עַד דְּקָפֵי טַחְלֵיהּ. טְחוֹל שֶׁלּוֹ צָף בַּיַּיִן: בַּר תְּלָתָא טַרְפֵי. בֶּן ג' שָׁנִים, שֶׁטְּעָנָה אוֹתוֹ מִשֶּׁנִּקְלַט ג' עָלִין חֲדָשִׁין: לְרַבָּנַן. לְתַלְמִידָיו: אִמְרוּ נַחְמָן אִיקְלַע לְגַבַּן. הַרְבּוּ בִּסְעוּדָה כְּאִילּוּ אֲנִי סוֹעֵד אֶצְלְכֶם: בַּר מֵהַהִיא עָרְמָה. דִּמְפָרֵשׁ וְאָזֵיל: וְלָא אֶפְשָׁר לֵיהּ. לִקְנוֹת יַיִן: לִשְׁקוֹל זוּזָא מַכָּא. זוּז רַע וּפָחוּת, שֶׁאֵינוֹ יוֹצֵא בְּהוֹצָאָה: וְלֵיזִיל לְשַׁב חֲנָוָתָא. וְדֶרֶךְ הַלּוֹקְחִים לְטוֹעֲמוֹ תְּחִלָּה שֶׁיְּהֵא טוֹב, וְיִטְעוֹם. וּכְשֶׁיִּתֵּן לוֹ הַזּוּז וְהַחֶנְוָנִי יִמְלָאֶנּוּ רַע וְלֹא יְקַבְּלֶנּוּ – וְהוּא יֵלֵךְ לַחֲנוּת אַחֶרֶת וְיַעֲשֶׂה כֵּן: וְאִי לָא. דְּאֵין לוֹ זוּז רַע: וְלֵישׁוּף מִשְׁחָא בְּצִידְעֵיהּ. בְּרַקָּתוֹ, וְהַתְּמָרִים וְהַשּׁוּמָּן מְחַמְּמִין אוֹתוֹ: בִּישָׁא מִי הָוֵה טָבָא. חוֹם הַשֶּׁמֶשׁ שֶׁהוּא קָשֶׁה לָאָדָם, כְּלוּם מֵטִיב לוֹ?! הֵיכָא דְּכָרֵיךְ זִיקָא. *אינדרו"ן שֶׁיֵּשׁ בּוֹ חַלּוֹנוֹת, וְהָרוּחַ נִכְנֶסֶת בָּהֶם, נִכְרֶכֶת וּמִתְגַּלְגֶּלֶת בָּאינדרו"ן: דִּילְמָא שָׁפֵי לֵיהּ אוּמָּנָא. מְרִיקוֹ מִדָּמוֹ. כְּמוֹ "הַשּׁוֹפֶה יַיִן לַחֲבֵירוֹ" (ב"מ דף ס.): וּמוֹקֵי לֵיהּ אַרְבִּיעָתָא. לֹא הִנִּיחַ בּוֹ דָּם אֶלָּא כְּדֵי חַיָּיו, דְּהַיְינוּ רְבִיעִית, וַהֲדַר אָתֵי לֵיהּ זִיקָא וְשָׁאֵיף לֵיהּ מִדָּם הַנּוֹתָר בְּגוּפוֹ, וּמְחַסְּרוֹ מִשִּׁיעוּרוֹ, וּמִסְתַּכֵּן: שַׁב לְבֵינֵי וַאֲרִיחָא. עוֹבִי הַחוֹמָה ז' לְבֵינִים מוּטָּלִין לְרָחְבָּן זֶה אֵצֶל זֶה, דְּכָל לְבֵינָה ג"ט, וַאֲרִיחָא – אָרִיחַ, חֲצִי לְבֵינָה – טֶפַח וּמֶחֱצָה: אַרְגִּישׁ בְּנַפְשֵׁיהּ. הִרְגִּישׁ בְּעַצְמוֹ שֶׁהוּא נֶחֱלָשׁ: חֲסַר חַד אֲרִיחָא. הַחוֹמָה הָיְתָה חֲסֵרָה מֵעוֹבְיָהּ אָרִיחַ:

תוספות

רבא משמיה דרב יהודה אמר שבעה. לכאורה משמע דרבא לטעמיה, דבפרק "הדר" (עירובין דף סח.) גבי ההוא ינוקא דאישתפוך חמימיה, אמר להו רבא: נישיילוה לאימיה, אם צריכה – ניחיימו אגב אימיה. דמסתמא ביום שמיני היה, קודם מילה שהיה צריך חמין למולו דלאחר מילה – מסוכן הוא, ובלא אימיה ביום שמיני מחללין עליו שבת. והיינו לאחר שבעה, דבנסתם הקבר בעינן צריכה, מיהו, ללישנא דאמרי לה לרבא שלשים תיקשי: למה צריכה? ועוד, דבקונטרס פי' התם: ניחיימו אגב אימיה – ע"י גוי. וכן פירש ר"ח. לכך יש לפרש דאביי ורבא ואמרי לה, מר אמר חדא, ומר אמר חדא ולא פליגי, וכולהו קיימו כנהרדעי*: מי

רבינו חננאל

צריכה אני מחללין עליה את השבת אמרה איני צריכה אין מחללין עליה את השבת ומסקינן לה לשמעתא דא"ל מרימר לרבינא הלכתא כי הא דמר זוטרא ספק נפשות להקל והוצרכנו לדקדק מאימתי פתיחת הקבר כדי לחלל באותו העת את השבת לעשות צרכי החיה. ואמר אביי משתשב על המשבר. ואמר רב הונא בריה דרב יהושע משעה שהדם שותת ויורד כו' ודייקי מדלא אמר רב הונא עד שיתחיל הדם להיות שותת ש"מ קודם שתשב על המשבר קאמר וכאביי עבדינן *ולא מחללי שבתא אלא עד שיהא שותת. קדם שותת ויורד ותשב על המשבר אבל דהא דאמר אביי משום רב יהודה עד מתי פתיחת הקבר ג' ימים בלבד אין הלכה כמותו. ולא כרבא דאמר משמיה דרב יהודה שבעה. אלא קיי"ל כנהרדעא דאמרי חיה ג' ז' ושלשים. ג' בין אמרה צריכה אני בין אמרה איני צריכה מחללין עליה את השבת. ז' אמרה צריכה אני מחללין עליה את השבת אמרה איני צריכה אין מחללין עליה את השבת. סתמא עבדינן כמר זוטרא לקולא. שלשים אפילו אמרה צריכה אני אין מחללין עליה את השבת. אלא עושין לה ע"י ארמאי כדרב עולא בריה דרב עילאי דאמר כל צרכי הולד נעשין ע"י ארמאי בשבת וכדרב המנונא דאמר דבר שאין בו סכנה אומר לנכרי ועושה. חיה לא תטבול בתוך שלשים יום שמא תצטנן אמר רבא לא אמרן אלא שאין בעלה עמה. אבל בעלה [עמה בעלה] מחממה. אמר רב יהודה אמר שמואל עושין מדורות לחיה בשבת סבור מינה לחיה אין לחולה לא [בימות הגשמים אין] בימות החמה לא וכו' ומסקינן משמא דשמואל הקיז דם ונצטנן עושין לו מדורה ואפילו בתקופת תמוז. שמעינן מינה אפילו לחולה ואפילו בימות החמה. שמואל צלחו ליה תכתקא דשאגא. פי' שמואל הקיז דם ולא היה לו עצים מוכנים להדליק ולהתחמם בהן ובקעו לו שידה שהיו עציה עצי שאגא והן יקרים להודיע שאם יתמהמה עד שיביאו לו עצים יסתכן וכדתרגם ויבקע עצי העולה וצלח אעי דעלתא. רב יהודה צלחו ליה פתורא פי' שולחן העשוי מעצי יַוָנָם והן יקרים פי' יאבנוס. ורבה צלחו ליה שרשיפא והוא הדום לכסא וכולן טעם אחד. שאם לא ימהרו להתחמם יסתכנו

*) נ"ל ולא מחללי שבתא עד שתהא הדם שותת ויורד ותשב על המשבר וכו' וכ"כ הרי"ף כאן משמיה דרבוותא ופשוט דכוונתו על דברי רבינו כאן:

עין משפט נר מצוה

לג א ב ג מיי' פ"ב מהל' שבת הלכה יג סמג לאוין סה טוש"ע א"ח סימן של סעיף ג:
לד ד מיי' שם טוש"ע שם ס"ד:
לה ה מיי' שם הלכה י סמג שם טוש"ע א"ח סי' שכח סעיף יז:
לו ו מיי' שם הלכה יד סמג שם טוש"ע א"ח סימן של סעיף ו:
לז ז מיי' וסמג שם טוש"ע א"ח סימן שכח סעיף יח:

גי' רא"ש אמרה איני צריכה אין מחללין לא אמרה איני צריכה מחללין

[וע"ע תוס' בגיטין ח: ד"ה אע"ג]

[שם ע"ש]
*[עיין רש"י גיטין ח: ד"ה כדאמר רבא]

ס"א ז"ח וכ"ג לא איתמר אמר ר"ח כו'

[לקמן קמ.]

[ועי' פסחים קיב.]

דברים כ

מסורת הש"ס

גי' רא"ש אמרה צריכה אני מחללי לא אמרה צריכה אין כו'

כן גי' הערוך בערך שרפרף אולם הגאון מהרי"ף הגיה כאן שנ"ל רבה

[יומא פג. פד: כתובות טו. ב"ק מד: ל. ב"ב נ: סנהדרין עט.]

בס"י הגירסא לא אמרה צריכה וכן לקמן

[ביצה כב.]

[ובביצה שם וכן בשאלתות פרש' שמות סי' לח איתא ואמר רב המנונא דבר שאין בו וכו']

עירובין עט:

אין זה בלעז כ"א לשון תלמו' אכסדרא דבי רב כאינדרונא מעלית' מנחות לג:

[חולין קיא.]

ס"א טבת

הגהות הב"ח

(א) רש"י ד"ה פתורא דיונה וכו' בויי"ש. נ"ב עלי ברותים:

גליון הש"ס

גמרא משעה שתשב על המשבר. עיין פ"ז מ"ד דאהלות בר"ש:

בדבר אחר – קשה לדבר אחר. רב ושמואל דאמרי תרווייהו: האי מאן דעביד מילתא – לישהי פורתא והדר ליקום. דאמר מר: *ה' דברים קרובין למיתה יותר מן החיים, ואלו הן: אכל ועמד, שתה ועמד, ישן ועמד, הקיז דם ועמד, שימש מטתו ועמד. אמר שמואל: פורסא דדמא – כל תלתין יומין. ובין הפרקים – ימעט, ובין הפרקים – יחזור וימעט. ואמר שמואל: פורסא דדמא – חד בשבתא, ארבעה ומעלי שבתא. אבל שני וחמישי – לא, דאמר מר: מי שיש לו זכות אבות – יקיז דם בשני ובחמישי, שב"ד של מעלה ושל מטה שוין כאחד. בתלתא בשבתא מאי טעמא לא – משום דקיימא ליה מאדים *בזווי, מעלי שבתא נמי קיימא בזווי! כיון דדשו ביה רבים – "שומר פתאים ה'" (תהלים קטז). אמר שמואל: ד' דהוא ד', ד' דהוא ארביסר, ד' דהוא עשרים וארבעה, ד' דליכא ארבע בתריה – סכנתא. ר"ח ושני לו – חולשא, שלישי לו – סכנה; מעלי יומא טבא – חולשא, מעלי יומא דעצרתא – סכנתא. וגזרו רבנן אכולהו מעלי יומא טבא משום יומא טבא דעצרת. דנפיק ביה זיקא ושמיה טבוח – דאי לא קבלו ישראל תורה – הוה טבח להו לבשרייהו ולדמייהו. אמר שמואל: אכל חטה והקיז דם לא הקיז אלא לאותה חטה והנ"מ – לרפואה, אבל לאוקולי – מיקל. המקיז דם, שתייה – לאלתר, אכילה – עד חצי מיל. איבעיא להו: "שתייה לאלתר" מעלי, אבל בתר הכי – קשי, או דילמא: לא קשי ולא מעלי? תיקו. איבעיא להו: "אכילה עד חצי מיל" הוא דקמעלי, הא בתר הכי ומקמי הכי – קשי, או דילמא: לא קשי ולא מעלי? תיקו. *מכריז רב: מאה קרי – בזוזא, מאה רישי – בזוזא, מאה שפמי – ולא כלום. אמר רב יוסף: כי הוינן בי רב הונא, יומא דמפגרי ביה רבנן אמרי "האידנא יומא דשפמי הוא" ולא ידענא מאי קאמרי.§ "וקושרין הטבור".§ ת"ר: *קושרין הטבור, ר' יוסי אומר: אף חותכין, וטומנין השליא כדי שיחם הולד. אמר רשב"ג: בנות מלכים טומנות בספלים של שמן, בנות עשירים בספוגים של צמר, בנות עניים במוכין. *אמר רב נחמן אמר רבה בר אבוה אמר רב: הלכה כר' יוסי. ואמר רב נחמן אמר רבה בר אבוה אמר רב: מודים חכמים לר' יוסי בטבור של שני תינוקות שחותכין, מ"ט – דמנתחי אהדדי. ואמר רב נחמן אמר רבה בר אבוה אמר רב: כל האמור בפרשת תוכחה עושין לחיה בשבת, שנאמר: "ומולדותיך ביום הולדת אותך לא כרת שרך ובמים לא רחצת למשעי והמלח לא המלחת והחתל לא חתלת" (יחזקאל טז). "ומולדותיך ביום הולדת" – מכאן שמיילדים את הולד בשבת, "לא כרת שרך" – מכאן שחותכין הטבור בשבת, "ובמים לא רחצת למשעי" – מכאן שרוחצין הולד בשבת, "והמלח לא המלחת" – מכאן שמולחין הולד בשבת, "והחתל לא חתלת" – מכאן שמלפפין הולד בשבת.§

הדרן עלך מפנין

רש"י

בדבר אחר. חזיר: קשה לדבר אחר. לרעת, שהחזירים מנוגעים הם כדאמרינן בקידושין (ד' מט:): "י' קבים נגעים ירדו לעולם, תשעה נטלו חזירים": אכל ועמד. מהר לעמוד פתאום אחר שאכל שובעו: פורסא דדמא. זמן הקזה, כמו "בפרוס הפסח" (שקלים פ"ג מ"א): בין הפרקים. פירקי שנותיו, כגון לאחר מ' שנה: ימעט. בהקזה. לא יקיז בכל חדש, אלא לג' חדשים: ובין הפרקים יחזור וימעט. לאחר ששים – יקיז לג' חדשים, לפי שאין כחו עליו, ואין דמו חם, וגופו מצטנן כשמחסר דמו: שב"ד של מעלה ושל מטה שוין. אדם נדון בכל יום, וב"ד יושבין בעיירות בב' ובה' – מתקנת עזרא ואילך (ב"ק ד' פב.), וכיון דיום הדין ופקידה היא – עונותיו נזכרים: דקיימא ליה מאדים בזווי. שמזל מאדים משמש בו בשעות זוגות. ומזל מאדים ממונה על החרב ועל הדבר ועל הפורעניות. והזוגות קשין, שהן רשות לשדים, כדאמר בפסחים (ד' קי:), והפורעניות מוכנין. שצ"מ חנכ"ל סדר השעות. כשנתלו המאורות והמזלות, שעה ראשונה של ד' בשבת שימש שבתאי, ובשניה צדק, ואחריו מאדים, ואחריו חמה, ואחריו נוגה, ואחריו כוכב, ואחריו לבנה – נמצאו ז' המזלות לז' השעות, וחוזרים חלילה לעולם. נמצא בסדר זה לעולם סימני מזלות המשמשין בתחלת לילי השבוע – כלנ"ש חל"ס: מוצאי שבת – שעה ראשונה שלו כוכב, תחלת ליל שני – צדק, וכן בסדר הזה. וסדר תחלת סימני הימים – חל"ס כלנ"ש: שעה ראשונה של אחד בשבת – חמה, ושל שני בשבת – לבנה, ושל שלישי בשבת – מאדים, נמצא מאדים חוזר בו חלילה בשעה שמינית ביום, והיא זוגות. אבל שאר ימים – אין מאדים בזוגות שלהם אם לא בלילה, ובלילה אין דרך להקיז: מעלי שבתא נמי קיימא מאדים בזווי. שהרי שעה ראשונה של יום נוגה, לפי הסדר של חל"ס כלנ"ש תחלת הימים, וכיון שתחלתו נוגה וסדר הליכתן שצ"ם חנכ"ל – נמצאו מתחילין לחזור חלילה בשעה רביעית, נמצא מאדים בשעה ששית: כיון דדשו ביה רבים. הורגלו בו מפני דוחקן, שיהיו קרובים לסעודת שבת, ואמרינן בפירקין דלעיל (ד' קיח:): כבוד שבת בדגים גדולים, ובמסכת ע"ז (ד' כט:) אמרינן: שני לדם דג: ארבע דהוא ד'. ד' בשבת שהוא ד' לחדש, או ארביסר לחדש, או כ"ד לחדש – כולהון קשה להקזה: ד' דליכא ד' בתריה. שאין ד' ימים עד סוף החדש. ואיפא דאמרי: דליכא ד' בשבת בתריה באותו חדש, ואינו כן: ה"ג: ר"ח ושני לו חולשא, שלישי לו סכנתא: אכל חטה והקיז דם לא הקיז אלא לחטה. שהאוכל מכביד את האדם, והקזה שאחר אכילה אינו מועיל אלא לאותו כובד: וה"מ. במקיז לרפואה: אבל אקולי. מי שיש לו דם המכביד עליו, אפי' לאחר אכילה – מקיז ומיקל: מאה רישי בזוזא. כלומר: אם יהיו בזול מאד – קנה ראשי בהמה; ואם לאו – אל תקח, שאינן בריאין לאכול: מאה קרי. דלועין: מאה שפמי. כמו: "על שפם" (ויקרא יג), גרוויינו"ן בלע"ז, שפתים של בהמה: יומא דמפגרי ביה רבנן. שהיו התלמידים מתעצלין מלבא בבית המדרש קרי ליה "יומא דשפמי", כלומר: היום הזה אבד לו, ואין בו תועלת: וטומנין את השליא. כדמפרש רשב"ג, שהיא רפואה להתחמם הולד: ספוגין של צמר. צמר מנופץ: של שני תינוקות. תאומים, וקשורין טבורן זה בזה: משום דמנתחי מהדדי. זה אילך וזה אילך, ונמצאו מסוכנין: בפרשת תוכחה. שהוכיח יחזקאל לישראל את חסדי הקב"ה שעמהן: תוכחה. לשון "לכו ונוכחה" (ישעיה א), להתווכח ולהודיע מי הוא שסרח על שכנגדו: למשעי. לטוח ולהחליק בשרו: שמולחין. ובשרו מתקשה: מלפפין. אנמליו"ן בלע"ז. ולאו היינו חסודי יניקא דאמרן לעיל בפרק "כל הכלים" (דף קכג.), דהא שמעינן ליה לרב נחמן דאסר. אלא *לפופי בעלמא, כמו שעושין בחגורות ופסיקיאות: הדרן עלך מפנין

תוספות

מי שיש לו זכות אבות. וקודם תקנת עזרא, אע"פ שהיו דנין בכל יום שהיו צריכים – לא היו קובעים ליֵשב בכל יום*:

דקאי מאדים בזווי. ברביעי נמי קאי מאדים בזווי בסוף היום, אלא לא חשו חכמים לכך דאין דרך להקיז כל כך בסמוך ללילה:

דליכא ארבע בתריה. שאין ד' ימים עד סוף החדש, כדפירש בקונטרס. דליכא למימר רביעי בשבת – דהא ד' דהוא עשרין וארבע היינו דליכא רביעי בתריה:

מאה רישי בזוזא מאה קרי בזוזא. לפירוש הקונטרס תימה: מה שייך הכא? ור"ח גרים: מאה קרני בזוזא. ומפרש: מאה רישי – מאה ראשי בני אדם, (ונראה) שהיה מנהג קצוב לספר לגלח בזוזא, וכן מנהג ק' קרני להקיז בזוזא, כמו "קרנא דאומנא" (לקמן דף קנד:). אבל מאה שפמי – לתקן השפה בולא כלום, דבשכר גילוח והקזה היה מתקן השפה, וביום שהיה מתקן שפמו לא היה נוטל כלום. ועל כן היה למשל כל מי שהיה יגע ולא עלה בידו שכרו – היו קורין אותו יומא דשפמי:

מפגרי רבנן. תשש כחם, והיו מתחלשין ולא יכלו למיגרס. כדכתיב (ש"א ל) "וירדוף דוד הוא וארבע מאות איש (עמו) ויעמדו מאתים איש אשר פגרו מעבור את נחל הבשור":

כל האמור בפרשת תוכחה. לאו מקרא מפיק, אלא: מסתמא, כיון שבא בפרשת תוכחה – אם כן לער הוא אם אין עושין, והקילו חכמים לעשות. ובכולן אין בהן איסורא דאורייתא:

הדרן עלך מפנין

רבינו חננאל

יסתכנו. פי' זוזא מכא. זוז מעוך שנמעך מטבע הצורה ונראה כאסימון. דעביד מלתא. באותו היום שמקיז דם. פורסא דדמא כל תלתין יומין. פי' גבול הדם לבחורים כל שלשים יום. בין הפרקים הגיע לחמשים שנה ימעט. יוציא משנים חדשים [או] ג' חדשים. פעם אחת עוד בין הפרקים בא בימים יחזור ימעט מששה חדשים לששה חדשים או משנה לשנה וזה הפי' קיבלנוהו מרבותינו קבלה: **בתלתא** קאי מאדים בזווי. פי' בשתי שעות שהן זוגות יום שלישי שעה שמינית מאדים ושעה שתים ועשרים מאדים ושכך סידור הכוכבים חל"ם כצנ"ש בימים נמצא יום אחד שעה ראשונה כוכב חמה יום שני שעה ראשונה כוכב לבנה. יום ג' שעה ראשונה כוכב מאדים יום ד' שעה ראשונה כוכב [כוכב]. יום ה' שעה ראשונה כוכב צדק יום ו' שעה ראשונה כוכב נוגה יום ז' שעה ראשונה כוכב שבתי וסידורן חל"ם בימים כצנ"ש חל"ם בלילות וסידוריהן חנכ"ל שצ"ם. וכיון שביום ג' עומד מאדים בשעה שמינית והן זוגות ובשעה כ"ב והן זוגות חיישינן לסכנה. וכיוצא בזה בשני ובחמישי משום הכי חיישינן לסכנה. כי מאדים הוא ממונה על הדם ואקשינן עלה והא יום ו' הוא דמעלי שבתא דקאי מאדים בשעה ששית ובשעה עשרים והן זוגות. ואמרת פורסא דדמא חד בשבא וארבעה ומעלי שבתא. ולא מצאו לו פירוק. והשיב אע"פ שהוא כן כיון דרשו בה רבים להקיז ביום ששי שומר פתאים ה'. מאה רישי בזוזי מאה קרני בזוזא שפמי ולא כלום פי' היה מנהג קצוב כי הספר מגלח מאה ראשי בני אדם נוטל שכרו זוז אחד וכן (א' מדוגמא) [חמשים] מאה קרן כלומר מאה קרן של זכוכית והוא ריבדא דכוסילתא נוטל בשכרו בק' קרן זוז אחד. אבל לתקן הזקן וליטול השפה ולתקנו לא היה מנהג ליקח האומן כלום אלא אותן בני אדם שמגלח ראשם או עושה להן ריבדא דכוסילתא נוטל שכרו כאשר אמרנו מתקן זקנם ונוטל שפמם בחנם. וכן היה הדין ויום שהיה האומן עושה השפמות לא היה נוטל שכר והיה הולך לביתו ריקם. ועל כן היה למשל כל מי שהיה יגע ולא [היה] עולה בידו (סבר) [שכר] היה קורא אותו יומא דשפמי. מיפגרי תשש כחם והוו מתחלשי יגעים ויעפים ולא יכלי למיגרס כדכתיב וירדף דוד הוא וארבע מאות איש ויעמדו מאתים איש אשר פגרו מעבור וגו' הוו אמרי יומא דשפמי*): **וקושרין** את הטיבור. ר' יוסי אומר אף חותכין את הטיבור כל צרכי מילה עושין בשבת אמר רב נחמן אמר רבה בר אבוה הלכה כרבי יוסי שחותכין בשבת טיבור תינוק אחד וכ"ש טיבור ב' תינוקות שבזה אפילו חכמים מודים שמחתך מ"ט משום (דמתחזי) [דמנתחו] אהדדי. ואמר רב נחמן אמר רבה בר אבוה אמר דבכל האמור בפרשת תוכחה עושין לחיה בשבת שנא' ומולדותיך ביום הולדת אותך מיכן שמיילדין לחיה בשבת לא כרת שרך מיכן שחותכין את הטיבור בשבת ובמים לא רוחצת למשעי מיכן שמרחיצין את הוולד בשבת והחתל לא חתלת מיכן שמלפפין הולד בשבת ואמרינן בתלמוד א"י ומחללין עליה את השבת שמואל אמר עושין לה מדורה אפילו בתקופת תמוז וקושרין את הטיבור כהדא אמתיה דבר קפרא נפקא מילדה בשבתא אתת ושאלת לר' וא' לה אזלון ושאלון לחייתא. אמרה ליה ליכא חייא. אמר לה זילי עבידי כמנהגך אמרה ליה ליכא מנהג אמר לה איזיל חתיך כר' יוסי כבמתניתא וכל צרכי חיה עושין בשבת תני השליא הזאת בשבת עשירים טומנין אותה בשמן והעניים בתבן ובחול אלו ואלו טומנין אותה בארץ כדי ליתן ערבון בארץ [לארץ]: **הדרן עלך מפנין**

*) עיין בערוך ערך פגר.

עין משפט נר מצוה

[וע"ע תוספות כתובות ג. ד"ה שכתי דינין]

לח א מיי' פ"ד מהלכות דעות הלכה יח:

לט ב מיי' שם הל' ג:

מ ג מיי' שם הלכה יט טוש"ע א"ח סי' רמ סעיף טו:

מא ד מיי' פ"ד מהלכות דעות הלכה יח:

מב ה ש"ע א"ח סימן תמח סעי' ו בהג"ה:

מג ו מיי' פ"ב מהלכות שבת הלכה יא יג סמג לאוין סה טוש"ע א"ח סימן של סעיף ז:

[ומכאן עד יומא דשפמי תמלא פירוש יפה בערוך ערך פגר בשינוי הנוסח]

מסורת הש"ס

גיטין ע.

[ועיין תוספות עירובין ע. ד"ה ואין]

[תוספ' פט"ו]

[לפני הרא"ש והטור לא היה כתוב הא דאמר רב נחמן הלכה כר' יוסי ועיין ב"י א"ח סימן של]

[וכן איתא לעיל סו: לפופי יעוקא בשבת שפיר דמי וע"ש בפרש"י וכן עוד לקמן קמז: ובפרש"י שם]

גליון הש"ס

גמרא כיון דדשו ביה רבים שומר פתאים. עיין תה"ד סי' רי"ח: רש"י ד"ה מלפפים וכו' בחגורות ופסיקיאות. עיין לקמן דף קמז ע"ב רש"י ד"ה כותחרי דלרה וע"ש. ועי' בתשובת חלמת הקדש חלק א"ח סי' ח:

רבי אליעזר אומר: אם לא הביא כלי מע"ש – מביאו בשבת מגולה. ובסכנה מכסהו ע"פ עדים. ועוד אמר *ר"א: כורתים עצים לעשות פחמין לעשות (כלי) ברזל. *כלל אמר ר"ע: אכל מלאכה שאפשר לעשותה מע"ש – אינה דוחה את השבת, (ומילה) שאי אפשר לעשותה מע"ש – דוחה את השבת.§

גמ' איבעיא להו: טעמא דר"א משום חבובי מצוה, או דילמא משום חשדא? למאי נפקא מינה – לאתויי מכוסה ע"פ עדים. אי אמרת משום חבובי מצוה, מגולה – אין, מכוסה – לא. אלא אי אמרת משום חשדא – אפי' מכוסה שפיר דמי. מאי? איתמר, א"ר לוי: לא אמרה ר"א אלא לחבובי מצוה. תניא נמי הכי: מביאו מגולה, ואין מביאו מכוסה, דברי ר"א. אמר רב אשי: מתני' נמי דיקא, דקתני: "ובשעת הסכנה מכסהו ע"פ עדים", בסכנה – אין, שלא בסכנה – לא. שמע מינה: משום חבובי מצוה, שמע מינה. תניא אידך: מביאו מגולה ואין מביאו מכוסה, דברי ר"א. ר' יהודה אומר משום ר"א: נוהגין היו בשעת הסכנה שהיו מביאין מכוסה ע"פ עדים. איבעיא להו: עדים דקאמר – איהו וחד, או דילמא: הוא ותרי? ת"ש: ובסכנה מכסהו ע"פ עדים, אי אמרת בשלמא הוא ותרי – שפיר, אלא אי אמרת הוא וחד – מאי עדים? שראוים להעיד במקום אחר.§ "ועוד אמר ר"א". *ת"ר: במקומו של ר"א היו כורתין עצים לעשות פחמין לעשות ברזל בשבת. במקומו של ר' יוסי הגלילי היו אוכלין בשר עוף בחלב. לוי איקלע לבי יוסף רישבא קריבו ליה רישא *דטווסא בחלבא לא אכל. כי אתא לקמיה דרבי א"ל: אמאי לא תשמתינהו? א"ל: אתריה דר' יהודה בן בתירה הוה, ואמינא: דילמא דרש להו כר' יוסי הגלילי. *דתנן, ר' יוסי הגלילי אומר, נאמר: °"לא תאכלו כל נבלה", ונאמר: °"לא תבשל גדי בחלב אמו" את שאסור משום נבלה – אסור לבשל בחלב, עוף שאסור משום נבלה יכול יהא אסור לבשל בחלב – ת"ל: "בחלב אמו" – יצא עוף שאין לו חלב אם. א"ר יצחק: עיר אחת היתה בא"י שהיו עושין כר"א, והיו מתים בזמנן. ולא עוד אלא שפעם אחת גזרה מלכות הרשעה גזרה על ישראל על המילה, ועל אותה העיר לא גזרה.§ תניא, רשב"ג אומר: כל מצוה שקיבלו עליהם בשמחה כגון מילה, דכתיב: °"שש אנכי על אמרתך כמוצא שלל רב" – בעדיין עושין אותה בשמחה, וכל מצוה שקבלו עליהם בקטטה, גכגון עריות – דכתיב: °"וישמע משה את העם בוכה למשפחותיו" *"על עסקי משפחותיו" – עדיין עושין אותה בקטטה, דליכא כתובה דלא רמו בה תיגרא. תניא, ר"ש בן אלעזר אומר: כל מצוה שמסרו ישראל עצמן עליהם למיתה בשעת גזרת המלכות, כגון עבודה זרה ומילה – עדיין היא מוחזקת בידם, וכל מצוה שלא מסרו ישראל עצמן עליה למיתה בשעת גזרת המלכות, כגון תפילין – עדיין היא מרופה בידם. *דא"ר ינאי: תפילין צריכין גוף נקי כאלישע בעל כנפים. מאי היא? אמר אביי: שלא יפיח בהם, רבא אמר: שלא יישן בהם. ואמאי קרו ליה "אלישע בעל כנפים"? שפעם אחת גזרה מלכות הרשעה גזרה על ישראל, שכל המניח תפילין על ראשו – יקרו את מוחו. והיה אלישע מניח תפילין ויצא לשוק. וראהו קסדור אחד, רץ מלפניו ורץ אחריו. כיון שהגיע אצלו – נטלן מראשו ואחזן בידו. א"ל: מה בידך? אמר לו: כנפי יונה. פשט את ידו ונמצאו בה כנפי יונה. לפיכך היו קוראין אותו "בעל כנפים". *מאי שנא כנפי יונה דא"ל, ולא א"ל שאר עופות? משום דדמיא כנסת ישראל ליונה, שנאמר: °"כנפי יונה נחפה בכסף ואברותיה בירקרק חרוץ", מה יונה זו כנפיה מגינות עליה, אף ישראל – מצות מגינות עליהן.§ א"ר אבא בר רב אדא א"ר יצחק: פעם אחת שכחו ולא הביאו איזמל מערב שבת, והביאוהו בשבת [דרך גגות ודרך חצירות] שלא

(ס"א / ס"א ל"ג / ס"א ל"ג / דברים יד / שם / תהלים קיט / במדבר יא / תהלים סח)

רש"י

רבי אליעזר אומר אם לא הביא כלי. איזמל למול את התינוק. וקאי אמתניתין דפרקין דלעיל* דסליק מיניה, "וכל צרכי מילה עושין בשבת": מגולה. בפני הכל. ובגמרא מפרש אמאי מצריך ליה לגלויי: ובסכנה. שגזרו ארמאים על המילה: מכסהו ע"פ עדים. שיעידו שאיזמל של מצוה הוא מביא, ולא יחשדוהו: כלל אמר ר"ע. נחלק על ר"א במכשירי מצוה שאין דוחין, הואיל ואפשר לעשותן מע"ש: [ושאי אפשר לעשות מע"ש. כגון] מילה עצמה, שא"א לה ליעשות, דזמנה ביום השמיני – דוחה שבת: גמ' טעמא דר"א. דקאמר: מגולה אין, מכוסה לא: משום חיבוב מצוה. להודיע שחביבה מצוה עליו, שמחלל שבת עליה: משום חשדא. שלא יחשדוהו שהוא נושא שאר חפציו. וסיפא דמתני' דקתני ובסכנה מכסהו ע"פ עדים – ודאי משום חשדא הוא. אלא רישא מיבעיא לן: דווקא מגולה קאמר, אבל מכוסה ע"פ עדים שלא בשעת הסכנה – לא, ומשום חיבוב מצוה, או לאו דווקא מגולה, דטעמיה משום חשדא – וה"ה למכוסה על פי עדים: אי אמרת בשלמא הוא ותרי שפיר. היינו דמיקרו עדים. אלא הוא וחד – מי מיקרי עדים? איהו לגביה נפשיה מי מיקרי עד? ומשני: שראוים להעיד במקום אחר. לעולם הכא עדות לא שייכא, דלאפוקי מחשדא בעלמא הוא, ואין כאן לא דיני ממונות ולא דיני נפשות שיהו שנים(א). ומאי קרו להו עדים – דאיכא גילוי מילתא ע"י השני, ושנים קרו עדים בעדות אחריתי שאינו נוגע בה: לעשות ברזל. לאיזמל של מילה: היו אוכלין בשר עוף בחלב. כדלקמן: רישבא. צייד עופות: נאמר לא תאכלו כל נבלה ונאמר. באותו פסוק עצמו: "לא תבשל גדי", משמע: כל האסור משום נבלה – נוהג בו איסור בשר בחלב: שש אנכי על אמרתך. אמירה יחידה שקדמה לשאר אמירות, והיא מילה, שישראל עושין וששים עליה. דכל שאר מצות אינן מוכיחות כל שעה, כגון תפילין ומזוזה וציצית – דאינן כשהוא בשדה וערום בבית המרחץ. אבל זו מעיד עליהם לעולם. כדאמרינן במנחות (דף מג:) בדוד, שראה עצמו בבית המרחץ ונצטער, אמר: אוי לי שאני ערום מכל מצות. כיון *שנסתכל במילה – נתיישבה דעתו: בשמחה. שעושין משתה: על עסקי משפחותיו. שנאסר להם קרובות: מרופה. רפיא: דא"ר ינאי תפילין צריכות גוף נקי. שלא יפיח. אלמא: לא זהירי בהו. ושמעינן מינה דלא מסרו עליה אלא אלישע לבדו: יקרו. פוריי"ר בלע"ז. לשון "יקרוה עורבי נחל" (משלי ל) ולשון "תנקר לא נעלה" (במדבר טז): את מוחו. שכנגד תפילין: קסדור. ממונה: מגינות *עליהן. אינה נלחמת בחרטומיה, אלא בכנפיה: דרך

תוספות

רבי אליעזר אומר אם לא הביא כלי כו' מביאו בשבת מגולה. °וא"ת: ויביאו התינוק אצל כלי, דהשתא ליכא איסור שבת כלל, דהאי נושא את עצמו! וי"ל: דקטן צריך לאמו הוא, ואחר המילה היה צריך להחזירו לאמו, ואז הוי כפות(ב) לפי שהוא חולה, כדאמרינן ביומא (דף סו:): אפי' תימא ר' נתן – חולה שאני. וגם אמו שהיא מסוכנת לא תוכל לבא אצל התינוק. ועוד י"ל: כיון דיותר בקל יביא הכלי משיביא התינוק – שרי ר"א כדי למהר המצוה. כדמוכח בגמרא, דאמר: פעם אחת שכחו ולא הביאו איזמל מע"ש והביאו בשבת שלא ברצונו, שהביאו דרך חצרות וגגות וקרפיפות, והיו יכולין להביא דרך רה"ר. אלמא דשרי ר"א דרך רה"ר דהוי דאורייתא(ג) °כדי למהר המצוה, אע"פ שיכול לעשות [בענין] דליכא אלא איסורא דרבנן:

שש אנכי. במדרש (שוחר טוב) "למנצח על השמינית" כתיב, הנדרש על המילה שהיא בשמיני. וכן אמרי'(ד) (פר"א פ' כ"ט): "ויעש אברהם משתה גדול ביום הגמל את יצחק" ביום "ה"ג" מל את יצחק, דהיינו ביום השמיני דמילה, כמנין ה"ג. ר"ת: אמר ליה כנפי יונה. הרי שלא מסר עצמו לומר "תפילין הן". רבינו שמואל: שלא

עין משפט נר מצוה

א א מיי' פ"ב מהלכות מילה הלכה ו סמג עשין כח טוש"ע א"ח סי' שלא סעיף ו וטוש"ע י"ד סימן רסו סעיף ב:

ב ב טוש"ע י"ד סימן רסה סעיף יב:

ג ג מיי' פכ"ב מהלכות איסורי ביאה הל' יח סמג לאוין קכד:

פסחים סו. סט: יבמות יד. מנחות עב. נו.

רבינו חננאל

פרק יט

רבי אליעזר אומר אם לא הביא כלי מערב שבת מביאו בשבת מגולה וכו' ואיבעיא לן האי דקתני ר' אליעזר אומר מביאו מגולה משום חבובי מצוה הוא או משום שלא יחשדוהו שהוציא חפציו טמונים לפיכך מגליהו שיראו שסכין של מצוה הוא. ופשטנא דמשום חבובי מצוה הוא היכא דליכא סכנה ותוב איבעיא לן האי דתנא במתניתא רבי יהודה משום רבי אליעזר [אומר] נוהגים היינו בסכנה מביאין אותו (בסכנה) מכוסה ע"פ עדים הני עדים שנים אחרים זולתו המביאו או דלמא הוא ואחרים ולא איפשטא בהדיא: לוי איקלע לבי יוסף רישבא קריבו ליה רישא דטווסא בחלבא לא אכל כי אתא לקמיה דר' א"ל מ"ט לא שמתינהו א"ל אתרא דר' יהודה בן בתירא ואמרי דלמא דריש להו כרבי יוסי הגלילי דסבר יצא עוף שאין לו חלב אם: א"ר יצחק עיר אחת היתה בא"י שהיו עושין כר' אליעזר והיו מתיה מתין בזמנן ולא עוד אלא שפעם אחת גזרה מלכות הרשעה גזרה על ישראל על המילה ועל אותה העיר לא גזרה*) כל השבח ואין הלכה כר"א ולא כר' יוסי הגלילי שמתיר בשר עוף בחלב ולא כרבי ינאי שאמר תפילין צריכין גוף נקי כאלישע בעל כנפים ומפרשי רבנן כי לא אמר רבי ינאי אלא בשעת הגזרה וסמיך דהוא עריק ועבדי ליה נס אמר ראבין בר רב אדא א"ר יצחק פעם אחת שכחו ולא הביאו איזמל מע"ש והביאוהו

*) נראה דצ"ל לאחר כל השבח הזה מ"מ אין הלכה כר"א וכו'.

גליון הש"ס

גמ' בשלמא הוא ותרי. עיין תשובת הרא"ש ח"א סי' פ"ט: תוס' ד"ה רבי אליעזר וכו' וא"ת ויביאו התינוק. עיין לעיל דף לד ע"א תוספות ד"ה אבל אדם: בא"ד כדי למהר המצוה. עיין עירובין דף קג ע"ב תוס' ד"ה מה לי:

מסורת הש"ס

[קכח:]

[נזכר לקמן קלו. ובעירובין קב: קג.]

יבמות יד. חולין קטז. ע"ש

[נ"ל דטווסא עיין בערוך פירושו]

חולין קיג.

יומא עה.

[נ"ל שנזכר]

לעיל מט.

[ברכות נג: לעיל מט. וש"נ]

*[נ"ל עליה]

הגהות הב"ח

(א) רש"י ד"ה ומשני וכו' ומאי קרי להו: (ב) תוס' ד"ה ר' אליעזר וכו' ואז הוי כפות. נ"ב עיין בפרק המצניע דף לד ע"ב: (ג) בא"ד כדי למהר המצוה. נ"ב עיין בסוף עירובין דף קג ע"ב בתוספות ד"ה מה לי: (ד) ד"ה שש וכו' וכן אמרי' במדרש ויעש אברהם:

שלא ברצון ר"א. מתקיף לה רב יוסף: "שלא ברצון ר"א"?! אדרבה, ר"א הוא דשרי! וכי תימא שלא ברצון ר"א – דשרי אפילו ברה"ר, אלא ברצון רבנן – דאסרו דרך רה"ר, ושרו דרך גגות דרך חצירות וקרפיפות. ומי שרי?! *והתניא: א כשם שאין מביאין אותו דרך רה"ר – כך אין מביאין אותו לא דרך גגות ולא דרך קרפיפות ולא דרך חצירות. אלא אמר רב אשי: שלא ברצון ר"א ומחלוקתו, אלא ברצון ר"ש. *דתנן, ר"ש אומר: אחד ב גגות(א) ואחד קרפיפות ואחד חצירות – כולן רשות אחד הן לכלים ששבתו בתוכן, ולא לכלים ששבתו בתוך הבית. בעא מיניה רבי זירא מר' אסי: מבוי שלא נשתתפו בו, מהו לטלטל בכולו? מי אמרינן כחצר דמי, מה חצר – אע"ג דלא ערבו מותר לטלטל בכולו, האי נמי – אע"ג דלא נשתתפו בו מותר לטלטל בכולו. או דילמא: לא דמי לחצר, דחצר אית ליה ד' מחיצות, האי – לית ליה ד' מחיצות. א"נ, חצר – אית ליה דיורין, האי – לית ביה דיורין. שתיק ולא א"ל ולא מידי. זימנין אשכחיה דיתיב וקא אמר: אמר ר"ש בן לקיש משום ר' יהודה הנשיא: פעם אחת שכחו ולא הביאו איזמל מע"ש, והביאוהו בשבת, והיה הדבר קשה לחכמים: היאך מניחין דברי חכמים ועושין כר"א. חדא – דר"א שמותי *הוא, ועוד – יחיד ורבים *הלכה כרבים. וא"ר אושעיא: שאילית את רבי יהודה הגוזר, ואמר לי: מבוי שלא נשתתפו בו הוה, ואייתוהו מהאי רישא להאי רישא. א"ל: ס"ל למר מבוי שלא נשתתפו(ב) מותר לטלטל בכולו? וא"ל: אין. א"ל: והא זימנין בעאי מינך ולא אמרת לי(ג) הכי! *דילמא אגב שיטפך רהיט לך גמרך? א"ל: אין, אגב שיטפא רהיטא לי גמרי *איתמר, אמר רבי זירא אמר רב: מבוי שלא נשתתפו בו – אין מטלטלין בו אלא בד' אמות. אמר אביי: הא מילתא אמרה רבי זירא ולא פירשה, עד דאתא רבה בר אבוה ופירשה, דאמר רב נחמן אמר רבה בר אבוה אמר רב: ג מבוי שלא נשתתפו בו, עירבו חצירות עם בתים – אין מטלטלין בו אלא בד' אמות, לא עירבו חצירות עם בתים – מותר לטלטל בכולו. אמר ליה רב חנינא חוזאה לרבה: מאי שנא כי עירבו חצירות עם בתים – דניתקו חצירות ונעשו בתים. ורב לטעמיה, *דאמר רב: ד אין המבוי ניתר בלחי וקורה עד שיהו בתים

דרך גגות ודרך חצירות. שלא עירבו זו עם זו, ואיכא איסורא דרבנן: שלא ברצון ר"א ומחלוקתו. קאמר. דר"א אפילו ברה"ר שרי, ואינהו דאייתו דרך חצרות גלי אדעתייהו דאין מכשירי מילה דוחין שבת. ושלא ברצון החלוקין עליו דאסרי דרך חצרות, דהעמידו חכמים דבריהם דאיסור (*) שבת אף במקום כרת: אלא ברצון ר"ש. שמתיר אף לדבר הרשות: דתנן ר"ש אומר אחד גגות כו' כולן. ואפילו הן של בעלים הרבה – מטלטלין מזה לזה, דלא אסרו מרשות לרשות אלא בתים: קרפיפות. אם של בית סאתים הוא – מטלטל בכולו, ואם יותר ולא הוקף לדירה – קרי ליה רשות אחת לגבי חבירו, או לגבי חצר, לטלטל ב' אמות בזה וב' אמות בזה, להוציא ולהכניס מזה לזה: ששבתו בתוכן. שכשקדש היום היו בתוכו ולא בתוך הבית. דאילו שבתו כלים בבית – לא מיבעיא היכא דלא עירבו בני בתי החצר, דאפילו מבית לחצר לא יוציאו כלי הבית, אלא אפילו עירבו, ומטלטל מבית לחצר – לא יוציאו כלי הבית מחצר זו לחברתה שלא עירבו עמה: שלא נשתתפו בו. עירוב דחצירות במבוי קרי שיתוף: מהו לטלטל. בתוכו בכולו כלים ששבתו בתוכו. ולהוציא מן החצר לתוכו – פשיטא לן דאסור, וכן ממנו לחצר: מה חצר אע"ג דלא עירבו. הרבה בתים שבחצר ביחד, ואסור להכניס ולהוציא מבתים לחצר ומחצר לבתים: מותר לטלטל בכולו. מה שנמצא בתוכו, או בגדיו שהוציאן מן הבית לתוכו דרך מלבוש – פושטן ומטלטלן בכולו לדברי הכל. דג' מחלוקות הן בעירובין, בפרק "כל גגות": לדברי ר' מאיר – גגין רשות לעצמן ומטלטלין מזה לזה, ואפילו של בעלים הרבה, וחצרות רשות לעצמן לטלטל מזו לזו בלא עירוב כלים ששבתו בתוכם, אבל לא מגגין לחצרות, וקרפיפות רשות לעצמן. ולדברי חכמים – גגין וחצרות רשות אחת, וקרפיפות רשות אחת. ולדברי ר"ש – כולן רשות אחת, חוץ מן הבתים: א"נ חצר אית ביה דיורין. כלומר: עשויה להשתמש בה תדיר: האי אין בו דיורין. שהדיורין בבתים הן. והבתים פתוחין לחצרות, וחצירות למבוי: זמנין. פעם אחרת: אשכחיה. רבי זירא לר' אסי: שמותי הוא. ברכוהו, כדאמרינן ב"הזהב" (ב"מ דף נט:). ובתלמוד ירושלמי *מפ': שמותי הוא – מתלמידי שמאי היה: וא"ר אושעיא. לאותן שהיה קשה עליהן מה ששמעו: שאילית את רבי יהודה הגוזר. המל את התינוקות: ואייתוהו מהאי רישא. שהיה התינוק בבית שבראש המבוי, ואיזמל בבית שבראש האחר שכנגדו, עד כאן דברי ר' אסי: א"ל. רבי זירא: אלמא ס"ל למר מדאמר ליה להא, ולא קשיא לך ביה מידי – סבירא לך מותר לטלטל בכולו: הכי גרסינן: והא זמנין בעאי מינך ולא אמרת דילמא אגב שיטפא אתיא לך. כשהיית שטוף בגרסתך לחזור על שמועה זו דר"ל, עם מרוצת גרסתך אתיא לך הך דר' אושעיא בהדה, דאיתמר עלה: ולא פירשה. אימתי מותר ואימתי אסור: עירבו חצרות. שבמבוי עם בתיהם, שבני הבתים מוציאין לחצרותיהן שעירבו בתים הפתוחים לחצר יחד, וכן בני חצר האחרת. אבל בני החצרות לא נשתתפו במבוי: אין מטלטלין. במבוי, אפי' כלים ששבתו בתוכו, אלא בד': לא עירבו חצרות עם בתיהן. שאסורים בני הבתים להוציא מבתיהן לחצריהם: מותר לטלטל בכולו. כלים ששבתו בתוכו. ולקמיה מפרש טעמא: ונעשו בתים. בטלו לגבי הבתים, ואין שם חצרות עליהם: בתים

שלא ברצון ר"א דשרי אפי' ברה"ר. קשה לרשב"א: הא אמרינן לקמן בפירקין (דף קלג.): כל מקום שאתה מוצא עשה ולא תעשה, אם אתה יכול לקיים את שניהם – מוטב כו'. והכא, כיון דאפשר לקיים את שניהם להביאו דרך גגות וחצירות וקרפיפות – אמאי יביאו אותו דרך רה"ר? וליכא למימר דלגבי מילה דגלי רחמנא בה דדחי שבת, כדדרשינן לקמן לא אמרינן הכי – דהא לקמן(ד) גבי בשר אפי' במקום בהרת יקוץ כו', אמרינן כדר"ל, דאמר ר"ל כל מקום שאתה מוצא כו': ומי שרי והתניא. וא"ת: ולוקמי שהביאו דרך חצר מעורבת, דהוי כרצון חכמים ושלא כרצון ר"א, דשרי אפי' דרך רה"ר! וי"ל דבכה"ג לא הוה(ה) שרי ר"א מן רה"ר, כיון שיכול להביאו דרך חצר מעורבת בהיתר גמור. א"נ: לישנא ד"שכחו" לא משמע כן, דאי היתה מעורבת – לא ה"ל למימר שכחו. אלא לא חשו להביאו מע"ש, כיון דבשבת אפשר להביאו בהיתר גמור. אבל כי מסיק ברצון ר"ש – אתי שפיר דקאמר שכחו, שאם היו נזכרין מע"ש – היו מביאין, משום דפליגי רבנן עליה: ברצון ר"ש. ה"ה דהוה מצי למימר ברצון ר"מ, שהביאו דרך גגות מגג לגג או דרך חצרות מחצר לחצר, כדמוכח בפרק "כל גגות" (עירובין דף פט.) דאית ליה: כל גגות העיר רשות אחת הן, וכן חצרות וקרפיפות. אלא נקט ר' שמעון, דקי"ל כוותיה: לכלים ששבתו לתוכו. וכן היה אותו איזמל: דרבי אליעזר שמותי הוא. מכ"ש. וכן מוכח בירושלמי במסכת תרומות בפרק "סאה תרומה", דתנן התם: סאה תרומה טמאה שנפלה למאה סאין טהורין, בית שמאי אוסרים וב"ה מתירין כו' עד לאחר שהודו ר"א אומר: תירום ותישרף. ואמר בגמרא:(ו) בן פזי ורבי אייבו בר נגרי הוו יתבין ואמרי: תנינן, אחר שהודו ר"א אומר תירום ותישרף. מי הודה למי? א"ר אסי: מתניתין אמרה כן לאחר שהודו, ר"א אומר תירום ותישרף. ר"א לאו שמותי הוא? הרי משמע דשמותי הוא מתלמידי ב"ש, דמינה קא פשיט דב"ש הודו לב"ה. ר"ת*: ניתקו חצרות ונעשו בתים. עי"ש: ותשיב כאילו אין כאן חצר כלל, שהחצר נעשה בית. וכשלא עירבו – חשיבי בתים כליתנהו. וחיהו, חצר לא חשיב כליתא, אע"פ שאסור לטלטל *) מתוכו למבוי, כיון שאין(ז) דרך מפסיק בינו למבוי – לא חשוב [כסתום]. אבל בתים – כסתומות חשיבי, כיון שהחצר מפסיק בינם למבוי. ודוקא היכא דלא נשתתפו בעינן בתים וחצרות פתוחין לתוכו, אבל נשתתפו – לא בעינן. ומשני: אפשר דמבטלי רשות גבי חד, דהשתא איכא בית דלא חשיב כסתום. ולא אמר נמי ניתקו חצרות כולם – כיון דשאר הבתים אסורין בחצר. ופריך: בית איכא, בתים ליכא. ולא מצי למימר דבטלי רשות גבי תרי, שהם היו אוסרין זה על זה. ולא מצי למימר שהשנים עירבו – דהא מדקאמר רב "לא עירבו" – משמע לא עירבו כלל: אפשר

ד א מיי' פ"ב מהלכות מילה הלכה ו סמג עשין כח טוש"ע א"ח סימן שלא סעיף ו וטוש"ע י"ד סימן רסו סעיף ב:
ה ב מיי' פ"ג מהלכות עירובין הלכה יח סמג עשין דרבנן א טוש"ע א"ח סימן שעב סעיף ב:
ו ג מיי' פ"ה מהלכות עירובין הלכה טו סמג שם טוש"ע א"ח סימן שפו:
ז ד מיי' פי"ז מהלכות שבת הלכה יז סמג שם טוש"ע א"ח סימן שסג סעיף כו:

גליון הש"ס

רש"י ד"ה מותר לטלטל בכולו וכו' פושטן ומטלטלן. תמוה לי הא מ"מ כיון דשבתו בבית אסור לטלטלן וכלתיות לחצר עירובין דף לא כסתמות ומודלת ועיינ"ג: תוספות ד"ה לר"א שמותי וכו' וכן מוכח בירושלמי. עיין ביצה דף לו ע"ב תוספות ד"ה ואומר:

נ"ל שבות
פסחים נב.
עירובין כג: לה. עד. פט. נה.
[לעיל מ: ברכות ט. וש"נ]
[נדה נג:]
עירובין נה.
סוף פרק ט דשביעית
עירובין ה. [ע"ש נ"ע] וב"מ עג.
[נדה ז:]
[וע"ע תוספות נדה ז: ד"ה שמותי הוא]

הגהות הב"ח

(א) גמ' אחד גגות ואחד חצרות ואחד קרפיפות רשות אחת: (ב) שם שלא נשתתפו בו מותר: (ג) שם ולא אמרת לי דילמא כצ"ל ותיבת הכי נמחק: (ד) תוס' ד"ה שלא וכו' דהא לקמן. נ"ב דף קלג: עי"ש: (ה) ד"ה ומי שרי וכו' ר"א דרך רה"ר כיון: (ו) ד"ה דרבי אליעזר וכו' ואמר בגמרא רבי יהודה בן פזי: (ז) ד"ה ניתקו וכו' כיון שאין דרך מפסיק:

רבינו חננאל

בשבת שלא כרצון רבי אליעזר ושקלינן וטרינן בה ואוקמא רב אשי שלא כרצון ר' אליעזר דשרי אפילו דרך רה"ר ושלא ברצון מחלוקתו והם החכמים שחולקים על ר' אליעזר ואומרים אפילו דרך גגות ודרך חצירות וכו' דרבי עקיבא סבירא ליה כוותיהון אלא כרצון ר' שמעון דשרי דרך גגות דתנן ר' שמעון אומר אחד גגות ואחד חצירות ואחת קרפיפות כו'. בעא ר' זירא מר' אמי מבוי שלא נשתתפו בו מהו לטלטל בכולו כו' ושתק ר' אמי ולא השיב לו זמנין אשכחיה דאמר אמר ר"ל משום רבי יהודה נשיאה פעם אחת שכחו ולא הביאו אזמל מע"ש והביאוהו בשבת והיה הדבר קשה לחכמים היאך מניחין דברי חכמים ועושין כר' אליעזר שהן דברי יחיד ועוד רבי אליעזר שמותי הוא כלומר מתלמידי שמאי הוא. א"ר אושעיא שאילית את ר' יהודה הגוזר פי' המל ואמר לי מבוי שלא נשתתפו בו הוה ואתיוה מהאי רישא להאי רישא אמינא ליה סבירא ליה למר מבוי שלא נשתתפו בו מותר לטלטלו בכולן א"ל אין כו'. אתמר ר' זירא אמר רב מבוי שלא נשתתפו בו אין מטלטלין בו אלא בארבע. ר' זירא לא פירש שמועה זו עד דאתא רב נחמן אמר רבה בר אבוה ופרשה משמיה דרב הכי מבוי שלא נשתתפו בו אם עירבו חצרות עם בתיהם אין מטלטלין בו אלא בארבע לא עירבו חצרות עם בתיהם מותר לטלטל בכולו א"ל רב חנינא חוזאה לרבא מפני מה כי עירבו עם בתיהם אין מטלטלין באותו מבוי אלא בארבע דניתקו חצרות ונעשו בתים כלומר כיון שעירבו נעשו בתי החצר והחצר רשות אחת ורב לטעמיה דאמר אין מבוי ניתר בלחי וקורה עד שיהו בתים

*) פי' ר"ל לדבריו דס"ל דבתים אין לה וא"כ אינו ניתר בלחי וקורה ולא ס"ל ר"ש דרשות א' הן וא"כ גם חצר אין לה וא"כ היאך אמר וחצירות איכא ועי' בטוא"ח סימן שעב וברמב"ם פ"ג מה"ע ומשכחת ליה לר"ש מבוי דניתר בלחי וקורה כמ"ש התוספות לקמן דבטלי רשות לגבי תרי ואותן תרי עירבו יחד וכוונת התוספות להקשות בין על עירבו ובין על לא עירבו וכדי שלא תאמר דזהו שמקשה המקשה באומרו בתים איכא חצרות ליכא בעירבו ע"כ פירשו התוספות דמ"ש ניתקו חצירות פירוש והשיב כאילו כו'.

*בָּתִּים וַחֲצֵרוֹת פְּתוּחִין לְתוֹכוֹ. וְהָכָא, בָּתִּים – אִיכָּא, חֲצֵרוֹת – לֵיכָּא. כִּי לָא עֵירְבוּ נַמִי, לֶיחֱזִינְהוּ לְהָנֵי בָּתִּים כְּמַאן דִּסְתִימִי דָּמוּ, וַחֲצֵרוֹת – אִיכָּא, וּבָתִּים – לֵיכָּא! אֶפְשָׁר דִּמְבַטְּלִי לֵיהּ רְשׁוּתָא דְּכוּלְּהוּ לְגַבֵּי חַד. סוֹף סוֹף, בַּיִת – אִיכָּא, בָּתִּים – לֵיכָּא! אֶפְשָׁר דְּמִצַּפְרָא וְעַד פַּלְגָא דְיוֹמָא לְגַבֵּי חַד, מִפַּלְגֵיהּ דְּיוֹמָא וּלְפַנְיָא לְגַבֵּי חַד. סוֹף סוֹף, בְּעִידָּנָא דְּאִיתֵיהּ לְהַאי – לֵיתֵיהּ לְהַאי! אֶלָּא אָמַר רַב אַשִׁי: מִי גָּרַם לַחֲצֵרוֹת שֶׁיֵּאָסְרוּ – בָּתִּים, וְלֵיכָּא. אָמַר ר' חִיָּיא בַּר אַבָּא א"ר יוֹחָנָן: °לֹא לַכֹּל אָמַר ר' אֱלִיעֶזֶר מַכְשִׁירֵי מִצְוָה דּוֹחִין אֶת הַשַּׁבָּת, שֶׁהֲרֵי שְׁתֵּי הַלֶּחֶם חוֹבַת הַיּוֹם הֵן וְלֹא לְמָדָן ר"א אֶלָּא מִגְּזֵירָה שָׁוָה. דְּתַנְיָא, ר' אֱלִיעֶזֶר אוֹמֵר: מִנַּיִין לְמַכְשִׁירֵי שְׁתֵּי הַלֶּחֶם שֶׁדּוֹחִין אֶת הַשַּׁבָּת – נֶאֶמְרָה הֲבָאָה בָּעוֹמֶר, וְנֶאֶמְרָה הֲבָאָה בִּשְׁתֵּי הַלֶּחֶם. מָה הֲבָאָה הָאֲמוּרָה בָּעוֹמֶר – מַכְשִׁירִין דּוֹחִין אֶת הַשַּׁבָּת, אַף הֲבָאָה הָאֲמוּרָה בִּשְׁתֵּי הַלֶּחֶם – מַכְשִׁירִין דּוֹחִין אֶת הַשַּׁבָּת. מוּפְנֵי, דְּאִי לָא מוּפְנֵי – אִיכָּא לְמִיפְרַךְ: מָה לָעוֹמֶר – שֶׁכֵּן אִם מָצָא קָצוּר – קוֹצֵר, תֹּאמַר בִּשְׁתֵּי הַלֶּחֶם שֶׁאִם מָצָא קָצוּר – אֵינוֹ קוֹצֵר. לָאֵי, אַפְנוּיֵי מוּפְנֵי. מִכְּדֵי כְּתִיב: °"וַהֲבֵאתֶם אֶת עוֹמֶר רֵאשִׁית קְצִירְכֶם אֶל הַכֹּהֵן", *"בְּיוֹם הֲבִיאֲכֶם" לָמָּה לִי? ש"מ – לְאַפְנוּיֵי. וְאַכַּתִּי, מוּפְנֶה מִצַּד אֶחָד הוּא, וְשָׁמְעִינַן לֵיהּ לְר' אֱלִיעֶזֶר *דְּאָמַר: מוּפְנֶה מִצַּד אֶחָד – לְמֵידִין וּמְשִׁיבִין! °'תָּבִיאוּ' רִבּוּיָא הוּא. לְמַעוּטֵי מַאי? אִילֵימָא לְמַעוּטֵי לוּלָב – *וְהָתַנְיָא: לוּלָב וְכָל מַכְשִׁירָיו דּוֹחִין אֶת הַשַּׁבָּת, דִּבְרֵי ר"א! וְאֶלָּא לְמַעוּטֵי סוּכָּה – וְהָתַנְיָא: סוּכָּה וְכָל מַכְשִׁירֶיהָ דּוֹחִין אֶת הַשַּׁבָּת, דִּבְרֵי ר"א! וְאֶלָּא לְמַעוּטֵי מַצָּה – וְהָתַנְיָא: מַצָּה וְכָל מַכְשִׁירֶיהָ דּוֹחִין אֶת הַשַּׁבָּת, דִּבְרֵי רַבִּי אֱלִיעֶזֶר! וְאֶלָּא לְמַעוּטֵי שׁוֹפָר – וְהָתַנְיָא: שׁוֹפָר וְכָל מַכְשִׁירָיו דּוֹחִין אֶת הַשַּׁבָּת, דִּבְרֵי ר"א! אָמַר רַב אַדָּא בַּר אַהֲבָה: לְמַעוּטֵי צִיצִית לְטַלִּיתוֹ, וּמְזוּזָה לְפִתְחוֹ. תַּנְיָא נַמִי הָכִי: וְשָׁוִין, שֶׁאִם צִיֵּיץ טַלִּיתוֹ וְעָשָׂה מְזוּזָה לְפִתְחוֹ – שֶׁהוּא חַיָּיב. מַאי טַעְמָא? אָמַר רַב יוֹסֵף: לְפִי שֶׁאֵין קָבוּעַ לָהֶם זְמַן. אָמַר לֵיהּ אַבַּיֵי: אַדְּרַבָּה, מִדְּאֵין קָבוּעַ לָהֶם זְמַן – כָּל

ויקרא כג | שם

רש"י

בָּתִּים וַחֲצֵרוֹת. שְׁנֵי בָתִּים פְּתוּחִים לִשְׁתֵּי חֲצֵרוֹת, שְׁתַּיִם לְכָל חָצֵר, וּשְׁתֵּי חֲצֵרוֹת פְּתוּחוֹת לַמָּבוֹי: כְּמַאן דִּסְתִימִי דָּמֵי. דְּהָא לְגַבֵּי מָבוֹי כְּמַאן דִּסְתִימִי הָווּ, דְּהָא חֲצֵרוֹת מַפְסִיקוֹת בֵּינְתַיִם, שֶׁאֵין הַבָּתִּים מוֹצִיאִין לָהֶם: אֶפְשָׁר דִּמְבַטְּלִי. בְּנֵי הַבָּתִּים שֶׁבֶּחָצֵר רְשׁוּת שֶׁיֵּשׁ לָהֶם בֶּחָצֵר לְגַבֵּי חַד מִינַּיְיהוּ, וְהָוֵי כָּל הֶחָצֵר שֶׁלּוֹ, וּמוּתָּר לְהוֹצִיא מִבֵּיתוֹ לֶחָצֵר: סוֹף סוֹף בַּיִת אִיכָּא. בְּכָל חָצֵר, בָּתִּים לֵיכָּא, וְרַב בָּעֵי שְׁנֵי בָתִּים לְכָל חָצֵר: אֶלָּא אָמַר רַב אַשִׁי. טַעְמָא לָאו מִשּׁוּם בָּתִּים וַחֲצֵרוֹת פְּתוּחוֹת לְתוֹכוֹ הוּא. דְּרַב בֵּין עֵירְבוּ בֵּין לֹא עֵירְבוּ, מִכֵּיוָן דִּפְתִיחֵי שְׁתֵּי חֲצֵרוֹת לַמָּבוֹי, וּשְׁנֵי בָתִּים לְכָל חָצֵר – תּוֹרַת מָבוֹי עָלָיו, וְנִיתָּר בְּלֶחִי וְקוֹרָה. וְהַיְינוּ טַעְמָא דְּכִי עֵירְבוּ בַּחֲצֵרוֹת וְלֹא נִשְׁתַּתְּפוּ בַּמָּבוֹי אָסוּר לְטַלְטֵל בּוֹ, וְכִי לֹא עֵירְבוּ – שָׁרֵי: מִי גָּרַם לַחֲצֵירוֹת שֶׁיֵּאָסְרוּ. עַל הַמָּבוֹי, לְהַצְרִיכוֹ שִׁיתּוּף לְהוֹצִיא מִן הַחֲצֵירוֹת לְתוֹכוֹ: בָּתִּים. הוּא דְּגַרְמֵי לוֹ, דְּאִי לָאו מִשּׁוּם בָּתִּים – הָווּ לְהוּ חֲצֵרוֹת וּמָבוֹי רְשׁוּת אַחַת. דְּרַב דַּאֲמַרָהּ לְהָא מִלְּתָא – כְּר"ש סְבִירָא לֵיהּ, דְּאָמַר בְּעֵירוּבִין (דף עד.): גַּג וְחָצֵר וְקַרְפֵּף וּמָבוֹי כּוּלָּן רְשׁוּת אַחַת הֵן, וּמְטַלְטְלִין מִזֶּה לָזֶה. וְאָמַר רַב עֲלָהּ: הֲלָכָה כְּר' שִׁמְעוֹן, וְהוּא שֶׁלֹּא עֵירְבוּ בָּתִּים עִם הַחֲצֵרוֹת, דְּלָא שְׁכִיחִי מָאנֵי דְּבָתִּים בֶּחָצֵר. הִלְכָּךְ, לְעִנְיַן טִלְטוּל בְּתוֹכוֹ נַמִי, כִּי לֹא עֵירְבוּ חֲצֵרוֹת עִם הַבָּתִּים – שָׁרֵי, דַּהֲוָה לְהוּ כְּמוֹ שֶׁנִּשְׁתַּתְּפוּ בּוֹ. דְּמִי גָּרַם לוֹ לַמָּבוֹי לֵיאָסֵר וּלְהִצְטָרֵךְ לְשִׁיתּוּף – בָּתִּים גָּרְמוּ לוֹ, וְאֵינָם, שֶׁהֲרֵי נִסְתַּלְּקוּ מִמֶּנּוּ, וּמוּתָּר לְהוֹצִיא מִן הַחֲצֵרוֹת לַמָּבוֹי כְּאִילּוּ נִשְׁתַּתְּפוּ. וּבְנִשְׁתַּתְּפוּ לָא מְסַפְּקָא לָן דְּמוּתָּר לְטַלְטֵל בְּכוּלָּן: לֹא לַכֹּל אָמַר רַבִּי אֱלִיעֶזֶר. לֹא בְּכָל מַכְשִׁירֵי מִצְוָה אָמַר כֵּן. וּלְקַמָּן מְפָרֵשׁ הֵי מַכְשִׁירֵי מִצְוָה אָתָא לְמַעוּטֵי: שְׁתֵּי הַלֶּחֶם. דַּעֲצֶרֶת חוֹבַת יוֹם הֵן, וְאֵין לְאַחֲרָן עַד לְמָחָר: וְלֹא לְמָדָן רַבִּי אֱלִיעֶזֶר. דְּאַפִּיָּיתָם תִּדְחֶה שַׁבָּת, אֶלָּא בִּגְזֵירָה שָׁוָה. וְאִי בְּכָל מַכְשִׁירֵי מִצְוָה שֶׁעִיקַּר הַמִּצְוָה נוֹהֶגֶת בַּשַּׁבָּת אָמַר מַכְשִׁירֶיהָ כְּמוֹתָהּ, לָמָּה לִי גְּזֵירָה שָׁוָה? מָה הֲבָאָה הָאֲמוּרָה בָּעוֹמֶר מַכְשִׁירֶיהָ. דְּהַיְינוּ קְצִירָה טְחִינָה וְהַרְקָדָה שֶׁלּוֹ דּוֹחִין אֶת הַשַּׁבָּת, כִּדְאָמְרִינַן בִּמְנָחוֹת (דף עב.): "בֶּחָרִישׁ וּבַקָּצִיר תִּשְׁבּוֹת" – מָה חָרִישׁ רְשׁוּת, אַף קָצִיר רְשׁוּת. יָצָא קְצִירַת הָעוֹמֶר שֶׁהִיא מִצְוָה: שֶׁכֵּן[א] מָצָא קָצוּר. שֶׁלֹּא לְשֵׁם עוֹמֶר – מִצְוָה לִקְצוֹר לִשְׁמָהּ, דִּכְתִיב: "וּקְצַרְתֶּם וַהֲבֵאתֶם". הִלְכָּךְ, קְצִירָה גּוּפָהּ מִצְוָה הִיא. תֹּאמַר בִּשְׁתֵּי הַלֶּחֶם, שֶׁלֹּא נֶאֱמַר בָּהֶן קְצִירָה? לָאֵי. בֶּאֱמֶת: מִצַּד אֶחָד. הֲבָאָה דְּעוֹמֶר מוּפְנָה, הֲבָאָה דִּשְׁתֵּי הַלֶּחֶם אֵינָהּ מוּפְנָה, דִּצְרִיכָה לְגוּפָהּ: וְשָׁמְעִינַן לֵיהּ לְרַבִּי אֱלִיעֶזֶר דְּאָמַר. גְּזֵירָה שָׁוָה שֶׁאֵינָהּ מוּפְנָה מִשְּׁנֵי צְדָדֶיהָ אֶלָּא מִצַּד אֶחָד – לְמֵדִין מִמֶּנָּה אִם אֵין לְהָשִׁיב, אֲבָל אִם יֵשׁ לְהָשִׁיב – מְשִׁיבִין. וּבְמַסֶּכֶת יְבָמוֹת בְּפֶרֶק "מִצְוַת חֲלִיצָה"* שָׁמְעִינַן לֵיהּ דְּאָמַר הָכִי. דְּקָתָנֵי: חֲלִיצָה בִּשְׂמֹאל פְּסוּלָה, וְרַבִּי אֱלִיעֶזֶר מַכְשִׁיר, דְּלָא יָלֵיף רֶגֶל רֶגֶל מִמְּצוֹרָע. וּפָרְכִינַן: וְרַבִּי אֱלִיעֶזֶר לָא יָלֵיף מִמְּצוֹרָע? וְהָא תַּנְיָא, ר"א אוֹמֵר: מִנַּיִין לִרְצִיעָה שֶׁהִיא בְּאוֹזֶן יְמָנִית – נֶאֱמַר כָּאן אוֹזֶן, וְנֶאֱמַר לְהַלָּן אוֹזֶן וכו'. וּמְשַׁנֵּינַן: אֹזֶן אֹזֶן – מוּפְנָה, רֶגֶל רֶגֶל – לֹא מוּפְנָה. וְהַאי לָאו מוּפְנָה דְּקָאָמְרִינַן – מִשְּׁנֵי צְדָדִין קָאָמַר. דְּרֶגֶל דִּכְתִיב בַּחֲלִיצָה אִיצְטְרִיכָא לְגוּפָהּ, אֲבָל מִצַּד אֶחָד מוּפְנֶה הוּא, דְּפָרָשַׁת מְצוֹרָע מוּפְנֶה הוּא, הַהִיא דְּעָנִי, דְּכוּלְּהוּ כְּתִיבִין בִּמְצוֹרָע עָשִׁיר: תָּבִיאוּ רִיבּוּיָא הוּא. דְּהָא אַ"וְהִקְרַבְתֶּם מִנְחָה חֲדָשָׁה" סָמֵיךְ, וּמָצֵי לְמִיכְתַּב "מִמּוֹשְׁבוֹתֵיכֶם לֶחֶם תְּנוּפָה", וְ"תָבִיאוּ" יְתֵירָה הוּא: לְמַעוּטֵי מַאי. הָא דְּאָמַר רַבִּי יוֹחָנָן לְעֵיל: לֹא לַכֹּל אָמַר רַבִּי אֱלִיעֶזֶר. לְמַעוּטֵי הֵי מַכְשִׁירִים אָתֵי, דְּלָא דָּחֵי שַׁבָּת? וְכָל מַכְשִׁירָיו. כְּגוֹן לְקוֹצְצוֹ מִן הַמְחוּבָּר: לְמַעוּטֵי צִיצִית. שֶׁלֹּא יִתְלֶנָּה בְּטַלִּיתוֹ בְּשַׁבָּת, כִּדְמְפָרֵשׁ טַעְמָא וְאָזֵיל: כָּל

תוספות

אפשר דמבטלי רשות כו'. וא"ת: כי עירבו חצרות נמי עם בתים, מצינן למימר שיש חצר למבוי, כגון שביטלו אותו של חצר זה לרשות דכולהו שיש להם במבוי, לבני חצר אחרת, ויכולין לטלטל מן החצר למבוי. הא לא בעי לאקשויי, דאיכא למ"ד בעירובין (דף סו:): אין ביטול רשות מחצר לחצר. ועוד: דבלאו הכי פריך שפיר:

מפלגא דיומא לפניא. רב לטעמיה, דאמר במסכת עירובין (דף סח:): מבטלין וחוזרין ומבטלין:

מי גרם לחצרות. אנן קי"ל דאפילו עירבו חצרות עם בתים מותר לטלטל[ב]. דהא רב דאסר בעירבו – לטעמיה, דפסיק כרבי שמעון דוקא בלא עירבו, אבל רבי יוחנן פסיק כר"ש, בין עירבו בין לא עירבו, וכר' יוחנן קי"ל:

לא לכל אמר רבי אליעזר מכשירי מצוה דוחין את השבת. לקמן מפרש דאתא למעוטי ציצית ומזוזה. וה"פ: לא[ג] כל מצות הנוהגות בשבת אמר ר' אליעזר שמכשירין ידחו שבת, שהרי שתי הלחם כו'. ומשמע לכאורה דאי לא דאשכחן דמצריך ר' אליעזר ג"ש, הוה גמרינן לציצית ומזוזה ממילה, ונימא דמכשיריה דחו שבת. ותימה הוא: היכי שייך למילף ציצית ומזוזה ממילה? דמילה דין הוא דמכשיריה דוחין שבת, דהיא עצמה דוחה שבת. אבל ציצית ומזוזה אין במצותן דחיית שבת:

תאמר בשתי הלחם שאם מצא קצור אינו קוצר. תימה: מאי קא פריך? דהיא גופה נילף מינה: מה העומר שאף על פי שמצא קצור – קוצר, אף שתי הלחם אם מצא קצור – קוצר. ונילף מינה תרתי: מכשירין וקצירה! ותירץ ר"ת: דהא לא דמי דנילף מינה קצירה, שהרי בעצרת יהיו כל החיטין והשעורין קצורים. ולא משמע דאתיא ג"ש אלא[ד] מכשירין דדחו שבת. א"נ, י"ל: דהא לא מצי למימר נילף קצירה, דמהיכא נפקא לן קצירת העומר דדחיא שבת – מדכתיב: "בחריש ובקציר תשבות" כדדרשינן במנחות בשילהי "ר' ישמעאל" (דף עב.): מה חריש רשות, אף קציר רשות, יצא קצירת העומר שהיא מצוה. וגלי רחמנא דליכא למילף אלא לגבי העומר, דכתיב ביה נמי "קציר", ולא לגבי שתי הלחם דלא כתיב בהו קציר. ועל כרחיך ודאי היינו טעמא דיליף גבי עומר קצירה משום דכתיב ביה קציר, דאי לאו הכי – מ"מ דיליף טפי גבי עומר מגבי שתי הלחם, דהכא נמי נימא יצא קצירת שתי הלחם שהיא מצוה:

ושוין שאם צייץ טליתו כו' מ"ט כו'. תימה: מה צריך טעם לזה? אלא משום דלא אשכחן דרבינהו קרא, דכל אינך מצרכינן קרא לקמן, דלא גמרי מהדדי. ומיהו, יש לומר: דאיכא למילף ציצית ומזוזה מסוכה, דמאי פרכת – שכן נוהגת בלילות כבימים, מזוזה נמי נוהג בלילות כבימים. וכן ציצית, לרבנן דפליגי עליה דרבי שמעון בפרק "התכלת" (מנחות דף מג.), דלא דרשי "וראיתם אותו" פרט לכסות לילה, אלא פרט לכסות סומא. ולהאי טעמא דפרישית, דמסוכה יליף – צריך לומר דציצית[ה] אם עבר זמנה בטלה. דאי לאו הכי – איכא למפרך: מה לסוכה שכן אם עבר זמנה בטלה. דמסתבר, דמילה אם עבר זמנה – לא בטלה. שאותה מילה עצמה שהוא מיחייב בשמיני הוא עושה בתשיעי. שאם מל בשמיני לא היה חוזר ומל בתשיעי. אבל[ו] סוכה ציצית ומזוזה – בכל יומא מיחייב בהן, אפילו קיימם היום – חייב לקיימם למחר. הלכך, כשעבר היום ולא עשאם – מצות היום לא יקיים עוד לעולם. ואם תאמר: ומסוכה היכי מצי למילף, וכן כל הנך דלקמן, דפריך ניכתוב רחמנא בהאי וניתי הנך וניגמרו מיניה. אדרבה, נגמר מכיבוד אב ואם, ומבנין בית המקדש דלא דחו שבת, כדאיתא

רבינו חננאל

בתים וחצרות פתוחין לתוכו והכא כיון שערבו כאלו אין שם חצר וכולן (בתים) [חצרות] נינהו ואפי' נשתתפו כיון שאין שם בתים אין שתוף מועיל באותו מבוי. כך יש לומר כי לא עירבו נמי כיון שהן אסורין להוציא מן הבית לחצר חשוב אותן הבתים כאלו סתומין הן שאין להם רשות להשתמש מן הבתים לחצר וחצר איכא בית ליכא. לטעמיה דרב היאך מטלטלין במבוי שאין לו בית ומפרק יתכן שיבטלו כל בני החצר רשותם לגבי חד וכיון שמבטלין רשותם לגביה יש לו להוציא מן הבית לחצר כדתנן נתנו לו רשותם הוא מותר והם אסורים וקיי"ל הא דתנן נתנו לו רשותם רשותם מעיקרא מקודם *) שיבטל הויא רשותא לגביהו ואקשינן וכיון שבטלו כל בני חצר רשותם לגבי חד נעשו כל הבתים שלו וכולן כבית אחד הן חשובין ורב לא אמר אלא בתים ומיעוטי בתי' שנים והכא ליכא שני בתים והיאך מתיר רב. ופרקינ' עוד כגון שבני חצר בטלו רשותן מן הבקר עד חצי היום לגבי ראובן בפירוש ומחצי היום ולהלן לגבי שמעון שנמצאו ראובן ושמעון שניהם מותרין בחצר זו דהא שמעינן לרב דאמר מבטלין וחוזרין ומבטלין ואקשינן תוב סוף סוף בעת שמותר לזה להשתמש בחצר זה אסור לחבירו ואותה העת אין שם בחצר אלא בית ראובן בלבד ומחצי היום ולהלן בית שמעון לבדו ואין לראובן בה רשות להשתמש. ומ"מ לא תמצא ב' בתים מותרין בחצר זו בעת אחת. ופירק רב אשי פירוק אחר ואמר מי גרם לחצרות הללו הפתוחות למבוי להיאסר בהן טלטול בתים מפני אלו הבתים שהן פתוחין לתוכן ולא עירבו שאלו לא היו בהן בתים מותרין היו השובתים שם לטלטל בה בכולה. שהן כמו קרפף שמותר השובת בו לטלטל בכולן וגם המבוי לא נאסר בהן טלטול אי לא מפני הבתים שהן פתוחים לתוכה ואינם. כלומר כיון שלא עירבו תחשבם כאלו סתומים הם ואינם כלל. הלא אילו היו סתומין היה הטלטול מותר בהם עכשיו יהיה מותר ועמדו דברי רב ועיקר דברי רב אשי ופירושם בעירובין פרק הדר עם הנכרי בחצר ופירשנום שם. ושמעינן מינה דרבנן פליגי על ר' שמעון דשרי דרך גגות ודרך חצירות ודרך קרפיפות ואע"ג דאמר רב הלכתא כר' שמעון בפרק כל גגות העיר רשות אחת הן לגבי

רב נסים גאון

ואכתי מופנה מצד א' הוא ושמעי' ליה לר' אליעזר דאמר מופנה מצד אחד למידין ומשיבין. דע שאע"פ שלא מצאנו לר' אליעזר בפירוש שאמר דבר זה יודעים אנחנו אותו מדבריהם במס' נדה בפרק המפלת (דף כב) מופנה מצד אחד לר' ישמעאל למידין ואין משיבין לרבנן למידין ומשיבין והואיל ור' אליעזר **) עומד כר' ישמעאל כי אנו מוצאין ר' יהושע חברו של ר' אליעזר אומר (ע"ז דף כט במשנה) ישמעאל אחי ועם זה לא נתיחד בחלוקה בזה הדבר אלא ר' ישמעאל והשאר שוו כולם בדבר אחד כי מופנה מצד אחד למידין ומשיבין ידענו כי ר' אליעזר בכלל החכמים ששוו עומד וסובר כמותן שאילו היה חולק עליהן בדבר זה היה נזכר עם ר' ישמעאל וכיון שלא הוזכרה החלוקה אלא בר' ישמעאל בלבד נתברר כי ר' אליעזר אינו שוה לו וכרבנן סבירא ליה ומיכן אמרנו ושמעינן ליה לר' אליעזר דאמר מופנה מצד אחד למידין ומשיבין לפי שכל החכמים שהיו באותו הדור שוו בדבר זה חוץ מר' ישמעאל שהוזכר בפירוש שהוא חולק: איצטריך

**) אין הלשון מדויק ואמנם כוונתו שוודאי ר"א היה בדורו של ר' יהושע ואם איתא דבר כותיה היה להזכירו עם ר"י ועי' ברש"י כאן בד"ה ושמעינן וביבמות קד ע"א ד"ה לא מופני וצ"ע.

מסורת הש"ס

[עירובין ה. יב: עג: עד.]

[נ"ל מיום]

יבמות ע:

סוכה מג.

הגהות הב"ח

(א) רש"י ד"ה שכן אם מצא: (ב) תוס' ד"ה מי גרם וכו' מותר לטלטל בכולו דהא רב: (ג) ד"ה לא לכל וכו' וה"פ לא לכל מצות: (ד) ד"ה תאמר וכו' אלא לענין מכשירין: (ה) ד"ה ושוין וכו' לציצית ומזוזה אם עבר: (ו) בא"ד אבל ציצית ומזוזה כצ"ל ותיבת סוכה נמחק:

גליון הש"ס

גמ' לא לכל אר"א מכשירי מצוה. עי' בס' בני חייא בסוף הספר בלקוטי': רש"י ד"ה ור"א וכו' מופנה הוא הכתוב לענין. עי' ברש"י יבמות דף ע ע"ב ד"ה ושמעי' לי' לר"א וכו' וצ"ע: תוס' ד"ה תאמר וכו' דאיכא למ"ד בעירובין. עי' עירובין דף עג ע"ב תוס' ד"ה אלא פשיטא: ד"ה ושוין וכו' אלא פרט לכסות סומא. וכ"כ רש"י סוכה יא ע"א ד"ה לפרזומא ועיין בספר המכתב פ"ג מהל' ציצית:

כל שעתא ושעתא זמניה הוא! אלא אמר רב נחמן א"ר יצחק, ואיתימא רב הונא בריה דרב יהושע: *הואיל ובידו להפקירן.§ אמר מר: לולב וכל מכשיריו דוחין את השבת, דברי ר"א. מנא ליה לר"א הא? אי מעומר ושתי הלחם – שכן צורך גבוה! אלא אמר קרא: °'ביום', *'ביום' – אפילו בשבת. ולמאי הלכתא? אילימא לטלטול – איצטריך קרא למישרי טלטול?! אלא למכשיריו. ורבנן – ההוא מיבעי ליה: 'ביום' ולא בלילה. ור"א, ביום ולא בלילה מנא ליה? נפקא ליה °מ"ושמחתם לפני ה' אלהיכם שבעת ימים", ימים ולא לילות. ורבנן – איצטריך, ס"ד אמינא: נילף שבעת ימים(א) מסוכה, מה להלן – ימים ואפילו לילות, אף כאן – ימים ואפילו לילות, קמ"ל. וליכתוב רחמנא בלולב וניתו הנך ונילפו מיניה! משום דאיכא למיפרך: מה ללולב שכן טעון ארבעה מינים.§ "סוכה וכל מכשיריה דוחין את השבת דברי רבי אליעזר". מנא ליה לר"א הא? אי מעומר ושתי הלחם – שכן צורך גבוה הוא! אי מלולב – שכן טעון ארבעה מינים! אלא: גמר שבעת ימים(ב) מלולב, מה להלן – מכשיריו דוחין את השבת, אף כאן נמי – מכשיריו דוחין את השבת. וליכתוב רחמנא בסוכה, וניתי הנך וניגמור מיניה! משום דאיכא למיפרך: מה לסוכה – שכן נוהגת בלילות כבימים.§ "מצה וכל מכשיריה דוחין את השבת, דברי ר"א". מנא ליה לר"א הא? אי מעומר ושתי הלחם – שכן צורך גבוה! אי מלולב – שכן טעון ארבעה מינים! אי מסוכה – שכן נוהגת בלילות כבימים! אלא: גמר 'חמשה עשר', 'חמשה עשר' מחג הסוכות, מה להלן – מכשיריה דוחין את השבת, אף כאן – מכשיריה דוחין את השבת. וליכתוב רחמנא במצה וניתו הנך וליגמור מיניה! משום דאיכא למיפרך: מה למצה – שכן נוהגת בנשים כבאנשים.§ "שופר וכל מכשיריו דוחין את השבת, דברי ר"א". מנא ליה לר"א הא? אי מעומר ושתי הלחם – שכן צורך גבוה, אי מלולב – שכן טעון ארבעה מינים! אי מסוכה – שכן נוהגת בלילות כבימים! אי ממצה – שכן נוהגת בנשים כבאנשים! אלא: אמר קרא °"יום תרועה יהיה לכם" – ביום, אפילו בשבת. ולמאי? אילימא לתקיעה – הא *תנא דבי שמואל: "כל מלאכת עבודה לא תעשו" – יצתה תקיעת שופר ורדיית הפת, שהיא חכמה ואינה מלאכה, אלא למכשירין. ורבנן – ההוא מיבעי ליה: ביום ולא בלילה. ור"א, ביום ולא בלילה מנא ליה? נפקא ליה °מ"ביום הכפורים תעבירו שופר בכל ארצכם" וגמרי מהדדי. וליכתוב רחמנא בשופר, וליתו הנך וליגמרו מיניה! מתקיעת שופר דראש השנה ליכא למיגמר – שכן מכנסת זכרונות של ישראל לאביהן שבשמים, מתקיעות [שופר] דיוה"כ ליכא למיגמרי – *דאמר מר: תקעו ב"ד שופר נפטרו עבדים לבתיהם ושדות חוזרות לבעליהן.§ (אמר מר) "מילה וכל מכשיריה דוחין את השבת, דברי רבי אליעזר" מנא ליה לר"א הא? אי מכולהו גמר – כדאמרינן. ועוד: מה להנך –

שכן

תורה אור

ויקרא כג

שם

במדבר כט

ויקרא כה

ר"ה ח:

כל שעתא זמניה הוא. וכיון שיש לו טלית, בכל יום שמשהא בלא ציצית עובר בעשה, ואפילו מונחת בקופסא. הלכך, כל יומא רמיא מצותיה עליה: הואיל ובידו להפקירן. ונפקי מרשותיה, ולאו עליה רמיא חובתיה: אי מעומר ושתי הלחם. וגמר במה מצינו: ביום ואפילו בשבת. מדלא כתיב "בראשון" – לדרשא אתא, בכל יום שהוא ראשון לחג: ולמאי איצטריך לרבויי. להאי ואפילו בשבת, אי נימא לטלטל כדמשמע קרא – לקיחה טלטול בעלמא הוא, ועדיין במתן תורה לא נאסר טלטול, דאיצטריך קרא למישרי להאי: אלא למכשיריו. דאיסורא דאורייתא הוא: מה להלן ימים ואפילו לילות. כדילפינן במסכת סוכה (דף מג.): וליכתוב רחמנא בלולב. דמכשירין דחו: וניתו. עומר ושתי הלחם מיניה, ולמה ליה דכתביה בכולהו? אי מלולב. במה מצינו מלולב, שהוא מצוה ומכשיריו דוחין, אף סוכה שהיא מצוה מכשיריה דוחין: גמר ז' ימים כו'. ובג"ש קאתי ליה. ואע"ג דאינה מופנה משני צדדים, דהא גבי לולב חד "שבעת ימים" הוא דכתיב, ודרשינן לר' אליעזר למעוטי לילות, כיון דגלי רחמנא בעומר ושתי הלחם ולולב – גילוי מילתא בעלמא הוא, ולא פרכינן עלה. גימגום(ג): וניתו הנך. עומר ושתי הלחם מינה: אי מסוכה שכן נוהגת בלילות כבימים. ואילו מצה, לילה הראשון חובה, ותו לא, כדאמרינן בפסחים (דף קכ.): ונכתוב רחמנא. בהדיא במצה, ונגמרו הנך כולהו מיניה: בנשים כבאנשים. כדילפינן בפסחים (ד' מג:): "לא תאכל עליו חמץ שבעת ימים" וגו', כל שישנו בבל תאכל חמץ – ישנו בקום אכול מצה. ונשים איתנהו בבל תאכל חמץ, דכל מצות לא תעשה, בין שהזמן גרמא בין שאין הזמן גרמא, חייבות. לאפוקי סוכה ולולב דליתנהו בנשים, דמצות עשה שהזמן גרמא היא: ולמאי. האי קרא, הי מילתא דתרועה אתא למישרי בשבת? אי לתקיעה – לא איצטריך, דאפילו תקיעת הרשות לית בה איסורא דאורייתא: מלאכת עבודה. של טורח: וגמרי מהדדי. במסכת ראש השנה (דף לג:): שאין תלמוד לומר "בחדש השביעי", דהא בכמה קראי כתב לן דיוה"כ בחודש השביעי, מה ת"ל "בחודש השביעי" – שיהו כל תרועות משל חדש השביעי שוות: נפטרו עבדים לבתיהם. קריאת דרור דיובל תלויה בה, הלכך חשיבא: אי מכולהו. מאחת מכולן: כדאמרינן. איכא למיפרך בכל הנך, חדא לד חמור החמור בה לעיל:

שאם

כדאיתא בפ"ק דיבמות (דף ו.)! וי"ל: דהכא הכי גמרי: מה מצינו בהנך שמצות נוהגות בשבת, ומכשיריה דחו שבת – אף כל שמצות נוהגות בשבת מכשיריה דחו שבת. הלכך לא שייך למילף מכיבוד, דהיינו המצוה עצמה ולא מכשיריה. ד"שחוט לי' 'בשל לי'" – היינו כיבוד עצמו, כשמתקן לו מאכלו. והבנין נמי הוי מצוה אחת, שצוה הקדוש ברוך הוא לבנות בית המקדש: **סד"א** נילף שבעת ימים משבעת ימים מסוכה. וא"ת: היכי תיסק אדעתיה לדון ג"ש? הא אין אדם דן ג"ש מעצמו אא"כ למדה מרבו! וי"ל: דשמא בעלמא ניתנה למדרש*: **קמ"ל**°. ולא ידענא השתא האי שבעת ימים למאי אתיא. דאע"ג דדרשינן בפ"ק דפסחים (דף ה.): מה שביעי שביעי לחג, אף ראשון ראשון לחג – הא איכא למידרש משבעה בלא ימים:

שכן טעון ארבעה מינים. אף על גב דעומר ושתי הלחם נמי מביאין עמהן כבשים ויין לניסוך ושמן למנחות – שאני ד' מינין שבלולב דמעכבין זה את זה, כדאמר בפרק "הקומץ" (מנחות דף כז.). ובפרק "התכלת" (שם דף מה:) [אמרינן]: הכבשים אין מעכבין לא את העומר, ולא את שתי הלחם. *והיינו טעון ד' מינין – שאין מצות לולב כלל בלא ד' מינין. אבל באלו יכולה להיות מצותן בלא ד' מינין. הר"ב פור"ת: **אי** מעומר כו'. הכא לא דייקא תלמודא למילף מביניהו. דהכי אורחיה דתלמודא: זימנין דייק וזימנין לא דייק. ואי הוה דייק – הוה משכח פירכ', הרב פור"ת. א"נ: מילתא דאתיא במה הצד טרח וכתב לה קרא, כמו מילתא דאתיא בקל וחומר. והאי דקאמר תלמודא: "ניכתוב רחמנא בהאי ותיתי אידך מיניה" – פירוש: ומאי צריך קרא? היינו משום דאי בלא מה הצד הוה מצי למילף הך מצוה מאידך – לא הוה כתב רחמנא קרא, כיון דהוה פשוט כל כך, דלא דמי למילתא דאתיא בק"ו דהוא פשוט יותר: **שבעת** ימים(ד) מלולב. מופנה הוה משני צדדים; גבי לולב לא איצטריך – דאע"ג דדרשינן ימים ולא לילות, מיהו לא הוה צריך למיכתב שבעת כלל, דהוה מצי למיכתב: "ושמחת לפני וגו' בימים" והוי לשון שבעת מיותר לג"ש. וא"ת: ור' אליעזר, היכי דריש ימים ולא לילות, כיון דאית ליה ג"ש – היא גופה נילף מסוכה, מה להלן ימים אפילו לילות – אף לולב ימים ואפי' לילות! ויש לומר: דלית לן למילף בג"ש מילתא דלשון ג"ש גופא מוכחא דאינו כן, דימים משמע ולא לילות:

ואי מסוכה שכן נוהגת בלילות כבימים. משמע דבעי למימר: תאמר במצה שאינה נוהגת בלילות כבימים; ואדרבה, עיקר מצותה בלילה הראשון שנאמר: "בערב תאכלו מצות" (שמות יב), והכי הוה מצי למימר: שכן נוהגת בימים ובלילות:

נפקא ליה מביום הכפורים. וגמרינן מהדדי, כדדרשינן בראש השנה*: שיהו כל התקיעות של חודש השביעי שוות כדפירש בקונטרס, ורבנן סברי דלא שייך לאקשויי, אלא לומר שסדר תקיעות יהיו שוין. דלענין סדר תקיעות מייתי לה התם, אבל לזמן דיוס – ודאי לא איתקש, דע"כ זמנם אינו שוה, שזה בראש חודש וזה בעשור לחודש:

והתניא

[כדאיתא בפ' התכלת מה:]

פי' מהרש"א

רבינו חננאל

אומל לא שרינן בכי האי גוונא דבהדיא קיי"ל הלכתא כרבנן*) וכבליה דרבי עקיבא דאמר כל מלאכה שאפשר לה לעשות מע"ש אינ' דוחה את השבת והבאת אזמל כיון שאפשר לו להביאו מע"ש ולא הביאו אין הבאתו דוחה את השבת אפילו לענין עשיית פסח דכרת הוא לא מייתינן אזמל למול בנו או עבדו כדי שיותר לו לעשות פסח ולא שנא להו לרבנן לא דרך רה"ר ולא דרך גגות וקרפיפות וחצרות הכל אחד הוא ובכל אסור ואשכחנן בתלמוד א"י עובדא ולא הביאוהו בשבת. ואמרינן בכל מקום (רב עביד) מעשה רב דגמרינן מינה. וזה הוא המעשה. ר' שמואל בר אבודומי הוה ליה עובדא למגזר לרב ששעא בריה אנשיון למיתי אזמל שאל לר' [מנא]. אמר להון ידחה למחר. שאל לר' יצחק בן אלעזר אמר להון משחוק [קונדיטון] לא אנשיתון ומיתי אזמל אנשיתון ידחה למחר: **א"ר** חייא בר אבא. א"ר יוחנן לא לכל א"ר אליעזר מכשירי מצוה דוחין את השבת שהרי שתי הלחם חובת היום הן ולא למדם ר' אליעזר אלא מג"ש נאמרה הבאה בעומר שנאמר והבאתם את עומר וגו' ונאמרה הבאה בשתי הלחם שנאמר ממושבותיכם תביאו לחם תנופה שתים וגו'. מנין שהעומר דוחה שבת. גרסינן באחרית פרק ר' ישמעאל אומר העומר היה בא בשבת מג' סאין וכו'. ת"ר תקריב את מנחת בכוריך מה ת"ל לפי שמצות העומר להביא מן הקמה מניין שאם לא מצא קמה יביא מן העומרין ת"ל תקריב כו' עד תקריב לפי שמצותו לקצור בלילה. מניין שאם קצר ביום כשר ודוחה שבת ת"ל תקריב כל שהוא תקריב מ"מ תקריבו אפי' רשבת אפילו ביום בטומאה. ותוב תניא (בתו"כ) בסוף פרשת אמור אל הכהנים (ובפסחיםעז:ובמנחותע"ב) וכ' אומר וידבר משה את מועדי ה' מה ת"ל לפי שלא למדנו שדוחין את השבת אלא הפסח והתמיד שכתוב בהן במועדו מניין לרבות העומר והקרב עמו. שתי הלחם והקרב עמהן שידחו שבת ת"ל וידבר משה את מועדי ה' קבעו מועד אחד לכולן ופשוטה היא זו ההלכה כולה. ואפי' ר' אליעזר שמתיר במכשירי מצוה מודה. שאם ציית טליתו ועשה מזוזה בפתחו בשבת שהוא חייב ואמרינן מ"ש הני ואוקימנא הואיל ובידו להפקירן. פי' כי הציצית הוא חובת הבגד וכיון שהפקיר אינו בגדו וכן הבית

[דף לג:]

*) עיין היטב ברי"ף כאן דדחה כל הראיות שהביא רבינו ע"ש.

מסורת הש"ס

[עי' תוספות מנחות מד. ד"ה טלית]

סוכה מג.

לעיל קיז: ע"ש ר"ה כט:

הגהות הב"ח

(א) גמ' נילף שבעת ימים משבעת ימים מסוכה: (ב) שם אלא גמר שבעת ימים משבעת ימים מלולב: (ג) רש"י ד"ה גמר ז' ימים וכו' גימגום הס"ד ואחר כך מ"ה ונכתוב רחמנא בהדיא בסוכה וניתי הנך עומר ושתי הלחם ולולב מינה: (ד) תוס' ד"ה שבעת ימים משבעת ימים מלולב מופנה הוה משני לדדין דגבי לולב נמי לא איצטריך:

גליון הש"ס

רש"י ד"ה כל שעתא וכו' ואפי' מונחת בקופסא. עי' מנחות דף מד ע"א תוס' ד"ה טלית: תוס' ד"ה קמ"ל ולא ידענא. כעין זה לעיל דף קיח ע"ב תד"ה אלו היו וש"נ:

שֶׁכֵּן אִם עָבַר זְמַנָּהּ בָּטְלָה. אֶלָּא, הַיְינוּ טַעְמָא דְּרַבִּי אֱלִיעֶזֶר, דְּאָמַר קְרָא: °"וּבַיּוֹם הַשְּׁמִינִי יִמּוֹל בְּשַׂר עָרְלָתוֹ" – וַאֲפִילּוּ בְּשַׁבָּת. וְלִיכְתּוֹב רַחֲמָנָא בְּמִילָה, וְלֵיתוּ הָנָךְ וְלִיגְמוֹר מִינֵּיהּ! מִשּׁוּם דְּאִיכָּא לְמִיפְרַךְ: מַה לְּמִילָה שֶׁכֵּן נִכְרְתוּ עָלֶיהָ שְׁלֹשׁ עֶשְׂרֵה בְּרִיתוֹת.§ ע"כ לָא פְּלִיגִי רַבָּנַן עֲלֵיהּ אֶלָּא בְּמַכְשִׁירֵי מִילָה, אֲבָל מִילָה גּוּפָהּ – דִּבְרֵי הַכֹּל דּוֹחָה שַׁבָּת. מְנָלַן? אָמַר עוּלָּא: הֲלָכָה. וְכֵן אָמַר רַבִּי יִצְחָק: הֲלָכָה. מֵיתִיבִי: *מִנַּיִן לְפִיקּוּחַ נֶפֶשׁ שֶׁדּוֹחֶה אֶת הַשַּׁבָּת – רַבִּי אֶלְעָזָר בֶּן עֲזַרְיָה אוֹמֵר: מַה מִּילָה שֶׁהִיא אַחַת מֵאֵיבָרָיו שֶׁל אָדָם – דּוֹחָה אֶת הַשַּׁבָּת, קַל וָחוֹמֶר לְפִיקּוּחַ נֶפֶשׁ שֶׁדּוֹחֶה אֶת הַשַּׁבָּת. וְאִי סָלְקָא דַּעְתָּךְ הֲלָכָה, קַל וָחוֹמֶר מֵהֲלָכָה מִי אָתֵי?! וְהָתַנְיָא, *אָמַר לוֹ רַבִּי אֶלְעָזָר (*בֶּן עֲזַרְיָה): עֲקִיבָא, עֶצֶם כִּשְׂעוֹרָה מְטַמֵּא הֲלָכָה, וּרְבִיעִית דָּם – קַל וָחוֹמֶר, וְאֵין דָּנִין קַל וָחוֹמֶר מֵהֲלָכָה! אֶלָּא אָמַר רַבִּי אֶלְעָזָר: אָתְיָא 'אוֹת' 'אוֹת'. אֶלָּא מֵעַתָּה, תְּפִילִּין דִּכְתִיב בָּהֶן אוֹת – לִידְחֵי שַׁבָּת! אֶלָּא אָתְיָא 'בְּרִית' 'בְּרִית'. גָּדוֹל, דִּכְתִיב בֵּיהּ בְּרִית – לִידְחֵי שַׁבָּת! אֶלָּא: אָתְיָא 'דּוֹרוֹת' 'דּוֹרוֹת'. צִיצִית דִּכְתִיב בֵּיהּ דּוֹרוֹת לִידְחֵי שַׁבָּת! אֶלָּא אָמַר רַב נַחְמָן בַּר יִצְחָק: דָּנִין 'אוֹת' 'בְּרִית' וְ'דוֹרוֹת' מֵ'אוֹת' 'בְּרִית' וְ'דוֹרוֹת' – לְאַפּוֹקֵי הָנָךְ דְּחַד חַד הוּא דִּכְתִיב בְּהֶן. וְר' יוֹחָנָן אָמַר: אָמַר קְרָא 'בַּיּוֹם' – *בַּיּוֹם אֲפִילּוּ בַּשַּׁבָּת. אֲמַר לֵיהּ רֵישׁ לָקִישׁ לְרַבִּי יוֹחָנָן: אֶלָּא מֵעַתָּה, מְחוּסְּרֵי כַּפָּרָה דִּכְתִיב בְּהוּ 'בַּיּוֹם' – הָכִי נַמִי דְּדָחוּ שַׁבָּת! הַהוּא מִיבָּעֵי לֵיהּ: 'בַּיּוֹם' – וְלֹא בַּלַּיְלָה. הַאי נַמִי מִיבָּעֵי לֵיהּ 'בַּיּוֹם' וְלֹא בַּלַּיְלָה! הַהוּא מִ"בֶּן שְׁמוֹנַת יָמִים" נָפְקָא. הַאי נַמִי מִ'בְּיוֹם צַוּוֹתוֹ' נָפְקָא! אע"ג דְּנָפְקָא מִ'בְּיוֹם צַוּוֹתוֹ' אִצְטְרִיכָא, סד"א: הוֹאִיל וְחָס רַחֲמָנָא עֲלֵיהּ לְאַתּוֹיֵי בְּדַלּוּת, בַּלַּיְלָה נַמִי לֵיתֵי, קמ"ל. מַתְקִיף לָהּ רָבִינָא: אֶלָּא מֵעַתָּה – יְהֵא זָר כָּשֵׁר בָּהֶן, וִיהֵא אוֹנֵן כָּשֵׁר בָּהֶן! הָא אַהַדְרֵיהּ קְרָא. רַב אַחָא בַּר יַעֲקֹב אָמַר: אָמַר קְרָא 'שְׁמִינִי', שְׁמִינִי אֲפִילּוּ בַּשַּׁבָּת. הַאי שְׁמִינִי מִיבָּעֵי לֵיהּ לְמַעוֹטֵי שְׁבִיעִי! שְׁבִיעִי – מִבֶּן שְׁמוֹנַת יָמִים נָפְקָא. וְאַכַּתִּי מִיבָּעֵי לֵיהּ, חַד – לְמַעוֹטֵי שְׁבִיעִי, וְחַד – לְמַעוֹטֵי תְּשִׁיעִי; דְּאִי מֵחַד הֲוָה אָמִינָא: שְׁבִיעִי הוּא – דְּלָא מְטָא זִמְנֵיהּ, אֲבָל מִשְּׁמִינִי וְאֵילָךְ – זִמְנֵיהּ הוּא! אֶלָּא מְחַוַּורְתָּא כִּדְרַבִּי יוֹחָנָן. תַּנְיָא כְּוָותֵיהּ דְּרַבִּי יוֹחָנָן, וּדְלָא כְּרַב אַחָא בַּר יַעֲקֹב: 'שְׁמִינִי יִמּוֹל' – אֲפִילּוּ בַּשַּׁבָּת. וּמָה אֲנִי מְקַיֵּים °"מְחַלְלֶיהָ מוֹת יוּמָת" – בִּשְׁאָר מְלָאכוֹת חוּץ מִמִּילָה, אוֹ אֵינוֹ אֶלָּא אֲפִי' מִילָה, וּמָה אֲנִי מְקַיֵּים 'שְׁמִינִי יִמּוֹל' – חוּץ מִשַּׁבָּת – ת"ל: 'בַּיּוֹם' – אֲפִילּוּ בַּשַּׁבָּת. אָמַר רָבָא: הַאי תַּנָּא, מֵעִיקָּרָא מַאי קָא נִיחָא לֵיהּ, וּלְבַסּוֹף מַאי קָא קַשְׁיָא לֵיהּ? הָכִי קָאָמַר: 'שְׁמִינִי יִמּוֹל' אֲפִילּוּ בַּשַּׁבָּת, וּמָה אֲנִי מְקַיֵּים "מְחַלְלֶיהָ מוֹת יוּמָת" – בִּשְׁאָר מְלָאכוֹ' חוּץ מִמִּילָה, אֲבָל מִילָה דָּחְיָא. מ"ט – ק"ו הוּא וּמַה צָּרַעַ' שֶׁדּוֹחָה אֶת הָעֲבוֹדָה, וַעֲבוֹדָה

ויקרא יב
שמות לא

רש"י

שֶׁאִם עָבַר זְמַנָּן בְּטֵלִין. הִילְכָּךְ דָּחוּ: וּבַיּוֹם הַשְּׁמִינִי יִמּוֹל וַאֲפִילּוּ בְּשַׁבָּת. וּמִילָה גּוּפָהּ דְּדָחְיָא שַׁבָּת אָמְרִינַן לְקַמָּן הֲלָכָה לְמֹשֶׁה מִסִּינַי, אִיַּיתַּר לֵיהּ 'בַּיּוֹם' לְמַכְשִׁירֶיהָ: י"ג בְּרִיתוֹת. נֶאֶמְרוּ לְאַבְרָהָם בְּפָרָשַׁת מִילָה (בראשית יז): וְהָא תַּנְיָא. בְּמַסֶּכֶת נָזִיר: עֲקִיבָא עֶצֶם כִּשְׂעוֹרָה הֲלָכָה. שֶׁהָיָה ר"ע דָּן ק"ו: מִנַּיִן לִרְבִיעִית דַּם הַמֵּת שֶׁהַנָּזִיר מְגַלֵּחַ עַל אֲהִילָהּ, ק"ו: מָה עֶצֶם כִּשְׂעוֹרָה, שֶׁאֵינוֹ מְטַמֵּא בְּאֹהֶל – נָזִיר מְגַלֵּחַ עַל מַגָּעוֹ וּמַשָּׂאוֹ, רְבִיעִית דָּם שֶׁמְּטַמְּאָה בְּאֹהֶל, דִּכְתִיב: "וְעַל כָּל נַפְשֹׁת מֵת לֹא יָבֹא" – אֵינוֹ דִּין שֶׁהַנָּזִיר מְגַלֵּחַ עָלֶיהָ?! וְאָמַר לֵיהּ רַבִּי אֶלְעָזָר: עֲקִיבָא, עֶצֶם כִּשְׂעוֹרָה הֲלָכָה לְמֹשֶׁה מִסִּינַי שֶׁיְּהֵא נָזִיר מְגַלֵּחַ עָלֶיהָ, וּרְבִיעִית דָּם אַתָּה בָּא לִלְמוֹד מִמֶּנָּה בְּק"ו – וְאֵין דָּנִין קַל וָחוֹמֶר מֵהֲלָכָה, דְּלֹא נִיתְּנָה תּוֹרָה שֶׁבְּעַל פֶּה לִידָּרֵשׁ בְּי"ג מִדּוֹת: אָתְיָא אוֹת אוֹת. בְּשַׁבָּת כְּתִיב (שמות לא): "כִּי אוֹת הִיא", וּבְמִילָה כְּתִיב (בראשית יז): "וְהָיָה לְאוֹת בְּרִית". מַה לְּהַלָּן שַׁבָּת – אַף כָּאן שַׁבָּת: אֶלָּא מֵעַתָּה. אִי הָךְ ג"ש דְּאוֹת הָאֲמוּרָה בְּשַׁבָּת נֶאֶמְרָה בְּסִינַי לִידָּרֵשׁ, שֶׁתֵּיבָה זוֹ לִדְרָשָׁה נֶאֶמְרָה – לִיגְמַר מִינָּהּ נַמִי לִתְפִילִּין: אֶלָּא אָתְיָא בְּרִית בְּרִית. הַהוּא דְּאוֹת אוֹת לֹא נֶאֶמְרָה בְּסִינַי, וְאֵין אָדָם דָּן גְּזֵירָה שָׁוָה מֵעַצְמוֹ. אֶלָּא הָךְ דִּבְרִית בְּרִית נֶאֶמְרָה בְּסִינַי, וּבְשַׁבָּת כְּתִיב בְּרִית (שמות לא): "לְדוֹרוֹתָם בְּרִית עוֹלָם": גָּדוֹל. בֶּן שְׁלֹשׁ עֶשְׂרֵה, דְּהָוֵי מִילָה שֶׁלֹּא בִּזְמַנָּהּ: דִּכְתִיב בֵּיהּ בְּרִית. "וְעָרֵל זָכָר אֲשֶׁר לֹא יִמּוֹל וגו' אֶת בְּרִיתִי הֵפַר" (בראשית יז), וְהַאי קְרָא בְּגָדוֹל כְּתִיב, מִדְּמִחַיֵּיב לֵיהּ כָּרֵת. שֶׁאִם לֹא מָלוֹ אָבִיו חַיָּיב לָמוּל אֶת עַצְמוֹ, וְלִידְחֵי שַׁבָּת. וַאֲנַן אָמְרִינַן לְקַמָּן דַּאֲפִילּוּ יוֹם טוֹב אֵינָהּ דּוֹחָה אֶלָּא בִּזְמַנָּהּ: דּוֹרוֹת דּוֹרוֹת. בְּשַׁבָּת כְּתִיב: "לְדוֹרוֹתָם בְּרִית עוֹלָם", וּבְמִילַת קָטָן כְּתִיב (שם): "וּבֶן שְׁמֹנַת יָמִים יִמּוֹל לָכֶם כָּל זָכָר לְדוֹרוֹתֵיכֶם": בַּיּוֹם וַאֲפִילּוּ בְּשַׁבָּת. מִדְּלָא כְּתִיב: "בַּשְּׁמִינִי יִמּוֹל", וּלְר' אֱלִיעֶזֶר דְּאַפְּקֵיהּ לְמַכְשִׁירִין – מִילָה עַצְמָהּ הֲלָכָה הִיא. וּפִיקּוּחַ נֶפֶשׁ לָא אָתְיָא לֵיהּ בְּק"ו מִמִּילָה, אֶלָּא מִקְּרָאֵי נָפְקָא לֵיהּ, כִּדְאָמְרִינַן בְּפֶרֶק בַּתְרָא דְּיוֹמָא*: מְחוּסְּרֵי כַּפָּרָה. כָּל טְמֵאִין שֶׁהוּזְקְקוּ לְקָרְבָּן: זָב וְזָבָה, יוֹלֶדֶת וּמְצוֹרָע, נֶאֱמַר בָּהֶן: "וּבַיּוֹם הַשְּׁמִינִי": בְּיוֹם צַוֹּתוֹ. אֶת בְּנֵי יִשְׂרָאֵל לְהַקְרִיב אֶת קָרְבְּנֵיהֶם" (ויקרא ז) – בַּיּוֹם וְלֹא בַּלַּיְלָה: אֶלָּא מֵעַתָּה. מִשּׁוּם דְּהוּכְשַׁר לְהָבִיא בְּדַלּוּת, מַכְשִׁירִין בָּהּ שְׁאָר פְּסוּלִין: יְהֵא זָר וְאוֹנֵן כָּשֵׁר בָּהֶן. אוֹנֵן עַד שֶׁלֹּא נִקְבַּר מֵתוֹ פָּסוּל לַעֲבוֹדָה, דִּכְתִיב (שם כא) בְּכֹהֵן גָּדוֹל: "לְאָבִיו וּלְאִמּוֹ לֹא יִטַּמָּא, וּמִן הַמִּקְדָּשׁ לֹא יֵצֵא וְלֹא יְחַלֵּל". וְהָכִי מַשְׁמַע: אַף בַּיּוֹם שֶׁמֵּתוּ אָבִיו וְאִמּוֹ אֵינוֹ צָרִיךְ לָצֵאת מִן הַמִּקְדָּשׁ, אֶלָּא מַקְרִיב אוֹנֵן וְלֹא יְחַלֵּל – וַעֲבוֹדָתוֹ לֹא תְּהֵא מְחוּלֶּלֶת בְּכָךְ. הָא אַחֵר שֶׁלֹּא יָצָא – חִילֵּל: הָא אַהַדְרֵיהּ קְרָא. לְפְסוּל בָּהֶן לַיְלָה, דִּכְתִיב בְּהוּ "וּבַיּוֹם" כִּדְאָמְרִינַן. וְכֵיוָן דִּלְעִנְיַן לַיְלָה תּוֹרַת כָּל הַקָּרְבָּנוֹת עֲלֵיהֶן – לְעִנְיַן זָר וְאוֹנֵן נַמִי תּוֹרַת קָרְבָּן עֲלֵיהֶן: שְׁמִינִי. כָּל שֶׁהוּא שְׁמִינִי, וַאֲפִילּוּ בַּשַּׁבָּת. "וּבַיּוֹם" – לְמַעוֹטֵי לַיְלָה: תַּנְיָא כְּוָותֵיהּ דְּר' יוֹחָנָן. דְּיָלֵיף מִ"וּבַיּוֹם": מֵעִיקָּרָא מַאי נִיחָא לֵיהּ. לְאוֹקְמֵי שְׁמִינִי דַּוְקָא וַאֲפִילּוּ בַּשַּׁבָּת, וְדָחֵי "מְחַלְלֶיהָ מוֹת יוּמָת" אֵצֶל שְׁאָר מְלָאכוֹת, מֵאֵיזֶה טַעַם נִרְאָה לוֹ כֵּן? וּלְבַסּוֹף. כְּשֶׁהֵיפֵךְ דְּבָרָיו, וְאָמַר: אוֹ אֵינוֹ אֶלָּא אֲפִי' מִילָה בִּכְלַל "מְחַלְלֶיהָ מוֹת יוּמָת", דְּהוּא דַּוְקָא, וְדָחֵי "שְׁמִינִי יִמּוֹל" אֵצֶל שְׁאָר יָמִים: מַאי קַשְׁיָא לֵיהּ. בְּטַעְמָא הָרִאשׁוֹן: אֲבָל מִילָה דָּחְיָא. שַׁבָּת בְּק"ו, וְתִיגְמַר מִינֵּיהּ לְמִידְחֵי מְחַלְלֶיהָ מוֹת יוּמָת אֵצֶל שְׁאָר מְלָאכוֹת, וּלְמֵימַר שְׁמִינִי דַּוְקָא קָאָמַר, וַאֲפִי' בְּיוֹם שַׁבָּת: וּמַה צָּרַעַת שֶׁדּוֹחָה אֶת הָעֲבוֹדָה. אַזְהָרָה שֶׁהִזְהִירָה תּוֹרָה עַל הַצָּרַעַת שֶׁלֹּא לָקוֹץ בַּהַרְתּוֹ, כִּדְתַנְיָא (מכות דף כב.): "הִשָּׁמֶר בְּנֶגַע הַצָּרַעַת" – אַזְהָרָה בְּקוֹצֵץ בַּהַרְתּוֹ הַכָּתוּב מְדַבֵּר. וְהֶחְמִירָה תּוֹרָה בְּאַזְהָרָה זוֹ לִדְחוֹת הָעֲבוֹדָה, כִּדְקַיְימָא לָן בִּפְסָחִים (דף סז.) דְּטוּמְאַת מֵת נִדְחֵית בְּקָרְבַּן צִבּוּר, וְלֹא זָבִין וּמְצוֹרָעִי', וּבְטֵלִים לַעֲשׂוֹת פֶּסַח. וְלָא אָמְרִינַן: יָקוֹצוּ בַּהַרְתָּן וְיֹאכְלוּ פְּסָחִים, אוֹ הַכֹּהֵן יָקוֹץ בַּהַרְתּוֹ וְיַעֲבוֹד, אִם הַכֹּהֲנִים טְמֵאִין בְּצָרַעַת וְהַקָּהָל טְהוֹרִין: וַעֲבוֹדָה

[תוספ' פט"ז] יומא פה: מכילתא פרשת כי תשא
פסחים פא: נזיר נז.
[בפסחים ובנזיר ליתא]
[סנהדרין נט:]
[דף פה:]

תוספות

והתניא אמר ליה רבי אלעזר כו'. ול"ג: והתנן. דכל זה אינו במשנה: **ההיא** מבן שמונת ימים נפקא. תימה: דתניא בת"כ, ומייתי לה בפרק "הערל" (יבמות עב:): השמיני ימול. דתניא: יכול בין ביום ובין בלילה, ת"ל: ביום. אין לי אלא שנימול לח', נימול לט' לי' ולי"א מניין שאינו נימול אלא ביום, ת"ל: וביום. ובפ"ב דמגילה (דף כ:) נמי אמר: אין מוהלין אלא ביום, דכתיב: "וביום השמיני". ויש לומר דסמיך א"בן שמנת ימים" ודרשא פשוטה נקט: **אלא** מעתה יהא זר ואונן כשר בהן. לאו דווקא נקט זר, דהא בכולהו בזב וזבה ויולדת ומצורע כתב בהו כהן:

הא אהדריה קרא. והוה ליה דבר שיצא מן הכלל לידון בדבר החדש, לאתויי בדלות, שאי אתה יכול להחזירו לכללו, לפסול לילה ואונן, עד שיחזירנו הכתוב לכללו בפירוש. הרי החזירה בפירוש – ופסל לילה, וה"ה אונן. וקשה: ואמאי לא קאמר דאהדריה קרא, מדכתיב כהן ולא זר? ושמא לשום דרשא אחריתי אתא:

תניא כוותיה דרבי יוחנן ודלא כרב אחא בר יעקב. ודלא כרב נחמן בר יצחק דאמר: אתיא "אות" "ברית" "דורות" לא הוי דאיהו מודה דדרשינן "ביום" כדדרשינן בברייתא. ואות ברית דורות – אתא למכשירין. וביום – למילה גופה. ולית ליה למילה הלכה, אע"ג דר' יוחנן אית ליה *הלכה לר' אליעזר, [כדפי' רש"י. והאי ברייתא דדרשי ביום – אתיא כרבנן, דביום] איצטריך למילה גופה. ולהכי לא קאמר אלא דלא כרב אחא, דברייתא מוכחא בהדיא דלא בעיא למדרש "שמיני ימול". מ"ר: **מה** צרעת שדוחה את העבודה. תימה, ולימא קל וחומר איפכא: ותדחה עבודה את הצרעת שיקוץ בהרתו כדי לעשות עבודה ומה שבת שדוחה את המילה, ומילה דוחה את הצרעת – עבודה דוחה אותה לצרעת שנדחה מפני מילה – אינו דין שתהא עבודה דוחה אותה! והא דאמרינן בפסחים בפרק "אלו דברים" (דף סז.): "וישלחו מן המחנה כל צרוע וכל זב וכל טמא לנפש" אם טמאי מתים משתלחין, זבים ומצורעים לא כ"ש? אלא יש לך שעה שזבין ומצורעים משתלחים ואין טמאי מתים משתלחים, ואיזה – זה פסח הבא בטומאה

[דף קלג.]

רבינו חננאל

כיוצא בו. עד כאן לא פליגי ר' אליעזר ורבנן אלא במכשירי מילה אבל במילה עצמה דברי הכל דחיא שבת. מנלן עולא ור' אסי ור' יצחק נפחא כולהי אימרי הלכה ומותבינן עליהן. מניין לפקוח נפש שדוח' שבת נענה ר' אלעזר בן עזריה ואמר ומה מילה שהיא אחד מאבריו של אדם דוחה שבת ק"ו לפקוח נפש שדוחה את השבת ואי ס"ד הלכה ק"ו מהלכה (מייתי) [מי אתי]. והתניא א"ל ר' עקיבא עצם כשעורה הלכה ורביעית דם ק"ו ואין דנין ק"ו מהלכה וכו' לבטלו וזה מפורש בנזיר פר' כ"ג ונזיר אין מטמאין לקרוביהן וכו'. ובטלו דברי מי שאמר הלכה היא ובא ר' אלעזר ללמדו בג"ש באות אות משבת. ונדחו דבריו ובא רב נחמן בר יצחק ולמדו באות ברית ודורו' בשבת כתיב לעשות את השבת לדורותם ברית עולם ביני ובין בני ישראל אות היא לעולם במילה כתיב ואתה את בריתי תשמור אתה וזרעך אחריך לדורותם וכתיב ונמלתם את בשר ערלתכם והיתה לאות ברית ביני וביניכם. ר' יוחנן אמר אמר קרא וביום השמיני ימול בשר ערלתו ביום אפילו בשבת אקשינן עליה ר"ל אי הכי אפילו מחוסרי כפרה כגון מצורע והזבה דכתי' בהן וביום השמיני יקח שני כבשים וגו' ובזבה כתיב וביום השמיני תקח לה שתי תורים הכי נמי כיון דכתיב בהו וביום יקריבו קרבנותיהם אפילו בשבת והא קיי"ל אין קרבן יחיד דוחה את השבת ופירק לו זה שכתוב במחוסרי כפרה וביום למעוטי לילה. עוד הקשה לו ר"ל וכל קושיא שהקשה לו פירק ר' יוחנן וחזר רבינא להתקיף על פירוק ר' יוחנן ופריק סד"א הואיל וחס רחמנא עליה לאתויי בדלות בלילה נמי ליתי קמ"ל וביום. התקיף רבינא אי הכי אמ' דחס עליהן או אינו כשר בהן ולא יטריחם להמתין עד שימצאו כהן טהור כשר לטהרם ופריק הא אהדריה קרא כלומר אע"פ שחס עליו והקל בקרבנו החזיר לטהרת הכהן שנאמר והביא אותם ביום השמיני לטהרתו אל הכהן וגו' ואתא רב אחא בר יעקב עוד להוציאו שהמילה מותרת בשבת מדכתיב וביום השמיני ימול כלומר איזה יפול שמיני אין לך לא להקדים ולא לאחר ונתקשה ולא עמדו דבריו ואמרינן אלא מחוורתא כר' יוחנן דאפקיה מן וביום. וסוגיא דשמעתיה כר' יוחנן ודתניא כוותי'. ולא כר' אחא בר יעקב:

רב נסים גאון

איצטריך סלקא דעתך אמינא הואיל וחס רחמנא עליה לאיתויי בדלות בלילה נמי ליתי קמ"ל מתקיף לה רבינא [אלא] מעתה יהא זר ואונן כשר בהן חייבנו הקב"ה בתורת הקרבנות שנקרבים ביום ולא בלילה שנאמר (ויקרא ז) אשר צוה ה' את משה ביום צותו את בני ישראל ופירש ביום צותו למדנו לכל הקרבנות כולם שאינן כשירין אלא ביום ובפרק הקורא את המגילה (דף כ) שנינו כל היום כשר לסמיכה לשחיטה כו' ובתלמוד אמרו לסמיכה ולשחיטה דכתיב (ויקרא ג) וסמך ושחט ואיתקש סמיכה לשחיטה ובשחיטה כתיב (שם יט) ביום זבחכם לקמיצה והגשה והזייה בבולהי כתיב ביום צותו והזהיר האונן והזר עם כל המנויין במשנה שלא יקרבו להקריב קרבן כמו שאמרה המשנה (זבחים דף טו) כל הזבחים שקיבל דמן זר ואונן כולם פסולין ובגמ' גרסי זר מנלן דתני לוי (ויקרא כב) דבר אל אהרן ואל בניו וינזרו למעוטי מאי כו' אלא הכי קאמר וינזרו מקדשי בני ישראל ולא יחללו כלומר בני ישראל ראוי להם שיתרחקו מן הקדשים ולא יקריבו אותן שלא יחללום שאם יקרבו אליהם ויקריבו אותם מחללים אותם ואמר עוד (במדבר יח) וזר לא יקרב ונאמר בעונש (שם) והזר הקרב יומת ובאונן עוד אמרו מנלן דכתיב (ויקרא כא) ומן המקדש לא יצא ולא יחלל הא אחר שלא יצא חילל וכשאמרנו כי המחוסר כפרה והוא המצורע שלשלמו ימי טהרתו ועדיין לא הקריב קרבן לא נאמר בו וביום השמיני אלא לחייב הקרבת קרבנו ביום ולא בלילה הקשינו לאמר כי דבר זה ידוע הוא לפי שכתב כן במקום אחר ביום צותו וממנו ידענו חיוב הקרבת כל הקרבנות ביום ולא בלילה והואיל וכן אין אנו צריכין לשנותו לנו עוד ופירק האומר דבר זה ואמר שמה שאמר כאן וביום השמיני אינו לשנות אלא שאנו צריכין לאותו דבר מפני שמצאנו שהקל כאן על המצורע ואמר בו (ויקרא יד) ואם דל הוא ואין ידו משגת מה שלא הקל על זולתו מכלל הטמאים והם זב וזבה ואילמלי שאמר בו וביום השמיני לחייב הקרבת קרבנו ביום היה עולה על דעתנו הואיל והיקל עליו הכתוב שדי לו בשתי תורים או ב' בני יונה לחטאתו ולעולתו ושינה בינו ובין שאר הטמאות בדבר זה והם הנזכרים אחריו הזב והזבה כמו כן נמי ראוי שיקריב קרבנותיו בלילה ולא היינו לומדין משפטו משאר הקרבנות שנאמר בהן ביום צותו הילכך הוצרכנו להשמיענו וביום השמיני כדי שירחיק מדעתנו סברא זו התקיף (רבא) [רבינא] ואמר הואיל ואתה אומר כי לפי שהקל עליו הכתוב שיביא שתי תורים או שני בני יונה מה שאין כן בזולתו לא נלמוד משאר הקרבנות כלום ממשפטו מפני שיצא מכללם מחמת שייחדו הכתוב בדבר זה ואילמלא שאמר הכתוב וביום השמיני היינו מתירים הקרבת קרבנותיו בלילה לפי דבר זה ראוי להיות הזר והאונן וכל המנויין

ח א מיי' פ"א מהל' מילה הלכה ט ופ"י מהל' טומאת צרעת הלכה ה סמג עשין כח טוש"ע י"ד סי' רסו סעיף א:
ט ב מיי' פ"א מהלכות מילה שם סמג שם טוש"ע שם סעיף ב:

תורה אור

וַעֲבוֹדָה דּוֹחָה אֶת הַשַּׁבָּת – מִילָה דּוֹחָה אוֹתָהּ. שַׁבָּת שֶׁנִּדְחֵית מִפְּנֵי הָעֲבוֹדָה – אֵינוֹ דִּין שֶׁתְּהֵא מִילָה דּוֹחָה אוֹתָהּ? וּמַאי 'אוֹ אֵינוֹ' דְּקָאָמַר – הֲדַר אָמַר: וּמִמַּאי דְּצָרַעַת חֲמוּרָה, דִּילְמָא שַׁבָּת חֲמוּרָה? שֶׁכֵּן יֵשׁ בָּהּ עוֹנָשִׁין וְאַזְהָרוֹת הַרְבֵּה. (*אִי נַמִּי) וּמִמַּאי מִשּׁוּם דַּחֲמִירָא צָרַעַת הִיא – דִּילְמָא מִשּׁוּם גַּבְרָא הוּא דְּלָא חֲזֵי? וּמָה אֲנִי מְקַיֵּים 'שְׁמִינִי יִמּוֹל' – חוּץ מִשַּׁבָּת, תַּלְמוּד לוֹמַר 'בַּיּוֹם' – אֲפִילּוּ בַּשַּׁבָּת. § תָּנוּ רַבָּנַן: [א]מִילָה דּוֹחָה אֶת הַצָּרַעַת בֵּין בִּזְמַנָּהּ בֵּין שֶׁלֹּא בִּזְמַנָּהּ. [ב]יוֹם טוֹב אֵינָהּ דּוֹחָה אֶלָּא בִּזְמַנָּהּ בִּלְבַד. מְנָהָנֵי מִילֵּי? דְּתָנוּ רַבָּנַן: "יִמּוֹל (ויקרא יב) בְּשַׂר עָרְלָתוֹ" – וְאַף עַל פִּי שֶׁיֵּשׁ שָׁם בַּהֶרֶת יָקוּץ. וּמָה אֲנִי מְקַיֵּים "הִשָּׁמֶר בְּנֶגַע הַצָּרַעַת" (דברים כד) – בִּשְׁאָר מְקוֹמוֹת חוּץ מִמִּילָה. אוֹ אֵינוֹ אֶלָּא אֲפִילּוּ מִילָה, וּמָה אֲנִי מְקַיֵּים "יִמּוֹל בְּשַׂר עָרְלָתוֹ" – בִּזְמַן שֶׁאֵין בָּהּ בַּהֶרֶת? ת"ל: 'בָּשָׂר' – וְאַף עַל פִּי שֶׁיֵּשׁ שָׁם בַּהֶרֶת. אָמַר רָבָא: הַאי תַּנָּא, מֵעִיקָּרָא מַאי נִיחָא לֵיהּ וּלְבַסּוֹף מַאי קַשְׁיָא לֵיהּ? הָכִי קָאָמַר: "יִמּוֹל בְּשַׂר עָרְלָתוֹ" – וְאַף עַל פִּי שֶׁיֵּשׁ בַּהֶרֶת, וּמָה אֲנִי מְקַיֵּים "הִשָּׁמֶר בְּנֶגַע הַצָּרַעַת" – בִּשְׁאָר מְקוֹמוֹת חוּץ מִמִּילָה, אֲבָל מִילָה דּוֹחָה אֶת הַצָּרַעַת. מ"ט? דְּאַתְיָא מִקַּל וָחוֹמֶר; וּמָה שַׁבָּת חֲמוּרָה – מִילָה דּוֹחָה אוֹתָהּ, צָרַעַת לֹא כָּל שֶׁכֵּן? וּמַאי "אוֹ אֵינוֹ" דְּקָאָמַר – הֲדַר קָאָמַר: מִמַּאי דְּשַׁבָּת חֲמִירָא, דִּילְמָא צָרַעַת חֲמִירָא? שֶׁכֵּן דּוֹחָה אֶת הָעֲבוֹדָה, וַעֲבוֹדָה דּוֹחָה אֶת הַשַּׁבָּת! ת"ל: 'בָּשָׂר' – וְאַף עַל פִּי שֶׁיֵּשׁ שָׁם בַּהֶרֶת. לִישָּׁנָא אַחֲרִינָא: מִילָה דּוֹחָה אֶת הַצָּרַעַת מ"ט – דְּאָתֵי עֲשֵׂה וְדָחֵי לֹא תַעֲשֶׂה, וּמַאי "אוֹ אֵינוֹ" דְּקָאָמַר – הֲדַר קָאָמַר: אֵימַר דְּאָמְרִינַן דְּאָתֵי עֲשֵׂה וְדָחֵי אֶת לֹא תַעֲשֶׂה – לֹא תַעֲשֶׂה גְּרֵידָא, הַאי עֲשֵׂה וְלֹא תַעֲשֶׂה הוּא. וּמָה אֲנִי מְקַיֵּים "יִמּוֹל בְּשַׂר עָרְלָתוֹ" – בִּזְמַן שֶׁאֵין בָּהּ בַּהֶרֶת! ת"ל: 'בָּשָׂר' – וְאַף עַל פִּי שֶׁיֵּשׁ שָׁם בַּהֶרֶת. תִּינַח גָּדוֹל דִּכְתִיב בְּהוּ 'בָּשָׂר', קָטָן נַמִּי כְּתִיב בֵּיהּ 'בָּשָׂר', בֵּינוֹנִי מְנָלַן? אָמַר אַבָּיֵי: אָתְיָא מִבֵּינַיָּא; מִגָּדוֹל לָא אָתְיָא – שֶׁכֵּן עָנוּשׁ כָּרֵת, מִקָּטָן לָא אָתְיָא – שֶׁכֵּן מִילָה בִּזְמַנָּהּ, הַצַּד הַשָּׁוֶה שֶׁבָּהֶן – שֶׁכֵּן נִימּוֹלִין וְדוֹחִין אֶת הַצָּרַעַת, אַף כֹּל שֶׁנִּימּוֹלִין דּוֹחִין אֶת הַצָּרַעַת. רָבָא אָמַר: מִילָה בִּזְמַנָּהּ דּוֹחָה לָא צְרִיכָא קְרָא, מִקַּל וָחוֹמֶר אָתְיָא: וּמָה שַׁבָּת דַּחֲמִירָא – דּוֹחָה, צָרַעַת לֹא כָּל שֶׁכֵּן! אֲמַר לֵיהּ רַב סָפְרָא לְרָבָא: מִמַּאי דְּשַׁבָּת חֲמִירָא, דִּילְמָא צָרַעַת חֲמִירָא? שֶׁכֵּן דּוֹחָה אֶת הָעֲבוֹדָה, וַעֲבוֹדָה דּוֹחָה אֶת הַשַּׁבָּת! הָתָם, לָאו מִשּׁוּם דַּחֲמִירָא צָרַעַת, אֶלָּא מִשּׁוּם דְּגַבְרָא הוּא דְּלָא חֲזֵי. אַמַּאי? וְיָקוֹץ בַּהַרְתּוֹ וְיַעֲבוֹד! מְחוּסַּר טְבִילָה הוּא. תִּינַח – נְגָעִים טְמֵאִים, נְגָעִים *טְהוֹרִים – מַאי אִיכָּא לְמֵימַר? אֶלָּא א"ר אַשִׁי: *הֵיכָא אָמְרִינַן דְּאָתֵי עֲשֵׂה וְדָחֵי ל"ת – כְּגוֹן מִילָה בְּצָרַעַת, א"נ צִיצִית וְכִלְאַיִם, דִּבְעִידָּנָא דְּמִתְעַקַּר לָאו – קָא מוֹקִי' עֲשֵׂה. הָכָא, בְּעִידָּנָא דְּמִתְעַקַּר לְלָאו – לָא קָא מוֹקִים עֲשֵׂה. וְהָא דְּרָבָא וְרַב סָפְרָא תַּנָּאֵי

וְאַבַּיֵי

רש"י

וַעֲבוֹדָה. חֲמוּרָה הִיא, שֶׁדּוֹחָה שַׁבָּת בִּתְמִידִין וּמוּסָפִין וְקָרְבְּנוֹת צִבּוּר שֶׁזְּמַנָּם קָבוּעַ: מִילָה דּוֹחָה אוֹתָהּ. אֶת הַצָּרַעַת, כִּדְתַנְיָא לְקַמָּן: "יִמּוֹל בְּשַׂר עָרְלָתוֹ", אֲפִילּוּ בִּמְקוֹם בַּהֶרֶת יָקוּץ: וּמָה אוֹ אֵינוֹ דְּקָאָמַר. דְּמַשְׁמַע אוֹ אֵינוֹ כֵּן כְּמוֹ שֶׁאָמַרְנוּ, אֶלָּא אֲפִי' מִילָה נַמִּי בִּכְלַל מְחַלְּלֶיהָ, מַאי קַשְׁיָא לֵיהּ דְּקָא הָדַר בֵּיהּ? הֲדַר אָמַר תַּנָּא. לְנַפְשֵׁיהּ, מִמַּאי דְּצָרַעַת חֲמוּרָה מִשַּׁבָּת, דְּתֵימָא ק"ו: דִּילְמָא שַׁבָּת חֲמוּרָה כו'. דְּהַאי דְּצָרַעַת דּוֹחָה עֲבוֹדָה – מִמַּאי דְּמִשּׁוּם חוּמְרָא דְּצָרַעַת הִיא? דִּילְמָא הָא דְּלָא אָמְרִינַן לֵיהּ יָקוּץ – מִשּׁוּם דְּגַבְרָא דְּלָא חֲזֵי הוּא, כִּדְלְקַמָּן. דְּאִי נַמִּי קָיֵיץ – מְחוּסַּר טְבִילָה וְהֶעֱרֵב שֶׁמֶשׁ, וְהַיּוֹם לֹא יַעֲבוֹד[א], וּטְבוּל יוֹם דִּמְצוֹרָע כִּמְצוֹרָע. הִילְכָּךְ: מְחַלְּלֶיהָ מוֹת יוּמָת – אֲפִילּוּ בְּמִילָה. וְעַל כָּרְחָךְ "שְׁמִינִי יִמּוֹל" תִּדְחֶה אֶלָּא שְׁאָר יָמִים: בֵּין שֶׁלֹּא בִּזְמַנָּהּ. כְּגוֹן קָטָן חוֹלֶה וְהִמְתִּינוּ לוֹ עַד שֶׁיַּבְרִיא: בָּשָׂר. רִיבּוּיָא הוּא, וְלִדְרָשָׁה: ה"ג: ל"א מַאי טַעְמָא אָתֵי עֲשֵׂה וְדָחֵי לֹא תַעֲשֶׂה. מ"ט מִילָה דּוֹחָה צָרַעַת – דְּאָתֵי עֲשֵׂה דִּימּוֹל וְדָחֵי לֹא תַעֲשֶׂה דְּהִשָּׁמֶר[ב] לְךָ. דְּהָכִי קי"ל בְּפ"ק דִּיבָמוֹת (דף ג:), דְּאָתֵי עֲשֵׂה וְדָחֵי לֹא תַעֲשֶׂה: הַאי עֲשֵׂה וְלֹא תַעֲשֶׂה הוּא. "הִשָּׁמֶר" לֹא תַעֲשֶׂה הוּא, וְ"לַעֲשׂוֹת כְּכֹל אֲשֶׁר יוֹרוּ" (דברים כד) הַיְינוּ עֲשֵׂה: תִּינַח גָּדוֹל. בַּר עוֹנָשִׁין דִּכְתִיב בֵּיהּ בָּשָׂר – "וְעָרֵל זָכָר אֲשֶׁר לֹא יִמּוֹל אֶת בְּשַׂר עָרְלָתוֹ" (בראשית יז), וְהַאי בַּר עוֹנָשִׁין מִשְׁתַּעֵי, מִדְּמִחַיֵּיב לֵיהּ כָּרֵת. וְקָטָן נַמִּי, בִּזְמַנָּהּ בַּיּוֹם הַשְּׁמִינִי כְּתִיב בֵּיהּ בָּשָׂר – "וּבַיּוֹם הַשְּׁמִינִי יִמּוֹל בְּשַׂר עָרְלָתוֹ": בֵּינוֹנִי. כְּגוֹן שֶׁלֹּא בִּזְמַנָּהּ וְלָאו בַּר עוֹנָשִׁין, וְאָבִיו מְצוּוֶּה עָלָיו, נָפְקָא לָן מֵ"הִמּוֹל לָכֶם כָּל זָכָר" (קדושין דף כט.): אָתְיָא מִבֵּינַיָּא. הַצַּד הַשָּׁוֶה שֶׁבָּהֶן – שֶׁנִּימּוֹלוּ וְדוֹחִין אֶת הַצָּרַעַת. אַף אֲנִי אָבִיא בֵּינוֹנִי שֶׁנִּימּוֹל וְיִדְחֶה הַצָּרַעַת: לָא צְרִיכָא קְרָא כו'. וְכִי אָתְיָא קְרָא – לְשֶׁלֹּא בִּזְמַנָּהּ שֶׁל בֵּינוֹנִי: דְּגַבְרָא לָא חֲזֵי. קס"ד מִפְּנֵי שֶׁהוּא טָמֵא, וְהַיְינוּ דְּפָרֵיךְ: וְיָקוֹץ וְיִטְהַר וְיַעֲבוֹד: מְחוּסַּר טְבִילָה. וְלָא חֲזֵי לַעֲבוֹדָה בְּהַאי יוֹמָא, וּמִשּׁוּם לְמָחָר דְּלֵיתָא לַעֲבוֹדָה קַמָּן – לָא מַדְחֵי: נְגָעִים טְהוֹרִין. כְּגוֹן בֹּהַק וּפָרְחָה בְּכוּלֵּיהּ, וּבְכוּלְּהוּ אִיתְרַבּוּ לְאִיסּוּר קְלִיָּה בְּסִפְרֵי: אֵין לִי אֶלָּא מִשֶּׁנִּזְקַק לְטוּמְאָה, עַד שֶׁלֹּא נִזְקַק לְטוּמְאָה מִנַּיִין? ת"ל: "כְּכֹל אֲשֶׁר יוֹרוּ": אֶלָּא אָמַר רַב אַשִׁי. הָא דְּאָמְרִינַן שַׁבָּת חֲמִירָא מִצָּרַעַת, אע"ג דְּדָחְיָיה צָרַעַת לַעֲבוֹדָה – לָאו חוּמְרָא דִּידָהּ הוּא, אֶלָּא הַיְינוּ טַעְמָא: כִּי אָמְרִינַן אָתֵי עֲשֵׂה וְדָחֵי לֹא תַעֲשֶׂה – כְּגוֹן מִילָה בְּצָרַעַת, דִּבְשַׁעַת קְלִיָּה דְּמִיעֲקַר לָאו מְקַיֵּים עֲשֵׂה. וְכֵן צִיצִית דְּכִלְאַיִם, בִּשְׁעַת לְבִישָׁה מִיעֲקַר לָאו וּמְקַיֵּים עֲשֵׂה. אֲבָל צָרַעַת הַנִּקְלֶפֶת מִשּׁוּם עֲבוֹדָה, בְּעִידָּנָא דְּמִיעֲקַר לָאו דִּקְלִיָּה אַכַּתִּי לָא מְקַיֵּים עֲשֵׂה דַּעֲבוֹדָה, הִילְכָּךְ מִידַּחְיָא עֲבוֹדָה מִמֵּילָא, וְלָאו חוּמְרָא דְּצָרַעַת הוּא: תַּנָּאֵי

תוספות

בטומאה. אלמא: דצרעת דוחה את העבודה! נימא דהיינו כל זמן שהיא עליו, ובק"ו נילף שיקוץ בהרתו כדי לעשות עבודה. ועוד קשה: לימא, רציחה תוכיח שדוחה את העבודה ואינו דוחה שבת, אף אני אביא מילה. וכי תימא מילה עדיפא שדוחה צרעת הדוחה את העבודה – אכתי נימא: קבורת מת מצוה תוכיח, דעדיפא ממילה שדוחה את המילה מ"ולאחותו" הדוחה את הצרעת הדוחה את העבודה הדוחה את השבת – אפילו הכי לא דחיא שבת! ויש לומר: דהכי נמי הוה מצי למימר איפכא, ורציחה תוכיח או קבורת מת מצוה תוכיח. אלא דניחא ליה לומר שיהא דוחה, דנפקא ליה מ"ביום" דמילה דחיא שבת. ועושה מתחילה ק"ו להעמיד דבריו, וסותרו אחר כך שאינו ק"ו כלל, [א]ופריך ליה מיניה וביה: **הדר אמר ממאי דשבת חמירא דילמא צרעת חמירא.** תימה: דבברייתא דלעיל מסיק איפכא, דלאו משום דצרעת חמירא, אלא משום [ג]גברא דלא חזי. ורבא גופיה סבירא ליה הכי לקמן. ועוד: למאי דקאמר השתא מנלן דצרעת דוחה את העבודה, אימא דעבודה דוחה הצרעת מק"ו: ומה שבת חמורה [צרעת לא כ"ש! ואומר ר"י: דלהאי לישנא] צריך לומר דגרסינן רבה הכא, ולית ליה דרבא דלקמן, דטעמא משום דגברא לא חזי וסבירא ליה כרב ספרא דפליג עליה דרבא לקמן. והא דפשיט להו לרבה ורב ספרא דצרעת דוחה עבודה – מצי למימר דמקרא נפקא להו. אבל רבא דס"ל גברא לא חזי – לדידיה לא בעי קרא. ועוד נראה לרשב"א: [ב]דאפי' ליכא קרא דצרעת דוחה עבודה – אתי שפיר אפילו לרב ספרא. דלא קאמר רב ספרא שיהא הטעם ודאי דצרעת דוחה עבודה משום חומרא דצרעת, אלא איכא למימר הכי ואיכא למימר הכי. הילכך, בברייתא דלעיל סתר ק"ו, דקאמר: וממאי דצרעת חמירא דילמא משום גברא דלא חזי. והכא ולקמן על מילתא דרבא דחינן בע"א: ממאי דשבת חמירא, דילמא צרעת חמירא שכן דוחה את העבודה. וזיל הכא קא מדחי ליה, וזיל הכא קא מדחי ליה. ומהאי טעמא נמי ליכא למילף ביה ק"ו דעבודה תדחי צרעת, דשבת דחמורה דוחה צרעת לא כ"ש – דדילמא אין לתלות משום חומרא אלא משום [ג]גברא לא חזי: **האי עשה ולא תעשה הוא.** "השמר" היינו לאו ו"לעשות" היינו עשה כדפי' בקונטרס. ואע"ג דאמר בסוף פרק הקומץ (מנחות דף לו:): השמר דלאו לאו השמר דעשה עשה – מכל מקום לאו מלות עשה הוא אלא לא תעשה[ד]) דאמר רחמנא הזהר פן תקוץ בהרת. תימה: היכי מצינן למימר דלעשות אתא לעשה, הא אמר לקמן דאיצטריך לעשות אי אתה עושה אבל אתה עושה בסיב שעל גבי רגלו! ויש לפרש דעשה שמעינן מדכתיב [ד]לשמור. ואם תאמר, והא אמר בסמוך: היכא אמרינן דאתי עשה ודחי את לא תעשה – כגון מילה בצרעת, אלמא דליכא בצרעת אלא לאו! ואר"ת דלא נקטינן אלא לסימנא בעלמא.

ואם תאמר: והא דקי"ל דאין עשה דוחה את לא תעשה ועשה, נגמר ממילה בצרעת דדחי! וי"ל: מה למילה °שכן נכרתו עליה י"ג בריתות*: **רבא אמר מילה בזמנה לא צריכא קרא.** והילכך, האי "בשר" דכתיב בה, אם אינו ענין לזמנה תנהו ענין לשלא בזמנה. ו"או אינו" דקתני, הוה מפרש רבא כלישנא אחרינא:

[וע"ע תוס' כתובות מ. ד"ה ניתי]

רבינו חננאל

ת"ר מילה דוחה צרעת בין בזמנה בין שלא בזמנה. פי' כתיב בצרעת השמר בנגע הצרעת ואמרו חכמים כ"מ שנאמר השמר פן ואל אינו אלא בל"ת. כלומר השמר אזהרה הוא שלא לעשות וכיון דכתיב השמר הנה הזהיר שלא לחתוך הצרעת (מכל מקום) [בכל מקום] שהיא והתיר במילה אם יש צרעת בערלה מותר לו לחתוך הערלה והצרעת עמה בין ביום השמיני שהוא זמן המילה כדכתיב וביום השמיני ימול בשר ערלתו. בין אירע לו אונס כגון חולי לקטן וכדומה לו ולא מל בשמיני חייב לימול כל זמן שיסור האונס והיא הנקראת מילה שלא בזמנה כלומר שאינה ביום השמיני וגם במילה שאינה ביום השמיני יש למל לחתוך הערלה אע"פ שיש בה צרעת והתורה שהזהירה שלא לחתוך הצרעת לגבי מילה התירה. ובאנו לברר זה הפי' שפירשנו מזו הברייתא. דת"ר ימול בשר ערלתו ואע"פ שיש שם בהרת ומה אני מקיים השמר בנגע הצרעת בשאר מקומות חוץ ממילה או אינו אלא אפי' מילה ומה אני מקיים ימול בשר ערלתו בזמן שאין שם בהרת ת"ל בשר אע"פ שיש שם בהרת לא תעשה בצרעת שנאמר השמר פן עשה שנא' ולעשות ופשוטה היא תינח גדול כתיב ביה בשר שנאמר וערל זכר אשר לא ימול את בשר ערלתו ונכרתה הנפש ההיא מעמיה את בריתי הפר. מדכתיב ונכרתה שמעינן מינה שהוא גדול ואם לא מל אותו אביו ונשאר ערל וגדל חייב למול עצמו קטן נמי כתיב ביה בשר שנאמר וביום השמיני ימול בשר ערלתו. ודרשת בשר אע"פ שיש שם בהרת אלו השנים הגדול שהוא בר עונשין והקטן שהוא בן שמונה ימים שכתב בהם בשר מילה דוחה את ערלתם אבל בינוני שאינו לא גדול בן עונשין ולא קטן בן שמונת ימים אלא בינוני שהוא מבן שמונה ימים ולמעלה הן חסר והן יתר עד שיגיע להתחייב בעונשים מנ"ל שמילתו דוחה צרעת. ופירק אביי ואמר אתיא מביניא כלומר משניהם מן הגדול ומן הקטן. ודברים פשוטין הן. ודברי רבא ורב ספרא פשוטין הן. אמר רב אשי היכא אמרינן דאתי עשה ודוחה לא תעשה כגון מילה בצרעת כלומר אם יש צרעת בערלה בחתיכת הערלה והצרעת עליה נתקיימה המילה שפיר וכן כלאים בציצית. אבל זה שאמר ויקוץ בהרתו ויעבור חתיכת הצרעת להכשיר הכהן לעבוד עבודה אינו דומה לאלו שיתכן שיתחוך הצרעת מעליו והוא לא יעשה עבודה והנה נעקרה אזהרתו שלא לחתוך הצרעת שהוא לאו כמו שפירשנו למעלה. ולא נתקיימה עבודתו שהוא עשה נגעים טהורין שפוסלין בכהנים מפורש בבכורות פ"ז (מה:) דתנן הכושי והגיחור והלווקר

רש"ל מ"ז והג"י גרס א"נ ממאי ויש ליישב אותה הגירסא דמקשה שני קושיות וה"פ דהוכחה שלו היא כיון דלא אמרינן דיקוץ בהרתו ויעבוד כמו שפרש"י והא ודאי די"ל ק"ו איפכא דיקוץ בהרתו בשביל עבודה כמו שהקשו התוס' אך כאשר חזינן בשום פעם דאי אפשר לו לקוץ הבהרת ואעפ"כ לא יעבוד ודאי לאו חומרא דעבודה הוא אלא חומרא דצרעת ולפי זה מקשה הכא דילמא שבת חמירא שכן יש בה כו' וא"כ דשבת חמירא מצרעת אסור לו לקוץ בהרת בשבת וא"כ שוב לא יכול ללמוד הק"ו איפכא דיקוץ בהרתו משום עבודה הא כבר נתנה העבודה לידחות מפני הצרעת בשבת וממילא נתבטל גם הק"ו הזה:

הגהות הב"ח

(א) רש"י ד"ה דילמא שבת וכו' לטבול יום: (ב) ד"ה ה"ג ל"א וכו' דהשמר דהכי כצ"ל ותיבת לך נמחק: (ג) תום' ד"ה הדר וכו' אלא משום דגברא:

גליון הש"ס

גמ' ת"ל ביום אפי' בשבת. עיין חולין דף חד ע"ב ברש"י ד"ה שודא וצ"ע: שם ואע"פ שיש שם בהרת. עיין בר"ש רפ"ב דחלה: תום' ד"ה האי וכו' שכן נכרתו עליה י"ג בריתות. עי' יבמות ה' ע"א תוד"ה שכן:

[ע' תוס' שבועות ז. ד"ה בקולן] ביצה ח: כתובות מ.

א) גיר' הרש"ל ופריך ליה מיניה וביה ונוכל לומר דהאי תנא בלאו אינו דקאמר כולה ופריך ואימא איפכא או מת מצוה תוכיח עכ"ל ואין הגירסא זו מוכרחת דא"א לפרש כן בדברי רבה שעליו הקשו תוס': ב) ואפילו לסברא זו גרסי' רבה: ג) וע' תוס' בעירובין דף נו. ד"ה השמר: ד) גיר' רש"ל ועי"ל תרי לעשות כתיבי בקרא זה חדא לעשה וחדא לעושה בסיב וכו' וכן פירש"י השמר לא תעשה הוא ולעשות ככל אשר יורו היינו עשה וא"ת והא אמר כו':

רב נסים גאון

המגויין במשנה שפסולין להקריב כשרים להקריב קרבנותיו של מצורע לפי שיצא מכללם ונבדל מהם חוץ מהקרבת קרבן בלילה שאמר בו הכתוב וביום השמיני בלבד ועמד זה הקושיא וזו ההתקפה ואמרנו קשיא ומקצת הגורסין אין מעמידין הדבר אלא שגורסין כך כיון דאהדריה קרא אהדריה כלומר אילו לא כתב וביום היינו אומרים מדחם רחמנא עליה לאיתויי בדלות בלילה נמי ליתי ויהא זר ואונן כשר בקרבנותיו והיינו

תַּנָּאֵי הִיא; דְּתַנְיָא: "בָּשָׂר" וְאַף עַל פִּי שֶׁיֵּשׁ שָׁם בַּהֶרֶת יִמּוֹל, דִּבְרֵי רַבִּי יֹאשִׁיָּה. רַבִּי יוֹנָתָן אוֹמֵר: אֵינוֹ צָרִיךְ, שַׁבָּת חֲמוּרָה – דּוֹחָה, צָרַעַת – לֹא כ"ש?! § אָמַר מָר: 'בָּשָׂר' אע"פ שֶׁיֵּשׁ שָׁם בַּהֶרֶת יִמּוֹל דִּבְרֵי רַבִּי יֹאשִׁיָּה. הָא לָמָּה לִי קְרָא? דָּבָר שֶׁאֵין מִתְכַּוֵּין הוּא, וְדָבָר שֶׁאֵין מִתְכַּוֵּין – מוּתָּר! אָמַר אַבָּיֵי: לָא נִצְרְכָא אֶלָּא לְרַבִּי יְהוּדָה, דְּאָמַר: דָּבָר שֶׁאֵין מִתְכַּוֵּין אָסוּר. רָבָא אָמַר: אֲפִילּוּ תֵּימָא ר"ש, מוֹדֶה ר"ש בִּפְסִיק רֵישֵׁיהּ וְלֹא יָמוּת. וְאַבָּיֵי לֵית לֵיהּ הַאי סְבָרָא?! וְהָא אַבָּיֵי וְרָבָא דְּאָמְרִי תַּרְוַיְיהוּ: מוֹדֶה רַבִּי שִׁמְעוֹן בִּפְסִיק רֵישֵׁיהּ וְלֹא יָמוּת! בָּתַר דִּשְׁמַעָהּ מֵרָבָא סְבָרָהּ. אִיכָּא דְּמַתְנֵי לְהָא דְּאַבָּיֵי וְרָבָא אַהָא: "הִשָּׁמֶר בְּנֶגַע הַצָּרַעַת לִשְׁמוֹר מְאֹד וְלַעֲשׂוֹת", "לַעֲשׂוֹת" – אִי אַתָּה עוֹשֶׂה, אֲבָל(א) עוֹשֶׂה אַתָּה בְּסִיב שֶׁעַל גַּבֵּי רַגְלוֹ וּבְמוֹט שֶׁעַל גַּבֵּי כְּתֵיפוֹ. וְאִם עָבְרָה – עָבְרָה. וְהָא לָמָּה לִי קְרָא? דָּבָר שֶׁאֵין מִתְכַּוֵּין הוּא, וְדָבָר שֶׁאֵין מִתְכַּוֵּין מוּתָּר! אָמַר אַבָּיֵי: לָא נִצְרְכָא אֶלָּא לְרַבִּי יְהוּדָה, דְּאָמַר: דָּבָר שֶׁאֵין מִתְכַּוֵּין אָסוּר. וְרָבָא אָמַר: אֲפִילּוּ תֵּימָא רַבִּי שִׁמְעוֹן, וּמוֹדֶה רַבִּי שִׁמְעוֹן בִּפְסִיק רֵישֵׁיהּ וְלֹא יָמוּת. וְאַבָּיֵי לֵית לֵיהּ הַאי סְבָרָא?! וְהָא אַבָּיֵי וְרָבָא דְּאָמְרִי תַּרְוַיְיהוּ: מוֹדֶה ר' שִׁמְעוֹן בִּפְסִיק רֵישֵׁיהּ וְלֹא יָמוּת! לְבָתַר דִּשְׁמַעָהּ מֵרָבָא – סְבָרָהּ. וְאַבָּיֵי אַלִּיבָּא דְּרַבִּי שִׁמְעוֹן, הַאי 'בָּשָׂר' מַאי עָבֵיד לֵיהּ? אָמַר רַב עַמְרָם: בְּאוֹמֵר: לָקוֹץ בַּהַרְתּוֹ הוּא מִתְכַּוֵּין. תֵּינַח גָּדוֹל, קָטָן מַאי אִיכָּא לְמֵימַר? אָמַר רַב מְשַׁרְשְׁיָא: בְּאוֹמֵר אֲבִי הַבֵּן לָקוֹץ בַּהֶרֶת דִּבְנוֹ הוּא קָא מִתְכַּוֵּין. וְאִי אִיכָּא אַחֵר – לִיעֲבֵיד אַחֵר, דְּאָמַר ר"ש בֶּן לָקִישׁ: כָּל מָקוֹם שֶׁאַתָּה מוֹצֵא עֲשֵׂה וְלֹא תַעֲשֶׂה, אִם אַתָּה יָכוֹל לְקַיֵּים שְׁנֵיהֶם – מוּטָב, וְאִם לָאו – יָבֹא עֲשֵׂה וְיִדְחֶה לֹא תַעֲשֶׂה! דְּלֵיכָּא אַחֵר. § אָמַר מָר: יוֹם טוֹב אֵינָהּ דּוֹחָה אֶלָּא בִּזְמַנָּהּ בִּלְבַד. מְנָא הָנֵי מִילֵּי? אָמַר חִזְקִיָּה, וְכֵן תָּנָא דְּבֵי חִזְקִיָּה, אָמַר קְרָא: "לֹא תוֹתִירוּ מִמֶּנּוּ (א)עַד בֹּקֶר" שֶׁאֵין ת"ל 'עַד בֹּקֶר'. מַה ת"ל 'עַד בֹּקֶר' – בָּא הַכָּתוּב לִיתֵּן לוֹ בֹּקֶר שֵׁנִי לִשְׂרֵיפָתוֹ. אַבָּיֵי אָמַר: אָמַר קְרָא "עוֹלַת שַׁבַּת בְּשַׁבַּתּוֹ" – וְלֹא עוֹלַת חוֹל בַּשַּׁבָּת, וְלֹא עוֹלַת חוֹל בְּיוֹ"ט. רָבָא אָמַר: אָמַר קְרָא "הוּא לְבַדּוֹ יֵעָשֶׂה לָכֶם", 'הוּא' – וְלֹא מַכְשִׁירִין, 'לְבַדּוֹ' – וְלֹא מִילָה שֶׁלֹּא בִּזְמַנָּהּ, דְּאָתְיָא מִקַּ"ו. רַב אַשִׁי אָמַר: 'שַׁבָּתוֹן' עֲשֵׂה הוּא, וַהֲוָה לֵיהּ יוֹ"ט עֲשֵׂה וְל"ת, וְאֵין עֲשֵׂה דּוֹחֶה אֶת לֹא תַעֲשֶׂה וַעֲשֵׂה. § "כְּלָל אָמַר ר"ע וכו'". § אָמַר רַב יְהוּדָה אָמַר רַב: הֲלָכָה כְּר"ע. וּתְנַן נַמִי גַּבֵּי פֶּסַח כִּי הַאי גַּוְונָא: כְּלָל אָמַר ר"ע: כָּל מְלָאכָה שֶׁאֶפְשָׁר לַהּ לַעֲשׂוֹתָהּ מֵעֶ"שׁ – אֵינָהּ דּוֹחָה אֶת הַשַּׁבָּת, שְׁחִיטָה שֶׁאִי אֶפְשָׁר לַעֲשׂוֹתָהּ מֵעֶ"שׁ – דּוֹחָה אֶת הַשַּׁבָּת. וְאָמַר רַב יְהוּדָה אָמַר רַב: הֲלָכָה כְּר"ע. וּצְרִיכָא, דְּאִי אַשְׁמְעִינַן גַּבֵּי מִילָה – הָתָם הוּא דְּמַכְשִׁירִין(ג) אֶפְשָׁר לַעֲשׂוֹת מֵאֶתְמוֹל לֹא דָּחוּ שַׁבָּת, דְּלֵיכָּא כָּרֵת. אֲבָל פֶּסַח דְּאִיכָּא כָּרֵת – אֵימָא לִידְחוּ שַׁבָּת. וְאִי אַשְׁמְעִינַן גַּבֵּי פֶּסַח – מִשּׁוּם דְּלֹא נִכְרְתוּ עָלֶיהָ י"ג בְּרִיתוֹת, אֲבָל מִילָה דְּנִכְרְתוּ עָלֶיהָ י"ג בְּרִיתוֹת – אֵימָא לִידְחוּ שַׁבָּת, צְרִיכָא. §

מתני' עוֹשִׂין כָּל צָרְכֵי מִילָה [בַּשַּׁבָּת]; מוֹהֲלִין וּפוֹרְעִין וּמוֹצְצִין, וְנוֹתְנִין עָלֶיהָ אִיסְפְּלָנִית וְכַמּוֹן. אִם לֹא שָׁחַק מֵעֶ"שׁ – לוֹעֵס בְּשִׁינָּיו וְנוֹתֵן, אִם לֹא טָרַף יַיִן וְשֶׁמֶן מֵעֶ"שׁ – יִנָּתֵן זֶה בְּעַצְמוֹ וְזֶה בְּעַצְמוֹ. וְאֵין עוֹשִׂין לָהּ חָלוּק לְכַתְּחִילָּה, אֲבָל כּוֹרֵךְ עָלֶיהָ סְמַרְטוּט. אִם לֹא הִתְקִין מֵעֶ"שׁ – כּוֹרֵךְ עַל אֶצְבָּעוֹ וּמֵבִיא, וַאֲפִי' מֵחָצֵר אַחֶרֶת. §

גמ'

רש"י

תַּנָּאֵי הִיא. דְּאִיכָּא דְּנָפְקָא לֵיהּ מִילָה בִּזְמַנָּהּ מִקַּ"ו כְּרַבָּנָן, וְכִי אָתָא קְרָא – לְשֶׁלֹּא בִּזְמַנָּהּ, וְאִיכָּא דְּלָא נָפְקָא לֵיהּ בְּקַ"ו, וְאִיצְטְרִיךְ לְמִילָה בִּזְמַנָּהּ כְּרַב סַפְרָא, וְשֶׁלֹּא בִּזְמַנָּהּ אָתְיָא מִבֵּינַיָּא: לר' יְהוּדָה. רַבִּי יֹאשִׁיָּה דְּמַצְרִיךְ קְרָא לְהָכִי – כְּרַבִּי יְהוּדָה סְבִירָא לֵיהּ: מוֹדֶה ר' שִׁמְעוֹן בִּפְסִיק כו'. הִילְכָּךְ, אִי לָא רַבֵּי קְרָא – תורה אור

לָא עָבְדִי: סְבָרָהּ. נָתַן בָּהּ דַּעְתֵּיהּ, וְקִבֵּל מִמֶּנּוּ: ה"ג: לַעֲשׂוֹת עוֹשֶׂה אַתָּה בְּסִיב שֶׁעַל רַגְלוֹ וּבְמוֹט שֶׁעַל גַּבֵּי כְּתֵיפוֹ. וְאֵינוֹ צָרִיךְ לְהִזָּהֵר (*) מִלִּדְחוֹת סִיב שֶׁקּוֹשֵׁר מִנְעָלוֹ בְּרַגְלוֹ וּמַלְבִּישׁוֹ מַשְׂאוֹי עַל כְּתֵיפוֹ: וְאִם עָבְרָה. הַבַּהֶרֶת בְּכָךְ – עָבְרָה, וְאֵינוֹ חוֹשֵׁשׁ לָהּ. לְהָכִי כְּתִיב "לַעֲשׂוֹת", שֶׁמּוּתָּר לַעֲשׂוֹת מְלַאכְתּוֹ: וְאַבָּיֵי אַלִּיבָּא דְּר' שִׁמְעוֹן. מֵעִיקָּרָא, מִקַּמֵּי דִּסְבָרָהּ, הַאי "בָּשָׂר" מַאי עָבֵיד לֵיהּ? בְּאוֹמֵר לָקוֹץ. גָּדוֹל שֶׁהוּא בַּר עוֹנָשִׁין, וְאוֹמֵר לַמּוֹהֵל לָקוֹץ בַּהַרְתּוֹ בְּכַוָּונָה לִיטַּהֵר: קָטָן. דְּלָא יָדַע לְכַוּוֹנֵי, מַאי אִיכָּא לְמֵימַר? וְעַל כָּרְחִיךְ בְּתַרְוַיְיהוּ כְּתִיב "בָּשָׂר", כִּדְאָמְרִי' לְעֵיל, וּ"בָשָׂר" דִּכְתִיב גַּבֵּי קָטָן בַּיּוֹם הַשְּׁמִינִי ל"ל? בְּאוֹמֵר אֲבִי הַבֵּן לָקוֹץ. דְּמִתְכַּוֵּין לְטַהֲרוֹ, וְהוּא מוּזְהָר דְּלָא לֶיעֱבַד בְּיָדַיִם וּבְמִתְכַּוֵּין: וְאִי אִיכָּא אַחֵר. שֶׁאֵינוֹ חוֹשֵׁשׁ לְטַהֲרוֹ – לֶיעֱבַד אַחֵר, וְלָא לֵיקוּ חַד לְהָתָם, וְאַף עַל גַּב דְּרַבְּיֵיהּ קְרָא; שֶׁהֲרֵי אַתָּה יָכוֹל לְקַיֵּים עֲשֵׂה בְּלֹא עֲקִירַת לָאו לְר' שִׁמְעוֹן, דְּהָא אַחֵר לָא מִיכַּוֵּין וְלָא עָבַר. וְאָמַר רֵישׁ לָקִישׁ כו', וּרְבוּיָא לְמַאי אֲתָא: שֶׁאֵין תַּלְמוּד לוֹמַר עַד בֹּקֶר. תְּנָיֵינָא, "וְהַנּוֹתָר מִמֶּנּוּ עַד בֹּקֶר", דְּמָצֵי לְמִכְתַּב "וְהַנּוֹתָר בָּאֵשׁ תִּשְׂרֹפוּ"(ג), אֶלָּא אַשְּׂרֵיפָה קָאֵי, וְהָכִי קָאָמַר: וְהַנּוֹתָר מִמֶּנּוּ בִּזְמַן שֶׁאֲסַרְתִּי לָךְ, דְּהַיְינוּ בֹּקֶר רִאשׁוֹן, כְּשֶׁיָּבֹא בֹּקֶר שֵׁנִי שֶׁהוּא חוּלּוֹ שֶׁל מוֹעֵד – תִּשְׂרְפוּ. אֲבָל בְּיוֹ"ט – לֹא. אַלְמָא: מִידֵּי דְּחוֹל לָא עָבְדִינַן בְּיוֹ"ט. וּפֶסַח קָרְבַּן י"ד בְּנִיסָן הוּא, שֶׁהוּא חוֹל. וּמִילָה שֶׁלֹּא בִּזְמַנָּהּ נַמִי מִידֵּי דְּחוֹל הוּא, דִּבְשַׁבָּת זוֹ לֹא הָיָה זְמַנָּהּ: וְלֹא עוֹלַת חוֹל בְּיוֹ"ט. אֵבְרֵי תָמִיד שֶׁל עֶרֶב יוֹ"ט אֵין קְרֵבִין בְּיוֹ"ט, וּמִילָה שֶׁלֹּא בִּזְמַנָּהּ נַמִי כְּעוֹלַת חוֹל בְּיוֹ"ט דָּמֵי: דְּאָתְיָא בְּקַ"ו. שֶׁתִּדְחֶה; וּמַה צָּרַעַת שֶׁדּוֹחָה עֲבוֹדָה – מִילָה שֶׁלֹּא בִּזְמַנָּהּ דּוֹחָה אוֹתָהּ, כִּדְאָמְרִינַן לְעֵיל(ד), שַׁבָּת שֶׁנִּדְחֵית מִפְּנֵי עֲבוֹדָה, אֵינוֹ דִּין שֶׁמִּילָה שֶׁלֹּא בִּזְמַנָּהּ דּוֹחָה אוֹתָהּ, לְהָכִי אִיצְטְרִיךְ לְבַדּוֹ: וְאֵין עֲשֵׂה. דְּמִילָה דּוֹחֶה לֹא תַעֲשֶׂה וַעֲשֵׂה. אֲבָל בִּזְמַנָּהּ, אִיתְרַבִּי מִ"בַּיּוֹם" אֲפִילּוּ בַּשַּׁבָּת: גַּבֵּי פֶּסַח. כָּל מְלָאכָה שֶׁאֶפְשָׁר לָהּ לַעֲשׂוֹת מֵעֶ"שׁ, כְּגוֹן הֲבָאָתוֹ מִחוּץ לַתְּחוּם וַחֲתִיכַת יַבַּלְתּוֹ: וּצְרִיכָא. לְמֵימַר בְּתַרְוַיְיהוּ הֲלָכָה כְּר"ע, דְּמַכְשִׁירִין לָא דָּחוּ: מִילָה בִּזְמַנָּהּ לֵיכָּא כָּרֵת. דְּקָטָן לָאו בַּר עוֹנָשִׁין הוּא וַאֲבוּהּ, לָא מִיחַיַּיב עֲלֵיהּ כָּרֵת:

מתני' מוֹהֲלִין. חוֹתֵךְ אֶת הָעָרְלָה: וּפוֹרְעִין. אֶת הָעוֹר הַמְכַסֶּה רֹאשׁ הַגִּיד: וּמוֹצְצִין. אֶת הַדָּם. וְאַף עַל גַּב דְּהָוְיָא עֲשִׂיַּית חַבּוּרָה, שֶׁאֵין הַדָּם נִיתָּק מֵחִיבּוּרוֹ אֶלָּא עַל יְדֵי(ה) הַמְּצִיצָה: אִיסְפְּלָנִית. תַּחְבּוֹשֶׁת: לוֹעֵס בְּשִׁינָּיו. כַּמָּה דְּאֶפְשָׁר לְשַׁנּוּיֵי מְשַׁנֵּינַן: לֹא טָרַף יַיִן וְשֶׁמֶן. כָּךְ הָיוּ רְגִילִין, וְהִיא רְפוּאָה, שֶׁמְּעָרְבִין וְטוֹרְפִין בִּקְעָרָה יַיִן וְשֶׁמֶן יַחַד, כְּדֶרֶךְ שֶׁטּוֹרְפִין בֵּיצִים בִּקְעָרָה: חָלוּק. כְּעֵין כִּיס דָּחוּק הָיוּ עוֹשִׂין וּמַלְבִּישִׁים אֶת רֹאשׁ הַגִּיד עַד הָעֲטָרָה וְקוֹשְׁרִים שָׁם, כְּדֵי שֶׁלֹּא יַחֲזוֹר הָעוֹר לְכַסּוֹת אֶת הַגִּיד: לֹא הִתְקִין. לֹא הִזְמִין: כּוֹרֵךְ עַל יָדוֹ. דֶּרֶךְ מַלְבּוּשׁ, לְשַׁנּוֹתוֹ מִדֶּרֶךְ הוֹלָכָה בְּחוֹל:

תוספות

ואביי אליבא דר' שמעון. ולרבי יונתן לא מיבעיא ליה, דמוקי ליה בינוני. ולאביי נמי דאמר לעיל דבינוני אתי מבינייא, מצי למימר דסבר ר' יונתן מילתא דאתי בק"ו טרח וכתב לה קרא:

באומר לקוץ בהרתו הוא מתכוין. וא"ת: אם כן, אמאי קאמר אביי: לא נצרכא אלא לרבי יהודה – הא לר"ש נמי איצטריך, כדאמר הכא! ויש לומר: דלשון ברייתא משמע דמיירי בלא מתכוין, מדלא קתני בשר, אע"ג דמתכוין לקוץ בהרת ימול:

ותנן נמי גבי פסח כה"ג אמר רב יהודה אמר רב הלכה כר"ע. והכא לא פריך הילכתא למשיחא – משום דנפקא מינה גבי מילה. אע"ג דגבי מילה נמי פסיק הכי – מ"מ לאלומי פיסקא דמילה פסיק נמי גבי פסח אגב דפסיק גבי מילה, דתילף מינה שפסק ברור הוא לכל דבר(ב):

וצריכא דאי אשמועינן. אדרב יהוד' קאי, דפסיק כר"ע הכא והתם. דאי אדרבי עקיבא – א"כ בפ' "שתי הלחם" (מנחות דף נו.) דקתני נמי: "כלל אמר ר"ע", הוה ליה למימר וצריכא. וכן פירש בקונטרס(ג):

עושין כל צרכי מילה בשבת. אע"ג דלעיל נמי קתני (ו)בשילהי "מפנין" (ד' קכח.) – התם תני לה אגב גררא דמילי דתינוק, אבל הכא עיקר:

גדול

רבינו חננאל

והננס והחרש והשוטה והשכור ובעלי נגעים טהורין פסולין באדם וכשרין בבהמה כו' פי' כל זמן שיש בכהן נגעים טהורים פסול לעבודה חתכו טהר מיד ואין צריך טבילה: **מודה** ר' שמעון בפסיק רישי' ולא ימות פי' כי ר' שמעון מודה בדבר שהוא ברור כגון אדם שחותך ראש אדם ואומר שאין כוונתו להמיתו אלא להוציא את ממונו שאין שומעין לו אלא דנין אותו דין כל הורג נפש כך כל דבר שמתברר (מעשין) [שיעשה] לאותה מלאכה אין אומרין שלא היתה כוונתו לכך. וכה"ג אפילו ר' שמעון מודה. ואביי אליבא דר' שמעון קודם שישמע מרבא. מודה ר' שמעון בפסיק רישיה ולא ימות דהוה מוקים ליה כר' יהודה ולא כר' שמעון הוה אמר דר"ש פליג נמי בהא דסבר ר' שמעון חתיכות הערלה והצרעת עליה דבר שאין מתכוון הוא שאין כוונתו לחתוך הצרעת אלא למול בנו וכי האי לר' שמעון שרי ולא צריך קרא למשרייה אם כן אבי אליבא דר' שמעון האי בשר ערלתו מאי עביד ליה אמר רב משרשיה באומר לקוץ בהרתו הוא מתכוין כלומר בדבר מוכיח שמתכוין לקוץ בהרתו בא הכתוב להתירו ואקשינן תינח גדול שיש בו דעת יש לומר בן מתכוין לקוץ בהרתו קטן שאין בו דעת למה כתוב בו בשר להתיר חתיכת צרעת במילה ואמרי' קטן נמי מתכוין אביו בזה במולו לבנו לחתוך בהרת בנו ואמרי' בעת שיש בהרת בערלה הקטן ימול אחר זולתו אבי הבן. שהאחר אין מתכוין לחתוך הבהרת ודבר שאין מתכוין לר' שמעון שרי ולא הוה צריך קרא למשריה דאמר רבי שמעון בן לקיש כל מקום שאתה מוצא עשה ולא תעשה פי' כגון זה עשה שנאמר וביום השמיני ימול בשר ערלתו. לא תעשה השמר בנגע הצרעת שהוא לאו כאשר פירשנו למעלה. ואם יש בהרת בערלה וימול אחר זולתו אבי הבן נתקיימה המילה שהוא עשה ונתקיימה חתיכת הצרעת שלא בכוונה שלא הזהירה התורה אלא במתכוין והאחר לא נתכוון ואין כאן עשה ולא לא תעשה ואם אין כאן אחר ... ופרקינן דליכא אחר ואם נאמר להמתין עד שיבא אחר ביטלנו וביום השמיני ימול בשר ערלתו: ובאנו לפרש עוד תשלום הברייתא: **אמר** מר י"ט אינו דוחה אלא בזמנו. פי' אין מילה דוחה י"ט אלא הנימול ביום ח' שהוא זמנו בלבד ואמרינן מנא הני מילי ופירשו חזקיה*) מן הקדשים שמטונן שריפה והוא עשה כדכתיב

*) חסר קצת וכצ"ל ופי' חזקיה דילפינן זה מנותר מן הקדשים וכו'.

עין משפט נר מצוה

י א מיי' פ"ו מהלכות טומאת צרעת הלכה ח סמג לאוין רסב:

יא ב מיי' פ"ג מהלכות עולות הלכה ו:

יב ג מיי' פ"א מהלכות קרבן פסח הלכה יח סמג עשין רנג:

יג ד מיי' פ"ב מהלכות מילה הל' ו סמג עשין כח טוש"ע א"ח סי' שלא סעיף א וטוש"ע י"ד סי' רסו סעיף ב:

יד ה מיי' שם הל' ז סמג שם וטוש"ע א"ח שם סעיף ז וטוש"ע י"ד שם סעיף ג:

מסורת הש"ס

[יומא לד:]

נ"ל מלדחוק

[שם]

לעיל עה. קג. קיח. קכ: ולק' קמא: [ביצה לו.] סוכה לג: כתובות ו. בכורות כה.

יבמות כ: נזיר מא. נח. מנחות מ.

לעיל כד: פסחים פג: תמורה ד: ע"ש

[פסחים סט:]

פסחים סו. סט: יבמות יד. מנחות עב. ודף נו.

[לעיל קכח:]

[ע' תוס' עמוד ב ד"ה לועס]

דברים כד | ויקרא יג | שמות יב | במדבר כח | שמות יב | ויקרא כג

גליון הש"ס

רש"י ד"ה שאין ת"ל וכו' י"ד בניסן הוא שהוא חול. עיין בטורי אבן במגילה בחבוני מלואים לקמן דף מז ע"ב ד"ה אף כאן:

הגהות הב"ח

(א) גמ' אבל אתה עושה אותו בסיב: (ב) שם ... (ג) רש"י ... לאפשר לעשות: (ג) רש"י מאי דדחי שבת כ"כ תוס' במנחות]. ד"ה שאין ת"ל וכו' באש תשרפו אלמא לאשריפה קאי וכו' דחול הוא דבי"ט זו לא: (ד) ד"ה לאתויי וכו' כדאמרינן לעיל י"ט ... שנדחית: (ה) ד"ה ומוצצין וכו' אלא ע"י (המגילה) תז"מ ונ"ב ס"א חבורה: (ו) תום' ד"ה עושין וכו' קתני לה בשילהי:

א) [נ"ל עד בקר והנותר ממנו עד בקר באש תשרופו וכ"ה בפסחים: ב) [וע"ע תוס' יומא יג. ד"ה הלכה ותוס' זבחים מ"ה ד"ה הלכתא]. ג) [ואמילתא דר"ע לא בעי צריכותא דאשמעי' בכל דוכתא ...

(*) נ"ל מלדחוק

רב נסים גאון

והיינו מפרישין אותו לענין דיניו מכלל הקרבנות אבל הואיל ונאמר בו וביום השמיני באר לנו בזה חזרתו לכלל הקרבנות בכל עניניו והשבתו אליהן בכל תנאותיהן חוץ מקרבן עולה ויורד המפורש בו בלבד וזה שהוצרכתי לפרש דבר זה לפי שראיתיו מסובך אצל כל התלמידים וביארתיו כדי שיתגלה ויתברר: **אימור** דאמרי' אתי עשה ודחי לא תעשה גרידא לא תעשה ועשה מי דחי לא תעשה גרידא הוא לא תעשה הכי יחיד *)שאין עמו כרת כמו (דברים כה) לא תחסום שור בדישו (שם כב) לא תחרוש בשור ובחמור (ויקרא יט) לא תקיפו פאת ראשכם ודומה להם ויתוסף עם זה מה שנאמר במבטא השמר פן ואל כגון (דברים כד) השמר בנגע הצרעת (שמות לד) פן תכרת ברית ליושב הארץ (שם טז) אל יצא איש ממקומו גם הן אזהרות לאו ומי שיעבר עליהם עובר על לא תעשה כמו שאמרו בתלמוד (עירובין דף נו וש"נ) השמר פן ואל אינו אלא לשון לא תעשה ומה שנמצא בתורה ממצות לא תעשה מה שאין בו כרת ולא מיתת בית דין ולא ניתוסף עליו עשה אותו דבר הוא הנקרא לאו גרידא ודינו שכשאירע עם מצות עשה במקום אחד נקיים מצות עשה ולא נחוש לאזהרת לאו ועיקר זה מצוי במסכת יבמות בפ' א' (דף ג) וכן אמרו שם אימור דאמרי' דאתי עשה ודחי לא תעשה גרידא לא תעשה ועשה מי דחי ותו לא תעשה גרידא מגלן דדחי דכתיב (דברים כב) לא תלבש שעטנז וכתיב גדילים תעשה לך ידענו כי זה לא תעשה אינו שוה בכל דבר אלא מיוחד הוא וכי הציווי שנאמר אחריו הוא תנאי עליו ולא בא להזהיר אלא על לבישת כלאים חוץ ממצות ציצית אבל מה שהוא מעורב מחוטי פשתן עם תכלת של צמר שהיא מצוה אינו נכנס בזו האזהרה אלא מותר הוא ואמרו חכמים שדבר זה עיקר הוא שנסמך עליו וכי כל אזהרה שאין עמה כרת שבתורה כך היא דרכה שבעת שאירע חיוב מצות עשה נדחה האזהרה שהיא לא תעשה ונקיים הציווי שהוא עשה ותבוא מצות עשה ותדחה לא תעשה כי האזהרה של לאו על זה התנאי נאמרה ובזה הפירוש שפירשנו יסיר מלבך ספק גדול שמסתפקין בו בני אדם ושואלין עליו והוא שאומרין מאחר שאנו יודעין שאזהרת לאו קשה מציווי עשה היאך יבא עשה וידחה האזהרה של לאו שהיא חמורה

*) נ"ל לא תעשה יחידי שאין עמו כרת.

עין משפט נר מצוה

טו א מיי' פ"ב מהלכות מילה הל' ד ו טוש"ע א"ח סי' שלא סעיף ב וטוש"ע י"ד סי' רסו סעיף ב:

טז ב מיי' פ"ז מהל' ס"ת הלכה ד ופ"ז מהל' לולב הל' ו סמג עשין כח ולאוין שסד טוש"ע א"ח סימן תרנו:

יז ג מיי' פ"א מהלכות דעות הלכה ו:

[שייך לעמוד א במשנה]

יח ד מיי' פ"ג מהלכות קידוש החדש הל' ד:

יט ה מיי' פ"ה מהל' תמידין ומוספין הל' ד סמג עשין קצ:

כ ו מיי' פ"ב מהלכות שגגות הלכה ט:

כא ז מיי' פ"ב מהל' מילה הל' ב סמג עשין כח טוש"ע י"ד סי' רסד סעיף ג:

כב ח טוש"ע א"ח סי' ד סעיף כ:

גמרא

תורה אור

גמ' מכדי קתני כולהו, 'כל צורכי מילה' לאתויי מאי? לאתויי הא, דת"ר: [א]המל, כל זמן שהוא עוסק במילה – חוזר בין על הציצין המעכבין את המילה בין על הציצין שאין מעכבין את המילה. פירש, על ציצין המעכבין את המילה – חוזר, על ציצין שאין מעכבין את המילה – אינו חוזר. מאן תנא "פירש אינו חוזר"? אמר רבה בר בר חנה אמר רבי יוחנן: רבי ישמעאל בנו של ר' יוחנן בן ברוקה היא. דתניא: *ארבעה עשר שחל להיות בשבת – מפשיט (*אדם) הפסח עד החזה, דברי רבי ישמעאל בנו של ר' יוחנן בן ברוקה. וחכ"א: מפשיטין את כולו. ממאי?! עד כאן לא קאמר ר' ישמעאל בנו של ר' יוחנן בן ברוקה התם(א) – משום דלא בעינן °"זה אלי ואנוהו", אבל הכא דבעינן "זה אלי ואנוהו" – הכי נמי, *דתניא: "זה אלי ואנוהו" – [ב]התנאה לפניו במצות; עשה לפניו סוכה נאה, ולולב נאה, ושופר נאה, ציצית נאה, ספר תורה נאה וכתוב בו לשמו בדיו נאה, בקולמוס נאה, בלבלר אומן וכורכו בשיראין נאין. אבא שאול אומר: "ואנוהו" – הוי דומה לו: [ג]מה הוא חנון ורחום – אף אתה היה חנון ורחום. אלא אמר רב אשי: הא מני – רבי יוסי היא, דתנן: *[ד]בין שנראה בעליל ובין שלא נראה בעליל – מחללין עליו את השבת, רבי יוסי אומר: נראה בעליל – אין מחללין עליו את השבת. ממאי?! דילמא עד כאן לא קאמר ר' יוסי התם(ב) – דלא ניתנה שבת לידחות, אבל הכא דניתנה שבת לידחות – הכי נמי! אלא אמרי נהרדעי: רבנן דפליגי עליה דרבי יוסי היא, דתנן: *[ה]ארבעה כהנים נכנסין, שנים בידם שני סדרים, ושנים בידם שני בזיכין. וארבעה מקדימין לפניהם, שנים – ליטול שני סדרים, ושנים – ליטול שני בזיכין. המכניסין עומדים בצפון ופניהם לדרום, והמוציאין עומדים בדרום ופניהם לצפון. אלו מושכים ואלו מניחין, טפחו של זה בצד טפחו של זה, משום שנאמר °"לפני (ה') תמיד". ר' יוסי אומר: אפילו אלו נוטלין ואלו מניחין – אף זה היה תמיד. ת"ר: מהלקטין את המילה, ואם לא הילקט – ענוש כרת. מני? א"ר כהנא: אומן. מתקיף לה רב פפא: אומן לימא להו "אנא עבדי פלגא דמצוה – אתון עבדיתו פלגא דמצוה"! אלא אמר רב פפא: גדול. מתקיף לה רב אשי: גדול בהדיא כתיב ביה °"וערל זכר אשר לא ימול"! אלא אמר רב אשי: לעולם אומן, [ו]וכגון דאתא בין השמשות דשבת, ואמרו ליה: לא מספקת, ואמר להו: מספקינא. ועבד ולא איסתפק, ואישתכח דחבורה הוא דעבד, וענוש כרת.§ "מוצצין וכו'".§ אמר רב פפא: [ז]האי אומנא דלא מייץ – סכנה הוא, ועברינן ליה. פשיטא, מדקא מחללי עליה שבתא – סכנה הוא! מהו דתימא: האי דם מיפקד פקיד, קמ"ל: חבורי מיחבר. ודומיא דאיספלנית וכמון, מה איספלנית וכמון – כי לא עביד סכנה הוא, אף ה"נ – כי לא עביד – סכנה הוא.§ "ונותנין עליה איספלנית".§ אמר אביי, *אמרה לי אם: איספלניתא דכולהון כיבי – שב מינאי תרבא וחדא קירא. רבא אמר: קירא וקלבא רישינא. דרשה רבא במחוזא, קרעינהו בני מניומי אסיא למנייהו. אמר להו: שבקי לכו חדא, דאמר שמואל: [ח]האי מאן דמשי אפיה ולא נגיב טובא – נקטרו ליה חספניתא

שמות טו | ס"ס כה | בראשית יז | [קידושין לא: ע"ש נסמן]

תוספות

גדול בהדיא כתיב ביה. אע"ג דבכמה דוכתין תניא מה שבהדיא בפסוק, איבעי(ז) למתני: גדול שלא מל ענוש כרת:

*__לועם__ בשיניו. אף על גב דאחר מילה חולה שיש בו סכנה הוא, מ"מ כמה דאפשר לשנויי משנינן: הכא

רש"י

גמ' מכדי קתני. במתניתין: כולהו. כל דברים העושים למילה, מוהלין ופורעין ומוצצין כו' למה ליה? דתנן כללא ברישא: עושין כל צרכי מילה: ציצין. שיורי ערלה, ובמתני'(ג) מפרש אלו הן ציצין המעכבין. ויש שאינן מעכבין, כגון בשר שאינה חופה רוב העטרה אלא מיעוטה. ומה היא עטרה – שורה גבוה המקפת בגיד סביב, שממנה הגיד משפע ויורד לצד הקרקע, ומשפע ויורד לצד הגוף: המל. בשבת: כל זמן שהוא עוסק בה. שלא סילק ידו, אם ראה שנשתיירו בה ציצין, בין מעכבין את המילה, שאינה כשרה עד שיתכסם, בין שאין מעכבין – חוזר וחותך, דכולה חדא מילתא היא, והרי ניתנה שבת לדחות אצלה: פירש. שסילק ידיו: על המעכבין חוזר. שהרי הן כמילה עצמה: ועל שאין מעכבין אינו חוזר. דהוי כהתחלה בפני עצמה, ועל אלו לא ניתן לחלל את השבת. והיינו דקתני כל צרכי מילה ואפילו ציצין שאין מעכבין – חוזר עליהם כל זמן שלא פירש: מאן תנא פירש אינו חוזר. ומשום דפירש חשיב ליה חזרה מילתא לנפשה, והואיל ולא עיכוב מצוה נינהו – לא הדר: מפשיט הפסח עד החזה. (ד)והיינו פירש. דתנן במסכת תמיד (פ"ד מ"ג) גבי הפשיטו, שהיה מתחיל מן הרגלים, והיה מפשיט ויורד עד שמגיע לחזה; הגיע לחזה, חתך את הראש ונתנו למי שזכה בו, ואח"כ הכרעיים, ומירק והפשיט כו'. שמעי' מיניה, משהגיע לחזה סילק ידיו מן ההפשט, והתחיל להתעסק בניתוח קצת. וגבי עולה דכולה כליל – מירק והפשיט, ומנתח הידים תחילה אחר הראש. וגבי פסח נמי, משהפשיט עד החזה, דיכול להוציא אימוריו(ה) בלא נימין – קורעו ומוציאן מיד, והוה ליה פירש מן ההפשט. וקאמר רבי ישמעאל: שוב אינו גומר ומפשיט. משום דכיון דפירש, הויא חזרה מילתא דאתחלתא לנפשה ושלא לצורך גבוה, דומיא דציצין דלא מעכבין: דלא בעינן זה אלי ואנוהו. דאחר נטילת האימורין אין הידור מצוה ביפוי בשר, אבל יפוי מילה מצוה היא: הוי דומה לו. ולשון אנוהו: אני והוא, אעשה עצמי כמותו לדבק בדרכיו: בין שנראה. החדש: בעליל. בגילוי לכל, ויש לדעת שראוהו בית דין והקרובים להם, ואין צריך לרואין חוץ לתחום לחלל שבת ולבא ולהעיד לפני ב"ד – מחללין: ר' יוסי אומר כו'. אלמא, אע"ג דאיכא מצוה, כיון דלאו לצורך גבוה הוא – לא מחללינן. והכא נמי פירש, דהוי אתחלתא דחילול כי הכא, בלא צורך גבוה – לא מחללינן: לא ניתנה שבת לדחות. אפילו בהתחלתה, דהא נראה בעליל. אבל הכא, כיון שניתנה שבת לדחות, להתחיל בה המילה – הכי נמי דכי פירש והדר לאו (ו)אתחלתא לנפשה היא, והוי כאילו שלא פירש, וגומר כל מצותו: רבנן דפליגי עליה דרבי יוסי. גבי לחם הפנים: ארבעה כהנים נכנסין. להיכל בשבת, לסדור לחם הפנים: שני סדרים. שתים ועשרות של לחם: שני בזיכין. שתי כפות מלאות לבונה, כדכתיב (ויקרא כד): "ונתת על המערכת לבונה זכה": מקדימין לפניהם שנים ליטול. מן השלחן אחד סדרים הישנים: ושנים ליטול שני בזיכין. והשלחן היה נתון ארכו ממזרח למערב, ואלו עומדין מזה לרוחב השלחן בצפון, ואלו עומדין לנגדו לדרום. ודווקא מכניסין לצפון, דכל צפון ענין חשיבות היא. כדאמרינן במסכת סוכה (דף נו.) גבי חילוק לחם הפנים למשמרה הנכנסת והיוצאת; הנכנסין חולקין בצפון כדי שיראו(ז) נכנסין: רבי יוסי אומר אפילו אלו נוטלין. תחילה, ומסלקין כולה מן השלחן, ולאחר שעה מניחין אלו: אף זה תמיד. ומה אני מקיים תמיד – שלא ילין שלחן בלא לחם. ולרבנן, אי שקלי ושבקי ליה והדר מסדרי – לא מיקרי להו תמיד, אלא התחלה אחריתי, ונמצא שמתעכב שלחן בלא לחם. וגבי פירש נמי, כי הדר אתי – מילתא אחריתי היא. ולרבי יוסי דאמר כי שבקי והדר מתחלי נמי תמיד הוא, דחדא מילתא הוא – הכא נמי פירש חוזר, אע"פ שאין מעכבין – דכולה גמר מילתא היא: מהלקטין. בציצין המעכבין: מני. כרת זו של מי הוא: אמר רב כהנא אומן. ענוש כרת. ובשבת קאי, שחילל שבת ולא עשה מצוה: ונימא אנא עבדי פלגא. כלומר: הואיל וכשהתחיל ברשות התחיל, וחבורה שעשה ברשות עשה, אמאי חייב? נימא להו: לכו אתם וסיימו המלאכה: אלא אמר רב פפא. בגדול שמל קמייהו, ובחול וענוש כרת דקאמר – משום מילה קאמר, דעדיין ערל הוא: וכגון דאתא בין השמשות. דכל היום כשר למילה, *ואמרו ליה: לא מספקת לגמור ביום כהילכתה, ותעשה חבורה בשבת בלא מצוה, וענוש כרת. ומיהו, מיתה ליכא – דלא אתרו ביה למיתה, ולא קבל עליו התראה. וכרת איכא, דאתחלה ברשות לא התחיל, ולא ניתנה שבת לדחות אלא בשעה זו: מהו דתימא. מתניתין לא אשמעינן דמחלל שבתא עלה, דדם מיפקד פקיד – מופקד ועומד שם כנתון בכלי, ובמציצה אין חבורה, ואין כאן איסור תורה, ומשום הכי שרי, ולאו משום סכנה. ואומנא דלא מייץ בחול – לאו סכנתא היא, ולא ניעבריה: קא משמע לן דדם חיבורי מיחבר. כשיוצא ע"י מציצה, ואפילו הכי שרי, משום סכנה, מדקתני במתני' גבי איספלנית וכמון: שב מינאי תרבא. ז' מנות של חלב: וחדא דקירא. שעוה: קירא וקלבא רישינא. הוא זפת של עץ שמוציאים ממנו שלא ע"י האור, והיא לבנה: קרעינהו למנייהו. שהפסיד להם לגלות רפואה זו: שבקי לכו חדא. שלא גיליתי: חספניתא

רבינו חננאל

והנותר ממנו עד בוקר באש תשרופו ואין שריפת קדשים דוחה י"ט דתנינן בגמרא בפ' כיצד צולין את הפסח. דתנן העצמות והגידים והנותר ישרפו בששה עשר חל ששה עשר להיות בשבת ישרפו בי"ז שאינו דוחה את השבת ולא את יו"ט וקיימא לן דמילה שלא בזמנה אפילו יו"ט אינו דוחה דתנן שני יו"ט של ר"ה נימול לי"ב ללמדך שאין עשה דוחה י"ט כן המילה שלא בזמנה אינה דוחה י"ט ואין לומר אי הכי אפי' מילה בזמנה כי מילה בזמנה בפירוש אמרה תורה וביום ואפי' בשבת וכ"ש י"ט אביי פירשו מעולת שבת בשבתו כו' רבא אמר הוא ולא מכשיריו פי' עשיית אוכל נפש דוחה י"ט ולא מכשירי אוכל נפש. כגון חטיבת עצים מן היער לבשל ביו"ט וכדומה (לו) [הוא] לבדו ולא מילה שלא בזמנה הבאה בק"ו וזהו ק"ו שאמר רבא ומה אוכל נפש שאע"פ שהיא באזהרת שמחה אינה (מנוח שדוחה) [דוחה] יו"ט לשחוט ולבשל ולאפות וכיוצא בהן מילה שלא בזמנה שאע"פ שהיא בלא זמנה מצוה היא ומעכבתו מלאכול בתרומה. אינו דין שדוחה י"ט בא לבדו למעט המילה שלא בזמנה. רב אשי אמר שבת שבתון עשה הוא וי"ט עשה ול"ת עשה שבתון ולא תעשה כל מלאכה לא תעשה נמצא כתיב ביו"ט עשה ול"ת והמילה עשה בלבד. ולא אתי עשה דמילה ודחי את לא תעשה ועשה דיו"ט: **מתני'** כלל א"ר עקיבא כל מלאכה שאפשר [לעשות] מע"ש דוחה את השבת וכו'. אמר רב יהודה אמר רב הלכה כר' עקיבא: **מתני'** עושין כל צרכי מילה בשבת מוהלין ופורעין כו' אמרינן כי מכדי קתני מוהלין ופורעין ומוצצין כו' עושין כל צרכי מילה למה לי לאתויי הא דתנו רבנן המל כל זמן שעוסק במילה חוזר בין על ציצין המעכבין את המילה בין על הציצין שאינן מעכבין את המילה פירש על ציצין המעכבין את המילה חוזר על שאין מעכבין אינו חוזר. ואמרינן מאן תנא פירש ואתא רבה בר בר חנה לאוקומה כר' (שמעון) [ישמעאל] בר' יוחנן בן

מסורת הש"ס

לעיל קטז: מנחות סג: [תוספתא פסחים פ"ד]

[נזיר ב: ע"ש] סוכה יא: מכילתא פרשת בשלח [מס' סופרים פ"ג הל' יג]

ר"ה כא: מנחות סד.

מנחות ז. לט:

פסחים ז. יומא כח: (מגילה כ.)

הגהות הב"ח

(א) גמ' התם אלא משום דלא: (ב) שם ר' יוסי התם אלא משום דלא ניתנה בשבת: (ג) רש"י ד"ה ציצין וכו' ובמתני'. נ"ב לקמן דף קלז סוף ע"א: (ד) ד"ה מפשיטין את הפסח עד וכו': (ה) שם להוצי' אימוריו נ"ב ע"ל בפרק כ"ב דף קטז בסוף הדף: (ו) ד"ה ושנים ליטול וכו' כדי שיראו שהן נכנסין: (ז) תום' ד"ה גדול וכו' איבעי ליה למיתני:

רב נסים גאון

חמורה ממנו ומדרך הידוע שהחמור דוחה הקל ולא עוד אלא שפעמים שעולה על דעתן שיש בענין הזה ענין חורה בדבר הראשון והתשובה הוא מה שהקדמנו שהאזהרה של לאו כך נאמרה מיוחדת וכי הציווי של עשה תנאי הוא בה וכן אמרו רז"ל (ספרי פ' תצא) מחלליה מות יומת וביום השבת שני כבשים בני שנה שניהן בדיבור אחד נאמרו ערות אשת אחיך ויבמה יבוא עליה שניהן בדיבור אחד נאמרו מה שאי אפשר לבשר ודם לומר שנא' אחת דיבר אלהים שתים זו שמענו הבן דבר זה ושמור אותו כי הוא ספק גדול והרי גלינו אותו ומזה העיקר אמרו רז"ל בתלמוד כל מקום שאתה מוצא עשה ולא תעשה אם אתה יכול לקיים את שניהם מוטב ואם לאו יבא עשה וידחה לא תעשה וסבר (רבינא) [רבא] כי לא תעשה שבקודש מוצא מזה העיקר וכי לא ידחה מפני עשה ולא שוה עמו רב אשי בדבר זה כמו שנאמר בשחיטת קדשים בפרק דם חטאת (דף לז) אמאי וניתי עשה ונידחי לא תעשה אמר רבינא אין עשה דוחה את לא תעשה שבמקדש דתניא כו' רב אשי אמר יקדש עשה הוא ואין עשה דוחה את לא תעשה ועשה ובמס' נזירות בפ"ב נזירין (דף נח) אמרו עוד (ומאי דקא מודי ליה) [ומאן דמוקים] לקרא למידחא לא תעשה ועשה לאו גרידא מנא ליה יליף מגדילים דאמר קרא לא תלבש שעטנז הא גדילים תעשה לך מהן וכל מה שתמצא בתלמוד דאתי עשה ודחי לא תעשה מזה העיקר שהקדימו הוא וזה הדין בלאו גרידא בלבד אבל לא תעשה ועשה וכל שכן לא תעשה שיש בו כרת אין עשה דוחה אותם ואנו מבארין לך זה ונאמר

חספניתא. פניו מתבקעות. ואני אומר שהוא מין שחין שקורין אינייר"א, והוא "(בגרב) ובחרס" שכתוב בתורה (דברים כח). *וחספניתא תרגום של חרס: במיא דסילקא. מרק תרדין: חזי לחולה. שאין בו סכנה: יבטלו. דהאי נמי חולה הוא: אבל לכולי עלמא שרי. ר"מ, וסתם מתני' ר"מ, ואמאי תנן: "נותן זה בעצמו וזה בעצמו": התם. גבי שאר חולים: לא בעו ליכא. לטרפו ולערבו יפה יפה: ולא לילך. לא יערבנו כל כך: ומתרץ: היינו דקתני נותן זה בעצמו וזה בעצמו. שמערב ואינו לוכך: אין מסננין את החרדל. בי"ט: במסננת שלו. טעמא מפרש לקמיה, דמיחזי כבורר, שמשליך הפסולת שלו:

*חספניתא. מאי תקנתיה? לימשי טובא במיא דסילקא.§ "לא שחק מערב שבת".§ תנו רבנן: דברים שאין עושין למילה בשבת עושין לה ביו"ט: [א]שוחקין לה כמון, וטורפין לה יין ושמן. א"ל אביי לרב יוסף: מאי שנא כמון בי"ט – דחזי לקדרה, יין ושמן חזי נמי בשבת לחולה! דתניא: *אין טורפין יין ושמן לחולה בשבת. אמר ר"ש בן אלעזר משום ר"מ: אף טורפין יין ושמן. א"ר שמעון בן אלעזר: פעם אחת חש רבי מאיר במעיו, ובקשנו לטרוף לו יין ושמן, ולא הנחנו. אמרנו לו: דבריך יבטלו בחייך?! אמר לנו: אע"פ שאני אומר כך, וחבירי אומרים כך – °מימי לא מלאני לבי לעבור על דברי חבירי. הוא ניהו דמחמיר אנפשיה, אבל לכולי עלמא – שרי! התם לא בעי ליכא, הכא בעי ליכא. הכא נמי, ניעביד ולא לילך! היינו דקתני: נותן זה בפני עצמו וזה בפני עצמו.§ ת"ר: [ב]אין מסננין את החרדל במסננת שלו ואין ממתקין אותו בגחלת. א"ל אביי לרב יוסף: מאי שנא מהא *דתנן: נותנים ביצה במסננת של חרדל? א"ל: התם – לא מיחזי כבורר, הכא – מיחזי כבורר. ואין ממתקין אותו בגחלת. והתניא: ממתקין אותו בגחלת! לא קשיא: [ג]כאן בגחלת של מתכת כאן בגחלת של עץ. א"ל אביי לרב יוסף: מ"ש *מבישרא אגומרי? א"ל: התם – לא אפשר, הכא – אפשר. א"ל אביי לרב יוסף: מהו לגבן? א"ל: [ד]אסור. מ"ש מלישה? א"ל: התם – לא אפשר, הכא – אפשר. והא אמרי נהרדעי: גבינה בת יומא מעליא! הכי קאמרי: דאפילו גבינה בת יומא מעליא.§ "אין עושין לה חלוק כו'".§ אמר אביי, *אמרה לי אם: [ה]האי חלוק דינוקא – לפניה לסיטרא *לעילאי, דילמא מידביק (א)גרדא מיניה ואתי לידי כרות שפכה. אימיה דאביי עבדא כיסתתא לפלגא. אמר אביי: האי ינוקא דלית ליה חלוק – לייתי בליתא דאית ליה שיפתא, וליכרכיה לשיפתא לתתאי, ועייף ליה לעילאי. ואמר אביי, אמרה לי אם: האי ינוקא דלא ידיע מפקתיה – לשייפיה מישחא, ולוקמיה להדי יומא, והיכא דזיג ליקרעיה בשערתא שתי וערב. אבל בכלי מתכות – לא, משום דזריף. ואמר אביי, אמרה לי אם: האי ינוקא דלא מייץ – מיקר (ב)דקר פומיה, מאי תקנתיה – לייתו כסא גומרי, ולינקטיה ליה להדי פומיה, דחיים פומיה ומייץ. ואמר אביי, אמרה לי אם: האי ינוקא דלא *מנשתיה – לינפפיה בנפוותא ומנשתיה. ואמר אביי, אמרה לי אם: האי ינוקא דלא *מעוי – ליתו סליתא דאימיה, ולישרקיה עילויה ומעוי. ואמר אביי, אמרה לי אם: האי ינוקא דקטין – לייתו לסילתא דאימיה, ולישרקיה עילויה מקוטנא לאולמא. ואי אלים – מאולמא לקוטנא. ואמר אביי, אמרה לי אם: [ו]האי ינוקא דסומק – דאכתי לא איבלע ביה דמא[א], ליתרחו ליה עד דאיבלע ביה דמא ולימהלוה. [ז]דירוק ואכתי לא נפל ביה דמיה – ליתרחו עד דנפל ביה דמיה, ולימהלוה. *דתניא, א"ר נתן: פעם אחת הלכתי לכרכי הים ובאת אשה אחת לפני, שמלה בנה ראשון ומת, שני ומת, שלישי הביאתו לפני. ראיתיו שהוא אדום, אמרתי לה: המתיני לו עד שיבלע בו דמו. המתינה לו עד שנבלע בו דמו, ומלה אותו וחיה. והיו קורין אותו "נתן הבבלי" על שמי. שוב פעם אחת הלכתי למדינת קפוטקיא, ובאת אשה אחת לפני, שמלה בנה ראשון ומת, שני ומת, שלישי הביאתו לפני. ראיתיו שהוא ירוק, הצצתי בו ולא ראיתי בו דם ברית. אמרתי לה: המתיני לו עד שיפול בו דמו. והמתינה לו, ומלה אותו וחיה, והיו קורין שמו "נתן הבבלי" על שמי.§

מתני'

א] [גי' הערוך ליתרחוהו ועי' במוסף הערוך ערך תרח וברש"י גיטין סח: ד"ה תרחי גבי].

ואין ממתקין אותו בגחלת. כדרך שרגילין לכבות לתוכו את הגחלת, או אבן ניסוקת: נותנין ביצה במסננת של חרדל. ומסננה בתוכו, לייפות מראיתו: לא מיחזי כבורר. שכולה יוצאה דרך המסננת, ואין משתייר שם פסולת: בגחלת של עץ. אסור, דשייך בה כיבוי לפי שעושה פחם. גחלת של מתכת לא שייך בה כיבוי דאינו נעשה פחם: ומ"ש מבישרא אגומרי. שצולין בי"ט ואע"ג דמכבה: לא אפשר. לצלות מאתמול, דדיומא שביחא טפי. אבל חרדל אפשר מאתמול: לגבן. גבינה: מאי שנא מלישה. שלשין פת ביום טוב, והאי נמי לישה דמיא: לא אפשר. דפת חמה מעליא טפי. הכא – אפשר מאתמול: אימא אף גבינתא בת יומא מעליא. וכ"ש דאתמול: לפניה לסטריה לעילאי. לאימרא שבשפת פיה יהפוך ויקפל למעלה שלא תהא סמוכה לבשרו. מפני שראש מקום חתך הבגד שם הוא, ויוצאין ממנו גרדין שקורין פיינד"ן, ודלמא מדביקא גרדתא מיניה במכה, וכשבא להפשיט החלוק מעל המילה ישמוט ויקרע את ראש הגיד, ומשוי ליה כרות שפכה: אימיה דאביי. אומנתו: עבדא. לתינוקות הבאים לידה לתקן מילתן: כיסתתא לפלגא. דמילה, כיס היתה עושה של בגד לפנים בתוך החלוק, ותופרתו מתוכו בתוך החלוק ומגיע למטה עד חצי החלוק, כדי לחוץ בין האימרא ובין המילה: לייתי בליתא. מעט שחק של בגד שיהא בו אימרא, לפי שהאימרא מהדקה יפה בבשר שלא ישמט החלוק מן הגיד: וליכרכיה לשפתיה לתתאי. לתחתית ראש הגיד יתן השפה, וראש השני החלק יהא למעלה: ולעפפיה לעילאי. אותו ראש העליון החלוק יקפל ויקפול כלפי חוץ מפני הגרדין, שלא ידבקו במכה: דלא ידיע ביה מפקתיה. שאין ניכר בו נקב בית הרעי, ששם הוצאת זבלו: לישייפיה מישחא. שהשמן מגהיל הבשר: ולוקמיה להדי יומא. נגד השמש: והיכא דזיג. שצלול כזכוכית, בידוע שהחלל כנגדו: בשערתא. בראש השעורה שהוא חדוד: דזריף. מנפחו, אינפליי"ר בלע"ז: דלא מייץ. שלא יכול לינק: מיקר הוא דקר פומיה. נצטננו שפתיו, ואין בו כח למוץ בהן: לייתו כסא דגומרי. תשטח גחלים על דף או על כלי: ולוקמה להדי פומיה. ויעמיד אצל פיו: דחיים פומיה. שיתחמם פיו: ומייץ. וינק: דלא מנשתא. שאין נשימה ניכרת בו, שאין דופק כנגד לבו כדרך כל אדם: לינפפיה בניפוותא. יניפו עליו בנפה שקורין וא"ן: דלא מעוי. אין רוחו נכנס ויוצא יפה, אליינ"א בלע"ז: סילתא דאימיה. שיליא שנולדה עמו: ולישרקיה עליה. יחליקנה על בשרו. כמו אישתרוקי אישתריקו (ע"ג ד' מ:) אשאולדי"ר: דקטין. שהוא דק: מקוטנא לאולמא. השליא ראשה א' קצר וראשה אחד רחב. יחליקוה עליו. מראש הקצר יתחילו, וימשכו לצד הרחב. כלומר: כן ירחיב זה ויתעבה: ואי אלים. ולא מחמת בריאות, אלא נפוח – לישרקיה עליה מאולמא לקוטנא: דסומק. כל בשרו אדום: לא איבלע ביה דמיה. בבשרו, דעכשיו כל דמו מלוי בין עור לבשר, וכשמוהלין אותו יוצא כל דמו: ליתרחו ליה. ימתינו מלמולו: לא נפל ביה דמא. לא בא בו דם, ומתוך כך חלש הוא ואין בו כח, וממהר לחלוש ולמות: לכרכי הים. ה"ג: ראיתיו שהיה ירוק. הצצתי בו ולא היה בו דם ברית, תרתי לגריעותא. חדא, דהאי מהיל ליה לא נפק מיניה דמא, והטפת דם ברית מצוה, כדכתיב (זכריה ט): "גם את בדם בריתך". ועוד, דמסוכן הוא, ומשום חולשא, שלא נולד בו עדיין דם:

מתני'

[ובתרגום שלפנינו ליתא ובע"ז כט: פירש רש"י חוספניתא סדקין שבפני אדם]

הכא מיחזי כבורר. מיהו, בורר לא הוי, שגם הפסולת ראוי לאכילה. ולא דמי למשמרת דריש "תולין" (לקמן ד' קלז:), דהיכא למ"ד חייב משום בורר: מי

עין משפט נר מצוה

כג א מיי' פ"ב מהלכות מילה הל' יוד סמג עשין כח טוש"ע י"ד סי' רסו סעיף ו:

כד ב ג מיי' פ"ג מהל' י"ט הלכה יז סמג לאוין עה טוש"ע א"ח סי' תקי סעיף ג: [וכרב אלפס ביצה פ"ב קנג: ע"ש וברא"ש שם סי' כג]:

כה ד שם סעיף ה:

כו ה טוש"ע י"ד סי' רסד סעיף ג בהג"ה:

כז ו ז מיי' פ"א מהל' מילה הלכה יז טוש"ע י"ד סי' רסג סעיף א:

מסורת הש"ס

[פי' כעין קרום הצומח בעור הפנים ומתקלף. ערוך]

[תוספ' פי"ג]

[לקמן קלט:]

[ביצה כג.]

[קידושין לא: ושם נסמן]

[גי' הערוך בערך סטר אבראי]

[פי' שאין יכול להשתין ערוך ע' שתס]

[פי' שאין מוציא הבל מחוטמו ערוך]

[חולין מז: תוספ' פט"ו ע"ש]

הגהות הב"ח

(א) גמ' דילמא מידביק גרדתא מיניה: (ב) שם מיקר הוא דקר:

גליון הש"ס

גמ' מימי לא מלאני לבי. לעיל דף קיח ע"ב:

רבינו חננאל

ברוקה. ולא קמה ופשוטה היא ובא רב אשי להעמידה כר' יוסי דנראה בעליל ואיפשטא במנחות בתחלת פ' ר' ישמעאל הכי לאו א"ר יוסי התם כיון דאפשר לא טרחינן הכא נמי כיון דאפשר לא טרחינן ונדחת גם זו ואתו נהרדעי ואוקמוה כרבנן דפליגי עליה דר' יוסי במנחות פרק שתי הלחם נילושות דתנן ד' כהנים נכנסים ב' בידם ב' סדרים וב' בידם ב' בזיכין וד' מקדמין לפניהם ב' ליטול ב' סדרים וב' ליטול ב' בזיכין המכניסין עומדין בצפון ופניהם לדרום והמוציאין עומדים בדרום ופניהם לצפון. אלו מושכין ואלו מניחין טפחיים של זה בצד טפחו של זה שנא' לפני תמיד. ר' יוסי אומר אפילו אלו נוטלין ואלו מניחין אף זו היתה תמיד. שמעינן מדבריהם שאו' אלו מושכין ואלו מניחין. פי' מושכין את לחם הפנים לא שמערין אותו מעל השלחן כולו אלא מושכין אותו מעט מעט ומתגלה מקצת השלחן ובאותו מקצת המגולה מניחין הלחם המכניסין החדש. וכן עושין טפחו של זה בצד טפחו של זה וסבירא להו שאם נטלו הישן מעל השלחן אין מחזירין אותו אלא כיון שסילק הלחם הישן ונשאר השלחן שעה אחת בלא לחם עברו על הכתוב לפני תמיד ואע"פ שיש לו רשות להדר הא חדש [הוא] מהא שמעינן שהפורש מן המצוה אין לו עוד לחזור עליה להדרה. ומצאנו בתלמוד א"י המל ימול מיכן לשתי מילות אחת למילה ואחת לפריעה. אחת למילה ואחת לציצין כדברי ר' עקיבא ולר' ישמעאל דסבירא ליה דברה תורה כלשון בני אדם נפקא ליה מהא דא"ר יהודה בן פזי אז אמרה חתן דמים למולות מיכן ב' מילות למילה ולפריעה למילה ולציצין:

ת"ר מהלקטין את המילה ואם לא הלקטו ענוש כרת. פי' מהלקטין יש מי שאומר מלקטן הציצין המעכבין את המילה כולן וכן סבירא לן ויש מי שאומר מהלקטין מלשון ילקוט שהערלה היא כמו ילקוט ובתוכו העטרה וצריך לחתוך הילקוט כולו לגלות העטרה ואם לא חתכו כולו כאלו לא מל והמל אם לא הילקט בשבת כל הציצין המעכבין את המילה כאלו לא מל וחילל השבת וענוש כרת. והאי דאמרו לא מספקת אינה התראה ואינו מתכוון לחלל את השבת אלא לעשות מצוה מכוון וכיון שלא עשה חייב (כדרבי) [כרת] מפני שלא הניח כיון שנכנסה השבת מוצצין. אע"ג דהאי דם מחבר הוא כיון דאי' סכנה דמיא לאספלנית וכמון ועבדינן לה בשבת פי' אספלנית: רטייה קירא שעוה והיא פסולת הדבש: חספניתא כעין קרום הצומח בעור הפנים ומתקלף ובלשון ישמעאל אל כופה סילקא בלשון ישמעאל סלק: טורפין. מערבין. פי' סילתא שיליא

רב נסים גאון

ונאמר כי כל מצות לא תעשה שבתורה שענש בה כרת לא דחיא לה מצות עשה כי התנאי שנא' בערות אשת אחיך שהוא היתר היבום בה שנאמר (דברים כה) יבמה יבא עליה לא בא אלא באשת אח גרידתא שאינה ערוה אלא משום אשת אח בלבד אבל באחות אשתו שהיא אשת אחיו ודומה לה מן ט"ו נשים המנויין במשנה לא נאמר בהן תנאי להתיר הייבום ואילו נשאו ראובן ושמעון שתי אחיות ומת ראובן ובן אין לאשתו על שמעון לא חליצה ולא ייבום ולא אתי עשה דאמר רחמנא יבמה יבא עליה ודחי (ויקרא יח) ואשה אל אחותה לא תקח שענש בה הכתוב כרת ובזה אמרה המשנה ט"ו נשים פוטרות צרותיהן וכו' ואמרו בתלמוד (יבמות דף ח) בסוף הדבר רבא אמר ערוה לא צריכא קרא דאין עשה דוחה את לא תעשה שיש בו כרת וכמו כן אם יהיה לא תעשה שאין בו כרת אבל נוסף עליו עשה שנמצא באותה מצוה עשה ולא תעשה אין לנו נמי לדחותה במצות עשה לפי שיצאת מן כלל לאו גרידא מפני הציווי שנתוסף עליה ואפילו שתי מצות עשה שהן זו כנגד זו ואין אחת מכרעת מחברתה אין לנו לדחות אחת מהן מפני האחרת כמו שנאמר בתלמוד בפרק תמיד נשחט (פסחים דף נט) בשלמא לתנא קמא יבא עשה דפסח שיש בה כרת וידחה עשה דהשלמה שאין בו כרת אלא לר' ישמעאל בנו של ר' יוחנן בן ברוקא מכדי האי עשה והאי עשה מאי אולמיה דהאי עשה מהאי עשה וכל שכן אם יהיה עשה ולא תעשה שמן הדין לקיים אותם יותר מלקיים העשה בלבד שכנגדם אלא אם יהיה דבר מיוחד שייחדו הכתוב או החכמים שנעשה כמו שהוא מפורש ואנו מזכירים עיקר שתקיש לו כל מה שתמצא מזה הענין ונאמר אמר הקב"ה ביום אחד לחודש השביעי שהוא יום ראש השנה (ויקרא כג) יהיה לכם שבתון זה מקרא מלא בציווי השביתה ואמר עוד מלאכת עבודה לא תעשו הזהיר בו מלעשות מלאכות מיוחדות נמצא עלינו בקידוש היום עצמו עשה ולא תעשה עוד ציונו בו לתקוע בשופר שנאמר (במדבר כט) יום תרועה יהיה לכם ובעת שלא תיקננו השופר מערב יום טוב והוצרכנו ביום טוב עצמו לתקוע בשופר לקיים המצוה ואי אפשר להיות דבר זה אלא עד שנחתוך השופר ונתקן אותו ונחלל קדושת היום ראוי לנו שנניח מצות שופר שהיא עשה ולא נחלל היום שיש בחיוב קידושו עשה ולא תעשה שאי אפשר שיבא עשה בלבד וידחה עשה ולא תעשה יחדו וכגון זה מילה שלא בזמנה והוא מי שנתאחר לאחר יום ח' מחמת חולי שאירע לתינוק או מפני הספק כמו ששנינו (לקמן דף קלז) בין השמשות ערב שבת נימול לי' יום טוב אחר שבת נמול לי"א וכשתהיה מילה שלא בזמנה אינה מותרת ביום טוב כי יום טוב יש בו עשה ולא תעשה ולא יבוא עשה של מילה ודחי עשה ולא תעשה של יום טוב אלא בזמנה שהוא יום ח' ודאי שבו נאמר (ויקרא יב) וביום השמיני ימול ואמרו בפירוש וביום ואפי' בשבת אבל שלא בזמנה אפי' יום טוב אינה דוחה שאין עשה דוחה את לא תעשה ועשה אלא נזיר מצורע כי פירש בראיות ברורות שעשה ידחה את לא תעשה ועשה שבו וביאור זה כי הקב"ה צוה הנזיר שיגדל שער ראשו מאחר שהקדים האזהרה

מתני' מַרְחִיצִין אֶת הַקָּטָן, בֵּין לִפְנֵי הַמִּילָה וּבֵין לְאַחַר הַמִּילָה. וּמְזַלְּפִין עָלָיו בַּיָּד, אֲבָל לֹא בַּכְּלִי. ר"א בֶּן עֲזַרְיָה *אוֹמֵר: מַרְחִיצִין אֶת הַקָּטָן בַּיּוֹם הַשְּׁלִישִׁי שֶׁחָל לִהְיוֹת בַּשַּׁבָּת, שֶׁנֶּאֱמַר: °"וַיְהִי בַיּוֹם הַשְּׁלִישִׁי בִּהְיוֹתָם כֹּאֲבִים" (בראשית לד). סָפֵק וְאַנְדְּרוֹגִינוֹס – אֵין מְחַלְּלִין עָלָיו אֶת הַשַּׁבָּת. וְרַבִּי יְהוּדָה מַתִּיר בְּאַנְדְּרוֹגִינוֹס.§ **גמ'** וְהָא אָמְרַתְּ רֵישָׁא 'מַרְחִיצִין'! רַב יְהוּדָה וְרַבָּה בַּר אֲבוּהּ דְּאָמְרִי תַּרְוַיְיהוּ: "כֵּיצַד" תָּנֵי; מַרְחִיצִין אֶת הַקָּטָן בֵּין לִפְנֵי מִילָה בֵּין לְאַחַר מִילָה, כֵּיצַד – מְזַלְּפִין עָלָיו בַּיָּד, אֲבָל לֹא בַּכְּלִי. אָמַר רָבָא: וְהָא 'מַרְחִיצִין' קָתָנֵי! אֶלָּא אָמַר רָבָא, הָכִי קָתָנֵי: מַרְחִיצִין אֶת הַקָּטָן בֵּין מִלִּפְנֵי מִילָה בֵּין לְאַחַר הַמִּילָה, בַּיּוֹם הָרִאשׁוֹן – כְּדַרְכּוֹ, וּבַיּוֹם הַשְּׁלִישִׁי שֶׁחָל לִהְיוֹת בַּשַּׁבָּת – מְזַלְּפִין עָלָיו בַּיָּד, אֲבָל לֹא בַּכְּלִי. ר"א בֶּן עֲזַרְיָה אוֹמֵר: מַרְחִיצִין אֶת הַקָּטָן בַּיּוֹם הַשְּׁלִישִׁי שֶׁחָל לִהְיוֹת בַּשַּׁבָּת, שֶׁנֶּאֱמַר: "וַיְהִי בַיּוֹם הַשְּׁלִישִׁי בִּהְיוֹתָם כֹּאֲבִים". תַּנְיָא כְּוָותֵיהּ דְּרָבָא: מַרְחִיצִין הַקָּטָן בֵּין לִפְנֵי מִילָה בֵּין לְאַחַר מִילָה, בְּיוֹם רִאשׁוֹן – כְּדַרְכּוֹ, וּבַיּוֹם הַשְּׁלִישִׁי שֶׁחָל לִהְיוֹת בַּשַּׁבָּת – מְזַלְּפִין עָלָיו בַּיָּד, ר"א בֶּן עֲזַרְיָה אוֹמֵר: מַרְחִיצִין אֶת הַקָּטָן בַּיּוֹם הַשְּׁלִישִׁי שֶׁחָל לִהְיוֹת בַּשַּׁבָּת, וְאע"פ שֶׁאֵין רְאָיָה לַדָּבָר – זֵכֶר לַדָּבָר, שֶׁנֶּאֱמַר: "וַיְהִי בַיּוֹם הַשְּׁלִישִׁי בִּהְיוֹתָם כֹּאֲבִים". וּכְשֶׁהֵן מְזַלְּפִין – אֵין מְזַלְּפִין לֹא בְּכוֹס וְלֹא בִּקְעָרָה וְלֹא בִּכְלִי, אֶלָּא בַּיָּד. אֲתָאן לְתַנָּא קַמָּא. מַאי "אע"פ שֶׁאֵין רְאָיָה לַדָּבָר זֵכֶר לַדָּבָר"? מִשּׁוּם דְּגָדוֹל – לָא סָלֵיק בִּישְׂרָא הַיָּיא, קָטָן – סָלֵיק בֵּיהּ בִּישְׂרָא הַיָּיא, הַהוּא דַּאֲתָא לְקַמֵּיהּ דְּרָבָא, אוֹרֵי לֵיהּ כִּשְׁמַעְתֵּיהּ. אִיחֲלַשׁ רָבָא. אֲמַר: אֲנָא בַּהֲדֵי תַּרְגִּימְנָא דְּסָבֵי לָמָּה לִי? אֲמַרוּ לֵיהּ רַבָּנַן לְרָבָא: וְהָתַנְיָא כְּוָותֵיהּ דְּמָר! אֲמַר לְהוּ: מַתְנִיתִין כְּוָותַיְיהוּ דַּיְקָא. מִמַּאי – מִדְּקָאָמַר: "רַבִּי אֶלְעָזָר בֶּן עֲזַרְיָה אוֹמֵר: מַרְחִיצִין אֶת הַקָּטָן בַּיּוֹם הַשְּׁלִישִׁי שֶׁחָל לִהְיוֹת בַּשַּׁבָּת". אִי אָמְרַתְּ בִּשְׁלָמָא תַּנָּא קַמָּא מְזַלְּפִין קָאָמַר – הַיְינוּ דְּקָאָמַר לֵיהּ ר"א בֶּן עֲזַרְיָה מַרְחִיצִין, אֶלָּא אִי אָמְרַתְּ תַּנָּא קַמָּא מַרְחִיצִין בַּיּוֹם הָרִאשׁוֹן קָאָמַר, וּמְזַלְּפִין בַּיּוֹם הַשְּׁלִישִׁי – הַאי "רַבִּי אֶלְעָזָר בֶּן עֲזַרְיָה אוֹמֵר מַרְחִיצִין?" "אַף מַרְחִיצִין" מִיבְּעֵי לֵיהּ! כִּי אֲתָא רַב דִּימִי אָמַר רַבִּי אֶלְעָזָר: הֲלָכָה כר"א בֶּן עֲזַרְיָה. הָווּ בָּהּ בְּמַעַרְבָא: הַרְחָצַת כָּל גּוּפוֹ אוֹ הַרְחָצַת מִילָה? אֲמַר לְהוּ הַהוּא מֵרַבָּנַן, וְרַבִּי יַעֲקֹב שְׁמֵיהּ: מִסְתַּבְּרָא, הַרְחָצַת כָּל גּוּפוֹ. דְּאִי ס"ד הַרְחָצַת מִילָה – מִי גָּרַע מֵחַמִּין עַל גַּבֵּי מַכָּה, דְּאָמַר רַב: אֵין מוֹנְעִין חַמִּין וְשֶׁמֶן מֵעַל גַּבֵּי מַכָּה בַּשַּׁבָּת. מַתְקִיף לָהּ רַב יוֹסֵף: וְלָא שָׁנֵי לָךְ בֵּין חַמִּין שֶׁהוּחַמּוּ בַּשַּׁבָּת לְחַמִּין שֶׁהוּחַמּוּ מע"ש?! מַתְקִיף לָהּ רַב דִּימִי: וּמִמַּאי דְּהָכָא בְּחַמִּין שֶׁהוּחַמּוּ בַּשַּׁבָּת פְּלִיגִי, דִּילְמָא בְּחַמִּין שֶׁהוּחַמּוּ בְּעֶ"שׁ פְּלִיגִי?! אֲמַר אַבַּיֵּי: אֲנָא בְּעַאי דְּאִישְׁנֵי לֵיהּ, וְקַדֵּים וְשָׁנֵי לֵיהּ רַב יוֹסֵף: מִפְּנֵי שֶׁסַּכָּנָה הוּא לוֹ. אִיתְּמַר נַמִי, כִּי אֲתָא רָבִין א"ר אֲבָהוּ א"ר אֶלְעָזָר, וְאָמְרִי לָהּ א"ר אֲבָהוּ א"ר יוֹחָנָן: [א]הֲלָכָה כר"א בֶּן עֲזַרְיָה, בֵּין בְּחַמִּין שֶׁהוּחַמּוּ בַּשַּׁבָּת בֵּין בְּחַמִּין שֶׁהוּחַמּוּ מע"ש, בֵּין הַרְחָצַת כָּל גּוּפוֹ, בֵּין הַרְחָצַת מִילָה – מִפְּנֵי שֶׁסַּכָּנָה הִיא לוֹ.§ גּוּפָא, אָמַר רַב: אֵין מוֹנְעִין חַמִּין וְשֶׁמֶן מֵעַל גַּבֵּי מַכָּה בַּשַּׁבָּת. וּשְׁמוּאֵל אָמַר: נוֹתֵן חוּץ לַמַּכָּה, וְשׁוֹתֵת וְיוֹרֵד לַמַּכָּה. מֵיתִיבִי: [ב]אֵין נוֹתְנִין שֶׁמֶן וְחַמִּין עַל גַּבֵּי מוֹךְ לִיתֵּן עַל גַּבֵּי מַכָּה בַּשַּׁבָּת! הָתָם מִשּׁוּם סְחִיטָה. תָּא שְׁמַע: אֵין נוֹתְנִין חַמִּין וְשֶׁמֶן עַל גַּבֵּי מוֹךְ שֶׁעַל גַּבֵּי מַכָּה בַּשַּׁבָּת! הָתָם נַמִי מִשּׁוּם סְחִיטָה. תַּנְיָא כְּוָותֵיהּ דִּשְׁמוּאֵל: [ג]אֵין נוֹתְנִין חַמִּין וָשֶׁמֶן עַל גַּבֵּי מַכָּה בַּשַּׁבָּת, אֲבָל נוֹתְנִין חוּץ לַמַּכָּה, וְשׁוֹתֵת וְיוֹרֵד לַמַּכָּה. תָּנוּ רַבָּנַן: [ד]נוֹתְנִין עַל גַּבֵּי הַמַּכָּה מוֹךְ יָבֵשׁ וּסְפוֹג יָבֵשׁ, אֲבָל לֹא גֶּמִי יָבֵשׁ וְלֹא כְּתִיתִין יְבֵשִׁין. קַשְׁיָא כְּתִיתִין אַכְּתִיתִין! לָא קַשְׁיָא, [ה]הָא – בַּחֲדָתֵי, הָא – בְּעַתִּיקֵי, אָמַר אַבַּיֵּי: שְׁמַע מִינַּהּ – הָנֵי כְּתִיתִין מַסּוּ.§ "סָפֵק וְאַנְדְּרוֹגִינוֹס כו'".§ תָּנוּ רַבָּנַן: °'עָרְלָתוֹ' (ויקרא יב) – עָרְלָתוֹ וַדַּאי דּוֹחָה אֶת הַשַּׁבָּת, וְלֹא

רש"י

מתני' וּמְזַלְּפִין עָלָיו. אֶת הַסַּמִּין: בַּיָּד. אֲבָל לֹא בִּכְלִי. וּבַגְּמָ' פָּרֵיךְ: הָא אָמְרַתְּ רֵישָׁא מַרְחִיצִין, דְּמַשְׁמַע כְּדַרְכּוֹ, וַהֲדַר תָּנֵי אֲפִילּוּ לְזַלֵּף עָלָיו בִּכְלִי אָסוּר: סָפֵק. כְּגוֹן סָפֵק בֶּן ח' חֳדָשִׁים [וְסָפֵק בֶּן ט'], דְּהוּא כְּאֶבֶן בְּעָלְמָא וְאֵין מִילָתוֹ דּוֹחָה שַׁבָּת (וְסָפֵק בֶּן ט'): ר' יְהוּדָה מַתִּיר בְּאַנְדְּרוֹגִינוֹס. דְּאִיתְרַבֵּי מִקְּרָאֵי, כִּדְמְפָרֵשׁ בַּגְּמָ' לְקַמָּן: **גמ'** וְהָא אָמְרַתְּ רֵישָׁא מַרְחִיצִין. וַאֲפִילּוּ כְּדַרְכּוֹ: בֵּיצַד קָתָנֵי. מַרְחִיצִין דְּרֵישָׁא לָאו כְּדַרְכּוֹ הוּא, דְּתָנָא סֵיפָא לְפָרוּשֵׁי כֵּיצַד מַרְחִיצִין – כְּגוֹן לְזַלֵּף בַּיָּד, וַאֲפִילּוּ בְּיוֹם רִאשׁוֹן: תַּנְיָא כְּוָותֵיהּ דְּרָבָא כו'. ה"ג: בַּיּוֹם הַשְּׁלִישִׁי מְזַלְּפִין עָלָיו בַּיָּד. וְלָא גָּרְסִינַן אֲבָל לֹא בִּכְלִי: אֲתָאן לְת"ק. הָךְ סֵיפָא תַּנָּא קַמָּא אֲמָרָהּ. דְּאִילּוּ ר"א – אֲפִילּוּ הַרְחָצָה כְּדַרְכּוֹ שָׁרֵי: מִשּׁוּם דְּגָדוֹל לָא סָלֵיק בִּישְׂרָא הַיָּיא. הַיְינוּ טַעְמָא דְּמַעֲשֵׂה שְׁכֶם לָאו רְאָיָה גְּמוּרָה הִיא, מִשּׁוּם דְּגָדוֹל אֵין מַכָּה שֶׁבִּבְשָׂרוֹ מַעֲלָה אֲרוּכָה מַהֵר, אֲבָל קָטָן נִתְרַפֵּא מִידֵי סַכָּנָתוֹ מַהֵר: אוֹרֵי לֵיהּ כִּשְׁמַעְתֵּיהּ. הִתִּיר לוֹ הָרְחִיצָה כְּדַרְכּוֹ בְּיוֹם רִאשׁוֹן שֶׁחָל לִהְיוֹת בַּשַּׁבָּת: אִיחֲלַשׁ. נַעֲשָׂה חוֹלֶה, וְהָיָה דּוֹאֵג שֶׁמָּא עַל כָּךְ נֶעֱנַשׁ: אֲמַר בַּהֲדֵי תַּרְגְּמָנָא דְּסָבֵי לָמָּה לִי. מֶה הָיָה לִי לַחֲלוֹק כְּנֶגֶד זְקֵנִים הַלָּלוּ, רַב יְהוּדָה וְרַבָּה בַּר אֲבוּהּ, שֶׁפֵּירְשׁוּ שֶׁאָסוּר לְהַרְחִיץ: אִי אָמְרַתְּ בִּשְׁלָמָא ת"ק מְזַלְּפִין. בְּיוֹם רִאשׁוֹן קָאָמַר, וְלָא אַיְירֵי בְּהַרְחָצָה כְּלָל אֶלָּא בְּזִילּוּף – הַיְינוּ דְּאָתָא ר"א בֶּן עֲזַרְיָה וּפָלֵיג, וְאָמַר מַרְחִיצִין: אֶלָּא אִי אָמְרַתְּ. תַּנָּא קַמָּא נַמִי מַרְחִיצִין אָמַר בִּשְׁנֵי הַיָּמִים, וְלָא פָּלֵיג ר"א אֶלָּא אַיּוֹם שְׁלִישִׁי, דְּקָאָמַר ת"ק מְזַלְּפִין, אַף מַרְחִיצִין בַּיּוֹם הַשְּׁלִישִׁי מִיבָּעֵי לֵיהּ: הָווּ בָּהּ. דַּיְיקִי בָּהּ: דְּאִי ס"ד הַרְחָצַת מִילָה מִי גָּרַע מֵחַמִּין עַל גַּבֵּי מַכָּה. דְּשָׁרֵי, וְהָכָא אָסְרִי רַבָּנַן בִּשְׁלִישִׁי (*לְגַמְרֵי): וְלָא שָׁנֵי כו'. וְהָכָא גַּבֵּי מִילָה בְּהוּחַמּוּ בַּשַּׁבָּת עָסְקִינַן. הִלְכָּךְ, בִּשְׁלִישִׁי דְּלֵיכָּא סַכַּנְתָּא – לָא: אֲמַר אַבַּיֵּי אֲנָא בְּעַאי דְּאִישְׁנֵי לֵיהּ. אֲנִי הָיִיתִי רוֹצֶה לְתָרֵץ אַתְקַפְתָּא זוֹ כִּדְשַׁנֵּי לֵיהּ רַב יוֹסֵף, מִפְּנֵי שֶׁסַּכָּנָה הִיא לוֹ: וְקַדֵּים רַב יוֹסֵף וְשַׁנְיָיא לֵיהּ. דְּוַדַּאי מַתְנִיתִין חַמִּין שֶׁהוּחַמּוּ בַּשַּׁבָּת נַמִי שָׁרֵי בַּיָּמִים הָרִאשׁוֹנִים. וּלְר"א אַף בִּשְׁלִישִׁי, מִפְּנֵי שֶׁמְּנִיעַת חַמִּין סַכָּנָה הִיא לוֹ: אֵין נוֹתְנִין כו'. קס"ד גְּזֵרָה מִשּׁוּם שְׁחִיקַת סַמָּנִין כִּשְׁמוּאֵל. דְּטַעְמֵיהּ מִשּׁוּם הָכִי הוּא, וְהַיְינוּ דְּקָאָמַר: אֲבָל נוֹתֵן חוּץ לַמַּכָּה, דְּלָא מוֹכְחָא מִילְּתָא דִּלְרְפוּאָה: מוֹךְ יָבֵשׁ וּסְפוֹג יָבֵשׁ. דְּלָאו לִרְפוּאָה הִיא, אֶלָּא שֶׁלֹּא יִשְׂרְטוּ בְּגָדָיו הַקָּשִׁים מַכָּתוֹ: אֲבָל לֹא כְּתִיתִין יְבֵשִׁים (א) וְגֶמִי יָבֵשׁ. חֲתִיכוֹת בְּגָדִים דַּקּוֹת, מִשּׁוּם דְּמַסּוּ, וְגָזְרוּ מִשּׁוּם שְׁחִיקַת סַמָּנִין: קַשְׁיָא כְּתִיתִין אַכְּתִיתִין. רֵישָׁא שָׁרֵי מוֹךְ יָבֵשׁ, דְּהַיְינוּ כְּתִיתִין, וְסֵיפָא אָסַר כְּתִיתִין: חַדְתֵי. חֲדָשִׁים שֶׁלֹּא הָיוּ עַל גַּבֵּי מַכָּה מֵעוֹלָם – מַסּוּ, עַתִּיקֵי לָא מַסּוּ: ה"ג. שְׁמַע מִינַּהּ הָנֵי כְּתִיתִין מַסּוּ: עָרְלָתוֹ וַדַּאי דּוֹחָה הַשַּׁבָּת. דְּבַהַאי קְרָא "וּבַיּוֹם הַשְּׁמִינִי" יָלְפִינַן מִינֵּיהּ אֲפִילּוּ בַּשַּׁבָּת, כְּתִיב בְּסֵיפֵיהּ "עָרְלָתוֹ", דְּמַשְׁמַע מִיעוּטָא: עָרְלָתוֹ שֶׁל זֶה, וְלֹא שֶׁל אַחֵר. וּלְמַעוּטֵי סָפֵק אָתָא: אַנְדְּרוֹגִינוֹס

תוספות

מי גרע מחמין על גבי מכה. והיכי אסרי רבנן בשלישי, אע"ג דאיכא למימר דרב אמרה למילתיה כר"א בן עזריה, דפסקינן לעיל הלכתא כוותיה משמע ליה דלכ"ע קאמר. ועוד, דאפילו לר"א בן עזריה פריך, דמשמע דשרי בשלישי משום סכנה, מדמייתי קרא: "ויהי ביום השלישי" ורב איירי במכה שאין בה סכנה: **ואין** מונעין חמין ושמן. פירש ה"ר יוסף פורת בשם רבינו שמואל: דבמעורבת יחד איירי, דאי כל חד באפי נפשיה – מאי קמ"ל בשמן, מתני' היא בפ' "שמנה שרצים" (לעיל דף קיא.): אבל סך הוא את השמן. והיינו – אפילו על גבי מכה, מדקתני: בני מלכים סכין ע"ג מכותיהן שמן וורד. מכלל דבשאר שמן – מותר לאחר אפילו ע"ג מכה. ושמואל נמי, היכי הוה פליג:

ולא

רבינו חננאל

מקוטמא לאולמא ממקום הדק לעבה: ת"ר דברים שאין עושין למילה בשבת עושין לה ביו"ט שוחקין כמון וטורפין לה יין ושמן יין בפ"ע ושמן בפ"ע אבל ע"י ליכא [אסור]. פי' ליכא עירוב יין ושמן להוליך השמן בתוך היין על [ידי] עירובו. (אבל) א"ל אביי לרבה מהו לגבן. פי' לגבן ביו"ט לקפות גבינה לקבץ פיתותי החלב הקפוי ולעשותם חריץ של גבינה. א"ל אסור לגבן. א"ל והלא גיבון כמו לישת העיסה שנותן מים בקמח ומולל בידיו ועושה פתיתין ומוסיף מים ומקבץ הפתיתין ועושה אותם עיסה. כך מקפה החלב בטוכמסו ואחר שיקפה בכלי ויעמוד מכנים ידו ופיתתו. ואח"כ מכנים ידו ומגבן מתוך הכים. הנה גיבון ולישה מלאכתן שוה מפני מה זה מותר וזה אסור ופירק לו קמח אי אפשר לאוכלו אלא ע"י לישה ביומו. והחלב אפשר לאכלו חלב או לעשותו גבינה בערב. אקשינן עלה והא אמרו נהרדעי גבינה בת יומא מעליא והנה היא כמו הלישה וכשם שהפת חמה מעליא כך הגבינה בת יומא מעליא ופריק ליה הכי קאמר אפילו בת יומא מעליא מכלל שבת שנים ושלשה ימים מעליא טפי ואפילו בת יומא מעליא: **אין** עושין למילה חלוק לכתחילה אבל כורך עליה סמרטוט: **מתניתין** מרחיצין את הקטן בין לפני המילה ובין לאחר המילה ומזלפין עליו אבל לא בכלי. ואקשי היאך קתני מזלפין מכלל שרחיצה אסורה והא רישא דמתניתין קתני מרחיצין ופרק' רב יהודה ורבה בר אבוה אמר כך סידור המשנה מרחיצין את הקטן בין לפני המילה ובין לאחר המילה. והרחצה זו כיצד היא ע"י זילוף היא ביד אבל לא בכלי. ואקשי עליהו רבה והא מרחיצין קתני וזילוף אינה רחיצה ופריק רבא משנתנו הא דקתני מרחיצין ביום ראשון של מילה אם היא שבת רחיצה כדרכו בין לפני המילה בין לאחר המילה וביום השלישי שחל להיות בשבת מזלפין ביד אבל לא בבלי ותניא כוותיה דרבא ואע"ג דתניא כוותיה לפום דקדוקא דמתניתין לא מיתוקמה כתירוציה דהא רבה כנפשיה אורי כשמעתיה ואיחלש ועיין במתניתין שפיר וחזא דלכאורה כתירוציה רהטא. וכי עיין בה

עין משפט נר מצוה

בח א מיי' פ"ב מהל' מילה הלכה ח ופ"ב מהל' שבת הלכה יד סמג עשין כח טוש"ע א"ח סי' של סעיף ט:

בט ב ג מיי' פכ"א מהל' שבת הלכה כו טוש"ע א"ח סי' שכח סעיף כב:

ל ד ה מיי' שם טוש"ע שם סעיף כג:

מסורת הש"ס

לעיל פו. ע"ש

רש"ל מ"ז וא"ל למתוק וקאי למאי דהסכים רבה לפי הסבר דקיקא כוותיה ולא התיר ת"ק אפי' לזלף ביום ג'

הגהות הב"ח

(א) רש"י ד"ה אבל לא כתיתין יבשים חתיכות כנ"ל ותיבות וגמי יבש נמחק:

רב נסים גאון

האזהרה עליו שלא יגלחנו שנאמר (במדבר ו) גדל פרע שער ראשו אחר שאמר תער לא יעלה על ראשו הרי הוא בדבר זה מוזהר בלאו ומצווה בעשה וחייב המצורע בעת טהרתו לגלח כל שער שבגופו שנאמר (ויקרא יד) והיה ביום השביעי יגלח את כל שערו וכשיתנגע הנזיר בצרעת ויגיע יום ז' שהוא חייב לגלח בו אמרו חכמים שמצות גילוח של צרעת דוחה עשה ולא תעשה שיש עליו לענין נזירותו וכי מה שאמר הכתוב לענין מצורע את ראשו אחר שאמר יגלח את כל שערו לא בא אלא לענין נזיר שנאמר בו תער לא יעבור על ראשו לומר כי זו המצוה אינו חייב בה אלא בעת שלא תהיה בו צרעת אבל בעת שיהיה בגופו צרעת יגלח את ראשו אפי' שער ראשו שהזהרתיו שלא יגלחנו בימי נזירותו חייב לגלח אם היה צרוע נתקיים לנו מזה שבנזיר מצורע לבדו יבא עשה ודחי לא תעשה ועשה ובראש מס' יבמות (דף ה) אמרו אלא דקיימא לן דאין עשה דחי לא תעשה ועשה ליגמר מנזיר דאתי עשה ודחי לא תעשה ועשה אלא מנזיר לא גמרינן שכן ישנן בשאלה ובארו כי דבר זה הוא מיוחד בו לבדו ולא בזולתו וכי בכל התורה כולה לא אתי עשה ודחי לא תעשה ועשה והזהר לשמור אלו העיקרים שפירשנו שמהן מתבארים לך כל דבר כשתמצא בתלמוד מעין אלו הענינים: **תינח** גדול דכתיב ביה בשר קטן נמי כתיב ביה בשר בינוני מנלן פי' כבר ידענו כי הקטנים פטורים ממצות והשכר והעונש הם תלויין בחיוב המצות ומאחר שנדע כי לא חייב הכתוב במצות אלא לפי שיש בו עניני החיוב כגון שהביא ב' שערות ושהגיע למספר שני האנשים ושיצא מגבול הנערות אז הוא בן עונשין וכיון שראינו שענש הכתוב מי שלא נימול שנאמר (בראשית יז) וערל זכר אשר לא ימול את בשר ערלתו ונכרתה וגו' ידענו כי דבר זה מיוחד הוא באנשים גדולים ולא בנערים ומצאנו כתב בו בשר ערלתו להודיענו שהמילה דוחה את הצרעת על דרך העיקר שהקדמנו דאתי עשה ודחי לא תעשה וכי בעת שתהיה בערלה בהרת ימול ויחתוך אותה וידחה מה שכתוב (דברים כד) השמר בנגע הצרעת והוצרכנו שיבאר לנו דבר זה להסיר מדעתנו מה שהיה עולה עליו שמה היינו סוברים כי זה שכתב (שם) לשמור מאד ולעשות הוא דבר מוסף על הלאו והוה ליה לא תעשה ועשה ואין המילה דוחה אותן שאין עשה דוחה את לא תעשה ועשה והסיר ממנו סברא זו והודיענו שהוא לא תעשה בלבד והמילה דוחה אותה וזהו שאמרו תינח גדול דכתב ביה בשר והקטן נמי שהוא בן ח' ימים נאמר בו וביום השמיני ימול בשר ערלתו ידענו כי המילה ביום ח' תדחה (עוד) את הצרעת נשאר לנו לשאול על הבינוני והוא שעברו עליו ח' ימים ולא נימול מפני מאורע שאירע לו כגון שהיה חולה או שהיה בו ספק התהיה המילה ראויה בו בעת שיש בהרת בערלתו או לא ולפיכך אמרו בינוני מנלן ובאה התשובה משם אביי דאתיא מבנייא ומשם רבא מילה בזמנה [לא] צריכא קרא כו' ופירוש על דעת אביי שהמילה מותרת בבינוני במקום שיש בהרת נלמוד מגדול וקטן כמו ששנינו (ריש ספרא) בבנין אב משני כתובים הצד השוה שבהן כו' וכן הוא הילוך הדבר בכאן כי הבינוני לא יתכן שנלמוד מן הגדול לפי שהגדול ענוש כרת לכך התירו בו הכתוב חתיכת הבהרת אבל הבינוני שאין בו חיוב כרת אין דבר זה מותר בו וכמו כן לא נלמוד דבר זה מן הקטן כי הקטן מילתו בזמנה ביום ח' והיא דוחה את השבת ולפיכך התיר הכתוב חתיכת הבהרת אבל הבינוני שאין מילתו בזמנה לא ומאחר שלא יכולנו ללמוד דבר זה מאחד מהן חיברנו אותם ביחד וקיימנו דבר עיקר מהם שהבינוני מותר לחתוך בהרת מערלתו וכן הילוכו של דבר בענין זה בינוני מנלן אמר אביי אתיא מבניינא מה לגדול שכן ענוש כרת קטן יוכיח שאינו ענוש כרת מה לקטן שכן מילה בזמנה גדול יוכיח שאין מילה בזמנה וחזר הדין הצד השוה שבהן שמילתו דוחה את הצרעת אף אני אביא בינוני שתהא מילתו דוחה את הצרעת ורבא לא הוצרך לדבר זה כי הוא סובר כי בשר ערלתו שנאמר בבן שמנת ימים לא בא להתיר מילת בן שמונת ימים במקום שיש בהרת כי זה נלמדנו מקל וחומר השתא שבת חמורה דוחה צרעת קלה לא כל שכן והואיל ואינו צריך לבן ח' ימים הועיל להתיר המילה בבינוני במקום שיש בהרת: **לא** צריכא אפי' ר' יהודה דאמר דבר שאינו מתכוין אסור כבר פירשנו זה בפ' כירה. לבדו ולא מילה שלא בזמנה

ולא ספק דוחה את השבת. ערלתו ודאי דוחה את השבת, [א]ולא אנדרוגינוס דוחה את השבת. רבי יהודה אומר: אנדרוגינוס דוחה את השבת וענוש כרת. ערלתו ודאי דוחה את השבת, [ב]ולא נולד בין השמשות דוחה את השבת. ערלתו ודאי דוחה את השבת, [ג]ולא נולד כשהוא מהול דוחה את השבת. שב"ש אומרים: צריך להטיף ממנו דם ברית, וב"ה אומרים: אינו צריך. *א"ר שמעון בן אלעזר: לא נחלקו ב"ש וב"ה *[ד]על נולד כשהוא מהול שצריך להטיף ממנו דם ברית, מפני שערלה כבושה היא. על מה נחלקו – על גר שנתגייר כשהוא מהול, שבית שמאי אומרים: [ה]צריך להטיף ממנו דם ברית, ובה"א: א"צ להטיף ממנו דם ברית.§ אמר מר: "ולא ספק דוחה את השבת". לאתויי מאי? לאתויי הא דתנו רבנן: *[ו]בן שבעה מחללין עליו את השבת, ובן ח' אין מחללין עליו את השבת. ספק בן ז' ספק בן ח' – אין מחללין עליו את השבת. *בן שמונה הרי הוא כאבן, ואסור לטלטלו. אבל אמו שוחה ומניקתו מפני הסכנה. איתמר, רב אמר: הלכה כת"ק, ושמואל אמר: הלכה כר"ש בן אלעזר. רב אדא בר אהבה אתיליד ליה ההוא ינוקא כשהוא מהול, אהדריה אתליסר מוהלאי עד דשוייה כרות שפכה. אמר: תיתי לי דעברי אדרב. אמר ליה רב נחמן: ואדשמואל לא עבר?! אימר דאמר שמואל בחול, בשבת מי אמר(א)? הוא סבר: ודאי ערלה כבושה היא. דאיתמר, רבה אמר: חיישינן שמא ערלה כבושה היא, רב יוסף אמר: ודאי ערלה כבושה היא. אמר רב יוסף: מנא אמינא לה – דתניא, רבי אליעזר הקפר אומר: לא נחלקו ב"ש וב"ה על נולד כשהוא מהול – שצריך להטיף ממנו דם ברית, על מה נחלקו – לחלל עליו את השבת. ב"ש אומרים: מחללין עליו את השבת, וב"ה אומרים: אין מחללין עליו את השבת. לאו מכלל דת"ק סבר "מחללין עליו את השבת"? ודילמא: ת"ק דברי הכל אין מחללין קאמר? אם כן, רבי אליעזר הקפר טעמא דב"ש אתא לאשמעינן?! דילמא ה"ק: *לא נחלקו ב"ש וב"ה בדבר זה.§ *)אמר ר' אסי: כל שאמו טמאה לידה – נימול לשמונה, וכל שאין אמו טמאה לידה – אין נימול לשמונה, שנאמר: °"אשה כי תזריע וילדה זכר וטמאה וגו' וביום השמיני ימול בשר ערלתו". א"ל אביי: דורות הראשונים יוכיחו, שאין אמו טמאה לידה – ונימול לשמונה! א"ל: *נתנה תורה ונתחדשה

ויקרא יב

*) [נ"ל אמר רבה אמר ר' אסי כל שאמו וכו' וכן איתא בשאלתות פ' לך לך סי' ט וכ"א ברי"ף והרא"ש].

רש"י

אנדרוגינוס. ספק הוא. ונולד בין השמשות נמי ספק זמנו הוא ספק אינו זמנו. וכן נולד מהול, ספק שמא ערלה כבושה היא, העור דבוק בבשר. ולקמיה פריך: ספק קמא לאתויי מאי? הואיל ותני כל הני ספיקי: רבי יהודה אומר כו'. לקמיה יליף מילתיה: שב"ש אומרים צריך להטיף כו'. ואפילו הכי מודו דשבת לא דחי: שצריך להטיף. חיישינן שמא ערלה כבושה היא: על גר. דליכא שום ספק ערלה, כגון ערבי מהול: בן ח' אין מחללין עליו. שהרי כמת הוא, ואין מילתו מצוה. ואי קשיא: א"כ לאו חילול הוא, שהרי הוא כמחתך בבשר מת – לקמן נמי מוקי האי חילול במכשירי מילה, ואליבא דר' אליעזר: מפני הסכנה. מפני שחלב הרבה(ב) בדדיה, ומביאה לידי חולי: כת"ק. אליבא דב"ה, דאמר א"צ להטיף ממנו דם ברית: אהדריה אתליסר מוהלאי. שיטיפו ממנו דם ברית, ולא רצו משום דשבת הואי, ואפילו לב"ש ספק הוא ואין מחללין: עד דשוייה כרות שפכה. והוא עצמו מלו, ועשאו כרות שפכה, שחתך מן הגיד: אדרב. דאמר: א"צ להטיף: בשבת מי אמר. הא ספיקא הוא: והוא סבר. רב אדא סבר דודאי ערלה כבושה היא, ומחללינן: חיישינן. הא דאמר ר"ש בן אלעזר: לדברי הכל צריך להטיף – אספיקא קאמר, ובחול, שמא ערלה כבושה היא. ולענין שבת נמי ודאי לא מחללינן: ודאי ערלה כבושה היא. ומחללינן: לאו מכלל דת"ק. דר' אליעזר הקפר סבר דברי הכל מחללין, ואנא דאמרי כוותיה: ה"ג: וממאי דילמא מכלל דת"ק סבר דברי הכל אין מחללין א"כ רבי אליעזר טעמא דב"ש אתא לאשמעינן כו'. א"כ דתנא לעיל מיניה אמר דברי הכל אין מחללין, ר' אליעזר הקפר דאתא לאיפלוגי ולמימר דלאו דברי הכל הוא, דהא לב"ש מחללין – מאי רבותא אשמעינן דב"ש פליגי בה? הא ב"ש במקום ב"ה אינה משנה! *ומשנינן: דילמא הכי קאמר ר' אליעזר לת"ק, דאמר בשבת לדברי הכל אין מחללין, ופלוגתייהו בחול, דלב"ה א"צ להטיף ממנו דם ברית – הא ליתא, דלא נחלקו בדבר זה. אלא ודאי צריך, ובשבת הוא דפליגי, וטעמא דב"ה אתא לאשמעינן, דבחול צריך, ולאפוקי מת"ק דאמר לב"ה לא צריך: כל שאין אמו טמאה לידה. כגון יוצא דופן, וגויה שילדה ולמחר נתגיירה – אין בנה ממתין עד שמנה, אלא נימול מיד: דורות הראשונים. מאברהם עד מתן תורה, שנתנה מילה ולא נהגו טומאה: ונתחדשה

תוספות

ולא ספק דוחה את השבת. נראה לר"י: דאסמכתא בעלמא הוא, ולא איצטריך קרא להכי דהיכי תיסוק אדעתיה לחלל את השבת, ולא ידענא אם הוא בר חיוב מילה או לא, כדמפרש לקמן דספק נולד לז' או לח'. ומשום נולד בין השמשות לא איצטריך נמי קרא, דמוטב דתיבטל מצות מילה בשמיני מספיקא בשב ואל תעשה ואל יחלל שבת בידים מספק. אלא נראה לר"י: דעיקר האי קרא אתא לאנדרוגינוס, שאינו דוחה שבת, ונולד כשהוא מהול. ומיהו, לא מחד "ערלתו" נפקי, דאין סברא לומר שקולים ויבואו שניהם, אלא תרי קראי כתיבי; חד במילה בזמנה: "וביום השמיני ימול בשר ערלתו", וחד במילה שלא בזמנה *)דגדול: "וערל זכר אשר לא ימול בשר ערלתו" (בראשית יז). א"נ קרא אתא לאנדרוגינוס, ונולד כשהוא מהול מסברא ידעינן דאין צריך להטיף דם ברית, ר"י. אי נמי: עיקר קרא לנולד כשהוא מהול, ולאנדרוגינוס לא צריך קרא. דהא נפקא ליה לר' יהודה לקמן דאנדרוגינוס טעון מילה מדכתיב: "כל זכר", ורבנן הוו דרשי לדרשה אחריתי:

לא נחלקו על נולד כשהוא מהול שצריך להטיף ממנו דם ברית כו' על מה נחלקו על גר שנתגייר. השתא משמע דיותר יש להצריך הטפה לנולד כשהוא מהול, מלנתגייר כשהוא מהול. דהא לנולד כ"ע מודו, ובגר איכא פלוגתא וא"כ לקמן דפסיק רב הלכה כת"ק, ומשמע דכוותיה קי"ל מדקאמר רב אדא בר אהבה תיתי לי דעברי אדרב. וכיון דקי"ל כת"ק בנולד כשהוא מהול, שאין צריך להטיף ממנו דם ברית – כ"ש גר שנתגייר כשהוא מהול. וה"ג לא פסקו כן, אלא פסקו דקטן א"צ, וגר צריך. ובקטן ודאי כדין פסקו כשמועתנו. ובגר נמי נראה לר"י שסמכו אההיא דיבמות דפרק "החולץ" (דף מו:), דתניא: הרי שבא ואמר מלתי ולא טבלתי, מטבילין אותו ומה בכך, דברי רבי יהודה. ור' יוסי אומר: אין מטבילין. ואת"ל דא"צ להטיף ממנו דם ברית, בנתגייר כשהוא מהול. לרבי יוסי אמאי אין מטבילין הרי הוא מהול לפנינו, מאי נפקא מינה אם לא מלו אותו ב"ד, לא יהא אלא ערבי מהול וגבעוני מהול? אלא ודאי צריך להטיף ממנו דם ברית, ולכך אין מטבילין דאינו גר עד שימול ויטבול. ונראה לרשב"א לתת טעם בדבר, שהרי הסברא הפוכה מסברא דשמעתין. והיינו טעמא: דבין קטן שנולד כשהוא מהול ובין גר שנתגייר כשהוא מהול – דין הוא דשניהם היו טעונים הטפת דם ברית, אי לאו דדרשינן הכא דקטן אין צריך להטיף ממנו, משום דכתיב "ערלתו". ודוקא בקטן דגלי – גלי, בגר דלא גלי – לא גלי. ור"ת פסק איפכא מה"ג:

בן שמנה הרי הוא כאבן ואסור לטלטלו. נראה לר"י דעכשיו מותר לטלטל כל תינוקות, שאין אנו בקיאין, וכולם כמו ספק בן ח' ספק בן ט' ופעמים שהאשה מתעברת סמוך לטבילתה, ופעמים שאינה מתעברת. ומותר למולו בשבת ממ"נ, כדאמרינן לקמן (דף קלו.): אפילו הוא בן שמנה ודאי כגון שלא בא על אשתו אלא פעם אחת ופירש, וילדה לסוף ח' – אפילו הכי נראה לר"י דמותר לטלטלו ולמולו בשבת אם אין ריעותא בשערו ובציפרניו, כדאמר בפרק "הערל" (יבמות דף פ:), דאמרינן: האי בר שבעה הוא ואישתהויי אישתהי: מפני הסכנה. סכנת חלב כשיש הרבה בדדין, ולא חיישינן שמא תטלטל אותו. ולא(ג) ידע רשב"א מאי איריא מפני הסכנה, דאפילו לא יהא אלא לצערא בעלמא מותר*, אפילו (ד) היא לחלוב עצמה ולהוציא חלב שבדדין, אע"פ שהיא מלאכה שאינה צריכה לגופה – דחמיר איסורא טפי מאיסור טלטול – נראה דשרי, מידי דהוה אמפיס מורסא, דשרינן משום צערא: מכלל דת"ק סבר ד"ה מחללין. ר' אליעזר הקפר ור"ש בן אלעזר תרווייהו קיימי את"ק. וה"ק ליה ר"א הקפר לר"ש בן אלעזר: לא כך יש להשיב על דברי ת"ק, אלא הכי אית לן למימר: לא נחלקו כו'. והשתא דייק שפיר, מכלל דת"ק סבר וכו'. פירוש רשב"א:

כתנאי

*) נ"ל דגדול ובכלך אם אינו ענין לשלא בזמנו שאף לודאי אינו דוחה.

עין משפט נר מצוה

לא א ב ג מיי' פ"א מהל' מילה הלכה יא סמג עשין כח טוש"ע א"ח סי' שלא סעי' ה וטוש"ע י"ד סי' רסו סעיף ח וסעיף י:

לב ד מיי' שם הלכה א סמג שם טוש"ע יד סי' רסג סעי' ד:

לג ה מיי' וסמג שם ומיי' פי"ד מהל' איסורי ביאה הלכה ה טוש"ע י"ד סי' רסח סעי' א:

לד ו מיי' פ"א מהל' מילה הלכה יד ופכ"ה מהל' שבת הלכה ו טוש"ע א"ח סי' של סעי' ז ח וי"ד סי' רס"ו סעי' יא בהג"ה:

מסורת הש"ס

(תוספ' פט"ז) יבמות עא. (תוספ' פט"ז) יבמות פ. ב"ק כ. [יבמות מו:] [לעיל מב. יבמות כח. ב"ק לב. סוכה טו.] [ב"ק קי:]

הגהות הב"ח

(א) גמ' מי אמרו הוא סבר: (ב) רש"י ד"ה מפני הסכנה וכו' שחלב הרבה. נ"ב וכמש' יבמות דף ע פירש"י משום סכנת שניים: (ג) תוס' ד"ה מפני הסכנה וכו' ולא ידע רשב"א מאי איריא כצ"ל ותיבת באי"ד רשב"א נמחק: (ד) בא"ד אפי' חלוב בעצמה כצ"ל ותיבת היא נמחק:

רבינו חננאל

יאות איתברר ליה כתירוציה דרב יהודה ורבה בר אבוה. דאי כתירוצ' דידיה דאוקמא למתניתין שאמרו חכמים מרחיצין ביום ראשון בשבת כדרכו ומזלפין ביום שלישי שחל להיות בשבת ר' אלעזר בן עזריה אומר אף מרחיצין ביום שלישי שחל להיות בשבת היה צריך לומר מפני שאמרו חכמים יום ג' שחל להיות בשבת מזלפין בא הוא ואמר מזלפין ואף מרחיצין אלא מכיון (כולא) [דלא] אמר כך שמעינן מינה שלא הזכירו חכמים ביום ג' שחל להיות בשבת לא רחיצה ולא זילוף. ומומילא שמעינן דלית להו לרבנן ביום השלישי לא רחיצה ולא זילוף. ר' אלעזר בן עזריה אומר מרחיצין את המילה ביום השלישי שחל להיות בשבת שנאמר ויהי ביום השלישי בהיותם כואבים וכ"ש ביום ראשון וקיי"ל כר' אלעזר בן עזריה דאמרי' א"ר אבהו א"ר יוחנן הלכה כר' אלעזר בן עזריה בין בחמין שהוחמו בשבת ובין חמין שהוחמו בע"ש. בין הרחצת כל גופו בין הרחצת מילה. מפני שסכנה היא לו: גופא אמר רב אין מונעין חמין ושמן מע"ג מכה בשבת ושמואל אמר נותנין חוץ למכה ושותת ויורד למכה. ואע"ג דקיי"ל רב ושמואל הלכה כרב באיסורי הכא הלכה כשמואל דתניא כוותיה. אין נותנין חמין ושמן ע"ג מכה בשבת אבל נותן חוץ למכה ושותת ויורד למכה. תני רב נותנין ע"ג מכה מוך יבש וספוג יבש אבל לא גמי יבש ולא כתיתין יבשין. קשיא כתיתין אכתיתין. רישא קתני נותנין ע"ג המכה מוך יבש והוא כתיתין והדר תני ולא כתיתין יבשין ופרקינן לא קשיא הא בחדתי והוא מוך יבש מותר שאין חשובין כרטיה. אבל כתיתין ישנין אסורין. ועלה אמר אביי ש"מ האי נקרא מסו. פי' נקרא היא כתיתין והן סמרטוטין יבשים שיש עליהם טינוף צואה ריעי. כדגרסינן בע"ז ליתו נקרא מקיקלתא כו': ת"ר ערלתו ערלתו ודאי דוחה את השבת ולא ספק דוחה את השבת ערלתו ודאי דוחה את השבת ולא אנדרוגינוס דוחה את השבת וכו' אמר מר ולא ספק דוחה את השבת לאתויי הא דתנו רבנן בן ז' מחללין עליו את השבת בן ח' אין מחללין עליו את השבת ספק בן ח' אין מחללין עליו את השבת בן ח' הרי הוא כאבן ואסור לטלטלו בשבת. אבל אמו שוחה עליו ומניקתו מפני הסכנה. (צריך לכתוב תשלום הברייתא כמות שהיא בתוספתא). אתמר רב אמר הלכתא כת"ק דברייתא דאמר הא דתני ולא נולד כשהוא מהול דוחה את השבת שבית שמאי אומרים צריך להטיף ממנו דם ברית וב"ה אומרים אין צריך להטיף ממנו דם ברית ושמואל אמר הלכה כר' שמעון בן אלעזר שאמר לא נחלקו בית שמאי ובית הלל על הנולד מהול שצריך להטיף ממנו דם ברית דכיון שר' שמעון בן אלעזר סתמא א' יש לומר לא אמר אלא בחול אבל בשבת לא אמר דומיא דסיפא דקתני סיפא על מה נחלקו על גר שנתגייר כשהוא מהול שב"ש אומרים צריך להטיף ממנו דם ברית וב"ה אין צריך וברור הוא שאין מילה לגר בשבת ועל זה אמר שמואל הלכה כר' שמעון בן אלעזר והוא בחול ולא בשבת. וחלקו עוד בנולד כשהוא מהול רבה ורב יוסף רבה אמר חיישינן שמא ערלה כבושה היא ורב יוסף אמר ודאי ערלה כבושה היא וראינו דברי רבה שהן שוין בשבת דרב אמר הלכה כת"ק ודקדקנו דברי ת"ק שאמר ולא נולד כשהוא מהול דוחה את השבת ועל זה חלוקת ב"ש וב"ה ועליו אמרו ב"ה אין צריך להטיף ממנו דם ברית בשבת. ויש לומר אפילו בחול דהא סתם קאמר אין צריך להטיף ממנו דם ברית ומסתברא כרבה דאמר שמא ערלה כבושה היא. ומשמא אין מחללין את השבת ובירור דבר זה דברי רבה שאמר מנא אמינא לה. דתניא ר' אליעזר הקפר ב"ר אומר לא נחלקו ב"ש [וב"ה על הנולד כשהוא מהול שצריך להטיף ממנו דם ברית ועל מה נחלקו לחלל עליו את השבת שבית

רב נסים גאון

בזמנה דאתיא מקל וחומר וגם זה פירשנו בפ' במה מדליקין: מילה דנכרתו עליה י"ג בריתות. מפורשין הן בתורה (בראשית יז) ואלו הן ואתה את בריתי תשמר ואתנה בריתי אני הנה בריתי והקימותי את בריתי לברית עולם ואתה את בריתי תשמור והיתה בריתי בבשרכם לברית עולם את בריתי הפר והקימותי את בריתי לברית עולם את בריתי אקים את יצחק*): ולא שאני לך בין חמין שהוחמו בשבת לחמין שהוחמו מערב שבת. תמצא נשיאות ונתינות שבדבר זה ומה שנאמר עליו בפ' כירה (ד' לח) דתנן מעשה שעשו אנשי טבריא שהביאו סילון של צונן לתוך אמה של חמין אמרו להם חכמים אם בשבת כחמין שהוחמו בשבת אסורין ברחיצה [וכו'] ומותרין בשתיה ואוקימנה כר' שמעון דאסורין להשתטף בהן כל גופו ולענין חמין שהוחמו מערב שבת אמר שמואל לא הותרו לרחוץ בהן אלא פניו ידיו ורגליו ותניא כוותיה דשמואל חמין שהוחמו מערב שבת למחר רוחץ בהן פניו ידיו ורגליו אבל לא ירחוץ בהן כל גופו ולר' שמעון מותר להשתטף בהן כל גופו ובפרק חבית (דף קמז) תמצא שיחזק דבר זה של ר' שמעון שמתיר להשתטף בהן כל גופו אסור לרחוץ בהן כל גופו: בן ח' הרי הוא כאבן. לפי מה שנולד לח' חדשים אי אפשר לו לחיות כל עיקר ותמצא פירושו בבראשית דר' אושעיא (פרשה יד) וייצר בב' יצירות יצירה לאדם ויצירה לחוה יצירה

*) פה חסרון וכפל ובלי סדרים והמעיין בפרשה ימצאם במלואם וכסדרם.

עין משפט
נר מצוה

לה א מיי' שם הלכה יא טוש"ע א"ח סי' שלא סעיף ה וי"ד סי' רסו סעיף י:

לו ב מיי' שם הלכה ז סמג עשין כח טוש"ע י"ד סי' רסב סעיף ג וסימן רסו סעיף י:

לז ג ד מיי' שם הלכה ד ה סמג שם טוש"ע י"ד סי' רסז סעיף א:

לח ה מיי' שם הלכה יג ופ"א מהל' יבום וחליצה הלכה כב ופ"ב מהל' רוצח ושמירת נפש הלכה ו ופ"א מהל' אבל הלכה ו סמג עשין נא ועשין דרבנן ב טוש"ע י"ד סי' שמ סעיף ל וסי' שעג סעיף ד וסי' שעח סעיף ו וטוש"ע אה"ע סי' קנו סעיף ד:

לט ו מיי' פ"ד מהל' מאכלות אסורות הלכה ד (ופ"ג מהל' איסורי מזבח הלכה ח) סמג לאוין עה וקלג עשין קעת:

תורה אור

וְנִתְחַדְּשָׁה הֲלָכָה. אִינִי?! וְהָא אִיתְּמַר: יוֹצֵא דוֹפֶן *וּמִי שֶׁיֵּשׁ לוֹ שְׁתֵּי עָרְלוֹת, רַב הוּנָא וְרַב חִיָּיא בַּר רַב. חַד אָמַר: מְחַלְּלִין עָלָיו אֶת הַשַּׁבָּת; וְחַד אָמַר: [א]אֵין מְחַלְּלִין. עַד כָּאן לָא פְּלִיגִי – אֶלָּא לְחַלֵּל עָלָיו אֶת הַשַּׁבָּת, [ב]אֲבָל לִשְׁמוֹנָה – וַדַּאי מַהֲלִינַן לֵיהּ! *הָא בְּהָא תַּלְיָא. כְּתַנָּאֵי: יֵשׁ יְלִיד בַּיִת שֶׁנִּימּוֹל לְאֶחָד וְיֵשׁ יְלִיד בַּיִת שֶׁנִּימּוֹל לִשְׁמֹנָה, יֵשׁ מִקְנַת כֶּסֶף שֶׁנִּימּוֹל לְאֶחָד, וְיֵשׁ מִקְנַת כֶּסֶף שֶׁנִּימּוֹל לִשְׁמֹנָה. יֵשׁ מִקְנַת כֶּסֶף שֶׁנִּימּוֹל לְא', וְיֵשׁ מִקְנַת כֶּסֶף שֶׁנִּימּוֹל לִשְׁמוֹנָה, כֵּיצַד? [ג]לָקַח שִׁפְחָה מְעוּבֶּרֶת וְאח"כ יָלְדָה – זֶהוּ מִקְנַת כֶּסֶף הַנִּימּוֹל לִשְׁמוֹנָה, לָקַח שִׁפְחָה וּוְלָדָהּ עִמָּהּ – זוֹ הִיא מִקְנַת כֶּסֶף שֶׁנִּימּוֹל לְאֶחָד. וְיֵשׁ יְלִיד בַּיִת שֶׁנִּימּוֹל לִשְׁמֹנָה, [ד]כֵּיצַד? לָקַח שִׁפְחָה וְנִתְעַבְּרָה אֶצְלוֹ וְיָלְדָה – זֶהוּ יְלִיד בַּיִת הַנִּימּוֹל לִשְׁמֹנָה. רַב חָמָא אוֹמֵר: יָלְדָה וְאח"כ הִטְבִּילָהּ – זֶהוּ יְלִיד בַּיִת שֶׁנִּימּוֹל לְאֶחָד, הִטְבִּילָהּ וְאַחַר כָּךְ יָלְדָה – זֶהוּ יְלִיד בַּיִת הַנִּימּוֹל לִשְׁמֹנָה. וְתַנָּא קַמָּא לָא שָׁנֵי לֵיהּ בֵּין הִטְבִּילָהּ וְאח"כ יָלְדָה, בֵּין יָלְדָה וְאח"כ הִטְבִּילָהּ, דְּאע"ג דְּאֵין אִמּוֹ טְמֵאָה לֵידָה – נִימּוֹל לִשְׁמֹנָה. (אֲמַר רָבָא): בִּשְׁלָמָא לְר' חָמָא – מַשְׁכַּחַת לָהּ יְלִיד בַּיִת נִימּוֹל לְא', יְלִיד בַּיִת נִימּוֹל לְח'. מִקְנַת כֶּסֶף נִימּוֹל לְא', וּמִקְנַת כֶּסֶף נִימּוֹל לְח'. יָלְדָה וְאח"כ הִטְבִּילָהּ – זֶהוּ יְלִיד בַּיִת שֶׁנִּימּוֹל לְאֶחָד, הִטְבִּילָהּ וְאח"כ יָלְדָה – זֶהוּ יְלִיד בַּיִת שֶׁנִּימּוֹל לְח'. מִקְנַת כֶּסֶף נִימּוֹל לִשְׁמֹנָה – כְּגוֹן שֶׁלָּקַח שִׁפְחָה מְעוּבֶּרֶת וְהִטְבִּילָהּ וְאח"כ יָלְדָה, מִקְנַת כֶּסֶף נִימּוֹל לְאֶחָד – כְּגוֹן °שֶׁלָּקַח זֶה שִׁפְחָה וְזֶה עוּבָּרָהּ. אֶלָּא לְת"ק בִּשְׁלָמָא כּוּלְּהוּ מַשְׁכַּחַת לְהוּ, אֶלָּא יְלִיד בַּיִת נִימּוֹל לְאֶחָד הֵיכִי מַשְׁכַּחַת לָהּ? א"ר יִרְמְיָה: בְּלוֹקֵחַ שִׁפְחָה לְעוּבָּרָהּ. הָנִיחָא *לְמ"ד קִנְיַן פֵּירוֹת לָאו כְּקִנְיַן הַגּוּף דָּמֵי, אֶלָּא לְמ"ד קִנְיַן פֵּירוֹת כְּקִנְיַן הַגּוּף דָּמֵי – מַאי אִיכָּא לְמֵימַר? אָמַר רַב מְשַׁרְשְׁיָא: בְּלוֹקֵחַ שִׁפְחָה ע"מ שֶׁלֹּא לְהַטְבִּילָהּ. *תַּנְיָא, ר"ש בֶּן גַּמְלִיאֵל אוֹמֵר: [ה]כֹּל שֶׁשָּׁהָה ל' יוֹם בָּאָדָם – אֵינוֹ נֵפֶל, שֶׁנֶּאֱמַר: °"וּפְדוּיָו מִבֶּן חֹדֶשׁ תִּפְדֶּה" (במדבר יח). [ו]שְׁמוֹנַת יָמִים בַּבְּהֵמָה אֵינוֹ נֵפֶל, שֶׁנֶּאֱמַר: °"וּמִיּוֹם הַשְּׁמִינִי וָהָלְאָה יֵרָצֶה לְקָרְבַּן" וגו' (ויקרא כב). הָא לֹא שָׁהָה – סְפֵיקָא הָוֵי.
מִימְהַל

רש"י

וְנִתְחַדְּשָׁה הֲלָכָה. דְּמִי שֶׁאִמּוֹ טְמֵאָה לֵידָה נִימּוֹל בְּח', וְלֹא אַחֵר: יוֹצֵא דוֹפֶן. שֶׁנִּקְרַעַת אִמּוֹ: שְׁתֵּי עָרְלוֹת. שְׁנֵי עוֹרוֹת זֶה עַל זֶה*. וְאָמְרִי לָהּ שְׁנֵי גִּידִין: אֲבָל לִשְׁמוֹנָה וַדַּאי מַהֲלִינַן. וְאע"ג דְּיוֹצֵא דוֹפֶן אֵין אִמּוֹ טְמֵאָה לֵידָה: הָא בְּהָא תַּלְיָא. וְחִילּוּל שַׁבָּת תָּלֵי בְּמִילָה לְח'. דְּמִי שֶׁנִּימּוֹל לְח' – דּוֹחֶה שַׁבָּת, וּמִי שֶׁאֵינוֹ נִימּוֹל לְח' – אֵינוֹ דּוֹחֶה הַשַּׁבָּת. דְּכִי כְּתִיב: "וּבַיּוֹם הַשְּׁמִינִי" דְּיָלְפִינַן מִינֵּיהּ וַאֲפִילּוּ בַּשַּׁבָּת – בְּנִימּוֹל לְח' כְּתִיב: כְּתַנָּאֵי. הָא דְּרַב אַסִי: ה"ג הָא מִילְּתָא בִּשְׁאִלְתּוֹת דְּרַב אַחַאי*: כֵּיצַד, לָקַח שִׁפְחָה[(א)] וְאַחַר כָּךְ יָלְדָה – זֶהוּ מִקְנַת כֶּסֶף שֶׁנִּימּוֹל לִשְׁמוֹנָה. לָקַח שִׁפְחָה וּוְלָדָהּ עִמָּהּ – זֶהוּ מִקְנַת כֶּסֶף שֶׁנִּימּוֹל לְאֶחָד. לָקַח שִׁפְחָה וְנִתְעַבְּרָה אֶצְלוֹ וְיָלְדָה – זֶהוּ יְלִיד בַּיִת שֶׁנִּימּוֹל לְח'. רַבִּי חָמָא אוֹמֵר: הִטְבִּילָהּ וְאַחַר כָּךְ יָלְדָה – זֶהוּ יְלִיד בַּיִת שֶׁנִּימּוֹל לְח'. יָלְדָה וְאח"כ הִטְבִּילָהּ – זֶהוּ יְלִיד בַּיִת שֶׁנִּימּוֹל לְא'. בִּשְׁלָמָא לְר' חָמָא מַשְׁכַּחַת לָהּ יְלִיד בַּיִת, כִּדְקָתָנֵי. מִקְנַת כֶּסֶף שֶׁנִּימּוֹל לִשְׁמוֹנָה – כְּגוֹן שֶׁלָּקַח שִׁפְחָה וְאַחַר כָּךְ יָלְדָה. נִימּוֹל לְא' נַמִּי – כְּגוֹן שֶׁלָּקַח שִׁפְחָה וּוְלָדָהּ עִמָּהּ. אֶלָּא לְת"ק כו'. וּבַסְּפָרִים שֶׁלָּנוּ כְּתִיב: נִימּוֹל לְאֶחָד נַמִּי – כְּגוֹן שֶׁלָּקַח זֶה שִׁפְחָה וְזֶה עוּבָּרָהּ. וְנִרְאֶה בְּעֵינַי דְּהָא דְּלָא גָּרֵיס בִּשְׁאִלְתּוֹת כְּגוֹן שֶׁלָּקַח זֶה שִׁפְחָה וְזֶה עוּבָּרָהּ – מִשּׁוּם דְּקַשְׁיָא לֵיהּ מַאי דּוֹחֲקֵיהּ לְאוֹקְמֵיהּ בִּשְׁנֵי לָקוֹחוֹת, וּלְשַׁנּוּיֵי גִּירְסָא דְּסֵיפָא מֵרֵישָׁא, דְּקָתָנֵי לָקַח שִׁפְחָה וּוְלָדָהּ זֶהוּ מִקְנַת כֶּסֶף שֶׁנִּימּוֹל לְא': יֵשׁ יְלִיד בַּיִת שֶׁנִּימּוֹל לְא'. דִּתְרֵי קְרָאֵי כְּתִיבֵי בִּילִיד בַּיִת וּמִקְנַת כֶּסֶף, חַד כְּתִיב בֵּיהּ ח' וְחַד לָא כְּתִיב בֵּיהּ ח' (בראשית יז): "הִמּוֹל יִמּוֹל יְלִיד בֵּיתְךָ וּמִקְנַת כַּסְפֶּךָ" וְלָא מְפָרֵשׁ בֵּיהּ לְח' יָמִים, וּכְתִיב (שם): "וּבֶן שְׁמוֹנַת יָמִים יִמּוֹל לָכֶם כָּל זָכָר לְדוֹרוֹתֵיכֶם יְלִיד בַּיִת וּמִקְנַת כֶּסֶף". וּמִסְתַּבְּרָא דְּהַאי דִּמְפָרֵשׁ בֵּיהּ לִשְׁמֹנָה – הַיְינוּ הֵיכָא דְּדָמֵי לְיִשְׂרָאֵל מְעַלְיָא, שֶׁנּוֹלַד בְּבֵיתוֹ שֶׁל יִשְׂרָאֵל מִשֶּׁקְּנָאוֹ, דְּדוּמְיָא דְּ'לָכֶם' בָּעֵינַן, דִּכְתִיב בְּהַהוּא קְרָא: "יִמּוֹל לָכֶם כָּל זָכָר", וַהֲדַר: "יְלִיד בַּיִת וּמִקְנַת כֶּסֶף" – הִלְכָּךְ, לָקַח שִׁפְחָה מְעוּבֶּרֶת וְיָלְדָה – הֲרֵי זֶה מִקְנַת כֶּסֶף, דְּגוּף שָׁלֵם הוּא בִּמְעֵי אִמּוֹ וּקְנָאוֹ, שֶׁנִּימּוֹל לְח', דְּדוּמְיָא דְּ'לָכֶם' הוּא, שֶׁנּוֹלַד בִּרְשׁוּתוֹ שֶׁל יִשְׂרָאֵל. לָקַח שִׁפְחָה וּוְלָדָהּ עִמָּהּ, שֶׁכְּבָר יְלָדַתּוּ, וְאע"פ שֶׁלֹּא עָבְרוּ עָלָיו ח' לְלֵידָתוֹ – מָלוֹ מִיָּד, כִּדְכְתִיב: "הִמּוֹל יִמּוֹל" וגו', דְּלָאו דּוּמְיָא דְּ'לָכֶם' הוּא. לָקַח שִׁפְחָה וְנִתְעַבְּרָה אֶצְלוֹ – לָא הָוֵי עוּבָּר מִקְנַת כֶּסֶף אֶלָּא יְלִיד בַּיִת שֶׁנִּימּוֹל לְח', דְּדוּמְיָא דְּ'לָכֶם' הוּא. וּלְקַמֵּיהּ מְפָרֵשׁ יְלִיד בַּיִת הַנִּימּוֹל לְאֶחָד אַלִּיבָּא דְּת"ק: רַבִּי חָמָא אוֹמֵר. הִטְבִּילָהּ לְשֵׁם עַבְדוּת וְחָלָה עָלֶיהָ שֵׁם תּוֹרַת שִׁפְחַת יִשְׂרָאֵל דְּנִתְחַיְּיבָה בְּכָל מִצְוֹת שֶׁהָאִשָּׁה חַיֶּיבֶת בָּהֶן, וְהָוְיָא טְמֵאָה לֵידָה – זֶהוּ יְלִיד בַּיִת שֶׁנִּימּוֹל לְח': יָלְדָה וְהִטְבִּילָהּ זֶהוּ יְלִיד בַּיִת שֶׁנִּימּוֹל לְאֶחָד. דְּכָל שֶׁאֵין אִמּוֹ טְמֵאָה לֵידָה אֵין מַמְתִּינִין לוֹ לְח', כְּרַב אַסִי: בִּשְׁלָמָא לְרַבִּי חָמָא. דְּשָׁנֵי בֵּין הִטְבִּילָהּ וְאַחַר כָּךְ יָלְדָה לְיָלְדָה וְאח"כ הִטְבִּילָהּ: מַשְׁכַּחַת לָהּ. כּוּלְּהוּ. יְלִיד בַּיִת נִימּוֹל לְאֶחָד – יָלְדָה וְאח"כ הִטְבִּילָהּ. יְלִיד בַּיִת נִימּוֹל לְח' – הִטְבִּילָהּ וְאח"כ יָלְדָה. וּשְׁנֵיהֶם כְּשֶׁנִּתְעַבְּרָה אֶצְלוֹ, דְּלָא הָוֵי מִקְנַת כֶּסֶף. מִקְנַת כֶּסֶף נִימּוֹל לְח' – כְּגוֹן שֶׁלָּקַח שִׁפְחָה מְעוּבֶּרֶת וְיָלְדָה לְאַחַר שֶׁהִטְבִּילָהּ. מִקְנַת כֶּסֶף הַנִּימּוֹל לְא' – כְּגוֹן שֶׁלָּקַח זֶה שִׁפְחָה וְזֶה עוּבָּרָהּ; דְּכֵיוָן דְּאֵין לְבַעַל הָעוּבָּר חֵלֶק בְּאִמּוֹ, לָאו דּוּמְיָא דְּ'לָכֶם' הוּא. ה"ה נַמִּי דְּמָצֵי לְפַלּוּגֵי בְּמִקְנַת כֶּסֶף בֵּין יָלְדָה וְאַחַר כָּךְ הִטְבִּילָהּ בֵּין הִטְבִּילָהּ וְאַחַר כָּךְ יָלְדָה, וּלְמֵימַר: מִקְנַת כֶּסֶף נִימּוֹל לְח' – כְּגוֹן שֶׁלָּקַח שִׁפְחָה מְעוּבֶּרֶת וְעוּבָּרָהּ, וְיָלְדָה וְאַחַר כָּךְ הִטְבִּילָהּ. אֶלָּא רְבוּתָא אַשְׁמְעִינַן, דַּאֲפִילּוּ בְּהִטְבִּילָהּ וְאח"כ יָלְדָה מַשְׁכַּחַת לָהּ. וְהָא דְּשָׁנֵי מִקְנַת כֶּסֶף נִימּוֹל לְא' לְרַבִּי חָמָא מִלְּת"ק, וְלָא אָמַר כְּגוֹן שֶׁלָּקַח שִׁפְחָה וּוְלָדָהּ עִמָּהּ – מִשּׁוּם דְּאִם כֵּן יָלְדָה קוֹדֶם טְבִילָה הִיא, וּמַאי אִירְיָא נוֹלַד קוֹדֶם שֶׁלְּקָחָהּ? אֲפִילּוּ נוֹלַד מִשֶּׁלְּקָחָהּ נַמִּי לְרַבִּי חָמָא נִימּוֹל לְא': אֶלָּא יְלִיד בַּיִת נִימּוֹל לְא' הֵיכִי מַשְׁכַּחַתְּ לָהּ. הָא וַדַּאי דּוּמְיָא דְּ'לָכֶם' הוּא, הוֹאִיל וְלָאו בְּטוּמְאַת לֵידָה תַּלְיָא לְדִידֵיהּ: בְּלוֹקֵחַ שִׁפְחָה לְעוּבָּרָהּ. וַאֲפִילּוּ מִיִּשְׂרָאֵל, דַּהֲוָי' טְמֵאָה לֵידָה, שֶׁכְּבָר טָבְלָה – לָאו דּוּמְיָא דְּ'לָכֶם' הוּא, הוֹאִיל וְאֵין לוֹ חֵלֶק בְּאִמּוֹ: הָנִיחָא כו'. פְּלוּגְתָּא דְּר"ל וְרַבִּי יוֹחָנָן בְּבָבָא בַּתְרָא (דף קלו.): שֶׁלְּקָחָהּ עַל מְנָת שֶׁלֹּא לְהַטְבִּילָהּ. דְּלָא שַׁיְיכָא בָּהּ תּוֹרַת חִיּוּבָא דְּמִצְוֹת כְּלָל, דְּלָאו דּוּמְיָא דְּ'לָכֶם' הוּא. אֲבָל לְטוּמְאַת לֵידָה לָא חָיְישִׁינַן בְּיָלְדָה וְאח"כ הִטְבִּילָהּ: וּפְדוּיָו. בִּבְכוֹר אָדָם כְּתִיב: מִבֶּן חֹדֶשׁ. מִדְּתָלֵי בְּהָכִי שְׁמַע מִינָּהּ עַכְשָׁיו נִתְבָּרֵר שֶׁהוּא בֶּן קַיָּימָא, וְלֹא קוֹדֶם לָכֵן: הָא לֹא שָׁהָה. שְׁלֹשִׁים יוֹם בְּאָדָם וּבִבְהֵמָה ח' יָמִים – סְפֵיקָא הָוֵי. הַתַּלְמוּד פָּרֵיךְ עֲלָהּ:
מִימְהַל

תוספות

כתנאי יש יליד בית כו'. תימה: היכי משמע ליה מתוך הך ברייתא דרבי חמא תלי טעמא בטומאת לידה? לעולם אימא לך דסבר יוצא דופן נימול לח', והאי דמצריך טבילה בשפחה – משום דבענין אחר אינה חשובה גיורת עד שתטבול, כדנפקא לן ביבמות בפרק "החולץ" (דף מו.):

כגון שלקח זה שפחה וזה עוברה. פירש בקונטרס: דהוי מצי למימר כגון שלקח שפחה מעוברת וילדה קודם טבילה. אלא רבותא נקט, דאפילו בטבלה ואח"כ ילדה משכחת לה מקנת כסף נימול לא'. וקשה לר"י: דא"כ ת"ק דלעיל ה"ל למינקט נמי הך רבותא, ואמאי קאמר [(ג)] מקנת כסף נימול כו'. אפילו לקח מעוברת נמי! אלא שלקח זה שפחה וזה עוברה אלא ודאי לקח זה שפחה וזה עוברה הוי שפיר דומיא ד'לכם' וכגירסת שאילתות דרב אחאי. נראה לר"י דגרס: כגון שלקח שפחה וולדה עמה. מיהו תימה לר"י: דהוה מצי למינקט רבותא אפילו בלא ולדה עמה, כגון שלקח שפחה מעוברת וילדה קודם טבילה! וי"ל: דניחא ליה למינקט כדקתני בברייתא במילתיה דת"ק. ועוד אומר ר"י: דמשום דהנך קראי נימול לאחד ונימול לשמונה דיליד בית ומקנת כסף כתיבי בפרשת "לך לך", הלכך ניחא לאשכוחינהו בכה"ג דשייך קודם מתן תורה דלא הוה טבילה. ואע"ג דיליד בית נימול לא' לר' חמא לא משכחת לה אלא אחר מתן תורה, בילדה ואח"כ טבלה – מיהו כל מה שיכול לקיים לפני מתן תורה מקיים: כגון שלקחה ע"מ שלא להטבילה. וכדמפר' ביבמות, בפרק "החולץ" (דף מח:) דלקח על מנת שלא לגיירו יכול להשהותו הרבה:

כל ששהה שלשים יום באדם וח' ימים בבהמה. אינן שוין. דיום שמנה כלאחר שמנה, כדמוכח לקמן. דעבד להו עיגלא תילתא ביומא דשבעה, וקאמר: אי איתרחיתו עד לאורתא הוה אכלינן מיניה. ויום שלשים כלפני שלשים, כדתנן בבכורות בפ' "יש בכור לנחלה" (דף מט.). ואפילו רבי עקיבא דפליג, לא קאמר אלא דמספקא אם הוא כלפני שלשים או כלאחר שלשים, ולענין אבילות אפילו ר"ע מודה דהוה כלפני שלשים, משום דהלכה כדברי המיקל באבל:

מסורת הש"ס

[עי' רש"י יבמות עב. ד"ה מי שיש לו]
[יבמות עב.]
[פרשת לך לך סימן טו]
[מגילה ו: נזיר יח: תמור' יח.]
ב"ק פח: נ. ב"מ נו. ב"ב נ. קלו: קלז. יבמו' לו: [גיטין מז: מח. ערכין כו:]
[יבמות שם ודף פ:] נדה מד: [תוספ' פט"ז]

הגהות הב"ח

(א) רש"י ד"ה ה"ג הא מילתא וכו' כילד לקח שפחה מעוברת ואח"כ וכו' שנימול לשמונה כגון שלקח שפחה מעוברת והטבילה ואח"כ ילדה: (ב) תום' ד"ה כגון שלקח זה וכו' הך רבותא ואמאי קאמר לקח שפחה וולדה עמה זו היא מקנת כסף שנימול לאחד אפילו לקח מעוברת נמי:

גליון הש"ס

גמ' שלקח זה שפחה וזה עוברה. עיין בשער המלך פי"ב מהל' נדה הלכה י ובקצות החושן סי' רט סעיף א ובספר כתובה בדף יא בתד"ה א"ה: שם שמנת ימים בבהמה. עי' מנחות דף לז ע"א תד"ה שומע אני:

רבינו חננאל

שמאי] אומרים מחללין ובה"א אין מחללין ודייק רבה מדברי ר' אליעזר הקפר מכלל דת"ק סבר דברי הכל אין מחללין ואמר רבה אנא דאמרי כת"ק לדברי הכל ואקשינן על הדין דוקיא דרבה א"כ ר' אליעזר הקפר טעמא דב"ש אתא לאשמעינן כלומר אם ת"ק אמר דברי הכל מחללין ור' אליעזר הקפר אמר כי ב"ה סבירא להו אין מחללין למה חלק על ת"ק. ת"ק אמר דברי הכל אין מחללין והוא עוד אמר כי בה"א אין מחללין והלכה כמותם. לא בא אלא לפרש טעמא דב"ש מה הוצרך לזה. והא בהדיא קיי"ל ב"ש במקום ב"ה אינה משנה פריק רבה דלמא ת"ק אמר לא נחלקו אלא בלהטיף ממנו דם ברית ור' אליעזר הקפר אמר לא נחלקו בזה אלא לחלל עליו את השבת נחלקו. וביקש רבה להעמיד דבריו כר"ה אליבא דתנא [קמא] ולא נתברר אבל עמדו דבריו כב"ה אליבא דר' אליעזר הקפר ונמצאו דבריו ודברי רב שאמר הלכה כת"ק דבר אחד. וקיי"ל הלכתא כב"ה באיסורי. ועוד רבה ורב יוסף הלכתא כרבה בר משדה קנין ומחצה הלכך כוותייהו עבדינן וקיי"ל הנולד כשהוא מהול צריך להטיף ממנו דם ברית בחול שמא ערלה כבושה היא. ואם חל ח' שלו בשבת אין מחללין עליו את השבת וכן הלכה. ומעשה דרב אדא בר אהבה ברור הוא והזכירוהו בתלמוד א"י כלשון הזה. רב אדא בר אהבה איתיליד ליה חד בר (בן) [כי] ממסמס ביה מית רבי אבין אמר פצוע דכא נעשה ונתענה עליו ומת. גר שנתגייר כשהוא מהול אין לו תקנה אבל הוא בעצמו לא: **אמר** רבה אמר רב אסי כל שאמו טמאה לידה נימול לשמונה כו' מסתברא שלא בא רבה אלא למעט בן הנכרית שאין אמו טמאה לידה. אם יקנהו אין נימול לח' שבן בת ישראל ובן הגיורת ובן השפחה אמה טמאה לידה שכך שנינו בענין אשה כי תזריע בני ישראל בענין הזה. ואין הגוים בענין הזה או בני ישראל אין לי אלא בני ישראל מניין לרבות את הגיורת ואת השפחה בין משוחררת ובין שאינה משוחררת ת"ל אשה כי תזריע וילדה זכר וטמאה גו' הא אפילו שפחה טמאה ומקשינן עלה וכל שאמו טמאה לידה נימול לשמונה ומי שאין אמו טמאה לידה אינו נימול לשמונה. והרי יוצא דופן שאין אמו טמאה לידה דתניא וילדה עד שתלד ממקום הולד פרט ליוצא דופן ר' שמעון אומר יוצא דופן הרי הוא כילוד וחייבין עליו קרבן ובלבד שהוא פטור מחמש סלעים ואתמר יוצא דופן ומי שיש לו ב' ערלות רב הונא ורב חייא בר רב חד אמר מחללין עליו את השבת וחד אמר אין מחללין עליו את השבת. עד כאן לא פליגי לחלל עליו את השבת אבל ודאי לשמונה מהלינן ליה. ופרקי' הא בהא תליא האומר מחללין עליו את השבת סבר נימול לח' והאומר אין מחללין סבר אינו נימול לשמונה ואמרי דדברי רבה כתנאי זה התנא שאמר לקח שפחה ועוברה עמה נימול לח'. פי' קנה שפחה גויה ועוברה נמצא זה העובר מקנת כסף וקודם שיטבלנה עודה בגיותה ילדתו כיון שיגיע ליום שמיני חייב למולו ואע"פ שילדתו בגיותה שאינה טמאה לידה ואמר התנא זהו מקנת כסף הנימול [לשמונה]. דלא כרבה ורב אחא אמר ילדה כו'. קיי"ל דכולהו תנאי מא"י אינון לפיכך קרי להו רבי בר מתלת דוכתי. ואע"ג דתנאי אינון קרי להו רב. רב אבא בהאשה שנפלו לה נכסים. ורב אבא נמי בג' שאכלו כאחד. ורב חמא בהדא דוכתא. ורב אחא אמר ילדה ואח"כ הטבילה אינו נימול לשמונה מאחר שאין אמו טמאה לידה אינו נימול לשמונה אלא ליום אחד כרבה. וזהו שאמר רבה לרב חמא דבעי טבילה משכחת לה יליד בית נימול לשמונה כגון שהטבילה ואח"כ ילדה. מקנת כסף נימול לשמונה כגון שלקח שפחה ועוברה עמה. וגם זו הטבילה ואח"כ ילדה ומפני מה לא פירש בה טבילה כיון שההפרש מקודם לזה בין הטבילה ואח"כ ילדה ובין ילדה ואח"כ הטבילה. (מימי) [מי] לא שמעת לה לקח שפחה ועוברה עמה. זהו מקנת כסף שנימול לשמונה. לקח

רב נסים גאון

יצירה לט' ויצירה לז' רב הונא אמר נוצר לט' ונוצר לז' חי לח' אינו חי: **הניחא** למאן דאמר קנין פירות [לאו] בקנין הגוף דמי אלא למאן דאמר קנין פירות (לאו) בקנין הגוף דמי. ומחלוקתם היא על זה בין ר' יוחנן ובין ריש לקיש ותמצא מחלוקתם בהרבה מקומות מן התלמוד במס' גיטין בפרק השולח גט לאשתו (דף מז) איתמר המוכר שדהו לפירות ר' יוחנן אמר מביא וקורא ריש לקיש אמר מביא ואינו קורא ר' יוחנן אמר מביא וקורא קנין פירות כקנין הגוף דמי ריש לקיש אמר מביא ואינו קורא קנין פירות לאו כקנין הגוף דמי ובבבא בתרא בפרק יש נוחלין (קלו) מכר הבן בחיי האב וכו' ובמס' יבמות בפרק החולץ (לו) כמו כן וזאת

מִימְהַל הֵיכִי מָהֲלִינַן לֵיהּ? אָמַר רַב אַדָּא בַּר אַהֲבָה: א)מָלִין אוֹתוֹ מִמַּה נַפְשָׁךְ; אִם חַי הוּא – שַׁפִּיר קָא מָהֵיל, וְאִם לָאו – מְחַתֵּךְ בְּבָשָׂר הוּא. וְאֶלָּא הָא דְּתַנְיָא: סָפֵק בֶּן ז' סָפֵק בֶּן ח' – אֵין מְחַלְּלִין עָלָיו אֶת הַשַּׁבָּת, אַמַּאי? נִימְהֲלֵיהּ מִמַּה נַפְשָׁךְ! אִם חַי הוּא – שַׁפִּיר קָא מָהֵיל, וְאִם לָאו – מְחַתֵּךְ בְּבָשָׂר הוּא! אָמַר מָר בְּרֵיהּ דְּרָבִינָא; אֲנָא וְרַב נַחוּמֵי בַּר זְכַרְיָה תַּרְגִּימְנָא: מִימְהִיל – הָכִי נַמִי מָהֲלִינַן לֵיהּ, לֹא נִצְרְכָה אֶלָּא לְמַכְשִׁירֵי מִילָה, *וְאַלִּיבָּא דְּרַבִּי אֱלִיעֶזֶר. אָמַר אַבַּיֵי: כְּתַנָּאֵי °"וְכִי יָמוּת מִן הַבְּהֵמָה אֲשֶׁר הִיא לָכֶם לְאָכְלָה" לְהָבִיא ב)בֶּן שְׁמֹנָה שֶׁאֵין שְׁחִיטָתוֹ מְטַהַרְתּוֹ, רַבִּי יוֹסֵי בְּרַבִּי יְהוּדָה וְר' אֶלְעָזָר בְּר"ש אוֹמְרִים: שְׁחִיטָתוֹ מְטַהַרְתּוֹ. מַאי לָאו בְּהָא קָא מִיפַּלְגִי, דְּמָר סָבַר: חַי הוּא, וּמ"ס: מֵת הוּא. אָמַר רָבָא: אִי הָכִי, אַדְּמִיפַּלְגִי לְעִנְיַן טוּמְאָה וְטָהֳרָה – לִיפַּלְגִי לְעִנְיַן אֲכִילָה! אֶלָּא, דְּכוּלֵּי עָלְמָא מֵת הוּא, וְרַבִּי יוֹסֵי בְּרַבִּי יְהוּדָה וְרַבִּי אֶלְעָזָר בְּרַבִּי שִׁמְעוֹן סָבְרִי: כִּטְרֵפָה; טְרֵפָה, לָאו ג)אַף עַל גַּב דְּמֵתָה הִיא – שְׁחִיטָתָהּ מְטַהַרְתָּהּ, הָכָא נַמִי – לָא שְׁנָא. וְרַבָּנַן: לָא דָּמֵי לִטְרֵפָה, טְרֵפָה – הָיְתָה לָהּ שְׁעַת הַכּוֹשֶׁר, הַאי – לֹא הָיְתָה לָהּ שְׁעַת הַכּוֹשֶׁר. וְכ"ת טְרֵפָה מִבֶּטֶן מַאי אִיכָּא לְמֵימַר? הָתָם, יֵשׁ בְּמִינָהּ שְׁחִיטָה, ד)הָכָא – אֵין בְּמִינָהּ שְׁחִיטָה. אִיבַּעְיָא לְהוּ: מִי פְּלִיגִי רַבָּנַן עֲלֵיהּ דְּרַבָּן שִׁמְעוֹן בֶּן גַּמְלִיאֵל אוֹ לָא? אִם תִּמְצֵי לוֹמַר "פְּלִיגִי" – הֲלָכָה כְּמוֹתוֹ אוֹ אֵין הֲלָכָה כְּמוֹתוֹ? ת"ש: *ה)עֵגֶל שֶׁנּוֹלַד בְּיוֹם טוֹב – שׁוֹחֲטִין אוֹתוֹ בְּיו"ט. הָכָא בְּמַאי עָסְקִינַן – ו)דְּקִים לֵיהּ בְּגַוֵּויהּ שֶׁכָּלוּ לוֹ חֳדָשָׁיו. ת"ש: *וְשָׁוִין, ז)שֶׁאִם נוֹלַד הוּא וּמוּמוֹ עִמּוֹ – שֶׁזֶּה מִן הַמּוּכָן. ה"נ: שֶׁכָּלוּ לוֹ חֳדָשָׁיו. ת"ש, דְּאָמַר רַב יְהוּדָה אָמַר שְׁמוּאֵל: הֲלָכָה כְּרַבָּן שִׁמְעוֹן בֶּן גַּמְלִיאֵל. *הֲלָכָה – מִכְּלָל דִּפְלִיגִי, שמ"מ. אָמַר אַבַּיֵי: ח)נָפַל מִן הַגַּג אוֹ אֲכָלוֹ אֲרִי – דִּבְרֵי הַכֹּל חַי הוּא, כִּי פְּלִיגִי – שֶׁפִּיהֵק וָמֵת. מָר סָבַר: חַי הוּא, וּמָר סָבַר: מֵת הוּא. לְמַאי נָפְקָא מִינַּהּ – ט)לִפְטוֹר מִן הַיִּבּוּם. נָפַל מִן הַגַּג אוֹ אֲכָלוֹ אֲרִי דִּבְרֵי הַכֹּל חַי הוּא?! וְהָא רַב פַּפָּא וְרַב הוּנָא בְּרֵיהּ דְּרַב יְהוֹשֻׁעַ אִיקְלְעוּ לְבֵי בְּרֵיהּ דְּרַב אִידִי בַּר אָבִין, וַעֲבִיד לְהוּ עִיגְלָא תִּילְתָּא בְּיוֹמָא דְּשִׁבְעָה. וְאָמְרִי לֵיהּ: י)אִי אִיתְרְחִיתוּ לֵיהּ עַד לְאוֹרְתָּא – הֲוָה אָכְלִינַן מִינֵּיהּ, הַשְׁתָּא – לָא אָכְלִינַן מִינֵּיהּ! אֶלָּא, כְּשֶׁפִּיהֵק וָמֵת – דִּבְרֵי הַכֹּל מֵת הוּא, כִּי פְּלִיגִי – בְּנָפַל מִן הַגַּג וַאֲכָלוֹ אֲרִי. מָר סָבַר: מֵת הוּא, וּמָר סָבַר: חַי הוּא. בְּרֵיהּ דְּרַב דִּימִי בַּר יוֹסֵף אִתְיְלִיד לֵיהּ הַהוּא יָנוֹקָא, בְּגוֹ תְּלָתִין יוֹמִין שְׁכִיב. יָתֵיב קָמִתְאַבֵּיל עִילָּוֵיהּ. אֲמַר לֵיהּ אֲבוּהּ: צְוָורוֹנִיתָא קָבָעֵית לְמֵיכַל?! אֲמַר לֵיהּ: כ)קִים לִי בֵּיהּ שֶׁכָּלוּ לוֹ חֳדָשָׁיו. רַב אָשֵׁי אִיקְלַע בֵּי רַב כָּהֲנָא, אִיתְרַע בֵּיהּ מִילְּתָא בְּגוֹ תְּלָתִין יוֹמִין. חַזְיֵיהּ דְּיָתֵיב וְקָא מִתְאַבֵּל עִילָּוֵיהּ, אֲמַר לֵיהּ: לָא סָבַר לֵיהּ מָר לְהָא דְּאָמַר רַב יְהוּדָה אָמַר שְׁמוּאֵל "הֲלָכָה כְּרַבָּן שִׁמְעוֹן בֶּן גַּמְלִיאֵל"? אֲמַר לֵיהּ: קִים לִי בְּגַוֵּיהּ שֶׁכָּלוּ לוֹ חֳדָשָׁיו. *אִיתְּמַר, מֵת*) בְּתוֹךְ שְׁלֹשִׁים, וְעָמְדָה וְנִתְקַדְּשָׁה. אָמַר רָבִינָא מִשְּׁמֵיהּ דְּרָבָא: אִם

*) [עי' תוס' בכורות מט. ד"ה מת ותוס' יבמות לו: ד"ה מת וכו' שכתבו דרש"י דהכא גורס בסוף שלשים].

תורה אור: ויקרא יא

רש"י

מִימְהַל הֵיכִי מָהֲלִינַן. שֶׁהוּא קָטָן בַּיּוֹם הַשְּׁמִינִי בְּשַׁבָּת, דִּילְמָא נֵפֶל הוּא וְלָא חֲזֵי לָמוּל, וְעוֹשֶׂה חַבּוּרָה שֶׁלֹּא לְשֵׁם מִצְוָה: אִם חַי הוּא. כְּלוֹמַר: אִם כָּלוּ לוֹ חֳדָשָׁיו – שַׁפִּיר קָא מָהֵיל: מְחַתֵּךְ בְּבָשָׂר. שְׁחוּטָה הוּא, וְלֹא חַבּוּרָה הִיא: לֹא נִצְרְכָה. הָא דְּקָתָנֵי: "אֵין מְחַלְּלִין" אֶלָּא לְעִנְיַן מַכְשִׁירֵי מִילָה לְרַבִּי אֱלִיעֶזֶר, דְּאָמַר דָּחוּ שַׁבָּת – ה"מ דְּקִים לֵיהּ בְּגַוֵּיהּ שֶׁכָּלוּ לוֹ חֳדָשָׁיו – שֶׁעָבְרוּ °ט' חֳדָשִׁים מִשֶּׁשִּׁמְּשָׁה עַד שֶׁיְּלָדַתּוּ, וְלֹא שִׁמְּשָׁה כָּל יְמֵי עִיבּוּרָהּ. אֲבָל סָפֵק – אֵין מַכְשִׁירָיו דּוֹחִין, דִּילְמָא לָאו בַּר מִימְהַל הוּא, וּמְחַלֵּל שַׁבָּת בַּעֲשׂוֹתוֹ פֶּחָמִים וּבַרְזֶל: כְּתַנָּאֵי. נֵפֶל גָּמוּר אִם חָשׁוּב כְּמֵת, כִּדְקָאָמַר רַב אַדָּא בַּר אַהֲבָה, דְּאֵינוֹ אֶלָּא מְחַתֵּךְ בְּבָשָׂר. אוֹ לֹא, וְהָוְיָא חַבּוּרָה: לְאָכְלָה לְהָבִיא בֶּן ח'. דְּכוּלֵּיהּ קְרָא דָּרֵישׁ לֵיהּ בְּתוֹרַת כֹּהֲנִים: "מִן הַבְּהֵמָה" – מִקְצָת בְּהֵמָה מְטַמְּאָה, וּמִקְצָת אֵינָהּ מְטַמְּאָה, פְּרָט לִטְרֵפָה שֶׁשְּׁחָטָהּ. וּמִדְּמַמְעִיט טְרֵפָה שֶׁשְּׁחָטָהּ – מִכְּלָל דִּבְטְהוֹרָה קָאֵי. "אֲשֶׁר הִיא לָכֶם" – לְהָבִיא בְּהֵמָה טְמֵאָה. לְפִי שֶׁפָּרָשָׁה רִאשׁוֹנָה דִּכְתִיב בָּהּ: "לְכָל הַבְּהֵמָה אֲשֶׁר הִיא מַפְרֶסֶת פַּרְסָה וְאֵינֶנָּה מַעֲלַת גֵּרָה" וגו' – מוֹקֵי לָהּ הָתָם בְּאֵבֶר מִן הַחַי הַכָּתוּב מְדַבֵּר. וּפָרָשָׁה זוֹ בְּמֵתָה וַדַּאי. "לְאָכְלָה" – לְהָבִיא בֶּן ח' חֳדָשִׁים, שֶׁאַף שְׁחִיטָתוֹ מִיתָה וּמְטַמְּאָה: מָר סָבַר חַי הוּא. לְפִיכָךְ שְׁחִיטָתוֹ מְטַהַרְתּוֹ: לְעִנְיַן אֲכִילָה. אִי מוּתָּר בַּאֲכִילָה בִּשְׁחִיטָתוֹ, אִם לָאו: טְרֵפָה. שְׁחִיטָתָהּ מְטַהַרְתָּהּ מִלְּטַמֵּא כִּדְפָרֵישִׁית: הָיְתָה לָהּ שְׁעַת הַכּוֹשֶׁר. לִשָּׁחֵט וְלִיטָּהֵר קוֹדֶם שֶׁנִּטְרְפָה: מִי פְּלִיגִי. לְמַכְשִׁירֵי וָלָד שֶׁל בְּהֵמָה בְּתוֹךְ ח' יָמִים: שׁוֹחֲטִים אוֹתוֹ בְּיו"ט. וְאֵינוֹ מוּקְצֶה, שֶׁהֲרֵי בֵּין הַשְּׁמָשׁוֹת נַמִי הָיָה מוּכָן אַגַּב אִמּוֹ. מִיהוּ, שָׁמְעִינַן מִינָּהּ דְּמוּתָּר לְבוֹ בַּיּוֹם: וְשָׁוִין. רַבִּי יְהוּדָה וְרַבִּי שִׁמְעוֹן, שֶׁנֶּחְלְקוּ בְּרוֹאִין מוּמִין בְּיו"ט בְּמַסֶּכֶת בֵּיצָה, שֶׁאִם נוֹלַד הַיּוֹם הוּא וּמוּמוֹ עִמּוֹ – שֶׁהוּא מִן הַמּוּכָן, וּמוּתָּר לְבַקֵּר מוּמוֹ בְּיו"ט, דְּלָא דָּמֵי כִּמְתַקֵּן בְּיו"ט, דְּלָא אִיתַּחְזַק בְּאִיסּוּרָא. וּמוֹקְמִינַן לָהּ הָתָם כְּגוֹן דְּיָתְבִי דַּיָּינֵי הָתָם, וְרָאוּהוּ בִּשְׁעַת לֵידָה מִיָּד: נָפַל מִן הַגַּג אוֹ אֲכָלוֹ אֲרִי. שֶׁמֵּת מֵחֲמַת מִיתָה הַבָּאָה לוֹ בְּתוֹךְ ל' מִמָּקוֹם אַחֵר – דִּבְרֵי הַכֹּל בְּחֶזְקַת כָּלוּ לוֹ חֳדָשָׁיו קָאֵי, דְּאִי לָאו הָךְ מִיתָה לָא הֲוָה מֵת. הִילְכָּךְ, חַי הוּא. וּבְאָדָם הָוֵי וָלָד, וּפוֹטֵר אֶת אִמּוֹ מִן הַחֲלִיצָה. וְגַבֵּי בְּהֵמָה נַמִי, סְתָם וְלַד בְּהֵמָה שֶׁשָּׁחַט בְּתוֹךְ ח' – מוּתָּר בַּאֲכִילָה, דְּלָא חָזֵינָא בֵּיהּ רֵיעוּתָא, וְרוֹב הַוּוֹלָדוֹת אֵינָן מַפִּילוֹת: שֶׁפִּיהֵק. °בייל"ר בְּלַעַ"ז. כְּלוֹמַר: לְאַחַר לֵידָתוֹ לֹא רָאוּ בּוֹ אֶלָּא חִיּוּת מְעַט, שֶׁפִּיהֵק וָמֵת, וְגַבֵּי אָדָם קָאֵי: ה"ג: וְעַבְדוּ(א) עִגְלָא תִּילְתָּא בְּיוֹמָא דְּשִׁבְעָה: אִיתְרַחִיתוּ. מִלְּשָׁחֲטוֹ עַד אוֹרְתָּא, שֶׁהוּא לֵיל שְׁמִינִי: הֲוָה אָכְלִינַן מִינֵּיהּ. דְּמִקְצָת הַיּוֹם כְּכוּלּוֹ, כִּדְכְתִיב (ויקרא כב): "וְהָיָה שִׁבְעַת יָמִים תַּחַת אִמּוֹ" – הָא לַיְלָה חָזֵי. וּמִיהוּ, מִיּוֹם הַשְּׁמִינִי הוּא דְּיֵרָצֶה – לְאוֹרְתָּא לָאו בַּת הַקְרָבָה הִיא, כִּדְכְתִיב (שם ז): "בְּיוֹם צַוֹּתוֹ לְהַקְרִיב". אֲבָל מִכְּלַל נֵפֶל נָפְקֵי לֵיהּ, וַחֲזֵי לְאַקְדּוּשֵׁי, כִּדְאָמְרִינַן בִּזְבָחִים (דף יב.): לַיְלָה לִקְדוּשָּׁה, יוֹם לְהַרְצָאָה. וְהִלְכָּךְ, לְעִנְיַן חוּלִּין – חֲזֵי מֵאוֹרְתָּא לְמִישְׁחֲטֵיהּ וּמֵיכַל. אַלְמָא: מַאן דְּס"ל כְּרשב"ג פָּלֵיג בְּמִיתָה הַבָּאָה לוֹ מִמָּקוֹם אַחֵר, וְאָמַר סְפֵיקָא הוּא: שְׁכִיב בְּגוֹ תְּלָתִין. לְלֵידָתוֹ: א)צְוָורוֹנִיתָא. מַטְעַמִּים שֶׁמַּאֲכִילִין אֶת הָאָבֵל: קָא בָּעֵית לְמֵיכַל. לְכָךְ אַתָּה מִתְאַבֵּל חִנָּם: אִיתְרַע מִילְּתָא. אִגַּלּוּיֵי בְּגוֹ תְּלָתִין יוֹמִין. לְלֵידַת הַוָּלָד: מֵת הַוָּלָד ב)בְּתוֹךְ ל'. לְלֵידָתוֹ, וְלֹא הָיָה לְאָבִיו בֵּן אֶלָּא הוּא, ג)וְנוֹלַד לְאַחַר מִיתַת אָבִיו, וְעַל יָדוֹ הָיוּ פּוֹטְרִין אִמּוֹ מִן הַחֲלִיצָה אִם הָיָה בַּר קַיָּימָא: וְעָמְדָה וְנִתְקַדְּשָׁה. לְאַחַר זְמַן, לְפִי שֶׁסְּבוּרָה שֶׁאֵינָהּ זְקוּקָה לְיָבָם: אִם

א) [במו"ק כ: גרס רש"י צוורוניתא [illegible]] ב) [illegible] ג) [illegible] ד) [illegible]

תוספות

מימהל היכי מהלינן ליה. מכאן משמע דלא איירי רשב"ג בבן שמנה(ב) דוקא, אלא בסתם ולדות. וכן משמע לקמן, דאמר ת"ש: עגל שנולד בי"ט שוחטין אותו בי"ט. ודחי: דכלו לו חדשיו. ואת"ל דלא איירי רשב"ג אלא בודאי בן שמנה – הוה ליה לדחויי: הכ"ע – בסתם ולדות. ועוד אמר לקמן: נפל מן הגג ואכלו ארי – דברי הכל חי הוא. ואי בודאי בן ח' איירי, היכי תיסק אדעתיה לומר ד"ה חי הוא? ובכולהו דלקמן נמי, דמוקמינן בדקים ליה בגוויה שכלו לו חדשיו. וקשה לר"י, מהא דאמרינן בפ' "הערל" (יבמות דף פ:): איזהו בן ח' – כל שלא כלו לו חדשיו, רבי אומר: שערו וצפרניו מוכיחין עליו כו'. דאמר: האי בר שבעה הוא, ואישתהויי אישתהי. ופריך: (ג) הא דעבד רבה תוספאה עובדא באשה שהלך בעלה למדינת הים, ואישתהי עד תריסר ירחי שתא, כמאן – כרבי. כיון דאיכא רשב"ג, דאמר אישתהי. *דתני כל ששהה כו' – כרבי עבד. אלמא משמע בהדיא, דבודאי בן ח' איירי, מדמוכח מיניה דמשתהי כרבי. ומנא ליה, דילמא לעולם ס"ל דלא משתהי, ובסתם ולדות איירי רשב"ג כדפרישית. ואור"י דע"כ בודאי בן ח' נמי איירי דהא בתוספתא דמכילתין מיתני מילתיה דרשב"ג בתר מילתיה דרבנן, ורבי דיבמות ואפלוגתייהו קאי דאיירי בבן ח'. וא"ת ובשמעתין, מנלן דבסתם ולדות ס"ל לרשב"ג: הא לא שהה – ספיקא הוי. דילמא קסבר ולד מעליא הוי, ולא איירי כלל בסתם ולדות, אלא בודאי בן ח'? ויש לומר: דדייקינן מדקתני "כל ששהה", דכל משמע לרבות סתם דווקא שהה, הא לא שהה – ספיקא הווי. והא דמבעיא לן לקמן אי פליגי רבנן עליה דרשב"ג – היינו בסתם ולדות, דבן ח' ודאי בהדיא קתני לה בתוספתא. וא"ת: והיכי פשיט לקמן מדאמר רב יהודה אמר שמואל הלכה כרשב"ג – מכלל דפליגי בסתם ולדות. תאמר דלעולם לא פליגי בסתם ולדות, וכי פסיק רב יהודה כוותיה – הנ"מ בודאי בן ח'! וי"ל: דא"כ ה"ל למיתני הלכה כר'(ד), דליכא למימר דלא קאמר הלכה כרבי משום דבעי הוכחת סימנין שערו וצפרניו, אבל רשב"ג לא בעי – דהא פשיטא דבן ח' שלא גמרו שערו וצפרניו לכ"ע לא חי. ומדנקט רשב"ג – ש"מ דבסתם ולדות איירי, ופסק בכולא מילתא כוותיה. והשתא נמי אין צריך לדקדק(ה) מכל, דבלאו הכי יש להוכיח דבסתם ולדות איירי, כמו שהוכחתי(ו)). ר"י: צודניתא. גרס בערוך*), לשון לידה ומזונות: ואם

*) [ערך צד ג]

רבינו חננאל

זה שפחה וזהו עובר זהו יליד בית שנימול לאחר דברי הכל הוא. כי פליגי בילדה ואח"כ הטבילה ת"ק סבר גם זה יליד בית נימול לשמונה. ורב אחא סבר זה יליד בית נימול לאחד. ושאר השמועה פשוטה היא: **תניא** רשב"ג אומר כל ששהה באדם שלשים יום אינו נפל שנאמר ופדויו מבן חדש תפדה. שמונת ימים בבהמה אינו נפל שנאמר ומיום השמיני והלאה ירצה וגו'. הא לא שהה ספק הוי וזה שאנו מלין כל קטן בן ח' ימים הלא אמר רשב"ג קודם ל' יום ספק נפל הוא ואין מחללין עליו את השבת ומלין אתו בן ח' ימים שמא נפל הוא. ופרקי' מלין אותו ממה נפשך אי חי הוא שפיר קא מהיל. ואי נפל הוא מחתך בבשר הוא ולא מלאכה היא ומקשינן אלא הא דתניא ספק בן ז' או בן ח' אין מחללין עליו את השבת אמאי (נימא) [נימהליה] ליה ממ"נ ופרקינן מימהל ה"נ ומהלינן ליה לא נצרכה אלא למכשירי מילה ואליבא דר' אליעזר ולית הלכתא הכי דשנויא היא ואשינויא לא סמכינן ואם יש להקשות עוד אי הכי אם המילה היתה בשר היא ואינה מלאכה אפילו מילה שאינה בזמנה יהא נימול בשבת מחתך בבשר הוא. ופירקו כי מילה דחי מלאכה היא כי כיון שחותך הערלה מתקנו לאכול תרומה ולשחוט עליו אביו את הפסח: **לאכלה** להביא בן ח' שאין שחיטתו מטהרתו פי' זו בהמה נפל טהורה שנולדה לפ' חדשים היא. ומיבעיא לן רשב"ג פליגי רבנן עליה או לא ופשטנו דפליגי רבנן עליה והלכתא

כוותיה דאמר רב יהודה אמר שמואל הלכה כרשב"ג ואי לא דפליגי הלכה למה. [illegible] אמר אביי נפל מן הגג ואכלו אריה. דברי הכל כמו חי הוא. [כי] פליגי שפיהק ומת ומקשינן עליה מדרב פפא ורב הונא בריה דרב יהושע דאיקלעו לבי בריה דרב אידי בר אבין ועביד להו עיגלא תלתא ביומא דשבעא ואמרו ליה אי אתרחיתו עד לאורתא הוה אכלינן מיניה [illegible]

עין משפט נר מצוה

מ א מיי' פ"א מהל' מילה הלכה יד סמג עשין כח טוש"ע י"ד סי' רסו סעיף יא בהג"ה:

מא ב ג ד מיי' פ"ב מהל' שאר אבות הטומאות הלכה ז:

מב ה ו מיי' פ"ב מהל' יום טוב הלכה [illegible] סמג לאוין עה טוש"ע א"ח סי' [illegible] סעיף ה:

מג ז מיי' שם הלכה [illegible] טוש"ע שם סעיף [illegible]:

מד ח ט מיי' פ"א מהל' יבום הלכה [illegible] סמג עשין [illegible] טוש"ע אה"ע סי' [illegible] סעיף [illegible]:

מה י מיי' פ"ד מהל' מאכלות אסורות הלכה [illegible] סמג לאוין [illegible] טוש"ע י"ד סי' [illegible] סעיף [illegible]:

[ר"ל מדקתני כל ששהה ולא תני אם שהה כרבי עבדי]

מו כ מיי' פ"א מהל' אבלות הלכה [illegible] סמג עשין [illegible] טוש"ע י"ד סי' [illegible] [illegible] וכן ברא"ש כאן והתם סי' לג]:

מסורת הש"ס

[לעיל קל.]

חולין נח: ביצה ו:

חולין שם ביצה כו:

[לעיל קו: וש"נ]

הגהות הב"ח

(א) רש"י ד"ה ה"ג ועביד להו עגלא תלתא: (ב) תוס' ד"ה מימהל וכו' בבן שמונה [illegible]: (ג) בא"ד ופריך אלא הא [illegible]: (ד) בא"ד [illegible]: (ה) בא"ד אין צריך לדקדק [illegible]

גליון הש"ס

[illegible]

רב נסים גאון

וזאת אחת מג' הלכות כרשב"ג [illegible] הלכה כר' יוחנן לבד מהני תלת: **אמר** אביי כתנאי [illegible] לאכלה להביא בן ח' שאין שחיטתו מטהרתו [illegible] (ויקרא יא) וכי ימות מן הבהמה יש מן הבהמה מטמאה ויש מן הבהמה שאין מטמאה [illegible]

מז א מיי' פ"ב מהל' יבום הלכה כא סמג עשין נ טוש"ע אה"ע סי' קסל סעיף ז:

מח ב מיי' פ"א מהל' ערכין הלכה ה:

אם אשת ישראל היא – חולצת, אם אשת כהן היא – אינה חולצת. ורב *שרביא משמיה דרבא אמר: אחת זו ואחת זו – חולצת. אמר ליה רבינא לרב שרביא: באורתא אמר רבא הכי, לצפרא הדר ביה. אמר ליה: שריתוה? יהא רעוא דתשרו תרבא. §"ר' יהודה מתיר וכו'". אמר רב שיזבי אמר רב חסדא: לא לכל אמר רבי יהודה אנדרוגינוס זכר הוא, שאם אתה אומר כן – בערכין יערך! ומנלן דלא מיערך – *דתניא: °"הזכר" – ולא טומטום ואנדרוגינוס. יכול לא יהא בערך איש, אבל יהא בערך אשה – תלמוד לומר: "הזכר ואם נקבה היא". זכר ודאי, נקבה ודאית, ולא טומטום ואנדרוגינוס.

ויקרא כז

[יבמות איתא משרשיא]

בכורות מב. ערכין ז: נדה כח:

רש"י

אם אשת ישראל היא. אם אינו כהן זה שנתקדשה לו, ומותר בחלוצה: חולצת. מן הספק, ואח"כ תנשא. ואם כהן הוא, שאם תחלוץ תהא אסורה לו – סמכינן אדרבנן, ואמרינן לאו נפל הוא, ואינה חולצת: לאורתא אמר רבא הכי. כדקאמרת, דאחת זו ואחת זו חולצת: ולצפרא הדר ביה. ואמר אשת כהן אינה חולצת: אמר ליה. רב שרביא לרבינא: שריתוה. בלא חליצה, ועבריתו אדרבן שמעון – יהא רעוא דתשרון חלב באכילה: לא לכל אמר ר"י. לא לכל דבר אמר ר"י דאנדרוגינוס זכר הוא, אלא לענין מילה בלבד, דיליף ליה מריבויא דקרא כדלקמן: שאם אתה אומר. זכר הוא לכל דבר: בערכין יערך. האומר "ערכו עלי" – יעריכהו: הזכר. ה' יתירה קדריש. וגבי נקבה דריש "ואם" יתירה, ולא טומטום ואנדרוגינוס: וקא

תורה אור

תוספות

ואם אשת כהן היא אינה חולצת. הקשה ה"ר משה מבהייס: ותחלוץ, ומה בכך? הא אמרי' בס"פ שני דיבמות (דף כג.) דספק חלוצה, היכא דנכנסה, שריא, דתנן התם: אם קדמו וכנסו – אין מוציאין מידם ואמרינן בגמ', *תני שילא: אפילו שניהם כהנים. מ"ט? חלוצה דרבנן, ועל ספק חלוצה לא גזרו. ואומר רבי: דהאי דאינה חולצת בשמעתין – לא משום שאם חלצה (לא) יהא מחויב להוציאה, אלא כיון דאפשר בלא חליצה – מוטב שלא תחלוץ, שלא להוציא לעז על בניה. כעין שמצינו בפרק בתרא דיבמות (דף קיט.), דתנן: האשה שהלך בעלה וצרתה למדינת הים, ובאו ואמרו לה מת בעליך – לא תנשא ולא תתייבם עד שתדע שמא מעוברת צרתה. ואמר בגמ': *ולעולם? אמר זעירי: ג' לעצמה, ט' לחבירתה, וחולצת ממ"נ. פי': שאם נתעברה צרתה וילדה – מותרת לשוק בלא חליצה, ואם לא נתעברה – הרי חליצה פוטרת. ר' יוחנן אמר: לעצמה ג', לחבירתה לעולם. ופריך: ותחלוץ ממ"נ! ומשני: גזירה שמא יהא ולד של קיימא, ונמצא מצריכה כרוז לכהונה. ולירכה! דילמא איכא דהוי בחליצה ולא הוה בהכרזה, ואמרו: קא שרו חלוצה לכהונה. אלמא אנו מעגנין אשה זו לעולם משום טעמא דנמצא מצריכה כרוז לכהונה, ולכך אין אנו מניחים לחלוץ. וכל שכן הכא שיש לימנע יותר מחליצה, ואיכא למיחש טפי שלא יאמרו קא שרו חלוצה לכהן. מ"ר: ואם אשת כהן היא אינה חולצת. דחי הוא, אפילו כי לא שהה, כרבנן. כדאי' ב"החולץ" (יבמות דף לו: ושם). והא דאמרינן לעיל דהלכה כרשב"ג – היינו דוקא באשת ישראל, אבל באשת כהן – לא קי"ל כוותיה להצריכה חליצה, הואיל ואשת כהן היא. מ"ר: **דתניא** הזכר ולא טומטום ואנדרוגינוס. השתא משמע דדריש מלשון זכר ונקבה, ולא מיתורא דה' ד"הזכר ואם נקבה". דאם לא כן – מאי קפריך בסמוך: ומ"ש גבי מילה, מאי קרא נריך במילה לרבות אנדרוגינוס? והא אדרבה, נריך מיעוט גבי ערכין למעוטי אנדרוגינוס! אלא ע"כ לאו מיתורא דקרא ממעט ליה מערך איש ואשה, אלא ממשמעות דזכר ונקבה, הלכך, נריך קרא במילה לרבות אנדרוגינוס. וכ"מ נמי דגבי קידוש ממעט אנדרוגינוס בלא שום ייתור, כדמוכח בפרק "טרף בקלפי" ביומא (דף מג. ושם), דאמר, תנן התם: הכל כשרים לקדש כו'. ומפרש: אשה מנלן? אמר קרא: ונתן ולא ונתנה כו'. ומההיא טעמא דממעט אשה ממעט אנדרוגינוס. וקשה לרבי: דבנדה פרק "המפלת" (דף כח: ושם) מייתינן הך מילתא דערכין, וקאמר: טעמא דכתב רחמנא "הזכר ואם נקבה" הא מזכר ונקבה לחוד – לא הוה ממעט להו, אלמא מיתורא דואם וה' דהזכר קדריש! ואומר רבי: דודאי מיתורא קדריש, כדמשמע התם. והא דאיצטריך "כל זכר" גבי מילה לרבות אנדרוגינוס – כי היכי דלא נילף מערכין. ומשום הכי, גבי קידוש לא נריך קרא למעט אנדרוגינוס, דילפינן מערכין. וממילה לא ילפינן – דאית לן למילף מערכין לחומרא, ופסול לקדש. והא דאמר רב ב"המפלת" (גם זה שם): טומטום ואנדרוגינוס שראו לובן ואודם כאחת – אין חייבין על ביאת מקדש, ושורפין עליו את התרומה. ונפקא ליה התם ביאת מקדש מדכתיב: "מזכר ועד נקבה תשלחו" – זכר ודאי נקבה ודאית, ולא טומטום ואנדרוגינוס. ופריך התם: וכל היכא דכתיב זכר ונקבה למעוטי טומטום ואנדרוגינוס, והתניא כו', דטעמא דכתב רחמנא "הזכר ואם נקבה כו'". והשתא מאי קפריך? דבלא יתור נמי שפיר ממעט טומטום ואנדרוגינוס, משום דילפינן מערכין! וי"ל: דכי גמרי מערכין – לחומרא, כמו גבי קידוש, אבל לקולא, לפוטרו מביאת מקדש כשראה לובן ואודם כאחת – לא ילפינן מערכין. אלא אדרבה, ילפינן ממילה לחומרא, לחייבו על ביאת מקדש. מיהו, קשה לרבי מהא דתני בבכורות, בפרק "אלו מומין" (דף מב. ושם): "הזכר" ולא הנקבה, כשהוא אומר למטה 'זכר' שאין תלמוד לומר – להוציא טומטום ואנדרוגינוס. והשתא, אמאי איצטריך קרא למעט טומטום ואנדרוגינוס שאינם קדושים לעולה? תיפוק ליה משום דילפינן מערכין לחומרא, דהיינו חומרא – שאין קדושה חלה עליהם, וצריך להביא קרבן אחר! ובדוחק אומר ר"י: דאדרבה, היא קולא שאם לא מצא אלא אנדרוגינוס – יהא יושב ובטל, כעין שמצינו גבי סוכה בפרק "לולב הגזול" (דף לו:), דתניא ר' יהודה אומר: אין סוכה נוהגת אלא בד' מינים שבלולב והדין נותן, ומה לולב שאינו בלילות כבימים כו', אמרו לו: כל דין שאתה דן שתחילתו להחמיר וסופו להקל אינו דין לא מצא ד' מינין יהא יושב ובטל. ומיהו, לא דמיא שפיר להתם, דהתם ודאי סופו להקל, שאם לא ימצא ד' מינים כל ימי סוכה – נמצא המצוה עוברת, וא"א לעשותה עוד אפילו ימצא אחרי כן. אבל גבי קרבן, אם אינו מוצא עכשיו אלא אנדרוגינוס – אחר זמן ימצא, וא"כ תחילתו *וסופו להחמיר הוא! ועוד אומר רבי: דההוא קרא ד"הזכר" גבי עולת נדבה הוא דכתיב, ולא גבי חובה, הלכך לא שייך התם יהא יושב ובטל, כיון שאינו מחויב שום קרבן. מ"ר: **הזכר** ולא טומטום ואנדרוגינוס. בבכורות בפרק (א) "אלו מומין" (מב. ושם) אמר: סמי מכאן טומטום. דתנן התם: טומטום ואנדרוגינוס אין שוחטין עליו לא במקדש ולא במדינה. רבי ישמעאל אומר: אין מום גדול מזה, וחכ"א: אינו בכור, אלא נגזז ונעבד. ואמר בגמ', אר"ח: מחלוקת באנדרוגינוס, אבל טומטום – דברי הכל ספיקא הוא, וקדוש מספיקא. אמר ליה(ב): אלא מעתה בערכין יערך, אלמה תניא: הזכר ולא טומטום ואנדרוגינוס! ואיחוי: תני מכאן טומטום. ומשמע דהכי פריך: אלמה תניא הזכר ולא טומטום, (ג) וכיון דאמרת דספיקא היא, אצטריך קרא למעוטי ספיקא?! ומאי קשיא, דבשלמא בההיא סוגיא דלעיל דהתם פריך גבי אנדרוגינוס: איצטריך קרא למעוטי ספיקא – שפיר פריך, שהרי אין סברא לומר שיהא ספק לפסוק, דודאי ברור למקרא אם הוא זכר או נקבה. ואם הוא אמת שהפסוק חושבו זכר – למה יחזורו שלא יהא קדוש לעולה? ואם קרא חשיב ליה נקבה – א"צ לכתוב למעטו. (ד) *אלא טומטום ודאי צריך קרא, שיש מהן זכרים ויש מהן נקבות. וכי האי גוונא – שייך שפיר למקרא למעטו, כיון שהוא ספק לנו אם הוא זכר או נקבה. כעין שמצינו גבי מעשר בהמה, דתנן בפ' בתרא דבכורות (דף נח:), ומייתי לה בפ"ק דב"מ (דף ו:): קפץ אחד מן המנויין לתוכן – כולן פטורין. ומפרש התם טעמא: דעשירי ודאי אמר רחמנא, ולא עשירי ספק. וכן בנגעים: ספק בהרת קדמה לשער לבן, או שער לבן קדם לבהרת, ונפקא לן בשלהי מסכת נזיר (דף סה.) דטהור, מדכתיב: "לטהרו או לטמאו" – שפתח הכתוב תחילה בטהרה. ונראה לר', דה"פ מילתא דרב חסדא; אבל טומטום קדוש מספיקא, משום דלכל כמה דמלינן לאוקמי קרא למעט אנדרוגינוס דממעטי להו רבנן, מדכתיב "הזכר" כדדריש התם לעיל – לית לן לאוקמי לקרא למעוטי טומטום. משום דאם הוא זכר ודאי – אין סברא למעוטי, ואם הוא נקבה – אין צריך קרא. דהשתא פריך שפיר מערכין, דלא הוה לן למעוטי טומטום? כיון דאיכא לאוקמי קרא לאנדרוגינוס – לית לן למעוטי טומטום מיניה. דליכא למימר "ואם נקבה" לאנדרוגינוס לא איצטריך, דכבר מיעטנוה מהזכר – (ה)מ"מ הוה אמינא; נהי דמעטיה קרא מערך איש, מיהו לא גרע מאשה, ויהא לו לכל הפחות ערך אשה. הלכך לאנדרוגינוס נמי אצטריך "ואם נקבה", לפיכך הוצרכו לתרץ: סמי מכאן טומטום. והא דתני בפ"ק דחגיגה (דף ד. ושם): "זכורך" להוציא טומטום ואנדרוגינוס. ולא פריך מינה בבכורות לרב חסדא, ולישני: סמי מכאן טומטום! ונראה לר': משום דקרא יתירא (ו) למעט טומטום, דתרי "זכורך" כתיבי. והא דפריך בפ"ק דחגיגה: בשלמא אנדרוגינוס איצטריך, סד"א הואיל ואית ליה זכרות – ליחייב, קמ"ל דבריה הוא בפני עצמו. אלא טומטום ספיקא הוא, איצטריך קרא למעוטי ספיקא – ומשני: כשבילין מבחוץ. ונראה לרבי: דשפיר פריך, דהתם ודאי לא הוה צריך קרא למעוטי טומטום, דפשיטא בלא קרא דלא מייתי עולת ראייה, דהיכי נעביד? מספיקא לא מייתי על תנאי דאם נקבה הוא תהא עולת נדבה – דהא עולת ראייה לא בעי סמיכה, ואסור לסמוך משום עבודה בקדשים. [ועולת נדבה בעי סמיכה]. ואם לא יסמוך – טוב שלא יביא, כמו שמצינו גבי פסח בפסחים פרק "האשה" (דף פח:), דתניא: חבורה שנתערבו עורות פסחיהן ונמצא יבלת באחת מהן – כולן יצאו לבית השריפה, ופטורין מלעשות פסח שני כו'. עד דפריך: ונייתי מותר הפסח! ומשני: משום סמיכה. דאילו מותר הפסח בעי סמיכה ואילו פסח לא בעי סמיכה. אלמא: משום סמיכה נמנעים מלעשות פסח, כ"ש מלהביא עולת ראייה. ובבכורות על מילתא דרב חסדא לא הוה מצי לשנויי כשבילין מבחוץ, דכ"ש דלא הוה ליה לקרא למעוטיה. מ"ר. וקשה לי: לרב חסדא אמאי ממעט רב בנדה טומטום

[שם כד.]

[דף קיט:]

[גיר' רש"א וסופו להחמיר הוא הלכך לא שייך התם יושב ובטל ועוד סבר רבי כו' ולא גבי חובה והוי קולא כיון שאינו מחויב שום קרבן]

ס"א אלא טומטום די"ל שהמקרא חושבו לא זכר ולא נקבה דיש מהם זכרים כו'

הגהות הב"ח

(א) תום' ד"ה הזכר וכו' בבכורות בפרק על אלו מומין וכו' אין לך מום גדול: (ב) בא"ד אמר ליה רבא אלא מעתה וכו': (ג) בא"ד דכיון דאמרת: (ד) בא"ד אלא טומטום דיש לומר שאין המקרא חושבו לא זכר ולא נקבה דיש מהן זכרים: (ה) בא"ד מהזכר דמ"מ ה"א נמי: (ו) בא"ד דקרא יתירה איכא למעט:

רבינו חננאל

ודבי ר' אושעיא איזה בן ח' כל שלא יצאו לו חדשיו. ר' אומר סימנים ניכרין בו שערו וצפרניו שלא גמרו וכדרך שבן שמנה חדשים באדם נפל כך בן ח' בבהמה גסה ובן ד' בדקה נפל. רשב"ג אומר כל ששהה באדם ל' יום אינו נפל וכו'. והלכתא כת"ק דאמר בן שמנה אין שחיטתו מטהרתו אלא אמרינן מת היה ונבילה היא ומטמאה שאין שחיטה מועלת בנבילה דתנינן מתניתין סתמא כוותיה בפרק בהמה המקשה לילד ופירשנוהו שם. מי יש במינו שחיטה מי אין במינו שחיטה בן ח' חי אין שחיטתו מטהרתו. לפי שאין למינו שחיטה. וסוגיא דשמעתא שאין שחיטתו מטהרתו בפחות משמנה ימים אלא ברמוחזק לן שכלו חדשיו כגון שהיתה בהמה קשורה לו בביתו ט' חדשים לגסה וד' לדקה וילדה וברי לן שלא עלה [עליה] זכר בביתו וזה ששנינו במשנתנו סתם תינוק בן יום א' מטמא בזיבה. ומטמא בנגעים ומטמא בטמא מת. וזוקק ליבום ופוסל מן היבום ומאכיל בתרומה ופוסל בתרומה ונוחל ומנחיל וההורגו חייב והרי הוא לאביו ולאמו ולכל קרוביו כחתן שלם ואמרינן בגמרא למאי [illegible] אמר רב פפא לענין אבלות לימא מתניתין דלא כרשב"ג דתניא רשב"ג אומר כל ששהה באדם ל' יום אינו נפל' [illegible] (ספק) ספיקא הוי. ומפרקינן דקים ליה ביה שכלו לו חדשיו. ודין כל השנוים במשנה זאת דינם אחד במוחזק לן ביה שכלו לו חדשיו ומיהא הוו (מיתא) [מתאבלין] באלי בריה דרב דימי בריה דרב יוסף ורב כהנא בינוקא דשכיב בגו תלתין יומין דהוו מוחזקין שכלו לו חדשיו: **אתמר** מת בתוך ל' ועמדה ונתקדשה אמר רבינא משמיה דרבא אם אשת ישראל היא חולצת אם אשת כהן היא אינה חולצת ורב שרביא משמיה דרבא אמר אחת זו ואחת זו חולצת. א"ל רבינא לרב שרביא באורתא אמר רבא הכי כי דאמרת לצפרא הדר ביה. א"ל יהא רעוא דתשרי תרבא כלומר עתה תאסר ואחר שעה תתירה. יהי רצון שתתיר אף החלב. והלכתא כרבינא משמא דרבא. והאמר רבינא והדר ביה רבא מההיא: ר' יהודה מתיר באנדרוגינוס פי' למולו בשבת אמר רב שיזבי אמר רב חסדא לא לכל

רב נסים גאון

ולאחר כן אמרו לאכלה להביא בן ח' שאין שחיטתו מטהרתו כלומר בן ח' חדשים בבהמה גסה טהורה על דעת כמו שאמרו בפרק א' ממסכת בכורות (דף ח) בבהמה גסה יולדת לט' חדשי[ם] ומה שתלד בהמה גסה טהורה בחודש ח' הרי הוא כמת ולא תועיל בו השחיטה להוציאו מידי נבילה לענין הטומאה כמו שמועלת בטריפה מכאן הראיה שהקדמנו ממה שאמרו ויש מן הבהמה שאינה מטמאה פרט לטריפה ששחטה

גמרא

(א)*וסתם ספרא רבי יהודה. אמר רב נחמן בר יצחק: אף אנן נמי תנינא *א"הכל כשרים לקדש, חוץ מחש"ו. רבי יהודה מכשיר בקטן, ופוסל באשה ואנדרוגינוס" – ש"מ. ומאי שנא מילה – משום דכתיב °"המול לכם כל זכר".§

מתני' *מי שהיו לו שני תינוקות, אחד למול אחר השבת ואחד למול בשבת. ושכח, ומל את של אחר השבת בשבת – חייב. אחד למול בע"ש, ואחד למול בשבת, ושכח ומל את של ע"ש בשבת, רבי אליעזר מחייב חטאת, ורבי יהושע פוטר.§ **גמ'** רב הונא מתני "חייב" – רב יהודה מתני פטור. רב הונא מתני "חייב" – דתניא, אמר ר"ש בן אלעזר: לא נחלקו רבי *אליעזר ור' יהושע על מי שהיו לו ב' תינוקות, אחד למול בשבת ואחד למול אחר השבת, ושכח ומל את של אחר השבת בשבת – שהוא חייב. על מה נחלקו – על מי שהיו לו ב' תינוקות, א' למול בע"ש וא' למול בשבת, ושכח ומל את של ע"ש בשבת. שר' אליעזר מחייב חטאת, ורבי יהושע פוטר. ושניהם לא למדוה אלא מעבודה זרה. ר' אליעזר סבר: כעבודה זרה, מה עבודה זרה אמר רחמנא "לא תעביד" וכי עביד – מיחייב, ה"נ – לא שנא. ורבי יהושע; התם – דלאו מצוה, הכא – מצוה. רב יהודה מתני: "פטור" – דתניא, א"ר מאיר: ב"לא נחלקו ר"א ורבי יהושע על מי שהיו לו ב' תינוקות אחד למול בע"ש ואחד למול בשבת, ושכח ומל את של ע"ש בשבת – שהוא פטור. על מה נחלקו – על מי שהיו לו ב' תינוקות, אחד למול אחר השבת וא' למול בשבת, ושכח ומל את של אחר השבת בשבת. שר"א מחייב חטאת, ורבי יהושע גפוטר. ושניהם לא למדוה אלא מעבודה זרה. ר"א סבר: כעבודה זרה, מה עבודה זרה אמר רחמנא "לא תעביד", וכי עביד – מיחייב, ה"נ – לא שנא. ור' יהושע: התם – לא טריד מצוה, הכא – טריד מצוה. *תני ר' חייא, אומר היה ר"מ: לא נחלקו רבי *אליעזר ורבי יהושע על מי שהיו לו ב' תינוקות א' למול בע"ש וא' למול בשבת, ושכח ומל את של ע"ש בשבת – שהוא חייב. על מה נחלקו – על מי שהיו לו ב' תינוקות, א' למול אחר השבת וא' למול בשבת. ושכח ומל של אחר השבת בשבת, *שר"א מחייב חטאת ור' יהושע פוטר. השתא, רבי יהושע סיפא דלא קא עביד מצוה – פוטר, רישא דקא עביד מצוה מחייב?! אמרי דבי ר' ינאי: רישא – כגון שקדם ומל של שבת בע"ש, דלא ניתנה שבת לידחות. סיפא – ניתנה שבת לידחות. א"ל רב אשי לרב כהנא: רישא נמי, ניתנה שבת לידחות לגבי תינוקות דעלמא! להאי גברא מיהא לא איתיהיב.§

מתני' *דקטן נימול לשמונה לתשעה ולעשרה ולאחד עשר ולי"ב, לא פחות ולא יותר. הא כיצד: כדרכו – לשמונה, נולד לבין השמשות – נימול לט', ביה"ש של ע"ש – נימול לעשרה, יו"ט לאחר השבת – נימול לאחד עשר, ב' ימים של ר"ה – נימול לשנים עשר. קטן החולה – אין מוהלין אותו עד שיבריא.§ **גמ'** *אמר שמואל: החלצתו חמה – נותנין לו כל ז' להברותו. איבעיא להו: מי בעינן מעת לעת? ת"ש: דתני *לודא "יום הבראתו כיום הולדו". מאי לאו, מה יום הולדו – לא בעינן מעת לעת, אף יום הבראתו לא בעינן מעת לעת. לא, עדיף יום הבראתו מיום הולדו. דאילו יום הולדו – לא בעינן מעת לעת, ואילו יום הבראתו – בעינן מעת לעת.§

מתני' *ואלו הן ציצין המעכבין את המילה: בשר החופה את רוב העטרה, ואינו אוכל בתרומה. זואם היה בעל בשר – מתקנו מפני מראית העין.

מל

כראשית יז | יבמות עא.

רש"י

והא סתם ספרא הוא, דתורת כהנים תניא לה, וסתם ספרא רבי יהודה*: לקדש. מי חטאת, לתת אפר על המים: מכשיר בקטן ופוסל באשה. טעמיה מפרש בסדר יומא בפ"ג: ובאנדרוגינוס. שמע מינה דרבי יהודה כאשה משוי ליה: כל זכר. ריבויא הוא:

מתני' ושכח ומל את של אחר השבת בשבת חייב. דטעה בדבר מצוה ולא עשה מצוה הוא, ועבד ליה חבורה שלא לצורך. ודהא אפילו רבי יהושע מודה: אחד למול בשבת ואחד למול בע"ש ושכח ומל את של ע"ש בשבת ר"א מחייב חטאת. דמילה שלא בזמנה אינה דוחה שבת. ואע"ג דטעה בדבר מצוה, שהיה טרוד באותו של שבת ומתוך כך טעה בזה, ואף בזה עשה מצוה – שהרי ראוי הוא למול, אלא שאינו דוחה שבת – ס"ל לר"א: טעה בדבר מצוה, ועשה מצוה שיש בה חיוב חטאת – חייב. ורבי יהושע פוטר, דס"ל: טעה בדבר מצוה ועשה מצוה – פטור: **גמ'** רב הונא מתני. במתניתין, ברישא חייב לדברי הכל, כדתנינן לה אנן: ורב יהודה מתני ברישא פטור. דמוקי לה בשכח ומל את של ע"ש בשבת, ופלוגתא היא בשל אחר השבת בשבת: שהוא חייב. דאע"ג דטריד במצוה וטעה בה, כיון דלאו מצוה, שעדיין לא הגיע זמנו למול – חייב: אלא מע"ז. שהוקשו כל חטאות שבתורה לחטאת ע"ז, דכתיב: "תורה אחת יהיה לכם" וגו', בפרשת "שלח לך אנשים" גבי קרבן ע"ז: ור' יהושע התם. עובד עבודה זרה לא עשה מצוה: ה"ג: רב יהודה מתני פטור. דתניא: אמר ר"מ, לא נחלקו ר"א ורבי יהושע על שהיו לו שני תינוקות אחד למול ע"ש כו': ה"ג ורבי יהושע התם לא טריד במצוה הכא טריד במצוה. טרוד להתעסק במצוה גמורה, שהרי אחד מהם זמנו היום, וטרוד לבו למהר ולעשות. ומתוך טרדו טעה, ומל את זה שאין בו מצוה כלל: ושכח ומל של ע"ש בשבת שהוא חייב. לקמיה מתרץ לה: דלא ניתנה שבת לידחות. שאין לו תינוק שיהא זמנו היום, הלכך לא היה טרוד היום במצוה, שלא היה מוטל עליו כלום לעשות, ולא היה לו לטעות: **מתני'** נולד בין השמשות נימול לט'. שהרי ליום שמיני של מחר הוא נימול, ושמא בין השמשות יום הוא ונימול לט': היה היום ע"ש. א"א למולו בשבת הבאה דשמא ט' הוא, והויא ליה מילה שלא בזמנה ואינה דוחה שבת, וצריך להמתין עד לאחר השבת שהוא עשירי: חל יו"ט להיות אחר השבת. אין מילה שלא בזמנה דוחה אותו, ונימול לי"א: **גמ'** חלצתו חמה. נשלף ממנו החולי ויצא מגופו: דתני לודא. שם חכם: יום הבראתו כיום הולדו. ממתינין לו כיום הולדו: מאי לאו. יום הולדו דווקא קאמר, דלא בעינן מעת לעת: לא. "כיום הולדו" דקתני – למיתב ליה ז'. מיהו, עדיף יום הבראתו מהא, דבעינן מעת לעת. ומהא ליכא למשמע מידי: **מתני'** ציצין. רצועות של בשר שנשארו מן הערלה: עטרה. היא שפה גבוה המקפת את הגיד סביב, וממנה משפע ויורד לראשו: ואינו אוכל בתרומה. אם כהן הוא, דילפינן ביבמות (דף ע.) שערל אסור בתרומה: ואם היה בעל בשר. שהיה שמן, ונראה בשר שלמעלה מערלתו לאחר שניטלה ערלה כולה, כאילו אותו בשר חוזר וחופה את הגיד: מתקנו. ומשפע באיזמל מאותו עובי: מפני מראית העין. שלא יהא נראה כערל:

פרע

תוספות

טומטום שראה לובן ואודם מביאת מקדש? וכ"ת: משום דליכא קרא יתירא (ג) דדריש לה לטומטום, דכתיב: "מזכר ועד נקבה תשלחו", ואי למעוטי אנדרוגינוס גרידא – לא ה"ל למיכתב אלא זכר – לא היא, דאי לא כתב אלא זכר א"כ ה"א אשה לא מחייב' בביאת מקדש, מדכתיב "זכר" ולא כתיב אדם. ושמא י"ל: דלית ליה לרב דר"ת, דאיכא אמורא נמי דפליג עליה בבכורות. וא"ת: ומאי איצטריך רב למעוטי אנדרוגינוס? והא איהו ס"ל בפרק "הערל" ביבמות (דף פג.) דאנדרוגינוס ספיקא הוא, (ג)ואיצטריך קרא למעוטי ספק?! מיהו, הא לא קשיא, דה"א: כשראה לובן ואודם כאחת – יתחייב ממ"נ. אבל הא תימה: כיון דסבר רב אנדרוגינוס ספיקא הוא, אמאי קאמר רב: מזכר ועד נקבה, זכר ודאי נקבה ודאית, ואם הוא זכר – ימעט אותו מזכר, ואם הוא נקבה – ימעט אותו מנקבה! ומיהו, י"ל: דמשום טומטום נקטיה, דפעמים הוי זכר, ופעמים הוי נקבה:

הזכר ולא טומטום ואנדרוגינוס. תימה לרבי: דבפרק "אלו מומין" (בכורות דף מב.) גבי בכור מצריך הזכר הזכרים – למעוטי טומטום ואנדרוגינוס, משמע התם דמ"הזכר" לחודיה לא הוה ממעט לה, והכא ממעטין ליה מ"הזכר" לחודיה:

עין משפט נר מצוה

מט א מיי' פ"ו מהל' פרה הלכה ב סמג עשין רלב:

נ ב ג מיי' פ"ב מהל' שגגות הלכה ח:

נא ד מיי' פ"א מהל' מילה הלכה יב סמג עשין כח טוש"ע י"ד סי' רסו סעיף ח:

נב ה מיי' שם הלכה טז סמג שם טוש"ע י"ד סי' רסב סעיף ב:

נג ו ז מיי' פ"ב מהל' מילה הלכה ג ה סמג שם טוש"ע י"ד סי' רסד סעיף ה ו:

רבינו חננאל

א"ר יהודה אנדרוגינוס זכר הוא. שאם אי אתה אומר כך יערך ומנ"ל דלא מערך דתניא הזכר ולא טומטום ואנדרוגינוס כו' ופשוטה היא ומסקינן בה ומאי שנא גבי מילה דכתיב המול לכם כל זכר כל לרבות. ויש מי שאומר הלכתא כרבנן דאמרי ספק ואנדרוגינוס אין מחללין עליו את השבת ואין הלכה כר' יהודה ומדחזינן רב חסדא דריש לטעמיה דר' יהודה ש"מ הלכתא כוותיה: **מתניתין** מי שהיו לו ב' תינוקות אחד למול אחר השבת ואחד למול בשבת ושכח ומל את של אחר השבת בשבת חייב וכו' [ואמרינן בגמ'] רב הונא מתני חייב ורב יהודא מתני פטור פי' רב הונא מתני חייב דמוקים ליה למתניתין לר"ש דאמר ר"ש לא נחלקו ר' אליעזר (ור"ש) [ור' יהושע] על מי שהיו לו*) דקיי"ל סתם משנה ר' מאיר ובהא תנא דבי ר' חייא פליגי עליה ורב הונא דמוקים לה כר' שמעון כוותיה עבדינן וחלוקת ר' אליעזר ור' יהושע דברים ברורין הן. (שנים) ושניהם מע"ז למדוה דהא איתקשא כל התורה כולה לע"ז ר' אליעזר סבירא כע"ז מה ע"ז אמרה תורה לא תעבוד ואם תעבוד ע"ז בשגגה מכל מקום חייב חטאת. כן אמרה תורה בשבת. המחלל השבת בשגגה מ"מ חייב חטאת. ור' יהושע סבר התם לגבי ע"ז לא נתכוין לקיים המצוה הכא בשבת נתכוין לקיים מצות מילה. לפיכך פטור הוא והלכתא כר' יהושע וכדמתניתין ר' שמעון: **אחד** למול ערב שבת ואחד למול בשבת ושכח ומל את של שבת בע"ש ואת של ע"ש בשבת פטור כי מ"מ מצוה עשה. ואע"פ שמל בט'. אבל בזמן ששכח ומל את של אחר השבת בשבת כיון שלא עשה מצוה כי בו' מלו אפילו ר' יהושע מודה שחייב חטאת. וכן הלכה וכל היכא דפליג ר' אליעזר ור' יהושע הלכה כר' יהושע חוץ ממקומות ידועים. וזה אינו מהם. וכן רב הונא הלכתא כוותיה דשכיח גבי ריש גלותא וגרסינן הלכתא כוותין או הלכתא כוותייכו כו': **מתניתין** קטן נימול לשמונה לתשעה כו' קטן חולה אין מלין אותו עד שיבריא. אמר שמואל חלצתו חמה נותנין לו כל ז' להברותו והלכתא כשמואל דיהבינן ליה מאחר שחלצתו חמה שבעת ימים

*) [נראה לעין דחסר פה כמה תיבות וכצ"ל על מי שהיו לו שני תינוקות אחד למול בשבת ואחד למול אחר השבת ושכח ומל של אחר השבת בשבת שהוא חייב וכו' ורב יהודה מתני פטור דתניא אמר ר"מ וכו' ומהדר לאוקמי מתני' כר"מ משום דקיי"ל דסתם משנה ר"מ וכו'].

מסורת הש"ס

[סנהדרין פו.]

[עירובין לו: וש"נ]

יומא מג. יבמות עב: ערכין ג. פרה פ"ה מ"ד

פסחים עב. כריתות יט:

[נ"ל אליעזר]

פסחים עב. ע"ש [נ"ל אליעזר]

[יבמות לד.]

ערכין ח:

יבמות עא.

ג"ז שם:

הגהות הב"ח

(א) גמ' וסתם ספרא ר' יהודה. נ"ב ול"ע מן מס' נדה דף מו: (ב) תום' ד"ה הזכר יתירא למעוטי לה לטומטום: (ג) בא"ד ספיקא הוא וכי איצטריך:

רב נסים גאון

אף אנן נמי תנינא הכל כשרין לקדש חוץ מחרש שוטה וקטן כו'. זו המשנה במס' פרה בפרק ה' ולענין קידוש מי חטאת נתכוונה. *)לומר שבעת שישארו ציצין המעכבין את המילה הרי הוא ערל עדיין ואם הוא כהן אסור לוכל בתרומה כמו ששנינו בבהמה המקשה לילד: (עב) בפרק בשחיטת חולין ששחטה ותמצא כמותה במס' יבמות (דף ע) הערל וכל הטמאין לא יאכלו בתרומה והזכירו בתלמוד המחלוקת שהיתה בין ר' אליעזר ובין ר' עקיבא בתורת כהנים במה שכתוב (ויקרא כב) איש איש מזרע אהרן ומה שכתוב (שם) תושב כהן ר' אליעזר גמר לערל בגזירה שוה לערל מפסח ור' עקיבא אמר איש איש לרבות את הערל: אבל

*) זה לפרש את המשנה אלו הן ציצין כו'.

נד א מיי' פ"ב מהל' מילה הלכה ד סמג עשין כח טוש"ע י"ד סי' רסד סעיף ד:
נה ב מיי' שם הלכה ג טוש"ע שם סעי' ה:
נו ג מיי' שם הלכה ה טור וש"ע שם סעיף ו:
נז ד מיי' פ"ג מהל' מילה הלכה א סמג שם טוש"ע י"ד סי' רסה סעיף א:
נח ה מיי' שם הלכה ד סמג שם טוש"ע י"ד סי' רסח סעיף ה:
נט ו מיי' שם הלכה ה סמג שם טוש"ע י"ד סי' רסז סעיף יב:
א ז מיי' פכ"א מהל' שבת הלכה יז ופ"ג מהל' י"ט הלכה יז סמג לאוין סה עה טוש"ע א"ח סי' שטו סעי' ט וסי' שיט סעיף ט וסי' תקי סעיף ד:

מל ולא פרע את המילה – כאילו לא מל.§ **גמ'** *אמר רבי אבינא א"ר ירמיה בר אבא אמר רב: ב בשר החופה את רוב גובהה של עטרה.§ "ואם היה בעל בשר וכו'".§ אמר שמואל: קטן המסורבל בבשר, רואין אותו, כ"ז שמתקשה ונראה מהול – אינו צריך למול, ואם לאו – צריך למול. במתניתא תנא, *רשב"ג אומר: ג קטן המסורבל בבשר רואין אותו, כל זמן שמתקשה ואינו נראה מהול – צריך למולו, ואם לאו – אינו צריך למולו. מאי בינייהו? איכא בינייהו: נראה ואינו נראה.§ "מל ולא פרע".§ ת"ר: * ד המל אומר: "אקב"ו על המילה". אבי הבן אומר: "אקב"ו להכניסו בבריתו של אברהם אבינו". העומדים (א) אומרים: כשם שנכנס לברית כך יכנס לתורה לחופה ולמע"ט. והמברך אומר: "אשר קידש ידיד מבטן, חוק בשארו שם, וצאצאיו חתם באות ברית קדש. על כן בשכר זאת, אל חי חלקנו, (ב) צוה* להציל ידידות שארינו משחת, למען בריתו אשר שם בבשרנו בא"י כורת הברית". ה המל את הגרים אומר: "ברוך אתה ה' אלהינו מלך העולם אקב"ו על המילה". והמברך אומר: "אקב"ו למול את הגרים ולהטיף מהם דם ברית, שאילמלא דם ברית לא נתקיימו שמים וארץ שנאמר: °אם לא בריתי יומם ולילה חוקות שמים וארץ לא שמתי [ירמיהו לג] בא"י כורת הברית". ו המל את העבדים אומר: "אקב"ו על המילה", והמברך אומר: "אקב"ו למול את העבדים ולהטיף מהם דם ברית *שאילמלא דם ברית חוקות שמים וארץ לא נתקיימו, שנאמ': 'אם לא בריתי יומם ולילה חוקות שמים וארץ לא שמתי' בא"י כורת הברית".§ [נדרים לב.]

הדרן עלך רבי אליעזר דמילה

רבי אליעזר אומר: תולין את המשמרת ביו"ט, ונותנין לתלויה בשבת. וחכ"א: ז אין תולין את המשמרת בי"ט, ואין נותנין לתלויה בשבת, אבל נותנין לתלויה ביו"ט.§ **גמ'** השתא ר"א, אוסופי אהל עראי לא מוספינן, למיעבד לכתחלה שרי?! מאי היא – דתנן, *פקק החלון, ר"א אומר: בזמן שקשור ותלוי – פוקקין בו, ואם לאו – אין פוקקין בו. וחכ"א: בין כך ובין כך – פוקקין בו. ואמר רבה בר בר חנה א"ר יוחנן: *הכל מודים שאין עושין אהל עראי בתחלה בי"ט, ואין צ"ל בשבת. לא נחלקו אלא להוסיף, שר"א אומר: אין מוסיפין בי"ט, ואין צ"ל בשבת. וחכ"א: מוסיפין בשבת, ואין צ"ל ביום טוב. ר"א סבר לה כרבי יהודה, דתניא: *אין בין יום טוב לשבת אלא אוכל נפש בלבד, רבי יהודה מתיר אף מכשירי אוכל נפש. אימר דשמעינן ליה לר' יהודה – במכשירין שאי אפשר לעשותם מערב יום טוב, במכשירין שאפשר לעשותם מעיו"ט מי שמעת ליה?! דר"א עדיפא מדרבי יהודה.§ "וחכ"א".§ איבעיא להו: תלה מאי? אמר רב יוסף: תלה – חייב חטאת. א"ל אביי: אלא מעתה, תלא כוזא בסיכתא הכי נמי דמיחייב?! אלא

[שולי הגליון: שבת קלט: עירובין קב. | ביצה לב: | תוספ' סוכה פ"א | מגילה ז: ביצה כח:]

רש"י

פרע. גילה: **גמ'** רוב גובהה. לא תימא רוב העטרה דקתני מתני' רוב היקפה, אלא אפילו רוב גובהה במקום אחד: קטן המסורבל בבשר. פלטר"י בלע"ז, שהשמן ועב, ולאחר שנימול נראה כמכוסה: כל זמן שמתקשה. ומתוך הקישוי מתפשט בשרו. כדשמואל גרסינן: ונראה מהול. במתניתא גרסינן: ואינו נראה מהול: **איכא** בינייהו נראה ואינו נראה. לשמואל, נראה מהול – הוא דאין צריך למולו; הא נראה ואינו נראה – צריך. למתניתא, אינו נראה – הוא דצריך; הא נראה ואינו נראה – אינו צריך: **אשר** קידש ידיד מבטן. יצחק קרי ידיד, על שם "אשר אהבת" (בראשית כב): **מבטן.** דקודם שנולד נתקדש למצוה זו, דכתיב (שם יז): "אבל שרה אשתך וגו' והקימותי את בריתי אתו", היינו מילה: **בשארו.** בבשרו: **שם.** חק של מילה: **וצאצאיו.** אחריו: **חתם באות.** זו של ברית קדש: **צוה** להציל ידידות שארינו משחת. מגיהנם, דכתיב: "גם את בדם בריתך שלחתי אסיריך מבור אין מים בו" (זכריה ט):

הדרן עלך ר' אליעזר דמילה

תולין את המשמרת. שמסננין בה שמרי יין, ומותח פיה לכל צד בעגול, ונעשה כאהל על חלל הכלי שקורין אשטנד"א. ואע"ג דעביד אהל, שרי בי"ט, כדמפרש בגמרא. אבל בשבת – מיתלא לכתחילה לא, אבל אם תלויה היא – נותנין לתוכה שמרים ומסנן, דאין דרך בורר בכך: **גמ'** פקק החלון. כגון ארובת הגג: **אלא** להוסיף. כגון פקק זה שאינו אלא תוספת עראי על האהל: **סבר** ליה כרבי יהודה. הלכך הכא שרי, דמכשירי אוכל נפש הוא: **שאי** אפשר לעשותן מעי"ט. כגון שפוד שנרצם בי"ט: **עדיפא.** חזקה, דהוא שרי אפילו מכשירין שאפשר מעיו"ט: **תלה** כוזא בסיכתא. תלה כלי קטן במגוד: ה"ג דמיחייב. והכא מאי חיובא איכא באהל עראי? בנין גמור לא הוי, ומדרבנן הוא דמיתסר: אלא

תוספות

מל ולא פרע את המילה כאילו לא מל. תימה: אמאי איצטריך למיתני הא? כיון דכבר תנא דבשר החופה את רוב העטרה מעכב המילה, וכי לא פרע – עדיין רוב עטרה מכוסה: **אבי** הבן אומר כו'. רבינו שמואל גרים אבי הבן ברישא, והדר המל אומר. וכבר הנהיג לעשות כן לברך אבי הבן קודם המילה, משום ד"להכניסו" – להבא משמע, כדאמרינן בפ"ק דפסחים (ד' ז. ושם): ב"לבער" – כ"ע לא פליגי דלהבא משמע. ועוד: *דכל המצות מברך עליהן עובר לעשייתן. ור"ת החזיר המנהג לקדמותו, וגרס המל ברישא, והדר אבי הבן, כמו שכתוב בכל הספרים. וכן מוכח כולה סוגיא מדקאמר; העומדים שם אומרים: כשם שהכניסו לברית. מכלל שכבר הכניסו. ועוד: דגבי גר דבסמוך גרס ברישא המל כו', והדר המברך אומר: אקב"ו למול את הגרים. ונראה הוא שזהו כנגד ברכת אבי הבן, והתם א"א לשנות הגירסא. שיש בלותה ברכה "להטיף מהן דם ברית כו' ברוך כורת הברית" – משמע דכל זה הוא אחר המילה. ועוד: דהמברך מברך לעולם אחר המילה, כמו במילת קטן. והיא דפסחים ה"פ: ב"לבער" כ"ע לא פליגי דלהבא משמע טפי מלשעבר, ומיהו: לשעבר נמי משמע. כי פליגי ב"על ביעור", מר סבר: דמשמע מעיקרא טפי מלהבא, ומר סבר: להבא נמי משמע כמו מעיקרא. והא דאמרינן דכל המצות מברך עובר לעשייתן – ה"מ כשהמברך עצמו עושה המצוה: **ידיד** מבטן. אומר ר"ת שהוא אברהם אבינו, שנקרא "ידיד", שנאמר (ירמיה יא): "מה לידידי בביתי" כדדרשינן במנחות בפרק "כל המנחות" (ד' נג: ושם). ושלשת האבות נזכרים: "חוק בשארו שם" – הוא יצחק, ו"צאצאיו חתם באות ברית קדש" – הוא יעקב וצאצאיו הוא ובניו, כמו שתרגם יונתן "הצאצאים והצפיעות" – בניא ובני בניא, (ישעיה כב) כלומר: יוצאי חלציו*): **במצותיו** וצונו למול את העבדים. שנאמר "יליד בית ומקנת כסף" (בראשית יז):

הדרן עלך ר' אליעזר דמילה

תולין. אבל נותנין לתלויה ביום טוב. וצריך לפרש ולומר שאם היה עושהו מאתמול – לא היה טוב כל כך וזוק. והא דתניא בפרקין דלעיל (ד' קלז. ושם) דאין מסננין את החרדל במסננת שלו בי"ט – אם היה עושהו מאתמול לא היה מתקלקל: **דרבי** אליעזר עדיפא מדר"י. תימה: ולר"א תיקשה ליה הנהו קראי דדריש בפ"ק דמגילה (ד' ז:) דקאמר: ורבי יהודה, כתיב "הוא" וכתיב "לכם", ולא קשיא; כאן – במכשירין שאפשר וכו'. וכ"ת: ר"א הוה דריש "הוא" לדרשה אחרינא – א"כ מנ"ל התם דרבי יהודה הוה מפליג? ניתא דרבי יהודה הוה דריש ליה לדרשה אחריתי כר' אליעזר! ונראה דבדאורייתא מודה ר' אליעזר דמכשירין דאפשר אסורים, *וכי שרי להו הכא – ה"מ באהל עראי, דאינו אלא מדרבנן, גזירה אטו אהל קבע, כדאמרינן בביצה בפרק "המביא" (ד' לב:). מיהו קשה: מנ"ל דעדיפא? דילמא בהא מודה אפילו רבי יהודה!

*) [ועי' תוס' מנחות נג. ד"ה בן]

[ועי' תוס' דפסחים מח: ד"ה מה לאיש רבות]

רבינו חננאל

מעת לעת להבראותו. וזה מפורש ביבמות בפר' הערל וכל הטמאים: **מתני'** ואלו הן ציצין המעכבין את המילה. א"ר אבינא א"ר ירמיה בר אבא אמר רב בשר החופה את רוב גובהה של עטרה וכו' וכן הלכתא. ואם הוא בעל בשר מתקנו מפני מראית העין כלומר אע"פ שהציצין הללו אינן חופין רוב גובהה של עטרה מתקנו מפני שלא יהא נראה כערלה: **אמר** שמואל קטן המסורבל בבשר רואין אותו כל זמן שמתקשה [ונראה מהול אין צריך למול במתניתא תנא רשבג"א קטן המסורבל בבשר רואין אותו כ"ז שמתקשה] שאינו נראה מהול צריך למול ואמרי' מאי ביניהם איכא ביניהם [נראה] ואינו נראה צריך למול לרשב"ג דאמר ואינו נראה מהול כלל צריך למול אבל אם נראה ואיוו וראה איוו צריך למול. פי' מסורבל מסובב בבשר כדכתי' כפיתו סרבלתהון וכו'. מל ולא פרע את המילה וכו'. פי' מי שמל ולא פרע את המילה כלומר לא קרע את העור וגילה את העטרה כאלו לא מל:

הדרן עלך ר' אלעזר אם לא הביא. עז ותהלה לאל אבי. שית עזר גלילין, חלץ באור והחלין. בפ' ר' אליעזר תולין:

ר' אליעזר אומר תולין את המשמרת ביו"ט וכו' ואקשי' עלה השתא ר' אליעזר להוסיף באהל עראי מחמיר ואמר אין מוסיפין לכתחלה (שאי) [מאי היא]. דתנן פקק החלון ר' אליעזר אומר בזמן שקשור ותלוי פוקקין בו כו' ופקק זה כגון מסך לסתום בו חללו של חלון ואמר רבה בר בר חנה א"ר יוחנן הכל מודים שאין עושין אהלי עראי בתחלה ביו"ט ואין צריך לומר בשבת לא נחלקו אלא להוסיף שר' אליעזר אומר אין מוסיפין ביו"ט ואין צ"ל בשבת וחכ"א מוסיפין בשבת ואין צ"ל ביו"ט ומפרקינן ר' אליעזר סבר לה כר' יהודה דתניא אין בין יו"ט לשבת אלא אוכל נפש בלבד. ר' יהודה אומר אף מכשירי אוכל נפש וזה שמתיר ר' אליעזר לעשות אהל לכתחלה ביו"ט לתלות המשמרת מפני שהוא מכשירי אוכל נפש כדי לשמר היין לשתות בשמחת יו"ט ונמצא ר' אליעזר מיקל מר' יהודה שר' יהודה אינו מתיר אלא במכשירין שאי אפשר לעשותן מעיו"ט אבל במכשירין שאפשר לעשותן מעיו"ט כגון שימור היין וכדומה לו אוסר ור' אליעזר מתיר אפילו בזה. ואין הלכה

מסורת הש"ס

יבמות מז: עא:
[תוספ' פט"ז]
[מנחות מב. תוספ' ברכות פ"ו כל הענין עד סופו]
הג"ה יעב"ץ ז"ל ניקד נוה כחיר"ק

הגהות הב"ח

(א) גמ' העומדין שם אומרים כשם שהכניסתו לברית כך תכניסהו לתור' כצ"ל וכן בתוס': (ב) שם חלקנו צורנו צוה: